Global Literary Theory

Global Literary Theory: An Anthology comprises a selection of classic, must-read essays alongside contemporary and global extracts, providing an engaging and timely overview of literary theory.

The volume is thoroughly introduced in the General Introduction and Part Introductions and each piece is contextualized within the wider sphere of global theory. Each part also includes annotated suggestions for further reading to help the reader navigate the extensive literature on each topic.

The volume engages with the "internationalizing" of the curriculum as well as the globalization of literature and theory. Alongside these key themes, the volume also extends its coverage to include:

- The core topics and theorists from formalism and structuralism to postmodernism and deconstruction
- Digital humanities and humanities computing and their relevance to globalization and literary theory
- The religious turn in literary theory and philosophy
- New textualities such as auto/biography, travel writing and ecocriticism
- Oppositional texts which "write back" against the canon

In addition, the book's Companion Website features an interactive world map incorporating biographies of every theorist in the book, as well as biographies of additional influential theorists.

Crucially, this anthology shows that ethnic studies, postcolonial studies, and globalization are not simply niche areas of literary study but are of concern across the contemporary humanities and that new voices are always emerging, and being discovered, from around the globe. As such, this volume offers a refocusing of essential literary theory, extending the canon in line with ongoing debates concerning contemporary cultural and geographic borders.

Richard J. Lane is a professor of English at Vancouver Island University, Canada, where he is the Director of the Literary Theory Research Group and the Seminar for Advanced Studies in the Humanities. He has written several books and articles on literary theory and has experience of teaching and presenting on literary theory at universities across the US, Canada and the UK.

"*Global Literary Theory: An Anthology* is a dynamic and illuminating synthesis of the fast moving and diverse field of literary theory. It introduces and subtly contextualizes a wide range of theoretical approaches from Russian formalism to postcolonialism, queer theory and globalization theory while never losing sight of their historical matrix and ongoing dialogue. We are reminded for example that the collapse of English literature's 'civilizing mission' was the catalyst for literary studies' replenishment by a variety of transformative and politicized theoretical approaches and that Derridean deconstruction cannot be thought of in isolation from his liminal Algerian heritage. Much more than a synopsis, *Global Literary Theory* is a superb intervention into the ongoing transnational conversation that constitutes contemporary literary theory."

Dr Ned Curthoys, *Australian National University, Australia*

Global Literary Theory

An Anthology

Edited by

Richard J. Lane

Routledge
Taylor & Francis Group

LONDON AND NEW YORK

First published 2013
by Routledge
2 Park Square, Milton Park, Abingdon, Oxon OX14 4RN

Simultaneously published in the USA and Canada
by Routledge
711 Third Avenue, New York, NY 10017

Routledge is an imprint of the Taylor & Francis Group, an informa business

British Library Cataloguing in Publication Data
A catalogue record for this book is available from the British Library

Library of Congress Cataloging in Publication Data
Global literary theory : an anthology / edited by Richard J. Lane.
    p. cm.
1. Literature—Philosophy.   2. Criticism.   3. Literature—History and
criticism—Theory, etc.   I. Lane, Richard J., 1966–
PN45.G5276 2013
801—dc23

                                                    2012025049

ISBN: 978-0-415-78301-9 (hbk)
ISBN: 978-0-415-78302-6 (pbk)

Typeset in Perpetua and Bell Gothic
by RefineCatch Limited, Bungay, Suffolk

Contents

viii   CONTENTS

Permissions

The editor and publisher gratefully acknowledge the permission granted to reproduce the following copyright material in this book:

Shklovsky, Viktor, "Art as Technique" from Lee T. Lemon and Marion J. Reis, eds., *Russian Formalist Criticism: Four Essays* pp.5–24. Reprinted by permission of the University of Nebraska Press © 1965 by the University of Nebraska Press.

Propp, Vladimir, "Morphology of the Folk-Tale", from *Morphology of the Folk-Tale* (translated by Laurence Scott, revised and edited with a preface by Louis A. Wagner) pp.25–28. Reprinted by permission of the University of Texas Press © 1968.

Da Silva, Francisco Vaz, "Red as Blood, White as Snow, Black as Crow: Chromatic Symbolism of Womanhood in Fairy Tales" in *Marvels & Tales: Journal of Fairy-Tale Studies,* Vol. 21, No. 2, pp.240–52. © 2007 Wayne State University Press. Reprinted with the permission of Wayne State University Press.

Saussure, F. de., "Nature of the Linguistic Sign", from Charles Bally and Albert Sechehaye, eds., *Course in General Linguistics,* pp.65–70. Reprinted by permission of the Philosophical Library Inc., New York © 1959.

Jakobson, Roman, "Two Aspects of Language", from Linda R. Waugh and Monique Monville-Burston, eds., *On Language* (Harvard University Press, 1990) pp.116–22; pp.125–27; pp.129–31. © Roman Jakobson Trust, University of Arizona.

Barthes, Roman, "Myth Today", from Susan Sontag, ed., *Barthes: Selected Writings,* pp.93–102; pp.130–33. ©1983 Fontana/Collins.

Kristeva, Julia, "The Semiotic Activity", in *Screen,* Vol. 14 Issue 1–2 Spring/Summer 1973, OUP, pp.25–39. Reprinted by permission of Oxford University Press.

Ahluwalia, Pal, *Out Of Africa: Poststructuralism's Colonial Roots,* pp.73–86. © Routledge, 2010. Reprinted by permission of the publisher.

Derrida, Jacques, *Writing and Difference* (translated, with an introduction and additional notes by Alan Bass), pp.278–93. Reprinted by permission of the University of Chicago Press © 1978.

Poovey, Mary, "Feminism and Deconstruction", from *Feminist Studies,* Vol. 14 No. 1, Spring 1988, pp.51–65. Reprinted by permission of Feminist Studies Inc.

Plates in Chapter 73

Plate 5: page from Lombard's scriptorium: reproduced with permission of Bibliothèque Nationale de France.

Every effort has been made to trace copyright holders and obtain their permission for use of copyright material. The publisher apologizes for any errors or omissions in the above list and would be grateful if notified of any corrections that should be incorporated in future reprints or editions of this book.

Acknowledgements

I could not have embarked upon this project without the expert guidance at Routledge of Polly Dodson and Holly Davis. It has been a pleasure working with them on all aspects of this anthology. Background research was provided by my research assistant Emily Marroquin, who is also my co-director of the Seminar for Advanced Studies in the Humanities at the Literary Theory Research Group, Vancouver Island University. I would like to acknowledge all of the participants at the Seminar for Advanced Studies, who have contributed to the creation of a collegial environment in which to explore and discuss literary theory. I have also greatly benefited from discussions concerning various aspects of theory with Professor Jens Zimmermann (Trinity Western University), Professor Richard Kearney (Boston College), Professor Stephen Ross (University of Victoria), Professor Emile Fromet de Rosnay (University of Victoria), Professor Natasha Duquette (Biola University), Professor George Pavlich (University of Alberta), Professor Sally Carpentier (Vancouver Island University) and Professor Ian Whitehouse (Vancouver Island University). More recent discussions concerning the digital humanities and humanities computing have been vital in my understanding of global literary theory; thanks go to Professor Raymond Siemens (Founder and Director of the Electronic Textual Cultures Lab, the University of Victoria) and Professor Jentery Sayers (the University of Victoria); my own research in the digital humanities is supported by the Canada Foundation for Innovation; the British Columbia Knowledge Development Fund; the Electronic Textual Cultures Lab, University of Victoria; the Faculty of Arts and Humanities, Vancouver Island University; the Director, Vancouver Island University Cowichan Campus; and the Vice President Academic's Office at Vancouver Island University. However, during the compiling, editing and writing of this anthology, the most generous support was given by my wife, Sarah.

The editor and publisher would like to acknowledge and thank the reviewers who provided valuable feedback throughout the writing process. They are:

Professor David Wills, University at Albany, USA
Professor Suvir Kaul, University of Pennsylvania, USA
Professor Madhavi Menon, American University, USA
Professor John Maynard, New York University, USA

Professor Alexander C. Y. Huang, Pennsylvania State University, USA
Professor Bob Eaglestone, Royal Holloway University of London, UK
Dr Paul Young, University of Exeter, UK
Dr Christopher Pittard, Portsmouth University, UK
Dr John Fitzsimmons, Central Queensland University, Australia
Dr Brett Jenkins, Murdoch University, Australia
Professor John Frow, University of Melbourne, Australia
Dr Edward Curthoys, Australian National University, Australia
Professor Carole Ferrier, University of Queensland, Australia
Dr Paul Sheehan, Macquarie University, Australia

General introduction

Criticism in the global village

One of the most enduring phrases first used in 1959 by the Canadian literary critic and media theorist Marshall McLuhan is the "global village", defined by the *Oxford English Dictionary* as the "world considered as a single community brought together by high technology and international communications." The word "Globe" goes back further, in English, to Thomas Elyot's *Bibliotheca Eliotae* published in 1542: "Some do suppose that he [sc. Archimedes] fyrste inuented the makynge of materiall spheris and the globe." (*OED*) What do these two thinkers—Elyot and McLuhan—have to do with a global literary theory anthology? And how can two thinkers separated by four hundred years even be connected? Both Elyot and McLuhan share deep roots in humanism (a belief in the positive values of art, learning and culture), and an awareness of culture's global reach—in Elyot's case, working for the court of King Henry VIII and travelling to Rome to advocate for Henry's divorce from Catherine of Aragon, and in McLuhan's case, theorizing the contemporary world of high speed global electronic communications and television that can bring people and ideas closer together. Both thinkers coined new language, with Elyot writing in the vernacular—the newly invigorated English language used instead of courtly or church Latin—especially with his books *The Governor* (1531) and his *Dictionary* (1538), and McLuhan writing in the new vernacular of technology in books such as *The Gutenberg Galaxy: The Making of Typographic Man* (1962) and *Understanding Media: The Extensions of Man* (1964). Elyot's ideas and language influenced Shakespeare and many of the writers of his age (we still use a substantial number of Elyot's new English words, such as "context", "edify" and "mutilate"[1]), while today, people of all backgrounds also use words and phrases from McLuhan such as "the medium is the message" or "cool" and "hot" media. Elyot's and McLuhan's educations involved what we now call "the classics": the great works of Greek and Latin culture, such as the philosophy of Aristotle (especially his *Poetics*) and Plato, the theories of the sublime put forward by Longinus, the epics of Homer, and the drama of Sophocles. Elyot translated Plutarch's (45–120 CE) *De educatione puerorum* (The Education or Bringing-Up of Children) and also drew upon Plato, Aristotle and the theologian Saint Thomas Aquinas in *The Governer*.[2] McLuhan had a conventional, humanistic education in the liberal arts, studying English literature at The University of

Manitoba and The University of Cambridge, and even after his reinvention as a media theorist and guru, he still believed in core humanistic values, especially those based upon dialogue and a "communal process" of reaching understanding.[3]

It is apparent, even with such a short overview, that both Elyot and McLuhan share innovative and humanistic approaches to language, literature and the global technologies and politics of their time. Writing about and theorizing literary texts involves here a deep knowledge of the classics, an interest in how texts function at the level of content and form, an engagement in a range of societal discourses (the politics of the state, the university, the media, and so on), and a purposeful goal or teleology for literary humanistic study: improving one's self, one's knowledge or simply one's social connections. But there is a difference between Elyot and McLuhan that is highly relevant for a global literary theory anthology: that between publication of *The Gutenberg Galaxy* and *Understanding Media*, McLuhan had charted the *distance* between the world of print technologies that Elyot and virtually all other humanists belong to, and the new world of electronic technologies and media that revolutionized the study of texts and transformed global communications. Through this revolution, linear, visual *print narratives*, often expressing nationalistic notions of humanistic progress and transcendence (universal truths or metanarratives), give way to mosaic-like acoustic/oral electronic or global *digital space*, with a concomitant "incredulity" towards, or suspicion of, traditional metanarratives.[4] This shift is theorized under a whole host of different names (and overlapping, interrelated concepts): postmodernism, poststructuralism, globalization, the hyperreal, the semiotic, the post-humanist, or it is simply described as the realm of "theory".

Humanist beginnings

Literary theory has complex roots, stretching back to the very beginnings of Western aesthetics and philosophy. With the emphasis upon the "literary", one way of exploring these roots is to focus on more recent beginnings within university literary critical or "English" studies, and what these effectively replaced: the study of classics and rhetoric.[5] In the UK, English literature was advocated as a morally uplifting and calming force for good, which would keep colonial British society—with its hierarchical and divisive class structure—running smoothly. English studies had three direct functions: to educate or inculcate English values into the men who were preparing to work overseas for the India Civil Service; as an important, civilizing supplement to increased technical and scientific training needed for Britain's burgeoning and innovative industrial base; and to provide an alternative to classics for the women who were beginning to enter higher education en masse.[6] The "bible" of this phase of English studies was—beyond the literary greats such as the works of Shakespeare, Milton, and Wordsworth—Matthew Arnold's *Culture and Anarchy* (1869). As Baldick notes, Arnold is considered the "founder" of "English literary criticism . . . not for any specific judgement upon authors or poems but for his emphatic readjustment of literary-critical discussion towards questions of literature's social function, and consequently the social function of criticism itself."[7] Criticism is to engage in the study of high poetry, which Arnold believes is the one mode of thought and expression that transcends all others, including religion, science and philosophy. For Arnold, poetry—and thoughtful, sensitive engagement with it—enables mankind to understand and interpret life, and to be consoled and sustained in the process.[8] Poetry and criticism would "humanize" an otherwise restless mass of people throughout the colonies, directing them away from barbarous and dangerous pursuits, such as political activism (demonstrations, anarchic riots) or intense individualism (breaking away from established spiritual authority, moral and artistic guidance). If religion had failed to provide social and political checks and balances, then poetry would have to take its place. Arnold's two "remedies" were education and the inculcation of high culture.[9] In other words, if religious impulses had become increasingly secularized, then culture needed to be sacrilized.[10] This project had already been underway globally for some considerable time, with the teaching of English literature in the colonies, through which Western values were inculcated as being universal and transcendent. As Ania Loomba notes, "Knowledge of the East is a specialisation for the European, but knowledge of the West for the Asian or African becomes synonymous [under colonialism] with education, knowledge, culture *per se*. If we add to this the dominant representation of literature as a repository of some fixed and unchanging human essence, we can begin to approach the significance of the European text in the colonial context, which also resulted in specific kinds of teaching and critical practices."[11]

After the First World War, the Arnoldian approach to literary studies was further institutionalized with the publication of an official report called *The Teaching of English in England* (1921), the result of a government educational committee's inquiry into pedagogy, subsequently known as the Newbolt Report. The committee argues for English studies as a mode of strengthening national cohesion and identity, creating a common, indigenous bond or "unity"; however, this binding force is also cast in *global*, visionary terms, as a mode of "grace" that "binds together by passion and knowledge the vast empire of human society."[12] Ironically, the seeds of the destruction of such a global humanist vision are sown in the report itself, especially where it argues that English professors should function like ambassadors and "missionaries" who go out into the (presumably "uncivilized") field to undertake "propaganda work, organisation and the building up of a staff of assistant missionaries."[13] While the report's intention is to elevate the study of morally and aesthetically great literature to the extent that humans throughout the world will increasingly worship it, this description of propaganda and organization can very simply be adopted for different aims, such as the instilling of opposing ideologies, or the adoption of scientific, lab-based approaches to the arts, as with today's social-science approaches to the arts, or the study of digital humanities and humanities computing.

The findings of the Newbolt Report fed into the rise of a new literary critical methodology known as New Criticism. In the UK, the chief practitioners were I.A. Richards, William Empson, F.R. Leavis and Q.D. Leavis; in the US, Monroe C. Beardsley, René Wellek (although he denied he was part of this loosely structured movement), Cleanth Brooks, W.K. Wimsatt and John Crowe Ransom. Richards had been disturbed by his students' inability to engage deeply in poetic texts and decided that this was due to the rise of mass culture, the media and post-War propaganda which was being used for commercial purposes; he developed a mode of "practical criticism" that would provide psychological and aesthetic tools, such as "synaesthesis" (harmonizing differences through the beauty of aesthetic experiences), to recover a sense of artistic value. His key texts were *The Foundations of Aesthetics* (1922, with James Wood and C.K. Ogden), *The Meaning of Meaning* (1923), *Principles of Literary Criticism* (1924) and *Practical Criticism* (1929). One of Richards' students, F.R. Leavis, reacted even more strongly against mass culture, that powerful force that his wife Q.D. Leavis analyzed in her *Fiction and the Reading Public* (1932). As with Arnold and the authors of the Newbolt Report, Leavis believed that the health of the nation resided in the cultural elite who were "the consciousness of the race", and he argued—in texts such as *Mass Civilisation and Minority Culture* (1930), and *For Continuity* (1933)—that this elite were needed to maintain standards and the best of Western tradition.

The critical writing of poet T.S. Eliot was also an important foundation for Leavis, especially Eliot's notion that it is literature that "contains a unique knowledge not available to science."[14] For Leavis, it is the great poets of the age—T.S. Eliot, Ezra Pound, and Gerard Manley Hopkins—who are the most alive, and the role of English studies becomes one of exposing people from industrialized, mass culture, to literary expressions and a higher mode of thinking that should be emulated.[15] In *The Great Tradition: George Eliot, Henry James, Joseph Conrad* (1948), and *D.H. Lawrence: Novelist* (1955), Leavis added major modern novelists to his pedagogic project. But it was in the journal *Scrutiny*, launched by Leavis and others in 1932, that more extensive guidance and articulation of his project was made available to teachers of English. In a debate between Leavis and René Wellek published in *Scrutiny*, Wellek praised Leavis except for his unwillingness to provide a more theoretical systematic account of poetry.[16] Leavis replied that such an account would not be literary criticism, but "philosophy", and that the critic's job was to "feel into" or intuit the literary text's "concrete fullness".[17] As Jefferson and Robey summarize Leavis's position: "The critic should not try to argue his case in conceptual terms, but attempt to convey directly this experience to the reader."[18] In a global context, Leavis's defence of the major modern English novelists and the importance of the English tradition can also be read as a reaction against mass or popular culture which in this period was synonymous with Americanization; ironically, this defence appears to have some parallels with other less powerful cultures attempting to safeguard local values from globalizing American ones; as Bill Ashcroft notes, "In some respects Leavis' battle reflects the predicament of decolonizing countries trying to carve a cultural space for themselves against an overwhelming imperial presence."[19]

Debates about methodology are crucial to the rise of English studies because Wellek shared many of Leavis's values—such as belief in the autonomy and primacy of the literary text, and the unifying value of the canon—while developing a more theoretically rigorous methodology, derived in part from his experiences of the Prague Linguistic Circle which he was part of between 1935 and 1939. Wellek's *Theory of Literature* (co-authored with Austin Warren, 1949), and six volume study *A History of Modern Criticism: 1750–1950* (1955–86), provided—against his will it must be said—the "philosophical foundation" for American New Criticism.[20] New critics share a set of approaches to literature, including a fundamental belief in the autonomy and unity of literary works, as well as the text's "resistance to paraphrase" which is in part explained by the irreducibility of literary language: its irony, connotation, paradox, and ambiguity, all forging a balanced and harmonious whole which is held in tension.[21] Studying *how* such a tension is achieved involves "close reading", that is to say, the detailed examination of the literary devices, the structural balances, and the range of meanings of a text.

An exemplary approach to close reading is found in I.A. Richards' student William Empson's *Seven Types of Ambiguity* (1930), where an ambiguity is "any verbal nuance, however slight, which gives room for alternative reactions to the same piece of language."[22] The global reach of New Criticism (and Practical Criticism) was rapidly achieved; New Critical tenets form the basis of close literary reading to this day, while Richards and Empson branched out internationally in other ways: Richards and Charles K. Ogden developed the Basic English project, a list of 850 English words that would lead, in their opinion, to international harmony through the communication of universal truths, while Empson produced a remarkable range of poems and criticism as a professor at Tokyo University in Japan, and at Peking National University, in China. As Castle summarizes, "It is hard to underestimate both the canon-forming impetus behind the New Criticism and the extent to which it transformed the nature of scholarship and teaching."[23] And yet, even though the methodology lives on in English composition classrooms, the New Criticism canons would begin to be dismantled during the second half of the twentieth century, and their humanist values would be repeatedly attacked and eventually overthrown.

The theoretical turn

What became known alternatively as "the theoretical turn", "the rise of theory", and in some quarters "the theory wars" began, roughly speaking, in the 1960s: literary criticism underwent a profound shift whereby three new domains of study began to directly compete with humanism.

These three domains are: language (linguistics, semiotics, structuralism, and so on); gender and sexuality; and history.[24] What each domain shares is a questioning of the previously held norms upon which the entire structure of English studies was built, aesthetic norms such as the redeeming qualities of the literary canon, or the belief in the individual artistic genius expressing universal themes and truths through poetic writing, and social norms, such as the *common sense* approach to culture based on patriarchal and what became known as "Eurocentric" or "Western" values. In the 1960s, there was widespread rejection of such norms driven by counter-cultural forces, such as the student uprisings protesting the Vietnam War, or simply changes in society driven by the rise of new technologies of sexuality (the invention of the contraceptive pill), communications (television), and art (the synthesis of drug culture, music, and advertising, to create postmodernism and popular culture). Even scientific norms were under attack, being theorized via the concept of the "paradigm" by Thomas Kuhn in *The Structure of Scientific Revolutions* (1962), where he suggests that most scientists work within an agreed upon, shared set of principles (a paradigm), which eventually will be countered and entirely overturned (the paradigm change or shift).[25] Kuhn argues that science does not work with universal empirical truths; rather, science is what Jean-François Lyotard calls "performative" — in other words, if it works, it is considered to be true. In *The Postmodern Condition: A Report on Knowledge* (1979), Lyotard discusses this performativity in terms of the predominance of language games and a widespread social incredulity towards universal truths, or "metanarratives". Other "new age" thinkers would go even further than Kuhn, and would apply the new sciences, such as quantum physics, to the arts (and vice versa), positing analogies and crossovers between previously separate realms of knowledge.

If science was now perceived to have a performative, if not entirely subjective, "narrative" or language-game status, then so did human identity. With the rise of more liberal approaches to sexuality in the 1960s and 1970s, alongside the development of a more militant feminism and complex theories of decentred subjectivity, the notion of a stable, self-present and expressive human subject came under attack. While this had been occurring throughout the modernist period (roughly the end of the nineteenth-century to the Second World War) — for example, with the translation into English of the works of Freud, the attempt to understand the post-traumatic condition in soldiers known as "shell shock", and the painterly aesthetics of psychological states with techniques such as cubism, or in literature, stream-of-consciousness and interior monologue — it was the turn to European theories of linguistics, semiotics and psychoanalysis that brought even bigger intellectual systems into play. A sense of global political crisis — with reaction to events such as the Cuban Missile Crisis, the Cold War in general, and again, the Vietnam War — also led to a socialist backlash within Western universities; ironically, given that the Cold War pitted North America and Western Europe against the Communist Soviet Union and its satellite countries in a dangerous economic and militaristic technological stalemate, the socialist critique of Capitalism from "within" the West continued to grow increasingly vocal. If liberal humanism had once posited great art as an antidote to the ills of mass culture as well as the crisis of cultural and political upheaval, for many involved in leftist activism and a rejection of traditional values, humanism and poetry were beginning to look antiquated and offered an untenable solution. As the Marxist critic Terry Eagleton suggests: "That this brand of transcendental humanism is indeed no more than a myth was becoming painfully evident throughout the 1960s — the period in which literary theory as we have it today first took off the ground."[26]

Such a historical overview still begs the question, in what way is literary theory really that different from literary criticism? Culler makes an astute observation: that theory is not really about the study of literary texts; rather, it is *a transgressing of disciplinary boundaries*: theory "has come to designate works that succeed in challenging and reorienting thinking in fields other than those to which they apparently belong."[27] So, literary studies undergoes a theoretical turn when it starts more aggressively trespassing on other academics' disciplinary territory: "This simple explanation is an unsatisfactory definition but it does seem to capture what has happened since the 1960s: writings from outside the field of literary studies have been taken up by people in literary studies because their analyses of language, or mind, or history, or culture, offer new and persuasive accounts of textual and cultural matters."[28] Another descriptive metaphor for theory that is even stronger than "trespassing", is "hijacking", e.g. "the hijack of culture by literary studies."[29] There is a sense here that theory is a heightened mode of critical activity: not just the analysis of a text, but a more disruptive deconstruction of texts and textuality in general (Barthes, Derrida, De Man, Kristeva); not just an analysis of subjectivity, but a more powerful interrogation of the foundational concept of the sovereign or self-present subject (Lacan, Irigaray, Butler, Žižek); not just an awareness of the historical dimensions of literature, but a radical shift into *historicism* where history is nothing but textual or discursive representation (Foucault, Greenblatt, Dollimore, Sinfield); not just a critique of patriarchal expressions within literature, but a feminist/queer theorist revision of gender and sexuality per se (Butler, Cixous, Haraway, Weeks, Foucault, Sedgwick); and finally, not just an awareness of the political and international backgrounds to literature, but a Marxist-based postcolonial attack upon the colonial contexts and roots of literary production (Eagleton, Jameson, Spivak, Said, Bhabha). In each of these cases, criticism has become more highly charged, conjoining intellectual theorizing with political and social awareness and responsibility.[30]

Exploring the above theorists from a more conventional categorizing approach, another family resemblance is that of shared European origins: for example deconstruction and poststructuralism build upon the insights of the Swiss linguist Ferdinand de Saussure (1857–1913), as well as the research produced by the Moscow Linguistic Circle (founded 1915), the Petrograd Society for the Study of Poetic Language (founded 1916) and the Prague Linguistic Circle (founded 1926). Psychoanalytical theory and feminism/gender studies critique and develop the work of Sigmund Freud (1856–1939), an Austrian medical researcher who developed an entirely new field in texts such as his "Project for a Scientific Psychology" (1895), and *The Interpretation of Dreams* (1900); other important early thinkers in relation to subjectivity and psychoanalysis/gender studies are the Swiss psychiatrist Carl Gustav Jung (1875–1961) and the Austrian psychiatrist Alfred Adler (1870–1937). Postcolonial theory draws even more widely upon a global range of thinkers and activists as Brennan notes, including "resistance intellectuals from Latin America throughout the nineteenth century, China of the 1920s, India of the 1940s, Algeria of the 1950s, Vietnam of the 1960s, Central America of the 1970s, and so on."[31] Examining the history of literary theory, then, reveals that theory has always had a political context, either as a coded critique of the repressive regimes in which earlier theoretical movements operated (such as Soviet Russia), or more openly with resistance intellectuals such as Frantz Fanon (1925–61) working with the guerrilla organization, the National Liberation Front, in French occupied Algeria. In one of the key texts of the politicized theoretical turn, called *Critical Practice* (1980), Catherine Belsey sketches how students of literature should proceed in relation to this politicized awareness: "As readers and critics we can choose actively to seek out the process of production of the text: the organization of the discourses which constitute it and the strategies by which it smoothes over the incoherences and contradictions of the ideology inscribed in it. A form of criticism which refuses to reproduce the pseudo-knowledge offered by the text provides a real knowledge of the work of literature."[32] Theory, then, works "against the grain", no longer simply accepting, or reproducing, the apparently unified expressive humanist values of texts—what Belsey calls "pseudo-knowledge"—but interrogating them, uncovering problematic systems of thought and behaviour that may need to be rejected or overturned, as well as the logical flaws and contradictions at the level of form and content through which the text can be teased apart. Clearly this is not a neutral, simple turn from one mode of doing literary criticism to an interdisciplinary and transdisciplinary approach to textuality: in effect, the theoretical turn is more of a declaration of war than a gentle disagreement with humanism.

Theory as a new global discipline

The theory wars were concurrent with the global decolonization of Empire, as well as a shift from class-based politics in the West, to identity "as the fulcrum of political mobilization and social movements."[33] High "philosophical" theory, such as deconstruction and poststructuralist psychoanalysis, was put at the service of other theories of identity, such as feminism, queer theory, and postcolonial studies. In effect, the shift to identity studies was in itself a form of decolonization: texts, belief systems, and entire nations were judged to be "colonized" by White, patriarchal, Eurocentric values. Postcolonial theory thus fulfilled two widespread new pedagogic injunctions: to understand *and* to decolonize identity, or as Robert Young puts it, to not only focus "on forces of oppression and coercive domination that operate in the contemporary world" but also "to develop new forms of engaged theoretical work that contributes to the development of dynamic ideological and social transformations."[34] Edward Said's monumental study of the colonial knowledge archive and practice of dominance, called *Orientalism* (1978), began to be applied more widely within literary theory studies. In fact this fulfilled Said's more general observation made while commenting upon Foucault in *The World, the Text, and the Critic* (1983), that "writing itself is a systematic conversion of the power relationship between controller and controlled . . . [and] a way of disguising the awesome materiality of so tightly a controlled production."[35] Similarly, Homi Bhabha's conception of cultural hybridity, derived in part from the study of colonial, anti-colonial, theoretical and diasporic migrant discourses and cultures, leads to a more generally applicable theory: not just a postcolonial study of liminality and in-between "third spaces" of diasporic, migratory being, but instead a postcolonial enunciation concerning knowledge production and representation per se. In other words, Bhabha's postcolonial theory—collected for the most part in *The Location of Culture* (1994)— replaces the old-fashioned notion of a unified literary criticism as having the "capacity to produce a cross-referential, generalizable unity that signifies a progression or evolution of ideas-in-time, as well as a critical self-reflection on their premises or determinants" with a theoretical "Third Space of enunciation, which makes the structure of meaning and reference an ambivalent process, [and] destroys this mirror of representation in which cultural knowledge is customarily revealed as an integrated, open, expanding code."[36] As Bhabha continues, "Such an intervention quite properly challenges our sense of the historical identity of culture as a homogenizing, unifying force, authenticated by the originary Past, kept alive in the national tradition of the People. In other words, the disruptive temporality of enunciation displaces the narrative of the Western nation which Benedict Anderson so perceptively describes as being written in homogenous, serial time."[37]

Gayatri Spivak's work on Third World "subalterns" (non-elite people who do not have access to power-knowledge mechanisms, such as self-representation or any level of authority) provides a useful warning to those engaged in speaking for colonial subjects via the potentially privileged perspective of theory; in her book *In Other Worlds: Essays in Cultural Politics* (1987), Spivak examines the dangers of essentializing and misrepresenting subaltern subjects—"migrants, shantytown dwellers, displaced tribes, refugees, untouchable castes, the homeless"[38]—as well as the Orientalist tendencies in Western theorists who represent the Other, such as French feminist and poststructural psychoanalyst Julia Kristeva in *About Chinese Women* (1977). Spivak offers practical alternatives with her theoretically inflected postcolonial re-reading of the canon, for example in "Three Women's Texts and a Critique of Imperialism" (1985); her major study of postcolonial thought in *A Critique of Postcolonial Reason: Toward a History of the Vanishing Present* (1999); and the shift towards comparative studies and a reorientation of the humanities within a global context in her *Death of a Discipline* (2003).[39] The double-bind with global postcolonial studies is that firstly, it so often functions from within the West, and secondly, that the global marketplace for postcolonial authors and artists usually involves writing in English, and heavy marketing and consumption of the global artistic product in countries such as the US and the UK. Colonial centres of power, in other words, have been transformed into cultural centres. This has led to debates concerning the location(s) of postcoloniality, such as Aijaz Ahmad's critique of Fredric Jameson's "Third World literature in the Era of Multinational Capitalism" (1986), where Ahmad accuses Jameson of "dehistoricizing" the particularities and differences of global space, or George Elliott Clarke's critique of Paul Gilroy's *The Black Atlantic: Modernity and Double Consciousness* (1993), where Clarke complicates W.E.B. Du Bois's theory of African American "double consciousness" (a split identity, between African and American; between racist stereotype and actual person; between African spirituality/myth and American materiality) to argue that African Canadian experience involves a more global "poly-consciousness".[40]

Theory's postcolonial turn is thus not only global in outlook, but it shares with globalization studies "an ethical program",[41] one which involves reorienting the entire field of the humanities: "it seeks to reorient cultural values attendant upon learning to understand and appreciate aesthetically the cultural achievements of those outside the European sphere. It seeks to show how earlier scholars in the West have been narrowly obsessed, culturally limited, and tendentiously ignorant of many of the world's most consequential artistic and intellectual creations."[42] This ethical project is vast, and is still underway. In relation to understanding contemporary theory, two broad re-conceptualizations are needed: first, to go back to the known or registered global roots of theory — for example, the Eastern European linguistics or the Russian Formalists — not just in the conventional sense of registering these roots as "beginnings" before quickly moving on to Western versions of, say, Formalism and Structuralism, but to more thoroughly understand the history and culture of these intellectual locations in and of themselves; second, to uncover the hidden, forgotten or effaced global roots of theory — for example, uncovering the significance of Algeria for the poststructuralists Derrida and Cixous — not as a way of producing an additional set of historical "data" about theory, but rather to re-examine the *constitutive* elements of theory. As Ahluwalia argues: "questions that have become so much a part of the post-structuralist canon — otherness, difference, irony, mimicry, parody, the lamenting of modernity and the deconstruction of the grand narratives of European culture arising out of the Enlightenment tradition — are possible *because* of their postcolonial connection."[43] Another important example of such a doubled re-conceptualization is that of "Afro-modernity", charted in the work of Arjun Appadurai, Paul Gilroy and George Elliott Clarke, among others; while the African American slave experience was initially foreclosed from theories of modernity, Gilroy argues that studying it actually leads to a profound re-thinking of those theories; Afro-modernity, then, "is no mere mimicry of Western modernity but an innovation upon its precepts, forces, and features. Its contours have arisen from the encounters between people of African descent and Western colonialism not only on the African continent but also in the New World, Asia, and ultimately Europe itself."[44]

What is being sketched here is an intellectual and social "recoil" as theory is unravelled and re-constituted from a global perspective. In some ways this merely produces a new dialogue, an expanded academic conversation that includes more participants, but in other ways, this recoil may fundamentally change the way we think of theory itself. As such, thinking theory "globally" is part of the "post-theory" landscape, the world "after theory" as Terry Eagleton puts it, when theory has become normalized and in many respects "neutralized" with its incorporation into the university curriculum. The post-theory landscape is not only diverse, but its practitioners are often travelling in opposing directions, such as the post-secular turn to religion in which humanistic and religious "big questions" are once more being asked, or digital humanities and humanities computing, in which canonical texts are being given a new lease of life, versus theorists of cybernetic, post-human existence, with a pronounced shift away from religion, metaphysics and conventional notions of the text, the subject, the body, and sexuality, functioning within virtual worlds and inorganic machine structures. These are just some of the examples of the post-theory landscape—"mediascape" might be a better word—and how these interests play out globally will be of real importance.

A Note on This Text, or, A Guide to Reading Globally

The extracts within this anthology are part of the wider academic conversation concerning theory: its origins, its practitioners, and its critics. The global re-reading of theory is represented in key extracts in individual sections which also contain representative, more "standard" extracts by Western theorists; the "global" extracts, however, also function "across" the anthology, in other words, crossing the at times artificial boundaries between theoretical movements. Ahluwalia (Part II), for example, looks at the Algerian roots of Derrida's theory of deconstruction, but Ahluwalia's bigger argument also applies to Fanon (Part VI) and Cixous (Part IX). Asian culture and philosophy is examined throughout the anthology, with extracts on Levinas and Laozi (Nuyen, in Part II); New Historicism and "the poetics of Chinese culture" (Berg, in Part V); race, colonialism and history in China (Karl, in Part VI); Asian American feminism (Shah, in Part IX); and the internet in China (Kang, in Part X). African American theory has deep global roots, for example with the African tradition of the "signifying monkey" explored by Gates, or the importance of the "slave sublime" theorized by Gilroy (both in Part VI). Some subjects in the anthology are examined from global perspectives, less as a critique of Western theory or values, and more as a recognition of how different indigenous groups have adopted and adapted new technologies of textuality and culture, for example Sundaram on "pirate electronic cultures" in India; Rose on rap music and "black cultural production" in America; and Vizenor on Native American notions of trickster postmodernism (all in Part III). "Global" does not necessarily mean "non-Western" as the Canadian media theorist McLuhan (Part III), and the African Canadian critic George Elliott Clarke make clear (Part VI). But extracts within the anthology do at times re-assess more traditional Western theoretical fields or disciplines from a global—meaning "world"—perspective, such as Scully on "race and ethnicity in women's and gender history" (Part VI). There are many postcolonial theorists who work with a critique of colonialism "from within", and thus perceive indigenous cultures as having connections with the oppressed peoples of the world, rather than their own Western colonizers, for example, the indigenous peoples of Australia, New Zealand, the US and Canada; two examples in the anthology are by Wisker and King (both in Part VII). Clearly, *identity* plays a major part in the global perspective on literary theory, and while critics such as Terry Eagleton are anxious that the turn to identity is a turn away from practical politics, this concept is important for a diverse range of theorists around the world. Gender, sexualities, and feminist studies have led the way here, and there are numerous extracts within the anthology that engage in the global conversation about identity, including Bhadra and Spivak on the "subaltern" (Part VII); Butler, Žižek, Foucault, Sedgwick, Nigianni and Walters, et al., on gender and sexualities (Part VIII); and Homans and Shah on alternatives to mainstream or "whitestream" feminism (Part IX). New technologies are transforming the humanities throughout the world, and theorists come at this topic from myriad perspectives: extracts include Sundaram on "electronic cultures" in India (Part III); Byrne on the internet and race in "computer-mediated public spheres" (Part VI); and Kang on "the internet in China" (Part X). Ever since the Rushdie Affair in 1989, when the diasporic Indian author Salman Rushdie was made subject to a "Fatwa" or legal ruling by the Ayatollah Khomeini that he should be sentenced to death for blasphemy for his novel *The Satanic Verses* (1988), there has been a widespread literary theoretical debate concerning the role of Islamic fundamentalism in global culture and politics. Extracts touching upon this debate go beyond stereotypes, for example Sardar's distinguishing between "traditionalism" (fundamentalism) and "tradition" (a more flexible cultural authenticity) in the Islamic critique of postmodernism (Part III); Ahmed and Hastings' "Islam in the age of postmodernity" (Part XI); or Cooke on "Arab women's literary history" (Part IX). Finally, the anthology ends with an entire section (Part XI) on globalization and global studies from a literary theory perspective, with extracts on "literary studies and globalization" (Gupta); "postcolonial studies and globalization theory" (Brennan); postcolonial perspectives "on globalization" (Xie); Islam and postmodernity (Ahmed & Hastings); and "the transnational book" and "the migrant writer" (Walkowitz).

Notes

1   Alistair Fox, "Sir Thomas Elyot", in David A. Richardson, ed., *Dictionary of Literary Biography Volume 136, Sixteenth-Century British Nondramatic Writers: Second Series*, Detroit: Gale Research, 1994. Electronic version.

2   Alistair Fox, "Sir Thomas Elyot", electronic version.

3   Marshall McLuhan, "The Humanities in the Electronic Age", quoted in Richard Cavell, *McLuhan in Space: A Cultural Geography*, Toronto: University of Toronto Press, 2003, p.67.

4   See Jean-François Lyotard, "What is Postmodernism?" From *The Postmodern Condition: A Report on Knowledge*, trans. Geoff Bennington and Brian Massumi, Minneapolis: University of Minnesota Press, 1989 and Richard Cavell, *McLuhan in Space*.

5   Suman Gupta, *Globalization and Literature*, Cambridge: Polity, 2009, p.127.

6   Chris Baldick, *The Social Mission of English Criticism 1848–1932*, Oxford: Clarendon Press, 1987, p.61; Suman Gupta, *Globalization and Literature*, pp.127–28.

7   Chris Baldick, *The Social Mission of English Criticism 1848–1932*, p.18.

8   Chris Baldick, *The Social Mission of English Criticism 1848–1932*, p.18.

9   Steven Marcus, "*Culture and Anarchy* Today", in Matthew Arnold, *Culture and Anarchy*, Samuel Lipman, ed., New Haven & London: Yale University Press, 1994, pp.165–85; p.167.

10 Steven Marcus, "*Culture and Anarchy* Today", p.169. See, also, Charles Taylor, *A Secular Age*, Cambridge, Massachusetts & London, England: The Belknap Press of Harvard University Press, 2007.

11 Ania Loomba, *Gender, Race, Renaissance Drama*, Manchester & New York: Manchester University Press, 1989, p.19.

12 Quoted in Chris Baldick, *The Social Mission of English Criticism 1848–1932*, p.96.

13 Quoted in Chris Baldick, *The Social Mission of English Criticism 1848–1932*, p.97.

14 Donald J. Childs, "New Criticism", in Irena R. Makaryk, ed., *Encyclopedia of Contemporary Literary Theory: Approaches, Scholars, Terms*, Toronto: University of Toronto Press, 2000, pp.120–24; p.120.

15 Richard J. Lane, "Frank Raymond Leavis (1895–1978)", *Fifty Key Literary Theorists*, London & New York: Routledge, 2006, p.201

16 Ann Jefferson and David Robey, "Introduction", in Ann Jefferson and David Robey, eds., *Modern Literary Theory: A Comparative Introduction*, p.11.

17 Quoted in Ann Jefferson and David Robey, "Introduction", p.12.

18 Jefferson and Robey, p.12.

19 Bill Ashcroft, *On Postcolonial Futures: Transformations of a Colonial Culture*, London and New York: Continuum, 2001, p.12.

20 Sarah Lawhill, "Wellek René", in Irena R. Makaryk, ed., *Encyclopedia of Contemporary Literary Theory: Approaches, Scholars, Terms*, Toronto: University of Toronto Press, 2000, pp.484–86; p.485.

21 Donald J. Childs, "New Criticism", pp.120–22.

22 William Empson, *Seven Types of Ambiguity*, London: Penguin, 1995, p.19.

23 Gregory Castle, *The Blackwell Guide to Literary Theory*, Oxford: Blackwell, 2007, p.27.

24 Jonathan Culler, *Literary Theory: A Very Short Introduction*, p.121.

25 See, also, Patricia Waugh's discussion of Kuhn, in her "Introduction" to *Literary Theory and Criticism: An Oxford Guide*, Oxford: Oxford University Press, 2006, pp.18–19.

26 Terry Eagleton, *The Significance of Theory*, Oxford: Basil Blackwell, 1990, p.30; see, also, Terry Eagleton, *Literary Theory: An Introduction*, Minneapolis: University of Minnesota Press, 1983.

27 Jonathan Culler, *Literary Theory: A Very Short Introduction*, Oxford: Oxford University Press, 2000, p.3.

28 Jonathan Culler, *Literary Theory: A Very Short Introduction*, p.3.

29 Quoted in Suman Gupta, *Globalization and Literature*, p.88.

30 Suman Gupta, *Globalization and Literature*, p.90.

31 Timothy Brennan, "From development to globalization: postcolonial studies and globalization theory", in Neil Lazarus, ed., *The Cambridge Companion to Postcolonial Literary Studies*, Cambridge: Cambridge University Press, 2004, pp.120–38; p.131.

32 Catherine Belsey, *Critical Practice*, London & New York: Methuen, 1980, p.129.

33 Suman Gupta, *Globalization and Literature*, pp.92–93.

34 Robert Young, quoted in Suman Gupta, *Globalization and Literature*, p.110.

35 Edward Said, *The World, The Text, And The Critic*, London: Faber and Faber, 1984, p.47.

36 Homi K. Bhabha, *The Location of Culture*, London & New York: Routledge, 1994, pp.36–37.

37 Homi K. Bhabha, *The Location of Culture*, p.37.

38 Gregory Castle, *The Blackwell Guide to Literary Theory*, p.322.

39 Richard J. Lane, "Gayatri Chakravorty Spivak (1942–)", in *Fifty Key Literary Theorists*, London & New York: Routledge, 2006, pp.246–51.

40 See Aijaz Ahmed, "Jameson's Rhetoric of Otherness and the 'National Allegory'", *Social Text* 17 (Autumn 1987): 3–25, and George Elliott Clarke, *Odysseys Home: Mapping African-Canadian Literature*. Toronto: University of Toronto Press, 2002.

41 Timothy Brennan, "From development to globalization: postcolonial studies and globalization theory", p.131.

42 Timothy Brennan, "From development to globalization: postcolonial studies and globalization theory", p.132.

43 Pal Ahluwalia, *Out of Africa: Post-structuralism's colonial roots*, Abingdon, Oxon & New York: Routledge, 2010, p.2.

44 Hanchard, quoted in Pal Ahluwalia, *Out of Africa: Post-structuralism's colonial roots,* p.15.

PART I

Formalism, structuralism

CONTEMPORARY LITERARY THEORY is conventionally traced back to Russian Formalism and Structuralism, two distinct, but related movements. In many respects, this is simply a practical choice: some of the more complex ideas in later theoretical approaches, such as deconstruction and poststructuralism, are built upon these earlier critical movements. But locating the origins of theory is also a politically strategic choice, one which conventionally roots literary theory in a European cultural and intellectual context. This potential "Eurocentrism" (positing European values and perspectives over those of other nations) is called into question by later methodologies, such as postcolonial studies (see Part VII). Upon closer examination, the European intellectual beginnings of literary theory were *not* one of privilege and hegemony: at times these scholars struggled with political upheaval, state hostility to their work, exile, and the impact of two world wars.

The Formalist project, while subject to political attack, sought to create a scientific study of literature, one which focused on the literary text itself, analyzing and formulating that previously elusive quality called "literariness". Instead of examining what surrounded a text, for example, society, culture, politics, and instead of assessing a text's place in history, the Formalists focused on *literary qualities*, mainly the self-reflective devices that made literariness different from everyday communicative speech or writing. The most famous such device explored by the Formalists is that of "defamiliarization" or making a text strange, that is to say, the way in which literature makes us aware of, and think about (if not struggle with), its unusual or simply different way of saying something, so much so that we pay attention to language itself, as if we were seeing it—or hearing it—for the first time (the awkwardness of this sentence, for example, slows down the reader and *defamiliarizes* the sentence structure). Such close attention to language demands deep knowledge of linguistics and rhetoric, which Formalist scholars developed through the Moscow Linguistic Circle (founded 1915), the Petrograd Society for the Study of Poetic Language, or OPOYAZ (founded 1916), and later when one of the key Formalists, Roman Jakobson (1896–1982), moved to Czechoslovakia, through the Prague Linguistic Circle (founded 1926). A linguistic approach to literature did already exist in Russia prior to Formalism, with the outstanding philological research (historical and comparative linguistics) of scholars Alexander Potebnya (1835–91) and Alexander Veselovsky (1838–1906). Potebnya argued that the essence of poetic language was metaphor, while Veselovsky suggested that the use of motifs (core themes) defined the literary text.[1] While both positions were attacked by the Formalists, what these thinkers achieved was to focus on the literary text itself, rather than the surrounding framework. The results of the first main Formalist phase were presented in the two volumes of *Studies on the Theory of Poetic Language* (1916 and 1917), and in *Poetics: Studies on the Theory of Poetic Language* (1919).

Roman Jakobson, in his essay "Linguistics and Poetics", argued that literariness is defined by the "poetic function" of texts, whereby "language itself becomes the aesthetic center" of a literary work.[2] The word for this function used by Jakobson is "texture". Viktor Shklovsky (1893–1984) developed the concept of *ostranenie*, variously translated into English as "defamiliarization", "dehabitualization", "making strange", or "bestrangement". What he argued was that the wider function of art was to shake people from their complacency and habitualized ways of being and perceiving. In his essay "Art as Technique" (1917), Shklovsky observes that "I personally feel that defamiliarization is found almost everywhere form is found."[3] Shifting the focus of study thereby from poetry to prose meant looking at structured literary devices that function through time, or as Boris Eichenbaum (1886–1959) put it in an important survey of Formalism called "The Theory of the 'Formal Method'", "We had to move from questions about 'technique-in-general' to the study of the specific devices of composition, to inquiry about plot, and so on."[4] The distinction between story and plot in prose narrative was regarded by the Formalists as central, "story" being the temporally connected events in a narrative, and "plot" being the artistic intervention, the deliberate rearranging of story events to create interesting effects. These effects can appear to be generated by the internal logic of a story (they appear natural), or, they clash with the apparently natural story world, "laying bare" or *foregrounding* the story's formal artistry. Shklovsky analyzes the way in which the eighteenth-century English author Sterne "slows down" narrative progression in his novel *Tristram Shandy*, "laying bare" or revealing the artistic devices that make up plot. This novel is perhaps the most extreme example of "laying bare" in English literature (for example, it includes a blank page so that the reader can draw the female protagonist); yet at the same time, it reveals that this is how all novels actually function (foregrounding the usually hidden artistic "mechanics" or techniques), and so Shklovsky concludes that it is the most "typical" novel in existence. Narrative voice can work to formally intervene in a story, and for Eichenbaum this process is the central driving force of a novel; in Eastern European literature, the use of narrational "*Skaz*", which effectively is a reproduction of oral speech forms, is one of the main examples explored in detail by Eichenbaum.

Ironically, the Russian Formalists came under attack from their own society: their emphasis upon literariness was at odds with the revolutionary changes—the Russian Revolution of 1917—that eventually transformed the country into the Union of Soviet Socialist Republics, or the USSR. The formation in 1922 of this official Communist state meant that university academics were now supposed to ideologically conform to the Marxist-Leninist viewpoint of the world. The international revolutionary Leon Trotsky (1879–1940) criticized the Formalists in his book *Literature and the Revolution* (1923), and this was followed the next year by a more serious attack by the Soviet Commissar of Education, Anatoly Lunacharsky, who accused the Formalists of being "decadent"[5] and their theories of being the last remaining gasp of the defeated pre-revolutionary Russian bourgeoisie. The Russian intellectual Mikhail Bakhtin (1895–1975), writing under the pseudonym of "P.N. Medvedev", in his book *The Formal Method in Literary Scholarship* (1928), also attacked the Formalists for not attending to the social base from which Marxists believe that literature is derived. To illuminate the seriousness of these criticisms, it is worth noting that Bakhtin, primarily known in the West for his work on carnival and dialogism in literature, was actually at odds with Marxism. He was arrested in 1929 for being a Christian, and sentenced to serve time in a prison camp; his friends arranged for his exile instead, which saved his life.[6] The general response to this sustained, ongoing

Marxist assault upon the Formalists was a transformation in their approach, with special emphasis upon their "scientific" methodology, i.e., their claim of producing neutral, empirical raw literary data, that would then be available for Marxist dialectical processing. Under the direction of Iurii Nikolaevich Tynianov (1894–1943), Formalism turned to concepts of dynamic form and historical evolution, the latter being one of the intellectual preoccupations of Marxism. Tynianov explored this shift in *The Problems of Verse Language* (1924), and with Roman Jakobson, in *Problems in the Study of Literature and Language* (1928).

The shift from Russian Formalism to Structuralism is historically complex, but one key route was via Tynianov's influence on the folklorist Vladimir Propp (1895–1970), a scholar who studied and worked at the University of St. Petersburg. Like the other Formalists, Propp was eventually made to publically recant for his non-Marxist approach to literature,[7] but before he did so he published his highly influential *Morphology of the Folktale* (1928), in which he formulated the concept of the literary "function" through analysis of Russian fairytales. Propp discovered that story and character variations are actually generated by thirty-one underlying structural functions (significant actions performed by characters) which are consistently repeated in identical sequences; these functions are the stable "elements in a tale" regardless of which characters perform them. Propp's *Morphology of the Folktale* was translated into English in 1958, and was reviewed by the French structuralist anthropologist Claude Lévi-Strauss (1908–2009) in his essay "Structure and Form: Reflections on a Work by Vladimir Propp" (1960). The American anthropologist and folklorist Alan Dundes (1934–2005) applied Propp's ideas in *The Morphology of North American Indian Folktales* (1964), and Propp's work also influenced theorists Claude Bremond, A.J. Greimas and Tzvetan Todorov. All of these thinkers applied structuralist methodologies, which is why Propp's work appealed to them. But understanding the relationships between Formalism and Structuralism also involves a return to the founder of the structuralist movement, the linguist Ferdinand de Saussure (1857–1913).

Best known for his assertion that the semiotic sign is arbitrary (meaning is constructed, not intrinsic), Saussure developed this thesis in his wider study of linguistics. Trained at the universities of Geneva, Leipzig and Berlin, Saussure taught at the Ecole Pratique des Hautes Etudes, Paris, and the University of Geneva, where he gave a series of lectures on general linguistics between 1907 and 1911. Student notes from these lectures were collated and posthumously published as the *Course in General Linguistics* (1916, translated into English 1959, with a new English translation in 1983). Saussure proposed a science of signs, called semiotics, in which historical developments were put aside to examine the inner workings of signs themselves; he suggested that signs were composed of sound units (signifiers) and concepts (signifieds), and that the connection between the two was, as mentioned, entirely arbitrary. In this system there is also no intrinsic or natural connection between a sign and an object in the world. Instead of such a connection, Saussure proceeds to identify the structural space of semiotics: the *langue* (language system or framework – its code) versus *parole* (individual speech utterances), as well as the difference between *diachronic* (sequences in time) and *synchronic* (word selection or choices in the present) aspects of expression. The key point is that all signs exist in structured social networks, and that meaning does not transcend these networks; rather, it is generated by them.

The Russian linguist Sergej Karcevskij (1884–1955) attended Saussure's Geneva seminars, and upon his return to Russia in 1917, disseminated these new ideas through the Moscow Linguistic Circle.[8] Jakobson, in particular, discussed Saussure's ideas with the members of the Moscow Linguistic Circle, but he was also influenced by the Polish linguists Baudouin and Kruszewski, as well as the American philosopher Charles Sanders Peirce (1839–1914). Ironically, as the critic John E. Joseph points out, "A history of structuralism written in structuralist terms would relegate authors to the background."[9] While this is an acute observation, following key authors in the development of structuralist thought is nonetheless a useful approach. Jakobson, for example, discussed Saussure's ideas while in New York, in person with Claude Lévi-Strauss, who was also fascinated by the work of Propp. In 1944 Lévi-Strauss delivered a paper on the "structural analysis in linguistics and culture" to the Linguistic Circle of New York, in which he argues that linguistics is a science that should be emulated in the development of anthropology.[10] Lévi-Strauss took his own advice in a series of groundbreaking works of structuralist anthropology, including the *Elementary Structures of Kinship* (1949), *Tristes Tropiques* (1955), and his collected papers, published as *Structural Anthropology* (1958). This innovative structuralist anthropology treated indigenous kinship systems (marital and other family relationships and taboos), as a linguistic system: the anthropologist was in effect now looking for the underlying codes and conventions, in this case the signs or "tokens" (women) which held the system together (through marriage). Lévi-Strauss argued that this structuralist approach could be applied to all aspects of culture and society, and, as with Propp's "morphological" approach, the apparent diversity and differences of all cultures could be reduced to a handful of core or universal attributes, for example, thinking through binary opposites (good/evil, male/female, etc), or "totemism" (relating social and belief structures with the natural world).[11] These underlying attributes and processes are unconscious, so it is not surprising that the subsequent intersection of structuralism and psychoanalysis in French theory would be so productive, especially in its later poststructuralist manifestation (Julia Kristeva, Jacques Lacan, Gilles Deleuze, and so on).

Saussure's notion of a "science of signs" clearly found widespread application in Lévi-Strauss's work, but in terms of literary theory, it is another French thinker—Roland Barthes (1915–80)—who arguably had a greater impact. Barthes' PhD thesis, *The Fashion System* (begun in 1957, published 1967), examined the way in which the socially constructed values of the fashion world, the "vestimentary code", effaces its own artificiality and arbitrariness in a highly successful process of making overconsumption appear natural. Thus, fashion changes appear to "naturally" follow the seasons, or the annual rhythms of the fashion show, which work not so much to introduce new styles, but to make the old ones appear outmoded and ready to be discarded. The result is that consumers buy more clothes than they actually need, and in the process, the vestimentary code which drives the system remains invisible. Barthes is not so far from Lévi-Strauss than at first appears, since he thinks of the fashion system as a large-scale "potlatch", an anthropological term derived from indigenous Native groups around the world, whereby goods and other valuable possessions are deliberately destroyed in a ritualistic way, creating in the process social prestige and title. The notion that sign systems efface their own artificiality, is also applied by Barthes to modern myths (advertising, wrestling, etc.) in *Mythologies* (1957), a highly successful collection of his essays. Barthes was also responsible, however, for a significant shift in literary critical through his application of structuralism in *Writing Degree Zero* (1953), *S/Z* (1970), *The Pleasure of the Text* (1973), and his infamous essay from 1968 called "The Death of the Author". In each of these works, Barthes was developing the structuralist concept of writing known as *écriture*: not a communicative mode, but a counter-cultural, self-reflexive writing that speaks the voice of semiotic textuality (not the author), that is to say, of language itself. The author is no longer a transcendent origin—merely a partner—in the structuring of language. Another key partner is the reader, who not only experiences the text's intensities and pleasures, but creates meaning through interpretation and other emotional and artistic responses.

Julia Kristeva (1941–), who studied with Barthes, further developed and radicalized structuralist insights, forming a bridge with poststructuralism, especially in her early works, later translated into English as *Revolution in Poetic Language* (1974) and *Desire in Language: A Semiotic Approach to Literature and Art* (1980). Other major structuralist practitioners were semiotician A.J. Greimas (1917–92) (Barthes had met him when working in Egypt), who went on to publish *Structural Semantics: An Attempt at a Method* (1966), and *The Social*

Sciences: A Semiotic View (1970), and Michel Foucault (1920–84), who developed an "archaeology" of the human sciences in books such as *Madness and Civilization: A History of Insanity in the Age of Reason* (1971), *The Archaeology of Knowledge* (1972), and *The Order of Things: An Archaeology of the Human Sciences* (1974). Barthes's PhD student, Tzvetan Todorov (1939–), synthesized and further developed Formalist and Structuralist thought, notably in his thesis *Literature et signification* (1967) and *The Fantastic: A Structural Approach to a Literary Genre* (1973). Todorov spent time in the US, and did much work in bridging French and American structuralism. In the realm of structural analysis of narrative, Gérard Genette (1930–) is noted for his narrative and discourse theories, notably *Figures I, II,* and *III* (1966, 1969, and 1972), an unsurpassed reading of Marcel Proust's modernist novel *Remembrance of Things Past*. Many of the major French structuralists would either deny the label (as Foucault did), or expand and radicalize structuralist thought by going in myriad new directions (deconstruction, poststructuralism, feminism, sexualities, and so on). Yet many contemporary theories begin with these thinkers, and they continue to have relevance in the twenty-first century.

Further reading: a selection

The way into theory can initially be quite daunting, especially in the act of going beyond shorter extracts, but there are many excellent introductory texts available aimed at students, such as the books in the Routledge Critical Idiom and Critical Thinkers series. Culler, Eagleton and Hawkes provide accessible, best-selling guides to literary theory, with sections that cover Formalism and Structuralism. Eagleton and Jameson adopt a Marxist perspective, the latter offering a complex but rewarding account of the field. Sturrock divides his book on Structuralism into thematized sections, on language, social sciences, literature, and so on, offering useful focus. Another accessible method is the comparative approach, which Pomorska adopts in her comparison of Formalism and Anglo-American New Criticism. In-depth author studies are valuable, and there are many such books in this list, varying from the highly biographical to some more focused on the history of ideas. Applying theory can help elucidate complex critical concepts, and Lothe and Rimon-Kenan do this with narrative theories, in relation to literature and film. Finally, there is nothing better than reading the primary texts themselves, such as the key Formalist essays provided by Lemon and Reis.

Bradford, Richard. *Roman Jakobson: Life, Language, Art*. London & New York: Routledge, 1995.
Broekman, Jan M. *Structuralism: Moscow-Prague-Paris*. Dordrecht, Holland & Boston, MA: D. Reidel, 1974.
Culler, Jonathan. *Literary Theory: A Very Short Introduction*. Oxford: Oxford University Press, 2000.
Culler, Jonathan. *Barthes: A Very Short Introduction*. Oxford: Oxford University Press, 2002.
Eagleton, Terry. *Literary Theory: An Introduction*. Anniversary Edition. Oxford: Blackwell & Minneapolis: University of Minnesota Press, 2008.
Eribon, Didier. *Michel Foucault*. Trans. Betsy Wing. Cambridge, MA: Harvard University Press, 1991.
Hawkes, Terence. *Structuralism and Semiotics*. London: Methuen, 1986.
Jameson, Fredric. *The Prison-House of Language: A Critical Account of Structuralism and Russian Formalism*. Princeton & London: Princeton University Press, 1972.
Lavers, Annette. *Roland Barthes: Structuralism and After*. Cambridge, MA: Harvard University Press, 1982.
Leach, Edmund. *Claude Lévi-Strauss*. Chicago: University of Chicago Press, 1989.
Lechete, John. *Julia Kristeva*. London & New York: Routledge, 1990.
Lemon, Lee T. and Marion J. Reis, ed. *Russian Formalist Criticism: Four Essays*. Trans. Lee T. Lemon and Marion J. Reis. Lincoln: University of Nebraska Press, 1965.
Lothe, Jakob. *Narrative in Fiction and Film: An Introduction*. Oxford: Oxford University Press, 2000.

Pomorska, Krystyna. *Russian Formalism and Anglo-American New Criticism*. The Hague, Netherlands: Mouton, 1971.

Rimmon-Kenan, Shlomith. *Narrative Fiction: Contemporary Poetics*. London & New York: Methuen, 1983.

Stacy, R.H. *Russian Literary Criticism: A Short History*. Syracuse, NY: Syracuse University Press, 1974.

Sturrock, John. *Structuralism*. Malden, MA & Oxford: Blackwell, 2003.

Warner, Elizabeth A. *Vladimir Propp, 1895–1970: The Study of Russian Folklore and Theory*. Hull: Hull University Press, 1999.

Notes

1   Lee T. Lemon and Marion J. Reis, "Introduction" to *Russian Formalist Criticism: Four Essays*, trans. Lee T. Lemon and Marion J. Reis, Lincoln: University of Nebraska Press, 1965, pp.xi–xiii.

2   Roman Jakobson, *Language in Literature*, ed. Krystyna Pomorska and Stephen Rudy, Cambridge, MA & London: the Belknap Press of Harvard University Press, 1987, p.71.

3   Viktor Shklovsky, "Art as Technique", in *Russian Formalist Criticism: Four Essays*, p.18.

4   Boris Eichenbaum, "The Theory of the 'Formal Method'", in *Russian Formalist Criticism: Four Essays*, p.115.

5   Lee T. Lemon and Marion J. Reis, "Introduction" to "The Theory of the 'Formal Method'" in *Russian Formalist Criticism: Four Essays*, p.100.

6   See Richard J. Lane, *Fifty Key Literary Theorists*, London & New York: Routledge, 2006, pp.9–14.

7   As Andrzej Karcz puts it in the opening to an in-depth study of Polish Formalism: "the Russian school of Formalism was silenced as heresy by Stalinist pressures in the Soviet Union"; see *The Polish Formalist School and Russian Formalism*, Rochester, NY: University of Rochester Press & Kraków, Poland: Jagiellonian University Press, 2002, p.9.

8   John E. Joseph, "The exportation of structuralist ideas from linguistics to other fields: An overview", in Sylvain, Auroux, ed. et. al., *History Of The Language Sciences: An International Handbook On Evolution Of The Study Of Language From The Beginnings To The Present*, volume 2, Berlin: De Gruyter Mouton, 2001, pp.1880–1908; p.1885.

9   John E. Joseph, "The exportation of structuralist ideas from linguistics to other fields: An overview", p.1881.

10   John E. Joseph, "The exportation of structuralist ideas from linguistics to other fields: An overview", p.1890.

11   Gary Ferraro and Susan Andreatta, *Cultural Anthropology: An Applied Perspective*, Belmont, CA: Wadsworth, 2010, p.80.

Chapter 1

Viktor Shklovsky

ART AS TECHNIQUE

Theorists often write most powerfully when reacting to previous critical ideas or methods. Viktor Shklovsky (1893–1984), one of the founders in Moscow (1917) of the Society for the Study of Poetic Language, reacts to the notion that literary language or art is purely metaphorical—or "thinking in images"—as suggested by the Russian philologist Alexander Potebnya (1835–91). While Potebnya did teach the Formalists to look for the distinctive "literariness" of literature, Shklovsky argues that such a metaphorical approach reduces literature to a mechanical process of clarifying "the unknown by means of the known." The outcome is not poetic, it is practical and functional, whereas for Shklovsky, literary language always foregrounds, or makes apparent, its intrinsic strangeness and difficulty. Shklovsky therefore argues that the core literary process is *ostranenie*, variously translated into English as "defamiliarization", "dehabitualization", "making strange", or "bestrangement". Any number of poetic techniques can work to defamiliarize a situation, which means that such a theory of literature is not entirely reductive. However, rather than clarifying or explaining something in real life (the approach of "thinking in images"), regarding literature as defamiliarization enables people to see what had become habitualized and subsequently *invisible* to them. This is where Shklovsky turns to "the general laws of perception" and the argument that over time our perception becomes automatic. When we learn to drive a car, we might be overwhelmed by all the actions and perceptions that we have to be constantly aware of; over time, as these actions and perceptions become second nature, they fade into the background. Shklovsky suggests that such a process is efficient, and when applied to language this efficiency is proven by the fact that we often speak in fragments or incomplete sentences. Habitualization, in other words, creates a linguistic shorthand. But there is a negative side to this efficient process, in that what was once vividly perceived has faded away: "Habitualization devours works, clothes, furniture, one's wife, and the fear of war." Shklovsky's playful sentence makes a serious point: if life becomes entirely automatic, then what is the point in living? Vivid perception is rich, sensual, and energizing, precisely *because* it is also difficult and challenging. Art, for Shklovsky, "exists that one may recover the sensation of life; it exists to make one feel things, to make the stone *stoney*." Imagine reading a difficult poem for the first time: the language is unfamiliar, the forms are difficult, and one has to spend an inordinate length of time re-reading the poem to make any sense of it. Yet in that process, the aesthetic richness of the language emerges.

As Shklovsky says: "*Art is a way of experiencing the artfulness of an object; the object is not important.*" What he means is that rushing through the poem to the end to try and "get it" misses the point: the meaning is embedded in, and generated by, the friction that the poem creates. One example of this friction is when a writer describes an object or event as if seen for the first time helping us to see what has become habitual through "fresh eyes", whereby life itself is enriched.

"**ART IS THINKING IN IMAGES.**" This maxim, which even high school students parrot, is nevertheless the starting point for the erudite philologist who is beginning to put together some kind of systematic literary theory. The idea, originated in part by Potebnya, has spread. "Without imagery there is no art, and in particular no poetry," Potebnya writes.[1] And elsewhere, "Poetry, as well as prose, is first and foremost a special way of thinking and knowing."[2]

Poetry is a special way of thinking; it is, precisely, a way of thinking in images, a way which permits what is generally called "economy of mental effort," a way which makes for "a sensation of the relative ease of the process." Aesthetic feeling is the reaction to this economy. This is how the academician Ovsyaniko-Kulikovsky,[3] who undoubtedly read the works of Potebnya attentively, almost certainly understood and faithfully summarized the ideas of his teacher. Potebnya and his numerous disciples consider poetry a special kind of thinking—thinking by means of images; they feel that the purpose of imagery is to help channel various objects and activities into groups and to clarify the unknown by means of the known. Or, as Potebnya wrote:

> The relationship of the image to what is being clarified is that: (a) the image is the fixed predicate of that which undergoes change—the unchanging means of attracting what is perceived as changeable. . . . (b) the image is far clearer and simpler than what it clarifies.[4]

In other words:

> Since the purpose of imagery is to remind us, by approximation, of those meanings for which the image stands, and since, apart from this, imagery is unnecessary for thought, we must be more familiar with the image than with what it clarifies.[5]

It would be instructive to try to apply this principle to Tyutchev's comparison of summer lightning to deaf and dumb demons or to Gogol's comparison of the sky to the garment of God.[6]

"Without imagery there is no art"—"Art is thinking in images." These maxims have led to far-fetched interpretations of individual works of art. Attempts have been made to evaluate even music, architecture, and lyric poetry as imagistic thought. After a quarter of a century of such attempts Ovsyaniko-Kulikovsky finally had to assign lyric poetry, architecture, and music to a special category of imageless art and to define them as lyric arts appealing directly to the emotions. And thus he admitted an enormous area of art which is not a mode of thought. A part of this area, lyric poetry (narrowly considered), is quite like the visual arts; it is also verbal. But, much more important, visual art passes quite imperceptibly into nonvisual art; yet our perceptions of both are similar.

Nevertheless, the definition "Art is thinking in images," which means (I omit the usual middle terms of the argument) that art is the making of symbols, has survived the downfall of the theory which supported it. It survives chiefly in the wake of Symbolism, especially among the theorists of the Symbolist movement.

Many still believe, then, that thinking in images—thinking in specific scenes of "roads and landscape" and "furrows and boundaries"[7]—is the chief characteristic of poetry. Consequently, they should have expected the history of "imagistic art," as they call it, to consist of a history of changes in imagery. But we find that images change little; from century to century, from nation to nation, from poet to poet, they flow on without changing. Images belong to no one: they are "the Lord's." The more you understand an age, the more convinced you become that the images a given poet used and which you thought his own were taken almost unchanged from another poet. The works of poets are classified or grouped according to the new techniques that poets discover and share, and according to their arrangement and development of the resources of language; poets are much more concerned with arranging images than with creating them. Images are given to poets; the ability to remember them is far more important than the ability to create them.

Imagistic thought does not, in any case, include all the aspects of art nor even all the aspects of verbal art. A change in imagery is not essential to the development of poetry. We know that frequently an expression is thought to be poetic, to be created for aesthetic pleasure, although actually it was created without such intent—e.g., Annensky's opinion that the Slavic languages are especially poetic and Andrey Bely's ecstasy over the technique of placing adjectives after nouns, a technique used by eighteenth-century Russian poets. Bely joyfully accepts the technique as something artistic, or more exactly, as intended, if we consider intention as art. Actually, this reversal of the usual adjective-noun order is a peculiarity of the language (which had been influenced by Church Slavonic). Thus a work may be (1) intended as prosaic and accepted as poetic, or (2) intended as poetic and accepted as prosaic. This suggests that the artistry attributed to a given work results from the way we perceive it. By "works of art," in the narrow sense, we mean works created by special techniques designed to make the works as obviously artistic as possible.

Potebnya's conclusion, which can be formulated "poetry equals imagery," gave rise to the whole theory that "imagery equals symbolism," that the image may serve as the invariable predicate of various subjects. (This conclusion, because it expressed ideas similar to the theories of the Symbolists, intrigued some of their leading representatives—Andrey Bely, Merezhkovsky and his "eternal companions" and, in fact, formed the basis of the theory of Symbolism.) The conclusion stems partly from the fact that Potebnya did not distinguish between the language of poetry and the language of prose. Consequently, he ignored the fact that there are two aspects of imagery: imagery as a practical means of thinking, as a means of placing objects within categories; and imagery as poetic, as a means of reinforcing an impression. I shall clarify with an example. I want to attract the attention of a young child who is eating bread and butter and getting the butter on her fingers. I call, "Hey, butterfingers!" This is a figure of speech, a clearly prosaic trope. Now a different example. The child is playing with my glasses and drops them. I call, "Hey, butterfingers!"[8] This figure of speech is a poetic trope. (In the first example, "butterfingers" is metonymic; in the second, metaphoric—but this is not what I want to stress.)

Poetic imagery is a means of creating the strongest possible impression. As a method it is, depending upon its purpose, neither more nor less effective than other poetic techniques; it is neither more nor less effective than ordinary or negative parallelism, comparison, repetition, balanced structure, hyperbole, the commonly accepted rhetorical figures, and all those methods which emphasize the emotional effect of an expression (including words or even articulated sounds).[9] But poetic imagery only externally resembles either the stock imagery of fables and ballads or thinking in images—e.g., the example in Ovsyaniko-Kulikovsky's *Language and Art* in which a little girl calls a ball a little watermelon. Poetic imagery is but one of the devices of poetic language. Prose imagery is a means of abstraction: a little watermelon instead of a lampshade, or a little watermelon instead of a head, is only the abstraction of one of the object's characteristics, that of roundness. It is no different from saying that the head and the melon are both round. This is what is meant, but it has nothing to do with poetry.

The law of the economy of creative effort is also generally accepted. [Herbert] Spencer wrote:

> On seeking for some clue to the law underlying these current maxims, we may see shadowed forth in many of them, the importance of economizing the reader's or the hearer's attention. To so present ideas that they may be apprehended with the least possible mental effort, is the desideratum towards which most of the rules above quoted point. . . . Hence, carrying out the metaphor that language is the vehicle of thought, there seems reason to think that in all cases the friction and inertia of the vehicle deduct from its efficiency; and that in composition, the chief, if not the sole thing to be done, is to reduce this friction and inertia to the smallest possible amount.[10]

And R[ichard] Avenarius:

> If a soul possess inexhaustible strength, then, of course, it would be indifferent to how much might be spent from this inexhaustible source; only the necessarily expended time would be important. But since its forces are limited, one is led to expect that the soul hastens to carry out the apperceptive process as expediently as possible—that is, with comparatively the least expenditure of energy, and, hence, with comparatively the best result.

Petrazhitsky, with only one reference to the general law of mental effort, rejects [William] James's theory of the physical basis of emotion, a theory which contradicts his own. Even Alexander Veselovsky acknowledged the principle of the economy of creative effort, a theory especially appealing in the study of rhythm, and agreed with Spencer: "A satisfactory style is precisely that style which delivers the greatest amount of thought in the fewest words." And Andrey Bely, despite the fact that in his better pages he gave numerous examples of "roughened" rhythm[11] and (particularly in the examples from Baratynsky) showed the difficulties inherent in poetic epithets, also thought it necessary to speak of the law of the economy of creative effort in his book[12]—a heroic effort to create a theory of art based on unverified facts from antiquated sources, on his vast knowledge of the techniques of poetic creativity, and on Krayevich's high school physics text.

These ideas about the economy of energy, as well as about the law and aim of creativity, are perhaps true in their application to "practical" language; they were, however, extended to poetic language. Hence they do not distinguish properly between the laws of practical language and the laws of poetic language. The fact that Japanese poetry has sounds not found in conversational Japanese was hardly the first factual indication of the differences between poetic and everyday language. Leo Jakubinsky has observed that the law of the dissimilation of liquid sounds does not apply to poetic language.[13] This suggested to him that poetic language tolerated the admission of hard-to-pronounce conglomerations of similar sounds. In his article, one of the first examples of scientific criticism, he indicates inductively the contrast (I shall say more about this point later) between the laws of poetic language and the laws of practical language.[14]

We must, then, speak about the laws of expenditure and economy in poetic language not on the basis of an analogy with prose, but on the basis of the laws of poetic language.

If we start to examine the general laws of perception, we see that as perception becomes habitual, it becomes automatic. Thus, for example, all of our habits retreat into the area of the unconsciously automatic; if one remembers the sensations of holding a pen or of speaking in a foreign language for the first time and compares that with his feeling at performing the action for the ten thousandth time, he will agree with us. Such habituation explains the principles by which, in ordinary speech, we leave phrases unfinished and words half expressed. In this process, ideally realized in algebra, things are replaced by symbols. Complete words are not expressed in rapid speech; their initial sounds are barely perceived. Alexander Pogodin offers the example of a boy considering the sentence "The Swiss mountains are beautiful" in the form of a series of letters: *T, S, m, a, b.*[15]

This characteristic of thought not only suggests the method of algebra, but even prompts the choice of symbols (letters, especially initial letters). By this "algebraic" method of thought we apprehend objects only as shapes with imprecise extensions; we do not see them in their entirety but rather recognize them by their main characteristics. We see the object as though it were enveloped in a sack. We know what it is by its configuration, but we see only its silhouette. The object, perceived thus in the manner of prose perception, fades and does not leave even a first impression; ultimately even the essence of what it was is forgotten. Such perception explains why we fail to hear the prose word in its entirety (see Leo Jakubinsky's article[16]) and, hence, why (along with other slips of the tongue) we fail to pronounce it. The process of "algebrization," the over-automatization of an object, permits the greatest economy of perceptive effort. Either objects are assigned only one proper feature—a number, for example—or else they function as though by formula and do not even appear in cognition:

> I was cleaning a room and, meandering about, approached the divan and couldn't remember whether or not I had dusted it. Since these movements are habitual and unconscious, I could not remember and felt that it was impossible to remember—so that if I had dusted it and forgot—that is, had acted unconsciously, then it was the same as if I had not. If some conscious person had been watching, then the fact could be established. If, however, no one was looking, or looking on unconsciously, if the whole complex lives of many people go on unconsciously, then such lives are as if they had never been.[17]

And so life is reckoned as nothing. Habitualization devours works, clothes, furniture, one's wife, and the fear of war. "If the whole complex lives of many people go on unconsciously, then such lives are as if they had never been." And art exists that one may recover the sensation of life; it exists to make one feel things, to make the stone *stony*. The purpose of art is to impart the sensation of things as they are perceived and not as they are known. The technique of art is to make objects "unfamiliar," to make forms difficult, to increase the difficulty and length of perception because the process of perception is an aesthetic end in itself and must be prolonged. *Art is a way of experiencing the artfulness of an object; the object is not important.*

The range of poetic (artistic) work extends from the sensory to the cognitive, from poetry to prose, from the concrete to the abstract: from Cervantes' Don Quixote—scholastic and poor nobleman, half consciously bearing his humiliation in the court of the duke—to the broad but empty Don Quixote of Turgenev; from Charlemagne to the name "king" [in Russian "Charles" and "king" obviously derive from the same root, *korol*]. The meaning of a work broadens to the extent that artfulness and artistry diminish; thus a fable symbolizes more than a poem, and a proverb more than a fable. Consequently, the least self-contradictory part of Potebnya's theory is his treatment of the fable, which, from his point of view, he investigated thoroughly. But since his theory did not provide for "expressive" works of art, he could not finish his book. As we know, *Notes on the Theory of Literature* was published in

1905, thirteen years after Potebnya's death. Potebnya himself completed only the section on the fable.[18]

After we see an object several times, we begin to recognize it. The object is in front of us and we know about it, but we do not see it[19]—hence we cannot say anything significant about it. Art removes objects from the automatism of perception in several ways. Here I want to illustrate a way used repeatedly by Leo Tolstoy, that writer who, for Merezhkovsky at least, seems to present things as if he himself saw them, saw them in their entirety, and did not alter them.

Tolstoy makes the familiar seem strange by not naming the familiar object. He describes an object as if he were seeing it for the first time, an event as if it were happening for the first time. In describing something he avoids the accepted names of its parts and instead names corresponding parts of other objects. For example, in "Shame" Tolstoy "defamiliarizes" the idea of flogging in this way: "to strip people who have broken the law, to hurl them to the floor, and to rap on their bottoms with switches," and, after a few lines, "to lash about on the naked buttocks." Then he remarks:

> Just why precisely this stupid, savage means of causing pain and not any other—why not prick the shoulders or any part of the body with needles, squeeze the hands or the feet in a vise, or anything like that?

I apologize for this harsh example, but it is typical of Tolstoy's way of pricking the conscience. The familiar act of flogging is made unfamiliar both by the description and by the proposal to change its form without changing its nature. Tolstoy uses this technique of "defamiliarization" constantly. The narrator of "Kholstomer," for example, is a horse, and it is the horse's point of view (rather than a person's) that makes the content of the story seem unfamiliar. Here is how the horse regards the institution of private property:

> I understood well what they said about whipping and Christianity. But then I was absolutely in the dark. What's the meaning of "his own," "his colt"? From these phrases I saw that people thought there was some sort of connection between me and the stable. At the time I simply could not understand the connection. Only much later, when they separated me from the other horses, did I begin to understand. But even then I simply could not see what it meant when they called me "man's property." The words "my horse" referred to me, a living horse, and seemed as strange to me as the words "my land," "my air," "my water."
>
> But the words made a strong impression on me. I thought about them constantly, and only after the most diverse experiences with people did I understand, finally, what they meant. They meant this: In life people are guided by words, not by deeds. It's not so much that they love the possibility of doing or not doing something as it is the possibility of speaking with words, agreed on among themselves, about various topics. Such are the words "my" and "mine," which they apply to different things, creatures, objects, and even to land, people, and horses. They agree that only one may say "mine" about this, that, or the other thing. And the one who says "mine" about the greatest number of things is, according to the game which they've agreed to among themselves, the one they consider the most happy. I don't know the point of all this, but it's true. For a long time I tried to explain it to myself in terms of some kind of real gain, but I had to reject that explanation because it was wrong.
>
> Many of those, for instance, who called me their own never rode on me—although others did. And so with those who fed me. Then again, the

coachman, the veterinarians, and the outsiders in general treated me kindly, yet those who called me their own did not. In due time, having widened the scope of my observations, I satisfied myself that the notion "my," not only in relation to us horses, has no other basis than a narrow human instinct which is called a sense of or right to private property. A man says "this house is mine" and never lives in it; he only worries about its construction and upkeep. A merchant says "my shop," "my dry goods shop," for instance, and does not even wear clothes made from the better cloth he keeps in his own shop.

There are people who call a tract of land their own, but they never set eyes on it and never take a stroll on it. There are people who call others their own, yet never see them. And the whole relationship between them is that the so-called "owners" treat the others unjustly.

There are people who call women their own, or their "wives," but their women live with other men. And people strive not for the good in life, but for goods they can call their own.

I am now convinced that this is the essential difference between people and ourselves. And therefore, not even considering the other ways in which we are superior, but considering just this one virtue, we can bravely claim to stand higher than men on the ladder of living creatures. The actions of men, at least those with whom I have had dealings, are guided by *words*—ours, by deeds.

The horse is killed before the end of the story, but the manner of the narrative, its technique, does not change:

Much later they put Serpukhovsky's body, which had experienced the world, which had eaten and drunk, into the ground. They could profitably send neither his hide, nor his flesh, nor his bones anywhere.

But since his dead body, which had gone about in the world for twenty years, was a great burden to everyone, its burial was only a superfluous embarrassment for the people. For a long time no one had needed him; for a long time he had been a burden on all. But nevertheless, the dead who buried the dead found it necessary to dress this bloated body, which immediately began to rot, in a good uniform and good boots; to lay it in a good new coffin with new tassels at the four corners, then to place this new coffin in another of lead and ship it to Moscow; there to exhume ancient bones and at just that spot, to hide this putrefying body, swarming with maggots, in its new uniform and clean boots, and to cover it over completely with dirt.

Thus we see that at the end of the story Tolstoy continues to use the technique even though the motivation for it [the reason for its use] is gone.[20]

In *War and Peace* Tolstoy uses the same technique in describing whole battles as if battles were something new. These descriptions are too long to quote; it would be necessary to extract a considerable part of the four-volume novel. But Tolstoy uses the same method in describing the drawing room and the theater:

The middle of the stage consisted of flat boards; by the sides stood painted pictures representing trees, and at the back a linen cloth was stretched down to the floor boards. Maidens in red bodices and white skirts sat on the middle of the stage. One, very fat, in a white silk dress, sat apart on a narrow bench to which a green pasteboard box was glued from behind. They were all singing something.

When they had finished, the maiden in white approached the prompter's box. A man in silk with tight-fitting pants on his fat legs approached her with a plume and began to sing and spread his arms in dismay. The man in the tight pants finished his song alone; then the girl sang. After that both remained silent as the music resounded; and the man, obviously waiting to begin singing his part with her again, began to run his fingers over the hand of the girl in the white dress. They finished their song together, and everyone in the theater began to clap and shout. But the men and women on stage, who represented lovers, started to bow, smiling and raising their hands.

In the second act there were pictures representing monuments and openings in the linen cloth representing the moonlight, and they raised lamp shades on a frame. As the musicians started to play the bass horn and counter-bass, a large number of people in black mantles poured onto the stage from right and left. The people, with something like daggers in their hands, started to wave their arms. Then still more people came running out and began to drag away the maiden who had been wearing a white dress but who now wore one of sky blue. They did not drag her off immediately, but sang with her for a long time before dragging her away. Three times they struck on something metallic behind the side scenes, and everyone got down on his knees and began to chant a prayer. Several times all of this activity was interrupted by enthusiastic shouts from the spectators.

The third act is described:

> . . . But suddenly a storm blew up. Chromatic scales and chords of diminished sevenths were heard in the orchestra. Everyone ran about and again they dragged one of the bystanders behind the scenes as the curtain fell.

In the fourth act, "There was some sort of devil who sang, waving his hands, until the boards were moved out from under him and he dropped down."[21]

In *Resurrection* Tolstoy describes the city and the court in the same way; he uses a similar technique in "Kreutzer Sonata" when he describes marriage—"Why, if people have an affinity of souls, must they sleep together?" But he did not defamiliarize only those things he sneered at:

> Pierre stood up from his new comrades and made his way between the campfires to the other side of the road where, it seemed, the captive soldiers were held. He wanted to talk with them. The French sentry stopped him on the road and ordered him to return. Pierre did so, but not to the campfire, not to his comrades, but to an abandoned, unharnessed carriage. On the ground, near the wheel of the carriage, he sat cross-legged in the Turkish fashion, and lowered his head. He sat motionless for a long time, thinking. More than an hour passed. No one disturbed him. Suddenly he burst out laughing with his robust, good natured laugh—so loudly that the men near him looked around, surprised at his conspicuously strange laughter.
>
> "Ha, ha, ha," laughed Pierre. And he began to talk to himself. "The soldier didn't allow me to pass. They caught me, barred me. Me—me—my immortal soul. Ha, ha, ha," he laughed with tears starting in his eyes.
>
> Pierre glanced at the sky, into the depths of the departing, playing stars. "And all this is mine, all this is in me, and all this is I," thought Pierre. "And all

this they caught and put in a planked enclosure." He smiled and went off to his comrades to lie down to sleep.[22]

Anyone who knows Tolstoy can find several hundred such passages in his work. His method of seeing things out of their normal context is also apparent in his last works. Tolstoy described the dogmas and rituals he attacked as if they were unfamiliar, substituting everyday meanings for the customarily religious meanings of the words common in church ritual. Many persons were painfully wounded; they considered it blasphemy to present as strange and monstrous what they accepted as sacred. Their reaction was due chiefly to the technique through which Tolstoy perceived and reported his environment. And after turning to what he had long avoided, Tolstoy found that his perceptions had unsettled his faith.

The technique of defamiliarization is not Tolstoy's alone. I cited Tolstoy because his work is generally known.

Now, having explained the nature of this technique, let us try to determine the approximate limits of its application. I personally feel that defamiliarization is found almost everywhere form is found. In other words, the difference between Potebnya's point of view and ours is this: An image is not a permanent referent for those mutable complexities of life which are revealed through it; its purpose is not to make us perceive meaning, but to create a special perception of the object—*it creates a "vision" of the object instead of serving as a means for knowing it.*

The purpose of imagery in erotic art can be studied even more accurately; an erotic object is usually presented as if it were seen for the first time. Gogol, in "Christmas Eve," provides the following example:

> Here he approached her more closely, coughed, smiled at her, touched her plump, bare arm with his fingers, and expressed himself in a way that showed both his cunning and his conceit.
>
> "And what is this you have, magnificent Solokha?" and having said this, he jumped back a little.
>
> "What? An arm, Osip Nikiforovich!" she answered. "Hmm, an arm! *He, he, he!*" said the secretary cordially, satisfied with his beginning. He wandered about the room.
>
> "And what is this you have, dearest Solokha?" he said in the same way, having approached her again and grasped her lightly by the neck, and in the very same way he jumped back.
>
> "As if you don't see, Osip Nikiforovich!" answered Solokha, "a neck, and on my neck a necklace."
>
> "Hmm! On the neck a necklace! *He, he, he!*" and the secretary again wandered about the room, rubbing his hands.
>
> "And what is this you have, incomparable Solokha?" . . . It is not known to what the secretary would stretch his long fingers now.

And Knut Hamsun has the following in "Hunger": "Two white prodigies appeared from beneath her blouse."

Erotic subjects may also be presented figuratively with the obvious purpose of leading us away from their "recognition." Hence sexual organs are referred to in terms of lock and key,[23] or quilting tools,[24] or bow and arrow, or rings and marlinspikes, as in the legend of Stavyor, in which a married man does not recognize his wife, who is disguised as a warrior. She proposes a riddle:

"Remember, Stavyor, do you recall
How we little ones walked to and fro in the street?
You and I together sometimes played with a marlinspike—
You had a silver marlinspike,
But I had a gilded ring?
I found myself at it just now and then,
But you fell in with it ever and always."
Says Stavyor, son of Godinovich,
"What! I didn't play with you at marlinspikes!"
Then Vasilisa Mikulichna: "So he says.
Do you remember, Stavyor, do you recall,
Now must you know, you and I together learned to read and write;
Mine was an ink-well of silver,
And yours a pen of gold?
But I just moistened it a little now and then,
And I just moistened it ever and always."[25]

In a different version of the legend we find a key to the riddle:

Here the formidable envoy Vasilyushka
Raised her skirts to the very navel,
And then the young Stavyor, son of Godinovich,
Recognized her gilded ring. . . . [26]

But defamiliarization is not only a technique of the erotic riddle—a technique of euphemism—it is also the basis and point of all riddles. Every riddle pretends to show its subject either by words which specify or describe it but which, during the telling, do not seem applicable (the type: "black and white and 'red'—read—all over") or by means of odd but imitative sounds ("'Twas brillig, and the slithy toves/Did gyre and gimble in the wabe").[27]

Even erotic images not intended as riddles are defamiliarized ("boobies," "tarts," "piece," etc.). In popular imagery there is generally something equivalent to "trampling the grass" and "breaking the guelder-rose." The technique of defamiliarization is absolutely clear in the widespread image—a motif of erotic affectation—in which a bear and other wild beasts (or a devil, with a different reason for nonrecognition) do not recognize a man.[28]

The lack of recognition in the following tale is quite typical:

A peasant was plowing a field with a piebald mare. A bear approached him and asked, "Uncle, what's made this mare piebald for you?"

"I did the piebalding myself."

"But how?"

"Let me, and I'll do the same for you."

The bear agreed. The peasant tied his feet together with a rope, took the ploughshare from the two-wheeled plough, heated it on the fire, and applied it to his flanks. He made the bear piebald by scorching his fur down to the hide with the hot ploughshare. The man untied the bear, which went off and lay down under a tree.

A magpie flew at the peasant to pick at the meat on his shirt. He caught her and broke one of her legs. The magpie flew off to perch in the same tree under which the bear was lying. Then, after the magpie, a horsefly landed on the mare, sat down, and began to bite. The peasant caught the fly, took a stick, shoved it up its rear, and let it go. The fly went to the tree where the bear and the magpie were. There all three sat.

The peasant's wife came to bring his dinner to the field. The man and his wife finished their dinner in the fresh air, and he began to wrestle with her on the ground.

The bear saw this and said to the magpie and the fly, "Holy priests! The peasant wants to piebald someone again."

The magpie said, "No, he wants to break someone's legs."

The fly said, "No, he wants to shove a stick up someone's rump."[29]

The similarity of technique here and in Tolstoy's "Kholstomer," is, I think, obvious.

Quite often in literature the sexual act itself is defamiliarized; for example, the *Decameron* refers to "scraping out a barrel," "catching nightingales," "gay wool-beating work" (the last is not developed in the plot). Defamiliarization is often used in describing the sexual organs.

A whole series of plots is based on such a lack of recognition; for example, in Afanasyev's *Intimate Tales* the entire story of "The Shy Mistress" is based on the fact that an object is not called by its proper name—or, in other words, on a game of nonrecognition. So too in Onchukov's "Spotted Petticoats," tale no. 525, and also in "The Bear and the Hare" from *Intimate Tales,* in which the bear and the hare make a "wound."

Such constructions as "the pestle and the mortar," or "Old Nick and the infernal regions" (*Decameron*), are also examples of the technique of defamiliarization. And in my article on plot construction I write about defamiliarization in psychological parallelism. Here, then, I repeat that the perception of disharmony in a harmonious context is important in parallelism. The purpose of parallelism, like the general purpose of imagery, is to transfer the usual perception of an object into the sphere of a new perception—that is, to make a unique semantic modification.

In studying poetic speech in its phonetic and lexical structure as well as in its characteristic distribution of words and in the characteristic thought structures compounded from the words, we find everywhere the artistic trademark—that is, we find material obviously created to remove the automatism of perception; the author's purpose is to create the vision which results from that deautomatized perception. A work is created "artistically" so that its perception is impeded and the greatest possible effect is produced through the slowness of the perception. As a result of this lingering, the object is perceived not in its extension in space, but, so to speak, in its continuity. Thus "poetic language" gives satisfaction. According to Aristotle, poetic language must appear strange and wonderful; and, in fact, it is often actually foreign: the Sumerian used by the Assyrians, the Latin of Europe during the Middle Ages, the Arabisms of the Persians, the Old Bulgarian of Russian literature, or the elevated, almost literary language of folk songs. The common archaisms of poetic language, the intricacy of the sweet new style [*dolce stil nuovo*],[30] the obscure style of the language of Arnaut Daniel with the "roughened" [*harte*] forms *which make pronunciation difficult*—these are used in much the same way. Leo Jakubinsky has demonstrated the principle of phonetic "roughening" of poetic language in the particular case of the repetition of identical sounds. The language of poetry is, then, a difficult, roughened, impeded language. In a few special instances the language of poetry approximates the language of prose, but this does not violate the principle of "roughened" form.

> Her sister was called Tatyana.
> For the first time we shall
> Wilfully brighten the delicate
> Pages of a novel with such a name.

wrote Pushkin. The usual poetic language for Pushkin's contemporaries was the elegant style of Derzhavin; but Pushkin's style, because it seemed trivial then, was unexpectedly difficult for them. We should remember the consternation of Pushkin's contemporaries over the vulgarity of his expressions. He used the popular language as a special device for prolonging attention, just as his contemporaries generally used Russian words in their usually French speech (see Tolstoy's examples in *War and Peace*).

Just now a still more characteristic phenomenon is under way. Russian literary language, which was originally foreign to Russia, has so permeated the language of the people that it has blended with their conversation. On the other hand, literature has now begun to show a tendency towards the use of dialects (Remizov, Klyuyev, Essenin, and others,[31] so unequal in talent and so alike in language, are intentionally provincial) and of barbarisms (which gave rise to the Severyanin group[32]). And currently Maxim Gorky is changing his diction from the old literary language to the new literary colloquialism of Leskov.[33] Ordinary speech and literary language have thereby changed places (see the work of Vyacheslav Ivanov and many others). And finally, a strong tendency, led by Khlebnikov, to create a new and properly poetic language has emerged. In the light of these developments we can define poetry as *attenuated, tortuous* speech. Poetic speech is *formed speech*. Prose is ordinary speech—economical, easy, proper, the goddess of prose [*dea prosae*] is a goddess of the accurate, facile type, of the "direct" expression of a child. I shall discuss roughened form and retardation as the general *law* of art at greater length in an article on plot construction.[34]

Nevertheless, the position of those who urge the idea of the economy of artistic energy as something which exists in and even distinguishes poetic language seems, at first glance, tenable for the problem of rhythm. Spencer's description of rhythm would seem to be absolutely incontestable:

> Just as the body in receiving a series of varying concussions, must keep the muscles ready to meet the most violent of them, as not knowing when such may come: so, the mind in receiving unarranged articulations, must keep its perspectives active enough to recognize the least easily caught sounds. And as, if the concussions recur in definite order, the body may husband its forces by adjusting the resistance needful for each concussion; so, if the syllables be rhythmically arranged, the mind may economize its energies by anticipating the attention required for each syllable.[35]

This apparently conclusive observation suffers from the common fallacy, the confusion of the laws of poetic and prosaic language. In *The Philosophy of Style* Spencer failed utterly to distinguish between them. But rhythm may have two functions. The rhythm of prose, or of a work song like "Dubinushka," permits the members of the work crew to do their necessary "groaning together" and also eases the work by making it automatic. And, in fact, it is easier to march with music than without it, and to march during an animated conversation is even easier, for the walking is done unconsciously. Thus the rhythm of prose is an important automatizing element; the rhythm of poetry is not. There is "order" in art, yet not a single column of a Greek temple stands exactly in its proper order; poetic rhythm is similarly disordered rhythm. Attempts to systematize the irregularities have been made, and such attempts are part of the current problem in the theory of rhythm. It is obvious that the systematization will not work, for in reality the problem is not one of complicating the rhythm but of disordering the rhythm—a disordering which cannot be predicted. Should the disordering of rhythm become a convention, it would be ineffective as a device for the roughening of language. But I will not discuss rhythm in more detail since I intend to write a book about it.[36]

Notes

1   Alexander Potebnya, *Iz zapisok po teorii slovesnosti* [*Notes on the Theory of Language*] (Kharkov, 1905), p. 83.

2   *Ibid.*, p. 97.

3   Dmitry Ovsyaniko-Kulikovsky (1835–1920), a leading Russian scholar, was an early contributor to Marxist periodicals and a literary conservative, antagonistic towards the deliberately meaningless poems of the Futurists. *Ed. note.*

4   Potebnya, *Iz zapisok po teorii slovesnosti,* p. 314.

5   *Ibid.*, p. 291.

6   Fyodor Tyutchev (1803–73), a poet, and Nicholas Gogol (1809–52), a master of prose fiction and satire, are mentioned here because their bold use of imagery cannot be accounted for by Potebnya's theory. Shklovsky is arguing that writers frequently gain their effects by comparing the commonplace to the exceptional rather than vice versa. *Ed. note.*

7   This is an allusion to Vyacheslav Ivanov's *Borozdy i mezhi* [*Furrows and Boundaries*] (Moscow, 1916), a major statement of Symbolist theory. *Ed. note.*

8   The Russian text involves a play on the word for "hat," colloquial for "clod," "duffer," etc. *Ed. note.*

9   Shklovsky is here doing two things of major theoretical importance: (1) he argues that different techniques serve a single function, and that (2) no single technique is all-important. The second permits the Formalists to be concerned with any and all literary devices; the first permits them to discuss the devices from a single consistent theoretical position. *Ed. note.*

10   Herbert Spencer, *The Philosophy of Style* [(Humboldt Library, Vol. XXXIV; New York, 1882), pp. 2–3. Shklovsky's quoted reference, in Russian, preserves the idea of the original but shortens it].

11   The Russian *zatrudyonny* means "made difficult." The suggestion is that poems with "easy" or smooth rhythms slip by unnoticed; poems that are difficult or "roughened" force the reader to attend to them. *Ed. note.*

12   *Simvolizm,* probably. *Ed. note.*

13   Leo Jakubinsky, "O zvukakh poeticheskovo yazyka" ["On the Sounds of Poetic Language"], *Sborniki,* I (1916), p. 38.

14   Leo Jakubinsky, "Skopleniye odinakovykh plavnykh v prakticheskom i poeticheskom yazykakh" ["The Accumulation of Identical Liquids in Practical and Poetic Language"], *Sborniki,* II (1917), pp. 13–21.

15   Alexander Pogodin, *Yazyk, kak tvorchestvo* [*Language as Art*] (Kharkov, 1913), p. 42. [The original sentence was in French, *"Les montaignes de la Suisse sont belles,"* with the appropriate initials.]

16   Jakubinsky, *Sborniki,* I (1916).

17   Leo Tolstoy's *Diary,* entry dated February 29, 1897. [The date is transcribed incorrectly; it should read March 1, 1897.]

18   Alexander Potebnya, *Iz lektsy po teorii slovesnosti* [*Lectures on the Theory of Language*] (Kharkov, 1914).

19   Victor Shklovsky, *Voskresheniye slova* [*The Resurrection of the Word*] (Petersburg, 1914).

20   See below, pp. 85–86, for a discussion of the motivational aspects of defamiliarization. *Ed. note.*

21   The Tolstoy and Gogol translations are ours. The passage occurs in Vol. II, Part 8, Chap. 9 of the edition of *War and Peace* published in Boston by the Dana Estes Co. in 1904–12. *Ed. note.*

22   Leo Tolstoy, *War and Peace,* IV, Part 13. Chap. 14. *Ed. note.*

23   [Dimitry] Savodnikov, *Zagadki russkovo naroda* [*Riddles of the Russian People*] (St. Petersburg, 1901), Nos. 102–7.

24   *Ibid.*, Nos. 588–91.

25   A. E. Gruzinsky, ed., *Pesni, sobrannye P[avel] N. Rybnikovym* [*Songs Collected by P. N. Rybnikov*] (Moscow, 1909–10), No. 30.

26   *Ibid.*, No. 171.

27   We have supplied familiar English examples in place of Shklovsky's wordplay. Shklovsky is saying that we create words with no referents or with ambiguous referents in order to force attention to the objects represented by the similar-sounding words. By making the reader go through the extra step of interpreting the nonsense word, the writer prevents an automatic response. A toad is a toad, but "tove" forces one to pause and think about the beast. *Ed. note.*

28   E. R. Romanov, "Besstrashny barin," *Velikorusskiye skazki* (Zapiski Imperskovo Russkovo Geograficheskovo Obschestva, XLII, No. 52). Belorussky sbornik, "Spravyadlivy soldat" ["The Intrepid Gentleman," *Great Russian Tales* (Notes of the Imperial Russian Geographical Society, XLII, No. 52). White Russian Anthology, "The Upright Soldier" (1886–1912)].

29   D[mitry] S. Zelenin, *Velikorusskiye skazki Permskoy gubernii* [*Great Russian Tales of the Permian Province* (St. Petersburg, 1913)], No. 70.

30   Dante, *Purgatorio,* 24:56. Dante refers to the new lyric style of his contemporaries. *Ed. note.*

31   Alexy Remizov (1877–1957) is best known as a novelist and satirist; Nicholas Klyuyev (1885–1937) and Sergey Essenin (1895–1925) were "peasant poets." All three were noted for their faithful reproduction of Russian dialects and colloquial language. *Ed. note.*

32   A group noted for its opulent and sensuous verse style. *Ed. note.*

33   Nicholas Leskov (1831–95), novelist and short story writer, helped popularize the *skaz,* or yarn, and hence, because of the part dialect peculiarities play in the *skaz,* also altered Russian literary language. *Ed. note.*

34   Shklovsky is probably referring to his *Razvyortyvaniye syuzheta* [*Plot Development*] (Petrograd, 1921). *Ed. note.* Victor Shklovsky, "Iskusstvo, kak priyom," *Sborniici,* II (1917).

35   Spencer, [p. 169. Again the Russian text is shortened from Spencer's original].

36   We have been unable to discover the book Shklovsky promised. *Ed. note.*

Chapter 2

Vladimir Propp

THE METHOD AND THE MATERIAL AND THE FUNCTIONS OF DRAMATIS PERSONAE

A striking assertion that the Russian Formalist scholar Vladimir Propp (1895–1970) makes in his book on the morphology (or form) of folktales, is that they can all be reduced to thirty-one "functions" or significant actions performed by characters. Even more striking is that these functions always occur in a predefined sequential order, regardless of how many functions are present in a particular story ("sequential" implies here that a particular story always takes place chronologically). In other words, Propp's Formalist method enables him to analyze the basic structure of folktales in an empirical sense, without entirely reducing them to abstract principles. After a historical overview, Propp—whose work influenced the American anthropologist and folklorist Alan Dundes and in France the structuralist anthropologist Claude Lévi-Strauss—begins with what he calls "The Method and Material". Here he notes that the apparent diversity of folktales is an illusion, since multiple characters (he calls them "dramatis personae"), often with different names in different stories, adopt identical functions. This observation provides a key to Propp's method: across a large number of texts, a small number of events and sequences are repeated. Distilling these repetitions gives the basic form and function of every folktale in existence. As Propp puts it: "the number of functions is extremely small, whereas the number of personages is extremely large." However, Propp is careful to note that functions are contextual, and that while they usually express an action, they take place within a narrative context. The meaning of a function is thus a composite of the action and its contextual situation within a story. In other words, Propp's Formalism does not just consist of identifying every marriage proposal or quest within a story, because given a different context, these actions may have entirely different meanings. Propp argues that the functions of a story are the stable "elements in a tale" regardless of which characters perform them. Further, the number of functions can be defined, their actual sequence is always identical, and that this means that all folktales are "of one type in regard to their structure". In an extensive chapter within his book, called "The Functions of Dramatis Personae", Propp delineates and analyzes each of the thirty-one functions, beginning with a summary, abbreviated definition, and a symbol. For example, function twenty-one is summarized as: "The Hero is Pursued. (Definition: *pursuit, chase*. Designation: Pr.)". Each function is given generic examples. In the case of function twenty-one, Propp lists seven sequential components, Pr^1 to Pr^7: 1. The pursuer flies after the hero; 2. He demands the guilty person; 3. He pursues the hero, rapidly transforming himself into various animals, etc.; 4. Pursuers (dragons' wives, etc.) turn into alluring objects and place themselves in the path of the hero; 5. The pursuer tries to devour the hero; 6. The pursuer attempts to kill the hero; and 7. He tries to gnaw through a tree in which the hero is taking refuge. Propp's important contribution to the study of folktales derives partly from his combination of empirical observation and aesthetic sensitivity, apparent in his conclusion that "one function develops out of another with logical and artistic necessity".

The method and material

Let us first of all attempt to formulate our task. As already stated in the foreword, this work is dedicated to the study of *fairy* tales. The existence of fairy tales as a special class is assumed as an essential working hypothesis. By "fairy tales" are meant at present those tales classified by Aarne under numbers 300 to 749. This definition is artificial, but the occasion will subsequently arise to give a more precise determination on the basis of resultant conclusions. We are undertaking a comparison of the themes of these tales. For the sake of comparison we shall separate the component parts of fairy tales by special methods; and then, we shall make a comparison of tales according to their components. The result will be a morphology (i.e., a description of the tale according to its component parts and the relationship of these components to each other and to the whole).

What methods can achieve an accurate description of the tale? Let us compare the following events:

1. A tsar gives an eagle to a hero. The eagle carries the hero away to another kingdom.[1]
2. An old man gives Súčenko a horse. The horse carries Súčenko away to another kingdom.
3. A sorcerer gives Iván a little boat. The boat takes Iván to another kingdom.
4. A princess gives Iván a ring. Young men appearing from out of the ring carry Iván away into another kingdom, and so forth.[2]

Both constants and variables are present in the preceding instances. The names of the dramatis personae change (as well as the attributes of each), but neither their actions nor functions change. From this we can draw the inference that a tale often attributes identical actions to various personages. This makes possible the study of the tale *according to the functions of its dramatis personae.*

We shall have to determine to what extent these functions actually represent recurrent constants of the tale. The formulation of all other questions will depend upon the solution of this primary question: how many functions are known to the tale?

Investigation will reveal that the recurrence of functions is astounding. Thus Bába Jagá, Morózko, the bear, the forest spirit, and the mare's head test and reward the stepdaughter. Going further, it is possible to establish that characters of a tale, however varied they may be, often perform the same actions. The actual means of the realization of functions can vary, and as such, it is a variable. Morózko behaves differently than Bába Jagá. But the function, as such, is a constant. The question of *what* a tale's dramatis personae do is an important one for the study of the tale, but the questions of *who* does it and *how* it is done already fall within the province of accessory study. The functions of characters are those components which could replace Veselóvskij's "motifs," or Bédier's "elements." We are aware of the fact that the repetition of functions by various characters was long ago observed in myths and beliefs by historians of religion, but it was not observed by historians of the tale (cf. Wundt and Negelein[3]). Just as the characteristics and functions of deities are transferred from one to another, and, finally, are even carried over to Christian saints, the functions of certain tale personages are likewise transferred to other personages. Running ahead, one may say that the number of functions is extremely small, whereas the number of personages is extremely large. This explains the two-fold quality of a tale: its amazing multiformity, picturesqueness, and color, and on the other hand, its no less striking uniformity, its repetition.

Thus the functions of the dramatis personae are basic components of the tale, and we must first of all extract them. In order to extract the functions we must define them. Definition must proceed from two points of view. First of all, definition should in no case depend on the personage who carries out the function. Definition of a function will most often be given in the form of a noun expressing an action (interdiction, interrogation, flight, etc.). Secondly, an action cannot be defined apart from its place in the course of narration. The meaning which a given function has in the course of action must be considered. For example, if Iván marries a tsar's daughter, this is something entirely different than the marriage of a father to a widow with two daughters. A second example: if, in one instance, a hero receives money from his father in the form of 100 rubles and subsequently buys a wise cat with this money, whereas in a second case, the hero is rewarded with a sum of money for an accomplished act of bravery (at which point the tale ends), we have before us two morphologically different elements—in spite of the identical action (the transference of money) in both cases. Thus, identical acts can have different meanings, and vice versa. *Function is understood as an act of a character, defined from the point of view of its significance for the course of the action.*

The observations cited may be briefly formulated in the following manner:

1. *Functions of characters serve as stable, constant elements in a tale, independent of how and by whom they are fulfilled. They constitute the fundamental components of a tale.*
2. *The number of functions known to the fairy tale is limited.*

If functions are delineated, a second question arises: in what classification and in what sequence are these functions encountered?

A word, first, about sequence. The opinion exists that this Sequence is accidental. Veselóvskij writes, "The selection and *order* of tasks and encounters (examples of motifs) already pre-supposes a certain *freedom*." Šklóvskij stated this idea in even sharper terms: "It is quite impossible to understand why, in the act of adoption, the *accidental* sequence [Šklóvskij's italics] of motifs must be retained. In the testimony of witnesses, it is precisely the sequence of events which is distorted most of all." This reference to the evidence of witnesses is unconvincing. If witnesses distort the sequence of events, their narration is meaningless. The sequence of events has its own laws. The short story too has similar laws, as do organic formations. Theft cannot take place before the door is forced. Insofar as the tale is concerned, it has its own entirely particular and specific laws. The sequence of elements, as we shall see later on, is strictly *uniform*. Freedom within this sequence is restricted by very narrow limits which can be exactly formulated. We thus obtain the third basic thesis of this work, subject to further development and verification:

3. *The sequence of functions is always identical.*

As for groupings, it is necessary to say first of all that by no means do all tales give evidence of all functions. But this in no way changes the law of sequence. The absence of certain functions does not change the order of the rest. We shall dwell on this phenomenon later. For the present we shall deal with groupings in the proper sense of the word. The presentation of the question itself evokes the following assumption: if functions are singled out, then it will be possible to trace those tales which present identical functions. Tales with identical functions can be considered as belonging to one type. On this foundation, an index of types can then be created, based not upon theme features, which are somewhat vague and diffuse, but upon exact structural features. Indeed, this will be possible. If we further compare structural types among themselves, we are led to the following completely unexpected phenomenon: functions cannot be distributed around mutually exclusive axes. This phenomenon, in all its concreteness, will become apparent to us in the succeeding and final chapters of this book. For the time being, it can be interpreted in the following manner: if we designate with the letter A a function encountered everywhere in first position, and similarly designate with the letter B the function which (if it is at all present) *always follows A,* then all functions known to the tale will arrange themselves within a *single* tale, and none will fall out of order, nor will any one exclude or contradict any other. This is, of course, a completely unexpected result. Naturally, we would have expected that where there is a function A, there cannot be certain functions belonging to other tales. Supposedly we would obtain several axes, but only a single axis is obtained for all fairy tales. They are of the same type, while the combinations spoken of previously are subtypes. At first glance, this conclusion may appear absurd or perhaps even wild, yet it can be verified in a most exact manner. Such a typological unity represents a very complex problem on which it will be necessary to dwell further. This phenomenon will raise a whole series of questions.

In this manner, we arrive at the fourth basic thesis of our work:

4.   *All fairy tales are of one type in regard to their structure.*

We shall now set about the task of proving, developing, and elaborating these theses in detail. Here it should be recalled that the study of the tale must be carried on strictly deductively, i.e., proceeding from the material at hand to the consequences (and in effect it is so carried on in this work). But the *presentation* may have a reversed order, since it is easier to follow the development if the general bases are known to the reader beforehand.

Before starting the elaboration, however, it is necessary to decide what material can serve as the subject of this study. First glance would seem to indicate that it is necessary to cover all extant material. In fact, this is not so. Since we are studying tales according to the functions of their dramatis personae, the accumulation of material can be suspended as soon as it becomes apparent that the new tales considered present no new functions. Of course, the investigator must look through an enormous amount of reference material. But there is no need to inject the entire body of this material into the study. We have found that 100 tales constitute more than enough material. Having discovered that no new functions can be found, the morphologist can put a stop to his work, and further study will follow different directions (the formation of indices, the complete systemization, historical study). But just because material can be limited in quantity, that does not mean that it can be selected at one's own discretion. It should be dictated from without. We shall use the collection by Afanás'ev, starting the study of tales with No. 50 (according to his plan, this is the first fairy tale of the collection), and finishing it with No. 151.[4] Such a limitation of material will undoubtedly call forth many objections, but it is theoretically justified. To justify it further, it would be necessary to take into account the degree of repetition of tale phenomena. If repetition is great, then one may take a limited amount of material. If repetition is small, this is impossible. The repetition of fundamental components, as we shall see later, exceeds all expectations. Consequently, it is theoretically possible to limit oneself to a small body of material. Practically, this limitation justifies itself by the fact that the inclusion of a great quantity of material would have excessively increased the size of this work. We are not interested in the quantity of material, but in the quality of its analysis. Our working material consists of

100 tales. The rest is reference material, of great interest to the investigator, but lacking a broader interest.

Notes

1   "*Car' daet udal'cu orla. Orel unosit udal'ca v inoe carstvo*" (p. 28). Actually, in the tale referred to (old number 104a = new number 171), the hero's future bride, Poljuša, tells her father the tsar that they have a *ptica-kolpalica* (technically a spoonbill, although here it may have meant a white stork), which can carry them to the bright world. For a tale in which the hero flies away on an eagle, see 71a (= new number 128). [L.A.W.]
2   See Afanás'ev, Nos. 171, 139, 138, 156.
3   W. Wundt, "Mythus und Religion," *Völkerpsychologie*, II, Section I; Negelein, *Germanische Mythologie*. Negelein creates an exceptionally apt term, *Depossedierte Gottheiten*.
4   Tales numbered 50 to 151 refer to enumeration according to the older editions of Afanás'ev. In the new system of enumeration, adopted for the fifth and sixth editions and utilized in this translation (cf. the Preface to the Second Edition, and Appendix V), the corresponding numbers are 93 to 270. [L.A.W.]

The functions of dramatis personae

In this chapter we shall enumerate the functions of the dramatis personae in the order dictated by the tale itself.

For each function there is given: (1) a brief summary of its essence, (2) an abbreviated definition in one word, and (3) its conventional sign. (The introduction of signs will later permit a schematic comparison of the structure of various tales.) Then follow examples. For the most part, the examples far from exhaust our material. They are given only as samples. They are distributed into certain groups. These groups are in relation to the definition as *species* to *genus*. The basic task is the extraction of *genera*. An examination of *species* cannot be included in the problems of general morphology. Species can be further subdivided into *varieties*, and here we have the beginning of systemization. The arrangement given below does not pursue such goals. The citation of examples should only illustrate and show the presence of the function as a certain *generic* unit. As was already mentioned, all functions fit into one consecutive story. The series of functions given below represents the morphological foundation of fairy tales in general.

A tale usually begins with some sort of initial situation. The members of a family are enumerated, or the future hero (e.g., a soldier) is simply introduced by mention of his name or indication of his status. Although this situation is not a function, it nevertheless is an important morphological element. The species of tale beginnings can be examined only at the end of the present work. We shall designate this element as the *initial situation,* giving it the sign α.

After the initial situation there follow functions:

I.   One of the members of a family absents himself from home.
*(Definition: **absentation***. Designation: β.)

1.   *The person absenting himself can be a member of the older generation* (β^1). Parents leave for work (113). "The prince had to go on a distant journey, leaving his wife to the care of strangers" (265). "Once, he (a merchant) went away to foreign lands" (197). Usual forms of absentation: going to work, to the forest, to trade, to war, "on business."

2. *An intensified form of absentation is represented by the death of parents (β^2).*
3. *Sometimes members of the younger generation absent themselves (β^3).* They go visiting (101), fishing (108), for a walk (137), out to gather berries (244).

II. An interdiction is addressed to the hero. *(Definition:* interdiction. *Designation: γ.)*

1. (γ^1). "You dare not look into this closet" (159). "Take care of your little brother, do not venture forth from the courtyard" (113). "If Bába Jagá comes, don't you say anything, be silent" (106). "Often did the prince try to persuade her and command her not to leave the lofty tower," etc. (265). Interdiction not to go out is sometimes strengthened or replaced by putting children in a stronghold (201). Sometimes, on the contrary, an interdiction is evidenced in a weakened form, as a request or bit of advice: a mother tries to persuade her son not to go out fishing: "you're still little," etc. (108). The tale generally mentions an absentation at first, and then an interdiction. The sequence of events, of course, actually runs in the reverse. Interdictions can also be made without being connected with an absentation: "don't pick the apples" (230); "don't pick up the golden feather" (169); "don't open the chest" (219); "don't kiss your sister" (219).
2. *An inverted form of interdiction is represented by an order or a suggestion,* (γ^2) "Bring breakfast out into the field" (133). "Take your brother with you to the woods" (244).

Here for the sake of better understanding, a digression may be made. Further on the tale presents the sudden arrival of calamity (but not without a certain type of preparation). In connection with this, the initial situation gives a description of particular, sometimes emphasized, prosperity. A tsar has a wonderful garden with golden apples; the old folk fondly love their Ivášečka, and so on. A particular form is agrarian prosperity: a peasant and his sons have a wonderful hay-making. One often encounters the description of sowing with excellent germination. This prosperity naturally serves as a contrasting background for the misfortune to follow. The spectre of this misfortune already hovers invisibly above the happy family. From this situation stem the interdictions not to go out into the street, and others. The very absentation of elders prepares for the misfortune, creating an opportune moment for it. Children, after the departure or death of their parents, are left on their own. A command often plays the role of an interdiction. If children are urged to go out into the field or into the forest, the fulfillment of this command has the same consequences as does violation of an interdiction not to go into the forest or out into the field.

III. The interdiction is violated *(Definition:* violation. *Designation: δ.)*

The forms of violation correspond to the forms of interdiction. Functions II and III form a *paired* element. The second half can sometimes exist without the first (the tsar's daughters go into the garden [β^3]; they are *late* in returning home). Here the interdiction of tardiness is omitted. A fulfilled order corresponds, as demonstrated, to a violated interdiction.

At this point a new personage, who can be termed the *villain,* enters the tale. His role is to disturb the peace of a happy family, to cause some form of misfortune, damage, or harm. The villain(s) may be a dragon, a devil, bandits, a witch, or a step-mother, etc. (The question of how new personages, in general, appear in the course of action has been relegated to a special chapter.) Thus, a villain has entered the scene. He has come on foot, sneaked up, or flown down, etc., and begins to act.

IV.   The villain makes an attempt at reconnaissance.
      (Definition: **reconnaissance.** *Designation:* ε.)

1.   *The reconnaissance has the aim of finding out the location of children, or sometimes of precious objects, etc.* (ε^1). A bear says: "Who will tell me what has become of the tsar's children? Where did they disappear to?" (201); a clerk: "Where do you get these precious stones?" (197);[1] a priest at confession: "How were you able to get well so quickly?" (258);[2] a princess: "Tell me, Iván the merchant's son, where is your wisdom?" (209);[3] "What does the bitch live on?" Jágišna thinks. She sends One-Eye, Two-Eye and Three-Eye on reconnaissance (101).[4]

2.   *An inverted form of reconnaissance is evidenced when the intended victim questions the villain* (ε^2). "Where is your death, Koščéj?" (156). "What a swift steed you have! Could one get another one somewhere that could outrun yours?" (160).

3.   *In separate instances one encounters forms of reconnaissance by means of other personages* (ε^3).
      [. . .]

Notes

1   "'Gde vy èti samocvetnye kamni berete?' (114)" (p. 38). The textual reference should be 115 (= new no. 197). [L.A.W.]

2   "'Otčego tak skoro sumel ty popravit'sja?' (114)" (p. 38). The textual reference should be 144 (= new no. 258). [L.A.W.]

3   "'Skaži, Ivan—kupečeskij syn, gde tvoja mudrost'?' (120)" (p. 38). The textual reference should be 120b (= new no. 209). [L.A.W.]

4   "Čem suka živet? dumaet Jagišna.' Ona posylaet na razvedku Odnoglazku, Dvuglazku, Treglazku (56)." Texts 56 and 57 (= new nos. 100 and 101) have been somewhat confused. The three daughters named are present in tale 56, but their mother is not called Jagišna, and the indicated question does not appear. On the other hand, in tale 57 Jagišna asks, "Čem suka živa živet?" but here she has only two daughters to send out, a two-eyed one and a three-eyed one. [L.A.W.]

Chapter 3

Francisco Vaz Da Silva

RED AS BLOOD, WHITE AS SNOW, BLACK AS CROW

Chromatic symbolism of womanhood in fairy tales

In the *Morphology of the Folktale,* the Russian Formalist Vladimir Propp observed that there were thirty-one functions (or actions) found in varying combinations in all folktales, and that these functions always took place in a predetermined sequence (see Chapter 2). While critics have long since applied Propp's theory to many different types of literature, what is significant about Francisco Vaz Da Silva's essay on "Chromatic Symbolism" is that he returns to Propp's specialist interest—the fairy tale—and applies an analogous insight from the work of Brent Berlin and Paul Kay concerning universal colour terms. Berlin and Kay suggest that although humans can discriminate many thousands of colour variations, there are eleven basic colour categories upon which all languages draw. Da Silva, a faculty member at the Lisbon University Institute's department of anthropology and author of *Metamorphosis: The Dynamics of Symbolism in European Fairy Tales* (2002), explores the way in which these universal colour categories, like Propp's functions, follow set or progressive sequences in fairy tales, with attention to one of the best known fairy tales of all: "Snow White". Colours function within texts as semiotic codes, which is to say that they reflect and articulate deep cultural values. In "Snow White" there is a tricolour pattern of white, black, and red, and Da Silva's thesis is that this pattern represents "a transcultural basic scheme". The white–black–red chromatic trio is also a powerful vehicle for expressing patriarchal notions of gender, one which Da Silva argues can be found in cultures around the world. The contrast of red and white is usually seen through a black frame, traced from medieval literature to seventeenth-century fairy tales. The colour red affirms "a blood link between a mother and a daughter", while the three drops of blood in "Snow White" represent the sexual cycles throughout a woman's life. Red-on-white stains signify the crossing of the threshold from an otherworldly innocence to the realm of procreation. Black relates to enchantment and death as well as being the prerequisite for re-birth (it therefore represents *potentiality*). Within Christian systems of representation, the image of the black Madonna appears to fit into this chromatic symbolism, and, as Da Silva argues, "the same tricolor symbolism underlies African ritual on the one hand, and representations of ideal womanhood in European fairy tales and folklore on the other." Da Silva suggests that the point of this tricolour symbolism is that it represents both an idealized patriarchal notion of women as fecund, reproductive subjects and "what men at all times and places have tried to appropriate by means of ritual action". Colour as a sensory experience functions in ways that are analogous to Propp's morphological observations, including the notion of sequential order. Da Silva's approach exceeds the simple analysis of symbols, through noting the possibility of a wider transcultural existence of the basic tricolour pattern, and the way in which the patriarchal fixing of the female subject depends upon sequential chains of signifiers. Da Silva refers in his essay to Angela Carter, an author who specializes in deconstructing fairy tales; a key to her feminist dismantling of such idealized, patriarchal notions of gender is the unexpected intervention in traditional patterns of events in her rewriting of traditional tales.

T HIS ARTICLE IS INTENDED AS A MODEST follow-up on a classic study by Brent Berlin and Paul Kay. In *Basic Color Terms: Their Universality and Evolution,* these two linguists showed that despite the proven ability of humans to discriminate thousands of color percepts, "a total universal inventory of exactly eleven basic term categories exists from which the eleven or fewer basic color terms of any given languages are always drawn" (2). This means that, as they put it, such "eleven basic color categories are pan-human perceptual universals" (108).[1] To my mind, this conclusion is eerily reminiscent of Vladimir Propp's discovery that thirty-one functions are all that the human imagination needs to produce the myriad extant variations in fairy tales. So the question arises of whether fairy tales use colors, as they use functions, in a patterned way. To answer, one must pursue Propp's sort of exploration of fairy-tale universal beyond formalism, in the realm of sensory experience—or, rather, of its encoding in color categories.

Encouragingly, fairy tales make striking use of colors. Max Lüthi once remarked that whereas "[t]he real world shows us a richness of different hues and shadings . . . [b]y contrast, the folktale prefers clear, ultrapure colors" (27). And he gave a well-known example: "Snow White is as white as snow, as red as blood, and as black as ebony" (28). While in the following discussion I shall take advantage of the example of the three colors of Snow White, I must part ways with Lüthi's ideas regarding the abstract style of fairy tales, for my purpose is to call attention to the role of colors as concrete semiotic markers. Indeed, in taking up the colors of Snow White (and some of her sisters), I would like to explore chromatic codes as a means to uncover folk notions regarding womanhood.

Basic chromatic trio

But how, precisely, does an exploration of chromatic codes regarding womanhood fit with Berlin and Kay's study on basic color terms? Let me backtrack a little. These authors have shown that natural languages encode basic color categories according to a single progressive sequence of color discriminations, so any given category supposes all previous ones. Specifically, they found that if a given language contains only two color terms, these refer to white and black. But if a language contains three terms, then it contains (in addition to the previous ones) a word for red. And so on and so forth concerning—in the following order—green or yellow, then blue, then brown, and finally purple, pink, orange, and gray.

But why would color terms follow such a strict order everywhere? Anthropologist Marshall Sahlins, while strengthening the case for a physiological basis of the universal scheme of color categories, also suggested that "colors are in practice semiotic codes" (171). This is why, Sahlins surmises, Berlin and Kay found strong cross-cultural regularities in the foci of basic color categories—for, if colors are to carry meanings, then "hues are socially relevant in their most distinctive perceptible form" (175). In principle, this argument applies to Lüthi's observation on the distinctiveness of fairy-tale colors.

In itself, the point that colors are convenient semiotic markers will not surprise anyone who is familiar with traffic lights or with the gender-specific assignments of blue and pink for babies. But, more ambitiously, I wish to focus on Snow White's tricolor pattern as one particular instance of a transcultural basic scheme. Berlin and Kay have shown the primacy of white, black, and red in most color terminologies (21); and, as one might expect, a fundamental chromatic trio tends to convey foundational notions.

Here is an interesting example. Victor W. Turner has shown in a classic study that the Ndembu of Zambia possess "primary terms" for only white, red, and black (60, 68). And he suggested these three colors stand for a totalizing tripartite mode of classification. Such "three principles of being" stand for, among others, heaven and chieftainship (white), blood spilling as in war (red), and sexual desire and regeneration (black).

This example inevitably leads to another, for Turner's description of an all-encompassing, tripartite classification recalls Georges Dumézil's views on a triadic Indo-European world-view. Indeed, Dumézil's scheme includes a chromatic trio of white, red, and black/dark blue/green (see Puhvel 159–60, 191; Zahan 131–32). And although languages of the Indo-European family typically present eleven-term basic color lexicons, the corresponding cultures still use the basic chromatic trio—as in depictions of Snow White's complexion.[2]

Therefore, examination of the basic chromatic trio should propitiate cross-cultural comparison. But Dumézil's elucidation of Indo-European triadic chromaticism (unlike that of Turner regarding the Ndembu of Zambia) is, unfortunately, rather scant. And although Dumézil recognizes a trivalent goddess who synthesizes the three Indo-European functions and stands for "the very ideal of womanhood in society" (Religion 307), the French savant does not have much to say about three-color embodiment in such a goddess—or about ideal womanhood, either.[3]

However, there is another way to elicit chromatic symbolism of ideal womanhood. As Snow White's complexion hints, European fairy tales express Dumézil intuition of a link between trivalent goddesses and ideal womanhood in terms of association between tricolor heroines and feminine perfection.

So, then, the following discussion examines the basic chromatic trio in European fairy tales from the perspective suggested by Snow White's tricolor complexion. It is hoped that this will reveal something about the workings of symbolism in fairy tales while facilitating comparative research on chromatic codes. Overall, this article calls attention to the importance of tapping yet unheeded aspects of fairy tales to help advance research and problem solving in the wider realm of the humanities.

Tricolor ideal womanhood: fairy-tale heroines

Twelfth-century Chrétien de Troyes has famously let us know that the sight of three drops of blood on snow reminds Perceval of his sweetheart. In *Conte du Graal*, Perceval, on beholding three drops of blood on white snow, thinks of the "fresh color" of the face of his sweetheart. Specifically, "the red on white in her face was just like those three drops of blood . . . on the snow" (302–3).

Five centuries later, the complete chromatic trio surfaced in a fairy tale. Giambattista Basile's tale 4.9, "The Crow," presents a prince who finds a white marble slate on which a crow has just been killed, and who exclaims: "Oh, Heavens! Would that I could have a wife as red and white as this stone, and with hair and eyebrows as black as the feathers of this crow." Instantly, he decides he must have "the original of the stone" (3: 488–89, 592). The same tricolor leitmotif appears in tale 5.9, "The Three Citrons," concerning a prince who does not want to hear about taking a wife until—having cut a finger over ricotta cheese, after watching some jackdaws—he decides to search for a woman who is like ricotta stained with blood. Likewise, a tale collected by François Luzel in Brittany presents a prince who, on beholding the contrast presented by a crow and its blood on snow, decides to marry the (as yet unknown) princess whose face is just as white, red, and black (131–37).

Such appears to be the proper background for understanding the Grimms' "Snow White" queen, who, on beholding three drops of her own blood on the snow, wishes to have a daughter "as white as snow, as red as blood, and as black as" ebony (Grimm 249). Presently, let us ask what the tricolor image tells us about the fairy-tale ideal maiden.

Consideration of all the above examples implies acknowledging that red-and-white is actually the basic contrast. Both the medieval image of three blood drops on snow and the Italian representation of blood on ricotta mention these two colors exclusively. Likewise, in "Snow White" it is the beauty of "red on white snow" that actually captures the queen's attention. But, of course, the queen sees the red-and-white contrast through a black frame. Similarly, Basile's hero sheds mesmerizing blood on ricotta on seeing black jackdaws. So the red-and-white contrast is the focus of the scene, and the black element is peripheral, to the point that it may vanish while the other two remain in sight.

Before proceeding with the elucidation of this chromatic articulation, it is important to know that the red-on-white contrast used to be important in daily life. Lucien Gerschel, in a classic contribution on colors and dyeing, showed that European sources throughout many centuries contrast the relative dullness of natural hemp or wool colors to the expensive production of bright white and its even more luxurious tinting with purple. This means that for a very long time, dyeing amounted to tinting white with red. Such equivalence still shows in the fact that the Spanish term *colorado* ("colored") means red. Similarly, the Portuguese term *colorau* designates a vermilion paste, and the derived term *corado* ("colored") designates blush—precisely that "touch of vermillion set on white," to be seen in the face of his sweetheart, to which Perceval compares the three drops of blood he sees on snow (Troyes 302).

Red . . .

Let us proceed. Such drops are surely important; but what could they stand for? Another Portuguese name for red-on-white blush, rosetas ("small roses"), points us the way of Briar-Rose—that floral maiden in the Grimms' no. 50 who pricks her finger at fifteen years old, then falls into a long sleep, which (as Charles Perrault's variant specifies) does not diminish "one bit of her complexion: her cheeks were carnation and her lips were coral" (Lang 56).

So now we face a slightly different question: what do such carnation cheeks and coral lips stand for? Basile's usual bluntness delivers a clear answer. Says he, Eros tinged the white face of the maiden with red, and Venus tainted with menstrual blood her lips—which Basile likens to roses, destined to pierce with their briars a thousand enamored hearts (3: 596). This establishes a clear association between red on a white face, roses, and menses. From here, it remains to inquire on the relationship between roses and three drops of blood reminiscent, as we know, of vermilion-on-white in the face of Perceval's sweetheart.

Recall that we have met three blood drops in "Snow White," where the queen sheds her own blood just before wishing for a tricolor daughter.[4] Again, we find them in no. 89, "The Goose Girl," in the Grimms' collection. Here a mother sets three drops of her own blood on a white handkerchief, which she gives to her daughter as the latter sets off to marry. Both cases, then, affirm a blood link between a mother and her daughter. Predictably (in view of the association between roses and menses), such a link may be told with flowers as well. For example, a Portuguese oral version of "Snow White" presents a mother named Rose and her daughter, called Flower of the Rose, of whom the former is envious to the point of trying to kill her (Barbosa 107). Note that both are roses, but only the younger maiden is the bloom, which casts the older woman on the side of briars. So, we may ask, what do briars indicate about a woman by the time her daughter is old enough to be the rose bloom? What the bloom represents is clear, for one version of "Sleeping Beauty" by Basile shows a maiden become pregnant after eating a leaf from a blooming rose. But let us look on the side of briars (2.8, "The Young Slave").

At this point we need to take a broader view of the flower metaphor encompassing both blooms and briars. For this purpose, let us extend our view for a moment. Shakespeare, in *Twelfth Night,* links "roses of spring" and "maidhood," and states, "[W]omen are as roses, whose fair flow'r being once display'd doth fall that very hour." And in *All's Well That Ends Well* he describes a maiden not as yet "husbanded" as "a fresh uncropped flower," defloration of whom would take her "roses" and barely leave her "thorns" to prick herself (Shakespeare 364, 372, 375, 388, 392). The same ancient symbolism of passage from roses to thorns underlies Ovid's description of the Roman festival of *Floralia* (April 28 through May 3) in *Fasti* 5.331–54. After associating the acts of wine drinking and of "pluck[ing] the rose," the poet sets to explain why "a crowd of drabs" frequent these games. Says he, the goddess Flora "warns us to use life's flower, while it still blooms; for the thorn, she reminds us, is flouted when the roses have fallen away" (Frazer 1: 271).

What can we learn from these examples? While Ovid appears to generically take the rose for the prime of womanhood and the thorn for life past its bloom, Shakespeare is more precise. On the one hand, he links plucked roses to lost maidenhood; on the other, he hints that the pricking leftover stands for other bloodsheds in a woman's life. Let us look in this perspective at "Little Briar-Rose." If to prick oneself at fifteen years old stands for the first spilling of blood, then the subsequent period of thorny unavailability should amount to the forbidding aspect of a blood condition. Indeed, all taken together, the contributions of Ovid, Shakespeare, and the Grimms suggest that red flowers stand for the fruitful aspect of womb blood as well as for youth, that most fruitful time in life, whereas thorns symbolize the leftovers of both: the monthly flux and life past its prime.

On the side of fairy tales this implies two things. First, Briar-Rose—or, rather, the thorny rose she impersonates—expresses the ambivalence of feminine blood. The bloom metaphor of womb blood affirms this medium is fruitful, whereas the use of pricking thorns to designate a blood condition implies marital unavailability. Second, the envy of a woman called Rose for her Flower-of-the-Rose daughter entails that the latter casts the former on the sterile side of spines, not blooms.

Now we are ready to grasp the constant meaning of three blood drops. Recall that Briar-Rose pricks one finger at fifteen years old, then becomes impenetrably surrounded by thorns until the right time comes for the elected husband to pass through her barrier—now displaying "large and beautiful flowers"—so as to deflower her, as Basile (5.5, "Sun, Moon, and Talia") specifies and independent oral variants confirm (see Braga 90–92; Curtin 57–61). Of course, both the pricked finger and the subsequent defloration entail bleeding. And it is as Snow White's mother pricks her finger that she conceives (both literally and figuratively) of a girl.

Thus, pricked fingers as well as thorns represent feminine bleeding in connection with potential fertility. Which suggests that three blood drops match the three bleedings punctuating a woman's destiny at puberty, defloration, and birth giving (cf. Verdier 252). "Red as blood," then, sets the dynamic frame of a shared destiny in which related women interact, both for good and for evil. Overall, women are like roses; but whereas a good mother passes on her blood drops and takes briars as they come, the bad one clings to rosebuds out of season.

. . . white . . .

After a lengthy discussion of the semantics of redness, the examination of whiteness risks sounding minimal. Not that this color is not important—in tales as elsewhere, white stands for luminosity and untainted sheen, thus for luminous heaven as much as for purity. Hence, the dove that keeps watch over Snow White fits with her glass coffin in regard of the idea of heavenly light. In the same vein, in tale no. 21 in the Grimms' collection, white doves represent Cinderella's dead mother watching over her daughter from heaven.

But, precisely, our theme denies such untainted otherworldliness. White is pertinent regarding our heroine insofar as it is tinged with red. The whole point of Snow White's sleep in the glass coffin is that she still has "pretty red cheeks," and even in her bier she remains "as white as snow, as red as blood, and her hair was as black as ebony" (Grimm 256). In sum, the purity of whiteness is there to be tinted.

We may understand this in at least two ways, which are by no means contradictory. First, the ideal woman born by supernatural intervention, or else actually searched for in some unearthly kingdom beyond water, is otherworldly (which white represents). But her destiny is incarnation and motherhood (which red epitomizes). Second, this is a theme of passage from the purity of infancy (white) to the mature realm of procreation (red). In both perspectives, the red-on-white stain embodies a threshold.

Angela Carter has keenly expressed the life-cycle dimension of this chromatic threshold regarding another fairy-tale theme. First she depicts a girl, "thirteen going on fourteen, the hinge of your life, when you are . . . nor child nor woman . . . untouched, invincible, immaculate. Like snow" (*Curious* 64–65). Then she asserts that the destiny of this girl, who can't bleed as yet, is to take on a "scarlet shawl, the colour of poppies, the colour of sacrifices, the colour of her menses" (*Bloody* 117). This girl is none other than Red Riding Hood, whose trials and tribulations Carter depicts in terms of a red-on-white hinge. Therefore, as in real-world ancient techniques of dyeing studied by Gerschel, so in the symbolic realm of fairy tales (of which Carter was a most penetrating commentator) white is the precondition for red—its chromatic background.

. . . and black

Finally we come to black, which (as you may recall) appears ancillary to the basic white-and-red contrast. Apparently, there is little to say about this color besides the fact that black appears primarily in the shape of an otherworldly bird (crow, raven) that has been killed. In itself this fact is important, for it relates black to death and the otherworld.

But there is more to it. Consider Basile's tale 5.9, "The Three Citrons," which engages blackness in interesting ways. At first sight it would appear there is no trace of death here, for the prince becomes mesmerized by the bicolor contrast of blood on ricotta cheese after seeing live jackdaws. However, when he decides to search for the bicolor woman, the dark element is made clear as he declares he must set on his search or else end up wandering with the shades.

Now let us focus on the maiden he seeks. She is fair as cream and red as a strawberry, with apparently no trace of blackness. But on suffering enchantment she is replaced by a black slave, who in turn presents some remarkable features. First, on looking at herself on a mirroring surface, the black slave sees the bicolor face of the maiden; second, the dark slave is called Lucia ("light"); and third, she introduces herself to the prince as the fair bride turned black, on the grounds that being bewitched, she turns black every other year. There is structural truth to this explanation, for the black usurper's appearance in the plot precisely matches the enchantment of the red-on-white bride. In other words, the black usurper appears to personify the heroine's enchantment. She is, in sum, the black aspect of the white-and-red heroine that appeared to be missing.

So, then, let us say blackness connotes enchantment as well as death. In fairy tales the two notions are intertwined. Enchantment is something like reversible death, and death itself appears in tones of enchantment.

Death and rebirth

Constantly, such enchantment-like death is prerequisite for rebirth. Let us heed N. J. Girardot's remarks on the death symbolism of time spent by Snow White in the dark forest. In his view, the fate of the tricolor heroine enacts "the idea of a union of the red (menstrual blood) and white (semen) through the agency of the black (the ritual 'death' involved in the initiation and marriage union)." At the very least, the association between symbolic death and blackness is certainly correct. The death of Snow White happens in the dwelling place of chthonian creatures, and Girardot again has a point as he argues that these dwarfs in the dark forest are not only "malevolent and destructive beings" but also "creative agents of growth and rebirth" (289–90). This articulation is nicely expressed in a German version mentioned by the Grimms. Here, the malevolent queen takes Snow White to the dwarfs' cave in hopes that they will kill her; but what they end up doing, instead, is elevating the inert maiden out of their cave and putting her in a silver coffin up on a tree (Hunt 407). The Grimms' text actually expands this lesson. The dwarfs' business is to draw ore from the mountains, so they routinely bring to light gleaming "copper and gold." In the same vein, they will not bury the maiden in the "dark earth" *(schwarze Erde)* but choose, instead, to elevate her to light by putting her in a glass coffin on top of a mountain (Grimm 252).

In sum, chthonian dwarfs in the dark forest are in the business of drawing luminous entities out of darkness. Thus, both the black slave called Lucia and dwarfs drawing solarlike ore out of darkness stand for the notion that darkness prefigures new light, for enchantment is, at bottom, a reversible death.

Such primacy of death and darkness over life and light is, beyond fairy tales, a standard feature of cyclic models regarding conspicuous natural phenomena. Consider the dark moon, out of which the "new" moon (as Romance languages call it) reappears periodically; or the black earth taking in the dead, as well as seeds, so as to generate new life.

And, of course, equivalence between such phenomena and women's cycles is a staple of symbolic thought. There is hardly any need to elaborate on the widespread correspondence between women's cycles and the moon's returns. And regarding equivalence between wombs and fields, recall that the term "husbandman" refers to him who casts seed in both the earth and the uterus. This analogy is old, of course, for it underlies Sophocles's depiction of Oedipus's fault in terms of "plowing" the place where he had been "sown," thus replacing his father in the "furrows" of Jocasta, whom the poet likens to "mother earth" having cropped twice at once (Sophocles 234, 236).

Poetic proclivities aside, my point is that ancient equivalence between women's cycles and paradigms of life springing out of death entails that women themselves operate rebirth from death.

Tricolor ideal womanhood: madonna

In terms of chromatic symbolism, this would mean women bring forth white from black by means of their sex-specific fertility, epitomized by red. Such general conclusion is borne out, even beyond fairy-tale heroines, by the paradigmatic image of ideal womanhood in Christendom.

Consider that artists have garbed the Virgin Mary in red and blue for centuries. This chromatic pattern is not too hard to fathom if we consider the foregoing discussion on rose symbolism, and if we heed François Rabelais's point that "blue signifies heaven and heavenly things" (62). In this light, blue-and-red figurations of Mary suggest she brings together celestial essence and womb blood. This is true in two senses. First, although Mary was heavenly begotten, she is still a woman able to conceive. Second, in Mary's earthly womb the godhead incarnated in human flesh. (Significantly, in Portuguese *encarnado* means both "incarnate" and "red.") In sum, Mary's blue-and-red figurations intimate the incarnation of celestial essence in womb blood, which is arguably the core value of Mary in Christian dogma (see Vaz da Silva).

Rabelais also ascribes white to celestial light, which suggests that blue and white share a heavenly connotation (60–61). This helps explain the shift of Mary's garb to white after the dogma of the Immaculate Conception, in 1854, emphasized the celestial purity of the Mother of Jesus.

Even garbed in white, though, the pure Virgin relates conspicuously to roses, rosaries, and flowers in enclosed gardens. The reason for this is clear once you recall that the popular expression "defloration" supposes that virgins possess flowers. In this frame of mind, the white mantle of virginal purity implies the virtuous accumulation of red flowers, which justifies constant association of Mary to roses (see Albert-Llorca 54, 193–205). Therefore, while the famous Portuguese Virgin of *Fátima* appears white-dressed, she presents conspicuous blush cheeks popularly named *rosetas* (from "roses").

So the Virgin Mary, like the ideal fairy-tale heroine, is a maiden in flowers whose face shows red on white. The fact that the destiny of the fairy-tale maiden is defloration while that of the Madonna hinges on the intactness of her flowers delineates two variations within a single conceptual framework of tricolor feminine perfection. Which suggests that the Virgin, too, ought to present a discreet black streak.

This would explain that black Madonna denominations have persisted to this day throughout Europe, even though a black Virgin Mary is strange from a canonical perspective. To understand what is at stake in such representations, consider the testimony of someone with firsthand experience. Carlo Levi, who lived among south Italian peasants, lucidly describes the black Madonna of Viggiano in terms that are rather remote from the official image of Mary. She appears, he says, as a "fierce, pitiless, mysterious, ancient earth goddess" endowed with a "black, scowling face" and "large, inhuman eyes." From daily acquaintance, he comes to see her as "a subterranean deity, black with the shadows of the bowels of the earth, a peasant Persephone or lower-world goddess of the harvest" (117, 119–21). From a comparative perspective, this point is certainly well taken, for David Shulman independently points out that Indian dark goddesses to this day may claim "to represent the earth in its character of the universal womb from which life issues, and to which life returns, in violence" (139; cf. Gimbutas xviii–xix, 110, 159, 255–56, 319). In sum, occasional representations of the usually white-and-red Virgin in disquieting black are in accord with the streak of death-connoting darkness we found at the core of fairy-tale representations of ideal womanhood.

Granted, a tricolor image of femininity composed of ostensible white-and-red, underlain by discreet black, may seem strange. But recall Freud's insight on "the three forms taken by the figure of the mother in the course of a man's life—the mother herself, the beloved one who is chosen after her pattern, and lastly the Mother Earth who receives him once more" (247).

Correspondence between Freud's death-related earth aspect and the black streak we have examined is obvious. So is the fit between the sexual aspect and red; indeed, Sahlins has noted the Western tendency to understand red "as harlotry as opposed to the prudery of blue or the purity of white" (178). Which brings us to the harmony between maternity and white.

Indeed, the cleanliness of white fits the purity of ideal motherhood, ultimately impersonated by the Madonna. Moreover, whiteness is a fitting symbol for milk and, thus, the nurturing aspect of motherliness.

Taken in separation, the white and red elements of womanhood have given rise to the rather pathological cultural antinomy southern Europeans express in terms of the *mamma* and the *puttana*. Conversely, their articulation synthesizes the nurturing and fertile aspects of maternity, as shown in the fairy-tale heroine and in Madonna imagery. And then, beyond this worldly aspect of femininity, occasional glimpses arise of the realm of death and new life hinging on a streak of black.

A comparative sketch

Throughout this discussion I have argued that the use of "pure colors" (Lüthi 24) in fairy tales has little do with empty abstraction; rather, it is part of a general encoding of cultural values in sensory-based categories.

Indeed, the chromatic symbolism found in fairy tales is not peculiar to this genre—nor, indeed, to Western cultures. In the aforementioned paper on color classification in Africa, Turner has made a few points worth considering. He notices that red is regularly paired with white in action contexts, whereas "black is seldom directly expressed." Both white and red are "associated with activity"; by contrast, black represents "that which is hidden" and tends to appear as "the null member" in the triad. In clearer terms, both white and red stand for life—for they represent life-giving elements, such as milk and semen on the one hand, and blood and its attendant power on the other—whereas black symbolizes darkness and death. But whenever black is displayed openly, it refers to "ritual death" and the inherent notion of "regeneration." Indeed, Turner clarifies that "'to die' often means . . . to reach the terminus of a cycle of growth"; death is like "a blackout, a period of powerlessness and passivity between two living states." Therefore, black stands for "potentiality, as opposed to actuality" (71–74, 79, 80–81).

These points strikingly fit the foregoing discussion, which suggests that the basic chromatic trio presents constant semantic values across genres and cultures. But, of course, such constant values allow for culture-specific variations and elaborations. Thus, the same tricolor symbolism underlies African ritual on the one hand, and representations of ideal womanhood in European fairy tales and folklore on the other. One way to understand this parallelism (while shunning the easy way of falling back on the myth-ritual hypothesis) would be to admit that the life-eliciting power of womanhood, as expressed in European tricolor symbolism, is what men at all times and places have tried to appropriate by means of ritual action.

Whatever the value of this speculation, in this article I have presented a strictly inductive way of examining the workings of symbolism in fairy tales, and suggested how such procedure facilitates comparative research. However, the field is vast, and research has yet to begin systematically. Chromaticism in fairy tales is a promising field of research; even so, patterned use of colors constitutes but one of several intertextual dimensions waiting to be unraveled before a basic command of the semantics of fairy tales is at hand.

Notes

1   Berlin and Kay (6) deem "basic" color terms that are monolexemic, designate values not included in any other color term, do not designate a narrow class of objects, and are psychologically salient for informants.

2   In fact, Luc de Heusch claims that chromatic systems in Bantu Africa show deep-set similarities to the tripartite Indo-European scheme.

3   Granted, there is a triadic color clue elsewhere. Dumézil examines a feminine Indo-European personification of royalty endowed with trivalent traits and variously associated to white, red, and dark. Thus, Indian Mādhavī is associated to white (*Types* 327n3), her Irish counterpart Medb is linked to red (337), and Irish representations of a loathly bride turning into a shining maiden associate the loathly shape to blackness (335–36). Still, these piecemeal associations fail to meet the Dumézilian principle that any group of three functions must be given as an organic whole in order to be recognized as such.

4   G. Ronald Murphy (123) suggests that the Grimms have changed the queen's drops of blood from "several" to "three" in order to allude to the German version of the episode in which Perceval beholds such drops. In the German text the three red drops on white are the very image of Parzifal's beloved wife—of her beautiful body, cheeks, and chin, and colors (see von Eschenbach 208). But, of course, we can also look closer to home—that is, in the inner logic of modern fairy tales.

Works cited

Albert-Llorca, Marlène. *Les Vierges miraculeuses: Légendes et rituels.* Paris: Gallimard, 2002.

Barbosa, Bernardino. "Contos Populares de Évora." *Revista Lusitana* 20 (1917): 107–18.

Basile, Giambattista. *Il Pentamerone ossia la fiaba delle fiabe.* Trans. Benedetto Croce. 3 vols. Roma: Laterza, 1974.

Berlin, Brent, and Paul Kay. *Basic Color Terms: Their Universality and Evolution.* 1969. Berkeley: U of California P, 1991.

Braga, Joaquim Teófilo. *Contos Tradicionais do Povo Português.* 3rd ed. Vol. 1. Lisboa: Dom Quixote, 1987.

Carter, Angela. *The Bloody Chamber.* London: Vintage, 1995.

—. *The Curious Room: Collected Dramatic Works.* Ed. Mark Bell. London: Vintage-Random House, 1997.

Curtin, Jeremiah. *Myths and Folk Tales of Ireland.* New York: Dover, 1975. Rpt. of *Myths and Folk-Lore of Ireland.* 1890.

de Heusch, Luc. *Rois nés d'un cœur de vache.* Paris: Gallimard, 1982.

Dumézil, Georges. *La religion romaine archaïque avec un appendice sur La religion des Étrusques.* 2nd ed. Paris: Payot, 1974.

—. *Types épiques indo-européens: Un héros, un sorcier, un roi.* Vol. 2 of *Mythe et épopée.* 4th ed. Paris: Gallimard, 1986.

Eschenbach, Wolfram von. *Parzival.* Trans. Danielle Buschinger, Wolfgang Spiewok, and Jean-Marc Pastré. Paris: 10/18, 1989.

Frazer, James George. *The Fasti of Ovid.* London: Macmillan, 1929. 4 vols. Hildesheim: Olms, 1973.

Freud, Sigmund. *Art and Literature: Jensen's "Gradiva," Leonardo da Vinci and Other Works.* Harmondsworth: Penguin, 1990.

Gerschel, Lucien. "Couleur et teinture chez divers peuples indo-européens." *Annales* 21.3 (1966): 608–31.

Gimbutas, Marija. *The Language of the Goddess.* London: Thames, 1989.

Girardot, N. J. "Initiation and Meaning in the Tale of Snow White and the Seven Dwarves." *Journal of American Folklore* 90.357 (1977): 274–300.

Grimm, Jacob, and Wilhelm Grimm. *The Complete Grimm's Fairy Tales.* Trans. Margaret Hunt. Ed. James Stern. 1944. New York: Pantheon, 1980.

Hunt, Margaret, ed. *Grimm's Household Tales, with the Author's Notes.* 1884. 2 vols. Detroit: Singing Tree Press, 1968.

Lang, Andrew, ed. *The Blue Fairy Book.* 1889. New York: Dover, 1965.

Levi, Carlo. *Christ Stopped at Eboli.* Trans. Frances Frenaye. Harmondsworth: Penguin, 1982.

Lüthi, Max. *The European Folktale: Form and Nature.* Trans. John D. Niles. Philadelphia: Institute for the Study of Human Issues, 1982.

Luzel, François-Marie. *Les contes de Luzel: Contes inédits.* Ed. Françoise Morvan. Vol. 1. Rennes: Presses Universitaires de Rennes/Terre de Brume, 1995.

Murphy, G. Ronald. *The Owl, the Raven, and the Dove: The Religious Meanings of the Grimms' Magic Fairy Tales.* New York: Oxford UP, 2000.

Puhvel, Jaan. *Comparative Mythology.* Baltimore: Johns Hopkins UP, 1989.

Rabelais, François. *Gargantua and Pantagruel.* Trans. J. M. Cohen. Harmondsworth: Penguin, 1955.

Sahlins, Marshall. "Colors and Cultures." *Symbolic Anthropology: A Reader in the Study of Symbols and Meanings.* Ed. Janet L. Dolgin, David S. Kemnitzer, and David M. Schneider. New York: Columbia UP, 1977. 165–80.

Shakespeare, William. *The Complete Works.* Glasgow: HarperCollins, 1994.

Shulman, David Dean. *Tamil Temple Myths: Sacrifice and Divine Marriage in the South Indian Âaiva Tradition.* Princeton, NJ: Princeton UP, 1980.

Sophocles. *The Three Theban Plays: Antigone, Oedipus the King, Oedipus at Colonus.* Trans. Robert Fagles. 2nd ed. Harmondsworth: Penguin, 1984.

Troyes, Chrétien de. *Le Conte du Graal ou Le Roman de Perceval.* Trans. Charles Méla. Paris: Livre de Poche, 1990.

Turner, Victor W. *The Forest of Symbols: Aspects of Ndembu Ritual.* Ithaca: Cornell UP, 1977.

Vaz da Silva, Francisco. "The Madonna and the Cuckoo: An Exploration in European Symbolic Conceptions." *Comparative Studies in Society and History* 46.2 (2004): 273–99.

Verdier, Yvonne. *Façons de dire, façons de faire: La laveuse, la couturière, la cuisinière.* Paris: Gallimard, 1979.

Zahan, Dominique. "L'homme et la couleur." *Les coordonées de l'homme et la culture matérielle.* Vol. 1.1 of *Histoire des mœurs.* Ed. Jean Poirier. Paris: Gallimard, 1990. 115–80.

Chapter 4

Ferdinand de Saussure

NATURE OF THE LINGUISTIC SIGN

Ferdinand de Saussure's work on linguistics is the foundation for much of the literary theory that eventually followed. "Foundation" might appear an odd word, because in Saussure's case it is a particularly slippery one: Saussure argued that meaning is arbitrary and differential (something means something because it is not something else, and *not* because it has any intrinsic value). Further, signs only function because they are culturally constructed, not being natural or organically pre-existent concepts or names. Contemporary ideas concerning networked systems, hypertext, semiotically produced virtual realities, and so on, can all be traced back to Saussure's *Course in General Linguistics* (1916), which is in itself an elusive text, being composed of student's notes taken from his lectures that he delivered at the University of Geneva (1907 to 1911). In the "Nature of the Linguistic Sign", Saussure has three propositions, the first one being that the sign is composed of a signified (a concept) and a signifier (the sound pattern or form of the sign, be it mentally or physically expressed). He begins by *rejecting* the notion that language is a collection of pre-existent names for things, what he calls "nomenclature" – which literally means to "call names". His main objection is that language as naming leads to the notion "that ideas already exist independently of words", whereas after Saussure, theorists came to believe that we create ideas in and through language. Or, to put this another way, language doesn't represent meaning, it creates or produces it. To prove his point, Saussure shows how signs are not "links" between names and things, but are in fact composed of concepts (signifieds) and sound patterns (signifiers). In his second proposition he argues that signs are arbitrary (this becomes his *first principle* for understanding how signs function). What this means is that even the link between the signified and the signifier is not natural or organic: it is socially constructed. There is no reason why the signifier "sister" (or *soeur* in French, the example Saussure gives) should be connected with the concept of being a sister. The signifier could be something entirely different, but only if society as a whole has agreed to its conventional usage. Such a point is more apparent in English in the medieval era, when the spellings of words—or signifiers—had not become uniform; it was only in the Elizabethan era that English spelling gradually stabilized and became fixed. Saussure is careful to look at cases which appear to contradict his thesis, for example onomatopoeic words, which means words which sound like the thing they describe ("tick-tock" for the tick-tocking of an antique clock); one only has to turn to the same word in another language to see that even onomatopoeia is arbitrary: a woofing dog goes "*oua oua*" in French. Also, Saussure shows how so-called onomatopoeic words, and his other example, that of exclamations, change over time. Saussure stresses in his third proposition that signifiers are linear, and that they are formed in time as chains, which is another fundamental law—or the *second principle*—of the functioning of the sign.

1. Sign, signified, signifier

Some people regard language, when reduced to its elements, as a naming-process only—a list of words, each corresponding to the thing that it names. For example:

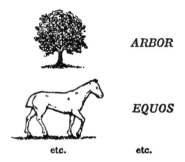

This conception is open to criticism at several points. It assumes that ready-made ideas exist before words; it does not tell us whether a name is vocal or psychological in nature (*arbor*, for instance, can be considered from either viewpoint); finally, it lets us assume that the linking of a name and a thing is a very simple operation—an assumption that is anything but true. But this rather naive approach can bring us near the truth by showing us that the linguistic unit is a double entity, one formed by the associating of two terms.

We have seen in considering the speaking-circuit that both terms involved in the linguistic sign are psychological and are united in the brain by an associative bond. This point must be emphasized.

The linguistic sign unites, not a thing and a name, but a concept and a sound-image.[1] The latter is not the material sound, a purely physical thing, but the psychological imprint of the sound, the impression that it makes on our senses. The sound-image is sensory, and if I happen to call it "material," it is only in that sense, and by way of opposing it to the other term of the association, the concept, which is generally more abstract.

The psychological character of our sound-images becomes apparent when we observe our own speech. Without moving our lips or tongue, we can talk to ourselves or recite mentally a selection of verse. Because we regard the words of our language as sound-images, we must avoid speaking of the "phonemes" that make up the words. This term, which suggests vocal activity, is applicable to the spoken word only, to the realization of the inner image in discourse. We can avoid that misunderstanding by speaking of the *sounds* and *syllables* of a word provided we remember that the names refer to the sound-image.

The linguistic sign is then a two-sided psychological entity that can be represented by the drawing:

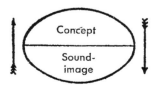

The two elements are intimately united, and each recalls the other. Whether we try to find the meaning of the Latin word *arbor* or the word that Latin uses to designate the concept "tree," it is clear that only the associations sanctioned by that language appear to us to conform to reality, and we disregard whatever others might be imagined.

Our definition of the linguistic sign poses an important question of terminology. I call the combination of a concept and a sound-image a *sign,* but in current usage the term generally designates only a sound-image, a word, for example (*arbor,* etc.). One tends to forget that *arbor* is called a sign only because it carries the concept "tree," with the result that the idea of the sensory part implies the idea of the whole.

Ambiguity would disappear if the three notions involved here were designated by the names, each suggesting, and opposing the others. I propose to retain the word *sign* [*signe*] to designate the whole and to replace *concept* and *sound-image* respectively by *signified* [*signifié*] and *signifier* [*signifiant*]; the last two terms have the advantage of indicating the opposition that separates them from each other and from the whole of which they are parts. As regards *sign,* if I am satisfied with it, this is simply because I do not know of any word to replace it, the ordinary language suggesting no other.

The linguistic sign, as defined, has two primordial characteristics. In enunciating them I am also positing the basic principles of any study of this type.

2. Principle I: the arbitrary nature of the sign

The bond between the signifier and the signified is arbitrary. Since I mean by sign the whole that results from the associating of the signifier with the signified, I can simply say: *the linguistic sign is arbitrary.*

The idea of "sister" is not linked by any inner relationship to the succession of sounds *s-ö-r* which serves as its signifier in French; that it could be represented equally by just any other sequence is proved by differences among languages and by the very existence of different languages: the signified "ox" has as its signifier *b-ö-f* on one side of the border and *o-k-s* (*Ochs*) on the other.

No one disputes the principle of the arbitrary nature of the sign, but it is often easier to discover a truth than to assign to it its proper place. Principle I dominates all the linguistics of language; its consequences are numberless. It is true that not all of them are equally obvious at first glance; only after many detours does one discover them, and with them the primordial importance of the principle.

One remark in passing: when semiology becomes organized as a science, the question will arise whether or not it properly includes modes of expression based on completely natural signs, such as pantomime. Supposing that the new science welcomes them, its main concern will still be the whole group of systems grounded on the arbitrariness of the sign. In fact, every means of expression used in society is based, in principle, on collective behavior or—what amounts to the same thing—on convention. Polite formulas, for instance, though often imbued with a certain natural expressiveness (as in the case of a Chinese who greets his emperor by bowing down to the ground nine times), are nonetheless fixed by rule; it is this rule and not the intrinsic value of the gestures that obliges one to use them. Signs that are wholly arbitrary realize better than the others the ideal of the semiological process; that is why language, the most complex and universal of all systems of expression, is also the most characteristic; in this sense linguistics can become the master-pattern for all branches of semiology although language is only one particular semiological system.

The word *symbol* has been used to designate the linguistic sign, or more specifically, what is here called the signifier. Principle I in particular weighs against the use of this term. One characteristic of the symbol is that it is never wholly arbitrary; it is not empty, for there is the rudiment of a natural bond between the signifier and the signified. The symbol of justice, a pair of scales, could not be replaced by just any other symbol, such as a chariot.

The word *arbitrary* also calls for comment. The term should not imply that the choice of the signifier is left entirely to the speaker (we shall see below that the individual does not have the power to change a sign in any way once it has become established in the linguistic community); I mean that it is unmotivated, i.e. arbitrary in that it actually has no natural connection with the signified.

In concluding let us consider two objections that might be raised to the establishment of Principle I:

1.   *Onomatopoeia* might be used to prove that the choice of the signifier is not always arbitrary. But onomatopoeic formations are never organic elements of a linguistic system. Besides, their number is much smaller than is generally supposed. Words like French *fouet* 'whip' or *glas* 'knell' may strike certain ears with suggestive sonority, but to see that they have not always had this property we need only examine their Latin forms (*fouet* is derived from *fāgus* 'beech-tree,' *glas* from *classicum* 'sound of a trumpet'). The quality of their present sounds, or rather the quality that is attributed to them, is a fortuitous result of phonetic evolution.

As for authentic onomatopoeic words (e.g. *glug-glug, tick-tock,* etc.), not only are they limited in number, but also they are chosen somewhat arbitrarily, for they are only approximate and more or less conventional imitations of certain sounds (cf. English *bow-bow* and French *ouaoua*). In addition, once these words have been introduced into the language, they are to a certain extent subjected to the same evolution—phonetic, morphological, etc.—that other words undergo (cf. *pigeon,* ultimately from Vulgar Latin *pīpiō,* derived in turn from an onomatopoeic formation): obvious proof that they lose something of their original character in order to assume that of the linguistic sign in general, which is unmotivated.

2.   *Interjections,* closely related to onomatopoeia, can be attacked on the same grounds and come no closer to refuting our thesis. One is tempted to see in them spontaneous expressions of reality dictated, so to speak, by natural forces. But for most interjections we can show that there is no fixed bond between their signified and their signifier. We need only compare two languages on this point to see how much such expressions differ from one language to the next (e.g. the English equivalent of French *aïe!* is *ouch!*). We know, moreover, that many interjections were once words with specific meanings (cf. French *diable!* 'darn!' *mordieu!* 'golly!' from *mort Dieu* 'God's death,' etc.).[2]

Onomatopoeic formations and interjections are of secondary importance, and their symbolic origin is in part open to dispute.

3. Principle II: the linear nature of the signifier

The signifier, being auditory, is unfolded solely in time from which it gets the following characteristics: (a) it represents a span, and (b) the span is measurable in a single dimension; it is a line.

While Principle II is obvious, apparently linguists have always neglected to state it, doubtless because they found it too simple; nevertheless, it is fundamental, and its consequences are incalculable. Its importance equals that of Principle I; the whole mechanism of language depends upon it. In contrast to visual signifiers (nautical signals, etc.) which can offer simultaneous groupings in several dimensions, auditory signifiers have at their command only the dimension of time. Their elements are presented in succession; they form a chain. This feature becomes readily apparent when they are represented in writing and the spatial line of graphic marks is substituted for succession in time.

Sometimes the linear nature of the signifier is not obvious. When I accent a syllable, for instance, it seems that I am concentrating more than one significant element on the same point. But this is an illusion; the syllable and its accent constitute only one phonational act. There is no duality within the act but only different oppositions to what precedes and what follows.

Notes

1   The term sound-image may seem to be too restricted inasmuch as beside the representation of the sounds of a word there is also that of its articulation, the muscular image of the phonational act. But for F. de Saussure language is essentially a depository, a thing received from without (see p. 13). The sound-image is par excellence the natural representation of the word as a fact of potential language, outside any actual use of it in speaking. The motor side is thus implied or, in any event, occupies only a subordinate role with respect to the sound-image. [Ed.]

2   Cf. English *goodness!* and *zounds!* (from *God's wounds*). [Tr.]

Chapter 5

Roman Jakobson

TWO ASPECTS OF LANGUAGE AND TWO TYPES OF APHASIC DISTURBANCES

Speakers of language are on the whole word users, not word coiners, according to Roman Jakobson, one of the founders in the early twentieth century of the influential Moscow Linguistic Circle and Prague Linguistic Circle, as well as becoming a leading Harvard and MIT professor. In his essay extracted here, he focuses on the range of word choices that we make when we use language, and what happens when our ability to make these choices breaks down. Jakobson posits two axes in his example of Alice (in Wonderland) choosing to say "pig" rather than "fig": the vertical axis of concurrence or selection (Alice chooses "p" rather than "f") and the horizontal axis of concatenation or combination, which means the building of the word through time. Both axes depend upon utilizing linguistic codes, which "limits" the word user's potential choices. At the phonemic level (speech sounds), word users have no choice with the pre-assigned linguistic code, but as users combine words into sentences, there is slightly more freedom to come up with original expressions. Jakobson observes that for Saussure, signs function along the linear combinatory line, which denies a role for selection; instead, Jakobson argues that language users are aware that in reality these two axes are co-present, and that this can be proven by studying individuals with neurolinguistic problems, namely "aphasia" (a breakdown in language skills). Utilizing empirical research data, Jakobson divides aphasics into those who suffer from the Similarity Disorder or the Contiguity Disorder, where "Metaphor is alien to the similarity disorder, and metonymy to the contiguity disorder". For example, if we are having trouble following a speaker who is explaining a concept, we might ask her "what do you mean?" The speaker responds by using a metalinguistic phrase: that is to say a phrase which explains *in different words* what she just said. The speaker is using language to reflect upon and re-phrase language! Those suffering from the similarity disorder can no longer do this, and this reduces the set of words available to them to explain a complex situation or concept. With the contiguity disorder, "Word order becomes chaotic" and grammatical rules are "dissolved". In this situation, the extent and variety of sentences is severely reduced. Jakobson theorizes from this overall study that the two fundamental aspects of language are metaphor and metonymy, and that all language users, including literary writers, can be analyzed according to these aspects, or "poles" as he calls them, to see if one or the other dominates. In the combination of these aspects, myriad creative possibilities emerge; what Jakobson calls "an impressive range of possible configurations." In literature, Jakobson argues that the metaphorical pole dominates in Romanticism and Symbolism, whereas Realism depends most heavily on the metonymic pole. The flat narrative style of postmodern writing, and some postcolonial authors, is also largely dependent upon metonymy. In painting, the Surrealists utilized the metaphorical pole, whereas the Cubists utilized the metonymic; Jakobson also discusses film (this approach applies equally well to other media), and even the Freudian interpretation of dreams. As Jakobson suggests, "The dichotomy discussed here appears to be of primal significance and consequence for all verbal behaviour and for human behaviour in general."

The linguistic problems of aphasia

If aphasia is a language disturbance, as the term itself suggests, then any description and classification of aphasic syndromes must begin with the question of what aspects of language are impaired in the various species of such a disorder. This problem, which was approached long ago by Hughlings Jackson (1915), cannot be solved without the participation of professional linguists familiar with the patterning and functioning of language.

To study adequately any breakdown in communication we must first understand the nature and structure of the particular mode of communication that has ceased to function. Linguistics is concerned with language in all its aspects—language in operation, language in drift (see Sapir 1921:chap. 7), language in the nascent state, and language in dissolution.

There are psychopathologists who assign a high importance to the linguistic problems involved in the study of language disturbances;[1] some of these questions have been touched upon in the best treatises on aphasia.[2] Yet, in most cases, this valid insistence on the linguist's contribution to the investigation of aphasia has been ignored. For instance, one book, dealing to a great extent with the complex and intricate problems of infantile aphasia, calls for the coordination of various disciplines and appeals for cooperation to otolaryngologists, pediatricians, audiologists, psychiatrists, and educators; but the science of language is passed over in silence, as if disorders in speech perception had nothing whatever to do with language (Myklebust 1954).

Linguists are also responsible for the delay in undertaking a joint inquiry into aphasia. Nothing comparable to the minute linguistic observations of infants of various countries has been performed with respect to aphasics. Nor has there been any attempt to reinterpret and systematize from the point of view of linguistics the multifarious clinical data on diverse types of aphasia. That this should be true is all the more surprising in view of the fact that, on the one hand, the amazing progress of structural linguistics has endowed the investigator with efficient tools and methods for the study of verbal regression and, on the other, the aphasic disintegration of the verbal pattern may provide the linguist with new insights into the general laws of language.

The application of purely linguistic criteria to the interpretation and classification of aphasic facts can substantially contribute to the science of language and language disturbances, provided that linguists remain as careful and cautious when dealing with psychological and neurological data as they have been in their traditional field. First of all, they should be familiar with the technical terms and devices of the medical disciplines dealing with aphasia; then, they must submit the clinical case reports to thorough linguistic analysis; further, they should themselves work with aphasic patients in order to approach the cases directly and not only through a reinterpretation of prepared records which have been quite differently conceived and elaborated.

There is one level of aphasic phenomena where amazing agreement has been achieved between those psychiatrists and linguists who have tackled these problems, namely the disintegration of the sound pattern.[3] This dissolution exhibits a time order of great regularity.

Aphasic regression has proved to be a mirror of the child's acquisition of speech sounds: it shows the child's development in reverse. Furthermore, comparison of child language and aphasia enables us to establish several *laws of implication*. The search for this order of acquisitions and losses and for the general laws of implication cannot be confined to the phonemic pattern but must be extended also to the grammatical system.[4]

The twofold character of language

Speech implies a selection of certain linguistic entities and their combination into linguistic units of a higher degree of complexity. At the lexical level this is readily apparent: the speaker selects words and combines them into sentences according to the syntactic system of the language he is using; sentences in their turn are combined into utterances. But the speaker is by no means a completely free agent in his choice of words: his selection (except for the rare case of actual neology) must be made from the lexical storehouse which he and his addressee possess in common. The communication engineer most properly approaches the essence of the speech event when he assumes that in the optimal exchange of information the speaker and the listener have at their disposal more or less the same "filing cabinet of *prefabricated* representations": the addresser of a verbal message selects one of these "preconceived possibilities," and the addressee is supposed to make an identical choice from the same assembly of "possibilities already foreseen and provided for" (MacKay 1952:183). Thus the efficiency of a speech event demands the use of a common code by its participants.

"'Did you say *pig* or *fig*?' said the Cat. 'I said *pig*,' replied Alice" (Carroll 1866:chap. 6). In this peculiar utterance the feline addressee attempts to recapture a linguistic choice made by the addresser. In the common code of the Cat and Alice (spoken English), the difference between a stop and a continuant, other things being equal, may change the meaning of the message. Alice had used the distinctive feature stop versus continuant, rejecting the latter and choosing the former of the two opposites; and in the same act of speech she combined this solution with certain other simultaneous features, using the gravity and the tenseness of /p/ in contradistinction to the acuteness of /t/ and to the laxness of /b/. Thus all these attributes have been combined into a bundle of distinctive features, the so-called phoneme. The phoneme /p/ was then followed by the phonemes /I/ and /g/, themselves bundles of simultaneously produced distinctive features. Hence the *concurrence* of simultaneous entities and the *concatenation* of successive entities are the two ways in which we speakers combine linguistic constituents.

Neither such bundles as /p/ or /f/ nor such sequences of bundles as /pɪg/ or /fɪg/ are invented by the speaker who uses them. Neither can the distinctive feature stop versus continuant nor the phoneme /p/ occur out of context. The stop feature appears in combination with certain other concurrent features, and the repertory of combinations of these features into phonemes such as /p/, /b/, /t/, /d/, /k/, /g/ is limited by the code of the given language. The code sets limitations on the possible combinations of the phoneme /p/ with other following and/or preceding phonemes; and only part of the permissible phoneme sequences are actually utilized in the lexical stock of a given language. Even when other combinations of phonemes are theoretically possible, the speaker, as a rule, is only a word user, not a word coiner. When faced with individual words, we expect them to be coded units. In order to grasp the word *nylon* one must know the meaning assigned to this vocable in the lexical code of modern English.

In any language there exist also coded word groups called "phrase words." The meaning of the idiom *how do you do* cannot be derived by adding together the meanings of its lexical constituents; the whole is not equal to the sum of its parts. Word groups which in this respect behave like single words are a common but nonetheless only marginal case. In order to comprehend the overwhelming majority of word groups, we need be familiar only with the constituent words and with the syntactic rules of their combination. Within these limitations we are free to put words in new contexts. Of course, this freedom is relative, and the pressure of current clichés upon our choice of combinations is considerable. But the freedom to compose quite new contexts is undeniable, despite the relatively low statistical probability of their occurrence.

Thus, in the combination of linguistic units, there is an ascending scale of freedom. In the combination of distinctive features into phonemes, the freedom of the individual speaker is zero: the code has already established all the possibilities which may be utilized in the given language. Freedom to combine phonemes into words is circumscribed; it is limited to the marginal situation of word coinage. In forming sentences with words, the speaker is less constrained. And finally, in the combination of sentences into utterances, the action of compulsory syntactic rules ceases, and the freedom of any individual speaker to create novel contexts increases substantially, although again the numerous stereotyped utterances are not to be overlooked.

Any linguistic sign involves two modes of arrangement:

1. *Combination.* Any sign is made up of constituent signs and/or occurs only in combination with other signs. This means that any linguistic unit at one and the same time serves as a context for simpler units and/or finds its own context in a more complex linguistic unit. Hence any actual grouping of linguistic units binds them into a superior unit: combination and contexture are two faces of the same operation.

2. *Selection.* A selection between alternatives implies the possibility of substituting one for the other, equivalent in one respect and different in another. Actually, selection and substitution are two faces of the same operation.

The fundamental role which these two operations play in language was clearly realized by Ferdinand de Saussure. Yet of the two varieties of combination—concurrence and concatenation—it was only the latter, the temporal sequence, which was recognized by the Geneva linguist. Despite his own insight into the phoneme as a set of concurrent distinctive features (*éléments différentiels des phonèmes*), the scholar succumbed to the traditional belief in the linear character of language "which excludes the possibility of pronouncing two elements at the same time" (1966:170).

In order to delimit the two modes of arrangement we have described as combination and selection, de Saussure states that the former "is *in presentia*: it is based on two or several terms jointly present in an actual series," whereas the latter "connects terms *in absentia* as members of a virtual mnemonic series" (p. 123). That is to say, selection (and, correspondingly, substitution) deals with entities conjoined in the code but not in the given message, whereas, in the case of combination, the entities are conjoined in both or only in the actual message. The addressee perceives that the given utterance (message) is a *combination* of constituent parts (sentences, words, phonemes) *selected* from the repository of all possible constituent parts (the code). The constituents of a context are in a state of *contiguity,* while in a substitution set signs are linked by various degrees of *similarity* which fluctuate between the equivalence of synonyms and the common core of antonyms.

These two operations provide each linguistic sign with two sets of "interpretants," to utilize the effective concept introduced by Charles Sanders Peirce (1932, 1934). There are two references which serve to interpret the sign—one to the code and the other to the context, whether coded or free, and in each of these ways the sign is related to another set of linguistic signs, through an *alternation* in the former case and through an *alignment* in the latter. A given significative unit may be replaced by other, more explicit signs of the same code, whereby its general meaning is revealed, while its contextual meaning is determined by its connection with other signs within the same sequence.

The constituents of any message are necessarily linked with the code by an internal relation and with the message by an external relation. Language in its various aspects deals with both modes of relation. Whether messages are exchanged or communication proceeds unilaterally from the addresser to the addressee, there must be some kind of contiguity between the participants of any speech event to assure the transmission of the message. The separation in space, and often in time, between two individuals, the addresser and the addressee, is bridged by an internal relation: there must be a certain equivalence between the symbols used by the addresser and those known and interpreted by the addressee. Without such an equivalence the message is fruitless: even when it reaches the receiver it does not affect him.

The similarity disorder

It is clear that speech disturbances may affect in varying degrees the individual's capacity for combination and selection of linguistic units, and indeed the question of which of these two operations is chiefly impaired proves to be of far-reaching significance in describing, analyzing, and classifying the diverse forms of aphasia. This dichotomy is perhaps even more suggestive than the classical distinction between *emissive* and *receptive* aphasia,[5] indicating which of the two functions in speech exchange, the encoding or the decoding of verbal messages, is particularly affected.

Head (1926) attempted to classify cases of aphasia into definite groups, and to each of these varieties he assigned "a name chosen to signify the most salient defect in the management and comprehension of words and phrases." Following this device, we distinguish two basic types of aphasia—depending on whether the major deficiency lies in selection and substitution, with relative stability of combination and contexture; or conversely, in combination and contexture, with relative retention of normal selection and substitution. In outlining these two opposite patterns of aphasia, I shall utilize mainly Goldstein's data (1948).

For aphasics of the first type (selection deficiency), the context is the indispensable and decisive factor. When presented with scraps of words or sentences, such a patient readily completes them. His speech is merely reactive: he easily carries on conversation but has difficulties in starting a dialogue; he is able to reply to a real or imaginary addresser when he is, or imagines himself to be, the addressee of the message. It is particularly hard for him to perform, or even to understand, such a closed discourse as the monologue. The more his utterances are dependent on the context, the better he copes with his verbal task. He feels unable to utter a sentence which responds neither to the cue of his interlocutor nor to the actual situation. The sentence "it rains" cannot be produced unless the utterer sees that it is actually raining. The deeper the utterance is embedded in the verbal or nonverbalized context, the higher are the chances of its successful performance by this class of patients.

Likewise, the more a word is dependent on the other words of the same sentence and the more it refers to the syntactic context, the less it is affected by the speech disturbance. Therefore words syntactically subordinated by grammatical agreement or government are more tenacious, whereas the main subordinating agent of the sentence, namely the subject, tends to be omitted. As long as beginning is the patient's main difficulty, it is obvious that he will fail precisely at the starting point, the cornerstone of the sentence pattern. In this type of language disturbance, sentences are conceived as elliptical sequels to be supplied from antecedent sentences uttered, if not imagined, by the aphasic himself or received by him from the other partner in the colloquy, actual if not imaginary. Key words may be dropped or superseded by abstract anaphoric substitutes (cf. Bloomfield 1933:chap. 15). A specific noun, as Freud (1953:22) noticed, is replaced by a very general one, for instance *machin* or *chose* (thing) in the speech of French aphasies. In a dialectal German sample of "amnesic aphasia" observed by Goldstein (1948:246–48), *Ding* (thing) or *Stückel* (piece) was substituted for all inanimate nouns, and *überfahren* (perform) for verbs which were identifiable from the context or situation and therefore appeared superfluous to the patient.

Words with an inherent reference to the context, such as pronouns and pronominal adverbs, and words serving merely to construct the context, such as connectives and auxiliaries, are particularly prone to survive. A typical utterance of a German patient, recorded by Quensel and quoted by Goldstein (p. 302), will serve as illustration: "Ich bin doch hier unten, na wenn ich gewesen bin ich wees nicht, we das, nu wenn ich, ob das nun doch, noch, ja. Was Sie her, wenn ich, och ich weess nicht, we das hier war ja." (But I am here below, well if I have been I know not, who that, now if I, if that now but, still, yes. What you here, if I, oh I know not, who that here was yes.) Thus only the framework, the connecting links of communication, is spared by this type of aphasia at its critical stage.

[. . .]

The contiguity disorder

From 1864 on it was repeatedly pointed out in Hughlings Jackson's pioneer contributions to the modern study of language and language disturbances:

> It is not enough to say that speech consists of words. It consists of words referring to one another in a particular manner; and, without a proper interrelation of its parts, a verbal utterance would be a mere succession of names embodying no proposition. (1868:66)
>
> Loss of speech is the loss of power to propositionize . . . Speechlessness does not mean entire wordlessness. (1879:114)

Impairment of the ability to propositionize or, generally speaking, to combine simpler linguistic entities into more complex units, is actually confined to one type of aphasia, the opposite of the type discussed in the preceding section. There is no wordlessness, since the entity preserved in most of such cases is the word, which can be defined as the highest among the linguistic units compulsorily coded—we compose our own sentences and utterances out of the word stock supplied by the code.

This contexture-deficient aphasia, which could be termed the "contiguity disorder," diminishes the extent and variety of sentences. The syntactic rules organizing words into higher units are lost; this loss, called "agrammatism," causes the degeneration of the sentence into a mere "word heap," to use Jackson's image (1866). Word order becomes chaotic; the ties of grammatical coordination and subordination, whether concord or government, are dissolved. As might be expected, words endowed with purely grammatical functions, like conjunctions, prepositions, pronouns, and articles, disappear first, giving rise to the so-called telegraphic style, whereas in the case of a similarity disorder they are the most resistant. The less a word depends grammatically on the context, the stronger is its tenacity in the speech of aphasics with a contiguity disorder and the earlier it is dropped by patients with a similarity disorder. Thus the "kernel subject word" is the first to fall out of the sentence in cases of similarity disorder, and conversely, it is the least destructible in the opposite type of aphasia.

The type of aphasia affecting contexture tends to give rise to infantile one-sentence utterances and one-word sentences. Only a few longer, stereotyped, ready-made sentences manage to survive. In advanced cases of this disease, each utterance is reduced to a single one-word sentence. While contexture disintegrates, the selective operation goes on. "To say what a thing is, is to say what it is like," Jackson notes (1879:125). The patient confined to the substitution set (once contexture is deficient) deals with similarities, and his approximate identifications are of a metaphoric nature, contrary to the metonymic ones familiar to the opposite type of aphasics. *Spyglass* for *microscope* or *fire* for *gaslight* are typical examples of such quasi-metaphoric expressions, as Jackson termed them, since, in contradistinction to rhetoric or poetic metaphors, they present no deliberate transfer of meaning.

In a normal language pattern, the word is at the same time both a constituent part of a superimposed context, the sentence, and itself a context superimposed on ever smaller constituents, morphemes (minimum units endowed with meaning) and phonemes. We have discussed the effect of contiguity disorder on the combination of words into higher units. The relationship between the word and its constituents reflects the same impairment, yet in a somewhat different way. A typical feature of agrammatism is the abolition of inflection: there appear such "unmarked" categories as the infinitive in the place of diverse finite verbal forms and, in languages with declension, the nominative instead of all the oblique cases. These defects are due partly to the elimination of government and concord, partly to the loss of ability to dissolve words into stem and desinence. Finally, a paradigm (in particular a set of grammatical cases such as *he-his-him* or of tenses such as *he votes-he voted*) present the same semantic content from different points of view associated with each other by contiguity; so there is one more impetus for aphasics with a contiguity disorder to dismiss such sets.

Also, as a rule, words derived from the same root, such as *grant-grantor-grantee,* are semantically related by contiguity. The patients under discussion are inclined to drop either the derivative words or the combination of a root with a derivational suffix, and even a compound of two words becomes irresolvable for them. Patients who understood and uttered such compounds as *Thanksgiving* or *Battersea,* but were unable to grasp or say *thanks* and *giving* or *batter* and *sea,* have often been cited. As long as the sense of derivation is still alive, so that this process is still used for creating innovations in the code, one can observe a tendency toward oversimplification and automatism: if the derivative word constitutes a semantic unit which cannot be entirely inferred from the meaning of its components, the Gestalt is misunderstood. Thus the Russian word *mokr-íca* signifies "wood-louse," but a Russian aphasic interpreted it as "something humid," especially "humid weather," since the root *mokr-*means "humid" and the suffix-*ica* designates a carrier of the given property, as in *nelépica* (something absurd), *svetlíca* (light room), *temníca* (dungeon, lit. dark room).

[. . .]

The metaphoric and metonymic poles

The varieties of aphasia are numerous and diverse, but all of them lie between the two polar types just described. Every form of aphasic disturbance consists in some impairment, more or less severe, of the faculty either for selection and substitution or for combination and contexture. The former affliction involves a deterioration of metalinguistic operations, while the latter damages the capacity for maintaining the hierarchy of linguistic units. The relation of similarity is suppressed in the former, the relation of contiguity in the latter type of aphasia. Metaphor is alien to the similarity disorder, and metonymy to the contiguity disorder.

The development of a discourse may take place along two different semantic lines: one topic may lead to another either through their similarity or through their contiguity. The metaphoric way would be the most appropriate term for the first case and the metonymic way for the second, since they find their most condensed expression in metaphor and metonymy respectively. In aphasia one or the other of these two processes is restricted or totally blocked—an effect which makes the study of aphasia particularly illuminating for the linguist. In normal verbal behavior both processes are continually operative, but careful observation will reveal that under the influence of a cultural pattern, personality, and verbal style, preference is given to one of the two processes over the other.

In a well-known psychological test, children are confronted with some noun and told to utter the first verbal response that comes into their heads. In this experiment two opposite linguistic predilections are invariably exhibited: the response is intended either as a substitute for or as a complement to the stimulus. In the latter case the stimulus and the response together form a proper syntactic construction, most usually a sentence. These two types of reaction have been labeled "substitutive" and "predicative."

To the stimulus *hut* one response was *burnt out;* another, *is a poor little house.* Both reactions are predicative; but the first creates a purely narrative context, while in the second there is a double connection with the subject *hut:* on the one hand, a positional (namely, syntactic) contiguity, and on the other, a semantic similarity.

The same stimulus produced the following substitutive reactions: the tautology *hut;* the synonyms *cabin* and *hovel;* the antonym *palace;* and the metaphors *den* and *burrow.* The capacity of two words to replace one another is an instance of positional similarity; in addition, all these responses are linked to the stimulus by semantic similarity (or contrast). Metonymical responses to the same stimulus, such as *thatch, litter,* or *poverty,* combine and contrast the positional similarity with semantic contiguity.

In manipulating these two kinds of connection (similarity and contiguity) in both their aspects (positional and semantic) – selecting combining, and ranking them – an individual exhibits his personal style, his verbal predilections and preferences.

In verbal art the interaction of these two elements is especially pronounced. Rich material for the study of this relationship is to be found in verse patterns which require a compulsory parallelism between adjacent lines, for example in biblical poetry or in the Finnic and, to some extent, the Russian oral traditions. This provides an objective criterion of what in the given speech community acts as a correspondence. Since on any verbal level – morphemic, lexical, syntactic, and phraseological—either of these two relations (similarity and contiguity) can appear, and each in either of two aspects, an impressive range of possible configurations is created. Either of the two gravitational poles may prevail. In Russian lyrical songs, for example, metaphoric constructions predominate while in the heroic epics the metonymic way is preponderant.

In poetry there are various motives which determine the choice between these alternants. The primacy of the metaphoric process in the literary schools of Romanticism and Symbolism has been repeatedly acknowledged, but it is still insufficiently realized that it is the predominance of metonymy which underlies and actually predetermines the so-called Realist trend, which belongs to an intermediary stage between the decline of Romanticism and the rise of Symbolism and is opposed to both. Following the path of contiguous relationships, the Realist author metonymically digresses from the plot to the atmosphere and from the characters to the setting in space and time. He is fond of synecdochic details. In the scene of Anna Karenina's suicide Tolstoj's artistic attention is focused on the heroine's handbag; and in *War and Peace* the synecdoches "hair on the upper lip" and "bare shoulders" are used by the same writer to stand for the female characters to whom these features belong.

The alternative predominance of one or the other of these two processes is by no means confined to verbal art. The same oscillation occurs in sign systems other than language.[6] A salient example from the history of painting is the manifestly metonymic orientation of

Cubism, where the object is transformed into a set of synecdoches; the Surrealist painters responded with a patently metaphoric attitude. Ever since the productions of D. W. Griffith, the art of the cinema, with its highly developed capacity for changing the angle, perspective, and focus of shots, has broken with the tradition of the theater and ranged an unprecedented variety of synecdochic close-ups and metonymic setups in general. In such motion pictures as those of Charlie Chaplin and Eisenstein (1950), these devices in turn were overlaid by a novel, metaphoric montage with its lap dissolves—the filmic similes (see Balazs 1952).

The bipolar structure of language (or other semiotic systems) and, in aphasia, the fixation on one of these poles to the exclusion of the other require systematic comparative study. The retention of either of these alternatives in the two types of aphasia must be confronted with the predominance of the same pole in certain styles, personal habits, current fashions, etc. A careful analysis and comparison of these phenomena with the whole syndrome of the corresponding type of aphasia is an imperative task for joint research by experts in psychopathology, psychology, linguistics, poetics, and semiotics, the general science of signs. The dichotomy discussed here appears to be of primal significance and consequence for all verbal behavior and for human behavior in general.[7]

To indicate the possibilities of the projected comparative research, I choose an example from a Russian folktale which employs parallelism as a comic device: "Thomas is a bachelor; Jeremiah is unmarried" (*Fomá xólost; Erjóma neženát*). Here the predicates in the two parallel clauses are associated by similarity: they are in fact synonymous. The subjects of both clauses are masculine proper names and hence morphologically similar, while on the other hand they denote two contiguous heroes of the same tale, created to perform identical actions and thus to justify the use of synonymous pairs of predicates. A somewhat modified version of the same construction occurs in a familiar wedding song in which each of the wedding guests is addressed in turn by his first name and patronymic: "Gleb is a bachelor; Ivanovič is unmarried." While both predicates here are again synonyms, the relationship between the two subjects is changed: both are proper names denoting the same man and are normally used contiguously as a mode of polite address.

Notes

1.   See, for instance, the discussion of aphasia in the *Nederlandsche Vereeniging voor Phonetische Wettenschappen*, with papers by the linguist J. van Ginneken and by two psychiatrists, F. Grewel and V. W. D. Schenk (1941:1035–1043); see furthermore F. Grewel (1949:726ff.).
2.   See works by A. R. Luria (1947), Kurt Goldstein (1948), and André Ombredane (1951).
3.   The aphasic impoverishment of the sound pattern has been observed and discussed by the linguist Marguerite Durand together with the psychopathologists T. Alajouanine and A Ombredane (1939) and by R. Jakobson (the first draft, presented to the International Congress of Linguists at Brussels in 1939 [1939e; see N. Trubetzkoy (1949:317–379)], was later developed into an outline [1941a]).
4.   A joint inquiry into certain grammatical disturbances was undertaken at the Bonn University Clinic by a linguist, G. Kandler, and two physicians, F. Panse and A. Leischner (see their joint report, 1952).
5.   [See Chapter 29 and RJ 1955a, 1964b, 1966c, 1975c.]
6.   See the remarkable studies of A. Gvozdev (1929, 1948, 1949).
7.   I ventured a few sketchy remarks on the metonymic turn in verbal art (1927, 1935b), in painting (1919), and in motion pictures (1933b), but the crucial problem awaits a detailed investigation.

Chapter 6

Roland Barthes

MYTH TODAY

For Roland Barthes myth is a semiological system, or, a system of signs that make up a type of language. Saussure argued that the signs, composed of signifiers and signifieds, are arbitrary (what Barthes calls "healthy"); for Barthes, the language of myth is not arbitrary, it is motivated, ideologically loaded, and responsible for transforming "history into Nature". Immediately, it can be seen why Barthes's work is so important for structuralism and poststructuralism (for example in books such as *Writing Degree Zero* (1953), *Mythologies* (1957) and *S/Z* (1970), among many others), since he brings together relatively abstract Saussurian semiotics with astute political analysis. As he suggests, arbitrary networks of signs simply generate meaning, whereas the language of myth *distorts* meaning. This is a big claim, but then the language of myth is vast, because anything can function as a mythical sign, not just speech and writing, but "photography, cinema, reporting, sport, shows, publicity" and so on. Barthes accounts for the differences between an arbitrary semiological system and a motivated one, by suggesting that myth "*is a second-order semiological system.*" The basic building blocks of myth are signs (signifiers and signifieds working together as a whole unit). These units, however, function within myth as the myth's signifiers. We can think of two "levels" here: on the first level, is a linguistic system ("the language-object") which functions just as Saussure argued; on the second level, there is the new language of myth (the "metalanguage") which incorporates signs as a beginning point, to make up a bigger more devious system of distorted signification. Barthes gives two main examples, the first being a linguistic one, the words found in a Latin grammar book which translated say "because my name is lion". At the level of the language-object, this collection of signifiers (words or sound patterns) all co-exist with their signifieds (concepts), to make a coherent unit; at the level of the metalanguage, the linguistic unit says something beyond the literal meaning: it addresses the schoolchild reading the grammar book and says "I am a grammatical example." This statement becomes the new signified, or meaning, at the higher level of myth. The overall combination of signifiers and signifieds is called by Barthes the "signification", and this is where things get complicated. Barthes explores the complications by producing a phenomenology of myth: how myth works upon readers, how myth manipulates them yet can still be deconstructed. Myth doesn't hide anything in its doubled semiological system: everything is in plain view. In Barthes's second example, a black soldier saluting a French flag, the distortion created by myth is that colonial peoples, subjected to imperial France, are loyal subjects who would happily fight for their imperial masters. In this myth, the history of colonialism is effaced, and a new notion of colonial subjectivity is produced. In fact myth, for Barthes, is like a machine: in this case a turnstile, in which arbitrary signs are rotated into the realm of the metalanguage that then makes them mean something new. There is also a certain slipperyness caused by this turnstile, as the semiotic chains are both arrested, fixed in place (colonial subjects should all be loyal to the centre!), yet kept mobile as more and more material is made to work for the myth. What is political and historical is processed by myth to appear natural and universal. Myth is therefore a mode of "*depoliticized speech*".

W**HAT IS MYTH, TODAY?** I shall give at the outset a first, very simple answer, which is perfectly consistent with etymology: *myth is a type of speech.*[1]

Myth is a type of speech

Of course, it is not *any* type: language needs special conditions in order to become myth: we shall see them in a minute. But what must be firmly established at the start is that myth is a system of communication, that it is a message. This allows one to perceive that myth cannot possibly be an object, a concept, or an idea; it is a mode of signification, a form. Later, we shall have to assign to this form historical limits, conditions of use, and reintroduce society into it: we must nevertheless first describe it as a form.

It can be seen that to purport to discriminate among mythical objects according to their substance would be entirely illusory: since myth is a type of speech, everything can be a myth provided it is conveyed by a discourse. Myth is not defined by the object of its message, but by the way in which it utters this message: there are formal limits to myth, there are no "substantial" ones. Everything, then, can be a myth? Yes, I believe this, for the universe is infinitely fertile in suggestions. Every object in the world can pass from a closed, silent existence to an oral state, open to appropriation by society, for there is no law, whether natural or not, which forbids talking about things. A tree is a tree. Yes, of course. But a tree as expressed by Minou Drouet is no longer quite a tree, it is a tree which is decorated, adapted to a certain type of consumption, laden with literary self-indulgence, revolt, images, in short with a type of social *usage* which is added to pure matter.

Naturally, everything is not expressed at the same time: some objects become the prey of mythical speech for a while, then they disappear, others take their place and attain the status of myth. Are there objects which are *inevitably* a source of suggestiveness, as Baudelaire suggested about Woman? Certainly not: one can conceive of very ancient myths, but there are no eternal ones; for it is human history which converts reality into speech, and it alone rules the life and the death of mythical language. Ancient or not, mythology can only have a historical foundation, for myth is a type of speech chosen by history: it cannot possibly evolve from the "nature" of things.

Speech of this kind is a message. It is therefore by no means confined to oral speech. It can consist of modes of writing or of representations; not only written discourse, but also photography, cinema, reporting, sport, shows, publicity, all these can serve as a support to mythical speech. Myth can be defined neither by its object nor by its material, for any material can arbitrarily be endowed with meaning: the arrow which is brought in order to signify a challenge is also a kind of speech. True, as far as perception is concerned, writing and pictures, for instance, do not call upon the same type of consciousness; and even with pictures, one can use many kinds of reading: a diagram lends itself to signification more than a drawing, a copy more than an original, and a caricature more than a portrait. But this is the point: we are no longer dealing here with a theoretical mode of representation: we are dealing with *this* particular image, which is given for *this* particular signification. Mythical speech is made of a material which has *already* been worked on so as to make it suitable for communication: it is because all the materials of myth (whether pictorial or written) presuppose a signifying consciousness, that one can reason about them while discounting their substance. This substance is not unimportant: pictures, to be sure, are more imperative than writing, they impose meaning at one stroke, without analyzing or diluting it. But this is no longer a constitutive difference. Pictures become a kind of writing as soon as they are meaningful: like writing, they call for a *lexis*.

We shall therefore take *language, discourse, speech,* etc., to mean any significant unit or synthesis, whether verbal or visual: a photograph will be a kind of speech for us in the same way as a newspaper article; even objects will become speech, if they mean something. This generic way of conceiving language is in fact justified by the very history of writing: long before the invention of our alphabet, objects like the Inca *quipu,* or drawings, as in pictographs, have been accepted as speech. This does not mean that one must treat mythical speech like language; myth in fact belongs to the province of a general science, coextensive with linguistics, which is *semiology*.

Myth as a semiological system

For mythology, since it is the study of a type of speech, is but one fragment of this vast science of signs which Saussure postulated some forty years ago under the name of *semiology*. Semiology has not yet come into being. But since Saussure himself, and sometimes independently of him, a whole section of contemporary research has constantly been referred to the problem of meaning: psychoanalysis, structuralism, eidetic psychology, some new types of literary criticism of which Bachelard has given the first examples, are no longer concerned with facts except inasmuch as they are endowed with significance. Now to postulate a signification is to have recourse to semiology. I do not mean that semiology could account for all these aspects of research equally well: they have different contents. But they have a common status: they are all sciences dealing with values. They are not content with meeting the facts: they define and explore them as tokens for something else.

Semiology is a science of forms, since it studies significations apart from their content. I should like to say one word about the necessity and the limits of such a formal science. The necessity is that which applies in the case of any exact language. Zhdanov made fun of Alexandrov the philosopher, who spoke of *"The spherical structure of our planet." "It was thought until now,"* Zhdanov said, *"that form alone could be spherical."* Zhdanov was right: one cannot speak about structures in terms of forms, and vice versa. It may well be that on the plane of "life," there is but a totality where structures and forms cannot be separated. But science has no use for the ineffable: it must speak about "life" if it wants to transform it. Against a certain quixotism of synthesis, quite platonic incidentally, all criticism must consent to the *ascesis,* to the artifice of analysis; and in analysis, it must match method and language. Less terrorized by the specter of "formalism," historical criticism might have been less sterile; it would have understood that the specific study of forms does not in any way contradict the necessary principles of totality and History. On the contrary: the more a system is specifically defined in its forms, the more amenable it is to historical criticism. To parody a well-known saying, I shall say that a little formalism turns one away from History, but that a lot brings one back to it. Is there a better example of total criticism than the description of saintliness, at once formal and historical, semiological and ideological, in Sartre's *Saint-Genet*? The danger, on the contrary, is to consider forms as ambiguous objects, half form and half substance, to endow form with a substance of form, as was done, for instance, by Zhdanovian realism. Semiology, once its limits are settled, is not a metaphysical trap: it is a science among others, necessary but not sufficient. The important thing is to see that the unity of an explanation cannot be based on the amputation of one or other of its approaches, but, as Engels said, on the dialectical coordination of the particular sciences it makes use of. This is the case with mythology: it is a part both of semiology inasmuch as it is a formal science, and of ideology inasmuch as it is a historical science: it studies ideas-in-form.[2]

Let me therefore restate that any semiology postulates a relation between two terms, a signifier and a signified. This relation concerns objects which belong to different categories, and this is why it is not one of equality but one of equivalence. We must here be on our guard, for despite common parlance which simply says that the signifier *expresses* the signified, we are dealing, in any semiological system, not with two, but with three different terms. For what we grasp is not at all one term after the other but the correlation which unites them: there are, therefore, the signifier, the signified, and the sign, which is the associative total of the first two terms. Take a bunch of roses: I use it to signify my passion. Do we have here, then, only a signifier and a signified, the roses and my passion? Not even that: to put it accurately, there are here only "passionified" roses. But on the plane of analysis, we do have three terms; for these roses weighted with passion perfectly and correctly allow themselves to be decomposed into roses and passion: the former and the latter existed before uniting and forming this third object, which is the sign. It is as true to say that on the plane of experience I cannot dissociate the roses from the message they carry, as to say that on the plane of analysis I cannot confuse the roses as signifier and the roses as sign: the signifier is empty, the sign is full, it is a meaning. Or take a black pebble: I can make it signify in several ways, it is a mere signifier; but if I weigh it with a definite signified (a death sentence, for instance, in an anonymous vote), it will become a sign. Naturally, there are between the signifier, the signified, and the sign, functional implications (such as that of the part to the whole) which are so close that to analyze them may seem futile; but we shall see in a moment that this distinction has a capital importance for the study of myth as semiological schema.

Naturally these three terms are purely formal, and different contents can be given to them. Here are a few examples: for Saussure, who worked on a particular but methodologically exemplary semiological system—the language or *langue*—the signified is the concept, the signifier is the acoustic image (which is mental), and the relation between concept and image is the sign (the word, for instance), which is a concrete entity.[3] For Freud, as is well known, the human psyche is a stratification of tokens or representatives. One term (I refrain from giving it any precedence) is constituted by the manifest meaning of behavior, another, by its latent or real meaning (it is, for instance, the substratum of the dream); as for the third term, it is here also a correlation of the first two: it is the dream itself in its totality, the parapraxis (a mistake in speech or behavior) or the neurosis, conceived as compromises, as economies effected thanks to the joining of a form (the first term) and an intentional function (the second term). We can see here how necessary it is to distinguish the sign from the signifier: a dream, to Freud, is no more its manifest datum than its latent content: it is the functional union of these two terms. In Sartrean criticism, finally (I shall keep to these three well-known examples), the signified is constituted by the original crisis in the subject (the separation from his mother for Baudelaire, the naming of the theft for Genet); Literature as discourse forms the signifier; and the relation between crisis and discourse defines the work, which is a signification. Of course, this tri-dimensional pattern, however constant in its form, is actualized in different ways: one cannot therefore say too often that semiology can have its unity only at the level of forms, not contents; its field is limited, it knows only one operation: reading, or deciphering.

In myth, we find again the tri-dimensional pattern which I have just described: the signifier, the signified, and the sign. But myth is a peculiar system, in that it is constructed from a semiological chain which existed before it: it *is a second-order semiological system*. That which is a sign (namely the associative total of a concept and an image) in the first system, becomes a mere signifier in the second. We must here recall that the materials of mythical speech (the language itself, photography, painting, posters, rituals, objects, etc.), however different at the start, are reduced to a pure signifying function as soon as they are caught by myth. Myth sees in them only the same raw material; their unity is that they all come down to the status of a mere language. Whether it deals with alphabetical or pictorial writing, myth wants to see in them only a sum of signs, a global sign, the final term of a first semiological chain. And it is precisely this final term which will become the first term of the greater system which it builds and of which it is only a part. Everything happens as if myth shifted the formal system of the first significations sideways. As this lateral shift is essential for the analysis of myth, I shall represent it in the following way, it being understood, of course, that the spatialization of the pattern is here only a metaphor:

Language		1. Signifier	2. Signified	
		3. Sign I SIGNIFIER		II SIGNIFIED
MYTH		III SIGN		

It can be seen that in myth there are two semiological systems, one of which is staggered in relation to the other: a linguistic system, the language (or the modes of representation which are assimilated to it), which I shall call the *language-object,* because it is the language which myth gets hold of in order to build its own system; and myth itself, which I shall call *metalanguage,* because it is a second language, *in which* one speaks about the first. When he reflects on a metalanguage, the semiologist no longer needs to ask himself questions about the composition of the language-object, he no longer has to take into account the details of the linguistic schema; he will only need to know its total term, or global sign, and only inasmuch as this term lends itself to myth. This is why the semiologist is entitled to treat in the same way writing and pictures: what he retains from them is the fact that they are both *signs,* that they both reach the threshold of myth endowed with the same signifying function, that they constitute, one just as much as the other, a language-object.

It is now time to give one or two examples of mythical speech. I shall borrow the first from an observation by Valéry.[4] I am a pupil in the second form in a French *lycée.* I open my Latin grammar, and I read a sentence, borrowed from Aesop or Phaedrus: *quia ego nominor leo.* I stop and think. There is something ambiguous about this statement: on the one hand, the words in it do have a simple meaning: *because my name is lion.* And on the other hand, the sentence is evidently there in order to signify something else to me. Inasmuch as it is addressed to me, a pupil in the second form, it tells me clearly: I am a grammatical example meant to illustrate the rule about the agreement of the predicate. I am even forced to realize that the sentence in no way *signifies* its meaning to me, that it tries very little to tell me something about the lion and what sort of name he has; its true and fundamental signification is to impose itself on me as the presence of a certain agreement of the predicate. I conclude that I am faced with a particular, greater, semiological system, since it is co-extensive with the language: there is, indeed, a signifier, but this signifier is itself formed by a sum of signs, it is in itself a first semiological system (*my name is lion*). Thereafter, the formal pattern is correctly unfolded: there is a signified (*I am a grammatical example*) and there is a global signification, which is none other than the correlation of the signifier and the signified; for neither the naming of the lion nor the grammatical example is given separately.

And here is now another example: I am at the barber's, and a copy of *Paris-Match* is offered to me. On the cover, a young Negro in a French uniform is saluting, with his eyes uplifted, probably fixed on a fold of the tricolor. All this is the *meaning* of the picture. But, whether naïvely or not, I see very well what it signifies to me: that France is a great Empire, that all her sons, without any color discrimination, faithfully serve under her flag, and that there is no better answer to the detractors of an alleged colonialism than the zeal shown by this Negro in serving his so-called oppressors. I am therefore again faced with a greater semiological system: there is a signifier, itself already formed with a previous system (*a black soldier is giving the French salute*); there is a signified (it is here purposeful mixture of Frenchness and militariness); finally there is a presence of the signified through the signifier.

Before tackling the analysis of each term of the mythical system, one must agree on terminology. We now know that the signifier can be looked at, in myth, from two points of view: as the final term of the linguistic system, or as the first term of the mythical system. We therefore need two names. On the plane of language, that is, as the final term of the first system, I shall call the signifier: *meaning* (*my name is lion, a Negro is giving the French salute*); on the plane of myth, I shall call it: *form*. In the case of the signified, no ambiguity is possible: we shall retain the name *concept*. The third term is the correlation of the first two: in the linguistic system, it is the *sign;* but it is not possible to use this word again without ambiguity, since in myth (and this is the chief peculiarity of the latter), the signifier is already formed by the *signs* of the language. I shall call the third term of myth the *signification*. This word is here all the better justified since myth has in fact a double function: it points out and it notifies, it makes us understand something and it imposes it on us.

[. . .]

Myth is depoliticized speech

And this is where we come back to myth. Semiology has taught us that myth has the task of giving a historical intention a natural justification, and making contingency appear eternal. Now this process is exactly that of bourgeois ideology. If our society is objectively the privileged field of mythical significations, it is because formally myth is the most appropriate instrument for the ideological inversion which defines this society: at all the levels of human communication, myth operates the inversion of *anti-physis* into *pseudo-physis*.

What the world supplies to myth is a historical reality, defined, even if this goes back quite a while, by the way in which men have produced or used it; and what myth gives in return is a *natural* image of this reality. And just as bourgeois ideology is defined by the abandonment of the name "bourgeois," myth is constituted by the loss of the historical quality of things: in it, things lose the memory that they once were made. The world enters language as a dialectical relation between activities, between human actions; it comes out of myth as a harmonious display of essences. A conjuring trick has taken place; it has turned reality inside out, it has emptied it of history and has filled it with Nature, it has removed from things their human meaning so as to make them signify a human insignificance. The function of myth is to empty reality: it is, literally, a ceaseless flowing out, a hemorrhage, or perhaps an evaporation, in short, a perceptible absence.

It is now possible to complete the semiological definition of myth in a bourgeois society: *myth is depoliticized speech*. One must naturally understand *political* in its deeper meaning, as describing the whole of human relations in their real, social structure, in their power of making the world; one must above all give an active value to the prefix *de-:* here it represents an operational movement, it permanently embodies a defaulting. In the case of the soldier Negro, for instance, what is got rid of is certainly not French imperiality (on the contrary, since what must be actualized is its presence); it is the contingent, historical, in one word: *fabricated,* quality of colonialism. Myth does not deny things, on the contrary, its function is to talk about them; simply, it purifies them, it makes them innocent, it gives them a natural and eternal justification, it gives them a clarity which is not that of an explanation but that of statement of fact. If I *state the fact* of French imperiality without explaining it, I am very near to finding that it is natural and *goes without saying:* I am reassured. In passing from history to Nature, myth acts economically: it abolishes the complexity of human acts, it gives them the simplicity of essences, it does away with all dialectics, with any going back beyond what is immediately visible, it organizes a world which is without contradictions because it is without depth, a world wide open and wallowing in the evident, it establishes a blissful clarity: things appear to mean something by themselves.[5]

However, is myth always depoliticized speech? In other words, is reality always political? Is it enough to speak about a thing naturally for it to become mythical? One could answer with Marx that the most natural object contains a political trace, however faint and diluted, the more or less memorable presence of the human act which has produced, fitted up, used, subjected, or rejected it.[6] The language-object, which *"speaks things,"* can easily exhibit this trace; the metalanguage, which *speaks of things,* much less easily. Now myth always comes under the heading of metalanguage: the depoliticization which it carries out often supervenes against a background which is already naturalized, depoliticized by a general metalanguage which is trained to *celebrate* things, and no longer to *"act them."* It goes without saying that the force needed by myth to distort its object is much less in the case of a tree than in the case of a Sudanese: in the latter case, the political load is very near the surface, a large quantity of artificial nature is needed in order to disperse it; in the former case, it is remote, purified by a whole century-old layer of metalanguage. There are, therefore, strong myths and weak myths; in the former, the political quantum is immediate, the depoliticization is abrupt; in the latter, the political quality of the object has *faded* like a color, but the slightest thing can bring back its strength brutally: what is more *natural* than the sea? And what more "political" than the sea celebrated by the makers of the film *The Lost Continent*?

Notes

From *Mythologies.*

1   Innumerable other meanings of the word "myth" can be cited against this. But I have tried to define things, not words.
2   The development of publicity, of a national press, of radio, of illustrated news, not to speak of the survival of a myriad rites of communication which rule social appearances makes the development of a semiological science more urgent than ever. In a single day, how many really non-signifying fields do we cross? Very few, sometimes none. Here I am, before the sea; it is true that it bears no message. But on the beach, what material for semiology! Flags, slogans, signals, signboards, clothes, suntan even, which are so many messages to me.
3   The notion of *word* is one of the most controversial in linguistics. I keep it here for the sake of simplicity.
4   *Tel Quel,* II.
5   To the pleasure principle of Freudian man could be added the clarity principle of mythological humanity. All the ambiguity of myth is there: its clarity is euphoric.
6   Cf. Marx and the example of the cherry tree (*The German Ideology*).

Chapter 7

Julia Kristeva

THE SEMIOTIC ACTIVITY

The foundational semiotic moment for feminist, psychoanalyst and poststructuralist Julia Kristeva, occurs as far back as the philosophical movement known Stoicism, initiated by Zeno of Citium (c.334–262 BC) in c. 300 BC. Kristeva argues that the Stoics replaced the Platonic "idea" (*eidos*, or eternal form) with that of the "sign" (*semeion*), thereby inaugurating a new basis for knowledge: a science base instead of a philosophical one. In the process, the Stoics repressed materialism, or questions of "being, essence, evidence", in favour of the semiotic "processes of signifying". Even though for Kristeva the whole of Western thought adopts this Stoic sign, which also created a new metaphysics (one of transcendent signifieds, a positing of presence rather than absence, and even for Kristeva Christian monotheism rather than polytheism, or the worship of many gods), it is still one that situates all of its systems "within a semiotic problematic". With the shift in the twentieth century into the human sciences, Kristeva suggests that once again the semiotic "science of signs" becomes important, and this can be seen in the work of linguists such as Peirce and Saussure. Kristeva points out that semiotics in its contemporary guise should not be regarded as entirely analogous with the logical "purity" of mathematics and logic; rather, she argues that it belongs to social, i.e., political, and psychological domains. Three different types of semiotic approaches emerge in the modern world for Kristeva: an attempt to logically unify all knowledge; an attempt to find the core codes that drive all systems; and an interrogation of the entire history of the metaphysical concept of the sign. The first two approaches are called by Kristeva "metasemiology" since they try and transcend knowledge domains, the third approach is called "analytical semiotics" or "semanalysis". Kristeva is in effect describing a deconstructive or poststructuralist notion of semiotics, and this becomes clear in the remainder of her essay, which charts the second half of the twentieth century and three "factors" that initiate this shift into poststructuralism: the Marxist concept of work (dialectical materialism); Freud's psychoanalytical approach to interpretation; and a postcolonial understanding of other linguistic and semiotic systems. For Kristeva, then, Marxism, psychoanalysis, and postcolonial studies all foreground the material basis for culture, whereby semiotic signs produce realities, be they social, psychic, or political. Instead of metaphysics being knowledge of higher things, Kristeva calls contemporary semiotic "gnosiology" (or epistemology – the study of knowledge systems) *material*, but in the deconstructive sense of difference and absence rather than presence (meaning is produced by differential networks of arbitrary signs). This material semiotics will "neutralize" metaphysics, and deconstruct logocentric systems, i.e., those dependent upon transcendent signifieds. In other words, Kristeva turns to Derrida's work to describe contemporary semiotics. Literature is what she calls the "specific object" of this new understanding of the sign, because it always exceeds and remains irreducible to any interpretive approach: nothing transcends its constant production and dispersal of meaning across its texts. Kristeva suggests that literature cannot be "recuperated" by rationality because it is essentially a "signifying practice": so the Stoic concept of the sign has finally been presented with something that it cannot comprehend.

THE TERM *SEMIOTICS* TODAY calls to mind a tradition rather than a homogeneous body of doctrine. The period of the Stoics, the Middle Ages with its *modi significandi,* the eighteenth century with Locke, Leibniz, Condillac and the Ideologists, and finally the beginning of the twentieth century with the axiomatic method that became imperative in logic and mathematics and then entered Saussurian and, later, Hjelmslevian and structural linguistics – these are the *great moments* of that *semiotic activity* which marks our Western *episteme* from its Greek beginnings to its positivist apotheosis. Yet it is clear that if this semiotic activity has always been present in the organisation of our knowledge, it is only very recently, within no more than the last few years, that it has emerged once more into the scientific and even ideological consciousness, taking its place in this resurgence amongst those events that characterise radically modern thought.

How is this emergence today of semiotics to be explained? To try to answer that question is, in fact, to try to answer a question that, because posed in metaphysical terms, is considerably more awkward: 'What is semiotics?'. In this paper I shall attempt to outline the terms of an answer by following briefly through history the determination and the impact of the semiotic enterprise in its 'great moments' in the Western *episteme.* I shall then go on to consider the situation of contemporary semiotics in relation to the fact of its emergence (what is it that today troubles and revives semiotic thinking?) and, at the same time, to consider to what extent it can break with its past in order to allow the recasting of those disciplines which were permitted by its inaugural gesture – logic and, closer to us, the human sciences. For, and here I am anticipating the thesis that I am going to stress at the end of this paper, if the *raison d'être* of the semiotic enterprise from the time of the Stoics to the present day has always been to found scientific abstraction in posing the *sign* and in so doing allowing the constitution of science (including linguistic science) as systematisation and formalisation, semiotics is now called upon to question these foundations, the foundations of science (and of linguistics), and to work towards the constitution of a *theory of knowledge* in which the project of linguistics, duly questioned, will itself be integrated. In other words, having provided the positive foundations of metaphysics and/or science, semiotics now offers itself as the area of the interrogation, analysis and criticism of metaphysics and/or science that they may be refounded in a new theoretical gesture (of which all that may be said is that it is practised as a critique of metaphysics).

As is well known, the Stoics were the first to construct a theory of the sign (*semeion*): there is no such theory in Aristotle who speaks of 'immediate truths', of first principles known intuitively by the *nous.* Between the *sound* (name) and the *thing* the Stoics locate an intermediary which is the *signification.* This intermediary they call the *lekton* or the expressible, a non-corporeal entity, situated on the side of language, that it has been found possible to translate by the Saussurian term *signifié.* The step taken here by the Stoics, at first sight elementary, is of crucial importance. Why? Because it poses in a clear and definite manner the opposition real/language and places the *signification* in the position of *necessary relation* between the two. The fundamental problem that determines Western thinking over the whole of its history, the relation matter/spirit is thus resolved by the establishment of a mediation, the *sense* hidden in the *sign*. It will henceforth be possible to put matter (point of emphasis of the Epicurian materialists, the principle opponents of the Stoics) between brackets and at the same time positivise the (platonic) *idea* by positing the domain of *signification*. The Stoic postulate of the sign thus neutralises and deflects Epicurus's materialism and, in a play of dialectic, recuperates, in scientificising it, Plato's idealism. What then does *signification* mean in Stoic doctrine?

The doctrine of the Stoics is above all *logical*: they formulate their famous syllogisms ('if there is sunshine, it is daylight: there is sunshine, therefore it is daylight') concerning compound, conditional or disjunctive propositions, syllogisms which display, in other words, the mechanism of a *proof*. The *sign* is also a *proof*, but if the syllogism was a proof within the process of reasoning, the sign installs the proof, so to speak, vertically, by posing a relation of necessity not between the premises of a conditional proposition and its conclusion, but between the out-there and that which speaks it, the thing and the word. That relation is the *lekton*, the expressible, the *signifié*, the sense. It can thus be seen that the sound is not identical with the thing, the word is not a (platonic) identity in relation to its out-side: their relation is not intrinsic, it is a relation of concommitance, of succession, of metonymy. The sign is no longer an *evidence* (as was the Idea, an *a-letheia*), but a *sequence* the two terms of which (referent-sound) are in a relation of *necessary induction* (through the *lekton*).

It is for this reason that the logic of the Stoics that has been called an inducive [*sic*] logic is at the same time a *semiology*. It has been found possible to say that 'the semiology logically precedes the theory of demonstration which cannot be established without it'[1] and indeed the Stoics do present semiology as a justification of their inductive logic. We ought perhaps, however, at a deeper level and in order to put things in their proper places, to see in the Stoic semiology a procedure subsequent to their logical doctrine, an inversion of that doctrine which, elaborated first of all within the area of the processes of judgement, is orientated in the direction of the material and infinite out-there which is thus recuperated withinto the process of judgement. Not withinto language, but withinto a certain language; that of the process of judgement, the rule of inductive judgement is thus at the basis of our theory of the sign; what we call semeiosis is *not the signifying activity in all its complexity, but only one of the signifying acts such as the structure of judgement allows it to filter through.*

It can be understood here why the theory of the sign, the matrix of the sign (object-*lekton*-sound) is indispensable that may be constructed on it all logic, and thus all reasoning, and hence all science (since fundamentally it is only a deductive reasoning compelled by the principles of identity and non-contradiction in the terms of a sequence). The semiotic gesture is thus the founding gesture of science. The Stoic *sign* in place of the platonic *idea* means the replacement of Philosophy by Science. I shall not here consider the complicity of sign and idea, of Zeno and Plato, but will call attention to what distinguishes the semiotic gesture from that of philosophy, for it is precisely this that today renders the semiotic problem urgently contemporary. This distinction may be grasped in two ways: 1. the semiotic project founds that of science; 2. the semiotic project replaces the fundamental philosophical question, that of Being (as Hegel and Heidegger have constantly emphasised), with the question of signifying, with, that is, the question of the relation out-there/language, infinite/finite, or matter/sense. Now what is this question if not that posed throughout its history by *materialism*? Not that Stoicism is a materialism; on the contrary it is the *repression* of the materialism of Epicurus and Democritus, a successful repression indeed and the more interesting in that it offers, in the sign, the very mechanism mounted in the discussion with the materialist thinkers of Antiquity in order to occult the infinity of matter and substitute in its place the probative finitude of the lekton – projection of the syllogism.

Semiotics is not, therefore, a philosophy; its domain is not that of being, essence, evidence. It is, basically, a theory of the processes of signifying, a *theory of knowledge* that may become either idealist or materialist according to the answer it gives to the problems of the relation matter/sense, according to the way in which it posits the object language, etc. Its problem is that of the materialists, that of out-there and language, and it is thus that it cuts across linguistics, serving as a lever not only for the reformulation of the object of linguistics but also as a point of support for any radical materialism, for any gnosiology aiming at elaboration as materialist.

We begin to understand here that what has been long sought for under the name of 'matter' is probably that which the matrix of the sign came to occult: not a so-called 'substance', but an infinity and plurality given to the mobile 'subject' in the modes of a significance that is diversified and not enclosed in the specific matrices of the sign. The Stoic sign that will be adopted by the whole of Western thought (Hegel and Saussure included) elides the plurality of the outside (out-of-sign) that it begins by posing, puts it between brackets and evolves in the *signifié* that immediately becomes primordial and absolute: a transcendental *signifié*, origin and refuge of transcendence. The term *transcendental signifié* is Jacques Derrida's and indicates how the pyramid of the sign (*référent-signifié-signifiant*) ends by resolving itself into the hypostasis of the signified that culminates in a God. It is not by chance that the historical period that sees the establishment of the doctrine of the sign by the Stoics coincides with the passage in Greek religion to monotheism, the repression of polytheism that paves the way for Christianity. With the sign is established that 'sobria ebreitas' described by Philo Judæus: a rational mastery over infinity for which must be found the finitude that will evoke it. It can be seen how the interrogation of the sign carried out today by Derrida shows clearly what Hegel and after him, though in a way which hardly begins to approach the problem, dialectical materialism, try to analyse: the congenitally metaphysical nature of philosophy and non-critical science, of idea and sign. Hegel called attention to this metaphysics and today the semiotic interrogation, interrogation of the sign, is able to demonstrate it in showing explicitly how the sign elides the real on behalf of a transcendental *Signifié*. Henceforth it will be necessary to combat this transcendence of the Logos and, faced with the sign, to think another concept that avoids transcendence and metaphysics (identity, noncontradiction) and suggests the material infinity in its movement of differentiation. It is to this end that Derrida speaks of *écriture* and *différance*.

We can understand, therefore, why today, when materialism reappears once again on the scene of Western theory, confronting the wavering of the idealism consecrated by the Christian religion, this materialism takes the form of a semiotics (in the sense of an interrogation of the sign). It can indeed only operate on the terrain of a semiotics, on that terrain where the problem is posed, in all its radicality, of the infinite outside and the finite sign-language that sign-ifies it. It is there in the juncture of the sign, and not in the zone of being or non-being, that is located a thinking intent on reformulating the kernel elements of our culture. We can understand too why, when the science of language is stifling in an ever more refined formalisation which nonetheless continues to go round in circles in the old framework inherited from the grammarians of Alexandria or Port-Royal, semiotics offers itself as a possible way out to the extent to which it takes hold by the root of that which has blocked our thinking and compelled it to evolve according to the principles of identity and non-contradiction, according to the figures of the syllogism, of subject and predicate, etc; it takes hold of the sign.

Because of its importance for our whole civilisation the semiotic question, if it has founded science, has not ceased to be a necessarily ideological question: it touched the religion of the Middle Ages and the humanist and libertarian ideology of the eighteenth century.

Let us briefly call to mind here the theories of the Modistae of the Middle Ages. From the work of St Augustine, but also alongside that work in the work of linguists such as Siger de Courtrai or Scaliger, is developed a complex reflection on the *modes of signifying* which present in various ways (active, passive, etc) a *senefiance* understood as the process of signification. The complexity of these texts, written in a difficult Latin, renders them arid reading today and this doubtless deprives us of some of the most fully worked-out studies of signification. It remains no less true, however, that the medieval sign hypostasises what I have referred to as a transcendental signified and makes of it a divine transcendence, absolute God, on the foundation of which unfolds the purely Christian doctrine. The quarrels between nominalism and realism, the problem of universals, are situated within a semiotic problematic: it is indeed a question of the value of the signifying unity, of the nature of the existence of a signifying unity or unities on the basis of an ideal immanence.

Nearer to us, Leibniz, in opposition to Descartes, also takes up the tradition of the Stoics (in his *Théodicée* he even acknowledges his kinship with Stoicism). His *Nouveaux Essais sur l'Entendement Humain* poses the question of the relation word/thing/idea, and in another context his attempt to construct a 'calculus ratiocinator' that would embrace the totality of signifying activity is well known. Combining mathematics, logic and linguistics, he proposes an *ars characteristica* – theory and art of the formation of signs in which all considerations corresponding to the idea must be drawn from the sign alone, and an *ars combinatoria* – a general computation providing a formal method for deriving consequences of signs. Setting out from the Stoic doctrine which, basing itself on the sign, established a deductive system that operated with minimal elements or *terms,* in accordance with strict rules, Leibniz became the precursor of the symbolic logic which will be developed at the beginning of the twentieth century and which will become one aspect of semiotics in the wider sense of the term.

Yet if the Leibnizian semiotic could lead to Carnap and his book *Der Logische Aufbau der Welt,* the eighteenth-century with Locke, Condillac and the French Ideologists generally proposes another aspect of the semiotic problem. This is, as Locke puts it, the relation between the word and the reality of things: the sign excludes the real thing and finds its area of activity between the word and the 'idea', but the question of its relation to the real remains posed and it is precisely this that sensualism will attempt to work out. The theory of knowledge appropriate to mechanistic materialism (from Condillac to Diderot) will be a theory of the sign: its development through the senses, its functioning in discourse, its transgression in art through another basic unity that avoids the univocity of the sign and also its transcendence and that is often designated as a *hieroglyph.* It may be said without exaggeration that the sensualists and the ideologists of the eighteenth century are already consciously semioticians. I am thinking here of the theories of the sign and the hieroglyph to be found in Rousseau and Diderot, as well as of that later science of signs announced by Destutt de Tracy in his *Eléments d'Idéologie:* 'The whole of our knowledge is formed of ideas; these ideas never appear to us except in the clothing of signs'; (grammar is) 'the science of signs'; 'every system of signs is a language: let us now add that every practice of a language, every emission of signs, is a discourse and let our grammar be the analysis of all types of discourse'. One cannot but see in this postulate the project of a grammar which is nothing other than a general semiology.

In our own century the semiotic enterprise takes on first of all the aspect of formal logic, or, better, let us say that the project of the Stoics finds its apogee in the symbolic logic of Boole, Frege, Peano, Peirce, Russell, Whitehead and later the Vienna Circle. After having founded science, the logico-semiotic enterprise of the Stoics has thus objectivised itself in a particular science: symbolic logic.

These two results – (1) the foundation of the project of science (2) the constitution of symbolic logic – have evidently not exhausted the whole range of possibilities contained originally in the semiotic enterprise. They leave untouched the domain of linguistic signification and of all forms of signifying practice – art, literature, religion, mythology, social relations, etc. How is one to approach diversity of signifying activity of which a foresight was allowed in the setting up of on the one hand *science* as rigorous intellection (obeying the laws of inductive and deductive logic) and on the other a *symbolic logic* which, elaborating explicatory models of, for example, the systems of mathematics, claimed to master artificial semiotic systems, How is one to master the signifying activity of language, the arts, social practice? In other words, how is a *human science* to be founded?

It is in the work done towards finding an answer to this question that the semiotic enterprise once again becomes crucial. Peirce and Saussure, more or less contemporaneously, posit the necessity for a science of signs the scope of which must be – in order to render it scientific – the whole of human activity. It can be said that consciously or unconsciously modern semiotics stems from the enormous impact of the positivist philosophy of Comte and of axiomatic method, which impact *demands* that such a positivism and such an axiomatisation be applied to the, as yet, imprecisely defined domain of language or to that of the 'human' in general. It is doubtless not by chance that Peirce, the first semiotician, is an axiomatician, and it was doubtless necessary that the foundation by Saussure of linguistics as a science (as against philology and comparative grammar) be simultaneous with the foundation of semiology by the same Saussure. It may be said that the birth of linguistics is a birth of semiotics overdetermined by axiomatic method. This is made clear in Peirce: 'Logic, in its general sense, is . . . only another name for *semiotic,* the quasi-necessary, or formal, doctrine of signs'.[3] Similarly, in Saussure, even if his project does not take this openly logical form, the reflection is determined, in the last instance, by axiomatics, for if Saussure's principal endeavour is orientated towards the definition of the sign as basic unit which brackets out the referent in order to operate only within the 'arbitrary' relation between *signifiant* and *signifié,* is this not an indication that Saussure is aiming at the isolation of a formal entity (and the definition of the sign as arbitrary is the symptom of this formality) that will permit him, in exactly the same way as the Stoics, to found a science (which cannot but be formal): 'Signs that are wholly arbitrary realise better than the others the ideal of the semiological process; that is why language, the most complex and universal of all systems of expression, is also the most characteristic; in this sense linguistics can become the master-pattern for all branches of semiology although language is only one particular semiological system'.[4] Thus, in creating formal linguistics, Saussure revived semiology as a science of signs that had at once to justify linguistics as a science and include it within the terms of a reflection that goes beyond the narrow framework of the study of *langue;* a reflection on the modes of signification.

Saussurian semiology was a warning both against the *contraction* of the object of linguistics and against extreme *technocratisation,* a warning forgotten for a good many years and which has only recently been remembered. This warning was expressed by Saussure in two brief observations: (1) Saussure never envisaged the linguistics he founded as a self-sufficient discipline. He stressed this firmly: if linguistics is the master-pattern of all semiology, *langue,* that object analysed by the Greek grammarians and formalised by the Stoics, is only one particular system of signs and, as such, only one part of semiology, 'if I have succeeded in assigning linguistics a place among the sciences, it is because I have related it to semiology'.[5] (2) This semiology is not, however, a neutral domain in which axiomatisation is to guard its formal purity (as in mathematics and symbolic logic). Semiology concerns itself with a social domain and its formalisation (permitted by the establishment of the concept of the sign) must be justified by some (psychological or sociological) theory. The semiotic model is not innocent, it is supported by a *theory* or an ideology, and if this is true of semiotics, it is also true of linguistics which is only one of its subsections: 'A science that studies the life of signs within society is thus conceivable; it would be a part of social psychology and consequently of general psychology . . . To determine the exact place of semiology is the task of the psychologist'.[6]

The Saussurian project may be resumed as follows: there is no linguistics other than as a part of semiotics which in turn is only a part of a general theory of psychological and sociological functioning. As far as linguistics is concerned, this formulation means that *linguistics can only find its full object as a part of semiotics which is part of a gnosiology*. Any other isolation of linguistics constrains it to dealing with a truncated, restricted, limited object, ignorant of this abstraction.

Today, faced with the massive enterprise of structural and even generative linguistics and even while recognising their achievement, it can be said that, linguistics not having taken into consideration Saussure's warning, we are witnessing a fragmentation of the body of *langue* which is pushing formalisation to its ultimate refinement but which is failing to achieve that which linguistics has taken as its object: the explication of the complexity of the act of signification. The resort to semiotics is thus a necessity for the linguist, restoring to him that complexity, demanding of him an act of epistemological and theoretical reflection on his object of study and the concepts and formalisations he uses in his work. It is in this sense that Benveniste, noting the extreme formalisation-atomisation of *langue* in contemporary linguistics (American structuralism), stresses the urgency of the need for the semiotic approach which the linguist must join to his method in order to renew his vision of language: 'It is from progress made in the analysis of symbols that may notably be expected a better understanding of the complex processes of signification in language and probably in areas outside language as well. And since this functioning is unconscious, as is the structure of behaviour, psychologists, sociologists and linguists are usefully combining forces in this research'.[7]

The role of support for and means of the recasting of linguistics is, however, only one of the roles that the semiotic enterprise is called upon to fulfil today. There is one other crucial role that the philosophy of science has not failed to stress: the role of semiotics in the constitution of a general *theory of discourse* and hence of an *epistemology*. The question has been posed since Husserl's *Logische Untersuchungen* which founded a reflection on the sign and the various types of sign. Heavily influenced by Husserl, the Linguistic Circle of Copenhagen, with Brøndal and Hjelmslev, turned towards the construction of a semiotics conceived as a system of formalisation or different discourses and composed, as system, of several strata of formalisation (denotation, connotation, etc), and completed by a *meta-semiology:* 'In conformity with Saussure's terminology we can define a *semiology* as a metasemiotic with a non-scientific semiotic as an object semiotic. And finally, we can use the designation *metasemiology* of a meta-(semiotic scientific) whose object semiotics are semiologies'.[8] Semiology is thus assigned the task of formalising, hence of rendering explicitly not only the foundations of linguistics, but also the foundations of the discourse that treats of linguistics, of, that is, semiology. Epistemology of linguistics and epistemology of the epistemology of linguistics, metasemiology is elaborated as the ultimate metalanguage that exhausts all possible formalisations. In the Hjelmslevian project semiology thus becomes the supreme means of the unification of the formalisation of different languages. It is as such that it can tackle 'the task of analysing various – geographical and historical, political and social, sacred, psychological – content-purports that are attached to nation (as content for national language), region (as content for regional language), the value-forms of styles, personality (as content for physiognomy; essentially a task for individual psychology), mood, etc. Many special sciences, in the first place, presumably, sociology, ethnology and psychology, must be thought of as making their contribution here'.[9]

This definition of the purpose of semiology as that of furnishing the final, unifying formalisation of the various types of language is found again in the thinking of Morris. He regards semiotics as the epistemological control point, thus *unifying* the projects of the other sciences. In other words, semiology must analyse and formalise the process of signification that founds not only linguistics but all science: 'Semiotic is not merely a science among sciences but an organon or instrument of all the sciences. This function can be performed in two ways. One is by making training in semiotic a regular part of the equipment of the scientist. In this way a scientist would become critically conscious of his linguistic apparatus and develop careful habits in its use. The second way is by specific investigations of the languages of the special sciences. The linguistically expressed result of all the sciences is part of the subject matter of descriptive semiotic'. These considerations are made in the perspective of 'a unification of the sciences on the basis of the concept of the sign'; 'The significance of semiotic lies in the fact that it is a step in the unification of science, since it supplies the foundations for any special science of signs, such as linguistics, logic, mathematics, rhetoric and (to some extent at least) aesthetics.'[10]

Reference to semiotics is present in the work of the Linguistic Circle of Prague, but here it is a question of a typology of signifying systems rather than of a semiology as apex of the pyramid of modes of discourse. The task of semiology will be to reveal the particularities of signifying systems, to determine that which makes them irreducibly different from one another. Hence the great importance that will be attached to the study of the specificity of art ('the organising distinction of art, and by which it is distinguished from other semiological structures, is the direction of its aim not towards the *signifié* but towards the sign itself'[11]). This tendency towards the establishment of a typology of signifying systems, supported by Roman Jakobson, is being developed today by the semiotic researches carried out in Soviet Russia and in Europe in general, while in the USA semioticians tend to prolong rather the positivist spirit of Morris's semiotic thinking. Semiotics as typology of signifying systems is more *historical* and more *sociological,* or, better, by its rigour and its scientific character it replaces the old humanist forms of discourse in the domains of history and sociology. It is precisely as a semiology of this tendency that Lévi-Strauss's structural anthropology may be understood and it can be said that typological semiotics is the method with which the attempt is today being made to develop the 'human sciences'.

Two conceptions of semiotics, which are moreover complementary and fundamentally similar, thus seem to be developing at the moment: (1) semiotics as point of control and unification of forms of discourse (including scientific discourse); (2) semiotics as typology of signifying systems. Following on from this second tendency, a third becomes henceforth possible. Without attempting to unify in a gesture of metaphysical mastery all possible modes of discourse, as Hjelmslev and Morris wanted, but taking as its point of departure the differences between the various sign systems, semiotics could begin to investigate its very constitutive kernel element; the sign and the scientific discourse it permits (as we have seen in our discussion of the Stoics). Semiotics could then try to analyse that which it has never dared call into question no matter what form it has taken during its history: the matrix of the Stoic sign. This would be to call into question semiotics itself, but without the claim of metasemiology to furnish the final rules of the semiotic project. Such a semiotics, that I will call an *analytical* semiotics, a *semanalysis,* would, on the contrary, attempt to analyse, that is, to dissolve, the constitutive centre of the semiotic enterprise such as it was posited by the Stoics, and this would mean the interrogation of the fundamental matrix of our civilisation grasped in its ideological, neuralgic locus.

It is necessary to stress the novelty of this crucial moment of the semiotic activity in which it undertakes the analysis of its own gesture. A long period, stretching from Zeno to Saussure and his successors, seems now to be closed and theory today seeks a different path from that suggested by the Stoics. As in fifth century BC Greece, the discussion now centres on the fundamental elements of the system of knowledge, elements capable of leading it in various directions. What is involved here through the calling into question of the sign is the whole gnosiology (theory of knowledge) as it has been thought in the West since Zeno.

It is easy to see, then, why semiotics as semanalysis imposes itself so forcefully on contemporary thinking. The reason is – and I repeat – that a semiotic activity orientated directly towards the matrix of the sign, foundation of our culture, is the only means of thinking the constants of that culture and of posing once more, in order perhaps to formulate them in a new way, the problems of the signifying act, its relation to the material infinity, rationality, scientificity, and so on.

Is this new calling into question necessary? And if so, why today?

The necessity for this new calling into question of the constants of our culture, and hence of rationality, scientificity and every individual science, is to be felt in every domain. Linguistics – to take only that science here as example – today finds itself so fragmented and so restricted in all its parts (by the very demands of scientific procedure) to a narrow reductive abstraction that the complexity of the linguistic act – of the signifying act – disappears. Faced with this disappearance linguistics, fragmented and locked in its reductive abstraction, turns to semiotics for help – to semiotics not as some miraculous synthesis or some magical return to material complexity or signifying plenitude, but as a theory of knowledge, as a reformulation of intellection starting with the element that determines it: the sign.

But why is this development from gnosiology to semiotics taking place today? What is it, in other words, that in the second half of our century demands the reconsideration of the gnosiological question from the site of the semiotics?

Let us call to mind at this point three factors exerting crucial pressure on modern history: the Marxist concept of 'work' within the context of dialectical materialism: the Freudian concept of the 'unconscious'; the dramatic eruption onto the world theatre of long oppressed nations, such as China and India with their linguistic and scriptural systems, their complex signifying practices which depart from the principles of sign and semeiosis established by the Greeks (I am thinking, for example, of the hieroglyphic writing of the Chinese and of the hypersemiotic practices of the Indians, their sacred texts, their rites, their mastery of the body). Without insisting any further here on the influence exerted on our culture by these hypersemiotic practices of the East, I will stop for a moment to consider the concepts of *work* and the *unconscious* in connection with the constitution of a semanalysis.

In his study of the capitalist system of exchange Marx showed that it is a semiotic system in which *money,* through a series of mutations, becomes the *general equivalent* or the *sign* of the work invested in the exchanged object. The economic system is thus a semiotic system: a chain of communication with a sender and a receiver and an object of exchange – money – which is the *sign* of a piece of *work*. The system of exchange only concerns the sign, but on this side and that of the sign open the zones of *work* which the sign represents, but also, and principally, occults. What takes place in this zone of work which supports the semiotic process but which is not reducible to it? Marx's economic theory does not offer an exhaustive answer to this question and only *poses* the concept of pre-sign work.

Now correlatively to this introduction in economic theory of the concept of work, *dialectical materialism* begins to examine the problem of the relation real-signification, and consequently the metaphysical basis of all sciences, the point of departure for which were the premises of an idealist philosophy. The initial moment of this examination by dialectical materialism was the thesis written by the young Marx on Democritus and Epicurus (remember that it was in opposition to Epicurus's theory that the Stoics asserted themselves in Greece).[12] Later, Engels in his *Dialektik der Natur* invokes the necessity for a scientific project which takes account of the dialectic between infinite and finite, totality (to be studied) and object (of study). These problems can be seen to continue the preoccupations of Hegel in his *Wissenschaft der Logik*. Hegel posed these problems as an idealist philosopher preoccupied with Being and Idea of which the real was merely a formation. Engels reverses the problematic and poses Hegel's questions, it may be said, no longer as a philosopher but as a 'semiotician': the infinite is no longer the idea but matter, and the finite is the real object which, in scientific theory, becomes the sign of the infinite dialectically realised in a finitude. The relation infinite-finite becomes a relation matter-sign. If the problematic is thus 'semiotic', it is not so in a positivist fashion; it is analytically semiotic, it is gnosiological. Its object is that which precedes, determines and decentres the sign, namely 'matter' qua movement and work. (Was this not the problematic of Heraclitus, Epicurus, Democritus, the pre-Stoics?)

On *another* plane complementary to that of dialectical materialism is situated *Freudian psychoanalysis.* Freud's discovery of the unconscious as *other scene* (*anderer Schauplatz*) distinct from that of communication and ordinary logic, as, similarly, Freudian method which consists in tapping the unconscious through language, has permitted in our own period the description of the unconscious as 'structured like a language'[13] and the search for the particularities of that linguistic structure. Freud indicates clearly that the signifying activity operative in the unconscious is neither a calculation nor a judgement, but a transformation, a *work;* indeed he entitles one of his texts *The Work of the Dream*[14] and specifies that the semantic and syntagmatic permutation in dream narrative denotes less a fixed sense than a transformation, a signifying work in which the subject is included. Language is thus posited as the object of psychoanalysis, no longer, however, as closed system with a given sense but as system of the *production* of signification and of the subject. In this same moment, and for the first time, the relation of the subject to his discourse is studied with precision. Such a conception of the functioning of the process of signification connects to the critique carried through by dialectical materialism of the metaphysical character of a certain rationalism or scientism constructed on the basis of the principle of identity and non-contradiction: founding principle of the sign and its system.

A semanalysis will therefore base itself on these two radical concepts in order to undertake the epistemological criticism of the sign and its system. It will be the area of the application of dialectical materialism and psychoanalysis, towards the constitution, starting from an analysis of languages, of a gnosiology.

It is clear that in such a perspective, the perspective, that is, of the consideration of the process of signification as a work and a production that exceeds the sign, the fixed sense and the closed structure, a reformulation of the smallest elements of our analytical apparatus becomes imperative: minimal units, modes of junction, etc. This reformulation is only just beginning (as, for instance, in Derrida's texts devoted to *écriture*). It is a question, therefore, of assigning, without totally abandoning them, notions such as sign, subject, structure, etc. to their exact place in the working of the process of signification, by postulating to begin with, and in order to delimit invasion by metaphysics, that every process of signification is a *formal play of differences,* that is, of *traces.*

To speak of traces does not, however, mean that I am trying to reintroduce a substantialism that linguistics has taken a long time to eliminate. To speak of traces means the neutralisation of the metaphysical conception of a Logos given immediately in the *phone* to the self-present Subject, and the postulation in place of the old – phonetising and phonetic – logocentrism of a new concept of *écriture:*

> It may be called *gramme* or *différance.* The play of differences supposes syntheses and inter-references such that there is no question at any moment of a single element being *present* in itself and referring only to itself . . . without referring to another element which is itself not simply present. This concatenation means that every element – phoneme or grapheme – is constituted from the trace in it of the other elements of the chain or system. This concatenation, this tissue, is the *text* that can only be produced in the transformation of another text. Nothing, neither in the elements nor in the system, is anywhere simply present or absent.

> Throughout there is nothing but differences of differences and traces of traces.
> The *gramme* is, then, the most general concept of semiology . . . and it is
> appropriate not merely to the field of writing in the narrow or classic sense, but
> also to that of linguistics . . . *Différance* is the systematic play of differences, of
> the traces of differences, of the *spacing* through which the elements relate to one
> another. It is the developing space of the chain of speech – that previously has
> been called temporal and linear . . .[15]

Such a theoretical conception of signification, a conception implicit in the formalisations of
contemporary linguistics, can and must be extended over the vast field of signifying practices
(myth, religion, art, etc), and this is the task of semanalysis.

It is impossible today to forecast the possible results of this extension. One thing,
however, seems to be certain: in order to achieve its elaboration this semanalysis needs to
provide itself with a *specific object* which the traditional modes of analysis are incapable of
grasping in all its specificity. That object is to be found in the so called literary or poetic text.
Why? This specific type of signifying practice carried out through *langue* but remaining
irreducible to its categories has always troubled science. Under the name of magic, madness,
or, in more ornamental fashion, literature, it has been submitted to various attempts at
recuperation into rationality but has always resisted as bearer of a surplus of signification that
the system of the sign is unable to contain. It may well be that this surplus is seen more
distinctly when focused in the light not of an attempt at containment in a sign system, but of
a semanalysis orientated towards that pre-signifying and pre-conscious work, a work that the
text exposes. We may thus begin to encompass semanalysis in giving it as object the 'text' –
a concept that it is first of all necessary to define as particular domain of signifying
practice, domain in which signification is engendered in relation to an infinite material
exterior and in relation to its own constituents in an activity of the generation of sense before
its production.

The conceptualisation of such a problematic is currently being worked through. But
literary practice itself has always been elaborated in terms of a work of research on the laws
of its own production, and so of the production of sense in language in general. This is even
more evident in modern times in the work of Joyce, Mallarmé, Artaud: literature becomes a
veritable exploration of the generation of sense, of the production of sense in language.

If semanalysis occupies itself with this modern literature, it is not with the aim of
constituting a particular branch of semiotics destined for the study of literature and as the
necessary replacement of classical rhetoric. If semanalysis concerns itself with the text, it is
solely that it may provide itself with an object where the specificities of the signifying act are
most clearly manifested, an activity that the Stoic system of the sign was unable to think. It is
in this way that semanalysis will be able to work out the concepts and methods that will serve
in the elaboration of what has been referred to here as a materialist gnosiology.

The exact sciences – mathematics, logic, linguistics – can furnish concepts and models
for this semanalysis which will to a certain extent be transformed and displaced in the process
of the semanalytical reflection and will be operative as subverted premises. They will thus
find their rightful place as branches of a general theory of signification, branches which once
reintegrated into the whole cannot but be modified.

Notes

1   V. Brochard, 'La logique des Stoïciens': *Etudes de philosophie ancienne et de philosophie moderne* Paris
    1954 p 231.

2   cf Jacques Derrida, *De la grammatologie* Paris 1967; *L'écriture et la différence* Paris 1967.

3   'Logic as Semiotic: The Theory of Signs': *The Philosophy of Peirce: Selected Writings* cd J Buchler London 1940 p 98.

4   *Course in General Linguistics* London 1960 p 68.

5   *Ibid* p 16.

6   *Ibid* p 16.

7   cf E Benveniste, *Problèmes de linguistique générale* Paris 1966 p 13.

8   L Hjelinslev, *Prolegomena to a Theory of Language* Madison 1963 p 120.

9   *Ibid* P 125.

10   Charles W. Morris, *Foundations of the Theory of Signs: International Encyclopedia of Unified Science* Vol. I Chicago 1955 pp 135, 80.

11   cf Jan Mukarovsky 'La dénomination poétique et la fonction esthétique de la langue' (1936) *Poétique* No 3 pp 392–98.

12   cf Marx, *Differenz der demokritischen und epikureischen Naturphilosophie: Werke* Sup Vol I Berlin 1968 pp 257–373.

13   cf J. Lacan *Ecrits* Paris 1966 (eg p 594, p 838).

14   The text is, of course, the sixth chapter of *Die Traumdeutung*: 'Der Traumarbeit'.

15   J. Derrida, 'Sémiologie et grammatologie': *Informations sur les sciences sociales* VII-3 p 142.

PART II

Deconstruction and poststructuralism

WHILE DECONSTRUCTION AND POSTSTRUCTURALISM are closely related (and often conflated – see Chapter 11), the former is a methodological approach to analyzing texts and arguments derived from the work of Jacques Derrida, while the latter describes a hybrid discourse that usually incorporates deconstructive ideas into a wider field of enquiry. Deconstructionists look for the logical flaws and blind spots, or aporias, in textual arguments, so that they can undermine the hierarchies which fix systems of thinking and being into place. The main target of a deconstructionist argument is the "metaphysics of presence", that is to say, the notion that systems are grounded—or transcended—in a self present entity, such as God, the liberal humanist concept of "man", or the notion of universal truth. Poststructuralism, on the other hand, is any theoretical approach that involves a deconstructive understanding of texts and arguments, but usually combined with a number of other methodologies to create a more hybrid theory, which is then usually put into the service of a more political project, such as feminism, queer theory, postcolonialism, and so on.

The roots of deconstruction and poststructuralism go back to the early twentieth century, with the rise of Formalism and Structuralism, picking up from them the notion of a "scientific" approach to humanism, as well as drawing upon the shift into linguistics, semiotics, and structuralist notions of anthropology and psychoanalysis. However, it was in the 1960s that key groundbreaking texts were first published, including Jacques Derrida's *Edmund Husserl's Origin of Geometry: An Introduction* (1962), Jacques Lacan's *Écrits* (1966), and Michel Foucault's *The Order of Things* (1966). Each of these texts presented a new way of critically incorporating radical structuralist methodologies into broad domains of thought: Derrida begins his deconstruction of phenomenology (a philosophy that examines worldly being), Foucault declares the end of humanism and the associated central concept of "man", and Lacan develops the complex implications of his argument that the unconscious is structured like a language. Deconstruction came into particular prominence with the publication of three more books by Derrida in 1967: *Of Grammatology* (which was translated into English in 1976 by the postcolonial and poststructuralist critic Gayatri Chakravorty Spivak), *Speech and Phenomena and Other Essays on Husserl's Theory of Signs*, and *Writing and Difference*.

Leftist thought was particularly strong in France, and this is usually associated with the student uprisings in Paris, in May of 1968, but even such activist political intellectualism was reinventing itself along deconstructive lines. For example, Jean Baudrillard, who was part of the leftist Utopie Group of radical architecture theorists led by Henri Lefebvre, wrote in 1967 that only "the multiple play of oppositions" when examining previously stable concepts and values, "founds a logic of cultural signification".[1] In a lecture the previous year, given at the International Colloquium on Critical Languages and the Sciences of Man, at the Johns Hopkins University in Baltimore, USA, Derrida had mapped out in detail the semiological notion that structures are nothing but decentred networks of signs. This broad sketch, however, can too easily mask the fact that in Derrida's deconstruction there is one special mode of writing that appears to offer deconstructive resources which are *already* encoded within the text: that is to say, literary writing. Deconstruction offers "the vision of writing as an envelopment of the languages of science and philosophy" and furthermore hints at "writing as a concept that could unhinge metaphysics and institute a generalized critique of the Western ideology of presence. Literature ... would become the privileged locus of such an unhinging."[2] To understand, then, how literature became so important for deconstruction and poststructuralism, involves re-tracing one's footsteps, back to the launch in 1960 of a highly critical and creative journal publication called *Tel Quel*.

Launched by the French publishing house Seuil and edited by the writer and critic Philippe Sollers (Philippe Joyaux), *Tel Quel* sought to examine "literary quality", publishing material by a wide range of experimental authors such as Borges, Defoe, T.S. Eliot, Pound, and Woolf. The journal also published the transgressive writings of Antonin Artaud and Georges Bataille.[3] The distinctive critical vision of the journal, however, arose in 1963, with a review of Michel Foucault's book *Raymond Roussel*. As Ffrench notes, this review "shifts the perspective" of the journal to "radical questions of textual space, auto-referentiality and infinity" as well as "fiction as a textual space rather than a phenomenal space."[4] Key contributions on this new understanding of textuality include Sollers' article "Logique de la fiction" (1963), and in the 1970s, multiple articles on the central literary text for *Tel Quel* theorists: James Joyce's *Finnegans Wake*. During the early years, Derrida was one of the major theorists of the deconstructive conception of textuality, while Julia Kristeva broadened the field through a synthesis of structuralism, deconstruction, psychoanalytical theory, and feminism.

In *Of Grammatology*, which is a close reading of the philosopher and writer Jean Jacques Rousseau (1712–78), Derrida's main strategic move is to question the metaphysical hierarchy of speech being prioritized and valued more highly than writing. This is important because the notion of a self-present speech is one of the mainstays of metaphysical thought. Derrida deconstructs this binary opposition of speech/writing, to suggest that speech is actually a form of writing, and that both depend upon the play of "différance" to generate meaning. Derrida's new word, or neologism, "différance" expresses two ideas, that of difference ("difference" means "to differ") and that of deferral and delay ("différer" means "to defer, to delay"). Meaning is always on the move, it is always networked, and created through the differential play of semiotic systems; it is never fixed in one place. Meaning, then, is always something generated through its dissemination and deferral, and when looked at closely enough from a deconstructive perspective, it has always already moved on, or is located elsewhere. In effect, this is what Saussure had argued by saying that signs are arbitrary, and that they only signify something because a cultural system has artificially constructed or assigned a meaning to them; there is no self-present, intrinsic value. Deconstruction, then, analyzes arguments closely, to occupy metaphysical concepts (usually those created by hierarchical binary oppositions) from within. These metaphysical concepts are not totally replaced, rather they are placed "under erasure", that is to say, they are continually re-used in their deconstructive form.[5]

Deconstruction also generates "undecidables", or, terms that resist becoming new conceptual grounds. "Undecidables" also *reveal* the workings of "différance". In his book *Dissemination* (1972), Derrida explores the undecidable term "pharmakon" from Plato's *Phaedrus*; the term can mean "poison" or "medicine/cure" depending upon the translation, and thus it in effect self-deconstructs an argument whenever it is used. There are many such undecidables in decon-struction (pharmakon; supplement; hymen; trace; etc.), and they all generate one important effect: that of textual multiplicity. Critic Rodolphe Gasché explains further: "They are undecid-able because they suspend the decidable opposition between what is true and false ... Their undecidability, their 'floating indetermination,' permits the substitution and the play of the con-ceptual binary oppositions."[6] Deconstruction is always produced via close textual engagement, and a mode of writing that foregrounds undecidables. This new "grammatology" reveals that all of the excluded topics and modes of argumentation that metaphysics had banished from its conceptual world actually helped maintain metaphysical philosophy's belief systems in the first place. The difference between a metaphysical "inside" which banished art, poetry, music, to the exile of the "outside" was in fact an illusion. In highly playful texts such as *Glas* (1974), Derrida explores the interweaving of philosophical and artistic writing,[7] in this case with a book in two main columns: one on the idealist philosopher of the dialectic, Hegel, the other on the transgressive dramatist and writer, Jean Genet. In *Glas*, Derrida also strips away any last ves-tiges of natural signs in Saussure, showing that even Saussure's non-arbitrary symbols and onomatopoeias (words that sound like the thing they describe) are entirely constructed by the arbitrary semiotic code. Some critics, such as Gregory L. Ulmer, regard *Glas* as being a new form of an aesthetic "applied grammatology", but in many respects all that Derrida is doing is crossing the philosophy/art boundary to show that each "side" is already implicated in the other.[8] In the later Derrida, deconstructive insights are developed in relation to the anthropo-logical and economic concept of the gift; the topic of hospitality; the concept of the foreigner; and other work on the theological turn in contemporary theory and philosophy, among many other topics.

If the work of Derrida defines in broad brush strokes the deconstructive project, Kristeva's intense engagement with multiple domains of thought is similarly productive in the realm of poststructuralism. Another key journal played a part in the rise of poststructuralism, that of *Psychanalyse*, which as early as 1953 had published Jacques Lacan's structuralist psychoana-lytical theories, notably his essay "Discours de Rome". *Psychanalyse* published work by the Hegelian Jean Hyppolite, and the linguist Émile Benveniste, "who elaborated a critique of Saussure focused on the subject and subjectivity that would be crucial for theorists like Kristeva in the move away from structuralism, precisely towards a more psychoanalytic perspective on language."[9] If Derrida examined the logical results of the science of signs, Kristeva examined this science via its moments of "excess".[10] Structuralism appeared to ignore the question of subjectivity, and in its most formalist mode, deconstruction sometimes appears to its critics to do the same thing, but for Kristeva, her development of a poststructuralist critique of structur-alism involved re-thinking the entire semiotic and structuralist field from the perspective of subjectivity. As Ffrench puts it: "Kristeva articulates linguistics with psychoanalysis in order to provide a theory of the relation between the linguistic and the pre-linguistic."[11] Reading Kristeva, then, involves engaging in some quite technical language, such as her concept of the semiotic "chora" that Kristeva calls an underlying "figuration" or, something which at a bodily, rhythmic level, generates patterns and has a naturally deconstructive force. This is just one of many terms coined or reworked by Kristeva ("chora" actually derives from Plato's *Timaeus*) in her first two major books *Séméiotiké: Recherches pour une sémanalyse* (1969) and *Le Texte du roman: Approche sémiologique d'une structure discursive transformationelle* (1970). A third key text was Kristeva's thesis, defended in 1973, and published the following year as *La Révolution du langage poétique: L'Avant-garde à la fin du XIXe siècle* (translated as *Revolution in Poetic Language*, in 1984).

Overall, Kristeva replaces the science of signs with a poststructuralist *sémanalyse*, in which the symbolic realm of science and logic is always threatened, undermined and deconstructed by a *bodily* semiotic realm of desire and drives. These two realms are always in relation, and at a textual level the bodily *geno-text* is what generates and simultaneously transgresses or deconstructively re-assesses the scientific *pheno-text*. Other key Kristevan poststructuralist terms are "intertextuality" that is to say a notion of textual networks that are interrelated at the smallest level of meaning, the components that Kristeva calls the text's *ideologemes*, or, "the smallest component in a system."[12] This approach to the multiplicity and interrelatedness of textuality is partly based upon the work of Mikhail Bakhtin, and his notion that multiple voices create a "polyphony" in literary texts. Kristeva's work began to be translated into English in 1980, with the publication of *Desire in Language: A Semiotic Approach to Literature and Art*. Apart from the groundbreaking *Revolution in Poetic Language* (trans. 1984), mentioned above, three more translated texts in the 1980s made Kristeva's thought more freely available: *Powers of Horror: An Essay on Abjection* (1980), *Tales of Love* (1983), and *In The Beginning Was Love: Psychoanalysis and Faith* (1985).

The intersection of psychoanalytical and other poststructuralist theories was not of course solely manifested in the work of Kristeva. Among many other theorists, notable contributions were made by Gilles Deleuze (1925–95) and Pierre Félix Guattari (1930–92), in particular two books: *Anti-Oedipus: Capitalism and Schizophrenia* (1972) and *A Thousand Plateaus: Capitalism and Schizophrenia* (1980). Building upon Guattari's essays published as *Psychanalyse et transversalité* (1972) and Deleuze's work on Nietzsche, published as *Nietzsche and Philosophy* (1962), a new theory of "machinic" subjectivity is presented in their joint works. In the process, Deleuze and Guattari critically threw off the structuralist interest in Sigmund Freud, to produce a poststructuralist account of desiring machines, where psychic flaws and fragmentation are celebrated, not regarded as something in need of a cure. Desiring machines are produced via coupling and breaks, producing energy flows and interruptions, and the concept of the "body without organs" where the concept of a hierarchical body, with "higher" controlling and functioning organs, such as the brain, or the face (the latter is central in the ethical work of Emmanuel Levinas), is rejected in favour of intensities of desire, neither representing some inner world, or transcending the moment. Another key practitioner of the intersection of psychoanalysis and other emerging theories is Shoshana Felman (1942–), who also acts as a mediator, translator, and theorist, working between European and North American poststructuralism. These multiple roles are apparent in her special edition of *Yale French Studies* (1977), re-published as *Literature and Psychoanalysis, The Question of Reading: Otherwise* (1982), in which essays by the American critics Barbara Johnson, Gayatri Chakravorty Spivak, Fredric Jameson and Felman herself, reveal the rise of theory in a North American context. In *Writing and Madness (Literature/ Philosophy/ Psychoanalysis)* (French 1978; English 1985; new edition 2003), Felman explores the parallel realms of the psychoanalytically excluded and transgressive, literary strangeness, excess and illusion. Of note is the fact that even though Felman was a professor at Yale University's department of French and Comparative Literature, she was never officially recognized as a member of the most prominent North American group of deconstructionists and poststructuralists, the Yale School, which deconstructionist and translator Barbara Johnson subsequently renamed the "Male School".[13] Yet the official, and unofficial, members of this group of theorists played a major part in introducing and developing a sophisticated theoretical approach in North America, and this warrants one more brief detour through the strangely recursive history of deconstruction and poststructuralism.

The "Structuralism" issue of *Yale French Studies* in 1966 was the first of two important sites of dialogue concerning the new theories that were being developed in France, the second being the previously mentioned International Colloquium on Critical Languages and the Sciences of Man, at the Johns Hopkins University in Baltimore, USA. The papers from the colloquium were published in 1970 as *The Languages of Criticism and the Sciences of Man*, with an interesting shift in title for the 1972 reprint, which was called *The Structuralist Controversy*. As Wallace Martin observes "In retrospect, the editors [of *The Structuralist Controversy*] questioned the very existence of structuralism as a meaningful concept", and found in the same volume "evidence . . . of the ensuing moment of theoretical deconstruction."[14] At Yale the main practitioners of deconstruction were Jacques Derrida as a visiting professor, and Paul de Man, Geoffrey Hartman, J. Hillis Miller, and Harold Bloom. What all of these critics were doing in a *loosely* related way (thus, the subsequent questioning of the viability of the "School" title), was applying a new deconstructive logic to literary texts and genres, with emphasis upon Romanticism. The deconstructive logic is revealed most clearly, as with Derrida's work and that of the *Tel Quel* critics, in readings of literature. In two groundbreaking texts, *Blindness and Insight: Essays in the Rhetoric of Contemporary Criticism* (1971) and *Allegories of Reading: Figural Language in Rousseau, Nietzsche, Rilke, and Proust* (1979), de Man argued that textual moments of insight and blindness (aporias) have to be confronted in deconstructive readings of literary texts. Drawing upon Nietzsche's insight that all texts are merely a mobile "army" of metaphors, de Man observes that the subsequent instability, or forever moving textual ground, means that questions of grammar or rhetoric cannot take priority, so that a science of signs (or, taken to its limits, a deconstructive grammatology) is both constitutive and an impossibility: "Literature as well as criticism—the difference between them being delusive— is condemned (or privileged) to be forever the most rigorous and, consequently, the most unreliable language in terms of which man [*sic*] names and transforms himself."[15] In other words, deconstruction reveals how signification works, yet destabilizes one's certainties, at the same time. The notion of permanently "misreading" texts can lead to euphoria or anxiety, such psychological states being relevant to the Yale School's investigation of Romanticism and related figures. Bloom's big "misreading" thesis is found in *The Anxiety of Influence: A Theory of Poetry* (1973), where he argues that misreading is a necessary process for poets to "clear imaginative space for themselves."[16] Bloom expands upon this notion in his *A Map of Misreading* (1975). The blurring of literature and criticism mentioned by de Man is explored—and celebrated—by Hartman in *The Fate of Reading: And Other Essays* (1975), and he subsequently develops a "paralanguage" or deconstructive echo of the literary text, in his *Criticism in the Wilderness: The Study of Literature Today* (1980). Such a performative, aesthetic approach to deconstruction is apparent in his *Saving the Text: Literature/ Derrida/ Philosophy* (1981). Miller also advocates and celebrates deconstructive indeterminacy in *Fiction and Repetition* (1982) and *The Linguistic Moment* (1985).

The Yale School came under attack after the death of de Man, and the discovery of his Second World War writings in Belgium, in favour of Nazi ideology. As Felman notes, "This discovery—and the furor this discovery provoked—displaced the intellectual debate from de Man's theory and pathbreaking methodology of reading to his personality and his political behaviour . . . This displacement in turn gave rise to a general assault on deconstruction and the Yale School, an assault that left the picture of the school's historic contribution more confused, more blurred, and more misunderstood than it had ever been."[17] Hartman responded to this attack in his *Minor Prophecies: The Literary Essay in the Culture Wars* (1991) as did Derrida himself in *Memoires for Paul de Man* (1986). Yet the shift into an obsession with biographical, historical and ethical issues in relation to de Man is in itself indicative of a broadening of deconstructive applications and approaches that was already underway. Deconstruction has never "ended" as such, it has merely transmogrified into the broader methodologies of poststructuralism. While purists, for example, still refer to the early and "later" Derrida—i.e., his later shift into more ethical and theological issues—poststructuralism is in some ways the name for a more diverse, hybrid discourse, that has thoroughly assimilated deconstructive methodologies, which accounts for this later series of interests in Derrida's, and a wide range of other critics', own writing.

Further reading: a selection

The secondary reading in this area is extensive, but there are definitely "classics" in the field, such as Bennington's deconstructive overview of Derrida's thought, with a fascinating response from Derrida written along the bottom of each page; Bennington doesn't just explain deconstruction, he demonstrates its modes of argumentation and expression. Norris's best-selling introduction offers a critical approach that readers continue to engage with favourably. Another good way "in" to deconstruction is through comparative approaches and applications, such as deconstruction and the following: feminism (Elam), architecture (Wigley), ethics (Critchley), and theology (Hart). McQuillan's reader offers an extensive collection of essays, including key texts by Derrida. Wider coverage of Yale School deconstruction is available through the reprinting of key essays in Arac, Godzich and Wallace, while the European poststructuralist thinkers are covered in depth by Ffrench. For deconstructionists and poststructuralists, literature is highly valued, partly because it is seen as being theoretically complex, doing many of the things theorists aspire to. Felman examines psychoanalytical and poststructuralist theories of literature, Wheedon focuses on feminist critical practice, and Davis on narrative and stories. Johnson examines gender, feminism and deconstructive literary readings, while Rapaport offers a strong critique of what he regards as "misreadings" of deconstruction and poststructuralism. Rapaport looks at the key postcolonial critic, Gayatri Spivak, in his chapter "Deconstructing Otherwise", and Hiddleston also uses the postcolonial lens to read key poststructuralist critics such as Derrida, Cixous, Kristeva and Lyotard, etc., ending with an outstanding chapter on Spivak.

Arac, Jonathan, Wlad Godzich, and Wallace Martin, eds. *The Yale Critics: Deconstruction in America*, Minneapolis: University of Minnesota Press, 1983.

Attridge, Derek, Geoffrey Bennington and Robert Young, eds. *Post-Structuralism and the Question of History*. Cambridge: Cambridge University Press, 1987.

Bennington, Geoffrey and Jacques Derrida. *Jacques Derrida*. Trans. Geoffrey Bennington. Chicago & London: University of Chicago Press, 1993.

Critchley, Simon. *The Ethics of Deconstruction: Derrida and Levinas*. Oxford: Blackwell, 1992.

Davis, Colin. *After Poststructuralism: Reading, Stories and Theory*. London & New York: Routledge, 2004.

Elam, Diane. *Feminism and Deconstruction: Ms. en Abyme*. London & New York: Routledge, 1994.

Felman, Shoshana. *Writing and Madness: (Literature / Philosophy / Psychoanalysis)*. Trans. Martha Noel Evans and Shoshana Felman. Palo Alto, CA: Stanford University Press, 2003.

Ffrench, Patrick. *The Time of Theory: A History of Tel Quel (1960–1983)*. Oxford: Clarendon Press, 1995.

Gasché, Rodolphe. *The Tain of the Mirror: Derrida and the Philosophy of Reflection*. Cambridge, Massachusetts & London, England: Harvard University Press, 1986.

Hart, Kevin. *The Trespass of the Sign: Deconstruction, Theology and Philosophy*. USA: Fordham University Press, 2000.

Hiddleston, Jane. *Poststructuralism and Postcoloniality: The Anxiety of Theory*. Liverpool: Liverpool University Press, 2010.

Johnson, Barbara. *A World of Difference*. Baltimore, Maryland: the Johns Hopkins University Press, 1989.

McQuillan, Martin. *Deconstruction: A Reader*. London & New York: Routledge, 2001.

Norris, Christopher. *Deconstruction: Theory and Practice*. Third Edition. London & New York: Routledge, 2002.

Rapaport, Herman. *The Theory Mess: Deconstruction in Eclipse*. New York: Columbia University Press, 2001.

Wheedon, Chris. *Feminist Practice and Poststructuralist Theory*. Second Edition. Oxford: Blackwell, 1997.

Wigley, Mark. *The Architecture of Deconstruction: Derrida's Haunt*. Cambridge, MA: MIT Press, 1995.

Notes

1   Jean Baudrillard, *Utopia Deferred: Writings for* Utopie *(1967–1978)*, trans. Stuart Kendall, New York: Semiotext(e), 2006, p.33; see also, Richard J. Lane, *Jean Baudrillard*, London & NY: Routledge, 2009 (second edition), pp.18–19.

2   Patrick Ffrench, *The Time of Theory: A History of* Tel Quel *(1960–1983)*, Oxford: Clarendon Press, 1995, p.17.

3   Patrick Ffrench, *The Time of Theory: A History of* Tel Quel *(1960–1983)*, p.52.

4   Patrick Ffrench, *The Time of Theory: A History of* Tel Quel *(1960–1983)*, p.58.

5   For more on this process, see Richard J. Lane, *Functions of the Derrida Archive: Philosophical Receptions*, Budapest: Akadémiai Kiadó, 2003, p.78.

6   Rodolphe Gasché, *The Tain of the Mirror: Derrida and the Philosophy of Reflection*, Cambridge, Massachusetts & London, England: Harvard University Press, 1986, p.241.

7   Richard J. Lane, *Functions of the Derrida Archive: Philosophical Receptions*, p.105.

8   Richard J. Lane, *Functions of the Derrida Archive: Philosophical Receptions*, p.101.

9   Patrick Ffrench, *The Time of Theory: A History of* Tel Quel *(1960–1983)*, p.22.

10   Patrick Ffrench, *The Time of Theory: A History of* Tel Quel *(1960–1983)*, p.163.

11   Patrick Ffrench, *The Time of Theory: A History of* Tel Quel *(1960–1983)*, p.165.

12   Richard J. Lane, *Fifty Key Literary Theorists*, London & New York: Routledge, 2006, p.189.

13   Barbara Johnson, *A World of Difference*, Baltimore, Maryland: the Johns Hopkins University Press, 1989, p.32.

14   Jonathan Arac, Wlad Godzich and Wallace Martin, eds., *The Yale Critics: Deconstruction in America*, Minneapolis: University of Minnesota Press, 1983, xv.

15   Paul de Man, *Allegories of Reading: Figural Language in Rousseau, Nietzsche, Rilke, and Proust*, New Haven & London: Yale University Press, 1979, p.19.

16   Harold Bloom, *The Anxiety of Influence: A Theory of Poetry*, New York: Oxford University Press, 1973, p.5.

17   Shoshana Felman, *Writing and Madness: (Literature / Philosophy / Psychoanalysis)*, trans. Martha Noel Evans and Shoshana Felman, Palo Alto, CA: Stanford University Press, 2003, p.9.

Chapter 8

Pal Ahluwalia

DERRIDA

Poststructuralism is often presented via its conceptual history, that is to say the philosophical and aesthetic movements it emerged from, or reacted to. Less frequently included in this narrative is the question of colonial history, and yet as Pal Ahluwalia shows, there is a profound connection between colonial/postcolonial Africa and "French" theory, especially in relation to those theorists born in Algeria: Louis Althusser, Hélène Cixous, and Jacques Derrida as well as numerous others who studied or lectured there, such as Michel Foucault. The Algerian War of Independence becomes more important from this perspective than the May 1968 student protests in Paris, which is one of the usual historical reference points to explain the emergence of French theory. Ahluwalia, an expert in concepts and histories of diaspora, exile and migration (reflected in his UNESCO chair in Transnational Diasporas and Reconciliation Studies, appointed in 2008), argues that key poststructuralist concepts, such as "otherness, difference, irony, mimicry, parody", emerge from colonial and postcolonial Africa, and this is apparent in the case of Derrida, who was born in 1930 into a family of "Sephardic Jewish" heritage, in El-Biar, Algeria. During the Second World War, Algerian Jews had their citizenship revoked, and along with the anti-Semitism that Derrida suffered, this created a feeling of uncertain—if not fragmented—identity, a theme that would emerge in his later work on the paradoxes of hospitality and the experience of being a "foreigner". Ahluwalia argues that even though Derridean deconstruction denies any stable point of origin, it is this sense of *displacement* in Derrida's early life that becomes significant in the development of a deconstructive methodology. So, deconstruction's double movement—first, the questioning or dismantling of a binary opposition or hierarchical structure (argument, text, etc.), second, showing how deconstructive devices are already at work in a system or text—can also be termed "displacement". Ahluwalia suggests that this movement mimics the relationship of the colonial subject and his or her colonial masters: displacement can be negative, but through postcolonial "interrogation, engagement, transformation" the master is in turn subject to intense critique and is himself displaced. In Derrida's biography, there is a continual displacement between being Algerian, Jewish, a French subject, and so on, that creates a diasporic postcolonial identity, one registered in a famous quotation from Derrida's book *Glas*: "In Algeria, in the middle of a mosque that the colonialists had changed into a synagogue, the *Torah* . . . is carried about." The many themes of

Deconstruction are present in this quotation—such as the role of the master text, or phallogocentrism; the Jewish conception of a holy text that has nothing outside of it; the shifting from one system of thought to another seen in the displacement of the mosque by the synagogue; and so on—but as Ahluwalia points out, these themes are first and foremost colonial and/or postcolonial. But what Ahluwalia calls the "excavation of Derrida's postcolonial roots" is not meant to recuperate some absent origin or to "rescue" deconstruction from postcolonial critique, rather, what appeared at the margins (Algeria, otherness, anti-Semitism . . .), is shown to be at the heart of Western theoretical discourse. For Ahluwalia, Algeria is the ghost that haunts all of Derrida's writing.

> I was born in Algeria, but already my family, which had been in Algeria for a long time, before the French colonization, was not simply Algerian. The French language was not the language of its ancestors. I lived in the pre-independent Algeria, but not all that long before Independence. All of this makes for a landscape that is very, very . . . full of contracts, mistures, crossings. The least statement on this subject seems to me to be a mutilation in advance.
>
> (Jacques Derrida)

> The home of the Jews and the poet is the text; they are the wanderers, born only of the book. But the freedom of the poet depends, in Derrida's interpretation, on the breaking of the tablets of law (slaying Moses again). . . . Both the poet and the Jew must write and must comment, because both poetry and commentary are forms of exiled speech, but the poet need not be faithful nor bound to any original text.
>
> (Susan Handelman)

THE PLACE OF ALGERIA IN DERRIDA'S WORK is the place of origins, and consequently it is the place of the scandalous, the erased, the deferred. There can be no more contentious issue in the philosopher's oeuvre, no more deconstructed concept, than origins: the origin of writing, of meaning, of the text. The rejection of origin itself as an ultimate locus, a beginning, a final arbiter of meaning, lies at the 'centre' of the philosophy and practice of deconstruction. It is no surprise, therefore, that the historical facts of Derrida's upbringing in colonial Algeria have not been widely known; indeed, that the events of his own origin have been systematically elided, excluded and glossed over. Christopher Norris has argued that Derrida's biographical details and his formative experiences are not relevant to an understanding of his work. They only become relevant 'to his *writing* insofar as they take the form of a relentless interrogation of philosophy by one who – for whatever reason – shares rather few of philosophy's traditional beliefs'. This explains 'Derrida's reluctance to supply that familiar kind of background information which relates "life" to "work" through a presupposed logic of one-way causal influence' (Norris 1987: 12).

The location of Derrida the person, however, like the location of other settler Algerians, specifically focuses the 'location' of Derrida's theory. Perhaps no other writer so comprehensively brings into view the question of the status of origins in intellectual work. Do we need to be bound to an understanding of origins as transcendent, or fixed, an immutable beginning? Why should Algeria matter? How do we negotiate the difficult terrain between essentialist notions of influence and presumptions of the text's disassociation from the world?

The fact that Derrida is Algerian raises a number of questions that circulate around the heresy of origin. How different would his work have been had he not been born in Algeria? For example, it is possible simply to read Derrida's work without acknowledging his colonial roots. As Derrida himself has noted, 'I do not believe that anyone can detect *by reading,* if I do not declare it, that I am a "French Algerian"' (1998: 46). What happens when his Algerian locatedness is taken into account? What impact did his formative years have on his later work? What of deconstructive theory or Derridean logocentrism? Does his overall project reflect his colonial roots and the tensions that arise out of being relocated within a new culture? Is the fate of Derrida of belonging and not belonging in both French and Algerian culture, of occupying that in-between space, part of his own alterity that inevitably makes its way into his writings, relevant to understanding his work? Does his profound influence on contemporary thought need to be contextualised against the backdrop of Algeria and the experience of colonisation? Is it the sense of exile, of being on the margins that allows him to challenge Western theory? Is there a different way of reading and enjoying Derrida's oeuvre whilst taking into account his own Algerian subjectivity? Does his work reflect its postcolonial source, or the tension arising from his experience of displacement? This chapter seeks to understand the effects of Derrida's colonial origin upon his theory and considers the implications for his theory of the suppression of that origin. These are not questions that need to be bound to egregious notions of influence; rather, they approach Derrida's own *texts* in their cultural location, their worldliness. In this respect, these questions are not so much about Derrida's theory as about the locatedness of theory itself.

Origins

Jacques Derrida's Algerian heritage is of long standing. He was born on July 15, 1930, the third son of Aime Derrida and Georgette (Safar) Derrida in El-Biar, Algeria, into a prosperous Sephardic Jewish family whose roots could be traced to those who had fled the Spanish Inquisition.[1] The Derrida family initially lived in a house in La Rue Saint-Augustin but in 1934 moved to a house that was named 'Pardes', 13, Rue d' Aurelle-de-Paladines also in El-Biar (Bennington and Derrida 1993: 325; Powell 2006). It was from this location that he attended school. However, the outbreak of the Second World War was to have a profound impact on the young Derrida, as Algerian Jews were subjected to persecutions despite the absence of any German occupation. It was as a young child that Derrida experienced anti-Semitism when the head teacher at school during roll call declared, 'French culture is not made for little Jews' (Bennington and Derrida 1993: 326). Considering his origins, whether in a literal or metaphoric sense, it is not possible to escape the profound and formative experience of his Jewishness. It has been suggested that Derrida's identity as a Sephardic Jew underlies 'the depth, rigor, and passion of the attack that he launches on the Western tradition' (Megill 1985: 276). Yet, Gideon Ofrat has pointed out recently that, 'beyond a few fitful glimmers, the decisive sway Derrida's philosophy has exercised over Western creativity and critical ideas these past twenty years, called for no illumination of its Jewish aspect' (2001: 1). Nevertheless, it is important to add to this: to recognise that in Derrida's case this very 'Jewishness' has been energised and directed by the pressure of a continually suppressed colonial background. It is a suppression that Derrida himself engaged in, living up to his own pronouncement that 'there is nothing outside the text' by not wanting anything personal to appear in print and, from 1962 to 1979, he went so far as not even to allow himself to be photographed for a publication (Stephens 1991). It is the scars of a colonial background that alert us to the return of the colonial into European thought. It is this colonial background that locates and energises the disruption of European modernity.

In 1941, Derrida joined Lycee Ben Aknoun where at the very beginning of the next school year he was to experience anti-Semitism on a personal level when he was expelled because of his religion. This experience, no doubt, left an indelible mark:

It's an experience which leaves nothing intact, something you can never again cease to feel. The Jewish children were expelled from school. In the principal's office: 'Go back home, your parents will explain.' Then the Allies land, and it's the period of what was called the two-headed government (de Gaulle-Giraud): racial laws were maintained for a period of almost six months, under a 'free' French government, friends who no longer knew you, the insults, the Jewish lycée with teachers expelled without a murmur of protest from the colleagues. I was enrolled there, but I skipped classes for a year.

(cited in David 1988: 74)

Although Derrida never forgot that moment of double marginalisation, the moment became more embedded in his theory than in his speech, for Algeria itself remains the repressed, the silent, the forgotten origin of his autobiography.

In 1943, Derrida enrolled at Lycee Emile-Maupas, a Jewish school ran by teachers who had been excluded from the public school system. It was later in that year that he was allowed to return to Lycee Ben Aknoun but the experience of expulsion, anti-Semitism as well as a desire to play professional soccer all contributed to his failing the baccalaureate exam in 1947. It was at this time that he attended a philosophy class at Lycee Gautier in Algiers and considered a career as a teacher. Nevertheless, he passed the baccalaureate in June 1948 and signed up in the advanced literature class at Lycee Bugeaud in Algiers. In 1950, he went to France for the very first time but it was not until 1952 that he was admitted finally to the Ecole Normale Supérieure where he met Louis Althusser. The next year he met Foucault and attended his lectures. In 1957, he returned to Algeria to do his military service and was seconded to a school in Kolea, where he taught French and English. In addition, he translated press articles and often met Pierre Bourdieu in Algiers.

Derrida's Algerian origins and his Jewish background are testimony to the importance of his identity, to his feelings of nonbelonging and otherness. It is here that the personal becomes political and inevitably part of Derrida's overall project. The issues of the other, the excluded, the margins, boundaries are all personal in his case. As Derrida himself writes,

The phenomena which interest me are precisely those that blur the boundaries, cross them, and make their historical artifice appear, also their violence, meaning the relations that are concentrated there and actually capitalize themselves there interminably. Those who are sensitive to all stakes of 'creolization' . . . assess this better than others.

(Derrida 1998: 9)

The powerful symbolism evoked by the frontier as a site where memory is sanctified is important for rethinking and re-examining the impact of the colonial experience on the imaginary of identity. The following excerpt from an interview with Catherine David of *Le Nouvel Observateur* (N.O.), nevertheless, illustrates the difficulties that Derrida had in contending with Algeria.

N.O.:   Just now you spoke about Algeria, where it all began for you . . .
JD: Ah, you want me to tell you things like "I-was-born-in-El-Biar-in-the-suburbs-of-Algiers-in-a-petit-bourgeois-Jewish-family-which-was-assimilated-but . . . " Is this really necessary?
N.O.:   How old were you when you left Algeria?
JD: Please, now . . . I came to France when I was nineteen. Before then, I had never been much past El-Biar. The war came to Algeria in 1940, and

with it, already then, the first concealed rumblings of the Algerian War. As a child, I had the instinctive feeling that the end of the world was at hand, a feeling which at the same time was most natural, and, in any case, the only one I ever knew. Even for a child incapable of analyzing things, it was clear that all this would end in fire and blood. No one could escape that violence and fear even if around it . . .

N.O.:   You have quite precise memories of that fear?

JD: Yes . . . in 1940, the singular experience of the Algerian Jews. Incomparable to that of European Jews, the persecutions were nonetheless unleashed in the absence of any German occupier.

N.O.:   You suffered personally?

JD: It's an experience which leaves nothing intact . . . The Jewish children were expelled from school. In the principal's office: 'Go home, your parents will explain'. Then the Allies land, and . . . racial laws were maintained for a period of almost six months, under a 'free' French government. Friends who no longer knew you, the insults, the Jewish lycée with teachers expelled without a murmur of protest from their colleagues. I was enrolled there, but I skipped classes for a year.

N.O.:   Why?

JD: From that moment – how can I say it – I felt displaced in a Jewish community, closed unto itself, as I would in the other (which they used to call 'the Catholics') . . . A paradoxical effect, perhaps of this bludgeoning was the desire to be integrated into the non-Jewish community, a fascinated but painful and distrustful desire, one with a nervous vigilance, a painstaking attitude to discern signs of racism in its most discreet formations or in its loudest denials. Symmetrically, oftentimes I felt an impatient distance with regard to various Jewish communities, when I have the impression that they close in upon themselves, when they pose themselves as such. From all of which comes a feeling of non-belonging that I have doubtless transposed . . .

N.O.:   In philosophy?

JD: Everywhere.

(David 1988: 74–75)

The autobiographical details that can be gleaned from this exchange, and often recalled by Derrida in several of his later writings and interviews, reveal the complexities faced by the Jewish community in Algeria. The Algerian Jews were essentially nonindigenous 'natives' much like the Indians of Southern and Eastern Africa (Ahluwalia 1995; Ahluwalia and Zegeye 2001). These nonindigenous 'natives' occupied a particularly ambivalent space between the coloniser and the colonised.[2] These subject races were 'virtual citizens' who received preferential treatment under the law. As Mahmood Mamdani points out, they were

> deprived of rights of citizenship, yet considered to have the potential of becoming full citizens. Though colonized, they came to function as junior clerks in the juggernaut that was the civilizing mission. Without being part of colonial rulers, they came to be integrated into the machinery of colonial rule as agents, whether in the state apparatus or in the marketplace. As such, they came to be seen as both instruments and beneficiaries of colonialism, however coerced the instrumentality and petty the benefits.

(2001:27)

For Derrida, coming from this community has contributed to concerns with identity that are best reflected in his self-designation as a Jewish 'Franco-Maghrebin'. This hyphenated designation, he reminds us, 'does not pacify or appease anything, not a single torment, not a single torture' (Derrida 1998: 11). The anti-Semitism that he describes in the foregoing interview revolves around the question of citizenship, which for these 'virtual citizens' is at the behest of the colonial power. In a recent interview, Derrida spoke about this explicitly:

> The Jewish community in Algeria was there long before the French colonizers.
> So on the one hand, Algerian Jews belonged to the colonized people, and on the
> other they assimilated with the French. During the Nazi occupation, there were
> no German soldiers in Algeria. There was only the French and the Vichy regime,
> which produced and enforced laws that were terribly repressive. I was expelled
> from school. My family lost its citizenship. When you're in such a marginal, and
> unsafe and shaky situation, you are more attentive to the question of your legal
> authorization. You are a subject whose identity is threatened, as are your rights.
>
> (Rosenfeld 1998)

The question of citizenship dates back to the latter part of the nineteenth century when, as France's control appeared precarious, the French exploited their relationship with the Jewish population in order to ensure their continued rule. In 1870, they were granted full French citizenship by the Crémieux decree and from that time, they identified themselves with the European French (Wood 1998). The effect of granting citizenship was that the *colons* now had an ally community. Relations between the French and the Jewish Algerians, however, were complex, accommodating when the need arose, but generally marked by a great deal of anti-Semitism.[3] The precarious position of the Algerian Jews was made clear in 1940 under the Vichy regime when their citizenship was revoked. It is clearly an experience that has left an indelible mark on Derrida, a mark that makes him highly conscious of what it means to be a French citizen. It is not surprising that in his deliberations on hospitality and citizenship he noted:

> Usually, the foreigner the foreign citizen, the foreigner to the family or the
> nation, is defined on the basis of birth: whether the citizenship is given or refused
> on the basis of territorial law or the law of blood relationship, the foreigner is a
> foreigner by birth, is a born foreigner.
>
> (Dufourmantelle and Derrida 2000: 87)

The link between the Sephardim and postcolonial identity is uncannily deep. In 1492, the very year that Columbus sailed uninvited for American shores Ferdinand and Isabella expelled the Jews from Spain. Just days after the last ship of Jewish exiles set sail southward, Columbus sailed westward. The Sephardic Jews expelled by Spain were those Oriental Jews who had spread through North Africa and Spain from the beginning of the dispersion. For several generations the Derrida family were considered indigenous Algerian Jews, revealing that Derrida's African roots were indeed very deep. The link between the discovery of America and the expulsion of the Sephardic Jews is a potent symbol in Derrida's own cultural history. More intriguing, it seems symbolic in the origin of Derrida's philosophy, an overde-termination that would be hard to invent. However, the connection returns with material force in Derrida's own life. This historical experience of the Algerian Jews who occupied such a unique place within colonial Algeria had a profound impact on Derrida's views about citizenship and belonging. In an interview, when he was asked a question about his identity, he responded: 'Each time this identity announces itself, each time a belonging circumscribes me, if I may put it this way, someone or something cries: Look out for the trap, you're caught, take off, get free, disengage yourself. Your engagement is elsewhere' (Weber 1995: 340).

Derrida's relationship with Algeria, or his 'nostalgeria' as he calls it, has at best remained ambivalent.

> No doubt these are the years during which the singular character of J.D.'s 'belonging' to Judaism is imprinted on him: wound, certainly, painful and prac- ticed sensitivity to antisemitism and any racism, 'raw' response to xenophobia, but also impatience with gregarious identification, with the militancy of belong- ing in general, even if it is Jewish. In short, a double rejection – of which there are many signs, well before *Circumfession*.
>
> (Bennington and Derrida 1993: 326–27)

While condemning France's colonial policy in Algeria he hoped, until the last moment, for a compromise that would induce indigenous Algerians and the *pieds-noirs* to live together peacefully. He even tried to prevent his parents from leaving Algiers in 1962, but soon realised that history had outrun such hopes for a transformed postcolonial state (Bennington and Derrida 1993: 330). In this tendency, we find a desperate desire for the stability of home that seems so at odds with his theory. For him, as we shall see, home, the beginning-point, became 'where you are'. Derrida would go back twice: in 1971, to lecture at the University of Algiers and in 1984, to visit his old home, but effectively Algeria disappeared from his life. It remains, however, the origin of origins, the ultimately deferred, unarticulated, palimpsestic and avoidable site of marginality and displacement.

Origin and displacement

For Derrida there are no ontological origins. It is from this perspective that the very origins of writing need to be considered. How does it actually appear? Clearly, this is a question about origins. However, Derrida argues, 'But a meditation upon the trace should undoubtedly teach us that there is no origin, that is to say, simple origin; that the questions of origin carry with them a metaphysics of presence' (1976: 74). The corollary of the anxiety of origin in Derrida's work is the predominance of displacement, a concept that is usually associated with Freud's interpretation of dreams, but which has expanded from a technical psychoanalytic term to a process encompassing a wide range of deconstructive strategies in post-structuralist theory. As Krupnick points out, displacement is not theoretically articulated by Derrida, but deconstruction itself proceeds by way of displacement, first reversing a binary opposition and then displacing it (1983: 1). For Derrida, it is not simply the case that the binary oppositions of metaphysics should be neutralised. Rather, deconstruction entails a reversal and displacement, because within familiar philosophical binaries there is always a violent hierarchy. One term of the binary is always superior to the other. It is the task of deconstruction to disrupt that hierarchy, to place the superior term under erasure. As Spivak points out, the task for deconstruction is:

> To locate the promising marginal text, to disclose the undecidable moment, to pry it loose with the positive lever of the signifier, to reverse the resident hierarchy, only to displace it; to dismantle in order to reconstitute what is always already inscribed.
>
> (1976: lxxvi)

The hierarchical opposition between speech and writing is not eliminated; rather it is *displaced,* cut loose from its metaphysical grounding. Post-structuralism itself is a 'displacement' of structuralism, which does not mean a 'replacement' or unfolding through time: 'It is more a question of an interrogation of structuralism's methods and assumptions' a transformation (Krupnick 1983: 4). In this respect, the term, used in this way, also provides a succinct account of the relationship between colonialism and postcolonialism: displacement as interrogation, engagement, transformation rather than a chronological development from its hegemonic precursor. The binary opposition so prevalent within postcolonial studies, that of the coloniser and colonised, is one that Derrida was all too familiar with. The Algerian War of Independence was testimony of how the superior term could be disrupted, placed under erasure and yet never erased.

Nevertheless, there is another way, a more historical, social and cultural way, in which the term 'displacement' forms a link between Derrida's post-structuralist project and his colonial origins. This is the sense of displacement as an *experience:* the experience of being out of place, *unheimlich.* The word itself thus comes to embody in its different uses both the concept of interrogation central to deconstruction, and the concept of cultural disarticulation that emerges as a fundamental feature of postcolonial experience in language, place and culture. As Ofrat argues, 'Derrida identifies this consciousness of estrangement from roots and tradition, of amnesia, with deconstruction. The eternal estrangement between writing and origin is a person's sentence of estrangement between his culture and its sources' (2001: 17–18).

This connection is itself a 'displacement' rather than a history, an etymology. In this displacement, we find the political paradox of deconstruction. For if, as Krupnick claims, deconstruction as Derrida 'practices it allies itself with the voiceless, the marginal, the repressed' (1983: 2), then it would seem that the occlusion of origins, the elision of the material location that Algeria metonymises, disables the political efficacy of that alliance, for it has 'no conviction that the old . . . order can be transcended' (2). It is in this aporia in Derrida's deconstructive strategy, the gap between the alliance with the marginalised and emancipatory potential of that alliance, that we find the repression of his own colonial origin – Algeria.

In Derrida's Algeria, we find a double cultural displacement. No matter how long-standing his family's residence in Algeria, a sense of cultural displacement was impossible to avoid. The very character of French colonialism – with its prodigious propulsion towards assimilation, its legislation of colonies as departments of France, its overwhelming linguistic and cultural centralisation – far from giving colonies a sense of cultural integrity, installed a spiritual and cultural displacement (in *all* cultural groups) even more strongly than in British colonies. This displacement was all the more disabling in those *pieds-noirs* and Jewish Algerians whose link to the soil of that country seemed to weaken their links with a France that most never visited. For the cultural and political hegemony of French colonialism allowed little room for the kind of postcolonial identity construction that occurred in British colonies. The lingering 'nostalgia for a different Algeria', which characterises the refusal of *pieds-noirs* to accept the changing political status of Algeria, is a poignant demonstration of the manner in which French colonialism kept Algerian culture in a permanent state of displacement. The radical strategy of *négritude* that arose in Francophone rather than the Anglophone colonies was a resounding testament to the incorrigible nature of Francophone cultural hegemony.[4]

When we consider Derrida's location in this hegemony, the displacement that he shared with other French Algerians was intensified, layered by the marginality of his own Jewishness. We cannot talk about Derrida's roots without talking about his Jewishness. However, by the same token, we cannot talk about his Jewishness without talking about his colonial roots, his Algerian origins. The experience of exclusion, of being sent home on his first day of school at

Lycee Ben Akoun in 1942, even though the Germans did not occupy the country, was an experience that affected him for the rest of his life. Derrida remembers this as a formative moment, when the radical instability of his own identity was forced upon him. After the Allied landing in France racial laws were nevertheless maintained for a period of almost six months in Algeria, 'under a "free" French government, friends who no longer knew you, the insults, the Jewish lycee with teachers expelled without a murmur of protest from the colleagues' (David 1988: 74). Even in the case of his Jewishness, the sense of displacement was exacerbated by his Algerian location.

The colonial and the diasporic are thus deeply embedded in Derrida's work, not as causes but as displacements, for arguably the strategy of displacement that pervades his work is itself a displacement of the dis-location, the displacement, of his colonial and cultural origin. In *Glas* Derrida speaks of a formative moment of dislocation:

> In Algeria, in the middle of a mosque that the colonialists had changed into a synagogue, the *Torah* once out from *derriére les rideaux,* is carried about in the arms of a man or child. . . . Children who have watched the pomp of this celebration, especially those who were able to give a hand, perhaps dream of it long after, of arranging there all the bits of their life.
>
> What am I doing here? Let us say that I work at the origin of literature by miming it. Between the two.
>
> (Derrida 1974: 268–69)

Here, we find the young Derrida, and Algeria itself, disappearing into the third person, displaced into the region 'between the two' worlds, a displacement into which his own deconstruction of European modernity plunges. Spivak interprets this passage as 'the Jewish child's inspiration of the absence of the father or Truth behind the veil, an inspiration that allows him to place his autobiography in that place producing the "origin of literature"' (Handelman 1983: 98).

By placing his autobiography in the place of the Father his 'story' takes on the patriarchal power of the Father as it elides the disturbing biographical history of his Algerian identity. What Derrida is 'miming' is the centrality of the *Torah.* Writing this many years later, he recreates, re-reads, reinterprets, reinscribes a reality that is deeply inflected with Algeria. That a mosque has been taken over by colonial authorities to be made into a synagogue encapsulates the ambivalent location of Algerian identity that Jewishness works to suppress. This form of displacement was a common feature of colonial authority and in ethnic oppositions of various kinds. One could say that Derrida's displacement of the *Torah* is paradoxically a displacement of the colonial marginality that resists incorporation into the universalist space 'between the two'. Miming the *Torah,* he reinscribes its patriarchal dominance. The key point about this is that Algeria, the place of identity, is outside, permanently displaced by the Word.

What becomes most resonant in this passage is the deep anxiety of origin that permeates Derrida's thinking. Susan Handelman uses this autobiographical passage from *Glas* to launch into a compelling exposition of Derrida's debt to the tradition of heretic hermeneutics that characterises rabbinical interpretation of the *Torah.* 'To place his own autobiography in place of the *Torah* is, first of all, to displace the most primary and authoritative Jewish text – and yet, at the same time, paradoxically to continue it' (Handelman 1983: 98). Displacement may be taken, as Handelman explains, as a key term for Jewish hermeneutics in general.

While most readers of Derrida interpret his deconstruction of European logocentrism as an extension of a Nietzschean tradition of deconstruction, Handelman sees this as an extension of that displacement which is the very mode of Rabbinical interpretation.

> To be both master and servant of the Book is itself a paradoxical condition; it
> defines the creative tension of the Rabbinic relation to the text. For the Jews as
> the 'People of the Book,' the central issue is how to deal with a canonical, divine
> Text that claims to be the essence of reality. In other words, the central problem
> is that of interpretation . . . As a solution, the Rabbis created a system of
> interpretation that *itself* became another equally authoritative canon, another
> Scripture.
>
> (Handelman 1983: 99)

The palimpsestic 'text' of interpretation becomes as authoritative as the original text. This is
a strong foretaste of the displacement and deferral that characterises Derrida's work. For
what is remarkable about this heretic tradition is that the Rabbis 'accomplished in their
"canonical" hermeneutic . . . a "revolution from within," freely reshaping and re-creating the
Scriptures that had been handed down to them' (1983: 100). This question raised by the
Rabbinical text is surely one source of the dissolution of boundaries in Derrida: the boundary
between literature and philosophy, the boundary between the text and context, the boundary
between the signifier and signified. It is this question that perhaps underlies his most notorious
statement: 'there is nothing outside the text'. The interpretation of this statement, Benson
argues, is that 'Derrida wants to insist both that understanding is contextual and that texts (or
the world) have a meaning which cannot be simply constructed however we like' (2000: 40).

Derrida is not so much the disrupter of tradition, but one who subscribes to a different
tradition. According to Handelman, the great problem of Jewish thought, especially for those
thinkers who absorbed Western philosophy yet still retain their affiliations to the *Torah,* was
the desire on one hand for 'an all-encompassing Scripture, a Writing that weaves together the
fragments of reality', yet, on the other hand, the reality of a text that 'simultaneously disseminates endless new meanings' through its interpreters (1983: 102). It is because of this,
she argues, that:

> Derrida, as part of this heretic hermeneutic, is obsessed (like Freud and Bloom)
> with the question of origins, and with the need to undo, re-write, or usurp
> origin – above all, through acts of revisionary interpretation. This is, of course,
> also a displacement of the 'father' – the authoritative originating principle.
> Derrida's target is all the fathers of philosophy. His project: to deconstruct the
> entire Western tradition of 'onto-theology', to undo 'logocentrism', to send
> the Word into the exile of writing.
>
> (1983: 102)

Although Handelman puts up a convincing case, it is important to remember that Derrida is
often read as belonging either to a Jewish or Greek tradition. However, Geoffrey Bennington,
suggests that such a reading can be problematic, and offers a 'non-dialectical way out',
arguing that he is 'neither Jew nor Greek, but "Egyptian", in a non-biographical sense'
(Bennington and Derrida 1993: 99). Bennington's sentiment is one that Derrida articulates
in an interview:

> I consider my own thought paradoxically, as neither Greek nor Jewish. I often
> feel that the questions I attempt to formulate on the outskirts of the Greek
> philosophical tradition have as their "other" the model of the Jew, that is, the
> Jew-as-other. And yet the paradox is that I have never actually invoked the
> Jewish tradition in any "rooted" or direct manner. Though I was born a Jew, I do
> not work or think within a living Jewish tradition. So that if there is a Judaic

dimension in my thinking which may from time to time have spoken in or through me, this has never assumed the form of an expert fidelity or debt to that culture. In short, the ultimate site (*lieu*) of my questioning would be neither Hellenic nor Herbaic if such were possible. It would be a non-site beyond both the Jewish influence of my youth and the Greek philosophic heritage which I received during my academic education in French universities.

(Kearney 1984: 107)

This is a major concern given Derrida's obsession with origins. A crucial part of Derrida's hermeneutic is to usurp origin. Nevertheless, this neglects Derrida's own origin. For his origin – not filiative, but geographical, cultural – is the place of displacement. Derrida's *place* of origin – Algeria – is already the displacement of the Father – France – a displacement that is the source and scene of actual violence. Algeria as origin is not merely usurped and displaced in Derrida's work. It is also, paradoxically, the origin of displacement, the origin of disruption. The binary of Algeria/France is not so much reversed as erased in Derrida's thinking, an erasure that, while usurping origins and giving free reign to the play of signifiers, underlies the great problems deconstruction has in placing itself in the world. 'If psychoanalysis might be seen as one attempt to cure the neurosis of the Jew-in-exile', says Handelman, 'deconstractionism could be thought of as another' (1983: 123). Displacement, as it appears in deconstruction 'is both the *condition* and *answer* to exile' (127).

This erasure of location, of the place of 'origin', is linked in Derrida to the deconstruction of history, the narrative of the past. The end of history for Derrida is, in an important sense, the end of identity, a deconstruction of origin, which, for the historical subject Jacques Derrida, is the end of Algeria and the beginning of indeterminacy.

However, for Derrida, by its very provisionality, its anxious political cultural and historical nature, Algeria becomes the source deferred, the origin beyond history and hence confirms the provisionality of all sources. Algeria thus is located in Derrida's thinking as the paradoxical place of displacement. Despite Derrida's difficulty with Algeria as his own place of origin, it seems too easy, too facile, to equate Derrida's sense of non-belonging with the principles of displacement, difference and deconstruction that characterise his work. Nevertheless, it is impossible, or at least problematic to ignore Derrida's Jewishness and Algerianness with his suspicion of origin. Even more poignantly, the absence of the originary is the absence of a discourse from which and within which it may be spoken. If one day 'I had to tell my story', says Derrida,

> . . . nothing in this narrative would start to speak of the things itself if I did not come up against the fact: for lack of capacity, competence, or self-authorization, I have never yet been able to speak of what my birth, as one says, should have made closest to me: the Jew, the Arab.
>
> (1989:31)

The trope of displacement in deconstruction continually rehearses the refrain of loss and displacement in Derrida's life.

> Older forms of thinking and feeling *must* change with such a displacement. Displacement itself takes on a new sense. It refers not to an essentially conservative 'reformulation' that has the effect of keeping the best of the old while adapting to new circumstances. Instead, displacement now refers to a violent intervention intended to shake and demoralize the old order.
>
> (Krupnik 1983: 12)

The confluence of Jewish and Algerian displacement occurs in the complex phenomenon of 'diaspora'. In diaspora, the concurrently desolating and empowering impetus of exile drives the intellectual's propensity to break new conceptual ground. In some cases, as Said points out, this propensity leads (in the case of Auerbach and Adorno for instance) to the exile's prominent place in the advancement of Western culture (Said 1984). However, more often, by loosening the intellectual's ties with tradition, by making ambivalent that connection with 'home', it leads to a critical and disruptive questioning of that tradition. It is not surprising then that the most vigorous dismantling of the assumptions of Western intellectual orthodoxy comes from its margins.

The link between Derrida's sense of 'non-belonging' and the centrality of displacement in his theory is not a simple causal definition of origins. Rather, it illustrates the true importance of Said's term 'worldliness'. For the 'worldliness' of Derrida's texts may be located as a structure of attitude and reference rather than a controlling influence. The world of this worldliness is a colonial world, the colonial world of French Algeria, the filiative world of the 'not quite French'. This introduces into his work the ambivalence of colonial identity itself, a marginality from which Derrida could launch his disruption of the dominance and logocentric integrity of Western philosophy. The very lesson of grammatology, David Keller points out, 'is that meaning is the result of différance, and différance is social/cultural/political/historical. Meaning does not have a specific Origin' (2001: 71).

Notes

1   A town hall document dated October 21, 1871, confirms that Georgette Safar's grandfather 'born in Algiers during the year eighteen hundred and thirty-two fulfills the conditions for citizenship' prescribed by the 1871 decree, and 'has declared that he takes the name of Safar as family name and as first name that of Mimoun'. Seven witnesses had vouched for the parents of 'the above named', who had 'just signed in Hebrew'. They 'had been established in Algeria before eighteen hundred and thirty'. Until the Cremieux decree of 1875, the 'indigenous Jews' of Algeria were not French citizens. They would lose their citizenship and become indigenous again under the Vichy government (Bennington and Derrida 1993: 325).

2   For a detailed analysis of this, see Mamdani (1996); Ahluwalia (2001b).

3   Frantz Fanon, in *A Dying Colonialism* (1989), examined the Jewish population in Algeria at some length. Writing at the height of war, when the FLN was trying to attract support from minorities, he was particularly concerned to show that the Algerian Jewish population was not homogenous and sought to explain their diversity through a socioeconomic analysis.

4   For a detailed analysis of the negritude movement, see Ahluwalia (2001a).

References

Ahluwalia, Pal. (1995) *Plantations and the Politics of Sugar in Uganda*, Kampala: Fountain Publishers.

—— (2001a) *Politics and Post-Colonial Theory: African Inflections*, London: Routledge.

—— (2001b) 'When Does a Settler Become a Native?: Citizenship and Identity in a Settler Society', *Pretexts*, Vol. 10, No. 1, pp. 63–73.

Bennington, Geoffrey and Derrida, Jacques. (1993) *Jacques Derrida*, Chicago: Chicago University Press.

Benson, Bruce Ellis. (2000) 'Traces of God', *Books and Culture*, September 2000, Vol. 6, No. 5, pp. 42–45.

David, Catherine. (1988) 'An Interview with Derrida', in Wood, David and Bernasconi, Robert (eds) *Derrida and Différance*, Evanston, IL: Northwestern University Press.

Derrida, Jacques. (1974) *Glas*, Paris: Galilée.

— (1976) *Of Grammatology*, trans. Gayatri Spivak, Baltimore: Johns Hopkins University Press.

— (1978) *The Post Card: From Socrates to Freud and Beyond*, trans. Alan Bass, Chicago: University of Chicago Press.

— (1986) 'Racism's Last Word', in Harry Louis Gates (ed.) *'Race', Writing and Difference*, trans. Peggy Kamuf, Chicago: University of Chicago Press.

— (1989) 'How Not to Speak', in Sanford Budick and Wolfgang Iser (eds), trans. Ken Frieden, *Languages of the Unsayable*, New York: Columbia University Press.

— (1998) *Monolingualism of the Other, or the Prosthesis of Origin*, trans. Patrick Mensah, Stanford, CA: Stanford University Press.

— (2007) *Learning to Live Finally: An Interview with Jean Birnbaum*, trans. Pascale-Ann Brault and Michael Naas, Hoboken, New Jersey: Melville House Publishing.

Dufourmantelle, Anne and Derrida, Jacques. (2000) *Of Hospitality*, trans. Rachel Bowlby, Stanford: Stanford University Press.

Handelman, Susan A. (1983) 'Jacques Derrida and the Heretic Hermeneutic', in Krupnick, Mark. (ed.) *Displacement: Derrida and After*, Bloomington: Indiana University Press.

Kearney, Richard. (1984) *Dialogues with Contemporary Continental Thinkers*, Manchester: Manchester University Press.

Keller, David. (2001) 'Deconstruction: Fad or Philosophy?', *Humanitas*, Vol. XIV, No. 2, pp. 58–75.

Krupnick, Mark. (ed.) (1983) *Displacement: Derrida and After*, Bloomington: Indiana University Press.

Mamdani, Mahmood. (1996) *Citizen and Subject: Contemporary Africa and the Legacy of Late Colonialism*, Princeton: Princeton University Press.

— (2001) *When Victims Become Killers: Colonialism, Nativism and the Genocide in Rwanda*, Oxford: James Currey.

Megill, Allan. (1985) *Prophets of Extremity: Nietzsche, Heidegger, Foucault, Derrida*, Berkeley: University of Berkeley Press.

Norris, Christopher. (1987) *Derrida*, Cambridge: Harvard University Press.

Ofrat, G. (2001) *The Jewish Derrida*, trans. Peretz Kidron, Syracuse: Syracuse University Press.

Powell, Jason. (2006) *Jacques Derrida: A Biography*, London: Continuum.

Rosenfeld, Michael. (1998) 'An Interview with Jacques Derrida', *Cardozo Life*, Fall 1998.

Rudey, John. (1992) *Modern Algeria: The Origins and Development of a Nation*, Bloomington: Indiana University Press.

Running-Johnson, Cynthia. (1999) 'The Self and the "Other(s)" in Cixous' *Sihanouk*', in Jacobus, Lee A. and Barreca, Regina (eds) *Hélène Cixous: Critical Impressions*, Amsterdam: Gordon and Breach Publishers.

— (2001) 'Cixous's Left and Right Hands of Writing in *Tambours sur la digue* and *Osnabrück*', *French Forum*, Vol. 26, No. 3, pp. 111–22.

Rushdie, Salman. (1991) *Imaginary Homelands*, New York: Penguin

Rye, Gill. (2002) 'New Women's Writing in France', *Modern and Contemporary France*, Vol. 10, No. 2, pp. 165–75.

Said, Edward. (1984) 'The Mind of Winter: Reflections on a Life in Exile', *Harpers*, No. 269, September, pp. 49–55.

Spivak, Gayatri. (1976) 'Introduction', in Jacques Derrida, *Of Grammatology*, trans. Gayatri Spivak, Baltimore: Johns Hopkins University Press.

Stephens, M. (1991) Deconstructing Jacques Derrida, *Los Angeles Times Magazine*, 21 July.

Weber, Elizabeth. (ed.) (1995) *Points … Interviews 1974–1994*, Stanford, CA: Stanford University Press.

Wood, Nancy. (1998) 'Remembering the Jews of Algeria', *Parallax*, Vol. 4, No. 2, pp. 169–83.

Chapter 9

Jacques Derrida

STRUCTURE, SIGN AND PLAY
IN THE DISCOURSE OF
THE HUMAN SCIENCES

Jacques Derrida, the founder of deconstruction and a prolific theorist and continental philosopher, opens his essay with a deconstructive demonstration: he uses a metaphysical word—"event"—to describe historical change, one which undermines metaphysics, and thus metaphysical words. The "event" in question is thinking "the structurality of structure", or, the semiological notion that structures are decentred networks of signs. To clarify, Derrida argues that all of Western philosophy (metaphysics) relies on notions of origin, centre, presence, transcendence, and so on, to explain how structures are formed, maintained, and how they develop or progress to a higher state. With the rise of sceptical thinkers such as the founder of psychoanalysis Sigmund Freud, and philosophers Friedrich Nietzsche (1844–1900) and Martin Heidegger (1889–1976), Derrida argues that the notion of a grounded structure or system is repeatedly called into question. Nietzsche creates a radically playful anti-metaphysics, declaring the death of God; Heidegger questions the concept of "Being as presence" and develops a methodology based on dismantling (*Abbau*) and destruction (*Destruktion*); Freud critiques notions of self-presence, personal knowledge and mastery, revealing a decentred subjectivity. Even more destabilizing is the rise of semiology, with the Saussurian idea of arbitrary differential networks of signs (see Chapter 4). Yet with the latter example, Derrida starts to add his deconstructive caveat: if metaphysical structures depend upon binary oppositions such as centre versus structure, or nature versus culture—a *hierarchy* of binary oppositions that creates value—then after the "event" of semiology, one cannot simply say that there is nothing but a chain of empty signifiers, thereby appearing to break free of metaphysics, because the critic has to use terms which still carry metaphysical associations. So the only way of performing a critique is to re-think and utilize these terms in strategically different ways. Such an awareness of decentred structures is foregrounded for Derrida in the structuralist ethnographical work of Claude Lévi-Strauss. Ethnology reveals both a dislocation of Eurocentric thought; yet it is simultaneously founded upon, and utilizes Eurocentric concepts and methodologies. Rethinking ethnography, then, involves using metaphysical and empirical procedures to self-reflexively decentre and deconstruct them. Lévi-Strauss observes key concepts that escape the previous ways of thinking, such as the universal incest prohibition, one that exceeds the binary opposition of nature/culture. In other words, the incest prohibition should occupy one side or the other of this opposition, but

Lévi-Strauss discovers it is both natural and cultural, which means that the prohibition appears "outside" of the opposition (it exceeds it), and yet also, paradoxically, founds the opposition in the first place. Derrida argues that systems of thought thus contain their own self-deconstructive concepts and terms, and so structures that once appeared to have centres, contain their own deconstructive tools for revealing that the concept of a centre is a "function" rather than an actuality. Lévi-Strauss argues this by suggesting that his own empirical and theoretical work on myth should be in itself seen as a form of myth; in other words, however scientific the methodology, the ground shifts beneath one's feet to reveal the playful, elusive network of signs that create meaning. In fact for the old metaphysical notion of "centre" Derrida eventually turns to its binary flipside, "play", which he argues is constitutive of structures in general.

We need to interpret interpretations more than to interpret things. (Montaigne)

PERHAPS SOMETHING HAS OCCURRED in the history of the concept of structure that could be called an "event," if this loaded word did not entail a meaning which it is precisely the function of structural—or structuralist—thought to reduce or to suspect. Let us speak of an "event," nevertheless, and let us use quotation marks to serve as a precaution. What would this event be then? Its exterior form would be that of a *rupture* and a redoubling.

It would be easy enough to show that the concept of structure and even the word "structure" itself are as old as the *epistēmē*—that is to say, as old as Western science and Western philosophy—and that their roots thrust deep into the soil of ordinary language, into whose deepest recesses the *epistēmē* plunges in order to gather them up and to make them part of itself in a metaphorical displacement. Nevertheless, up to the event which I wish to mark out and define, structure—or rather the structurality of structure—although it has always been at work, has always been neutralized or reduced, and this by a process of giving it a center or of referring it to a point of presence, a fixed origin. The function of this center was not only to orient, balance, and organize the structure—one cannot in fact conceive of an unorganized structure—but above all to make sure that the organizing principle of the structure would limit what we might call the *play* of the structure. By orienting and organizing the coherence of the system, the center of a structure permits the play of its elements inside the total form. And even today the notion of a structure lacking any center represents the unthinkable itself.

Nevertheless, the center also closes off the play which it opens up and makes possible. As center, it is the point at which the substitution of contents, elements, or terms is no longer possible. At the center, the permutation or the transformation of elements (which may of course be structures enclosed within a structure) is forbidden. At least this permutation has always remained *interdicted* (and I am using this word deliberately). Thus it has always been thought that the center, which is by definition unique, constituted that very thing within a structure which while governing the structure, escapes structurality. This is why classical thought concerning structure could say that the center is, paradoxically, *within* the structure and *outside it*. The center is at the center of the totality, and yet, since the center does not belong to the totality (is not part of the totality), the totality *has its center elsewhere*. The center is not the center. The concept of centered structure—although it represents coherence itself, the condition of the *epistēmē* as philosophy or science—is contradictorily coherent. And as always, coherence in contradiction expresses the force of a desire.[1] The concept of centered structure is in fact the concept of a play based on a fundamental ground, a play constituted on the basis of a fundamental immobility and a reassuring certitude, which itself is beyond the reach of play. And on the basis of this certitude anxiety can be mastered, for anxiety is invariably the result of a certain mode of being implicated in the game, of being caught by the game, of being as it were at stake in the game from the outset. And again on the basis of what we call the center (and which, because it can be either inside or outside, can also indifferently be called the origin or end, *archē* or *telos*), repetitions, substitutions, transformations, and permutations are always *taken* from a history of meaning [*sens*]—that is, in a word, a history—whose origin may always be reawakened or whose end may always be anticipated in the form of presence. This is why one perhaps could say that the movement of any archaeology, like that of any eschatology, is an accomplice of this reduction of the structurality of structure and always attempts to conceive of structure on the basis of a full presence which is beyond play.

If this is so, the entire history of the concept of structure, before the rupture of which we are speaking, must be thought of as a series of substitutions of center for center, as a linked chain of determinations of the center. Successively, and in a regulated fashion, the center receives different forms or names. The history of metaphysics, like the history of the West, is the history of these metaphors and metonymies. Its matrix—if you will pardon me for demonstrating so little and for being so elliptical in order to come more quickly to my principal theme—is the determination of Being as *presence* in all senses of this word. It could be shown that all the names related to fundamentals, to principles, or to the center have always designated an invariable presence—*eidos, archē, telos, energeia, ousia* (essence, existence, substance, subject) *alētheia,* transcendentality, consciousness, God, man, and so forth.

The event I called a rupture, the disruption I alluded to at the beginning of this paper, presumably would have come about when the structurality of structure had to begin to be thought, that is to say, repeated, and this is why I said that this disruption was repetition in every sense of the word. Henceforth, it became necessary to think both the law which somehow governed the desire for a center in the constitution of structure, and the process of signification which orders the displacements and substitutions for this law of central presence—but a central presence which has never been itself, has always already been exiled from itself into its own substitute. The substitute does not substitute itself for anything which has somehow existed before it. Henceforth, it was necessary to begin thinking that there was no center, that the center could not be thought in the form of a present-being, that the center had no natural site, that it was not a fixed locus but a function, a sort of nonlocus in which an infinite number of sign-substitutions came into play. This was the moment when language invaded the universal problematic, the moment when, in the absence of a center or origin, everything became discourse—provided we can agree on this word—that is to say, a system in which the central signified, the original or transcendental signified, is never absolutely present outside a system of differences. The absence of the transcendental signified extends the domain and the play of signification infinitely.

Where and how does this decentering, this thinking the structurality of structure, occur? It would be somewhat naïve to refer to an event, a doctrine, or an author in order to designate this occurrence. It is no doubt part of the totality of an era, our own, but still it has always already begun to proclaim itself and begun to *work*. Nevertheless, if we wished to choose several "names," as indications only, and to recall those authors in whose discourse this occurrence has kept most closely to its most radical formulation, we doubtless would have to cite the Nietzschean critique of metaphysics, the critique of the concepts of Being and truth, for which were substituted the concepts of play, interpretation, and sign (sign without present truth); the Freudian critique of self-presence, that is, the critique of consciousness, of the subject, of self-identity and of self-proximity or self-possession; and, more radically, the Heideggerean destruction of metaphysics, of onto-theology, of the determination of Being as presence. But all these destructive discourses and all their analogues are trapped in a kind of circle. This circle is unique. It describes the form of the relation between the history of metaphysics and the destruction of the history of metaphysics. There is no sense in doing without the concepts of metaphysics in order to shake metaphysics. We have no language—no syntax and no lexicon—which is foreign to this history; we can pronounce not a single destructive proposition which has not already had to slip into the form, the logic, and the implicit postulations of precisely what it seeks to contest. To take one example from many: the metaphysics of presence is shaken with the help of the concept of *sign*. But, as I suggested a moment ago as soon as one seeks to demonstrate in this way that there is no transcendental or privileged signified and that the domain or play of signification henceforth has no limit, one must reject even the concept and word "sign" itself—which is precisely what cannot be done. For the signification "sign" has always been understood and determined, in its meaning, as sign-of, a signifier referring to a signified, a signifier different from its signified. If one erases the radical difference between signifier and signified, it is the word "signifier" itself which must be abandoned as a metaphysical concept. When Lévi-Strauss says in the preface to *The Raw and the Cooked* that he has "sought to transcend the opposition between the sensible and the intelligible by operating from the outset at the level of signs,"[2] the necessity, force, and legitimacy of his act cannot make us forget that the concept of the sign cannot in itself surpass this opposition between the sensible and the intelligible. The concept of the sign, in each of its aspects, has been determined by this opposition throughout the totality of its history. It has lived only on this opposition and its system. But we cannot do without the concept of the sign, for we cannot give up this metaphysical complicity without also giving up the critique we are directing against this complicity, or without the risk of erasing difference in the self-identity of a signified reducing its signifier into itself or, amounting to the same thing, simply expelling its signifier outside itself. For there are two heterogenous ways of erasing the difference between the signifier and the signified: one, the classic way, consists in reducing or deriving the signifier, that is to say, ultimately in *submitting* the sign to thought; the other, the one we are using here against the first one, consists in putting into question the system in which the preceding reduction functioned: first and foremost, the opposition between the sensible and the intelligible. For the *paradox* is that the metaphysical reduction of the sign needed the opposition it was reducing. The opposition is systematic with the reduction. And what we are saying here about the sign can be extended to all the concepts and all the sentences of metaphysics, in particular to the discourse on "structure." But there are several ways of being caught in this circle. They are all more or less naïve, more or less empirical, more or less systematic, more or less close to the formulation—that is, to the formalization—of this circle. It is these differences which explain the multiplicity of destructive discourses and the disagreement between those who elaborate them. Nietzsche, Freud, and Heidegger, for example, worked within the inherited concepts of metaphysics. Since these concepts are not elements or atoms, and since they are taken from a syntax and a system, every particular borrowing brings along with it the whole of metaphysics. This is what allows these destroyers to destroy each other reciprocally—for example, Heidegger regarding Nietzsche, with as much lucidity and rigor as bad faith and misconstruction, as the last metaphysician, the last "Platonist." One could do the same for Heidegger himself, for Freud, or for a number of others. And today no exercise is more widespread.

What is the relevance of this formal schema when we turn to what are called the "human sciences"? One of them perhaps occupies a privileged place—ethnology. In fact one can assume that ethnology could have been born as a science only at the moment when a decentering had come about: at the moment when European culture—and, in consequence, the history of metaphysics and of its concepts—had been *dislocated,* driven from its locus, and forced to stop considering itself as the culture of reference. This moment is not first and foremost a moment of philosophical or scientific discourse. It is also a moment which is political, economic, technical, and so forth. One can say with total security that there is nothing fortuitous about the fact that the critique of ethnocentrism—the very condition for ethnology—should be systematically and historically contemporaneous with the destruction of the history of metaphysics. Both belong to one and the same era. Now, ethnology—like any science—comes about within the element of discourse. And it is primarily a European science employing traditional concepts, however much it may struggle against them. Consequently, whether he wants to or not—and this does not depend on a decision on his part—the ethnologist accepts into his discourse the premises of ethnocentrism at the very moment when he denounces them. This necessity is irreducible; it is not a historical contingency. We ought to consider all its implications very carefully. But if no one can escape this necessity, and if no one is therefore responsible for giving in to it, however little he may do so, this does not mean that all the ways of giving in to it are of equal pertinence. The quality and fecundity of a discourse are perhaps measured by the critical rigor with which this relation to the history of metaphysics and to inherited concepts is thought. Here it is a question both of a critical relation to the language of the social sciences and a critical responsibility of the discourse itself. It is a question of explicitly and systematically posing the problem of the status of a discourse which borrows from a heritage the resources necessary for the deconstruction of that heritage itself. A problem of *economy* and *strategy*.

If we consider, as an example, the texts of Claude Lévi-Strauss, it is not only because of the privilege accorded to ethnology among the social sciences, nor even because the thought of Lévi-Strauss weighs heavily on the contemporary theoretical situation. It is above all because a certain choice has been declared in the work of Lévi-Strauss and because a certain doctrine has been elaborated there, and precisely, in a *more or less explicit manner,* as concerns both this critique of language and this critical language in the social sciences.

In order to follow this movement in the text of Lévi-Strauss, let us choose as one guiding thread among others the opposition between nature and culture. Despite all its rejuvenations and disguises, this opposition is congenital to philosophy. It is even older than Plato. It is at least as old as the Sophists. Since the statement of the opposition *physis/nomos, physis/technē,* it has been relayed to us by means of a whole historical chain which opposes "nature" to law, to education, to art, to technics—but also to liberty, to the arbitrary, to history, to society, to the mind, and so on. Now, from the outset of his researches, and from his first book (*The Elementary Structures of Kinship*) on, Lévi-Strauss simultaneously has experienced the necessity of utilizing this opposition and the impossibility of accepting it. In the *Elementary Structures,* he begins from this axiom or definition: that which is *universal* and spontaneous, and not dependent on any particular culture or on any determinate norm, belongs to nature. Inversely, that which depends upon a system of *norms* regulating society and therefore is capable of *varying* from one social structure to another, belongs to culture. These two definitions are of the traditional type. But in the very first pages of the *Elementary Structures* Lévi-Strauss, who has begun by giving credence to these concepts, encounters what he calls a *scandal,* that is to say, something which no longer tolerates the nature/culture opposition he has accepted, something which *simultaneously* seems to require the predicates of nature and of culture. This scandal is the *incest prohibition.* The incest prohibition is universal; in this sense one could call it natural. But it is also a prohibition, a system of norms and interdicts; in this sense one could call it cultural:

> Let us suppose then that everything universal in man relates to the natural order, and is characterized by spontaneity, and that everything subject to a norm is cultural and is both relative and particular. We are then confronted with a fact, or rather, a group of facts, which, in the light of previous definitions, are not far removed from a scandal: we refer to that complex group of beliefs, customs, conditions and institutions described succinctly as the prohibition of incest, which presents, without the slightest ambiguity, and inseparably combines, the two characteristics in which we recognize the conflicting features of two

mutually exclusive orders. It constitutes a rule, but a rule which, alone among all the social rules, possesses at the same time a universal character.[3]

Obviously there is no scandal except within a system of concepts which accredits the difference between nature and culture. By commencing his work with the *factum* of the incest prohibition, Lévi-Strauss thus places himself at the point at which this difference, which has always been assumed to be self-evident, finds itself erased or questioned. For from the moment when the incest prohibition can no longer be conceived within the nature/culture opposition, it can no longer be said to be a scandalous fact, a nucleus of opacity within a network of transparent significations. The incest prohibition is no longer a scandal one meets with or comes up against in the domain of traditional concepts; it is something which escapes these concepts and certainly precedes them—probably as the condition of their possibility. It could perhaps be said that the whole of philosophical conceptualization, which is systematic with the nature/culture opposition, is designed to leave in the domain of the unthinkable the very thing that makes this conceptualization possible: the origin of the prohibition of incest.

This example, too cursorily examined, is only one among many others, but nevertheless it already shows that language bears within itself the necessity of its own critique. Now this critique may be undertaken along two paths, in two "manners." Once the limit of the nature/culture opposition makes itself felt, one might want to question systematically and rigorously the history of these concepts. This is a first action. Such a systematic and historic questioning would be neither a philological nor a philosophical action in the classic sense of these words. To concern oneself with the founding concepts of the entire history of philosophy, to deconstitute them, is not to undertake the work of the philologist or of the classic historian of philosophy. Despite appearances, it is probably the most daring way of making the beginnings of a step outside of philosophy. The step "outside philosophy" is much more difficult to conceive than is generally imagined by those who think they made it long ago with cavalier ease, and who in general are swallowed up in metaphysics in the entire body of discourse which they claim to have disengaged from it.

The other choice (which I believe corresponds more closely to Lévi-Strauss's manner), in order to avoid the possibly sterilizing effects of the first one, consists in conserving all these old concepts within the domain of empirical discovery while here and there denouncing their limits, treating them as tools which can still be used. No longer is any truth value attributed to them; there is a readiness to abandon them, if necessary, should other instruments appear more useful. In the meantime, their relative efficacy is exploited, and they are employed to destroy the old machinery to which they belong and of which they themselves are pieces. This is how the language of the social sciences criticizes *itself*. Lévi-Strauss thinks that in this way he can separate *method* from *truth,* the instruments of the method and the objective significations envisaged by it. One could almost say that this is the primary affirmation of Lévi-Strauss; in any event, the first words of the *Elementary Structures* are: "Above all, it is beginning to emerge that this distinction between nature and society ('nature' and 'culture' seem preferable to us today), while of no acceptable historical significance, does contain a logic, fully justifying its use by modern sociology as a methodological tool."[4]

Lévi-Strauss will always remain faithful to this double intention: to preserve as an instrument something whose truth value he criticizes.

On the one hand, he will continue, in effect, to contest the value of the nature/culture opposition. More than thirteen years after the *Elementary Structures, The Savage Mind* faithfully echoes the text I have just quoted: "The opposition between nature and culture to which I attached much importance at one time . . . now seems to be of primarily methodological importance." And this methodological value is not affected by its "ontological" nonvalue (as might be said, if this notion were not suspect here): "However, it would not be enough to reabsorb particular humanities into a general one. This first enterprise opens the way for others which . . . are incumbent on the exact natural sciences: the reintegration of culture in nature and finally of life within the whole of its physico-chemical conditions."[5]

On the other hand, still in *The Savage Mind,* he presents as what he calls *bricolage* what might be called the discourse of this method. The *bricoleur,* says Lévi-Strauss, is someone who uses "the means at hand," that is, the instruments he finds at his disposition around him, those which are already there, which had not been especially conceived with an eye to the operation for which they are to be used and to which one tries by trial and error to adapt them, not hesitating to change them whenever it appears necessary, or to try several of them at once, even if their form and their origin are heterogenous—and so forth. There is therefore a critique of language in the form of *bricolage,* and it has even been said that *bricolage* is critical language itself. I am thinking in particular of the article of G. Genette, "Structuralisme et critique littéraire," published in homage to Lévi-Strauss in a special issue of *L'Arc* (no. 26, 1965), where it is stated that the analysis of *bricolage* could "be applied almost word for word" to criticism, and especially to "literary criticism."

If one calls *bricolage* the necessity of borrowing one's concepts from the text of a heritage which is more or less coherent or ruined, it must be said that every discourse is *bricoleur.* The engineer, whom Lévi-Strauss opposes to the *bricoleur,* should be the one to construct the totality of his language, syntax, and lexicon. In this sense the engineer is a myth. A subject who supposedly would be the absolute origin of his own discourse and supposedly would construct it "out of nothing," "out of whole cloth," would be the creator of the verb, the verb itself. The notion of the engineer who supposedly breaks with all forms of *bricolage* is therefore a theological idea; and since Lévi-Strauss tells us elsewhere that *bricolage* is mythopoetic, the odds are that the engineer is a myth produced by the *bricoleur.* As soon as we cease to believe in such an engineer and in a discourse which breaks with the received historical discourse, and as soon as we admit that every finite discourse is bound by a certain *bricolage* and that the engineer and the scientist are also species of *bricoleurs,* then the very idea of *bricolage* is menaced and the difference in which it took on its meaning breaks down.

This brings us to the second thread which might guide us in what is being contrived here.

Lévi-Strauss describes *bricolage* not only as an intellectual activity but also as a mythopoetical activity. One reads in *The Savage Mind,* "Like *bricolage* on the technical plane, mythical reflection can reach brilliant unforeseen results on the intellectual plane. Conversely, attention has often been drawn to the mythopoetical nature of *bricolage.*"[6]

But Lévi-Strauss's remarkable endeavor does not simply consist in proposing, notably in his most recent investigations, a structural science of myths and of mythological activity. His endeavor also appears—I would say almost from the outset—to have the status which he accords to his own discourse on myths, to what he calls his "mythologicals." It is here that his discourse on the myth reflects on itself and criticizes itself. And this moment, this critical period, is evidently of concern to all the languages which share the field of the human sciences. What does Lévi-Strauss say of his "mythologicals"? It is here that we rediscover the mythopoetical virtue of *bricolage.* In effect, what appears most fascinating in this critical search for a new status of discourse is the stated abandonment of all reference to a *center,* to a *subject,* to a privileged *reference,* to an origin, or to an absolute *archia.* The theme of this decentering could be followed throughout the "Overture" to his last book, *The Raw and the Cooked.* I shall simply remark on a few key points.

1. From the very start, Lévi-Strauss recognizes that the Bororo myth which he employs in the book as the "reference myth" does not merit this name and this treatment. The name is specious and the use of the myth improper. This myth deserves no more than any other its referential privilege: "In fact, the Bororo myth, which I shall refer to from now on as the key myth, is, as I shall try to show, simply a transformation, to a greater or lesser extent, of other

myths originating either in the same society or in neighboring or remote societies. I could, therefore, have legitimately taken as my starting point any one representative myth of the group. From this point of view, the key myth is interesting not because it is typical, but rather because of its irregular position within the group."[7]

2. There is no unity or absolute source of the myth. The focus or the source of the myth are always shadows and virtualities which are elusive, unactualizable, and nonexistent in the first place. Everything begins with structure, configuration, or relationship. The discourse on the acentric structure that myth itself is, cannot itself have an absolute subject or an absolute center. It must avoid the violence that consists in centering a language which describes an acentric structure if it is not to shortchange the form and movement of myth. Therefore it is necessary to forego scientific or philosophical discourse, to renounce the *epistēmē* which absolutely requires, which is the absolute requirement that we go back to the source, to the center, to the founding basis, to the principle, and so on. In opposition to *epistemic* discourse, structural discourse on myths—*mythological* discourse—must itself be *mythomorphic*. It must have the form of that of which it speaks. This is what Lévi-Strauss says in *The Raw and the Cooked,* from which I would now like to quote a long and remarkable passage:

> The study of myths raises a methodological problem, in that it cannot be carried out according to the Cartesian principle of breaking down the difficulty into as many parts as may be necessary for finding the solution. There is no real end to methodological analysis, no hidden unity to be grasped once the breaking-down process has been completed. Themes can be split up *ad infinitum.* Just when you think you have disentangled and separated them, you realize that they are knitting together again in response to the operation of unexpected affinities. Consequently the unity of the myth is never more than tendential and projective and cannot reflect a state or a particular moment of the myth. It is a phenomenon of the imagination, resulting from the attempt at interpretation; and its function is to endow the myth with synthetic form and to prevent its disintegration into a confusion of opposites. The science of myths might therefore be termed "anaclastic," if we take this old term in the broader etymological sense which includes the study of both reflected rays and broken rays. But unlike philosophical reflection, which aims to go back to its own source, the reflections we are dealing with here concern rays whose only source is hypothetical. . . . And in seeking to imitate the spontaneous movement of mythological thought, this essay, which is also both too brief and too long, has had to conform to the requirements of that thought and to respect its rhythm. It follows that this book on myths is itself a kind of myth.[8]

This statement is repeated a little farther on: "As the myths themselves are based on secondary codes (the primary codes being those that provide the substance of language), the present work is put forward as a tentative draft of a tertiary code, which is intended to ensure the reciprocal translatability of several myths. This is why it would not be wrong to consider this book itself as a myth: it is, as it were, the myth of mythology."[9] The absence of a center is here the absence of a subject and the absence of an author: "Thus the myth and the musical work are like conductors of an orchestra, whose audience becomes the silent performers. If it is now asked where the real center of the work is to be found, the answer is that this is impossible to determine. Music and mythology bring man face to face with potential objects of which only the shadows are actualized. . . . Myths are anonymous."[10] The musical model chosen by Lévi-Strauss for the composition of his book is apparently justified by this absence of any real and fixed center of the mythical or mythological discourse.

Thus it is at this point that ethnographic *bricolage* deliberately assumes its mythopoetic function. But by the same token, this function makes the philosophical or epistemological requirement of a center appear as mythological, that is to say, as a historical illusion.

Nevertheless, even if one yields to the necessity of what Lévi-Strauss has done, one cannot ignore its risks. If the mythological is mythomorphic, are all discourses on myths equivalent? Shall we have to abandon any epistemological requirement which permits us to distinguish between several qualities of discourse on the myth? A classic, but inevitable question. It cannot be answered—and I believe that Lévi-Strauss does not answer it—for as long as the problem of the relations between the philosopheme or the theorem, on the one hand, and the mytheme or the mythopoem, on the other, has not been posed explicitly, which is no small problem. For lack of explicitly posing this problem, we condemn ourselves to transforming the alleged transgression of philosophy into an unnoticed fault within the philosophical realm. Empiricism would be the genus of which these faults would always be the species. Transphilosophical concepts would be transformed into philosophical naïvetés. Many examples could be given to demonstrate this risk: the concepts of sign, history, truth, and so forth. What I want to emphasize is simply that the passage beyond philosophy does not consist in turning the page of philosophy (which usually amounts to philosophizing badly), but in continuing to read philosophers *in a certain way*. The risk I am speaking of is always assumed by Lévi-Strauss, and it is the very price of this endeavor. I have said that empiricism is the matrix of all faults menacing a discourse which continues, as with Lévi-Strauss in particular, to consider itself scientific. If we wanted to pose the problem of empiricism and *bricolage* in depth, we would probably end up very quickly with a number of absolutely contradictory propositions concerning the status of discourse in structural ethnology. On the one hand, structuralism justifiably claims to be the critique of empiricism. But at the same time there is not a single book or study by Lévi-Strauss which is not proposed as an empirical essay which can always be completed or invalidated by new information. The structural schemata are always proposed as hypotheses resulting from a finite quantity of information and which are subjected to the proof of experience. Numerous texts could be used to demonstrate this double postulation. Let us turn once again to the "Overture" of *The Raw and the Cooked,* where it seems clear that if this postulation is double, it is because it is a question here of a language on language:

> If critics reproach me with not having carried out an exhaustive inventory of South American myths before analyzing them, they are making a grave mistake about the nature and function of these documents. The total body of myth belonging to a given community is comparable to its speech. Unless the population dies out physically or morally, this totality is never complete. You might as well criticize a linguist for compiling the grammar of a language without having complete records of the words pronounced since the language came into being, and without knowing what will be said in it during the future part of its existence. Experience proves that a linguist can work out the grammar of a given language from a remarkably small number of sentences. . . . And even a partial grammar or an outline grammar is a precious acquisition when we are dealing with unknown languages. Syntax does not become evident only after a (theoretically limitless) series of events has been recorded and examined, because it is itself the body of rules governing their production. What I have tried to give is an outline of the syntax of South American mythology. Should fresh data come to hand, they will be used to check or modify the formulation of certain grammatical laws, so that some are abandoned and replaced by new ones. But in no instance would I feel constrained to accept the arbitrary demand for a total

mythological pattern, since, as has been shown, such a requirement has no meaning.[11]

Totalization, therefore, is sometimes defined as *useless,* and sometimes as *impossible.* This is no doubt due to the fact that there are two ways of conceiving the limit of totalization. And I assert once more that these two determinations coexist implicitly in Lévi-Strauss's discourse. Totalization can be judged impossible in the classical style: one then refers to the empirical endeavor of either a subject or a finite richness which it can never master. There is too much, more than one can say. But nontotalization can also be determined in another way: no longer from the standpoint of a concept of finitude as relegation to the empirical, but from the standpoint of the concept of *play.* If totalization no longer has any meaning, it is not because the infiniteness of a field cannot be covered by a finite glance or a finite discourse, but because the nature of the field—that is, language and a finite language—excludes totalization. This field is in effect that of *play,* that is to say, a field of infinite substitutions only because it is finite, that is to say, because instead of being an inexhaustible field, as in the classical hypothesis, instead of being too large, there is something missing from it: a center which arrests and grounds the play of substitutions. One could say—rigorously using that word whose scandalous signification is always obliterated in French—that this movement of play, permitted by the lack or absence of a center or origin, is the movement of *supplementarity.* One cannot determine the center and exhaust totalization because the sign which replaces the center, which supplements it, taking the center's place in its absence—this sign is added, occurs as a surplus, as a *supplement.*[12] The movement of signification adds something, which results in the fact that there is always more, but this addition is a floating one because it comes to perform a vicarious function, to supplement a lack on the part of the signified. Although Lévi-Strauss in his use of the word "supplementary" never emphasizes, as I do here, the two directions of meaning which are so strangely compounded within it, it is not by chance that he uses this word twice in his "Introduction to the Work of Marcel Mauss," at one point where he is speaking of the "overabundance of signifier, in relation to the signifieds to which this overabundance can refer":

> In his endeavor to understand the world, man therefore always has at his disposal a surplus of signification (which he shares out amongst things according to the laws of symbolic thought—which is the task of ethnologists and linguists to study). This distribution of a *supplementary* allowance [*ration supplémentaire*]—if it is permissible to put it that way—is absolutely necessary in order that on the whole the available signifier and the signified it aims at may remain in the relationship of complementarity which is the very condition of the use of symbolic thought.[13]

(It could no doubt be demonstrated that this *ration supplémentaire* of signification is the origin of the *ratio* itself.) The word reappears a little further on, after Lévi-Strauss has mentioned "this floating signifier, which is the servitude of all finite thought":

> In other words—and taking as our guide Mauss's precept that all social phenomena can be assimilated to language—we see in *mana, Wakau, oranda* and other notions of the same type, the conscious expression of a semantic function, whose role it is to permit symbolic thought to operate in spite of the contradiction which is proper to it. In this way are explained the apparently insoluble antinomies attached to this notion. . . . At one and the same time force and action, quality and state, noun and verb; abstract and concrete, omnipresent and

localized—*mana* is in effect all these things. But is it not precisely because it is none of these things that *mana* is a simple form, or more exactly, a symbol in the pure state, and therefore capable of becoming charged with any sort of symbolic content whatever? In the system of symbols constituted by all cosmologies, *mana* would simply be a zero symbolic value, that is to say, a sign marking the necessity of a symbolic content *supplementary* [my italics] to that with which the signified is already loaded, but which can take on any value required, provided only that this value still remains part of the available reserve and is not, as phonologists put it, a group-term.

Lévi-Strauss adds the note:
    "Linguists have already been led to formulate hypotheses of this type. For example: 'A zero phoneme is opposed to all the other phonemes in French in that it entails no differential characters and no constant phonetic value. On the contrary, the proper function of the zero phoneme is to be opposed to phoneme absence.' (R. Jakobson and J. Lutz, "Notes on the French Phonemic Pattern," *Word* 5, no. 2 [August 1949]: 155). Similarly, if we schematize the conception I am proposing here, it could almost be said that the function of notions like *mana* is to be opposed to the absence of signification, without entailing by itself any particular signification."[14]

The *overabundance* of the signifier, its *supplementary* character, is thus the result of a finitude, that is to say, the result of a lack which must be *supplemented*.

It can now be understood why the concept of play is important in Lévi-Strauss. His references to all sorts of games, notably to roulette, are very frequent, especially in his *Conversations*,[15] in *Race and History*,[16] and in *The Savage Mind*. Further, the reference to play is always caught up in tension.

Tension with history, first of all. This is a classical problem, objections to which are now well worn. I shall simply indicate what seems to me the formality of the problem: by reducing history, Lévi-Strauss has treated as it deserves a concept which has always been in complicity with a teleological and eschatological metaphysics, in other words, paradoxically, in complicity with that philosophy of presence to which it was believed history could be opposed. The thematic of historicity, although it seems to be a somewhat late arrival in philosophy, has always been required by the determination of Being as presence. With or without etymology, and despite the classic antagonism which opposes these significations throughout all of classical thought, it could be shown that the concept of *epistēmē* has always called forth that of *historia,* if history is always the unity of a becoming, as the tradition of truth or the development of science or knowledge oriented toward the appropriation of truth in presence and self-presence, toward knowledge in consciousness-of-self. History has always been conceived as the movement of a resumption of history, as a detour between two presences. But if it is legitimate to suspect this concept of history, there is a risk, if it is reduced without an explicit statement of the problem I am indicating here, of falling back into an ahistoricism of a classical type, that is to say, into a determined moment of the history of metaphysics. Such is the algebraic formality of the problem as I see it. More concretely, in the work of Lévi-Strauss it must be recognized that the respect for structurality, for the internal originality of the structure, compels a neutralization of time and history. For example, the appearance of a new structure, of an original system, always comes about—and this is the very condition of its structural specificity—by a rupture with its past, its origin, and its cause. Therefore one can describe what is peculiar to the structural organization only by not taking into account, in the very moment of this description, its past conditions: by omitting to posit the problem of the transition from one structure to another, by putting history between brackets. In this "structuralist" moment, the concepts of chance and discontinuity are indispensable. And Lévi-Strauss does in fact often appeal to them, for example, as concerns that structure of structures, language, of which he says in the "Introduction to the Work of Marcel Mauss" that it "could only have been born in one fell swoop":

> Whatever may have been the moment and the circumstances of its appearance on the scale of animal life, language could only have been born in one fell swoop. Things could not have set about acquiring signification progressively. Following a transformation the study of which is not the concern of the social sciences, but rather of biology and psychology, a transition came about from a stage where nothing had a meaning to another where everything possessed it.[17]

This standpoint does not prevent Lévi-Strauss from recognizing the slowness, the process of maturing, the continuous toil of factual transformations, history (for example, *Race and History*). But, in accordance with a gesture which was also Rousseau's and Husserl's, he must "set aside all the facts" at the moment when he wishes to recapture the specificity of a structure. Like Rousseau, he must always conceive of the origin of a new structure on the model of catastrophe—an overturning of nature in nature, a natural interruption of the natural sequence, a setting aside *of* nature.

Besides the tension between play and history, there is also the tension between play and presence. Play is the disruption of presence. The presence of an element is always a signifying and substitutive reference inscribed in a system of differences and the movement of a chain. Play is always play of absence and presence, but if it is to be thought radically, play must be conceived of before the alternative of presence and absence. Being must be conceived as presence or absence on the basis of the possibility of play and not the other way around. If Lévi-Strauss, better than any other, has brought to light the play of repetition and the repetition of play, one no less perceives in his work a sort of ethic of presence, an ethic of nostalgia for origins, an ethic of archaic and natural innocence, of a purity of presence and self-presence in speech—an ethic, nostalgia, and even remorse, which he often presents as the motivation of the ethnological project when he moves toward the archaic societies which are exemplary societies in his eyes. These texts are well known.[18]

Turned towards the lost or impossible presence of the absent origin, this structuralist thematic of broken immediacy is therefore the saddened, *negative,* nostalgic, guilty, Rousseauistic side of the thinking of play whose other side would be the Nietzschean *affirmation,* that is the joyous affirmation of the play of the world and of the innocence of becoming, the affirmation of a world of signs without fault, without truth, and without origin which is offered to an active interpretation. *This affirmation then determines the noncenter otherwise than as loss of the center.* And it plays without security. For there is a *sure* play: that which is limited to the *substitution* of *given* and *existing, present,* pieces. In absolute chance, affirmation also surrenders itself to *genetic* indetermination, to the *seminal* adventure of the trace.

There are thus two interpretations of interpretation, of structure, of sign, of play. The one seeks to decipher, dreams of deciphering a truth or an origin which escapes play and the order of the sign, and which lives the necessity of interpretation as an exile. The other, which is no longer turned toward the origin, affirms play and tries to pass beyond man and humanism, the name of man being the name of that being who, throughout the history of metaphysics or of ontotheology—in other words, throughout his entire history—has dreamed of full presence, the reassuring foundation, the origin and the end of play. The second interpretation of interpretation, to which Nietzsche pointed the way, does not seek in ethnography, as Lévi-Strauss does, the "inspiration of a new humanism" (again citing the "Introduction to the Work of Marcel Mauss").

There are more than enough indications today to suggest we might perceive that these two interpretations of interpretation—which are absolutely irreconcilable even if we live them simultaneously and reconcile them in an obscure economy—together share the field which we call, in such a problematic fashion, the social sciences.

For my part, although these two interpretations must acknowledge and accentuate their difference and define their irreducibility, I do not believe that today there is any question of *choosing*—in the first place because here we are in a region (let us say, provisionally, a region of historicity) where the category of choice seems particularly trivial; and in the second, because we must first try to conceive of the common ground, and the *différance* of this irreducible difference. Here there is a kind of question, let us still call it historical, whose *conception, formation, gestation,* and *labor* we are only catching a glimpse of today. I employ these words, I admit, with a glance toward the operations of childbearing—but also with a glance toward those who, in a society from which I do not exclude myself, turn their eyes away when faced by the as yet unnamable which is proclaiming itself and which can do so, as is necessary whenever a birth is in the offing, only under the species of the nonspecies, in the formless, mute, infant, and terrifying form of monstrosity.

Notes

1   TN. The reference, in a restricted sense, is to the Freudian theory of neurotic symptoms and of dream interpretation in which a given symbol is understood contradictorily as both the desire to fulfill an impulse and the desire to suppress the impulse. In a general sense the reference is to Derrida's thesis that logic and coherence themselves can only be understood contradictorily, since they presuppose the suppression of *différance*, "writing" in the sense of the general economy. Cf. "La pharmacie de Platon," in *La dissemination*, pp. 125–26, where Derrida uses the Freudian model of dream interpretation in order to clarify the contractions embedded in philosophical coherence.

2   *The Raw and the Cooked*, trans. John and Doreen Wightman (New York: Harper and Row, 1969), p. 14. [Translation somewhat modified.]

3   *The Elementary Structures of Kinship*, trans. James Bell, John von Sturmer, and Rodney Needham (Boston: Beacon Press, 1969), p. 8.

4   Ibid., p. 3.

5   *The Savage Mind* (London: George Weidenfeld and Nicholson; Chicago: University of Chicago Press, 1966), p. 247.

6   Ibid., p. 17.

7   *The Raw and the Cooked*, p. 2.

8   Ibid., pp. 5–6.

9   Ibid., p. 12.

10   Ibid., pp. 17–18.

11   Ibid., pp. 7–8.

12   TN. This double sense of supplement—to supply something which is missing, or to supply something additional—is at the center of Derrida's deconstruction of traditional linguistics in *De la grammatologie*. In a chapter entitled "The Violence of the Letter: From Lévi-Strauss to Rousseau" (pp. 149ff.), Derrida expands the analysis of Lévi-Strauss begun in this essay in order further to clarify the ways in which the contradictions of traditional logic "program" the most modern conceptual apparatuses of linguistics and the social sciences.

13   "Introduction à l'oeuvre de Marcel Mauss," in Marcel Mauss, *Sociologie et anthropologie* (Paris: P.U.F., 1950), p. xlix.

14   Ibid., pp. xlix–1.

15   George Charbonnier, *Entretiens avec Claude Lévi-Strauss* (Paris: Plon, 1961).

16   *Race and History* (Paris: Unesco Publications, 1958).

17   "Introduction à l'oeuvre de Marcel Mauss," p. xlvi.

18   TN. The reference is to *Tristes tropiques*, trans. John Russell (London: Hutchinson and Co., 1961).

Chapter 10

Mary Poovey

FEMINISM AND DECONSTRUCTION

Bringing feminism and deconstruction together may lead to both being transformed. Mary Poovey, who has published widely on feminist and economic theory in books such as *Uneven Developments* (1989), *Making a Social Body* (1995), and *A History of the Modern Fact* (1998), argues that taking a deconstructive, antihumanist stance means that essentialist (biologically located) notions of female identity are called into question, and instead "woman" becomes a relational term (i.e., understood in relation to "man"). Deconstruction clearly undermines the hierarchy and implicit power relations in such binary oppositions, arguing instead for an endless play of terms within a system. Therefore biological existence cannot be a material anchor-point or a transcendent signified which is outside of, or fixes all of the values in a system. The danger here, for Poovey, is that such a conservative mode of deconstruction, while arguing for the importance of the semiotics of gender and sexuality, denies actual (historical) female experience of sexuality and sociality, i.e., the "experiential basis" of North American feminism. Derrida and other critics have worked on a solution to this problem, arguing that the binary term "woman" has in fact the power to deconstruct the entire metaphysical structure of power relations, via its role in producing "undecidables" (ecriture; the supplement; différance; hymen — see section introduction), terms which reveal subversively multiple positions of meaning within otherwise tightly structured systems of thought. Such terms are expressed as a "middle voice", one which is both constitutive and highly disruptive. Poovey points out that French feminists such as Luce Irigaray and Hélène Cixous argue that this middle voice is "feminine language", for example Cixous's notion of maternal "white ink" or Irigaray's notion of female genitalia dividing the unified subject. The problem is, such a notion of feminine language, apart from reproducing some elements of essentialism, also portrays a pre-existent notion of "woman" which again can preclude what Poovey calls the "concrete, class- and race-specific facts of historical women." Deconstruction, in other words, is useful, but it needs to undergo feminist critique. Poovey argues that deconstruction offers three main strategic tools: first, it demystifies institutions and concepts that appear to be natural or neutral in being; second, it challenges and potentially dismantles "hierarchical and oppositional logic"; and third it offers the notion of the middle voice or "in-between" undecidable term, which can be used to rethink power structures created through binary thinking. Two key examples given by Poovey are "coverture" – married women being normative – which produced an opposition between married and unmarried women that inadvertently gave the latter more freedoms and rights, and the notion that gender is a social construct (something developed in more detail by Judith Butler – see Chapter 51). But deconstruction often works in generalities that thereby miss the specificity of given situations, say those of black women, and in effect it needs to deconstruct "itself", rather than operating as an inviolable master discourse. Poovey suggests, then, that deconstruction has its uses, but only if it is "historicized" and, ironically, deconstructed. A feminist deconstruction maintains its strategies of critique and demystification, while acknowledging the real experiences of historical women, in all of their difference and diversity: it provides for collective strength and political action, without reducing all women to a homogenous undifferentiated category.

THERE ARE AS MANY DECONSTRUCTIONS as there are feminisms. To discuss the relationship between "deconstruction" and "feminism" is therefore to beg – or defer – the question of definition. It requires that I posit two entities that have no existence as such so as to examine a relationship that indisputably does exist in contemporary criticism – particularly literary criticism. In this essay, I will posit these two, overly simplified, provisional entities for the purposes of discussion, but my primary project here will be to suggest some of the reasons why the difficulties of definition multiply when these two nouns are brought into conjunction. I want to try to explain both why deconstruction calls feminism into question and how feminism can use deconstruction. In the process, I will suggest that feminism must rewrite deconstruction so as to incorporate its strategies into a political project and that this rewriting will necessarily transform feminism – possibly, it will take us (conceptually) "beyond" feminism altogether.

First of all, the problem: to accept the antihumanist premises of deconstruction is already to question the possibility that women, as opposed to "woman," exist.[1] This is not to say that biological females do not exist but, rather, that neither sexuality nor social identity is given exclusively in or through the body, however it is sexed. Instead of reflecting a unitary "self," identity is relational; as such, "woman" is only a position that gains its (provisional) definition from its placement in relation to "man." This formulation of the problem follows from the philosophical program of deconstruction as it has been practiced by Jacques Derrida in particular. Part of Derrida's critique of Western metaphysics has involved a demystification of presence or identity. By demonstrating that the idea of presence depends upon language, which simultaneously stands for and stands *in the place of* the things words represent, Derrida argues that presence is always elusive and relational – not the ground of truth but the illusion produced by the endless substitution of signifiers with which we (hopefully, but futilely) try to capture it.[2] One effect of the demystification of presence – and one of the strategies by which Derrida has achieved this demystification – is the deconstruction of binary oppositions. Presence, in other words, seems fixed and its ontological integrity ensured because it seems to stand in opposition to another fixed term – absence. Yet Derrida has argued that the interdependence of these terms means that neither can be autonomous and that both of them really take their definition relationally, from the chain of signifiers to which they belong. None of the members of this linguistic chain has priority, and the "ground" that produces the effect of meaning and essence is the play of substitutions to which I have already alluded. The project of deconstruction, then, is not to reverse binary oppositions but to problematize the very idea of opposition and the notion of identity upon which it depends. Deconstruction therefore undermines identity, truth, being as such; it substitutes endless deferral or play for these essences.

From the perspective of this project, a feminism that bases its epistemology and practice on women's experience is simply another deluded humanism, complicit with the patriarchal institutions it claims to oppose.[3] To argue that women's biological nature grounds a set of experiences and feelings is obviously to fall into this humanistic trap, but even to maintain that all women necessarily occupy the position of "other" to man and that their social oppression follows from this binary split is to risk reducing position to essence, because it retains both the concept of unified identity and the oppositional logic that currently dictates our "knowledge" of sex difference and the nature of woman. To take deconstruction to its logical conclusion would be to argue that "woman" is *only* a social construct that has no basis in nature, that "woman," in other words, is a term whose definition depends upon the context in which it is being discussed and not upon some set of sexual organs or social experiences. This renders the experience women have of themselves and the meaning of their social relations problematic, to say the least. It also calls into question the experiential basis upon which U.S. feminism has historically grounded its political programs. The challenge for those of us who are convinced both that real historical women do exist and share certain experiences *and* that deconstruction's demystification of presence makes theoretical sense is to work out some way to think both women and "woman." It isn't an easy task.

One approach to this problem has been offered by Derrida himself (as well as by other deconstructive critics like Jean-François Lyotard, Roland Barthes, and Michel Serres). In such texts as *Spurs: Nietzsche's Styles* and "The Double Session," Derrida has investigated the possibility that "woman," as that which is constituted in the position of "other," can subvert or problematize the entire metaphysics based on presence and identity. Although I do not intend to analyze the specific argument or strategy Derrida works out in these essays, his basic program is to explore and exploit that principle which subverts the structure of binary opposition – what he calls variously "différance," "writing," or "supplementarity." As the play of substitution, différance can be provisionally figured as whatever problematizes opposition or represents the in-between (the hymen, for example, which is the boundary between inside and outside and is therefore both; or masturbation, whose accompanying fantasies both do and do not make the loved one present).[4] Alternatively, this principle can be conceptualized as a mode of speech, which Derrida calls the "middle voice." "Différance is not simply active," Derrida writes; "it rather indicates the middle voice, it precedes and sets up the opposition between activity and passivity."[5] As Frances Bartkowski explains this middle voice, it "is one in which the subject and object are often the same; it is most often found in the reflexive form where the subject-verb-object relationship is de-centered. It abolishes distance, and may therefore be seen as the form in which a distinct erotic component is present."[6]

This middle voice, as a figuration of that which disrupts the structure of binary oppositions and therefore the identity of the terms the structure supports and depends upon, has been theorized by French feminists such as Luce Irigaray and Hélène Cixous as a specifically feminine language. This is an elaboration of the Derridean flirtation with the feminine as writing ("if style were a man . . . then writing would be a woman").[7] Because it is the form in which most Americans have encountered and felt challenged to grapple with deconstructive ideas and strategies, I will focus on this version of deconstruction instead of Derrida's own intermittent adoption of a "feminine" stand.

With the publication in 1976 of Cixous's "Laugh of the Medusa" in *Signs,* the ideas of French feminists first began to be accessible to U.S. audiences. Because of many Americans' linguistic insularity and the stylistic difficulty of these writings, their popularity necessarily depended upon their being available in translation. The appearance of Cixous's essay was followed by *Signs'* publication of two pieces by Luce Irigaray, "When Our Lips Speak Together" (1980) and "And the One Doesn't Stir without the Other" (1981) and by the publication, in 1980, of an entire anthology of French feminist texts, *New French Feminisms,* edited by Elaine Marks and Isabelle de Courtivron.[8] Almost as soon as these texts entered U.S. libraries and bookstores, commentaries began to appear. Such early works as Carolyn

Burke's 1978 "Report from Paris: Women's Writing and the Women's Movement" and her 1981 "Irigaray through the Looking Glass," Ann Rosalind Jones's 1980 "Writing the Body: Toward an Understanding of l'Écriture Féminine," and Jane Gallop's *The Daughter's Seduction: Feminism and Psychoanalysis* (1982) helped U.S. audiences interpret these elusive, often stylistically experimental writings. Soon Americans were embracing French ideas, as in the collaboratively edited 1981 issue of *Yale French Studies* entitled *Feminist Readings: French Texts/ American Contexts*.[9] As French feminism (often unjustifiably homogenized into a single "school" by U.S. readers – as I am doing here) has made its way onto undergraduate as well as graduate syllabi, its dissemination and assimilation have continued. Two significant recent events have been the publication in 1985 by Cornell University Press of Luce Irigaray's *Speculum of the Other Woman* (translated by Gillian G. Gill) and Toril Moi's sweeping critique of U.S. feminism in the name of the kind of feminism Moi associates with Julia Kristeva (*Sexual/ Textual Politics: Feminist Literary Theory*).[10]

The commercial success of French feminist texts is a measure of the appeal this theory holds for U.S. feminist audiences. For U.S. feminist academics, the attraction of French feminism resides not so much in its philosophical dismantling of binary thinking (which it shares with deconstruction) as in its argument that the in-between mode of speech Derrida describes is *feminine* discourse – a special language that seems to articulate, if not derive from, the female body and female sexuality in particular. Calling for "woman" to "write her self," Hélène Cixous set the stage for this essentialistic interpretation of French feminism with her emphasis on "white ink." In "The Laugh of the Medusa," Cixous associates this "ink" with "mother's milk," and, even though she problematizes the literal connection between female biology and the kind of writing this "ink" produces, her text certainly allows for the interpretation that such writing must be done by women because it expresses what is biologically unique to them. Woman, Cixous states, "must write about women and bring women to writing, from which they have been driven away as violently as from their bodies – for the same reasons, by the same law, with the same fatal goal." She writes that "a woman's body, with its thousand and one thresholds of ardor . . . will make the old single-grooved mother tongue reverberate with more than one language."[11] Luce Irigaray also authorizes this return to biology and essentialism in her creation of a myth of female desire and in basing "feminine" language on the physical properties of female genitalia. "Woman's desire most likely does not speak the same language as man's desire," she writes. "Woman finds pleasure more in touch than in sight. . . . The value accorded to the only definable form [by the dominant, male imaginary] excludes the form involved in female autoeroticism. The *one* of form, the individual sex, proper name, literal meaning – supercedes, by spreading apart and dividing, this touching of *at least two* (lips) which keeps woman in contact with herself."[12]

The reason French feminists postulate a feminine language "based on" the female body is that they maintain values are reproduced in language and that a language that privileges identity, singularity, and linearity perpetuates the oppression and nonrepresentation of woman. By the definition of this "economy of the same" (the phrase is Irigaray's), woman is not-man; as such, she is "other" to that which is the norm. As one example of this, woman's sexuality has been theorized as lack because it has been conceptualized in terms of male sexuality; in keeping with this, woman has been rendered semantically passive because she has been relegated to the position of the object, not the subject of desire.[13] The project of French feminists, then, is to develop a different language so that women can tell a different story. "If we continue to speak the same language to each other, we will reproduce the same story," Irigaray explains in "When Our Lips Speak Together." This language celebrates plurality and semantic indeterminacy, the slippage engendered by contradiction, the waywardness of digression because these are "like" female genitals, which are multiple instead of singular. Woman, Irigaray argues, in "This Sex Which Is Not One," is indefinitely other in herself. That is undoubtedly the reason she is called temperamental, incomprehensible, perturbed, capricious – not to mention her language in which "she" goes off in all directions and in which "he" is unable to discern the coherence of any meaning. . . . In her statements – at least when she dares speak out – woman retouches herself constantly. She just barely separates from herself some chatter, an exclamation, a half-secret, a sentence left in suspense – When she returns to it, it is only to set out again from another point of pleasure or pain. One must listen to her differently in order to hear an *"other meaning" which is constantly in the process of weaving itself, at the same time ceaselessly embracing words and yet casting them off to avoid becoming fixed, immobilized.* For when "she" says something, it is already no longer identical to what she means. Moreover, her statements are never identical to anything. Their distinguishing feature is one of contiguity. They touch (*upon*). And when they wander too far from this nearness, she stops and begins again from "zero": her body-sex organ.[14]

Whether any women "really" speak like this is no more the point than whether male sexuality is "really" singular. Instead, the endeavor is to imagine some organization of fantasy, language, and reality other than one based on identity and binary oppositions, which is currently the dominant mode and therefore equated with the dominant sex, men. If French feminism shares with deconstruction the project of demystifying the dominant symbolic economy, then, it differs from the general practice of deconstruction in focusing primarily upon the recuperative project of recovering that which might have come "before" the economy of the same and which therefore may not have been appropriated by men.[15] I place "before" in quotation marks here because this enterprise, like any other quest for origins within a system that critiques presence and originality, will necessarily be not only speculative but projective and fictional. Yet the fact that postulating a "before" is critical to French feminism reinforces the essentialism that the analogy to the female body also encourages. That is, in theorizing the possibility that a language might have existed (and might exist again) that had not (yet) been organized into binary oppositions, noncontradictory logic, and self-identical terms, French feminists open the door to the idea of some "natural" language that "accurately" articulates the human subject and especially the human body. That this body is biologically female and therefore "multiple" instead of male and "singular" does not mitigate the essentialism that deconstruction targets as a ruse of metaphysics. French feminism, then, when given the reading many Americans have given it, can be said to play back into the very mystification and binary opposition that it is deconstruction's (other) goal to dismantle or deconstruct.

The problem that French feminism inadvertently introduces for U.S. feminists in particular has been addressed by Jonathan Culler – even though Culler's explicit subject is not French feminism but the three "moments" of U.S. feminist criticism. Culler argues that asking women to read as "woman" – or, by extension, to write as "woman" – is to make a self-contradictory request, for "it appeals to the condition of being a woman as if it were a given and simultaneously urges that this condition be created or achieved." One cannot read or write outside the dominant economy, in other words, because one has been constituted as a subject *by* that economy; in order for there to be a "feminine" reading or writing, some position that is "outside" the economy would have to exist. Failing that, this "outside" would have to be produced as a desirable but ultimately unattainable goal – and even then, it would still necessarily be conceptualized in terms derived from and allowed by the dominant system of representation. According to Culler, so powerful is the appeal of this (nonexistent) point of reference and so convincing is the impression that women *are* outside the dominant representational system that nearly every feminist sooner or later reproduces it and the essentialism it implies. "Even the most sophisticated theorists make this appeal," Culler charges, "even the most radical French theorists . . . always have moments . . . when they speak as women."[16]

So we are back to the problem with which I began. Is it possible to be a woman if one accepts the philosophical program of deconstruction, or must a deconstructive critic be a "woman"? By way of proposing my answer to this question, I want to outline what I see as the positive contributions deconstruction makes to a feminism that is interested not only in the idea of "woman" but also in the concrete, class- and race-specific facts of historical women. I will conclude with an analysis of the limitations of deconstruction and some suggestions about how and why feminism must finally use deconstructive strategies to demystify the category of "woman" whose seductive appeal threatens to prevent some kinds of questions from being asked.

From the perspective of a feminist interested in history and such social determinants as race and class, the primary contribution of deconstruction is not its recuperative program but the project of demystification. Because deconstruction reveals the figurative nature of all ideology, it can expose the artifice inherent in such categories as "nature" and gender. This, in turn, opens the possibility for (although, as I will argue in a moment, it does not presuppose or mandate) a genuinely historical practice — one that could analyze and deconstruct the specific articulations and institutionalizations of these categories, their interdependence, and the uneven processes by which they have been deployed and altered. Given this emphasis, deconstructive strategies could enable feminists to write a history of the various contradictions within institutional definitions of woman that would show how these contradictions have opened the possibility for change. The fact that the nineteenth-century legal principle of "coverture," for example, institutionalized the married woman as *the* normative "woman" meant that unmarried women enjoyed rights which "naturally" belonged to men. Despite other institutional and ideological constraints upon their behavior, this contradiction within the category "woman" facilitated the entry of increasing numbers of (middle-class) women into waged work, *and* it helped expose the artificiality of an opposition that aligned legal and property rights with sex.

The second contribution deconstruction can make is to challenge hierarchical and oppositional logic. Because the practice of deconstruction transforms binary oppositions into an economy in which terms circulate rather than remain fixed, it could (although it does not usually or necessarily) mobilize another ordering system in which the construction of false unities intrinsic to binary oppositions would not prevail. In other words, in its demystifying mode, deconstruction does not simply offer an alternative hierarchy of binary oppositions; it problematizes and opens to scrutiny the very nature of identity and oppositional logic and therefore makes visible the artifice necessary to establish, legislate, and maintain hierarchical thinking. Given this emphasis, deconstructive strategies could enable us to chart more accurately the multiple determinants that figure in any individual's social position and (relative) power and oppression. All women may currently occupy the position "woman," for example, but they do not occupy it in the same way. Women of color in a white-ruled society face different obstacles than do white women, and they may share more important problems with men of color than with their white "sisters." By deconstructing the term "woman" into a set of independent variables, this strategy can show how consolidating all women into a falsely unified "woman" has helped mask the operations of power that actually divide women's interests as much as unite them.

Deconstruction's third contribution is the idea of the "in-between." Even as an ad hoc strategy, the "in-between" constitutes one tool for dismantling binary thinking. Once the binary construct is revealed to be artificial, the identity of the two, apparently fixed terms and the rigidity of the "structure" that prevents other possibilities from being formulated could be destabilized. Such a strategy would not abolish either the hierarchical thinking that lurks within binary oppositions or power more generally conceived. But it would enable us to rethink "power" (along with identity) so as to perceive its fragmentary quality. We could then see (and make the most of) the power various groups of women do currently wield and expose the limitations of the power that seems to be (but is not) the "property" of some unified ruling group.[17]

Thus, just to provide one more concrete example, deconstruction provides the tools for exposing the fact that the opposition between the "sexes," like the definitions of "women" and "men," is a social construction, not a reflection or articulation of biological fact. In so doing, deconstruction sets up the possibility that the supposedly fixed opposition of masculine/ feminine might lose its social prominence because we could begin to recognize that there is no necessary connection between anatomical sexuality and gender stereotypes or roles. This, in turn, might legitimate behaviors that do not seem to "derive from" sex (boys might be allowed to be more nurturing, for example). This social liberation of the concept from its natural "referent" might, in turn, open the door for examining even the fixity of the anatomical categories upon which the binary opposition seems to be based. Instead of relegating all biological variants into the two categories, "male" and "female" (with "abnormal" absorbing everything that is "left over"), this practice might enable us both to multiply the categories of sex and to detach reproduction from sex – a hitherto unthinkable concept increasingly made possible by new reproductive technologies. Such a focus on the social construction of sexual identity goes beyond the more common understanding of social construction many feminists now endorse, because it deconstructs not only the relationship between women and certain social roles but also the very term "woman." Such a reconceptualization of sex and the individual is the radical – and logical – extension of deconstruction's program. It would challenge the very basis of our current social organization. In so doing, it would necessarily feel like a loss, but it might also create the conditions of possibility for as yet unimagined organizations of human potential.

This brave new world of the reconceptualized subject may be implied by deconstruction, but it does not follow necessarily from its current practice. Indeed, as it is most typically practiced – both in its recuperative and its demystifying modes – deconstruction tends to work against the kinds of historically specific, political practices to which I have just alluded. It must be obvious to anyone familiar with deconstruction today that its politics, when they are visible, are most typically conservative. One reason for this is the popularity of what I have called deconstruction's recuperative project. I have already suggested that the particular formulation of the subversive position as a "feminine" language allows for the kind of biologism all too compatible with conservative arguments about female nature. Beyond this, however, the relegation of the "feminine" to a unified *position* has two limiting consequences. On the one hand, it subordinates the diversity of the real historical women who occupy that position to the likeness they share by virtue of their placement as "other." And on the other hand, it works against any analysis of who comes to occupy that position, why certain groups occupy it at various times, or the relationships among those groups. Just to give one example of this second problem, the deconstructive project can be (and has been) used to analyze the marginalization of peoples of color as well as women, and the recuperative emphasis of deconstruction has been invoked to describe the subversive operations of black "signifyin(g)" or "jive."[18]

Yet although this emphasis on placement and subversive languages undoubtedly provides a vocabulary for conceptualizing the positive effects of difference and therefore for undermining negative stereotypes, it does not facilitate our understanding of the relationship between women and blacks, for example, nor does it account for the specific kinds of oppression or subversiveness women or blacks (or black women) may suffer or exercise when assigned to that position. In providing no tools for analyzing specificity, moreover, the recuperative mode of deconstruction provides no model of change. If we cannot describe why a particular group came to occupy the position of "other" or how its tenure in that position differs from the effect such positioning has on other groups, we have no basis upon which to posit or by which to predict any other state of affairs. We have no basis, in other words, for political analysis or action.

The more fundamental limitation of deconstruction follows from the reluctance of deconstructive critics to examine the artifice — and historical specificity — of their own practice. To committed deconstructive critics, everything seems subject to deconstruction's dismantling gaze except deconstruction itself. Insofar as it purports to be a master strategy instead of the methodological counterpart to a historically specific conceptualization of language and meaning, deconstruction — even in its demystifying mode — participates in the very process it claims to expose. The very project of deconstructing binary logic is inextricably bound to a preoccupation with the *structures* of language and conceptualization, after all, instead of, for example, an interest in the social relations or institutions by which language and ideas (including deconstruction) are produced, distributed, and reinforced. As long as it is viewed only according to its own implicit definition — as an ahistorical master strategy — deconstruction must remain outside of politics, because no stable position (other than its own) can exist. This gives deconstruction an apparently unassailable hold on the conceptualization of meaning. But this, I suggest, is not because deconstruction is "true" or because it *necessarily* superseded politics but only because it has refused the historicizing tendency it contains but has not so far turned upon itself.

My original problem, then, returns with a vengeance born of my political commitment to the future as well as the present. Because of its ability to dismantle binary logic and deconstruct identity, I do think deconstruction has provided and continues to offer an essential tool for feminist analysis. But in order for this double-edged blade not to reproduce the system it purports to cut apart, deconstruction itself must be historicized and subjected to the same kind of scrutiny with which it has dismantled Western metaphysics. As part of this historicizing project, we should examine the extent to which deconstruction's feminization of philosophy is implicated in the feminization — and appropriation — of other practices traditionally considered masculine (and therefore unacceptably explicit in their aggression). I would also like to see some analysis of the kinds of questions deconstruction precludes by conceptualizing its questions in terms of structures and play and more analysis of the political interests deconstruction currently serves — as well as the interests in which it could be enlisted.[19] Ultimately, my prediction is that feminists practicing deconstructive and other poststructuralist techniques from an explicitly political position will so completely rewrite deconstruction as to leave it behind, for all intents and purposes, as part of the historicization of structuralism already underway in several disciplines.

For the present, however, and looking toward the future, I propose that materialist feminists need to pursue two projects simultaneously. On the one hand, we need to recognize that "woman" *is* currently both a position within a dominant, binary symbolic order *and* that that position is arbitrarily (and falsely) unified. On the other hand, we need to remember that there *are* concrete historical women whose differences reveal the inadequacy of this unified category in the present and the past. The multiple positions real women occupy — the positions dictated by race, for example, or by class or sexual preference — should alert us to the inadequacy of binary logic and unitary selves without making us forget that this logic *has* dictated (and still does) some aspects of women's social treatment. At the same time, however, this emphasis must also lead us to question the ahistorical nature of what has been taken as the basis of feminism. For, if the position "woman" *is* falsely unified and if one's identity is *not* given (solely or necessarily) by anatomy, then woman — or even women — cannot remain a legitimate rallying point for political actions. Real historical women have been (and are) oppressed, and the ways and means of that oppression need to be analyzed and fought. But at the same time, we need to be ready to abandon the binary thinking that has stabilized women as a group that *could* be collectively (although not uniformly) oppressed.

I suggest, then, that materialist feminists need to do battle on two fronts. We must recognize that what (most) women now share is a positional similarity that masquerades as a natural likeness and that has historically underwritten oppression, *and* we must be willing to give up the illusory similarity of nature that reinforces binary logic even though such a move threatens to jeopardize what seems "special" about women. My argument is that the structural similarity that pretends to reflect nature masks the operation of other kinds of difference (class and race, for example) precisely by constructing a "nature" that seems desirable, because it gives women what seems to be (but is not) a naturally constructive and politically subversive role. In the long run, materialist feminists will need to write not only the history of women's oppression but also the future of gender difference(s). We will need to turn from campaigns that reproduce the essentialism of sex difference to projects that call into question the very essentialism upon which our history has been based. In this sense, conceptualizing the issue in terms of real women is part of the solution, but it is also part of the problem. Deconstruction is a critical component of the political work I am outlining here, but unless it is deployed upon itself, it will trap us in a practice that once more glorifies the "feminine" instead of giving us the means to explode binary logic and make the social construction of (sexed) identities a project of pressing political concern. If deconstruction took feminism seriously, it wouldn't look like deconstruction anymore. If feminism took deconstruction at its word, we could begin to dismantle the system that assigns to all women a single identity and a marginal place.

Notes

1   Here is Alice A. Jardine on the problematic notion of "woman."

> "The problem" attendant upon French theorists' use of "woman" or "the feminine" as a metaphor for that which disrupts the paternal order of signification is that within the increasing use of quotation marks around the word "woman," women as thinking, writing subjects are placed in the position of constantly wondering whether it is a question of women or of woman, of their written bodies or of their *written* bodies. To refuse "woman" or the "feminine" as cultural concepts is, ironically, to return to metaphysical – anatomical – definitions of sexual identity. To accept a metaphorization of woman, on the other hand, means risking once again the absence of women as subjects in the struggles against theories of metaphysical presence. The attempt to analyze, to separate ideological and cultural determinations of "the feminine" from "the real woman" – seemingly the most logical path to follow – may also be the most interminable where *women* become literally and figuratively impossible.

See her "Pre-Texts for the Transatlantic Feminist," *Yale French Studies* 62 (1981): 223–24. Jardine discusses this dilemma at greater length in *Gynesis: Configurations of Woman and Modernity* (Ithaca: Cornell University Press, 1985), esp. 31–49. Jonathan Culler also discusses this issue, but, although his analysis of "Reading As a Woman" illuminates the problem, he finally defers tackling the intersection of feminism and deconstruction. The telling footnote reads, in part: "The relation between feminism and deconstruction is a complicated question. . . . Derrida's *Éperons* . . . is a relevant but in many ways unsatisfying document in this case." All Culler has to add are "some brief indications" about how the conjunction might be more satisfactorily addressed. See Culler's *On Deconstruction: Theory and Criticism after Structuralism* (Ithaca: Cornell University Press, 1982), 61, n.10.

Helpful analyses of feminism and deconstruction include Gayatri Chakravorty Spivak's "French Feminism in an International Frame," *Yale French Studies* 62 (1981): 154–84, and "Displacement and the Discourse of Woman," in *Displacement: Derrida and After,* ed. Mark Krupnick (Bloomington:

Indiana University Press, 1983), 169–95; Jane Gallop, "Annie Leclerc Writing a Letter, with Vermeer," in *The Poetics of Gender,* ed. Nancy K. Miller (New York: Columbia University Press, 1986), 137–56; Frances Bartkowski, "Feminism and Deconstruction: 'A Union Forever Deferred,'" *Enclitic* 4 (Fall 1980): 70–77; Myra Love, "Christa Wolf and Feminism: Breaking the Patriarchal Connection," *New German Critique* 16 (Winter 1979): 31–53; and Elizabeth A. Meese, *Crossing the Double-Cross: The Practice of Feminist Criticism* (Chapel Hill: University of North Carolina Press, 1986), esp. 72–87.

2   See Jacques Derrida, ". . . *That Dangerous Supplement* . . .," in *Of Grammatology,* trans. Gayatri Chakravorty Spivak (Baltimore and London: Johns Hopkins University Press, 1974), 141–64.

3   See Alice A. Jardine, "Opaque Texts and Transparent Contexts: The Political Difference of Julia Kristeva," in *Poetics of Gender,* 97–98; Spivak, "French Feminism in an International Frame," 175–76; and Beverly Brown and Parveen Adams, "The Feminine Body and Feminist Politics," *m/f* no. 3 (1979): esp. 35–38.

4   See Jacques Derrida, "The Double Session," in *Dissemination,* trans. Barbara Johnson (Chicago: University of Chicago Press, 1981), 173–285, and ". . . *That Dangerous Supplement* . . .," 144–52.

5   Derrida, quoted in Bartkowski, 72.

6   Bartkowski, 72.

7   Jacques Derrida, *Spurs: Nietzsche's Styles,* trans. Barbara Harlow (Chicago: University of Chicago Press, 1978), 57.

8   Hélène Cixous, "The Laugh of the Medusa: Viewpoint," trans. Keith Cohen and Paula Cohen, *Signs* 1 (Summer 1976): 875. Luce Irigaray, "When Our Lips Speak Together," trans. Carolyn Burke, *Signs* 6 (Autumn 1980): 69–79, and "And the One Doesn't Stir without the Other," *Signs* 7 (Autumn 1981): 60–67; Elaine Marks and Isabelle de Courtivron, *New French Feminisms: An Anthology* (Amherst: University of Massachusetts Press, 1980). Future references to *New French Feminisms* are to the 1981 Schocken edition.

9   Carolyn Burke, "Report from Paris: Women's Writing and the Women's Movement," *Signs* 3 (Summer 1978): 843–55, and "Irigaray through the Looking Glass," *Feminist Studies* 7 (Summer 1981): 288. Ann Rosalind Jones, "Writing the Body: Toward an Understanding of *l'Écriture Féminine,*" *Feminist Studies* 7 (Summer 1981): 247–63; Jane Gallop, *The Daughter's Seduction: Feminism and Psychoanalysis* (Ithaca: Cornell University Press, 1982); See *Feminist Readings: French Text s/American Contexts,* ed. Colette Gaudin et al., special issue of *Yale French Studies* 62 (1981).

10   Luce Irigaray, *Speculum of the Other Woman,* trans. Gillian G. Gill (Ithaca: Cornell University Press, 1985); and Toril Moi, *Sexual/Textual Politics: Feminist Literary Theory* (London and New York: Methuen, 1985).

11   Hélène Cixous, "The Laugh of the Medusa," in *New French Feminisms,* 245, 256. All future references are to this edition.

12   Luce Irigaray, "This Sex Which Is Not One," trans. Claudia Reeder, in *New French Feminisms,* 101.

13   Ibid., 99–106.

14   Irigaray, "When Our Lips Speak Together," 69; "This Sex Which Is Not One," 103.

15   Julia Kristeva postulates a signifying mode in which every individual engages before the acquisition of language. This "heterogeneous," "maternally connotated" mode, which she calls "le sémiotique," is "detected genetically in the first echolalias of infants as rhythms and intonations anterior to the first phonemes, morphemes, lexemes, and sentences; this heterogeneousness . . . is later reactivated as rhythms, intonations, glossalalias in psychotic discourse." See her "From One Identity to an Other," in *Desire in Language: A Semiotic Approach to Literature and Art,* trans. Thomas Gora, et al. (New York: Columbia University Press, 1980), 133. Other feminists, like Sherry Ortner, have speculated that the "before" is phylogenetic–a literal presocial state of nature more or less preserved in "primitive" societies. See "Is Woman to Man As Nature is to Culture?" in *Women, Culture, and Society,* ed. Michelle Rosaldo and Louise Lamphere (Stanford: Stanford University Press, 1974).

16   Culler, 49, 63.

17   See Brown and Adams, 47.

18   See esp. Hortense J. Spillers, "Interstices: A Small Drama of Words," in *Pleasure and Danger: Exploring Female Sexuality,* ed. Carol S. Vance (Boston: Routledge & Kegan Paul, 1984), 73–100.

19   See Bartkowski, 76–77.

Chapter 11

Tilottama Rajan

PHENOMENOLOGY AND/AS DECONSTRUCTION

In untangling the intertwined threads of European deconstruction and North American poststructuralism, Tilottama Rajan is "desynonymizing" two words that are used interchangeably by most critics. The reason for doing this is that North American poststructuralism largely adopts the Saussurian, semiological and structuralist aspects of Derrida's work, yet does not on the whole engage in, or explore, the phenomenological backgrounds of deconstruction. Rajan, a distinguished professor and Canada Research Chair in English and Theory at the University of Western Ontario, argues that the early deconstructive texts by Derrida emerge from encounters with phenomenologists Edmund Husserl (1859–1938), Martin Heidegger (1889–1976), Maurice Merleau-Ponty (1908–61), and Jean-Paul Sartre (1905–80). All four explored questions of consciousness, perception, and being. The North American reception of deconstruction, mainly occurring through the work of the Yale School, posits a world of signs and literary texts (the "rhetoric of blindness", and so on), rather than modes of subjectivity. The conflation of a wider conception of poststructuralism (Lacan, Foucault, Deleuze and Guattari, etc.), with Yale School deconstruction is understandable since Derrida's essay "Structure, Sign, and Play in the Human Sciences" became a key text or "gateway" into the entire field in question. Rajan also notes that the notion that deconstruction is mainly an engagement with literary texts, fails to situate it correctly as a philosophical response to the rise of the social sciences, and of course it also fails to comprehend its debt to existentialist phenomenology. The conflation of deconstruction with poststructuralism can be seen most clearly in the "linguistic turn" of philosophy and theory, which Rajan traces via the work of the American theorist Paul de Man, especially in his analysis of the early Sartre, and his move away from such philosophy. The core thesis developed by Rajan is that deconstruction "transposes" phenomenology "into linguistic models" that continue with the core ontological and ethical questions of being in the world. Such questions—for example, the role and existential meaning of death, or, the "analytic of finitude"—are avoided or forgotten by poststructuralists in favour of narrow structural and semiological concerns. Derrida is partly responsible for this effacement of core ontological and ethical questions, although they do return in the "later" Derrida, particularly in his work on religion. His deconstruction of Husserl's phenomenology—for example his conflation of consciousness and spirit—creates a set of assumptions about other phenomenological approaches, particularly those of Sartre and

Merleau-Ponty, just as Foucault rejects existentialist phenomenology. Yet as Rajan points out, many key Derridean concepts can be traced back to this excluded or *abjected* philosophy, such as Sartre's notion of self-presence being "an impalpable fissure" that "has slipped into being", just as Derrida will later call this "fissure" the "gram" or trace of a trace. Rajan traces Derrida's negative approach to consciousness through the early French reception of Hegel's *Phenomenology of Spirit*, particularly that of translator Jean Hyppolite's commentary, *Genesis and Structure of Hegel's Phenomenology of Spirit* (1946, Engl. trans. 1974); Hyppolite transforms understanding of Hegel's philosophy into a mobile, ever-moving machine in which consciousness is always "nonidentical", related to absence, dispersal, and dissemination. As with Sartre's analogous exploration of consciousness and the Other, the crossing back and forth of phenomenology and semiological notions of language, is apparent from the beginning, and may be productively returned to.

Desynonymizing deconstruction and poststructuralism

The terms *deconstruction* and *poststructuralism* surface simultaneously in the early stages of the Anglo-American assimilation of French theory.[1] They are used interchangeably to refer to the same general group of theorists, though they are also indexed separately, reflecting an untheorized awareness of their difference. In books published in the eighties deconstruction is most often identified with Derrida and de Man and sometimes more extensively with the *Tel Quel* group and the American Heideggerians William Spanos and Joseph Riddel.[2] As such it may name an operation—of dismantling, unworking, or desedimentation—that is transportable to the work of other theorists not specifically called deconstructive (such as Foucault).[3] Or it may refer not just to a critical activity but to a certain view of language as *écriture* that privileges literature as what de Man calls "the most advanced and refined mode of deconstruction."[4] Hence the view, polemically proclaimed by Habermas, that deconstruction involves the "leveling of the genre distinction" between philosophy and literature, and then between criticism and literature, in "one comprehensive, all-embracing context of texts. . . . a 'universal text'."[5] The term *poststructuralism* has a wider provenance, being used to describe the work of Lacan, Foucault, Deleuze and Guattari, and on occasion that of Michel Serres, Paul Ricoeur, and Gerard Genette, as well as more recently Baudrillard and Lyotard.[6] On this basis we could describe deconstruction as an approach that, while not confined to literary theory, privileges the philosophical category literature, as Blanchot uses the term. This usage is most sympathetically glossed by Foucault, who notes that the word *literature* "is of recent date" as is the isolation, after romanticism, of a "'literary'" language increasingly "differentiated from the discourse of ideas . . . [and] the values that were able to keep it in general circulation." Literature in this sense is left with nothing "to do but to curve back in a perpetual return upon itself, as if its discourse could have no other content than the expression of its own form" (OT: 300).

Poststructuralism, we could then say, is a broader interdisciplinary movement that exceeds this separatism of literature, thus holding out possibilities of escape from the prison-house of language with which deconstruction is often associated.[7] But there are at least two problems with this distinction. First, Derrida is also referred to as a poststructuralist, even when he is being criticized for an ultratextualism that privileges the category "text/text-uality" if not exactly literature.[8] Derrida, who uses the term *deconstruction* but not the Anglo-American term *poststructuralism,* is also placed under the second heading because of the initial gateway status of "Structure, Sign, and Play in the Human Sciences" in the translation of his work from France to North America.[9] Similarly the evolution of Barthes's work as an over-turning of his earlier structuralism leads him to be described as poststructuralist, even though his interest in textuality leads him to be discussed in books on deconstruction.[10] When both terms are used to describe the same theorist, then, it would seem that poststructuralism (or ultra-, neo-, or superstructuralism)[11] names a relationship to structuralism that is not foregrounded in the term *deconstruction*.

Second, it is incorrect to tie deconstruction's focus on *écriture* to a privileging of the literary; on the contrary deconstruction is arguably not a development internal to literary studies but to philosophy. Indeed, the literariness of deconstruction, and hence a certain taint of formalism that has led to its overthrow by new historicism and now cultural studies, are largely North American phenomena—results of the brief hegemony enjoyed by "Yale" deconstruction[12] and even more so of its temporary co-optation into an apparatus of pedagogical reproduction that has been described by John Guillory in *Cultural Capital*. Deconstruction in America is associated with the privileging of literary studies; in fact its institutional impetus in France comes from an attempt to rethink philosophy in the face of the rising power of the social sciences.[13] For his part, Derrida disavows any exclusive focus on literature; he speaks of his "first desire . . . to go in the direction of the literary event," towards Mallarmé and Blanchot, but then of the necessity "not to close oneself up in philosophy as such or even in literature."[14] Moreover, if we can, indeed, divide Derrida and de Man as exemplars of deconstruction from Foucault as a practitioner of poststructuralism, we must ask why literature is also important to the early Foucault, not to mention to Baudrillard.[15] Either the distinction between the two terms is untenable, or there is a difference between them that cannot be so easily aligned with a division of theorists.

Because *poststructuralism* is an Anglo-American term, or at least because it does not originate in France,[16] we could simply conclude that the duplication of terms is careless. I suggest, however, that we see it as what Stanley Corngold, commenting on de Man, calls an "error." Whereas mistakes are "without true value. . . . the skew of error implies a truth": "Error functions as a movement informing both human existence and the thought adequate to existence that is literary language. The notion of error is implicated in the very definition of the trope."[17] Thus the duplication of deconstruction as poststructuralism is not simply wrong. Rather, the redundant coinage of the second term points to an aspect of the Anglo-American appropriation of French theory not accounted for by the term *deconstruction*. Conversely, this duplication also points to a resistance of deconstruction to being economized within "poststructuralism." In short, it points to a palimpsestic history within this theory that the doubled terminology helps to unpack and that is covered over by the asymmetry between the time of the appearance of the works discussed in this study (which spans five decades) and their condensed, achronological translation into English. Among the peculiarities of this translation, the history of which would require a different kind of study, it is worth mentioning two examples. One is the translation of Baudrillard, which has proceeded backward from the later to the earlier work.[18] The other is the framing of early translations of Derrida and Foucault by the discovery of Saussure and structuralism, whilst the translation of Blanchot and Levinas has had to wait till much later.

While the doubling of deconstruction and poststructuralism occurs in Anglo-American commentary, my interest is in its heuristic value for reading French theory itself. In other words, this error discloses a difference within a theoretical corpus that was too rapidly mediated to the English-speaking world for the genealogical entanglements that are perhaps still overlooked in France as well to be fully grasped. Poststructuralism combined with the American appropriation of Derrida into literary studies to cover over certain aspects of deconstruction that this study explores. The term names the fact that deconstruction in England and America was perceived almost entirely as a problematizing of or emancipation from structuralism, which retained the latter's dismissal of phenomenology and its rhetoric of the end of man. In commentaries of the eighties, Derrida is invariably approached through

Saussure. When it is recognized that his work began with Husserl and not Saussure, phenomenology is metonymized with structuralism as a thought reducible to Husserl and a naive foil to deconstruction. In the process we forget one part of the intellectual context in which deconstruction emerged as a return of a phenomenological project—a "humanisme de l'autre homme" in Levinas' phrase[19]—that acquires renewed urgency if we return to it through deconstruction.

The linguistic turn of phenomenology: Sartre, de Man, and the image

In the early work of de Man, we can see that the linguistic turn we associate with structuralism also occurs as a radicalization of phenomenology.[20] De Man is often viewed as Derrida's American "disciple," but as Lindsay Waters points out his career developed quite autonomously until they met in 1966 (when de Man was forty-seven).[21] De Man's early work is an unusually pure case of the emergence of deconstruction from phenomenology. Although Derrida's linguistic turn can be seen as early as the *Origin of Geometry* and arguably develops from Blanchot, at a certain stage (in *Of Grammatology*) it becomes caught up and energized by a critique of Saussure and structuralism. In de Man's early work there are few references to structuralism; indeed, his marginalization of Derrida's discussion of Saussure in his review of *Of Grammatology* (1970) shows his disinterest in linguistics, even though he is everywhere concerned with language.[22] In *Allegories of Reading* de Man does indeed refashion himself as a poststructuralist by building his work around a linguistics of tropes and speech-act theory. But as I argue elsewhere, at this point he is systematically rewriting his earlier "vocabulary of intent and desire" in a "more linguistic terminology."[23] The terms *presence/absence*, *immanence/transcendence* and the Benjaminian pair *symbol/allegory* are thus translated into a vocabulary of figure/reference and metaphor/metonymy that claims a greater technical rigor.[24]

The importance of Heidegger for de Man is well known, though by 1955 de Man already expresses reservations about him similar to those of Derrida in the "Ends of Man" (1968).[25] Less well known, however, is that de Man's theory of the intentional structure of the romantic image—which predates *Of Grammatology* by seven years—draws strongly on Sartre's theory of the image in *Imagination* and *The Psychology of Imagination,* as well as on his division between the *pour-soi* and the *en-soi.* Sartre ontologizes intentionality so as to make it part of the "destruction" of the cogito. Intentionality as a "mode of existence of consciousness," in Levinas's phrase, means simply that consciousness is conscious *of* something and thus "in contact with the world." For Husserl it is simply "an animating act which gives to the hyletic phenomena a transcendent meaning." In this act the subject is constituted through a subject-object relationship in which the amorphous world of sense available to the pre-thetic consciousness is focused and given a sense (as meaning). Intentionality, in other words, is a way of knowing linked to the postulate of an ego.[26] But for Sartre intentionality strikes at the very core of human being. To be conscious of something means that consciousness is *not* that of which it is conscious; that it is not means that it is lacking in relation to an in-itself that *is*. This in-itself has being, while consciousness as intentionality is a nothingness that desires being.

The "consequences for images are immediately apparent," Sartre says: "An image, too, is an image *of* something" that it is not, a lack of presence. Imagination is thus radically different from "perception."[27] Following Sartre de Man also embarks on a "phenomenology of poetic language" as negativity—a phrase he later edits out of "The Intentional Structure."[28] For de Man too there is a radical difference between consciousness as *pour-soi* and the natural object as *en-soi,* wherein the latter as an object of "nostalgia" is also a temptation to "permanence" and "lethargy."[29] The natural object does not originate by imitation or desire; it is defined by its "identity," "safe in its immediate being" (RR: 4). The image by contrast is pure nothingness, "always constitutive, able to posit regardless of presence but . . . unable to give a foundation to what it posits except as an intent of consciousness" (RR: 6).[30] Language is a form of unhappy consciousness: "Critics who speak of a 'happy relationship' between matter and consciousness" forget that the constitution of this relationship in "language indicates that it does not exist in actuality" (RR: 8). This nonbeing (non-être) of language is what accounts for the "annihilating power" (l'action destructive) of thought (RR: 6, 8), which in turn makes the theory of consciousness the site of an ethics as well as an ontology. The "demands of consciousness" (RR: 8) require a constant vigilance against the bad faith that mistakes words for things; or as Derrida later says: "Writing is dangerous from the moment that representation there claims to be presence and the sign of the thing itself" (OGr: 144).

De Man grows critical of Sartre for abandoning the "theoretical poetics" of his early work for a positivist investment in "experience." Whereas Sartre had once insisted on the "radical distinction between perception and imagination," he later fails to separate "direct experience and the knowing of this experience." This is why de Man praises Heidegger for leading "the problem of history back" from "the naive forms it had taken in the interior of activisms and political determinisms" to "the ontological level."[31] But in fact de Man's work up to Blindness and Insight (1971) is a classic case of filtering Heidegger through the pre-Marxist Sartre, as described in Chapter 3. De Man turns to Heidegger to avoid Sartre's "unphilosophical undertaking" in What Is literature? yet finds in Heidegger the complacency that also disturbs Levinas. Analyzing the convergence of metaphors of building and vegetation, he sees Heidegger as succumbing to the "temptation to permanence,"[32] the phrase he later uses in "The Intentional Structure" to describe the natural object as in-itself (RR: 4, 6). As such Heidegger's thought involves a "beatitude that properly speaking is a lethargy."[33] Inasmuch as Dasein approximates the lethargy of being in-itself, the "demands of consciousness" require, in Sartre's words, a subject that is not what it is and is what it is not (BN: 28). Indeed, de Man's "vigilance" leads him to criticize the bad faith of Heidegger and Malraux in specifically Sartrean terms. The temptation to permanence consists in "the death of the mind," in refusing to think the negation and in assimilating it to death pure and simple, "in refusing the effort and the pain of interiorizing the exterior negation that is organic death."[34] For this reason, in leading the problem of literature back from an "empirical" to an "ontological" level in his own criticism, de Man adopts a Sartrean vocabulary that refuses the shelter of being: a vocabulary of "absence," "nonbeing," "nothingness," and the "void."[35]

De Man's early work suggests that the critique of representation, as a refusal of presence, largely precedes the advent of structuralism. Indeed, it takes place through a distinction between imagination and perception that derives from Sartre, not Saussure, albeit intensified by Blanchot. But this genealogy is by no means confined to de Man, who himself notes that a "grounding in phenomenology" was seminal for Foucault in The Order of Things.[36] Indeed, we also find in Of Grammatology a similar Sartrean vocabulary of "void," "emptiness," and the "abyss of representation" associated with the supplement as "lack" (OGr: 145, 163, 184). We find the same posing of "imagination" as "at bottom the relationship with death" against "the thing itself," "immediate presence," and "originary perception" (184, 157) and the same insistence on the radical division between imagination and perception (SP: 44). And we likewise find a deconstruction of representation that occurs as much at the site of the "image" as of the "sign" (OGr: 144–51, 182–87). This analysis is, moreover, mobilized by a Sartrean psychoanalytic that sees the "imaginary" (l'imaginaire) as a form of bad faith: hence the "danger" and "seducti[veness]" of the image (151), which takes the sign for the real, and hence also what Derrida calls auto-affection or what Sartre calls the "shut . . . consciousness" of the Imaginary.[37]

In the remainder of this chapter I begin by tracing the compatibility of phenomenology with deconstruction as a general style of thinking so as to suggest why it matters that we distinguish deconstruction from poststructuralism. Deconstruction is a transposition of phenomenological into linguistic models that retains the ontological concerns of the former. Those concerns derive not only from Heidegger but also from Sartre via Levinas and Blanchot. When Derrida speaks of language he speaks of death, as he repeatedly makes clear: "Death is the movement of difference to the extent that that movement is necessarily finite" (OGr: 143); and again death is the "master-name for the supplementary series" that keeps language in motion as a process of "metonymic substitutions" (183). Death here entails not just an ontology but an ethics that has to do with the "dispossession" we experience through language (166, 142). These ontological and ethical concerns are not ones admitted by structuralism. They are elided by poststructuralism[38] whether in the liberatory surpassing of "metaphysics" I discuss in the next chapter or in the ascetic, resistant forms more fully explored in this book. De Man's later work exemplifies the second case. When he writes that "death is a displaced name for a linguistic predicament" (RR: 81) he reverses Derrida; he affiliates himself with a poststructuralist refusal of interiority that, because of its own history, virtually solicits its own deconstruction.

To forget deconstruction's links to phenomenology is to disconnect it from this analytic of finitude at the core of its focus on language. This forgetting partly explains why the linguistic turn has been taken for a "critical aestheticism." Reading Derrida through his "American followers," William Spanos associates deconstruction, as well as structuralism and the New Criticism, with "spatial form" and with an "antitranscendental transcendental literary rhetoric:"

> Because of its commitment to the textuality of texts—the absolute absence of reference in the signifier, the deconstructive mode . . . transforms all texts into self-canceling, free-floating signifying systems that hover above time . . . into an undifferentiated global anti-Book . . . a universalist discourse in reverse.[39]

Spanos's comments do not fully do justice to Derrida. They do describe a tendency in certain forms of poststructuralism, though they neglect the pathos that often attends the loss of temporality. But to complicate things further, the meaning of the term *poststructuralism* has also changed since it first surfaced in the early seventies. While it once carried the taint of ultratextualism and a loss of agency, it has now become a general term for oppositional presentisms that reclaim precisely this rhetoric of agency. In this refashioning of poststructuralism, the neglect of a deconstruction linked to phenomenology has also played a crucial role.

Beyond Husserl: the French connections of phenomenology

Derrida, as I suggest in Chapter 4, plays a key role in turning phenomenology towards deconstruction. Indeed, he himself describes his work as "radicaliz[ing] phenomenology in order to go further even than the structuralist objection."[40] Yet curiously the proscription of phenomenology in the late sixties has much to with influential statements by Derrida. In "Semiology and Grammatology" (1968) he characterizes "phenomenological meaning" as disconnected from any materiality that cannot be contained within the "concept" (P: 22):

> Meaning is the phenomenality of the phenomenon. . . . This layer of pure meaning, or a pure signified, refers . . . to a layer of prelinguistic or presemiotic

(preexpressive, Husserl calls it) meaning whose presence would be conceivable outside and before the work of *différance*. . . . Such a meaning . . . given to consciousness in perceptive intuition—would not be, from the outset, in the position of a signifier. (30, 32)

As is well known, Derrida further associates phenomenology with voice as the pure interiority of consciousness and thus with a pneuma without psyche or a presence freed from the trace: "the voice is consciousness itself. When I speak, not only am I conscious of being present for what I think, but I am conscious also of keeping as close as possible to my thought, or the 'concept'" (22).

Derrida's view, however, rests on a "reduction" of phenomenology to Husserl that forgets its diversity as "the sum," in Ricoeur's words, both of "Husserl's work and of the heresies issuing from it."[41] To begin with Derrida neglects a difference that is seminal to his own work: between transcendental and existential phenomenology or, in Foucault's version, between "a philosophy of knowledge, of rationality and of concept" represented by Husserl and one of "experience, of sense and of subject" exemplified by Sartre and Merleau-Ponty.[42] Transcendental phenomenology, as Ricoeur says, "studies the conditions of the appearances of things to the structure of human subjectivity"; it is thus a form of neo-Kantianism that will prove curiously complicit with structuralism in the figural economy of the careers studied here. One need not be surprised, then, that in "Semiology and Grammatology" Derrida places this "phenomenology" in metonymic proximity to Saussurian linguistics. But, as Ricoeur says, the phenomenology "termed 'existential' . . . becomes a method and is placed in the service of a dominating problem-set, namely, the problems concerning existence" and the "investigation of the various aspects of man's insertion in the world." Derrida is not unaware of this difference (P: 32–34), already highlighted by Levinas in the thirties.[43]

Ricoeur's use of the term *method* in connection with existential phenomenology is significant in that it cuts through the conventional privileging of transcendental phenomenology on the grounds that the latter alone is sensitive to the rigor of method. By 1969 Foucault, for instance, has come to see existential phenomenology as a subjectivism and a positivism that avoids the rigor of method,[44] although earlier he had seen its emphasis on "actual experience" in more complex terms that are perhaps inflected by Georges Batailles notion of "inner experience."[45] Foucault's later dismissal of existential phenomenology rests on its conflation with "existentialism," which is not a phenomenology but an applied ethics or pragmatic anthropology. For this reason Jean Wahl prefers the term "philosophies of existence" to describe a range of anti-idealisms from Schelling to Levinas.[46] Method in these cases is precisely the condition of possibility for a disclosure of the idealism of method. Thus Levinas's work on Husserl criticizes transcendental phenomenology on the very grounds of "method." He complains that Husserl brackets ontology for epistemology when a method is always "deep[ly]" implicated in "an ontology."[47] Husserl's autonomization of method becomes the spur to an existential counter-method that criticizes the technical as self-certainty. Method is likewise the basis on which Jean Hyppolite's *Genesis and Structure in Hegel's Phenomenology of Spirit* (1946) shifts Hegel from the transcendental to the existential side. And both Levinas and Hyppolite were important early models for Derrida's own work in intellectual history up to *Speech and Phenomena*.

Derrida's dismissal of phenomenology as a philosophy of consciousness also rests on a second metonymic reduction that assumes the identity of consciousness with what he later calls "spirit." Yet as Sartre says, the "being of consciousness" is a "being such that in its being, its being is in question" (BN: 120). This nonbeing of consciousness has to do precisely with the term *presence,* which Sartre in the section of *Being and Nothingness* on "Presence to Self" foregrounds some twenty-five years before Derrida. As Christina Howells points out, "presence" for Sartre is "'a way of *not coinciding with oneself,* of escaping identity'. It is not *plenitude.*"[48] Presence "supposes that an impalpable fissure has slipped into being. If being is present to itself, it is because it is not wholly itself" (124). Moreover, Sartre rigorously refuses to positivize nonpresence or difference as the space between two terms that can be "apprehended in themselves and include as such elements of positivity" (125). If we ask

> *what it is* which separates the subject from himself, we are forced to admit that it is *nothing.* Ordinarily what separates is a distance in space, a lapse of time, a psychological difference, or simply the individuality of two co-presents—in short a *qualified* reality. . . . [But the] separation which separates [consciousness] from itself can not be grasped or even conceived in isolation. If we seek to reveal it, it vanishes. . . . The fisssure within consciousness is a nothing [that has] being only as we do not see it. (124–25)

Indeed, what Sartre describes here exceeds the opposition presence/absence and beckons towards a new vocabulary: Derrida's gram, in which nothing is "simply present or absent" because there are only "differences and traces of traces" (P: 26).

In short, Derrida's absorption of consciousness into the "series" spirit/mind/ego[49] neglects the care taken by French phenomenology to desynonymize these various terms. Sartre separates consciousness from being as well as from the "transcendental ego." Ricoeur distinguishes it from spirit in terms of phenomenology's already doubled genesis in Hegel and Husserl. "Spirit" names the being-in-itself that consciousness lacks; it "is not directed toward another who is lacking to it" but claims to be "entirely complete within itself." In effect Ricoeur uses the term *consciousness* to problematize the spirit that Derrida takes consciousness to be. Unlike spirit, "consciousness aims at another that it is not, another placed before it, outside it." To be sure, Husserl speaks of consciousness in the ways Derrida suggests. But, as Ricoeur argues, Husserl's is "a phenomenology of consciousness that is raised above itself into a phenomenology of mind," whereas Hegel's is a "phenomenology of spirit in the element of consciousness. . . . The theory of *Geist* continues to be a *phenomenological* description [emphasis mine] because spirit is identical to itself only in the final moment. . . . All the earlier developments . . . [are] only consciousness and not yet spirit."[50] Or as Ricoeur says elsewhere, Hegel (and here we could also read Sartre) introduced into the field of phenomenological analysis the "negative" experiences of disappearance, contradiction, struggle, and frustration that impart the tragic tone to his phenomenology. This tone is utterly foreign to Husserl's works.

Ricoeur's partition of consciousness from spirit, his reference to "the suppression of consciousness by spirit,"[51] obviously draws on the French Hegelians' shift of focus from the *Logic* to the *Phenomenology* and, within this shift, on the prominence given by the *Phenomenology's* translator Jean Hyppolite to the unhappy consciousness. And here it is important to distinguish Hyppolite's commentary on Hegel, *Genesis and Structure Of Hegel's Phenomenology of Spirit,* from Alexandre Kojève's lectures on the *Phenomenology,* given in the thirties but not published till 1947. Kojève was a Stalinist; Hyppolite, though always left-leaning, was more cautious in relating philosophy to politics—and much closer in this respect to Foucault, Derrida, and Lyotard. Kojève, despite his emphasis on man as a "negating-negativity," directs the negative outward as an aggressive "anthropogenetic" desire; he focuses on Hegel as a thinker of history and on, in particular, the Battle of Jena and the Napoleonic period as inaugurating the famous "end of history." Correspondingly, he emphasizes the master-slave relationship so as to recuperate negativity within an "anthropology."[52] As Judith Butler says, Kojève maintains a "dualistic ontology that severs human beings into natural and social dimensions;" on this basis he makes negation into "an action of human origin that is applied externally to the realm of the nonhuman" so as to transform the natural into the social.[53] In effect, Kojève follows the Kantian division of "pragmatic" from "physiological" anthropology that gave "anthropology" a bad name in French theory after the war. Physiological anthropology, according to Kant, is concerned with "what Nature makes of man," whereas pragmatic anthropology "aims at what man makes, can, or should make of himself as a freely acting being" or with man as "his own ultimate purpose." In this binary, the pragmatic as the basis of civil society is used to protect human freedom from the entire realm of what later came to be called the "unthought."[54]

Hyppolite also accepts the Hegelian formulation that "human beings are what they are not and are not what they are." But whereas Kojève "infers from this non-coincidence a dualistic world" in which negation is a creative power exerted by the free subject upon an external object, Hyppolite—and Sartre in *Being and Nothingness*—internalizes negation so as to establish "duality (inner-negation) as a monistic principle."[55] This radical difference between the two is evident in Hyppolite's emphasis on the unhappy consciousness rather than the master-slave relationship. It is also evident in the way the two thinkers position Hegel and philosophy. Kojève frames Hegel's career against the Battle of Jena. For him philosophy is the philosophy of history; in fact it *is* history, destiny. For Hyppolite, whether "Hegel was conscious of it or not" the *Phenomenology* conveyed "not a completed system but the history of [its] own philosophical development," its own autobiography in which the commentary on Hegel is also implicated within its "own philosophical journey,"[56] the work on Hegel being the unworking of both Hegel and his critics. Foucault will later refer to the seminality of this method for his own generation: "Instead of conceiving philosophy as a totality ultimately capable of dispersing and regrouping itself in the movement of the concept, Jean Hyppolite transformed it into an endless task, against the background of an infinite horizon, . . . uncertain, mobile all along its line of contact with non-philosophy" (AK: 236).

For Hyppolite, then, consciousness, and, indeed, the very cogito of philosophy, are imbued with nonpresence. "Consciousness," he writes, "is not a thing, a determinate Dasein; it is always beyond itself; it goes beyond, or transcends itself." And again: "Self-certainty cannot be in-itself without losing itself and becoming a thing. It is a perpetual transcendence toward a never given adequation with itself. Consciousness is never what it is."[57] To say that consciousness is nonidentical is perhaps nothing new; for instance Peter Dews, following Manfred Frank, has traced an intellectual history linking deconstruction and post-Kantian idealism in ways that arguably normalize the former.[58] But we could go further and argue that "consciousness" is the site at which French philosophy first encounters the (non)structures of aporia, supplementarity, chiasmic exchange, and *différance* later named within the field of writing. Foucault does, indeed, make this claim for the originality of Hyppolite as not simply conceptual but as having to do with his relation to writing. Foucault's words can be adapted to Sartre and "the alterations he worked, not within [phenomenology], but upon it, and upon philosophy" as previously conceived in its Husserlian separation from "non-philosophy" (AK: 236). For instance, although Sartre may not use the term *aporia,* the aporia is at the heart of his intellectual syntax. This syntax constantly puts its own statements under erasure in doubled, self-reversing formulations, such as the famous description of the *pour-soi* as "being what it is not and not being what it is" (BN: 28) or the vertiginous account of consciousness as a "reflection-reflecting" caught in a perpetual circle, "circuit," or *"dédoublement"* (214–15). Sartre's way of writing in *Being and Nothingness* makes it impossible for him to say anything without unsaying it. Again, although Sartre does not speak of a *supplement,* it is prefigured in the way he conceives the relation between the *pour-soi* and *en-soi,* which is unlike anything in Hegel. For it is not simply the case that nothingness "needs being" to posit itself as negation, whereas being is self-sufficing.[59] On the contrary, the for-itself is also the "nothingness whereby 'there is' being" (251). Or, as Sartre later puts it, lacking difference and distance, the in-itself as absolute identity cannot "found" itself or become "present" to itself; in "a project to found itself" it must therefore "g[i]ve itself the modification of the for-itself" (789–90), thus supplementing itself with its own supplement.[60]

Sartre likewise encounters, in the famous scene in the park in which he meets the Other, "a decentralization of the world which undermines the centralization" effected by the cogito (343). That he apprehends this "disintegration" or "original dispersion" (343, 215) phenomenologically as an ungraspable experience rather than as what de Man calls "a linguistic predicament" (RR: 81) does not mean that it is any less a "decentering" of the cogito (BN: 83) than the one effected by language. Indeed, the Sartrean consciousness has a profoundly linguistic structure as spacing and reference. The *pour-soi* is a "reference to itself" that can never escape "from the chains of this reference" to become a "*seen* reference" or a "reference which is what it is" (216). As "distance" and difference (125) the *pour-soi* has no referent and does not "refer us elsewhere to another being," but is "only a perpetual reference of self to self" (125–26). This latency of the linguistic as the basis for a deconstruction of self-consciousness and perception is disseminated throughout Sartre's text, even if he does not systematically thematize it.[61] There are, for instance, his discussions of perception as figure, which unravel the collusion of *Gestalt* psychology with structuralism (42, 466).[62] There are also his frequent accounts of consciousness as a "reflected-reflecting" that "refers to a reflecting without there being any object of which the reflection would be the reflection" (178–79)—accounts that rely for their unsettling of a classical reflectionism on aporias of grammar.[63] Sartre's brief but pregnant discussion of language as the discourse of the other,[64] which culminates a much more extensive discussion of the subject as a barred subject divided between the Symbolic and the Real, is equally important.[65] In short the transposition of phenomenological into linguistic insights in deconstruction occurs because in some sense the linguistic is already embedded in phenomenology.

Levinas's critique of phenomenology

Derrida's generation is not alone in ignoring the radicality of existential phenomenology. One of the major sources for his view is Levinas, who also defines "consciousness" as the suppression of alterity and "an adequation between thought and what it thinks."[66] Levinas associates phenomenology as a philosophy of consciousness with the twin motifs of light and intentionality. Although intentionality was to become a major locus for phenomenology's self-deconstruction in the work of Sartre, Levinas reads it strictly through Husserl.[67] Intentionality is "an animating act, which gives to the transcendent phenomena a transcendent meaning."[68] As "consciousness of" something, it is not, like Merleau-Ponty's "perception," a nonthetic connection in which the self is exscribed upon the world; it is rather a directed, focusing activity in which the predication of an object constitutes the subject. On this basis Levinas associates intentionality with the "sphere of intelligibility" and "vision:" "the structure of a *seeing* having the *seen* for its object" (TO: 97). Moreover, because an epistemology always conceals an ethics, intentionality as "aiming" is a "moment of egoism or egotism" (97–98): in "thought understood as vision, knowledge, and intentionality, intelligibility thus signifies the reduction of the other to the Same" (99).

Light, which Derrida evokes as "the *phenomenological* metaphor" (M: 131), is Levinas's figure for this clarity or phenomenality of cognition that he also associates as early as 1940 with "representation":

> Every intention is a self-evidence being sought, a light that tends to make itself known. To say that at the basis of every intention—even affective or relative intentions—representation is found, is to conceive the whole of mental life on

the model of light. . . . The theory of intentionality in Husserl, linked so closely to his theory of self-evidence . . . identifies mind with intellection, and intellection with light.

Light, intention, and representation form a matrix that allows Levinas to see phenomenology as blind to the unthought: "phenomenology describes [only] that which appears." While it may deal with states (*états d'âme*) such as fear and anguish that are nonpredicative or "without an object,"[69] a "descriptive phenomenology" always grasps them phenomenally in their coming to light rather than materially in their unintelligibility. And for Levinas phenomenology is always descriptive; as such, it "stages *personages*" and "presupposes an ego" (EE: 66). This process of hypostasis explains why light is also related to "property" and (self) possession. Light is "a condition for phenomena" and "makes objects into a world, that is, makes them belong to us. . . . Illuminated space all collects about a mind which possesses it. In this sense it is already like the product of a synthesis. Kant's space is essentially a lit up space: it is in all its dimensions accessible, explorable" (48).

Levinas's criticisms of Husserl in the thirties are undertaken from what he sees as a Heideggerian perspective. Yet in the forties he comes to see Heidegger too as a philosopher of light, opposing him to Blanchot as a figure for "night."[70] As Derrida later says, in spite of everything it leads us to "question, and to redistribute, [Heideggerian] *Dasein* still occupies a place analogous to that of the transcendental subject."[71] Inasmuch as Heidegger had provided Levinas with the means to criticize Husserl, the condensing of the two conveys Levinas's dismissal of the entire phenomenological tradition, both transcendental and existential. With this identification of the Germans Levinas claims to leave phenomenology behind, therein also modelling Derrida's exit from all Western philosophy, metonymically reduced to logocentrism and ontotheology. In Levinas's case this condensation of phenomenologies also takes the form of a placement of both "knowledge" and "experience" under the heading of "intention." Experience is "assimilable to a knowledge [*savoir*]" and is constructed through "protentions" and "retentions." Levinas's dismissal of experience—and his reading of this category through Husserl—is all the more significant, given that in 1929 it was experience that had allowed him to critique Husserl, by insisting on the reinsertion of the "phenomenon" into "consciousness" or "the individual and affective life of which [it] is the object."[72]

Notes

1   One notes the following titles: Josué V. Harari (ed.), *Textual Strategies: Perspectives in Post-Structuralist Criticism*, John Sturrock (ed.), *Structuralism and Since: From Lévi-Strauss to Derrida*; Christopher Norris, *Deconstruction*; Edith Kurzweil, *The Age of Structuralism: Lévi-Strauss to Foucault*; Robert Young (ed.), *Untying the Text: A Post-Structuralist Reader,* Jonathan Arac, Wlad Godzich, and Wallace Martin (eds.), *The Yale Critics: Deconstruction in America*; Vincent Leitch, *Deconstructive Criticism: An Advanced Introduction*; Stephen W. Melville, *Philosophy beside Itself: On Deconstruction and Modernism*; Peter Dews, *Logics of Disintegration: Post-Structuralist Thought and the Claims of Critical Theory*; and Richard Machin and Christopher Norris (eds.), *Post-Structuralist Readings of English Poetry*. See also Frank Lentricchia, *After the New Criticism,* 156–211, 282–317. In most of these studies, *deconstruction* and *poststructuralism* are not distinguished, although each term has different yet overlapping resonances. See Lentricchia, who discusses Derridean deconstruction in a chapter entitled "History or the Abyss: Post-structuralism" (157–77); Leitch, who frequently refers to the authors he treats in *Deconstructive Criticism* as poststructuralist (e.g. 102–3); and Donald Pease who uses both terms to describe Hillis Miller ("J. Hillis Miller: The Other Victorian at Yale," in *The Yale Critics,* 88). Young says that a "straightforward identification of deconstruction with poststructuralism" is simplistic, but then does not really distinguish them (15). I discuss later on Norris's distinction between the two terms—a shift from his initial identification of them in *Deconstruction*.

2   See Leitch, 73–85, 87–102, 105–15, 286.

3   See Harari who sees poststructuralism as continuing from structuralism and sees deconstruction as providing a set of tools for the former (445–46, 34–37).

4   De Man, *Allegories*, 17.

5   Habermas, *Modernity*, 185, 189, 190, 192, 199.

6   Kurzweil describes Kristeva, Derrida, Ricoeur, and Deleuze and Guattari as poststructuralists and notes that Althusser, Foucault, and Barthes all "reneged on their structuralisms" (9–10, 240–44). Dews's book on "poststructuralist thought" deals with Derrida, Lacan, Foucault, and Lyotard. Harari's collection of "poststructuralist perspectives" includes Foucault, Derrida, de Man, Deleuze, Eugenio Donato, Serres, Genette, and Barthes. Finally, Baudrillard and Lyotard are associated with poststructuralism by Pefanis (2, 50, 85, 147n13).

7   Thus Eagleton includes Derrida, Barthes, Foucault, Lacan, and Kristeva under the heading of poststructuralism, making a point of their different disciplinary orientations (134). He defines "deconstruction" as a more narrowly literary critical movement (145). Although he does not reduce Derrida to his American appropriation into literary criticism, Michael Ryan also sees deconstruction as narrower than the work it affected: the work of "such overtly politicized intellectuals as Julia Kristeva, Gilles Deleuze, and Michel Foucault" (103). Young associates deconstruction with "textual aestheticism" (19). Leitch also notes the view that deconstruction is confined to the literary sphere, using the term "poststructuralism" to refer to the "wider social and cultural contexts" taken up by Jameson, Said, and Foucault (142), although Leitch does not rigorously distinguish the two terms.

8   See Lentricchia, *After the New Criticism*, 157–77; Jonathan Culler, "Jacques Derrida," in *Structuralism*, ed. Sturrock, 55. Other deconstructive theorists are also loosely referred to as poststructuralist: for instance Hillis Miller (by Pease in *The Yale Critics*, 88) and Joseph Riddel (by Lentricchia, 159).

9   The inaugural status of this essay is evident in Lentricchia's discussion of Derrida (157–60). "Structure, Sign, and Play" was first delivered as a lecture at the international colloquium on "Critical Languages and the Sciences of Man" at Johns Hopkins in 1966, and published a year later in *L'Ecriture et la différance* (WD: 278–93). It is also the essay by which Derrida is often represented in anthologies of literary theory, which also represent de Man by "Semiology and Rhetoric" (e.g., Richter). Until the translation of *Of Grammatology* in 1976, Derrida's other translated work (except for "White Mythology"—1974) appeared in philosophical—specifically phenomenological—contexts: journals, collections, and the Northwestern series in Phenomenology and Existential Philosophy, which published SP (1973). In other words, in the world of "theory" Derrida until 1976 would have been known largely by "Structure, Sign, and Play" and perhaps by "The Ends of Man" (delivered as a lecture in New York in 1968). "Structure, Sign, and Play" would then have framed the reading of OGr as an overturning of structuralism that continued its focus on the sign, even though Derrida might have been known to a very small circle of philosophers as a late phenomenologist. (Indeed de Man, as we shall see, sees the importance of OGr as lying in its discussion of Rousseau rather than of Saussure).

10   For the former see Lentricchia, *After the New Criticism*, 163; for the latter see Leitch, 102–13, 198–204.

11   Frank, *What Is Neostructuralism?*; Harland, *Superstructuralism*. "Ultrastructuralism" is used by Dosse (11.17).

12   See Gasché, who polemically argues that "deconstructive criticism" has "little in common" with Derrida's thought and originates "in New Criticism; it is a continuation of this American-bred literary scholarship" (*Tain*, 3).

13   This transference to literary studies is inaugurated by de Man in "Criticism and Crisis," first published in 1967 and reprinted as the opening essay of *Blindness and Insight* (1971). De Man specifically evokes the crisis I take up later in this chapter, a crisis provoked by the rise of the social sciences and Lévi-Straussian structuralism in the French university system but going back three decades to Husserl's *Crisis*. But, importantly, he reframes the crisis of philosophy as one that is resolved by literature: not literature in a Blanchotian sense but the implementation of this philosophical category in literary *criticism* (14–19). Although de Man later reextends his focus on literature to larger epistemological, historiographical, and ontological questions—as when he invokes the division into the trivium and quadrivium in the opening chapter of *Allegories* and more extensively in *Aesthetic Ideology*—at this point he insists on his credentials as a literary critic: "My interest in criticism is subordinate to my interest in primary literary texts" (viii).

14   Derrida, *Points*, 79.

15   On the importance of literature to the early Baudrillard see Genosko, xi.

16   Dosse notes its American origins (11.17); Žižek describes it as an "Anglo-Saxon and German invention" in *Looking Awry* (142). Frank coins the related term "neostructuralism," which is equated with poststructuralism on the back cover of the translation of *What Is Neostructuralism?* which deals

among others with Derrida, Foucault, Lacan, and Deleuze and Guattari. Habermas also uses the term *poststructuralism* in 1985, although only once (*Modernity,* 106).

17   Stanley Corngold, "Error in Paul de Man," in *The Yale Critics,* 92.

18   One of the earliest translations of Baudrillard is *Simulations* (1983), which begins with an essay from *Simulacra and Simulation* (1981), *followed* by the second chapter of the earlier *Symbolic Exchange and Death* (1976). The translation provides no bibliographical information, thus leading us to assume that texts arguably drawn from different stages of Baudrillard's work are part of a single text. The effect is to fold what I shall argue is the deconstructive Baudrillard into the bitterly poststructuralist Baudrillard. *Simulations,* which was preceded by English translations of *The Mirror of Production* (1973) in 1975 and *For a Critique of the Political Economy of the Sign* (1972) in 1981, was followed by translations of *In the Shadow of the Silent Majorities* (1978), also in 1983, *Forget Foucault* (1977) in 1987, *America* (1986) and *The Ecstasy of Communication* (1987) in 1988, *Seduction* (1979), and *Fatal Strategies* (1983) in 1990. It is only very recently that Baudrillard's earliest work has been made available to an English-speaking public, with the translation of *Symbolic Exchange and Death* (1976) in 1993, of *The System of Objects* (1968) in 1996, and of *The Consumer Society* (1970) in 1998.

19   Levinas, *Humanisme de l'autre homme.* My use of the phrase is suggestive because deconstruction as defined in this study is more concerned with the ontic than Levinas himself is (TO: 39)—a concern that reflects its crossing of Sartre with Heidegger.

20   I do not deal with de Man extensively in this book, partly because my focus is on French theory and partly because I have discussed his position between phenomenology and poststructuralism elsewhere (see n. 24). Nevertheless as a migrant European intellectual, de Man cannot entirely be fitted into his American identity as a literary critic, which he initially emphasized (see n. 13), but later resisted once he had attained the security of being a public intellectual figure. De Man has a borderline status as an American and European figure. Whereas Miller and Hartman are literary critics, de Man really is a philosopher—of language—which is why I discuss him at various points in this study.

21   Norris, *Deconstruction;* Waters, "Introduction: Paul de Man: Life and Works" (de Man, *Critical Writings,* lii–liii).

22   De Man, *Critical Writings,* 214–17.

23   De Man, *Blindness and Insight,* 276.

24   Rajan, "The Erasure of Narrative in Post-Structuralist Representations of Wordsworth," 350–70; "Displacing Post-Structuralism," 451–74. De Man's translation of Harold Bloom's psychological terminology into rhetorical terms as a way or making manifest what he sees as latent in Bloom's work is revealingly autobiographical in this respect (*Blindness and Insight,* 267–76).

25   De Man, *Critical Writings,* 34–39; *Blindness and Insight,* 250–55.

26   Levinas, *Theory of Intuition,* 41, 43, 39, 50–51.

27   Sartre, *Imagination,* 133–34. See also *The Psychology of Imagination,* which opens with a section entitled "The Intentional Structure of the Image" and posits an absolute division between imagination and perception, 153–56.

28   De Man, "Structure intentionelle de l'image romantique," 69 (trans. mine). Other changes that de Man makes in translating this article for inclusion in Harold Bloom's *Romanticism and Consciousness* and then *The Rhetoric of Romanticism* include the excision of the terms "existential" (71; RR: 4) and, at five places, "being" (72–73; RR: 5–6).

29   De Man, *Critical Writings,* 38–39.

30   Derrida uses almost the same language seven years later: "Imagination alone has the power of *giving birth to itself.* It creates nothing because it is imagination. But it receives nothing that is alien or anterior to it. It is not affected by the 'real'" (OGr: 186). Compare Sartre's notion of the image as doubly negative: first because it "freely" posits by negating the real, but second because it is thereby nothing and is "deprived of the category of the real" (*Psychology,* 229, 238–39).

31   De Man, *Critical Writings,* 104, 155, 34.

32   Ibid., 105, 32.

33   Ibid., 39.

34   Ibid., 39, 32–33.

35   De Man, *Blindness and Insight,* 50, 18–19, 69, 127, 207.

36   Ibid., 17, 71, 49.

37   Sartre, *Psychology,* 215. It is important to recognize that bad faith for Sartre does not imply the possibility of good faith; good faith is, if anything, even more profoundly in bad faith than bad faith itself.

38   Even if the word *poststructuralism* is not actually used by French theorists, Foucault does locate himself as not being a structuralist, as do even early French commentators on his work (e.g. Piaget, 108–15). Derrida places himself in a phenomenological context in his discussion of Rousseau, which makes

considerable use of the perception/imagination distinction, but OGr also places itself after Saussure and Lévi-Strauss. And in *Allegories of Reading,* de Man positions himself against formalism and speech-act theory, not phenomenology.

39   Spanos, *Heidegger and Criticism,* 43, 87, 97–100; see also 30–33, and more generally 84–131. While sympathizing with Spanos's attempt to establish a position outside poststructuralism (which he too equates with deconstruction), I would disagree with his absolute dismissal of Derrida and de Man, and his sense—on which he wavers (6)—that Heidegger provides an adequate basis for thinking the limitations of a postmodernism and technology deeply implicated in capitalism. Moreover, Spanos's "destruction" is more transformative than the deconstruction I analyze here; indeed this need for a transformative critique is very much a product of the American academy. Curiously, Heidegger appeals to Spanos for precisely the reasons that affirmative poststructuralisms remain popular on this side of the Atlantic: Heidegger is more amenable than Derrida to the "radical, emancipatory task of contemporary oppositional intellectuals" (82)—a point we can see if we contrast the affirmative Kojèvian tone of Heidegger's 1966 essay "The End of Philosophy and the Task of Thinking" (in *Basic Writings*) to the greater caution of "The Ends of Man" (1968). Destruction is aimed only against the past and the forgetting it has gone through and does not deconstruct its own amnesias. In this sense Heidegger's phenomenology—if it can be called that—is radically different from French phenomenology.

40   Interview with Vincent Descombes, quoted by Dosse (11.19). Dosse nevertheless presents Derrida as a poststructuralist who adopted the strategy of deconstruction (11.17–27).

41   Ricoeur, *Husserl,* 4.

42   Foucault, "Introduction" to Canguilhem, *Normal,* 8–9.

43   Ricoeur, *Husserl,* 203; Levinas, *Discovering Existence,* 39.

44   Canguilhem, *Normal,* 8–9.

45   Thus in OT, in the section on "Man and His Doubles," Foucault notes that "the analysis of actual experience is a discourse of mixed nature." On the one hand, the belief that one can grasp experience leads to a certain positivism in which "the empirical, in man, [is made to] stand for the transcendental." On the other hand, this empiricism is "simultaneously promising and threatening." For the "phenomenological project continually resolves itself, before our eyes, into a description-empirical despite itself-of actual experience," wherein empiricism as an anti-idealism doubles back on itself so as to interrupt the positivity of a naive (or undoubled) empiricism (321, 328). In *Inner Experience,* published in 1943 and then expanded in 1954, Bataille similarly tries to reconceptualize the term *experience* by thinking it in terms of a transgression of the bounded ego. Inner experience is paradoxically the same as the "absolute exteriority" or "thought from the outside" that Foucault associates with Blanchot in his 1966 monograph, in which be picks up Levinas's phrase to describe Blanchot (*Proper Names,* 133).

46   Wahl, *Philosophies of Existence.* Wahl notes considerable "diversities" an indeed "grave conflicts" among these philosophies. Heidegger and Jaspers refuse the designation "existentialist," while Sartre, Merleau-Ponty, and Marcel accept it (3–4). Heidegger, for his part, is concerned with existence only insofar as it illuminates "being" (3–4). The common denominator for all these thinkers is an "empiricism" that relates to "the element[s] of *facticity*" and affectivity, and that goes back to Schelling (7, 29), as well as "an intimate union of the existential and the ontological" (45). Wahl includes Levinas among the group (103), while Levinas himself speaks of his debt to Wahl (*Éthique:* 47).

47   Levinas, *Theory of Intuition,* liv, 124.

48   Howells, "Sartre and Derrida: Qui perd gagne," 148. See also my roughly contemporaneous appendix on Sartre, Derrida, and de Man in *Dark Interpreter,* 267–71. Howells is virtually the only commentator to have emphasized Sartre's importance for Derrida in the face of the latter's dismissals of him; see also her "Derrida and Sartre: Hegel's Death Knell" (169–81), and her recent *Derrida* (27–28, 86–94).

49   Derrida, *Of Spirit,* 18.

50   Ricoeur, "Hegel and Husserl," 229–31.

51   Ricoeur, *Husserl,* 206; "Hegel and Husserl," 228.

52   Kojève, 6, 39, 41–44, 158–61. Thus for Kojève "the Negativity which *is* Man" is the "Action of Fighting and Work by which Man preserves himself in spatial being while *destroying it*" (5, 155).

53   Butler, *Subjects of Desire,* 92.

54   Kant, *Anthropology,* 3. Kant relegates to the realm of the physiological anything that is in excess of man's free cognition of himself: in other words, the entire realm of the "unthought" that is the object of the phenomenology discussed here and by which Kant himself remains fascinated even as he tries to keep it outside the bounded ego of pragmatic anthropology.

55   Butler, *Subjects of Desire,* 93. Hyppolite himself identifies Sartre with Kojève. But although the Kojèvian influence on Sartre is conspicuous in *The Psychology of Imagination* and returns in *Critique of*

Dialectical Reason, I would argue that BN is closer to the work of Hyppolite, providing a psychoanalysis of its own troping of desire and negation into forms of mastery. It is significant that Kojève describes his work as a "phenomenological *anthropology*" (39), whereas Sartre subtitles BN *A Phenomenological Essay on Ontology.* As I argue in the next chapter, BN contains an anthropology, but inscribed as a figure within an excessive, unreadable ontology.

56   Hyppolite, *Genesis,* 52.

57   Ibid., 16, 203; see more generally 56, 62, 190–215. I have not included in this brief genealogy Wahl's *Le Malheur de la conscience dans la philosophie de Hegel.* Although Wahl foregrounds the unhappy consciousness well before Hyppolite does, his religious perspective leads him to make it the mere "darkened image of happy consciousness" and thus to positivize negativity (147–48).

58   Dews, 19–31. Dews also points to the importance of Merleau-Ponty, particularly for Lyotard (31–44). Frank, *Neostructuralism,* 87–101.

59   Descombes, 48–50. Descombes does go on to make the point I make here (51), but in so doing locates a philosophical inconsistency in BN which I see as strategic.

60   LaCapra is one of the few commentators to note the functioning of a certain supplementary in Sartre's thought, although typically he dismisses Sartre's writing as "the scene of relatively blind internal contestation." Nevertheless LaCapra is unusual in at least relating Sartre to contemporary French theory, albeit only as a "foil" and antithetical stimulus for it (25, 221–22, 42).

61   I obviously disagree with the common view that Sartre neglected language or spoke of it only in the most simplified and unreflexive fashion; see for example La Capra, 25–26; Lacan, *Speech and Language in Psychoanalysis,* 300–301. It is not clear whether Sartre had read Saussure or Lacan. However, his comments on the term *language* as not being restricted to the "articulated word" and extending to semiotic phenomena generally (BN: 486) and his extensive discussions of "reflection" in ways that imbue the philosophical concept with the figurality of the mirror place Sartre in the same intellectual ambience as Saussure and Lacan, perhaps in advance of the latter, who by 1943 had published only his short essay on the mirror stage.

62   Sartre's use of the terms *figure* and *ground* will be discussed in Chapter 3. While these terms, drawn from *Gestalt* psychology, could be seen as part of a phenomenological debate about "perception," as Piaget points out *Gestalt* psychology, which initially developed in the ambience of phenomenology, was subsumed into structuralism as part of its "positive" or constructionist side, as distinct from the "negative" side taken over by Foucault and others who accept the structurality of structure and the death of the subject (114–15, 46–52). Inasmuch as structuralism absorbs *Gestalt* theories of perception into its linguistic model, Sartre, one could argue, redeploys a linguistic sense of figure as constructed in order to deconstruct the hypostasis effected by perception (in Levinas's terms) in ways that contribute to de Man's notion of deconstruction as a "disfiguration." Sartre, moreover, sees perception and language as analogous and speaks of their collusion in the process of hypostasis (BN: 410).

63   Ideally, Sartre writes, reflection would be "pure reflection" or "the simple presence of the reflective for-itself to the for-itself reflected-on" (BN: 218). Reflection as "simultaneously an objectivation and an interiorization" (216) would then be a dialectic that allows self-consciousness to be self-constituting: "By reflection the for-itself, which has lost itself outside itself, attempts to put itself inside its own being" (216). However, as Sartre describes it, reflection is the permanent disintegration of such identity (217; cf. also 122, 126).

64   Sartre writes: "Language by revealing to us abstractly the principal structures of our body-for-others (even though the existed body is ineffable) impels us to place our alleged mission wholly in the hands of the Other" (BN: 463). Later he continues: "Language is not a phenomenon added onto being-for-others; It *is* originally being-for-others" (485).

65   The terms are Lacan's, but Sartre's work is, I would argue, the switch-point that makes it possible for Lacan to develop the concept of the Real through a deconstruction of Husserl's theory of intuition. Sartre's extensive exploration (in the section on "The Body") of how the body is not directly known but is known only as it is named by the "language" and "concepts" of the other (BN: 463–65) prefigures Lacan's understanding of the Symbolic as an order constituted by the bar s/S. Sartre does nevertheless preserve a place for intuition, and also for a Real that exceeds language and is absolutely inaccessible to language, but that conveys our irreducibility to discourse. Intuition is what gives us noncognitive access to "the existed body," the body as "non-thetically existed" (465, 468). The usefulness of intuition, given the remoteness of Sartre's use of the term from its origin in Husserl, is that this body, which can only be "alienated" through language and can only be known as other, is nevertheless "present to intuition" (567), but as materiality rather than phenomenality: "the *body which is suffered* serves as a nucleus, as matter for the alienating means which surpass it" (465). This is not the place for an extensive tracing of Sartre's influence on Lacan. But if Sartre's account of intuition versus

knowledge through language and concepts lays the basis for Lacan's distinction between the Real and the Symbolic, Sartre's account of the Imaginary in *The Psychology of Imagination* is arguably also important for Lacan.

66   Levinas, *Éthique*, 52, 58.

67   Only at two points does Levinas concede the radical potential of intentionality. In *God, Death* he writes: "Phenomenology seems to make possible the thinking of nothingness (*le néant*) thanks to the idea of intentionality as an access to something other than oneself, and an access that can be had in a non-theoretical manner (thus, in sentiments, actions, etc., which are irreducible to serene representation). . . . Anxiety, which has no object, has the non-object as its object: nothingness" (68–69). In *Éthique* he speaks of a "non-theoretical intentionality" and thus of a "Husserlian possibility which can be developed beyond what Husserl himself has said on the ethical problem and on the relation with the other which for him remains representational (even though Merleau-Ponty has tried to interpret it otherwise)" (22–23).

68   Levinas, *Theory of Intuition*, 39.

69   Levinas, *Discovering Existence*, 61; *Éthique*, 79, 31.

70   Levinas, *Theory of Intuition*, 154–55; *Éthique*, 29–30. Levinas's first criticisms of *Heidegger* as well as Husserl can be found in TO: 40–48. See also *Éthique* (31–33). *God, Death* (31–55), and *Proper Names* (127–39). Although Levinas rarely speaks of Heidegger's politics, they are undoubtedly at issue in his reassessment of Heidegger, although in the subtle ways analyzed by Bourdieu, who sees politics as embedded in ontology and linguistics in *The Political Ontology of Martin Heidegger.*

71   Derrida, *Points*, 273.

72   Levinas, *God, Death*, 19; *Discovering Existence*, 33.

Chapter 12

A.T. Nuyen

LEVINAS AND LAOZI ON THE DECONSTRUCTION OF ETHICS

Anh Tuan Nuyen, a professor in the Department of Philosophy at the National University of Singapore, brings together an ancient Chinese philosopher—Laozi (?604–?531 BC)—with a contemporary Western philosopher—Emmanuel Levinas (1905–95)—through the lens of Derridean deconstruction, revealing striking parallels in their conception of ethics. Laozi (a name which means "Old Master") is commonly thought to have written the *Daode jing*, the essence of Taoist thought and belief, although scholars have traced the text back to more ancient oral cultures. The *Daode jing* is a deep book of wisdom concerning the "way" (the "dao"), or the unnameable "rule of life" which transcends the ephemeral or transient aspects of the world. Nuyen argues that both Laozi and Levinas "speak of ethics deconstructively". To explain this, Nuyen first gives an overview of deconstruction, focusing on Derrida's idea of *différance*, a neologism (new word) coined by Derrida to express the way in which meaning is structured via differential networks that are productive yet also subject to undecidability, i.e., they cannot be anchored or pinned down by a self-present value or transcendental signified. Nuyen observes that Derrida, in his critique of metaphysics, sought the "other of language", that is to say, an unnamable and undecidable other (not a transcendental signified, such as Rationality or God) which always disrupts human systems of ethical thought. For Nuyen, Laozi and Levinas share an analogous notion of an other which undermines ethical laws and closed systems of being. Quoting the first two lines of the *Daode jing*, Nuyen rejects the notion that its paradoxical wording expresses a negative theology or ethics, rather, these lines speak with a deconstructive "middle voice", one of force, power and a totally different conception of virtue (or *de*). In Levinas's terms, this other voice of *de* (one which does not use words or language) is the absolutely foreign other which disrupts and facilitates my coming to understand my self. The *de* is thus not foundational, in the sense of being a rule, but it is primordial, in the sense of being active as a force prior to the engagement of rule-bound systems. Being open to the other, being engaged in an ethics that accepts the deconstructive force of the "foreigner" to oneself, leads not to self-destruction but to self-constitution (or subject formation) in an ethical sense. For Levinas, this openness to the other is self-confirming, just as the wise person in the *Daode jing* puts himself last, yet is thereby affirmed and preserved (he comes out first). While Nuyen is careful to acknowledge and map some of the differences between Laozi and Levinas, he argues that they share a "non-foundationalist ethics" even if Levinas's thought is ultimately humanist, whereas Laozi's is not. Nuyen suggests that some of the differences are interpretive, and that looked at deconstructively, these two thinkers are closer together than may be at first apparent, such as Laozi's notion of passivity being paralleled with Levinas's "disinterested" behaviour, where both positively cast aside personal desires or interests. Such an observation has bigger implications in that criticism of the apparent passivity of the *Daode jing* needs to be reassessed in the light of the attainments for self and others in a deconstructive notion of ethics.

T HE AIM OF THIS CHAPTER is to argue that we can understand the *Daodejing* better if we understand it as a deconstruction of ethics similar to Levinas's attempt to pull the metaphysical rug of Being from underneath ethics. The idea that Daoist philosophy is deconstructive is not new. Indeed, many commentators have argued that it bears comparison with Derrida's deconstruction in the main aspects of both (Yeh, 1983; Cheng, 1990; Chien, 1990; Ownes, 1993; Nuyen, 1995). However, these efforts tend to focus on the metaphysical issues, hence on Chuangzi, leaving the ethics of Daoism, and the ethics of the *Daodejing* in particular, unexplored. I shall argue in this chapter that the "deconstructive way," as one commentator has put it (Yeh, 1983), is seen most clearly if we focus on the ethical issues. With this in mind, it is more productive to read the *Daodejing* through the lens of Levinas rather than Derrida. It is not my intention to make a direct comparison of Levinas and Laozi, reading one as the other, nor to show that Levinas's philosophy can be construed as Daoist, nor that Daoist philosophy is Levinasian. There are sufficient profound dissimilarities between Levinas and Laozi, and between Levinas's ethics and the ethics of the *Daodejing,* to discourage such efforts. Rather, I aim to show that in both Levinas and Laozi, there is an ethics that is deconstructive, or more precisely, that both speak of ethics deconstructively. In Section I, I shall explain what it means to "speak of ethics deconstructively." In Section II, I shall show how both Levinas and Laozi do so. Specifically, I want to show that, in the *Daodejing, de* stands to *dao* as Levinas's ethic of responsibility stands to the otherwise of Being, to the *saying* from beyond essence.

I

Deconstruction is many things to many people. To one commentator, at one extreme, it is an "oxymoronic blend of prolixity, turgidity, and lightness . . .," it has "uncouth density" and consists of "sterile stratagems" (Verges, 1992, 386, 390). To some literary critics, who stand at one other extreme, it is a way of reading texts that is imaginative, innovative, and liberating, a way of reading that is not dictated by the presumption of a true, or correct, meaning that each text must have. To the former, deconstruction is not just destruction but total annihilation, annihilation of meaning, truth, value, and so of ethics as well. If such critics were right, a deconstructive ethics, Levinasian or otherwise, would indeed be oxymoronic. I have elsewhere (Nuyen, 1993) argued against this extreme view of deconstruction, and I will simply assume here that it is mistaken. I shall also ignore the views of deconstructionist literary critics, as they are not particularly relevant to the task at hand. What, then, is deconstruction?

I shall use the term "deconstruction" to refer to a group of interrelated ideas made well known by Derrida. On the negative side is Derrida's rejection of the idea that the meaning of a term is dictated by the one who utters it, and that of a text by the one who authors it, an idea that led Plato to privilege speech over writing, a tendency that Derrida calls "phonocentrism." Generalizing from this, Derrida claims that traditional philosophy is structuralist in nature, in that it always presupposes a structure that requires to be present in its center something – God, rationality, substance, ideology, etc. – that guarantees meaning, truth, and value. Derrida refers to this idea as the "metaphysics of presence." From the philosophical point of view, it is rationality that is typically present in the center of a philosophical structure, a view that Derrida calls "logocentrism." A concerted attack on the metaphysics of presence and logocentrism can be found in Derrida's earlier works, particularly *Speech and Phenomena* (Derrida, 1973), *Of Grammatology* (Derrida, 1976) and *Writing and Difference* (Derrida, 1978a). But this attack cannot be taken in isolation from other key, positive, ideas in Derrida's deconstructive package. Indeed, taken in isolation, it has resulted in a version of deconstruction derided by Derrida's detractors and uncritically embraced by many of his followers. One such key idea is *différance*. What is often not noticed by Derrida's detractors and uncritical followers is that Derrida accepts that there are such things as meanings, truth, and values. What makes Derrida different from traditional philosophers is that he takes a deconstructive view of meanings, truth, and values, taking them to be the outcomes of *différance*.

What, then, is *différance*? It is a neologism constructed by Derrida from the ordinary French word *différence*. It is not an easy thing to explain what it is, and to make matters worse, Derrida insists that *différance* "is neither a *word* not a *concept*" (Derrida, 1973, 130). The idea of *différance* – "neither a word nor a concept" but at least an idea – is inspired by the work of the Swiss linguist Ferdinand de Saussure. For Saussure, the meaning of a word (e.g. "dog") is not determined by any extra-linguistic entity (e.g. the animal dog) but by the differences between that word and other words close to it in terms of the sound images (e.g. the sounds of "fog," "log", etc.) and in terms of the mental images signified by them (e.g. the mental images of a cat, a wolf, a fox, etc.). Indeed, Derrida borrows from Saussure the words "signifier" and "signified" (used by Saussure to refer respectively to the sound image and the mental image of a word). In Derrida's hands, the "signifiers" are the words themselves and the "signifieds" are the extra-linguistic entities whose presence (or presence in the intention of the speaker) is supposed for the determination of meanings (together with the metaphysical presence of the speaker). Inspired by Saussure, Derrida insists that meanings are determined by the signifiers themselves, by the words of the text: "There is nothing outside the text" (Derrida, 1976, 158). They are determined by the "play of differences" in the words themselves, in the way they signify, and in the way we use them for our own purposes, whatever they may be. The play of differences, in turn, is made possible by the fact that part of the meaning of a word is the very thing, or things, that the word excludes, for example, the "day" that "night" excludes, the "oak tree" that the "acorn" excludes. Very often, what is excluded is merely deferred, like the day that is deferred from what now is the night, the oak tree that is deferred from the present acorn. "*Différance*" is meant, partly, to capture the idea that there are both differing and deferring in language. It is the differings and deferrings of language that produce meanings, truths and values: *différance* "could be said to designate the productive and primordial constituting causality, the process of scission and division whose differings and differences would be the constituted products or effects" (Derrida, 1973, 137). What is deferred, or excluded, can be called upon to undermine the unity of meaning, to blur the sharp line that divides the two terms of a binary opposition, thus leading to a multiplicity of meanings. For many literary critics, this constitutes deconstructive reading.

However, this is not all there is to deconstruction. It is important to stress at this point – and this is something that commentators often overlook – that "there is nothing outside the text" only as far as meanings are concerned. This notorious statement is neither an endorsement of anti-realism nor a confirmation of idealism. Indeed, Derrida insists that a text, or language generally, must have an "other" outside of it:

> I never cease to be surprised by critics who see my work as a declaration that there is nothing beyond language, that we are imprisoned in language; it is in fact saying the exact opposite. The critique of logocentrism is above all else the search for the "other," and the "other of language."
>
> (Kearney, 1984, 123)

More importantly, this "other" leaves a "trace" within the text, inhabiting in the in-between of words and concepts, and of the binary oppositions of words and concepts. It is an absent remainder of, or an "undecidable" within, language. It is as silent as the ending "-*ance*" in *différance*. As such, it often plays a subversive function, disrupting the signification process and undermining the authority of the speaker. This "other" can only be hinted at in language. Yet, precisely because it can be hinted at, the hinting itself can serve to disrupt the semantic, the declarative, and the axiomatic functions of language, in just the same way as does the "deferred," the textual "other," as we saw above. This "metaphysical other" can also serve to *deconstruct* claims of meanings, truth, and values.

The deconstruction of claims of meanings and truth has been widely practiced and is thus quite well known, but that of values, particularly ethical values, is less so. Yet it is precisely traditional ethical theories that are ripe for deconstruction. Like the rest of traditional philosophy, traditional ethical theories are constructed each as a structure with a center, in which resides a value-dispensing entity, such as a God in Christian ethics, a rational being in Kantian ethics, an ideal observer in consequentialism, and so on. To use another metaphor, a traditional ethical theory is typically constructed on a foundation. For Cartesians, the roots of any ethical foundation will have to go all the way down to the first philosophy that bears the name of the thinking being, the *res cogitans*. To be sure, the entity at the center, or the center of the foundation, of a traditional moral theory – God, the noumenal self, the ideal observer – is typically characterized as an "other" to the moral agent. But this "other" is quite unlike the Derridean "other." This "other" is not a "trace" that is undecidable, that inhabits the in-between, that "remains undecided between the active and the passive [and] recalling something like a middle voice" (Derrida, 1982, 9). Instead, this "other" is typically fully conceptualized, fully articulated either as an active or a passive, even when it is characterized as the Infinite, or the Transcendental, or the Ideal. As we shall see, what both Laozi and Levinas have done is on the one hand to reject the idea that we can conceptualize, or characterize, or speak of, or name, the "other," and on the other hand to show that this non-conceptualizable, this unnamable "other" disrupts and undermines our ethical theorizing. To do this is precisely to deconstruct, in the Derridean sense, the ethical claims of traditional theories. This is the sense in which Laozi and Levinas are said to speak deconstructively of ethics.

More particularly, I am suggesting that both Laozi and Levinas gesture at an other that deconstructs ethical claims and judgments made on the basis of ethical principles, or moral laws, posited in traditional moral theories. Before elaborating on this claim, it is important to stress that I am not suggesting that there is no difference between Derrida's talk of the other and Levinas's. It is beyond the scope of this chapter to compare and contrast Derrida's other with Levinas's. Suffice it to point out that (1) Derrida draws some differences between himself and Levinas on the notion of the other (Derrida, 1978a) and (2) Levinas has a more complex notion of the other, speaking of, as we shall see, both the other (*l'autre*) and the Other (*l'Autrui*). My purpose in invoking Derrida here is to explain the sense of "speaking deconstructively." To repeat, I use this phrase to refer to the strategy of invoking some undecidable element that is both outside a particular structure of thought and apt to disrupt this structure. I will call any element that plays this deconstructive role a "Derridean other" without suggesting that it *is* Derrida's other (hence "Derridean" rather than "Derrida's"). Thus, insofar as Levinas, or Laozi, speaks of an element that plays a deconstructive role, Levinas, or Laozi, speaks of a Derridean other. For my purpose, the similarity between Derrida and Levinas does not go beyond the deconstructive force of something outside the text, something otherwise than being. Thus there is no suggestion that since Levinas deconstructs traditional ethical theories and makes his ethics of responsibility "first philosophy," Derrida must likewise be said to have in mind some kind of ethics as first philosophy, even though there is certainly an ethical side to his deconstruction.

Returning to my claim above, there is ample textual evidence to support it. In the case of Laozi, the evidence lies in the very first two lines of the *Daodejing*: "The [D]ao that can be told of is not the eternal [D]ao; The name that can be named is not the eternal name" (Chan, 1963, 139). With these two lines, the *Daodejing* begins with a paradox: It discusses that which cannot be told of and named. We can, of course, interpret the first two lines in such a way as to dissolve the paradox. We can, for instance, read them as saying that the *dao* is a negativity, a non-being, as opposed to the positive being that originates from it, and as such the *dao* cannot be told of, or named, in the way that anything with a positive being can be told of or named. Read this way, the *dao* does not "remain(s) undecided between the active and the passive," to use Derrida's words cited above. It is not a Derridean "other." I have elsewhere argued that this reading is mistaken (Nuyen, 1995). The main point of my claim is that reading the first two lines of the *Daodejing* this way is to miss the fundamental point that the *dao* is truly *unnamable,* not even as the "nameless," which is a name. The *dao* of Laozi is not the negative non-being in the simple sense of the opposite of the positive being. In various chapters of the *Daodejing* (e.g. chs. 25 and 42), we are told that the *dao* is beyond and prior to the positive *yang* and the negative *yin,* before heaven and earth, truly "undecided between the active and the passive." Yet the *dao* speaks, albeit with an indeterminable "middle voice" (to use another Derridean phrase). As I shall argue, it speaks through the *de,* making *de* not just a virtuous way but also a power, or a potency, to disrupt and to undermine our traditional ways of seeing our ethical relationships with others. This is the sense in which Laozi speaks deconstructively of ethics. This is the sense in which the ethical message in the *Daodejing* is a deconstructive one. I shall look more closely at that message in Section II.

Turning now to Levinas, textual evidence that justifies my reading is not hard to find. It can be seen even in the title of one of Levinas's books: *Otherwise than Being or Beyond Essence.* This title speaks of an "other" that is other than the active and the passive, other than Being and hence also non-Being, "other otherwise," as Levinas puts it. For Levinas, this "other," *l'autre,* is that which makes the person that I encounter a truly Other, *l'Autrui,* beyond my thematization and conceptualization, a being that is "absolutely foreign to me – refractory to every typology, to every genus, to every characterology, to every classification" (Levinas, 1969, 73). By contrast, traditional ethical theories treat the Other as a being like me, possessing rationality and deserving respect, and where necessary deserving to be a recipient of my benevolence. Thus, in traditional ethical theories, the Other is essentially the Same: You and I are the same in being both moral agents. For Levinas, the Other "*is not under a category*" (*ibid.,* 69, emphasis original) by virtue of a Derridean "other" that is "other otherwise." As we shall see, because of this Derridean "other," my commerce with the Other can only be ethical. This Derridean "other" deconstructs the foundation of traditional ethical theories, putting ethics itself first before all else, thus making it "first philosophy." This is the sense in which Levinas speaks deconstructively of ethics. If I am right, we are justified in reading Laozi through Levinas, as I propose to do in Section II.

II

In various works, Levinas argues that it is the radical otherness of those with whom I interact – biblically referred to by Levinas as the stranger, the homeless, the neighbor, the widow, the orphan, or generally as the Other (*l'Autrui*) – that disrupts and undermines, or deconstructs, as Derrida would put it, my understanding of myself as a being having a particular essence, which is binarily opposed to something else having some other essence – a man as opposed to a woman, a husband as opposed to a bachelor, a professional as opposed to a manual worker, and so on. We feel this deconstructive effect in the very phenomenology of subjectivity. Thus I encounter myself as a subject when and only when I am aware of myself as a unique identity, completely separated from what is not myself, and this awareness comes to me only when I am aware of others as completely other. As Levinas puts it in *Otherwise than Being*, subjectivity is constituted as a "node and denouement" of being and the otherwise than being, "of essence and the essence's other" (Levinas, 1981, 10). Clearly, then, Levinas is here speaking of an other that inhabits the in-between of being and the otherwise of being, between essence and the beyond of essence, an other that deconstructs being. Subjectivity results from such deconstruction.

Levinas goes on to argue that each of us has a desire for subjectivity, a primordial desire designated by Levinas simply as "Desire," which expresses itself every time we utter "I." Given that subjectivity can only be confirmed by the separation of the "I" from the "not-I" as mentioned above, the desire for subjectivity can only be fulfilled when the "I" maintains the separation between it and the Other, and it can do so by maintaining the radical alterity of the Other, maintaining the Other's otherness. The trouble is that the "I" exists in the world as a being and has the tendency to totalize others, absorbing them into its being, its essence. This tendency has to be resisted, or deconstructed. To maintain the Other in its radical alterity, I must avoid making myself the standard of reference in my dealings with them, avoid calculating everything in terms of my interests, my enjoyment, and my welfare. As Levinas puts it, I have to behave in such a way that "the good of this world break forth from the exclusive property of enjoyment," or from the "egoist and solitary enjoyment" (Levinas, 1969: 76). The enjoyment in which "I am absolutely for myself" (*ibid.*, 134) "assuredly does not render the concrete man" (*ibid.*, 139). This breaking away from "egoist and solitary enjoyment" is what makes my commerce with the Other ethical. Ethics, then, deconstructs the being of the "I" and reveals to it its subjectivity. Fortunately, in my day-to-day commerce with my fellow beings, which is typically conducted in language, I already realize that they possess an alterity that cannot be absorbed into the totality of my being. As Levinas puts it, the "relationship of language implies transcendence, radical separation, the revelation of the other to me" (*ibid.*, 73). In my day-to-day commerce, I already realize that the Other possesses a radical alterity, an absolute otherness that can confirm my subjectivity. All I have to do is to make this commerce ethical.

How am I to make my commerce with the Other ethical? Levinas's answer is that I have to be responsible for the Other. It is this "responsibility [that] confirms the subjectivity" of the "I" (Levinas, 1969, 245). Levinas goes on: "To utter 'I,' to affirm the irreducible singularity [of my subjectivity] . . . means to possess a privileged place with regard to responsibilities for which no one can replace me and from which no one can release me. To be unable to shirk: this is the I" (*ibid.*). The responsibility for the Other that defines subjectivity is not one that the "I" chooses to take on in an ethical decision. It is a primordial responsibility that produces the "I" in the first place and thus is prior to freedom. It possesses an "antecedence to my freedom, . . . to the present and to representation, is a passivity more passive than all passivity, an exposure to the other without this exposure being assumed" (Levinas, 1981, 15). How am I to be responsible for the Other? By exposing myself "to outrage, to wounding" (*ibid.*), by taking on the burdens of others as a "hostage who substitutes himself for the others" (*ibid.*), by offering others "even the bread out of one's own mouth and the coat from one's shoulders" (*ibid.*, 55).

We have seen how ethics arises, for Levinas, in the process of deconstruction of the being of the "I," of its essence. We have seen that the deconstructive force comes from the radical otherness of the Other, which serves precisely the deconstructive function of the Derridean "other." We have seen that the metaphysical "Desire" for subjectivity is fulfilled when we turn toward this "other" in our maintenance of the radical alterity of the Other. While this alterity, this otherness, cannot be named or told of in our thematization and conceptualization, we do come face to face with it in our ethical commerce with the Other. The deconstruction of the totality of being is the endless reaching out for this "other." Thus Levinas effectively confirms Derrida's statement cited earlier, namely: "The critique of logocentrism is above all else the search for the 'other,' and the 'other of language'." Indeed, what Derrida means by "language" here is arguably what Levinas calls "the *said*" and what he means by "the other of language" is arguably what Levinas calls "the *saying*." In traditional ethical theories, the subject, the "I," first arises, as for example in a Cartesian *cogito,* full of being and possessive of an essence that is its identity, and subsequently arrives at ethical principles and makes ethical choices, guided by the *logos* that is part of its essence. This traditional "I" *says* what is ethical and what is not, and its ethics is part of the *said.* In deconstructing this traditional "I," its logocentrism, in rejecting the *said* of traditional ethics, Levinas shows how an "I" emerges in its ethical commerce with the Other. He shows that ethics is not part of the *said,* based on a foundation that is also part of the *said.* Rather, ethics is the reaching out for the other of the *said,* the reaching out for the *saying.* In his religious writings, or in the religious moments of his writings on ethics, Levinas equates this with the reaching out for God, the true God that is beyond what is thematized and conceptualized in the *said* of traditional theology, the God that "comes to mind" in His *saying.* The metaphysical Desire for subjectivity translates into the Desire for the Infinite, for God, a "metaphysical desire [that] tends toward *something else entirely,* toward the *absolutely other*" (Levinas, 1969. 33, emphasis original). To be ethical and to be religious are one and the same thing.

Just as Levinas's God cannot be conceptualized and thematized, Laozi's *dao* cannot be named and spoken of. That which can be named and spoken of is not the real, or the constant, or the eternal *dao.* The first two lines of the *Daodejing* suggest that we may profit from reading it through Levinas. The fact that Levinas links ethics to the Infinite adds strength to this notion given the juxtaposition of *dao* and *de* in the very title of Laozi's work. In particular, it can be argued that, like Levinas, Laozi speaks deconstructively of ethics. As we have seen, this means deconstructing traditional ethical teachings, particularly those that name and speak of the *dao* as some principle that can be incorporated into a foundation of an ethical discourse. Just as Levinas urges an ethics not explicable in the words of the *said* but, precisely for that reason, one that allows us to remain within the proximity of the *saying* of the other, of the Infinite, of God, Laozi urges that we follow "the teaching that uses no words" (*bu yan zhi jiao*) (*Daodejing,* ch. II; Lau, 1963, 58), the *de* that allows us to remain in proximity of the *dao.* It is through the teaching of this *de* that we can comport ourselves according to the *dao,* and we need to comport ourselves with it because the *dao* is the very ground of our existence, being "the beginning of heaven and earth" and "the mother of the myriad creatures" (*Daodejing,* ch. I; Lau, 1963, 57).

With Levinas in mind, the second line of *Daodejing* ("always allow yourself to have desires in order to observe [the *dao*'s] manifestations" [ch. I; Lau, 1963, 57]) can be given a Levinasian reading as a claim for the need to develop a metaphysical desire for the *dao* that parallels the metaphysical desire for the Infinite in Levinas. The first line ("rid yourself of desires in order to observe its secrets") then becomes the equivalent of the Levinasian thesis that the desires for the enjoyment that is "absolutely for myself" have to be rid of because they will only entrench me within the totality of my being, within the worldly affairs, and thus will effectively turn me away from the Infinite, from the secrets of the *dao.* Traditional ethical theories, the teachings that use words, as Laozi would say, may succeed in making the enjoyment that is absolutely for myself conform to certain ethical principles, but the pursuit of it is still absolutely for myself, even if the "myself" is seen as some ethical self. To follow the teachings that use words, one needs to make choices of certain actions over others, and perform them so as to conform to their ethical principles. But in doing this, the "manifestations" of the *dao* will be missed and its "secrets" will remain secret. Instead, what we are to do is to follow "the teaching that uses no words," that is, to accept being virtuous as a primordial responsibility that arises prior to freedom, prior to choices, and prior to actions that manifest those choices. This, I take it, is the Levinasian take on the idea of "Taking no action" (*wuwei*) that is a recurrent theme in the *Daodejing*. *Wuwei* is thus a "passivity more passive than all passivity," as Levinas says about ethical responsibility. The teaching that uses no words, Laozi's *de*, is a teaching of a primordial responsibility for my fellow human beings that falls on me without my choosing. *De* is not founded on anything *said* and yet allows us to hear the *saying* of the *dao,* to observe its manifestations. Furthermore, *de* carries with it the deconstructive power of the *dao,* and to follow *de* is to deconstruct the entity that is constructed in the midst of worldly affairs, full of being and pregnant with essence. The "nothing" of the *dao* that is at the heart of *de* deconstructs this entity to produce a "something," namely an ethical "I," a virtuous individual. In this something, the nothingness of the *dao* manifests itself. Thus, we are told that "Something and Nothing produce each other" (*Daodejing,* ch. II; Lau, 1963, 58).

I have suggested that the "Something" that is produced by the "Nothing" is a virtuous being who follows the teaching that uses no words. But how does the virtuous "Something" in turn produce the "Nothing"? The answer lies in Levinas's account of ethical conduct as an opening up to the Other in such a way as to maintain their radical alterity, their otherness. To be ethical, as we have seen, is the same thing as to be religious in the sense of tending "toward *something else entirely,* toward the *absolutely other.*" For Laozi, the "absolutely other" is the "Nothing" that is unnameable, a "mystery upon mystery" (*Daodejing,* ch. I; Lau, 1963, 57). By contrast, to be "absolutely for myself" is to be trapped in the totality of one's being, to remove oneself from the "node and denouement" of being and the otherwise than being where one's subjectivity is located. Indeed, one is still trapped even if one follows the teachings of traditional ethical theories, the teachings that use words, insofar as such teachings spin out of being and totalize all else. So trapped, both "Something" – the "I" in its full subjectivity – and "Nothing" – the "absolutely other" that is a "mystery upon mystery" – are snuffed out. To be responsible for others, to accomplish *de,* is to break out from the totality of one's being, thus allowing the "Something" to be realized, together with the "Nothing." For Levinas, acting ethically toward others is not self-effacing but the exact opposite, namely self-confirming. In a similar way, we find Laozi arguing that "the sage puts his person last and it comes out first," that he treats his person "as extraneous to himself and it is preserved" (*Daodejing*. ch. VII; Lau, 1963, 63). Being ethical, or virtuous, the sage puts his person last in his commerce with his fellow human beings, going out of himself as if his person is extraneous to himself in the service of others. Yet, in doing so, he confirms his subjectivity as a "Something," preserving his person. Being selfless, "without thought of self (*wusi*)," he manages "to accomplish his private ends (*si*)" of confirming his own subjectivity, of satisfying the metaphysical desire for the absolutely other, for knowledge of the secrets of the *dao*. We are now in a position to see why in "bestow(ing) all he has on others" and "giv(ing) all he has to others," "he has yet more," and having given all, "he is richer still" (*Daodejing,* ch. LXXXI; Lau, 1963, 143). For Levinas, in "giving the bread out of one's mouth and the coat from one's shoulders," what one gains is one's own subjectivity. To have this is to have more than egoist enjoyment, to be richer than one without subjectivity.

It may be objected at this point that the virtuous sage in Laozi is nothing like the ethical person in Levinas. Thus it may be said that while the latter immerses himself or herself in feeding the hungry and comforting the distressed, the former is counseled not to "contend" (*zheng*) with "the myriad creatures" (*Daodejing,* ch. VIII; Lau, 1963, 64). There are two possible ways of cashing out this objection. One is to say that while Levinas's ethics is humanistic, Laozi's is not. The second way is to say that for Levinas, the ethical person seeks to benefit others by acting, whereas for Laozi, he or she is counseled to benefit others by taking no action. It may be said further that the difference between Levinas and Laozi rests on a more fundamental difference between them on the idea of the other. My response to these two points consists in admitting the second without conceding the first. Levinas and Laozi do indeed differ on the notion of the other (no less than both, each in his own way, differing from Derrida). For one thing, Laozi's other has to do with the *dao,* and there is really nothing that corresponds to it in Levinas. Further, it seems that for Laozi, the *dao* plays a regulative role, adjusting the cosmic forces and guiding human actions (albeit in a way characterized as *wuwei* – more on *wuwei* later). Such metaphysical realism is totally absent in Levinas. However, what is important for my purpose here is that, from the human point of view, both Laozi's *dao* and Levinas's other play the same deconstructive role, leading to the same kind of non-foundationalist ethics.

Turning to the first objection, again from the human point of view, the claim that Levinas's ethics is humanistic and Laozi's is not is mistaken. It might be thought that such a claim finds support in chapter 25 of the *Daodejing,* where we find the well-known passage: "Man models himself on earth, Earth on heaven, Heaven on the way, And the way on that which is naturally so" (Lau, 1963, 82). Thus the "modeling chain" seems to lead beyond mere human relations. However, I read this passage as saying simply that man should model himself on earth, and what earth and heaven do is their business, as we, from the human point of view, have no way of knowing how they model themselves. Modeling on earth, in turn, means modeling on the earthly manifestations, on the way things are on earth, including inter-human relationships. Read this way, Laozi's ethics seems to be just as humanistic as Levinas's.

As for the claim that Laozi's virtuous sage is nothing like Levinas's ethical agent in that the latter seeks to benefit others by *acting,* and the former is counseled to do so by *taking no action,* this objection does not take account of Levinas's description of ethical behavior as "dis-inter-ested" behavior (Levinas, 1998, 36). For Levinas, seeking to benefit others out of some interest, even if it is an interest in their welfare, is egoistic. He calls it an "inter-ested move-ment of consciousness," or a movement among (*inter*) the manifestations of being (*esse*) (*ibid.,* xv). To go over to the Other with an interest, even if it is an interest dictated by an ethical theory, is to return to oneself. A truly ethical movement, by contrast, has to be dis-inter-ested, that is, one not based on any articulated interest. It is only by such movement that there is no return to being, that there is satisfaction of the desire for what is otherwise than being, for what is infinite and transcendent. With this in mind, we can read "not con-tending with the myriad creatures," or "taking no action" to mean not seeking to benefit others as a means of satisfying an interest, even if it is specified by an ethical teaching that uses words. The truly virtuous person acts to benefit others in a disinterested way, such that the benefits are conferred without the beneficiaries noticing any action having been taken. This is a plausible reading of "taking no action" to benefit others, more plausible than the interpreta-tion that one should do absolutely nothing. This reading is confirmed by passages where one is advised to act to benefit others in such a way that the "people all say, 'It happened to us naturally'" (*Daodejing,* ch. XVII; Lau, 1963, 73), where we learn that the sage "excels in saving people" (*Daodejing,* ch. XXVII; Lau, 1963, 84) but in saving them he "leaves no wheel tracks," "uses no counting rods . . . no bolts . . . no cords" (*ibid.*). Indeed, "the people will benefit a hundredfold" if one does not act out of some determinate interest, including, or perhaps particularly, the interest in cultivating "benevolence" (*ren*) and "rectitude" (*yi*) as spoken of in the teaching that uses words (*Daodejing,* ch. XIX; Lau, 1963, 75). Paradoxically, then, the "man of the highest virtue" is one who "does not keep to virtue" (*Daodejing*, ch. XXXVIII; Lau, 1963, 99). Following Levinas, "not keeping to virtue" can be read as "having no interest in being virtuous." This, arguably, is the most plausible way of making sense of the seemingly paradoxical advice to "(e)xterminate the sage, discard the wise, . . .; Exterminate benevolence, discard rectitude, . . ." (*Daodejing*, ch. XIX; Lau, 1963, 75). What we are to "exterminate" and "discard" is what is *said*. The ethical conduct, or the virtuous behavior, that is spoken of in the teaching that uses the words of the *said* has been deconstructed by Levinas and Laozi, and the outcome is an ethics more in tune with the *saying* of the Infinite, the "secrets" of the *dao*.

If I am right in this point of comparison between the writings of Levinas and the *Daodejing*, then we can defend the teachings of the latter against the charge that they amount to a withdrawal from the world. Daoism is often compared negatively with Confucianism on this score. Against the former, the latter is often praised for its advocacy of social engagement. However, if we read Laozi's "taking no action" as "taking no interested action," or as maintaining a disinterested stance in the Levinasian sense, then a different slant can be put on Laozi's teachings. In Levinas, disinterestedness is not an indifference toward the others or toward the Infinite, or a withdrawal from them. Indeed, Levinas insists that his notion of disinterestedness "does not signify indifference, but allegiance to the other" (Levinas, 1998, 36). In the same way, we can say that Laozi does not advocate indifference, or withdrawal from social engagement. On the contrary, what is advocated is allegiance to the *dao by way of* acting to benefit our fellow human beings but in such a way as to "leave no wheel tracks." Interestedness has to be deconstructed and the way to deconstruct it is to be responsible for others without consciously deciding to assume the responsibility, or to be virtuous without actively following the sage and the wise, without consciously following their teachings on benevolence and rectitude.

If I am correct in my reading of the *Daodejing* through the writings of Levinas, the enigmatic first two lines of this work can be compared with Isaiah 65:1, quoted by Levinas: "I am sought of them that asked not for me, I am found of them that sought me not." To ask for the Way by name is not to seek the real Way; to speak of what one takes to be the Way is not to speak of the eternal Way. There are those who teach of the Way in words, some of whom go on to build ethical theories on the foundation of the Way that they speak of in words. What they say need to be deconstructed if we are to experience the manifestations of the Way. In practice, the deconstruction of the *said* is conducted in the ethical commerce with the Other, in "excelling in saving people." Seeking to be responsible for the Other is seeking God without asking for Him; excelling in saving people is finding the Way without seeking it. The true sage is one who "knows without having to stir, (i)dentifies without having to see, (a)ccomplishes without having to act" (*Daodejing*, ch. XLVII; Lau, 1963, 108). In following the true sage, we get "close to the way" (*Daodejing*, ch. VIII; Lau, 1963, 64) because the Way also benefits the "myriad creatures [but] claims no authority; . . . gives them life yet claims no possession; . . . benefits them yet exacts no gratitude; . . . accomplishes its task yet lays claim to no merit" (*Daodejing*, ch. II, Lau, 1963, 58). We get close to the Way "by means of this" (*Daodejing*, ch. LIV; Lau, 1963, 115). If I am right, it can be said that despite the heavy emphasis on ethics, on *de*, the *Daodejing* is still ultimately a work on ontology, on the nature of the *dao*, and more importantly, on how to attain it. Again if I am right, we can read the *Daodejing* as suggesting that the way to attain the *dao* is the *wuwei* way, that is, not taking any direct actions to attain it, such as inquiring into its nature, seeking its manifestations, measuring its effects and so on. (Any such action would be deconstructed by the *dao* in any case.) Rather, the way to attain it is through ethical action, through *de*.

I have argued in this chapter that the *Daodejing* can be read as a deconstruction of the *de* in the "teachings that use words" similar to the deconstruction of ethics found in the writings of Levinas. For both Laozi and Levinas, ethics is not something that we reason out on the basis of certain suppositions about ourselves and the world, not something that can be said, or learned from the "teachings that use words." What is said gets deconstructed by the unthematizable other, by the unnameable *dao*. The deconstructive process reveals, in passivity, in *wuwei*, an ethical conduct by which one accomplishes subjectivity, attains sagehood, and comes face to face with the other, the Infinite, the *dao*, without speaking of it or naming it. In a passivity more passive than all passivity, in *wuwei*, everything is accomplished. This is indeed a miracle. The Infinite, the *dao*, through its deconstructive potency, its *de*, is capable of it. As Levinas puts it, the "miracle of creation lies in creating a moral being" (Levinas, 1969, 89).

References

Chan, Wing-tsit (1963) *The Way of Lao Tzu*, Indianapolis, IN: Bobbs-Merrill.

Cheng, Chung-ying (1990) "A Taoist interpretation of 'différance' in Derrida," *Journal of Chinese Philosophy*, 17, 19–30.

Chien, Chi-hui (1990) " 'Theft's way': a comparative study of Chuang Tzu's Tao and Derridean trace," *Journal of Chinese Philosophy*, 17, 31–49.

Derrida, J. (1973) *Speech and Phenomena*, trans. D.B. Allison, Evanston, IL: Northwestern University Press.

— (1978a) *Writing and Difference*, trans. Alan Bass, Chicago, IL: University of Chicago Press.

— (1982) *Margins of Philosophy*, trans. Alan Bass, Chicago, IL: University of Chicago Press.

Kearney, R. (1984) *Dialogues with Contemporary Continental Thinkers*, Manchester: Manchester University Press.

Lau, D.C. (1963) *Lao Tzu: Tao Te Ching*, Harmondsworth: Penguin.

Levinas, E. (1969) *Totality and Infinity*, trans. A. Lingis, Pittsburgh, PA: Duquesne University Press.

— (1981) *Otherwise than Being or Beyond Essence*, trans. A. Lingis, The Hague: Martinus Nijhoff.

— (1998) *Of God Who Comes to Mind*, trans. B. Bergo, Stanford, CA: Stanford University Press.

Nuyen, A.T. (1993) "The Unbearable Slyness of Deconstruction," *Philosophy*, 68, 392–6.

— (1995) "Naming the unnameable: The being of the *Tao*," *Journal of Chinese Philosophy*, 22, 487–97.

Ownes, W.D. (1993) "Tao and différance: The existential implications," *Journal of Chinese Philosophy*, 20, 261–77.

Verges, F.G. (1992) "The unbearable lightness of deconstruction," *Philosophy*, 67, 386–93.

Yeh, M. (1983) "The deconstructive way: a comparative study of Derrida and Chuang Tzu," *Journal of Chinese Philosophy*, 10, 95–125.

Chapter 13

Julia Kristeva

GENOTEXT AND PHENOTEXT

Julia Kristeva's essay demands quite some background reading and knowledge of her own poststructuralist system of thought, through which she makes significant contributions to feminist and psychoanalytical theory, but armed with a few key terms, it is possible for the reader to understand her argument. Two of those key terms are found in her first sentence: the "semiotic chora" and the "symbolic". The semiotic chora is what Kristeva calls an underlying "figuration" or, something which at a bodily, rhythmic level, generates patterns and deconstructive meanings before more structured language and laws take over in the realm of the "symbolic". Her technical word for deconstructive meanings is "signifiance": it is the poststructuralist notion that texts playfully undermine or transgress fixed systems of thought. The semiotic chora is found in the realm of the unconscious, and is ordered (not constrained) by social processes, such as family upbringing, gender, and ideology. The *genotext* and *phenotext* are always in relation to one another: the *genotext* is the underlying semiotic expression of the chora, one which leads to "the advent of the symbolic". Importantly for feminism, what underlies the logical algebraic world of the symbolic is the body, especially the maternal body—chora, after all, means "receptacle" as is found in Plato's book *Timaeus*. So the *genotext* expresses the bodily drives of desire and needs—human affects in other words—yet it is always implicated in family and social structures, as explained by discoveries such as Sigmund Freud's concept of pre-Oedipal relations (the Oedipus Complex signifies a transition from desire-for-the-mother to the realm of the symbolic law-of-the-father). Kristeva argues that genotext traces can be found in the rhythmic and melodic aspects of a text, as well as in narrative expressions of desire and fantasy that defer denotation, or the communication of factual and stabilized signification. While the genotext can thus be seen to be at work, it is not actually linguistic (for example, it is the *rhythm* in language, not the language itself). Genotext processes may be fleetingly glimpsed and subject to changes in social and psychological constraints. The language that does function at the level of communication is the phenotext; unlike the wholeness of the genotext, the phenotext is divided, yet in its divisions it manages to communicate ideas and concepts. Kristeva notes that any signifying system needs both genotext and phenotext operations. The phenotext even expresses the social constraints that have been previously imposed upon the more freely moving genotext, so even in the most apparently ordered and fixed of phenotexts, glimpses of more transgressive processes can be seen. According to Kristeva, avant-garde writing, such as that of Mallarmé and Joyce, do express more fully the semiotic chora: we can see this in Joyce's "stream-of-consciousness" writing in his modernist novel *Ulysses*. Kristeva does warn that such experimental aesthetics tend not to be highly political, and thus in these novels transgression operates in non-ideological ways. The "revolutionary" potential of accessing the semiotic chora emerges for Kristeva in more recent poststructuralist writing, i.e., the type of writing that comes after modernism. She mentions the work of Jacques Lacan as a key example of a poststructuralist psychoanalytical thinker who searches for and reveals the semiotic chora in a wide social range of discourses.

I N LIGHT OF THE DISTINCTION we have made between the semiotic *chora* and the symbolic, we may now examine the way texts function. What we shall call a *genotext* will include semiotic processes but also the advent of the symbolic. The former includes drives, their disposition, and their division of the body, plus the ecological and social system surrounding the body, such as objects and pre-Oedipal relations with parents. The latter encompasses the emergence of object and subject, and the constitution of nuclei of meaning involving categories: semantic and categorial fields. Designating the genotext in a text requires pointing out the transfers of drive energy that can be detected in phonematic devices (such as the accumulation and repetition of phonemes or rhyme) and melodic devices (such as intonation or rhythm), in the way semantic and categorial fields are set out in syntactic and logical features, or in the economy of mimesis (fantasy, the deferment of denotation, narrative, etc.). The genotext is thus the only transfer of drive energies that organizes a space in which the subject is not *yet* a split unity that will become blurred, giving rise to the symbolic. Instead, the space it organizes is one in which the subject will be *generated* as such by a process of facilitations and marks within the constraints of the biological and social structure.

In other words, even though it can be seen in language, the genotext is not linguistic (in the sense understood by structural or generative linguistics). It is, rather, a *process,* which tends to articulate structures that are ephemeral (unstable, threatened by drive charges, "quanta" rather than "marks") and nonsignifying (devices that do not have a double articulation). It forms these structures out of: a) instinctual dyads, b) the corporeal and ecological continuum, c) the social organism and family structures, which convey the constraints imposed by the mode of production and d) matrices of enunciation, which give rise to discursive "genres" (according to literary history), "psychic structures" (according to psychiatry and psychoanalysis), or various arrangements of "the participants in the speech event" (in Jakobson's notion of the linguistics of discourse).[1] We may posit that the matrices of enunciation are the result of the repetition of drive charges (a) within biological, ecological, and socio-familial constraints (b and c), and the stabilization of their facilitation into stases whose surrounding structure accommodates and leaves its mark on symbolization.

The genotext can thus be seen as language's underlying foundation. We shall use the term *phenotext* to denote language that serves to communicate, which linguistics describes in terms of "competence" and "performance." The phenotext is constantly split up and divided, and is irreducible to the semiotic process that works through the genotext. The phenotext is a structure (which can be generated, in generative grammar's sense); it obeys rules of communication and presupposes a subject of enunciation and an addressee. The genotext, on the other hand, is a process; it moves through zones that have relative and transitory borders and constitutes a *path* that is not restricted to the two poles of univocal information between two full-fledged subjects. If these two terms—genotext and phenotext—could be translated into a metalanguage that would convey the difference between them, one might say that the genotext is a matter of topology, whereas the phenotext is one of algebra. This distinction may be illustrated by a particular signifying system: written and spoken Chinese, particularly classical Chinese. Writing represents-articulates the signifying process into specific networks or spaces; *speech* (which may correspond to that writing) restores the diacritical elements necessary for an exchange of meaning between two subjects (temporality, aspect, specification of the protagonists, morpho-semantic identifiers, and so forth).[2]

The signifying process therefore includes both the genotext and the phenotext; indeed it could not do otherwise. For it is in language that all signifying operations are realized (even when linguistic material is not used), and it is on the basis of language that a theoretical approach may attempt to perceive that operation.

In our view, the process we have just described accounts for the way all signifying practices are generated.[3] But every signifying practice does not encompass the infinite totality of that process. Multiple constraints—which are ultimately sociopolitical—stop the signifying process at one or another of the theses that it traverses; they knot it and lock it into a given surface or structure; they discard *practice* under fixed, fragmentary, symbolic *matrices,* the tracings of various social constraints that obliterate the infinity of the process: the phenotext is what conveys these obliterations. Among the capitalist mode of production's numerous signifying practices, only certain literary texts of the avant-garde (Mallarmé, Joyce) manage to cover the infinity of the process, that is, reach the semiotic *chora,* which modifies linguistic structures. It must be emphasized, however, that this total exploration of the signifying process generally leaves in abeyance the theses that are characteristic of the social organism, its structures, and their political transformation: the text has a tendency to dispense with political and social signifieds.

It has only been in very recent years or in revolutionary periods that signifying practice has inscribed within the phenotext the plural, heterogeneous, and contradictory process of signification encompassing the flow of drives, material discontinuity, political struggle, and the pulverization of language.

Lacan has delineated four types of discourse in our society: that of the hysteric, the academic, the master, and the analyst.[4] Within the perspective just set forth, we shall posit a different classification, which, in certain respects, intersects these four Lacanian categories, and in others, adds to them. We shall distinguish between the following signifying practices: narrative, metalanguage, contemplation, and text-practice.

Let us state from the outset that this distinction is only provisional and schematic, and that although it corresponds to actual practices, it interests us primarily as a didactic implement [*outil*]—one that will allow us to specify some of the modalities of signifying dispositions. The latter interest us to the extent that they give rise to different practices and are, as a consequence, more or less coded in modes of production. Of course narrative and contemplation could also be seen as devices stemming from (hysterical and obsessional) transference neurosis; and metalanguage and the text as practices allied with psychotic (paranoid and schizoid) economies.

Notes

1   See "Shifters. Verbal Categories, and the Russian Verb," in Roman Jakobson, *Selected Writings* (Mouton: The Hague and Paris, 1971), vol. 2:130–47.

2   See Joseph Needham, *Science and Civilisatien in China,* 4 vols. (Cambridge: Cambridge University Press, 1960), vol. 1.

3   From a similar perspective, Edgar Morin writes: "We can think of magic, mythologies, and ideologies both as mixed systems, making affectivity rational and rationality affective, and as outcomes of

combining: a) fundamental drives, b) the chancy play of fantasy, and c) logico-constructive systems. (To our mind, the theory of myth must be based on triunic syncretism rather than unilateral logic)" He adds, in a note, that "myth does not have a single logic but a synthesis of three kinds of logic." "Le Paradigme perdu: La Nature humaine," paper presented at the "Invariants biologiques et universaux culturels" Colloquium, Royaumont, September 6–9, 1972.

4   Lacan presented this typology of discourse at his 1969 and 1970 seminars.

PART III

Media, culture and postmodernism

IN THE *DIALECTIC OF ENLIGHTENMENT* (1944), Theodor Adorno and Max Horkheimer present a powerful, scathing attack upon the "culture industry" (see Chapter 31), arguing that society is kept in check by the capitalist mass entertainment industries of "movies, radio, jazz, and magazines."[1] Authentic culture, for Adorno and Horkheimer, is what would now be called by some "high culture", that is to say, painting, sculpture, architecture, classical music, dance, opera, and great works of literature, with emphasis upon poetry and drama. For Walter Benjamin, these are all arts that produce unique works that exist singularly in space and time: there is only one original Sistine Chapel painted by Michelangelo in the Vatican, Rome, just as there is only one painting by Picasso called *Guernica*, which is in the Renia Sofia (the modern art museum) in Madrid, Spain. With the rise of photography and film in the nineteenth century, however, Benjamin and others began to theorize a new artistic phenomenon: mass reproducibility. Just as the Industrial Revolution was driven by the invention and widespread use of machines to more efficiently perform repetitive tasks, so with photography and film, the techniques of the factory production line could be applied to the mass reproduction of images (and eventually sound; the first movies were silent). But this new mechanistic process meant that the notion of a unique work of art, and the fetish of the artwork's associated aura, gave way to the era of the copy, and the mechanized delivery of these copies literally "into" people's lives and homes. Instead of travelling to the authentic work of art (a trip to the Vatican in Italy, for example), the copy comes to the viewer, either meeting him or her halfway in the movie theatre, or sticking with Adorno and Horkheimer's list, the radio waves beamed into the home. While Benjamin stresses the revolutionary potential of the technical reproducibility of art, suggesting that it is now something available to the masses (used for example to reject the high cultural pageantry of the fascist Nazi rallies that were occurring in his lifetime), for Adorno and Horkheimer, the sophisticated capitalist nations of the west, especially the USA, rapidly created a modern culture industry, to instead *pacify* the masses and to train them to become ideal consumers of products they did not really need. These two lenses: mass culture as a Marxist or other *revolutionary form* or mass culture as a capitalist *pacifying mechanism*, remain potential positions that critics often adopt when discussing contemporary culture.

For today's readers, there are at least two striking omissions from Adorno and Horkheimer's mass entertainment industry list: television and the internet. Although the technology for producing a televised picture had existed as early as 1897, when the Nobel prize-winning physicist Ferdinand Braun (1850–1918) invented the Cathode Ray Tube, it was not until 1926 that the first public demonstration by John Logie Baird (1888–1946) of the "mechanical" television took place in Scotland. Over the next decade, other countries were soon involved in producing and transmitting mechanical television, which produced vague visual "shadow-grams", with a shift into fully electrical—and higher quality—television in 1936. At the BBC's launch of the EMI-Marconi electrical system at Alexandra Palace in London in 1936, newspaper journalists excitedly reported on the images that were transmitted into a house at St. John's Wood: "People gathered in the room watched the flickerless reception, which was clear to view whether the lights were on or off."[2] Even at this early stage, however, television was perceived as a threat, and saboteurs had attempted to wreck the occasion by filling a power outlet in the studio with lead.[3] While anxieties about the detrimental influence of watching too much television remain to this day, it was not until the 1960s and 1970s, that the revolutionary potential of mainstream television became apparent. The Vietnam War (1959–73) became known as the first "televised war" as powerful uncensored images of death and destruction were transmitted into people's homes. This media revolution, alongside the new "rock" journalism of magazines such as *Rolling Stone*, contributed to the public's reaction against American involvement in this war.[4] Television in this instance is what the semiotician and theorist Umberto Eco calls "paleo-television", or television which "refers to the world outside itself, to the reality outside television."[5] Never again would wartime journalists be given such unfettered freedom to generate raw footage of events on the ground; since the Vietnam War, "embedded" journalists have had carefully controlled access to battles and military engagements.

Another mode of television which began to predominate in the 1980s was what Umberto Eco calls "neo-television", or, television with an obsession with itself. As Strinati notes, neo-television "is television which is about television. Its concern is with the world of television, its conventions, programmes and personalities, rather than with its capacity to open a window onto the real world outside television."[6] Neo-television may simply be a synonym for postmodernism, since theorists such as Lyotard and Baudrillard have clarified that with the rise of a fully immersive and self-reflective media culture, the new televisual simulated worlds stop taking the form of a copy or pale reflection of the "outside" world, and instead begin to feel more real than the real itself. This transition to what Baudrillard calls "the hyperreal" can be sketched in multiple ways, although one of the most common is to suggest that it is a positive shift from the modern world of elitist distinctions between high and low cultures, to the postmodern world, where there is a democratic flattening of aesthetic and cultural hierarchies in favour of popular culture forms. Another approach to this shift suggests that hyperreal postmodern culture is, more negatively, a manifestation of late capitalism, and it is merely an intensification of the commodification of the world, which means making all objects and subjects available for consumption. Regardless of one's position here, the inward, implosive television-based cultural turn that takes place during the 60s, 70s, and 80s, involves an intense process of cultural recycling.[7] Baudrillard argues that high Culture with a capital "C" has been replaced by mass culture, "where the latter is cyclical, produced by the medium (television) rather than autonomous human subjects."[8] More positively, Marshall McLuhan argues that television and modern media are prosthetic "extensions" of human beings, which as Richard Cavell observes, has serious implications: "Whereas the mechanical era had extended the human body, the electronic era was extending the central nervous system towards 'the technological simulation of consciousness' . . . and, in the process, was 'abolishing space and time' . . . as separate and unrelated categories."[9]

Televisual technologies regarded as prostheses leads to a cybernetic subjectivity: that is to say, hybrid humans or animals that are part organic, part high-tech machine. Such cybernetic beings are imagined in advance through "speculative" or science fiction, and with the rise of film and television such rich imaginative worlds can be designed and built at least in prototype form, although there is usually a technological lag in terms of everyday implementation. With this example alone, another one of the defining features of the shift into a postmodern world is apparent: the "copy" (here, imaginative science fiction cybernetic technologies) precedes the "original" (the actual making of fully functional technologies available for purchase in the everyday world). For Baudrillard, this reversal takes place because postmodernism is a world where "the code" is more important than an object in nature. The code could be the binary code of computer software that generates immersive virtual realities, the genetic code of DNA and RNA that can be manipulated to produce life-forms, or the semiotic code of all signifying systems (society, culture, art, etc.).

As the science fiction writer William Gibson has shown in his novels and short stories, most notably in *Neuromancer* (1984) where he coined the term "cyberspace", postmodern culture is often more accurately called "counter-culture". The flattening of hierarchies that took place with the shift into media-based popular culture worlds was partly driven by the rise of a new category of voracious consumer, and producer of new forms: the teenager. Youth culture is, as always, open to commodification, but it also represents a subversive, fragmented, and highly mobile hybrid form of aesthetics and politics. In the UK, Dick Hebdige's *Subculture: The Meaning of Style* (1979), the Centre for Contemporary Cultural Studies at the University of Birmingham's *The Empire Writes Back: Race and Racism in 70s Britain* (1982), and Paul Gilroy's "*There Ain't No Black in the Union Jack": The Cultural Politics of Race and Nation* (1987), all examine ways in which popular cultural forms, such as punk, reggae, hip-hop, and rap, can codify and express resistance to the state in relation to issues of class, gender and ethnicity. Subcultures often adopt a language of their own, or even more subversively, create a double-discourse whereby the language of the state or of some other authority, is given new meaning, a "subversive potential in the ability to switch between the languages of oppressor and oppressed."[10] While the British Centre for Contemporary Cultural Studies examined counter-cultures in the era of Britain's apparent post-industrial decline, in the US, it was industrial *transformation* and high-tech computerization that led to many highly skilled young black Americans finding themselves without jobs.[11] Graffiti artists, hip hop and rap artists, all found themselves in a post-industrial urban environment, with many high-tech jobs having migrated west to the fast-emerging markets of California's Silicon Valley, with basic industrial production often being re-situated overseas in Mexico and the Far East. Counter-cultural black artists reacted by using "the tools of obsolete industrial technology to traverse contemporary cross-roads of lack and desire in urban Afrodiasporic communities"[12] to build new communities (crews, posses, etc.) and new markets. The commercial success of rap, for example, does not necessarily mean its counter-cultural messages are reduced; if anything, they are globalized: "rap . . . draws international audiences [as well as White producers/audiences] because it is a powerful conglomeration of voices from the margins of American society speaking about the terms of that position."[13] Within the rap world of hyperbolic masculinity and misogyny, female rappers have become an important dialogic voice, engaging in and often contesting previously male-dominated rap codes.

Counter-cultural popular art forms are incessantly questioning; they embody what Lyotard argues is a shared feature of postmodernism: an incredulity towards metanarratives. What this means is that the broad overarching western narratives of philosophy, religion, high art, and morality are no longer regarded by postmodernists as expressing universal truths. If anything, within postmodernism, the opposite is often the case: the metanarratives are regarded as hegemonic and oppressive. Counter-cultural voices, in other words, express their suspicion of universals because such voices emerge from minority, marginal or oppressed cultures that have experienced poverty, exclusion and other modes of impoverished life. Opposed to metanarratives, then, are small, locally produced micronarratives (music, poetry, activist journalism, street art), claiming a space for potentially liberating lived experiences. Metanarratives are also regarded by postmodernists as expressing pejorative values, such as sexism, racism, or colonialism (see Parts VI and VII), and furthermore, they are seen to uphold these negative values by *producing knowledge* that then facilitates the transmission of further such viewpoints. While McLuhan's famous slogan "the medium is the message" might still apply to televisual and internet entertainment—i.e., it implies that the medium is contentless, yet this does not matter for postmodern audiences or consumers who fetishize the technological form—there is no doubt that television and internet news is the new arena for the production of, and opposition to, hegemonic metanarratives. A case in point is the media response to the attack on the Trade Towers in the US (9/11), when much of the western media initially recycled what Edward Said calls "Orientalist" notions of Islam (see Chapters 17 and 46). Orientalism is a western metanarrative that creates a body of knowledge to prove that non-western nations are less advanced and in other ways inferior in their social, economic and belief systems. Paradoxically, the weaker, inferior Other, is, in this case, also perceived as a dangerous threat to the west, one which needs to be understood to be kept at bay. Orientalists, then, appear to immerse themselves in understanding the Other, yet for Said, this is in actuality an immensely well-researched reinforcement of the western stereotypes of the Orient (an old-fashioned term for the Middle East and the Far East). After 9/11, the western media appeared to initially trot out Orientalist notions of Islam, terrorism, totalitarianism, and so on, before more critical voices began to question this media-based reinforcement and production of the Orientalist metanarrative. Oppositional media that offer critical micronarratives proliferate on the internet, and in locally produced televisual news stations such as Al Jazeera. The importance of televisual and internet media reveals how the world has indeed become what McLuhan termed "the global village", that is to say, telecommunications are instantaneous and thus transform notions of time and space, collapsing distances through the high-speed transmission of data which is shared within, and indeed can create, local communities. While globalization is studied in more depth in Part XI, it is important to note that it is media-based postmodern culture that has been one of the main vehicles of globalization. Social networking on the internet, for example, is global, but these same networks can be used for local ends, such as farmers in the Developing World getting a better deal for their crops through text-message-based access to market price fluctuations.[14]

The globalization of postmodernism leads to both resistance to its perceived western or capitalist values, and an embracing of postmodern techniques (sampling, montage, flattening of hierarchies, technological innovation, production of virtual or hyperreal worlds). In many respects, non-western forms of postmodernism are more culturally pervasive at the local, community level, such as the Indian film industry known as "Bollywood" which has become a powerful media production force. Bollywood films are thoroughly hybrid in construction, "combining melodrama, action, comedy, social commentary and romance, violently juxtaposing intensely tragic scenes with jolly song and dance numbers, jolting the viewer from one extreme of feeling to another."[15] Diasporic Indian communities throughout the western world often consume more Bollywood films through video, DVD and internet-streaming technologies, than any other form of media, and Bollywood production values are now influencing other national cinemas. Bollywood's postmodern complexity means that it deconstructs the First World/Third World Cinema binary opposition; instead, Bollywood is a melange of local political and ethnic cultural tensions and issues, such as its use of Hindi as its main language, combined with a global range of entertainment modes and genres, from the indigenous to the international. Other forms of Indian media—such as music and computer software—have similarly proliferated, although commentators point out that in this instance, the postmodern technologies of sampling, copying, and mass distribution leads to a culture of "recycling" in "gray areas" of illegality. In other words, the global issue of copyright and intellectual property managements is directly in conflict with postmodernism's basic structure (its hybrid form). Sundaram calls this structure a "preponderant *non-legality*" which he observes in India "at the level of technocultural services to the vast majority of the population in cities and towns, [where] the actors in this space have simply ignored the state as the regulator of everyday life."[16] Copyright and patent infringement takes place globally; what it reveals is less something profound concerning legality and more the fact that within postmodernism, intellectual property rights become even more important as "the code" is of significant commercial value. Recycling and sampling might be a counter-cultural way of life, but the original creators of the sampled materials are resolutely modern in their notions of ownership regardless of the postmodern attitudes of the new consumers.

Further reading: a selection

Contemporary media, popular culture and postmodernism are so interrelated that it is sometimes difficult separating them. John Mepham, in Smythe, suggests four narratives of postmodernism: the historical, the philosophical, the ideological, and the aesthetic (textual strategies). The further reading on the topic usually takes one or more of these narratives or perspectives, and they are useful ways into the topic. Brooker gives key primary essays on modernism and postmodernism, while Connor provides an overview that includes literature, architecture, visual arts, film and television as well as cultural politics. Delany considers how a city, in this case Vancouver, can be postmodern, from architecture to literature; the essays in Delany are varied and highly accessible. López and Potter present essays critical of postmodernism, suggesting that there are other more viable ways of perceiving the world, including a return to realism. Out of the extensive reading on popular culture and media, several texts stand out for ease of access, such as Fiske, Freccero and Strinati. Gilroy, Nielsen and Rose examine black British and American cultural politics and aesthetics, while Skelton and Allen, and Thussu, examine the ways in which globalization and international studies have transformed notions of culture and media.

Brooker, Peter, ed. *Modernism/Postmodernism*. London & New York: Longman, 1996.

Caputo, John D. and Michael J. Scanlon, eds. *Augustine and Postmodernism: Confessions and Circumfession*. Bloomington & Indianapolis: Indiana University Press, 2005.

Connor, Steven. *Postmodernist Culture: An Introduction to Theories of the Contemporary*. Oxford: Blackwell, 1990.

Curran, James and Myung-Jin Park, eds. *De-Westernizing Media Studies*. Abingdon, Oxon: Routledge, 2005.

Delany, Paul, ed. *Vancouver: Representing the Postmodern City*. Vancouver: Arsenal Pulp Press, 1994.

Eagleton, Terry. *After Theory*. New York: Basic Books, 2003.

Fiske, John. *Understanding Popular Culture*. Second Edition. Abingdon, Oxon, & New York: Routledge, 2010.

Freccero, Carla. *Popular Culture: An Introduction*. New York & London: New York University Press, 1999.

Gilroy, Paul. *"There Ain't No Black in the Union Jack": The Cultural Politics of Race and Nation*. Chicago: University of Chicago Press, 1991.

Kellner, Douglas, ed. *Baudrillard: A Critical Reader*. Oxford: Blackwell, 1995.

López, José and Garry Potter, eds. *After Postmodernism: An Introduction to Critical Realism*. London & New York: Athlone, 2001.

Nielsen, Aldon Lynn. *Black Chant: Languages of African-American Postmodernism*. Cambridge & New York: Cambridge University Press, 1997.

Rayner, Philip, Peter Wall and Stephen Kruger, eds. *Media Studies: The Essential Resource*. London & New York: Routledge, 2004.

Rose, Tricia. *Black Noise: Rap Music and Black Culture in Contemporary America*. Hanover & London: Wesleyan University Press, 1994.

Skelton, Tracey and Tim Allen, eds. *Culture and Global Change*. London & New York: Routledge, 2000.

Smyth, Edmund J. ed. *Postmodernism and Contemporary Fiction*. London: Batsford, 1991.

Strinati, Dominic. *An Introduction to Studying Popular Culture*. London & New York: Routledge, 2000.

Thussu, Daya Kishan, ed. *Internationalizing Media Studies*. Abingdon, Oxon & New York: Routledge, 2009.

Notes

1   Theodor Adorno and Max Horkheimer, *Dialectic of Enlightenment*, trans. John Cumming, London: Verso, 1992, 132.

2   *The Times* newspaper, <http://www.tvhistory.tv/1936%20QF.htm> from <http://www.tvhistory.tv/index.html> accessed March 29th, 2011.

3   <http://www.tvhistory.tv/1936-Aug-Radiolympia-Report.JPG> accessed March 29th, 2011.

4   See Fredric Jameson, "Postmodernism and Consumer Society" in Fredric Jameson, *The Cultural Turn: Selected Writings on the Postmodern, 1993–1998*, London & New York: Verso, 1998, 1–20.

5   Dominic Strinati, *An Introduction to Studying Popular Culture*, London & New York: Routledge, 2000, p.233.

6   Dominic Strinati, *An Introduction to Studying Popular Culture*, p.233.

7   Richard J. Lane, "Culture", in *The Baudrillard Dictionary*, Richard G. Smith, ed., Edinburgh: Edinburgh University Press, 2010, 44–46, p.45.

8   Richard J. Lane, "Culture", in *The Baudrillard Dictionary*, p.45.

9   Richard Cavell, *McLuhan in Space: A Cultural Geography*, Toronto: University of Toronto Press, 2003, p.81.

10   Paul Gilroy, *"There Ain't No Black in the Union Jack"*: The Cultural Politics of Race and Nation, Chicago: University of Chicago Press, 1991, p.194.

11   Tricia Rose, *Black Noise: Rap Music and Black Culture in Contemporary America*, Hanover & London: Wesleyan University Press, 1994, pp.34–35.

12   Tricia Rose, *Black Noise: Rap Music and Black Culture in Contemporary America*, p.35.

13   Tricia Rose, *Black Noise: Rap Music and Black Culture in Contemporary America*, p.19.

14   See, for example, <http://www.guardian.co.uk/katine/2009/jan/04/katine-uganda-africa-mobile-phones> and <http://www.guardian.co.uk/katine/katine-chronicles-blog/2010/jan/14/mobile-phones-africa> , accessed April 4th 2011.

15   Heather Tyrrell, "Bollywood versus Hollywood: Battle of the dream factories", in *Culture and Global Change*, Tracey Skelton and Tim Allen, eds., London & New York: Routledge, 2000, 260–73, p.262.

16   Ravi Sundaram, "Recycling Modernity: Pirate Electronic Cultures in India", *Third Text*, 47 (Summer 1999): 59–65; p.64.

Chapter 14

Walter Benjamin

THE WORK OF ART IN THE AGE OF ITS TECHNOLOGICAL REPRODUCIBILITY (SECOND VERSION)

Karl Marx (1818–83) predicted vast social changes that would be brought about by capitalism, and by the time of Walter Benjamin's essay (1935–36), these were manifesting themselves not just in the "base" (or, the material productive forces in which human lives are embedded) but also in the "superstructure" (legal, political, intellectual and cultural aspects of life). Benjamin, a German-Jewish scholar whose work bridges Marxism and messianism, as well as literature and politics, asks how art will change under the current conditions of production, not to serve the rising political force in Germany of fascism, but to resist it, and to bring about revolutionary transformation. In this second version of his essay, Benjamin presents nineteen theses on his topic; the extract gives the first eight. In his second thesis, Benjamin notes that even though artworks have always been reproducible—i.e., single copies can be made, however laboriously— it is "technological" reproduction that emerges in the nineteenth century as something new. In other words, hand-made copies are replaced by mass-produced, rapidly made machine copies. This process culminates for Benjamin in the technologies of photography and film, with his acute observation that the eye can move more rapidly than the hand. Past notions of authenticity, such as artworks having a "unique existence in a particular place", and a physical, historical identity, are replaced by new ideas, since technological reproduction is not dependent upon singular time and space: the "copy" can be produced and consumed anywhere, and it is not limited to a physical reality. The new technologies are also prosthetic: the camera eye can see deeper into the close-up world (such as macro photography), and slow-motion film reveals movements never before observed by the human eye. In other words, the copy outperforms the original. In his third and fourth theses Benjamin also introduces another marker of old-fashioned authenticity: the concept of the "aura", which he defines as "A strange tissue of space and time: the unique apparition of a distance, however near it may be." A more literal translation of the German would call the aura a "one-time appearance" intertwined with the far and near, which could be expressed as the unique occasion whereby in a particular place a person saw something beautiful or moving, either in the distance (say, a mountain range), or up close (a branch casting a shadow). In the modern era of technological reproducibility, the aura withers away: the "masses" want to get closer to the artwork, and they also want to "overcome" its uniqueness and authenticity, perhaps because historically such grand works of art were always out of reach because of class disempowerment and poverty. Modern artworks are transitory and repeatable, and they wrench themselves away from older traditions, organizing human perception in new ways, such as through the delights of distraction. While authentic or auratic works of art belonged in the cult world of ritual and exclusivity, modern works are potentially political. Benjamin describes this as a shift from cult to exhibition value, i.e., from a closed, hierarchical, secret and magical world, to an open, technological society, where humans learn, through shifts in perception, how to operate the machines that will one day give them mastery over nature. While the aura does not fade away entirely—such as its continuing presence in portrait photography—Benjamin notes how film can be used practically, such as with documentary evidence at crime scenes, and is open to positive manipulation: it can be creatively re-edited, and continually improved.

> The true is what he can; the false is what he wants.

> —Madame de Duras[1]

I

When Marx undertook his analysis of the capitalist mode of production, that mode was in its infancy.[2] Marx adopted an approach which gave his investigations prognostic value. Going back to the basic conditions of capitalist production, he presented them in a way which showed what could be expected of capitalism in the future. What could be expected, it emerged, was not only an increasingly harsh exploitation of the proletariat but, ultimately, the creation of conditions which would make it possible for capitalism to abolish itself.

Since the transformation of the superstructure proceeds far more slowly than that of the base, it has taken more than half a century for the change in the conditions of production to be manifested in all areas of culture. How this process has affected culture can only now be assessed, and these assessments must meet certain prognostic requirements. They do not, however, call for theses on the art of the proletariat after its seizure of power, and still less for any on the art of the classless society. They call for theses defining the tendencies of the development of art under the present conditions of production. The dialectic of these conditions of production is evident in the superstructure, no less than in the economy. Theses defining the developmental tendencies of art can therefore contribute to the political struggle in ways that it would be a mistake to underestimate. They neutralize a number of traditional concepts—such as creativity and genius, eternal value and mystery—which, used in an uncontrolled way (and controlling them is difficult today), allow factual material to be manipulated in the interests of fascism. *In what follows, the concepts which are introduced into the theory of art differ from those now current in that they are completely useless for the purposes of fascism. On the other hand, they are useful for the formulation of revolutionary demands in the politics of art* [Kunstpolitik].

II

In principle, the work of art has always been reproducible. Objects made by humans could always be copied by humans. Replicas were made by pupils in practicing for their craft, by masters in disseminating their works, and, finally, by third parties in pursuit of profit. But the technological reproduction of artworks is something new. Having appeared intermittently in history, at widely spaced intervals, it is now being adopted with ever-increasing intensity. Graphic art was first made technologically reproducible by the woodcut, long before written language became reproducible by movable type. The enormous changes brought about in literature by movable type, the technological reproduction of writing, are well known. But they are only a special case, though an important one, of the phenomenon considered here from the perspective of world history. In the course of the Middle Ages the woodcut was supplemented by engraving and etching, and at the beginning of the nineteenth century by lithography.

Lithography marked a fundamentally new stage in the technology of reproduction. This much more direct process—distinguished by the fact that the drawing is traced on a stone, rather than incised on a block of wood or etched on a copper plate—first made it possible for graphic art to market its products not only in large numbers, as previously, but in daily changing variations. Lithography enabled graphic art to provide an illustrated accompaniment to everyday life. It began to keep pace with movable-type printing. But only a few decades after the invention of lithography, graphic art was surpassed by photography. For the first time, photography freed the hand from the most important artistic tasks in the process of pictorial reproduction—tasks that now devolved upon the eye alone. And since the eye perceives more swiftly than the hand can draw, the process of pictorial reproduction was enormously accelerated, so that it could now keep pace with speech. Just as the illustrated newspaper virtually lay hidden within lithography, so the sound film was latent in photography. The technological reproduction of sound was tackled at the end of the last century. *Around 1900, technological reproduction not only had reached a standard that permitted it to reproduce all known works of art, profoundly modifying their effect, but it also had captured a place of its own among the artistic processes. In gauging this standard, we would do well to study the impact which its two different manifestations—the reproduction of artworks and the art of film—are having on art in its traditional form.*

III

In even the most perfect reproduction, *one* thing is lacking: the here and now of the work of art—its unique existence in a particular place. It is this unique existence—and nothing else—that bears the mark of the history to which the work has been subject. This history includes changes to the physical structure of the work over time, together with any changes in ownership. Traces of the former can be detected only by chemical or physical analyses (which cannot be performed on a reproduction), while changes of ownership are part of a tradition which can be traced only from the standpoint of the original in its present location.

The here and now of the original underlies the concept of its authenticity, and on the latter in turn is founded the idea of a tradition which has passed the object down as the same, identical thing to the present day. *The whole sphere of authenticity eludes technological—and of course not only technological—reproduction.* But whereas the authentic work retains its full authority in the face of a reproduction made by hand, which it generally brands a forgery, this is not the case with technological reproduction. The reason is twofold. First, technological reproduction is more independent of the original than is manual reproduction. For example, in photography it can bring out aspects of the original that are accessible only to the lens (which is adjustable and can easily change viewpoint) but not to the human eye; or it can use certain processes, such as enlargement or slow motion, to record images which escape natural optics altogether. This is the first reason. Second, technological reproduction can place the copy of the original in situations which the original itself cannot attain. Above all, it enables the original to meet the recipient halfway, whether in the form of a photograph or in that of a gramophone record. The cathedral leaves its site to be received in the studio of an art lover; the choral work performed in an auditorium or in the open air is enjoyed in a private room.

These changed circumstances may leave the artwork's other properties untouched, but they certainly devalue the here and now of the artwork. And although this can apply not only to art but (say) to a landscape moving past the spectator in a film, in the work of art this process touches on a highly sensitive core, more vulnerable than that of any natural object. That core is its authenticity. The authenticity of a thing is the quintessence of all that is transmissible in it from its origin on, ranging from its physical duration to the historical testimony relating to it. Since the historical testimony is founded on the physical duration, the former, too, is jeopardized by reproduction, in which the physical duration plays no part. And what is really jeopardized when the historical testimony is affected is the authority of the object, the weight it derives from tradition.

One might focus these aspects of the artwork in the concept of the aura, and go on to say: what withers in the age of the technological reproducibility of the work of art is the latter's aura. This process is symptomatic; its significance extends far beyond the realm of art. *It might be stated as a general formula that the technology of reproduction detaches the reproduced object from the sphere of tradition. By replicating the work many times over, it substitutes a mass existence for a unique existence. And in permitting the reproduction to reach the recipient in his or her own situation, it actualizes that which is reproduced.* These two processes lead to a massive upheaval in the domain of objects handed down from the past—a shattering of tradition which is the reverse side of the present crisis and renewal of humanity. Both processes are intimately related to the mass movements of our day. Their most powerful agent is film. The social significance of film, even—and especially—in its most positive form, is inconceivable without its destructive, cathartic side: the liquidation of the value of tradition in the cultural heritage. This phenomenon is most apparent in the great historical films. It is assimilating ever more advanced positions in its spread. When Abel Gance fervently proclaimed in 1927, "Shakespeare, Rembrandt, Beethoven will make films. . . . All legends, all mythologies, and all myths, all the founders of religions, indeed, all religions, . . . await their celluloid resurrection, and the heroes are pressing at the gates," he was inviting the reader, no doubt unawares, to witness a comprehensive liquidation.[3]

IV

Just as the entire mode of existence of human collectives changes over long historical periods, so too does their mode of perception. The way in which human perception is organized—the medium in which it occurs—is conditioned not only by nature but by history. The era of the migration of peoples, an era which saw the rise of the late-Roman art industry and the Vienna Genesis, developed not only an art different from that of antiquity but also a different perception. The scholars of the Viennese school Riegl and Wickhoff, resisting the weight of the classical tradition beneath which this art had been buried, were the first to think of using such art to draw conclusions about the organization of perception at the time the art was produced.[4] However far-reaching their insight, it was limited by the fact that these scholars were content to highlight the formal signature which characterized perception in late-Roman times. They did not attempt to show the social upheavals manifested in these changes in perception—and perhaps could not have hoped to do so at that time. Today, the conditions for an analogous insight are more favorable. And if changes in the medium of present-day perception can be understood as a decay of the aura, it is possible to demonstrate the social determinants of that decay.

What, then, is the aura? A strange tissue of space and time: the unique apparition of a distance, however near it may be.[5] To follow with the eye—while resting on a summer afternoon—a mountain range on the horizon or a branch that casts its shadow on the beholder is to breathe the aura of those mountains, of that branch. In the light of this description, we can readily grasp the social basis of the aura's present decay. It rests on two circumstances, both linked to the increasing emergence of the masses and the growing intensity of their movements. Namely: *the desire of the present-day masses to "get closer" to things, and their equally passionate concern for overcoming each thing's uniqueness [Überwindung des Einmaligen jeder Gegebenheit] by assimilating it as a reproduction.* Every day the urge grows stronger to get hold of an object at close range in an image [*Bild*], or, better, in a facsimile [*Abbild*], a reproduction. And the reproduction [*Reproduktion*], as offered by illustrated magazines and newsreels, differs unmistakably from the image. Uniqueness and permanence are as closely entwined in the latter as are transitoriness and repeatability in the former. The stripping of the veil from the object, the destruction of the aura, is the signature of a perception whose "sense for sameness in the world"[6] has so increased that, by means of reproduction, it extracts sameness even from what is unique. Thus is manifested in the field of perception what in the theoretical sphere is noticeable in the increasing significance of statistics. The alignment of reality with the masses and of the masses with reality is a process of immeasurable importance for both thinking and perception.

V

The uniqueness of the work of art is identical to its embeddedness in the context of tradition. Of course, this tradition itself is thoroughly alive and extremely changeable. An ancient statue of Venus, for instance, existed in a traditional context for the Greeks (who made it an object of worship) that was different from the context in which it existed for medieval clerics (who viewed it as a sinister idol). But what was equally evident to both was its uniqueness— that is, its aura. Originally, the embeddedness of an artwork in the context of tradition found expression in a cult. As we know, the earliest artworks originated in the service of rituals— first magical, then religious. And it is highly significant that the artwork's auratic mode of existence is never entirely severed from its ritual function. In other words: *the unique value of the "authentic" work of art always has its basis in ritual.* This ritualistic basis, however mediated it may be, is still recognizable as secularized ritual in even the most profane forms of the cult of beauty. The secular worship of beauty, which developed during the Renaissance and prevailed for three centuries, clearly displayed that ritualistic basis in its subsequent decline and in the first severe crisis which befell it. For when, with the advent of the first truly revolutionary means of reproduction (namely photography, which emerged at the same time as socialism), art felt the approach of that crisis which a century later has become unmistakable, it reacted with the doctrine of *l'art pour l'art*—that is, with a theology of art. This in turn gave rise to a negative theology, in the form of an idea of "pure" art, which rejects not only any social function but any definition in terms of a representational content. (In poetry, Mallarmé was the first to adopt this standpoint.)[7]

No investigation of the work of art in the age of its technological reproducibility can overlook these connections. They lead to a crucial insight: for the first time in world history, technological reproducibility emancipates the work of art from its parasitic subservience to ritual. To an ever-increasing degree, the work reproduced becomes the reproduction of a work designed for reproducibility.[8] From a photographic plate, for example, one can make any number of prints; to ask for the "authentic" print makes no sense. *But as soon as the criterion of authenticity ceases to be applied to artistic production, the whole social function of art is revolutionized. Instead of being founded on ritual, it is based on a different practice: politics.*

VI

Art history might be seen as the working out of a tension between two polarities within the artwork itself, its course being determined by shifts in the balance between the two. These two poles are the artwork's cult value and its exhibition value.[9] Artistic production begins with figures in the service of magic. What is important for these figures is that they are present, not that they are seen. The elk depicted by Stone Age man on the walls of his cave is an instrument of magic, and is exhibited to others only coincidentally; what matters is that the spirits see it. Cult value as such even tends to keep the artwork out of sight: certain statues of gods are accessible only to the priest in the cella; certain images of the Madonna remain covered nearly all year round; certain sculptures on medieval cathedrals are not visible to the viewer at ground level. *With the emancipation of specific artistic practices from the service of ritual, the opportunities for exhibiting their products increase.* It is easier to exhibit a portrait bust that can be sent here and there than to exhibit the statue of a divinity that has a fixed place in the interior of a temple. A panel painting can be exhibited more easily than the mosaic or fresco which preceded it. And although a mass may have been no less suited to public presentation than a symphony, the symphony came into being at a time when the possibility of such presentation promised to be greater.

The scope for exhibiting the work of art has increased so enormously with the various methods of technologically reproducing it that, as happened in prehistoric times, a quantitative shift between the two poles of the artwork has led to a qualitative transformation in its nature. Just as the work of art in prehistoric times, through the exclusive emphasis placed on its cult value, became first and foremost an instrument of magic which only later came to be recognized as a work of art, so today, through the exclusive emphasis placed on its exhibition value, the work of art becomes a construct [*Gebilde*] with quite new functions. Among these, the one we are conscious of—the artistic function—may subsequently be seen as incidental. This much is certain: today, film is the most serviceable vehicle of this new understanding. Certain, as well, is the fact that the historical moment of this change in the function of art—a change which is most fully evident in the case of film—allows a direct comparison with the primeval era of art not only from a methodological but also from a material point of view.

Prehistoric art made use of certain fixed notations in the service of magical practice. In some cases, these notations probably comprised the actual performing of magical acts (the carving of an ancestral figure is itself such an act); in others, they gave instructions for such procedures (the ancestral figure demonstrates a ritual posture); and in still others, they provided objects for magical contemplation (contemplation of an ancestral figure strengthens the occult powers of the beholder). The subjects for these notations were humans and their environment, which were depicted according to the requirements of a society whose technology existed only in fusion with ritual. Compared to that of the machine age, of course, this technology was undeveloped. But from a dialectical standpoint, the disparity is unimportant. What matters is the way the orientation and aims of that technology differ from those of ours. Whereas the former made the maximum possible use of human beings, the latter reduces their use to the minimum. The achievements of the first technology might be said to culminate in human sacrifice; those of the second, in the remote-controlled aircraft which needs no human crew. The results of the first technology are valid once and for all (it deals with irreparable lapse or sacrificial death, which holds good for eternity). The results of the second are wholly provisional (it operates by means of experiments and endlessly varied test procedures). The origin of the second technology lies at the point where, by an unconscious ruse, human beings first began to distance themselves from nature. It lies, in other words, in play.

Seriousness and play, rigor and license, are mingled in every work of art, though in very different proportions. This implies that art is linked to both the second and the first technologies. It should be noted, however, that to describe the goal of the second technology as "mastery over nature" is highly questionable, since this implies viewing the second technology from the standpoint of the first. The first technology really sought to master nature, whereas the second aims rather at an interplay between nature and humanity. The primary social function of art today is to rehearse that interplay. This applies especially to film. *The function of film is to train human beings in the apperceptions and reactions needed to deal with a vast apparatus whose role in their lives is expanding almost daily.* Dealing with this apparatus also teaches them that technology will release them from their enslavement to the powers of the apparatus only when humanity's whole constitution has adapted itself to the new productive forces which the second technology has set free.[10]

VII

In photography, exhibition value begins to drive back cult value on all fronts. But cult value does not give way without resistance. It falls back to a last entrenchment: the human countenance. It is no accident that the portrait is central to early photography. In the cult of remembrance of dead or absent loved ones, the cult value of the image finds its last refuge. In the fleeting expression of a human face, the aura beckons from early photographs for the last time. This is what gives them their melancholy and incomparable beauty. But as the human being withdraws from the photographic image, exhibition value for the first time shows its superiority to cult value. To have given this development its local habitation constitutes the unique significance of Atget, who, around 1900, took photographs of deserted Paris streets.[11] It has justly been said that he photographed them like scenes of crimes. A crime scene, too, is deserted; it is photographed for the purpose of establishing evidence. With Atget, photographic records begin to be evidence in the historical trial [*Prozess*]. This constitutes their hidden political significance. They demand a specific kind of reception. Free-floating contemplation is no longer appropriate to them. They unsettle the viewer; he feels challenged to find a particular way to approach them. At the same time, illustrated magazines begin to put up signposts for him—whether these are right or wrong is irrelevant. For the first time, captions become obligatory. And it is clear that they have a character altogether different from the titles of paintings. The directives given by captions to those looking at images in illustrated magazines soon become even more precise and commanding in films, where the way each single image is understood seems prescribed by the sequence of all the preceding images.

VIII

The Greeks had only two ways of technologically reproducing works of art: casting and stamping. Bronzes, terra cottas, and coins were the only artworks they could produce in large numbers. All others were unique and could not be technologically reproduced. That is why they had to be made for all eternity. *The state of their technology compelled the Greeks to produce eternal values in their art.* To this they owe their preeminent position in art history— the standard for subsequent generations. Undoubtedly, our position lies at the opposite pole from that of the Greeks. Never before have artworks been technologically reproducible to such a degree and in such quantities as today. Film is the first art form whose artistic character is entirely determined by its reproducibility. It would be idle to compare this form in detail with Greek art. But on one precise point such a comparison would be revealing. For film has given crucial importance to a quality of the artwork which would have been the last to find approval among the Greeks, or which they would have dismissed as marginal. This quality is its capacity for improvement. The finished film is the exact antithesis of a work created at a single stroke. It is assembled from a very large number of images and image sequences that offer an array of choices to the editor; these images, moreover, can be improved in any desired way in the process leading from the initial take to the final cut. To produce *A Woman of Paris*, which is 3,000 meters long, Chaplin shot 125,000 meters of film.[12] *The film is therefore the artwork most capable of improvement. And this capability is linked to its radical renunciation of eternal value*. This is corroborated by the fact that for the Greeks, whose art depended on the production of eternal values, the pinnacle of all the arts was the form least capable of improvement—namely sculpture, whose products are literally all of a piece. In the age of the assembled [*montierbar*] artwork, the decline of sculpture is inevitable.

Notes

This version of the essay "Das Kunstwerk im Zeitalter seiner technischen Reproduzierbarkeit" (first published in Volume 7 of Benjamin's *Gesammelte Schriften,* in 1989) is a revision and expansion (by seven manuscript pages) of the first version of the essay, which was composed in Paris in the autumn of 1935. The second version represents the form in which Benjamin originally wished to see the work published; it served, in fact, as the basis for the first publication of the essay—a somewhat shortened form translated into French—in the *Zeitschrift für Sozialforschung* in May 1936. The third version of the essay (1936–39) will appear in Walter Benjamin, *Selected Writings: Volume 4, 1938–1940* (Cambridge, Mass.: Harvard University Press, forthcoming).

1   Madame Claire de Duras, née Kersaint (1778–1828), the wife of Duc Amédée de Duras, field marshal under Louis XVIII, was the author of two novels, *Ourika* (1823) and *Edouard* (1825). She presided over a brilliant salon in Paris. Benjamin cites Madame de Duras in the original French.

2   The German political philosopher Karl Marx (1818–83) analyzed the capitalist mode of production in his most famous and influential work, *Das Kapital* (3 vols., 1867, 1885, 1895), which was carried to completion by his collaborator Friedrich Engels (1820–95).

3   Abel Gance, "Le Temps de l'image est venu!" (It Is Time for the Image!), in Léon Pierre-Quint, Germaine Dulac, Lionel Landry, and Abel Gance, *L'Art cinématographique,* vol. 2 (Paris, 1927), pp. 94–96. [Benjamin's note. Gance (1889–1981) was a leading French film director whose epic films *J'Accuse* (1919), *La Roue* (1922), and *Napoléon* (1927) made innovative use of such devices as superimposition, rapid intercutting, and split screen.—*Trans.*]

4   Alois Riegl (1858–1905) was an Austrian art historian who argued that different formal orderings of art emerge as expressions of different historical epochs. He is the author of *Stilfragen: Grundlegungen zu einer Geschichte der Ornamentik* (Questions of Style: Toward a History of Ornament; 1893) and *Die spätrömische Kunst-Industrie nach den Funden in Österreich-Ungarn* (1901). The latter has been translated by Rolf Winks as *Late Roman Art Industry* (Rome: Giorgio Bretschneider Editore, 1985). Franz Wickhoff (1853–1909), also an Austrian art historian, is the author of *Die Wiener Genesis* (The Vienna Genesis; 1922), a study of the sumptuously illuminated, early sixth-century A.D. copy of the biblical book of Genesis preserved in the Austrian National Library in Vienna.

5   "Einmalige Erscheinung einer Ferne, so nah sie sein mag." At stake in Benjamin's formulation is an interweaving not just of time and space—*einmalige Erscheinung,* literally "one-time appearance"—but of far and near, *eine Ferne* suggesting both "a distance" in space or time and "something remote," however near it (the distance, or distant thing, that appears) may be.

6   Benjamin is quoting Johannes V. Jensen, *Exotische Novellen,* trans. Julia Koppel (Berlin: S. Fischer, 1919), pp. 41–42. Jensen (1873–1950) was a Danish novelist, poet, and essayist who won the Nobel Prize for Literature in 1944. See "Hashish in Marseilles," in Benjamin, *Selected Writings, Volume 2: 1927–1934* (Cambridge, Mass.: Harvard University Press, 1999), p. 677.

7   Stéphane Mallarmé (1842–98), French poet, translator, and editor, was an originator and leader of the Symbolist movement, which sought an incantatory language divorced from all referential function. Among his works are *L'Aprèsmidi d'un faune* (Afternoon of a Faun; 1876) and *Vers et prose* (Poetry and Prose; 1893).

8   In film, the technological reproducibility of the product is not an externally imposed condition of its mass dissemination, as it is, say, in literature or painting. *The technological reproducibility of films is based directly on the technology of their production. This not only makes possible the mass dissemination of films in the most direct way, but actually enforces it.* It does so because the process of producing a film is so costly that an individual who could afford to buy a painting, for example, could not afford to buy a [master print of a] film. It was calculated in 1927 that, in order to make a profit, a major film needed to reach an audience of nine million. Of course, the advent of sound film [in that year] initially caused a movement in the opposite direction: its audience was restricted by language boundaries. And that coincided with the emphasis placed on national interests by fascism. But it is less important to note this setback (which in any case was mitigated by dubbing) than to observe its connection with fascism. The simultaneity of the two phenomena results from the economic crisis. The same disorders which led, in the world at large, to an attempt to maintain existing property relations by brute force induced

film capital, under the threat of crisis, to speed up the development of sound film. Its introduction brought temporary relief, not only because sound film attracted the masses back into the cinema but also because it consolidated new capital from the electricity industry with that of film. Thus, considered from the outside, sound film promoted national interests; but seen from the inside, it helped internationalize film production even more than before. [Benjamin's note. By "the economic crisis," Benjamin refers to the devastating consequences, in the United States and Europe, of the stock market crash of October 1929.—*Trans.*]

9   This polarity cannot come into its own in the aesthetics of Idealism, which conceives of beauty as something fundamentally undivided (and thus excludes anything polarized). Nonetheless, in Hegel this polarity announces itself as clearly as possible within the limits of Idealism. We quote from his *Vorlesungen zur Philosophie der Geschichte* [Lectures on the Philosophy of History]: "Images were known of old. In those early days piety required them for worship, but it could do without *beautiful* images. Such images might even be disturbing. In every beautiful image, there is also something external— although, insofar as the image is beautiful, its spirit still speaks to the human being. But religious worship, being no more than a spiritless torpor of the soul, is directed at a *thing*. . . . Fine art arose . . . in the church . . ., though art has now gone beyond the ecclesiastical principle." Likewise, the following passage from the *Vorlesungen über die Ästhetik* [Lectures on Aesthetics] indicates that Hegel sensed a problem here: "We are beyond the stage of venerating works of art as divine and as objects deserving our worship. Today the impression they produce is of a more reflective kind, and the emotions they arouse require a more stringent test." [Benjamin's note. The German Idealist philosopher Georg Wilhelm Friedrich Hegel (1770–1831) accepted the chair in philosophy at the University of Berlin in 1818. His lectures on aesthetics and the philosophy of history (delivered 1820–29) were later published by his editors, with the text based mainly on notes taken by his students.—*Trans.*]

10 The aim of revolutions is to accelerate this adaptation. Revolutions are innervations of the collective—or, more precisely, efforts at innervation on the part of the new, historically unique collective which has its organs in the new technology. This second technology is a system in which the mastering of elementary social forces is a precondition for playing [*das Spiel*] with natural forces. Just as a child who has learned to grasp stretches out its hand for the moon as it would for a ball, so humanity, in its efforts at innervation, sets its sights as much on currently utopian goals as on goals within reach. For in revolutions, it is not only the second technology which asserts its claims vis-à-vis society. Because this technology aims at liberating human beings from drudgery, the individual suddenly sees his scope for play, his field of action [*Spielraum*], immeasurably expanded. He does not yet know his way around this space. But already he registers his demands on it. For the more the collective makes the second technology its own, the more keenly individuals belonging to the collective feel how little they have received of what was due them under the dominion of the first technology. In other words, it is the individual liberated by the liquidation of the first technology who stakes his claim. No sooner has the second technology secured its initial revolutionary gains than vital questions affecting the individual—questions of love and death which had been buried by the first technology—once again press for solutions. Fourier's work is the first historical evidence of this demand. [Benjamin's note. Charles Fourier (1772–1837), French social theorist and reformer, urged that society by reorganized into self-contained agrarian cooperatives which he called "phalansteries." Among his works are *Théorie des quatre mouvements* (Theory of Four Movements; 1808) and *Le Nouveau Monde industriel* (The New Industrial World; 1829–30). He is an important figure in Benjamin's *Passagen-Werk* (Arcades Project). The term *Spielraum*, in this note, in note 22, and in the text, literally means "playspace," "space for play."—*Trans.*]

11 Eugène Atget (1857–1927), recognized today as one of the leading photographers of the twentieth century, spent his career in obscurity making pictures of Paris and its environs. See Benjamin's "Little History of Photography," in Walter Benjamin, *Selected Writings: Volume 2, 1927–1934* (Cambridge, Mass.: Harvard University Press, 1999), pp. 518–19 (trans. Edmund Jephcott and Kingsley Shorter).

12 *A Woman of Paris* (1923)—which Benjamin refers to by its French title, *L'Opinion publique*—was written and directed by Charlie Chaplin (Charles Spencer Chaplin; 1899–1977), London-born actor who was on stage from the age of five. He came to the United States with a vaudeville act in 1910 and made his motion picture debut there in 1914, eventually achieving worldwide renown as a comedian. He was the director of such films as *The Kid* (1921), *The Circus* (1928), *City Lights* (1931), *Modern Times* (1936), and *The Great Dictator* (1940). See Benjamin's short pieces "Chaplin" (1929) and "Hitler's Diminished Masculinity" (1934) in Volume 2 of this edition.

Chapter 15

Marshall McLuhan and Quentin Fiore

"TIME" HAS CEASED, "SPACE" HAS VANISHED. WE NOW LIVE IN A *GLOBAL* VILLAGE

While Marshall McLuhan's rather awkward compound word "allatonceness" never caught on, his phrase the "global village" has increased in popularity ever since he first used it in 1959 (Wyndham Lewis, an author McLuhan admired, had called the earth "one big village" in 1948). McLuhan, a literary critic who became an infamous and prophetic media theorist, argues that a world dominated by the visual linearity of print has been replaced by "acoustic space", that is to say, a permanently connected, dynamic and sensation-based realm of instantaneous electronic communication, brilliantly visualized here by graphic designer Quentin Fiore. When McLuhan says that time and space have "ceased" he means that in some ways these are meaningless terms when any event or sensation can be simultaneously experienced by multiple people in multiple locations around the globe. It has become normal, from the perspective of the internet and satellite communications, to think this way, but McLuhan prophetically mapped out this new networked world in the 1950s and 1960s. Shifting from linear print technologies ("visual") to multiple senses ("acoustic") is analogous to an earlier way of experiencing life: the oral cultures of the medieval era that proceeded the invention of moveable type with Gutenberg's (1400?–1468) printing experiments in 1438. In the global village, the interior, private space of reading is replaced with the communities of oral/aural cultures, leading to the notion of "tribal" existence. But McLuhan identifies a problem: people use outmoded notions of communication to articulate what is going on in an electronic age, one which immerses and envelops people in data. McLuhan argues that because linear reading and analysis have been replaced by data overload, people need to work with "pattern recognition" rather than bit-by-bit classification. This is a shift from analytical reflection to artistic process, engaging creatively and productively in situations and environments. The atomized individuals of print culture give way to the digital masses, with a concomitant surge of youthful immersion in popular culture. Democratic shifts in pedagogy lead to the 1960s and 1970s notion of the college "dropout" (rejecting the knowledge and methods of one's teachers as being politically and technologically outmoded and irrelevant) and the "teach-in" (whereby the students politicize their teachers and peers, taking over the role of the teacher). In fact McLuhan regards interaction as key, and this also involves learning to trust diverse sources—and senses—of information, shifting away from the visual (we trust the printed text) to the multimedia (different information modes, such as the speculative, graphical, aural, or countercultural).

Two modernist artists: John Cage and James Joyce are given as exemplary figures of aural society: Cage's democratic notion of sound and artistic expression means that everyone becomes an artist of equal validity, generating their own theatrical performances, just as the "oral linguistic music" of Joyce's *Finnegans Wake* derives from the vernacular of Ireland's Dublin. Authorship and copyright are deeply questioned once individuals can access new reproduction technologies. McLuhan's example is the photocopier machine, but more contemporary examples might be copying digital music or eBooks. Television "abolished writing" for McLuhan, extending our senses in active and corporate (or communal) participation of what we see and hear; now we are the screen onto which television projects its images, creating a new hyperreal or virtual world.

Ours is a brand-new world of allatonceness. "Time" has ceased, "space" has vanished. We now live in a global village . . . a simultaneous happening. We are back in acoustic space. We have begun again to structure the primordial feeling, the tribal emotions from which a few centuries of literacy divorced us.

We have had to shift our stress of attention from action to reaction. We must now know in advance the consequences of any policy or action, since the results are experienced without delay. Because of electric speed, we can no longer wait and see. George Washington once remarked, "We haven't heard from Benj. Franklin in Paris this year. We should write him a letter."

At the high speeds of electric communication, purely visual means of apprehending the world are no longer possible; they are just too slow to be relevant or effective.

Unhappily, we confront this new situation with an enormous backlog of outdated mental and psychological responses. We have been left d-a-n-g-l-i-n-g. Our most impressive words and thoughts betray us—they refer us only to the past, not to the present.

Electric circuitry profoundly involves men with one another. Information pours upon us, instantaneously and continuously. As soon as information is acquired, it is very rapidly replaced by still newer information. Our electrically-configured world has forced us to move from the habit of data classification to the mode of pattern recognition. We can no longer build serially, block-by-block, step-by-step, because instant communication insures that all factors of the environment and of experience coexist in a state of active interplay.

We have now become aware of the possibility of arranging the entire human environment as a work of art, as a teaching machine designed to maximize perception and to make everyday learning a process of discovery. Application of this knowledge would be the equivalent of a thermostat controlling room temperature. It would seem only reasonable to extend such controls to all the sensory thresholds of our being. We have no reason to be grateful to those who juggle these thresholds in the name of haphazard innovation.

An astronomer looking through a 200-inch telescope exclaimed that it was going to rain. His assistant asked, "How can you tell?" "Because my corns hurt."

Environments are not passive wrappings, but are, rather, active processes which are invisible. The groundrules, pervasive structure, and over-all patterns of environments elude easy perception. Anti-environments, or countersituations made by artists, provide means of direct attention and enable us to see and understand more clearly. The interplay between the old and the new environments creates many problems and confusions. The main obstacle to a clear understanding of the effects of the new media is our deeply embedded habit of regarding all phenomena from a fixed point of view. We speak, for instance, of "gaining perspective." This psychological process derives unconsciously from print technology.

Print technology created the public. Electric technology created the mass. The public consists of separate individuals walking around with separate, fixed points of view. The new technology demands that we abandon the luxury of this posture, this fragmentary outlook.

The method of our time is to use not a single but multiple models for exploration—the technique of the suspended judgment is the discovery of the twentieth century as the technique of invention was the discovery of the nineteenth.

The youth of today are not permitted to approach the traditional heritage of mankind through the door of technological awareness. This only possible door for them is slammed in their faces by a rear-view-mirror society.

The young today live mythically and in depth. But they encounter instruction in situations organized by means of classified information—subjects are unrelated, they are visually conceived in terms of a blueprint. Many of our institutions suppress all the natural direct experience of youth, who respond with untaught delight to the poetry and the beauty of the new technological environment, the environment of popular culture. It could be their door to all past achievement if studied as an active (and not necessarily benign) force.

The student finds no means of involvement for himself and cannot discover how the educational scheme relates to his mythic world of electronically processed data and experience that his clear and direct responses report.

It is a matter of the greatest urgency that our educational institutions realize that we now have civil war among these environments created by media other than the printed word. The classroom is now in a vital struggle for survival with the immensely persuasive "outside" world created by new informational media. Education must shift from instruction, from imposing of stencils, to discovery—to probing and exploration and to the recognition of the language of forms.

The young today reject goals. They want roles—R-O-L-E-S. That is, total involvement. They do not want fragmented, specialized goals or jobs.

We now experience simultaneously the dropout and the teach-in. The two forms are correlative. They belong together. The teach-in represents an attempt to shift education from instruction to discovery, from brainwashing students to brainwashing instructors. It is a big, dramatic reversal. Vietnam, as the content of the teach-in, is a very small and perhaps misleading Red Herring. It really has little to do with the teach-in, as such, anymore than with the dropout.

The dropout represents a rejection of nineteenth-century technology as manifested in our educational establishments. The teach-in represents a creative effort, switching the educational process from package to discovery. As the audience becomes a participant in the total electric drama, the classroom can become a scene in which the audience performs an enormous amount of work.

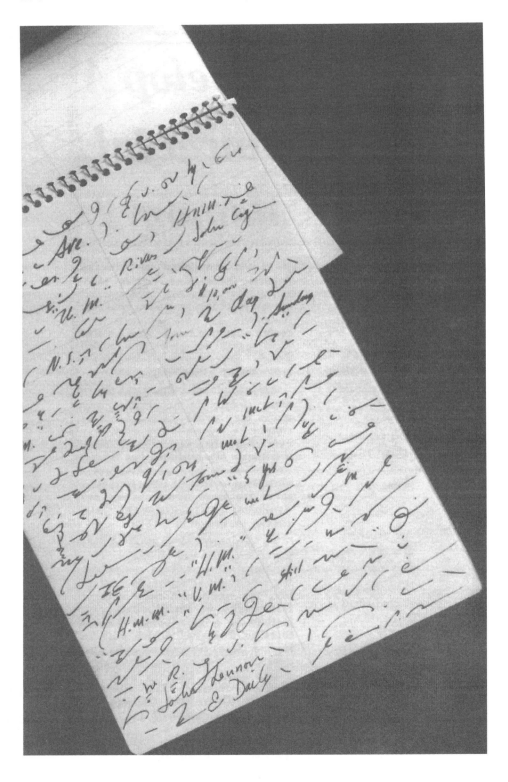

Most people find it difficult to understand purely verbal concepts. They <u>suspect</u> the ear; they don't trust it. In general we feel more secure when things are <u>visible</u>, when we can "see for ourselves." We admonish children, for instance, to "believe only half of what they <u>see</u>, and nothing of what they <u>hear</u>." All kinds of "shorthand" systems of notation have been developed to help us <u>see</u> what we <u>hear</u>.

We employ visual and spatial metaphors for a great many everyday expressions. We <u>insist</u> on employing visual metaphors even when we refer to purely psychological states, such as tendency and duration. For instance, we say <u>there</u>after when we really mean <u>then</u>after, always when we mean at all times. We are so visually biased that we call our wisest men <u>visio</u>naries, or <u>seers</u>!

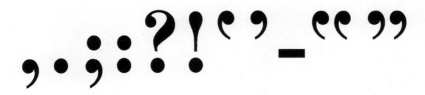

<u>Reminders</u>—(relics of the past)—in a world of the PRINTED word—efforts to **introduce** an AUDITORY dimension onto the <u>visual</u> organization of the **PAGE:** all effect <u>information</u>, **RHYTHM,** inflection, pauses. Until <u>recent</u> years, these EFFECTS were quite **elaborate**—they allowed for all sorts of **CHANGES** of type faces. The NEWSPAPER layout provides more variety of **AUDITORY** effects from typography than the **ordinary book page** does.

you

you

you

you

you

"Speak that I may see you."

Electrically-recorded voiceprints, like fingerprints, are now being accepted as evidence by some courts.

Five people were asked to say "you." One was asked to repeat it. Which two voiceprints were made by the same speaker?

Voiceprints at upper left, lower right.

John Cage:

"One must be disinterested, accept that a sound is a sound and a man is a man, give up illusions about ideas of order, expressions of sentiment, and all the rest of our inherited aesthetic claptrap."

"The highest purpose is to have no purpose at all. This puts one in accord with nature, in her manner of operation."

"Everyone is in the best seat."

"Everything we do is music."

"Theatre takes place all the time, wherever one is. And art simply facilitates persuading one this is the case."

"They [I Ching] told me to continue what I was doing, and to spread

JOY
and
revolution."

Listening to the simultaneous messages of Dublin, James Joyce released the greatest flood of oral linguistic music that was ever manipulated into art.

"The prouts who will invent a writing there ultimately is the poeta, still more learned, who discovered the raiding there originally. That's the point of eschatology our book of kills reaches for now in soandso many counterpoint words. What can't be coded can be decorded if an ear aye sieze what no eye ere grieved for. Now, the doctrine obtains, we have occasioning cause causing effects and affects occasionally recausing alter-effects."

Joyce is, in the "Wake," making his own Altamira cave drawings of the entire history of the human mind, in terms of its basic gestures and postures during all the phases of human culture and technology. As his title indicates, he saw that the wake of human progress can disappear again into the night of sacral or auditory man. The Finn cycle of tribal institutions can return in the electric age, but if again, then let's make it a wake or awake or both. Joyce could see no advantage in our remaining locked up in each cultural cycle as in a trance or dream. He discovered the means of living simultaneously in all cultural modes while quite conscious.

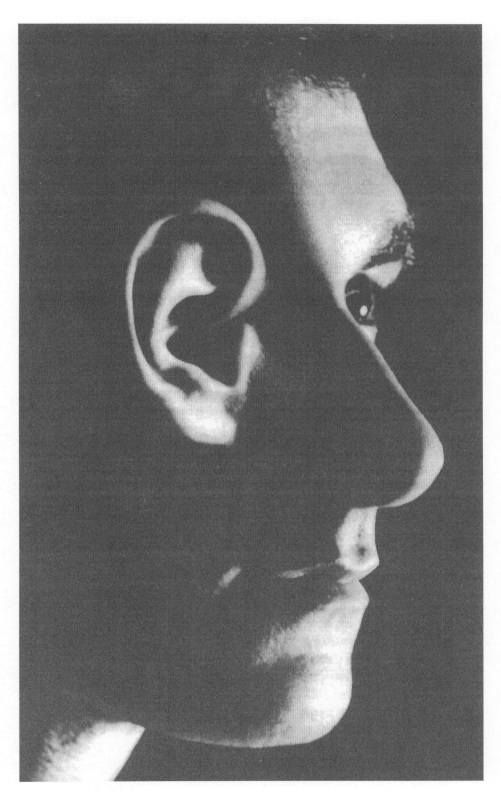

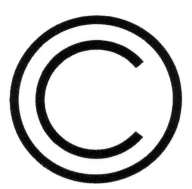

"Authorship"—in the sense we know it today, individual intellectual effort related to the book as an economic commodity—was practically unknown before the advent of print technology. Medieval scholars were indifferent to the precise identity of the "books" they studied. In turn, they rarely signed even what was clearly their own. They were a humble service organization. Procuring texts was often a very tedious and time-consuming task. Many small texts were transmitted into volumes of miscellaneous content, very much like "jottings" in a scrapbook, and, in this transmission, authorship was often lost.

The invention of printing did away with anonymity, fostering ideas of literary fame and the habit of considering intellectual effort as private property. Mechanical multiples of the same text created a public—a reading public. The rising consumer-oriented culture became concerned with labels of authenticity and protection against theft and piracy. The idea of copyright—"the exclusive right to reproduce, publish, and sell the matter and form of a literary or artistic work"—was born.

Xerography—every man's brain-picker—heralds the times of instant publishing. Anybody can now become both author and publisher. Take any books on any subject and custom-make your own book by simply xeroxing a chapter from this one, a chapter from that one—instant steal!

As new technologies come into play, people are less and less convinced of the importance of self-expression. Teamwork succeeds private effort.

A ditto, ditto device.
„   „   „   „

A ditto, ditto device.
„   „   „   „

A ditto, ditto device.
„   „   „   „

Even so imaginative a writer as Jules Verne failed to envisage the speed with which electric technology would produce informational media. He rashly predicted that television would be invented in the XXIXth Century.

Science-fiction writing today presents situations that enable us to perceive the potential of new technologies. Formerly, the problem was to invent new forms of labor-saving. Today, the reverse is the problem. Now we have to adjust, not to invent. We have to find the environments in which it will be possible to live with our new inventions. Big Business has learned to tap the s-f writer.

AU XXIXme SIÈCLE

Television completes the cycle of the human sensorium. With the omnipresent ear and the moving eye, we have abolished writing, the specialized acoustic-visual metaphor that established the dynamics of Western civilization.

In television there occurs an extension of the sense of active, exploratory touch which involves all the senses simultaneously, rather than that of sight alone. You have to be "with" it. But in all electric phenomena, the visual is only one component in a complex interplay. Since, in the age of information, most transactions are managed electrically, the electric technology has meant for Western man a considerable drop in the visual component, in his experience, and a corresponding increase in the activity of his other senses.

Television demands participation and involvement in depth of the whole being. It will not work as a background. It engages you. Perhaps this is why so many people feel that their identity has been threatened. This charge of the light brigade has heightened our general awareness of the shape and meaning of lives and events to a level of extreme sensitivity.

It was the funeral of President Kennedy that most strongly proved the power of television to invest an occasion with the character of corporate participation. It involves an entire population in a ritual process. (By comparison, press, movies, and radio are mere packaging devices for consumers.) In television, images are projected at you. You are the screen. The images wrap around you. You are the vanishing point. This creates a sort of inwardness, a sort of reverse perspective which has much in common with Oriental art.

Chapter 16

Tricia Rose

VOICES FROM THE MARGINS

Rap music and contemporary black cultural production

Mainstream media accounts of rap music often follow the simple binary logic of good/bad, liberating/ghettoizing, and so on, yet this is to simplify what Tricia Rose, Professor of Africana Studies at Brown University, calls instead the "contradictory articulations" of a powerful contemporary musical form. Rejecting binary logic, or either/or thinking, leads to a dialectically explosive form of thinking where extreme positions are registered and analyzed, but also potentially left in place. So Rose notes, for example, that black women rappers reject and critique sexism and economic deprivation while at the same time other, usually male rappers, often utilize a discourse of violence and misogyny. These contradictions are part of a more complex interweaving of social issues, cultural differences, and the overall politics of the street and the community, analyzed by Rose in books such as *Microphone Fiends* (co-ed., 1994), *Black Noise* (1994), *Longing to Tell* (2003), and *The Hip Hop Wars* (2008). Rose notes that popular culture is "polyvocal" (many voices), in other words, it articulates many different perspectives, including extremes, thereby expressing the diversity of actual communities. Since rap music emerges from and expresses black urban culture at the margins of mainstream society, its voices will be deliberately critical and counter-cultural. Many rap narratives express complex negotiations: with one's self-development as an autonomous and artistic individual, with urban gang and drug culture, with issues of sexuality and economics. The raw energy of rap often comes from the fact that, as Rose points out, "Rappers speak with the voice of personal experience." Rap narratives are not just part of a polyvocal community, they also draw deeply upon popular cultural media such as film, video, television and more recently the internet. The language used is often the vernacular: local street and alternative media languages made up mainly of highly creative slang and black history references. Sampled and quoted intertextual elements are often parodied and in other ways manipulated to re-code dominant whitestream media with black intensities of history, experience and hope. For a long time, however, rap music did not make it into the mainstream: Rose suggests that an album released in 1979 ("Rappers Delight") triggered the mainstream interest in the commodification of black rap. The rise of major rap artists during the 1980s and 1990s also involved the incorporation of rap culture into the movie industry, notably black filmmaker Spike Lee's *She's Gotta Have It* and *Do the Right Thing*. One of the ironies of entering the mainstream is that this alternative, countercultural musical form became popular among young white consumers. This is consistent with the history of white music incorporating and appropriating black creativity into its own whitestream versions, for example with the history of blues and jazz. White artists have a number of economic and other advantages over blacks, causing inequities, such as when MTV initially denied a space on their music cable channel for black performers. Yet once cable channels started to show black music videos, this media became extremely important as "a creative arena" for black artists in the wider sense of learning how to control and create using the audio-visual technologies of video and film. New alternative forms of rap music maintain its cultural autonomy, while mainstream black video and television production facilitates not just creative—but also media industry—control.

PUBLIC ENEMY'S "CAN'T TRUSS IT" opens with rapper Flavor Flav shouting "Confusion!" over a heavy and energetic bass line. The subsequent lyrics suggest that Flavor Flav is referring to lead rapper Chuck D's story about the legacy of slavery, that it has produced extreme cultural confusion. He could just as easily be describing the history of rap. Rap music is a confusing and noisy element of contemporary American popular culture that continues to draw a great deal of attention to itself. On the one hand, music and cultural critics praise rap's role as an educational tool, point out that black women rappers are rare examples of aggressive pro-women lyricists in popular music, and defend rap's ghetto stories as real-life reflections that should draw attention to the burning problems of rascism and economic oppression, rather than to questions of obscenity. On the other hand, news media attention on rap seems fixated on instances of violence at rap concerts, rap producers' illegal use of musical samples, gangsta raps' lurid fantasies of cop killing and female dismemberment, and black nationalist rappers' suggestions that white people are the devil's disciples. These celebratory and inflammatory aspects in rap and the media coverage of them bring to the fore several long-standing debates about popular music and culture. Some of the more contentious disputes revolve around the following questions: Can violent images incite violent action, can music set the stage for political mobilization, do sexually explicit lyrics contribute to the moral "breakdown" of society, and finally, is this really *music* anyway?

And, if these debates about rap music are not confusing enough, rappers engage them in contradictory ways. Some rappers defend the work of gangster rappers and at the same time consider it a negative influence on black youths. Female rappers openly criticize male rappers' sexist work and simultaneously defend the 2 Live Crew's right to sell misogynist music. Rappers who criticize America for its perpetuation of racial and economic discrimination also share conservative ideas about personal responsibility, call for self-improvement strategies in the black community that focus heavily on personal behavior as the cause and solution for crime, drugs, and community instability.

Rap music brings together a tangle of some of the most complex social, cultural, and political issues in contemporary American society. Rap's contradictory articulations are not signs of absent intellectual clarity; they are a common feature of community and popular cultural dialogues that always offer more than one cultural, social, or political viewpoint. These unusually abundant polyvocal conversations seem irrational when they are severed from the social contexts where everyday struggles over resources, pleasure, and meanings take place.

Rap music is a black cultural expression that prioritizes black voices from the margins of urban America. Rap music is a form of rhymed storytelling accompanied by highly rhythmic, electronically based music. It began in the mid-1970s in the South Bronx in New York City as a part of hip hop, an African-American and Afro-Caribbean youth culture composed of graffiti, breakdancing, and rap music. From the outset, rap music has articulated the pleasures and problems of black urban life in contemporary America. Rappers speak with the voice of personal experience, taking on the identity of the observer or narrator. Male rappers often speak from the perspective of a young man who wants social status in a locally meaningful way. They rap about how to avoid gang pressures and still earn local respect, how to deal with the loss of several friends to gun fights and drug overdoses, and they tell grandiose and sometimes violent tales that are powered by male sexual power over women. Female rappers sometimes tell stories from the perspective of a young woman who is skeptical of male protestations of love or a girl who has been involved with a drug dealer and cannot sever herself from his dangerous life-style. Some raps speak to the failures of black men to provide security and attack men where their manhood seems most vulnerable: the pocket. Some tales are one sister telling another to rid herself from the abuse of a lover.

Like all contemporary voices, the rapper's voice is imbedded in powerful and dominant technological, industrial, and ideological institutions. Rappers tell long, involved, and sometimes abstract stories with catchy and memorable phrases and beats that lend themselves to black sound bite packaging, storing critical fragments in fast-paced electrified rhythms. Rap tales are told in elaborate and ever-changing black slang and refer to black cultural figures and rituals, mainstream film, video and television characters and little-known black heroes. For rap's language wizards, all images, sounds, ideas, and icons are ripe for recontextualization, pun, mockery, and celebration. Kool Moe Dee boasts that each of his rhymes is like a dissertation, Kid-N-Play have quoted Jerry Lee Lewis's famous phrase "great balls of fire," Big Daddy Kane brags that he's raw like sushi (and that his object of love has his nose open like a jar of Vicks), Ice Cube refers to his ghetto stories as "tales from the darkside," clearly referencing the television horror show with the same name. Das Efx's raps include Elmer Fud's characteristic "OOOH I'm steamin'!" in full character voice along with a string of almost surreal collagelike references to Bugs Bunny and other television characters. At the same time, the stories, ideas, and thoughts articulated in rap lyrics invoke and revise stylistic and thematic elements that are deeply wedded to a number of black cultural storytelling forms, most prominently toasting and the blues. Ice-T and Big Daddy Kane pay explicit homage to Rudy Ray Moore as "Dolomite," Roxanne Shante toasts Millie Jackson, and black folk wisdom and folktales are given new lives and meanings in contemporary culture.

Rap's stories continue to articulate the shifting terms of black marginality in contemporary American culture. Even as rappers achieve what appears to be central status in commercial culture, they are far more vulnerable to censorship efforts than highly visible white rock artists, and they continue to experience the brunt of the plantationlike system faced by most artists in the music and sports industries. Even as they struggle with the tension between fame and rap's gravitational pull toward local urban narratives, for the most part, rappers continue to craft stories that represent the creative fantasies, perspectives, and experiences of racial marginality in America.

Rap went relatively unnoticed by mainstream music and popular culture industries until independent music entrepreneur Sylvia Robinson released "Rappers Delight" in 1979. Over the next five years rap music was "discovered" by the music industry, the print media, the fashion industry, and the film industry, each of which hurried to cash in on what was assumed to be a passing fad. During the same years, Run DMC (who recorded the first gold rap record *Run DMC* in 1984), Whodini, and the Fat Boys became the most commercially successful symbols of rap music's sounds and style.

By 1987, rap music had survived several death knells, Hollywood mockery, and radio bans and continued to spawn new artists, such as Public Enemy, Eric B. & Rakim, and L.L. Cool J. At the same time, women rappers, such as MC Lyte and Salt 'N' Pepa, encouraged by Roxanne Shante's early successes, made inroads into rap's emerging commercial audience. Between 1987 and 1990 a number of critical musical and industry changes took place. Public Enemy became rap's first superstar group, and media attention to its black nationalist political articulations intensified. The success of De La Soul's playful Afrocentricity, tongue in cheek spoof of rap's aggressive masculinity and manipulation of America's television culture encouraged the Native Tongues wing of rap that opened the door to such future groups as A Tribe Called Quest, Queen Latifah, Brand Nubian, and Black Sheep. Ice-T put the Los Angeles gangsta rap style on the national map, which encouraged the emergence of NWA, Ice Cube, Too Short, and others.

At the industry level, the effects of rap's infiltration were widespread. Black filmmaker Spike Lee's commercially successful use of b-boys, b-girls, hip hop music, and style in the contemporary urban terrain as primary themes in *She's Gotta Have It* and *Do the Right Thing* fired up Hollywood's new wave of black male ghetto films, most notably, *Colors*, *New Jack City*, *Boyz n the Hood*, *Juice* and *Menace II Society*. By 1989, MTV began playing rap music on a relatively regular basis, and multimillion unit rap sales by the Beastie Boys, Tone Loc, M.C. Hammer and Vanilla Ice convinced music industry executives that rap music, for all of its "blackness" in attitude, style, speech, music, and thematics, was a substantial success with white teenagers.

Rap's black cultural address and its focus on marginal identities may appear to be in opposition to its crossover appeal for people from different racial or ethnic groups and social positions. How can this black public dialogue speak to the thousands of young white suburban boys and girls who are critical to the record sales successes of many of rap's more prominent stars? How can I suggest that rap is committed culturally and emotionally to the pulse, pleasures, and problems of black urban life in the face of such diverse constituencies?

To suggest that rap is a black idiom that prioritizes black culture and that articulates the problems of black urban life does not deny the pleasure and participation of others. In fact, many black musics before rap (e.g., the blues, jazz, early rock 'n' roll) have also become American popular musics precisely because of extensive white participation; white America has always had an intense interest in black culture. Consequently, the fact that a significant number of white teenagers have become rap fans is quite consistent with the history of black music in America and should not be equated with a shift in rap's discursive or stylistic focus away from black pleasure and black fans. However, extensive white participation in black culture has also always involved white appropriation and attempts at ideological recuperation of black cultural resistance. Black culture in the United States has always had elements that have been at least bifocal—speaking to both a black audience and a larger predominantly white context. Rap music shares this history of interaction with many previous black oral and music traditions.

Like generations of white teenagers before them, white teenage rap fans are listening in on black culture, fascinated by its differences, drawn in by mainstream social constructions of black culture as a forbidden narrative, as a symbol of rebellion. Kathy Ogren's study of Jazz in the 1920s shows the extensive efforts made by white entertainers and fans to imitate jazz music, dance styles, and language as well as the alarm such fascination caused on the part of state and local authority figures. Lewis Erenberg's study of the development of the cabaret illustrates the centrality of jazz music to the fears over blackness associated with the burgeoning urban nightlife culture. There are similar and abundant cases for rock 'n' roll as well.[1]

Fascination with African-American culture is not new, nor can the dynamics and politics of pleasure across cultural "boundaries" in segregated societies be overlooked. Jazz, rock 'n' roll, soul, and R&B each have large devoted white audience members, many of whom share traits with Norman Mailer's "white negroes," young white listeners trying to perfect a model of correct white hipness, coolness, and style by adopting the latest black style and image. Young white listeners' genuine pleasure and commitment to black music are necessarily affected by dominant racial discourses regarding African Americans, the politics of racial segregation, and cultural difference in the United States. Given the racially discriminatory context within which cultural syncretism takes place, some rappers have equated white participation with a process of dilution and subsequent theft of black culture. Although the terms dilution and theft do not capture the complexity of cultural incorporation and syncretism, this interpretation has more than a grain of truth in it. There is abundant evidence that white artists imitating black styles have greater economic opportunity and access to larger audiences than black innovators. Historical accounts of the genres often position these subsequently better known artists as the central figures, erasing or marginalizing the artists and contexts within which the genre developed. The process of incorporation and marginalization of black practitioners has also fostered the development of black forms and practices that are less and less accessible, forms that require greater knowledge of black language and styles in order to participate. Be Bop, with its insider language and its "willfully harsh, anti-assimilationist sound" is a clear example of this response to the continuation of plantation system logic in American culture.[2] In addition to the sheer pleasure black musicians derive from developing a new and exciting style, these black cultural reactions to American culture suggest a reclaiming of the definition of blackness and an attempt to retain aesthetic control over black cultural forms. In the 1980s, this re-claiming of blackness in the popular realm is complicated by access to new reproduction technologies and revised corporate relations in the music industry.

In a number of ways, rap has followed the patterns of other black popular musics, in that at the outset it was heavily rejected by black and white middle-class listeners; the assumption was that it would be a short-lived fad; the mainstream record industry and radio stations rejected it; its marketing was pioneered by independent entrepreneurs and independent labels; and once a smidgen of commercial viability was established the major labels attempted to dominate production and distribution. These rap-related patterns were augmented by more general music industry consolidation in the late 1970s that provided the major music corporations with greater control over the market. By 1990 virtually all major record chain store distribution is controlled by six major record companies: CBS, Polygram, Warner, BMG, Capitol-EMI, and MCA.[3]

However, music industry consolidation and control over distribution is complicated by three factors: the expansion of local cable access, sophisticated and accessible mixing, production, and copying equipment, and a new relationship between major and independent record labels. In previous eras when independent labels sustained the emergence of new genres against industry rejection, the eventual absorption of these genres by larger companies signalled the dissolution of the independent labels. In the early 1980s, after rap spurred the growth of new independent labels, the major labels moved in and attempted to dominate the market but could not consolidate their efforts. Artists signed to independent labels, particularly Tommy Boy, Profile, and Def Jam continued to flourish, whereas acts signed directly to the six majors could not produce comparable sales. It became apparent that the independent labels had a much greater understanding of the cultural logic of hip hop and rap music, a logic that permeated decisions ranging from signing acts to promotional methods. Instead of competing with smaller, more street-savvy labels for new rap acts, the major labels developed a new strategy: buy the independent labels, allow them to function relatively autonomously, and provide them with production resources and access to major retail distribution.[4] Since the emergence of Public Enemy and their substantial cross-genre success in the late 1980s, rappers have generally been signed to independent labels (occasionally black owned and sometimes their own labels) and marketed and distributed by one of the six major companies. In this arrangement, the six majors reap the benefits of a genre that can be marketed with little up-front capital investment, and the artists are usually pleased to have access to the large record and CD chain stores that would otherwise never consider carrying their work.

In the 1980s, the trickle-down effect of technological advances in electronics brought significantly expanded access to mixing, dubbing, and copying equipment for consumers and black market retailers. Clearly, these advances provided aspiring musicians with greater access to recording and copying equipment at less expense. They also substantially improved the market for illegal dubbing of popular music for street corner sale at reduced cost. (Illegally recorded cassette tapes cost approximately $5.00, one-half the cost of label issues.) These lower quality tapes are usually sold in poorer, densely populated communities where reduced cost is a critical sales factor. Rap music is a particularly popular genre for bootleg tapes in urban centers.[5]

Even though actual sales demographics for rap music are not available, increasing sales figures for rap musicians (several prominent rap artists have sales over 500,000 units per album), suggest that white teenage rap consumers have grown steadily since the emergence of Public Enemy in 1988.[6] Middle-class white teenage rap consumers appear to be an increasingly significant audience. This can be inferred from location sales via market surveys and Soundscan, a new electronic scan system installed primarily in large, mostly suburban music chain stores. It is quite possible, however, that the percentage of white rap consumers in relation to overall sales is being disproportionately represented, because bootleg street sales coupled with limited chain music store outlets in poor communities makes it very difficult to assess the demographics for actual sales of rap music to urban black and Hispanic consumers. In addition to inconsistent sales figures, black teen rap consumers may also have a higher "pass-along rate," that is, the rate at which one purchased product is shared among consumers. In my conversations with James Bernard, an editor at *The Source* (a major hip hop culture magazine with a predominantly black teen readership), *The Source's* pass-along rate is approximately I purchase for every 11–15 readers. According to Bernard, this rate is at least three to four times higher than the average magazine industry pass-along rate. It is conceivable, then, that a similar pass-along rate exists among rap music CD and cassette consumption, especially among consumers with less disposable income.

Cable television exploded during the 1980s and had a significant effect on the music industry and on rap music. Launched in August 1981 by Warner Communications and the American Express Company, MTV became the fastest growing cable channel and as Garofalo points out, "soon became the most effective way for a record to get national exposure."[7] Using its rock format and white teen audience as an explanation for its almost complete refusal to play videos by black artists (once pressure was brought to bear they added Michael Jackson and Prince), MTV finally jumped on the rap music bandwagon. It was not until 1989, with the piloting of "Yo! MTV Raps" that any black artists began to appear on MTV regularly. Since then, as Jamie Malanowski reports, "'Yo MTV Raps' [has become] one of MTV's most popular shows, is dirt cheap to produce and has almost single-handedly dispelled the giant tastemaking network's reputation for not playing black artists."[8]

Since 1989, MTV has discovered that black artists in several genres are marketable to white suburban teenagers and has dramatically revised its formatting to include daily rap shows, Street Block (dance music), and the rotation of several black artists outside of specialized-genre rotation periods. However, MTV's previous exclusion of black artists throughout the mid-1980s, inspired other cable stations to program black music videos. Black Entertainment Television (BET), the most notable alternative to MTV, continues to air a wide variety of music videos by black artists as one of its programming mainstays. And local and syndicated shows (e.g., "Pump It Up!" based in Los Angeles and "Video Music Box" based in New York), continue to play rap music videos, particularly lower budget, and aggressively black nationalist rap videos deemed too angry or too antiwhite for MTV.

MTV's success has created an environment in which the reception and marketing of music is almost synonymous with the production of music videos. Fan discussions of popular songs and the stories they tell are often accompanied by a reading of the song's interpretation in music video. Music video is a collaboration in the production of popular music; it revises meanings, provides preferred interpretations of lyrics, creates a stylistic and physical context for reception; and valorizes the iconic presence of the artist. Can we really imagine, nonetheless understand, the significance of Michael Jackson's presence as a popular cultural icon without interpreting his music video narratives? The same holds true for Madonna, Janet Jackson, U2, Whitney Houston, Nirvana, and Guns N Roses among others. The visualization of music has far-reaching effects on musical cultures and popular culture generally, not the least of which is the increase in visual interpretations of sexist power relationships, the mode of visual storytelling, the increased focus on how a singer looks rather than how he or she sounds, the need to craft an image to accompany one's music, and ever-greater pressure to abide by corporate genre-formatting rules.

The significance of music video as a partner in the creation or reception of popular music is even greater in the case of rap music. Because the vast majority of rap music (except by the occasional superstar) has been virtually frozen out of black radio programming—black radio representatives claim that it scares off high-quality advertising—and because of its limited access to large performance venues, music video has been a crucial outlet for rap artist audiences and performer visibility. Rap music videos have animated hip hop cultural style and aesthetics and have facilitated a cross-neighborhood, cross-country (transnational?) dialogue in a social environment that is highly segregated by class and race.

The emergence of rap music video has also opened up a previously nonexistent creative arena for black visual artists. Rap music video has provided a creative and commercially viable arena where black film, video, set design, costume, and technical staff and trainees can get the crucial experience and connections to get a foot in the world of video and film production. Before music video production for black musicians, these training grounds, however exploitative, were virtually inaccessible to black technicians. The explosion of music video production, especially black music video, has generated a pool of skilled young black workers in the behind-the-scenes nonunion crews (union membership is overwhelmingly white and male), who are beginning to have an impact on current black film production.

Notes

1   See Kathy J. Ogren, *The Jazz Revolution: Twenties America and the Meaning of Jazz* (New York: Oxford University Press, 1989); Lewis A. Erenberg, *Steppin' Out: New York Night Life and the Transformation of American Culture, 1890–1930* (Chicago: University of Chicago Press, 1981); Nelson George, *The Death of Rhythm and Blues* (New York: Pantheon, 1988); Leroi Jones, *Blues People: The Negro Experience in White America and the Music That Developed from It* (New York: Morrow Quill, 1963), for discussions on the politics of black music in the United States.

2   Jones, *Blues People,* p. 181.

3   Russell Sanjek and David Sanjek, *American Popular Music Business in the 20th Century* (New York: Oxford University Press, 1991).

4   Reebee Garofalo, "Crossing Over: 1939–89," in Janette L. Dates and William Barlow, eds., *Split Image: African Americans in the Mass Media* (Washington, D.C.: Howard University Press, 1990), pp. 57–121.

5   At the last three annual New Music Seminars in New York, panels were devoted to the issue of bootleg record sales and their effect on rap music sales.

6   Although some evidence suggests that more adults are buying rap music, rap is still predominantly consumed by teenagers and young adults. See Janine McAdams and Deborah Russell, "Rap Breaking Through to Adult Market," *Hollywood Reporter,* 19 September 1991, pp. 4, 20. Chuck D and Ice-T have claimed that white teenagers consume approximately 50 to 70 percent of rap music. Ice-T claims that "more than 50 percent are going to white kids. Black kids buy the records, but the white

kids buy the cassette, the CD, the album, the tour jacket, the hats, everything. Black kids might just be buying the bootleg on the street. It's only due to economics." Alan Light, "Ice-T," *Rolling Stone,* 20 August 1992, pp. 31–32, 60. My research has yielded no source for these statistics other than speculation. Furthermore, these rappers may be specifically referring to their fan base; Ice-T and Public Enemy are both known for mixing rock and rap, making it more likely that white consumers would be drawn to their work.

7   Garofalo, "Crossing Over," p. 108. See also Serge Denisoff, *Inside MTV* (New Brunswick, N.J.: Transaction Books, 1987).

8   Jamie Malanowski, "Top Hip Hop," *Rolling Stone,* 13 July 1989, pp. 77–78.

Chapter 17

Edward Said

ISLAM AS NEWS

The background to Edward Said's work on "Islam as News" is the energy crisis of the 1970s, when the west woke up to the reality that not only did the Middle Eastern nations own much of the world's available oil resources, but that they could also control its supply. The US had come to Israel's defence when Egyptian and Syrian troops attempted to reclaim lost territory; in retaliation, OPEC (The Organization of Petroleum Exporting Countries) stopped supplying oil to the US, and it also raised prices for other consumers, leading to inflation, financial instability and crisis in the West. A second major energy price rise took place during the Iranian Revolution of 1978–79, during which there was also a major diplomatic incident, when young Islamic militants took the US Embassy staff hostage in Tehran. As Said argues, it is during such crises that the American media gets interested in "Islam", a stereotyping label which stands in for the diversity and difference of actual Muslim peoples around the world. Said, famous for critiquing the colonialist discursive field of "Orientalism" (a mode of study, denigrating and contributing to the colonialist control of mainly Islamic countries), argues that there are many ways in which Islam can be misrepresented, but he begins with an American television advertisement from 1980 in which OPEC and state leaders were anonymously paraded as a severe threat to America's energy sources; Said's point is that this stereotyping of the Arab Other partakes of a wider western tradition that he calls "Orientalism". Going back to the days of the European Empires, Orientalism is a body of western knowledge used to stereotype and subjugate those people who resided in what used to be called the "Orient" (the Middle East and Far East). The Orient was perceived to be both inferior yet paradoxically also a severe threat to the political and religious stability of the west; the European response was to use considerable resources in studying and consolidating their knowledge of this Other. Such Orientalist knowledge can be thought of as a mirror that the West holds up to see its own prejudices. Western ascendancy was shaken by the energy and political crises of the 1970s, especially the Islamic revolution in Iran. The new label for the Other used by Orientalists was "Islam": a label that quickly identifies (or more accurately speaking misidentifies) people and produces complex levels of meaning. Said notes how "The West" is a label that is not reduced to the dominant religion of Christianity, or any of its countercultural or past revolutionary impulses, but "Islam" is a religious label that stands in for all of the Muslim world. While he notes that Muslims were never really welcome in Europe, Said does point out that European Orientalism was at least based on experience of Muslim culture; the new Orientalism finding voice in the 1970s American media has no such comprehensive intellectual or experiental basis. Subsequently, American knowledge concerning "Islam" during this era is suspiciously prolix, both full and empty at the same time. Said's thesis was tested most dramatically during the crisis which followed the attack on the World Trade Towers on September 11, 2001; what happened in the media was an outpouring of Orientalist thoughts and feelings, except that now the label "Islam" was firmly attached to, or became synonymous with that of "terrorist". The critique of Orientalism is ongoing, often in an attempt to resist simplistic and degrading stereotypes of diverse peoples, but the power of the media is such that, as Said shows, sometimes the images do more damaging work than any amount of intellectual re-education can heal.

I. Islam and the West

In order to make a point about alternative energy sources for Americans, Consolidated Edison of New York (Con Ed) ran a striking television advertisement in the summer of 1980. Film clips of various immediately recognizable OPEC personalities—Yamani, Qaddafi, lesser-known robed Arab figures—alternated with stills as well as clips of other people associated with oil and Islam: Khomeini, Arafat, Hafez al-Assad. None of these figures was mentioned by name, but we were told ominously that "these men" control America's sources of oil. The solemn voice-over in the background made no reference to who "these men" actually are or where they come from, leaving it to be felt that this all-male cast of villains has placed Americans in the grip of an unrestrained sadism. It was enough for "these men" to appear as they have appeared in newspapers and on television for American viewers to feel a combination of anger, resentment, and fear. And it is this combination of feelings that Con Ed instantly aroused and exploited for domestic commercial reasons, just as a year earlier Stuart Eizenstat, President Carter's domestic policy adviser, had urged the president that "with strong steps we [should] mobilize the nation around a real crisis and with a clear enemy—OPEC."

There are two things about the Con Ed commercial that, taken together, form the subject of this book. One, of course, is Islam, or rather the image of Islam in the West generally and in the United States in particular. The other is the use of that image in the West and especially in the United States. As we shall see, these are connected in ways that ultimately reveal as much about the West and the United States as they do, in a far less concrete and interesting way, about Islam. But let us first consider the history of relationships between Islam and the Christian West before we go on to examine the current phase.

From at least the end of the eighteenth century until our own day, modern Occidental reactions to Islam have been dominated by a radically simplified type of thinking that may still be called Orientalist. The general basis of Orientalist thought is an imaginative and yet drastically polarized geography dividing the world into two unequal parts, the larger, "different" one called the Orient, the other, also known as "our" world, called the Occident or the West.[1] Such divisions always come about when one society or culture thinks about another one, different from it; but it is interesting that even when the Orient has uniformly been considered an inferior part of the world, it has always been endowed both with greater size and with a greater potential for power (usually destructive) than the West. Insofar as Islam has always been seen as belonging to the Orient, its particular fate within the general structure of Orientalism has been to be looked at first of all as if it were one monolithic thing, and then with a very special hostility and fear. There are, of course, many religious, psychological, and political reasons for this, but all of these reasons derive from a sense that so far as the West is concerned, Islam represents not only a formidable competitor but also a latecoming challenge to Christianity.

For most of the Middle Ages and during the early part of the Renaissance in Europe, Islam was believed to be a demonic religion of apostasy, blasphemy, and obscurity.[2] It did not seem to matter that Muslims considered Mohammed a prophet and not a god; what mattered to Christians was that Mohammed was a false prophet a sower of discord, a sensualist, a hypocrite, an agent of the devil. Nor was this view of Mohammed strictly a doctrinal one. Real events in the real world made of Islam a considerable political force. For hundreds of years great Islamic armies and navies threatened Europe, destroyed its outposts, colonized its domains. It was as if a younger, more virile and energetic version of Christianity had arisen in the East, equipped itself with the learning of the ancient Greeks, invigorated itself with a simple, fearless, and warlike creed, and set about destroying Christianity. Even when the world of Islam entered a period of decline and Europe a period of ascendancy, fear of "Mohammedanism" persisted. Closer to Europe than any of the other non-Christian religions, the Islamic world by its very adjacency evoked memories of its encroachments on Europe, and always, of its latent power again and again to disturb the West. Other great civilizations of the East—India and China among them—could be thought of as defeated and distant and hence not a constant worry. Only Islam seemed never to have submitted completely to the West; and when, after the dramatic oil-price rises of the early 1970s, the Muslim world seemed once more on the verge of repeating its early conquests, the whole West seemed to shudder.

Then in 1978 Iran occupied center stage, causing Americans to feel increasing anxiety and passion. Few nations so distant and different from the United States have so intensely engaged Americans. Never have Americans seemed so paralyzed, so seemingly powerless to stop one dramatic event after another from happening. And never in all this could they put Iran out of mind, since on so many levels the country impinged on their lives with a defiant obtrusiveness. Iran was a major oil supplier during a period of energy scarcity. It lies in a region of the world that is commonly regarded as volatile and strategically vital. An important ally, it lost its imperial regime, its army, its value in American global calculations during a year of tumultuous revolutionary upheaval virtually unprecedented on so huge a scale since October 1917. A new order which called itself Islamic, and appeared to be popular and anti-imperialist, was struggling to be born. Ayatollah Khomeini's image and presence took over the media, which failed to make much of him except that he was obdurate, powerful, and deeply angry at the United States. Finally, as a result of the ex-shah's entry into the United States on October 22, 1979, the United States Embassy in Teheran was captured by a group of students on November 4; many American hostages were held. This crisis nears its end as I write.

Reactions to what took place in Iran did not occur in a vacuum. Further back in the public's subliminal cultural consciousness, there was the longstanding attitude to Islam, the Arabs, and the Orient in general that I have been calling Orientalism. For whether one looked at such recent, critically acclaimed fiction as V. S. Naipaul's *A Bend in the River* and John Updike's *The Coup,* or at grade-school history textbooks, comic strips, television serials, films, and cartoons, the iconography of Islam was uniform, was uniformly ubiquitous, and drew its material from the same time honored view of Islam: hence the frequent caricatures of Muslims as oil suppliers, as terrorists, and more recently, as bloodthirsty mobs. Conversely, there has been very little place either in the culture generally or in discourse about non-Westerners in particular to speak or even to think about, much less to portray, Islam or anything Islamic sympathetically. Most people, if asked to name a *modern* Islamic writer, would probably be able to pick only Khalil Gibran (who wasn't Islamic). The academic experts whose specialty is Islam have generally treated the religion and its various cultures within an invented or culturally determined ideological framework filled with passion, defensive prejudice, sometimes even revulsion; because of this framework, *understanding* of Islam has been a very difficult thing to achieve. And to judge from the various in-depth media studies and interviews on the Iranian revolution during the spring of 1979, there has been little inclination to accept the revolution itself as much more than a defeat for the United States (which in a very specific sense, of course, it was), or a victory of dark over light.

V. S. Naipaul's role in helping to clarify this general hostility towards Islam is an interesting one. In a recent interview published in *Newsweek International* (August 18, 1980) he spoke about a book he was writing on "Islam," and then volunteered that "Muslim fundamentalism has no intellectual substance to it, therefore it must collapse." What Muslim fundamentalism he was referring to specifically, and what sort of intellectual substance he had in mind, he did not say: Iran was undoubtedly meant, but so too—in equally vague terms— was the whole postwar wave of Islamic anti-imperialism in the Third World, for which Naipaul has developed a particularly intense antipathy. In *Guerrillas* and *A Bend in the River*, Naipaul's last two novels, Islam is in question, and it is part of Naipaul's general (and with liberal Western readers, popular) indictment of the Third World that he lumps together the corrupt viciousness of a few grotesque rulers, the end of European colonialism, and postcolonial efforts at rebuilding native societies as instances of an over-all intellectual failure in Africa and Asia. "Islam" plays a major part according to Naipaul, whether it is in the use of Islamic surnames by pathetic West Indian guerrillas, or in the vestiges of the African slave trade. For Naipaul and his readers, "Islam" somehow is made to cover everything that one most disapproves of from the standpoint of civilized, and Western, rationality.[3]

It is as if discriminations between religious passion, a struggle for a just cause, ordinary human weakness, political competition, and the history of men, women, and societies seen *as* the history of men, women, and societies cannot be made when "Islam," or the Islam now at work in Iran and in other parts of the Muslim world, is dealt with by novelists, reporters, policy-makers, "experts." "Islam" seems to engulf all aspects of the diverse Muslim world, reducing them all to a special malevolent and unthinking essence. Instead of analysis and understanding as a result, there can be for the most part only the crudest form of us-versus-them. Whatever Iranians or Muslims say about their sense of justice, their history of oppression, their vision of their own societies, seems irrelevant; what counts for the United States instead is what the "Islamic revolution" is doing right now, how many people have been executed by the Komitehs, how many bizarre outrages the Ayatollah, in the name of Islam, has ordered. Of course no one has equated the Jonestown massacre or the destructive frenzy produced at the Who concert in Cincinnati or the devastation of Indochina with Christianity, or with Western or American culture at large; that sort of equation has been reserved for "Islam."

Why is it that a whole range of political, cultural, social, and even economic events has often seemed reducible in so Pavlovian a way to "Islam"? What is it about "Islam" that provokes so quick and unrestrained a response? In what way do "Islam" and the Islamic world differ for Westerners from, say, the rest of the Third World and from the Soviet Union? These are far from simple questions, and they must therefore be answered piecemeal, with many qualifications and much differentiation.

Labels purporting to name very large and complex realities are notoriously vague and at the same time unavoidable. If it is true that "Islam" is an imprecise and ideologically loaded label, it is also true that "the West" and "Christianity" are just as problematic. Yet there is no easy way of avoiding these labels, since Muslims speak of Islam, Christians of Christianity, Westerners of the West, and all of them about all the others in ways that seem to be both convincing and exact. Instead of trying to propose ways of going around the labels, I think it is more immediately useful to admit at the outset that they exist and have long been in use as an integral part of cultural history rather than as objective classifications: a little later in this chapter I shall speak about them as interpretations produced for and by what I shall call communities of interpretation. We must therefore remember that "Islam," "the West," and even "Christianity" function in at least two different ways, and produce at least two meanings, each time they are used. First, they perform a simple identifying function, as when we say Khomeini is a Muslim, or Pope John Paul II is a Christian. Such statements tell us as a bare minimum what something is, as opposed to all other things. On this level we can distinguish between an orange and an apple (as we might distinguish between a Muslim and a Christian) only to the extent that we know they are different fruits, growing on different trees, and so forth.

The second function of these several labels is to produce a much more complex meaning. To speak of "Islam" in the West today is to mean a lot of the unpleasant things I have been mentioning. Moreover, "Islam" is unlikely to mean anything one knows either directly or objectively. The same is true of our use of "the West." How many people who use the labels angrily or assertively have a solid grip on all aspects of the Western tradition, or on Islamic jurisprudence, or on the actual languages of the Islamic world? Very few, obviously, but this does not prevent people from confidently characterizing "Islam" and "the West," or from believing they know exactly what it is they are talking about.

For that reason, we must take the labels seriously. To a Muslim who talks about "the West" or to an American who talks about "Islam," these enormous generalizations have behind them a whole history, enabling and disabling at the same time. Ideological and shot through with powerful emotions, the labels have survived many experiences and have been capable of adapting to new events, information, and realities. At present, "Islam" and "the West" have taken on a powerful new urgency everywhere. And we must note immediately that it is always the West, and not Christianity, that seems pitted against Islam. Why? Because the assumption is that whereas "the West" is greater than and has surpassed the stage of Christianity, its principal religion, the world of Islam—its varied societies, histories, and languages notwithstanding—is still mired in religion, primitivity, and backwardness. Therefore, the West is modern, greater than the sum of its parts, full of enriching contradictions and yet always "Western" in its cultural identity; the world of Islam, on the other hand, is no more than "Islam," reducible to a small number of unchanging characteristics despite the appearance of contradictions and experiences of variety that seem on the surface to be as plentiful as those of the West.

A recent example of what I mean is to be found in an article for the "News of the Week in Review" section of the Sunday *New York Times,* September 14, 1980. The piece in question is by John Kifner, the able *Times* correspondent in Beirut, and its subject is the extent of Soviet penetration of the Muslim world. Kifner's notion is evident enough from his article's title ("Marx and Mosque Are Less Compatible Than Ever"), but what is noteworthy is his use of Islam to make what in any other instance would be an unacceptably direct and unqualified connection between an abstraction and a vastly complex reality. Even if it is allowed that, unlike all other religions, Islam is totalistic and makes no separation between church and state or between religion and everyday life, there is something uniquely—and perhaps deliberately—uninformed and uninforming, albeit conventional enough, about such statements as the following:

> The reason for Moscow's receding influence is disarmingly simple: Marx and mosque are incompatible. [Are we to assume, then, that Marx and church, or Marx and temple, are more compatible?]
>
> For the Western mind [this is the point, obviously enough], conditioned since the Reformation to historical and intellectual developments which have steadily diminished the role of religion, it is difficult to grasp the power exerted by Islam [which, presumably, has been conditioned neither by history nor by intellect]. Yet,

for centuries it has been the central force in the life of this region and, for the moment at least, its power seems on the upsurge.

In Islam, there is no separation between church and state. It is a total system not only of belief but of action, with fixed rules for everyday life and a messianic drive to combat or convert the infidel. To the deeply religious, particularly to the scholars and clergy but also to the masses [in other words, no one is excluded], Marxism, with its purely secular view of man, is not only alien but heretical.

Not only does Kifner simply ignore history and such complications as the admittedly limited but interesting series of parallels between Marxism and Islam (studied by Maxime Rodinson in a book that attempts to explain why Marxism seems to have made some inroads in Islamic societies over the years[4]) but he also rests his argument on a hidden comparison between "Islam" and the West, so much more various and uncharacterizable than simple, monolithic, totalitarian Islam. The interesting thing is that Kifner can say what he says without any danger of appearing either wrong or absurd.

Islam versus the West: this is the ground bass for a staggeringly fertile set of variations. Europe versus Islam, no less than America versus Islam, is a thesis that it subsumes.[5] But quite different concrete experiences with the West as a whole play a significant role too. For there is an extremely important distinction to be made between American and European awareness of Islam. France and England, for example, until very recently possessed large Muslim empires; in both countries, and to a lesser degree in Italy and Holland, both of which had Muslim colonies too, there is a long tradition of direct experience with the Islamic world.[6] This is reflected in a distinguished European academic discipline of Orientalism, which of course existed in those countries with colonies as well as in those (Germany, Spain, prerevolutionary Russia) that either wanted them, or were close to Muslim territories, or were once Muslim states. Today the Soviet Union has a Muslim population of about 50 million, and since the last days of 1979 has been in military occupation of Muslim Afghanistan. None of these things is comparably true of the United States, even though never before have so many Americans written, thought, or spoken about Islam.

The absence in America either of a colonial past or of a longstanding cultural attention to Islam makes the current obsession all the more peculiar, more abstract, more secondhand. Very few Americans, comparatively speaking, have actually had much to do with real Muslims; by comparision, in France the country's second religion in point of numbers is Islam, which may not be more popular as a result, but is certainly more known. The modern European burst of interest in Islam was part of what was called "the Oriental renaissance," a period in the late eighteenth and early nineteenth centuries when French and British scholars discovered "the East" anew—India, China, Japan, Egypt, Mesopotamia, the Holy Land. Islam was seen, for better or for worse, as part of the East, sharing in its mystery, exoticism, corruption, and latent power. True, Islam had been a direct military threat to Europe for centuries before; and true also that during the Middle Ages and early Renaissance, Islam was a problem for Christian thinkers, who continued for hundreds of years to see it and its prophet Mohammed as the rankest variety of apostasy. But at least Islam existed for many Europeans as a kind of standing religiocultural challenge, which did not prevent European imperialism from building its institutions on Islamic territory. And however much hostility there was between Europe and Islam, there was also direct experience, and in the case of poets, novelists, and scholars like Goethe, Gérard de Nerval, Richard Burton, Flaubert, and Louis Massignon, there was imagination and refinement.

Yet in spite of these figures and others like them, Islam has never been welcome in Europe. Most of the great philosophers of history from Hegel to Spengler have regarded

Islam without much enthusiasm. In a dispassionately lucid essay, "Islam and the Philosophy of History," Albert Hourani has discussed this strikingly constant derogation of Islam as a system of faith.[7] Apart from some occasional interest in the odd Sufi writer or saint, European vogues for "the wisdom of the East" rarely included Islamic sages or poets. Omar Khayyám Harun al-Rashid, Sindbad, Aladdin, Hajji Baba, Scheherazade, Saladin, more or less make up the entire list of Islamic figures known to modern educated Europeans. Not even Carlyle could make the Prophet widely acceptable, and as for the substance of the faith Mohammed propagated, this has long seemed to Europeans basically unacceptable on Christian grounds, although precisely for that reason not uninteresting. Towards the end of the nineteenth century, as Islamic nationalism in Asia and Africa increased, there was a widely shared view that Muslim colonies were meant to remain under European tutelage, as much because they were profitable as because they were underdeveloped and in need of Western discipline.[8] Be that as it may, and despite the frequent racism and aggression directed at the Muslim world, Europeans *did* express a fairly energetic sense of what Islam meant to them. Hence the representations of Islam—in scholarship, art, literature, music, and public discourse—all across European culture, from the end of the eighteenth century until our own day.

Little of this concreteness is to be found in America's experience of Islam. Nineteenth-century American contacts with Islam were very restricted; one thinks of occasional travelers like Mark Twain and Herman Melville, or of missionaries here and there, or of short-lived military expeditions to North Africa. Culturally there was no distinct place in America for Islam before World War II. Academic experts did their work on Islam usually in quiet corners of schools of divinity, not in the glamorous limelight of Orientalism nor in the pages of leading journals. For about a century there has existed a fascinating although quiet symbiosis between American missionary families to Islamic countries and cadres of the foreign service and the oil companies; periodically this has surfaced in the form of hostile comments about State Department and oil-company "Arabists," who are considered to harbor an especially virulent and anti-Semitic form of philo-Islamism. On the other hand, all the great figures known in the United States as important academic experts on Islam have been foreign-born: Lebanese Philip Hitti at Princeton, Austrian Gustave von Grunebaum at Chicago and UCLA, British H. A. R Gibb at Harvard, German Joseph Schacht at Columbia. Yet none of these men has had the relative cultural prestige enjoyed by Jacques Berque in France and Albert Hourani in England.

But even men like Hitti, Gibb, von Grunebaum, and Schacht have disappeared from the American scene, as indeed it is unlikely that scholars such as Berque and Hourani will have successors in France and England. No one today has their breadth of culture, nor anything like their range of authority. Academic experts on Islam in the West today tend to know about jurisprudential schools in tenth-century Baghdad or nineteenth-century Moroccan urban patterns but never (or almost never) about the whole civilization of Islam—literature, law, politics, history, sociology, and so on. This has not prevented experts from generalizing from time to time about the "Islamic mind-set" or the "Shi'a penchant for martyrdom," but such pronouncements have been confined to popular journals or to the media, which solicited these opinions in the first place. More significantly, the occasions for public discussions of Islam, by experts or by nonexperts, have almost always been provided by political crises. It is extremely rare to see informative articles on Islamic culture in the *New York Review of Books,* say, or in *Harper's.* Only when the stability of Saudi Arabia or Iran has been in question has Islam seemed worthy of general comment.

Consider therefore that Islam has entered the consciousness of most Americans—even of academic and general intellectuals who know a great deal about Europe and Latin America—principally if not exclusively because it has been connected to newsworthy issues like oil, Iran and Afghanistan, or terrorism.[9] And all of this by the middle of 1979 had come to be called either the Islamic revolution, or "the crescent of crisis," or "the arc of instability," or "the return of Islam." A particularly telling example was the Atlantic Council's Special Working Group on the Middle East (which included Brent Scowcroft, George Ball, Richard Helms, Lyman Lemnitzer, Walter Levy, Eugene Rostow, Kermit Roosevelt, and Joseph Sisco, among others): when this group issued its report in the fall of 1979 the title given it was "Oil and Turmoil: Western Choices in the Middle East."[10] When *Time* magazine devoted its major story to Islam on April 16, 1979, the cover was adorned with a Gérôme painting of a bearded muezzin standing in a minaret, calmly summoning the faithful to prayer; it was as florid and overstated a nineteenth-century period piece of Orientalist art as one could imagine. Anachronistically, however, this quiet scene was emblazoned with a caption that had nothing to do with it: "The Militant Revival." There could be no better way of symbolizing the difference between Europe and America on the subject of Islam. A placid and decorative painting done almost routinely in Europe as an aspect of one's general culture had been transformed by three words into a general American obsession.

But surely I am exaggerating? Wasn't *Time*'s cover story on Islam simply a piece of vulgarization, catering to a supposed taste for the sensational? Does it *really* reveal anything more serious than that? And since when have the media mattered a great deal on questions of substance, or of policy, or of culture? Besides, was it *not* the case that Islam had indeed thrust itself upon the world's attention? And what had happened to the experts on Islam, and why were their contributions either bypassed entirely or submerged in the "Islam" discussed and diffused by the media?

A few simple explanations are in order first. As I said above, there has never been any American expert on the Islamic world whose audience was a wide one; moreover, with the exception of the late Marshall Hodgson's three-volume *The Venture of Islam,* posthumously published in 1975, no general work on Islam has ever been put squarely before the literate reading public.[11] Either the experts were so specialized that they only addressed other specialists, or their work was not distinguished enough intellectually to command the kind of audience that came to books on Japan, Western Europe, or India. But these things work both ways. While it is true that one could not name an American "Orientalist" with a reputation outside Orientalism, as compared with Berque or Rodinson in France, it is also true that the study of Islam is neither truly encouraged in the American university nor sustained in the culture at large by personalities whose fame and intrinsic merit might make their experiences of Islam important on their own.[12] Who are the American equivalents of Rebecca West, Freya Stark, T. E. Lawrence, Wilfred Thesiger, Gertrude Bell, P. H. Newby, or more recently, Jonathan Raban? At best, they might be former CIA people like Miles Copeland or Kermit Roosevelt, very rarely writers or thinkers of any cultural distinction.

A second reason for the critical absence of expert opinion on Islam is the experts' marginality to what seemed to be happening in the world of Islam when it became "news" in the mid-1970s. The brutally impressive facts are, of course, that the Gulf oil-producing states suddenly appeared to be very powerful; there was an extraordinarily ferocious and seemingly unending civil war in Lebanon; Ethiopia and Somalia were involved in a long war; the Kurdish problem unexpectedly became pivotal and then, after 1975, just as unexpectedly subsided; Iran deposed its monarch in the wake of a massive, wholly surprising "Islamic" revolution; Afghanistan was gripped by a Marxist coup in 1978, then invaded by Soviet troops in late 1979; Algeria and Morocco were drawn into protracted conflict over the Southern Sahara issue; a Pakistani president was executed and a new military dictatorship set up. There were other things taking place too, most recently a war between Iran and Iraq, but let us be satisfied with these. On the whole I think it is fair to say that few of these happenings might have been illuminated by expert writing on Islam in the West; for not only had the experts not predicted them nor prepared their readers for them, they had instead provided a mass of literature that seemed, when compared with what was happening, to be about an impossibly distant region of the world, one that bore practically no relation to the turbulent and threatening confusion erupting before one's eyes in the media.

Notes

1   See Edward W. Said, *Orientalism* (London: Routledge and Kegan Paul, 1978), pp. 49–73.

2   See Norman Daniel, *The Arabs and Medieval Europe* (London: Longmans, Green & Co., 1975); also his earlier and very useful *Islam and the West: The Making of an Image* (Edinburgh: University Press, 1960). There is a first-rate survey of this matter, set in the political context of the 1956 Suez War, by Erskine B. Childers in *The Road to Suez: A Study of Western-Arab Relations* (London: MacGibbon & Kee, 1962), pp. 25–61.

3   I have discussed Naipaul in "Bitter Dispatches From the Third World," *The Nation,* May 3, 1980, pp. 522–25.

4   Maxime Rodinson, *Marxism and The Modern World,* trans. Michael Palis (London: Zed Press, 1979). See also Thomas Hodgkin, "The Revolutionary Tradition in Islam," *Race and Class* 21, no. 3 (Winter 1980): 221–37.

5   There is an elegant account of this theme, done by a contemporary Tunisian intellectual: see Hichem Djaït, *L'Europe et l'Islam* (Paris: Editions du Seuil, 1979). A brilliant psychoanalytic/structuralist reading of one "Islamic" motif in European literature—the seraglio—is to be found in Alain Grosrichard, *Structure du sérail: La Fiction du despotisme asiatique dans l'Occident classique* (Paris: Éditions du Seuil, 1979).

6   See Maxime Rodinson, *La Fascination de l'Islam* (Paris: Maspéro, 1980).

7   Albert Hourani, "Islam and the Philosophers of History," in *Europe and The Middle East* (London: Macmillan & Co., 1980), pp. 19–73.

8   As an instance, see the penetrating study by Syed Hussein Alatas, *The Myth of the Lazy Native: A Study of the Image of the Malays, Filipinos, and Javanese from the 16th to the 20th Century and in the Ideology of Colonial Capitalism* (London: Frank Cass & Co., 1977).

9   Not that this has always meant poor writing and scholarship: as an informative general account which answers principally to political exigencies and not mainly to the need for new knowledge about Islam, there is Martin Kramer, *Political Islam* (Washington, D.C.: Sage Publications, 1980). This was written for the Center for Strategic and International Studies, Georgetown University, and therefore belongs to the category of policy, not of "objective," knowledge. Another instance in the January 1980 (vol. 78, no. 453) special issue on "The Middle East, 1980" of *Current History.*

10   *Atlantic Community Quarterly* 17, no. 3 (Fall 1979): 291–305, 377–78.

11   Marshall Hodgson, *The Venture of Islam,* 3 vols. (Chicago and London: University of Chicago Press, 1974). See the important review of this by Albert Hourani, *Journal of Near Eastern Studies* 37, no. 1 (January 1978): 53–62.

12   One index of this is the report "Middle Eastern and African Studies: Developments and Needs" commissioned by the U.S. Department of Health, Education and Welfare in 1967, written by Professor Morroe Berger of Princeton, also president of the Middle East Studies Association (MESA). In this report Berger asserts that the Middle East "is not a center of great cultural achievement . . . and therefore does not constitute its own reward so far as modern culture is concerned. . . . [It] has been receding in immediate political importance to the U.S." For a discussion of this extraordinary document and the context that produced it, see Said, *Orientalism,* pp. 287–93.

Chapter 18

Ravi Sundaram

RECYCLING MODERNITY

Pirate electronic cultures in India

The key to understanding Ravi Sundaram's definition of "pirate electronic cultures" is that he does not simply mean the illegal copying and redistribution of electronic data. Instead, he draws a picture of an entire alternative local media culture, one that has developed independently of global media corporations or nationalist politics as defined by the Indian state. Writing in an era of inflation and economic crisis, Sundaram notes how "electronic capitalism" thrived when all other sectors of the Indian economy were in a period of decline. He notes that there are two "fables" or stories that exist within India to explain this success: first, the narrative of a vibrant technological industry (software industries, telephone call centres, and so on) that exists in a virtual realm and actual American time zone (i.e., so North Americans can use Indian call centres or call upon programming expertise when needed), and second, the narrative of inequality whereby Indian computing solutions remain inexpensive and its workers are paid low wages. The first fable is one of modernization (the developing world will catch up with the West), whereas the second fable follows the dependency theory: that the developing world can never catch up with the West because its resources are constantly drained away by more affluent countries (what the German economist André Gunder Frank [1929–2005] called "the development of underdevelopment"). Sundaram, who is a Senior Fellow at the Centre for the Study of Developing Societies, in Delhi, suggests that both fables belong to the world of the economic elite, and that a third option has arisen in India: a dispersed and mobile "technoculture" based upon recycling, innovation, non-legality, and orality, i.e., it often serves non-literate groups of people. This is a "pirate modernity" because old, often discarded technology is raided for cheap or free components to build local communications and entertainment networks which are outside of the control of global corporations and the state, for example, the state-controlled Soviet-style projects of India's first prime minister Jawaharlal Nehru (1889–1964). Partly driven by necessity—or survival—pirate electronic cultures are hybrid and encourage innovation; their modernity is not one of monumental cultural goals and ambitions, more that of technological speed and simultaneity: the collapsing of space and time by instant digital communications. At the time of writing the article Sundaram observes that India's entertainment industries produce their own legal and non-legal content, while computing content—software architecture—was lacking; that has since changed, and Indian software is now sold around the globe. Sundaram argues that pirate electronic cultures have been responsible for the "retreat of the state" when it comes to everyday cultural life, and that the "everyday" has become the new arena for class and economic struggle, production and consumption. The "electronic everyday" is urban (metropolitan centres and small towns), largely "non-legal", highly productive, and driven by the speed of instantaneous communications. Sundaram suggests that while Indian pirate electronic cultures are not postmodern since class struggle and inequality are still present, two Western theorists of postmodernism, Jean Baudrillard and Paul Virilio, have developed approaches relevant to local Indian modes of production and consumption. Baudrillard's critique of Marxism facilitates analysis of consumer consumption, rather than production, whereas Virilio's concept of "Chronopolitics" is relevant because it is a politics of time rather than space. Yet even these theorists get recycled—or pirated—in an Indian context when they are used to help describe unique, local, digital cultures.

MARX, NOW LONG FORGOTTEN BY MOST who spoke his name but a decade or two ago, once said the following in his brilliantly allegorical essay on the *Eighteenth Brumaire of Louis Bonaparte.* "Bourgeois revolutions . . . storm quickly from success to success; their dramatic effects out do each; men and things set in sparkling brilliants; ecstasy is the everyday spirit; but they are short-lived; soon they have attained their zenith, and a long crapulent depression lays hold of society before it learns soberly to assimilate the results of its storm-and-stress period."

In Asia, reeling under the current crisis, the moment of ecstasy has long passed, and the 'long crapulent depression' is here to stay. India, a poor cousin of the East Asians, tried to ignore the crisis through its traditional west-centredness. But the crisis has finally arrived in South Asia, the Indian rupee has dived steadily since last year and inflation is raging. But in the area of electronic capitalism, the mood is buoyant. Software stocks have risen 120% and soon software will become India's largest export.

Many fables have emerged as a response to the irruption of electronic capitalism in a country where 400 million still cannot read or write. The first fable is a domesticated version of the virtual ideology. In this Indianised version, propagated by the technocratic and programming élite, India's access to western modernity (and progress) would obtain through a vast virtual universe, programmed and developed by 'Indians'. The model: to develop techno-cities existing in virtual time with US corporations, where Indian programmers would provide low-cost solutions to the new global techno-space.

The second fable is a counter-fable to the first and quite familiar to those who live in the alternative publics of the net. This fable comes out of a long culture of Old-Left politics in India and draws liberally from 1960s dependency theory. The fable, not surprisingly, argues that India's insertion in the virtual global economy follows traditional patterns of unequal exchange. Indian programmers offer a low-cost solution to the problems of trans-national corporations. Indian software solutions occupy the lower end of the global virtual commodity chain, just as cotton farmers in South Asia did in the 19th century, from where they would supply Manchester mills with produce.

All fables are not untrue, but some are more 'true' than others. Thus the second fable claims, not unfairly, that most Indian software is exported, and there is very little available in the local languages (ironically the Indian language versions of the main programs are being developed by IBM and Microsoft).

The alternative vision posed by the second fable is typically nationalist. Here India would *first* concentrate on its domestic space and then forge international links. In a sense both fables suffer from a yearning for *perfection.* While the first promises a seamless transition to globalism, the second offers a world that is autarchic. Both are ideological, in the old 19th century sense of the term, which makes one a little uncomfortable. "Down with all the hypotheses that allow the belief in a true world", once wrote Nietzsche, angrily.

There is no doubt that for a 'Third World' country, India displays a dynamic map of the new technocultures. The problem for both the fables mentioned above is that they remain limited to the *élite* domains of techno-space in India. This domain is composed of young, upper-caste, often English-speaking programmers in large metropoles, particularly emerging techno-cities like Bangalore and Hyderabad. This is the story which *Wired* loves to tell its western audiences, but in a critical, innovative sense most of these programmers are not the future citizens of the counter net-publics in India.

What is crucial in the Indian scenario is that the dominant electronic public has cohered with the cultural-political imagination of a belligerent Hindu-nationalist movement. Hindu nationalism in India came to power using an explosive mix of anti-minority violence and a discourse of modernity that was quite contemporary. This discourse appealed to the upper-caste élites in the fast-growing cities and towns, using innovative forms of mechanical and electronic reproduction. Thus it was the Hindu nationalists who first used cheap audio-cassette tapes to spread anti-Muslim messages; further giant video-scapes were used to project an aesthetisised politics of hate. Some of the first Indian web-sites were also set up by the Hindu nationalists. To this landscape has been added that terrifying weapon, the nuclear bomb.

This is an imagination that is aggressive, technologically savvy, and eminently attractive to the cyber-élites. The cyber-élites may be uncomfortable with the Hindu nationalists' periodic rhetoric of 'national sufficiency', but such language is hyper-political and has less meaning on the ground.

Outside the universe of the cyber-élite is another one which speaks to a more energetic technoculture. This is a world of innovation and non-legality, of *ad hoc* discovery and electronic survival strategies. But before I talk about this, a story of my own.

Some years ago, I was on a train in Southern India where I met Selvam, a young man of 24, who I saw reading used computer magazines in the railway compartment. Selvam's story is fascinating, for it throws light on a world outside those of the techno-élite. Selvam was born in the temple town of Madurai in southern India, the son of a worker in the town court. After ten years in school, Selvam began doing a series of odd jobs, he also learnt to type at a night school after which he landed a job at a typists shop. It was there that Selvam first encountered the new technoculture Indian-style.

From the late 1980s, India witnessed a unique communicative transformation – the spread of public telephones in different parts of the country. Typically these were not anonymous card-based instruments as in the West or other parts of the Third World, but run by *humans*. These were called Public Call Offices (PCOs). The idea was that in a non-literate society like India the act of telecommunication had to be mediated by humans. Typically literates and non-literates used PCOs which often doubled as fax centres, xerox shops and typists shops. Open through the night, PCOs offered inexpensive, personalised services which spread rapidly all over the country.

Selvam's typing shop was such a PCO. Selvam worked on a used 286, running an old version of Wordstar, where he would type out formal letters to state officials for clients, usually peasants and unemployed. Soon Selvam graduated to a faster 486 and learnt programming by devouring used manuals, and simply asking around. This is the world of informal technological knowledge existing in most parts of India, where those excluded from the upper-caste, English speaking bastions of the cyber-élite learn their tools.

Selvam told me how the textile town of Coimbatore, a few hours from Madurai set up its own BBS, by procuring used modems, and connecting them later at night. Used computer equipment is part of a vast commodity chain in India, originating from various centres in India, but the main centre is Delhi.

Delhi has a history of single-commodity markets from the days of the Moghul empire. Various markets would specialise in a single commodity, a tradition which has continued to the present. The centre of Delhi's computer trade is the Nehru Place market. Nehru Place is a dark, seedy cluster of grey concrete blocks, which is filled with small shops devoted to the computer trade. Present here are the agents of large corporations, as well as software pirates, spare parts dealers, electronic smugglers and wheeler-dealers of every kind in the computer world.

This cluster of legality and non-legality is typical of Indian technoculture. When the cable television revolution began in the 1990s, all the cable operators were illegal, and many continue to be so even today. This largely disorganised, dispersed scenario makes it impossible for paid cable television to work in India. This is a pirate modernity, but one with no particular thought about counter-culture or its likes. It is a simple survival strategy.

The computer trade has followed the pirate modernity of cable television. Just as small town cable operators would come to the cable market in the walled city area of Delhi for equipment, so people from small towns like Selvam would come to Nehru Place to source computer parts, used computers, older black and white monitors, and mother-boards out of fashion in Delhi.

This is a world that is everyday in its imaginary, pirate in its practice, and mobile in its innovation. This is also a world that never makes it to the computer magazines, nor the technological discourses dominated by the cyber-élite. The old nationalists and Left view this world with fascination and horror, for it makes a muddle of simple nationalist solutions. One can call this a *recycled* electronic modernity. And it is an imaginary that is suspect in the eyes of all the major ideological actors in techno-space.

For the Indian proponents of a global virtual universe, the illegality of recycled modernity is alarming and 'unproductive'. Recycled modernity prevents India's accession to World Trade Organization conventions, and has prevented multinational manufacturers from dominating India's domestic computer market. For the nationalists, this modernity only reconfirms older patterns of unequal exchange and world inequality. In cyber-terms this means smaller processing power than those current in the West, lesser bandwidth, and no control over the key processes of electronic production.

I suspect that members of the electronic avant-gardes and the network counter-publics in the West will find recycled modernity in India baffling. For recycled modernity has no discrete spaces of its own in opposition to the main cyber-élites, nor does it posit a self-defined oppositional stance. This is a modernity that is fluid and mocking in definition. But is also a world of those dispossessed by the élite domains of electronic capital, a world which possesses a hunter-gatherer cunning and practical intelligence.

The term 'recycling' may conjure up images of a borrowed, unoriginal modern. Originality (the eternal search for 'newness') was of course Baudelairian modernity's great claim to dynamism. As social life progressed through a combination of dispersion and unity, the Baudelairian subject was propelled by a search for new visions of original innovation, both artistic and scientific. A lot of this has fallen by the wayside in the past few decades, but weak impulses survive to this day.

It is important to stress too that recycled modernity does not reflect a thought-out postmodern sensibility. Recycling is a strategy of both survival and innovation on terms entirely outside the current debates on the structure and imagination of the Net and technoculture in general. As globalists/virtualists push eagerly for a new economy of virtual space, and the nationalists call for a national electronic self-sufficiency, the practitioners of recycling keep working away in the invisible markets of India.

In fact given the evidence, it could even be argued that recycling's claim to 'modernity' is quite fragile. Recycling practices (today at least) lack modernity's self-proclaimed reflexivity: there is no sense of a means-ends action, nor is there any coherent project. This contrasts with the many historical legacies of modernity in India — one of which was

Nehruvian. The technological side of this modernity was monumental and future-oriented, it spoke in terms of projects, clear visions, argued goals. And the favourite instrument of this modernity was a state Plan, borrowed from Soviet models. Nehruvian modernity has been recently challenged by Hindu nationalism, which has also sought to posit its own claims to the modern, where an authoritarian state and the hegemony of the Hindu majority ally with a dynamic urban consumption regime.

Recycling practices' claim to modernity rely less on any architecture of mobility than on an engagement with speed. Speed constitutes recycling's great reference of activity, centred around sound, vision and data. This is the pirate modern's "eternal present" (Benjamin), one that is historically situated and mediated through various registers of difference. Speed in the time of the 'now' is the effort at acceleration propelled partly by global techno-capital. Temporal acceleration, which Reinhart Koselleck claims is one of modernity's central features, speaks to the deep yearnings of recycling's praxis. But this is a constantly shifting universe of adaptation to available tools of speed, the world info-bahn being but an infrequent visitor. Consider the practice of speed in a 'Third World' country like India, where both the givenness of access to the Net and the purchase of processing power do not exist in simultaneity. They have to be created, partly through developing new techniques, and partly through breaking the laws of global electronic capital.

Recycling's great limitation in the computer/Net industry is content. This actually contrasts with the other areas of India's culture industry – music and cinema. In the field of popular music, a pirate culture effectively broke the stranglehold of multinational companies in the music scene and opened up vast new areas of popular music which the big companies had been afraid to touch. Selling less from official music stores but from neighbourhood betel-leaf (*paan*) shops, the pirate cassettes have made India into one of the major music markets in the world. In the field of cinema and television, content has never been a problem with a large local film industry which has restricted Hollywood largely to English-language audiences.

What accounts for this great limitation in the Net and the computer components of recycled modernity? Recycling practices have, as we have shown, been very successful in expanding computer culture, by making it inexpensive and accessible. Most importantly recycling provided a practical education to tens of thousands of people left out of the upper-caste technical universities. But content providers are still at a discount. But perhaps not yet. The last time I went to Nehru Place I met a young man from eastern India busy collecting Linux manuals. In a few years the recyclers, bored with pirating Microsoft ware, will surely begin writing their own.

Thinking through the transitions: the city and the pirate modern

The emergence of a large 'pirate' electronic space in India gestures to a number of emergent practices in India in the 1980s and the 1990s. Though 'globalisation' is usually held out as a representational shorthand to capture this era, one can argue that in fact a number of complex, often unintended, factors cohered in making the 'contemporary'.

Globalisation discourses in the public sphere have tended to focus on the state and its regulatory regime as a major reference point. While neo-liberal critics of the old regime of state-centred accumulation have pushed, often successfully, for a dismantling of state controls, critics from both the right and the left have tended to defend a nationalist economic model which would retain regulatory controls.

In fact, one of the most interesting aspects of the 1990s in India has been the dramatic retreat of the state at the level of the everyday. The magnified imaginary of the regulatory national state which informed the architecture of Nehruvianism is little in evidence, with a number of competing actors on the ground.

The 'everyday' is something that needs to be clarified here. The state, for example, continues to retain a close grip on the means of legal violence, nor has the regulatory model disappeared. In fact this model has been grafted onto a corrupt liberalisation regime to award the larger contracts in infrastructure.

I would like to speak of the 'everyday' as a space where practices of quotidian consumption, mobility and struggle, are articulated. It is this space that has been largely absent even in those cultural discourses on technological globalisation which have tended to look at élite domains of consumption and identity.

Looking back at the 1990s without the benefit of long-term hindsight, one can posit a number of preliminary formulations on the transitions of the decade. For clarity, I will limit my argument to the electronic everyday, the world of phones, computers, communication, television and music cultures.

The first would be that this everyday has emerged within a distinct *urban* space, in India's fast growing metropolitan centres and small towns. The notion of a distinct urban culture has lacked a public register in the Indian case, but this 'new' everyday has in a sense announced the arrival, albeit hesitantly, of a wide-ranging cluster of forms which we could organise under the term 'urban experience'. Unknown to many of us who lived through the decade, the urban arrived in India in the 1990s. To be sure, the multiple crises of the Third World City are also reflected in this 'urban experience': large-scale inequalities, violence, collapse of infrastructure, and the rise of élite suburbia based on automobile transport. In the midst of all this is a pirate electronic space speaking to the new phone, television and communication cultures that offer a new mobility and employment to thousands in the grey economy.

Thus the second aspect of this everyday is its preponderant *non-legality*. Operating at the level of technocultural services to the vast majority of the population in cities and towns, the actors in this space have simply ignored the state as the regulator of everyday life. The thousands of small cable television operators, pirate audio-cassette shop owners and grey market computer companies have, with significant success, evaded state controls on their operations. Part of the problem has been the state's slow response in imposing regulatory mechanisms due to an inability to understand the new technologies. But when regulation has come, success has been uneven, with only the larger firms falling in line.

The third aspect of the everyday is that the networks of quotidian consumption are dominated by those who, in the older Marxist language, would be called 'petty-commodity producers'. Much of 20th century Marxism from Lenin to the structuralists has puzzled over the reproduction of petty-commodity production in contemporary capitalism. Often this sector has been seen as a derivative category distinct from the main dynamic of capitalist production, a form that is mired in 'circulation', not production. In fact in the expansion of the electronic everyday in India's cities in the 1990s, it is precisely this petty-commodity sector that was crucial. Dominated by small entrepreneurs often focused in their own locality, this sector laid non-legal cable television networks, set up small PCO and computer shops and distribution outlets of music cassettes. Along with this expansion came a host of other interventions in the locality: community advertising through inexpensive desktop-published flyers, informal credit networks that give liquidity for low-cost consumption goods like black and white television sets sold in poor parts of the city.

Many years ago, before he joined the academic star-system, Jean Baudrillard wrote *The Mirror of Production*, a critique of Marxist political economy. Despite its problems, some of which anticipate his later shifts, Baudrillard's text nevertheless managed to point to the anthropomorphic core of Marxism's critique of political economy. Marxism's primacy of production (the "realm of the concrete") led to a devaluing of the circuits of exchange and consumption. Exchange was always seen as exhibiting a lack, a space where labour-power was reified, and often generating "false needs". In the Indian case many of the critics of globalisation, by focusing on the élite consumption spaces (with their effects of waste and violence), tended to miss out on the profound transformations that were taking place in daily life in cities and towns. The Marxisant/nationalist heritage with its hostility and moral suspicion towards consumption in general, played no small part in this.

The last feature of the electronic everyday has been the insertion of a spatio-temporal experience in the locality through *speed*. As urban neighbourhoods get connected through phone lines, television, and increasingly PCO/internet access points, we can speak of flashes of what Paul Virilio has called the possibility of *arrival without departure* in late modernity. Virilio argues that temporal experiences have been fundamentally transformed with the arrival of the new telecommunication networks. Central to the transition is the transformation of modes of travel. Thus for Virilio the audio-visual is the "last vehicle" in modernity, after the railway, the automobile and the aeroplane. Further, a new form of chrono-politics is increasingly displacing the older forms of geopolitics.

Virilio's model is too extreme for the Indian case, but one can surely detect a transformation of the 'local' in the city with the spread of technocultural density. With the generalisation of modes of simultaneity through new technologies of transmission (live telecasts, sport events, long distance phone use by sections of the migrant poor), the 'locality' loses the old form of spatial security. The abolition of distance has, of course, been the great motive force of speed. In India this was pioneered by television (one can recall Heidegger's comments on television – "the peak of the abolition of every possibility of remoteness") but also through the phone network.

Chapter 19

Jean-François Lyotard

ANSWERING THE QUESTION:

What is postmodernism?

While Jean-François Lyotard, a significant continental philosopher and poststructuralist, is most famous for defining postmodernism as *an incredulity towards metanarratives*—i.e., no longer believing in, or being sceptical of, universal systems or truths—in answering the question "what is postmodernism?" he also reveals *an incredulity towards representation*. This can be explained by thinking about "realistic" art. Realism, to the uninitiated, is simply a reflection in writing or painting, of the world as it is; on deeper examination, realism is shown to be a way of representing the world *as it should be*. In other words, "realism" is an ideological construct. An historical example is the way in which during the Second World War the Nazi party banned avant-garde (experimental, conceptual, critical) art in favour of realism. What they had in mind with "realism" was paintings and sculptures of Aryan white muscular males heroically building the Third and Final Reich: the ethnically cleansed utopia that in fact was being built via the death and destruction of the Holocaust. In linking postmodernism to anti-representational art movements that are called the "avant-garde" Lyotard is making a strong political move. As such, the postmodern is temporally repositioned by Lyotard: no longer is it something that comes after the modern, now, it is the modern in its "nascent" state, or, in other words, an aesthetic which is born through the rejection and dismantling of the representational work that went before it. As Lyotard's examples show—Cézanne rejecting the methods of the French Impressionists; Picasso and Braque rejecting the methods of Cézanne, and so on—this state is constant. Something is only truly modern, then, if narratives of progression are abandoned; or, something is only truly modern if it is first postmodern. The political side of this involves Lyotard's rejection of any system that demands consensus, which would ultimately be a totalizing notion of human subjectivity and society: the anti-representational is also the anti-consensual. Lyotard's postmodernism, then, is anarchic, anti-systematic, inventing new local (not transcendent) rules of aesthetic and political game playing. Lyotard is not arguing, however, that modern aesthetics and postmodernism are identical. He distinguishes between two modes of the sublime to explain what he means: first, the modern aesthetic of the sublime is one where the "unpresentable" is alluded to at the level of content, and expressed via experimental form; second, the postmodern aesthetic of the sublime is one where the "unpresentable" is put forward without the pleasure of experimental form. What might the "unpresentable" be? It could be an Other that threatens unified systems of thought: something that needs to be expelled or cast outside of a system to maintain order and control. The sublime is that which overpowers reason, in a frightening, yet ultimately pleasurable sense, and for Lyotard, the sublime becomes important because the sublime event generates an aesthetic response that breaks free of rule-bound behaviour. The postmodern sublime, then, offers an ethics, one where the Other can be directly "presented" (not re-presented) as a disturbing yet ultimately creative force.

The postmodern

What, then, is the postmodern? What place does it or does it not occupy in the vertiginous work of the questions hurled at the rules of image and narration? It is undoubtedly a part of the modern. All that has been received, if only yesterday (*modo, modo,* Petronius used to say), must be suspected. What space does Cézanne challenge? The Impressionists'. What object do Picasso and Braque attack? Cézanne's. What presupposition does Duchamp break with in 1912? That which says one must make a painting, be it cubist. And Buren questions that other presupposition which he believes had survived untouched by the work of Duchamp: the place of presentation of the work. In an amazing acceleration, the generations precipitate themselves. A work can become modern only if it is first postmodern. Postmodernism thus understood is not modernism at its end but in the nascent state, and this state is constant.

Yet I would like not to remain with this slightly mechanistic meaning of the word. If it is true that modernity takes place in the withdrawal of the real and according to the sublime relation between the presentable and the conceivable, it is possible, within this relation, to distinguish two modes (to use the musician's language). The emphasis can be placed on the powerlessness of the faculty of presentation, on the nostalgia for presence felt by the human subject, on the obscure and futile will which inhabits him in spite of everything. The emphasis can be placed, rather, on the power of the faculty to conceive, on its "inhumanity" so to speak (it was the quality Apollinaire demanded of modern artists), since it is not the business of our understanding whether or not human sensibility or imagination can match what it conceives. The emphasis can also be placed on the increase of being and the jubilation which result from the invention of new rules of the game, be it pictorial, artistic, or any other. What I have in mind will become clear if we dispose very schematically a few names on the chessboard of the history of avant-gardes: on the side of melancholia, the German Expressionists, and on the side of *novatio,* Braque and Picasso, on the former Malevitch and on the latter Lissitsky, on the one Chirico and on the other Duchamp. The nuance which distinguishes these two modes may be infinitesimal; they often coexist in the same piece, are almost indistinguishable; and yet they testify to a difference (*un différend*) on which the fate of thought depends and will depend for a long time, between regret and assay.

The work of Proust and that of Joyce both allude to something which does not allow itself to be made present. Allusion, to which Paolo Fabbri recently called my attention, is perhaps a form of expression indispensable to the works which belong to an aesthetic of the sublime. In Proust, what is being eluded as the price to pay for this allusion is the identity of consciousness, a victim to the excess of time (*au trop de temps*). But in Joyce, it is the identity of writing which is the victim of an excess of the book (*au trop de livre*) or of literature.

Proust calls forth the unpresentable by means of a language unaltered in its syntax and vocabulary and of a writing which in many of its operators still belongs to the genre of novelistic narration. The literary institution, as Proust inherits it from Balzac and Flaubert, is admittedly subverted in that the hero is no longer a character but the inner consciousness of time, and in that the diegetic diachrony, already damaged by Flaubert, is here put in question because of the narrative voice. Nevertheless, the unity of the book, the odyssey of that consciousness, even if it is deferred from chapter to chapter, is not seriously challenged: the identity of the writing with itself throughout the labyrinth of the interminable narration is enough to connote such unity, which has been compared to that of *The Phenomenology of Mind.*

Joyce allows the unpresentable to become perceptible in his writing itself, in the signifier. The whole range of available narrative and even stylistic operators is put into play without concern for the unity of the whole, and new operators are tried. The grammar and vocabulary of literary language are no longer accepted as given; rather, they appear as academic forms, as rituals originating in piety (as Nietzsche said) which prevent the unpresentable from being put forward.

Here, then, lies the difference: modern aesthetics is an aesthetic of the sublime, though a nostalgic one. It allows the unpresentable to be put forward only as the missing contents; but the form, because of its recognizable consistency, continues to offer to the reader or viewer matter for solace and pleasure. Yet these sentiments do not constitute the real sublime sentiment, which is in an intrinsic combination of pleasure and pain: the pleasure that reason should exceed all presentation, the pain that imagination or sensibility should not be equal to the concept.

The postmodern would be that which, in the modern, puts forward the unpresentable in presentation itself; that which denies itself the solace of good forms, the consensus of a taste which would make it possible to share collectively the nostalgia for the unattainable; that which searches for new presentations, not in order to enjoy them but in order to impart a stronger sense of the unpresentable. A postmodern artist or writer is in the position of a philosopher: the text he writes, the work he produces are not in principle governed by preestablished rules, and they cannot be judged according to a determining judgment, by applying familiar categories to the text or to the work. Those rules and categories are what the work of art itself is looking for. The artist and the writer, then, are working without rules in order to formulate the rules of what *will have been done.* Hence the fact that work and text have the characters of an *event;* hence also, they always come too late for their author, or, what amounts to the same thing, their being put into work, their realization (*mise en oeuvre*) always begin too soon. *Post modern* would have to be understood according to the paradox of the future (*post*) anterior (*modo*).

It seems to me that the essay (Montaigne) is postmodern, while the fragment (*The Athaeneum*) is modern.

Finally, it must be clear that it is our business not to supply reality but to invent allusions to the conceivable which cannot be presented. And it is not to be expected that this task will effect the last reconciliation between language games (which, under the name of faculties, Kant knew to be separated by a chasm), and that only the transcendental illusion (that of Hegel) can hope to totalize them into a real unity. But Kant also knew that the price to pay for such an illusion is terror. The nineteenth and twentieth centuries have given us as much terror as we can take. We have paid a high enough price for the nostalgia of the whole and the one, for the reconciliation of the concept and the sensible, of the transparent and the communicable experience. Under the general demand for slackening and for appeasement, we can hear the mutterings of the desire for a return of terror, for the realization of the fantasy to seize reality. The answer is: Let us wage a war on totality; let us be witnesses to the unpresentable; let us activate the differences and save the honor of the name.

Chapter 20

Gerald Vizenor

A POSTMODERN INTRODUCTION

The striking parallels sketched by Gerald Vizenor between postmodern and indigenous, or tribal narratives, can help elucidate features of both. Importantly, Vizenor—who is the Distinguished Professor of American Studies at The University of New Mexico, and author of numerous books on Native culture, literature and theory—starts with Lyotard's phrase "wisps of narrative" or the small, local stories that indigenous and postmodernist discourses are entirely composed of. Elsewhere, Lyotard opposes small, or little narratives (postmodernism) with the big, overarching and transcendent metanarratives of the Enlightenment, metaphysics, religion, and so on. So even though indigenous literatures are often written from a faith perspective, this is not one that is considered to override and replace all other notions of the sacred. After a short but comprehensive survey of postmodernism, Vizenor notes (in "Pleasurable Misreading") how indigenous cultures have been commodified, reduced, stereotyped, and fantasized over, by the west, and yet, there is not a more "truthful" account of these cultures available in the sense of a fixed, universal truth (another metanarrative); rather, the playfulness and elusiveness of tribal discourse can be embraced through postmodern "misreading". A core notion here is that indigenous discourses are comic rather than tragic; for example, social sciences and anthropology usually misread indigenous culture via the tragic vision of decline, decimation, disease, and so on. Postmodernism, for Vizenor, offers a liberating break from such "hypotragic signs" (a kind of "deficient" tragedy based upon Western aesthetics), offering instead this notion of a "comic holotrope", or, a symbolically rich sign. After offering some examples of comic misreadings of indigenous culture ("Narrative dissidence"), Vizenor produces a theoretically dense section ("Comic signs and holotropes"). The key indigenous figure that binds Vizenor's ideas together is trickster: a mythological, but from an indigenous perspective, real being, who in fact brought about humanity, and through his transformative, playful and disturbing games, intervenes in history and society. Vizenor contends that trickster writing is produced via the "comic holotrope", a full yet tricky, playful, subversive and funny sign, but not a static sign: it is a sign of plenitude and promise, not one that can be captured, fixed, as if it were a moth to be pinned down, placed on display. The "comic holotrope" is a whole sign that expresses complete relationships, between the individual and the community, or, the empirical and the metaphysical, the profane and the secular. A key moment in Vizenor's *definition-in-process* of the trickster sign is that it is "a consonance in tribal discourse." This gives a major clue as to how the trickster sign can be, or initiates the process of becoming, a whole sign: the holotrope is acoustical as well as written. The holotrope *is a sounding*, one which is in accord and sympathy with "tribal discourse": it is an expression of that tribal discourse at the same time as it tries something new. Even when it does something new, it does it in good faith, in agreement and harmony. The consonance means that the trickster sign partakes of an oral culture, even though it appears written on the page, just as trickster is present in performative texts when they are simply being read.

Postmodern discourse

Native American Indian histories and literatures, oral and written, are imagined from "wisps of narratives." These narrative wisps, wrote Jean-François Lyotard, are

> stories that one tells, that one hears, that one acts out; the people does not exist as a subject but as a mass of millions of insignificant and serious little stories that sometimes let themselves be collected together to constitute big stories and sometimes disperse into digressive elements.[1]

The critical attention in this collection is postmodernism: new essays on narrative discourse, authors, readers, tricksters and comic world views rather than tragic themes, individualism and modernism.

Lyotard uses the word *postmodern* to describe "the condition of knowledge in the most highly developed societies" and to designate "the state of our culture following the transformations which, since the end of the nineteenth century, have altered the game rules for science, literature, and the arts." His studies "place these transformations in the context of the crisis of narratives."[2]

The word *postmodernism* is a clever condition: an invitation to narrative chance in a new language game and an overture to amend the formal interpretations and transubstantiation of tribal literatures.

Ihab Hassan, for instance, wrote that postmodernism sounds awkward and uncouth. The word "evokes what it wishes to surpass or suppress, modernism itself. The term thus contains its enemy within, as the terms romanticism and classicism, baroque and rococo, do not. . . . But if much of modernism appears hieratic, hypotactical, and formalist, postmodernism strikes us by contrast as playful, paratactical, and deconstructionist."[3]

Brian McHale, on the other hand, asserts,

> Nobody likes the term, yet people continue to prefer it over the even less satisfactory alternatives. . . . Postmodernism is not post modern, whatever that might mean, but post modern*ism*; it does not come *after the present* (a solecism), but after the *modernist movement*. . . . Postmodernism follows *from* modernism.

He wrote that a "superior construction of postmodernism would be one that produces new insights, new or richer connections, coherence of a different degree or kind, ultimately *more discourse*."[4]

Native American Indian literatures are tribal discourse, more discourse. The oral and written narratives are language games, comic discourse rather than mere responses to colonialist demands or social science theories.

Stephen Tyler, in his essay on postmodern anthropology, considers discourse as the "maker of the world, not its mirror. . . . The world is what we say it is, and what we speak of is the world." Tribal narratives are discourse and in this sense tribal literatures are the world rather than a representation. Tyler argues that one of the constant themes in the dominant culture has been the "search for apodictic and universal method. In our own times we see the triumph of formalism in all branches of thought. . . . Form, in other words, produces form; it is both process and structure." He points out that postmodern

> writing focuses on the outer flow of speech, seeking not the thought that "under-lies" speech, but the thought that *is* speech. . . . Modernists sought a form of writing more in keeping with "things," emphasizing, in imitation of modern science, the descriptive function of writing—writing as a "picture of reality."

Postmodern writing overturns

> modernist *mimesis* in favor of a writing that "evokes" or "calls to mind," not by completion and similarity but by suggestion and difference. The function of the text is not to depict or reveal within itself what it says. The text is "seen through" by what it cannot say. It shows what it cannot say and says what it cannot show.[5]

Pleasurable misreadings

The world is a text, Vincent Leitch argues in *Deconstructive Criticism,* and nothing stands behind this world of tropes because a literal language does not exist, except in illusions. The literal translations and representations of tribal literatures are illusions, consolations in the dominant culture. There can never be "correct" or "objective" readings of the text or the tropes in tribal literatures, only more energetic, interesting and "pleasurable misreadings."[6]

Native American Indian literatures have been pressed into cultural categories, transmuted by reductionism, animadversions and the hyper-realities of neocolonial consumerism. The concept of "hyperrealities" is borrowed from *Travels in Hyperreality* by Umberto Eco. He wrote that Americans live in a "more to come" consumer culture.

> This is the reason for this journey into hyperreality, in search of instances where the American imagination demands the real thing and, to attain it, must fabricate the absolute fake; where the boundaries between game and illusion are blurred. . . . [7]

Tribal cultures, in this sense, have been invented as "absolute fakes" and consumed in social science monologues. The consumers demand more cultures and new literatures; at the same time, postmodern criticism would liberate tribal narratives in a most "pleasurable misreading."

Native American Indian literatures are unstudied landscapes, wild and comic rather than tragic and representational, storied with narrative wisps and tribal discourse. Social science theories constrain tribal landscapes to institutional values, representationalism and the politics of academic determination. The narrow teleologies deduced from social science monologues and the ideologies that arise from structuralism have reduced tribal literatures to an "objective" collection of consumable cultural artifacts. Postmodernism liberates imagination and widens the audiences for tribal literatures; this new criticism rouses a comic world view, narrative discourse and language games on the past.

"The return to the past, to the traces, fragments, and debris of memory and history is both necessary and inconclusive," reasoned David Carroll.

The acceptance of representation in its simple sense is a kind of bureaucratic solution to the conflicts of history, an acquiescence to the demands and false security of realism without the will or the force to maintain the potentially irresolvable contradiction of the struggle.[8]

Monologic realism and representation in tribal literatures, in this sense, is a "bureaucratic solution" to neocolonialism and the consumption of narratives and cultures.

In a recent essay on narrative and politics David Carroll wrote,

Any narrative that predetermines all responses or prohibits any counter-narratives puts an end to narrative itself by suppressing all possible alternative actions and responses, by making itself its own end and the end of all other narratives.[9]

Narrative dissidence

Antonin Dvořák, the composer, and Oleg Cassini, the modern couturier, have in common their unusual interests in tribal cultures; now a source of "little dissident narratives" and ironic literature.[10] Separated in time by a century, these two men shared certain hyperrealities about Native American Indian cultures.

"The Americans expect great things of me," wrote Dvořák. "And the main thing is . . . to create a national music. Now, if the small Czech nation can have such musicians, they say, why could not they, too, when their country and people are so immense?"[11]

Patricia Hampl, in her sensitive meditation on the Czech composer, wrote that he arrived in Spillville, Iowa, in 1893, with his wife, six children, housemaid, and secretary.

They stayed the whole summer, an unusually hot one, past Dvořák's fifty-second birthday, which fell on the feast of the Nativity of Mary, September 8. He passed out cigars to the townspeople who gathered for a celebration in his honor. Two days later—quite suddenly it seemed to some people—he and his family packed up and were gone, back the long way they had come.[12]

Big Moon, the Kickapoo leader and healer, was in Spillville late that summer with other tribal people to sell medicinal herbs. Dvořák attended the tribal dances, listened to the music and even paid for a snake oil headache treatment; he consumed the hyperrealities that he believed were tribal, authentic, real and representational. A franchised composer at the turn of the last century, he was inspired and imagined a national music; meanwhile, most tribal cultures were enslaved on reservations. The tribal people he encountered were on the boundaries. Modern immigrants were surrounded by "native immigrants" that summer in a small town; their stories are narrative wisps in the national tenure on savagism and civilization.

"He believed the answer lay in the music of the slaves," Hampl wrote,

Negro spirituals, and in American Indian music, especially its insistent, patient rhythms . . . Maybe he could not perceive the American hesitation. In the old country "the peasants" were himself, his family. His people. In America there was a boundary. Black and white, red and white. We call it racism. He stepped over the line easily, perhaps thinking Indian drum beats were as accessible to white American composers as Czech folk music was to him. He didn't hear the heavier hit of the drum on the ear, the black wail it is impossible to borrow.[13]

Dvořák considered an opera based on *The Song of Hiawatha* by Henry Wadsworth Longfellow, a romantic colonialist poem. "He had read the poem in translation," Hampl wrote. "Naturally, its admiration for the indiginous culture appealed to Dvořák. So did Longfellow's lyrical, if rather didactic, restatement of landscape and the beauties of nature." But the idea "fizzled."[14]

Dvořák and his daughter Otilka, who was fifteen that summer, visited the Chicago World's Columbian Exposition. Behind the mechanical Uncle Sam on the midway, the barkers and pitch men, Otilka must have witnessed the ethnic exhibits, tribal dances and ceremonies. In 1893 the exhibits included a "Bedouin camp, a Winnebago Indian village, a Lapland village, a Persian palace, a Chinese market," and other cultural hyperrealities.[15]

Otilka returned to Spillville. Later that summer she was seen near the tribal camp on the boundaries, near the river where her father walked and recorded the sounds of water, birds and tribal music. She was seen "roaming around the woods, Big Moon by her side. Keeping company. . . . It was Big Moon with her in the woods by the Turkey River, and what of it?"[16] Dvořák was told about his daughter and the tribal leader who had danced for the composer and treated his headache. "Like so much, it depends on your attitude, your place in the story," wrote Hampl. "That night the Dvořáks started packing. They were gone the next day."[17]

Dvořák pursued the hyperrealities of tribal cultures, the structured ceremonies at the tenable borders of civilization in a small town. He imagined tribal music as an instance of nationalism and worried that his daughter was too close to savagism. This, the wilderness in flesh and bone too close to home, is where hyperrealities and dioramas transmute the landscape and narrative discourse.

"I see the rest," wrote Hampl. "Girl on a pony, gold light in the blue morning sky, a glade where a good-looking man, native to the place, puts his hand surely between two clumps of fern to expose for her the white wood mallow, a plant she had never seen before."[18]

Oleg Cassini, the personal couturier and costume designer, considered "looks and styles" and historical periods in his fashion career; unabashed hyperrealities abound in his recent autobiography. "I realized that there was one area I'd never really exploited: my lifelong obsession with American Indians."[19]

Cassini satisfied his obsession in an agreement with Peter MacDonald, the elected chairman of the Navajo Nation. Cassini announced at the National Press Club that he would build, as a joint venture with the tribal government, a "world-class luxury resort" on the reservation. The architecture and furnishings of the tourist resort would "have their base in authentic Navajo designs." MacDonald said that the designer resort would "reflect the unique culture and tradition of our people." Moreover, the tribal leader announced, "We are creating a Navajo Board of Standards for all new tourist facilities on the Reservation to assure that the Navajo name means quality."[20] Designer hyperrealities are valuable properties in a consumer culture, even on reservations.

In one instance Cassini stated his clever attention to cultural selection and tribal standards. "A good many of my American Indian dresses required intricate beading of a sort that was not available in Italy," he wrote in his autobiography.

> I'd been told Hong Kong was the place to find such material. . . . And then the show began. The line was modeled by girls with dark hair and the somatic characteristics of Indians; one wore beads and headdresses. Sometimes the models were barefoot, but generally they wore moccasins.[21]

These stories are serious and comic, numerous narrative wisps that controvert hyperrealities. Tribal literatures are burdened with colonialism and tragic world views; however, there is a curious humanism in tribal narratives on minacious consumerism. Serious attention to cultural hyperrealities is an invitation to trickster discourse, an imaginative liberation in comic narratives; the trickster is postmodern.

Mikhail Bakhtin considered consciousness and character identification in aesthetic events. In trickster discourse the trickster is a comic trope, a chance separation in a narrative.

> There are events that, in principle, cannot unfold on the plane of a single and unified consciousness, but presuppose two consciousnesses that do not fuse; they are events whose essential and constitutive element is the relation of a consciousness to *another* consciousness, precisely because it is *other*. Such are all events that are creatively productive, innovative, unique, and irreversible.[22]

Tribal narratives are creative productions rather than social science monologues; the trickster is a comic trope, chance in a narrative wisp, tribal discourse and an irreversible innovation in literature.

Comic signs and holotropes

The trickster is a communal sign in a comic narrative; the comic *holotrope* (the whole figuration) is a consonance in tribal discourse. Silence and separation, not monologues in social science methodologies, are the antitheses of trickster discourse. The instrumental language of the social sciences are tragic or *hypotragic* modes that withhold communal discourse. Comic signs and tragic modes are cultural variations, the mood and humor in a language game; but they are not structural opposition.

Comic world views are communal; chance is more significant than "moral ruin." Tragic modes are inventions and impositions that attend the "discoverers" and translators of tribal narratives. The notion of the "vanishing tribes" is a lonesome nuisance, to cite one *hypotragic* intrusion, that reveals racialism and the contradictions in humanism and historical determinism. More than a century ago, when politicians, missionaries and some intellectuals argued over monogenesis and the "separate creation of nonwhite races," the commissioner of Indian affairs "asserted that 'the fact stands out clear, well-defined, and indisputable, that Indians, not only as individuals but as tribes, are capable of civilization and christianization.'"[23]

These two capabilities, however, were not acceptable to most whites at the time; those who "saw cultures with primitive technologies, engaged in some limited agriculture yet dependent to a large extent upon hunting and gathering for food and apparel." It was common then

> to refer to Indian communities as hunter societies as opposed to white societies engaged in agriculture and domestic industries. . . . They contrasted the preliterate Indian societies . . . with the accomplishments of their own society and judged the Indian languages generally worthless even though of scientific interest . . . and they saw their own rapidly multiplying population overwhelming the static or declining numbers of the Indian tribes.[24]

The paternal rhetoric of liberal politics, however, promised that peace, wealth and power would be shared; but there was no salvation in the domination, revision or transvaluation of tribal cultures. In the *hypotragic* end there are tricksters and comedies—chance, humor and at best a communal discourse in a tribal narrative. The colonists strained to tame the wild, the tribes and the environment. Now, high technologies overbear postcolonial promises and transvaluations; the tragic mode is in ruin.

Comic signs in tribal narratives, and then tragic modes in translations and imposed histories, are seldom mentioned in social science research and "discoveries." To understand these variations and the problems of interpretation we must turn to the theories of imaginative literature. Literary criticism, however, has not considered tribal narratives until the past two decades. Arnold Krupat comments that "there has been a sufficient amount of sophisticated writing about Native American literature in the last ten years or so to constitute a New Indian Criticism."[25]

Even now, serious critical attention to tribal narratives is minimal; a dubious virtue, given the instrumental possession of tribal experience by romantic adventurers, missionaries and then social science. "Prior to the twentieth century," Michael Castro points out, "literary approaches to the Indian were dominated by two opposing and distancing stereotypes, the 'brutish savage' and the 'noble savage,' each serving underlying psychic needs of Western culture."[26] These stereotypes and several others, such as idiotism and "genetic code" alcoholism, are *hypotragic* impositions that deny a comic world view—the racist denial of tribal languages and ceremonies.

Histories read the past, or the past in the historical present; criticism reads the narrative; and the trickster reads neither. Here in trickster discourse the trickster unties the *hypotragedies* imposed on tribal narratives—tribal narratives have been underread in criticism and overread in social science. The tragic mode is not in structural opposition to the comic sign. Rather, it is a racial burden, a postcolonial overcompensation at best; these burdens are a dubious triumph. "Without a sense of the tragic, comedy loses heart, it becomes brittle, it has animation but no life," asserts Richard Sewall. "Without a recognition of the truths of comedy, tragedy becomes bleak and intolerable."[27] Without a doubt social science theories are "bleak" reminders of the *hypotragic* intrusion and postcolonial domination of tribal cultures and literature.

More than fifty years ago Aldous Huxley "wondered whether tragedy as a form of art might not be doomed." He witnessed colonial durance, the intrusions of "moral ruin" and the duress of romantic and tragic modes in the translation of comic tribal literature, but his concern centered on the classics. Meanwhile, social science studies reproduced new theories and contributed not so much to the doom of tragedies, but to a new insolence in tribal literature, an outbreak of *hypotragedies*. Huxley argues in "Tragedy and the Whole Truth"[28] that tragedies are more than "mere verisimilitude" and empirical evidence, more than facts; tragedies are not the "whole truth." The trickster, a semiotic sign in a third-person narrative, is never tragic or *hypotragic,* never the whole truth or even part truth. Social science on the other hand is never comic, never a chance and never tragic in the end. Causal research strains to discover the "whole truth" or the invented truth in theories and models; these "whole truth" models imposed on tribal experiences are *hypotragedies,* abnormal tragedies in this instance. They have no comic imagination, no artistic intent, no communal signification of mythic verism.

"To make a tragedy," Huxley writes, "the artist must isolate a single element out of the totality of human experience and use that exclusively as his material. Tragedy is something that is separated out from the Whole Truth. . . ." In *The Death of Tragedy,* George Steiner holds that tragedy is dead because of the promise of salvation, which is an argument similar to the "whole truth."

In his classical studies on tragedy and comedy Walter Kerr points out that "tragedy is the form that promises us a happy ending."[29] He argues that "comedy depends upon tragedy" and that there is hope in tragedy, while in comedy "there is no way out." He would not, it seems, agree with the notion of the "whole truth." Kerr writes, "In short, tragedy should report every conceivable experience man can have as he exercises his freedom totally in the hope of arriving at a new state of being."[30] Huxley declares, "For the fact is that tragedy and what I have called the Whole Truth are not compatible; where one is, the other is not."

Social science theories isolate certain elements in tribal narratives; the construction of human experience is modular. The trickster is a communal sign, never isolation; a concordance of narrative voices. The trickster is not tragic because the narrative does not promise a happy ending. The comic and tragic, the *hypotragic*, are cultural variations; the trickster is opposed by silence and isolation, not social science. The antithesis of the tragic in social science is chaos, rumors and wild conversations. The trickster livens chaos, but as Paul Watzlawick has argued, realities in social science rest "on the supposition that the world cannot be chaotic— not because we have any proof for this view, but because chaos would simply be intolerable." The comic trickster and social science, a tragic monologue, are contradictions but not antithetical; social science is a limited language game.[31]

"The comic rites are necessarily impious," muses Wylie Sypher, "for comedy is sacrilege as well as release. . . . We find ourselves reflected in the comedian, who satisfies our need for impieties."[32] Sypher maintains that the "high comic vision of life is humane, an achievement of man as a social being," which would include trickster narratives, comic *holotropes* and concordance in discourse. "So the comic spirit keeps us pure in mind by requiring that we regard ourselves skeptically. Indeed this spirit is an agent of that civilizing activity Matthew Arnold called 'criticism,' which is essential to 'culture.'"[33]

The trickster, then, is a comic and communal sign, a discourse in a narrative with no hope or tragic promises. The trickster is neither the "whole truth" nor an isolated *hypotragic* transvaluation of primitivism. The trickster is as aggressive as those who imagine the narrative, but the trickster bears no evil or malice in narrative voices. Malice and evil would silence the comic *holotropes;* there would be no concordance in the discourse. Neither the narrator, the characters, nor the audience would share the narrative event.

Arthur Koestler observes in "The Act of Creation" that there are various "moods involved in different forms of humor, including mixed or contradictory feelings; but whatever the mixture, it must contain a basic ingredient which is indispensible: an impulse, however faint, of aggression or apprehension. . . ."[34] He writes, "Replace aggression by sympathy," as liberal humanists and postcolonial interpreters have done with tribal cultures, "and the same situation will no longer be comic but pathetic, and evoke not laughter but pity."

Freedom is a sign, and the trickster is chance and freedom in a comic sign; comic freedom is a "doing," not an essence, not a museum being, not an aesthetic presence. The trickster as a semiotic sign is imagined in narrative voices, a communal rein to the unconscious, which is comic liberation; however, the trickster is outside comic structure, "making it" comic rather than inside comedy, "being it."[35] The trickster is agonistic imagination and aggressive liberation, a "doing" in narrative points of view and outside the imposed structures.

Jean-Paul Sartre reasoned that freedom, or comic liberation in this instance, is involvement, to be *engagé* [engager] in a free choice; "a freedom which would produce its own existence would lose its very meaning. . . ." Freedom determines "itself by its very upsurge as a 'doing'"[36] The trickster is a comic sign with no histories, no political or economic signification, and no being or presence in the narrative. The trickster is nothingness in a narrative voice, an encounter that centers imagination in comic *holotropes,* a communal being; nothingness in consciousness and comic discourse.

"Creativity occurs in an act of encounter," wrote Rollo May in *The Courage to Create,* "and is to be understood with this encounter as its center."[37] The trickster is an encounter in narrative voices, a communal sign and creative encounter in a discourse.

Tribal cultures, social science and the environment have at least three circumstances in common: science is a trope to power and rules memories; science measures humans and the earth in *hypotragic* isolation and monologues; the tribes and the wilderness vanish in tragic narratives. The wild environment and tricksters are comic and communal; science is a monologue with science not the environment, and the antitheses are silence and chaos. "In literature or in ecology, comedy enlightens and enriches human experience without trying to transform either mankind or the world," wrote Joseph Meeker in *The Comedy of Survival: Studies in Literary Ecology.* "The comic mode of human behavior represented in literature is the closest art has come to describing man as an adaptive animal."[38] The trickster animates this human adaptation in a comic language game and social science overcomes chaos in a monologue; the environment bears the comedies and tragedies.

Notes

1 Jean-François Lyotard, *Instructions païennes* quot. David Carroll, "Narrative, Heterogeneity, and the Question of the Political: Bakhtin and Lyotard," *The Aims of Representation,* ed. Murray Krieger (New York: Columbia University Press, 1987) 85.

2 Jean-François Lyotard, *The Postmodern Condition: A Report on Knowledge* (Minneapolis: University of Minnesota Press, 1984) xxiii.

3 Ihab Hassan, *The Postmodern Turn* (Columbus: Ohio State University Press, 1987), 87, 91.

4 Brian McHale *Postmodern Fiction* (New York: Methuen, 1987) 3–5.

5 Stephen Tyler, "Post-Modern Anthropology," *Discourse and the Social Life of Meaning,* ed. Phyllis Pease Chock and June Wyman (Washington: Smithsonian Institution Press, 1986) 37, 40, 45.

6 Vincent Leitch, *Deconstructive Criticism* (New York: Columbia University Press, 1983) 59.

7 Umberto Eco, *Travels in Hyperreality* (San Diego: Harcourt Brace Jovanovich, 1986) 8. In *Simulations* Jean Baudrillard argues that the "hyperreal" is the product of a synthesis of "models in a hyperspace without atmosphere . . . never again will the real have to be produced. . . ." The hyperreal is "sheltered from the imaginary, and from any distinction between the real and the imaginary, leaving room only for the orbital recurrance of models and the simulated generation of differences." Indians are simulations in the social sciences, conceivable models of tribal cultures. "For ethnology to live, its object must die." The posthumous savages, he writes, have "become referential simulacra, and the science itself a pure simulation." (New York: Semiotex(e), 1983) 3, 4, 13, 15.

8 David Carroll, *The Subject in Question* (Chicago: University of Chicago Press, 1982) 117.

9 Carroll, "Narrative," 77.

10 Carroll, "Narrative," 75. He wrote, "Hundreds, thousands of little dissident narratives of all sorts are produced in spite of all attempts to repress them, and they circulate inside and eventually, or even initially, outside the boundaries of the totalitarian state. The importance of these little narratives is not only that they challenge the dominant metanarrative and the state apparatus that would prohibit or discredit them, but that they also indicate the possibility of another kind of society, or another form of social relations. . . ."

11 Patricia Hampl, *Spillville* (Minneapolis: Milkweed Editions, 1987) 82.

12 Hampl 9.

13 Hampl 82.

14 Hampl 90.

15 Burton Benedict, ed., *The Anthropology of World's Fairs* (London: Scolar Press; Berkeley: The Lowie Museum of Anthropology, 1983) 58.

16 Hampl 92.

17 Hampl 94.

18 Hampl 98–99.

19 Oleg Cassini, *In My Own Fashion: An Autobiography* (New York: Simon and Schuster, 1987) 359.

20 Wayne King, "Navajos Plan Luxury Resort for Tourists on Reservation," *New York Times,* October 28, 1987.

21 Cassini 360, 61, 62.

22 Mikhail Bakhtin, *Mikhail Bakhtin: The Dialogical Principle* by Tzvetan Todorov (Minneapolis: University of Minnesota Press, 1984) 99–100.

23 Francis Paul Prucha, *The Indians in American Society* (Berkeley: University of California Press, 1985) 7.

24 Prucha 8–9.

25   Arnold Krupat, *For Those Who Come After: A Study of Native American Autobiography* (Berkeley: University of California Press, 1985) 4.

26   Michael Castro, *Interpreting the Indian: Twentieth-Century Poets and the Native American* (Albuquerque: University of New Mexico Press, 1983) xiv.

27   Richard Sewall, *The Vision of Tragedy* (New Haven: Yale University Press, 1959) 1.

28   Aldous Huxley, "Tragedy and the Whole Truth," *Virginia Quarterly Review,* April 1931: 177–82.

29   Walter Kerr, *Tragedy and Comedy* (New York: Simon & Schuster, 1968) 36.

30   Kerr 135.

31   Paul Watzlawick, ed., *The Invented Reality* (New York: W. W. Norton 1984) 63. John Berger provides an unusual distinction between opposition and separation. In *And Our Faces, My Heart Brief As Photos* (New York: Pantheon Books, 1894 89), he wrote, "The opposite of to love is not to hate but to separate. If love and hate have something in common it is because, in both cases, their energy is that of bringing and holding together—the lover with the loved, the one who hates with the hated. Both passions are tested by separation."

32   Wylie Sypher, "The Meaning of Comedy" *Comedy,* ed. Wylie Sypher (Baltimore: Johns Hopkins University Press, 1956) 223–24.

33   Sypher, 252–53.

34   Arthur Koestler, "The Act of Creation" *Bricks to Babel* (New York: Random House, 1980) 330.

35   Kerr 15.

36   Jean-Paul Sartre, *Being and Nothingness* (Secaucus, New Jersey: The Citadel Press, 1956) 461. "Adventures are stories, and one does not *live* a story," wrote Iris Murdoch in *Sartre: Romantic Rationalist.* Stories are told later, "one can only see it from the outside. The meaning of an adventure comes from its conclusion. . . . But when one is inside an event, one is not thinking of it. One can live or tell; not both at once. When one is living, nothing happens." (New York: Viking, 1987) 39–40. Trickster discourse reveals narrative contradictions in representation, simulation, comic adventures, liberation, and nothingness.

37   Rollo May, *The Courage to Create* (New York: W. W. Norton, 1975) 77.

38   Joseph Meeker, *The Comedy of Survival: Studies in Literary Ecology* (New York: Charles Scribner's Sons, 1972) 39, 192.

Chapter 21

Jean Baudrillard

THE PRECESSION OF SIMULACRA

The differences between an original and a copy disappear in Borges' fable which sociologist and postmodern theorist Jean Baudrillard opens his essay with: the map (or copy of reality) which is so detailed that it becomes indistinguishable from the original. Yet this notion of simulation is outmoded in today's postmodern society, and Baudrillard suggests that it is merely a "second-order" simulacra. Contemporary simulation is of another order, where even the notion of an original and a copy is antiquated: now simulations are the starting point for producing virtual realities, or, what Baudrillard calls the hyperreal. So the simulation precedes what we call "the real", but because it is a virtual reality, "the real" starts to decay, since elsewhere Baudrillard says it has been murdered. This algorithmic, digital hyperreal detaches itself from metaphysical and ethical questions: it is performative (if it works, it is good or true) and "operational". This world entirely composed of signs is portrayed by Baudrillard as a nightmarish double of the reality that it replaces, and this double exists in an electronic hyperspace which in Baudrillard's day meant orbital satellites, telecommunications and data banks, although now, internet "cloud computing" would be a better example. Baudrillard's rhetorical and hyperbolic language (for which he is famous in texts such as *Simulacra and Simulation* (1981), *The Gulf War Did Not Take Place* (1991) and *The Spirit of Terrorism* (2002)), implies the nightmare, using words such as "liquidation" and "artificial resurrection", crossing the extermination of the real with its Sci Fi re-embodiment. Baudrillard explores more concrete examples of simulation in relation to medicine, psychoanalysis and sexuality, in each case suggesting that professions which depend upon being able to tell the difference between reality and simulations are deeply undermined by postmodern hyperreality. In a dense section on religion, Baudrillard argues that the "iconoclasts", or Reformers who destroyed images of God in Christian churches, feared that the images *didn't* stand in for God, but maintained the secret that God did not exist. While this is a large and controversial claim, there is a grain of truth in Baudrillard's suggestion that those who did worship images were inadvertently modern, since now we exist in a world of semiotics or signs *producing the real* (the hypereal), *not standing in for*, the (metaphysical, or Platonic, etc.) real. In other words, this is a shift from a depth-model of signs, to a surface model where the sign refers to nothing but more signs, what Baudrillard calls a "weightless" system, or "an uninterrupted circuit without reference or circumference." This is also a shift from representation (the sign represents the real) to simulation, which is sketched in more detail in Baudrillard's "successive phases of the image". In "The End of the Panopticon" Baudrillard discusses reality television as an "exhumation" of the dead real, the family in question being sacrificial lambs led to the televisual slaughter. Baudrillard argues that what is real or true in reality television is not the corpse of reality, but television itself. This situation goes beyond Guy Debord's idea of the society of the spectacle: now, perspectival space has gone—the distance between the real and the copy—and it is impossible to distinguish between the medium and the message, e.g., Marshall McLuhan's notion that "the medium is the message". Another example related to this is the move from war to "deterrence"; during the Cold War the threat of actual nuclear war becomes more real than war itself. Deterrence is analogous to the flow of capital: it can be "traded" and "exchanged" at global summits, as strategic moves between nation states. What would happen, Baudrillard asks, if such a hyperreal system were to suffer an actual "explosion"?

> The simulacrum is never what hides the truth—it is truth that hides the fact that there is none.
> The simulacrum is true.
>
> —Ecclesiastes [*sic*]

IF ONCE WE WERE ABLE TO VIEW the Borges fable in which the cartographers of the Empire draw up a map so detailed that it ends up covering the territory exactly (the decline of the Empire witnesses the fraying of this map, little by little, and its fall into ruins, though some shreds are still discernible in the deserts—the metaphysical beauty of this ruined abstraction testifying to a pride equal to the Empire and rotting like a carcass, returning to the substance of the soil, a bit as the double ends by being confused with the real through aging)—as the most beautiful allegory of simulation, this fable has now come full circle for us, and possesses nothing but the discrete charm of second-order simulacra.[1]

Today abstraction is no longer that of the map, the double, the mirror, or the concept. Simulation is no longer that of a territory, a referential being, or a substance. It is the generation by models of a real without origin or reality: a hyperreal. The territory no longer precedes the map, nor does it survive it. It is nevertheless the map that precedes the territory—*precession of simulacra*—that engenders the territory, and if one must return to the fable, today it is the territory whose shreds slowly rot across the extent of the map. It is the real, and not the map, whose vestiges persist here and there in the deserts that are no longer those of the Empire, but ours. *The desert of the real itself.*

In fact, even inverted, Borges's fable is unusable. Only the allegory of the Empire, perhaps, remains. Because it is with this same imperialism that present-day simulators attempt to make the real, all of the real, coincide with their models of simulation. But it is no longer a question of either maps or territories. Something has disappeared: the sovereign difference, between one and the other, that constituted the charm of abstraction. Because it is difference that constitutes the poetry of the map and the charm of the territory, the magic of the concept and the charm of the real. This imaginary of representation, which simultaneously culminates in and is engulfed by the cartographer's mad project of the ideal coextensivity of map and territory, disappears in the simulation whose operation is nuclear and genetic, no longer at all specular or discursive. It is all of metaphysics that is lost. No more mirror of being and appearances, of the real and its concept. No more imaginary coextensivity: it is genetic miniaturization that is the dimension of simulation. The real is produced from miniaturized cells, matrices, and memory banks, models of control—and it can be reproduced an indefinite number of times from these. It no longer needs to be rational, because it no longer measures itself against either an ideal or negative instance. It is no longer anything but operational. In fact, it is no longer really the real, because no imaginary envelops it anymore. It is a hyperreal, produced from a radiating synthesis of combinatory models in a hyperspace without atmosphere.

By crossing into a space whose curvature is no longer that of the real, nor that of truth, the era of simulation is inaugurated by a liquidation of all referentials—worse: with their artificial resurrection in the systems of signs, a material more malleable than meaning, in that it lends itself to all systems of equivalences, to all binary oppositions, to all combinatory algebra. It is no longer a question of imitation, nor duplication, nor even parody. It is a question of substituting the signs of the real for the real, that is to say of an operation of deterring every real process via its operational double, a programmatic, metastable, perfectly descriptive machine that offers all the signs of the real and short-circuits all its vicissitudes. Never again will the real have the chance to produce itself—such is the vital function of the model in a system of death, or rather of anticipated resurrection, that no longer even gives the event of death a chance. A hyperreal henceforth sheltered from the imaginary, and from any distinction between the real and the imaginary, leaving room only for the orbital recurrence of models and for the simulated generation of differences.

The divine irreference of images

To dissimulate is to pretend not to have what one has. To simulate is to feign to have what one doesn't have. One implies a presence, the other an absence. But it is more complicated than that because simulating is not pretending: "Whoever fakes an illness can simply stay in bed and make everyone believe he is ill. Whoever simulates an illness produces in himself some of the symptoms" (Littré). Therefore, pretending, or dissimulating, leaves the principle of reality intact: the difference is always clear, it is simply masked, whereas simulation threatens the difference between the "true" and the "false," the "real" and the "imaginary." Is the simulator sick or not, given that he produces "true" symptoms? Objectively one cannot treat him as being either ill or not ill. Psychology and medicine stop at this point, forestalled by the illness's henceforth undiscoverable truth. For if any symptom can be "produced," and can no longer be taken as a fact of nature, then every illness can be considered as simulatable and simulated, and medicine loses its meaning since it only knows how to treat "real" illnesses according to their objective causes. Psychosomatics evolves in a dubious manner at the borders of the principle of illness. As to psychoanalysis, it transfers the symptom of the organic order to the unconscious order: the latter is new and taken for "real" more real than the other—but why would simulation be at the gates of the unconscious? Why couldn't the "work" of the unconscious be "produced" in the same way as any old symptom of classical medicine? Dreams already are.

Certainly the psychiatrist purports that "for every form of mental alienation there is a particular order in the succession of symptoms of which the simulator is ignorant and in the absence of which the psychiatrist would not be deceived." This (which dates from 1865) in order to safeguard the principle of a truth at all costs and to escape the interrogation posed by simulation—the knowledge that truth, reference, objective cause have ceased to exist. Now, what can medicine do with what floats on either side of illness, on either side of health, with the duplication of illness in a discourse that is no longer either true or false? What can psychoanalysis do with the duplication of the discourse of the unconscious in the discourse of simulation that can never again be unmasked, since it is not false either?[2]

What can the army do about simulators? Traditionally it unmasks them and punishes them, according to a clear principle of identification. Today it can discharge a very good simulator as exactly equivalent to a "real" homosexual, a heart patient, or a madman. Even military psychology draws back from Cartesian certainties and hesitates to make the distinction between true and false, between the "produced" and the authentic symptom. "If he is this good at acting crazy, it's because he is." Nor is military psychology mistaken in this regard: in this sense, all crazy people simulate, and this lack of distinction is the worst kind of subversion. It is against this lack of distinction that classical reason armed itself in all its categories. But it is what today again outflanks them, submerging the principle of truth.

Beyond medicine and the army, favored terrains of simulation, the question returns to religion and the simulacrum of divinity: "I forbade that there be any simulacra in the temples because the divinity that animates nature can never be represented." Indeed it can be. But what becomes of the divinity when it reveals itself in icons, when it is multiplied in simulacra? Does it remain the supreme power that is simply incarnated in images as a visible theology? Or does it volatilize itself in the simulacra that, alone, deploy their power and pomp of fascination— the visible machinery of icons substituted for the pure and intelligible Idea of God? This is precisely what was feared by Iconoclasts, whose millennial quarrel is still with us today.[3] This is precisely because they predicted this omnipotence of simulacra, the faculty simulacra have of effacing God from the conscience of man, and the destructive, annihilating truth that they allow to appear—that deep down God never existed, that only the simulacrum ever existed, even that God himself was never anything but his own simulacrum—from this came their urge to destroy the images. If they could have believed that these images only obfuscated or masked the Platonic Idea of God, there would have been no reason to destroy them. One can live with the idea of distorted truth. But their metaphysical despair came from the idea that the image didn't conceal anything at all, and that these images were in essence not images, such as an original model would have made them, but perfect simulacra, forever radiant with their own fascination. Thus this death of the divine referential must be exorcised at all costs.

One can see that the iconoclasts, whom one accuses of disdaining and negating images, were those who accorded them their true value, in contrast to the iconolaters who only saw reflections in them and were content to venerate a filigree God. On the other hand, one can say that the icon worshipers were the most modern minds, the most adventurous, because, in the guise of having God become apparent in the mirror of images, they were already enacting his death and his disappearance in the epiphany of his representations (which, perhaps, they already knew no longer represented anything, that they were purely a game, but that it was therein the great game lay—knowing also that it is dangerous to unmask images, since they dissimulate the fact that there is nothing behind them).

This was the approach of the Jesuits, who founded their politics on the virtual disappearance of God and on the worldly and spectacular manipulation of consciences—the evanescence of God in the epiphany of power—the end of transcendence, which now only serves as an alibi for a strategy altogether free of influences and signs. Behind the baroqueness of images hides the éminence grise of politics.

This way the stake will always have been the murderous power of images, murderers of the real, murderers of their own model, as the Byzantine icons could be those of divine identity. To this murderous power is opposed that of representations as a dialectical power, the visible and intelligible mediation of the Real. All Western faith and good faith became engaged in this wager on representation: that a sign could refer to the depth of meaning, that a sign could be exchanged for meaning and that something could guarantee this exchange— God of course. But what if God himself can be simulated, that is to say can be reduced to the signs that constitute faith? Then the whole system becomes weightless, it is no longer itself anything but a gigantic simulacrum—not unreal, but a simulacrum, that is to say never exchanged for the real, but exchanged for itself, in an uninterrupted circuit without reference or circumference.

Such is simulation, insofar as it is opposed to representation. Representation stems from the principle of the equivalence of the sign and of the real (even if this equivalence is Utopian, it is a fundamental axiom). Simulation, on the contrary, stems from the utopia of the principle of equivalence, *from the radical negation of the sign as value,* from the sign as the reversion and death sentence of every reference. Whereas representation attempts to absorb simulation by interpreting it as a false representation, simulation envelops the whole edifice of representation itself as a simulacrum.

Such would be the successive phases of the image:

it is the reflection of a profound reality;
it masks and denatures a profound reality;
it masks the *absence* of a profound reality;
it has no relation to any reality whatsoever: it is its own pure simulacrum.

In the first case, the image is a *good* appearance—representation is of the sacramental order. In the second, it is an evil appearance—it is of the order of maleficence. In the third, it plays at being an appearance—it is of the order of sorcery. In the fourth, it is no longer of the order of appearances, but of simulation.

The transition from signs that dissimulate something to signs that dissimulate that there is nothing marks a decisive turning point. The first reflects a theology of truth and secrecy (to which the notion of ideology still belongs). The second inaugurates the era of simulacra and of simulation, in which there is no longer a God to recognize his own, no longer a Last Judgment to separate the false from the true, the real from its artificial resurrection, as everything is already dead and resurrected in advance.

When the real is no longer what it was, nostalgia assumes its full meaning. There is a plethora of myths of origin and of signs of reality—a plethora of truth, of secondary objectivity, and authenticity. Escalation of the true, of lived experience, resurrection of the figurative where the object and substance have disappeared. Panic-stricken production of the real and of the referential, parallel to and greater than the panic of material production: this is how simulation appears in the phase that concerns us—a strategy of the real, of the neoreal and the hyperreal that everywhere is the double of a strategy of deterrence.

[. . .]

The end of the panopticon

It is still to this ideology of lived experience—exhumation of the real in its fundamental banality, in its radical authenticity—that the American TV verité experiment attempted on the Loud family in 1971 refers: seven months of uninterrupted shooting, three hundred hours of nonstop broadcasting, without a script or a screenplay, the odyssey of a family, its dramas, its joys, its unexpected events, nonstop—in short, a "raw" historical document, and the "greatest television performance, comparable, on the scale of our day-to-day life, to the footage of our landing on the moon." It becomes more complicated because this family fell apart during the filming: a crisis erupted, the Louds separated, etc. Whence that insoluble controversy: was TV itself responsible? What would have happened *if TV hadn't been there?*

More interesting is the illusion of filming the Louds as *if TV weren't there.* The producer's triumph was to say: "They lived as if we were not there." An absurd, paradoxical formula—neither true nor false: utopian. The "as if *we* were not there" being equal to "as if *you* were there." It is this utopia, this paradox that fascinated the twenty million viewers, much more than did the "perverse" pleasure of violating someone's privacy. In the "verité" experience it is not a question of secrecy or perversion, but of a sort of frisson of the real, or of an aesthetics of the hyperreal, a frisson of vertiginous and phony exactitude, a frisson of simultaneous distancing and magnification, of distortion of scale, of an excessive transparency. The pleasure of an excess of meaning, when the bar of the sign falls below the usual waterline of meaning: the nonsignifier is exalted by the camera angle. There one sees what the real never was (but "as if you were there"), without the distance that gives us perspectival space and depth vision (but "more real than nature"). Pleasure in the microscopic simulation that allows the real to pass into the hyperreal. (This is also somewhat the case in porno, which is fascinating more on a metaphysical than on a sexual level.)

Besides, this family was already hyperreal by the very nature of its selection: a typical ideal American family, California home, three garages, five children, assured social and professional status, decorative housewife, upper-middle-class standing. In a way it is this statistical perfection that dooms it to death. Ideal heroine of the American way of life, it is, as in ancient sacrifices, chosen in order to be glorified and to die beneath the flames of the medium, a modern *fatum*. Because heavenly fire no longer falls on corrupted cities, it is the camera lens that, like a laser, comes to pierce lived reality in order to put it to death. "The Louds: simply a family who agreed to deliver themselves into the hands of television, and to die by it," the director will say. Thus it is a question of a sacrificial process, of a sacrificial spectacle offered to twenty million Americans. The liturgical drama of a mass society.

TV verité. A term admirable in its ambiguity, does it refer to the truth of this family or to the truth of TV? In fact, it is TV that is the truth of the Louds, it is TV that is true, it is TV that renders true. Truth that is no longer the reflexive truth of the mirror, nor the perspectival truth of the panoptic system and of the gaze, but the manipulative truth of the test that sounds out and interrogates, of the laser that touches and pierces, of computer cards that retain your preferred sequences, of the genetic code that controls your combinations, of cells that inform your sensory universe. It is to this truth that the Loud family was subjected by the medium of TV, and in this sense it amounts to a death sentence (but is it still a question of truth?).

End of the panoptic system. The eye of TV is no longer the source of an absolute gaze, and the ideal of control is no longer that of transparency. This still presupposes an objective space (that of the Renaissance) and the omnipotence of the despotic gaze. It is still, if not a system of confinement, at least a system of mapping. More subtly, but always externally, playing on the opposition of seeing and being seen, even if the panoptic focal point may be blind.

Something else in regard to the Louds. "You no longer watch TV, it is TV that watches you (live)," or again: "You are no longer listening to Don't Panic, it is Don't Panic that is listening to you"—a switch from the panoptic mechanism of surveillance (*Discipline and Punish* [Surveiller et punir]) to a system of deterrence, in which the distinction between the passive and the active is abolished. There is no longer any imperative of submission to the model, or to the gaze "YOU are the model!" "YOU are the majority!" Such is the watershed of a hyperreal sociality, in which the real is confused with the model, as in the statistical operation, or with the medium, as in the Louds' operation. Such is the last stage of the social relation, ours, which is no longer one of persuasion (the classical age of propaganda, of ideology, of publicity, etc.) but one of deterrence: "YOU are information, you are the social, you are the event, you are involved, you have the word, etc." An about-face through which it becomes impossible to locate one instance of the model, of power, of the gaze, of the medium itself, because *you* are always already on the other side. No more subject, no more focal point, no more center or periphery: pure flexion or circular inflexion. No more violence or surveillance: only "information," secret virulence, chain reaction, slow implosion, and simulacra of spaces in which the effect of the real again comes into play.

We are witnessing the end of perspectival and panoptic space (which remains a moral hypothesis bound up with all the classical analyses on the "objective" essence of power), and thus to the *very abolition of the spectacular*. Television, for example in the case of the Louds, is no longer a spectacular medium. We are no longer in the society of the spectacle, of which the situationists spoke, nor in the specific kinds of alienation and repression that it implied. The medium itself is no longer identifiable as such, and the confusion of the medium and the message (McLuhan)[4] is the first great formula of this new era. There is no longer a medium in the literal sense: it is now intangible, diffused, and diffracted in the real, and one can no longer even say that the medium is altered by it.

Such a blending, such a viral, endemic, chronic, alarming presence of the medium, without the possibility of isolating the effects—spectralized, like these advertising laser sculptures in the empty space of the event filtered by the medium—dissolution of TV in life, dissolution of life in TV—indiscernible chemical solution: we are all Louds doomed not to invasion, to pressure, to violence and blackmail by the media and the models, but to their induction, to their infiltration, to their illegible violence.

But one must watch out for the negative turn that discourse imposes: it is a question neither of disease nor of a viral infection. One must think instead of the media as if they were, in outer orbit, a kind of genetic code that directs the mutation of the real into the hyperreal, just as the other micromolecular code controls the passage from a representative sphere of meaning to the genetic one of the programmed signal.

It is the whole traditional world of causality that is in question: the perspectival, determinist mode, the "active," critical mode, the analytic mode—the distinction between cause and effect, between active and passive, between subject and object, between the end and the means. It is in this sense that one can say: TV is watching us, TV alienates us, TV manipulates us, TV informs us . . . In all this, one remains dependent on the analytical conception of the media, on an external active and effective agent, on "perspectival" information with the horizon of the real and of meaning as the vanishing point.

Notes

1 Cf. J. Baudrillard, "L'ordre des simulacres" (The order of simulacra), in *L'échange symbolique et la mort* (Symbolic exchange and death) (Paris: Gallimard, 1976).

2 A discourse that is itself not susceptible to being resolved in transference. It is the entanglement of these two discourses that renders psychoanalysis interminable.

3 Cf. M. Perniola, *Icônes, visions, simulacres* (Icons, visions, simulacra) (1978), 39.

4 The medium/message confusion is certainly a corollary of that between the sender and the receiver, thus sealing the disappearance of all dual, polar structures that formed the discursive organization of language, of all determined articulation of meaning reflecting Jakobson's famous grid of functions. That discourse "circulates" is to be taken literally: that is, it no longer goes from one point to another, but it traverses a cycle that *without distinction* includes the positions of transmitter and receiver, now unlocatable as such. Thus there is no instance of power, no instance of transmission—power is something that circulates and whose source can no longer be located, a cycle in which the positions of the dominator and the dominated are exchanged in an endless reversion that is also the end of power in its classical definition. The circularization of power, of knowledge, of discourse puts an end to any localization of instances and poles. In the psychoanalytic interpretation itself, the "power" of the interpreter does not come from any outside instance but from the interpreted himself. This changes everything, because one can always ask of the traditional holders of power where they get their power from. Who made you duke? The king. Who made you king? God. Only God no longer answers. But to the question: who made you a psychoanalyst? the analyst can well reply: You. Thus is expressed, by an inverse simulation, the passage from the "analyzed" to the "analysand," from passive to active, which simply describes the spiraling effect of the shifting of poles, the effect of circularity in which power is lost, is dissolved, is resolved in perfect manipulation (it is no longer of the order of directive power and of the gaze, but of the order of tactility and commutation). See also the state/family circularity assured by the fluctuation and metastatic regulation of the images of the social and the private (J. Donzelot, *La police des familles* [The policing of families]).

Impossible now to pose the famous question: "From what position do you speak?"—"How do you know?" "From where do you get your power?" without hearing the immediate response: "But it is *of* you (from you) that I speak"—meaning, it is you who are speaking, you who know, you who are the power. Gigantic circumvolution, circumlocution of the spoken word, which is equal to a blackmail with no end, to a deterrence that cannot be appealed of the subject presumed to speak, leaving him without a reply, because to the question that he poses one ineluctably replies: but *you are* the answer, or: your question is already an answer, etc.—the whole strangulatory sophistication of intercepting speech, of the forced confession in the guise of freedom of expression, of trapping the subject in his own interrogation, of the precession of the reply to the question (all the violence of interpretation lies there, as well as that of the conscious or unconscious management of the "spoken word" [*parole*]).

This simulacrum of the inversion or the involution of poles, this clever subterfuge, which is the secret of the whole discourse of manipulation and thus, today, in every domain, the secret of any new power in the erasure of the scene of power, in the assumption of all words from which has resulted this fantastic silent majority characteristic of our time—all of this started without a doubt in the political sphere with the democractic simulacrum, which today is the substitution for the power of God with the power of the people as the source of power, and of power as *emanation* with power as *representation*. Anti-Copernican revolution: no transcendental instance either of the sun or of the luminous sources of power and knowledge—everything comes from the people and everything returns to them. It is with this magnificent recycling that the universal simulacrum of manipulation, from the scenario of mass suffrage to the present-day phantoms of opinion polls, begins to be put in place.

Chapter 22

Ziauddin Sardar

SURVIVING POSTMODERNISM

While Ziauddin Sardar's critique of postmodernism might appear extreme, conflating postmodernism with globalized capitalism, colonialism, secularism and a general embracing of "evil", it is important to register that first, there are myriad such cultural perspectives concerning postmodernism around the globe that similarly reject its value system, and second, that Sardar is not advocating a return to traditionalism or fundamentalism, but rather a continuation of non-Western, non-postmodern traditions. As an expert on science and Islam, as well as extensive publications and television programmes on media studies, cultural studies, theory, cyberfutures, and postmodernism, among many other topics, Sardar has long explored the traditional role of reason in Islam, and how this has been misunderstood by other cultures. In the extract, Sardar opens with the art of Chinese painters Lin Yong and Su Hua, suggesting that what they represent is Islamic and Chinese traditions as dynamic living forces which can "confront" the problems of Western modernity and postmodernism. Sardar distinguishes as mentioned between traditionalism and tradition. *Traditionalism* is what the West might call "fundamentalism": in responding to external pressures, such as secular, liberal, or capitalist values and demands, it tends to cling to a rigid notion of the past, freezing traditions into fixed, immutable values (ones that can never be changed or transformed), thus becoming oppressive for many people. Sardur sees *tradition* as something much more flexible and dynamic: still a "summation of the absolute frame of reference" of past values and axioms, but nonetheless subject to historical difference and development, and therefore future change. In many respects, traditionalism/fundamentalism emerges as a direct response to postmodernism, whereas tradition can be utilized to more positively counter global postmodern values. Through examining the poetry of the Indian political thinker and poet Sir Mohammad Iqbal (1877–1938), Sardur notes that a non-egotistical Islamic notion of Self is required to counter the shallow postmodern egotism of consumer culture; this Self is one created by God, and so deeply implicated in community that it is the "antithesis of western individualism". Iqbal's notion of the community informs Sardar's argument, since its members need to become educated in terms of cultural and religious history and values, before they can truly play a part in it (for example, elsewhere Iqbal argues they must become educated before they have the right to vote). Sardar calls this process the "recovery" of the Self, and argues that on a wider scale, it is what the turn to tradition involves, and can provide. For Sardar this is not a secular recovery: it is oppositional to secular postmodernism. So Sardar regards postmodern plurality and multiculturalism as "anti-human" since secularism theoretically accords all values (human and non-human, good and evil) equality. While this is debatable, Sardar does provide the example of postmodernism's attitude to other religions: they become subsumed in a consumerist notion of New Age "spirituality" while simultaneously being stripped of authenticity and efficacy. In his section "The Incredible Lightness of Authenticity" Sardar suggests some strategies of resistance beyond his earlier idea of returning the Orientalist gaze upon the west to map its deficiencies; in this section he argues that traditional systems need to be regarded as strengths, containing potential solutions to societal problems, and that local technologies need to be invented for indigenous development. In this, and other related ways, modernity is redefined in non-Western forms, creating a continuity with the past while rejecting a postmodern present or future.

T HE MINARET IS CLEARLY THERE. It looks as if serried ranks of people are huddled around, even on top of the minaret, in a representation in which the rules of realist perspective have been abandoned. The painting is, however, subtly Other. The Chinese painters Lin Yong and Su Hua have become famous in Pakistan for a series of works that draws on the tradition of Persian and Turkish miniatures to depict contemporary life in modern Pakistan.[1] 'Friday prayers', like the classic miniatures which illustrated the sixteenth-century masterpiece *Shahnama* ('Book of Kings'), uses a single plane to represent a number of dimensions. The congregation, the minaret of the mosque, and the *neem* tree in late autumn, all appear to exist in a single plane. Closer examination shows that we are actually outside looking in, taking an aerial view that encompasses what is outside the walls of the mosque and what is within its precincts. While the scene is clearly rural Pakistan, the painting is distinctively Chinese: with its characteristic brushstrokes, the *neem* tree rendered in the style of bamboo, the line of Chinese calligraphy at the left-hand corner, and the unmistakable signature. Other paintings by Lin Yong and Su Hua in the 'Pakistan' series can also be mistaken for representations of classic Islamic miniatures or Chinese paintings. 'Park', for example, seems like an illustration from an old Muslim text of fairytales or the work of an old Chinese master. In fact, it shows families and friends enjoying a day out in the Shalimar Gardens, Lahore in the mid-1980s. But while true to both Islamic and Chinese traditions, 'Friday prayers', 'Park' and the other paintings in the series are not products of an ossified and historically frozen past. There is here a technique that is entirely the work of tradition, it is a wholly identifiable 'gaze', which can embrace the conventions of other civilisations, whether they be the conventions of Persian miniatures or western realist portraiture, to produce a new kind of art, one that is intercommunicative, that engages many observers from many different backgrounds, without violating its unique point of origin. Here tradition is presented as a dynamic force: alive, innovative, life-enhancing. What we witness in these paintings is a thriving, dynamic culture ready to confront the problems of modernity and the nihilism of postmodernism: these parameters, as the paintings illustrate so breathtakingly, are common to both Islamic and Chinese traditions, and by corollary to all non-western traditions.

From the perspective of non-western societies, surviving postmodernism is all about moving forward to tradition. Cultural resistance to postmodernism begins with tradition, as did opposition to modernity. Non-western cultural resistance *to* postmodernism – which, as I have consistently argued, does not represent a discontinuity with history, a sharp break from modernity, but an extension of the grand western narrative of secularism and its associated ideology of capitalism and bourgeois liberalism – can come only from non-western traditions. More: tradition can actually transform non-western societies into cultures *of* resistance.

But tradition is a double-edged sword. Traditions of resistance have maintained non-western enclaves of cultural autonomy as heavily defended redoubts. But fortified earthworks cannot be moved. There is a cultural resistance that does not go forward and is coming perilously, indeed fatally, close to being a dead weight, submerging Other cultures in illusory pasts instead of anchoring them to the continuing flow of history. Non-western cultures must distinguish between tradition and traditionalism. Tradition is the summation of the absolute frame of reference provided by the values and axioms of a civilisation that remain enduringly relevant and the conventions that have been developed in history into its own distinctive 'gaze': patterns of organisation, ideas, lifeways, techniques and products. Tradition can be periodised, it can be studied as a work of human history wherein there has been change. *Most* significantly tradition *is,* and in its being is proactive, whether or not the bearers of a particular tradition have lived up to this challenge or not. Traditionalism, on the other hand, is a reflex-action, a response to external pressure. In retention it is passive; its only activity is to retain. It reifies formalist aspects of tradition as it operated in a defined past to be the guarantor of the survival of a community, while holding tenaciously to those practices and ideas of autonomous tradition that have continued in an embattled present. It can, and indeed has, become ossified, oppressive and backward-looking in many societies and cultures. This happens when tradition is romanticised and fixed in specific space-time coordinates. It is traditionalism that dominates fundamentalist activity throughout the non-west. By offering the past as the ultimate answer to contemporary problems it falsifies both tradition and the past and fails to generate or inculcate the acquisitive knowledge impulse that is the essence of any living tradition. Tradition is a way of knowing; traditionalism deals only with the imperishable content of what is known. Traditionalism has done a fine job in maintaining some aspects of the non-western heritage, in retaining something for Other cultures to fight for. It has developed ramparts and barricades that make today's citizens of the non-west conscious that there are lines that cannot be crossed or compromised. But in its preservational task, traditionalism, as personified by fundamentalist movements, has become a pathological factor of postmodern times: it can fight only to destroy and reinstall; it cannot build anew.

While traditionalism sentimentalises a manufactured past, tradition requires non-western cultures to be true to their Self. But this Self is not the 'I' of western individualism, what is known in Islamic parlance as *nafs:* subservience to *nafs* leads to selfishness, greed, perpetual desire and cynicism. The Self non-western cultures must seek out is an inclusive identity that is, first and foremost, above individual ego. Postmodernism celebrates egoism – and it is the ego that ultimately leads, as Mohammad Iqbal suggests, to the demonisation of the Other and the ensuing conflict:

> It makes from itself to be Other than itself,
> It makes itself from the form of Other,
> In order to multiply the pleasure of strife.[2]

Iqbal is hailed in the Indian subcontinent as 'the poet-philosopher of the east' and much of his poetry, like the work of so many eastern poets and philosophers before him, is devoted to the exploration of how the Self can be liberated from the ego. Two of his great epic poems, *Asrar-I Khudi* ('The Secrets of the Self') and *Rumuz-I-Bekhudi* ('The Mysteries of Selflessness') are devoted to the subject. In 'The Mysteries of Selflessness' Iqbal argues that the community and the individual are not discrete categories, but inseparable elements that become fused through a living consciousness of tradition. The semantic field of the term Self employed in the poems makes clear the parameters in which the poet is operating. *Khud* means self while the suffix 'i' signifies coming. The terms are related to *khuda,* which means the self existing God. The Self that Iqbal is discussing implicitly and explicitly refers to a concept of unitary creation. It reminds readers that within the Islamic framework *nafs,* the individual ego, is not the only concept that defines the individual human being. The more familiar and extensive concept is *fitrah,* which translates as innate human nature. The *fitrah* of all human beings gives us the qualitative measure of what it is to be human: to begin with knowledge, a propensity to make, to do and to learn, as well as to speak; a capacity to discern right from wrong; a capacity to recognise one's origin and purpose. It is the *fitrah* which makes human beings capable of experiencing a sense of belonging and necessitates community. Indeed, within the Islamic framework it is inconceivable for an individual to exist except in community, hence the full development and realisation of their humanity requires building mutual compatibility with the community. As the suffix in the term *khudi* indicates, neither the Self nor the community within which it must exist are static givens. The moral and ethical framework of values, origin and purpose endures; Self and, by implication, community must be created, striven for, reforged in each generation. Islam has never been interested in that quintessentially western concept of 'the good citizen'; the whole focus of Islamic discourse on politics, society and the individual concerns how to foster the holistic conception of the 'moral human being': only a good society can generate good people, while good people cannot be fulfilled without exerting themselves to achieve a good community. The notion of *fitrah* is the antithesis of western individualism, not because it denies individual personality, identity and responsibility – all these are basic ideas fundamental to an Islamic outlook – but because in the Islamic purview the individual is only conceivable within a web of essential relationships wherein their individuality is neither the dominant nor the only significant consideration if the person is to realise and be true to his or her innate nature.

A community, argues Iqbal, is like a child. A child acquires a sense of its worth when it learns to remember and link tomorrow with its yesterday, and hence 'createth its own history'. It is the personal history of the child that opens its 'Being's eye': 'so his memory maketh him aware of his own Self'. Similarly, it is its memory, its living history, its tradition, that makes a community 'self-aware'; and only through self-awareness can a collection of individuals actually become a community:

> Know, then, 'tis the connecting thread of days
> That stitches up thy life's loose manuscript;
> This selfsame thread sews us a shirt to wear,
> Its needle the remembrance of old yarns.
> What thing is history, O self-unaware?
> A fable? Or a legendary tale?
> Nay, 'tis the thing that maketh thee aware
> Of thy true self, alert to the task,
> A seasoned traveller; this is the source
> Of the soul's ardour, this is the nerve that knits
> The body of the whole community.[3]

Historical tradition is not static, it must be reinvented by each new generation as it takes over its cultural inheritance from those preceding it. Only through the interweaving of past and present can change attain meaningful form:

> The skilful vision that beholds the past
> Can recreate before thy wondering gaze
> The past anew; wine of a hundred years
> That bowl contains, an ancient drunkenness
> Flames in its juice; a cunning fowler it
> To snare the bird that from our garden flew.[4]

The constructive capacity of human nature, its innate ability to become skilled, refined – hence the word civilised – is all about making interconnections, maintaining continuity of meaning. This is the antithesis of rupture, fragmentation and discontinuity. It leads us to gaze anew upon the past, not as the pattern that must slavishly be repeated in the present and for the future but in its spiritual essence. In the conventions of Persian and Urdu poetry wine and all references to drinking and drunkenness refer to spiritual essence in the sense of perception and experience of the divine. What each generation must lay hold of is the passionate, intoxicated, creative essence of human skilfulness, the need to be doing and being which changes things in its environment, adapts and refines the material world and the human organisation of this world; to maintain the meaning of values, morality and ethics despite apparent differences. Living memory, reinterpreted history, dynamic tradition not only enable a community to survive and thrive, they are prerequisites for life:

> If thou desirest everlasting life,
> Break not the thread between the past and now
> And the far future. What is life? A wave
> Of consciousness of continuity,
> A gurgling wine that flames the revellers.[5]

The recovery of their Self is thus the strongest hurdle that Other societies can place before postmodernism. Although Iqbal's ideas are rooted in Islamic thought, its concepts and categories, they have a resonance and relevance for all non-western societies. It is not merely that Iqbal's poetry has been eagerly embraced by Indians and Chinese. It is the more general point that non-western cultures share a holistic instinct, which is derived from their diverse but intercommunicative individual traditions as illustrated by the paintings of Lin Yong and Su Hua. What all Others share today is what separates them from and impels their resistance to postmodernism. Each non-western tradition has to recover the Self that enables it to begin making its present and future anew within the continuity of its own history. This is not an isolated or lonely struggle: culturally alive non-western writers, academics and activists share many premises in their struggle for cultural renewal, though the cultural premises they draw from are different for each, according to the tradition from which they come. It is not a homogenisation of all Others that one is talking about, but a kind of solidarity through difference, a compatibility through plurality, which can strengthen them in their contest with the massed forces of postmodernism. The cultures of resistance that the non-west must seek to create are not about eradicating the individual in the search to re-establish the community as a viable thriving entity. It is rather the rejection of the notion that human beings can find and are fulfilled through the existential loneliness and angst of postmodern existence. The quest is to find a new dispensation, their own multiple and diverse cultural means beyond the straitjacket of western modernity and postmodernism where individual and community form a symbiotic whole.

The proliferation of cultures of resistance in the non-west will multiply the 'gazes' that are turned upon the west. It has been characteristic of the 'gaze' of Orientalism, for example, that the object of its interest has been seen to be passive. Indeed, the Other has always been a passive object for the west, a negative awaiting its overwriting in order to become human, predictable, able to be included in its processes of political, social and economic control. The outward vision of cultures of resistance, however, must be true to the Self of the non-west. Their 'gaze' must become not a languorous stare of incomprehension, but a sharpened vision, which can engage and hold a plurality of objects, styles and ideas in a critical, simultaneous moment; it is an outward look that takes things in their whole and divergent being and is prepared to deal with them as they are. Perhaps this was the reason why the non-west facilitated its own domination. It took the scions of the conquering west, as it took all things, on their own limited and finite terms expecting them to be flawed, and in so doing misconceived the nature of the danger posed. Now, having resisted and endured through that long onslaught of the category mistake, the non-west can make an active virtue from what was an immobilising error. To look on the west and see limitations, frailty and flaws is not to take the west on its own idealised terms but in the round, in its reality and in distinctly non-western terms.

As I have tried to show, while actively seeking plurality and representation for 'Other voices', postmodernism in fact dismembers Other cultures by attacking their immune system: eradicating identity, erasing history and tradition, reducing everything that makes sense of life for non-secular cultures into meaninglessness. It places the inhuman and degrading on a par with the humane and ethical. From the standpoint of the concept of *fitrah* by removing the innate capacity to distinguish between good and evil postmodernism can be classified as anti-human. It is thus the most pathological of all creeds of domination, the final solution of the cultural logic of secularism: the acquired inhuman domination syndrome (AIDS) of our time. The movement forward to the Self provides Other cultures with a much needed antidote to the virulent and ever-changing virus of postmodernism.

But the revival of Other traditions is necessary not only for resisting postmodernism. It is also essential for the creation of a genuinely pluralistic world. Postmodernism, with its globalising and secularising tendencies, turning all cultures into ahistorical, liberal, free markets, is set to eliminate any possibility of dialogue with cultures that are truly Other: who will be there to dialogue with once the earth and humanity are completely westernised? This is the subtext of the postmodern appropriation of multiculturalism, as I have tried to demonstrate. It is the appropriation of those facets which are conducive to the thrust of dominance, appropriation of elements that account for the losses suffered by the modern self. The corollary is that what postmodernism leaves behind, soundless and unmentioned, what they do not want of the totality of the Other or actively traduce, parody, ridicule and deride, is then useless. In the process the Other as a going concern is as comprehensively destroyed as ever it was under modernism and its colonial endeavour, it is as successfully fragmented and destabilised. What postmodernist multiculturalism wants of the Other has one further subversive twist of the knife. Postmodernism seeks to appropriate its own romanticised and unbalanced conception of the 'soul' of the Other, the psychic/spiritual power which is one way of describing aspects of non-western worldviews. Not only does the New Age agenda, which makes multiculturalism a respectable and marketable commodity, deform the reality of non-western worldviews, it also plays havoc within the non-west. It disproportionately empowers those who hold firmest to ossified traditionalism and pietistic outlooks, thus making it easier for the totalitarian power of the project of postmodernism to consume them entirely. It makes unholy allies of the old traditionalists and the new onslaught from the west, leaving no space for the new discourses of the non-west to occupy and develop. Tradition is either what the traditionalists say or what the west deems it to be through its scholarship or co-option. The traditionalists and the postmodernists justify each other's existence neatly by the virulence of their adversarial rhetoric. They fight, therefore they are. Recovery of the Self in non-western cultures needs more than sabre-rattling, and does not finds its *raison d'être* in the mere existence of the postmodernist threat. Cultures of resistance must be nurtured because they are the only humane answer to the pressing need for liveable options, sustainable choices for the people of the non-west. It is only in their Self that the Other can find hope, sanity and fulfilment. The survival and the flowering of non-western traditions make viable alternatives to the west conceivable, and genuine pluralism, with thriving cultures that are truly Other, a possibility.

All non-western cultures will change and are changing. The issue for them is to change within meaningful boundaries, reformulate traditions into contemporary configurations, rediscover their history and heritage in forms that empower and resist the onslaught of modernity and postmodernism and, on the basis of tradition, to author new answers to contemporary questions. This rethinking of the concept of tradition is a process of recovery of indigenous meaning and a development of inherent, autonomous potential to initiate stable but dynamic change. It requires serious attention to the way in which the corpus of traditional worldviews becomes fossilised and tradition confined and made into a preserve of private, domestic and exotic peasant 'culture'. More specifically, it requires releasing internal forces of dynamism and change that are intrinsic to all non-western cultures. For example, within Islam the dynamic principle of *ijtihad* – sustained and reasoned struggle for innovation and adjusting to change – has been neglected for centuries. A strategy for desirable futures for Islamic cultures would articulate methods for the rediscovery of this principle – a rediscovery which would lead to reformulation of Islamic tradition into contemporary configurations.[6] The highly complex and multidimensional concept of *han* in Korean thought represents similar notions of opening up new horizons for future life. As Tae-Chang Kim argues so forcefully, the fossilisation of the past in Korean tradition can be overcome by discovering new ways of practising traditional notions: '*han* is, *par excellence*, a horizon – opening force. *Han* has been underlying the Korean people's endless passion to try to go through the dark times of trials and tribulations and find a new alternative world.'[7] Other cultures have similar principles hidden from view. In other words, desirable futures can be conceived of and planned for only where plural processes of autonomous cultural adaptation are the accepted norm.

The incredible lightness of authenticity

Rethinking tradition also requires an appreciation of cultural authenticity and cultural autonomy. Cultural authenticity means that traditional physical, intellectual and spiritual environments and values should be respected and accorded their proper place in society. It is not a question of re-instituting Puritanism in all its stark determinism. What is most needed is the unabashed embrace of self-confidence, the pride that dares to walk its talk. The figure that really terrifies the west most is the unapologetic Other with the competence and the confidence to accommodate the contemporary world and amend it in ways undreamed of and unconsidered by the hosts of modernity and postmodernism. How could this be done? First, by seeing traditional systems as a source of strength and a reservoir of solutions for people's problems. Clearly this does not mean that all the urgent questions that beset non-western cultures can find ready answers in the past – that is the cloud cuckoo land of fundamentalists who substitute evangelical euphoria for thought. What the past offers is more complex. What makes the Other different from the west is a civilisational corpus of ways of knowing, being and doing defined by value parameters. These active principles have been in suspended animation often for centuries, under the onslaught of modernity and colonialism. They need the animation of thought, critically undertaken in the sincere belief that the value parameters matter and must be maintained. This is as much a leap of knowledge as it is a leap of faith. When the 'gaze' of tradition is turned upon the modern world as a knowledge enterprise, working through the value-defined categories and concepts of tradition, its geography looks radically different. This geo-morphing raises new questions, and renders old ideas fruitful repositories of new ways to think about what have so far been considered intractable problems. The stark truth is that no one in the non-west and certainly not the west itself has any idea of what potency this enterprise will release. It is not the form of the past that such an undertaking requires or seeks, but its conceptual power, the power that can integrate, synthesise and innovate within the parameters of enduring values to author meaningful change, change that delivers us into a future our forebears could not have imagined but where they would eventually recognise themselves as at home.

Meaningful change is the currency of cultural authenticity. It will include authentic mistakes, for which the non-west must accept responsibility, as well as food for thought that can stimulate the barren landscape of ideas of the west. The drive for cultural authenticity will be far easier if there is cultural autonomy. This is the crux of the problem. Postmodernism simply does not tolerate cultural autonomy, nor do the totalitarian reflexes of free market capitalism and liberal democracy. Creating the space, resources and empowerment needed to nurture the cultural autonomy that will permit cultural authenticity to mature will be hard. It is the only battlefield, and it most definitely cannot be won with landmines, small arms or artillery, let alone long-range bombers and high octane explosives. It is a work of imaginative reconstruction.

The second requirement, the detail of engineering cultural autonomy, is emphasising indigenous development stemming from traditions and encouraging the norms, language, beliefs, arts and crafts of a people – the very factors that provide meaning, identity and richness to people's lives. The corollary of all this is a sensible check on postmodern consumer goods that represent the omnipotence of technology – which induce dependency, thwart self-reliance and expose non-western societies to physical and mental domination. As A. K. N. Reddy has so elegantly pointed out, appropriate technology is more sophisticated intellectually and just as technological as the dominant consumer variant. The difference is that appropriate technology submits itself to more demanding criteria, ones that respect and integrate the values of indigenous cultures and humane social and economic considerations.[8] What is important is not the abandonment of technological advance but the refashioning of what criteria determine whether an advance has been made, and the devising of new criteria to generate new forms of local production processes and products to satisfy local needs. The very expression of cultural authenticity, leading to a degree of self-reliance, self-respect and pride, transforms a culture into a force of resistance. Desirable futures require articulation and implementation of strategies for cultural authenticity and hence transformation of traditions into cultures of resistance.

Postmodernism is at pains to discredit and destabilise the very concept of authenticity. It is either rendered as a romanticised notion that is unknowable to members of Other cultures themselves because they have been adulterated by colonialism, or ridiculed and derided as inferior. The battle to reassert cultural authenticity is the most precarious balancing act for non-western people. It must embrace the culturally authentic proposition that none of our civilisations is monolithic. This is not the meaning of tradition, certainly not the definition of tradition on which I have been operating. The balance comes in recognising that non-western authenticities will be, as they once were, multiple, that there will and indeed must be multiple ways of doing and being that can be elicited within the commonly held consensus of publicly agreed parameters.

Surviving postmodernism also demands strategies for cultural autonomy. Cultural autonomy does not mean isolating a culture from the outside world or shunning the benefits of modern society. It means the ability and the power to make one's own choices based on one's own culture and tradition. Contrary to popular belief, cultural autonomy does not compromise 'national sovereignty', it is not an invariant threat to unstable nation states. There are two dimensions of cultural autonomy. The external dimension requires non-western societies to seek their economic and political development with the accent firmly on local traditions and cultures. The internal dimension requires nation states to provide space and freedom for ethnic minorities within their boundaries to realise their full cultural potential, make their own choices and articulate their own cultural alternatives. Cultural autonomy has to be seen as a dialectical concept. It embraces both the macro level of cultural, religious or ethnic groups and the micro level of the human mind. It begins with the simple idea that cultures, and individuals within cultures, have a right to self-expression and leads to the burgeoning of pluralism and multiculturalism.

It is mere historic accident that the European definition of nationalism and hence the nation state should emphasise one unique and dominating cultural identity. In part, this is derived from the cultural homogeneity of European communities. Its other prop was the historic legacy of a system of thought that defined the only rightful citizen as the orthodox — that is, one who subscribed to the orthodox beliefs of the Church which underpinned the whole concept of governance in medieval Europe. When religious orthodoxy broke down in Reformation Europe, new political entities were formed. Where this did not happen, populations changed their religious affiliation to match that of the sovereign. The quest for liberty of conscience is the origin of both the movement for political enfranchisement and citizens' rights and the secularisation of thought and society in Europe. Even then it was a quest that did not imply an accepted place for multiculturalism and heterogeneity since dissenting citizens shared the same cultural ancestry and, in many respects, culture as the rest of the nation state.

The non-western experience has been quite different. Genuine heterogeneity of culture, within communities and systems of governance, has been an integral part, for example, of Islamic, Indian and southeast Asian history and experience. Recovery of tradition should focus on the rediscovery of the means of stable plurality within communities and states. Today, Asia is virtually the only place where this desperately needed human resource can be championed. Ironically, given contemporary events, it is the only logical place to search for working, historical models of pluralism and multiculturalism that are not based on secularism. It should also lead to the preservation of what is good and life-enhancing in traditional thought; legal, economic and political arrangements for the equal participation of all cultures in wealth and social opportunity; the elimination of distrust between cultural groups; the encouragement of meaningful communication between peoples and cultures; and the elimination of extremist positions and actions. Thus, strategies for cultural autonomy are the *sine qua non* for surviving postmodernism.

Just as we can document the transition in western discourse of the singular form of the terms culture and civilisation to the plural, so we need to effect a change in the usage and meaningful content of the term 'modernity'. At present, the term means, and implies, only one thing: the slavish replication of the process of social, cultural, political and economic transformation, which occurred in Europe and in western civilisation. Non-western societies need to redefine modernity in their own terms and cultural frameworks. This requires using traditional concepts and ideas as analytical tools, incorporating the knowledge of the past into the thought processes and products of today. As Susantha Goonatilake points out, 'Asians have tried to use the past, but in the nineteenth and twentieth centuries, they have largely emphasised the presumed "spiritual" aspects. It is in the more mundane, material aspects, however, that Asian cultural elements could be fruitfully used.'[9] Cultural elements from non-western history, traditions and lineages need to be identified in such areas as science, medicine, technologies, materials and agriculture, and reprocessed and incorporated into modern systems of distribution and dissemination.

In the contemporary information age the battle for norms and values is won not so much in the political arena as by the control of the tools of perception. For postmodernism the image is all and the imagist industries, film and the media, are genuine centres of power and influence. One cannot shut out the satellite feed, or close down or stand aside from the information superhighway, though the greatest part of the non-west will remain an unconnected branch line for a very long time. Countermanding the global information and image industry with alternative imagery and information is the essence of empowering cultural autonomy with cultural authenticity. For a brief moment it appeared as if Japan might be opening this enclosed conundrum through the power of the almighty yen by buying into the US entertainment industries: films, music, games, software. The strategy has been a resounding failure. Not only did Hollywood successfully use the Japanese as a convenient punchbag for its own excess, but the Japanese clearly had no concerted 'cultural' imprint ready to infiltrate into the axioms of Hollywood. Ownership and control are the failed headlines of the old left analysis of the media. They are only one facet to explain the supremacy of the western media industry. Its most insidious achievement is co-option of all points on the social and political scale within the west through cultural identity: the fact that there is such a thing as western civilisation and a western worldview which unifies owners and controllers with the operatives of the media, those who actually do the manufacturing of the cultural products.

Owners, controllers and operatives share a common conception that they 'understand' their audience, the arrogant notion that it is they, jointly and severally, who 'know' what should be produced, when in fact they are all merely serving the most basic and brutal of free market notions – you get only what is most profitable. But now the non-west is beginning to have a marked effect on the film industry. The audiences of Asia now affect the market value of Hollywood stars. The ability to make profits from films that flopped in America from non-western audiences is generating a genre of films driven by marquee value star names that are long on action, short on dialogue – a kind of all-purpose comic book, special effects-driven epic of global communication. Out of this morass of meaninglessness, opportunities that empower cultural authenticity and autonomy have to be effected. But such opportunities cannot be created from cringing apologetics and lack of self-confidence in one's own cultural identity which are the kiss of death for the non-west. Mouth-to-mouth resuscitation of indigenous cultural traditions demands concerted strategic thought and the investment of financial resources: serious efforts have to be made for the production of indigenous cultural products, local film production has to be encouraged, investment has to be made in making local television programmes. In short, wherever possible, meaningless western culture has to be replaced with products that impart indigenous cultural meaning. Cultural autonomy cannot be gained without human and financial commitment; it requires a *volte face* from the passive acceptance of the notion that 'things change' to actively changing things.[10]

Beyond the pursuit of cultural authenticity and cultural autonomy, resistance to postmodernism requires non-western cultures to come to terms with their own darker side. The point is not to indulge in the postmodern embrace that glories in evil, but to combat it and constrain the deformity it imposes on society. In as far as all cultures are human products, they have an unsavoury darker side. Many non-western cultures have an undeniably authoritarian streak that needs to be checked. For example, the argument that the 'individual' does not exist in the communal milieu of Asia as an absolute individual has become an excuse for the violation of the human integrity and the dignity of individuals. There is a place for political dissent in the Asian purview that needs both to be acknowledged and enhanced. Communal values embellish participatory governance; they should not be used as a licence for the ruthless suppression of dissenting voices. It is precisely because of the stability produced by strong extended family commitments, community structures and social concerns that non-western societies need to be open societies, with accountable political structures, actively promoting and encouraging all that is good and healthy in human endeavour. To achieve this, non-western societies have consciously to come to terms with the unsavoury side of their history. The Japanese, for example, have to do more than say 'no' to the west, abandon their old policy of 'Leave Asia, turn to the West' (*'Datsu-Ah, Nyuu-Oh'*) in favour of the new clarion call, 'Leave the West, turn to Asia' (*'Datsu-Oh, Nyuu-Ah'*), as the novelist and film director, Shintaro Ishihara, argues so well in *The Japan That Can Say No;*[11] they must also address the painful facts of their history if Japan is to play a prominent role in Asia and, through it, in non-western politics. Similarly, the corruption and abuse of power that has a certain history in non-western societies needs to be directly addressed. What Anwar Ibrahim has said about Asia applies equally to all Other cultures:

> We must have the courage to address the stark contradictions within our society. Although we take pride in religiosity continuing to be a major element in our lives, yet at the same time, and most paradoxically, our society seems to be indifferent to the moral decadence and the erosion of social fabric through widespread permissiveness and corruption. Of course, some would say that many of the vices rampant are but the inevitable consequences of abject poverty. No doubt there is a grain of truth in that. Yet, we cannot help feeling that if the practice of religion had been entrenched together with its moral and ethical dimensions, then this degeneration could have been kept in check.
>
> Our self-induced euphoria in respect of our remarkable economic growth must not blind us to the parallel rise in corruption, bribery, nepotism and the abuse of power. While some seem content to regard this as a necessary evil, we firmly hold that this is a fundamental issue at the core of our moral and ethical foundations. There can be no compromise on this.
>
> The experience of Southeast Asia in economics, social and political development is indeed rich and varied. Because we wanted our development to be indigenous, ASEAN remained neutral during the Cold War. Each member embarked on its own particular mode of democracy. However, some may have entertained the idea that authoritarianism is the most efficacious means for economic success. To them, democracy is, maybe, too cumbersome for orderly development. It may even be seen as inimical to political stability, which is a precondition for rapid economic growth and social well being. Even Asian, especially Confucian, values have now come to be invoked in support of that proposition. This notion has been effectively debunked by the experience of Malaysia and Thailand. Political liberality is *not* incompatible with strong economic performance. Both these countries have sustained economic growth for more than three decades while practicing open and vibrant forms of democracy. As for Asian values, they produced great civilisations in the past. However, if these values are to contribute towards a renaissance of Asia, they must serve as a source of liberation. Asian cultural renewal must mean the cultivation of all that is true, just and caring from our heritage, not perpetuating the narrow and oppressive order of the feudal past . . .[12]

Pre-eminently one is not saying that Other cultures are inherently virtuous, just as resolutely as I oppose the notion that they are inherently evil. Nor will a recovery of public consensus and concern for shared values as the glue of traditional cultures end for them the worry of wrestling with the problem of evil in our times – that is, their own evil in times they shape and determine for themselves. Consciously and deliberately one is looking to avoid utopian vision; utopias have always betrayed their adherents. It is the unglamorous realm of the real, with all its complexity, confusion and constraints, that one is seeking to influence with remedies of its own kind: complexity, a measure of confusion and constraints. The first lesson for the reconstructors of Other civilisations is they have no ready answers and an urgent need to confront and deal with their own limitations through the categories and concepts of their own knowledge systems. Only the people of the non-west can realise how far this is from being an instant panacea. It is a project that requires a willingness to accept complexity of argument, confusion of voices – a proof of diversity as well as concerned creativity and vibrancy of debate – and an acknowledgement of the limits within which such debate must range. However, in advance even what is an unbreachable barrier may not be instantly obvious. It is not a case of asking people to die on the barricades but making it possible for them to live within the boundaries. Cultural resistance, as for example in Iran and other places, has come to mean asking people to die for the utopian rhetoric of cultural authenticity rather than asking them to live according to what one believes as part of a complex rethinking of inherited tradition. Living one's resistance is far harder, not self-evident in the world we now inhabit, and likely to look and act quite contrary to the modes of inherited traditionalism still extant and powerfully authoritative within our societies.

The one characteristic of traditional lifeways that most urgently needs to be recaptured by culturally resistant Others is tolerance. Anecdotal evidence generates the argument that traditional societies used tolerance as the connective tissue of their existence. The importance of personal networks in the structuring of society, for example, makes for a measure of latitude, a tolerance of individual eccentricity or divergence from the norm precisely because the individual is known in a very real sense and maintains relations with all those who would otherwise abstractly condemn such behaviour in a stranger. In traditional worldviews individuals are never abstractions by dint of the conception of the structure and organisation of society. Analyses of Other cultures which have concentrated on building up ideal-types of how things are or were seldom chronicled the spaces such societies offered for the individual. Western scholarship provides documentation of what ideal marriage rules are preferred, how kinship networks and ascribed social positions are ideally operated, but only belatedly did it consider that at any one time there may be more unpreferred marriages than those that fulfil the 'rule' and that there may be multiple ways of operating and being innovative within or around the confines of ascription. Tolerance also develops from the inherent fact that no one person, group or institution within traditional civilisations possesses the absolute. The absolute values and qualities that generate and animate Other outlooks are transcendent. As has been argued within contemporary Muslim scholarship, it makes interpreters of us all. The absolute frame of reference is always there: all that successive generations of Muslims can do is stand in an interpretative relationship to that reference frame, and only learning, cogency and contextual importance can distinguish an individual opinion. Any individual opinion is always open to re-examination. Whether the challenge is accepted or not it is the responsibility of each new generation to strive to ensure they maintain the best possible interpretative relationship with Islam, or put another way, that they utilise the basic values and axioms of Islam as the adaptive instruments to determine change in society. The classical Muslim scholar would say: this is what I think, the best I can do under the circumstances, but God alone knows all. Today, as yesterday, cultural reformers must be content to agree that so long as one holds to the supreme importance of the formulation that God alone knows all there is, humility and tolerance of multiple discourses become an imperative. The necessity of a conscientious, interpretative search for truth that is common to all leads to the acknowledgement and acceptance of the fact that the truth that can be made knowable by human efforts is limited.

By declaring that there is no truth and no morality, that all is meaningless and that life itself is a meaningless problem; by announcing that religion and philosophy, history and tradition are symptoms of will to power and symbols of decadence; by raising doubt, cynicism and ambivalence to an arch value; by its acceptance of barbarism and embrace of evil and hence legitimisation of every act of cruelty, neglect and intolerance; by appropriating the knowledge, history and cultural products of the Others; by embarking on a crusade to transform Other cultures into ahistorical, identity-less masses and perpetual consumers of its cultural products; by isolating and further marginalising Other cultures by irony and ridicule; by attempting to subsume Other cultures into the Grand Narrative of bourgeois liberalism, free market capitalism and secularism; by giving a new life to the old tools of colonial domination and subjugation – by all these means, postmodernism has declared a war on non-western cultures and societies. Yet, while postmodernism may displace, fragment and even momentarily occupy Other cultures, the innate and powerful desire for historic meaning and identity in non-western societies cannot be eradicated. It is the urge of every culture to be true to its Self, to be self-confirming and self-propagating. It is this unfathomable urge – which has 'presence' as its prime value and forms the matrix of every idealism – that will lead to the return of dynamic tradition and give the twenty-first century its defining character. The invincible, life-denying forces of postmodernism are about to encounter the immovable object of life-enhancing tradition.

Notes

1   Lin Yong and Su Hua, *Pakistan,* Beijing,1985.
2   From the poem 'Will and the Way' by Sir Muhammad Iqbal, in Chughtai, *The Poet of the East and Chughtai,* Karachi, 1968.
3   Sir Muhammad Iqbal, *The Mysteries of Selflessness,* translated by A. J. Arberry, John Murray, London, 1953, p. 61. (First published 1910.)
4   Ibid., p. 62.
5   Ibid.
6   For a discussion of *ijtihad,* see Ziauddin Sardar, *The Future of Muslim Civilisation,* 2nd editon, Mansell, London, 1987.
7   Tae-Chang Kim, 'Coherence and Chaos in Our Uncommon Futures: A *Hun* Philosophical Perspective', in Mika Mannermaa et al., eds., *Coherence and Chaos in Our Uncommon Futures: Visions, Means, Actions,* World Future Studies Federation, Turku, 1994, p. 44.
8   A.K.N. Reddy, 'Appropriate Technology: A Reassessment', in Ziauddin Sardar, ed., *The Revenge of Athena: Science, Exploitation and the Third World,* Mansell, London, 1988.
9   Susantha Goonatilake, 'The Futures of Asian Cultures: Between Localisation and Gobalisation', *The Futures of Cultures,* Unesco Publishing, Paris, 1994.
10   Anwar Ibrahim, 'From Things Change to Change Things', in Ziauddin Sardar, ed., *An Early Crescent: The Future of Knowledge and the Environment in Islam and the West,* Mansell, London, 1989.
11   Shintaro Ishihara, *The Japan That Can Say No,* Simon and Schuster, New York, 1991.
12   Anwar Ibrahim, *New Strait Times,* 21 September 1994.

References

Goonatilake, Susantha, 'The futures of Asian cultures: between localisation and globalisation', in *The Futures of Cultures,* Unesco Publishing, Paris, 1994.

Ibrahim, Anwar, 'From things change to Change Things' in Ziauddin Sardar (ed.), *An Early Crescent: The Future of Knowledge and the Environment in Islam and the West,* Mansell, London, 1989.

Iqbal, Sir Muhammad, *The Mysteries of Selflessness,* translated by A. J. Arberry, John Murray, London, 1953 (original 1910).

Ishihara, Shintaro, *The Japan That Can Say No,* Simon and Schuster, New York, 1991.

Kim, TaeChang, 'Coherence and Chaos in Our Uncommon Futures: A Hun Philosophical Perspective' in Mika Mannermaa et al. (eds), *Coherence and Chaos in Our Uncommon Futures: Visions, Means, Actions,* World Future Studies Federation, Turku, 1994.

Lin Yong, Lin, and Su Hua, *Pakistan,* Beijing, 1985.

Sardar, Ziauddin, *The Future of Muslim Civilization,* Croom Helm, London, 1979; Mansell, London, 1987.

Sardar, Ziauddin (ed.), *The Revenge of Athena: Science, Exploitation and the Third World,* Mansell, London, 1988.

PART IV

Psychoanalysis and its critics

ONE OF THE MOST PROFOUND transformations of literary theoretical discourse was brought about by a field that might at first glance appear unrelated to literature: that of psychoanalysis. Yet from its very beginning, psychoanalysis dealt with stories (dreams, autobiographical accounts, philosophical and scientific narratives concerning subjectivity), personal and social myths which psychoanalysis would decode and rebuild, and actual literary characters, plots and structures that would guide this new approach to the mind. Some of the transformative ideas concerning family, sexuality, and culture first put forward by the founder of psychoanalysis, Sigmund Freud (1856–1939), derive from an ancient Greek story: that of Oedipus the King. As Jokasta, Oedipus's wife and mother shockingly says in Sophocle's *Oedipus Rex* (c.425 BC), "How many men, in dreams, have lain with their mothers! / No reasonable man is troubled by such things." Freud derived from Sophocles a modern version of these words spoken by Jokasta, called "The Oedipal Complex" whereby childhood sexual desires and rivalry (with the parents), are seen to be most powerfully expressed as the child passes through this stage into adulthood and wider societal structures. If Freud, then, derived many psychoanalytical insights from literary and mythological stories, it is equally important to observe that there are many different stories (or perspectives) concerning the beginnings of psychoanalysis, depending upon who is doing the telling. For those schooled in the Freudian tradition and its variants, the story begins in the year 1900 with the publication of Freud's *The Interpretation of Dreams*. For others, however, a slightly earlier text is more significant, namely Freud's "Project for a Scientific Psychology" (1895) with its emphasis upon sexuality, and speculation concerning parallels between physiological and psychic symptoms.[1] Another approach examines the extended critical process that Freud underwent, transforming himself from an investigator of neurological disease into an investigator of what we would now call psychiatric illness.

Freud was a medical student at the University of Vienna, as well as a researcher on the central nervous system, working under Ernst Brücke (1819–92). He also studied under Jean-Martin Charcot (1825–93) at the Salpêtrière in Paris, before returning to Vienna to set up his private practice. Freud's search for physical, neurological causes of disease took him in the new direction of a scientific enquiry into how the mind functioned, initially under the influence of Charcot who, "opened the way to taking mental illness seriously, with his diagnosis of hysteria and the use of hysteria."[2] Freud initially followed the theories of nineteenth-century medical positivism and vitalism, that is to say a scientific search for underlying life forces that drive subjectivity in a non-mechanistic way. The results of this period were published in his "Project for a Scientific Psychology" and a book jointly written with his professor and mentor, Josef Breuer (1842–1925) called *Studies in Hysteria* (1895). The patient Anna O led Freud and Breuer to the cathartic "talking cure" which can be seen as "the result of proceeding according to the physicalist or vitalist model of the psyche: tension is released . . . through talking and interpretation – that is, through a manipulation of meaning(s)."[3] The psychoanalytical critic and historian of French psychiatry, Elisabeth Roudinesco, argues that "the bourgeois conformism of Vienna at the end of the nineteenth century was reflected in Freud and Breuer's *Studies on Hysteria*",[4] while another French psychoanalytical critic, Jean Laplanche, suggests that it was the case of Emma, in "Project for a Scientific Pyschology" that reveals the shift from vitalism to an entirely new conception of mind since in Emma's case, Freud had to understand her displacement and repression of her original trauma, which was buried underneath a more recent memory of a traumatic scene.[5]

In Freud's first main phase, developing his emerging theories of the psyche, he worked with a dualistic model of mind, comprising areas of unconscious and conscious activity; later on he would develop a tripartite model of mind, composed of the ego (the conscious self which mediates between the id and superego), the id (the unconscious instincts and drives), and the superego (the conscience, judge or censor which controls the ego).[6] In either phase, accessing unconscious areas of mind involves intensive interpretation, the aim being a therapeutic outcome. Early texts in which his theories of interpretation were worked out, include Freud's *The Interpretation of Dreams, The Psychopathology of Everyday Life* (1901), *Three Essays on the Theory of Sexuality* (1905) and *Jokes and Their Relation to the Unconscious* (1905). Dreams, for Freud, are the disguised fulfilment of a repressed wish, which appear to our conscious selves as the manifest, or remembered dream; the analyst's task is to interpret the "dream-work" mechanisms of symbolization, dramatization, displacement, condensation, and secondary revision, to access the latent or hidden content of the original dream.[7] Another route to the unconscious is discovered through analysis of parapraxes, or "slips of the tongue", which punctuate our conversation and inadvertently reveal underlying thoughts and feelings. Similarly, jokes and loosely structured conversation about one's neurotic symptoms can be deeply revealing. What Freud specifically *rejected* was the use of hypnosis in attempting to access the unconscious, or in bringing about a cure; this is partly a reaction against what Freud perceived to be the faulty logic of his professors and mentors, and partly the way in which Freud could break free from them and start again on his own terms. For many people, however, the scandal of this fresh start was Freud's insistence that at the heart of psychiatry was sexuality, including powerful sexual drives (the libido) and childhood sexuality. Negative reactions from psychologists soon followed, with some arguing that Freud's work was merely intellectual speculation, while others more forcefully suggested that his concept of childhood sexuality was "a sickness."[8] Yet Freud persisted: he was creating a methodology that could make diagnostic and therapeutic sense of what psychologists perceived to be "senseless" material, and nowhere was his approach more welcomed than in the US, especially after his trip to lecture at Clark University in 1909. American psychiatrists had visited Europe to study the use of hypnosis, but were on the whole sceptical of this procedure; in the US, Freud offered a synthesis of his new findings and a rational approach to trauma, catharsis, and sexuality.[9] The American analysts enthusiastically embraced this early Freudianism, as did the British (led by Ernest Jones [1879–1958]) and the Germans (led by Karl Abrahams [1877–1925]), but in France opposition from leading psychologists, such as Hippolyte Bernheim and Pierre Janet, meant that acceptance was some time in coming.

The various national Freudian movements came into existence during a time of war: the two World Wars, with the Spanish Civil War in between. The most rigorous Freudian Institute, in Berlin, rapidly offered training and an internationally recognized analytical approach; Karl Abrahams was treating German soldiers for war neuroses, or what was known as "shell shock" from 1915,[10] an area of analysis that would eventually transform notions of trauma, gender, and at a more mundane level, the behaviour of human beings in highly stressful environments. The Berlin Institute, however, was co-opted by the Nazi party during the rise of fascism and Nazism in Germany, with many Jewish members fleeing to England and the US. This "gathering storm" over Europe led many thinkers of the age to explore mass psychosis, or, the concept of a "group" mind. In *The Crowd: A Study of Popular Mind* (1895), Gustave Le Bon (1841–1931) argued that crowd psychology reveals the underlying "primitive mind" or truth concerning societal drives and desires. Freud, in *Totem and Taboo* (1913), "Thoughts for the Times on War and Death" (1915), *Group Psychology and the Analysis of the Ego* (1921), and *Civilization and Its Discontents* (1930), explores the complex relationships between the individual and society, subsuming social psychology into that of the individual. Critics regard much of this work as in conflict with Freud's assertion of a primal narcissistic ego divorced from social relations.[11] Freudian psychoanalysis reveals, then, that the subject is always already in a relationship with the Other. Additionally, in this period, Freud developed concepts such as the death drive and the concept of a primal horde who murder the patriarchal father, thus relating the Oedipal Complex whereby the child desires his mother and must encounter his father as a rival (the female version of this is the Electra Complex), to a wider social and political vision.

Freudian psychoanalysis took many directions, especially after Freud's death in 1939, with rival approaches and leaders either modifying and developing Freud's insights, or exploring new pathways. Carl Gustav Jung (1875–1961) who was a friend and colleague of Freud's between 1907 and 1913 (travelling with him to Clark University in the US), is famous for developing the notion of a "collective unconscious", yet at a more practical level, his therapeutic use of word-association tests to trigger emotional responses (which uncovered otherwise hidden neuroses) paralleled Freud's interpretive methodology in his dream analysis,[12] contributing to a shared understanding of the psyche. Their differences, however, proved problematic: Jung rejected the idea that sexuality was an underlying cause of neurosis, and in his complex alternative system, the fragmented psyche sought balance in a teleological,[13] or goal-oriented series of processes (leading to a personal harmonious "individuation" or accepting and reconciling of internal opposites). Detractors accused Jung of obscurity and mysticism in his study of the occult, the metaphysical and mythological realms of psyche, while ignoring his contributions to gender and subjectivity, as well as his hermeneutical approach to creativity. Gender and sex differences had never been adequately accounted for by Freud, and a new generation of women analysts sought to rectify this situation, including Melanie Klein (1882–1960), whose work on object-relations focused on the relationships between the subject and his or her surrounding world, with emphasis upon mother–child relationships; Karen Horney (1885–1952), who went beyond Freud's notion of "penis envy" arguing that men suffered from "womb envy"; and Helene Deutsch (1884–1982), who developed a major new approach to motherhood in her *Psychology of Women* (two volumes, 1944 & 1945). Later critics, however, suggest that important as these early analysts undoubtedly are, they still offer a heteronormative account of female sexuality and gender construction, one which "relies on a biological hypothesis of natural heterosexual drives" which cannot be tested or proven/disproven within a clinical context, the latter revealing instead "extensive variations in psychosexual developmental processes and outcomes."[14] Feminist psychoanalysts who reject biological essentialism—such as Hélène Cixous (1937–), Luce Irigaray (1932–), Julia Kristeva (1941–), and Juliet Mitchell (1940–)—tend to critically follow the insights of Jacques Lacan (1901–81), especially his more fluid concepts, that the unconscious is structured like a language, that the ego is a fantasmatic, illusory construct, and that anatomy is not as important as the "structural conditions"[15] of the society in which women exist. A key text in the debates concerning Lacan and feminism is Juliet Mitchell and Jacqueline Rose's, eds., *Feminine Sexuality: Jacques Lacan and the École Freudienne* (1982, translated by Jacqueline Rose). Mitchell and Rose introduce and provide translations of key lectures by Lacan, arguing that he both facilitated a new feminist reworking of Freud, yet remained phallocentric. Rose suggests that "the relationship between psycho-analysis and feminism might seem to start at the point where Freud's account of sexual difference was rejected by analysts specifically arguing *for* women."[16]

Jacques Lacan's re-reading of Freud shifts psychoanalysis from a scientific model to a semiotic model of mind. Lacan's central insight—that the unconscious is structured like a language—derives in part from Freud, yet it was Lacan who registered the full poststructuralist implications of the mind's resistance to interpretation. For Lacan, subjectivity is always subject to splitting, misidentification, and the Saussurian linguistic slippage of signification (see Chapter 4). The symbolic "phallus" or law-of-the-father may be a controlling force in mature adult life, but since for Lacan this symbol can never be a fully transcendent signifier, there is space for a feminist critique, adoption and further development of Lacan's approach. Lacan posits three interrelated psychic realms or "orders": the Semiotic, the Symbolic and the Real. The Semiotic is the pre-linguistic realm of drives, desires, bodily functions, and image-identifications; the Symbolic is linguistic, and regulatory, representing a shift from identification with the mother, to that of society and the law-of-the-father; the Real is that which cannot be approached through language or any other system, yet nonetheless it impacts the subject. Lacan theorizes a "mirror stage" (see Chapter 25) which occurs in children at six to eighteen months of age, whereby the child moves from a formless, boundary-less world becoming a separate entity or being in a world of objects. The first main unified object the child sees is his or her reflection in the mirror: this splitting or doubling, an image identification with a separate or external entity, literally situated elsewhere, will have an effect on the child's entire life, regardless of later mental processes. Identification with the mother parallels this process, since she initially appeared fragmented and similarly formless, and then she provides another apparently unified external image. For Lacan, the mirror stage represents a series of fantasies and provides the groundwork for a socially based identity: "though the mirror-stage experience of localization of the body signals the beginning of a sense of identity, this unity has been found *outside* and, accordingly, the destiny of humans [for Lacan] is to (re-)experience themselves only in relationship to others."[17] The mirror stage comes to an end as the child enters the Oedipal conflict, and shifts from learning physical mobility to acquiring language and social skills, yet it is essential in understanding Lacan's approach, to recognize that the human subject doesn't simply progress towards a more "rational" being: "The imagistic and fantasmatic subject of identifications continues, nonetheless, to coexist (in a double inscription) with the subject of language and cultural codes throughout life."[18] Subjectivity, then, for Lacan is always elsewhere: at times it appears fixed, at other times it is in play. This can be comprehended in Lacan's concept of the self (the *moi*) which is a composite,[19] created by the gaze (mirroring, external objects, image identification) and by "scripting" (the effects of language, voice, writing, sound, symbols and tropes).[20] Subjectivity is composed of these part-objects (*objet a*), and it is the task of the analyst to both hear and speak the discourse of the *moi*. Thus Lacan's lectures are notorious for their punning and linguistic playfulness, which was his way of demonstrating in real time, his theories of mind at work.

The dynamics of the Lacanian conception of subjectivity are revealed in his interest in Hegel's dialectic of the master and the slave: the master only gains recognition of his status through the slave's existence, and through possession of the material goods produced by the slave. Through the potential "struggle to death" that led to one combatant giving-in and becoming a slave, there is direct recognition of the slave's identity; the master's identity is indirectly recognized (the material goods) and thereby is always frustratingly "outside" of the master. The master won the struggle, but in terms of direct recognition, he has lost. This eternal rivalry (the slave struggles for life and freedom; the master struggles to maintain prestige and recognition from the abject other) parallels the Lacanian subject's struggles with his or her composite ego, as well as an ongoing narcissistic internalized otherness.[21] Key theorists such as Judith Butler, Gilles Deleuze, Pierre Guattari, and Slavoj Žižek share this Lacanian interest in Hegel's dialectic and the master/slave passage. For Butler, in *Subjects of Desire: Hegelian Reflections in Twentieth-Century France* (1987), the key question in Hegel is that of re-instating desire and the fact that the subject always gains recognition from an external other (Hegel's notion of self-reflection); also, because the Hegelian subject is dialectical, it is a subject always on the move or in the process of formation and re-affirmation of identity, just as the master continues to re-affirm his identity in relation to the slave. In *Gender Trouble: Feminism and the Subversion of Identity* (1990; anniversary edition 1999), Butler utilizes this notion of continually having to re-affirm one's identity, to deconstruct theories of gender. She argues that gender is a performance, and that the apparent normativity of heterosexuality masks its instability and constant need for re-articulation. For Butler, homosexuality is not a secondary mode of being, and she argues that there is a formative psychological internalized prohibition of homosexual desire. Deleuze and Guattari, in a number of singly and jointly written books, such as *Anti-Oedipus: Capitalism and Schizophrenia* (1972), argue that Hegelian negation/resentment seen in the master/slave narrative, is now replaced by a Nietzschean affirmation of the will whereby the dialectic is replaced by a play of forces, celebrating desire, chance, and intensity. Žižek, in a comprehensive engagement with Butler's thought, in *The Ticklish Subject: The Absent Centre of Political Ontology* (1999), argues that by positioning gender differentiation and formation before the Symbolic (before language and law), Butler is repeating the very essentialist gesture she was trying to deconstruct.

Further reading: a selection

As so many psychoanalytical theories build upon the work of Freud, it is a good idea to start with one or more of the introductory overviews, such as Eliot or Thurschwell. Lear's biography of Freud is comprehensive and can be usefully paired with Roudinesco's biographical account of Lacan. The leap from theory to application can be daunting: De Berg and Wright both take practical approaches, examining, for example, Hamlet, fairy tales, and different approaches to literary critical methodologies. Alcorn approaches the literary text through the lens of narcissism, with chapters on rhetoric, reader response, character, plot, and imagery, with Conrad's *Heart of Darkness* as a main literary case study. As mentioned above feminist criticism of Freud has been extensive, with highlights being Gilman's book on Freud, race and gender, and Mitchell's "radical reassessment" of Freud from a feminist perspective. Fink, Grosz, Homer, Ragland-Sullivan, and Žižek all "introduce" Lacan, perhaps the most accessible for beginning readers being Homer's volume in the Routledge Critical Thinkers Series. Lane and Schultheis approach psychoanalysis through the lens of race and postcolonialism, with the former being an extensive collection of essays theoretical and applied, while the latter reads different postcolonial novelists in in-depth chapters. A classic text, bringing together Derrida and Lacan, is Muller and Richardson's case-study approach to Poe's "The Purloined Letter", the occasion of considerable and rewarding psychoanalytical theoretical debate.

Alcorn, Marshall W. *Narcissism and the Literary Libido: Rhetoric, Text and Subjectivity*. New York: New York University Press, 1994.

De Berg, Henk. *Freud's Theory and Its Use in Literary and Cultural Studies: An Introduction*. Rochester, NY: Camden House, 2003.

Elliot, Anthony. *Psychoanalytic Theory: An Introduction*. Second Edition. Durham, NC: Duke University Press, 2002.

Fink, Bruce. *The Lacanian Subject: Between Language and Jouissance*. Princeton, NJ: Princeton University Press, 1995.

Gilman, Sander L. *Freud, Race and Gender*. Princeton, NJ: Princeton University Press, 1993.

Grosz, Elisabeth. *Jacques Lacan: A Feminist Introduction*. London & New York: Routledge, 1990.

Homer, Sean. *Jacques Lacan*. London & New York: Routledge, 2005.

Lane, Christopher, ed. *The Psychoanalysis of Race*. New York: Columbia University Press, 1998.

Lear, Jonathan. *Freud*. Abingdon, Oxon: Routledge, 2005.

Mitchell, Juliet. *Psychoanalysis and Feminism: A Radical Reassessment of Freudian Psychoanalysis*. New York: Basic Books, 2000.

Mitchell, Juliet and Jacqueline Rose, eds. *Feminine Sexuality: Jacques Lacan and the École Freudienne*. Trans. Jacqueline Rose, New York: Norton, 1985.

Muller, John P. and William J. Richardson, eds. *The Purloined Poe: Lacan, Derrida, and Psychoanalysis*. Baltimore, MD & London: the Johns Hopkins University Press, 1988.

Ragland-Sullivan, Ellie. *Jacques Lacan and the Philosophy of Psychoanalysis*. Urbana & Chicago: University of Illinois Press, 1987.

Roudinesco, Elisabeth. *Jacques Lacan: An Outline of a Life and a History of a System of Thought*. Trans. Barbara Bray. Cambridge: Polity, 1997.

Schultheis, Alexandra W. *Regenerative Fictions: Postcolonialism, Psychoanalysis and the Nation as Family*. Houndmills, Basingstoke: Palgrave Macmillan, 2004.

Thurschwell, Pamela. *Sigmund Freud*. London & New York: Routledge, 2000.

Wright, Elizabeth. *Psychoanalytic Criticism: A Reappraisal*. Second Edition. London & New York: Routledge, 1998.

Žižek, Slavoj. *Looking Awry: An Introduction to Jacques Lacan through Popular Culture*. Cambridge, MA: MIT Press, 1991.

Notes

1   Edith Kurzwell, *The Freudians: A Comparative Perspective*, New Haven & London: Yale University Press, 1989, p.61.

2   John Lechte, *Fifty Key Contemporary Thinkers: From Structuralism to Postmodernity*, London & New York: Routledge, 2003, p.21.

3   John Lechte, *Fifty Key Contemporary Thinkers: From Structuralism to Postmodernity*, p.21.

4   Elisabeth Roudinesco, quoting André Breton, *Jacques Lacan*, trans. Barbara Bray, Cambridge: Polity, 1999, p.18.

5   John Lechte, *Fifty Key Contemporary Thinkers: From Structuralism to Postmodernity*, p.21; see, also, Jean Laplanche, *Life and Death in Psychoanalysis*, trans. Jeffrey Mehlman, Baltimore: the Johns Hopkins University Press, 1976.

6   See Andrew M. Colman, *A Dictionary of Psychology*, Oxford: Oxford University Press, 2009.

7   Henk De Berg, *Freud's Theory and Its Use in Literary and Cultural Studies*, Rochester, New York: Camden House, 2003, p.18.

8   Edith Kurzwell, *The Freudians: A Comparative Perspective*, p.20.

9   Edith Kurzwell, *The Freudians: A Comparative Perspective*, p.24.

10   Edith Kurzwell, *The Freudians: A Comparative Perspective*, p.43.

11   See, for example, Mikkel Borch-Jacobsen, *The Freudian Subject*, trans. Catherine Porter, London: Macmillan, 1989, section four, "The Primal Band".

12   J.J. Clarke, *In Search of Jung*, London & New York: Routledge, 1992, p.7.

13   J.J. Clarke, *In Search of Jung*, p.10.

14   Nancy Chodorow, *The Reproduction of Mothering: Psychoanalysis and the Sociology of Gender*, Berkeley and Los Angeles: University of California Press, 1978, 117.

15   Edith Kurzwell, *The Freudians: A Comparative Perspective*, p.164.

16   Juliet Mitchell and Jacqueline Rose, eds., *Feminine Sexuality: Jacques Lacan and the École Freudienne*, trans. Jacqueline Rose, New York: Norton, 1985, p.28.

17   Ellie Ragland-Sullivan, *Jacques Lacan and the Philosophy of Psychoanalysis*, Urbana & Chicago: University of Illinois Press, 1987, p.27.

18   Ellie Ragland-Sullivan, *Jacques Lacan and the Philosophy of Psychoanalysis*, p.29.
19   Ellie Ragland-Sullivan, *Jacques Lacan and the Philosophy of Psychoanalysis*, p.42.
20   Ellie Ragland-Sullivan, *Jacques Lacan and the Philosophy of Psychoanalysis*, p.44.
21   Ellie Ragland-Sullivan, *Jacques Lacan and the Philosophy of Psychoanalysis*, pp.47–48.

Chapter 23

Sigmund Freud

THE DREAM-WORK[1]

Readers of Sigmund Freud, the founder of psychoanalysis, have long been fascinated by his groundbreaking work on the interpretation of dreams, and his overall thesis that a dream is a disguised fulfilment of a suppressed wish. Freud approaches this topic of dream interpretation from many angles, and published various essays and a book on the subject. In "The Dream-Work" which comes from his *Introductory Lecture on Psychoanalysis* (1915–17), Freud distinguishes between the latent and the manifest dreams: the latent dream is the actual dream a person had, translated and transformed by dream work processes (condensation, displacement, symbolization, dramatization, secondary revision) into the manifest or remembered dream, the one which is reported to the psychoanalyst. The analytical task is to work backwards, decoding the dream-work processes to get at the latent dream itself. In "The Dream-Work" Freud starts by discussing condensation, which is composed of (1) omitting latent dream elements, (2) revealing only fragments of latent complexes, and (3) combining and fusing disparate latent elements that nonetheless have something in common. The latter process produces a composite image in the manifest dream, which Freud notes readily happens because our imagination already has the artistic capacity for such creativity. Freud suggests condensation is a sort of translation process which utilizes compression rather than individual articulation of concepts, etc., in the original text. With displacement, two processes are at work, both designed to "fool" the interpreter as such: a latent component is replaced by a "remote" (i.e., remotely connected) allusion, and an important latent element is replaced with an unimportant one, creating a decentred structure (or, a new and strange centre, which can throw the interpreter off balance). With symbolization, the latent dream's verbal images are turned into visual ones: this is what Freud calls "the essence of the formation of dreams" and he devotes a considerable part of his essay revealing the difficulties involved in doing this. Freud notes that overall, his approach enables psychoanalytical interpretation to make sense of what medical science thought of as senseless material. The "strange behaviour of the dream-work" can be decoded by attempting to understand its unusual logic. Freud does this, for example, with the way in which the dream-work processes "contraries" that were in the latent dream. He notes that such a logic is apparent in the development of language itself (this observation is taken up later by analysts such as Jacques Lacan), and that these are the "archaic" features of the dream-work. Throughout his lecture, however, Freud warns the reader about too quickly attempting to understand the manifest dream. For example, what appears sensible in the manifest dream is inevitably caused by a distortion of the latent dream; similarly components that appear connected in the manifest dream might be separate in the latent dream, or, they might represent other connections in the actual dream. Freud's point is that the coherence of the manifest dream is often brought about by "secondary revision", another dream-work process. The dream therefore needs interpretation by decoding: the manifest dream is less a guide and more of a con trick, yet the "con" follows a logic of its own that can be reverse engineered.

LADIES AND GENTLEMEN, – When you have thoroughly grasped the dream-censorship and representation by symbols, you will not yet, it is true, have completely mastered the distortion in dreams, but you will nevertheless be in a position to understand most dreams. In doing so you will make use of both of the two complementary techniques: calling up ideas that occur to the dreamer till you have penetrated from the substitute to the genuine thing and, on the ground of your own knowledge, replacing the symbols by what they mean. Later on we shall discuss some uncertainties that arise in this connection.

We can now take up once more a task that we tried to carry out previously with inadequate means, when we were studying the relations between the elements of dreams and the genuine things they stood for. We laid down four main relations of the kind: the relation of a part to a whole, approximation or allusion, the symbolic relation and the plastic representation of words. We now propose to undertake the same thing on a larger scale, by comparing the manifest content of a dream *as a whole* with the latent dream as it is revealed by interpretation.

I hope you will never again confuse these two things with each other. If you reach that point, you will probably have gone further in understanding dreams than most readers of my *Interpretation of Dreams*. And let me remind you once again that the work which transforms the latent dream into the manifest one is called the *dream-work*. The work which proceeds in the contrary direction, which endeavours to arrive at the latent dream from the manifest one, is our *work of interpretation*. This work of interpretation seeks to undo the dream-work. The dreams of infantile type which we recognize as obvious fulfilments of wishes have nevertheless experienced some amount of dream-work – they have been transformed from a wish into an actual experience and also, as a rule, from thoughts into visual images. In their case there is no need for interpretation but only for undoing these two transformations. The additional dream-work that occurs in other dreams is called 'dream-distortion', and this has to be undone by our work of interpretation.

Having compared the interpretations of numerous dreams, I am in a position to give you a summary description of what the dream-work does with the material of the latent dream-thoughts. I beg you, however, not to try to understand too much of what I tell you. It will be a piece of description which should be listened to with quiet attention.

The first achievement of the dream-work is *condensation*.[2] By that we understand the fact that the manifest dream has a smaller content than the latent one, and is thus an abbreviated transla-tion of it. Condensation can on occasion be absent; as a rule it is present, and very often it is enormous. It is never changed into the reverse; that is to say, we never find that the manifest dream is greater in extent or content than the latent one. Condensation is brought about (1) by the total omission of certain latent elements, (2) by only a fragment of some complexes in the latent dream passing over into the manifest one and (3) by latent elements which have something in common being combined and fused into a single unity in the manifest dream.

If you prefer it, we can reserve the term 'condensation' for the last only of these processes. Its results are particularly easy to demonstrate. You will have no difficulty in recalling instances from your own dreams of different people being condensed into a single one. A composite figure of this kind may look like A perhaps, but may be dressed like B, may do something that we remember C doing, and at the same time we may know that he is D. This composite structure is of course emphasizing something that the four people have in common. It is possible, naturally, to make a composite structure out of things or places in the same way as out of people, provided that the various things and places have in common something which is emphasized by the latent dream. The process is like constructing a new and transitory concept which has this common element as its nucleus. The outcome of this superimposing of the separate elements that have been condensed together is as a rule a blurred and vague image, like what happens if you take several photographs on the same plate.[3]

The production of composite structures like these must be of great importance to the dream-work, since we can show that, where in the first instance the common elements necessary for them were missing, they are deliberately introduced – for instance, through the choice of the words by which a thought is expressed. We have already come across condensations and composite structures of this sort. They played a part in the production of some slips of the tongue. You will recall the, young man who offered to '*begleitdigen*' ['*begleiten* (accompany)' + '*beleidigen* (insult)'] a lady. Moreover, there are jokes of which the technique is based on a condensation like this. But apart from these cases, it may be said that the process is something quite unusual and strange. It is true that counterparts to the construction of these composite figures are to be found in some creations of our imagination, which is ready to combine into a unity components of things that do not belong together in our experience – in the centaurs, for instance, and the fabulous beasts which appear in ancient mythology or in Böcklin's pictures. The 'creative' imagination, indeed, is quite incapable of *inventing* anything; it can only combine components that are strange to one another. But the remarkable thing about the procedure of the dream-work lies in what follows. The material offered to the dream-work consists of thoughts – a few of which may be objectionable and unacceptable, but which are correctly constructed and expressed. The dream-work puts these thoughts into another form, and it is a strange and incomprehensible fact that in making this translation (this rendering, as it were, into another script or language) these methods of merging or combining are brought into use. After all, a translation normally endeavours to preserve the distinctions made in the text and particularly to keep things that are similar separate. The dream-work, quite the contrary, tries to condense two different thoughts by seeking out (like a joke) an ambiguous word in which the two thoughts may come together. We need not try to understand this feature all at once, but it may become important for our appreciation of the dream-work.

But although condensation makes dreams obscure, it does not give one the impression of being an effect of the dream-censorship. It seems traceable rather to some mechanical or economic factor, but in any case the censorship profits by it.

The achievements of condensation can be quite extraordinary. It is sometimes possible by its help to combine two quite different latent trains of thought into one manifest dream, so that one can arrive at what appears to be a sufficient interpretation of a dream and yet in doing so can fail to notice a possible 'over-interpretation'.

In regard to the connection between the latent and the manifest dream, condensation results also in no simple relation being left between the elements in the one and the other. A manifest element may correspond simultaneously to several latent ones, and, contrariwise, a latent element may play a part in several manifest ones – there is, as it were, a criss-cross relationship. In interpreting a dream, moreover, we find that the associations to a single manifest element need not emerge in succession: we must often wait till the whole dream has been interpreted.

Thus the dream-work carries out a very unusual kind of transcription of the dream-thoughts: it is not a word-for-word or a sign-for-sign translation; nor is it a selection made according to fixed rules – as though one were to reproduce only the consonants in a word and to leave out the vowels; nor is it what might be described as a representative selection – one element being invariably chosen to take the place of several; it is something different and far more complicated.

The second achievement of the dream-work is *displacement*.[4] Fortunately we have made some preliminary examination of this: for we know that it is entirely the work of the dream-censorship. It manifests itself in two ways: in the first, a latent element is replaced not by a component part of itself but by something more remote – that is, by an allusion; and in the second, the psychical accent is shifted from an important element on to another which is unimportant, so that the dream appears differently centred and strange.

Replacing something by an allusion to it is a process familiar in our waking thought as well, but there is a difference. In waking thought the allusion must be easily intelligible, and the substitute must be related in its subject-matter to the genuine thing it stands for. Jokes, too, often make use of allusion. They drop the precondition of there being an association in subject-matter, and replace it by unusual external associations such as similarity of sound, verbal ambiguity, and so on. But they retain the precondition of intelligibility: a joke would lose all its efficiency if the path back from the allusion to the genuine thing could not be followed easily. The allusions employed for displacement in dreams have set themselves free from both of these restrictions. They are connected with the element they replace by the most external and remote relations and are therefore unintelligible; and when they are undone, their interpretation gives the impression of being a bad joke or of an arbitrary and forced explanation dragged in by the hair of its head. For the dream-censorship only gains its end if it succeeds in making it impossible to find the path back from the allusion to the genuine thing.

Displacement of accent is unheard-of as a method of expressing thoughts. We sometimes make use of it in waking thought in order to produce a comic effect. I can perhaps call up the impression it produces of going astray if I recall an anecdote. There was a blacksmith in a village, who had committed a capital offence. The Court decided that the crime must be punished; but as the blacksmith was the only one in the village and was indispensable, and as on the other hand there were three tailors living there, one of *them* was hanged instead.

The third achievement of the dream-work is psychologically the most interesting. It consists in transforming thoughts into visual images.[5] Let us keep it clear that this transformation does not affect *everything* in the dream-thoughts; some of them retain their form and appear as thoughts or knowledge in the manifest dream as well; nor are visual images the only form into which thoughts are transformed. Nevertheless they comprise the essence of the formation of dreams; this part of the dream-work is, as we already know, the second most regular one [pp. 160–61], and we have already made the acquaintance of the 'plastic' representation of words in the case of individual dream-elements.

It is clear that this achievement is not an easy one. To form some idea of its difficulties, let us suppose that you have undertaken the task of replacing a political leading article in a newspaper by a series of illustrations. You will thus have been thrown back from alphabetic writing to picture writing. In so far as the article mentioned people and concrete objects you will replace them easily and perhaps even advantageously by pictures; but your difficulties will begin when you come to the representation of abstract words and of all those parts of speech which indicate relations between thoughts – such as particles, conjunctions and so on. In the case of abstract words you will be able to help yourselves out by means of a variety of devices. For instance, you will endeavour to give the text of the article a different wording, which may perhaps sound less usual but which will contain more components that are concrete and capable of being represented. You will then recall that most abstract words are 'watered-down' concrete ones, and you will for that reason hark back as often as possible to the original concrete meaning of such words. Thus you will be pleased to find that you can represent the 'possession' of an object by a real, physical sitting down on it.[6] And the dream-work does just the same thing. In such circumstances you will scarcely be able to expect very great accuracy from your representation: similarly, you will forgive the dream-work for replacing an element so hard to put into pictures as, for example, 'adultery' ['*Ehebruch*', literally, 'breach of marriage'], by another breach – a broken leg ['*Beinbruch*'].[7] And in this way you will succeed to some extent in compensating for the clumsiness of the picture writing that is supposed to take the place of the alphabetic script.

For representing the parts of speech which indicate relations between thoughts – 'because', 'therefore', 'however', etc. – you will have no similar aids at your disposal; those constituents of the text will be lost so far as translation into pictures goes. In the same way, the dream-work reduces the content of the dream-thoughts to its raw material of objects and activities. You will feel pleased if there is a possibility of in some way hinting, through the subtler details of the pictures, at certain relations not in themselves capable of being represented. And just so does the dream-work succeed in expressing some of the content of the latent dream-thoughts by peculiarities in the *form* of the manifest dream – by its clarity or obscurity, by its division into several pieces, and so on. The number of part-dreams into which a dream is divided usually corresponds to the number of main topics or groups of thoughts in the latent dream. A short introductory dream will often stand in the relation of a prelude to a following, more detailed, main dream or may give the motive for it; a subordinate clause in the dream-thoughts will be replaced by the interpolation of a change of scene into the manifest dream, and so on. Thus the form of dreams is far from being without significance and itself calls for interpretation. When several dreams occur during the same night, they often have the same meaning and indicate that an attempt is being made to deal more and more efficiently with a stimulus of increasing insistence. In individual dreams a particularly difficult element may be represented by several symbols – by 'doublets'.[8]

If we make a series of comparisons between the dream-thoughts and the manifest dreams which replace them, we shall come upon all kinds of things for which we are unprepared: for instance, that nonsense and absurdity in dreams have their meaning. At this point, indeed, the contrast between the medical and the psychoanalytic view of dreams reaches a pitch of acuteness not met with elsewhere. According to the former, dreams are senseless because mental activity in dreams has abandoned all its powers of criticism; according to our view, on the contrary, dreams become senseless when a piece of criticism included in the dream-thoughts – a judgement that 'this is absurd' – has to be represented. The dream you are familiar with of the visit to the theatre ('three tickets for I florin 50') is a good example of this. The judgement it expressed was: 'it was absurd to marry so early.'[9]

Similarly, in the course of our work of interpretation we learn what it is that corresponds to the doubts and uncertainties which the dreamer so often expresses as to whether a particular element occurred in a dream, whether it was this or whether, on the contrary, it was something else. There is as a rule nothing in the latent dream-thoughts corresponding to these doubts and uncertainties; they are entirely due to the activity of the dream-censorship and are to be equated with an attempt at elimination which has not quite succeeded.

Among the most surprising findings is the way in which the dream-work treats contraries that occur in the latent dream. We know already that conformities in the latent material are replaced by condensations in the manifest dream. Well, contraries are treated in the same way as conformities, and there is a special preference for expressing them by the same manifest element. Thus an element in the manifest dream which is capable of having a contrary may equally well be expressing either itself or its contrary or both together: only the sense can decide which translation is to be chosen. This connects with the further fact that a representation of 'no' – or at any rate an unambiguous one – is not to be found in dreams.

A welcome analogy to this strange behaviour of the dream-work is provided for us in the development of language. Some philologists have maintained that in the most ancient languages contraries such as 'strong-weak', 'light-dark', 'big-small' are expressed by the same verbal roots. (What we term 'the antithetical meaning of primal words'.) Thus in Ancient Egyptian 'ken' originally meant 'strong' and 'weak'. In speaking, misunderstanding from the use of such ambivalent words was avoided by differences of intonation and by the accompanying gesture, and in writing, by the addition of what is termed a 'determinative' – a picture which is not itself intended to be spoken. For instance, 'ken' meaning 'strong' was written with a picture of a little upright man after the alphabetic signs; when 'ken' stood for 'weak', what followed was the picture of a man squatting down limply. It was only later, by means of slight modifications of the original homologous word, that two distinct representations were arrived at of the contraries included in it. Thus from 'ken' 'strong-weak' were derived 'ken' 'strong' and 'kan' 'weak'. The remains of this ancient antithetical meaning seem to have been preserved not only in the latest developments of the oldest languages but also in far younger ones and even in some that are still living. Here is some evidence of this, derived from K. Abel (1884).

In Latin, words that remained ambivalent in this way are 'altus' ('high' and 'deep') and 'sacer' ('sacred' and 'accursed').

As instances of modifications of the same root I may mention 'clamare' ('to cry'), 'clam' ('softly', 'quietly', 'secretly'); 'siccus' ('dry'), 'succus' ('juice'). And in German: 'Stimme' ['voice'], 'stumm' ['dumb'].

If we compare related languages, there are numerous examples. In English, 'to lock'; in German, 'Loch' ['hole'] and 'Lücke' ['gap']. In English, 'to cleave'; in German, 'kleben' ['to stick'].

The English word 'without' (which is really 'with-without') is used today for 'without' alone. 'With', in addition to its combining sense, originally had a removing one; this is still to be seen in the compounds 'withdraw' and 'withhold'. Similarly with the German 'wieder' ['together with' and 'wider' 'against'].

Another characteristic of the dream-work also has its counterpart in the development of language. In Ancient Egyptian, as well as in other, later languages, the order of the sounds in a word can be reversed, while keeping the same meaning. Examples of this in English and German are: 'Topf' ['pot']–'pot'; 'boat'–'tub'; 'hurry'–'Ruhe' ['rest']; 'Balken' ['beam']–'Kloben' ['log'] and 'club'; 'wait'–'täuwen' ['tarry']. Similarly in Latin and German: 'capere'–'packen' ['to seize']; 'ren'–'Niere' ['kidney'].

Reversals like this, which occur here with individual words, take place in various ways in the dream-work. We already know reversal of meaning, replacement of something by its opposite. Besides this we find in dreams reversals of situation, of the relation between two people – a 'topsy-turvy' world. Quite often in dreams it is the hare that shoots the sportsman. Or again we find a reversal in the order of events, so that what precedes an event causally comes after it in the dream – like a theatrical production by a third-rate touring company, in which the hero falls down dead and the shot that killed him is not fired in the wings till afterwards. Or there are dreams where the whole order of the elements is reversed, so that to make sense in interpreting it we must take the last one first and the first one last. You will remember too from our study of dream-symbolism that going or falling into the water means the same as coming out of it — that is, giving birth or being born, and that climbing up a staircase or a ladder is the same thing as coming down it. It is not hard to see the advantage that dream-distortion can derive from this freedom of representation.

These features of the dream-work may be described as *archaic*. They are equally characteristic of ancient systems of expression by speech and writing and they involve the same difficulties, which we shall have to discuss again later in a critical sense.

And now a few more considerations. In the case of the dream-work it is clearly a matter of transforming the latent thoughts which are expressed in words into sensory images, mostly of a visual sort. Now our thoughts originally arose from sensory images of that kind: their first material and their preliminary stages were sense impressions, or, more properly, mnemic images of such impressions. Only later were words attached to them and the words in turn linked up into thoughts. The dream-work thus submits thoughts to a *regressive* treatment and undoes their development; and in the course of the regression everything has to be dropped that had been added as a new acquisition in the course of the development of the mnemic images into thoughts.

Such then, it seems, is the dream-work. As compared with the processes we have come to know in it, interest in the manifest dream must pale into insignificance. But I will devote a few more remarks to the latter, since it is of it alone that we have immediate knowledge.

It is natural that we should lose some of our interest in the manifest dream. It is bound to be a matter of indifference to us whether it is well put together, or is broken up into a series of disconnected separate pictures. Even if it has an apparently sensible exterior, we know that this has only come about through dream-distortion and can have as little organic relation to the internal content of the dream as the façade of an Italian church has to its structure and plan. There are other occasions when this facade of the dream *has* its meaning, and reproduces an important component of the latent dream-thoughts with little or no distortion. But we cannot know this before we have submitted the dream to interpretation and have been able to form a judgement from it as to the amount of distortion that has taken place. A similar doubt arises when two elements in a dream appear to have been brought into a close relation to each other. This may give us a valuable hint that we may bring together what corresponds to these elements in the latent dream as well; but on other occasions we can convince ourselves that what belongs together in the dream-thoughts has been torn apart in the dream.

In general one must avoid seeking to explain one part of the manifest dream by another, as though the dream had been coherently conceived and was a logically arranged narrative. On the contrary, it is as a rule like a piece of breccia, composed of various fragments of rock held together by a binding medium, so that the designs that appear on it do not belong to the original rocks imbedded in it. And there is in fact one part of the dream-work, known as 'secondary revision',[10] whose business it is to make something whole and more or less coherent out of the first products of the dream-work. In the course of this, the material is arranged in what is often a completely misleading sense and, where it seems necessary, interpolations are made in it.

On the other hand, we must not over-estimate the dream-work and attribute too much to it. The achievements I have enumerated exhaust its activity; it can do no more than condense, displace, represent in plastic form and subject the whole to a secondary revision. What appear in the dream as expressions of judgement, of criticism, of astonishment or of inference — none of these are achievements of the dream-work and they are very rarely expressions of afterthoughts about the dream; they are for the most part portions of the latent dream-thoughts which have passed over into the manifest dream with a greater or less amount of modification and adaptation to the context. Nor can the dream-work compose speeches. With a few assignable exceptions, speeches in dreams are copies and combinations of speeches which one has heard or spoken oneself on the day before the dream and which have been included in the latent thoughts either as material or as the instigator of the dream. The dream-work is equally unable to carry out calculations. Such of them as appear in the manifest dream are mostly combinations of numbers, sham calculations which are quite senseless *quâ* calculations and are once again only copies of calculations in the latent dream-thoughts. In these circumstances it is not to be wondered at that the interest which had turned to the dream-work soon tends to move away from it to the latent dream-thoughts, which are revealed, distorted to a greater or less degree, by the manifest dream. But there is no justification for carrying this shift of interest so far that, in looking at the matter theoretically, one replaces the dream entirely by the latent dream-thoughts and makes some assertion about the former which only applies to the latter. It is strange that the findings of psychoanalysis could be misused to bring about this confusion. One cannot give the name of 'dream' to anything other than the product of the dream-work – that is to say, the *form* into which the latent thoughts have been transmuted by the dream-work.

The dream-work is a process of quite a singular kind, of which the like has not yet become known in mental life. Condensations, displacements, regressive transformations of thoughts into images – such things are novelties whose discovery has already richly rewarded the labours of psychoanalysis. And you can see once more, from the parallels to the dream-work, the connections which have been revealed between psychoanalytic studies and other fields – especially those concerned in the development of speech and thought. You will only be able to form an idea of the further significance of these discoveries when you learn that the mechanism of dream-construction is the model of the manner in which neurotic symptoms arise.

I am also aware that we are not yet able to make a survey of the whole of the new acquisitions which these studies have brought to psychology. I will only point out the fresh proofs they have provided of the existence of unconscious mental acts – for this is what the latent dream-thoughts are – and what an unimaginably broad access to a knowledge of unconscious mental life we are promised by the interpretation of dreams.

But now the time has no doubt come for me to demonstrate to you from a variety of small examples of dreams what I have been preparing you for in the course of these remarks.

Notes

1   [The whole of Chapter VI of *The Interpretation of Dreams* (over a third of the entire book) is devoted to the dream-work.]
2   [Condensation is discussed, with numerous examples, in Section A of Chapter VI of *The Interpretation of Dreams*.]
3   [Freud more than once compared the result of condensation with Francis Galton's 'composite photographs', e.g. in Chapter IV of *The Interpretation of Dreams*.]
4   [Displacement is the subject of Section B of Chapter VI of *The Interpretation of Dreams*; but it comes up for discussion at a great many other places in the book.]
5   [The main discussion of this is in Section C of Chapter VI of *The Interpretation of Dreams*.]
6   [The German word '*besitzen*' ('*to* possess') is more obviously connected with sitting than its English equivalent ('*sitzen*' = 'to sit').]
7   While I am correcting the proofs of these pages chance has put into my hands a newspaper cutting which offers an unexpected confirmation of what I have written above:

'DIVINE PUNISHMENT
'*A Broken Arm for a Broken Marriage.*
'Frau Anna M., wife of a militiaman, sued Frau Klementine K. for adultery. According to the statement of claim, Frau K. had carried on an illicit relationship with Karl M., while her own husband was at the front and was actually making her an allowance of 70 Kronen [about £3.50] a month. Frau

K. had already received a considerable amount of money from the plaintiff's husband, while she and her child had to live in hunger and poverty. Fellow-soldiers of her husband had informed her that Frau K. had visited taverns with M. and had sat there drinking till far into the night. On one occasion the defendant had asked the plaintiff's husband in the presence of several other soldiers whether he would not get a divorce soon from "his old woman" and set up with her. Frau K.'s caretaker also reported that she had repeatedly seen the plaintiff's husband in the house most incompletely dressed.

'Before a court in the Leopoldstadt [district of Vienna] Frau K. yesterday denied knowing M., so that there could be no question of her having intimate relations with him.

'A witness, Alberane M., stated, however, that she had surprised Frau K. kissing the plaintiff's husband.

'At a previous hearing, M., under examination as a witness, had denied having intimate relations with the defendant. Yesterday the Judge received a letter in which the witness withdrew the statements he had made on the earlier occasion and admitted that he had had a love-affair with Frau K. up till the previous June. He had only denied his relations with the defendant at the former hearing because she had come to him before the hearing and begged him on her knees to save her and say nothing. "Today", the witness wrote, "I feel compelled to make a full confession to the Court, for I have broken my left arm and this seems to me to be a divine punishment for my wrongdoing."

'The Judge stated that the penal offence had lapsed under the statute of limitations. The plaintiff then withdrew her claim and the defendant was discharged.'

8   [In philology the term is used of two different words with the same etymology: e.g. 'fashion' and 'faction', both from the Latin *'factio'*.]

9   [Absurdity in dreams is discussed in Section G of Chapter VI of *The Interpretation of Dreams*.]

10   [This is the subject of Section I of Chapter VI of *The Interpretation of Dreams*.]

Chapter 24

Sigmund Freud

THE "UNCANNY"

Sigmund Freud observes that while in a general sense the uncanny relates to the frightening (dread and horror), there must be some "core of feeling" that has led people to use such a specialist term. While Freud suggests that not much literature on the topic was available to him, there is enough to ascertain that paradoxically, the uncanny relates fear to the personally known (the familiar). Through linguistic analysis, Freud shows how the German word for uncanny—*unheimlich*—contains its opposite, or the homely (*Heimlich*), which is neatly summarized by Schelling's famous definition: "everything is *unheimlich* that ought to have remained secret and hidden but has come to light." Freud turns to literature to study some examples (as he so often does in his psychoanalytical essays, such as the essays "Psychopathic Characters on the Stage" and "Creative Writers and Day-Dreaming"), in particular the uncanny feeling that arises when something that should be inanimate shows signs of life, such as the doll Olympia in Hoffman's story "The Sand-Man". However, upon closer analysis of the story, Freud discovers that the more uncanny element is the protagonist's fear of having his eyes forcibly removed, which in Freudian symbolism represents an even deeper fear: that of castration. Another literary example of the uncanny is that of the double (or doppelgänger), that is to say, a duplicate or unrelated "twin" who appears indistinguishable from the original person. While the double was once seen as an "insurance" against death, for example with the idea of the soul as being a double of the individual, now it has become an early warning signal of impending destruction. From a psychoanalytical perspective, Freud argues that the double relates to an extremely "early mental stage", i.e., early in evolutionary and developmental terms. To explore the double further, Freud observes that it is a form of repetition, and he gives the amusing and revealing example of accidentally finding himself in the same red light district three times over, as he wanders around a city. Coincidences, i.e., too many "chance" repetitions occurring in a sequence, are also uncanny. These examples and others in the text all suggest that an innate repetition compulsion is somehow uncanny. Finally, Freud gives a number of examples of wish fulfilment as being uncanny: Polycrates, who is a character in a story by Herodotus, whose every wish comes true, one of Freud's patients, and the example of the "evil eye" (or "omnipotence of thoughts"). Freud suggests that these examples refer back to an earlier set of human beliefs known as "animism", or, the notion that the world is inhabited by magical spirits. Freud suggests that human beings pass through an analogous stage in their personal psychic development, going beyond this stage yet still incorporating fragments or traces of such beliefs within their mature psyches. At this point in his essay Freud reaches two conclusions: first, that it is the recurrence of repressed elements that are frightening, and therefore uncanny; and second, if they are repressed, that means they were once familiar to us, regardless of whether they were pleasurable or painful, good or bad, and further, this conclusion explains the linguistic paradox with which Freud started his essay.

I

It is only rarely that a psychoanalyst feels impelled to investigate the subject of aesthetics, even when aesthetics is understood to mean not merely the theory of beauty but the theory of the qualities of feeling. He works in other strata of mental life and has little to do with the subdued emotional impulses which, inhibited in their aims and dependent on a host of concurrent factors, usually furnish the material for the study of aesthetics. But it does occasionally happen that he has to interest himself in some particular province of that subject; and this province usually proves to be a rather remote one, and one which has been neglected in the specialist literature of aesthetics.

The subject of the 'uncanny'[1] is a province of this kind. It is undoubtedly related to what is frightening – to what arouses dread and horror; equally certainly, too, the word is not always used in a clearly definable sense, so that it tends to coincide with what excites fear in general. Yet we may expect that a special core of feeling is present which justifies the use of a special conceptual term. One is curious to know what this common core is which allows us to distinguish as 'uncanny' certain things which lie within the field of what is frightening.

As good as nothing is to be found upon this subject in comprehensive treatises on aesthetics, which in general prefer to concern themselves with what is beautiful, attractive and sublime – that is, with feelings of a positive nature – and with the circumstances and the objects that call them forth, rather than with the opposite feelings of repulsion and distress. I know of only one attempt in medico-psychological literature, a fertile but not exhaustive paper by Jentsch (1906). But I must confess that I have not made a very thorough examination of the literature, especially the foreign literature, relating to this present modest contribution of mine, for reasons which, as may easily be guessed, lie in the times in which we live; so that my paper is presented to the reader without any claim to priority.

In his study of the 'uncanny' Jentsch quite rightly lays stress on the obstacle presented by the fact that people vary so very greatly in their sensitivity to this quality of feeling. The writer of the present contribution, indeed, must himself plead guilty to a special obtuseness in the matter, where extreme delicacy of perception would be more in place. It is long since he has experienced or heard of anything which has given him an uncanny impression, and he must start by translating himself into that state of feeling, by awakening in himself the possibility of experiencing it. Still, such difficulties make themselves powerfully felt in many other branches of aesthetics; we need not on that account despair of finding instances in which the quality in question will be unhesitatingly recognized by most people.

Two courses are open to us at the outset. Either we can find out what meaning has come to be attached to the word 'uncanny' in the course of its history; or we can collect all those properties of persons, things, sense-impressions, experiences and situations which arouse in us the feeling of uncanniness, and then infer the unknown nature of the uncanny from what all these examples have in common. I will say at once that both courses lead to the same result: the uncanny is that class of the frightening which leads back to what is known of old and long familiar. How this is possible, in what circumstances the familiar can become uncanny and frightening, I shall show in what follows. Let me also add that my investigation was actually begun by collecting a number of individual cases, and was only later confirmed by an examination of linguistic usage. In this discussion, however, I shall follow the reverse course.

The German word *'unheimlich'* is obviously the opposite of *'heimlich'* ['homely'], *'heimisch'* ['native'] – the opposite of what is familiar; and we are tempted to conclude that what is 'uncanny' is frightening precisely because it is *not* known and familiar. Naturally not everything that is new and unfamiliar is frightening, however; the relation is not capable of inversion. We can only say that what is novel can easily become frightening and uncanny; some new things are frightening but not by any means all. Something has to be added to what is novel and unfamiliar in order to make it uncanny.

On the whole, Jentsch did not get beyond this relation of the uncanny to the novel and unfamiliar. He ascribes the essential factor in the production of the feeling of uncanniness to intellectual uncertainty; so that the uncanny would always, as it were, be something one does not know one's way about in. The better orientated in his environment a person is, the less readily will he get the impression of something uncanny in regard to the objects and events in it.

It is not difficult to see that this definition is incomplete, and we will therefore try to proceed beyond the equation 'uncanny' = 'unfamiliar'. We will first turn to other languages. But the dictionaries that we consult tell us nothing new, perhaps only because we ourselves speak a language that is foreign. Indeed, we get an impression that many languages are without a word for this particular shade of what is frightening.

I should like to express my indebtedness to Dr Theodor Reik for the following excerpts:

LATIN: (K. E. Georges, *Deutschlateinisches Wörterbuch*, 1898). An uncanny place: *locus suspectus;* at an uncanny time of night: *intempesta nocte.*
GREEK: (Rost's and Schenkl's Lexikons), ξένος (i.e. strange, foreign).
ENGLISH: (from the dictionaries of Lucas, Bellows, Flügel and Muret-Sanders). Uncomfortable, uneasy, gloomy, dismal, uncanny, ghastly; (of a house) haunted; (of a man) a repulsive fellow.
FRENCH: (Sachs-Villatte). *Inquiétant, sinistre, lugubre, mal à son aise.*
SPANISH: (Tollhausen, 1889). *Sospechoso, de mal agüero, lúgubre, siniestro.*

The Italian and Portuguese languages seem to content themselves with words which we should describe as circumlocutions. In Arabic and Hebrew 'uncanny' means the same as 'daemonic', 'gruesome'.

Let us therefore return to the German language. In Daniel Sanders's *Wörterbuch der Deutschen Sprache* (1860, I, 729), the following entry, which I here reproduce in full, is to be found under the word *'heimlich'*. I have laid stress on one or two passages by italicizing them.[2]

Heimlich, adj., subst. *Heimlichkeit* (pl. *Heimlichkeiten*): I. Also *heimelich, heimelig,* belonging to the house, not strange, familiar, tame, intimate, friendly, etc.

(*a*) (Obsolete) belonging to the house or the family, or regarded as so belonging (cf. Latin *familiaris,* familiar): *Die Heimlichen,* the members of the household; *Der heimliche Rat* (*Genesis,* xli, 45; *2 Samuel,* xxiii, 23; *1 Chronicles,* xii, 25; *Wisdom,* viii, 4), now more usually *Geheimer Rat* [Privy Councillor].
(*b*) Of animals: tame, companionable to man. As opposed to wild, e.g. 'Animals which are neither wild nor *heimlich*', etc. 'Wild animals . . . that are trained to be *heimlich* and accustomed to men.' 'If these young creatures are brought up from early days among

men they become quite *heimlich,* friendly' etc. So also: 'It (the lamb) is so *heimlich* and eats out of my hand.' 'Nevertheless, the stork is a beautiful, *heimelich* bird.'

(c) Intimate, friendlily comfortable; the enjoyment of quiet content, etc., arousing a sense of agreeable restfulness and security as in one within the four walls of his house.[3] 'Is it still *heimlich* to you in your country where strangers are felling your woods?' 'She did not feel too *heimlich* with him.' 'Along a high, *heimlich,* shady path . . ., beside a purling, gushing and babbling woodland brook.' 'To destroy the *Heimlichkeit* of the home.' 'I could not readily find another spot so intimate and *heimlich* as this.' 'We pictured it so comfortable, so nice, so cosy and *heimlich.*' 'In quiet *Heimlichkeit,* surrounded by close walls.' 'A careful housewife, who knows how to make a pleasing *Heimlichkeit (Häuslichkeit* [domesticity]) out of the smallest means.' 'The man who till recently had been so strange to him now seemed to him all the more *heimlich.*' 'The protestant land-owners do not feel . . . *heimlich* among their catholic inferiors.' 'When it grows *heimlich* and still, and the evening quiet alone watches over your cell.' 'Quiet, lovely and *heimlich,* no place more fitted for their rest.' 'He did not feel at all *heimlich* about it.' – Also, [in compounds] 'The place was so peaceful, so lonely, so shadily-*heimlich.*' 'The in- and outflowing waves of the current, dreamy and lullaby-*heimlich.*' Cf. in especial *Unheimlich* [see below]. Among Swabian Swiss authors in especial, often as a trisyllable: 'How *heimelich* it seemed to Ivo again of an evening, when he was at home.' 'It was so *heimelig* in the house.' 'The warm room and the *heimelig* afternoon.' 'When a man feels in his heart that he is so small and the Lord so great – that is what is truly *heimelig.*' 'Little by little they grew at ease and *heimelig* among themselves.' 'Friendly *Heimeligkeit.*' 'I shall be nowhere more *heimelich* than I am here.' 'That which comes from afar . . . assuredly does not live quite *heimelig (heimatlich* [at home], *freundnachbarlich* [in a neighbourly way]) among the people.' 'The cottage where he had once sat so often among his own people, so *heimelig,* so happy.' 'The sentinel's horn sounds so *heimelig* from the tower, and his voice invites so hospitably.' 'You go to sleep there so soft and warm, so wonderfully *heim'lig.*' – *This form of the word deserves to become general in order to protect this perfectly good sense of the word from becoming obsolete through an easy confusion with* II [see below]. Cf: '"The Zecks [a family name] are all 'heimlich'."* (in sense II) *"'Heimlich'? . . . What do you understand by 'heimlich'?" "Well, . . . they are like a buried spring or a dried-up pond. One cannot walk over it without always having the feeling that water might come up there again." "Oh, we call it 'unheimlich'; you call it 'heimlich'. Well, what makes you think that there is something secret and untrustworthy about this family?"'* (Gutzkow).

(d) Especially in Silesia: gay, cheerful; also of the weather.

II. Concealed, kept from sight, so that others do not get to know of or about it, withheld from others. To do something *heimlich,* i.e. behind someone's back; to steal away *heimlich; heimlich* meetings and appointments; to look on with *heimlich* pleasure at someone's discomfiture; to sigh or weep *heimlich;* to behave *heimlich,* as though there was something to conceal; *heimlich* love-affair, love, sin; *heimlich* places (which good manners oblige us to conceal) (I *Samuel,* v, 6). 'The *heimlich* chamber' (privy) (2 *Kings,* x, 27). Also, 'the *heimlich* chair'. 'To throw into pits or *Heimlichkeiten*'. – 'Led the steeds *heimlich* before Laomedon.' – 'As secretive, *heimlich,* deceitful and malicious towards cruel masters . . . as frank, open, sympathetic and helpful towards a friend in misfortune.' 'You have still to learn what is *heimlich* holiest to me.' 'The *heimlich* art' (magic). 'Where public ventilation has to stop, there *heimlich* machinations begin.' 'Freedom is the whispered watchword of *heimlich* conspirators and the loud battle-cry of professed revolutionaries.' 'A holy, *heimlich* effect.' 'I have roots that are most *heimlich,* I am grown in the deep earth.' 'My *heimlich* pranks.' 'If he is not given it openly and scrupulously he may seize it *heimlich* and unscrupulously.' 'He had achromatic telescopes constructed *heimlich* and secretly.' 'Henceforth I desire that there should be nothing *heimlich* any longer between us.' – To discover, disclose, betray someone's *Heimlichkeiten*; 'to concoct *Heimlichkeiten* behind my back'. 'In my time we studied *Heimlichkeit*.' 'The hand of understanding can alone undo the powerless spell of the *Heimlichkeit* (of hidden gold).' 'Say, where is the place of concealment . . . in what place of hidden *Heimlichkeit*?' 'Bees, who make the lock of *Heimlichkeiten*' (i.e. sealing-wax). 'Learned in strange *Heimlichkeiten*' (magic arts).

For compounds see above, Ic. Note especially the negative '*un-*': eerie, weird, arousing gruesome fear: 'Seeming quite *unheimlich* and ghostly to him.' 'The *unheimlich*, fearful hours of night.' 'I had already long since felt an *unheimlich*, even gruesome feeling.' 'Now I am beginning to have an *unheimlich* feeling' . . . 'Feels an *unheimlich* horror.' '*Unheimlich* and motionless like a stone image.' 'The *unheimlich* mist called hill-fog.' 'These pale youths are *unheimlich* and are brewing heaven knows what mischief.' '"*Unheimlich*" *is the name for everything that ought to have remained . . . secret and hidden but has come to light*' (Schelling). – 'To veil the divine, to surround it with a certain *Unheimlichkeit*.' – *Unheimlich* is not often used as opposite to meaning II (above).

What interests us most in this long extract is to find that among its different shades of meaning the word '*heimlich*' exhibits one which is identical with its opposite, '*unheimlich*'. What is *heimlich* thus comes to be *unheimlich*. (Cf. the quotation from Gutzkow: 'We call it "*unheimlich*"; you call it "*heimlich*".') In general we are reminded that the word '*heimlich*' is not unambiguous, but belongs to two sets of ideas, which, without being contradictory, are yet very different: on the one hand it means what is familiar and agreeable, and on the other, what is concealed and kept out of sight.[4] '*Unheimlich*' is customarily used, we are told, as the contrary only of the first signification of '*heimlich*', and not of the second. Sanders tells us nothing concerning a possible genetic connection between these two meanings of *heimlich*. On the other hand, we notice that Schelling says something which throws quite a new light on the concept of the *Unheimlich*, for which we were certainly not prepared. According to him, everything is *unheimlich* that ought to have remained secret and hidden but has come to light.

Some of the doubts that have thus arisen are removed if we consult Grimms' dictionary (1877, 4, Part 2, 873 ff.). We read:

> *Heimlich*; adj. and adv. *vernaculus, occultus*; MHG. *heimelich, heimlich*.
>
> (P. 874.) In a slightly different sense: 'I feel *heimlich*, well, free from fear' . . .
>
> [3] (*b*) *Heimlich* is also used of a place free from ghostly influences . . . familiar, friendly, intimate.
>
> (P. 875: *β*) Familiar, amicable, unreserved.
>
> 4. *From the idea of 'homelike', 'belonging to the house', the further idea is developed of something withdrawn from the eyes of strangers, something concealed, secret; and this idea is expanded in many ways* . . .
>
> (P. 876.) 'On the left bank of the lake there lies a meadow *heimlich* in the wood.' (Schiller, *Wilhelm Tell*, 1.4.) . . . Poetic licence, rarely so used in modern speech . . . *Heimlich* is used in conjunction with a verb expressing the act of concealing: 'In the secret of his tabernacle he shall hide me *heimlich*.' (*Psalms*, xxvii, 5.) . . . *Heimlich* parts of the human body, *pudenda* . . . 'the men that died not were smitten on their *heimlich* parts.' (I *Samuel*, v, 12.) . . .
>
> (*c*) Officials who give important advice which has to be kept secret in matters of state are called *heimlich* councillors; the adjective, according to modern usage, has been replaced by *geheim* [secret] . . . 'Pharaoh called Joseph's name "him to whom secrets are revealed"' (*heimlich* councillor). (*Genesis* xli, 45.)

(P. 878.) 6. *Heimlich*, as used of knowledge – mystic, allegorical: a *heimlich* meaning, *mysticus, divinus, occultus, figuratus*.

(P. 878.) *Heimlich* in a different sense, as withdrawn from knowledge, unconscious . . . *Heimlich* also has the meaning of that which is obscure, inaccessible to knowledge . . . 'Do you not see? They do not trust us; they fear the *heimlich* face of the Duke of Friedland.' (Schiller, *Wallensteins Lager*, Scene 2.)

9. *The notion of something hidden and dangerous, which is expressed in the last paragraph, is still further developed, so that 'heimlich' comes to have the meaning usually ascribed to 'unheimlich'.* Thus: 'At times I feel like a man who walks in the night and believes in ghosts; every corner is *heimlich* and full of terrors for him'. (Klinger, *Theater*, 3, 298.)

Thus *heimlich* is a word the meaning of which develops in the direction of ambivalence, until it finally coincides with its opposite, *unheimlich*. *Unheimlich* is in some way or other a subspecies of *heimlich*. Let us bear this discovery in mind, though we cannot yet rightly understand it, alongside of Schelling's definition of the *Unheimlich*. If we go on to examine individual instances of uncanniness, these hints will become intelligible to us.

II

When we proceed to review the things, persons, impressions, events and situations which are able to arouse in us a feeling of the uncanny in a particularly forcible and definite form, the first requirement is obviously to select a suitable example to start on. Jentsch has taken as a very good instance 'doubts whether an apparently animate being is really alive; or conversely, whether a lifeless object might not be in fact animate'; and he refers in this connection to the impression made by waxwork figures, ingeniously constructed dolls and automata. To these he adds the uncanny effect of epileptic fits, and of manifestations of insanity, because these excite in the spectator the impression of automatic, mechanical processes at work behind the ordinary appearance of mental activity. Without entirely accepting this author's view, we will take it as a starting-point for our own investigation because in what follows he reminds us of a writer who has succeeded in producing uncanny effects better than anyone else.

Jentsch writes: 'In telling a story, one of the most successful devices for easily creating uncanny effects is to leave the reader in uncertainty whether a particular figure in the story is a human being or an automaton, and to do it in such a way that his attention is not focused directly upon his uncertainty, so that he may not be led to go into the matter and clear it up immediately. That, as we have said, would quickly dissipate the peculiar emotional effect of the thing. E. T. A. Hoffmann has repeatedly employed this psychological artifice with success in his fantastic narratives.'

This observation, undoubtedly a correct one, refers primarily to the story of 'The Sand-Man' in Hoffmann's *Nachtstücken*,[5] which contains the original of Olympia, the doll that appears in the first act of Offenbach's opera, *Tales of Hoffmann*. But I cannot think – and I hope most readers of the story will agree with me – that the theme of the doll Olympia, who is to all appearances a living being, is by any means the only, or indeed the most important, element that must be held responsible for the quite unparalleled atmosphere of uncanniness evoked by the story. Nor is this atmosphere heightened by the fact that the author himself treats the episode of Olympia with a faint touch of satire and uses it to poke fun at the young man's idealization of his mistress. The main theme of the story is, on the contrary, something different, something which gives it its name, and which is always re-introduced at critical moments: it is the theme of the 'Sand-Man' who tears out children's eyes.

This fantastic tale opens with the childhood recollections of the student Nathaniel. In spite of his present happiness, he cannot banish the memories associated with the mysterious and terrifying death of his beloved father. On certain evenings his mother used to send the children to bed early, warning them that 'the Sand-Man was coming'; and, sure enough, Nathaniel would not fail to hear the heavy tread of a visitor, with whom his father would then be occupied for the evening. When questioned about the Sand-Man, his mother, it is true, denied that such a person existed except as a figure of speech; but his nurse could give him more definite information: 'He's a wicked man who comes when children won't go to bed, and throws handfuls of sand in their eyes so that they jump out of their heads all bleeding. Then he puts the eyes in a sack and carries them off to the half-moon to feed his children. They sit up there in their nest, and their beaks are hooked like owls' beaks, and they use them to peck up naughty boys' and girls' eyes with.'

Although little Nathaniel was sensible and old enough not to credit the figure of the Sand-Man with such gruesome attributes, yet the dread of him became fixed in his heart. He determined to find out what the Sand-Man looked like; and one evening, when the Sand-Man was expected again, he hid in his father's study. He recognized the visitor as lawyer Coppelius, a repulsive person whom the children were frightened of when he occasionally came to a meal; and he now identified this Coppelius with the dreaded Sand-Man. As regards the rest of the scene, Hoffmann already leaves us in doubt whether what we are witnessing is the first delirium of the panic-stricken boy, or a succession of events which are to be regarded in the story as being real. His father and the guest are at work at a brazier with glowing flames. The little eavesdropper hears Coppelius call out: 'Eyes here! Eyes here!' and betrays himself by screaming aloud. Coppelius seizes him and is on the point of dropping bits of red-hot coal from the fire into his eyes, and then of throwing them into the brazier, but his father begs him off and saves his eyes. After this the boy falls into a deep swoon; and a long illness brings his experience to an end. Those who decide in favour of the rationalistic interpretation of the Sand-Man will not fail to recognize in the child's phantasy the persisting influence of his nurse's story. The bits of sand that are to be thrown into the child's eyes turn into bits of red-hot coal from the flames; and in both cases they are intended to make his eyes jump out. In the course of another visit of the Sand-Man's, a year later, his father is killed in his study by an explosion. The lawyer Coppelius disappears from the place without leaving a trace behind.

Nathaniel, now a student, believes that he has recognized this phantom of horror from his childhood in an itinerant optician, an Italian called Giuseppe Coppola, who at his university town, offers him weather-glasses for sale. When Nathaniel refuses, the man goes on: 'Not weather-glasses? not weather-glasses? also got fine eyes, fine eyes!' The student's terror is allayed when he finds that the proffered eyes are only harmless spectacles, and he buys a pocket spy-glass from Coppola. With its aid he looks across into Professor Spalanzani's house opposite and there spies Spalanzani's beautiful, but strangely silent and motionless daughter, Olympia. He soon falls in love with her so violently that, because of her, he quite forgets the clever and sensible girl to whom he is betrothed. But Olympia is an automaton whose clock-work has been made by Spalanzani, and whose eyes have been put in by Coppola, the Sand-Man. The student surprises the two masters quarrelling over their handiwork. The optician carries off the wooden eyeless doll; and the mechanician, Spalanzani, picks up Olympia's bleeding eyes from the ground and throws them at Nathaniel's breast, saying that Coppola had stolen them from the student. Nathaniel succumbs to a fresh attack of madness, and in his delirium his recollection of his father's death is mingled with this new experience. 'Hurry up! hurry up! ring of fire!' he cries. 'Spin about, ring of fire – Hurrah! Hurry up, wooden doll!

lovely wooden doll, spin about—.' He then falls upon the professor, Olympia's 'father', and tries to strangle him.

Rallying from a long and serious illness, Nathaniel seems at last to have recovered. He intends to marry his betrothed, with whom he has become reconciled. One day he and she are walking through the city market-place, over which the high tower of the town hall throws its huge shadow. On the girl's suggestion, they climb the tower, leaving her brother, who is walking with them, down below. From the top, Clara's attention is drawn to a curious object moving along the street. Nathaniel looks at this thing through Coppola's spy-glass, which he finds in his pocket, and falls into a new attack of madness. Shouting 'Spin about, wooden doll!' he tries to throw the girl into the gulf below. Her brother, brought to her side by her cries, rescues her and hastens down with her to safety. On the tower above, the madman rushes round, shrieking 'Ring of fire, spin about!' – and we know the origin of the words. Among the people who begin to gather below there comes forward the figure of the lawyer Coppelius, who has suddenly returned. We may suppose that it was his approach, seen through the spy-glass, which threw Nathaniel into his fit of madness. As the onlookers prepare to go up and overpower the madman, Coppelius laughs and says: 'Wait a bit; he'll come down of himself.' Nathaniel suddenly stands still, catches sight of Coppelius, and with a wild shriek 'Yes! "Fine eyes – fine eyes"!' flings himself over the parapet. While he lies on the paving-stones with a shattered skull the Sand-Man vanishes in the throng.

This short summary leaves no doubt, I think, that the feeling of something uncanny is directly attached to the figure of the Sand-Man, that is, to the idea of being robbed of one's eyes, and that Jentsch's point of an intellectual uncertainty has nothing to do with the effect. Uncertainty whether an object is living or inanimate, which admittedly applied to the doll Olympia, is quite irrelevant in connection with this other, more striking instance of uncanniness. It is true that the writer creates a kind of uncertainty in us in the beginning by not letting us know, no doubt purposely, whether he is taking us into the real world or into a purely fantastic one of his own creation. He has, of course, a right to do either; and if he chooses to stage his action in a world peopled with spirits, demons and ghosts, as Shakespeare does in *Hamlet*, in *Macbeth* and, in a different sense, in *The Tempest* and *A Midsummer Night's Dream*, we must bow to his decision and treat his setting as though it were real for as long as we put ourselves into his hands. But this uncertainty disappears in the course of Hoffmann's story, and we perceive that he intends to make us, too, look through the demon optician's spectacles or spy-glass – perhaps, indeed, that the author in his very own person once peered through such an instrument. For the conclusion of the story makes it quite clear that Coppola the optician really *is* the lawyer Coppelius[6] and also, therefore, the Sand-Man.

There is no question, therefore, of any intellectual uncertainty here: we know now that we are not supposed to be looking on at the products of a madman's imagination, behind which we, with the superiority of rational minds, are able to detect the sober truth; and yet this knowledge does not lessen the impression of uncanniness in the least degree. The theory of intellectual uncertainty is thus incapable of explaining that impression.

We know from psychoanalytic experience, however, that the fear of damaging or losing one's eyes is a terrible one in children. Many adults retain their apprehensiveness in this respect, and no physical injury is so much dreaded by them as an injury to the eye. We are accustomed to say, too, that we will treasure a thing as the apple of our eye. A study of dreams, phantasies and myths has taught us that anxiety about one's eyes, the fear of going blind, is often enough a substitute for the dread of being castrated. The self-blinding of the mythical criminal, Oedipus, was simply a mitigated form of the punishment of castration — the only punishment that was adequate for him by the *lex talionis*. We may try on rationalistic grounds to deny that fears about the eye are derived from the fear of castration, and may argue that it is very natural that so precious an organ as the eye should be guarded by a proportionate dread. Indeed, we might go further and say that the fear of castration itself contains no other significance and no deeper secret than a justifiable dread of this rational kind. But this view does not account adequately for the substitutive relation between the eye and the male organ which is seen to exist in dreams and myths and phantasies; nor can it dispel the impression that the threat of being castrated in especial excites a peculiarly violent and obscure emotion, and that this emotion is what first gives the idea of losing other organs its intense colouring. All further doubts are removed when we learn the details of their 'castration complex' from the analysis of neurotic patients, and realize its immense importance in their mental life.

Moreover, I would not recommend any opponent of the psychoanalytic view to select this particular story of the Sand-Man with which to support his argument that anxiety about the eyes has nothing to do with the castration complex. For why does Hoffmann bring the anxiety about eyes into such intimate connection with the father's death? And why does the Sand-Man always appear as a disturber of love? He separates the unfortunate Nathaniel from his betrothed and from her brother, his best friend; he destroys the second object of his love, Olympia, the lovely doll; and he drives him into suicide at the moment when he has won back his Clara and is about to be happily united to her. Elements in the story like these, and many others, seem arbitrary and meaningless so long as we deny all connection between fears about the eye and castration; but they become intelligible as soon as we replace the Sand-Man by the dreaded father at whose hands castration is expected.[7]

We shall venture, therefore, to refer the uncanny effect of the Sand-Man to the anxiety belonging to the castration complex of childhood. But having reached the idea that we can make an infantile factor such as this responsible for feelings of uncanniness, we are encouraged to see whether we can apply it to other instances of the uncanny. We find in the story of the Sand-Man the other theme on which Jentsch lays stress, of a doll which appears to be alive. Jentsch believes that a particularly favourable condition for awakening uncanny feelings is created when there is intellectual uncertainty whether an object is alive or not, and when an inanimate object becomes too much like an animate one. Now, dolls are of course rather closely connected with childhood life. We remember that in their early games children do not distinguish at all sharply between living and inanimate objects, and that they are especially fond of treating their dolls like live people. In fact, I have occasionally heard a woman patient declare that even at the age of eight she had still been convinced that her dolls would be certain to come to life if she were to look at them in a particular, extremely concentrated, way. So that here, too, it is not difficult to discover a factor from childhood. But, curiously enough, while the Sand-Man story deals with the arousing of an early childhood fear, the idea of a 'living doll' excites no fear at all; children have no fear of their dolls coming to life, they may even desire it. The source of uncanny feelings would not, therefore, be an infantile fear in this case, but rather an infantile wish or even merely an infantile belief. There seems to be a contradiction here; but perhaps it is only a complication, which may be helpful to us later on.

Hoffmann is the unrivalled master of the uncanny in literature. His novel, *Die Elixiere des Teufels [The Devil's Elixir]*, contains a whole mass of themes to which one is tempted to ascribe the uncanny effect of the narrative;[8] but it is too obscure and intricate a story for us to venture upon a summary of it. Towards the end of the book the reader is told the facts, hitherto concealed from him, from which the action springs; with the result, not that he is at last enlightened, but that he falls into a state of complete bewilderment. The author has piled up too much material of the same kind. In consequence one's grasp of the story as a whole suffers, though not the impression it makes. We must content ourselves with selecting those themes of uncanniness which are most prominent, and with seeing whether they too can fairly be traced back to infantile sources. These themes are all concerned with the phenomenon of the 'double', which appears in every shape and in every degree of development. Thus we have characters who are to be considered identical because they look alike. This relation is accentuated by mental processes leaping from one of these characters to another — by what we should call telepathy — so that the one possesses knowledge, feelings and experience in common with the other. Or it is marked by the fact that the subject identifies himself with someone else, so that he is in doubt as to which his self is, or substitutes the extraneous self for his own. In other words, there is a doubling, dividing and interchanging of the self. And finally there is the constant recurrence of the same thing[9] – the repetition of the same features or character-traits or vicissitudes, of the same crimes, or even the same names through several consecutive generations.

The theme of the 'double' has been very thoroughly treated by Otto Rank (1914). He has gone into the connections which the 'double' has with reflections in mirrors, with shadows, with guardian spirits, with the belief in the soul and with the fear of death; but he also lets in a flood of light on the surprising evolution of the idea. For the 'double' was originally an insurance against the destruction of the ego, an 'energetic denial of the power of death', as Rank says; and probably the 'immortal' soul was the first 'double' of the body. This invention of doubling as a preservation against extinction has its counterpart in the language of dreams, which is fond of representing castration by a doubling or a multiplication of a genital symbol.[10] The same desire led the Ancient Egyptians to develop the art of making images of the dead in lasting materials. Such ideas, however, have sprung from the soil of unbounded self-love, from the primary narcissism which dominates the mind of the child and of primitive man. But when this stage has been surmounted, the 'double' reverses its aspect. From having been an assurance of immortality, it becomes the uncanny harbinger of death.

The idea of the 'double' does not necessarily disappear with the passing of primary narcissism, for it can receive fresh meaning from the later stages of the ego's development. A special agency is slowly formed there, which is able to stand over against the rest of the ego, which has the function of observing and criticizing the self and of exercising a censorship within the mind, and which we become aware of as our 'conscience'. In the pathological case of delusions of observation, this mental agency becomes isolated, dissociated from the ego, and discernible to the physician's eye. The fact that an agency of this kind exists, which is able to treat the rest of the ego like an object – the fact, that is, that man is capable of self-observation – renders it possible to invest the old idea of a 'double' with a new meaning and to ascribe a number of things to it – above all, those things which seem to self-criticism to belong to the old surmounted narcissism of earliest times.[11]

But it is not only this latter material, offensive as it is to the criticism of the ego, which may be incorporated in the idea of a double. There are also all the unfulfilled but possible futures to which we still like to cling in phantasy, all the strivings of the ego which adverse external circumstances have crushed, and all our suppressed acts of volition which nourish in us the illusion of free will.[12] [Cf. Freud, 1901b, P.F.L., 5, 316.]

But after having thus considered the *manifest* motivation of the figure of a 'double', we have to admit that none of this helps us to understand the extraordinarily strong feeling of something uncanny that pervades the conception; and our knowledge of pathological mental processes enables us to add that nothing in this more superficial material could account for the urge towards defence which has caused the ego to project that material outward as something foreign to itself. When all is said and done, the quality of uncanniness can only come from the fact of the 'double' being a creation dating back to a very early mental stage, long since surmounted – a stage, incidentally, at which it wore a more friendly aspect. The 'double' has become a thing of terror, just as, after the collapse of their religion, the gods turned into demons. (Heine, 'Die Götter im Exil'.)

The other forms of ego disturbance exploited by Hoffmann can easily be estimated along the same lines as the theme of the 'double'. They are a harking-back to particular phases in the evolution of the self-regarding feeling, a regression to a time when the ego had not yet marked itself off sharply from the external world and from other people. I believe that these factors are partly responsible for the impression of uncanniness, although it is not easy to isolate and determine exactly their share of it.

The factor of the repetition of the same thing will perhaps not appeal to everyone as a source of uncanny feeling. From what I have observed, this phenomenon does undoubtedly, subject to certain conditions and combined with certain circumstances, arouse an uncanny feeling, which, furthermore, recalls the sense of helplessness experienced in some dream-states. As I was walking, one hot summer afternoon, through the deserted streets of a provincial town in Italy which was unknown to me, I found myself in a quarter of whose character I could not long remain in doubt. Nothing but painted women were to be seen at the windows of the small houses, and I hastened to leave the narrow street at the next turning. But after having wandered about for a time without inquiring my way, I suddenly found myself back in the same street, where my presence was now beginning to excite attention. I hurried away once more, only to arrive by another *détour* at the same place yet a third time. Now, however, a feeling overcame me which I can only describe as uncanny, and I was glad enough to find myself back at the piazza I had left a short while before, without any further voyages of discovery. Other situations which have in common with my adventure an unintended recurrence of the same situation, but which differ radically from it in other respects, also result in the same feeling of helplessness and of uncanniness. So, for instance, when, caught in a mist perhaps, one has lost one's way in a mountain forest, every attempt to find the marked or familiar path may bring one back again and again to one and the same spot, which one can identify by some particular landmark. Or one may wander about in a dark, strange room, looking for the door or the electric switch, and collide time after time with the same piece of furniture – though it is true that Mark Twain succeeded by wild exaggeration in turning this latter situation into something irresistibly comic.[13]

If we take another class of things, it is easy to see that there, too, it is only this factor of involuntary repetition which surrounds what would otherwise be innocent enough with an uncanny atmosphere, and forces upon us the idea of something fateful and inescapable when otherwise we should have spoken only of 'chance'. For instance, we naturally attach no importance to the event when we hand in an overcoat and get a cloakroom ticket with the number, let us say, 62; or when we find that our cabin on a ship bears that number. But the impression is altered if two such events, each in itself indifferent, happen close together – if we come across the number 62 several times in a single day, or if we begin to notice that everything which has a number – addresses, hotel rooms, compartments in railway trains – invariably has the same one, or at all events one which contains the same figures. We do feel this to be uncanny. And unless a man is utterly hardened and proof against the lure of superstition, he will be tempted to ascribe a secret meaning to this obstinate recurrence of a number; he will take it, perhaps, as an indication of the span of life allotted to him.[14] Or suppose one is engaged in reading the works of the famous physiologist, Hering,[15] and within the space of a few days receives two letters from two different countries, each from a person called Hering, though one has never before had any dealings with anyone of that name. Not long ago an ingenious scientist (Kammerer, 1919) attempted to reduce coincidences of this kind to certain laws, and so deprive them of their uncanny effect. I will not venture to decide whether he has succeeded or not.

How exactly we can trace back to infantile psychology the uncanny effect of such similar recurrences is a question I can only lightly touch on in these pages; and I must refer the reader instead to another work,[16] already completed, in which this has been gone into in detail, but in a different connection. For it is possible to recognize the dominance in the unconscious mind of a 'compulsion to repeat' proceeding from the instinctual impulses and probably inherent in the very nature of the instincts – a compulsion powerful enough to overrule the pleasure principle, lending to certain aspects of the mind their daemonic character, and still very clearly expressed in the impulses of small children; a compulsion, too, which is responsible for a part of the course taken by the analyses of neurotic patients. All these considerations prepare us for the discovery that whatever reminds us of this inner 'compulsion to repeat' is perceived as uncanny.

Now, however, it is time to turn from these aspects of the matter, which are in any case difficult to judge, and look for some undeniable instances of the uncanny, in the hope that an analysis of them will decide whether our hypothesis is a valid one.

In the story of 'The Ring of Polycrates',[17] the King of Egypt turns away in horror from his host, Polycrates, because he sees that his friend's every wish is at once fulfilled, his every care promptly removed by kindly fate. His host has become 'uncanny' to him. His own explanation, that the too fortunate man has to fear the envy of the gods, seems obscure to us; its meaning is veiled in mythological language. We will therefore turn to another example in a less grandiose setting. In the case history of an obsessional neurotic,[18] I have described how the patient once stayed in a hydropathic establishment and benefited greatly by it. He had the good sense, however, to attribute his improvement not to the therapeutic properties of the water, but to the situation of his room, which immediately adjoined that of a very accommodating nurse. So on his second visit to the establishment he asked for the same room, but was told that it was already occupied by an old gentleman, whereupon he gave vent to his annoyance in the words: 'I wish he may be struck dead for it.' A fortnight later the old gentleman really did have a stroke. My patient thought this an 'uncanny' experience. The impression of uncanniness would have been stronger still if less time had elapsed between his words and the untoward event, or if he had been able to report innumerable similar coincidences. As a matter of fact, he had no difficulty in producing coincidences of this sort; but then not only he but every obsessional neurotic I have observed has been able to relate analogous experiences. They are never surprised at their invariably running up against someone they have just been thinking of, perhaps for the first time for a long while. If they say one day 'I haven't had any news of so-and-so for a long time', they will be sure to get a letter from him the next morning, and an accident or a death will rarely take place without having passed through their mind a little while before. They are in the habit of referring to this state of affairs in the most modest manner, saying that they have 'presentiments' which 'usually' come true.

One of the most uncanny and widespread forms of superstition is the dread of the evil eye, which has been exhaustively studied by the Hamburg oculist Seligmann (1910–11). There never seems to have been any doubt about the source of this dread. Whoever possesses something that is at once valuable and fragile is afraid of other people's envy, in so far as he projects on to them the envy he would have felt in their place. A feeling like this betrays itself by a look[19] even though it is not put into words; and when a man is prominent owing to noticeable, and particularly owing to unattractive, attributes, other people are ready to believe that his envy is rising to a more than usual degree of intensity and that this intensity will convert it into effective action. What is feared is thus a secret intention of doing harm, and certain signs are taken to mean that that intention has the necessary power at its command.

These last examples of the uncanny are to be referred to the principle which I have called 'omnipotence of thoughts', taking the name from an expression used by one of my patients.[20] And now we find ourselves on familiar ground. Our analysis of instances of the uncanny has led us back to the old, animistic conception of the universe. This was characterized by the idea that the world was peopled with the spirits of human beings; by the subject's narcissistic overvaluation of his own mental processes; by the belief in the omnipotence of thoughts and the technique of magic based on that belief; by the attribution to various outside persons and things of carefully graded magical powers, or 'mana'; as well as by all the other creations with the help of which man, in the unrestricted narcissism of that stage of development, strove to fend off the manifest prohibitions of reality. It seems as if each one of us has been through a phase of individual development corresponding to this animistic stage in primitive men, that none of us has passed through it without preserving certain residues and traces of it which are still capable of manifesting themselves, and that everything which now strikes us as 'uncanny' fulfils the condition of touching those residues of animistic mental activity within us and bringing them to expression.[21]

At this point I will put forward two considerations which, I think, contain the gist of this short study. In the first place, if psychoanalytic theory is correct in maintaining that every affect belonging to an emotional impulse, whatever its kind, is transformed, if it is repressed, into anxiety, then among instances of frightening things there must be one class in which the frightening element can be shown to be something repressed which *recurs*. This class of frightening things would then constitute the uncanny; and it must be a matter of indifference whether what is uncanny was itself originally frightening or whether it carried some *other* affect. In the second place, if this is indeed the secret nature of the uncanny, we can understand why linguistic usage has extended *das Heimliche* ['homely'] into its opposite, *das Unheimliche*; for this uncanny is in reality nothing new or alien, but something which is familiar and old-established in the mind and which has become alienated from it only through the process of repression. This reference to the factor of repression enables us, furthermore, to understand Schelling's definition of the uncanny as something which ought to have remained hidden but has come to light.

Notes

1   [The German word, translated throughout this paper by the English 'uncanny', is *'unheimlich'*, literally 'unhomely'. The English term is not, of course, an exact equivalent of the German one.]

2   [In the translation which follows, a few details, mainly giving the sources of the quotations, have been omitted.]

3   [It may be remarked that the English 'canny', in addition to its more usual meaning of 'shrewd', can mean 'pleasant', 'cosy'.]

4   [According to the *Oxford English Dictionary*, a similar ambiguity attaches to the English 'canny', which may mean not only 'cosy' but also 'endowed with occult or magical powers'.]

5   Hoffmann's *Sämtliche Werke*, Grisebach edition, 3. [A translation of 'The Sand-Man' is included in *Eight Tales of Hoffmann*, translated by J. M. Cohen, London, Pan Books, 1952.]

6   Frau Dr Rank has pointed out the association of the name with *'coppella'* = crucible, connecting it with the chemical operations that caused the father's death; and also with *'coppo'* = eye-socket.

7   In fact, Hoffmann's imaginative treatment of his material has not made such wild confusion of its elements that we cannot reconstruct their original arrangement. In the story of Nathaniel's childhood, the figures of his father and Coppelius represent the two opposites into which the father-imago is split by his ambivalence; whereas the one threatens to blind him – that is, to castrate him – the other, the 'good' father, intercedes for his sight. The part of the complex which is most strongly repressed, the death-wish against the 'bad' father, finds expression in the death of the 'good' father, and Coppelius is made answerable for it. This pair of fathers is represented later, in his student days, by Professor Spalanzani and Coppola the optician. The Professor is in himself a member of the father-series, and Coppola is recognized as identical with Coppelius the lawyer. Just as they used before to work together over the secret brazier, so now they have jointly created the doll Olympia; the Professor is even called the father of Olympia. This double occurrence of activity in common betrays them as divisions of the father-imago: both the mechanician and the optician were the father of Nathaniel (and of Olympia as well). In the frightening scene in childhood, Coppelius, after sparing Nathaniel's eyes, had screwed off his arms and legs as an experiment; that is, he had worked on him as a mechanician would on a doll. This singular feature, which seems quite outside the picture of the Sand-Man, introduces a new castration equivalent; but it also points to the inner identity of Coppelius with his

later counterpart, Spalanzani the mechanician, and prepares us for the interpretation of Olympia. This automatic doll can be nothing else than a materialization of Nathaniel's feminine attitude towards his father in his infancy. Her fathers, Spalanzani and Coppola, are, after all, nothing but new editions, reincarnations of Nathaniel's pair of fathers. Spalanzani's otherwise incomprehensible statement that the optician has stolen Nathaniel's eyes (see above), so as to set them in the doll, now becomes significant as supplying evidence of the identity of Olympia and Nathaniel. Olympia is, as it were, a dissociated complex of Nathaniel's which confronts him as a person, and Nathaniel's enslavement to this complex is expressed in his senseless obsessive love for Olympia. We may with justice call love of this kind narcissistic, and we can understand why someone who has fallen victim to it should relinquish the real, external object of his love. The psychological truth of the situation in which the young man, fixated upon his father by his castration complex, becomes incapable of loving a woman, is amply proved by numerous analyses of patients whose story, though less fantastic, is hardly less tragic than that of the student Nathaniel.

Hoffmann was the child of an unhappy marriage. When he was three years old, his father left his small family, and was never united to them again. According to Grisebach, in his biographical introduction to Hoffmann's works, the writer's relation to his father was always a most sensitive subject with him.

8   [Under the rubric 'Varia' in one of the issues of the *Internationale Zeitschrift für Psychoanalyse* for 1919 (5, 308), the year in which the present paper was first published, there appears over the initials 'S.F.' a short note which it is not unreasonable to attribute to Freud. Its insertion here, though strictly speaking irrelevant, may perhaps be excused. The note is headed: 'E. T. A. Hoffmann on the Function of Consciousness' and it proceeds: 'In *Die Elixiere des Teufels* (Part II, p. 210, in Hesse's edition) – a novel rich in masterly descriptions of pathological mental states – Schönfeld comforts the hero, whose consciousness is temporarily disturbed, with the following words: "And what do you get out of it? I mean out of the particular mental function which we call consciousness, and which is nothing but the confounded activity of a damned toll-collector – excise-man – deputy-chief customs officer, who has set up his infamous bureau in our top storey and who exclaims, whenever any goods try to get out: 'Hi! hi! exports are prohibited . . . they must stay here . . . here, in this country. . . .'"']

9   [This phrase seems to be an echo from Nietzsche (e.g. from the last part of *Also Sprach Zarathustra*). In *Beyond the Pleasure Principle* (1920g), *P.F.L.*, II, 292, Freud puts a similar phrase, 'this perpetual recurrence of the same thing', into inverted commas.]

10   [Cf. *The Interpretation of Dreams* (1900a), *P.F.L.*, 4, 474.]

11   I believe that when poets complain that two souls dwell in the human breast, and when popular psychologists talk of the splitting of people's egos, what they are thinking of is this division (in the sphere of ego psychology) between the critical agency and the rest of the ego, and not the antithesis discovered by psychoanalysis between the ego and what is unconscious and repressed. It is true that the distinction between these two antitheses is to some extent effaced by the circumstance that foremost among the things that are rejected by the criticism of the ego are derivatives of the repressed. – [Freud had already discussed this critical agency at length in his paper on narcissism (1914c), *P.F.L.*, II, 89–92, and it was soon to be further expanded into the 'ego ideal' and 'super-ego' in, respectively, *Group Psychology* (1921c), ibid., 12, 161–66, and *The Ego and the Id* (1923b), ibid., II, 367–79.]

12   In Ewers's *Der Student von Prag*, which serves as the starting-point of Rank's study on the 'double', the hero has promised his beloved not to kill his antagonist in a duel. But on his way to the duelling-ground he meets his 'double', who has already killed his rival. [Cf. Rank, 1914.]

13   [Mark Twain, *A Tramp Abroad*, London, 1880, I, 107.]

14   [Freud had himself reached the age of sixty-two a year earlier, in 1918.]

15   [Ewald Hering (1834–1918); cf. *P.F.L.,* II, 211–12, 322.]

16   [This was *Beyond the Pleasure Principle* (1920g), ibid., II, 283–86, 288–94, where the 'compulsion to repeat' is enlarged upon.]

17   [Schiller's poem based on Herodotus.]

18   'Notes upon a Case of Obsessional Neurosis' (1909d) [*P.F.L.*, 9, 113–14].

19   ['The evil eye' in German is *'der böse Blick'*, literally 'the evil look'.]

20   [The obsessional patient referred to just above – the 'Rat Man' (1909d), *P.F.L.*, 9, 113–14 and n. 2.]

21   Cf. my book *Totem and Taboo* (1912–13), Essay III, 'Animism, Magic and the Omnipotence of Thoughts', where the following footnote will be found: 'We appear to attribute an "uncanny" quality to impressions that seek to confirm the omnipotence of thoughts and the animistic mode of thinking in general, after we have reached a stage at which, in our *judgement*, we have abandoned such beliefs.' [*P.F.L.*, 13, 144 n. 1.]

Chapter 25

Jacques Lacan

THE MIRROR STAGE AS FORMATIVE OF THE *I* FUNCTION, AS REVEALED IN PSYCHOANALYTIC EXPERIENCE

As a child's identity is formed, the common understanding is often one of maturing and unifying subjectivity. With Jacques Lacan's "mirror stage", a key process to grasp is that of identity formation occurring via identification with a mirror image, one which is permanently exterior to the child. In other words, this image precedes the social development of the ego as a "fiction" which "will forever remain irreducible for any single individual". The mature human being then, according to Lacan, can never be entirely regulated by any organizing principle, since his or her core identity will always be situated elsewhere. Lacan, famous for re-reading Freud from a structuralist and poststructuralist perspective (as well as founding the *École Freudienne de Paris* in 1964), opens his essay on the Mirror Stage by saying that his psychoanalytic theory is at odds with those people who believe that identity is grounded by the *cogito*, as in René Descartes' famous maxim: "*cogito ergo sum*" or "I think therefore I am". Instead, Lacan believes in the eccentric or permanently displaced subject, playfully rewriting in his essay "The Agency of the Letter in the Unconscious" Descartes' maxim as: "I am not wherever I am the plaything of my thought: I think of what I am where I do not think to think". Lacan observes that young children (age six to eighteen months), at a stage of limited abilities, still appear to be able to recognize their own image in a mirror. In fact this event is more than recognition, it is a moment of "*Aha-Erlebnis*" or sudden insight (the word literally means an "aha-experience"). This insight occurs in a previously formless or shapeless subject—the infant who exists in a pre-linguistic, fragmented form—whereby through self-reflection, he or she gains an idealized, unified image. The pre-mirror stage infant could not dissociate bodily and conceptual experiences; after the mirror stage, she is a separate being, in a world full of separate objects such as the most important one of all, her mother. Lacan calls this process an "identification", or, the human child transformed through seeing an "imago" (literally a "likeness", but in this case meaning "an idealized image"). Whatever happens after the mirror stage, such as the transition from a pre-linguistic Imaginary realm into that of language and law—the Symbolic Order—Lacan argues that the subject will always remain split, as her new identity will forever be haunted by, but not quite coincide with her idealized image. So the imago and the ego may get closer and closer together, but their intersection point is off in infinity: they "asymptotic-ally approach" one another. This idealized image is called a "mirage" and a gestalt or "shape"/"pattern", which both brings the subject into being, and forever alienates her. Lacan suggests that this is why human beings are haunted by their doubles, either in dreams or other fantasies. Lacan offers some physiological evidence from the animal kingdom, although he also suggests that such evidence is relatively worthless! Instead, he moves on to suggest that his theory is about the human being forging a relationship between herself and reality (her *Innenwelt*, inner world, and *Umwelt*, environment). Human beings, in others words, are "dialectical", not centred by the *cogito*, always subject to the forces of the *imago* identification, and then by societal desires and demands. The fragmented subject comes back to haunt us in dreams and in psychological illnesses and breakdowns, and no matter how successfully the subject has negotiated key stages in life, such as the Oedipus or Jocasta Complex, he or she will always misrecognize his or her core being.

THE CONCEPTION OF THE MIRROR STAGE I introduced at our last congress thirteen years ago, having since been more or less adopted by the French group, seems worth bringing to your attention once again—especially today, given the light it sheds on the *I* function in the experience psychoanalysis provides us of it. It should be noted that this experience sets us at odds with any philosophy directly stemming from the *cogito*.

Some of you may recall the behavioral characteristic I begin with that is explained by a fact of comparative psychology: the human child, at an age when he is for a short while, but for a while nevertheless, outdone by the chimpanzee in instrumental intelligence, can already recognize his own image as such in a mirror. This recognition is indicated by the illuminative mimicry of the *Aha-Erlebnis,* which Köhler considers to express situational apperception, an essential moment in the act of intelligence.

Indeed, this act, far from exhausting itself, as in the case of a monkey, in eventually acquired control over the uselessness of the image, immediately gives rise in a child to a series of gestures in which he playfully experiences the relationship between the movements made in the image and the reflected environment, and between this virtual complex and the reality it duplicates—namely, the child's own body, and the persons and even things around him.

This event can take place, as we know from Baldwin's work, from the age of six months on; its repetition has often given me pause to reflect upon the striking spectacle of a nursling in front of a mirror who has not yet mastered walking, or even standing, but who—though held tightly by some prop, human or artificial (what, in France, we call a *trotte-bébé* [a sort of walker])—overcomes, in a flutter of jubilant activity, the constraints of his prop in order to adopt a slightly leaning-forward position and take in an instantaneous view of the image in order to fix it in his mind.

In my view, this activity has a specific meaning up to the age of eighteen months, and reveals both a libidinal dynamism that has hitherto remained problematic and an ontological structure of the human world that fits in with my reflections on paranoiac knowledge.

It suffices to understand the mirror stage in this context *as an identification,* in the full sense analysis gives to the term: namely, the transformation that takes place in the subject when he assumes [*assume*] an image—an image that is seemingly predestined to have an effect at this phase, as witnessed by the use in analytic theory of antiquity's term, "imago."

The jubilant assumption [*assomption*] of his specular image by the kind of being—still trapped in his motor impotence and nursling dependence—the little man is at the *infans* stage thus seems to me to manifest in an exemplary situation the symbolic matrix in which the *I* is precipitated in a primordial form, prior to being objectified in the dialectic of identification with the other, and before language restores to it, in the universal, its function as subject.

This form would, moreover, have to be called the "ideal-I"[1]—if we wanted to translate it into a familiar register—in the sense that it will also be the rootstock of secondary identifications, this latter term subsuming the libidinal normalization functions. But the important point is that this form situates the agency known as the ego, prior to its social determination, in a fictional direction that will forever remain irreducible for any single individual or, rather, that will only asymptotically approach the subject's becoming, no matter how successful the dialectical syntheses by which he must resolve, as *I*, his discordance with his own reality.

For the total form of his body, by which the subject anticipates the maturation of his power in a mirage, is given to him only as a gestalt, that is, in an exteriority in which, to be sure, this form is more constitutive than constituted, but in which, above all, it appears to him as the contour of his stature that freezes it and in a symmetry that reverses it, in opposition to the turbulent movements with which the subject feels he animates it. Through these two aspects of its appearance, this gestalt—whose power [*prégnance*] should be considered linked to the species, though its motor style is as yet unrecognizable—symbolizes the *I*'s mental permanence, at the same time as it prefigures its alienating destination. This gestalt is also replete with the correspondences that unite the *I* with the statue onto which man projects himself, the phantoms that dominate him, and the automaton with which the world of his own making tends to achieve fruition in an ambiguous relation.

Indeed, for imagos—whose veiled faces we analysts see emerge in our daily experience and in the penumbra of symbolic effectiveness[2]—the specular image seems to be the threshold of the visible world, if we take into account the mirrored disposition of the *imago of one's own body* in hallucinations and dreams, whether it involves one's individual features, or even one's infirmities or object projections; or if we take note of the role of the mirror apparatus in the appearance of *doubles,* in which psychical realities manifest themselves that are, moreover, heterogeneous.

The fact that a gestalt may have formative effects on an organism is attested to by a biological experiment that is so far removed from the idea of psychical causality that it cannot bring itself to formulate itself in such terms. The experiment nevertheless acknowledges that it is a necessary condition for the maturation of the female pigeon's gonad that the pigeon see another member of its species, regardless of its sex; this condition is so utterly sufficient that the same effect may be obtained by merely placing a mirror's reflective field near the individual. Similarly, in the case of the migratory locust, the shift within a family line from the solitary to the gregarious form can be brought about by exposing an individual, at a certain stage of its development, to the exclusively visual action of an image akin to its own, provided the movements of this image sufficiently resemble those characteristic of its species. Such facts fall within a realm of homeomorphic identification that is itself subsumed within the question of the meaning of beauty as formative and erogenous.

But mimetic facts, understood as heteromorphic identification, are of just as much interest to us insofar as they raise the question of the signification of space for living organisms—psychological concepts hardly seeming less appropriate for shedding light here than the ridiculous attempts made to reduce these facts to the supposedly supreme law of adaptation. We need but recall how Roger Caillois (still young and fresh from his break with the sociological school at which he trained) illuminated the subject when, with the term "legendary psychasthenia," he subsumed morphological mimicry within the derealizing effect of an obsession with space.

As I myself have shown, human knowledge is more independent than animal knowledge from the force field of desire because of the social dialectic that structures human knowledge as paranoiac; but what limits it is the "scant reality" surrealistic unsatisfaction denounces therein. These reflections lead me to recognize in the spatial capture manifested by the mirror stage, the effect in man, even prior to this social dialectic, of an organic inadequacy of his natural reality—assuming we can give some meaning to the word "nature."

The function of the mirror stage thus turns out, in my view, to be a particular case of the function of imagos, which is to establish a relationship between an organism and its reality—or, as they say, between the *Innenwelt* and the *Umwelt*.

In man, however, this relationship to nature is altered by a certain dehiscence at the very heart of the organism, a primordial Discord betrayed by the signs of malaise and motor uncoordination of the neonatal months. The objective notions of the anatomical incompleteness of the pyramidal tracts and of certain humoral residues of the maternal organism in the newborn confirm my view that we find in man a veritable *specific prematurity of birth*.

Let us note in passing that this fact is recognized as such by embryologists, under the heading "fetalization," as determining the superiority of the so-called higher centers of the central nervous system, and especially of the cerebral cortex which psychosurgical operations will lead us to regard as the intra-organic mirror.

This development is experienced as a temporal dialectic that decisively projects the individual's formation into history: the mirror stage is a drama whose internal pressure pushes precipitously from insufficiency to anticipation—and, for the subject caught up in the lure of spatial identification, turns out fantasies that proceed from a fragmented image of the body to what I will call an "orthopedic" form of its totality—and to the finally donned armor of an alienating identity that will mark his entire mental development with its rigid structure. Thus, the shattering of the *Innenwelt* to *Umwelt* circle gives rise to an inexhaustible squaring of the ego's audits.

This fragmented body—another expression I have gotten accepted into the French school's system of theoretical references—is regularly manifested in dreams when the movement of an analysis reaches a certain level of aggressive disintegration of the individual. It then appears in the form of disconnected limbs or of organs exoscopically represented, growing wings and taking up arms for internal persecutions that the visionary Hieronymus Bosch fixed for all time in painting, in their ascent in the fifteenth century to the imaginary zenith of modern man. But this form turns out to be tangible even at the organic level, in the lines of "fragilization" that define the hysteric's fantasmatic anatomy, which is manifested in schizoid and spasmodic symptoms.

Correlatively, the *I* formation is symbolized in dreams by a fortified camp, or even a stadium—distributing, between the arena within its walls and its outer border of gravel-pits and marshes, two opposed fields of battle where the subject bogs down in his quest for the proud, remote inner castle whose form (sometimes juxtaposed in the same scenario) strikingly symbolizes the id. Similarly, though here in the mental sphere, we find fortified structures constructed, the metaphors for which arise spontaneously, as if deriving from the subject's very symptoms, to designate the mechanisms of obsessive neurosis: inversion, isolation, reduplication, undoing what has been done, and displacement.

But were I to build on these subjective data alone—were I to so much as free them from the experiential condition that makes me view them as based on a language technique—my theoretical efforts would remain exposed to the charge of lapsing into the unthinkable, that of an absolute subject. This is why I have sought, in the present hypothesis grounded in a confluence of objective data, a *method of symbolic reduction* as my guiding grid.

It establishes a genetic order in *ego defenses,* in accordance with the wish formulated by Anna Freud in the first part of her major book, and situates (as against a frequently expressed prejudice) hysterical repression and its returns at a more archaic stage than obsessive inversion and its isolating processes, situating the latter as prior to the paranoiac alienation that dates back to the time at which the specular *I* turns into the social *I*.

This moment at which the mirror stage comes to an end inaugurates, through identification with the imago of one's semblable and the drama of primordial jealousy (so well brought out by the Charlotte Bühler school in cases of transitivism in children), the dialectic that will henceforth link the *I* to socially elaborated situations.

It is this moment that decisively tips the whole of human knowledge [*savoir*] into being mediated by the other's desire, constitutes its objects in an abstract equivalence due to competition from other people, and turns the *I* into an apparatus to which every instinctual pressure constitutes a danger, even if it corresponds to a natural maturation process. The very normalization of this maturation is henceforth dependent in man on cultural intervention, as is exemplified by the fact that sexual object choice is dependent upon the Oedipus complex.

In light of my conception, the term "primary narcissism," by which analytic doctrine designates the libidinal investment characteristic of this moment, reveals in those who invented it a profound awareness of semantic latencies. But it also sheds light on the dynamic opposition between this libido and sexual libido, an opposition they tried to define when they invoked destructive and even death instincts in order to explain the obvious relationship between narcissistic libido and the alienating *I* function, and the aggressiveness deriving therefrom in all relations with others, even in relations involving aid of the most good-Samaritan variety.

The fact is that they encountered that existential negativity whose reality is so vigorously proclaimed by the contemporary philosophy of being and nothingness.

Unfortunately, this philosophy grasps that negativity only within the limits of a self-sufficiency of consciousness, which, being one of its premises, ties the illusion of autonomy in which it puts its faith to the ego's constitutive misrecognitions. While it draws considerably on borrowings from psychoanalytic experience, this intellectual exercise culminates in the pretense of grounding an existential psychoanalysis.

At the end of a society's historical enterprise to no longer recognize that it has any but a utilitarian function, and given the individual's anxiety faced with the concentration-camp form of the social link whose appearance seems to crown this effort, existentialism can be judged on the basis of the justifications it provides for the subjective impasses that do, indeed, result therefrom: a freedom that is never so authentically affirmed as when it is within the walls of a prison; a demand for commitment that expresses the inability of pure consciousness to overcome any situation; a voyeuristic-sadistic idealization of sexual relationships; a personality that achieves self-realization only in suicide; and a consciousness of the other that can only be satisfied by Hegelian murder.

These notions are opposed by the whole of analytic experience, insofar as it teaches us not to regard the ego as centered on the *perception-consciousness system* or as organized by the "reality principle"—the expression of a scientific bias most hostile to the dialectic of knowledge—but, rather, to take as our point of departure the *function of misrecognition* that characterizes the ego in all the defensive structures so forcefully articulated by Anna Freud. For, while *Verneinung* [negation] represents the blatant form of that function, its effects remain largely latent as long as they are not illuminated by some reflected light at the level of fate where the id manifests itself.

The inertia characteristic of the *I* formations can thus be understood as providing the broadest definition of neurosis, just as the subject's capture by his situation gives us the most general formulation of madness—the kind found within the asylum walls as well as the kind that deafens the world with its sound and fury.

The sufferings of neurosis and psychosis provide us schooling in the passions of the soul, just as the balance arm of the psychoanalytic scales—when we calculate the angle of its threat to entire communities—provides us with an amortization rate for the passions of the city.

At this intersection of nature and culture, so obstinately scrutinized by the anthropology of our times, psychoanalysis alone recognizes the knot of imaginary servitude that love must always untie anew or sever.

For such a task we can find no promise in altruistic feeling, we who lay bare the aggressiveness that underlies the activities of the philanthropist, the idealist, the pedagogue, and even the reformer.

In the subject to subject recourse we preserve, psychoanalysis can accompany the patient to the ecstatic limit of the *"Thou art that"* where the cipher of his mortal destiny is revealed to him, but it is not in our sole power as practitioners to bring him to the point where the true journey begins.

Notes

1   I have let stand the peculiar translation I adopted in this article for Freud's *Ideal Ich* [*je-idéal*], without further comment except to say that I have not maintained it since.

2   See Claude Lévi-Strauss' essay, entitled "L'efficacité symbolique," in *Revue de l'histoire des religions* CXXXV, 1 (1949): 5–27.

Chapter 26

Shoshana Felman

JACQUES LACAN

Madness and the risks of theory
(the uses of misprision)

Cleverly modelling the rhetorical playfulness of Jacques Lacan's highly theoretical and creative psychoanalytical writing style, Shoshana Felman also introduces a new translation of a key term that Lacan uses, *méprise*, which in English she calls "misprision". In French, *méprise* means an error, mistake, or misunderstanding. Freud had famously observed that we can gain access to the unconscious through mistakes, such as slips-of-the-tongue, when we accidentally reveal what we desire or are secretly thinking about. Lacan takes over this approach, but Felman acutely observes that *méprise* also involves the power relations between the analyst and the patient. The word misprision literally means a failure or deliberate attempt to hide a crime against the authorities. It is no coincidence that Felman should be guiding the reader through the complexities of translation, theory and psychoanalysis, since it was through her edited collection of essays in *Yale French Studies* (1977) published as *Literature and Psychoanalysis, The Question of Reading: Otherwise* (1982), that major North American theorists came together to engage with Lacanian thought. Lacanian psychoanalysis is all about the law of the father (the authority par excellence) and the undermining of that law via mechanisms of bodily desire and powerful neuroses. The complicated opening of Felman's essay is a playful exploration of Lacan's insight that the unconscious is structured like a language, and from a poststructuralist perspective, this means that the psychoanalytical subject—the human being—is fictional in the sense of *accessing* subjectivity via language, and *producing* axioms (a universal or functional maxim or truth) through logic and other forms of language. Felman introduces Lacan's three co-constitutive realms of the Imaginary (pre-linguistic, bodily, image-based), the Symbolic (linguistic, cultural, law), and the Real (that area that cannot be encompassed by the Imaginary or the Symbolic, but nonetheless is part of our identities). Felman notes that psychoanalytical decoding of the Symbolic is blocked by the fictional image-identifications of the Imaginary (see Chapter 25). But this means that psychoanalytical knowledge is not really directly accessible, and that it is contradictory, not just because it can only be found in the breakdown of psychic order, the slips-of-the-tongue, dreams and fantasies, but because the concept of knowledge is itself a linguistic construct. The anchor of the ultimate knowing subjects— metaphysics, the cogito, God, and so on—are thus rejected by Lacan, and regarded as delusional fantasies or myth. The "logic" of psychoanalysis (the "grammar" of the unconscious, or "continuity"), then, is one of not just seeking errors, but engaging in misprision, through rhetorical strategies which mimic "the rhetoric of the unconscious" or its "discontinuity". These two combine to produce a deliberately contradictory "grammar of rhetoric". This strange-sounding discourse is not a metalanguage, i.e., a language rising above and commenting upon some inferior or lower mode of expression; instead, it is a language that desires to speak the psyche itself. It is an enthusiastic language, or, an enthusiasm (a passion, a sudden desire), that passes in time, to reveal that the psychoanalytic grammar of rhetoric, like the unconscious, was always subject to "Spaltung" (splitting or division). It was also always subject to "transference", that is to say, redirecting one's psychic energies onto another person or object, which is what the patient usually does when undergoing analysis. Felman notes then that Lacan's pedagogy is one of ambiguity and blindness, yet paradoxically, as with poetry, this leads to great insight.

Meaning and knowledge

"The truth pursued by science," writes Georges Bataille, "is true only on condition that it be devoid of meaning, and nothing can have meaning except insofar as it is fiction."[1] This proposition could define at once the doctrine and the difficulty of psychoanalysis, as a *practice*—and a *science*—of the *fiction* of the subject. "What is truth, if not a complaint?" says Lacan. Now, "it is not the meaning of the complaint that is important, but whatever might be found beyond that meaning, that might be definable as real." The "real," here, refers specifically to what is not dependent upon the idea the subject has of it: "that which is not affected by my thinking about it."[2] "There is no other truth," Lacan affirms, "than mathematicized truth, that is, *written* truth"; truth, in other words, "can hinge only on axioms: truth proceeds only from what has no meaning."[3] There is truth only where there is no meaning.

Does psychoanalysis, then, aspire to meaning—or to truth? What is the meaning *of* psychoanalysis? This question, whose urgency has become evident in the current field of theory (but we know—from psychoanalysis—that evidence is, precisely, that which is *least seen*), this now unavoidable question of *the meaning of psychoanalysis,* is in fact a contradiction in terms, since "meaning" is forever but a fiction and since it is psychoanalysis itself which has taught us that. But contradiction, as we know, is the mode of functioning par excellence of the unconscious, and consequently, also of the logic of psychoanalysis. To reckon with psychoanalysis is to reckon with contradiction, including its disequilibrium, without reducing it to the specular illusion of symmetry or of a dialectical synthesis. If, indeed, the specular illusion, the "Imaginary," to use the Lacanian term, is itself a constitutive principle of *meaning,* being precisely "that which *blocks* the decoding of the *Symbolic*," which in turn acts as a vehicle for the Real only by being "always encoded," then "the Imaginary is a dimension [*dit-mension,* a speech-dimension] as important as the others."[4] The Imaginary is an irreducible dimension because within language, the "sememe"—the semantic unit—is always occupied by the body: it makes up for the fact that there is nothing else to lead the body toward the Other. There is no *natural* relationship: the only relationship with the Other is by "the intermediary of what *makes sense* in language."[5] We must not, then, resolve the contradiction, but resolve to accept it: we must articulate the question of the *meaning* of psychoanalysis on the basis of its own contradiction: we must consider this contradiction not as a contingent fact, but as the condition that makes possible the very question of psychoanalysis: of psychoanalysis *as a question*. Psychoanalysis introduces into the field of theory nothing less than the necessity of a new kind of articulation of its own question: the subversive urgency of psychoanalysis, its momentousness for culture, lies in the need it has brought out and in the henceforth irreversible search it has inaugurated for *a new status of discourse.*

If, by its most radical dimension, psychoanalysis subverts the very status of meaning, even while it is thereby constrained to call itself in question and to subvert *its own* meaning, it does so because, as Lacan says, "meaning *knows itself*": meaning is, above all else, that which is present to itself; it is therefore a form of knowledge—knowledge of self—of consciousness. Now, if Freud's discovery of the unconscious "makes sense" (we see here again the pervasive problem of meaning that language cannot eliminate, the problem of the apprehension by consciousness of the unconscious which escapes it), this "id" (this "it") which speaks yields a *language* which *knows,* but without any subject being able to assume such a knowledge or being able to know that he/she knows. Lacan makes it clear that we are in no way dealing with the myth of "non-knowledge" [*non-savoir*] that a superficial avant-garde used to its advantage: for not only is it not *sufficient* not to know; the very ability not to know is not granted to us,[6] and cannot thus be taken for granted. What we are dealing with is a knowledge that is, rather, indestructible; *a knowledge which does not allow for knowing that one knows;*[7] a knowledge, therefore, that is not supported by *meaning* which, by definition, *knows itself.* The subject can get a hold on this unconscious knowledge only by the intermediary of his *mistakes*—the effects of non-sense his speech registers: in dreams, slips of the tongue, or jokes.

"A question suddenly arises (. . .): in the case of the knowledge yielded solely by the subject's mistake, what kind of subject could ever be in a position to know it in advance?"[8] The "subject who is presumed to know," that basic myth of Western culture, of the University, and of philosophic discourse, can only be "God Himself": a reflection in which the "knowledge" of consciousness contemplates itself, a phantom of potency produced by the narcissistic, self-inflating spell of the mirror. "Here he is, the God of the philosophers, dislodged from his latency in every theory. *Theoria,* might that not be the place in the world for the theology?"[9] The "subject presumed to know" lives in delusions and fantasies. By subverting this subject, psychoanalysis has radicalized a theory of non-transparency, a theory of what Baudelaire calls "the universal misunderstanding," and Proust "that perpetual error that we call, precisely, life." But within this theory, the position of psycho-analysis is itself problematic since it arises from the contradiction which determines its own discourse, namely: How can one construct a *theory* of the mistake essential to the very subject of theory as such? And if error is universal, how is one to escape error oneself? To what sort of listening or understanding can one appeal in a theory of radical *mis-understanding*? Lacan is fully aware of the untenable position he has nevertheless taken and taken on with an unparalleled intensity of effort and desire: "Retain at least what this text, which I have tossed out in your direction, bears witness to: my enterprise does not go beyond the act in which it is caught, and therefore, its only chance lies in its error—in its misprision [*elle n'a de chance que de sa méprise*]."[10] To my mind, the staggering originality of Lacan's work and discourse resides precisely in this untenable theoretical position. I would like, then, to attempt here an (overtly) brief meditation on this *méprise*—this misprision[11]—and on the significance of Lacan's gesture of giving it its chance.

Grammar and rhetoric

Misprision, for Lacan, is of course an outgrowth of "the trickiness of the unconscious," which in language "is revealed by the rhetorical overload Freud shows it utilizes to make its argument":[12] the symptom functions like a metaphor, desire like a metonymy; the narcissistic mechanisms of defense and resistance employ all kinds of "tropes" and "figures of speech"— periphrasis, ellipsis, denial, digression, irony, litotes, etc.[13] A theory of misprision will thus be a theory of the *rhetoric* of the unconscious: "On the basis of the manifestations of the unconscious with which I deal as an analyst, I came to develop a theory of the effects of the signifier through which I rejoin the preoccupations of rhetoric."[14] Alongside this inquiry into rhetoric, there is in Lacan's work a second project, focusing on *grammar:* "Such are the structural conditions which determine—as *grammar*—the system of encroachments constitutive of the signifier."[15] The accomplishment of this double project should thus establish a *grammar of rhetoric.*

The logical coherence of such a project may seem self-evident. However, for a logician like Charles Sanders Peirce, the logical affiliation between rhetoric and grammar cannot be taken for granted: in fact, Peirce makes a distinction between "pure rhetoric" and "pure grammar." What he calls "pure rhetoric" is the well-known process by which one sign engenders another: a system of reference from sign to sign in which meaning is but another sign, requiring for its establishment the intervention of a *third* element which Peirce calls the *interpretant.* "Pure grammar," on the other hand, postulates the possibility of a continuous, binary relationship between sign and meaning not requiring the intervention of a third element. In general, we think of grammar as a logical system *par excellence* and, as such, identical to itself, universal, and generative, that is, inscribing the possibility of infinite combinations and transformations stemming from a *single, unified model* without the intervention of another model that would interfere with or subvert the first.[16] By contrast, rhetoric can be perceived only through a *discontinuity* that subverts or, at the very least, contradicts the logical *continuity* of the grammatical model. Rhetoric, to borrow out of context a Lacanian expression, always has an "*incongruous dimension* which analysts have not yet entirely given up because of their justified feeling that their conformism is of value only on the basis of that dimension."[17]

But if the grammatical model of continuity and the rhetorical model of discontinuity are not congruent, how are we to understand, as a whole, the Lacanian project of establishing a *grammar of rhetoric?* It would seem that Lacan's scientific project is to reduce the rhetorical mystifications of the unconscious to the rigor of a grammar. The unconscious as an operation and psychoanalysis as a science would, as a result, be modeled on two different epistemologies and would be distinguished from each other just as grammar is distinguished from rhetoric. "If the symptom is a metaphor, it is not a metaphor to say so," Lacan affirms.[18] To "grammaticalize" rhetoric would then be to formalize it, to abstract a concept from it, to state a theory of rhetoric in a language itself rid of rhetoric: it would be to make the uttering of a statement coincide perfectly with what is stated, concerning, but also contradicting, rhetoric itself which is precisely "the law by which the utterance of a statement can never be reduced to the statement itself of whatever discourse."[19] Man pursues his dream, Lacan says elsewhere, "and as he does, it sometimes happens that he wishes to stop dreaming."[20] By the same token, Lacan himself, at times, dreams of dreaming no more: "If all that is articulated in sleep only enters into analysis through its narration, doesn't this presuppose that the structure of narration does not succumb to sleep?"[21] The task Lacan assigns himself is to break away from sleep so as to talk about it, to break away from the very mechanisms of the unconscious in order to *say the unconscious itself.*

Is this project feasible? Lacan is the first to recognize and to affirm that one cannot *get out of* the unconscious; therefore, it is not possible to say the unconscious itself, it is not possible to free oneself from its fundamental function as deception in order to enunciate, without deceiving oneself, the absolute law of deception: "We don't even know if the unconscious has a being in itself, and (. . .) it is because one could not say *that's it* that it was named the 'it' [*id*]. In fact, one could only say of the unconscious, *that's not it,* or rather, *that's it,* but *not for real.*"[22] Lacan formulates the same logical principle when he states "that no metalanguage can be spoken, or, more aphoristically, that there is no Other of the Other."[23] What, however, is a *grammar* (a formalized grammar) if not the epitome of metalanguage? Grammar is thus— and Lacan knows it—one more impossible desire: the desire to establish a norm, a rule of *correctness,* to avoid precisely the misprision inherent in the enterprise, to be for once a *non-dupe.* But who knows better than Lacan that "non-dupes err"?[24] Lacan's writing thus articulates the very torment which inhabits logic. And the chances taken by Lacan's text—what gives it a chance and what makes its chance ours—is the spark struck up in language by the inner tension of a discourse struggling with itself, struggling with its double, contradictory desire: the desire for grammar and its counterpart, the desire for rhetoric. It is precisely through this contradiction that Lacan's discourse rejoins the *Real:* "the real," says Lacan, "is the *impossible.*"

A shade of enthusiasm

Lacan's language registers this contradictory desire both as a complication and as a simplification: on the one hand, as the ironic and sophisticated complication of a theory of misprision which excepts—in all conscience—neither its author nor its recipients; and on the other hand, as the affective simplification of the pathos of failure which prevades that discourse,[25] a pathos countered by the intensity of Lacan's affirmations and by the urgency of his enthusiasm. "The originality we are allowed," says Lacan, "is limited to the scrap of enthusiasm we have brought (. . .) to what Freud was able to name."[26] The urgency of the enthusiasm in Lacan's text serves to wrest affirmation from uncertainty, from the doubt occasioned by its own contradictions and complications. It manifests, in the very midst of logic, the function of desire,[27] that "function of haste"[28] necessary to produce an affirmation within a plural logic. Each time the urgency passes, the enthusiasm inevitably subsides again into a sense of failure, in recognition of its own inescapable naïveté, of the blindness of its own intoxication. Lacan takes stock—within his desire for *grammar*—of his own unconscious *rhetoric.* "A shade of enthusiasm is the surest trace to leave behind in a writing to make it dated—in the worst sense of the word." That is the way Lacan introduces nothing less than his famous Rome Report, "The Function and Field of Speech and Language in Psychoanalysis": "We wish to discuss," writes Lacan, "the subject put in question by this report, since putting the subject here in its place, at the place in which we ourselves have not failed to illustrate it, is but to do justice to the place where it lies in wait for us."[29] The movement of Lacan's text thus obeys the principle outlined by Bachelard: "Let us begin by admiring. Later, we shall see whether it will be necessary, through criticism or reduction, to organize our disappointment."[30]

"A shade of enthusiasm" is thus the surest trace to leave behind in a writing to make it dated. But what does "to make dated" mean here? When we are dealing with Lacan, it means, first of all, to mark a memorable date, to introduce a new articulation into cultural discourse, a "renewal of the alliance with Freud's discovery."[31] But since this innovation, this "renewal of the alliance" rallies specifically to an elusive structure, consisting in the linguistic articulation of the very mechanisms of repression through which truth escapes, modernity can be attained only within a radical dimension of loss. Modernity is precisely what gets lost: what gets lost in and through the very welling up of the enthusiasm of having discovered it. Enthusiasm thus becomes the hallmark of the "missed chance," that peculiar movement through which we move away from that toward which we want to go. "If it is true that psychoanalysis rests on a fundamental conflict, on an initial radical drama as far as everything that might be included under the heading psychical is concerned, the innovation to which I have referred (. . .) makes no claim to a position of exhaustiveness with respect to the unconscious, since it is, itself, an intervention in the conflict (. . .). This indicates that the cause of the unconscious (. . .) must be conceived as, fundamentally, a lost cause. And it is the only chance one has of winning it."[32]

This radical dimension of loss is, therefore, nothing other than the loss of the security of a metalanguage, the loss of a "claim to a position of exhaustiveness" which would precisely be the claim of *grammar:* we are faced, once again, with the inescapable dimension of *rhetoric,* that "stumbling block" which forces discourse to discover that it can only define rhetoric rhetorically, by participating in it, i.e., by stumbling, by elaborating not a grammar of rhetoric but a *rhetoric of rhetoric:* "Stumbling, faltering, splitting. In a spoken or written sentence something slips (. . .). It's there that something else is asking to be realized— something which appears as intentional, of course, but partaking of *a strange temporality.*"[33] This "strange temporality" is the lack of a present, the non self-presence characteristic of the rhetorical mode. It is also in this sense that the rhetoric of desire and enthusiasm is bound to be *dated*: for this rhetoric is not contemporaneous with its own statement. "There is no present," writes Mallarmé, "no—a present does not exist. (. . .) Ill-informed is he who would proclaim himself his own contemporary."[34]

To say that enthusiasm makes a text "dated" is to say that the enthusiasm has had a future that has come to point to it as past; that, from its own enthusiasm, the text has gleaned both more and less than it had expected; that urgency—both emotional and logical—has inscribed in language a vanishing point where the writing becomes *self-transgressive*. It is to say that the text—as it must—has organized our disappointment, has disappointed its own enthusiasm, subverted its own fantasy, and recanted the authority of its own rhetoric.

Inescapably, enthusiasm is what passes; it is, therefore, *nothing:* nothing, in any case, other than what is doomed—like us—to pass. "It is here that is inscribed that final *Spaltung* by which the subject articulates himself in the Logos, and on which Freud was beginning to write, giving us, at the ultimate point of a work that has the dimensions of being, the solution of the 'infinite' analysis, when his death applied to it the word Nothing."[35]

> Nothing, this foam, virgin verse
> Denoting only its cut.[36]

"A shade [*un rien*] of enthusiasm" has a good chance of amounting to the *nothingness* [*rien*] of enthusiasm. But isn't that the source, precisely, both of the misprision and of the chance inherent in psychoanalytic *transference?* "At that turning point where the subject experiences the collapse of the assurance provided him by that fantasy whereby each individual fashions his view of the Real, what becomes evident is that the hold of desire is *nothing* but the hold of an un-being."[37]

In the "transference of intensity"[38] constitutive of desire's repetitions and structuring not just psychoanalytic treatment but also "that perpetual error that we call, precisely, life," what seeks realization is a kind of metaphoric operation, a desire for analogy—for metaphor. But the result is, each time, the abortion of the specular analogy, the failure of the metaphor to attain and name its proper meaning. "If the psychoanalyst cannot respond to the demand, it is only because to respond to it would of necessity be to disappoint it, since what is demanded is, in any case, Something-Else; and *that is precisely what one must come to understand.*"[39] While the analyst, in the transferential operation, occupies the precise place of the "nothing" of enthusiasm, the place of the primordial partial object—*l'objet petit a*—which materalizes the non-being of desire, the end point of analysis—the naming of the Nothing—teaches the subject that the blind metaphor of his destiny is deprived of any proper meaning since all it can name is a metonymy (*l'objet petit a*). That is to say that the psychoanalyst, in playing the role of the non-proper (*non-propre*) (which the analysand deceives himself into reading as a proper name [*nom propre*]), occupies the radically other position of the pre-eminently rhetorical; and that the therapeutic goal is then to deconstruct the grammatical illusion of identity—of the proper—in order to reconcile the subject to his own rhetoric.

Notes

1   G. Bataille, "L'Apprenti Sorcier," *Oeuvres complètes* (Paris: Gallimard, 1973), I, 526.
2   "Les Non-dupes errent" (seminari), April 23, 1974 (unpublished).
3   *Ibid.*, February II, 1973.
4   *Ibid.*, November 13, 1973.
5   *Ibid.*, June II, 1974.
6   *Ibid.*, April 23, 1974.
7   *Ibid.*, February 2, 1974.
8   "La Méprise du sujet supposé savoir," *Scilicet,* no. I (1968), 38.
9   *Ibid.*, p. 39.
10 *Ibid.*, p. 41.
11 "A misunderstanding, a mistake (arch.)" (*Oxford English Dictionary*). This is the closest, and the only perfectly accurate, English equivalent to Lacan's word, *méprise.*
12 "La Méprise du sujet supposé savoir," p. 32.
13 "The Agency of the Letter in the Unconscious," *Ecrits: A Selection,* trans. A. I Sheridan (New York: Norton, 1977), p. 156.
14 "La Métaphore du sujet," *Edits* (Paris: Seuil, 1966), p. 889.
15 "The Agency of the Letter," p. 152. Translation modified; emphasis added.
16 These comments, as well as the epistemological distinction between rhetoric and grammar, are based on the remarkable article by Paul de Man, "Semiology and Rhetoric," *Diacritics,* no. 3 (1973). Reprinted in *Allegones of Reading* (New Haven: Yale University Press, 1979).
17 "The Agency of the Letter," p. 152.
18 *Ibid.*, p. 175.
19 "La Métaphore du sujet," p. 889.
20 "Les Non-dupes errent" (seminar), March 12, 1974.
21 "De la psychanalyse dans ses rapports avec la réalité," *Scilicet,* no. 1, p. 35.
22 "La Méprise du sujet supposé savoir," p. 35.
23 "The Subversion of the Subject and the Dialectic of Desire in the Freudian Unconscious," *Ecrits: A Selection,* p. 311.
24 The title (translated) of Lacan's seminar of 1973–74.
25 Cf. "La Psychanalyse: Raison d'un échec," *Scilicet,* no. I, pp. 42–50.
26 "Introduction to 'Scilicet,'" *Scilicet,* no. 1 (1968), 5–6.
27 Cf. Lacan's insistence on "the desire of the analyst" in *The Four Fundamental Concepts of Psychoanalysis,* trans. A. Sheridan (New York: Norton, 1977), p. 158.
28 Cf. "Le Temps logique et l'assertion de certitude anticipée," *Ecrits,* pp. 197–229.
29 "Du sujet enfin en question," *Ecrits,* p. 229.
30 Georges Bachelard, *La Poétique de l'espace* (Paris: P.U.F., 1958), pp. 197–98.
31 *The Four Fundamental Concepts,* p. 128.
32 *Ibid.*, pp. 127–28.
33 *Ibid.*, p. 25.
34 "L'Action restreinte," *Oeuvres complètes,* p. 372.
35 Lacan, "The Direction of the Treatment and the Principles of Its Power," *Ecrits: A Selection,* p. 277.
36 Mallarmé, "Salut," *Selected Poems,* trans. C. F. MacIntyre (Berkeley: University of California Press, 1957), P. 2.
37 Lacan, "Le Psychanalyste de l'école," *Scilicet,* no. I (1968), 25. My italics.
38 Cf. Freud, *The Interpretation of Dreams,* in the *Standard Edition* (London: Hogarth, 1956), V, 560, 562–63, 564: "I am now in a position to give a precise account of the part played in dreams by the unconscious wish . . . the psychology of the neuroses [shows us] that an unconscious idea as such is quite incapable of entering the preconscious and that it can only exercise any effect there by establishing a connection with an idea which already belongs to the preconscious, by *transferring its intensity* on to it and by getting itself 'covered' by it. Here we have the fact of 'transference' . . . It will be seen that the day's residues . . . not only borrow something from the unconscious . . . namely the instinctual force which is at the disposal of the repressed wish—but that they also offer the unconscious something indispensable—namely the necessary point of attachment for a transference."
39 Lacan, "La Psychanalyse: Raison d'un échec," p. 44. My italics.

Chapter 27

Judith Butler

PASSING, QUEERING

Nella Larsen's psychoanalytic challenge

Nella Larsen (1891–1964), one of the writers of the Harlem Renaissance (1920 to 1940, comprising a great outpouring of African American artistic and intellectual works), provides the occasion for Judith Butler's exploration of the convergence of feminism, psychoanalysis and theories of race, in this case in Larsen's novel *Passing* (1929). Butler's essay opens with some complex theoretical language, but in essence she is questioning the notion that sexual difference explains all other differences, especially that of race (white/black, hegemonic (dominant) versus minority groups, and so on). Instead, she suggests that the normalizing of heterosexuality, which partly functions by making homosexuality a taboo, is related to the normalizing of hegemonic *race relations*, whereby there is a taboo on miscegenation, or, mixed race sexual reproduction. This argument relates to Butler's notion of performing gender (see Chapter 51), which she explores in her groundbreaking and highly influential book *Gender Trouble: Feminism and the Subversion of Identity* (1990; anniversary edition 1999). In her essay on Larsen and psychoanalysis, the focus is on two main literary characters—Clare and Irene—who "pass" themselves off as white instead of their mixed race or African American identities. They achieve this racial performance not just through what they do, but also more interestingly, through what they don't do, or say, throughout the novel. In other words, certain racializing behaviours are "disavowed", rejected and repulsed. This situation is complicated by the fact that Irene appears attracted to Clare, especially in light of Clare's desire for Irene's husband. This "triangular" relationship of desire is called by René Girard "mimetic desire", except in this case, it both reveals and hides Clare's repressed lesbian identity. In a key scene in the novel, Clare's racist husband is shocked to find her in the company of African Americans; Clare falls, is pushed, or commits suicide by jumping from a window, this trauma being a blank spot that cannot be directly narrated. Butler notes that in this scene of proximity and disavowal, Clare's husband constitutes his own whiteness through the binary opposite of "blackness"; in other words, as much as this man dislikes black characters, his hatred of them brings about his self-assured identity as a non-black person. Furthermore, blackness is exoticised and eroticised by him, gaining a sexual thrill from the "uncertain border between black and white". Butler is elucidating the connections between sexuality and race (as well as class), through her focus on the gaps and slippages revealed by this triangular or mimetic desire. Lesbian sexuality in the novel is what is "almost spoken" yet also "withheld from speech"; Butler calls this the "muteness of homosexuality" within a normative and normalizing society. She proves this psychic mechanism by observing the use of the word "queer" in the novel, which is the label used for the gaps and slippages in heternormative speech. While "queer" had a less sexual meaning in the era of the Harlem Renaissance, Butler teases out the underlying sense of difference that stands in for homosexuality, i.e., as this underlying world is brought to the surface in alternative ways. Such "queer" fissures in the text, and the obvious risk of moving outside of heteronormative family structures (such as marriage), takes on deep psychoanalytical and class meaning. In fact, Butler suggests that her analysis proves that sexual difference is not prior to racial or class difference, and that these are perhaps interrelated, or, more technically speaking, co-constitutive (working together) to form and police identity.

> Can identity be viewed other than as a by-product of a manhandling of life, one that, in fact, refers no more to a consistent pattern of sameness than to an inconsequential process of otherness?
>
> TRINH T. MINH-HA

A NUMBER OF THEORETICAL QUESTIONS have been raised by the effort to think the relationship between feminism, psychoanalysis, and race studies. For the most part, psychoanalysis has been used by feminist theorists to theorize sexual difference as a distinct and fundamental set of linguistic and cultural relations. The philosopher Luce Irigaray has claimed that the question of sexual difference is *the* question for our time.[1] This privileging of sexual difference implies not only that sexual difference should be understood as more fundamental than other forms of difference, but that other forms of difference might be *derived* from sexual difference. This view also presumes that sexual difference constitutes an autonomous sphere of relations or disjunctions, and is not to be understood as articulated through or *as* other vectors of power.

What would it mean to consider the assumption of sexual positions, the disjunctive ordering of the human as "masculine" or "feminine" as taking place not only through a heterosexualizing symbolic with its taboo on homosexuality, but through a complex set of racial injunctions that operate in part through the taboo on miscegenation? Further, how might we understand homosexuality and miscegenation to converge at and as the constitutive outside of a normative heterosexuality that is at once the regulation of a racially pure reproduction? To coin Marx, then, let us remember that the reproduction of the species will be articulated as the reproduction *of* relations of reproduction, that is, as the cathected site of a racialized version of the species in pursuit of hegemony through perpetuity, that requires and produces a normative heterosexuality in its service.[2] Conversely, the reproduction of heterosexuality will take different forms depending on how race and the reproduction of race are understood. And though there are clearly good historical reasons for keeping "race" and "sexuality" and "sexual difference" as separate analytic spheres, there are also quite pressing and significant historical reasons for asking how and where we might read not only their convergence, but the sites at which the one cannot be constituted save through the other. This is something other than juxtaposing distinct spheres of power, subordination, agency, historicity, and something other than a list of attributes separated by those proverbial commas (gender, sexuality, race, class) that usually mean that we have not yet figured out how to think the relations we seek to mark. Is there a way, then, to read Nella Larsen's text as engaging psychoanalytic assumptions not to affirm the primacy of sexual difference, but to articulate the convergent modalities of power by which sexual difference is articulated and assumed?

Consider, if you will, the following scene from Nella Larsen's *Passing* in which Irene descends the stairs of her home to find Clare, in her desirable way, standing in the living room.[3] At the moment Irene lights upon Clare, Brian, Irene's husband, appears to have found Clare as well. Irene thus finds Clare, finds her beautiful, but at the same time finds Brian finding Clare beautiful as well. The doubling will prove to be important. The narrative voice is sympathetic to Irene, but exceeds her perspective on those occasions on which Irene finds speaking to be impossible.

> She remembered her own little choked exclamation of admiration, when, on coming downstairs a few minutes later than she had intended, she had rushed into the living room where Brian was waiting and had found Clare there too. Clare, exquisite, golden, fragrant, flaunting, in a stately gown of shining black taffeta, whose long, full skirt lay in graceful folds about her slim golden feet; her glistening hair drawn smoothly back into a small twist at the nape of her neck; her eyes sparkling like dark jewels. (233)

Irene's exclamation of admiration is never voiced, choked back it seems, retained, preserved as a kind of seeing that does not make its way into speech. She would have spoken, but the choking appears to stifle her voice; what she finds is Brian waiting, Brian finding Clare as well, and Clare herself. The grammar of the description fails to settle the question of who desires whom: "she had rushed into the living room where Brian was waiting and had found Clare there too": is it Irene who finds Clare, or Brian, or do they find her together? And what is it that they find in her, such that they no longer find each other, but mirror each other's desire as each turns toward Clare. Irene will stifle the words that would convey her admiration. Indeed, the exclamation is choked, deprived of air; the exclamation fills the throat and thwarts her speaking. The narrator emerges to speak the words Irene might have spoken: "exquisite, golden, fragrant, flaunting." The narrator thus states what remains caught in Irene's throat, which suggests that Larsen's narrator serves the function of exposing more than Irene herself can risk. In most cases where Irene finds herself unable to speak, the narrator supplies the words. But when it comes to explaining exactly how Clare dies at the end of the novel, the narrator proves as speechless as Irene.

The question of what can and cannot be spoken, what can and cannot be publicly exposed, is raised throughout the text, and it is linked with the larger question of the dangers of public exposure of both color and desire. Significantly, it is precisely what Irene describes as Clare's flaunting that Irene admires, even as Irene knows that Clare, who passes as white, not only flaunts but hides—indeed, is always hiding *in* that very flaunting. Clare's disavowal of her color compels Irene to take her distance from Clare, to refuse to respond to her letters, to try to close her out of her life. And though Irene voices a moral objection to Clare's passing as white, it is clear that Irene engages many of the same social conventions of passing as Clare. Indeed, when they meet after a long separation, they are both in a rooftop cafe passing as white. And yet, according to Irene, Clare goes too far, passes as white not merely on occasion, but in her life, and in her marriage. Clare embodies a certain kind of sexual daring that Irene defends herself against, for the marriage cannot hold Clare, and Irene finds herself drawn by Clare, wanting to be her, but also wanting her. It is this risk taking, articulated at once as a racial crossing and sexual infidelity, that alternately entrances Irene and fuels her moral condemnation of Clare with renewed ferocity.

After Irene convinces herself that Brian and Clare are having an affair, Irene watches Clare work her seduction and betrayal on an otherwise unremarkable Dave Freeland at a party. The seduction works through putting into question both the sanctity of marriage and the clarity of racial demarcations:

> Scraps of their conversation, in Clare's husky voice, floated over to her: " . . .
> always admired you . . . so much about you long ago . . . everybody says so . . .
> no one but you. . . ." And more of the same. The man hung rapt on her words,
> though he was the husband of Felise Freeland, and the author of novels that
> revealed a man of perception and a devastating irony. And he fell for such
> pishposh! And all because Clare had a trick of sliding down ivory lids over
> astonishing black eyes and then lifting them suddenly and turning on a caressing
> smile. (254)

Here it is the trick of passing itself that appears to eroticize Clare, the covering over of
astonishing black by ivory, the sudden concession of the secret, the magical transformation of
a smile into a caress. It is the changeability itself, the dream of a metamorphosis, where that
changeableness signifies a certain freedom, a class mobility afforded by whiteness that
constitutes the power of that seduction. This time Irene's own vision of Clare is followed not
only by a choking of speech, but by a rage that leads to the shattering of her tea cup, and the
interruption of chatter. The tea spreads on the carpet like rage, like blood, figured as dark
color itself suddenly uncontained by the strictures of whiteness:

> Rage boiled up in her.
>   There was a slight crash. On the floor at her feet lay the shattered cup. Dark
> stains dotted the bright rug. Spread. The chatter stopped. Went on. Before her.
> Zulena gathered up the white fragments. (254)

This shattering prefigures the violence that ends the story, in which Clare is discovered by
Bellew, her white racist husband, in the company of African Americans, her color "outed,"
which initiates her swift and quite literal demise: with Irene ambiguously positioned next to
Clare with a hand on her arm, Clare falls from the window, and dies on the street below.
Whether she jumped or was pushed remains ambiguous: "What happened next, Irene Red-
field never afterwards allowed herself to remember. Never clearly. One moment Clare had
been there, a vital glowing thing, like a flame of red and gold. The next she was gone" (271).
     Prior to this moment, Bellew climbs the stairs to the Harlem apartment where the salon
is taking place and discovers Clare there; her being there is sufficient to convince him that she
is black. Blackness is not primarily a visual mark in Larsen's story, not only because Irene and
Clare are both light-skinned, but because what can be seen, what qualifies as a visible marking,
is a matter of being able to read a marked body in relation to unmarked bodies, where
unmarked bodies constitute the currency of normative whiteness. Clare passes not only
because she is light-skinned, but because she refuses to introduce her blackness into
conversation, and so withholds the conversational marker that would counter the hegemonic
presumption that she is white. Irene herself appears to "pass" insofar as she enters conversations
that presume whiteness as the norm without contesting that assumption. This dissociation
from blackness that she performs through silence is reversed at the end of the story in which
she is exposed to Bellew's white gaze in clear association with African Americans. It is only
on the condition of an association that conditions a naming that her color becomes legible. He
cannot "see" her as black before that association, and he claims to her face with unrestrained
racism that he would never associate with blacks. If he associates with her, she cannot be
black. But if she associates with blacks, she becomes black, where the sign of blackness is
contracted, as it were, through proximity, where "race" itself is figured as a contagion
transmissable through proximity. The added presumption is that if he were to associate with
blacks, the boundaries of his own whiteness, and surely that of his children, would no longer
be easily fixed. Paradoxically, his own racist passion *requires* that association; he cannot be

white without blacks and without the constant disavowal of his relation to them. It is only through that disavowal that his whiteness is constituted, and through the institutionalization of that disavowal that his whiteness is perpetually—but anxiously—reconstituted.[4]

Bellew's speech is overdetermined by this anxiety over racial boundaries. Before he knows that Clare is black, he regularly calls her "Nig," and it seems that this term of degradation and disavowal is passed between them as a kind of love toy. She allows herself to be eroticized by it, takes it on, acting as if it were the most impossible appellation for her. That he calls her "Nig" suggests that he knows or that there is a kind of knowingness in the language he speaks. And yet, if he can call her that and remain her husband, he cannot know. In this sense, she defines the fetish, an object of desire about which one says, "I know very well that this cannot be, but I desire this all the same," a formulation that implies its equivalence: "Precisely because this cannot be, I desire it all the more." And yet Clare is a fetish that holds in place both the rendering of Clare's blackness as an exotic source of excitation and the denial of her blackness altogether. Here the "naming" is riddled with the knowledge that he claims not to have; he notes that she is becoming darker all the time; the term of degradation permits him to see and not to see at the same time. The term sustains his desire as a kind of disavowal, one that structures not only the ambivalence in his desire for Clare, but also the erotic ambivalence by which he constitutes the fragile boundaries of his own racial identity. To reformulate an earlier claim, then: although he claims that he would never associate with African Americans, he requires the association and its disavowal for an erotic satisfaction that is indistinguishable from his desire to display his own racial purity.

In fact, it appears that the uncertain border between black and white is precisely what he eroticizes, what he needs in order to make Clare into the exotic object to be dominated.[5] His name, Bellew, like bellow, is itself a howl, the long howl of white male anxiety in the face of the racially ambiguous woman whom he idealizes and loathes. She represents the specter of a racial ambiguity that must be conquered. But "Bellew" is also the instrument that fans the flame, the illumination that Clare, literally "light," in some sense *is*. Her luminescence is dependent on the life he breathes into her; her evanescence is equally a function of that power.

> One moment Clare had been there, a vital glowing thing, like a flame of red and gold. The next she was gone.
>
> There was a gasp of horror, and above it a sound not quite human, like a beast in agony. (271)

"Nig! My God! Nig!" Bellew bellows, and at that moment Clare vanishes from the window. His speech vacillates between degradation and deification, but opens and closes on a note of degradation. The force of that vacillation illuminates, inflames Clare, but also works to extinguish her, to blow her out. Clare exploits Bellew's need to see only what he wants to see, working not so much the appearance of whiteness, but the vacillation between black and white as a kind of erotic lure. His final naming closes down that vacillation, but functions also as a fatal condemnation—or so it seems.

For it is, after all, Irene's hand that is last seen on Clare's arm, and the narrator, who is usually able to say what Irene cannot, appears drawn into Irene's nonnarrativizable trauma, blanking out, withdrawing at the crucial moment when we expect to learn whose agency it was that catapulted Clare from the window and to her death below. That Irene feels guilt over Clare's death is not quite reason enough to believe that Irene pushed her, since one can easily feel guilty about a death one merely wished would happen, even when one knows that one's wish could not be the proximate cause of the death. The gap in the narrative leaves open whether Clare jumped, Irene pushed, or the force of Bellew's words bellowed her out the window. It is, I would suggest, this consequential gap, and the triangulation that surrounds it, that occasions a rethinking of psychoanalysis, in particular, of the social and psychic status of "killing judgments." How are we to explain the chain that leads from judgment to exposure to death, as it operates through the interwoven vectors of sexuality and race?

Clare's fall: is this a joint effort, or is it at least an action whose causes must remain not fully knowable, not fully traceable? This is an action ambiguously executed, in which the agency of Irene and Clare is significantly confused, and this confusion of agency takes place in relation to the violating speech of the white man. We can read this "finale," as Larsen calls it, as rage boiling up, shattering, leaving shards of whiteness, shattering the veneer of whiteness. Even as it appears that Clare's veneer of whiteness is shattered, it is Bellew's as well; indeed, it is the veneer by which the white project of racial purity is sustained. For Bellew thinks that he would never associate with blacks, but he cannot be white without his "Nig," without the lure of an association that he must resist, without the specter of a racial ambiguity that he must subordinate and deny. Indeed, he reproduces that racial line by which he seeks to secure his whiteness through producing black women as the necessary and impossible object of desire, as the fetish in relation to which his own whiteness is anxiously and persistently secured.

There are clearly risks in trying to think in psychoanalytic terms about Larsen's story, which, after all, published in 1929, belongs to the tradition of the Harlem Renaissance and ought properly to be read in the context of that cultural and social world. Whereas many critics have read the text as a tragic story of the social position of the mulatto, others have insisted that the story's brilliance is to be found in its psychological complexity. It seems to me that perhaps one need not choose between the historical and social specificity of the novel, as it has been brought to light by Barbara Christian, Gloria Hull, Hazel Carby, Amritjit Singh, and Mary Helen Washington, and the psychological complexity of cross-identification and jealousy in the text as it has been discussed by Claudia Tate, Cheryl Wall, Mary Mabel Youmans, and Deborah McDowell.[6] Both Tate and McDowell suggest that critics have split over whether this story ought to be read as a story about race and, in particular, as part of the tragic genre of the mulatto, or whether it ought to be read as psychologically complex and, as both McDowell and Carby insist, an allegory of the difficulty of representing black women's sexuality precisely when that sexuality has been exoticized or rendered as an icon of primitivism. Indeed, Larsen herself appears to be caught in that very dilemma, withholding a representation of black women's sexuality precisely in order to avert the consequence of its becoming exoticized. It is this withholding that one might read in *Quicksand,* a novella published the year before *Passing,* where Helga's abstinence is directly related to the fear of being depicted as belonging to "the jungle." McDowell writes, "since the beginning of their 130-year history, black women novelists have treated sexuality with caution and reticence. This is clearly linked to the network of social and literary myths perpetuated throughout history about black women's libidinousness."[7]

The conflict between Irene and Clare, one that spans identification, desire, jealousy, and rage, calls to be contextualized within the historically specific constraints of sexuality and race that produced this text in 1929. And though I can only do that in a very crude way here, I would like briefly to sketch a direction for such an analysis. For I would agree with both McDowell and Carby not only that is it unnecessary to choose whether this novella is "about" race or "about" sexuality and sexual conflict, but that the two domains are inextricably linked, such that the text offers a way to read the racialization of sexual conflict.

Claudia Tate argues that "race . . . is not the novel's foremost concern" and that "the real impetus for the story is Irene's emotional turbulence" (142) and the psychological ambiguity that surrounds Clare's death. Tate distinguishes her own psychological account from those who reduce the novel to a "trite melodrama" (146) of black women passing for white. By underscoring the ambiguity of Clare's death, Tate brings into relief the narrative and psychic complexity of the novella. Following Tate, Cheryl Wall refuses to separate the psychological ambiguity of the story from its racial significance. Agreeing that "Larsen's most striking insights are into psychic dilemmas confronting certain black women," she argues that what appear to be "the tragic mulattoes of literary convention" are also "the means through which the author demonstrates the psychological costs of racism and sexism." For Wall, the figure of Clare never fully exists apart from Irene's own projections of "otherness" (108). Indeed, according to Wall, Irene's erotic relation to Clare participates in a kind of exoticism that is not fully different from Bellew's. Irene sees in Clare's seductive eyes "the unconscious, the unknowable, the erotic, and the passive," where, according to Wall, "[these] symbolize those aspects of the psyche Irene denies within herself" (108–9). Deborah McDowell specifies this account of psychological complexity and projection by underscoring the conflicted homoeroticism between Clare and Irene. McDowell writes, "Though, superficially, Irene's is an account of Clare's passing for white and related issues of racial identity and loyalty, underneath the safety of that surface is the more dangerous story—though not named explicitly—of Irene's awakening sexual desire for Clare" (xxvi). Further, McDowell argues that Irene effectively displaces her own desire for Clare in her "imagination of an affair between Clare and Brian" (xxviii), and that in the final scene "Clare's death represents the death of Irene's sexual feelings, for Clare" (xxix).

To understand the muted status of homosexuality within this text—and hence the displacement, jealousy, and murderous wish that follow—it is crucial to situate this repression in terms of the specific social constraints on the depiction of black female sexuality mentioned previously. In her essay, "The Quicksands of Representation," Hazel Carby writes,

> Larsen's representation of both race and class are structured through the prism of black female sexuality. Larsen recognized that the repression of the sensual in Afro-American fiction in response to the long history of the exploitation of black sexuality led to the repression of passion and the repression or denial of female sexuality and desire. But, of course, the representation of black female sexuality meant risking its definition as primitive and exotic within a racist society. Racist sexual ideologies proclaimed the black woman to be a rampant sexual being, and in response black women writers either focused on defending their morality or displaced sexuality onto another terrain. (174)

In contrast, McDowell sees Larsen as resisting the sexual explicitness found in black female blues singers such as Bessie Smith and Ma Rainey (xiii), but nevertheless wrestling with the problem of rendering public a sexuality that thereby became available to an exoticizing exploitation.[8] In a sense, the conflict of lesbian desire in the story can be read in what is almost spoken, in what is withheld from speech, but which always threatens to stop or disrupt speech. And in this sense the muteness of homosexuality converges in the story with the illegibility of Clare's blackness.

To specify this convergence let me turn first to the periodic use of the term *queering* in the story itself, where queering is linked to the eruption of anger into speech such that speech is stifled and broken, and then to the scene in which Clare and Irene first exchange their glances, a reciprocal seeing that verges on threatening absorption. Conversations in *Passing* appear to constitute the painful, if not repressive, surface of social relations. It is what Clare withholds in conversation that permits her to "pass"; and when Irene's conversation falters, the narrator refers to the sudden gap in the surface of language as "queer" or as "queering." At the time, it seems, *queer* did not yet mean homosexual, but it did encompass an array of meanings associated with the deviation from normalcy that might well include the sexual: of obscure origin, the state of feeling ill or bad, not straight, obscure, perverse, eccentric. As a verb-form *to queer* has a history of meaning: to quiz or ridicule, to puzzle, but also, to swindle and to cheat. In Larsen's text, the aunts who raise Clare as white forbid her to mention her race; they are described as "queer" (189). When Gertrude, another passing black woman, hears a racial slur against blacks, Larsen writes, "From Gertrude's direction came a queer little suppressed sound, a snort or a giggle" (202)—something queer, something short of proper conversation, passable prose. Brian's longing to travel to Brazil is described as an "old, queer, unhappy restlessness" (208), suggesting a longing to be freed of propriety.

That Larsen links queerness with a potentially problematic eruption of sexuality seems clear: Irene worries about her sons picking up ideas about sex at school; Junior, she remarks, "'picked up some queer ideas about things—some things—from the older boys.' 'Queer ideas?' [Brian] repeated. 'D'you mean ideas about sex, Irene?' 'Ye-es. Not quite nice ones, dreadful jokes, and things like that'" (219–20). Sometimes conversation becomes "queer" when anger interrupts the social surface of conversation. Upon becoming convinced that Brian and Clare are having an affair, Irene is described by Larsen this way:

> Irene cried out: "But Brian, I—'' and stopped, amazed at the fierce anger that had blazed up in her.
> Brian's head came round with a jerk. His brows lifted in an odd surprise.
> Her voice, she realized *had* gone queer. (249)

As a term for betraying what ought to remain concealed, *queering* works as the exposure within language—an exposure that disrupts the repressive surface of language—of both sexuality and race. After meeting Clare's husband on the street with her black friend Felise, Irene confesses that she has previously "passed" in front of him. Larsen writes, "Felise drawled: 'Aha! Been 'passing' have you? Well, I've queered that'" (259).

In the last instance, queering is what upsets and exposes passing; it is the act by which the racially and sexually repressive surface of conversation is exploded, by rage, by sexuality, by the insistence on color.

Irene and Clare first meet up after years apart in a cafe where they are both passing as white. And the process by which each comes to recognize the other, and recognize her as black is at once the process of their erotic absorption each into the other's eyes. The narrator reports that Irene found Clare to be "an attractive-looking woman . . . with those dark, almost black, eyes and that wide mouth like a scarlet flower against the ivory of her skin . . . a shade too provocative." Irene feels herself stared at by Clare, and clearly stares back, for she notes that Clare "showed [not] the slightest trace of disconcertment at having been detected in her steady scrutiny." Irene then "feel(s) her color heighten under the continued inspection, [and] slid her eyes down. What she wondered could be the reason for such persistent attention? Had she, in her haste in the taxi, put her hat on backwards?" From the start, then, Irene takes Clare's stare to be a kind of inspection, a threat of exposure which she returns first as scrutiny and distrust only then to find herself thoroughly seduced: "She stole another glance. Still looking. What strange languorous eyes she had!" (177). Irene resists being watched, but then falls into the gaze, averts the recognition at the same time that she "surrenders" to the charm of the smile.

The ambivalence wracks the motion of the narrative. Irene subsequently tries to move Clare out of her life, refuses to answer her letters, vows not to invite her anywhere, but finds herself caught up by Clare's seduction. Is it that Irene cannot bear the identification with Clare, or is it that she cannot bear her desire for Clare; is it that she identifies with Clare's passing but needs to disavow it not only because she seeks to uphold the "race" that Clare betrays but because her desire for Clare will betray the family that works as the bulwark for that uplifted race? Indeed, this is a moral version of the family that opposes any sign of passion even within the marriage, even any passionate attachment to the children. Irene comes to hate Clare not only because Clare lies, passes, and betrays her race, but because Clare's lying secures a tentative sexual freedom for Clare and reflects back to Irene the passion that Irene denies herself. She hates Clare not only because Clare has such passion, but because Clare awakens such passion in Irene, indeed, a passion *for* Clare: "In the look Clare gave Irene, there was something groping, and hopeless, and yet so absolutely determined that it was like an image of the futile searching and firm resolution in Irene's own soul, and increased the feeling of doubt and compunction that had been growing within her about Clare Kendry." She distrusts Clare as she distrusts herself, but this groping is also what draws her in. The next line reads: "She gave in" (231).

When Irene can resist Clare, she does it in the name of "race," where "race" is tied to the Du Boisian notion of uplift and denotes an idea of "progress" that not only is masculinist but, in Larsen's story, becomes construed as upward class mobility. This moral notion of "race" which, by the way, is often contested by the celebratory rhetoric of "color" in the text, also requires the idealization of bourgeois family life in which women retain their place in the family. The institution of the family also protects black women from a public exposure of sexuality that would be rendered vulnerable to a racist construction and exploitation. The sexuality that might queer the family becomes a kind of danger: Brian's desire to travel, the boys' jokes, all must be unilaterally subdued, kept out of public speech, not merely in the name of race, but in the name of a notion of racial progress that has become linked with class mobility, masculine uplift, and the bourgeois family. Ironically, Du Bois himself came to praise Larsen's *Quicksand* precisely for elevating black fiction beyond the kind of sexual exoticization that patrons such as Carl Van Vechten sought to promote.[9] Without recognizing that Larsen was struggling with the conflict produced, on the one hand, by such exotic and racist renderings and, on the other hand, by the moral injunctions typified by Du Bois, Du Bois himself praises her writings as an example of uplift itself.[10] And yet, one might argue that *Passing* exemplifies precisely the cost of uplift for black women as an ambiguous death-suicide whereas *Quicksand* exemplifies that cost as a kind of death in marriage, where both stories resolve on the impossibility of sexual freedom for black women.[11]

What becomes psychically repressed in *Passing* is linked to the specificity of the social constraints on black women's sexuality that inform Larsen's text. If, as Carby insists, the prospect of black women's sexual freedom at the time of Larsen's writing rendered them vulnerable to public violations, including rape, because their bodies continued to be sites of conquest within white racism, then the psychic resistance to homosexuality and to a sexual life outside the parameters of the family must be read in part as a resistance to an endangering public exposure.

To the extent that Irene desires Clare, she desires the trespass that Clare performs, and hates her for the disloyalty that that trespass entails. To the extent that Irene herself eroticizes Clare's racial trespass and Clare's clear lack of loyalty for family and its institutions of monogamy, Irene herself is in a double bind: caught between the prospect of becoming free from an ideology of "race" uncritical in its own masculinism and classism, on the one hand, and the violations of white racism that attend the deprivatization of black women's sexuality, on the other. Irene's psychic ambivalence toward Clare, then, needs to be situated in this historical double bind.[12] At the same time, we can see mapped within Larsen's text the incipient possibility of a solidarity among black women. The identification between Clare and Irene might be read as the unlived political promise of a solidarity yet to come.

McDowell points out that Irene imagines that Brian is with Clare and that this imagining coincides with the intensification of Irene's desire for Clare. Irene passes her desire for Clare through Brian; he becomes the fantasmatic occasion for Irene to consummate her desire for

Clare, but also to deflect from the recognition that it is her desire that is being articulated through Brian. Brian carries that repudiated homosexuality, and Irene's jealousy, then, can be understood as not only a rivalry with him for Clare, but the painful consequence of a sacrifice of passion that she repeatedly makes, a sacrifice that entails the displacement or rerouting of her desire through Brian. That Brian appears to act on Irene's desire (although this, importantly, is never confirmed and, so, may be nothing other than an imaginary conviction on Irene's part) suggests that part of that jealousy is anger that he occupies a legitimated sexual position from which he can carry out the desire which she invested in him, that he dares to act the desire which she relegated to him to act on. This is not to discount the possibility that Irene also desires Brian, but there is very little evidence of a passionate attachment to him in the text. Indeed, it is against his passion, and in favor of preserving bourgeois ideals that she clamors to keep him. Her jealousy may well be routed along a conventional heterosexual narrative, but—as we saw in Cather—that is not to foreclose the interpretation that a lesbian passion runs that course.

Freud writes of a certain kind of "jealousy" that appears at first to be the desire to have the heterosexual partner whose attention has wandered but is motivated by a desire to occupy the place of that wandering partner in order to consummate a foreclosed homosexuality. He calls this a "delusional jealousy . . . what is left of a homosexuality that has run its course and it rightly takes its position among the classical forms of paranoia. As an attempt at defense against an unduly strong homosexual impulse it may, in a man, be described in the formula: "*I* do not love him, *she* loves him!"[13] And, in a woman and in *Passing,* the following formula might apply: "I, Irene, do not love her, Clare: he, Brian, does!"

It is precisely here, in accounting for the sacrifice, that one reformulation of psychoanalysis in terms of race becomes necessary. In his essay on narcissism, Freud argues that a boy child begins to love through sacrificing some portion of his own narcissism, that the idealization of the mother is nothing other than that narcissism transferred outward, that the mother stands for that lost narcissism, promises the return of that narcissism, and never delivers on that promise. For as long as she remains the idealized object of love, she carries his narcissism, she is his displaced narcissism and, insofar as *she carries it,* she is perceived to *withhold it from him.* Idealization, then, is always at the expense of the ego who idealizes. The ego-ideal is produced as a consequence of being severed from the ego, where the ego is understood to sacrifice some part of its narcissism in the formation and externalization of this ideal.

The love of the ideal will thus always be ambivalent, for the ideal deprecates the ego as it compels its love. For the moment, I would like to detach the logic of this explanation from the drama between boy child and mother that is Freud's focus (not to discount that focus, but to bring into relief other possible foci), and underscore the consequence of ambivalence in the process of idealization. The one I idealize is the one who carries for me the self-love that I myself have invested in that one. And accordingly, I hate that one, for he or she has taken my place even as I yielded it, and yet I require that one, for he or she represents the promise of the return of my own self-love. Self-love, self-esteem is thus preserved and vanquished at the site of the ideal.

How can this analysis be related to the questions concerning the racialization of sexuality I have tried to pose? The ego-ideal and its derivative, the superego, are regulatory mechanisms by which social ideals are psychically sustained. In this way, the social regulation of the psyche can be read as the juncture of racial and gendered prohibitions and regulations and their forced psychic appropriations. Freud argues speculatively that this ego-ideal lays the groundwork for the superego and that the superego is lived as the psychic activity of "watching" and, from the perspective that is the ego, the experience of "being watched": "it (the super-ego) constantly watches the real ego and measures it by that (ego-) ideal." Hence, the superego stands for the measure, the law, the norm, one that is embodied by a fabrication, a figure of a being whose sole feature it is to watch, to watch in order to judge, as a kind of persistent scrutiny, detection, effort to expose, that hounds the ego and reminds it of its failures. The ego thus designates the psychic experience of being seen, and the superego that of seeing, watching, exposing the ego. Now, this watching agency is not the same as the idealization that is the ego-ideal; it stands back both from the ego-ideal and the ego, and measures the latter against the former and always, always finds it wanting. The superego is not only the measure of the ego, the interiorized judge, but the activity of prohibition, the psychic agency of regulation that Freud calls *conscience*.[14]

For Freud, this superego represents a norm, a standard, an ideal that is in part socially received; it is the psychic agency by which social regulation proceeds. But it is not just any norm; it is the set of norms by which the sexes are differentiated and installed. The superego thus first arises, says Freud, as a prohibition that regulates sexuality in the service of producing socially ideal "men" and "women." This is the point at which Lacan intervened in order to develop his notion of the symbolic, the set of laws conveyed by language itself that compel conformity to notions of "masculinity" and "femininity." And many psychoanalytic feminists have taken this claim as a point of departure for their own work. They have claimed in various ways that sexual difference is as primary as language, that there is no speaking, no writing, without the presupposition of sexual difference. And this has led to a second claim that I want to contest, namely, that sexual difference is more primary or more fundamental than other kinds of differences, including racial difference. It is this assertion of the priority of sexual difference over racial difference that has marked so much psychoanalytic feminism as white, for the assumption here is not only that sexual difference is more fundamental, but that there is a relationship called "sexual difference" that is itself unmarked by race. That whiteness is not understood by such a perspective as a racial category is clear; it is yet another power that need not speak its name. Hence, to claim that sexual difference is more fundamental than racial difference is effectively to assume that sexual difference is white sexual difference and that whiteness is not a form of racial difference.

Within Lacanian terms, the ideals or norms that are conveyed in language are the ideals or norms that govern sexual difference and that go under the name of the symbolic. But what requires radical rethinking is what social relations compose this domain of the symbolic, what convergent set of historical formations of racialized gender, of gendered race, of the sexualization of racial ideals, or the racialization of gender norms, makes up both the social regulation of sexuality and its psychic articulations. If, as Norma Alarcón has insisted, women of color are "multiply interpellated," called by many names, constituted in and by that multiple calling, then this implies that the symbolic domain, the domain of socially instituted norms, is composed of *racializing norms,* and that they exist not merely alongside gender norms, but are articulated through one another.[15] Hence it is no longer possible to make sexual difference prior to racial difference or, for that matter, to make them into fully separable axes of social regulation and power.

In some ways, this is precisely the challenge to psychoanalysis that Nella Larsen offers in *Passing.* And here is where I would follow Barbara Christian's advice to consider literary narrative as a place where theory takes place,[16] and would simply add that I take Larsen's *Passing* to be in part a theorization of desire, displacement, and jealous rage that has significant implications for rewriting psychoanalytic theory in ways that explicitly come to terms with race. If the watching agency described by Freud is figured as a watching judge, a judge who embodies a set of ideals, and if those ideals are to some large degree socially instituted and maintained, then this watching agency is the means by which social norms sear the psyche and expose it to a condemnation that can lead to suicide. Indeed Freud remarked that the superego, if left fully unrestrained, will fully deprive the ego of its desire, a deprivation that is psychic death and that Freud claims leads to suicide. If we rethink Freud's "super-ego" as the psychic force of social regulation, and we rethink social regulation in terms that include vectors of power such as gender and race, then it should be possible to articulate the psyche politically in ways that have consequences for social survival.

For Clare, it seems, cannot survive, and her death marks the success of a certain symbolic ordering of gender, sexuality, and race, as it marks as well the sites of potential resistance. It may be that as Zulena, Irene's black servant, picks up the shattered whiteness of the broken tea cup, she opens the question of what will be made of such shards. We might read a text such as Toni Morrison's *Sula* as the piecing together of the shattered whiteness that composes the remains of both Clare and Irene in Nella Larsen's text, rewriting Clare as Sula, and Irene as Nel, refiguring that lethal identification between them as the promise of connection in Nel's final call: "girl, girl, girlgirlgirl."[17]

At the close of Larsen's *Passing,* it is Bellew who climbs the stairs and "sees" Clare, takes the measure of her blackness against the ideal of whiteness and finds her wanting. Although Clare has said that she longs for the exposure in order to become free of him, she is also attached to him and his norm for her economic well-being, and it is no accident—even if it is figured as one—that the exposure of her color leads straightway to her death, the literalization of a "social death." Irene, as well, does not want Clare free, not only because Irene might lose Brian, but because she must halt Clare's sexual freedom to halt her own. Claudia Tate argues that the final action is importantly ambiguous, that it constitutes a "psychological death" for Irene just as it literalizes death for Clare. Irene appears to offer a helping hand to Clare, who somehow passes out the window to her death. Here, as Henry Louis Gates Jr. suggests, passing carries the double meaning of crossing the color line and crossing over into death: passing as a kind of passing on.[18]

If Irene turns on Clare to contain Clare's sexuality, as she has turned on and extinguished her own passion, she does this under the eyes of the bellowing white man; his speech, his exposure, his watching divides them against each other. In this sense, Bellew speaks the force of the regulatory norm of whiteness, but Irene identifies with that condemnatory judgment. Clare is the promise of freedom at too high a price, both to Irene and to herself. It is not precisely Clare's race that is "exposed," but blackness itself is produced as marked and marred, a public sign of particularity in the service of the dissimulated universality of whiteness. If Clare betrays Bellew, it is in part because she turns the power of dissimulation against her white husband, and her betrayal of him, at once a sexual betrayal, undermines the reproductive aspirations of white racial purity, exposing the tenuous borders that that purity requires. If Bellew anxiously reproduces white racial purity, he produces the prohibition against miscegenation by which that purity is guaranteed, a prohibition that requires strictures of heterosexuality, sexual fidelity, and monogamy. And if Irene seeks to sustain the black family at the expense of passion and in the name of uplift, she does it in part to avert the position for black women outside the family, that of being sexually degraded and endangered by the very terms of white masculinism that Bellew represents (for instance, she tells Clare not to come to the dance for the Negro Welfare Fund alone, that she'll be taken as a prostitute). Bellew's watching, the power of exposure that he wields, is a historically entrenched social power of the white male gaze, but one whose masculinity is enacted and guaranteed through heterosexuality as a ritual of racial purification. His masculinity cannot be secured except through a consecration of his whiteness. And although Bellew requires the specter of the black woman as an object of desire, he must destroy this specter to avoid the kind of association that might destabilize the territorial boundaries of his own whiteness. This ritualistic expulsion is dramatized quite clearly at the end of *Passing* when Bellew's exposing and endangering gaze and Clare's fall to death are simultaneous with Irene's offer of an apparently helping hand. Fearing the loss of her husband and fearing her own desire, Irene is positioned at the social site of contradiction: both options threaten to jettison her into a public sphere in which she might become subject, as it were, to the same bad winds. But Irene fails to realize that Clare is as constrained as she is, that Clare's freedom could not be acquired at the expense of Irene, that they do not ultimately enslave each other, but that they are both caught in the vacillating breath of that symbolic bellowing: "Nig! My God! Nig!"

If Bellew's bellowing can be read as a symbolic racialization, a way in which both Irene and Clare are interpellated by a set of symbolic norms governing black female sexuality, then the symbolic is not merely organized by "phallic power," but by a "phallicism" that is centrally sustained by racial anxiety and sexualized rituals of racial purification. Irene's self-sacrifice might be understood then as an effort to avoid becoming the object of that kind of sexual violence, as one that makes her cling to an arid family life and destroy whatever emergence of passion might call that safety into question. Her jealousy must then be read as a psychic event orchestrated within and by this social map of power. Her passion for Clare had to be destroyed only because she could not find a viable place for her own sexuality to live. Trapped by a promise of safety through class mobility, Irene accepted the terms of power that threatened her, becoming its instrument in the end. More troubling than a scene in which the white man finds and scorns his "Other" in the black women, this drama displays in all its painfulness the ways in which the interpellation of the white norm is reiterated and executed by those whom it would—and does—vanquish. This is a performative enactment of "race" that mobilizes every character in its sweep.

And yet, the story reoccupies symbolic power to expose that symbolic force in return, and in the course of that exposure began to further a powerful tradition of words, one that promised to sustain the lives and passions of precisely those who could not survive within the story itself. Tragically, the logic of "passing" and "exposure" came to afflict and, indeed, to end Nella Larsen's own authorial career, for when she published a short story, "Sanctuary," in 1930, she was accused of plagiarism, that is, exposed as "passing" as the true originator of the work.[19] Her response to this condemning exposure was to recede into an anonymity from which she did not emerge. Irene slipped into such a living death, as did Helga in *Quicksand*. Perhaps the alternative would have meant a turning of that queering rage no longer against herself or Clare, but against the regulatory norms that force such a turn: against both the passionless promise of that bourgeois family and the bellowing of racism in its social and psychic reverberations, most especially, in the deathly rituals it engages.

Notes

1   See Luce Irigaray, *Éthique de la différence sexuelle* (Paris: Editions de Minuit, 1984), 13.
2   Freud's *Totem and Taboo: Resemblances between the Lives of Savages and Neurotics* (New York: Moffat, Yard and Co., 1918) attests to the inseparability of the discourse of species reproduction and the discourse of race. In that text, one might consider the twin uses of "development" as the movement toward an advanced state of culture and the "achievement" of genital sexuality within monogamous heterosexuality.
3   Nella Larsen, *Passing* in *An Intimation of Things Distant: The Collected Fiction of Nella Larsen*, ed. Charles Larson, foreword by Marita Golden (New York: Anchor Books, 1992), 163–276.
4   This suggests one sense in which "race" might be construed as performative. Bellew produces his whiteness through a ritualized production of its sexual barriers. This anxious repetition accumulates the force of the material effect of a circumscribed whiteness, but its boundary concedes its tenuous status precisely because it requires the "blackness" that it excludes. In this sense, a dominant "race" is constructed (in the sense of *materialized*) through reiteration and exclusion.
5   This is like the colonized subject who must resemble the colonizer to a certain degree, but who is prohibited from resembling the colonizer too well. For a fuller description of this dynamic, see Homi Bhabha, "Of Mimicry and Man: The Ambivalence of Colonial Discourse," *October* 28 (spring 1984): 126.

6   Where references in the text are made to the following authors, they are to the following studies unless otherwise indicated: Houston A. Baker Jr., *Modernism and the Harlem Renaissance* (Chicago: Chicago University Press, 1987); Robert Bone, *The Negro Novel in America* (New Haven: Yale University Press, 1958); Hazel V. Carby, *Reconstructing Womanhood: The Emergence of the Afro-American Woman Novelist* (London: Oxford University Press, 1987); Barbara Christian, *Black Women Novelists: The Development of a Tradition, 1892–1976* (Westport, Ct.: Greenwood Press, 1980) and "Trajectories of Self-Definition: Placing Contemporary Afro-American Women's Fiction," in *Conjuring: Black Women, Fiction, and Literary Tradition,* ed. Marjorie Pryse and Hortense J. Spillers (Bloomington: Indiana University Press, 1985), 233–48; Henry Louis Gates Jr., *Figures in Black: Words, Signs, and the "Racial" Self* (New York: Oxford University Press, 1987); Nathan Huggins, *Harlem Renaissance* (New York: Oxford University Press, 1971); Gloria Hull, *Color, Sex, and Poetry: Three Women Writers of the Harlem Renaissance* (Bloomington: Indiana University Press, 1987); Deborah E. McDowell, introduction to Nella Larsen's *Quicksand; and, Passing* (New Brunswick: Rutgers University Press, 1986); Jacquelyn Y. McLendon, "Self-Representation as Art in the Novels of Nella Larsen," in *Redefining Autobiography in Twentieth-Century Fiction,* ed. Janice Morgan and Colette T. Hall (New York: Garland, 1991); Hiroko Sato, "Under the Harlem Shadow: A Study of Jessie Faucet and Nella Larsen," in *The Harlem Renaissance Remembered,* ed. Arno Bontemps (New York: Dodd, 1972), 63–89; Amritjit Singh, *The Novels of the Harlem Renaissance* (State College: Pennsylvania State University Press, 1976); Claudia Tate, "Nella Larsen's *Passing*: A Problem of Interpretation," *Black American Literature Forum* 14, no. 4 (1980): 142–46; Hortense Thornton, "Sexism as Quagmire: Nella Larsen's *Quicksand,*" *CLA Journal* 16 (1973): 285–301; Cheryl Wall, "Passing for What? Aspects of Identity in Nella Larsen's Novels," *Black American Literature Forum* 20, no. 1–2 (1986): 97–111; Mary Helen Washington, *Invented Lives: Narratives of Black Women, 1860–1960* (New York: Anchor-Doubleday, 1987).

7   Deborah E. McDowell, "'That nameless . . . shameful impulse': Sexuality in Nella Larsen's *Quicksand and Passing*" in *Black Feminist Criticism and Critical Theory Studies in Black American Literature,* ed. Joel Weixlmann and Houston A. Baker Jr., vol. 3 (Greenwood, Fla.: Penkevill Publishing Company, 1988), 141. Reprinted in part as introduction to *Quicksand and Passing.* All further citations to McDowell in the text are to this essay.

8   Jewelle Gomez suggests that black lesbian sexuality very often thrived behind the church pew. See Jewelle Gomez, "A Cultural Legacy Denied and Discovered: Black Lesbians in Fiction by Women," in *Home Girls: A Black Feminist Anthology,* ed. Barbara Smith. (Latham, N.Y.: Kitchen Table Press, 1983), 120–21.

9   For an analysis of the racist implications of such patronage, see Bruce Kellner, "'Refined Racism': White Patronage in the Harlem Renaissance," in *The Novels of the Harlem Renaissance,* ed. Amrit Singh (State College: Pennsylvania State University Press, 1976), 93–106.

10   McDowell writes, "Reviewing Claude McKay's *Home to Harlem* and Larsen's *Quicksand* together for *The Crisis,* for example, Du Bois praised Larsen's novel as 'a fine, thoughtful and courageous piece of work,' but criticized McKay's as so 'nauseating' in its emphasis on 'drunkenness, fighting, and sexual promiscuity' that it made him feel . . . like taking a bath." She cites "Rpt. in *Voices of a Black Nation: Political Journalism in the Harlem Renaissance,* ed. Theodore G. Vincent (San Francisco: Ramparts Press, 1973) 359," in McDowell, 164.

11   Indeed, it is the way in which Helga Crane consistently uses the language of the "primitive" and the "jungle" to describe sexual feeling that places her in a tragic alliance with Du Bois.

12   For an effort to reconcile psychoanalytic conflict and the problematic of incest and the specific history of the African American family postslavery, see Hortense J. Spillers, "'The Permanent Obliquity of an In(pha)llibly Straight': In the Time of the Daughters and the Fathers," in *Changing Our Own Words,* ed. Cheryl Wall (New Brunswick: Rutgers, 1989), 127–49.

13   Sigmund Freud, "Some Neurotic Mechanisms in Jealousy, Paranoia, and Homosexuality," in *The Standard Edition of the Complete Psychological Works of Sigmund Freud,* trans. and ed. James Strachey, 24 vols. (London: Hogarth Press, 1953–74), 18: 225.

14   Significantly, Freud argues that conscience is the sublimation of homosexual libido, that the homosexual desires that are prohibited are not thoroughly destroyed; they are satisfied by the prohibition itself. In this way, the pangs of conscience are nothing other than the displaced satisfactions of homosexual desire. The guilt about such desire is, oddly, the very way in which that desire is preserved.

This consideration of guilt as a way of locking up or safeguarding desire may well have implications for the theme of white guilt. For the question there is whether white guilt is itself the satisfaction of racist passion, whether the reliving of racism that white guilt constantly performs is not itself the very satisfaction of racism that white guilt ostensibly abhors. For white guilt—when it is not lost to self-pity—produces a paralytic moralizing that *requires* racism to sustain its own sanctimonious posturing. Precisely because white moralizing is itself nourished by racist passions, it can never be the basis on which to build and affirm a community across difference; rooted in the desire to be exempted from white racism, to produce oneself as the exemption, this strategy virtually requires that the white community remain mired in racism: hatred is merely transferred outward, and thereby preserved, but it is not overcome.

15   Norma Alarcón, "The Theoretical Subject(s) of *This Bridge Called My Back* and Anglo-American Feminism," in *Making Face, Making Soul: Haciendo Caras,* ed. Gloria Anzaldua (San Francisco: Aunt Lute, 1990), 356–69.

16   Barbara Christian, "The Race for Theory," in *The Nature and Context of Minority Discourse,* ed. A. R. Jan Mohared and D. Lloyd (New York: Oxford University Press, 1990). 37–49.

17   Toni Morrison, *Sula* (New York: Knopf, 1973), 174.

18   Henry Louis Gates Jr., *Figures,* 202.

19   I am thankful to Barbara Christian for pointing out to me the link between the theme of "passing" and the accusation of plagiarism against Larsen.

Chapter 28

Gilles Deleuze and Félix Guattari

THE MACHINES

Towards the end of this extract from *Anti-Oedipus*, Gille Deleuze and Félix Guattari say that their concept of the "desiring-machine" is not a metaphor. This is an important moment in their new definition of being: not that the human is *like* a machine, but that the human *is* a machine. Machines partake of energy flows: sometimes they are a break in that flow, perhaps an uncoupling, or a halt in a process, sometimes they facilitate that flow, through activity and production. Deleuze and Guattari argue that these machine processes are autonomous, networked, not controlled by some higher force. This concept of machines is anti-humanistic, but it is also anti-psychoanalytic in the conventional sense of Freudian and related psychoanalytical philosophies; it is this anti-psychoanalytical approach that Deleuze and Guattari are famous for, especially in books such as *Anti-Oedipus: Capitalism and Schizophrenia* (1972) and *A Thousand Plateaus: Capitalism and Schizophrenia* (1980). Freud believed that the fragmented, broken-down psyche could be healed, made whole again; Deleuze and Guattari believe that this is an oppressive narrative that creates a new fantasy or myth of a homogenous subject, one who conforms to the rules and regulations of the bourgeois family, the laws of the state, the church, and so on. Instead, the fragmented breaks (individuals) are reconceived as being merely the working parts of a machine, one which functions through desire. Deleuze and Guattari also reconceptualize the body, not just the psyche, with their notion of the "body without organs" drawn from the anti-humanistic work of drama theorist and radical philosopher, Antonin Artaud (1896–1948). What this means is that the concept of a hierarchical body, with "higher" controlling and functioning organs, such as the brain, or the face (the latter is central in the ethical work of Levinas), is rejected in favour of intensities of desire, neither representing some inner world, or transcending the moment. In other words, this is a passion stripped bare of its usual artistic, metaphysical and religious attributes. Desire simply is, in *Anti-Oedipus*, and if it drives anything within the system, it is not for some purpose or reason. The language of this theory can initially be daunting, for example, that of the code and the chain. Drawing upon Lacan and the mathematical work of Andrei A. Markov (1856–1922), the disjunctive code of the unconscious which Lacan suggests creates diverse and open-ended signifying chains, is akin to the generation of probabilities in the Markov chain (a mathematical chain of events that reveal that random variables generate further events in statistical patterns, i.e., outcomes which are dependent upon the previous events). All this means that the anti-Oedipal unconscious is not so much structured like a language, as simultaneously written and deconstructed. The theorists Roland Barthes and Julia Kristeva call such a self-deconstructive writing "signifiance". Deleuze and Guattari suggest that the closest psychoanalytical category for such a model of subjectivity (although it is a model without "subjects" per se, just desiring machines and intensities), is schizophrenia, and they call the disjunctive chains "schizzes". They do not mean this word to be used pejoratively, instead, "schizzes" represent an openness and a creativity, one which resists the straitjacket of conventional thinking.

I N WHAT RESPECT ARE desiring-machines really machines, in anything more than a metaphorical sense? A machine may be defined as a *system of interruptions* or breaks (*coupures*). These breaks should in no way be considered as a separation from reality; rather, they operate along lines that vary according to whatever aspect of them we are considering. Every machine, in the first place, is related to a continual material flow (*hylè*) that it cuts into. It functions like a ham-slicing machine, removing portions[1] from the associative flow: the anus and the flow of shit it cuts off, for instance; the mouth that cuts off not only the flow of milk but also the flow of air and sound; the penis that interrupts not only the flow of urine but also the flow of sperm. Each associative flow must be seen as an ideal thing, an endless flux, flowing from something not unlike the immense thigh of a pig. The term *hylè* in fact designates the pure continuity that any one sort of matter ideally possesses. When Robert Jaulin describes the little balls and pinches of snuff used in a certain initiation ceremony, he shows that they are produced each year as a sample taken from "an infinite series that theoretically has one and only one origin," a single ball that extends to the very limits of the universe.[2] Far from being the opposite of continuity, the break or interruption conditions this continuity: it presupposes or defines what it cuts into as an ideal continuity. This is because, as we have seen, every machine is a machine of a machine. The machine produces an interruption of the flow only insofar as it is connected to another machine that supposedly produces this flow. And doubtless this second machine in turn is really an interruption or break, too. But it is such only in relationship to a third machine that ideally—that is to say, relatively—produces a continuous, infinite flux: for example, the anus-machine and the intestine-machine, the intestine-machine and the stomach-machine, the stomach-machine and the mouth-machine, the mouth-machine and the flow of milk of a herd of dairy cattle ("and then . . . and then . . . and then . . ."). In a word, every machine functions as a break in the flow in relation to the machine to which it is connected, but at the same time is also a flow itself, or the production of a flow, in relation to the machine connected to it. This is the law of the production of production. That is why, at the limit point of all the transverse or transfinite connections, the partial object and the continuous flux, the interruption and the connection, fuse into one: everywhere there are breaks-flows out of which desire wells up, thereby constituting its productivity and continually grafting the process of production onto the product. (It is very curious that Melanie Klein, whose discovery of partial objects was so far-reaching, neglects to study flows from this point of view and declares that they are of no importance; she thus short-circuits all the connections.)[3]

"Connecticut, Connect-I-cut!" cries little Joey. In his study *The Empty Fortress*, Bruno Bettelheim paints the portrait of this young child who can live, eat, defecate, and sleep only if he is plugged into machines provided with motors, wires, lights, carburetors, propellers, and steering wheels: an electrical feeding machine, a car-machine that enables him to breathe, an anal machine that lights up. There are very few examples that cast as much light on the régime of desiring-production, and the way in which breaking down constitutes an integral part of the functioning, or the way in which the cutting off is an integral part of mechanical connections. Doubtless there are those who will object that this mechanical, schizophrenic life expresses the absence and the destruction of desire rather than desire itself, and presupposes certain extremely negative attitudes on the part of his parents to which the child reacts by turning himself into a machine. But even Bettelheim, who has a noticeable bias in favor of Oedipal or pre-oedipal causality, admits that this sort of causality intervenes only in response to autonomous aspects of the productivity or the activity of the child, although he later discerns in him a nonproductive stasis or an attitude of total withdrawal. Hence there is first of all, according to Bettelheim, an autonomous reaction to the total life experience, of which the mother is only a part. Also we must not think that the machines themselves are proof of the loss or repression of desire (which Bettelheim translates in terms of autism). We find ourselves confronted with the same problem once again: How has the process of the production of desire, how have the child's desiring-machines begun to turn endlessly round and round in a total vacuum, so as to produce the child-machine? How has the process turned into an end in itself? Or how has the child become the victim of a premature interruption or a terrible frustration? It is only by means of the body without organs (eyes closed tight, nostrils pinched shut, ears stopped up) that something is produced, counterproduced, something that diverts or frustrates the entire process of production, of which it is nonetheless still a part. But the machine remains desire, an investment of desire whose history unfolds, by way of the primary repression and the return of the repressed, in the succession of the states of paranoiac machines, miraculating machines, and celibate machines through which little Joey passes as Bettelheim's therapy progresses.

In the second place, every machine has a sort of code built into it, stored up inside it. This code is inseparable not only from the way in which it is recorded and transmitted to each of the different regions of the body, but also from the way in which the relations of each of the regions with all the others are recorded. An organ may have connections that associate it with several different flows; it may waver between several functions, and even take on the régime of another organ—the anorectic mouth, for instance. All sorts of functional questions thus arise: What flow to break? Where to interrupt it? How and by what means? What place should be left for other producers or antiproducers (the place of one's little brother, for instance)? Should one, or should one not, suffocate from what one eats, swallow air, shit with one's mouth? The data, the bits of information recorded, and their transmission form a grid of disjunctions of a type that differs from the previous connections. We owe to Jacques Lacan the discovery of this fertile domain of a code of the unconscious, incorporating the entire chain—or several chains—of meaning: a discovery thus totally transforming analysis. (The basic text in this connection is his *La lettre volée* [*The Purloined Letter*].) But how very strange this domain seems, simply because of its multiplicity—a multiplicity so complex that we can scarcely speak of *one* chain or even of *one* code of desire. The chains are called "signifying chains" (*chaînes signifiantes*) because they are made up of signs, but these signs are not themselves signifying. The code resembles not so much a language as a jargon, an open-ended, polyvocal formation. The nature of the signs within it is insignificant, as these signs have little or nothing to do with what supports them. Or rather, isn't the support completely immaterial to these signs? The support is the body without organs. These indifferent signs follow no plan, they function at all levels and enter into any and every sort of connection; each one speaks its own language, and establishes syntheses with others that are quite direct along transverse vectors, whereas the vectors between the basic elements that constitute them are quite indirect.

The disjunctions characteristic of these chains still do not involve any exclusion, however, since exclusions can arise only as a function of inhibiters and repressers that eventually determine the support and firmly define a specific, personal subject.[4] No chain is homogeneous; all of them resemble, rather, a succession of characters from different alphabets in which an ideogram, a pictogram, a tiny image of an elephant passing by, or a rising sun may suddenly make its appearance. In a chain that mixes together phonemes, morphemes, etc., without combining them, papa's mustache, mama's upraised arm, a ribbon, a little girl, a cop, a shoe suddenly turn up. Each chain captures fragments of other chains from which it "extracts" a surplus value, just as the orchid code "attracts" the figure of a wasp: both phenomena demonstrate the surplus value of a code. It is an entire system of shuntings along certain tracks, and of selections by lot, that bring about partially dependent, aleatory phenomena bearing a close resemblance to a Markov chain. The recordings and transmissions that have come from the internal codes, from the outside world, from one region to another of the organism, all intersect, following the endlessly ramified paths of the great disjunctive synthesis. If this constitutes a system of writing, it is a writing inscribed on the very surface of the Real: a strangely polyvocal kind of writing, never a biunivocalized, linearized one; a transcursive system of writing, never a discursive one; a writing that constitutes the entire domain of the "real inorganization" of the passive syntheses, where we would search in vain for something that might be labeled the Signifier—writing that ceaselessly composes and decomposes the chains into signs that have nothing that impels them to become signifying. The one vocation of the sign is to produce desire, engineering it in every direction.

These chains are the locus of continual detachments—schizzes[5] on every hand that are valuable in and of themselves and above all must not be filled in. This is thus the second characteristic of the machine: breaks that are a detachment (*coupures-détachements*), which must not be confused with breaks that are a slicing off (*coupures-prélèvements*). The latter have to do with continuous fluxes and are related to partial objects. Schizzes have to do with heterogeneous chains, and as their basic unit use detachable segments or mobile stocks resembling building blocks or flying bricks. We must conceive of each brick as having been launched from a distance and as being composed of heterogeneous elements: containing within it not only an inscription with signs from different alphabets, but also various figures, plus one or several straws, and perhaps a corpse. Cutting into the flows (*le prélèvement du flux*) involves detachment of something from a chain; and the partial objects of production presuppose stocks of material or recording bricks within the coexistence and the interaction of all the syntheses.

How could part of a flow be drawn off without a fragmentary detachment taking place within the code that comes to inform the flow? When we noted a moment ago that the schizo is at the very limit of the decoded flows of desire, we meant that he was at the very limit of the social codes, where a despotic Signifier destroys all the chains, linearizes them, biunivocalizes them, and uses the bricks as so many immobile units for the construction of an imperial Great Wall of China. But the schizo continually detaches them, continually works them loose and carries them off in every direction in order to create a new polyvocity that is the code of desire. Every composition, and also every decomposition, uses mobile bricks as the basic unit. *Diaschisis* and *diaspasis,* as Monakow put it: either a lesion spreads along fibers that link it to other regions and thus gives rise *at a distance* to phenomena that are incomprehensible from a purely mechanistic (but not a machinic) point of view; or else a humoral disturbance brings on a shift in nervous energy and creates broken, fragmented paths within the sphere of instincts. These bricks or blocks are the essential parts of desiring-machines from the point of view of the recording process: they are at once component parts and products of the process of decomposition that are spatially localized only at certain moments, by contrast with the nervous system, which is a great chronogeneous machine: a melody-producing machine of the "music box" type, with a nonspatial localization.[6] What makes Monakow and Mourgue's study an unparalleled one, going far beyond the entire Jacksonist philosophy that originally inspired it, is the theory of bricks or blocks, their detachment and fragmentation, and above all what such a theory presupposes: the introduction of desire into neurology.

The third type of interruption or break characteristic of the desiring-machine is the residual break (*coupure-reste*) or residuum, which produces a subject alongside the machine, functioning as a part adjacent to the machine. And if this subject has no specific or personal identity, if it traverses the body without organs without destroying its indifference, it is because it is not only a part that is peripheral to the machine, but also a part that is itself divided into parts that correspond to the detachments from the chain (*détachements de chaîne*) and the removals from the flow (*prélèvements de flux*) brought about by the machine. Thus this subject consumes and consummates each of the states through which it passes, and is born of each of them anew, continuously emerging from them as a part made up of parts, each one of which completely fills up the body without organs in the space of an instant. This is what allows Lacan to postulate and describe in detail an interplay of elements that is more machinic than etymological: *parere:* to procure; *separare:* to separate; *se parere:* to engender oneself. At the same time he points out the intensive nature of this interplay: the part has nothing to do with the whole; "it performs its role all by itself. In this case, only after the subject has partitioned itself does it proceed to its parturition . . . that is why the subject can procure what is of particular concern to it here, a state that we would label a legitimate status within society. Nothing in the life of any subject would sacrifice a very large part of its interests."[7]

Like all the other breaks, the subjective break is not at all an indication of a lack or need (*manque*), but on the contrary a share that falls to the subject as a part of a whole, income that comes its way as something left over. (Here again, how bad a model the Oedipal model of castration is!) That is because breaks or interruptions are not the result of an analysis; rather, in and of themselves, they are syntheses. Syntheses produce divisions. Let us consider, for example, the milk the baby throws up when it burps; it is at one and the same time the restitution of something that has been levied from the associative flux (*restitution de prélèvement sur le flux associatif*); the reproduction of the process of detachment from the signifying chain (*reproduction de détachement sur la chaîne signifiante*); and a residuum (*résidu*) that constitutes the subject's share of the whole. The desiring-machine is not a metaphor; it is what interrupts and is interrupted in accordance with these three modes. The first mode has to do with the connective synthesis, and mobilizes libido as withdrawal energy (*énergie de prélèvement*). The second has to do with the disjunctive synthesis, and mobilizes the Numen as detachment energy (*énergie de détachement*). The third has to do with the conjunctive synthesis, and mobilizes Voluptas as residual energy (*énergie résiduelle*). It is these three aspects that make the process of desiring-production at once the production of production, the production of recording, and the production of consumption. To withdraw a part from the whole, to detach, to "have something left over," is to produce, and to carry out real operations of desire in the material world.

Notes

1   The authors' word for this process is *prélèvement*. The French word has a number of meanings, including: a skimming or a draining off; a removal of a certain quantity as a sample or for purposes of testing; a setting apart of a portion or share of the whole; a deduction from a sum of money on deposit. In the English text that follows, in a number of cases the noun *prélèvement* or the corresponding verb *prélever* will be indicated in parentheses following its translation. (*Translators' note.*)

2   Robert Jaulin, *La mort sara* (Paris: Plon, 1967), p. 122.

3   "Children of both sexes regard urine in its positive aspect as equivalent to their mother's milk, in accordance with the unconscious, which equates all bodily substances with one another." Melanie Klein, *The Psycho-Analysis of Children*, trans. Alix Strachey, The International Psycho-Analytic Library, no. 22 (London: Hogarth Press and the Institute of Psycho-Analysis, 1954), p. 291. (First edition, 1932.)

4   See Jacques Lacan, "Remarque sur le rapport de Daniel Lagache," in *Ecrits* (reference note 36), of "an exclusion having its source in these signs as such being able to come about only as a condition of consistency within a chain that is to be constituted; let us also add that the one dimension limiting this condition is the translation of which such a chain is capable. Let us consider this game of lotto for just a moment more. We may then discover that it is only because these elements turn up by sheer chance within an ordinal series, in a truly unorganized way, that their appearance makes us draw lots" (p. 658).

5   A coined word (French *schize*), based on the Greek verb *schizein*, "to split," "to cleave," "to divide." (*Translators' note.*)

6   C. von Monakow and Mourgue, *Introduction biologique à l'étude de la neurologie et de la psycho-pathologie* (Paris: Alcan, 1928).

7   Jacques Lacan, "Position de l'inconscient," in *Ecrits* (Paris: Editions du Seuil), p. 843.

Chapter 29

Slavoj Žižek

HEGEL 1

Taking Deleuze from behind

Two modes of being stand behind Slavoj Žižek's reading of Deleuze: *univocity*, or, all things that exist are of equal value, and *equivocity*, that there are differences between beings and Being. To put this another way, with univocity, Deleuze argues that there is a single plane of existence via which desiring machines are constantly becoming; with equivocity, there is a hierarchy of differentiated existence, between creatures and a Creator, beings and God, where the transcendent term cannot be directly known. Later in the extract, Žižek calls this term outside the system that nonetheless drives it, the "Exception". Deleuze not only rejects such a hierarchical notion of existence, he utilizes his own unique mode of queer theory, or "philosophical buggery" as Žižek puts it, to occupy the work of thinkers who project any trace of equivocity. This procedure is different from deconstruction, according to Žižek, because if Derrida follows a "hermeneutics of suspicion", Deleuze utilizes "excessive benevolence" in his acts of ventriloquism, making major thinkers (Plato, Descartes, Kant, etc.) say the opposite to what they mean, producing "true monsters" of them and their work. Žižek himself bridges these positions through his Lacanian reading methodology, that is to say, being both deconstructive and "ventriloquist" (all statements are potentially expressive of Lacanian insights). Only one thinker fails to be "buggered" by Deleuze (to stick with Žižek's terminology), and that is Hegel. Žižek regards this failure on Deleuze's part to reveal a sort of incest prohibition, which means that rather than being different from Deleuze, Hegel must instead be "uncannily close". Hegel is supposed to be the absolute Other to Deleuze, but perhaps Deleuze fears the monstrous outcome which would follow the breaking of the incest taboo: that Deleuze "equals" Hegel. Hegel posited a dialectical system of thought that analyzed the relationships between the universal and the particular, the abstract and the concrete universal, and so on. The dialectic progresses via negation, whereas Deleuze argues for a realm of absolute positivity and total immanence (there is nothing outside of the machine system). Žižek argues that Hegel's negativity is the "positivization" of negativity, and that the dialectic is always about immanence (it is not driven by a higher force, it is a system that drives itself). In which case, Hegel and Deleuze once again, are similar in their philosophies. But Lacan's Real and Hegel's Absolute Knowledge/Spirit—the German word *Geist* can be translated both ways—appear to be outside this flat ontology, or single plane of what exists. Žižek counters this argument by suggesting that the Real and Absolute *Geist* are not absent causes, but more transgressively, they are within the system, as Symbolic forces without their status of exceptions to the rule. Another way of putting this is to think about the dialectic once more: instead of the end goal (the *telos*) being some transcendent moment, it was there from the start, driving the whole system, just never being directly accessible. The "goal" then is the system or processes that make up the system; the flat ontology already works in the present, just as the dialectic works in the present, through immanent "tensions" or differences in intensities. This is where Deleuze meets Hegel, who meets Lacan: the "traumatic core" of psychoanalysis does not exist on some other plane, in a hierarchical system of equivocity: it is here, now, as a transgressive aspect of a univocal and endless becoming.

I N HIS AUTOBIOGRAPHY, SOMERSET MAUGHAM reports how he was always an avid reader of great philosophers and found in all of them something interesting to learn, a way to get in contact with them—in all of them *except Hegel,* who remained totally foreign and impenetrable to him. The same figure of Hegel as the absolute Otherness, the philosopher from whom one has to differentiate oneself ("whatever this means, it is clear that it is incompatible with Hegelian absolute knowledge"), persists in contemporary philosophy up to Deleuze. Besides Hegel, there are three other philosophers who are obviously hated by Deleuze: Plato, Descartes, and Kant. However, with the last three, he nonetheless finds a way to read them "against the grain," to discover in their very theoretical practice procedures (of conceptual invention, of "staging" concepts) that offer a way to undermine their "official" position. Suffice it to recall the reading of Plato in the appendix to *The Logic of Sense,* which almost makes out of Plato the first anti-Platonist, the detailed reconstruction of the process of "montage" and staging that Descartes enacts in his construction of the concept of *cogito,* or the reading of Kant's multitude of the faculties of reason as opposed to the transcendental unity of the subject. In all three cases, Deleuze tries to enter the enemy's territory and twist, for his own ends, the very philosopher who should be his greatest enemy. However, there is no such operation with Hegel; Hegel is "thoroughly bad," unredeemable. Deleuze characterizes his reading of philosophers as guided by the tendency

> to see the history of philosophy as a sort of buggery or (it comes to the same thing) immaculate conception. I saw myself as taking an author from behind and giving him a child that would be his own offspring, yet monstrous. It was really important for it to be his own child, because the author had to actually say all I had him saying. But the child was bound to be monstrous too, because it resulted from all sorts of shifting, slipping, dislocations, and hidden emissions that I really enjoyed.[1]

Perhaps this unexpected reference to the *philosophical practice* of buggery provides the best exemplification of what Deleuze is effectively aiming at through his insistence on the univocity of Being: an attitude of perceiving disparate and incompatible events or propositions ("immaculate conception," "buggery," "philosophical interpretation") as occurring at the same ontological level. It is therefore crucial to perceive how the proper attitude toward propositions like "taking a philosopher from behind" is not one of an obscene, condescending, and dismissive sneer but one of completely naive seriousness: Deleuze is not trying to amuse us by way of generating a shocking effect. And the same goes for Foucault who, in his genealogy, locates at the same level of univocity philosophical statements, economic debates, legal theories, pedagogical injunctions, sexual advice. This practice of buggery is also what distinguishes Deleuze from the field of deconstruction; perhaps the most obvious sign of the gap that separates Deleuze from deconstruction is his fierce opposition to the latter's "hermeneutics of suspicion." He advised his students to trust the author you are studying. Proceed by feeling your way. . . . You must silence the voices of objection within you. You must let him speak for himself, analyze the frequency of his words, the style of his own obsessions.[2]

(It would just be good if Deleuze were to display some readiness to follow this approach also in his reading of Hegel.) Linked to this is the second feature separating Deleuze from deconstruction, which concerns his style of philosophical "indirect free speech." Both Deleuze and Derrida deploy their theories through a detailed reading of other philosophers, that is to say, they both reject the pre-Kantian, uncritical, direct deployment of philosophical systems. For both of them, philosophy today can be practiced only in the mode of metaphilosophy, as a reading of (other) philosophers. But, while Derrida proceeds in the mode of critical deconstruction, of undermining the interpreted text or author, Deleuze, in his buggery, imputes to the interpreted philosopher his own innermost position and endeavors to extract it from him. So, while Derrida engages in a "hermeneutics of suspicion," Deleuze practices an excessive benevolence toward the interpreted philosopher. At the immediate material level, Derrida has to resort to quotation marks all the time, signalling that the employed concept is not really his, whereas Deleuze endorses everything, directly speaking through the interpreted author in an indirect free speech *without* quotation marks. And, of course, it is easy to demonstrate that Deleuze's "benevolence" is much more violent and subversive than the Derridean reading: his buggery produces true monsters.

One should resist the temptation to submit Deleuzian notions of immanence and "pure presence" of the flux of becoming to a direct Derridean critique (deconstructive reading), reproaching Deleuze with "metaphysics of presence." It is not that such critique is simply wrong but, rather, that it misses the point by being too much "up to the point," by hitting its target all too directly. *Of course* Deleuze asserts presence against representation, and so forth, but precisely this "obvious" fact renders palpable that we are dealing here with a radical misunderstanding. What gets lost in such a critique is the fact that Derrida and Deleuze speak different, totally incompatible, languages, with no shared ground between them.

Deleuze is here deeply Lacanian: does Lacan not do the same in his reading of Kant "with Sade"? Jacques-Alain Miller once characterized this reading with the same words as Deleuze. The aim of Lacan is to "take Kant from behind," to produce the Sadean monster as Kant's own offspring. (And, incidentally, does the same not go also for Heidegger's reading of pre-Socratic fragments? Is he also not taking from behind Parmenides and Heraclitus? Is his extensive explanation of Parmenides' "Being and thought are the same" not one of the greatest buggeries in the history of philosophy?) The term "immaculate conception" is to be linked to the notion, from *The Logic of Sense,* of the flow of sense as infertile, without a proper causal power. Deleuzian reading does not move at the level of the actual imbrication of causes and effects; it stands to "realistic" interpretations as anal penetration does with regard to "proper" vaginal penetration. This is the "truth" of Deleuze's indirect free speech: a procedure of philosophical buggery. Deleuze even introduces variations into this topic of taking a philosopher from behind. He claims that, in his book on Nietzsche, things got turned around so that it was Nietzsche who took him from behind; Spinoza resisted being taken from behind, and so forth. However, Hegel is the absolute exception—as if this exception is constitutive, a kind of prohibition of incest in this field of taking philosophers from behind, opening up the multitude of other philosophers available for buggery. And what if we are effectively dealing here with the prohibition of incest? This would mean that, in an unacknowledged way, Hegel is uncannily *close* to Deleuze.

So, in short, why should we not risk the act of taking from behind Deleuze himself and engage in the practice of the *Hegelian buggery of Deleuze*? Therein resides the ultimate aim of the present booklet. What monster would have emerged if we were to stage the ghastly scene of the spectre of Hegel taking Deleuze from behind? How would the offspring of *this* immaculate conception look? Is Hegel really the one philosopher who is "unbuggerable," who cannot be taken from behind? What if, on the contrary, Hegel is the greatest and unique self-buggerer in the history of philosophy? What if the "dialectical method" is the one of permanent self-buggering? Sade once wrote that the ultimate sexual pleasure is for a man to penetrate himself anally (having a long and plastic enough penis that can be twisted around even when erect, so that it is possible to do it)—perhaps this closed circle of self-buggery is the "truth" of the Hegelian Circle. (There is, nonetheless, a distinction between Deleuze and Hegel-Lacan with regard to practicing philosophy as buggery: while Deleuze himself does the act of buggery, Hegel and Lacan adopt the position of a perverse observer who stages the spectacle of buggery and then watches for what the outcome will be. Lacan thus stages the scene of Sade taking Kant from behind—this is how one has to read "Kant *with* Sade"—to see the monster of Kant-Sade being born; and Hegel also is the observer of a philosophical edifice buggering itself, thus generating the monster of another philosophy.)

At a recent public discussion that followed a talk on the ethics of betrayal (the Nietzschean "noble betrayal" as the highest sign of love and respect, of fidelity even), the author (a Derridean) was asked about his own attitude toward Derrida: where is *his own* "noble betrayal" of Derrida, whom he never criticizes? The author's reply was that Derrida has no need of it, since he is all the time already betraying himself (questioning his own previous positions, etc.). But, does the same not go much more for Lacan? Is he not permanently changing his position, so that when, in his great negative statement, he pathetically proclaims that "there is no Other of the Other," and so forth, the question to be asked is But who was the poor idiot who *claimed* that there *is* an "Other of the Other" in the first place? The answer is always *Lacan himself a couple of years ago.* And, is not the highest case of this procedure Lacan's standardized attacks on Hegel in the style of "whatever I am saying, one thing is sure: it is not the Hegelian absolute knowledge, the Hegelian perfect circle of dialectical mediation?" What if this "not" is Lacan's version of "This is not my mother"? And, what if the same goes for Deleuze? What if this exceptional role of Hegel, this refusal to take him from behind, betrays a fear of excessive proximity? What if Deleuze has to elevate Hegel into an absolute Other who cannot be appropriated by free indirect speech because taking Hegel from behind would produce a monster unbearable for Deleuze himself?

Deleuze equals Hegel: is this the ultimate infinite judgment? Or, as Catherine Malabou puts it,[3] *Deleuze: Hegel = Ahab: White Whale* (the fixed exception, the One as the unity beneath multiplicity)—no complexity, no impersonal intensities, no multitudes, just Falsity embodied. This is why Deleuze even enjoins us to forget Hegel. This absolute rejection, this urge to "stupidize" Hegel, to present a straw man image of him (as amply demonstrated by Malabou), conceals, of course, a disavowed affinity. Fredric Jameson already drew attention to the fact that the central reference of *Anti-Oedipus,* the underlying scheme of its larger historical framework, is "The Pre-Capitalist Modes of Production," the long fragment from the *Grundrisse* manuscripts in which we encounter Marx at his most Hegelian (its entire scheme of the global historical movement relying on the Hegelian process from substance to subject). And, what about the other key Deleuzian concept literally taken over from Hegel, that of the "concrete universal"? (What Deleuze aims at with the "concrete universality" is the formal generative model of a process of BECOMING as opposed to the "abstract" universals [genuses and species] that serve to categorize modes of being, of established reality.) Is Deleuze's critique of the Platonic logic of ideal universal types designating the same quality (set of properties) in the elements comprised by the type not strangely close to Hegel's critique of abstract universality?

What is, effectively, the Hegelian "self-movement of the Notion" about? Recall a boring academic textbook that, apropos of a philosophical problem or discipline, enumerates the series of predominant opinions or claims: "The philosopher A claimed that soul is immortal, while the philosopher B claimed that there is no soul, and the philosopher C that soul is only the form of the body. . . ." There is something blatantly ridiculous and inadequate in presenting such a panoply of "opinions of philosophers"—why? We, the readers, somehow "feel" that this is not philosophy, that a "true" philosophy must systematically account for this very multitude of "opinions" (positions), not just enumerate them. In short, what we expect is to get a report on how one "opinion" arises out of the inconsistencies or insufficiencies of another "opinion" so that the chain of these "opinions" forms an organic Whole—or, as Hegel would have put it, the history of philosophy itself is part of philosophy, not just a comparative report on whether and how different "opinions" are right or wrong. This organic interweaving of "opinions" (positions) is what Hegel calls the "self-movement of the Notion." This is why, when someone—even if, like Francis Fukuyama, he claims to be a Hegelian—begins a sentence with "Hegel believes that . . .," he thereby automatically disqualifies himself not only as a Hegelian but also as a serious philosopher. Philosophy is emphatically *not* about the "beliefs" of different individual persons.

And, what is the Hegelian *Begriff* as opposed to the nominalist "notion," the result of abstracting shared features from a series of particular objects? Often, we stumble on a particular case that does not fully "fit" its universal species, that is "atypical"; the next step is to acknowledge that *every* particular is "atypical," that *the universal species exists only in exceptions,* that there is a structural tension between the Universal and the Particular. At this point, we become aware that the Universal is no longer just an empty neutral container of its subspecies but an entity in tension with each and every one of its species. The universal Notion thus acquires a dynamics of its own. More precisely, the true Universal *is* this very antagonistic dynamics between the Universal and the Particular. It is at this point that we pass from "abstract" to "concrete" Universal—at the point when we acknowledge that every Particular is an "exception," and, consequently, that the Universal, far from "containing" its particular content, *excludes* it (or is excluded *by* it). This exclusion renders the Universal itself particular (it is not truly universal, since it cannot grasp or contain the particular content), yet this very failure is its strength: the Universal is thus simultaneously posited as the Particular. The supreme political case of such a gesture is the moment of revolutionary "councils" taking over—the moment of "ahistorical" collective freedom, of "eternity in time," of what Benjamin called "dialectic in suspense." Or, as Alain Badiou would have put it in his Platonic terms, in such historical moments, the eternal Idea of Freedom appears/transpires. Even if its realization is always "impure," one should stick to the eternal Idea, which is not just a "generalization" of particular experiences of freedom but their inherent Measure. (To which, of course, Hegel would have retorted that the Thermidor occurs because such a direct actualization of freedom has to appear as Terror.) One should insert this appearance of Freedom into the series of exceptional temporalities, together with the Messianic time first formulated by Paul—the time when "the end is near," the time of the end of time (as Giorgio Agamben puts it) when, in an ontological "state of emergency," one should suspend one's full identification with one's sociosymbolic identity and act *as if* this identity is unimportant, a matter of indifference. (This exceptional temporality is to be strictly distinguished from the ecstatic-carnivalesque suspension of Order in which things are turned upside-down in a generalized orgy.)

This story of the Hegelian Deleuze goes on ad infinitum. When, with reference to Darwin, Deleuze emphasizes how variations within a universal kind are not the inessential, contingent particularities of a species (the "irrational," conceptually irrelevant differences between individuals) but the crucial moments of evolution, of the emergence of the New, is he not more Hegelian than he is ready to admit? What's more, is the Deleuzian "phase transition" not strangely close to the old Hegelian (and, later, dialectical-materialist) notion of the passage of quantity into new quality, namely, to the Hegelian critique of considering quantity independently of quality? (No wonder one of Deleuze's references here is Ilya Prigogine, who, unique among today's theoreticians, had the courage to point out that, taken in itself, outside its ideological role, the philosophy of dialectical materialism is not without its merits).[4] So, what if, like Ahab's "becoming-whale," Deleuze himself is caught in a strange "becoming-Hegel"? The difference between Hegel and Deleuze is here much more difficult to determine than it may appear: grosso modo, Deleuze wants to assert the primacy of the genetic process of differentiation against any mode of universal Being, whereas Hegel's aim is to introduce (self) movement into the very heart of conceptual universality. However, in this sense, is Hegel not also a "conceptual nominalist" like Deleuze? When Deleuze conceives of universality as individual, is he not again close to Hegel's notion of individuality as universal (in its self-relating negation of its particular properties)?

Deleuze's great anti-Hegelian motif is that of absolute positivity, his thorough rejection of negativity. For Deleuze, Hegelian negativity is precisely the way to subordinate difference to Identity, to reduce it to a sublated moment of identity's self-mediation ("identity of identity and difference"). The accusation against Hegel is thus double. Hegel introduces negativity into the pure positivity of Being, *and* Hegel introduces negativity in order to reduce differentiation to a subordinated/sublatable moment of the positive One. What remains unthinkable for Deleuze is simply a negativity that is *not* just a detour on the path of the One's self-mediation. One is tempted to defend Hegel here: is what Hegel ultimately does to negativity not the unheard-of *"positivization" of negativity itself*? Recall the most famous lines of all from the Sherlock Holmes stories, found in "The Silver Blaze": "'Is there any point to which you wish to draw my attention?' 'To the curious incident of the dog in the night time.' 'The dog did nothing in the night time.' 'That was the curious incident,' remarked Sherlock Holmes."

The absence itself is here perceived as a positive fact; we thus obtain a curious field in which absences accompany presences as just another set of positive facts. Perhaps this is how one should read Pascal: "A picture includes absence and presence, pleasant and unpleasant. Reality excludes absence and unpleasantness."[5] A picture (here synonymous with what Deleuze calls the flow of the Sense-Event) is an immaterial texture in which absences themselves have positive existence, in contrast to the bodily Real in which, as Lacan put it, nothing lacks, there are no absences. When, in February 2003, Colin Powell addressed the UN Security Council to advocate the attack on Iraq, the U.S. delegation asked the large reproduction of Picasso's "Guernica" on the wall behind the speaker's podium to be covered with a different visual ornament. Although the official explanation was that "Guernica" does not provide the adequate optical background for the televised transmission of Powell's speech, it was clear to everyone what the U.S. delegation was afraid of: that "Guernica," the painting supposed to be "about" the catastrophic results of the German aerial bombing of the Spanish city in the civil war, would give rise to the "wrong kind of associations" if it were to serve as the background to Powell advocating precisely the bombing of Iraq by the far superior U.S. Air Force. This is the power of negativity at its most elementary. If the U.S. delegation were to abstain from demanding that "Guernica" be covered up, probably no one would associate Powell's speech with the painting displayed behind him—the very change, the very gesture of concealing the painting, drew attention to it and imposed the "wrong association," confirming its truth.

Another subterranean link between Deleuze and Hegel is that of *immanence*. If there ever was a philosopher of unconditional immanence, it is Hegel. Is Hegel's elementary procedure not best encapsulated by his motto, from the introduction to *Phenomenology,* according to which the difference between For-us and In-itself is itself "for us": it is ourselves, in the immanence of our thought, who experience the distinction between the way things appear to us and the way they are in themselves. The distinction between appearance and transcendent reality is itself a fact of our experiential appearance; when we say that a thing is, in itelf, in a certain way, this means it *appears* to us in this mode of being. More generally, absolute immanence also determines the status of Hegel's critique of Kant and the Kantian handling of antinomies/contradictions. Far from denying us access to the Thing-in-itself, the antinomic or contradictory character of our experience of a Thing is what brings us into direct contact with it. This is also how Hegel would have approached Kafka. The Castle or Court "in themselves" are just a reified projection of the immanent movement of our thought-experience—it is not the inaccessible Thing-Castle that is refracted inadequately in our inconsistent experience. On the contrary, the spectre of the Thing-Castle is the *result* of the inherent-immanent refraction of our experience. And, finally, does the passage from one to another "shape of consciousness" in the *Phenomenology* also not rely on the turn toward absolute immanence? When Hegel refutes asceticism, he does not proclaim it inadequate to the objective state of things; he simply compares it with the immanent LIFE-PRACTICE of the ascetic subject—it is this practice (in Deleuzian terms: what an ascetic subject "does" with asceticism, on behalf of it) that refutes what asceticism "is."

The wager of Deleuze's concept of the "plane of consistency," which points in the direction of absolute immanence, is that of his insistence on the univocity of being. In his "flat ontology," all heterogeneous entities of an assemblage can be conceived at the same level, without any ontological exceptions or priorities. To refer to the well-known paradoxes of inconsistent classification, the plane of consistency would be something like a mixture of elements thrown together through a multitude of divergent criteria (recall Borges's famous taxonomy: brown dogs, dogs who belong to the emperor, dogs who don't bark, and so forth—up to dogs who do not belong to this list). It would be all too easy to counter here that the Lacanian Real is precisely that which resists inclusion within the plane of consistency, the absent Cause of the heterogeneity of the assemblage. Is it, rather, not that this "plane of consistency" is what Lacan called the "feminine" non-All set, with no exceptions and, for that very reason, no totalizing agency?[6] When, at the very end of *Seminar XI*, Lacan refers to Spinoza as the philosopher of the universal signifier and, as such, the true antipode of Kant,[7] he makes the same point: Spinoza is the philosopher of feminine *assemblage,* against Kant as the philosopher of the masculine Exception (the moral Law that suspends the imbrication of phenomenal causes and effects). The Spinozan One-Whole is thus a nontotalized Real, bringing us back to Lacan's fundamental thesis: the Real is not simply external to the Symbolic but, rather, the Symbolic itself deprived of its externality, of its founding exception.

What about Hegel? What if Hegel "feminized" Kant again by way of reducing the Kantian ontological opposition between phenomena and the Thing-in-itself to the absolutely immanent tension inhering within phenomena themselves? It is thus already with Hegel that the logic of Transgression, the idea that, to attain Truth or ultimate Reality, one has to violate the superficial order (with its rules) and force the passage to another dimension hidden beneath, is suspended. Hegel would undoubtedly fully endorse Deleuze's scathing remark about Bataille, the ultimate thinker of Transgression:

> "Transgression," a concept good for seminarists under the law of a Pope or a priest, the tricksters. Georges Bataille is a very French author. He made the little secret the essence of literature, with a mother within, a priest beneath, an eye above.[8]

In a late story by Somerset Maugham, an older Frenchmen has a paid young concubine. When he finds her in bed with a young man and she confesses that they really love each other, he proposes a unique solution. The two of them should marry; he will provide them with an apartment and a job for the young man—the price is that, twice a week, while the young man is at work, the old man will visit the young wife and make love to her. The solution is thus the reversal of the usual situation: instead of the young woman living with an old man and cheating on him with a young lover, she will live with the man whom she really loves and cheat on him with the old, unattractive man. Does this story not provide the clearest staging of the Bataillean transgression? Bataille's ultimate horizon is the tension between homogeneity and its heterogeneous excess—between the profane and the sacred, the domain of exchange, and the excess of pure expenditure. (And, insofar as Bataille's opposition of homogeneity and heterogeneity echoes Lacan's couple of S_2 and S_1, the chain of "ordinary" signifiers and the Master-Signifier, this is how one should also read the series of S_1 in Lacan's seminar *Encore*: not as an ordinal series but as the series of excesses themselves).[9] Or, to put it in Chesterton's terms: a miracle is no longer the irrational exception that disturbs the rational order, since *everything* becomes a miracle; there is no longer the need to assert excess against normality, since *everything* becomes an excess—excess is everywhere, in an unbearable intensity. Therein resides the true transgression. It occurs when the tension between the ordinary phenomenal reality and the transgressive Excess of the Real Thing is abolished. In other words, the truly subversive agent asserts the univocity of Being, assembling all the heterogeneous elements within the same "plane of consistency." Instead of the ridiculously pathetic fake heroism of forcing the established order toward its transcendent traumatic core, we get a profoundly indifferent enumeration that, without the blink of an eye, puts in the same series ethics and buggery.

Notes

1   Gilles Deleuze, *Negotiations* (New York: Columbia University Press, 1995), p. 6.
2   Quoted from André-Pierre Colombat, "Three Powers of Literature and Philosophy," in *A Deleuzian Century?* edited by Ian Buchanan (Durham, N.C.: Duke University Press, 1999), p. 204.
3   Catherine Malabou, "Who's Afraid of Hegelian Wolves?" in *Deleuze: A Critical Reader*, edited by Paul Patton (Oxford: Blackwell, 1996).
4   See Ilya Prigogine, *From Being to Becoming: Time and Complexity in the Physical Sciences* (New York: W. H. Freeman, 1981).
5   Pascal, *Pensées*, p. 107.
6   See chapter VI of Jacques Lacan, *Le séminaire, livre XX: Encore* (Paris: Editions du Seuil, 1975).
7   Jacques Lacan, *The Four Fundamental Concepts of Psycho-Analysis* (New York: Norton, 1977), p. 253.
8   Gilles Deleuze and Claire Parnet, *Dialogues II* (New York: Columbia University Press, 2002), p. 47.
9   See chapter XI of Jacques Lacan, *Le séminaire, livre XX: Encore.*

PART V

Marxism, critical theory and new historicism

HIGHLY INFLUENTIAL ON LATE NINETEENTH- and twentieth-century thought, the works of Karl Marx and his associate Friedrich Engels contributed to profound social and political transformation, nowhere more so than in the now defunct USSR, or Union of Socialist Soviet Republics—more simply known as Communist Russia. Marxism developed at a time of great economic inequality, and political upheaval, as eighteenth- and nineteenth-century aristocratic regimes were subsumed into newly arisen industrial societies. In the twentieth century, Marxism flourished during the Spanish Civil War, and as a reaction against Fascism in Germany and Italy during the Second World War; for many people it also offered an alternative to the increasingly powerful capitalist forces of American society, which the Frankfurt School, in particular, was deeply troubled by (see Chapter 31). During the Cold War, Marxism profoundly influenced western intellectual circles, especially in relation to civil rights, numerous anti-war and anti-colonial movements, and as the backbone of various alternative political movements from the 1960s onwards. More recently, Marxist ideas have informed anti-capitalist movements, green politics, and myriad approaches to diverse issues such as fair trade between the First and Third Worlds, as well as attempts to tackle the economic and technological roots of global climate change.

In *A Critique of Political Economy* (1859), Marx argued that "It is not the consciousness of men that determines their existence, but, on the contrary, their social existence that determines their consciousness."[1] Earlier, in *The Communist Manifesto* (1848), Marx and Engels had asked: "Does it require deep intuition to comprehend that man's ideas, views and conceptions, in one word, man's consciousness, changes with every change in the conditions of his material existence, in his social relations and in his social life?"[2] In these two quotations, we have the base-superstructure model: the "base" of material existence directly influences the "superstructure" of art, literature, religion, law and politics. By material existence, Marx and Engels mean more specifically the productive labour undertaken to satisfy one's needs, which in turn produces different modes of society. With the Industrial Revolution, feudal society (land-owners and landless peasants, with the latter providing physical labour in a largely agrarian world) was abruptly transformed into a factory-based, urbanized industrial society (capitalist bosses and workers, with the latter working the machines). Marx and Engels use the terms "bourgeoisie" (the ruling capitalists) and "proletariat" (the workers) for the two main classes that dominate during the Industrial Revolution. Whereas landless peasants had formerly been embedded in static rural society (villages, families in place for generations, with a Lord of the Manor, a church Minister, and so on, overseeing all), the industrial revolution had led to urbanization and concentration of the new factory workers; the proletariat, being more heavily concentrated in urban neighbourhoods, become more uniform, as they suffer from similar oppressive working conditions, such as minimum wages and long working hours. For Marx and Engels, this uniformity of experience naturally progresses to the organization of labour unions, with the potential for subsequent industrial action, which they argue is necessarily *political* action. Ironically, the new communications technologies that facilitate turning local struggles into national political action (in this period, the railways), are also an effect of the bourgeois need to constantly revolutionize technology per se, or what Marx and Engels call "the instruments of production."[3]

Marx and Engels argue that proceeding through a series of revolutions, the Bourgeoisie have taken over all of the political and social orders or society, reducing existence to a "money relation",[4] or, as Marx and Engels evocatively describe it: "All fixed, fast-frozen relations, with their train of ancient and venerable prejudices and opinions are swept away, all new-formed ones become antiquated before they can ossify. All that is solid melts into air, all that is holy is profaned, and man [*sic*] is at last compelled to face with sober senses, his real conditions of life, and his relations with his kind."[5] Alienated from their mode of production, with no actual financial gain beyond brute everyday survival, the proletariat are sleep-walkers, existing in a fantasy world or "false consciousness", one that can be "awakened" to reality and revolution. Such a Hegelian notion of historical progression is known as the Marxist dialectic, one which in this case (in *The Communist Manifesto*) is guided or mediated by the Communists, those men and women already awakened to the reality of class oppression, whose function is not to form a separate class, but to lead the otherwise inactive, or severely disadvantaged, proletariat. Once they have gained "political supremacy", the proletariat will revolutionize society by abolishing property, inheritance, private ownership of the means of production, centralizing banking, agriculture and industry through state control, and creating free education. In Marx and Engels' day, another key aim was the abolition of child labour, a labour force extensively used in the early stages of the Industrial Revolution.[6] The technical details of the economic, political and social theories sketched in *The Communist Manifesto* were published as Marx's *Capital* (vol. 1, 1867 – vols. 2 & 3 posthumously published).

Marxist literary theory developed in myriad ways, from orthodox Marxist applications of the dialectic to literary texts, to various post-Marxist political approaches to literature, ones which often stress ideological autonomy, the primacy of the material world, the historical conditions of literary or aesthetic production, and/or social justice issues. Marxist thinker Louis Althusser (1918–90) facilitated a shift from "base-superstructure" thinking (art is simply the outcome of economics) to a more complex and dynamic notion of structural relations (known as *structural Marxism*). Althusser, while agreeing with the notion that the economic base is that which "in the last instance determines the whole edifice"[7] also argued that ideological formations structure subjectivity through a process known as "interpellation" or the hailing of a subject into being (who accepts the call). Ideology, in other words, is definitely "superstructural", but it functions side-by-side with the economic base because it is not just physical skills that need to be reproduced to maintain a working class, but also their mental acquiescence to the ruling order. More specifically, Althusser identifies the Ideological State Apparatuses (ISAs) as being responsible for reproducing and maintaining the workers' submission to capitalism, namely religion, the arts, educational systems and the family. But ideology is not therefore something illusory or fantasmatic: it is real, made up of material practices that take place within the ISAs. Intriguingly, from a literary theoretical perspective, for Althusser it is "authentic" works of art that enable one to have an autonomous perspective on ideology, what in *Lenin and Philosophy* (1971) he called "*internal distantiation*".[8] Althusser also draws upon the work of Jacques Lacan (see Chapter 25), in particular the notion that ideology is "speculary", i.e., a mirror through which an imaginary notion of the real is constructed.[9]

In *The Political Unconscious: Narrative as a Socially Symbolic Act* (1981), American critic Fredric Jameson (see Chapter 32) provides an acute analysis of Althusser, specifically his critique of early mechanistic Marxist notions of causality in favour of his conception of "structural" causality, which means that the "effects" aren't simple add-ons, they are part of the production process itself. Jameson manages to synthesize both notions of causality with his notion of a political "unconscious", recuperating Marxism for literary and cultural studies, because it is regarded not as one interpretive methodology in a whole shopping mall of theoretical alternatives, but instead as the "untranscendable horizon" that sublates (or dialectically incorporates) all other critical approaches.[10] For Jameson, a dialectical approach is far more dynamic and open to differences than any other critical theory. As he argues in *Marxism and Form* (1971): "For a genuinely dialectical criticism, indeed, there can be no preestablished categories of analysis: to the degree that each work is the end result of a kind of inner logic or development in its own content, it evolves its own categories and dictates the specific terms of its own interpretation."[11] Thought, in other words, cannot be separated from the specificities of the literary object itself,[12] a material awareness of the object, and of the act of self-reflection. This awareness is necessarily "shocking" to the subject, being "the mark of an abrupt shift to a higher level of consciousness, to a larger context of being."[13]

The Frankfurt School, based at The Institute of Social Research at the University of Frankfurt, influenced the development of Marxist critical theory, especially the notion that a work's "inner logic" has to be followed to develop what is called "immanent criticism". Two thinkers explore this approach in great depth: Theodor Adorno and Walter Benjamin. The Institute of Social Research was founded in 1923 under the directorship of Carl Grünberg; in 1930, Max Horkheimer took over the directorship, and attracted a dynamic group of researchers to the Institute, including Adorno, Marcuse, and as a research associate, Walter Benjamin. Horkheimer stressed that the Institute would be interdisciplinary in nature, and that its members should develop "a dialectical penetration and development of philosophical theory and the praxis of individual scientific disciplines."[14] All aspects of society would be investigated to create a new approach to Marxism, one which detailed the structural relationships at work in the West, with focus on Fascist and later, American ideology. While the Institute's projects were disrupted by the rise to power of the Nazi party, and the emigration of most of the members to Geneva (in 1933) and then to Columbia University, New York (1935),[15] more positively this disruption offered new subjects and new perspectives, such as the threat to political emancipation brought about by the mind-numbing capitalist mass media, explored by Adorno and Horkheimer in *The Dialectic of Enlightenment* (1944).

A virtuoso example of immanent criticism is Adorno's *Aesthetic Theory* (1970), which also offers another alternative to the capitalist commodification of all art forms: the avant-garde modernist artwork, for example, the plays of Samuel Beckett. It is the *negative dialectics* of the avant-garde (also the title of a book by Adorno published in 1966) that offers a mode of resistance to the apparently inexhaustible capitalist system whereby all objects, subjects and processes are reduced to their "exchange-value". For example, Beckett's existentially bleak and often apparently meaningless plays, follow a negative dialectics—a presentation of unremitting negation that does not get synthesized and taken up to a higher level, as found in Hegelian dialectics—creating an interrogation of modern meaning-making or signifying processes in a world that appears without hope. As Adorno puts it: "Beckett's plays are absurd [i.e., the genre of Absurdism] not because of the absence of any meaning, for then they would be simply irrelevant, but because they put meaning on trial; they unfold its history."[16] There are two key points here: first, Adorno is not arguing for a postmodern lack of meaning, rather, there is still authentic reality, meaning, and identity, but only accessible via negative dialects, and second, even at the bleakest moment of modernism, a historical understanding is still available. Or as he puts it earlier on in *Aesthetic Theory*, "Authentic artworks are eloquent even when they refuse any form of semblance."[17]

Benjamin's more esoteric version of the Marxist dialectic is what he called a "dialectics at a standstill", that is to say, he believed that dialectical opposites could be brought together and maintained as opposites, held in tension, rather than being allowed synthesis. The point of this procedure is to create an explosive, revolutionary outcome, in thought and practice. Such a dialectic produces what Benjamin calls "dialectical images", that is to say, a methodology that in itself brings together Marxism and the modernist aesthetics/practices of the Surrealists.[18] Benjamin demonstrates his dialectics at a standstill in his work *The Arcades Project* (*Das Passagen-Werk* 1982; trans. 1999), which is ostensibly a study of the now defunct nineteenth-century Paris arcades, or glassed-over passages between streets that were filled with shops and other types of retail outlet. What Benjamin was actually doing with this work was creating bundles (called "convolutes") of quotes and commentaries that he juxtaposed to make dialectical images, in the process articulating a materialist, historical awareness of how commodity forms work, not just in the past, but also in the twentieth century. In other words, by turning outmoded objects into dialectical images, he created a shock awareness of how capitalism works today, which was also Benjamin's version of the Marxist "awakening" of the proletariat. Again, as with Adorno, while Benjamin is sometimes adopted by postmodernists, his approach suggests that there *is* an underlying reality that *can* be dialectically accessed, yet in Benjamin's case this includes an at times dense, mystical combination of Marxism, modernism, and Jewish Messianic theology. Examining various sections of *The Arcades Project*—topics covered include Sales Clerks, Fashion, Boredom, Advertising, Prostitution, Gambling, etc., but also Baudelaire, On The Theory of Knowledge, Theory of Progress, etc.—the reader can immediately see a difference between Adorno's application of his negative dialectic to the "high" culture of modernism, and Benjamin's crisscrossing or chiastic movement between "high" and "low". There may be some irony in the fact that Adorno's methodology should maintain such a hierarchy, with its rigorously policed boundaries between elite and popular cultures, whereas Benjamin's work maintains an encounter with materiality, and develops an alternative dialectic through low "elements".[19] As Lechte argues: "Grasping the force and significance of avant-garde art requires the use of concepts which can never do a work justice; for the materiality of the work constitutes its uniqueness, and this defies conceptualisation."[20]

Another strong critique of "high" culture, with the concomitant foregrounding of the material real, is New Historicism, emerging in the 1970s from a Marxist and Althusserian understanding of culture, transforming "ideology critique into discourse analysis."[21] Two of New Historicism's main practitioners—the critics Catherine Gallagher and Stephen Greenblatt—playfully articulate those lowly subjects previously excluded from discussions concerning literary and cultural production who have returned via "a social rebellion in the study of culture": "a rabble of half-crazed religious visionaries, semiliterate political agitators, coarse-faced peasants in hobnailed boots, dandies whose writings had been discarded as ephemera, imperial bureaucrats, freed slaves, women novelists dismissed as impudent scribblers, learned women excluded from easy access to the materials of scholarship, scandalmongers, provincial politicians, charlatans, and forgotten academics."[22] This is a veritable carnivalesque, a Bakhtinian overturning of hierarchical structures, and a re-evaluation of what counts as significant in cultural production. Instead of the high commodity of the Western canon, with its literary greats, New Historicism examines previously excluded, marginalized or non-literary texts. The resulting "broadening" of the textual field for analysis also reveals how the literary greats, which may initially appear aesthetically autonomous and detached from the material world, are in fact embedded in social and material relations, being "texts very much in and of their world."[23] Gallagher has developed this approach in texts such as *Nobody's Story: The Vanishing Acts of Women Writers in the Marketplace, 1670–1820* (1994) and *The Body Economic: Life, Death, and Sensation in Political Economy and the Victorian Novel* (2006). Major contributions by Greenblatt include *Renaissance Self-Fashioning: From More to Shakespeare* (1980), *Shakespearian Negotiations: The Circulation of Social Energy in Renaissance England* (1988), and a New Historicist biography, called *Will in the World: How Shakespeare Became Shakespeare* (2004). In 2000, Gallagher and Greenblatt jointly produced *Practicing New Historicism*.

Further links with Bakhtin's work are apparent in New Historicism's rejection of the "monological" critical work of the previous generation of historicists (for example, attempting to explain the genius of a single voice, such as Shakespeare's, in his historical setting), in favour of the "dialogical" approach of New Historicism (for example, being aware of the socially embedded nature of any speech utterance, as Bakhtin pointed out).[24] What Bakhtin offers New Historicism is a notion of semiotics grounded in the material reality of a world of social relations, thus rejecting Saussure's core thesis (and therefore the core thesis of structuralism and poststructuralism) that the sign is arbitrary. Emerson has summarized this difference between Saussure and Bakhtin with Bakhtin's "four 'social amendments'": "1. the sign and the effect of meaning it creates are a matter of the external world; 2. the external experience that is 'signified' by the sign is socially organised; 3. ideologies are not independent, isolated phenomena, they involve a relationship of communication and negotiation between different social groups within society; 4. 'the word' must be seen in the original, Greek sense of the term, as *logos*, a discursive given where not only *what* is said is important, but also *by* whom, *to* whom and *in which* situation."[25] The shift from ideology to discourse analysis, then, is not a movement towards more abstraction, but rather the belief that textual realities are always materially embedded.

Further reading

A good place to start is with the primary texts collected in Eagleton and Milne, a book which not only includes the thinkers covered in this section, but also additional important Marxist critics such as Bloch, Lukács and Williams. Singer's short introduction is a highly accessible collection of essays on Marx, while Eagleton's introduction to *Marxism and Literary Criticism* offers a similarly accessible bridge into Marxist literary studies, including sections on "the writer and commitment" and "the author as producer". Jameson is a prolific and important North American Marxist critic, and two of his books are listed below: in *Marxism and Form,* the thinkers covered are Adorno, Benjamin, Marcuse, Schiller, Bloch, Lukács, and Sartre, with a key concluding chapter called "Towards Dialectical Criticism"; in *The Political Unconscious,* Jameson brilliantly applies dialectical reasoning to readings of the authors Balzac, Gissing and Conrad. Reading Jameson can be a challenge for those new to Marxist thought, but his applications on literary and other topics are highly illuminating, and Dowling can act as a reliable and perceptive guide. Single author introductions recommended here include Bernard-Donals, Buck-Morss, Ferretter, Gilloch, Higgins, and Pieters. Interdisciplinary applications and global contexts are provided by Dawahare, Glaser and Walker, and Mandelker.

Bernard-Donals, Michael F. *Mikhail Bakhtin: Between Phenomenology and Marxism*. Cambridge & New York: Cambridge University Press, 1994.

Buck-Morss, Susan. *The Dialectics of Seeing: Walter Benjamin and the Arcades Project*. Cambridge, MA & London: the MIT Press, 1999.

Colebrook, Claire. *New Literary Histories: New Historicism and Contemporary Criticism*. Manchester & New York: Manchester University Press, 1997.

Dawahare, Anthony. *Nationalism, Marxism, and African American Literature Between the Wars: A New Pandora's Box*. Jackson, MS: University Press of Mississippi, 2003.

Dowling, William C. *Jameson, Althusser, Marx: An Introduction to the Political Unconscious*. London: Methuen & Ithaca, NY: Cornell University Press, 1984.

Eagleton, Terry. *Marxism and Literary Criticism*. London & New York: Routledge Classics, 2002.

Eagleton, Terry and Drew Milne, eds. *Marxist Literary Theory*. Oxford: Blackwell, 1999.

Ferretter, Luke. *Louis Althussser*. Abingdon, Oxon & New York: Routledge, 2006.

Gallagher, Catherine and Stephen Greenblatt. *Practicing New Historicism*. Chicago & London: University of Chicago Press, 2000.

Gilloch, Graeme. *Walter Benjamin: Critical Constellations*. Oxford: Polity, 2002.

Glaser, Daryl and David M. Walker, eds. *Twentieth Century Marxism: A Global Introduction*. Abingdon, Oxford: Routledge, 2007.

Held, David. *Introduction to Critical Theory: Horkheimer to Habermas*. Berkeley and Los Angeles: University of California Press, 1980.

Higgins, John. *Raymond Williams: Literature, Marxism and Cultural Materialism*. Abingdon, Oxon & New York: Routledge, 1999.

Jameson, Fredric. *Marxism and Form: Twentieth-Century Dialectical Theories of Literature*. Princeton, NJ: Princeton University Press, 1971.

Jameson, Fredric. *The Political Unconscious: Narrative as a Socially Symbolic Act*. London: Methuen, 1981.

Mandelker, Amy, ed. *Bakhtin in Contexts: Across the Disciplines*. Evanston, IL: Northwestern University Press, 1995.

Pieters, Jürgen. *Moments of Negotiation: The New Historicism of Stephen Greenblatt*. Amsterdam: Amsterdam University Press, 2001.

Singer, Peter. *Marx: A Very Short Introduction*. Oxford: Oxford University Press, 2000.

Notes

1   Quoted in Ian Adams and R.W. Dyson, *Fifty Major Political Thinkers*, London & New York: Routledge, 2003, p.124.

2   Karl Marx and Friedrich Engels, *The Communist Manifesto*, trans. Samuel Moore, London: Penguin, 1988, p.102.

3   Karl Marx and Friedrich Engels, *The Communist Manifesto*, p.83.

4   Karl Marx and Friedrich Engels, *The Communist Manifesto*, p.82.

5   Karl Marx and Friedrich Engels, *The Communist Manifesto*, p.83.

6   Karl Marx and Friedrich Engels, *The Communist Manifesto*, pp.104–5.

7   Quoted in Dominic Strinati, *An Introduction to Theories of Popular Culture*, p.150.

8   Quoted in John Thurston, "Althusser, Louis", in *Encyclopedia of Contemporary Literary Theory: Approaches, Scholars, Terms*, Irena R. Makaryk, ed., Toronto: University of Toronto Press, 2000, 230–33, p.232.

9   Quoted in John Thurston, "Althusser, Louis", p.232.

10   Fredric Jameson, *The Political Unconscious: Narrative as a Socially Symbolic Act*, London: Methuen, 1981, p.10.

11   Fredric Jameson, *Marxism and Form: Twentieth-Century Dialectical Theories of Literature*, Princeton, NJ: Princeton University Press, 1971, p.333.

12   Fredric Jameson, *Marxism and Form*, p.338.

13   Fredric Jameson, *Marxism and Form*, p.375.

14   Quoted in David Held, *Introduction to Critical Theory: Horkheimer to Habermas*, Berkeley and Los Angeles: University of California Press, 1980, p.32.

15   David Held, *Introduction to Critical Theory*, p.34.

16   Theodor W. Adorno, *Aesthetic Theory*, trans. Robert Hullot-Kentor, Minneapolis: University of Minnesota Press, 1997, p.153.

17   Theodor W. Adorno, *Aesthetic Theory*, p.104.

18   See Richard J. Lane, *Reading Walter Benjamin: Writing Through the Catastrophe*, Manchester & New York: Manchester University Press, 2005.

19   John Lechte, *Fifty Key Contemporary Thinkers*, p.180.

20   John Lechte, *Fifty Key Contemporary Thinkers*, p.180.
21   Catherine Gallagher and Stephen Greenblatt, *Practicing New Historicism*, Chicago & London: University of Chicago Press, 2000, p.9.
22   Catherine Gallagher and Stephen Greenblatt, *Practicing New Historicism*, pp.9–10.
23   Catherine Gallagher and Stephen Greenblatt, *Practicing New Historicism*, p.10.
24   Jürgen Pieters, *Moments of Negotiation: The New Historicism of Stephen Greenblatt*, Amsterdam: Amsterdam University Press, 2001, p.157.
25   Quoted in Jürgen Pieters, *Moments of Negotiation*, p.159, quotation modified by Lane.

Chapter 30

Karl Marx

THE COMMODITY

In this extract from chapter one of his three-volume book *Capital*, a book that continues to have a profound influence upon materialist thinking, Karl Marx starts explaining how human labour, or work, is turned into a commodity, something which can be assigned a value and exchanged. Marx will later argue that workers are essentially exploited by the capitalist bosses and owners of the surplus value produced by the workers (who are paid only a minimum wage or small share of that value), and that while the workers are responsible for literally *making* the world in which society can flourish, they are alienated from this world because of their fundamental exploitation. Marx, who along with Friedrich Engels wrote the *Communist Manifesto* (1848), begins by making a powerful statement: capitalist societies are wealthy, and this wealth appears in the form of diverse commodities. He first defines the commodity as something that satisfies human needs, whether such needs derive from physical or mental cravings, satisfied through consumption or as a means of further production. Yet right from the beginning, Marx is careful to point out that this is not just about individuals: through history, different commodities have been discovered, and through societal agreement, standards of measurement concerning commodities have been invented. A commodity which is useful is said to have "use-value", and for Marx, this is derived from the physical properties of the commodity, be it a metal or a precious stone, such as a diamond. Use-value is *not* connected to the labour involved in acquiring or producing the commodity, but it *is* realized or put into effect through use or consumption. While the use-value is thus materially inherent in the commodity, commodities can also be the "material bearers" or carriers of "exchange-value". Exchange-value is an abstract form, a "mode of expression" of the production of labour that went into acquiring or making a particular commodity. Thus if two different amounts of two types of commodity are said to have equal exchange-value, this third component (the labour value) is what is being expressed, not anything about the material goods themselves. For Marx, this reveals that a commodity only has use-value if human labour has been "objectified" or is "materialized" in it; the labour-value embodied here is socially agreed upon, and fluctuates according to processes such as industrialization and technological advances (Marx is thinking of the profound transformation from craft to factory production in the nineteenth-century Industrial Revolution). Marx points out, however, that some things can have a personal use-value, i.e., not "mediated" through labour, but directly satisfying ("Air, virgin soil, natural meadows, unplanted forests, etc."), in which case they are not commodities. To become a commodity the thing must be produced for others: what Marx calls the "social use-values" of things. The true "substance" of value, then, is human labour, but to become a commodity subject to, or available for exchange, *qualitative* differences of production are needed, meaning different skill levels and production techniques which contribute to the act of acquiring or making something. Labour, for Marx, is thus the bedrock of human activity; at an essential level it creates useful goods, "mediating" between human beings and nature.

1. The two factors of the commodity: use-value and value (substance of value, magnitude of value)

The wealth of societies in which the capitalist mode of production prevails appears as an 'immense collection of commodities'[1]; the individual commodity appears as its elementary form. Our investigation therefore begins with the analysis of the commodity.

The commodity is, first of all, an external object, a thing which through its qualities satisfies human needs of whatever kind. The nature of these needs, whether they arise, for example, from the stomach, or the imagination, makes no difference.[2] Nor does it matter here how the thing satisfies man's need, whether directly as a means of subsistence, i.e. an object of consumption, or indirectly as a means of production.

Every useful thing, for example, iron, paper, etc., may be looked at from the two points of view of quality and quantity. Every useful thing is a whole composed of many properties; it can therefore be useful in various ways. The discovery of these ways and hence of the manifold uses of things is the work of history.[3] So also is the invention of socially recognized standards of measurement for the quantities of these useful objects. The diversity of the measures for commodities arises in part from the diverse nature of the objects to be measured, and in part from convention.

The usefulness of a thing makes it a use-value.[4] But this usefulness does not dangle in mid-air. It is conditioned by the physical properties of the commodity, and has no existence apart from the latter. It is therefore the physical body of the commodity itself, for instance iron, corn, a diamond, which is the use-value or useful thing. This property of a commodity is independent of the amount of labour required to appropriate its useful qualities. When examining use-values, we always assume we are dealing with definite quantities, such as dozens of watches, yards of linen, or tons of iron. The use-values of commodities provide the material for a special branch of knowledge, namely the commercial knowledge of commodities.[5] Use-values are only realized [*verwirklicht*] in use or in consumption. They constitute the material content of wealth, whatever its social form may be. In the form of society to be considered here they are also the material bearers [*Träger*] of . . . exchange-value.

Exchange-value appears first of all as the quantitative relation, the proportion, in which use-values of one kind exchange for use-values of another kind.[6] This relation changes constantly with time and place. Hence exchange-value appears to be something accidental and purely relative, and consequently an intrinsic value, i.e. an exchange-value that is inseparably connected with the commodity, inherent in it, seems a contradiction in terms.[7] Let us consider the matter more closely.

A given commodity, a quarter of wheat for example, is exchanged for *x* boot-polish, *y* silk or *z* gold, etc. In short, it is exchanged for other commodities in the most diverse proportions. Therefore the wheat has many exchange values instead of one. But *x* boot-polish, *y* silk or *z* gold, etc., each represent the exchange-value of one quarter of wheat. Therefore *x* boot-polish, *y* silk, *z* gold, etc., must, as exchange-values, be mutually replaceable or of identical magnitude. It follows from this that, firstly, the valid exchange-values of a particular commodity express something equal, and secondly, exchange-value cannot be anything other than the mode of expression, the 'form of appearance',[8] of a content distinguishable from it.

Let us now take two commodities, for example corn and iron. Whatever their exchange relation may be, it can always be represented by an equation in which a given quantity of corn is equated to some quantity of iron, for instance 1 quarter of corn = x cwt of iron. What does this equation signify? It signifies that a common element of identical magnitude exists in two different things, in 1 quarter of corn and similarly in x cwt of iron. Both are therefore equal to a third thing, which in itself is neither the one nor the other. Each of them, so far as it is exchange-value, must therefore be reducible to this third thing.

A simple geometrical example will illustrate this. In order to determine and compare the areas of all rectilinear figures we split them up into triangles. Then the triangle itself is reduced to an expression totally different from its visible shape: half the product of the base and the altitude. In the same way the exchange values of commodities must be reduced to a common element, of which they represent a greater or a lesser quantity.

This common element cannot be a geometrical, physical, chemical or other natural property of commodities. Such properties come into consideration only to the extent that they make the commodities useful, i.e. turn them into use-values. But clearly, the exchange relation of commodities is characterized precisely by its abstraction from their use-values. Within the exchange relation, one use-value is worth just as much as another, provided only that it is present in the appropriate quantity. Or, as old Barbon says: 'One sort of wares are as good as another, if the value be equal. There is no difference or distinction in things of equal value . . . One hundred pounds worth of lead or iron, is of as great a value as one hundred pounds worth of silver and gold.'[9]

As use-values, commodities differ above all in quality, while as exchange-values they can only differ in quantity, and therefore do not contain an atom of use-value.

If then we disregard the use-value of commodities, only one property remains, that of being products of labour. But even the product of labour has already been transformed in our hands. If we make abstraction from its use-value, we abstract also from the material constituents and forms which make it a use-value. It is no longer a table, a house, a piece of yarn or any other useful thing. All its sensuous characteristics are extinguished. Nor is it any longer the product of the labour of the joiner, the mason or the spinner, or of any other particular kind of productive labour. With the disappearance of the useful character of the products of labour, the useful character of the kinds of labour embodied in them also disappears; this in turn entails the disappearance of the different concrete forms of labour. They can no longer be distinguished, but are all together reduced to the same kind of labour, human labour in the abstract.

Let us now look at the residue of the products of labour. There is nothing left of them in each case but the same phantom-like objectivity; they are merely congealed quantities of homogeneous human labour, i.e. of human labour-power expended without regard to the form of its expenditure. All these things now tell us is that human labour-power has been expended to produce them, human labour is accumulated in them. As crystals of this social substance, which is common to them all, they are values – commodity values [*Warenwerte*].

We have seen that when commodities are in the relation of exchange, their exchange-value manifests itself as something totally independent of their use-value. But if we abstract from their use-value, there remains their value, as it has just been defined. The common factor in the exchange relation, or in the exchange-value of the commodity, is therefore its value. The progress of the investigation will lead us back to exchange-value as the necessary mode of expression, or form of appearance, of value. For the present, however, we must consider the nature of value independently of its form of appearance [*Erscheinungs form*].

A use-value, or useful article, therefore, has value only because abstract human labour is objectified [*vergegenständlicht*] or materialized in it. How, then, is the magnitude of this value to be measured? By means of the quantity of the 'value-forming substance', the labour, contained in the article. This quantity is measured by its duration, and the labour-time is itself measured on the particular scale of hours, days etc.

It might seem that if the value of a commodity is determined by the quantity of labour expended to produce it, it would be the more valuable the more unskilful and lazy the worker who produced it, because he would need more time to complete the article. However, the labour that forms the substance of value is equal human labour, the expenditure of identical human labour-power. The total labour-power of society, which is manifested in the values of the world of commodities, counts here as one homogeneous mass of human labour-power, although composed of innumerable individual units of labour-power. Each of these units is the same as any other, to the extent that it has the character of a socially average unit of labour-power and acts as such, i.e. only needs, in order to produce a commodity, the labour time which is necessary on an average, or in other words is socially necessary. Socially necessary labour-time is the labour-time required to produce any use-value under the conditions of production normal for a given society and with the average degree of skill and intensity of labour prevalent in that society. The introduction of power-looms into England, for example, probably reduced by one half the labour required to convert a given quantity of yarn into woven fabric. In order to do this, the English hand-loom weaver in fact needed the same amount of labour-time as before; but the product of his individual hour of labour now only represented half an hour of social labour, and consequently fell to one half its former value.

What exclusively determines the magnitude of the value of any article is therefore the amount of labour socially necessary, or the labour-time socially necessary for its production.[10] The individual commodity counts here only as an average sample of its kind.[11] Commodities which contain equal quantities of labour, or which can be produced in the same time, have therefore the same value. The value of a commodity is related to the value of any other commodity as the labour-time necessary for the production of the one is related to the labour-time necessary for the production of the other. 'As exchange-values, all commodities are merely definite quantities of *congealed labour-time*.'[12]

The value of a commodity would therefore remain constant, if the labour-time required for its production also remained constant. But the latter changes with every variation in the productivity of labour. This is determined by a wide range of circumstances; it is determined amongst other things by the workers' average degree of skill, the level of development of science and its technological application, the social organization of the process of production, the extent and effectiveness of the means of production, and the conditions found in the natural environment. For example, the same quantity of labour is present in eight bushels of corn in favourable seasons and in only four bushels in unfavourable seasons. The same quantity of labour provides more metal in rich mines than in poor. Diamonds are of very rare occurrence on the earth's surface, and hence their discovery costs, on an average, a great deal of labour-time. Consequently much labour is represented in a small volume. Jacob questions whether gold has ever been paid for at its full value.[13] This applies still more to diamonds. According to Eschwege, the total produce of the Brazilian diamond mines for the eighty years ending in 1823 still did not amount to the price of 1½ years' average produce of the sugar and coffee plantations of the same country,[14] although the diamonds represented much more labour, therefore more value. With richer mines, the same quantity of labour would be embodied in more diamonds, and their value would fall. If man succeeded, without much labour, in transforming carbon into diamonds, their value might fall below that of bricks. In general, the greater the productivity of labour, the less the labour-time required to produce an article, the less the mass of labour crystallized in that article, and the less its value.

Inversely, the less the productivity of labour, the greater the labour-time necessary to produce an article, and the greater its value. The value of a commodity, therefore, varies directly as the quantity, and inversely as the productivity, of the labour which finds its realization within the commodity. (Now we know the *substance* of value. It is *labour*. We know the *measure of its magnitude*. It is *labour-time*. The *form*, which stamps *value* as *exchange-value*, remains to be analysed. But before this we need to develop the characteristics we have already found somewhat more fully.)[15]

A thing can be a use-value without being a value. This is the case whenever its utility to man is not mediated through labour. Air, virgin soil, natural meadows, unplanted forests, etc. fall into this category. A thing can be useful, and a product of human labour, without being a commodity. He who satisfies his own need with the product of his own labour admittedly creates use-values, but not commodities. In order to produce the latter, he must not only produce use-values, but use-values for others, social use-values. (And not merely for others. The medieval peasant produced a corn-rent for the feudal lord and a corn-tithe for the priest; but neither the corn-rent nor the corn-tithe became commodities simply by being produced for others. In order to become a commodity, the product must be transferred to the other person, for whom it serves as a use-value, through the medium of exchange.)[16] Finally, nothing can be a value without being an object of utility. If the thing is useless, so is the labour contained in it; the labour does not count as labour, and therefore creates no value.

2. The dual character of the labour embodied in commodities

Initially the commodity appeared to us as an object with a dual character, possessing both use-value and exchange-value. Later on it was seen that labour, too, has a dual character: in so far as it finds its expression in value, it no longer possesses the same characteristics as when it is the creator of use-values. I was the first to point out and examine critically this twofold nature of the labour contained in commodities.[17] As this point is crucial to an understanding of political economy, it requires further elucidation.

Let us take two commodities, such as a coat and 10 yards of linen, and let the value of the first be twice the value of the second, so that, if 10 yards of linen = W, the coat = $2W$.

The coat is a use-value that satisfies a particular need. A specific kind of productive activity is required to bring it into existence. This activity is determined by its aim, mode of operation, object, means and result. We use the abbreviated expression 'useful labour' for labour whose utility is represented by the use-value of its product, or by the fact that its product is a use-value. In this connection we consider only its useful effect.

As the coat and the linen are qualitatively different use-values, so also are the forms of labour through which their existence is mediated – tailoring and weaving. If the use-values were not qualitatively different, hence not the products of qualitatively different forms of useful labour, they would be absolutely incapable of confronting each other as commodities. Coats cannot be exchanged for coats, one use-value cannot be exchanged for another of the same kind.

The totality of heterogeneous use-values or physical commodities reflects a totality of similarly heterogeneous forms of useful labour, which differ in order, genus, species and variety: in short, a social division of labour. This division of labour is a necessary condition for commodity production, although the converse does not hold; commodity production is not a necessary condition for the social division of labour. Labour is socially divided in the primitive Indian community, although the products do not thereby become commodities. Or, to take an example nearer home, labour is systematically divided in every factory, but the workers do not bring about this division by exchanging their individual products. Only the products of mutually independent acts of labour, performed in isolation, can confront each other as commodities.

To sum up, then: the use-value of every commodity contains useful labour, i.e. productive activity of a definite kind, carried on with a definite aim. Use-values cannot confront each other as commodities unless the useful labour contained in them is qualitatively different in each case. In a society whose products generally assume the form of commodities, i.e. in a society of commodity producers, this qualitative difference between the useful forms of labour which are carried on independently and privately by individual producers develops into a complex system, a social division of labour.

It is moreover a matter of indifference whether the coat is worn by the tailor or by his customer. In both cases it acts as a use-value. So, too, the relation between the coat and the labour that produced it is not in itself altered when tailoring becomes a special trade, an independent branch of the social division of labour. Men made clothes for thousands of years, under the compulsion of the need for clothing, without a single man ever becoming a tailor. But the existence of coats, of linen, of every element of material wealth not provided in advance by nature, had always to be mediated through a specific productive activity appropriate to its purpose, a productive activity that assimilated particular natural materials to particular human requirements. Labour, then, as the creator of use-values, as useful labour, is a condition of human existence which is independent of all forms of society; it is an eternal natural necessity which mediates the metabolism between man and nature, and therefore human life itself.

Use-values like coats, linen, etc., in short, the physical bodies of commodities, are combinations of two elements, the material provided by nature, and labour. If we subtract the total amount of useful labour of different kinds which is contained in the coat, the linen, etc., a material substratum is always left. This substratum is furnished by nature without human intervention. When man engages in production, he can only proceed as nature does herself, i.e. he can only change the form of the materials.[18] Furthermore, even in this work of modification he is constantly helped by natural forces. Labour is therefore not the only source of material wealth, i.e. of the use-values it produces. As William Petty says, labour is the father of material wealth, the earth is its mother.[19]

Let us now pass from the commodity as an object of utility to the value of commodities.

We have assumed that the coat is worth twice as much as the linen. But this is merely a quantitative difference, and does not concern us at the moment. We shall therefore simply bear in mind that if the value of a coat is twice that of 10 yards of linen, 20 yards of linen will have the same value as a coat. As values, the coat and the linen have the same substance, they are the objective expressions of homogeneous labour. But tailoring and weaving are qualitatively different forms of labour. There are, however, states of society in which the same man alternately makes clothes and weaves. In this case, these two different modes of labour are only modifications of the labour of the same individual and not yet fixed functions peculiar to different individuals, just as the coat our tailor makes today, and the pair of trousers he makes tomorrow, require him only to vary his own individual labour. Moreover, we can see at a glance that in our capitalist society a given portion of labour is supplied alternately in the form of tailoring and in the form of weaving, in accordance with changes in the direction of the demand for labour. This change in the form of labour may well not take place without friction, but it must take place.

If we leave aside the determinate quality of productive activity, and therefore the useful character of the labour, what remains is its quality of being an expenditure of human labour-power. Tailoring and weaving, although they are qualitatively different productive activities, are both a productive expenditure of human brains, muscles, nerves, hands etc., and in this sense both human labour. They are merely two different forms of the expenditure of human labour-power. Of course, human labour-power must itself have attained a certain level of development before it can be expended in this or that form. But the value of a commodity represents human labour pure and simple, the expenditure of human labour in general. And just as, in civil society, a general or a banker plays a great part but man as such plays a very mean part,[20] so, here too, the same is true of human labour. It is the expenditure of simple labour-power, i.e. of the labour-power possessed in his bodily organism by every ordinary man, on the average, without being developed in any special way. *Simple average labour,* it is true, varies in character in different countries and at different cultural epochs, but in a particular society it is given. More complex labour counts only as *intensified,* or rather *multiplied* simple labour, so that a smaller quantity of complex labour is considered equal to a larger quantity of simple labour. Experience shows that this reduction is constantly being made. A commodity may be the outcome of the most complicated labour, but through its *value* it is posited as equal to the product of simple labour, hence it represents only a specific quantity of simple labour.[21] The various proportions in which different kinds of labour are reduced to simple labour as their unit of measurement are established by a social process that goes on behind the backs of the producers; these proportions therefore appear to the producers to have been handed down by tradition. In the interests of simplification, we shall henceforth view every form of labour-power directly as simple labour-power; by this we shall simply be saving ourselves the trouble of making the reduction.

Just as, in viewing the coat and the linen as values, we abstract from their different use-values, so, in the case of the labour represented by those values, do we disregard the difference between its useful forms, tailoring and weaving. The use-values coat and linen are combinations of, on the one hand, productive activity with a definite purpose, and, on the other, cloth and yarn; the values coat and linen, however, are merely congealed quantities of homogeneous labour. In the same way, the labour contained in these values does not count by virtue of its productive relation to cloth and yarn, but only as being an expenditure of human labour-power. Tailoring and weaving are the formative elements in the use-values coat and linen, precisely because these two kinds of labour are of different qualities; but only in so far as abstraction is made from their particular qualities, only in so far as both possess the same quality of being human labour, do tailoring and weaving form the substance of the values of the two articles mentioned.

Coats and linen, however, are not merely values in general, but values of definite magnitude, and, following our assumption, the coat is worth twice as much as the 10 yards of linen. Why is there this difference in value? Because the linen contains only half as much labour as the coat, so that labour-power had to be expended twice as long to produce the second as to produce the first.

While, therefore, with reference to use-value, the labour contained in a commodity counts only qualitatively, with reference to value it counts only quantitatively, once it has been reduced to human labour pure and simple. In the former case it was a matter of the 'how' and the 'what' of labour, in the latter of the 'how much', of the temporal duration of labour. Since the magnitude of the value of a commodity represents nothing but the quantity of labour embodied in it, it follows that all commodities, when taken in certain proportions, must be equal in value.

If the productivity of all the different sorts of useful labour required, let us say, for the production of a coat remains unchanged, the total value of the coats produced will increase along with their quantity. If one coat represents x days' labour, two coats will represent $2x$ days' labour, and so on. But now assume that the duration of the labour necessary for the production of a coat is doubled or halved. In the first case, one coat is worth as much as two coats were before; in the second case two coats are only worth as much as one was before, although in both cases one coat performs the same service, and the useful labour contained in it remains of the same quality. One change has taken place, however: a change in the quantity of labour expended to produce the article.

In itself, an increase in the quantity of use-values constitutes an increase in material wealth. Two coats will clothe two men, one coat will only clothe one man, etc. Nevertheless, an increase in the amount of material wealth may correspond to a simultaneous fall in the magnitude of its value. This contradictory movement arises out of the twofold character of labour. By 'productivity' of course, we always mean the productivity of concrete useful labour; in reality this determines only the degree of effectiveness of productive activity directed towards a given purpose within a given period of time. Useful labour becomes, therefore, a more or less abundant source of products in direct proportion as its productivity rises or falls. As against this, however, variations in productivity have no impact whatever on the labour itself represented in value. As productivity is an attribute of labour in its concrete useful form, it naturally ceases to have any bearing on that labour as soon as we abstract from its concrete useful form. The same labour, therefore, performed for the same length of time, always yields the same amount of value, independently of any variations in productivity. But it provides different quantities of use-values during equal periods of time; more, if productivity rises; fewer, if it falls. For this reason, the same change in productivity which increases the fruitfulness of labour, and therefore the amount of use-values produced by it, also brings about a reduction in the value of this increased total amount, if it cuts down the total amount of labour-time necessary to produce the use-values. The converse also holds.

On the one hand, all labour is an expenditure of human labour-power, in the physiological sense, and it is in this quality of being equal, or abstract, human labour that it forms the value of commodities. On the other hand, all labour is an expenditure of human labour-power in a particular form and with a definite aim, and it is in this quality of being concrete useful labour that it produces use-values.[22]

Notes

1   Karl Marx, *Zur Kritik der Politischen Ökonomie,* Berlin, 1859, p. 3 [English translation, p. 27].

2   'Desire implies want; it is the appetite of the mind, and as natural as hunger to the body . . . The greatest number (of things) have their value from supplying the wants of the mind' (Nicholas Barbon, *A Discourse on Coining the New Money Lighter. In Answer to Mr Locke's Considerations etc.,* London, 1696, pp. 2, 3).

3   'Things have an intrinsick vertue' (this is Barbon's special term for use-value) 'which in all places have the same vertue; as the loadstone to attract iron' (op. cit., p. 6). The magnet's property of attracting iron only became useful once it had led to the discovery of magnetic polarity.

4   'The natural worth of anything consists in its fitness to supply the necessities, or serve the conveniences of human life' (John Locke, 'Some Considerations on the Consequences of the Lowering of Interest' (1691), in *Works,* London, 1777, Vol. 2, p. 28). In English writers of the seventeenth century we still often find the word 'worth' used for use-value and 'value' for exchange-value. This is quite in accordance with the spirit of a language that likes to use a Teutonic word for the actual thing, and a Romance word for its reflection.

5   In bourgeois society the legal fiction prevails that each person, as a buyer, has an encyclopedic knowledge of commodities.

6   'Value consists in the exchange relation between one thing and another, between a given amount of one product and a given amount of another' (Le Trosne, *De l'intérêt social,* in *Physiocrates,* ed. Daire, Paris, 1846, p. 889).

7   'Nothing can have an intrinsick value' (N. Barbon, op. cit., p. 6); or as Butler says:

'The value of a thing
Is just as much as it will bring.'
          (Samuel Butler, *Hudibras,* Part 2, Canto 1, lines 465–66, 'For what is worth in
                        any thing, but so much money as 'twill bring?')

8   *Erscheinungsform.* This word appears in inverted commas in the original.

9   N. Barbon, op. cit., pp. 53 and 7.

10   'The value of them' (the necessaries of life) 'when they are exchanged the one for another, is regulated by the quantity of labour necessarily required, and commonly taken in producing them' (*Some Thoughts on the Interest of Money in General, and Particularly in the Publiek Funds,* London, pp. 36, 37). This remarkable anonymous work of the eighteenth century bears no date. However, it is clear from its contents that it appeared in the reign of George II, about 1739 or 1740.

11   'Properly speaking, all products of the same kind form a single mass, and their price is determined in general and without regard to particular circumstances' (Le Trosne, op. cit., p. 893).

12   Karl Marx, op. cit., p. 6 [English translation, p. 30].

13   William Jacob, *An Historical Enquiry in to the Production and Consumption of the Precious Metals,* London, 1831, Vol. 2, p.101.

14   This information comes from H. A. M. Merivale, *Lectures on Colonization and Colonies,* London, 1841, Cf. *Grundrisse,* p.833.

15   The passage in parentheses occurs only in the first edition.

16   [Note by Engels to the fourth German edition:] I have inserted the passage in parentheses because, through its omission, the misconception has very frequently arisen that Marx regarded every product consumed by someone other than the producer as a commodity.

17   Karl Marx, op. cit., pp. 12, 13, and passim [English translation, pp. 41, 42].

18   'All the phenomena of the universe, whether produced by the hand of man or indeed by the universal laws of physics, are not to be conceived of as acts of creation but solely as a reordering of matter. Composition and separation are the only elements found by the human mind whenever it analyses the notion of reproduction; and so it is with the reproduction of value' (use-value, although Verri himself, in this polemic against the Physiocrats, is not quite certain of the kind of value he is referring to) 'and wealth, whether earth, air and water are turned into corn in the fields, or the secretions of an insect are turned into silk by the hand of man, or some small pieces of metal are arranged together to form a repeating watch' (Pietro Verri, *Meditazioni sulla economia politica* – first printed in 1771 – in Custodi's edition of the Italian economists, *Parte moderna,* Vol. 15, pp. 21, 22).

19   *A Treatise of Taxes and Contributions,* published anonymously by William Petty, London, 1667, p.47.

20   Cf. Hegel, *Philosophie des Rechts,* Berlin, 1840, p. 250, para. 190. Hegel says here: 'In civil society as a whole, at the standpoint of needs, what we have before us is the composite idea which we call man. Thus this is the first time, and indeed the only time, to speak of man in this sense' (*Hegel's Philosophy of Right,* tr. T. M. Knox, Oxford, 1952, p. 127).

21   The reader should note that we are not speaking here of the wages or value the worker receives for (e.g.) a day's labour, but of the value of the commodity in which his day of labour is objectified. At this stage of our presentation, the category of wages does not exist at all.

22   In order to prove that 'labour alone is the ultimate and real standard by which the value of all commodities can at all times and places be estimated and compared', Adam Smith (here, as elsewhere occasionally, Marx quotes an English author in German. This explains certain slight divergences from the original English text) says this: 'Equal quantities of labour, at all times and places, must have the same value for the labourer. In his ordinary state of health, strength and activity; in the ordinary degree of his skill and dexterity, he must always lay down the same portion of his ease, his liberty, and his happiness' (*Wealth of Nations,* Bk I, Ch. 5 [pp. 104–5]). On the one hand, Adam Smith here (but not everywhere) confuses his determination of value by the quantity of labour expended in the production of commodities with the determination of the values of commodities by the value of labour, and therefore endeavours to prove that equal quantities of labour always have the same value. On the other hand, he has a suspicion that, in so far as labour manifests itself in the value of commodities, it only counts as an expenditure of labour-power; but then again he views this expenditure merely as the sacrifice of rest, freedom and happiness, not as also man's normal life-activity. Of course, he has the modern wage-labourer in mind. Adam Smith's anonymous predecessor, cited in note 9, is much nearer the mark when he says: 'One man has employed himself a week in providing this necessary of life. . . . and he that gives him some other in exchange, cannot make a better estimate of what is a proper equivalent, than by computing what cost him just as much labour and time: which in effect is no more than exchanging one man's labour in one thing for a time

328   KARL MARX

certain, for another man's labour in another thing for the same time' (*Some Thoughts on the Interest of Money in General etc.*, p. 39). [Note by Engels to the fourth German edition:] The English language has the advantage of possessing two separate words for these two different aspects of labour. Labour which creates use-values and is qualitatively determined is called 'work' as opposed to 'labour'; labour which creates value and is only measured quantitatively is called 'labour', as opposed to 'work'. (Unfortunately, English usage does not always correspond to Engels' distinction. We have tried to adopt it where possible.)

Chapter 31

Theodor Adorno and Max Horkheimer

THE CULTURE INDUSTRY

Enlightenment as mass deception

As western society became more industrialized and technological, letting go of religious beliefs and other long-held traditions, some thinkers feared a loss of cultural cohesion. Theodor Adorno and Max Horkheimer reject this fear with the observation that the opposite has occurred: the new culture industries homogenize every cultural product into one highly stable uniform whole. Planned industrial expansion is reflected not just in the throwaway consumer culture of processed food, but also in the realms of housing, movies and radio. Writing before television really took off in the US, Adorno and Horkheimer—two of the key members of the Frankfurt School—are nonetheless highly prophetic in their forecast concerning mass entertainment in a technological age, interpreted through the lens of Marxist critical theory. They present a version of Marx's notion that the workers in modern society are alienated: from their mode of production and from themselves. Technology holds society together by reducing everything to the standardized uniformity of the industrial production line, expressed through the core thesis that "A technological rationale is the rationale of domination itself." Consumer choice is an illusion: small product differences mask the fact that all products are essentially identical; and this is replicated in the realm of politics, where the differences between parties is minimal. The culture industry analyzes consumers to produce more propaganda, thus betraying and undermining any notion of "meaning" inherent in previously oppositional artworks. Ideas, once explored by artworks, have been "liquidated" and replaced by "effects" or technical details. Once, experimental form was the vehicle by which artworks were created to protest against any notion of standardization or conformity to industrial society, such as the Romantics asserting Nature as an antidote to the capitalist Industrial Revolution and its associated intense urbanization. But the "totality" or uniformity of the culture industry has brought such artistic protest to an end: the formulaic has replaced the unique, countercultural artwork. Adorno and Horkheimer argue further that the new media begin to create a new reality: "Real life is indistinguishable from the movies". Consumers are not given the time or space to engage in an intellectual, thoughtful response to an artwork; with the new media, responses are programmed in advance, becoming automatic. The suggestion is that people themselves become automatons, programmed to work well on factory production lines, and to behave themselves between shifts. Leisure, in other words, is another form of work, moulding human beings so that they conform to the status quo. Adorno and Horkheimer are in effect arguing that the culture industry plays a large part in forging the "false consciousness" that keeps workers pacified within a capitalist society, that is to say, the ideal consumer is also the ideal producer. An important illusion to be maintained here is that the culture industry continually produces new and surprising experiences, when in reality, the new masks the sameness of the organized conventions; apparently transgressive style, say that of jazz music, is in fact merely a "calculated mutation" to "confirm the validity of the system". Authentic culture, for Adorno and Horkheimer, is always "contrary" to the prevailing administrative politics of the day; the culture industry utilizes the schematic potential of a "common denominator" to transform what used to be oppositional so that it agrees with and reproduces the underlying demands of capitalism.

THE SOCIOLOGICAL THEORY THAT the loss of the support of objectively established religion, the dissolution of the last remnants of precapitalism, together with technological and social differentiation or specialization, have led to cultural chaos is disproved every day; for culture now impresses the same stamp on everything. Films, radio and magazines make up a system which is uniform as a whole and in every part. Even the aesthetic activities of political opposites are one in their enthusiastic obedience to the rhythm of the iron system. The decorative industrial management buildings and exhibition centers in authoritarian countries are much the same as anywhere else. The huge gleaming towers that shoot up everywhere are outward signs of the ingenious planning of international concerns, toward which the unleashed entrepreneurial system (whose monuments are a mass of gloomy houses and business premises in grimy, spiritless cities) was already hastening. Even now the older houses just outside the concrete city centers look like slums, and the new bungalows on the outskirts are at one with the flimsy structures of world fairs in their praise of technical progress and their built-in demand to be discarded after a short while like empty food cans. Yet the city housing projects designed to perpetuate the individual as a supposedly independent unit in a small hygienic dwelling make him all the more subservient to his adversary—the absolute power of capitalism. Because the inhabitants, as producers and as consumers, are drawn into the center in search of work and pleasure, all the living units crystallize into well-organized complexes. The striking unity of microcosm and macrocosm presents men with a model of their culture: the false identity of the general and the particular. Under monopoly all mass culture is identical, and the lines of its artificial framework begin to show through. The people at the top are no longer so interested in concealing monopoly: as its violence becomes more open, so its power grows. Movies and radio need no longer pretend to be art. The truth that they are just business is made into an ideology in order to justify the rubbish they deliberately produce. They call themselves industries; and when their directors' incomes are published, any doubt about the social utility of the finished products is removed.

Interested parties explain the culture industry in technological terms. It is alleged that because millions participate in it, certain reproduction processes are necessary that inevitably require identical needs in innumerable places to be satisfied with identical goods. The technical contrast between the few production centers and the large number of widely dispersed consumption points is said to demand organization and planning by management. Furthermore, it is claimed that standards were based in the first place on consumers' needs, and for that reason were accepted with so little resistance. The result is the circle of manipulation and retroactive need in which the unity of the system grows ever stronger. No mention is made of the fact that the basis on which technology acquires power over society is the power of those whose economic hold over society is greatest. A technological rationale is the rationale of domination itself. It is the coercive nature of society alienated from itself. Automobiles, bombs, and movies keep the whole thing together until their leveling element shows its strength in the very wrong which it furthered. It has made the technology of the culture industry no more than the achievement of standardization and mass production, sacrificing whatever involved a distinction between the logic of the work and that of the social system. This is the result not of a law of movement in technology as such but of its function in today's economy. The need which might resist central control has already been suppressed by the control of the individual consciousness. The step from the telephone to the radio has clearly distinguished the roles. The former still allowed the subscriber to play the role of subject, and was liberal. The latter is democratic: it turns all participants into listeners and authoritatively subjects them to broadcast programs which are all exactly the same. No machinery of rejoinder has been devised, and private broadcasters are denied any freedom. They are confined to the apocryphal field of the "amateur," and also have to accept organization from above. But any trace of spontaneity from the public in official broadcasting is controlled and absorbed by talent scouts, studio competitions and official programs of every kind selected by professionals. Talented performers belong to the industry long before it displays them; otherwise they would not be so eager to fit in. The attitude of the public, which ostensibly and actually favors the system of the culture industry, is a part of the system and not an excuse for it. If one branch of art follows the same formula as one with a very different medium and content; if the dramatic intrigue of broadcast soap operas becomes no more than useful material for showing how to master technical problems at both ends of the scale of musical experience—real jazz or a cheap imitation; or if a movement from a Beethoven symphony is crudely "adapted" for a film sound-track in the same way as a Tolstoy novel is garbled in a film script: then the claim that this is done to satisfy the spontaneous wishes of the public is no more than hot air. We are closer to the facts if we explain these phenomena as inherent in the technical and personnel apparatus which, down to its last cog, itself forms part of the economic mechanism of selection. In addition there is the agreement—or at least the determination—of all executive authorities not to produce or sanction anything that in any way differs from their own rules, their own ideas about consumers, or above all themselves.

In our age the objective social tendency is incarnate in the hidden subjective purposes of company directors, the foremost among whom are in the most powerful sectors of industry—steel, petroleum, electricity, and chemicals. Culture monopolies are weak and dependent in comparison. They cannot afford to neglect their appeasement of the real holders of power if their sphere of activity in mass society (a sphere producing a specific type of commodity which anyhow is still too closely bound up with easygoing liberalism and Jewish intellectuals) is not to undergo a series of purges. The dependence of the most powerful broadcasting company on the electrical industry, or of the motion picture industry on the banks, is characteristic of the whole sphere, whose individual branches are themselves economically interwoven. All are in such close contact that the extreme concentration of mental forces allows demarcation lines between different firms and technical branches to be ignored. The ruthless unity in the culture industry is evidence of what will happen in politics. Marked differentiations such as those of A and B films, or of stories in magazines in different price ranges, depend not so much on subject matter as on classifying, organizing, and labeling consumers. Something is provided for all so that none may escape; the distinctions are emphasized and extended. The public is catered for with a hierarchical range of mass-produced products of varying quality, thus advancing the rule of complete quantification. Everybody must behave (as if spontaneously) in accordance with his previously determined and indexed level, and choose the category of mass product turned out for his type. Consumers appear as statistics on research organization charts, and are divided by income groups into red, green, and blue areas; the technique is that used for any type of propaganda.

How formalized the procedure is can be seen when the mechanically differentiated products prove to be all alike in the end. That the difference between the Chrysler range and General Motors products is basically illusory strikes every child with a keen interest in varieties. What connoisseurs discuss as good or bad points serve only to perpetuate the semblance of competition and range of choice. The same applies to the Warner Brothers and Metro Goldwyn Mayer productions. But even the differences between the more expensive and cheaper models put out by the same firm steadily diminish: for automobiles, there are such differences as the number of cylinders, cubic capacity, details of patented gadgets; and for films there are the number of stars, the extravagant use of technology, labor, and equipment, and the introduction of the latest psychological formulas. The universal criterion of merit is the amount of "conspicuous production," of blatant cash investment. The varying budgets in the culture industry do not bear the slightest relation to factual values, to the meaning of the products themselves. Even the technical media are relentlessly forced into uniformity. Television aims at a synthesis of radio and film, and is held up only because the interested parties have not yet reached agreement, but its consequences will be quite enormous and promise to intensify the impoverishment of aesthetic matter so drastically, that by tomorrow the thinly veiled identity of all industrial culture products can come triumphantly out into the open, derisively fulfilling the Wagnerian dream of the *Gesamtkunstwerk*—the fusion of all the arts in one work. The alliance of word, image, and music is all the more perfect than in *Tristan* because the sensuous elements which all approvingly reflect the surface of social reality are in principle embodied in the same technical process, the unity of which becomes its distinctive content. This process integrates all the elements of the production, from the novel (shaped with an eye to the film) to the last sound effect. It is the triumph of invested capital, whose title as absolute master is etched deep into the hearts of the dispossessed in the employment line; it is the meaningful content of every film, whatever plot the production team may have selected.

The man with leisure has to accept what the culture manufacturers offer him. Kant's formalism still expected a contribution from the individual, who was thought to relate the varied experiences of the senses to fundamental concepts; but industry robs the individual of his function. Its prime service to the customer is to do his schematizing for him. Kant said that there was a secret mechanism in the soul which prepared direct intuitions in such a way that they could be fitted into the system of pure reason. But today that secret has been deciphered. While the mechanism is to all appearances planned by those who serve up the data of experience, that is, by the culture industry, it is in fact forced upon the latter by the power of society, which remains irrational, however we may try to rationalize it; and this inescapable force is processed by commercial agencies so that they give an artificial impression of being in command. There is nothing left for the consumer to classify. Producers have done it for him. Art for the masses has destroyed the dream but still conforms to the tenets of that dreaming idealism which critical idealism balked at. Everything derives from consciousness: for Malebranche and Berkeley, from the consciousness of God; in mass art, from the consciousness of the production team. Not only are the hit songs, stars, and soap operas cyclically recurrent and rigidly invariable types, but the specific content of the entertainment itself is derived from them and only appears to change. The details are interchangeable. The short interval sequence which was effective in a hit song, the hero's momentary fall from grace (which he accepts as good sport), the rough treatment which the beloved gets from the male star, the latter's rugged defiance of the spoilt heiress, are, like all the other details, ready-made clichés to be slotted in anywhere; they never do anything more than fulfill the purpose allotted them in the overall plan. Their whole *raison d'être* is to confirm it by being its constituent parts. As soon as the film begins, it is quite clear how it will end, and who will be rewarded, punished, or forgotten. In light music, once the trained ear has heard the first notes of the hit song, it can guess what is coming and feel flattered when it does come. The average length of the short story has to be rigidly adhered to. Even gags, effects, and jokes are calculated like the setting in which they are placed. They are the responsibility of special experts and their narrow range makes it easy for them to be apportioned in the office. The development of the culture industry has led to the predominance of the effect, the obvious touch, and the technical detail over the work itself—which once expressed an idea, but was liquidated together with the idea. When the detail won its freedom, it became rebellious and, in the period from Romanticism to Expressionism, asserted itself as free expression, as a vehicle of protest against the organization. In music the single harmonic effect obliterated the awareness of form as a whole; in painting the individual color was stressed at the expense of pictorial composition; and in the novel psychology became more important than structure. The totality of the culture industry has put an end to this. Though concerned exclusively with effects, it crushes their insubordination and makes them subserve the formula, which replaces the work. The same fate is inflicted on whole and parts alike. The whole inevitably bears no relation to the details—just like the career of a successful man into which everything is made to fit as an illustration or a proof, whereas it is nothing more than the sum of all those idiotic events. The so-called dominant idea is like a file which ensures order but not coherence. The whole and the parts are alike; there is no antithesis and no connection. Their prearranged harmony is a mockery of what had to be striven after in the great bourgeois works of art. In Germany the graveyard stillness of the dictatorship already hung over the gayest films of the democratic era.

The whole world is made to pass through the filter of the culture industry. The old experience of the movie-goer, who sees the world outside as an extension of the film he has just left (because the latter is intent upon reproducing the world of everyday perceptions), is now the producer's guideline. The more intensely and flawlessly his techniques duplicate empirical objects, the easier it is today for the illusion to prevail that the outside world is the straightforward continuation of that presented on the screen. This purpose has been furthered by mechanical reproduction since the lightning takeover by the sound film.

Real life is becoming indistinguishable from the movies. The sound film, far surpassing the theater of illusion, leaves no room for imagination or reflection on the part of the audience, who is unable to respond within the structure of the film, yet deviate from its precise detail without losing the thread of the story; hence the film forces its victims to equate it directly with reality. The stunting of the mass-media consumer's powers of imagination and spontaneity does not have to be traced back to any psychological mechanisms; he must ascribe the loss of those attributes to the objective nature of the products themselves, especially to the most characteristic of them, the sound film. They are so designed that quickness, powers of observation, and experience are undeniably needed to apprehend them at all; yet sustained thought is out of the question if the spectator is not to miss the relentless rush of facts. Even though the effort required for his response is semi-automatic, no scope is left for the imagination. Those who are so absorbed by the world of the movie—by its images, gestures, and words—that they are unable to supply what really makes it a world, do not have to dwell on particular points of its mechanics during a screening. All the other films and products of the entertainment industry which they have seen have taught them what to expect; they react automatically. The might of industrial society is lodged in men's minds. The entertainments manufacturers know that their products will be consumed with alertness even when the customer is distraught, for each of them is a model of the huge economic machinery which has always sustained the masses, whether at work or at leisure—which is akin to work. From every sound film and every broadcast program the social effect can be inferred which is exclusive to none but is shared by all alike. The culture industry as a whole has molded men as a type unfailingly reproduced in every product. All the agents of this process, from the producer to the women's clubs, take good care that the simple reproduction of this mental state is not nuanced or extended in any way.

The art historians and guardians of culture who complain of the extinction in the West of a basic style-determining power are wrong. The stereotyped appropriation of everything, even the inchoate, for the purposes of mechanical reproduction surpasses the rigor and general currency of any "real style," in the sense in which cultural *cognoscenti* celebrate the organic precapitalist past. No Palestrina could be more of a purist in eliminating every unprepared and unresolved discord than the jazz arranger in suppressing any development which does not conform to the jargon. When jazzing up Mozart he changes him not only when he is too serious or too difficult but when he harmonizes the melody in a different way, perhaps more simply, than is customary now. No medieval builder can have scrutinized the subjects for church windows and sculptures more suspiciously than the studio hierarchy scrutinizes a work by Balzac or Hugo before finally approving it. No medieval theologian could have determined the degree of the torment to be suffered by the damned in accordance with the *ordo* of divine love more meticulously than the producers of shoddy epics calculate the torture to be undergone by the hero or the exact point to which the leading lady's hemline shall be raised. The explicit and implicit, exoteric and esoteric catalog of the forbidden and tolerated is so extensive that it not only defines the area of freedom but is all-powerful inside it. Everything down to the last detail is shaped accordingly. Like its counterpart, avant-garde art, the entertainment industry determines its own language, down to its very syntax and vocabulary, by the use of anathema. The constant pressure to produce new effects (which must conform to the old pattern) serves merely as another rule to increase the power of the conventions when any single effect threatens to slip through the net. Every detail is so firmly stamped with sameness that nothing can appear which is not marked at birth, or does not meet with approval at first sight. And the star performers, whether they produce or reproduce, use this jargon as freely and fluently and with as much gusto as if it were the very language which it silenced long ago. Such is the ideal of what is natural in this field of activity, and its influence becomes all the more powerful, the more technique is perfected and diminishes the tension between the finished product and everyday life. The paradox of this routine, which is essentially travesty, can be detected and is often predominant in everything that the culture industry turns out. A jazz musician who is playing a piece of serious music, one of Beethoven's simplest minuets, syncopates it involuntarily and will smile superciliously when asked to follow the normal divisions of the beat. This is the "nature" which, complicated by the ever-present and extravagant demands of the specific medium, constitutes the new style and is a "system of non-culture, to which one might even concede a certain 'unity of style' if it really made any sense to speak of stylized barbarity."[1]

The universal imposition of this stylized mode can even go beyond what is quasi-officially sanctioned or forbidden; today a hit song is more readily forgiven for not observing the 32 beats or the compass of the ninth than for containing even the most clandestine melodic or harmonic detail which does not conform to the idiom. Whenever Orson Welles offends against the tricks of the trade, he is forgiven because his departures from the norm are regarded as calculated mutations which serve all the more strongly to confirm the validity of the system. The constraint of the technically-conditioned idiom which stars and directors have to produce as "nature" so that the people can appropriate it, extends to such fine nuances that they almost attain the subtlety of the devices of an avant-garde work as against those of truth. The rare capacity minutely to fulfill the obligations of the natural idiom in all branches of the culture industry becomes the criterion of efficiency. What and how they say it must be measurable by everyday language, as in logical positivism. The producers are experts. The idiom demands an astounding productive power, which it absorbs and squanders. In a diabolical way it has overreached the culturally conservative distinction between genuine and artificial style. A style might be called artificial which is imposed from without on the refractory impulses of a form. But in the culture industry every element of the subject matter has its origin in the same apparatus as that jargon whose stamp it bears. The quarrels in which the artistic experts become involved with sponsor and censor about a lie going beyond the bounds of credibility are evidence not so much of an inner aesthetic tension as of a divergence of interests. The reputation of the specialist, in which a last remnant of objective independence sometimes finds refuge, conflicts with the business politics of the Church, or the concern which is manufacturing the cultural commodity. But the thing itself has been essentially objectified and made viable before the established authorities began to argue about it. Even before Zanuck acquired her, Saint Bernadette was regarded by her latter-day hagiographer as brilliant propaganda for all interested parties. That is what became of the emotions of the character. Hence the style of the culture industry, which no longer has to test itself against any refractory material, is also the negation of style. The reconciliation of the general and particular, of the rule and the specific demands of the subject matter, the achievement of which alone gives essential, meaningful content to style, is futile because there has ceased to be the slightest tension between opposite poles: these concordant extremes are dismally identical; the general can replace the particular, and vice versa.

Nevertheless, this caricature of style does not amount to something beyond the genuine style of the past. In the culture industry the notion of genuine style is seen to be the aesthetic equivalent of domination. Style considered as mere aesthetic regularity is a romantic dream of the past. The unity of style not only of the Christian Middle Ages but of the Renaissance expresses in each case the different structure of social power, and not the obscure experience of the oppressed in which the general was enclosed. The great artists were never those who embodied a wholly flawless and perfect style, but those who used style as a way of hardening themselves against the chaotic expression of suffering, as a negative truth. The style of their works gave what was expressed that force without which life flows away unheard. Those very art forms which are known as classical, such as Mozart's music, contain objective trends which represent something different to the style which they incarnate. As late as Schönberg and Picasso, the great artists have retained a mistrust of style, and at crucial points have subordinated it to the logic of the matter. What Dadaists and Expressionists called the untruth of style as such triumphs today in the sung jargon of a crooner, in the carefully contrived elegance of a film star, and even in the admirable expertise of a photograph of a peasant's squalid hut. Style represents a promise in every work of art. That which is expressed is subsumed through style into the dominant forms of generality, into the language of music, painting, or words, in the hope that it will be reconciled thus with the idea of true generality. This promise held out by the work of art that it will create truth by lending new shape to the conventional social forms is as necessary as it is hypocritical. It unconditionally posits the real forms of life as it is by suggesting that fulfillment lies in their aesthetic derivatives. To this extent the claim of art is always ideology too. However, only in this confrontation with tradition of which style is the record can art express suffering. That factor in a work of art which enables it to transcend reality certainly cannot be detached from style; but it does not consist of the harmony actually realized, of any doubtful unity of form and content, within and without, of individual and society; it is to be found in those features in which discrepancy appears: in the necessary failure of the passionate striving for identity. Instead of exposing itself to this failure in which the style of the great work of art has always achieved self-negation, the inferior work has always relied on its similarity with others—on a surrogate identity.

In the culture industry this imitation finally becomes absolute. Having ceased to be anything but style, it reveals the latter's secret: obedience to the social hierarchy. Today aesthetic barbarity completes what has threatened the creations of the spirit since they were gathered together as culture and neutralized. To speak of culture was always contrary to culture. Culture as a common denominator already contains in embryo that schematization and process of cataloging and classification which bring culture within the sphere of administration. And it is precisely the industrialized, the consequent, subsumption which entirely accords with this notion of culture. By subordinating in the same way and to the same end all areas of intellectual creation, by occupying men's senses from the time they leave the factory in the evening to the time they clock in again the next morning with matter that bears the impress of the labor process they themselves have to sustain throughout the day, this subsumption mockingly satisfies the concept of a unified culture which the philosophers of personality contrasted with mass culture.

Note

1　　Nietzsche, *Unzeitgemässe Betrachtungen, Werke,* Vol. I (Leipzig, 1917), p. 187.

Chapter 32

Fredric Jameson

MASS CULTURE AS
BIG BUSINESS

Fredric Jameson's account of Adorno and Horkheimer is one of increasing complexity and theoretical density, even though it starts straightforwardly enough with a defence of their critique of the culture industry in the *Dialectic of Enlightenment*. Jameson, the leading Marxist critic in North America and author of some of the most influential works of Marxist literary theory such as *The Prison-House of Language* (1972) and *The Political Unconscious* (1981), notes that Adorno and Horkheimer separate mass culture from authentic art, with the former utilizing categories such as entertainment, amusement and pleasure, while the latter initially appears something deep and "humorless". Mass culture, in the *Dialectic of Enlightenment*, is another form of industrialized labour or work: it prepares the worker for the production line, and it mimics the processes of mechanized processes (it is the "afterimage" of work). Pleasure, in mass culture, rapidly becomes boredom, precisely because it makes no intellectual demands upon the consumer. This negative result also reveals that there is an association between work and leisure: they are dialectically mediated (simple repetition, for example, has the capacity to be boring *and* pleasurable, pacifying and exciting, and so on). Authentic art offers the promise of future happiness, not something that can be consumed in the present day. In the process of crafting that promise, it reveals the suffering of the world, the current absence of the hoped for future state, and the blissful knowledge of what could be. The culture industry, on the other hand, presents suffering as a temporary inconvenience which merely defers for a few brief moments, say in a the plot of a film, the achievement of happiness in the here and now. If authentic art dwells, for example, on the ritualized bliss of asceticism, the culture industry considers such self-denial "jovial renunciation", that is to say, a temporary and essentially empty and ironic gesture. Instead of Kant's perceptual schemata that is brought to bear on reality, under capitalism, the culture industry provides an equivalent, in the schemata of "sameness" found at work and experienced analogically through mass entertainment. So Jameson observes that the *Dialectic of Enlightenment* doesn't just address the culture industry as a process of commodification; rather Adorno and Horkheimer are closer to Marx, exploring "the effects of exchange itself", the new reality based upon the abstraction of equivalence. Equivalence (analyzed by Marx in his first chapter of *Capital*) is not a natural phenomena, but rather a mental act or what Jameson calls "an extraordinary cultural invention" whereby abstract, ideological notions of value create conformity and a homogenous culture. Difference, otherness, opposition, are all excluded by the workings of equivalence, which does in fact align like with unlike. In other words, for Marx, the workings of equivalence still creates inequalities, not an equal society. For Adorno and Horkheimer, the mimesis of authentic artworks escapes from this totalizing field of equivalence: mimesis in this instance does not mean copying or re-presenting some other object; it means expressing some inner truth that cannot be subject to equivalence or exchange. Mimesis becomes, in Adorno and Horkheimer's work, an alternative way of understanding the Enlightenment, not just how myth is turned into Enlightenment thought, but how the reverse can also happen.

A T ANY RATE, THE ADORNO-HORKHEIMER theory of the Culture Industry provides a theoretical description of mass cultural experience which can scarcely be reduced to sheer opinionated or elitist vituperation against 'bad art'. To be sure, the philosophers' argument commits them to differentiate mass-cultural 'experience' from the genuinely aesthetic type: this is achieved by separating 'entertainment', 'amusement', and even 'pleasure' itself off from what happens in art, which cannot be described in those terms. Indeed, the worst fears of those for whom a Germanic dialectic is virtually by definition humorless in its very essence[1] will be confirmed by the obsessive diatribes against laughter that appear and reappear throughout this book; a somewhat different light is shed on this odd prejudice by the realization that laughter is here conceived as essentially Homeric – that is, as a ferocious vaunting, with bared teeth, over the victim, as exemplified, for example, by Wyndham Lewis's Tyros; while we should also read into the record Adorno's frequent exception – from such denunciations of sheer malicious 'fun' – of the genuinely zany, such as the Marx Brothers, and his otherwise astonishing insistence on the deeper mindless silliness or 'simplicity' [*Albernheit*] of all true art.

The analysis of pleasure, however, takes place within a framework of the theory of the alienated labor process and has been prolonged by any number of contemporary discussions of the commodification and colonization of leisure:

> Amusement under late capitalism is the prolongation of work. It is sought after as an escape from mechanized work, and to recruit strength in order to be able to cope with it again. Meanwhile, however, mechanization so dominates the resting worker's leisure and happiness, and so profoundly determines the manufacture of amusement goods, that his experiences are inevitably mere after-images of the work process itself. The ostensible content is merely a faded foreground; what sinks in is the automatic succession of standardized operations. What happens at work, in the factory or in the office, can be evaded only by approximation to it in one's leisure time. All amusement suffers from this incurable malady. Pleasure hardens into boredom because, in order to remain pleasure, it must demand no effort and thereby moves rigorously in the worn grooves of association. (DA 123/137)

This concluding word, 'association', needs to be retained, and the historical weight of its philosophical connotation further developed, since, as we shall see, it functions as the mediation between the labor process and whatever pleasurable experience may be attributed to mass-cultural works in the first place. For even the most implacable theory of manipulation in mass culture (and the Adorno-Horkheimer theory is a good deal subtler than that) must somehow acknowledge the experiential moment in the mesmerization of the masses before the television set; if only then to dismiss it as the fix, addiction, false pleasure, or whatever. The great definition of art which Adorno and Horkheimer borrow from Stendhal and make their own – art as the *'promesse de bonheur'* – suggests, however, that for them much will be at stake in coming to terms theoretically with just such false happiness, just such deceptive pleasure (about which the utopian positions of a Bloch or a Marcuse will suggest that true happiness or pleasure is somehow inscribed within this false experience).[2]

In fact, Adorno and Horkheimer make the only really consequent and rigorous move open to them: they sunder pleasure decisively from happiness, while at the same time denying the possibility of either as some full experience or plenitude in its own right. Pleasure thereby becomes an evanescent natural release, which can never be sustained:

> pleasure [*Vergnügen*] always means not thinking about anything, forgetting suffering even where it is shown. Helplessness is its foundation. It is in fact flight; but not, as is often said, flight from a wretched reality, but on the contrary flight from any last thought of resistance left open by this last. (DA 130/144)

In this form, whatever is left of pleasure in the older sense comes to invest the position of the ultimate victims, 'the ones who suffer for everything anyhow'. As for the ultimate mystery of sexuality – so often taken as the very prototype of pleasure in general, and some-times inconsiderately (even by Adorno himself in passing) assimilated to the experience of art itself – it may be preferable, in true Lacanian fashion, to deny its relationship to pleasure altogether:

> Delight [*Lust*] is austere: *res severa verum gaudium*. The monastic theory that not asceticism but the sexual act denotes the renunciation of attainable bliss receives negative confirmation in the gravity of the lover who apprehensively stakes his life on the fleeting instant. In the Culture Industry, jovial renunciation takes the place of the pain that lies at the heart of ecstasy and asceticism alike. (DA 126–27/141)

Pain as the very truth of pleasure: with this deeply felt paradox we touch the central dialectic of Adorno's conception of experience and his notion of authenticity. The related but distinct notion of happiness also, as we shall see later on, follows this pattern, but as it were on a temporal or historical continuum, very much in the spirit of Bloch's 'not yet': happiness is possible, here and now, only as what does not yet exist, as what is not yet possible or achievable. The Stendhal formula takes on its power when we stress its constitutive incompletion: art is not bliss, but rather the latter's *promise*. The Frankfurt School then rewrite it in their own grimmer idiom: 'The secret of aesthetic sublimation is its representa-tion of fulfillment as a broken promise' (DA 125/140).[3] What is inauthentic in the offerings of the Culture Industry, then, is not the remnants of experience within them, but rather the ideology of happiness they simultaneously embody: the notion that pleasure or happiness ('entertainment' would be their spurious synthesis) already exists, and is available for consumption.

This is, then, one crucial thematic differentiation between 'genuine art' and that offered by the Culture Industry: both raise the issue and the possibility of happiness in their very being, as it were, and neither provides it; but where the one keeps faith with it by negation and suffering, through the enactment of its impossibility, the other assures us it is taking place ('Not Italy is offered, but eye-witness evidence of its existence' [DA 133/148]).

This is then the moment at which we must return to the implication of the word 'association' (already stressed above), but less in the sense of the tradition that emerges from Locke than, rather, in its final twist and solution in Kant himself, and in the theory of the categories and the mental schemata. This is of course the point at which, as has already been mentioned, the stereotypicality of Hollywood and Culture Industry products is, with malicious playfulness, attributed to the *Critique of Pure Reason* as its caricature and ultimate outcome; to be sure,

> Kant's formalism still expected a contribution from the individual, who was thought to relate the varied experiences of the senses to fundamental concepts; but industry robs the individual of his function. Its prime service to the customer is to do his schematizing for him. Kant said that there was a secret mechanism in the soul which prepared direct intuitions in such a way that they could be fitted into the system of pure reason. But today that secret has been deciphered. (DA 112/124)

The Kantian problematic is not, to be sure, exhausted by this particular application and appropriation of its mechanisms: for the question of perceptual schemata (and of their opposite number, something like a perceptual or aesthetic *nominalism*) persists in 'genuine art' and returns episodically in *Aesthetic Theory* as the problem of the 'universal' and the 'particular'. Here, however, schematism, in the Kantian sense, provides the crucial mediation between the labor process and 'degraded' entertainment, which seeks the same – repetition and the familiar – as its very element: Taylorization, the rationalization of the labor process and of mass production, is here to be grasped both in production and reception in well-nigh indistinguishable fashion (but the identification of reception with production is constant in Adorno, and holds for 'high art' as well, which will in some sense also constitute another more self-conscious version of this synthesis, and be characterized as something like a reception of production – but of advanced production, of 'high' technology).

Here we seem to pass beyond a straightforward analysis of mass-cultural artefacts in terms of commodification; or, to be more precise, the emphasis at this point shifts from the emphasis on the ideological dimension of the commodity – that is to say, on the 'religious' mysteries of commodity fetishism – to what may be called its existential or even metaphysical dimension in Marx – namely, the effects of exchange itself, and in particular of *equivalence* as a new form imposed on reality and on *abstraction* in the broadest epistemological sense as a historically emergent mode of organizing the world. This is, of course, the point at which the analysis of the Culture Industry loops back into the larger framework under which it was subsumed: the evocation of the 'dialectic of Enlightenment', of what Weber called rationalization and Lukács reification: the coming into being of 'identity' as a mental operation which, as we have seen in the preceding chapter, is at one and the same time a primary instrument of domination and embodiment of the will to power.

The first chapter of *Capital,* indeed, stages 'equivalence' as anything but a natural process, and shows it to be at one and the same time a creative mental act, an extraordinary cultural invention, which is also a brutal and revolutionary intervention into the objective world: nothing in the senses endorses the conceptual leap whereby the famous coat becomes equivalent 'in value' to the equally famous twenty yards of linen. Nor can a metaphysics of Number – according to which, eventually, one pound of iron shavings is discovered to be equivalent to one pound of feathers – ground this new value *form,* whose historical evolution culminates in the so-called 'general form of value' or money: it has not been sufficiently appreciated that Marx's four stages of value project a whole history of abstraction as such, of which the commodity form is but a local result (and Weber's rationalization, Simmel's intellectualization, and Lukács's reification constitute its global generalization, at the other end of time). Abstraction in this sense is the precondition of 'civilization' in all its complex development across the whole range of distinct human activities (from production to the law, from culture to political forms, and not excluding the psyche and the more obscure 'equivalents' of unconscious desire), whose very different histories the history of abstraction might therefore be called upon to underwrite.

'Equivalence' retains these senses in *Dialectic of Enlightenment,* where it excludes difference and heterogeneity, and 'excises the incommensurable' (15/12), transforming the unlike into the same, banishing the fear of the new and allowing comparable and measurable quantities to be manipulated. On the other hand, Adorno and Horkheimer also dispose of an alternate characterization of this primal process (which constitutes the very dynamic of 'enlightenment' as such, and of science and 'instrumental reason'): as we have seen, they also call it *mimesis,* and thereby open up a thematic alternative to the Marxian doctrine or problematic of equivalence – a second language or code which, intended to incorporate anthropology (since the grandest dialectical move in the book lies as we have seen in its assimilation of myth to enlightenment), secures mimetic activity as a genuine drive or impulse, and thereby draws this whole new theory into the mythic proper, reprojecting it as an anthropological narrative of the transformation of primal mimetic impulses into Western science. Now a 'scene of origins' will be necessary; so that the Ur-motivation of the mimetic is staged as fear and impotence before Nature, which ritual mimesis and, after it, science, are called upon to master (by domination of the self); while the evident break of 'modernity', the emergence of science – in, for example, the emblematic passage from perceptual 'science', *'pensée sauvage',* alchemy, into mathematical and non-representational thinking – is attributed to a mimetic taboo, or 'ban on graven images', which is itself, however, dialectically as profoundly mimetic (in the anthropological sense) as what it seeks to repress and cancel.

Habermas has shrewdly suggested[4] that this alternate mythic conceptuality – the code of the mimetic – is ultimately imposed on Adorno and Horkheimer by the inner logic of their positions: as reason and rationality are for them implacably identified as 'instrumental reason' (as *Verstand* rather than *Vernunft*) they no longer have any positive space for the development of conceptual alternatives to 'enlightenment' and are thereby forced back into a type of mythic thinking of their own. He also stresses the unrealized capacity of the notion of mimesis as inter-personality, and as the space for relations with other people (whom we understand by mutual imitation): this possibility, which for Habermas himself is clearly fundamental, is generally, however, in Adorno and Horkheimer, conceived as something fully as baleful as it might be socially and intellectually promising, let alone productive.

Meanwhile, it seems clear that the theory of the Culture Industry is itself unduly limited and restricted by these rather more metaphysical propositions about the mimetic impulse, which to be sure 'explain' the deeper power and attraction of a mass culture that has none of the power and attraction of Art; but explain it too easily and naturalistically (the schematisms of alienated labor invested by some deeper human 'drive'), thereby forestalling those more complex lines of speculation and inquiry that postmodern mass culture seems to demand.[5] In particular, the matter of repetition in contemporary mass culture has not only become a more complicated and interesting phenomenon than the one Adorno and Horkheimer had in mind: it would also seem to suggest mediations of a type they could obviously not elaborate with the originality of daily life in late capitalism, and in particular with the newer structures of an image or spectacle society (which are also scarcely even foreshadowed in Benjamin's alternate theory of mass culture, staged under the sign of the mechanically reproducible work of art). As for the 'stereotypical', the current revival of the term 'formulaic' to designate some of these mass-cultural structures suddenly opens up analogies with cultural production and reception in non- or pre-capitalist societies, which are equally excluded from the historical framework of *Dialectic of Enlightenment.*

Abbreviations

DA
Dialektik der Aufklärung (Frankfurt: Fischer, 1986, original 1944)
Dialectic of Enlightenment, trans. John Cumming (New York: Herder & Herder, 1972)

Notes

1   Terry Eagleton's complaint in *Against the Grain,* London 1986; see also MM 280/210: 'He who has laughter on his side has no need of proof.'
2   The Culture Industry 'builds the need for happiness in and exploits it. It thus has its moment of truth in the way in which it satisfies a substantial need developing out of the tendentially increasing renunciation demanded by society; but becomes the absolutely untrue in the way in which it offers that satisfaction.' (AT 461/430)
3   Actually, we owe this brilliant formula to the translator!
4   See above, Introduction, note 5.
5   Andreas Huyssens has pointed out (in *After the Great Divide,* Bloomington, IN 1986) the intimate relationship between the Wagner book and Adorno's theory of the Culture Industry. Indeed, the emergence of this last now proves to be endogamous, something that art does to itself in its disintegration during the imperialist period (Adorno suggests, in the light of the *Gesamtkunstwerk,* that Nietzsche should have called *his* Wagner book 'The Birth of Film out of the Spirit of Music'). In Benjamin's thought the stage of the 'reproducible work of art' follows that of the emergence of high modernism in the language and form of Baudelaire; in Adorno, both are simultaneous with Wagner. In addition, a rich discussion of 'phantasmagoria' (ch. 16) lays claim to prolong and continue Marx's notion of commodity fetishism in the aesthetic realm.

Chapter 33

Sue Vice

CARNIVAL AND THE GROTESQUE BODY

Bakhtin's study of "carnival" — a transgressive overturning of hierarchy in favour of normally oppressed people at the bottom of society — reveals how popular folk culture and humour can be a politically subversive force. In fact some critics now believe that Bakhtin's dissertation on carnival, called *Rabelais and His World* (1965; English trans. 1968), is a coded critique of totalitarian Stalinist society. Sue Vice opens by noting that carnival "has become textualized" moving from its earlier manifestation in great markets and fairs of medieval Europe, to become sometimes the content, sometimes the form, of texts. Intriguingly, carnival is highly theatrical and spectacular, but its participants simultaneously occupy the roles of actor and spectator. In other words, carnival is a malleable site of subjectivity, in which a person can both perform and observe the effects of his or her identity. Vice, a professor of English at The University of Sheffield, has explored such malleability of subjectivity through her publications on the modernist author Malcolm Lowry, and more recently on the topic of "false testimony" and the Holocaust. A doubled subjectivity is apparent in how carnival offers a parallel identity: one subject to whoever is in authority (the church, capitalist bosses, the totalitarian state), but also existing as a powerful oppositional emotional outlet ("reversal, parody, song, and laughter"). This second life is expressed through "grotesque realism", the study of which may in itself be a parody of the Stalinist demands of "Socialist Realism". Before covering grotesque realism in this extract, Vice examines carnival's "folk humour", that is to say, a type of excessive discourse and theatrical behaviour that is in opposition to the hegemony of the church and medieval feudal lords. Three categories of folk humour are: 1. ritual spectacles; 2. comic verbal compositions; and 3. various genres of billingsgate. Vice gives ten more "characteristics" of folk humour derived from Bakhtin's book the *Problems of Dostoevsky's Poetics* (1929). Carnival is a highly social, lived space in which previously held apart opposites (high/low; sacred/profane) can subversively meld together, especially through the foregrounding of debasing bodily functions, used to attack the sacred and the authoritative. Laughter and parody are powerful carnivalesque forces, leading to radical transformation, although "carnival time" which is cyclical and opposed to linear, teleological narratives (such as that of Christian theology), leads to communal, not necessarily individual, rebirth and renewal. Some critics see this latter aspect as emerging from Bakhtin's experiences of mass imprisonment and murder that happened under the terror of Stalinism. "Grotesque realism" is the genre that opposes all that is oppressive and transcendent, with that of the lowly bodily functions of sexuality and defecation, earthy laughter and the material body rather than lofty spirituality and authority. A central function of grotesque realism is that of "degredation", meaning not just being brought down to earth, but also being re-born. Vice suggests that much of the discourse used here by Bakhtin is gendered: the low is equated with the womb and the maternal body; the high with that of the masculine. Other critics see patterns of race and class stereotyping here. Vice ends with a contemporary example which reveals the complexity of the topic: analysis of a scene from James Joyce's *Ulysses* (1922).

Introduction

In both *Rabelais and His World* and *Problems of Dostoevsky's Poetics*, Bakhtin uses a relatively conventional literary critical approach to introduce his notion of carnival, first discussing earlier critics of a particular writer's work, then using his own theory to show more accurately, as he says, what that writer is about. In the case of Rabelais, Bakhtin emphasizes the forgotten tradition of 'popular humour', which can make sense of his particular discourse; and, in the case of Dostoevsky, Bakhtin sees polyphony's roots in a similar, although more distant, carnival past.[1]

This chapter examines Bakhtin's discussion of carnival as an element of popular history which has become textualized. Carnival is, as Julia Kristeva puts it, 'a signifier, but also a signified': it can be the subject or the means of representation in a text, or both. The carnivalesque may be detected in textual images, plot, or language itself. As carnival 'is a spectacle, but without a stage', in which the participant is 'both actor and spectator',[2] its textualization is not a straightforward matter, because the change of form at once introduces the equivalent of a stage, and a sharp distinction between actor (character and narrator) and spectator (reader). However, Bakhtin's work on representation in the early essay 'Author and Hero in Aesthetic Activity' can make some sense of this problem. Carnival's absence of footlights both encourages and prohibits linking it to drama, which is also considered in this chapter. Bakhtin's notion of carnival includes the literary genre of 'grotesque realism', which centres on the image of the grotesque body. Contemporary interest in the body as a critical category makes this part of Bakhtin's theory particularly compelling,[3] and raises questions of gender, and psychoanalysis, a discipline about which the Bakhtin circle had mixed feelings. The chapter concludes with a look at a critic who has used carnival and the categories of grotesque realism to reassess a modern novel, and a brief example of how this kind of criticism might work in relation to another text.

The origin of carnival's place in Bakhtin's writing is a piece of mythicized literary history: the historical carnivals which characterized the Middle Ages, up to the time of Rabelais in the sixteenth century, live on in 'transposed' (PDP 124)[4] form in literary texts. These carnivals are the precursors of the ones we know today: May Day holidays; the British Notting Hill Carnival; the Brazilian carnivals; New Orleans Mardi Gras; the Mexican Day of the Dead.[5] Bakhtin suggests that in the Middle Ages the carnival played a much more prominent role in the life of the ordinary people, who inhabited a dual realm of existence: one official, characterized by the authority of the church, the feudal system, work, and one unofficial, characterized by reversal, parody, song, and laughter. Bakhtin claims that the carnivalization of literature

> proved remarkably productive as a means for capturing in art the developing relationships under capitalism, at a time when previous forms of life, moral principles and beliefs were being turned into 'rotten cords' and the previously

concealed, ambivalent, and unfinalized nature of man and human thought was being nakedly exposed. (PDP 166)

However, even here it is obvious that matters are not as straightforward as they seem. The role of the church, for instance, as an oppressive force is used ironically, or double-voicedly, by Bakhtin, Robert Stam suggests, to appear to fit in with Stalinist anti-clericalism, but actually speaking against it. Stam points out that Bakhtin takes favourite Stalinist themes, including '"folk art"', the '"people"' and 'the oppressiveness of the church' and makes them 'boomerang against Soviet officialdom'. In this way, Bakhtin matches his own theory with practice, as he is deploying the 'strategy of subversive co-optation or the "anthropophagic" devouring of dominant discourses'. In a Stalinist atmosphere, this is certainly a carnival exhibiting only 'laughter's footsteps'.[6]

In the Prologue to *Rabelais,* Michael Holquist also suggests that Bakhtin's own historical moment informed his treatment of carnival, and that what has often been thought of as his nostalgic view of a brutal past actually conflicts, or engages dialogically, with a much more oppressive idealism, that of Stalinism (RW xix).[7] Terry Eagleton places a different emphasis on the same point: 'in what is perhaps the boldest, most devious gesture in the history of "Marxist criticism", Bakhtin pits against that "official, formalistic and logical authoritarianism" whose unspoken name is Stalinism the explosive politics of the body, the erotic, the licentious and semiotic.'[8] Bakhtin's book suffered from this conflict; he submitted *Rabelais* as a thesis in 1940, and it was published in the Soviet Union only twenty-five years later (RW xix). In another reversal, Bakhtin's formulation of grotesque realism is, as Holquist suggests, a point-by-point inversion of categories used in the Soviet Union in the 1930s to define Socialist Realism.[9] It is very tempting to see *Rabelais* as a dangerous joke at the expense of the Soviet authorities, and that it is they who are being lampooned obliquely when Bakhtin describes the medieval culture of *parodia sacra* (RW 14), the Feast of Fools (RW 78), carnival beatings (RW 265), donkeys' masses (RW 78), and Rabelais' complete reversal of the most authoritarian discourse by using it as the template for the 'absolutely gay and fearless talk, free and frank, [. . .] beyond all verbal prohibitions' of *Pantagruel's* Prologue. Bakhtin identifies this as a parody of ecclesiastical rhetoric: 'behind the abuses and curses are the Church's intolerance, intimidation, and *autos-da-fé*'. He goes further, and claims that Rabelais' Prologue, written in the manner of a street hawker, by its carnival reversal 'travesties the very foundations of medieval thought, the methods of establishing truth and conviction which are inseparable from fear, violence, morose and narrow-minded seriousness and intolerance' (RW 167). This tone of moral certainty suggests the importance of Rabelais' use of popular culture in his work in a particular context, and perhaps Bakhtin's idea of himself performing a similar role in his own.

Folk humour

Bakhtin describes the 'folk carnival humor' which Rabelais draws upon as a 'boundless world of humorous forms and manifestations [which] opposed the official and serious tone of medieval ecclesiastical and feudal culture'. All the elements of this popular humour–'folk festivities of the carnival type, the comic rites and cults, the clowns and fools, giant, dwarfs, and jugglers, the vast and manifold literature of parody' – can be categorized under three headings:

1   *Ritual spectacles:* carnival pageants, comic shows of the marketplace.
2   *Comic verbal compositions:* parodies both oral and written, in Latin and in the vernacular.
3   *Various genres of billingsgate:* curses, oaths, popular blazons. (RW 5)

These features can, according to Bakhtin, be traced in examples of carnivalesque literature.

In *Problems of Dostoevsky's Poetics*, Bakhtin adds detail to this list in his discussion of the 'transposition' of carnival's 'pageantry' into 'a language of artistic images that has something in common with its concretely sensuous nature' (PDP 122). The following are further characteristics of carnival, some of its literary form only, some of both this and its street form:

4 Carnival is 'a pageant without footlights and without a division into performers and spectators' (PDP 122), as its participants do not watch but '*live* in it', with its suspension of 'hierarchical structure and all the forms of terror, reverence, piety, and etiquette connected with it'.

5 Carnival allows '*free and familiar contact between people*' who would usually be separated hierarchically, and allows for 'mass action' (PDP 123).

6 Carnival *mésalliances* allow for unusual combinations: 'the sacred with the profane, the lofty with the low, the great with the insignificant, the wise with the stupid'.

7 Carnival profanation consists of 'a whole system of carnivalistic debasings and bringings down to earth', to the level of the body, particularly in the case of parodies of sacred texts.

8 Death and renewal are central to carnival, represented most often by the carnival act of 'the *mock crowning and subsequent decrowning of the carnival king*' (PDP 124); the two states are inseparable in the carnival view: crowning entails decrowning (PDP 125).

9 Carnival laughter is directed at exalted objects, and forces them to renew themselves; thus its debasing results in new life, and it is 'ambivalent' (PDP 126); '[m]uch was permitted in the form of laughter that was impermissible in serious form' (PDP 127).

10 Carnival parody survives in attenuated form in the 'narrowly formal literary' parody of modern times (PDP 128); in the original kind, '[e]verything has its parody, that is, its laughing aspect, for everything is reborn and renewed through death'.

11 Carnival in contemporary literature does survive generically, although its influence is usually limited to the work's content (PDP 132); its traces may be detected, for instance in representations of legends and unofficial history (Toni Morrison's *Beloved,* for instance), and certain kinds of laughter (PDP 165; Malcolm Lowry's *Under the Volcano*), image system (Angela Carter's *Nights at the Circus*), parody; within the individual character's 'ambivalent passions' (PDP 159; Bakhtin cites as examples George Sand's and Victor Hugo's novels).

12 A local carnival feature is its 'sense of a great city', such as St Petersburg (Dostoevsky), Paris (Balzac) (PDP 160), or London (Dickens).

Any list of carnival features should also include a thirteenth category, that of carnival time, which is characterized, as Bakhtin says, by '[m]oments of death and revival, of change and renewal [which] always led to a festive perception of the world'. The monologic authoritarianism of the feudal world explains the omnipresence of carnival, which was 'the people's second life' (PDP 8).[10] Carnival is the opposite of a time of terror or purges, as 'the true feast of time, the feast of becoming, change, and renewal. It was hostile to all that was immortalized and completed' (10). The important point about this is that renewal does not occur within the lifetime of an individual carnival subject, but within the body of the people as a whole: birth is always implicit within death. There are clearly positive elements in this cyclical, rather than linear, model of human life and history.[11] However, the idea of communal (rather than collective) survival, perhaps even at the expense of the individual, is exactly the problem the Russian critic Mikhail K. Ryklin identifies with this theory, in which he sees Bakhtin replacing the Stalinist purges' 'reality of denunciation and convulsions of suffering bodies, confessing their guilt under torture' by 'the coming-into-being of speech body-giants, gazing as if from the sidelines at the suffering of their chance individual incarnations'. In his 1993 article, Ryklin 'chillingly' describes *Rabelais and His World* as 'indirectly dedicated to the terror and dictated by it'. To point to the likely survival of the people as a whole or as an abstraction is, according to Ryklin, a way of blinding oneself to individual deaths – even when these deaths were murders, and suffered by friends and members of one's own circle. Read in such a light, Bakhtin's phrase 'The death of the individual is only a moment in the celebrating life of the folk and of humankind, a moment *necessary for their rejuvenation and completion*' sounds with extra intonation.[12] Bakhtin has allowed his theory to become infiltrated and deformed by Stalinist ideology, according to Ryklin, in contrast to Stam's sense that Bakhtin was manipulating the discourses of that ideology.

However, it is worth noting that Bakhtin sees the carnivalesque view of death as a way of combatting 'real' everyday and religious fears of death in the Middle Ages, conjured up by natural, 'divine and human power'. Such a 'victory over fear' was of course only 'ephemeral', as is the nature of carnival, but from these 'brief moments another unofficial truth emerged'. This suggests at least that Bakhtin sees the 'unofficial truth' of the people's bodily resurgence as directly proportional to the real threats those people lived under.

Ryklin interprets *Rabelais and His World* as what Caryl Emerson calls 'a requiem' for the individual body, which she says is 'no wonder, for subversion, revolution, and the myth of a collective "body of the people" that never hurts or dies no matter how much you torment it, understandably arouse less rapture in the ex-Soviet-Union than in the West'.[13] Ryklin suggests that Bakhtin has to adopt the theory of 'the life cycle that transcends the individual', to quote Nancy Glazener,[14] precisely because he lived in a regime where individuals were vanishing and being killed in huge numbers. Ryklin sees Bakhtin's attitude to carnival not as an apologia, which for someone who had suffered exile and censorship is unlikely, but as a rationalization based on his own position as a member of the intelligentsia under Stalin, which transformed him into a kind of hostage.[15] 'Only by opposing the ideal and imperishable image of folkness to terror as the catastrophe of the real folk could he survive', Ryklin says. Emerson points out that national history partly accounts for the different aspects of his theories Bakhtin is valued for in the West and Russia. While Western readers value his writings on 'the novel as subversive genre, carnival as permanent revolution, and culture as a battleground where marginal figures endlessly undermine all centers', in Russia his early essays on 'individuation and personality' are more widely read.[16]

The long history of carnival led to the development of a 'rich idiom' of related symbols, which were characterized by the 'pathos of change and renewal' and the 'gay relativity of prevailing truths and authorities', Bakhtin says. The combination of cyclical time with the other significant carnivalesque movement, the 'logic of the "inside out", [. . .] of the "turn-about", of a continual shifting from top to bottom', leads naturally to parody, as the carnivalesque was a parody of official life. Bakhtin is keen to point out that carnivalesque parody and travesty are quite different from 'the negative and formal parody of modern times', which only denies without renewing (PDP 10–11). This is a consistent thread in his argument: in modern versions of carnival laughter, 'billingsgate' profanations, and so on, only the downward half of the subverting movement has survived. This is particularly clear in Bakhtin's potted history of the fate of the carnivalesque in the centuries after the Renaissance.

Grotesque realism

Bakhtin describes the literary genre, originally medieval, of 'grotesque realism' as one opposed to all forms of high art and literature.[17] It includes parody and any other form of discourse which 'bring[s] down to earth' anything ineffable or authoritarian, a task achieved principally through mockery: 'The people's laughter which characterized all the forms of grotesque realism from immemorial times was linked with the bodily lower stratum. Laughter degrades and materializes' (RW 20). 'Degradation' is a typical and important operation of the grotesque. Its central trait is an ambivalent act: 'Degradation here means coming down to earth, the contact with the earth as an element that swallows up and gives birth at the same time' (RW 21). This ambivalence, particularly when it involves the new birth implicit in death, or the resurgence implicit in being toppled, is the characteristic principle of both grotesque realism and carnival itself. As well as working on the 'cosmic' level, degradation can be experienced at the level of the human body:

> To degrade also means to concern oneself with the lower stratum of the body,
> the life of the belly and the reproductive organs; it therefore relates to acts of
> defecation and copulation, conception, pregnancy, and birth. Degradation digs
> a bodily grave for a new birth. (RW 24)

Bakhtin points out that the terms 'upward' and 'downward' in grotesque realism do not have simply relative meanings, but 'strictly topographical' ones – and, one might add, what look like strictly gender-related ones. 'Downward' is earth, 'an element that devours, swallows up (the grave, the womb) and [is] at the same time an element of birth, or renascence (the maternal breasts)'; in its bodily aspect, 'the lower part is the genital organs, the belly, and the buttocks'. 'Upward' is heaven; 'the upper part' of the body 'is the face or the head' (RW 21).

Bakhtin suggests that the 'bodily element'[18] of carnival and grotesque realism concerns bodies in general and not bodies as distinguished by gender, which some critics see as transcending, others as succumbing to, the usual gender stereotypes. However, a familiar pattern seems to be described here. Earth and the reproductive body are associated with the feminine; heaven and the rational body with the masculine. Bakhtin concludes, 'Grotesque realism knows no other lower level; it is the fruitful earth and the womb. It is always conceiving'. This semi-metaphorical appropriation of the womb, and other aspects of the feminine, is admired by some critics as a way of retrieving categories which are usually ignored; and deplored by others, who see it as a 'de-femalising' of the female body, and point out that women's 'lives, like their bodies, are melted down into a generalised human existence'.[19] Ruth Ginsburg argues that Bakhtin's interest in pregnancy 'is a metaphoric appropriation of the feminine that has nothing to do with real or fictional females'.[20] The same critical split attends the apparent association of the grotesque itself with the feminine. If grotesque images are associated with the changes of time and 'copulation, pregnancy, birth, growth, old age, disintegration, dismemberment' (RW 25), then they seem to be closer to the feminine than to the masculine. Bakhtin, however, distinguishes the grotesque from its opposite, the classical, in terms of class rather than gender. 'Classic' aesthetics are associated with 'the ready-made [. . .] the finished, completed man, cleansed, as it were, of all the scoriae of birth and development' (RW 25). Rather than continue the masculine orientation this seems to have, Bakhtin gives a different interpretation of the coexistence of grotesque and classical in Renaissance realism: 'The ever-growing, inexhaustible, ever-laughing principle which uncrowns and renews is combined with its opposite: the petty, inert "material principle" of class society' (RW 24). Adding another dimension, Diane Roberts, in *The Myth of Aunt Jemima* racializes Bakhtin's binary of grotesque and classical within a single gender, and also across gender. The contest over the body was fuelled in the antebellum American South by a Bakhtinian polarity: 'Some bodies are "high", like the statue on the pedestal that so often represents white women in Southern culture, while some, like black women (and black men) are "low", represented by the unspeakable, "unclean" elements official culture would repress'.[21]

If the Kerch terracottas of laughing 'senile pregnant hags' discussed by Bakhtin (RW 25) are representative of grotesque realism, then Greek and Roman statues are representative of classical aesthetics. In James Joyce's *Ulysses* (1922), when Leopold Bloom visits a museum, he secretly tries to see if the statues of women have any orifices – it is as if he is looking for the grotesque body in the classical one, but cannot find it. Bloom thinks,

> Lovely forms of women sculpted Junonian. Immortal lovely. And we stuffing food in one hole and out behind: food, chyle, blood, dung, earth, food: have to feed it like stoking an engine. They have no. Never looked. I'll look today. Keeper won't see. Bend down let something fall see if she.[22]

Bloom is unable to utter the grotesque word for what he is looking for; and he fails in his quest to find out whether or not these statues have any such attributes, because he is looking for the grotesque in the wrong place – a museum. Bakhtin describes the 'artistic canon of antiquity' in terms that fit Bloom's statues well: '[a]s conceived by these canons, the body was [. . .] isolated, alone, fenced off from all other bodies', its 'apertures closed'. Bloom is inspired by thoughts of the grotesque cycle of eating and excreting to inspect the statues, but, as Bakhtin points out, 'inner processes of absorbing and ejecting were not revealed' in the classical body. 'The individual body was presented apart from its relation to the ancestral body of the people', a state of affairs symbolized by the divide between Bloom here pretending to drop something on the floor so he can look up at the statues' lower bodily regions, and the statues themselves. We have seen him defecate, and eat offal, and will see him take a bath, and masturbate, while the statues are 'Immortal lovely'; he is a grotesque representative confronting the fact that the 'ever unfinished nature of the [classical] body was kept hidden' (RW 28–29).

Abbreviations

PDP *Problems of Dostoevsky's Poetics*
RW *Rabelais and His World*

Notes

1   Bakhtin published a revised version of *Problems,* with a new chapter 4, in 1963; see Gary Saul Morson and Caryl Emerson, *Rethinking Bakhtin: Extensions and Challenges,* Northwestern University Press, Evanston, Illinois 1989, pp. 160–61. Ken Hirschkop points out that the English translation of *Rabelais and His World* translates the Russian adjective *narodnyi* as 'folk', but 'popular' is probably more appropriate; I have altered my own practice as a result. (I am grateful to Sally Eames, Anne Grigson and Isobel Wilson, students on the Sheffield University MA in Information Studies, who conducted bibliographical searches for works linking Bakhtin and Kristeva; to the British Academy, who partially funded my attendance at the Seventh Biennial Bakhtin Conference in Moscow, June 1995, where I gave a version of part of this chapter; and to David Shepherd and the Bakhtin Centre at the University of Sheffield, where I gave another version.)

2   Julia Kristeva, 'Word, Dialogue, and Novel', *Desire in Language: A Semiotic Approach to Literature and Art,* Basil Blackwell, Oxford 1980, p. 78.

3   See for instance Carroll Smith-Rosenberg, 'The Body Politic', in Elizabeth Weed, ed., *Coming to Terms,* Routledge, London 1989, pp. 101–21.

4   This is the translator's term, naturally.

5   See Peter Jackson, 'Street Life: The Politics of Carnival', *Society and Space* 6, 1988, pp. 213–27; I am grateful to Professor Jackson for this reference.

6   Robert Stam, *Subversive Pleasures: Bakhtin, Cultural Criticism and Film,* Johns Hopkins University Press, Baltimore, Maryland 1989, p. 158.

7   Michael Holquist, 'Introduction', RW xix.

8   Terry Eagleton, *Walter Benjamin, or Towards a Revolutionary Criticism,* New Left Books, London 1981, p. 144.

9   Holquist, 'Introduction', pp. xix, xvii.

10 Clair Wills, 'Upsetting the Public: Carnival, Hysteria and Women's Texts', in Ken Hirschkop and David Shepherd, eds, *Bakhtin and Cultural Theory,* Manchester University Press, Manchester 1989, p. 133.

11 See Wills, 'Upsetting the Public' on history as crisis, pp. 131, 133: and Ken Hirschkop on carnival and history, 'Introduction', in Hirschkop and Shepherd, *Bakhtin and Cultural Theory,* pp. 33–35.

12 Mikhail K. Ryklin, 'Bodies of Terror: Theses Toward a Logic of Violence', *NLH* 24 (1), winter 1993, pp. 54 (Bakhtin's italics), 56. Ken Hirschkop suggests a source for Bakhtin's emphasis on the collective which is different from Ryklin and Emerson's: the researches of Brian Poole suggest that this is 'the neo-Kantian Hermann Cohen's contrast of the "mortal individual" with the "immortal people" (the latter alone being the true subject of historical progress and ultimate redemption)'. Cohen is discussed in AA 240–41, n. 73.

13 Caryl Emerson, 'Preface' to Ryklin, 'Bodies of Terror', pp. 48, 46.

14 Nancy Glazener, 'Dialogic Subversion: Bakhtin, the Novel and Gertrude Stein', in Hirschkop and Shepherd, *Bakhtin and Cultural Theory,* p. 113.

15 Ryklin, 'Bodies of Terror', p. 55. This is an issue which has exercised critics: Sergey Bocharov quotes a conversation with Bakhtin, in which Bakhtin says the only way to have avoided betraying his homeland and culture would have been '"By perishing. I began writing an article to be called 'On Those Who Failed to Perish' [. . .] of course I destroyed it later"' (Bocharov, 'Conversations with Bakhtin', *PMLA* 109 (5), October 1994, p. 1020). Morson and Emerson reply to Wall and Thomson's review: Bakhtin, who 'spent much of his life eluding purges, who barely escaped what amounted to a death sentence, and who saw his friends (including Medvedev) arrested and disappear', could only have disapproved of Stalinist practices. (Medvedev was shot probably in early 1938; Volosinov was also a victim of Stalinist terror, but precise details of his fate are not known.)

16 Ryklin, 'Bodies of Terror', p. 55; Emerson, 'Preface', p. 46.

17 See for instance Ilkka Joki, 'David Mamet's Drama: The Dialogicality of Grotesque Realism', David Shepherd, ed., *Bakhtin, Carnival and Other Subjects, Critical Studies* 3 (2)–4 (1/2), 1993, pp. 80–98.

18 Ann Jefferson, 'Bodymatters: Self and Other in Bakhtin, Sartre and Bardies', in Hirschkop and Shepherd, *Bakhtin and Cultural Theory,* p. 166.

19 Jefferson, 'Bodymatters', and Mary Russo, *The Female Grotesque: Risk, Excess, and Modernity,* Routledge, London 1994, are more positive than Ruth Ginsburg, 'The Pregnant Text. Bakhtin's Ur-Chronotope: The Womb', in Shepherd, *Bakhtin, Carnival,* p. 168, and Jane Miller, *Seductions: Studies in Reading and Culture,* Virago, London 1990, p.149: see her discussion pp. 139–50.

20 Ginsbug, 'The Pregnant Text', p. 169.

21 Diane Roberts, *The Myth of Aunt Jemima: Representations of Race and Region,* Routledge, London 1994, p. 2.

22 James Joyce, *Ulysses: The Corrected Text,* ed. Hans Walter Gabler *et al.,* Penguin, Harmondsworth 1986, 8.928–32. Thanks to J. S. Bernstein for discussing this episode with me.

Chapter 34

Walter Benjamin

N

[On the theory of knowledge, theory of progress]

Walter Benjamin's thoughts on writing a materialist history are at their most charged in this section of *The Arcades Project* (1972, English trans. 1999), a book made up of thematically related quotations, aphorisms and commentary ostensibly about the outmoded spaces of the nineteenth-century Paris arcades, the glassed over passages between city streets that formed elegant shopping malls. As Marx notes [N5,3], a materialist understanding of reality can start from any historical or theoretical point; Benjamin, chooses the *outmoded* iron and glass technologies—and shopping experiences—of the Paris arcades because their "signs of decline" [N1,11] create a Surrealist x-ray of capitalism, one which can shine a light on the present-day. Benjamin, who mainly wrote using the essay form, ponders his own methodology: his rejection of the concept of progress (which masks people's true social and economic relations) leads him to seek another approach, that of montage (juxtaposing concepts and images), new perspectives, or, "a displacement of the angle of vision" [N1a,3], all with the aim of explosively bringing the past into the present, awakening people to the oppressive reality of their lives under capitalism. From a materialist perspective, what capitalism calls "progress" is for the working classes a "catastrophe". Benjamin thus has to modify the Marxist (and Hegelian) dialectic, which progresses to a particular endpoint (the telos), creating a dialectics at a standstill. What this means is that historical materialism "actualizes" [N2,2] in a dialectical image otherwise dormant or hidden facts, here dug up from the nineteenth-century Paris Arcades, but teaching us something revolutionary about the present day. Such a dialectical image brings the forward motion of the dialectic to a halt [N2,7], building up thereby its intensity and power, until with an explosive "lightning" flash [N1,1], true revolutionary insight is gained. This insight is called by Benjamin the "now of recognisability" [N3a,3 and N9,7], i.e., something can be seen that wasn't in the individual parts, but exists because those parts have been brought together. If the Surrealists thought that their technique of montage could give them unique access to the unconscious mind, the dialectic image which works in a similar way, enables people to wake up from their apolitical slumbers to see into the very heart of capitalist society and its workings. Benjamin compares this with Marcel Proust's project in his novel *Remembrance of Things Past*, where awakening is a "dialectical point of rupture", a new beginning brought about by evoking "the space of someone waking up". [N3a,3] With the dialectical image, the materialist historian gets at the truth of things, experiencing "the birth of authentic historical time" [N3,1], not "timeless truth" [N3,2], but revolutionary truth, one in which people can act in new ways, undergoing profound transformation. There is a messianic tinge to this theory, but Benjamin argues that he is really crossing Breton (Surrealism) with Le Corbusier (modernism), the resulting heightened graphicness conjoined with Marxism. [N2,6] The form of this extract clearly acts out the theory, thus the juxtapositions between blocks of text mimics the montage method, creating a new constellation of knowledge and revolution.

> Times are more interesting than people.
> —Honoré de Balzac, *Critique littéraire,* Introduction by Louis Lumet (Paris, 1912), p. 103 [Guy de la Ponneraye, *Histoire de l'Amiral Coligny*]

> The reform of consciousness consists *solely* in . . . the awakening of the world from its dream about itself.
> —Karl Marx, *Der historische Materialismus: Die Frühschriften* (Leipzig <1932 >), vol. 1, p. 226 (letter from Marx to Ruge; Kreuzenach, September 1843)[1]

IN THE FIELDS WITH WHICH WE ARE CONCERNED, knowledge comes only in lightning flashes. The text is the long roll of thunder that follows.   [N1, 1]

Comparison of other people's attempts to the undertaking of a sea voyage in which the ships are drawn off course by the magnetic North Pole. Discover *this* North Pole. What for others are deviations are, for me, the data which determine my course.—On the differentials of time (which, for others, disturb the main lines of the inquiry), I base my reckoning.   [N1, 2]

Say something about the method of composition itself: how everything one is thinking at a specific moment in time must at all costs be incorporated into the project then at hand. Assume that the intensity of the project is thereby attested, or that one's thoughts, from the very beginning, bear this project within them as their telos. So it is with the present portion of the work, which aims to characterize and to preserve the intervals of reflection, the distances lying between the most essential parts of this work, which are turned most intensively to the outside.   [N1, 3]

To cultivate fields where, until now, only madness has reigned. Forge ahead with the whetted axe of reason, looking neither right nor left so as not to succumb to the horror that beckons from deep in the primeval forest. Every ground must at some point have been made arable by reason, must have been cleared of the undergrowth of delusion and myth. This is to be accomplished here for the terrain of the nineteenth century.   [Nl, 4]

These notes devoted to the Paris arcades were begun under an open sky of cloudless blue that arched above the foliage; and yet—owing to the millions of leaves that were visited by the fresh breeze of diligence, the stertorous breath of the researcher, the storm of youthful zeal, and the idle wind of curiosity—they've been covered with the dust of centuries. For the painted sky of summer that looks down from the arcades in the reading room of the Bibliothèque Nationale in Paris has spread out over them its dreamy, unlit ceiling.   [N1, 5]

The pathos of this work: there are no periods of decline. Attempt to see the nineteenth century just as positively as I tried to see the seventeenth, in the work on *Trauerspiel.* No belief in periods of decline. By the same token, every city is beautiful to me (from outside its borders), just as all talk of particular languages' having greater or lesser value is to me unacceptable.   [N1, 6]

And, later, the glassed-in spot facing my seat at the Staatsbibliothek. Charmed circle inviolate, virgin terrain for the soles of figures I conjured.   [N1, 7]

Pedagogic side of this undertaking: "To educate the image-making medium within us, raising it to a stereoscopic and dimensional seeing into the depths of historical shadows." The words are Rudolf Borchardt's in *Epilegomena zu Dante,* vol. 1 (Berlin, 1923), pp. 56–57.   [N1, 8]

Delimitation of the tendency of this project with respect to Aragon: whereas Aragon persists within the realm of dream, here the concern is to find the constellation of awakening. While in Aragon there remains an impressionistic element, namely the "mythology" (and this impressionism must be held responsible for the many vague philosophemes in his book),[2] here it is a question of the dissolution of "mythology" into the space of history. That, of course, can happen only through the awakening of a not-yet-conscious knowledge of what has been.   [N1, 9]

This work has to develop to the highest degree the art of citing without quotation marks. Its theory is intimately related to that of montage.   [N1, 10]

"Apart from a certain *haut-goût* charm," says Giedion, "the artistic draperies and wall-hangings of the previous century have come to seem musty." <Sigfried>Giedion, *Bauen in Frankreich* (Leipzig and Berlin <1928>), p. 3. We, however, believe that the charm they exercise on us is proof that these things, too, contain material of vital importance for us—not indeed for our building practice, as is the case with the constructive possibilities inherent in iron frameworks, but rather for our understanding, for the radioscopy, if you will, of the situation of the bourgeois class at the moment it evinces the first signs of decline. In any case, material of vital importance politically; this is demonstrated by the attachment of the Surrealists to these things, as much as by their exploitation in contemporary fashion. In other words: just as Giedion teaches us to read off the basic features of today's architecture in the buildings erected around 1850, we, in turn, would recognize today's life, today's forms, in the life and in the apparently secondary, lost forms of that epoch.   [N1, 11]

"In the windswept stairways of the Eiffel Tower, or, better still, in the steel supports of a Pont Transbordeur, one meets with the fundamental aesthetic experience of present-day architecture: through the thin net of iron that hangs suspended in the air, things stream—ships, ocean, houses, masts, landscape, harbor. They lose their distinctive shape, swirl into one another as we climb downward, merge simultaneously." Sigfried Giedion, *Bauen in Frankreich* (Leipzig and Berlin), p. 7. In the same way, the historian today has only to erect a slender but sturdy scaffolding—a philosophic structure—in order to draw the most vital aspects of the past into his net. But just as the magnificent vistas of the city provided by the new construction in iron (again, see Giedion, illustrations on pp. 61–63) for a long time were reserved exclusively for the workers and engineers, so too the philosopher who wishes here to garner fresh perspectives must be someone immune to vertigo—an independent and, if need be, solitary worker.   [N1a, 1]

The book on the Baroque exposed the seventeenth century to the light of the present day. Here, something analogous must be done for the nineteenth century, but with greater distinctness.   [N1a, 2]

Modest methodological proposal for the cultural-historical dialectic. It is very easy to establish oppositions, according to determinate points of view, within the various "fields" of any epoch, such that on one side lies the "productive," "forward-looking," "lively," "positive" part of the epoch, and on the other side the abortive, retrograde, and obsolescent. The very contours of the positive element will appear distinctly only insofar as this element is set off against the negative. On the other hand, every negation has its value solely as background for the delineation of the lively, the positive. It is therefore of decisive importance that a new partition be applied to this initially excluded, negative component so that, by a displacement of the angle of vision (but not of the criteria!), a positive element emerges anew in it too—something different from that previously signified. And so on, ad infinitum, until the entire past is brought into the present in a historical apocatastasis.[3]   [N1a, 3]

The foregoing, put differently: the indestructibility of the highest life in all things. Against the prognosticators of decline. Consider, though: Isn't it an affront to Goethe to make a film of *Faust,* and isn't there a world of difference between the poem *Faust* and the film *Faust*? Yes, certainly. But, again, isn't there a whole world of difference between a bad film of *Faust* and a good one? What matter are never the "great" but only the dialectical contrasts, which often seem indistinguishable from nuances. It is nonetheless from them that life is always born anew.   [N1a, 4]

To encompass both Breton and Le Corbusier—that would mean drawing the spirit of contemporary France like a bow, with which knowledge shoots the moment in the heart.   [N1a, 5]

Marx lays bare the causal connection between economy and culture. For us, what matters is the thread of expression. It is not the economic origins of culture that will be presented, but the expression of the economy in its culture. At issue, in other words, is the attempt to grasp an economic process as perceptible *Ur*-phenomenon, from out of which proceed all manifestations of life in the arcades (and, accordingly, in the nineteenth century).   [N1a, 6]

This research—which deals fundamentally with the expressive character of the earliest industrial products, the earliest industrial architecture, the earliest machines, but also the earliest department stores, advertisements, and so on—thus becomes important for Marxism in two ways. First, it will demonstrate how the milieu in which Marx's doctrine arose affected that doctrine through its expressive character (which is to say, not only through causal connections); but, second, it will also show in what respects Marxism, too, shares the expressive character of the material products contemporary with it.   [N1a, 7]

Method of this project: literary montage. I needn't *say* anything. Merely show. I shall purloin no valuables, appropriate no ingenious formulations. But the rags, the refuse—these I will not inventory but allow, in the only way possible, to come into their own: by making use of them.   [N1a, 8]

Bear in mind that commentary on a reality (for it is a question here of commentary, of interpretation in detail) calls for a method completely different from that required by commentary on a text. In the one case, the scientific mainstay is theology; in the other case, philology.   [N2, 1]

It may be considered one of the methodological objectives of this work to demonstrate a historical materialism which has annihilated within itself the idea of progress. Just here, historical materialism has every reason to distinguish itself sharply from bourgeois habits of thought. Its founding concept is not progress but actualization.   [N2, 2]

Historical "understanding" is to be grasped, in principle, as an afterlife of that which is understood; and what has been recognized in the analysis of the "after-life of works," in the analysis of "fame," is therefore to be considered the foundation of history in general.   [N2, 3]

How this work was written: rung by rung, according as chance would offer a narrow foothold, and always like someone who scales dangerous heights and never allows himself a moment to look around, for fear of becoming dizzy (but also because he would save for the end the full force of the panorama opening out to him).   [N2, 4]

Overcoming the concept of "progress" and overcoming the concept of "period of decline" are two sides of one and the same thing.   [N2, 5]

A central problem of historical materialism that ought to be seen in the end: Must the Marxist understanding of history necessarily be acquired at the expense of the perceptibility of history? Or: in what way is it possible to conjoin a heightened graphicness <*Anschaulichkeit*>

to the realization of the Marxist method? The first stage in this undertaking will be to carry over the principle of montage into history. That is, to assemble large-scale constructions out of the smallest and most precisely cut components. Indeed, to discover in the analysis of the small individual moment the crystal of the total event. And, therefore, to break with vulgar historical naturalism. To grasp the construction of history as such. In the structure of commentary. □ Refuse of History □   [N2, 6]

A Kierkegaard citation in Wiesengrund, with commentary following: "'One may arrive at a similar consideration of the mythical by beginning with the imagistic. When, in an age of reflection, one sees the imagistic protrude ever so slightly and unobserved in a reflective representation and, like an antediluvian fossil, suggest another species of existence which washed away doubt, one will perhaps be amazed that the image could ever have played such an important role.' Kierkegaard wards off the 'amazement' with what follows. Yet this amazement heralds the deepest insight into the interrelation of dialectic, myth, and image. For it is not as the continuously living and present that nature prevails in the dialectic. Dialectic comes to a stop in the image, and, in the context of recent history, it cites the mythical as what is long gone: nature as primal history. For this reason, the images—which, like those of the *intérieur*, bring dialectic and myth to the point of indifferentiation—are truly 'antediluvian fossils.' They may be called dialectical images, to use Benjamin's expression, whose compelling definition of 'allegory' also holds true for Kierkegaard's allegorical intention taken as a figure of historical dialectic and mythical nature. According to this definition, 'in allegory the observer is confronted with the *facies hippocratica* of history, a petrified primordial landscape.'" Theodor Wiesengrund-Adorno, *Kierkegaard* (Tübingen, 1933), p. 60.[4] □ Refuse of History □   [N2, 7]

Only a thoughtless observer can deny that correspondences come into play between the world of modern technology and the archaic symbol-world of mythology. Of course, initially the technologically new seems nothing more than that. But in the very next childhood memory, its traits are already altered. Every childhood achieves something great and irreplaceable for humanity. By the interest it takes in technological phenomena, by the curiosity it displays before any sort of invention or machinery, every childhood binds the accomplishments of technology to the old worlds of symbol. There is nothing in the realm of nature that from the outset would be exempt from such a bond. Only, it takes form not in the aura of novelty but in the aura of the habitual. In memory, childhood, and dream. □ Awakening □   [N2a, 1]

The momentum of primal history in the past is no longer masked, as it used to be, by the tradition of church and family—this at once the consequence and condition of technology. The old prehistoric dread already envelops the world of our parents because we ourselves are no longer bound to this world by tradition. The perceptual worlds <*Merkwelten*> break up more rapidly; what they contain of the mythic comes more quickly and more brutally to the fore; and a wholly different perceptual world must be speedily set up to oppose it. This is how the accelerated tempo of technology appears in light of the primal history of the present. □ Awakening □   [N2a, 2]

It's not that what is past casts its light on what is present, or what is present its light on what is past; rather, image is that wherein what has been comes together in a flash with the now to form a constellation. In other words, image is dialectics at a standstill. For while the relation of the present to the past is a purely temporal, continuous one, the relation of what-has-been to the now is dialectical: is not progression but image, suddenly emergent.—Only dialectical images are genuine images (that is, not archaic); and the place where one encounters them is language. □ Awakening □   [N2a, 3]

In studying Simmel's presentation of Goethe's concept of truth,[5] I came to see very clearly that my concept of origin in the *Trauerspiel* book is a rigorous and decisive transposition of this basic Goethean concept from the domain of nature to that of history. Origin—it is, in effect, the concept of *Ur*-phenomenon extracted from the pagan context of nature and brought into the Jewish contexts of history. Now, in my work on the arcades I am equally concerned with fathoming an origin. To be specific, I pursue the origin of the forms and mutations of the Paris arcades from their beginning to their decline, and I locate this origin in the economic facts. Seen from the standpoint of causality, however (and that means considered as causes), these facts would not be primal phenomena; they become such only insofar as in their own individual development—"unfolding" might be a better term—they give rise to the whole series of the arcade's concrete historical forms, just as the leaf unfolds from itself all the riches of the empirical world of plants. [N2a, 4]

"As I study this age which is so close to us and so remote, I compare myself to a surgeon operating with local anesthetic: I work in areas that are numb, dead—yet the patient is alive and can still talk." Paul Morand, *1900* **(Paris, 1931), pp. 6–7.** [N2a, 5]

What distinguishes images from the "essences" of phenomenology is their historical index. (Heidegger seeks in vain to rescue history for phenomenology abstractly through "historicity.")[6] These images are to be thought of entirely apart from the categories of the "human sciences," from so-called habitus, from style, and the like. For the historical index of the images not only says that they belong to a particular time; it says, above all, that they attain to legibility only at a particular time. And, indeed, this acceding "to legibility" constitutes a specific critical point in the movement at their interior. Every present day is determined by the images that are synchronic with it: each "now" is the now of a particular recognizability. In it, truth is charged to the bursting point with time. (This point of explosion, and nothing else, is the death of the *intentio,* which thus coincides with the birth of authentic historical time, the time of truth.) It is not that what is past casts its light on what is present, or what is present its light on what is past; rather, image is that wherein what has been comes together in a flash with the now to form a constellation. In other words: image is dialectics at a standstill. For while the relation of the present to the past is purely temporal, the relation of what-has-been to the now is dialectical: not temporal in nature but figural <*bildlich*>. Only dialectical images are genuinely historical—that is, not archaic—images. The image that is read—which is to say, the image in the now of its recognizability—bears to the highest degree the imprint of the perilous critical moment on which all reading is founded. [N3, 1]

Resolute refusal of the concept of "timeless truth" is in order. Nevertheless, truth is not—as Marxism would have it—a merely contingent function of knowing, but is bound to a nucleus of time lying hidden within the knower and the known alike. This is so true that the eternal, in any case, is far more the ruffle on a dress than some idea. [N3, 2]

Outline the story of *The Arcades Project* in terms of its development. Its properly problematic component: the refusal to renounce anything that would demonstrate the materialist presentation of history as imagistic <*bildhaft*> in a higher sense than in the traditional presentation. [N3, 3]

A remark by Ernst Bloch apropos of *The Arcades Project:* "History displays its Scotland Yard badge." It was in the context of a conversation in which I was describing how this work—comparable, in method, to the process of splitting the atom—liberates the enormous energies of history that are bound up in the "once upon a time" of classical historiography. The history that showed things "as they really were" was the strongest narcotic of the century. [N3, 4]

"The truth will not escape us," reads one of Keller's epigrams.[7] He thus formulates the concept of truth with which these presentations take issue. [N3a, l]

"Primal history of the nineteenth century"—this would be of no interest if it were understood to mean that forms of primal history are to be recovered among the inventory of the nineteenth century. Only where the nineteenth century would be presented as originary form of primal history—in a form, that is to say, in which the whole of primal history groups itself anew in images appropriate to that century—only there does the concept of a primal history of the nineteenth century have meaning.   [N3a, 2]

Is awakening perhaps the synthesis of dream consciousness (as thesis) and waking consciousness (as antithesis)? Then the moment of awakening would be identical with the "now of recognizability," in which things put on their true—surrealist—face. Thus, in Proust, the importance of staking an entire life on life's supremely dialectical point of rupture: awakening. Proust begins with an evocation of the space of someone waking up.   [N3a, 3]

"If I insist on this mechanism of contradiction in the biography of a writer . . ., it is because his train of thought cannot bypass certain facts which have a logic different from that of his thought by itself. It is because there is no idea he adheres to that truly holds up . . . in the face of certain very simple, elemental facts: that workers are staring down the barrels of cannons aimed at them by police, that war is threatening, and that fascism is already enthroned. . . . It behooves a man, for the sake of his dignity, to submit his ideas to these facts, and not to bend these facts, by some conjuring trick, to his ideas, however ingenious." Aragon, "D'Alfred de Vigny à Avdeenko," *Commune,* 2 (April 20, 1935), pp. 808–9. But it is entirely possible that, in contradicting my past, I will establish a continuity with that of another, which he in turn, as communist, will contradict. In this case, with the past of Louis Aragon, who in this same essay disavows his *Paysan de Paris:* "And, like most of my friends, I was partial to the failures, to what is monstrous and cannot survive, cannot succeed. . . . I was like them: I preferred error to its opposite" (p. 807).   [N3a, 4]

In the dialectical image, what has been within a particular epoch is always, simultaneously, "what has been from time immemorial." As such, however, it is manifest, on each occasion, only to a quite specific epoch—namely, the one in which humanity, rubbing its eyes, recognizes just this particular dream image as such. It is at this moment that the historian takes up, with regard to that image, the task of dream interpretation.   [N4, 1]

The expression "the book of nature" indicates that one can read the real like a text. And that is how the reality of the nineteenth century will be treated here. We open the book of what happened.   [N4, 2]

Just as Proust begins the story of his life with an awakening, so must every presentation of history begin with awakening; in fact, it should treat of nothing else. This one, accordingly, deals with awakening from the nineteenth century.   [N4, 3]

The realization of dream elements in the course of waking up is the canon of dialectics. It is paradigmatic for the thinker and binding for the historian.   [N4, 4]

Raphael seeks to correct the Marxist conception of the normative character of Greek art: "If the normative character of Greek art is . . . an explicable fact of history, . . . we will have . . . to determine . . . what special conditions led to each renascence and, in consequence, what special factors of . . . Greek art these renascences adopted as models. For the totality of Greek art never possessed a normative character; the renascences . . . have their own proper history. . . . Only a historical analysis can indicate the era in which the abstract notion of a 'norm' . . . of antiquity was born. . . . This notion was created solely by the Renaissance—that is, by primitive capitalism—and subsequently taken up by classicism, which . . . commenced to assign it its place in a historical sequence. Marx has not advanced along this way in the full measure of the possibilities of historical materialism." Max Raphael, *Proudhon, Marx, Picasso* (Paris <1933>), pp. 178–79.   [N4, 5]

It is the peculiarity of *technological* forms of production (as opposed to art forms) that their progress and their success are proportionate to the *transparency* of their social content. (Hence glass architecture.)   [N4, 6]

An important passage in Marx: "It is recognized that where . . . the epic, for example, . . . is concerned, . . . certain significant creations within the compass of art are possible only at an early stage of artistic development. If this is the case with regard to different branches of art within the sphere of the arts, it is not so remarkable that this should also be the case with regard to the whole artistic realm and its relation to the general development of the society." Cited without references (perhaps *Theorien des Mehrwerts,* vol. 1?)[8] in Max Raphael, *Proudhon, Marx, Picasso* (Paris <1933>), p. 160.   [N4a, 1]

The Marxian theory of art: one moment swaggering, and the next scholastic.   [N4a, 2]

Proposal for a gradation of the superstructure, in A. Asturaro, *Il materialismo storico e la sociologia generale* (Genoa, 1904) (reviewed by Erwin Szabó in *Die neue Zeit*, 23, no. 1 [Stuttgart], p. 62): "Economy. Family and kinship. Law. War. Politics. Morality. Religion. Art. Science."   [N4a, 3]

Strange remark by Engels concerning the "social forces": "But when once their nature is understood, they can, in the hands of the producers working together, be transformed from master demons into willing servants." (!) Engels, *Die Entwicklung des Sozialismus von der Utopie zur Wissenschaft* (1882).[9]   [N4a, 4]

Marx, in the afterword to the second edition of *Das Kapital*: "Research has to appropriate the material in detail, to analyze its various forms of development, to trace out their inner connection. Only after this work is done can the actual movement be presented in corresponding fashion. If this is done successfully, if the life of the material is reflected back as ideal, then it may appear as if we had before us an a priori construction." Karl Marx, *Das Kapital*, vol 1, ed. Korsch (Berlin <1932>), p. 45.[10]   [N4a, 5]

The particular difficulty of doing historical research on the period following the close of the eighteenth century will be displayed. With the rise of the mass-circulation press, the sources become innumerable.   [N4a, 6]

Michelet is perfectly willing to let the people be known as "barbarians." "'Barbarians.' I like the word, and I accept the term." And he says of their writers: "Their love is boundless and sometimes too great, for they may devote themselves to details with the delightful awkwardness of Albrecht Dürer, or with the excessive polish of Jean-Jacques Rousseau, who does not conceal his art enough; and by this minute detail they compromise the whole. We must not blame them too much. It is . . . the luxuriance of their sap and vigor. . . . This sap wants to give everything at once—leaves, fruit, and flowers; it bends and twists the branches. These defects of many great workers are often found in my books, which lack their good qualities. No matter!" J. Michelet, *Le Peuple* (Paris, 1846), pp. xxxvi–xxxvii.[11]   [N5, 1]

Letter from Wiesengrund of August 5, 1935: "The attempt to reconcile your 'dream' momentum—as the subjective element in the dialectical image—with the conception of the latter as model has led me to some formulations . . .: With the vitiation of their use value, the alienated things are hollowed out and, as ciphers, they draw in meanings. Subjectivity takes possession of them insofar as it invests them with intentions of desire and fear. And insofar as defunct things stand in as images of subjective intentions, these latter present themselves as immemorial and eternal. Dialectical images are constellated between alienated things and incoming and disappearing meaning, are instantiated in the moment of indifference between death and meaning. While things in appearance are awakened to what is newest, death transforms the meanings to what is most ancient." With regard to these reflections, it should be kept in mind that, in the nineteenth century, the number of "hollowed-out" things increases at a rate and on a scale that was previously unknown, for technical progress is continually withdrawing newly introduced objects from circulation.   [N5, 2]

"The critic can start from any form of theoretical or practical consciousness, and develop out of the actual forms of existing reality the true reality as what it ought to be, that which is its aim." Karl Marx, *Der historische Materialismus: Die Frühschriften,* ed. Landshut and Mayer (Leipzig <1932>), vol. 1, p. 225 (letter from Marx to Ruge; Kreuzenach, September 1843).[12] The point of departure invoked here by Marx need not necessarily connect with the latest stage of development. It can be undertaken with regard to long-vanished epochs whose "ought to be" and whose aim is then to be presented—not in reference to the next stage of development, but in its own right and as preformation of the final goal of history.   [N5, 3]

Notes

In translating Convolute N, we have greatly benefited from the previous translation of this convolute, "Re the Theory of Knowledge, Theory of Progress," by Leigh Hafrey and Richard Sieburth, originally published in *Philosophical Forum* (Fall–Winter, 1983–84), and reprinted in *Benjamin: Philosophy, History, Aesthetics,* ed. Gary Smith (Chicago: University of Chicago Press, 1989), pp. 38–83.

1   Karl Marx, *Selected Writings,* ed. David McLellan (New York: Oxford University Press, 1977), p. 38.

2   Reference is to Louis Aragon, *Le Paysan de Paris* (Paris, 1926). [R.T.] On the not-yet-conscious knowledge of what has been, see K1, 2.

3   "Restoration of all things." Derived from Jewish apocalyptic, Stoic, and Neoplatonic-Gnostic traditions, the concept originally referred to the recurrence of a specific planetary constellation.

4   Adorno, *Kierkegaard: Construction of the Aesthetic,* trans. Robert Hullot-Kentor (Minneapolis: University of Minnesota Press, 1989), p. 54. The Kierkegaard passage is from *The Concept of Irony.* For the passage from Benjamin cited by Adorno, see Benjamin, *The Origin of German Tragic Drama,* trans. John Osborne (London: Verso, 1977), p. 166. The *facies hippocratica* is a death mask.

5   Georg Simmel, *Goethe* (Leipzig, 1913), esp. pp. 56–61; see also Benjamin, *GS,* vol. 1, pp. 953–54. [R.T.] "Origin" here translates *Ursprung.*

6   See Martin Heidegger, *Being and Time,* trans. John Macquarrie and Edward Robinson (New York: Harper and Row, 1962), Division 2, Chapter 5. On truth as "the death of the *intentio*" (parenthesis below), see Benjamin, *The Origin of German Tragic Drama,* p. 36. On time in the dialectical image, see Q°, 21 in "First Sketches."

7   This sentence could not be found among Keller's epigrams. [R.T.]

8   The passage occurs in the Introduction to the *Kritik der Politischen Ökonomie,* in Karl Marx and Friedrich Engels, *Werke* (Berlin, 1964), vol. 13, pp. 640ff. [R.T.] In English, "Introduction to a Critique of Political Economy," in Marx and Engels, *The German Ideology,* trans. anonymous (New York: International Publishers, 1970), pp. 149–50.

9   Friedrich Engels, *Socialism, Utopian and Scientific,* trans. Edward Aveling (1935; rpt. Westport, Conn.: Greenwood, 1977), p. 68. Rolf Tiedemann informs us that Benjamin wrote in his manuscript, instead of "aus dämonischen Herrschern," the truly "strange" words "und dämonischen Herrscher." The sentence would then read: "they can, in the hands of associated producers and master demons, be transformed into willing servants."

10   Marx, *Capital,* vol. 1, trans. Samuel Moore and Edward Aveling (1887; rpt. New York: International Publishers, 1967), p. 28. Marx distinguishes between *Forschung* (research) and *Darstellung* (presentation, application).

11   Jules Michelet, *The People,* trans. John P. McKay (Urbana: University of Illinois Press 1973), pp. 18–19.

12   Marx, *Selected Writings,* p. 37.

Chapter 35

Catherine Gallagher and Stephen Greenblatt

THE POTATO IN THE MATERIALIST IMAGINATION

In many respects Catherine Gallagher and Stephen Greenblatt's extract on the potato pits two modes of materialism against each other: that of the eighteenth and nineteenth centuries in Britain, and that of a more recent manifestation, found in New Historicist interpretations. The potato is an interesting material object which also functions as a sign: it is the "Ur-food" or imagined "original" earthy primitive Northern European food, not just growing from the soil, but subterranean: buried and growing underneath the ground. This imagined earliest foodstuff actually arrived in Europe from the Americas in the seventeenth century. So, this shows that it is more than just a dietary substance: it stands in for the most primitive food imagined, the food of peasants, and lowly people, which reveals in turn how food is a signifier of class. Gallagher and Greenblatt, leading proponents of the New Historicism movement explored in numerous books and articles on topics such as Shakespeare, the Renaissance, the body, and women writers in the marketplace, situate this signifier in debates concerning economics, class, and even subjectivity, in other words concerning the "autochthonous" body, or, the self-originating body that can miraculously appear from the same soil in which potatoes grow. Rejecting Raymond Williams' notion of food as being low down a scale of cultural signs, Gallagher and Greenblatt argue instead that the symbolism of the potato is culturally powerful and even threatening. They compare it to the Eucharistic Host which they explore in earlier chapters in their book, to suggest that the potato and the Host are both signs which "mark the limits of representation", which means that they help us see how class, gender and other categories of being are inherently unstable, and are culturally constructed. The potato is compared in the debates of the time to a semiotically and materially "rich" foodstuff: that of bread. The Eucharistic Host and bread are complex signs generated by, and embedded in, communities; the potato is seen by some as simple, isolated, primitive, outside of orderly theological or state-sanctioned community, indeed potentially outside of nascent capitalist economies because it can be grown by individuals, and it facilitates self-sufficiency. The issues here are made apparent by the English attitude to the politics of food in Ireland: the separate Catholic religion is made even more threatening (from the perspective of the English) when its adherents are autochthonous primitive beings, outside of English state control. The Irish were described by some English thinkers as creatures lower than animals, outside of the grain (or bread) economy. Whether the English wanted to improve or control the lives of the poor, the potato is central to the debate: it is a sign of debasement and want, as well as paradoxically being the opposite, a sign of plenitude and independence. The potato is a sign in a "moral economy" but New Historicism adds to earlier analyses by foregrounding the body and its material needs and significations. Food markets were used to control populations: being self-sufficient in food production took one outside of that control, breaking the exploitative bond between the classes; the potato is "economically extrinsic" and "extra-economic", which means that it makes no profit and is thus literally outside of an economic system, or at the least, marks a liminal space, one which is half inside, half outside, of societal control.

WHEN VICE PRESIDENT DAN QUAYLE was being ridiculed for misspelling "potato" by putting an "e" at the end, President Bush defended him by claiming that Chaucer had spelled the word that way. Bush thus revealed that he knew something about the history of the English language and its orthography but nothing about the history of the potato, which was not introduced into Europe until the seventeenth century. The English word derives from the Spanish pronunciation of the Haitian name for what we call the sweet potato, "batata." It was first used in English in 1597. Bush, though, is not the only American who assumes there were medieval potatoes: a medieval theme park in the Midwest advertises that it makes its potato pancakes from an authentic fourteenth-century recipe.

Belief in the medieval potato is not really surprising, given the strong association in the modern mind between potatoes and peasants, on the one hand, and peasants and medieval Europe, on the other. Indeed, despite its very late arrival on the scene, the potato represents something like an Ur-food even in the northern European imagination. We don't wish to make excuses for George Bush in this chapter, though; we intend, rather, to unearth the long-neglected British potato debate of the late eighteenth and early nineteenth centuries,[1] with the hope of exploring simultaneously the relation between the body history[2] that has deeply influenced new historicism and older forms of materialist thought.

The potato debate was basically a controversy over the relative merits of potatoes and grain as the staple food of the working poor. It raged with peculiar intensity during the 1790s and then again in the 1830s, both eras of dispute over poor-law policy. Most conceded that a unit of land producing potatoes would feed three times as many people as the same land bearing wheat, but they disagreed over the desirability of such an arrangement. Several issues were involved, such as the proper level of wages, the effect on population growth, the danger of setting wages according to the cheapest possible staple food, and the social consequences of having two standard foods, wheat bread for the middle classes and potatoes for the poor.

This list of abstract issues, however, gives little sense of the passion suffusing the potato debate, the vehemence with which the opposing parties predicted that either misery or abundance would accompany the spread of the tuber. The very idea of a potato debate seems mildly ridiculous because we've forgotten what the debaters knew—that the vast majority of people would live primarily on one food and that this food would cost the majority of their income. The cost of labor, most political economists agreed, was determined fundamentally by the cost of grain, and the supply of grain largely controlled the supply of laboring people. In the debaters' minds, therefore, bushels of the staple food became almost interchangeable with people themselves, and many insisted that potato people were radically different from grain people. If we take a look at the rhetoric of this debate, we can see that potato eaters often undergo a peculiarly quick transition from plant to person, as if they were literalizing the political economists' equations. In this debate, anxieties about the tuber generally sprout from this quick transition, from a perception of the potato's primeval, archaic power to conjure people right out of the ground. But this same, at times disturbingly close, link between soil and people led others to extol the plant as "the root of plenty." The potato, to put it briefly, became an icon of the autochthonous body for certain late-eighteenth- and early-nineteenth-century writers, and hence it seems an appropriate topic for launching a discussion of the modern materialist imagination.

The potato also gives us an opportunity to assert that representation knows no natural limits. That vegetable's very significance as a peculiarly primitive food, a thing representing mere subsistence and (in some minds) the virtual end of culture, gave it tremendous symbolic weight. But the potato did not restrict itself to one meaning; it was as ambivalent, arbitrary, historically over-determined, unstable, and opaque as any other signifier. Like all signifiers, it spoils the distinction between matter and idea, but its placement in the imagined ground of existence especially unsettles attempts to distinguish a physical material base from an ideological superstructure or a bodily need from a cultural exigency. When, for example, Raymond Williams tries to devise a scale on which phenomena could be ranged from the "less cultural" to the "more," he claims that food would be down at the "less cultural" end because any symbolic function it might have would be submerged in its primary purpose of sustaining life. Food, he admits, has "signifying" moments; one can analyze it semiotically, demonstrating the various social meanings of how and what people prepare and consume. Nevertheless, its nonsignifying, merely physiological utility takes precedence over its ideational meaning.[3] If Williams were right, the more an edible item was merely food to a people, the more it seemed simply to satisfy a bodily need, the less it would "signify" and the less "cultural" it would be. But the potato debate demonstrates that "mere food" is not only already a cultural category, but also an extremely potent and disturbing one. It was precisely by being *only food* that the potato became symbolically resonant.

The potato in the materialist imagination thus enjoys a certain uncanny resemblance to the elusive object of the previous chapter: the consecrated Host in the doctrine of the Real Presence. Both attempt to mark the limits of representation, to define the outer reaches of the realm of human signification. Just as the Host, by *being* rather than *meaning* the literal presence of Christ's body and blood, is placed beyond artistic representation, the potato conducts us to the nineteenth-century materialists' beyond, where the Real is the physical ground of our existence, as harsh and unremitting in its determinism as it is generally indifferent to our constructions of its import. Like the Host, the potato is a threshold phenomenon: the former gives access to the divine, independently of the intentions or control of the participants in the sacrament; the latter threatens to turn culture into nature or to overwhelm meaning with matter. Believing Catholics and nineteenth-century materialists alike seem to have needed a sign for the end of signification, and each found it in a bit of matter that could be thought of as a literal body.

To be sure, the literal body of Christ and the autochthonous body of the potato would occupy opposite extremes on the sort of spectrum imagined by Raymond Williams. In Williams's terms, the potato would have an excess of matter and the Eucharist an excess of signification: in its primal materiality, its lumpish absence of standard form, the potato seems the antithesis of the eucharistic Host, whose matter has been sublimated almost out of existence. And, indeed, a similar contrast is implied in the potato debate when potatoes are compared and contrasted to bread, just as the Eucharist had been. The common comparative term only strengthens the case for their diametrical difference. The Host is infinitely more than the physical accidents of the bread, whereas the potato is ever so much less. Indeed, compared to potatoes, bread is anything but accidental. The possibility of subsisting on the potato is what made it comparable to bread rather than to other roots (like carrots and parsnips).[4] It was understood, therefore, as a substitute for the very food that most commonly stood as a signifier for all food. Although bread has this general synechdochal function in European culture (even in Ireland people don't ask God to "Give us this day our daily potatoes"), the potato, introduced much later, is imagined to be the more *primitive* contender because it comes right out of the earth, haphazardly shaped, like a clot of dirt, but virtually ready to eat. If the eucharistic Host was the body made transcendent and immortal, the potato was rhetorically associated by its opponents with physical wretchedness, filth, and infirmity. Those who compared bread and potatoes frequently stressed that bread partook of several elements and required many differentiated stages of production. Wheat, which bears its grains aboveground, ripens all golden in the sunlit air, while potato tubers expand unseen in occulted darkness. Passing through few stages of civilized productive mediation, the potato makes a startlingly abrupt transition from ground to human being. The whole satisfyingly social and symbolic cycle of planting, germination, sprouting, growing, ripening, harvesting, thrashing, milling, mixing, kneading, and baking, which makes wheat into bread, is bypassed in tuber culture. Without being formed by human hands, baked in man-made ovens, passing through a differentiated society, or circulating in an economy, the very root of the potato plant itself becomes something like a hard, knobby little loaf of bread, a point succinctly made by one of the earliest words for the potato in English—"bread-root." Just as the Eucharist enacts Christ's continued dwelling among his communicants, bread represents the cooperation of the elements in human endeavors and the cooperation of people with one another in a society where the division of labor has been achieved but people nevertheless share the same food. In short, whereas the Eucharist partakes of divinity and bread of culture, the potato represented a presocial state of isolation in which the poor were cut off from civilization and undifferentiated both from each other and from nature.

The English had a word for this state: Ireland. Ireland was a place without bread, a land of spurious substitutes: potatoes and Communion wafers believed to be the literal body and blood of Christ, the one a cause of degrading carnality, the other a focus of mass delusion. Of course the believers didn't see it that way, but to them as well the potato and Host were on opposite sides of that rare commodity, bread. To the believer, the Host is spiritual, as opposed to bodily, nourishment. It gathers up the symbolic meanings of bread—including human community, mutual nurturance, and reliance on natural cycles of death and resurrection—saturates them with transcendent spirituality, and lets the physical gravity of bread—for example, bulk and nutrition—drop away like dross. Only a hint of bread remains in the Host, whose papery thinness and stamped impression recall a text or a coin (despite the anti-representationalism of the doctrine of the Real Presence) far more than they do any kind of food. Thus even for the believer, the Communion wafer and the potato, as spiritual and physical food, even as antimatter and matter, would have seemed an obvious pair of opposites.

But for those who feared what Ireland represented, the potato and the Host might seem destructively complementary opposites that canceled their mutual term of comparison: bread. The potato was often imagined to be the root of mere materiality, whereas the Host was the symbol of chimerical spirituality; together they might trick a people into thinking that they had no need for the middle term represented by bread—culture—because they were gathered by their religion into a transcendent mystical body. By believing the bizarre claim of the transubstantiation, that the consecrated Host *is* the body and blood of Christ, the Irish became victims of a misplaced concreteness that eradicated culture, the realm of transformation through labor and of exchanges that were recognizably symbolic. Perhaps it was because the Irish peasantry was in the grip of superstition, because they thought they could eat God's body, that they uncomplainingly lived on a hog's diet.

To our knowledge, no nineteenth-century writer explicitly made these connections: we have assembled in the foregoing paragraphs the complementary sides of English alarmism about the state of Ireland, but they do not truly make a single empirically available discourse. Generally, the anti-potato faction had little explicit interest in religion, and the debate we'll be describing was secular in tone, even downright materialist in its assumptions about human motivation and cultural practices. Nevertheless, the most horrific anti-potato rhetoric seems to borrow the extreme literalism of eucharistic doctrine when it turns to the relation between body and food. In William Cobbett's fulminations, for example, food and body are difficult to distinguish, as if, in potato eating, the Sacrament had been grotesquely inverted to produce bodies bearing an ugly resemblance to misshapen roots. Writing at the end of the potato debate in 1834 and synthesizing many of the potato opponents' images, the radical journalist portrays the Irish peasantry as people living underground, like their food, literally in the soil. The potato, he writes, "has chased bread from the cottages of this island," and with the disappearance of civilized food has come a descent into the very ground of existence. The potato eaters live, he tells his correspondent, in low mud huts full of holes:

> . . . no windows at all; but a hole or two holes in the wall; . . . the floor nothing but the bare earth; no chimney, but, a hole at one end of the roof a foot or two high at the end of the miserable shed; this hole is sometimes surrounded by a few stones . . .; in cold weather the poor, ragged half-naked creatures stop up the hole to keep in the smoke to keep them from perishing with cold! The fuel is *peat,* just such as that dug out of our moors, and never a stick of wood.[5]

Everything about this description makes the dwelling seem subterranean: the building materials of rough stone and mud, the fuel of peat ("as that dug out of our moors"), the strange combination of exposure and suffocation, and the repeated use of the word "hole." As Cobbett's description goes on, the underground imagery becomes even more insistent. "Hole" comes to describe the very dwelling just when "the root of all misery" (the potato) appears in the description:

> As to the *goods* in the hole, they are, an *iron pot,* a *rough table,* or board laid across two poles of stones, seats of stones. . . . The potatoes are taken up and turned out into a great dish, which dish is a shallow basket made of oziers with the bark on. The family squat round this basket and take out the potatoes with their hands; the pig stands and is helped by some one, and sometimes he eats out of the pot. He goes in and out and about the hole, like one of the family. (82–83)

Lest we think that the potato is merely incidental to this subterranean existence, Cobbett proclaims loudly and frequently that the tuber is the channel through which Irish landlords have brought the peasantry lower than the very ground:

> The people never could have been brought to this pass without the ever-damned potatoes! People CAN keep life in them by the means of this nasty, filthy hog-feed; and the tyrants make them do it, and have thus reduced them to the state of hogs, and worse than that of hogs. (83)

Through Cobbett's subterranean imagery, the Irish laborers have indeed been reduced to something quite a bit lower than pigs—something closely resembling potatoes.

As the shortest route through which the land can bear people, the potato triggered deep fears in many and hopes in some about the earth's fecundity. Cobbett's depictions of Irish cottiers eating the filthy root in their "holes" can be linked, for example, to persistent stories of exotic dirt-eating races; closer to home, they recall derogatory English medieval images of peasants eating dirt. The formulation is both insulting to peasants—"Peasants eat dirt, therefore peasants are dirt"—and reassuring to the landed classes—"Peasants can eat dirt, so we needn't worry about them." The complete idea has the structure of a cruel joke: the bad news is that the peasants eat dirt; the good news is that there's plenty of dirt. This absurd conflation of utter privation and abundance seems fundamental to the idea of autochthonous people, people who are part and parcel of the land, as medieval serfs were imagined to be.

A seventeenth-century mention of the Irish potato illustrates its affinity with the notion of a people who are so rooted in the soil that they cannot be eradicated even by the destruction of their grain supply. John Houghton writes of the plant's introduction to the British Isles:

> This I have been informed was brought first out of Virginia by Sir Walter Raleigh, and he stopping at Ireland, some was planted there, where it thrived well and to good purpose, for in three succeeding wars, when all the corn above ground was destroyed, this supported them; for the soldiers, unless they had dug up all the ground where they grew, and almost sifted it could not extirpate them.[6]

The rather sloppy use of pronouns in this passage underlines the main point: the "them" who cannot be extirpated short of digging up and sifting the ground could denote either the potatoes or the rebellious Irish.

As a tale of autochthonous people, though, this one is riddled with ironies. First, Irish survival is assured by a symptom of the very thing that seems to threaten it: English colonialism. Because an English colonist brought a food from an incipient colony on the other side of the Atlantic to plant in a far older colonial settlement near Cork, the Irish were later able to withstand the devastation wrought by subsequent English armies. According to the story, the colonizing drive of the seventeenth century both propelled English aggression and unexpectedly furnished provision against its deadliness. This first level of narrative irony is so satisfying that the story seems to have gone unquestioned for over a century even though some of its details are easy to refute: Raleigh was never in Virginia, and if he had been he wouldn't have found potatoes there in the late sixteenth century.[7]

A second level of irony emerges in another version of the Raleigh story, where the colonizer blunders doubly: he not only unwittingly provides the enemy with an underground food supply, but also misunderstands the sort of food he imports. Raleigh, the story goes, didn't even know what part of the potato to eat, and after tasting the bitter berries, told his gardener to destroy the plants. But, according to the operations of a peculiarly incongruous Irish providence, the roots nevertheless spread, merging, as in Houghton, with the very ground and becoming a symbol for the ineradicability of Irish Catholicism, which, despite its above-ground ruination, would maintain its subterranean vitality. The striking thing about this version of the story is that the potato is depicted as thoroughly accidental and therefore providential. Raleigh never meant to introduce a new staple food, only a variety of berry, and when the plant disappointed him, he tried to throw it away. The potato is thus the Englishman's garbage, that which has no value inside his economy, mysteriously transmogrified into salvational nutrition, manna from heaven hidden under the ground. The potato in this story is the bit of matter that not only foils the invader's intentions, but also eludes his economy of scarcity, escaping both his control and his conceptual categories and giving the Irish a foothold in what Bataille calls a general economy, where waste and wealth are indistinguishable.

These myths of the origin of the Irish potato, therefore, both use and disorganize ideas of the autochthonous relationship between ground and people. The people may be inextricable from the land, but only because the land harbors an alien stuff. Instead of being indigenous or natural, the nurturing element of this ground is foreign and accidental. Hence, instead of underlying history as the bedrock of human existence, this ground is interlaced with historical irony. The accidental potato, moreover, tosses a twist into the linear narrative of increasing English ascendancy and reminds us that what might have seemed reassuring in the autochthonous myth when applied to English peasants—the notion that to have the ground was to have the people—was positively threatening to Cromwellians and Orangemen in war-ridden seventeenth-century Ireland.

But by the late eighteenth century, when the great potato debate began, certain Englishmen had new reasons for promulgating the utopian dimension of the autochthonous myth, implying that the potato was as plentiful as the earth itself. The potato's English advocates started the potato debate; most of them wanted to keep wages down by shifting the English poor off of a diet of wheat bread and on to one of potatoes. It was in response to this proposal that Cobbett spread his belief in the magical destructive power of the plant, even reversing Houghton's image of the food as the ideal provision against invasion: "It is both my pleasure and my duty to discourage in every way that I can the cultivation of this damned root, being convinced that it has done more harm to mankind than the sword and pestilence united" (83). Although passages like these, which conjure ideas of potato armies and potato locusts making their way across the Irish Sea, are unique to Cobbett, the image on which he relied primarily, that of the potato pulling its eaters down into an undifferentiated organic muck, had a prior life in the utopian depictions of Ireland by a potato enthusiast, the prolific English agricultural writer and "improver" Arthur Young. Thirty years before Cobbett went to Ireland, Arthur Young revived Houghton's implicit characterization of the potato as an almost preternaturally compact and unfailing food supply. His descriptions of Irish cottiers at their meal emphasize the benevolent fecundity of the tuber:

> . . . [M]ark the Irishman's potatoe bowl placed on the floor, the whole family upon their hams around it, devouring a quantity almost incredible, the beggar seating himself to it with a hearty welcome, the pig taking his share as readily as the wife, the cocks, hens, turkies, geese, the cur, the cat, and perhaps the cow—and all partaking of the same dish. No man can often have been witness of it without being convinced of the plenty, and I will add the cheerfulness, that attends it.[8]

Where Cobbett saw human degradation, Young saw abundance, variety, and fertility. The profuseness of this potato-eating family is just an alternative reading of its dirt; to feed your animals and your family out of the same dish indicated to Young a generosity that only people who have plenty can afford to indulge. The various forms of animal life gathered round the "potatoe bowl" have, in a sense, sprung from it. The steaming potatoes in this passage are, to use Young's phrase, "the root of plenty," the always-abundant fleshy plant stuff out of which the animal world emerges. True, that world is undifferentiated—note the mixture of pigs and persons in the description of the "family on their hams" around the meal—but the lack of hierarchical arrangement in this passage implies, not regression to a degraded primitivism, but retrieval of a golden age, a peaceable kingdom, where all God's creatures inhabit the world harmoniously.

We might see the difference between Cobbett's vision and Young's, therefore, as the inversion of a single metamorphosis: if in Cobbett's descriptions the Irish cottiers lived the underground life of the potatoes, in Young's the potatoes turned into people with extraordinary ease. Cobbett expressed the dreadful half of the dirt-eater idea, and Young expressed its hopeful half. It would, however, be a mistake to characterize Cobbett and Young simply as inheritors of the older images of autochthonous populations. The residues of those images persist, but they are organized according to new ways—uniquely modern ways—of imagining the relationship between human bodies and the earth as the ground of material existence.

Both Young and Cobbett were concerned by what they saw as a worsening relationship between the land and the people who worked it in *England,* and they were interested in the role (or potential role) of the potato either to exacerbate or to ameliorate the new conditions. Arthur Young was an enlightened advocate of progress through scientific agriculture. Like many "improving" landlords of the eighteenth century, he believed that the ultimate good of agricultural communities would be served by the most efficient food production. Efficiency, he reasoned, was motivated by profit seeking; profit seeking necessitated private ownership and control of the land, which in turn required enclosures of what had been commons. Genuinely humanitarian desires for cheap food and a higher minimum standard of living led scientific agriculturalists like Young to propagandize in favor of enclosures as a step in the march of progress. Toward the end of the eighteenth century, however, this naive faith that higher profits for landlords would automatically create inexpensive and plentiful food for the working poor was somewhat shaken. Thousands of people had lost their common and forest rights, often their mainstay against starvation when the wheat crop failed, but they had not gained, it seemed, a proportional drop in the price of wheat when the harvest was good. In 1794 a disastrous harvest and widespread food rioting revealed the extent of destitution and absolute dependency among the agricultural poor. Young fastened on the potato partly as a way to compensate the poor for their loss of common rights, but mainly as a miraculous staple crop that would never fail if properly cultivated. The enclosures could continue. Progress could march on without trampling on the security or independence of the British laborer; if he were allotted three acres of subsistence tubers and a cow, he would be protected against the vicissitudes of the larger agricultural commodity market, indeed, provided against all contingencies: failed corn crops, wars, over-pasturing, or protectionist legislation. Far from turning away from the enlightenment optimism of his earlier writings, his belief that the benign market and new scientific principles would bring about an era of unprecedented plenty, Young supplemented it in the 1790s with an equally fervent faith in the reliability of that thoroughly *modern* staple, the potato:

> The great object is by means of milk and potatoes to take the mass of the country's "poor" from the consumption of wheat, and to give them substitutes equally wholesome and nourishing and as independent of scarcities natural and artificial, as the providence of the Almighty will permit.[9]

Young was, consequently, very far from believing the old autochthonous myth that the poor could always somehow scratch a living out of the earth. His modified utopia required active supervision by progressive thinkers, the spread of scientific methods, and a new spirit of self-reliance, even of individualism, among laborers. Young tried to make the potato stand for all of this. It was a symbol of mankind's improvability if not his complete perfectibility. Whereas in Houghton's story the potato was an occulted form of nature's bounty brought to light by history's irony or God's providence, in Young's view the potato was pliant nature's response to human ingenuity and scientific understanding. If it wouldn't completely solve the problem of scarcity—some experience of which seemed ordained by our material nature and God's will—it was at least a significant step in that direction. Inside this meliorist vision, therefore, the potato was transformed from the Ur-food to the innovative food; Young's potato-patch utopia might even be seen as a precursor of futuristic fantasies about human societies that free themselves from "scarcities natural and artificial" by making all of their food in chemistry labs. Implicit in his potato is the dream of a humanity that has subdued its material conditions to its will not through ascetic denial, but through the discovery and propagation of unfaltering supply. The potato is the bit of matter that promises Arthur Young a new material order, a secular transubstantiation in which the human body is no longer experienced as needy and hungry, and is hence no longer riotous and unpredictable.

Like most Enlightenment panaceas, though, Young's potato had to overcome the prejudices of the benighted, some of whom, like Cobbett, objected that it violated the principles of the moral economy, and others of whom, like Thomas Malthus and David Ricardo, insisted that it violated those of political economy.

The phrase "the moral economy" refers to a concept developed by E. P. Thompson in his 1971 essay "The Moral Economy of the Crowd"; and, before continuing with our analysis of the early-nineteenth-century potato debates, we will take a short historiographical detour into that essay. "The moral economy of the crowd," Thompson writes, was "a consistent traditional view of social norms and obligations, of the proper economic functions of several parties within the community"[10] that, in the last half of the eighteenth century, was frequently opposed to the free-market assumptions of early political economy. Thompson uses the concept to explain the food riots of the late 1790s, the very experiences that inspired Young's potato allotments. Thompson's argument is such an important protest against historians who disregard cultural factors when analyzing economic behavior, especially behavior in response to dietary changes, that we want to spend a few pages not only reviewing what he has to tell us about the struggle over working-class food in the period, but also analyzing the terms of his own argument. His essay interests us here both because it provides the crucial concept of the moral economy and because it marks out the analytical limits that even an English *cultural* materialist historian stayed within up until the 1970s.

We must admit at the outset that Thompson never mentions Arthur Young or any other potato debater in his essay on the 1790s; indeed, he entirely overlooks the potato, and this oversight, we suggest, might indicate the limitations of the culturalist historical materialism he practices. It is, of course, easy to pick out the defects of thirty-year-old essays, and Thompson's must be acknowledged as a triumph of cultural history. First, it explodes the "abbreviated and 'economistic' picture of the food riot, as a direct, spasmodic, irrational response to hunger" (258). The historical consciousness of the rioters, Thompson insists, must be reconstructed. "How," he asks, "is their behaviour modified by custom, culture, and reason?" (187). Hunger, in other words, is a necessary but hardly a sufficient explanation of food riots. Second, the essay argues that economic historians fail to historicize their own presuppositions; relying on the idea of "economic man" to analyze earlier societies, they assume a universality of motive that is blind to cultural difference. Thompson's analysis, in contrast, insists on putting economic beliefs and behavior back into a larger cultural context. Finally, the essay subtly rejects as anachronistic a simple class-conflict model of popular uprising in the eighteenth century, substituting instead a dynamic of conflicted negotiations inside the "bread nexus" that the moral economy took for granted. Hence, the historical consciousness of the rioters was not utterly distinct from that of their governors: their "definite, and passionately held, notions of the common weal . . . found some support in the paternalist traditions of the authorities; notions which the people re-echoed so loudly in their turn that the authorities were, in some measure, the prisoners of the people" (189).

These are no mean insights. And yet, since the intervening decades saw the development of what has come to be called the history of the body, something about Thompson's analysis seems lacking. The absence of the potato, we only half facetiously urge, marks his reluctance to submit the ideas of hunger and dearth to a more thorough cultural or historical analysis. Despite his vigilant anti-reductionism, he allows hunger and scarcity to stand as self-evident material stimuli on which a cultural analysis of response can be mounted. To be sure, he notes that the equation of provision with wheat and the equation of bread with white bread require quite a bit of cultural explanation; but he confines his discussion of the alternatives to "rougher" grain mixtures and concludes that by the 1790s millers and bakers could no longer produce, and laborers could no longer stomach, coarser household loaves. Although he draws almost exclusively on R. N. Salaman's *The History and Social Influence of the Potato*

(1949)[11] for evidence that the poor would accept nothing but white bread even at the height of the scarcity, he never mentions the widespread proposals and the practical attempts to substitute potatoes for wheat. Perhaps, recognizing the availability of alternative staple foods would make the crowd actions of the 1790s seem *too* culturally determined, *too* independent of material causes, and therefore not entirely "rational." Thompson's resistance to the potato is symptomatic of cultural materialism's desire for a moral economy of explanation that assumes the reasonableness of popular action and its conformity to an implied human norm. The delicate balance between cultural variety and normative humanity in Thompson's analysis depends on an unvarying physical substratum, which the potato threatens to contaminate.

Our debt to Thompson's analysis and our distance from it on the issue of the potato mark the continuity and discontinuity between cultural materialism and the body history that followed in its wake. Viewing the moral economy, body historians would look for more than a cultural grid determining responses to the physical stimulus of hunger; they would look at hunger as part of the bodily experience of that economy. Much in Thompson's analysis already points in this direction. He demonstrates that what was at stake in the riots was the preservation of the old bread nexus (as opposed to the newer cash nexus) because it provided the flash points, the friction that enabled the rough negotiations of crowd action. That is, his analysis indicates that the laborers were struggling for the preservation of the terms of the struggle, which provided the experience of cultural inclusion. The more extended and intricate the network through which people received their staple food, the more places of potential popular intervention: "[The corn] is harvested, threshed, taken to market, ground at the mill, baked, and eaten. But at every point in this process there are radiating complexities. . . ."[12] The "radiating complexities" were the integuments of the social body itself, and it was these from which Arthur Young's potato patches would have freed the laborer: "if each had his ample potatoe ground and a cow, the price of wheat would be of little more consequence to them than it is to their brethren in Ireland," wrote Young.[13] But Thompson's description of the moral economy shows us how far such a sensation of inconsequentiality would have been from the desires of the crowd. Having a secure provision in independent isolation could not possibly have accomplished what the rioters sought, which was the experience, through friction, of their incorporation in a social body organized around bread.

The moral economy was therefore not just a cultural mediator of responses to the physical stimulus of hunger; it was itself a physiological-cultural stimulus: both the experience of inclusion inside a corporate body and a cause of the sensation of hunger. When English people refused to eat potato stews because they were "swill"—not human food—and resisted even the moderate proposal that they should add potatoes to their home-baked bread, it seems extremely likely that they were increasing their hunger. But it is also possible that they remained hungry, as they claimed they did, even when they grudgingly ate such alternatives to bread. Abundant complaints that "*squashy* stuff"[14] (eaten in no matter how large a quantity) was simply not solid enough to satisfy working people should remind us that appetite, too, has a culture and a history. Our point is not that the rejection of the potato caused the dearth of the 1790s; but the vehement refusal to accept potato substitutes for white bread when they were available points to the need for a thorough historicization of what counted as food and what felt like hunger.

Tossing the potato into Thompson's analysis of the food riots in the 1790s could, therefore, strengthen the "culturalism" of his account, but only by moving the "cultural" further into the body, by making it more than a mental structure or a set of shared understandings equivalent to "consciousness." Generally ontological agnostics, body historians do not attempt to deny the importance of matter, but they do question the proposition that physical experience is uniform and stable across time and space. Perhaps paradoxically, though, they also tend to privilege the body as a place where culture has a peculiarly tenacious hold. Because the moral economy was a mode of physical existence, and not just a way of thinking, a body historian might argue, its disruption was met with unusually violent reaction.

Cobbett's letters from Ireland[15] are the most complete, if delayed, articulation of that reaction available, and their insistence on the physical perils of noninclusion represented by the potato bears out the body historians' hunches. The letters evince a horror about the breakdown of the bread nexus that was probably shared by the English poor, who energetically repulsed the potato in the 1790s. The Irish, Cobbett reports, may be filled with potatoes, but they are nevertheless permanently deprived of the sensation of a nurturing connection to the people who own the land and ultimately control them. Since they are outside of the "radiating complexities" of the bread market, the Irish that Cobbett depicts have no points of entry into a shared community or moral economy. Indeed, in Ireland, because of the potato, there is no community. For Cobbett, potato eating marks the border, not simply between going hungry and being satisfied, but between sharing in *civilization's* nourishment and being deprived of it. The potato threatens the physical life of the poor *as humans* because it is only food, mere subsistence, unorganized into a reciprocal economy of rights and duties, expectations and negotiations. Situated at the gateway to the merely physical, the potato signifies the awful possibility that a country's staple food might not form a bond, however contested, between land and labor, countryside and city, rich and poor. Cobbett images the potato as purely exploitative bondage, which reduces people not just to animals but to harshly misused animals, when he figures it as simultaneously food and muzzle, that which stops the mouth as it fills it. God's law, he claims, forbids feeding the laborer on

> . . . infamous potatoes and salt. The law of God forbids to muzzle the ox while he is treading out the corn. . . . [I]n order that the farmers should be merciful and just, even to the animals that they employed, God commands, in the 25th chapter of DEUTERONOMY, "Thou shallt not *muzzle* the ox when he treadeth out the corn"; that is, thou shalt not pinch him, thou shalt not take from him a share of that which he has caused to come. (184)

Because potatoes are not "a share" of the master's provision, not part of what the master eats or sells, which is grain, they cannot properly recompense the laborer. Hence, no matter how plentiful the potato, it would always be nugatory nourishment and a sign of expulsion from the social body. Indeed Cobbett's image denotes an even worse state than expulsion, for the tethered oxen, although outside a proper social organism, are nevertheless slavishly bound to the masters. Similarly, the cottiers are not free from the landowners' civilization; instead, their potato muzzles place them in a uniquely modern state of pure subjugation.

If the potato threatened to break the bread nexus, violating the moral economy by forcing the laboring poor to live on a cheap subsistence crop while they continued to produce a dearer cash crop for their landlords, the political economists portrayed it as no less menacing to the cash nexus. Indeed, the political economists' unanimous condemnation of Arthur Young's potato-allotment scheme shows that, in their minds, the cash nexus and a thoroughly commodified bread nexus were inseparable. If English working people were struggling to preserve the multiple places where they could intervene to shape the social organism by insisting on eating white bread, political economists saw the wheat market as the primary means of controlling the reproduction of laborers and keeping them fit and efficient. Food rioters and political economists, therefore, were united in their opposition to the potato as a staple food. Unlike the working-class activists, however, political economists did have a use for the potato precisely as a stigmatized food.

Thomas Malthus's response to Arthur Young (in the 1806 version *of An Essay on Population*) is a convenient guide to the political economists' potato. For the sake of argument, Malthus at first brackets the possibility of potato crop failures and concentrates simply on the misery that would follow from the very plenty Young predicted:

> The specific cause of the poverty and misery of the lower classes . . . in Ireland is, that from . . . the facility of obtaining a cabin and potatoes . . ., a population is brought into existence which is not demanded by the quantity of capital and employment in the country; and the consequence of which must therefore necessarily be . . . to lower in general the price of labour by too great competition; from which must result complete indigence to those who cannot find employment, and an incomplete subsistence even to those who can.[16]

The reader might be puzzled by the word "subsistence" here. After all, Young said that the potato would insure "subsistence," making the marketplace (in grain, labor, and all other commodities) irrelevant to the issue of survival. But by "subsistence" Malthus means more than, as he puts it, "mere food" (231); he means also "decent housing and decent clothing," which can only be secured when labor itself is a relatively scarce commodity. And labor can only be scarce when food is relatively expensive. Since in a normal Malthusian world, cheap food will create an excess population, the potato is the root of misery *because* it is the root of plenty. For Malthus, the bad news was that the people were being asked to eat potatoes, and the *worse* news was that there were plenty of potatoes. Plenty of potatoes translates immediately and ineluctably into plenty of people, but into very little of anything else.

In Malthus's view, the potato was dangerous not only because it was cheap and abundant, but also because it would be grown in allotments set aside from capitalist agricultural enterprise. Hence the potato occupied a dangerously liminal place, simultaneously outside and inside the cash nexus, and the people that it nurtured were seen as similarly liminal. As a noncash crop, the potato would always be an insensitive indicator of the economy's need for bodies; if the crops are healthy, potatoes will stay cheap until a large surplus population appears. In contrast, a cash crop like wheat will quickly register the presence of too many people, for if it were very plentiful and therefore very cheap for any length of time, either rising demand would make it more expensive or some of the land on which it grew would soon be turned into pasture to increase the farmer's profit. In either case, the price of grain would go up, encouraging sexual abstinence and discouraging any further swelling of the population. Because wheat is a cash crop, in other words, its price is a sensitive mechanism that can potentially adjust the supply of people to the needs of employers in the economy at large.

The danger of potatoes thus lies in their economically extrinsic position; the extra-economic bodies that potato allotments automatically produce are not so much "redundant" in relation to the immediate food supply as in relation to the need for "productive" labor— that is, profit-making labor. Although they are sprung right from the ground and can therefore hardly be considered out of place, these potato paupers are themselves a kind of dirt because they are *not* organized into an economy. In the terms available to political economists, they could only be thought of as labor, but they have nothing to labor at besides their own reproduction. Utterly stripped-down versions of humanity, they are mere stomachs and sexual organs, multiplying to exhaustion, as in this description of a cottier's life by the radical Malthusian Francis Place:

> Once in possession of the cabin, the garden, and the girl, the Irishman sets himself and his wife to work to provide themselves with food. . . . Thus they go

> on, until the increase of the family makes it impossible for them to provide food enough in ordinary seasons for the healthy support of themselves and their children. . . . [W]hile a rood of land capable of producing potatoes can be had, the population may continue to increase, and must remain in its present deplorable condition . . . ill clothed, idle, dirty, ragged, and wretched in the extreme.[17]

Place's language is reminiscent of the old autochthonous myth: the Irishman and his wife set to work raising potatoes, but come up with crop after crop of children; where there is "a rood of land," there will be filthy, ragged people. And yet this is a thoroughly modern, completely Malthusian picture of humanity.

For this minimal human creature was, we might say, Malthus's invention and was fast becoming central to economic thought. According to Malthus, there are two invariant facts about human beings: they must have food, and they must have sex. A lack of either causes misery. Indeed, unless they use some vicious birth-control device, they will go on having sex until they have multiplied beyond their food supply. Only the constant threat of starvation keeps the majority of people from rampant reproduction. This rudimentary person, as critics pointed out at the time, was really just an appetite-driven body incapable of mental activity beyond the most basic Benthamite calculation: that is, the pleasure of this immediate copulation will be less than the pain of that future hunger. And yet the sheer physicality of the creature made it irresistibly attractive to political economists, for its simple pain/pleasure mechanism rendered it both predictable and organizable into a "laboring population" that would expand or contract in relation to the needs of capital. To give Malthus his due, he did not normally think that any actual persons were merely human nature in the raw; he expected people to behave according to a wide range of other cultural imperatives, all of which he classified as tending toward either vice or misery. Nevertheless, unacculturated man—we'll call him *homo appetitūs*—looked like a reliable part of everybody and could hence serve as the material substratum on which the economic system might rest.

It looked reliable, that is, until the potato people came into view and demonstrated how easy it might be for such a completely physical being to slip out from under the very economic structure he was supposed to ground. The potato eaters seem to have literalized *homo appetitūs* in Malthus's mind and thereby to have liberated his anarchic potential. Unlike Adam Smith's *homo economicus* (a cooler character, with more complicated calculating capacities), *homo appetitūs*, at once antisocial and practically egoless, is decidedly *non*economical. One would expect such a creature to get as far outside of restraining economic systems as possible, and the potato patch presents a likely ground for his self-exile. The very physicality that seemed to ground political economy in physiological certainty, to make its practitioners "materialists" in the nineteenth-century sense of the term, becomes a principle of disorganization when it escapes from the labor market: Malthus is "strongly disposed to believe that the indolent and turbulent habits of the lower Irish can never be corrected while the potato system enables them to increase so much beyond the regular demand for labour."[18] The bodies that can copulate and eat regardless of the demand for labor will become at once lazy and menacing. Only in the context of the economy does *homo appetitūs* turn into *homo economicus*. In short, instead of the human body providing a predictable material ground for the economy, the economy is necessary to make the body reliable.

The threat that Malthus spies in the potato, moreover, is worse than the mere irrelevance of the marketplace to *homo appetitūs*, for no bodies inside a nation can actually be completely outside of its economy. Those seemingly redundant creatures multiplying on its margins press inward as potential labor, no matter how unwilling to work, cheapening the general price of labor until the difference between the industrious and the nonindustrious has disappeared. Hence, the potato is in fact no hedge against the marketplace, but is instead that unruly thing that, itself only very indirectly controlled by the price mechanisms of the larger economy, can profoundly disequilibriate it. The economy will recover its equilibrium, adjusting itself to overpopulation, and population growth will eventually slow, but only when people become too weak even to copulate. What Malthus saw when he looked at the potato was the destructive potential of the creatures his own imagination had conjured.

And that was his optimistic vision. His pessimistic one foresaw potato crop failures, persistent infant mortality, and perhaps eventual mass starvation. Political economists certainly shared the common belief that it was difficult to stop the potato once it got going, but they also insisted that its progress was often disturbingly fitful. The population that springs out of the potato patches is, like their food, ephemeral. Note, for example, how difficult it is to tell the failing crop from the dying people in this account, which is taken from Place's *Illustrations and Proofs of the Principle of Population:*

> One great drawback on potatoes, as food for the inhabitants of a country is, that in no crop is there a greater difference in good or bad years as to the quantity produced. Two or three good years will create people, the redundancy of which population will be repressed by subsequent years of failure. . . . [Y]ears of scarcity . . . are very frequent, and these periods put an end to the false part of the population . . . raised by years of plenty. (265)

The potato garden thus produces a "false" crop of children, which seldom survives to maturity.

At first sight, it might seem that the fear of overpopulation should be mitigated by the assurance of uncertain crops and infant starvation, but the two evils could easily coexist. Place's "false part of the population" is too large for the supply of potatoes, but that might be only a small fraction of the population that is redundant in relation to the demand for labor. On closer inspection, the continuity between the ideas of constantly multiplying and constantly dying potato eaters seems more salient than their superficial discrepancy. For both ideas point to the same hyper-physical humanity. If the potato liberates the sheer physicality of *homo appetitūs* from its regulation by the marketplace, it also exposes that physicality as merely organic, corruptible, and therefore quickly perishable.

And now we have arrived at our last point about the potato in the materialist imagination: it is too biologically immanent. It was seen as both cause and symbol of the body's vulnerability. David Ricardo wrote to Maria Edgeworth in 1823 that the case for or against the potato as the people's primary food had to rest on the crop's physical security, both its evenness of yield from year to year and/or the possibility of its achieving a nonperishable, storable form. He begins with the assumption that wheat is preferable because it can be turned into the relatively durable form of flour and stored, in times of plenty, to supply the dearth of later scanty grain harvests. (It should be mentioned here that wheat flour could not be stored against potato failures because, wheat being so much more expensive, potato-dependent people would not be able to afford flour.) Lacking any such "dry" instatiation, the potato becomes an extreme instance of the problem that food in general presents to the political economist:

> We cannot, I think, doubt that the situation of mankind would be much happier if we could depend with as much certainty on a given quantity of capital and labour producing a certain quantity of food, as we can depend upon the same quantity of capital and labour producing a certain quantity of manufactured goods. It is evident that in the latter case we calculate upon results almost with

absolute certainty; in the other case we must always be exposed to the uncertainty
of the seasons, which will render the crop fluctuating.[19]

This intractability of nature not only throws off economic calculations about the availability
of food, but also renders the cost of labor, and hence the cost of everything else, unpredictable.
Unfortunately, even manufacturing, admired here for its regularity, is made vulnerable,
through the workers' bodies, to an uncontrollable natural world. Under these imperfect
arrangements that link us biologically to the planet, the best we can do is choose a staple food
that can partially overcome its own organicism, its own tendency to decay. Ricardo is
convinced that the potato is unfit for such transcendence; he meets Edgeworth's assurances
that potato flour can be made and kept usable for years with undisguised skepticism and hints
that the potato could wipe out the progress an advanced economy has made in liberating
humankind from dependence on shifty nature. It is unredeemably organic, untransformable
into a long-term storable commodity. For Ricardo, as for Malthus, the potato occupies a
place that is at once extra-economic and rudimentary in his system; he fears that the root
might carry an unbearable load of biotic unpredictability into the economy's foundation,
which is the worker's body.

The lumpish intransigence of Ricardo's potato, its failure to undergo preservative
physical transformations, is imagistically matched by its failure to undergo metamorphoses in
the marketplace. As a "short crop" (440), some potatoes will be turned into cash, but the vast
majority, Ricardo notes, will be immediately consumed by their producers. You can make
nothing of potatoes but more people, who (Malthus might have chimed in) will only make
more potatoes. Moreover, since it is the cheapest staple, it has no *substitutes* when it disappears.
People living on wheat can replace their principal food with a cheaper one, but people already
living on the least expensive nourishment are left without anything affordable when their
crop fails. Bread eating and smooth commodity exchanges are thus paralleled by Ricardo; in
both, metamorphoses are delightfully plentiful. But the potato, in his account, stands
stubbornly apart from the transformative wonders of the economy and plays the part of a
memento mori.

Its liminal status inspired Malthus and other political economists to propose that the
potato be institutionalized as a badge of dishonor. Far from following Cobbett's advice and
discouraging the cultivation of the root of misery in England, Malthus acquiesced in Arthur
Young's plan to furnish parish relief solely in the form of potatoes. The potato, Malthus
hoped, would draw "a more marked line than at present between dependence and
independence."[20] The tuber should remain what it already was in the eighteenth-century
English imagination—a stigmatized food—but its meaning should be stabilized. It should, as
it had in the minds of the bread rioters, characterize the unincorporated, but it should also
define the new perimeters of the social body that mattered by equating the members of that
organism with the official economy. People were no longer to think that they could casually
cross over from productive laborer to part-time pauper. "Pauper" was to become a category
that would stick, and the potato would help by making "an useful distinction between those
who are dependent on parish relief and those who are not."[21] If you crossed the line, the
parish authorities would, as it were, throw in your face the very symbol of your own indolent,
turbulent, redundant, intransigent, and distressingly mortal body.

Let us conclude, then, by suggesting that imagery from the potato debate allows us to
trace a shift in cultural attitudes toward the age-old concept that our bodies have their source
in the soil. Both the potato's proponents and its opponents took this concept for granted. Its
proponents foresaw unprecedented prosperity based on the scientifically induced new
fertility of the soil. But the potato's opponents saw in it everything that is fearsome about our
biological contingency. For them, the food represented a shrunken humanity, unorganized

into a social totality or an economic system, mired instead in the boglike ground. The debate shows the extent to which the autochthonous body had become the locus of new, identifiably modern, hopes and fears. Above all, it had been soiled and transported to Ireland, where it could be imagined as both foreign and threateningly close. The anti-potato writers both produced and banished this ghastly nightmare of *merely* biological bodies, purposeless bodies that just multiply and die. Theirs is the bad dream of nineteenth-century materialism; it haunted the same thinkers who were making physical well-being the raison d'être of social and economic arrangements. By expatriating the autochthonous body, English materialism protected itself from its own reductio ad absurdum.

By using the potato to identify the problematic status of the body in nineteenth-century materialist thought, we hope to suggest more broadly why "materialism" has become a problematic term. We are not, to be sure, implying that our potato debaters exhaust the possible directions that the materialist imagination might take. But we do claim that they manifest a tendency typical of materialism to invoke the human body as the ground of all explanation and, therefore, to leave it unexamined as a historical phenomenon or a representational crux. In materialist history, bodies as representation cannot bear much scrutiny; indeed, they cannot actually carry much history. Hence the historians of the potato debate have tended to reproduce the blind spots of the original debaters. We hope we've turned the blind spots of those eyes into the roots of new insights.

Notes

1   This debate is discussed at length in Redcliffe N. Salaman's *The History and Social Influence of the Potato* (Cambridge: Cambridge University Press, 1949). Salaman's book is an unsurpassed achievement, and much of the evidence for our own, much quirkier, analysis comes from its pages.

2   The kind of body history referred to here began appearing in Europe and the United States in the 1960s. Drawing on medical and scientific history, the histories of sex, gender, and corporeal political discourse; of disciplinary institutions; of the family, food, exercise, sport, and work, these histories demonstrate that the body has not only been perceived, interpreted, and represented differently in different times, but also that it has been lived differently. Examples include Michel Foucault's *The History of Sexuality*, trans. Robert Hurley (New York: Pantheon Books, 1978–86); Barbara Duden's *The Woman Beneath the Skin: A Doctor's Patients in Eighteenth-Century Germany*, trans. Thomas Dunlap (Cambridge: Harvard University Press, 1991); and Thomas Laqueur's *Making Sex: Body and Gender from the Greeks to Freud* (Cambridge: Harvard University Press, 1990). See also these collections: Catherine Gallagher and Thomas Laqueur, eds., *The Making of the Modern Body: Sexuality and Society in the Nineteenth Century* (Berkeley: University of California Press, 1987); Michel Feher, Ramona Naddaff, and Nadia Tazi, eds., *Fragments for a History of the Human Body*, 3 vols. (New York: Zone Books, 1989).

3   Raymond Williams, *The Sociology of Culture* (New York: Schocken, 1982), pp. 209–10.

4   Biologists, by the way, no longer categorize the part of the potato plant we eat as a "root," but rather as a fleshy underground stem.

5   *Cobbett in Ireland: A Warning to England*, ed. Denis Knight (London: Lawrence and Wishert, 1984), p. 82.

6   John Houghton, *Houghton's Collection*, vol. II, p. 469. Quoted also in Salaman, *The History and Social Influence of the Potato*, p. 150.

7   Salaman thinks that, nevertheless, expeditions sponsored by Raleigh might have collected potato specimens that could have ended up on Raleigh's Irish estates.

8   Arthur Young, *A Tour in Ireland*, II (London, 1780), p. 23.

9   Arthur Young, *The Question of Scarcity Plainly Stated and Remedies Considered* (London: McMillan, 1800), p. 79.

10 E. P. Thompson, "The Moral Economy of the Crowd," in *Customs in Common: Studies in Traditional and Popular Culture* (New York: New Press, 1991), pp. 185–258. This quotation is from p. 188.

11 See Thompson, "The Moral Economy of the Crowd," p. 191 n. 5.

12 Thompson, "The Moral Economy of the Crowd," p. 193.

13   Young, *The Question of Scarcity*, p. 77.

14   The phrase comes from an anonymous poem of 1800; quoted in Thompson, "The Moral Economy of the Crowd," p. 232.

15   If by the 1830s the "cash nexus" had replaced the "bread nexus" as the central mechanism linking and creating conflict between country and city, laborers and governors, proletariat and bourgeois, and the moral economy was therefore merely a nostalgic memory, the bread nexus was nonetheless still a powerful ideal image of how things should be, which stood starkly opposed to the assumptions underlying the utilitarians' reform legislation. Hence, although it may be somewhat anachronistic to use Cobbett's potato rants as outbursts of the mentality of the food rioters of 1795, the anachronism throws into relief the threat that the tuber posed to "the moral economy of the crowd."

16   Thomas Malthus, *An Essay on Population*, I (1806; reprint, New York: E. P. Dutton & Co., 1967), p. 228.

17   Francis Place, *Illustrations and Proofs of the Principle of Population: Including an Examination of the Proposed Remedies of Mr. Malthus, and Reply to the Objections of Mr. Godwin and Others* (1822; reprint, London: George Allen and Unwin Ltd., 1967), p. 265.

18   Malthus, *An Essay on Population*, p. 230 n. 1.

19   "Ricardo to Miss Edgeworth. Bromesberrow Place, Ledbury, December 13th, 1822." Printed in *The Economic Journal. The Journal of the Royal Economic Society* xvii (1907): 433.

20   Malthus, *An Essay on Population*, p. 232.

21   Malthus, *An Essay on Population*, p. 232.

Chapter 36

Daria Berg

WHAT THE MESSENGER OF SOULS HAS TO SAY

New historicism and the poetics of Chinese culture

Examining a seventeenth-century Chinese novel called *Xingshi yinyuan zhuan* from a New Historicist perspective enables Daria Berg to articulate a wider conception of the genre called the *zhanghui xiaoshuo*, or "chapter-linked novel", which draws upon the vernacular, or local, personal stories of everyday life. While *Xingshi yinyuan zhuan* appears to be about the Chinese virago or a shrewish, violently tempered woman, and her exploits with her "hen-pecked" husband, the New Historicist approach leads Berg to the conclusion that what the novel really explores is the shifting hierarchies and social background of the time when the novel was written, in this instance, expressed through the conflicts that arise when people of different social backgrounds marry. Berg, who holds the chair of Chinese Culture and Society at the University of St. Gallen in Switzerland, has published extensively on Chinese fiction, gender, and class, and she brings this expertise to bear in the extract on her extensive exploration of the genre of the *zhanghui xiaoshuo*, with its blurring of fiction and history, merging the grotesque with the carnivalesque to produce a "hyperrealism" that is a polyvocal "textual orchestration of voices and visions." From a Chinese perspective, this genre initially meant a historical discourse that was drawn from the small sayings, the "gossip of the streets" that could have political and aesthetic force. Right from the beginning, the *zhanghui xiaoshuo* engaged in generic boundary blurring, although scholars eventually decided that these texts were "flawed" works of history, and they eventually became regarded as aesthetic objects. From a New Historicist perspective, which Berg summarizes and surveys, it is the generic boundary blurring between fact and fiction that opens up the genre to a wider notion of discourse, one which merely offers *versions* of history, not simply artistic representations. This is in line not only with the Structuralist notion of history as a form of narrative (Barthes), but also Greenblatt's polyphonic or many voices of historical production, the analysis of which he has called "cultural poetics". Berg explores three "main assumptions" of New Historicism before applying them to *Xingshi yinyuan zhuan*: (1) Literary and non-literary texts circulate inseparably; (2) All works of art are embedded in a network of negotiation and exchange; (3) Any critique is subjective and influenced by cultural contexts. Berg suggests that New Historicism does downplay the aesthetics of the text, which in this case are central to the genre of *zhanghui xiaoshuo* which relies heavily on satirical, grotseque and rhetorically playful writing. Berg's application reveals the importance of the alternative voices of Chinese history—voices that articulate the social destabilization and re-organization that occurred in the sixteenth century when the four social classes (in order of importance and position: scholar officials; farmers; artisans; merchants) began to be questioned. The marriage between the protagonists Sujie (the virago) and Di Xichen, in *Xingshi yinyuan zhuan* is, from a hierarchical and historical Confucian perspective, a "nightmare" since society has become "mixed" up. The novel, then, is as much about the unleashing and circulation of what New Historicists call "social energy" in this carnivalesque world, where the old hierarchies and values are questioned and in many respects, reversed. Aestheticized voices are returned central stage in their role in providing a historical perspective on this period of social change.

Portrait of a virago

Viragos abound in Chinese literature but stories about shrewish wives and henpecked husbands reach a climax in the *xiaoshuo* writings of the late Ming (1368–1644)/early Qing (1644–1911) era (Wu 1995). The *Yinyuan zhuan* is the first novel to focus on a wife's tyranny over her husband, and Xue Sujie, the main female protagonist, appears as one of the most violent and obnoxious viragos in Chinese literature (Wu 1986:142ff; 1995:110ff, 197). When Sujie batters her husband Di Xichen, for example, the narrative voice comments:

> Sujie charged at Di Xichen and gave him a clip round the ear – who would have thought that such a beautiful girl had hands like wood? She beat him until one side of his face became as red as the buttocks of a monkey, swelling so much that it looked like steamed loaves of bread. Di Xichen got extremely upset and took up the whip she had used to beat her chambermaid to use it on her. Before he managed to hit her, however, Sujie got hold of it and threw him down on to the floor, held down his head with her thighs and let the whiplashes rain down on him. Di Xichen yelled out for his mother and father, 'Help! Help!' (*YYZ*, 48:702)

Sujie, moreover, tortures Di Xichen with shoe needles and pliers (52:751–54, 59:855), makes him kneel throughout the night locked into the privy and ties him down there on a bench (60:867–68). She imprisons and starves him (63:902–3), bites a chunk out of his arm (73:1043), deals him six hundred blows with a club (95:1359–60) and pours hot charcoal down his collar (97:1385–86).

These scenes have both amused and astounded literary critics in the East and the West, who have marvelled at Sujie's antics. Unlike the viragos in other Chinese stories, Sujie does not even repent her misdeeds in hell. The depiction of the virago in *Yinyuan zhuan* makes full use of irony and satire, painting a grotesque picture of social dysfunction and the inversion of social hierarchies – but what interest does it hold for the twentieth-century reader and how do we interpret it?

Sujie has inspired some modern critics to write monographs about the phenomenon of the virago in Chinese literature (Wu 1995). In her study of the Chinese virago as a literary theme, Yenna Wu concludes that the shrewish wife is both a social phenomenon and a literary type (1986:63). Critics have struggled to spell out the author's intention in writing this work on the theme of the shrew and on retribution as marital destiny – this is what the title promises but the problem remains that principle and action do not match up properly (Wu 1986). The literary critics Wimsatt and Beardsley have warned about the pitfalls of intentional fallacy: 'the design or intention of the author is neither available nor desirable as a standard for judging the success of a work of literary art' (Wimsatt and Beardsley [1954] 1995:90).

Whatever the author's intention, and whether he succeeded in fulfilling it or not, the voices from the text may well have an altogether different story to tell.

This leads us to some more intriguing questions: How did the characters of Sujie and Di Xichen come to be conceived? What were the elements in the society of the time that led to the creation of such characters? What can the novel tell us about life at the time in which it emerged? What story do the voices in the text have to tell? Since critics have almost exclusively focused on the theme of the virago and the analysis of rhetorical figures within the text, very little has been done to answer these questions.[1] They demand an approach that enables us to fill the gaps in our understanding of the story in its cultural context.

The novel *Xingshi Yinyuan Zhuan*

The *Yinyuan zhuan* is a chapter-linked novel (*zhanghui xiaoshuo*) in an idiom approaching the vernacular. It appears as a comic novel, brimming with irony and satire and with a delight in the grotesque. One of the longest traditional novels ever written, the one hundred chapter-long narrative is a milestone in the history of the *xiaoshuo* between the sixteenth-century *Jin Ping Mei* (The Plum in the Golden Vase) and the eighteenth-century *Hongloumeng* (Dream of the Red Chamber; Story of the Stone). The action takes place mainly in Shandong province and is set in the fifteenth century, but detail and rhetoric rather refer to the time of its composition in the seventeenth century around the end of the Ming dynasty (Berg 1999; Wu 1999).

As the present title of the book, *Xingshi yinyuan zhuan,* and an earlier title, *E yinyuan* (Horrific Marriage Destinies) announce, the principle of *yuan,* 'destiny' or 'affinity' in Buddhist terminology, governs a network of relationships in human society. *Yuan* functions mainly in the specific usage of *yinyuan,* the affinity that brings men and women together. It works in both its positive sense as the source of love and marriage and its negative sense as predestined enmity and a bond of tragedy. The principle of *yuan* divides the plot into two parts, i.e. two sets of marriage destinies, but paradoxically it also links them. The first major protagonist kills with his arrow a fox demon on a hunt in Chapter 1. They are later reincarnated as the protagonist Di Xichen and his shrewish wife Xue Sujie to play out the tale of revenge for the fox's slaughter. Finally, in Chapter 100, Sujie shoots back the arrow at Di Xichen, fatally wounding him.

The novel, however, depicts not only the couple and their families but more than a dozen major protagonists, several hundred minor characters and masses of anonymous inhabitants of the fictional world. Apart from the marital partners, we encounter characters in the other Confucian ethical relationships such as rulers and subjects, fathers and sons, older and younger brothers and friends. We also see much more in sharp detail: doctors, patients, teachers, students, merchants and patrons of scholarship. We enter into the world of women, meeting not only shrewish but also virtuous ones and a multitude of mothers, daughters, sisters, aunts, maids, cooks and servants. In sum, a panoramic grand view of society unfolds before us and explodes the thematic framework of marriage destinies.

The author has so far remained anonymous and we know only his pen-name Xi Zhou Sheng, Scholar of the Western Zhou.[2] The text suggests that he was familiar with life in Shandong province and the capital Beijing in the 1630s and 1640s. The novel must have been composed sometime between 1628 and 1681 and it remains unclear whether it is a product of the Ming or the Qing dynasty. Its voices and visions, however, appear to be steeped in the late Ming world and reveal no explicit references to the dynastic change or the Qing reign. Internal evidence suggests that the current timeframe in the narrative corresponds to the last two decades of the Ming dynasty, from the late 1620s to the early 1640s, an era of political breakdown and social turmoil that also witnessed a burst of creative energy in literature and the arts.

In analysing the *Yinyuan zhuan,* the first task is to investigate the characteristics of this text. With its fierce scrutiny of provincial society, the *Yinyuan zhuan* appears as a novel of manners and has been called a 'novel of social realism' (Wu 1991:55), but the issue of realism has proven a major dilemma for literary critics. Andrew Plaks, for example, observes:

> Although in much of the book we get the sense of a thoroughgoing realism
> that is almost cinematographic in detail . . . this mimetic treatment gives way
> to various levels of unreality or distortion at many key points. (Plaks 1985:564)

Critics have been battling with the generic classifications of the novel. Labels for the novel range from 'photographic realism', not mimetic but rather a 'stylization of reality', to 'a conventional Buddhist tale of moral retribution' that fails 'to achieve realistic integrity' (Ch'en Shouyi 1961:573; Wu 1986:170; Hsia 1968:204–5). The guidelines to the *Yinyuan zhuan* refer to the paradox of fiction and realism in the text:

> First, Chao Yuan, Di Zongyu, Miss Tong and Miss Xue in this tale are not the
> real names for I do not wish to let the facts expose the people.
>   Second, for all the people with flawless moral conduct I use their real
> names. . . . (*YYZ,* 3:1537)

According to this claim the fictional and the historical coexist within the narrative as complementary parts rather than opposites. The narrative even becomes explicit in erasing the borders of history and fiction, reality and illusion by means of paradox when announcing: 'Virtue becomes vice, fiction becomes truth' (9:127). Puns on *zhen* (real) and *jia* (false) in the text (10:146) anticipate the eighteenth-century novel *Hongloumeng,* which develops this paradox further and declares as the reader enters into the realm of the novel:

> Truth becomes fiction when the fiction's true,
> Real becomes not-real when the unreal's real.
>   (*Hongloumeng* 1957:1:5; Cao Xueqin 1973:55)

In the *Yinyuan zhuan* the key notion *yuan* (destiny) itself takes part in the paradoxical play on reality and illusion, appearing as *jiayuan,* a false form of destiny (*YYZ,* 80:1134). Eventually *yuan* does turn out to play an ambiguous role as the denouement does not match up with the principles and promises involved in karmic retribution and marriage destinies.

The identification of the voice of the narrator in the *Yinyuan zhuan* also plays an important part in the analysis of the narrative play on fiction and history. According to the literary critics Gérard Genette and Mieke Bal, the text consists of several agents that reflect perceived reality by speaking and seeing: the speakers/narrators and the perceivers/focalizors (Genette 1980:189–91; Bal 1988:119–20).[3] The terms *narrator* and *focalizor* refer to a linguistic function and not a person, an 'it', a linguistic subject or agent and not a 'he' or 'she', a male or female person.[4] This also illustrates their difference to the biographical author or the implied author (Booth 1983:151; Bal 1988:120).[5] Narrator(s) and focalizor(s) can appear as either identical or different agents. In addition the text reflects another layer of voices and visions: those of the fictional characters/actors who also perform by speaking and perceiving.

The voice of the narrator in the *Yinyuan zhuan* frequently interferes in the action as an omniscient agent. It also intrudes into the story announcing its presence as a visible 'I' (wo). The 'I' in the story is but one version of the narrator, one of the several different possibilities of its manifestation. The narrative voice represents human follies and vices in carnivalesque imagery with warning and apocalyptic overtones. In deploring the current state of affairs and advertising a revival of Confucian norms and values, the narrator reveals itself as a Confucian conservative. But it also appears in many other guises – telling and commenting while shifting its tone of voice and parading once as a moralist, then as a preacher, teacher, satirist, humorist and caricaturist. It assumes the voices of an epic poet, scribe, reporter and commentator, and even eye-witness. Addressing both fictional characters and the implied reader directly, it functions as a mediator between the actors and the narratee. The narrative voice also stresses the topicality of events in the story. By referring to 'nowadays' (jin), it fabricates the illusion of topical references linking the world in the story to the contemporary present time of narrating in the seventeenth century (e.g. YYZ, 20:304).[6]

In the Yinyuan zhuan, then, fiction and history both divide and converge: the good characters retain their 'real' names and the bad characters assume pseudonyms. Some events masquerade as 'real' and others as unreal. The narrator claims to have personally witnessed certain scenes in the story while grotesque and carnivalesque imagery introduces a layer of hyper-realism. Ultimately both reality and illusion exist in written discourse solely in the perception of the narrator and actors. Fiction and history interweave in the textual orchestration of voices and visions, true to the xiaoshuo tradition of rhetoric.

Reading the Xiaoshuo: history and fiction from the Chinese perspective

As we set out to analyse the voices in the Yinyuan zhuan, let us first consider how Chinese readers would have read and understood the rhetoric of the xiaoshuo. In modern Chinese the term xiaoshuo generally translates into English as 'novel' or 'fiction' but the Chinese novel borrows a term with ancient roots that had little to do with creative fiction. The concept of xiaoshuo originally stems from historiography.

The term xiaoshuo was first used in the Zhuangzi (Book of Zhuangzi; attr. to Zhuang Zhou, 369–286 BC).[7] It also occurs in the Xunzi (Book of Xunzi; attr. to Xun Qing, c. 300–230 BC); the character xiao meaning 'minor or petty' and shuo denoting 'political advice or persuasion' (Xunzi yinde, 85/22/70). Xiaoshuo thus occurs in the meaning of small talk, chit-chat, petty talk or minor persuasions and both the Zhuangzi and Xunzi refer to the adornment or embellishment of such political advice (Wilhelm 1972:252).

The earliest definition of xiaoshuo as a literary genre occurs in Huan Tan's (43 BC–AC 28) Xinlun (New Treatise) which was written in c. 2 AD:[8]

> The xiaoshuo writers collect fragments and minor sayings and select parables they have heard to make short books. The xiaoshuo contain words that have a certain value for controlling oneself and regulating one's household. (Wenxuan, 31:6a)

The modern scholar Victor Mair reminds us of the difference between fiction and xiaoshuo:

> Where the Chinese term etymologically implies a kind of gossip or anecdote, the English word indicates something made up or created by an author or writer. 'Xiaoshuo' imports something, not of particularly great moment, that is presumed actually to have happened. . . . For this reason, many recorders of xiaoshuo are at great pains to tell us exactly from whom, when, where, and in what circumstances they heard their stories. (Mair 1983:21–22; transcription adapted by the author)

Mair here emphasizes the Chinese claim for historicity in writing *xiaoshuo* and points to the underlying difference in conception from the English term, placing *xiaoshuo* in the realm of historical discourse.

The grand historian of the Latter Han dynasty (25–220), Ban Gu (32–92), included an entry for *xiaoshuo* in the bibliography of the first dynastic history, the *Yiwenzhi* (Bibliographic Treatise) in the *Hanshu* (History of the [Former] Han Dynasty) which is based on the bibliographic catalogue *Qilüe* (Seven Epitomies) by Liu Xin (50 BC–AD 23) (*Hanshu*, 30:1744– 45). Ban Gu categorizes the school of *xiaoshuo* writers under philosophy and defines it in the following way:

> The trend of the *xiaoshuo jia* emerged from the Board of Petty Officials. It was created by those who picked up the gossip of the streets and the sayings of the alleys and repeated what they had heard wherever they went. (Translation adapted from Wilhelm 1972:251–52)

Although Ban Gu traces the genre of *xiaoshuo* to minor – i.e. not quite properly Confucian – persuasions and popular lore, the modern scholar Hellmut Wilhelm conjectures that it must have contained expository writings with political intent as in the *Zhuangzi* and *Xunzi*, rather than popular lore. His analysis of the early *xiaoshuo* from the Zhou dynasty (trad. 1122/hist. *c.* 1050–1221 BC) reveals that these texts came from the persuasion and from the (legendary) episode and must have concerned fictionalized history or historical legend (Wilhelm 1972:252–63).

During the Wei, Jin and Northern and Southern dynasties (220–581), *xiaoshuo* referred mainly to works of history and philosophy but never the *belles-lettres* (*wen*) (Cheng Yizhong 1987:44). The author of the first book-length study in Chinese literary criticism, Liu Xie (c. 465–520), classified literary writings including philosophy and history in his *Wenxin diaolong* (The Literary Mind and the Carving of Dragons) but did not recognize *xiaoshuo* as literature (Lu 1994:46–47).[9] Literary critics followed his example until the twentieth century.

The titles of traditional *xiaoshuo* texts include elements remindful of their historical association, such as *zhi* (record), *ji* (account) and *zhuan* (transmitted tale). Gan Bao's (fl. 320) preface to his early fourth-century collection of *zhiguai xiaoshuo* ('records of the strange', or 'writings recording abnormalities') entitled *Soushen ji* (In Search of the Supernatural) regards the texts as statements on historiography, defends the importance of committing historical information to writing and insists on their claim to truthfulness (*Jinshu*, 82:2151). The style of terse, documentary prose and the biographical structure in the *Soushen ji* are reminiscent of historiographical works. It also contains materials from the dynastic histories, from their commentaries and from ethnographic descriptions.

In his autobiography in the *Baopuzi* (He Who Embraces Simplicity) the Daoist philospher Ge Hong (c. 280–340), who also wrote *zhiguai xiaoshuo*, establishes their relation to historiography:

> I moreover composed a book on people who are not normally mentioned in books, which resulted in the *Shenxian zhuan* in 10 scrolls (*juan*), and I did the same for people who did not enter officialdom which resulted in the *Yinyu zhuan*, also in 10 scrolls. (*Baopuzi*, 203)

In his use of the term, *xiaoshuo* refers to an unofficial version of historiography.

Since Xun Xu (d. 289) and Li Chong (early fourth century), the dynastic histories list books under four categories: classics (*jing*), historical records (*shi*), philosophical writings (*zi*) and miscellaneous works (*ji*) (Drège 1991:109) The works classified as *xiaoshuo* all appear under philosophical writings (Lu Hsun 1982:3; Cheng Yizhong 1987:44–45; Lu 1994:49).[10] This categorization remained influential throughout the centuries – the eighteenth-century *Siku quanshu* (Complete Library of Four Branches of Books) collection still retained *xiaoshuo* in the same section and even twentieth-century scholars and bibliographers have tended to follow this classification, listing classical *xiaoshuo* under philosophical writings and vernacular *xiaoshuo* under miscellaneous works (Cheng Yizhong 1987:44; Dudbridge 1995:39).[11]

The only extant items from the *xiaoshuo* listed in the *Suishu* (History of the Sui Dynasty) are the *Yan Danzi* (Prince Dan of Yan), a historical narrative, and *Shishuo xinyu* (New Account of Tales of the World), which also contains anecdotes from historical sources and appears as a kind of *yeshi,* unofficial history. Stories about ghosts, spirits and the supernatural world from the Wei, Jin and Northern and Southern dynasties by contrast did not count as *xiaoshuo,* but would appear under *zazhuan* (miscellaneous traditions) in the history section (*shi*) in the *Jiu Tangshu* (Old History of the Tang Dynasty), under *zazhuan ji* (records of miscellaneous traditions) in the *Xin Tangshu* (New History of the Tang Dynasty), or under *zhuan ji* (records of traditions) in other works (Cheng Yizhong 1987:44). The early Tang dynasty (618–907) historians and bibliographers apparently found no reason to distinguish between *xiaoshuo* and historical records (Lu 1994:49, 130).

In 710 the historian Liu Zhiji (661–721) critically surveyed all aspects of historical scholarship in his work *Shitong* (Anatomy of Histories *or* Everything You Always Wanted to Know about Historiography) and established standards of critical procedure for historians.[12] The Chinese historian considered history to be a mirror of human affairs; its pattern of success or failure served a didactic function. The historian regarded his task as the 'faithful recording of events' (*shilu*) and was fascinated with the narration of events (*xushi*) (Lu 1994:130). Liu Zhiji praised the skilful narration of events in imperial historiography and criticized *xiaoshuo* texts from the historian's point of view. He regarded *xiaoshuo* texts (including *zazhuan, zaji* [miscellaneous records] and *dili* [geography] writings such as *Shishuo xinyu* and *Soushen ji*) as a branch of historiography, assessed them for veracity and reliability and concluded they were 'flawed works of history' (Pulleyblank 1961:135–66).[13] Tang scholars since Liu Zhiji thus began to view the *xiaoshuo* from the philosophy category and the *zazhuan* from the history category as one kind (Cheng Yizhong 1987:45f.).[14]

In the High Tang period the poet and painter Gu Kuang (d. *c.* 806) sketched in his preface to the *Guangyi ji* (Great Book of Marvels), a collection of tales by his contemporary and friend, the scholar-official Dai Fu, the state of the field of what later came to be known as *zhiguai xiaoshuo* (*Wenyuan yinghua,* 737:5b–7a).[15] He listed the names of 'men who recorded strange things' (*zhiguai zhi shi*) from the Han (206 BC–AD 220) to the Tang dynasty as belonging to one tradition, although he did not refer to their works as *xiaoshuo.* The imperial bibliographies (*Suishu, Jiu Tangshu*) classify the texts in Gu Kuang's list under 'miscellaneous traditions' (*zazhuan*), 'geography' (*dili*), 'miscellaneous histories' (*zashi*), 'miscellaneous schools of thought' (*zajia*), 'Daoism', 'standard histories', 'histories of usurping dynasties', and 'commonplaces' (*xiaoshuo jia*) (Dudbridge 1995:18–45). Gu Kuang's list gives insight into the way Tang readers and writers would have read and understood these tales: historical records, geographical writings and supernatural stories all form part of the same discourse charting the mental map of their world.

In the late Tang period, Gao Yanxiu regarded 'unofficial history writings' (*yeshi*) and 'miscellaneous records' (*zaji*) as *xiaoshuo,* thus identifying *xiaoshuo* as history rather than philosophy. Duan Chengshi (*c.* 803–63) was the first to call the *zhiguai* tales *xiaoshuo* (Cheng Yizhong 1987:46).

All these documents illustrate the lack of clear-cut boundaries between history and fiction in the Wei, Jin, Northern and Southern dynasties and Tang periods. The *xiaoshuo* texts retain the tradition of recording 'street gossip' as their source, and may have included oral narratives, family held records and other documents of regional sayings and customs (Cheng Yizhong 1987:50; Campany 1996:179; Nienhauser 1999:188).

Misleading terminology: *Zhiguai* and *Chuanqi*

Ever since the publication of Lu Xun's (1881–1936) *Zhongguo xiaoshuo shilüe* (A Brief History of Chinese Fiction) modern scholars have distinguished between prose narratives from the Wei, Jin and Northern and Southern dynasties under the label of *zhiguai* and Tang tales under the generic label of *chuanqi,* regarding the former as proto-fiction and the latter as the beginning of consciously creative fiction (DeWoskin 1977:51; Adkins 1980; Kao 1985:21ff.). Recent scholarship has shown, however, that this conception is erroneous and represents but a twentieth-century generic classification (Dudbridge 1999). The term *zhiguai*[16] has been used as a generic term only in modern times and it refers not just to texts from the Wei, Jin and Northern and Southern dynasties but to an unbroken tradition of 'recording the strange' (*zhiguai*), running from antiquity through the Tang dynasty right to the present day (Li Jianguo 1984:11; Dudbridge 1995:18).[17]

Similarly, the term *chuanqi* originally appeared as the title of a tale collection by the Tang writer Pei Xing (825–80) and was used in the Song dynasty (980–1279) by Chen Shidao (c. 1068–94) to describe writings in the style of Pei Xing. Although in the Ming era Hu Yinglin (1551–1602) used the term to refer to Tang dynasty tales (Cheng Yizhong 1987:49–50),[18] it was not adopted in a generic way until Lu Xun's criticism appeared in the twentieth century and it was not used for classification in catalogues. As far as Tang readers were concerned, no distinction existed between *zhiguai* and *chuanqi* and both referred to a 'literature of record' among historical documents (Dudbridge 1995; Campany 1996; Nienhauser 1999). Most recently, the sinologist Glen Dudbridge (1999) has argued that the traditional and modern scholars' instinct and urge to categorize these narratives have often made culturally sensitive interpretation impossible. The dominant genre of narrative in imperial China remained history writing and the poetics of narrative continued as a theory of historiography until the Ming/Qing era. Attitudes towards the reading of *xiaoshuo* began to change with the emergence of the long vernacular *xiaoshuo* in the late Ming era. Writers and critics began to emphasize that *xiaoshuo* narratives were self-consciously non-historical and creative works that required their own poetics rather than being judged as defective history or quasi-history (Lu 1994:134).[19]

The Ming/Qing discourse on the nature of *xiaoshuo* texts develops ideas first formulated in the Song period. Guanyuan Naideweng (fl. 1235) attempted to classify genres of storytelling (including *shuohua, huaben* and *xiaoshuo*) in his *Ducheng jisheng* (A Record of the Splendours of the Capital City) and discussed the nature of *xiaoshuo* as a mixture of *xu* (imaginary) and *shi* (real) and also *zhen* (true) and *jia* (false) (*Ducheng jisheng,* 82). The self-conscious mixing of reality and illusion became a common topos in the writing of the long vernacular *xiaoshuo* of the Ming/Qing era. The late Ming critic Xie Zhaozhe (1567–1624) commented on the style of *xiaoshuo* writings in his *Wuzazu* (Five Miscellanies) as follows:

> Fiction (*xiaoshuo*) and dramatic compositions should contain a mixture of the fictive (*xu*) and the real (*shi*). Then they become writings that capture the essence of literary games. One should try to construct feelings and scenes as perfectly as possible but not ask whether they really exist or not. (*Wuzazu,* 1287)

In the early seventeenth century the champion of popular literature, Feng Menglong (1574–1646), also discussed the dialectic of principle (*li*) and events (*shi*), and the mixing of true (zhen) and fictive (yan) in xiaoshuo writing. In his preface to the anthology Jingshi tongyan (Words to Warn the World) he states that events in fiction do not have to be completely real or completely fictive: 'The protagonists may not have done the things, and the things may not belong to the protagonists' (Xu, ZXX, 97). In Feng's view, the truthfulness of a story does not depend on whether the depicted events are historically verifiable; what matters is the principle and its containing some universal truth.

The delight in punning and playing with the notions of reality and illusion marks most of the great vernacular Ming/Qing novels and culminates in the self-reflexivity of the Hongloumeng, which emphasizes its fictionality while both the narrator and the commentator, Zhiyan zhai (Red Inkstone), insist on the truthfulness of the story (Yu 1988). As we have seen, the Yinyuan zhuan, too, celebrates this very paradox.

The historian as a messenger of souls

In exploring how the literary text communicates to us from the past and how the fictional artefact relates to historical 'reality', we need an approach that allows us to take into account the Chinese discourse on the nature of xiaoshuo texts and their cultural idiosyncrasies. The reality of seventeenth-century China that we can know today exists only as a narrated or perceived reality in the voices of various observers and in the reconstructed images from surviving sources. Each textual source represents a construct in itself and communicates its particular perception of the past. Literary texts clearly mark their representations of the world as images of artistic perception. The novel after all represents a literary construct that conveys its own particular perception of the world. It does not mirror 'historical reality'; rather it presents a version of perceived reality. Our interest in the Yinyuan zhuan focuses on this very issue: how written discourse communicates perceived reality and historical experience.

Recent literary criticism abandons the distinction of historical and literary sources in textual analysis. Twentieth-century literary theory rests on the assumption that all texts can equally be decoded and deconstructed. Bakhtin, for example, postulates the intrinsic relation between fiction and history:

> The boundaries between fiction and non-fiction, between literature and non-literature and so forth are not laid up in heaven. Every specific situation is historical. And the growth of literature is not merely development and change within the fixed boundaries of any given definition; the boundaries themselves are constantly changing. (cited in Gearhart 1984:i)

Suzanne Gearhart describes in her literary-historical approach to the French Enlightenment period the boundary separating history and fiction as 'open' (5–8). She points out that the study of the relationship of history and fiction is one of the most important critical tasks. Structuralist critics such as Gerard Genette, Roland Barthes and Tzvetan Todorov discard the older distinction between historical 'evidence' and fictional 'narrative' that Gallie and Collingwood proposed (Gallie 1964). Barthes has questioned the traditional opposition between history and fiction, maintaining that history is essentially a form of narrative (Barthes 1970; Gearhart 1984:204). Barthes argues that fictional discourse has an arbitrary relationship to historical reality but historical narratives are also arbitrary in this sense. Todorov regards both history and fiction as types of narrative. For Todorov neither history nor fiction exists outside of language. Both constitute forms of discourse. He argues that l'histoire (in the meaning of both history and story) is always a convention: 'It does not exist at the level of events themselves.' It is 'an abstraction because it is always perceived and narrated by someone. It does not exist "in itself"' (Todorov 1966:127; Belsey 1985:ix). In sum, fictional and non-fictional sources may differ in their style and rhetoric but both constitute forms of written discourse conveying particular perceptions.

The concept of perception is of crucial importance to our analysis. How does a text perceive the world? How can it communicate perceived reality? How does it represent historical experience? How does it relate to its context? The French cultural historian Emmanuel Le Roy Ladurie has compared the role of the modern historian to that of Arnaud Gélis, the messenger of souls in the mediaeval village of Montaillou whose task is to make the dead speak and to communicate between the living and the dead (Le Roy Ladurie 1982:601). His historical approach has inspired analytical approaches to both Western and Chinese literary narratives.

The Renaissance scholar Stephen Greenblatt tackles the problem of perception in textual analysis in terms of voices. Drawing on the image of the historian as a messenger of souls, he embarks on his study of literary texts from the English Renaissance period and their historical contexts with the 'desire to speak with the dead' (Greenblatt 1988:1). He cautions that this involves not one single voice of the other but many voices including one's own: the voices within the literary text, those from its contexts, and finally the critic's own voice that poses questions to the text and searches for answers (20). The concept of the multi-voiced or polyphonic novel in literary criticism is already familiar from the Russian critic Bakhtin (1984:5–46), but here the dialogue of voices refers to the work of literary criticism that looks at literature as historical records of the past. Greenblatt has referred to his style of analysis as new historicism, but he has come to prefer the term 'cultural poetics' to emphasize his concern with the integration of aesthetic and social discourse (Greenblatt 1990:147).

The new historicism merits a closer look as it offers some useful concepts in our search for an approach to the Chinese *xiaoshuo* that remains sensitive to indigenous concepts such as the perceived historicity of texts. The term was coined by Roy Harvey Pearce in his book *Historicism Once More* (1969). In 1973, Hayden White's book *Metahistory* had a powerful impact on historians by pointing out their unconscious reliance on rhetorical figures (White 1973). In the 1980s and 1990s, Renaissance scholars in America, notably Stephen Greenblatt, made the term fashionable when they embarked on a new historical and cultural approach to Shakespeare and his world.

The new historicists appear as a loose group of modern scholars including both historians and literary critics who share a reciprocal concern with the historicity of texts and the textuality of history (Montrose 1986:8; Veeser 1994). The new historicism tries to turn away from the formal, de-contextualized analysis that has dominated criticism in the 1980s and 1990s (Greenblatt 1990:163). While the old historicists (e.g. Leopold von Ranke) attempt to reconstruct history *wie es eigentlich gewesen ist* (as it actually happened), claiming to avoid all value judgements in their account of the past, the new historicism challenges the reading of fiction as an unproblematic documentary source from which one can easily build a picture of societies of the past (169).[20] New historicism instead pays attention to rhetoric as a ground for the contestation and negotiation of power relations and acknowledges the modern critic's engagement and partiality.

The new historicists reject any notion of history as an imitation of events in the world or a reflection of external reality and propose to treat both literature and history as forms of discourse. They acknowledge their debt to recent developments in literary, anthropological and social theory, in particular post-structuralism, but insist that the new historicism can be situated as a practice but is 'no doctrine at all' and that it remains 'unresolved and disingenuous about its relation to literary theory'[21] (146–47).

Independently from European Renaissance scholarship, Dudbridge has applied a similar approach to the study of traditional Chinese literature. He uses Le Roy Ladurie's concept of the historian as the messenger of souls in tracing the sequence of voices in his analysis of Tang dynasty tales and their historical context (Dudbridge 1995:1–17). Although Dudbridge does not use the term 'new historicism', his analysis similarly reacts against the old historicism that would regard anecdotal literature as a simple and straightforward testimony of past practices in the analysis of customs and beliefs. Instead, like the new historicists, he takes an interest in historical particularity, reading the tales as a literature of record, not of fantasy or creative fiction (16; cf. Greenblatt 1990:164).

In his analysis of the Chinese poetics of narrative, Sheldon Lu has also attempted to solve the 'dilemma of balancing respect for the historical character of literary texts and the desire to appropriate cross-cultural and transhistorical methodologies' by pointing to the new historicist's 'other sense of history' that understands history as a story or narrative and allows for the coexistence of multiple, competing and conflicting histories (Lu 1994:160–61).

It may be worth our while, then, to outline and critically evaluate some of the key assumptions shared by the new historicists that appear most relevant to our inquiry into the Chinese *xiaoshuo* and examine how useful these concepts would prove in an approach to Chinese texts.[22] Let us consider here three main assumptions.

(1)   Literary and non-literary texts circulate inseparably

New historicists assume that both literary and non-literary texts circulate inseparably, that both constitute forms of cultural discourse and require analysis that takes them into consideration simultaneously (Veeser 1994:16–17; Greenblatt 1990:170ff.). This appears as the most important and relevant concept to our inquiry into Chinese fiction as it provides a critical approach that remains sensitive to the Chinese conception of *xiaoshuo* texts and their perceived historicity. The new historicism abandons the distinction between a literary text and its cultural or historical backdrop and demands an investigation into the margins as well as the centre. This approach can provide us with an analytical tool for seeing both literary and non-literary texts in context and reconstructing resonance and significance within a cross-generic discourse (Greenblatt 1990:169).

One problem here lies in the stress on cultural significance at the expense of the role of aesthetics in textual analysis. The portrayal of the virago in the *Yinyuan zhuan* thrives on satire, irony, hyperbole and the grotesque. In order to analyse the text for its potential of yielding glimpses of perceived reality, we cannot afford to ignore its rhetoric. In dealing with the Chinese *xiaoshuo*, therefore, we face a dual task: on the one hand, we need to analyse the rhetoric and aesthetics of the text and, on the other, we shall use the aesthetics as a tool to reconstruct the perceptions in the voices that speak through the textual traces of the past.

(2)   All works of art are embedded in a network of negotiation and exchange

The new historicism assumes that all works of art are embedded in a network of negotiations and exchange that accompanies the production of a text. In Greenblatt's definition, art 'does not simply exist in all cultures; it is made up along with other products, practices, [and] discourses of a given culture.' In his use of the word, 'made up' means 'inherited, transmitted, altered, modified, [and] reproduced far more than it means invented' and he claims that 'as a rule, there is very little pure invention in culture' (1988:13). The work of art appears as a product of collective negotiation and exchange between a creator and the institutions or practices of society and involves currencies such as money and prestige and, as returns, pleasure and interest (1988:12; 1990:158). The new historicism is interested in reconstructing the historical circumstances of the production and consumption of texts and regards the context not as a fixed background, but rather as a dynamic network of social forces (1990:170). Greenblatt uses the term 'resonance' to refer to the dynamics of such forces in culture (161–83).

A focus on resonance could provide important insights into cultural practices in the Chinese context, too, as a detailed knowledge about the creation of a text and the motives of creation would help safeguard against the pitfalls of intentional fallacy and illuminate the position of the text in relation to power, authority and the contestations or manipulations involved in its creation. The problem with the *Yinyuan zhuan* however, as with so many other *xiaoshuo* texts, is that it remains difficult to analyse the historical circumstances of artistic production, since this requires exact knowledge about the authorship and dating of a text. In the case of the *Yinyuan zhuan,* we know next to nothing about the author and we face the additional difficulty of not even being able to determine whether the text is a product of the Ming or the Qing period.

Despite this problem, the concept of cultural embeddedness remains useful in the Chinese context insofar as it seeks to explore how other cultural structures resonate within imaginative literature (164–69). Artistic imagination appears as bound up with a collective, social energy (1988:12). Greenblatt defines this *energia* as a term from rhetoric (rather than physics) denoting the power of language to cause 'a stir to the mind' (6) Social energy circulates through anything produced by society, including dreams, desire, anxiety and experience (19). Although this concept has been formulated for the analysis of Renaissance culture in Europe, it may be applied to the Chinese context, too, as it can help us identify and define aspects of the culture out of which the *xiaoshuo* texts have emerged, even if we cannot recover the historical circumstances of the original production and consumption of those texts. Most recently, in his study of Tang dynasty tales, Dudbridge (1999:169–70) has also stressed the need to explore echo and resonance between texts in the analysis of *xiaoshuo* narratives – rather than questions of generic category which remain problematic. He also speaks of the 'energies in the surrounding intellectual culture' involved in the creation and reading of texts (154, 156).

Chinese writers themselves have acknowledged and pointed to the phenomenon that the concept of social energy describes. The late Ming scholar Feng Menglong, for example, maintained that *xiaoshuo* narratives have always existed side by side with other genres. Although society has attributed only marginal value to *xiaoshuo* stories, their power to affect and transform the readers exceeds that of the Confucian classics The Great Understanding or the Way, as Sheldon Lu paraphrases Feng, 'becomes accessible to us when we have truly recognised not only the relativity of each and every little narrative (*xiaoshuo*) but also the value and worth inherent in each narrative's partial truth and local knowledge (Lu 1994:168). Tracing the flow of social energy will show the permeability of boundaries between the literary and non-literary discourse and help to identify the voices and perceptions from the past.

(3)   Any critique is subjective and influenced by cultural contexts

The new historicism moreover holds that any critique or analysis of a text is inherently subjective and any reading is influenced by the cultural contexts both of the text and the critic. This self-consciousness about the critic's voice and position derives from concepts developed by Jacques Derrida and the theory of deconstruction (Veeser 1994:12, 31 n. 25), and manifests itself in the sense of ambivalence and embarrassment apparent in the self-confessions of new historicist critics, leading Greenblatt to conclude that 'there can be no single method, no overall picture, no exhaustive and definitive cultural poetics' (Greenblatt 1988:19). In diametrical opposition to the old historicism, the new historicism challenges the notion that any objective analysis or reconstruction of history is possible and instead proposes approaching textual traces from the past with a spirit of wonder (1990:170). This position ultimately negates the possibility of making any claims to accessing history through critical discourse.

For the present purpose, too, it remains important to stress that any form of analysis is bound to be subjective and to acknowledge the presence of the critic's voice in selecting and organizing his or her material. Instead of the concept of wonder, it may be more suitable in the present project to place more emphasis on the spirit of exploration in the historical inquiry into literary texts that seeks to recreate the perceptions from the past and their versions of historical experience.

Notes

1   Similar questions have been raised in an approach to late Ming literature by Allan Barr. See Barr 1997.
2   This has been interpreted as a nostalgic reference to the Golden Age of the Western Zhou dynasty (traditionally 1122 BC, historically ca. 1050–1770 BC) as a Confucian utopia (cf. Wu 1986:40).
3   Genette distinguishes between narration and focalization (also: point of view, points of perception, narrative perspective) (Genette 1980:189–91). Bal introduces the concept of the focalizor next to the narrator to distinguish between 'those who see' and 'those who speak' (Bal 1988:119–20).
4   While Scholes defines the narrator like a *histor* as a 'man of authority' (Scholes and Kellogg 1979:266), Bal (1988:118–21) points out that the narrator is not a storyteller but an 'it'.
5   On the concept of the implied author, see Booth 1983 (151). Bal defines the term as the 'result of investigation of the meaning of the text, and not the source of that meaning' (Bal 1988:120).
6   There are numerous other references; Chapters 23 to 29 depict the most important contrast of 'then' and 'now'.
7   In the phrase: 'If you parade your little theories [*xiaoshuo*] to fish for fame, you will be far from the Great Paradigm' (*Zhuangzi jishi*, 26:925).
8   On *Xinlun*, see also Pokora 1975.
9   Liu Xie mentions *xiaoshuo* only once in passing (Lu 1994:46–47).
10   Wei Zheng's (580–643) definition of *xiaoshuo* in the *Suishu* is based on the *Hanshu*: '*Xiaoshuo* were the talk of the street . . . all the talk of the street and the highways was recorded. Officers at court took charge of local records and prohibitions, while the officers in charge of civil affairs reported local sayings and customs' (translated in Lu Hsun 1982:4).
11   On categories, see also McMullen 1988 (159–60). On the problem of classification, see also Dudbridge 2000 (53–79).
12   On the title of the *Shitong*, see Quirin 1987 (173) and Durbridge 2000 (63). For the translation I am indebted to Glen Dudbridge, personal communication.
13   Liu Zhili's son Liu Suceng also collected historical narratives from the Wei, Jin and Northern and Southern dynasties and the early Tang in an anthology entitled *Xiaoshuo* (Cheng Yizhong 1987:45).
14   The *Xin Tangshu* (*Yiwenzhi*) classifies some *zazhuan ji* as *xiaoshuo*; the *Siku quanshu* also classifies some *zashi* as *xiaoshuo* while leaving them under philosophy. Zhang Xuecheng (1738–1801) established a *xiaoshuo* section in *Shikao shili*, continuing Liu Zhiji's tradition.
15   For an annotated critical translation and discussion of Gu Kuang's preface, see Dudbridge 1995 (18–45).
16   The term first appears in the *Zhuangzi* (*Zhuangzi jishi*, 1A:4).
17   Thematic and textual devices known from stories in the *zhiguai* tradition are apparent in the writings of contemporary writers such as Su Tong, Can Xue, Ge Fei, Yu Hua and even Wang Shuo (Wedell-Wedellsborg 1998).
18   On Hu Yinglin, see Nienhauser 1986 (439–441).

19   Sheldon Lu points out that writers began to celebrate verisimilitude – a resemblance to the real world or an internal psychological truthfulness – instead of historicity in the late imperial period and used new terms to describe the artistic quality of fictional writings such as 'realistic' (*bizhen*), 'exact picture' (*xiaoxiang*), 'exact image of the thing' (*xiaowu*), 'spiritual resemblance' (*chuanshen*), and 'picture-like' (*ruhua*) (Lu 1994:134).

20   While the old historicism adhered to the veneration of the past or tradition, the new historicism by contrast approaches its subject with a spirit of wonder and reacts against the canonization of certain texts and the celebration of literary authority, treating the power of certain authorities as suspicious.

21   Joel Fineman has, not without irony, drawn attention to the new historicism's 'programmatic refusal to specify a methodological program for itself – its characteristic air of reporting, haplessly, the discoveries it happened serendipitously to stumble upon in the undirected, idle rambles through the historical archives'. Louis Montrose states that the new historicists are 'actually quite heterogenous in their critical practices' while Catherine Gallagher calls the 'phenomenon' one of 'indeterminacy' and Veeser admits that 'the New Historicism is a phrase without an adequate referent' (in Veeser 1994: 1).

22   The present study here draws on Veeser's account of the new historicism that recognizes five key assumptions (Veeser 1994).

References

Adkins, Curtis P. (1980) 'The Hero in T'ang ch'uan-ch'i Tales', in: *Critical Essays on Chinese Fiction*, edited by Winston L.Y. Yang and Curtis P. Adkins. Hong Kong: The Chinese University Press.

Bakhtin, M. (1984) *Problems of Dostoevsky's Poetics*. Edited and translated by C. Emerson. Manchester University Press.

Bal, Mieke (1988) *Narratology. Introduction to the Theory of Narrative*. Translated by Christine van Boheemen. Toronto, Buffalo and London: University of Toronto Press.

Baopuzi. By Ge Hong, ed. Zhuzi jicheng.

Barr, Allan H. (1997) 'The Wanli Context of the "Courtesan's Jewel Box" Story', *Harvard Journal of Asiatic Studies* 57/1:107–41.

Barthes, Roland (1970) 'Historical Discourse', in: *Introduction to Structuralism*, edited by M. Lane. New York: Basic Books.

Belsey, Catherine (1985) *The Subject of Tragedy: Identity and Difference in Renaissance Drama*. Reprinted London: Methuen.

Berg, Daria (1999) 'Reformer, Saint and Saviour: Visions of the Great Mother in the Novel *Xingshi yinyuan zhuan* and its Seventeenth-Century Chinese Context', *Nan Nü: Men, Women, and Gender Studies in Early and Imperial China* 1/2:237–67.

Booth, Wayne (1983) *The Rhetoric of Fiction*. Reprinted Harmondsworth: Penguin.

Campany, Robert Ford (1996) *Strange Writing: Anomaly Accounts in Early Medieval China*. Albany: SUNY.

Cao Xueqin (1973) *The Story of the Stone*. Vol. 1. Translated by David Hawkes. Harmondsworth: Penguin.

Ch'en Shouyi (1961) *Chinese Literature – A Historical Introduction*. New York: Ronald.

Cheng Yizhong (1978) 'Lun Tangdai xiaoshuo de yanjin zhi ji', *Wenxue yichan* 5:44–52.

DeWoskin, Kenneth J. (1977) 'The Six Dynasties *chih-kuai* and the Birth of Fiction', in: *Chinese Narrative: Critical and Theoretical Essays*, edited by Andrew H. Plaks. Princeton, NJ: Princeton University Press.

Drège, Jean-Pierre (1991) *Les bibliothèques en Chine au temps des manuscrits: jusqu'au Xe siècle*. Paris: Ecole Française d'Extrême Orient.

Dudbridge, Glen (1995) *Religious Experience and Lay Society in T'ang China. A Reading of Tai Fu's 'Kuang-i chi'*. Cambridge: Cambridge University Press.

– (1999) 'A Question of Classification in Tang Narrative: The Story of Ding Yue', in: *India, Tibet, China: Genesis and Aspects of Traditional Narrative*, edited by Alfredo Cadonna. Florence: Leo S. Olschki.

– (2000) *Lost Books of Medieval China*. The 1999 Panizzi Lectures. London: The British Library.

Gallie, W.B. (1964) *Philosophy and the Historical Understanding*. New York: Schocken Books.

Gearhart, Suzanne (1984) *The Open Boundaries of History and Fiction: A Critical Approach to the French Enlightenment Period*. Princeton: Princeton University Press.

Genette, Gérard (1980) *Narrative Discourse: An Essay in Method*. Translated by Jane E. Lewin. Ithaca, NY: Cornell University Press.

Greenblatt, Stephen (1988) *Shakespearean Negotiations: The Circulation of Social Energy in Renaissance England*. Oxford: Clarendon Press.

– (1990) *Learning to Curse: Essays in Early Modern Culture*. New York and London: Routledge.

Hongloumeng. By Cao Xueqin, ed. Beijing: Renmin wenxue, 1957.

Hsia, C.T. (1968) *The Classic Chinese Novel. A Critical Introduction*. New York and London: Columbia University Press.

Jinshu. Ed. Beijing: Zhonghua, 1974.

Kao, Karl S.Y. (1985) *Classical Chinese Tales of the Supernatural and the Fantastic: Selections from the Third to the Tenth Century*. Bloomington: Indiana University Press.

Le Roy Ladurie, Emmanuel (1982) *Montaillou, village occitan de 1294 à 1324*. Revised edition, Paris: Gallimard.

Li Jianguo (1984) *Tangqian zhiguai xiaoshuo shi*. Tianjin: Nankai daxue.

Lu Hsun (1982) *A Brief History of Chinese Fiction*. Translated by Yang Hsien-Yi and Gladys Yang. Beijing: Foreign Language Press.

Lu Sheldon Hsiao-peng (1994) *From Historicity to Fictionality: The Chinese Poetics of Narrative*. Stanford: Stanford University Press.

Mair, Victor H. (1983) 'The Narrative Revolution in Chinese Literature: Ontological Presuppositions', *Chinese Literature, Essays, Articles and Reviews* 5:1–27.

McMullen, David (1988) *State and Scholars in T'ang China*. Cambridge: Cambridge University Press.

Montrose, Louis Adrian (1986) 'Renaissance Literary Studies and the Subject of History', *English Literary Renaissance* 16:5–12.

Nienhauser, William H. (ed. and comp.) (1986) *The Indiana Companion to Traditional Chinese Literature*. Bloomington: Indiana University Press.

– (1999) Review: Glen Durbridge, *Religious Experience and Lay Society in T'ang China. A Reading of Tai Fu's 'Kuang-i chi'*. Cambridge: Cambridge University Press, 1995. *T'oung Pao* 85:181–9.

Pearce, Roy Harvey (1969) *Historicism Once More*. Princeton, NJ: Princeton University Press.

Pokora, Timoteus (1975) *Hsin-lun (New Treatise), and Other Writings by Huan T'an (43 B.C.– 28 A.D.)*. Ann Arbor: Center for Chinese Studies, University of Michigan.

Quirin, Michael (1987) *Liu Zhiji und das Chun Qiu*. Würzburger Sino-Japonica 15. Frankfurt am Main and New York: p. Lang.

Scholes, Robert E., and Robert Kellogg (1979) *The Nature of Narrative*. New York: Oxford University Press.

Todorov, Tzvetan (1966) 'Les catégories du récit littéraire', *Communications* 8:125–51.

Veeser, Aram H. (1994) 'The New Historicism', in: *The New Historicism Reader*, edited by Aram H. Veeser. New York and London: Routledge.

Wedell-Wedellsborg, Anne (1998) 'Contemporary *zhiguai*? Modern Stories of the Strange and the Abnormal'. Paper delivered at the EACS Conference, Edinburgh, 10–13 September.

Wenxuan. By Xiao Tong, Jinling shuju edition, 1869.

White, Hayden (1973) *Metahistory: The Historical Imagination in Nineteenth-Century Europe*. Baltimore and London: Johns Hopkins University Press.

Wilhelm, Hellmut (1972) 'Notes on Chou Fiction', in: *Transition and Permanence: Chinese History and Culture*, edited by David C. Buxbaum and Frederick W. Mote. Hong Kong: Cathay.

Wimsatt, Jr, W.K., and Monroe C. Beardsley [1914] (1995) 'The Intentional Fallacy', reprinted in *Authorship: from Plato to the Postmodern*, edited by Sean Burke. Edinburgh: Edinburgh University Press.

Wu, Yenna (1986) 'Marriage Destinies to Awaken the World: A Literary Study of *Xingshi yinyuan zhuan*'. Ph.D. diss., Harvard University.

— (1991) 'Repetition in Xingshi yinyuan zhuan', *Harvard Journal of Asiatic Studies* 51/1:55–87.

— (1995) *The Chinese Virago: A Literary Theme*. Cambridge, MA, and London: Harvard University Press.

— (1999) *Ameliorative Satire and the Seventeenth-Century Chinese Novel Xingshi yinyuan zhuan – Marriage as Retribution, Awakening the World*. Lewiston: Edwin Mellen.

Xingshi yinyuan zhuan. By Xi Zhou Sheng, 3 vols., ed. Shanghai: Guji, 1981. Reprinted 1985. (=YYZ)

Xu. By Feng Menglong, reprinted in Zeng Zuyin *et al.* (eds. and annots.), *Zhongguo lidai xiaoshuo xuba xuanzhu*. Hubei: Chanjiang wenyi, 1982.

Xunzi yinde: A Concordance to Hsun Tzu. Ed. Harvard-Yenching Institute, Sinological Index Series, reprinted Taipei: Chinese Materials and Research Aids Service Center, Inc., 1966.

Yu, Anthony C. (1988) 'History, Fiction and the Reading of Chinese Narrative', *Chinese Literature, Essays, Articles and Reviews* 10:1–19.

Zhuangzi jishi. Ed. Guo Qingfan, Beijing: Zhonghua shuju, 1961.

PART VI

Race and ethnicity

LOCATING STUDIES ON RACE AND ETHNICITY can reveal much about the politics of identity, as well as changing conceptions of subjectivity. Moving in and out of different pseudo-scientific domains of study in the eighteenth and nineteenth centuries, and then shifting into the arts, humanities, and social sciences in the twentieth and twenty-first centuries, the categories "race" and "ethnicity" are in themselves unstable, highly contested, at times interchangeable, and yet increasing in importance, with "anti-racism" and associated discourses replacing early notions of race. Within literary studies, race has been regarded since the 1980s as part of the "holy trinity of literary criticism": that of race, class, and gender.[1] Race is a word used in the English language from 1508,[2] from the French, meaning a "group of people connected by common descent", sharing "hereditary characteristics" or "traits" (*OED*). Race was initially viewed from a biological perspective, beginning with the now outmoded notion that different races have natural, fixed attributes or personalities—an approach known as *biological determinism*.

Nineteenth-century ideas of race developed in anthropology and in eugenics, the latter being a pseudo-science which stereotyped and categorized people, suggesting that racial "stock" could be improved (or eradicated) by carefully controlled breeding programmes. Such theories were also used to explain successes in European colonization around the world, asserting that there were superior and inferior "races" of people. Author and critic Max Nordau, for example, writing towards the end of the nineteenth century, predicted that white Europeans would eventually dominate the planet, finding little resistance from non-whites: ". . . the coloured races . . . are of necessity doomed, first of all to be dislodged by the sons of the white race and then to be annihilated."[3] As he expands in language that many would now find deeply problematic: "the white race is better prepared for the struggle for existence than all the other races of men, and just as he requires the land of the savage to live upon will he take it without any hesitation. The black, red, or yellow specimens of humanity will then be nothing else than foes of the white race."[4] Similar racist ideas, expressing widely held beliefs, were used, for example, in colonized North America and Australia as the justification for the displacement of indigenous peoples; this was known in North America as the "vanishing Indian" thesis: that indigenous peoples would die out, or be completely assimilated into white cultures. Nordau's language is heavily weighted with assumptions that are nowhere proven: races are described via skin colour or types (phenotypical characteristics), people with certain skin types are "doomed", are "savages", and are natural enemies to white Europeans (he later goes on to suggest that climate is also an important factor in racial characteristics). This approach, however, did not just apply to non-European groups of people: it was also applied internally, most notoriously within Nazi Germany, in an attempt to exterminate Jewish and other peoples deemed racially or mentally inferior.

Such racist essentialism is now widely considered outmoded and based upon bad science, i.e., unproven notions of physical description and evolution that merely propped up systems of inequality, displacement and genocide (e.g., American slavery, European colonialism, the Holocaust in Nazi Germany). "Ethnicity" has now in many respects become the preferred term, because it is not based upon essentialism, but instead the notion that ethnic groups are social constructs. In 1949, a group of leading academics issued in Paris a "Statement on Race" which argued that since all human beings belonged to the same species, *Homo Sapiens*, the term "race" was meaningless, and should be replaced internationally with the phrase "ethnic group".[5] Sociologist Steve Fenton notes that in contrast with the essentialism of theories based upon the term "race", "the term 'ethnic' or 'ethnic group' is used primarily in contexts of *cultural* difference, where cultural difference is associated above all with an actual or commonly perceived shared ancestry, with language markers, and with national or regional origin."[6] Furthermore, "ethnicity" is not just a term that describes ethnic groups, but the social relationships that lead to a particular group believing that it is distinctive: "for ethnicity to spring to life it is necessary that *real or perceived differences of ancestry, culture and language are mobilised in social transactions*."[7] The term "race" persists, however, for a variety of reasons, including the fact that as long as individuals and groups still identify themselves using a discourse of race, it is clearly still a functioning concept, however negatively conceived, and however outmoded. Also, anti-racism texts and movements necessarily utilize a discourse of race to articulate an oppositional critique thereby sustaining, according to some critics, the very category—race—that they wish to remove from society!

Literary criticism turned serious attention to race and ethnicity in the late twentieth century, as part of an overall methodological shift towards cultural and identity studies alongside myriad postcolonial rewritings of the European canon, literary-critical studies of colonial history and of African American, Asian American and ethnic writers in the US. Rather than conceiving of these critical areas as being in direct causal or linear relationships, it is more accurate to regard them as sharing concerns, which at times intersect, and at other times work in parallel or even in isolation from one another. For example, African American studies returned to the history of slavery and the ensuing cultural challenges following emancipation, as well as the powerful, immensely creative works that flowed from the twentieth-century Harlem Renaissance, to reconceive notions of race and resistance to white culture. Henry Louis Gates, Jr, argues that the critical tools used to approach black American texts are themselves a product of a Eurocentric mindset and tradition, and in *Figures in Black: Words, Signs, and the "Racial" Self* (1987), he sets about interrogating "Euro-American" literary critical discourse: "by learning to read a black text within a black formal cultural matrix and explicating it with the principles of criticism at work in both the Euro-American and the African-American traditions, I believe that we critics can identify and produce richer structures of meaning than are possible otherwise."[8] To put this another way, as Gates does in his preface to *Black Literature and Literary Theory* (first published 1984), the challenge is "to posit a 'black self' in the very Western languages in which blackness itself is a figure of absence, a negation."[9] In *The Signifying Monkey: A Theory of African-American Literary Criticism* (1988), Gates turns away from European rhetoric and instead focuses on Nigerian Yoruba mythology, the trickster figure of Esu-Elegbara (see Chapter 38), as well as the African American figure of the "Signifying Monkey", both of whom offer an alternative "cultural matrix" of black Signifyin(g): the double-voiced oral/written texts of black American cultural production where the vernacular and high culture both utilize a double discourse.

Doubling is also essential to Paul Gilroy's approach to black identity, in *The Black Atlantic: Modernity and Double Consciousness* (1993), where he posits a diasporic (dispersed) and hybrid concept of black subjectivity. Again, this becomes a question of location, here, the transitional and transnational intersecting space of the Black Atlantic, the slavery and trade routes between Africa, the Caribbean, the Americas and the UK known as the "middle passage". Gilroy rethinks black aesthetics and subjectivity via this trope of diasporic identity, but he also argues that it is crucial to maintain an awareness of "race" in broader discussions of "western aesthetic judgement, taste, and cultural value" especially as these feed into the formation of cultural studies.[10] The concept of "double consciousness" comes from W.E.B. Du Bois's *The Souls of Black Folk* (1903); Gilroy notes how this concept is a "symbiosis between three modes of thinking, being, and seeing. The first is racially particularistic, the second nationalistic in that it derives from the nation state in which the ex-slaves but not-yet-citizens find themselves ... The third is diasporic or hemispheric, sometimes global and occasionally universalist."[11] What Gilroy aims for is a (largely successful) attempt at rethinking modernity via black double consciousness, that is to say, rejecting the essentialism that can be the result of a return to a racial/ethnic past (be it "Africa" or elsewhere), in favour of black subjectivity and aesthetics being a constitutive and yet critical factor in the emergence of modernity.

A key component in such a black aesthetic is music (see Chapter 16): in Du Bois's case the epiphanic experience of hearing the Jubilee Singers at Fisk University, "who once hid in a Brooklyn organ loft, lest pious Congregationalists see their black faces before they heard their heavenly voices."[12] Gilroy's earlier text, *"There Ain't No Black In The Union Jack": The Cultural Politics of Race and Nation* (1987), draws heavily in a syncretist fashion upon different modalities of black British music and related cultural expressions of a black British vernacular; in the third chapter of *The Black Atlantic*, Gilroy moves beyond syncretism to ask deeper philosophical and political questions about black slavery/post-slavery music as a communicative device that functions when language and written art forms are suppressed: "Thinking about music—a non-representational, non-conceptual form—raises aspects of embodied subjectivity that are not reducible to the cognitive and the ethical. These questions are also useful in trying to pinpoint the distinctive aesthetic components in black communication."[13] For some critics, however, regardless of approach, what the "Black Atlantic" theory excludes is another location entirely: that of black Canada. The Canadian critic George Elliott Clarke argues that the assertions of a new hybrid space of blackness are in some ways negated by relying heavily on African American sources, be they primary or secondary: "Gilroy's effort to dispense with African-American parochialism is complicated by his decision to focus his analyses on African-American writers and intellectuals, namely, Frederick Douglass, Martin Robinson Delany (who may also be classified as African-Canadian), Du Bois, Richard Wright, James Baldwin, and Toni Morrison. Though Gilroy essays, valiantly, to set these figures in a Pan-Atlantic context, he nevertheless succumbs to ideas that, once again, Americanize blackness."[14]

The tensions inherent in approaching questions of race and ethnicity from non-essentializing perspectives are manifold, for example, in the above discussion of race and ethnicity in relation to both a black "cultural matrix" and the "Black Atlantic", the category of "whiteness" remains unexamined and stable in the background, carrying with it a set of assumptions that are not explained or clarified. Critics have noted how this "naturalisation" of whiteness can lead to a lack of engagement in anti-racist initiatives,[15] and in a more general sense, facilitates a sense in which for many white people concerns of race and ethnicity always involve some problematic "other", i.e., a subjectivity that white people stand outside of. An unexamined concept of naturalized whiteness can also dovetail with outmoded narratives concerning nationalistic superiority and global economic hierarchy, or, to put it more simply, with unexamined power relations in today's world. Apparently essentializing accounts of race and ethnicity may sometimes mask more subversive, anti-essentializing intent. A case in point is W.E.B. Du Bois's groundbreaking history of Africans, called *The Negro* (1915), which shifts the idea of Africa away from outmoded colonialist notions of history and race in favour of focusing on African peoples themselves.[16] As Robert Gregg argues, in this text Du Bois relies "more heavily on the idea of race as a social construction, and, through his attention to migration, he came pretty close to throwing out a racial classification system altogether."[17] Apparently essentialist statements about race are undermined by the doubled subjectivity that Du Bois finds in his study: African subjects initiated and built important civilizations, yet at the same time, are stripped of their historical significance.[18] As Gregg summarizes, Du Bois's "definition of the color line in *The Negro* linked all colonized peoples, not just people of African descent. The Pan-African movement, Du Bois wrote, would 'not be merely a narrow racial propaganda.' With the resolution of the Cold War and the ascendency of the global market, bringing new and old color lines into sharp relief, Du Bois's sweeping vision of Africans and the diaspora seems more relevant now than at any time in the past hundred years."[19]

Another anti-essentializing approach to race and ethnicity is the work of Frantz Fanon, especially with his *Black Skin, White Masks* (French 1952; English trans. 1968), a psychological, existentialist and phenomenological investigation into racism and alienation (see Chapter 37), in which language itself both fixes (through the device of interpellation or "hailing") *and* divides the subject (the "white mask" of the colonizer's language never entirely hiding signs of difference, e.g., the racist's obsession with black skin). Postcolonial critic Homi K. Bhabha (see Chapter 47) calls *Black Skin, White Masks* "a meditation on the experience of dispossession and dislocation – psychic and social – which speaks to the condition of the marginalized, the alienated, those who have to live under the surveillance of a sign of identity and fantasy that denies their difference."[20] In *The Wretched of the Earth* (1961), Fanon takes a Marxist, anti-colonial approach to identity, based upon his experiences with the Algerian National Liberation Front who were trying to overthrow French rule. At the core of this book is the thesis that colonialism can only be overthrown by violent action in response, i.e., through the use of force; decolonization, then, meant the destruction of the entire colonial system of power and subjection.[21]

While Fanon has been criticized for not explicitly foregrounding questions of gender except in stereotypical terms, one of his best-known essays in *Studies in a Dying Colonialism* (1959), is on Arab women and veiling. For Fanon, colonial attempts to remove the veil equal a "destructuring" of Algerian culture. The veil becomes a sign of a failed European interpellation: colonial society is "frustrated" by the inability to physically see, and therefore fix the identities of, Algerian women. The veil becomes a symbol of threatening opposition when Algerian women joined in with the battle against the occupiers; now the veil moves from being "a symbol of resistance" to being "a technique of camouflage" as Bhabha puts it, since underneath it could be hidden weapons and explosives: "The veil that once secured the boundary of the home – the limits of woman – now masks the woman in her revolutionary activity, linking the Arab city and the French quarter, transgressing the familial and cultural boundary."[22] The indeterminacy of this sign for westerners means that they can also project their fantasies and neuroses about the female Other. In reality, the act of veiling is not homogenous, varying even within specific cultural groups, where "veiling is a multifaceted and polysemic institution, involving a multiplicity of forms and meanings."[23] What this example reveals, however, is that the intersection of race, ethnicity and gender leads to a more accurate analysis of identity within different groups (especially when class differences are also built in to the analysis). Critic bell hooks, in *Ain't I a Woman: Black Women and Feminism* (1981), powerfully reiterates slavery abolition campaigner Sojourner Truth's question from the 1951 Women's Rights Convention in Ohio, in response to a male delegate who had said that women could not have equal rights with men. Hooks takes on this question to argue that black women are marginalized from a white, middle-class feminist perspective, and from patriarchal sexism within black communities.[24] To move into a more inclusionary criticism of gender and race involves, however, learning to hear different voices, and re-learning how to critically respond in relation to texts that often do not come from the cultural, ethnic or class backgrounds of mainstream critical theorists.

Literary critical approaches to race and ethnicity were transformed in the twentieth century as key new areas developed, such as Canadian First Nations studies, Native American studies, Asian American studies, Chicano studies, and so on. What many of these approaches share is not just a focus and recovery of the writings of a particular ethnic group, but also a sense that new methodological approaches need to be taken to understand the literature in question. For example, Canadian and American indigenous peoples highly value orature, i.e., cultural knowledge transmitted through oral stories and performances; such orature feeds directly into contemporary indigenous literature. But this implies that a Eurocentric criticism based upon the valorization of the written Eurocentric canon does not have the capacity to fully comprehend indigenous texts. Salish writer Lee Maracle, for example, argues that readers need to be transformed by indigenous stories to understand them: "We attempt to story another being/phenomenon's behaviour and commit to its journey, its coming into being and going out of being, to this story. We then alter our conduct, our behaviour, to facilitate a common journey . . .".[25] Another important factor for indigenous authors in Canada and America is that of border-crossing, since aboriginal land-use patterns precede colonial borders imposed by Europeans. Related to this is Chicano/a identity, which derives from "both a hybrid and a border culture"[26] As Gloria Anzaldúa writes: "To live in the Borderlands means you / are neither *hispana india negra española / ni gabacha, eres mestiza, mulata*, half-breed / caught in the crossfire between camps / while carrying all five races on your back."[27] Within particular ethnic literary studies, immense diversity is often encountered, and it is imperative that critical approaches do not homogenize differences. A case in point is the term "Asian-American" studies, within which is found multiple ethnicities, such as Chinese, Japanese, Korean, Pacific, South Asian, and Vietnamese writers.[28] Differences may occur within a group, for example, between the older and younger generations of Canadian Asian writers; as critic Glenn Deer suggests, a new wave of Canadian Asian writing has a different sense of "spatial consciousness" and "urban mobility" where there is movement "beyond some of the earlier preoccupations with historically racialized enclaves."[29] Finally, shifts in what constitutes the literary text have recently involved switching critical attention from older modes of multimedia and popular culture, to computer-mediated modes, such as the internet, blogs, digital social networking sites, and so on, leading to new examinations of race and ethnicity performed through and within digitized worlds.

Further reading: a selection

One of the best places to start learning about race and ethnicity is a text such as Caliendo's and McIlwain's, which has focused essays on topics such as the origins of the concept of race, ethnicity, whiteness, gender and sexuality, media and popular culture, and so on, as well as a glossary of key terms, such as diaspora, Islamophobia, institutional racism and prejudice. Banton, Fenton and Hannaford go into considerable detail conceptually, sociologically and historically (Hannaford more specifically takes a history-of-ideas approach). Literary-critical texts in this area are extensive, and a small sample of these are given below, with a focus on gender and feminism (Abel, Christian, Afhsar, Maynard), black American, British and Canadian writing (Christian, Clarke, Gates, Gilroy, Gunning), Asian-American and British Asian authors (Gunning, Zamora), and new technologies (Everett, Leung). Christian's text "The Race for

Theory", collected in *New Black Feminist Criticism, 1985–2000*, is a classic for a number of reasons, not least the debates it initiated concerning essentialism versus notions of constructed subjectivity and identity. Gilroy (1987), Werbner and Modood address anti-racism, hybridity, multiculturalism and ethnic alliances, through a broad range of cultural texts.

Abel, Elizabeth, Barbara Christian and Helene Moglen, eds. *Female Subjects in Black and White: Race, Psychoanalysis, Feminism*. Berkeley & Los Angeles: University of California Press, 1997.

Afshar, Haleh and Mary Maynard, eds. *The Dynamics of "Race" and Gender: Some Feminist Interventions*. London: Taylor & Francis, 1994.

Banton, Michael. *Racial Theories*. Cambridge: Cambridge University Press, 1998.

Caliendo, Stephen M, and Charlton D. McIlwain, eds. *The Routledge Companion to Race and Ethnicity*. Abingdon, Oxon & New York: Routledge, 2011.

Christian, Barbara. *New Black Feminist Criticism, 1985–2000*. Gloria Bowles, M. Giulia Fabi, and Arlene R. Keiser, eds. Urbana & Chicago: University of Illinois Press, 2007.

Clarke, George Elliott. *Odysseys Home: Mapping African-Canadian Literature*. Toronto: University of Toronto Press, 2002.

Everett, Anna, ed. *Learning Race and Ethnicity: Youth and Digital Media*. Cambridge, MA: MIT Press, 2008.

Fenton, Steve. *Ethnicity*. Cambridge & Malden, MA: Polity, 2010.

Gates, Henry Louis, Jr. *Figures in Black: Words, Signs, and the "Racial" Self*. Oxford & New York: Oxford University Press, 1987.

Gates, Henry Louis, Jr., ed. *Black Literature and Literary Theory*. London & New York: Routledge, 1984.

Gilroy, Paul. *"There Ain't No Black In The Union Jack": The Cultural Politics of Race and Nation*. First published 1987. Chicago & London: University of Chicago Press, 1991.

Gilroy, Paul. *The Black Atlantic: Modernity and Double Consciousness*. Cambridge, MA: Harvard University Press, 1993.

Gunning, Dave. *Race and Antiracism in Black British and British Asian Literature*. Liverpool: Liverpool University Press, 2010.

Hannaford, Ivan. *Race: The History of an Idea in the West*. Baltimore & London: the Johns Hopkins University Press, 1996.

Leung, Linda. *Virtual Ethnicity: Race, Resistance and the World Wide Web*. Aldershot, Hants: Ashgate, 2005.

Miles, Robert. *Racism*. London & New York: Routledge, 1999.

Werbner, Pnina and Tariq Modood, eds. *Debating Cultural Hybridity: Multi-Cultural Identities and the Politics of Anti-Racism*. London & New Jersey: Zed, 1997.

Zamora, Maria C. *Nation, Race & History in Asian American Literature: Re-membering the Body*. New York: Lang, 2008.

Notes

1   Anthony Appiah and Henry Louis Gates, Jr., eds., *Identities*, Chicago & London: University of Chicago Press, 1995, p.1.

2   Michael Banton, *Racial Theories*, Cambridge: Cambridge University Press, 1998, p.17.

3   Max Nordau, *Paradoxes*, trans. J.R. McIlraith, London: Heinemann, 1896, p.337.

4   Max Nordau, *Paradoxes*, p.338.

5   Ivan Hannaford, *Race: The History of an Idea in the West*, Baltimore & London: the Johns Hopkins University Press, 1996, p.386.

6   Steve Fenton, *Ethnicity: Racism, Class and Culture*, Lanham, Maryland: Rowman & Littlefield, 1999, pp.3–4.

7   Steve Fenton, *Ethnicity: Racism, Class and Culture*, p.6.

8   Henry Louis Gates, Jr., *Figures in Black: Words, Signs, and the "Racial" Self*, Oxford & New York: Oxford University Press, 1987, p.xxi.

9   Henry Louis Gates, Jr., ed., *Black Literature and Literary Theory*, London & New York, Routledge, 1990, p.7.

10   Paul Gilroy, *The Black Atlantic: Modernity and Double Consciousness*, Cambridge, MA: Harvard University Press, 1993, p.9.

11   Paul Gilroy, *The Black Atlantic: Modernity and Double Consciousness*, p.127.

12   Quoted in Paul Gilroy, *The Black Atlantic: Modernity and Double Consciousness*, p.116.

13   Paul Gilroy, *The Black Atlantic: Modernity and Double Consciousness*, p.76.

14   George Elliott Clarke, *Odysseys Home: Mapping African-Canadian Literature*, Toronto: University of Toronto Press, 2002, p.82.

15   Alastair Bonnett, "Constructions of Whiteness in European and American Anti-Racism", in *Debating Cultural Hybridity: Multi-Cultural Identities and the Politics of Anti-Racism*, ed. Pnina Werbner and Tariq Modood, London & New Jersey: Zed, 1997, 173–92, pp.173–4.

16   Robert Gregg, "Afterword", in W.E.B. Du Bois, *The Negro*, Philadelphia: University of Pennsylvania Press, 2001, 245–72, p.259.

17   Robert Gregg, "Afterword", p.264.

18   Robert Gregg, "Afterword", p.267.

19   Robert Gregg, "Afterword", p.271.

20   Homi K. Bhabha, "Foreword: Remembering Fanon, Self, Psyche and the Colonial Condition", in Frantz Fanon, *Black Skin, White Masks*, trans. Charles Lam Markmann, London: Pluto, 1986, vii–xxv, p.xxiv.

21   Irene L. Gendzier, *Frantz Fanon: A Critical Study*, New York & Toronto: Pantheon, 1973, p.200.

22   Homi K. Bhabha, "Foreword: Remembering Fanon, Self, Psyche and the Colonial Condition", p.xxiii.

23   Shahla Haeri, "Obedience versus Autonomy: Women and Fundamentalism in Iran and Pakistan", in *The Globalization Reader*, ed. Frank J. Lechner and John Boli, Oxford: Blackwell, 2004, 348–56, p.355.

24   Ruth Robbins, *Literary Feminisms*, Houndmills, Basingstoke & London: Macmillan, 2000, p.188.

25   Quoted in Richard J. Lane, *The Routledge Concise History of Canadian Literature*, Abingdon, Oxon & New York: Routledge, 2011, p.204.

26   Candida N. Hepworth, "Chicano/a Literature: 'An Active Interanimating of Competing Discourses'", in *Post-Colonial Literatures: Expanding the Canon*, Deborah Madsen, ed., London: Pluto, 1999, 164–79, p.170.

27   Candida N. Hepworth, "Chicano/a Literature: 'An Active Interanimating of Competing Discourses'", p.170.

28   Julie Rivkin and Michael Ryan, eds., *Literary Theory: An Anthology*, Oxford: Blackwell, 2004, p.961.

29   Quoted in Richard J. Lane, *The Routledge Concise History of Canadian Literature*, p.142.

Chapter 37

Frantz Fanon

THE FACT OF BLACKNESS

It is always a shock to read the opening line of Frantz Fanon's text as he repeats the phrases which situate him as a human being in a nexus of racial prejudice, colonial history, and social/ psychological mythology. Fanon is interpellated (which means being hailed and identified) by the racist phrases, in the process being transformed from an individual eagerly seeking meaning, to an object of derision, scorn and fear. Fanon approaches this racist experience through multiple discourses (eugenics; psychoanalysis; history; phenomenology; aesthetics), the over-riding one being existentialism, following the philosophers Karl Jaspers and Jean Paul Sartre. The resulting hybrid discourse is rich in its allusions, intertexts and quotations, all of which provide temporary attempts at understanding how a person could be reduced to a series of racist stereotypes: temporary in the sense that the writing shares a particular experience with the reader, subjects it to analysis, and then moves on when the analysis proves inadequate to the experience itself. This procedure is existentialist, but it also follows the dialectical movement of consciousness in Hegel's *Phenomenology of Spirit*. Fanon, a leading psychiatrist, intellectual, writer, and eventually guerrilla fighter (for the Algerian National Liberation Front), argues that for a black person, interpellation leads to a fragmentation of subjectivity, one which is recomposed by white society. Attempting a bodily awareness, Fanon finds instead a "third-person consciousness", which is the "racial epidermal schema" (black versus white skin) that white society insists stands in for his physiological schema of self-understanding. Different versions of this schema exist: Fanon is identified with the history of slavery, with the indigenous people in the French colonies, but he rejects this in favour of asserting his own notion of subjectivity as a black man. Misidentified from without, Fanon compares these statements about his blackness to his own knowledge and self-certainty. Yet even with his own achievements registered, for example, his position as a doctor, there is always the racist epithet "negro" attached as a reduction and displacement of identity. Ironically, Fanon sees this as a doubly difficult position: reduced to the epithet, but always being subject to extra scrutiny within his profession, Fanon knows that this is a highly volatile subject position, liable to breakdown at the sign of a single error or mistake. What lies behind these existential experiences is the history of colonialism and the nineteenth-century pseudo-science of eugenics, which classified the world according to supposed hereditary qualities (criminality, low intelligence, disease); now known to be spurious science (Fanon calls it "a shameful science"), eugenics still feeds into racist discourse, in Fanon's time, and today. Perhaps, Fanon suggests, the answer to his dilemma lies in turning to the "Negritude" movement ("African" rather than white European culture). Here, and in his book *The Wretched of the Earth*, Fanon suggests that this option is also problematic, since he is once more reduced to a set of racial stereotypes: black "rhythm", the "irrational", the "tom-tom" beat of a "cosmic message" and so on; this parody collapses under its own weight, as Fanon reveals later on in *Black Skin, White Masks* that the Negritude approach merely makes him a developmental stage, which has the potential of fitting him right back into the prejudices from which he is trying to escape.

"**D**IRTY NIGGER!" OR SIMPLY, "Look, a Negro!"
I came into the world imbued with the will to find a meaning in things, my spirit filled with the desire to attain to the source of the world, and then I found that I was an object in the midst of other objects.

Sealed into that crushing objecthood, I turned beseechingly to others. Their attention was a liberation, running over my body suddenly abraded into nonbeing, endowing me once more with an agility that I had thought lost, and by taking me out of the world, restoring me to it. But just as I reached the other side, I stumbled, and the movements, the attitudes, the glances of the other fixed me there, in the sense in which a chemical solution is fixed by a dye. I was indignant; I demanded an explanation. Nothing happened. I burst apart. Now the fragments have been put together again by another self.

As long as the black man is among his own, he will have no occasion, except in minor internal conflicts, to experience his being through others. There is of course the moment of "being for others," of which Hegel speaks, but every ontology is made unattainable in a colonized and civilized society. It would seem that this fact has not been given sufficient attention by those who have discussed the question. In the *Weltanschauung* of a colonized people there is an impurity, a flaw that outlaws any ontological explanation. Someone may object that this is the case with every individual, but such an objection merely conceals a basic problem. Ontology—once it is finally admitted as leaving existence by the wayside—does not permit us to understand the being of the black man. For not only must the black man be black; he must be black in relation to the white man. Some critics will take it on themselves to remind us that this proposition has a converse. I say that this is false. The black man has no ontological resistance in the eyes of the white man. Overnight the Negro has been given two frames of reference within which he has had to place himself. His metaphysics, or, less pretentiously, his customs and the sources on which they were based, were wiped out because they were in conflict with a civilization that he did not know and that imposed itself on him.

The black man among his own in the twentieth century does not know at what moment his inferiority comes into being through the other. Of course I have talked about the black problem with friends, or, more rarely, with American Negroes. Together we protested, we asserted the equality of all men in the world. In the Antilles there was also that little gulf that exists among the almost-white, the mulatto, and the nigger. But I was satisfied with an intellectual understanding of these differences. It was not really dramatic. And then. . . .

And then the occasion arose when I had to meet the white man's eyes. An unfamiliar weight burdened me. The real world challenged my claims. In the white world the man of color encounters difficulties in the development of his bodily schema. Consciousness of the body is solely a negating activity. It is a third-person consciousness. The body is surrounded by an atmosphere of certain uncertainty. I know that if I want to smoke, I shall have to reach out my right arm and take the pack of cigarettes lying at the other end of the table. The matches, however, are in the drawer on the left, and I shall have to lean back slightly. And all these movements are made not out of habit but out of implicit knowledge. A slow composition of my *self* as a body in the middle of a spatial and temporal world—such seems to be the schema. It does not impose itself on me; it is, rather, a definitive structuring of the self and of the world—definitive because it creates a real dialectic between my body and the world.

For several years certain laboratories have been trying to produce a serum for "denegrification"; with all the earnestness in the world, laboratories have sterilized their test tubes, checked their scales, and embarked on researches that might make it possible for the miserable Negro to whiten himself and thus to throw off the burden of that corporeal malediction. Below the corporeal schema I had sketched a historico-racial schema. The elements that I used had been provided for me not by "residual sensations and perceptions primarily of a tactile, vestibular, kinesthetic, and visual character,"[1] but by the other, the white man, who had woven me out of a thousand details, anecdotes, stories. I thought that what I had in hand was to construct a physiological self, to balance space, to localize sensations, and here I was called on for more.

"Look, a Negro!" It was an external stimulus that flicked over me as I passed by. I made a tight smile.

"Look, a Negro!" It was true. It amused me.

"Look, a Negro!" The circle was drawing a bit tighter. I made no secret of my amusement.

"Mama, see the Negro! I'm frightened!" Frightened! Frightened! Now they were beginning to be afraid of me. I made up my mind to laugh myself to tears, but laughter had become impossible.

I could no longer laugh, because I already knew that there were legends, stories, history, and above all *historicity,* which I had learned about from Jaspers. Then, assailed at various points, the corporeal schema crumbled, its place taken by a racial epidermal schema. In the train it was no longer a question of being aware of my body in the third person but in a triple person. In the train I was given not one but two, three places. I had already stopped being amused. It was not that I was finding febrile coordinates in the world. I existed triply: I occupied space. I moved toward the other . . . and the evanescent other, hostile but not opaque, transparent, not there, disappeared. Nausea. . . .

I was responsible at the same time for my body, for my race, for my ancestors. I subjected myself to an objective examination, I discovered my blackness, my ethnic characteristics; and I was battered down by tom-toms, cannibalism, intellectual deficiency, fetishism, racial defects, slave-ships, and above all else, above all: "Sho' good eatin'."

On that day, completely dislocated, unable to be abroad with the other, the white man, who unmercifully imprisoned me, I took myself far off from my own presence, far indeed, and made myself an object. What else could it be for me but an amputation, an excision, a hemorrhage that spattered my whole body with black blood? But I did not want this revision, this thematization. All I wanted was to be a man among other men. I wanted to come lithe and young into a world that was ours and to help to build it together.

But I rejected all immunization of the emotions. I wanted to be a man, nothing but a man. Some identified me with ancestors of mine who had been enslaved or lynched: I decided to accept this. It was on the universal level of the intellect that I understood this inner kinship—I was the grandson of slaves in exactly the same way in which President Lebrun was the grandson of tax-paying, hard-working peasants. In the main, the panic soon vanished.

In America, Negroes are segregated. In South America, Negroes are whipped in the streets, and Negro strikers are cut down by machine-guns. In West Africa, the Negro is an animal. And there beside me, my neighbor in the university, who was born in Algeria, told me: "As long as the Arab is treated like a man, no solution is possible."

"Understand, my dear boy, color prejudice is something I find utterly foreign. . . . But of course, come in, sir, there is no color prejudice among us. . . . Quite, the Negro is a man like ourselves. . . . It is not because he is black that he is less intelligent than we are. . . . I had a Senegalese buddy in the army who was really clever. . . ."

Where am I to be classified? Or, if you prefer, tucked away?

"A Martinican, a native of 'our' old colonies."

Where shall I hide?

"Look at the nigger! . . . Mama, a Negro! . . . Hell, he's getting mad. . . . Take no notice, sir, he does not know that you are as civilized as we. . . ."

My body was given back to me sprawled out, distorted, recolored, clad in mourning in that white winter day. The Negro is an animal, the Negro is bad, the Negro is mean, the Negro is ugly; look, a nigger, it's cold, the nigger is shivering, the nigger is shivering because he is cold, the little boy is trembling because he is afraid of the nigger, the nigger is shivering with cold, that cold that goes through your bones, the handsome little boy is trembling because he thinks that the nigger is quivering with rage, the little white boy throws himself into his mother's arms: Mama, the nigger's going to eat me up.

All round me the white man, above the sky tears at its navel, the earth rasps under my feet, and there is a white song, a white song. All this whiteness that burns me. . . .

I sit down at the fire and I become aware of my uniform. I had not seen it. It is indeed ugly. I stop there, for who can tell me what beauty is?

Where shall I find shelter from now on? I felt an easily identifiable flood mounting out of the countless facets of my being. I was about to be angry. The fire was long since out, and once more the nigger was trembling.

"Look how handsome that Negro is! . . ."

"Kiss the handsome Negro's ass, madame!"

Shame flooded her face. At last I was set free from my rumination. At the same time I accomplished two things: I identified my enemies and I made a scene. A grand slam. Now one would be able to laugh.

The field of battle having been marked out, I entered the lists.

What? While I was forgetting, forgiving, and wanting only to love, my message was flung back in my face like a slap. The white world, the only honorable one, barred me from all participation. A man was expected to behave like a man. I was expected to behave like a black manor at least like a nigger. I shouted a greeting to the world and the world slashed away my joy. I was told to stay within bounds, to go back where I belonged.

They would see, then! I had warned them, anyway. Slavery? It was no longer even mentioned, that unpleasant memory. My supposed inferiority? A hoax that it was better to laugh at. I forgot it all, but only on condition that the world not protect itself against me any longer. I had incisors to test. I was sure they were strong. And besides. . . .

What! When it was I who had every reason to hate, to despise, I was rejected? When I should have been begged, implored, I was denied the slightest recognition? I resolved, since it was impossible for me to get away from an *inborn complex,* to assert myself as a BLACK MAN. Since the other hesitated to recognize me, there remained only one solution: to make myself known.

In *Anti-Semite and Jew* (p. 95), Sartre says: "They [the Jews] have allowed themselves to be poisoned by the stereotype that others have of them, and they live in fear that their acts will correspond to this stereotype. . . . We may say that their conduct is perpetually overdetermined from the inside."

All the same, the Jew can be unknown in his Jewishness. He is not wholly what he is. One hopes, one waits. His actions, his behavior are the final determinant. He is a white man, and, apart from some rather debatable characteristics, he can sometimes go unnoticed. He belongs to the race of those who since the beginning of time have never known cannibalism. What an idea, to eat one's father! Simple enough, one has only not to be a nigger. Granted, the Jews are harassed—what am I thinking of? They are hunted down, exterminated, cremated. But these are little family quarrels. The Jew is disliked from the moment he is tracked down. But in my case everything takes on a *new* guise. I am given no chance. I am overdetermined from without. I am the slave not of the "idea" that others have of me but of my own appearance.

I move slowly in the world, accustomed now to seek no longer for upheaval. I progress by crawling. And already I am being dissected under white eyes, the only real eyes. I am *fixed*. Having adjusted their microtomes, they objectively cut away slices of my reality. I am laid bare. I feel, I see in those white faces that it is not a new man who has come in, but a new kind of man, a new genus. Why, it's a Negro!

I slip into corners, and my long antennae pick up the catch-phrases strewn over the surface of things—nigger underwear smells of nigger—nigger teeth are white—nigger feet are big—the nigger's barrel chest—I slip into corners, I remain silent, I strive for anonymity, for invisibility. Look, I will accept the lot, as long as no one notices me!

"Oh, I want you to meet my black friend. . . . Aimé Césaire, a black man and a university graduate. . . . Marian Anderson, the finest of Negro singers. . . . Dr. Cobb, who invented white blood, is a Negro. . . . Here, say hello to my friend from Martinique (be careful, he's extremely sensitive). . . ."

Shame. Shame and self-contempt. Nausea. When people like me, they tell me it is in spite of my color. When they dislike me, they point out that it is not because of my color. Either way, I am locked into the infernal circle.

I turn away from these inspectors of the Ark before the Flood and I attach myself to my brothers, Negroes like myself. To my horror, they too reject me. They are almost white. And besides they are about to marry white women. They will have children faintly tinged with brown. Who knows, perhaps little by little. . . .

I had been dreaming.

"I want you to understand, sir, I am one of the best friends the Negro has in Lyon."

The evidence was there, unalterable. My blackness was there, dark and unarguable. And it tormented me, pursued me, disturbed me, angered me.

Negroes are savages, brutes, illiterates. But in my own case I knew that these statements were false. There was a myth of the Negro that had to be destroyed at all costs. The time had long since passed when a Negro priest was an occasion for wonder. We had physicians, professors, statesmen. Yes, but something out of the ordinary still clung to such cases. "We have a Senegalese history teacher. He is quite bright. . . . Our doctor is colored. He is very gentle."

It was always the Negro teacher, the Negro doctor; brittle as I was becoming, I shivered at the slightest pretext. I knew, for instance, that if the physician made a mistake it would be the end of him and of all those who came after him. What could one expect, after all, from a Negro physician? As long as everything went well, he was praised to the skies, but look out, no nonsense, under any conditions! The black physician can never be sure how close he is to disgrace. I tell you, I was walled in: No exception was made for my refined manners, or my knowledge of literature, or my understanding of the quantum theory.

I requested, I demanded explanations. Gently, in the tone that one uses with a child, they introduced me to the existence of a certain view that was held by certain people, but, I was always told, "We must hope that it will very soon disappear." What was it? Color prejudice.

> It [colour prejudice] is nothing more than the unreasoning hatred of one race for another, the contempt of the stronger and richer peoples for those whom they consider inferior to themselves, and the bitter resentment of those who are kept in subjection and are so frequently insulted. As colour is the most obvious outward manifestation of race it has been made the criterion by which men are

judged, irrespective of their social or educational attainments. The light-skinned races have come to despise all those of a darker colour, and the dark-skinned peoples will no longer accept without protest the inferior position to which they have been relegated.[2]

I had read it rightly. It was hate; I was hated, despised, detested, not by the neighbor across the street or my cousin on my mother's side, but by an entire race. I was up against something unreasoned. The psychoanalysts say that nothing is more traumatizing for the young child than his encounters with what is rational. I would personally say that for a man whose only weapon is reason there is nothing more neurotic than contact with unreason.

I felt knife blades open within me. I resolved to defend myself. As a good tactician, I intended to rationalize the world and to show the white man that he was mistaken.

In the Jew, Jean-Paul Sartre says, there is

> a sort of impassioned imperialism of reason: for he wishes not only to convince others that he is right; his goal is to persuade them that there is an absolute and unconditioned value to rationalism. He feels himself to be a missionary of the universal; against the universality of the Catholic religion, from which he is excluded, he asserts the "catholicity" of the rational, an instrument by which to attain to the truth and establish a spiritual bond among men.[3]

And, the author adds, though there may be Jews who have made intuition the basic category of their philosophy, their intuition

> has no resemblance to the Pascalian subtlety of spirit, and it is this latter—based on a thousand imperceptible perceptions—which to the Jew seems his worst enemy. As for Bergson, his philosophy offers the curious appearance of an anti-intellectualist doctrine constructed entirely by the most rational and most critical of intelligences. It is through argument that he establishes the existence of pure duration, of philosophic intuition; and that very intuition which discovers duration or life, is itself universal, since anyone may practice it, and it leads toward the universal, since its objects can be named and conceived.[4]

With enthusiasm I set to cataloguing and probing my surroundings. As times changed, one had seen the Catholic religion at first justify and then condemn slavery and prejudices. But by referring everything to the idea of the dignity of man, one had ripped prejudice to shreds. After much reluctance, the scientists had conceded that the Negro was a human being; *in vivo* and *in vitro* the Negro had been proved analogous to the white man: the same morphology, the same histology. Reason was confident of victory on every level. I put all the parts back together. But I had to change my tune.

That victory played cat and mouse; it made a fool of me. As the other put it, when I was present, it was not; when it was there, I was no longer. In the abstract there was agreement: The Negro is a human being. That is to say, amended the less firmly convinced, that like us he has his heart on the left side. But on certain points the white man remained intractable. Under no conditions did he wish any intimacy between the races, for it is a truism that "crossings between widely different races can lower the physical and mental level. . . . Until we have a more definite knowledge of the effect of race-crossings we shall certainly do best to avoid crossings between widely different races."[5]

For my own part, I would certainly know how to react. And in one sense, if I were asked for a definition of myself, I would say that I am one who waits; I investigate my surroundings, I interpret everything in terms of what I discover, I become sensitive.

In the first chapter of the history that the others have compiled for me, the foundation of cannibalism has been made eminently plain in order that I may not lose sight of it. My chromosomes were supposed to have a few thicker or thinner genes representing cannibalism. In addition to the *sex-linked,* the scholars had now discovered the *racial-linked.*[6] What a shameful science!

But I understand this "psychological mechanism." For it is a matter of common knowledge that the mechanism is only psychological. Two centuries ago I was lost to humanity, I was a slave forever. And then came men who said that it all had gone on far too long. My tenaciousness did the rest; I was saved from the civilizing deluge. I have gone forward.

Too late. Everything is anticipated, thought out, demonstrated, made the most of. My trembling hands take hold of nothing; the vein has been mined out. Too late! But once again I want to understand.

Since the time when someone first mourned the fact that he had arrived too late and everything had been said, a nostalgia for the past has seemed to persist. Is this that lost original paradise of which Otto Rank speaks? How many such men, apparently rooted to the womb of the world, have devoted their fives to studying the Delphic oracles or exhausted themselves in attempts to plot the wanderings of Ulysses! The pan-spiritualists seek to prove the existence of a soul in animals by using this argument: A dog lies down on the grave of his master and starves to death there. We had to wait for Janet to demonstrate that the aforesaid dog, in contrast to man, simply lacked the capacity to liquidate the past. We speak of the glory of Greece, Artaud says; but, he adds, if modern man can no longer understand the *Choephoroi* of Aeschylus, it is Aeschylus who is to blame. It is tradition to which the anti-Semites turn in order to ground the validity of their "point of view." It is tradition, it is that long historical past, it is that blood relation between Pascal and Descartes, that is invoked when the Jew is told, "There is no possibility of your finding a place in society." Not long ago, one of those good Frenchmen said in a train where I was sitting: "Just let the real French virtues keep going and the race is safe. Now more than ever, national union must be made a reality. Let's have an end of internal strife! Let's face up to the foreigners (here he turned toward my corner) no matter who they are."

It must be said in his defense that he stank of cheap wine; if he had been capable of it, he would have told me that my emancipated-slave blood could not possibly be stirred by the name of Villon or Taine.

An outrage!

The Jew and I: Since I was not satisfied to be racialized, by a lucky turn of fate I was humanized. I joined the Jew, my brother in misery.

An outrage!

At first thought it may seem strange that the anti-Semite's outlook should be related to that of the Negrophobe. It was my philosophy professor, a native of the Antilles, who recalled the fact to me one day: "Whenever you hear anyone abuse the Jews, pay attention, because he is talking about you." And I found that he was universally right—by which I meant that I was answerable in my body and in my heart for what was done to my brother. Later I realized that he meant, quite simply, an anti-Semite is inevitably anti-Negro.

You come too late, much too late. There will always be a world—a white world—between you and us. . . . The other's total inability to liquidate the past once and for all. In the face of this affective ankylosis of the white man, it is understandable that I could have made up my mind to utter my Negro cry. Little by little, putting out pseudopodia here and there, I secreted a race. And that race staggered under the burden of a basic element. What was it? *Rhythm!* Listen to our singer, Léopold Senghor:

> It is the thing that is most perceptible and least material. It is the archetype of the
> vital element. It is the first condition and the hallmark of Art, as breath is of life:

breath, which accelerates or slows, which becomes even or agitated according to the tension in the individual, the degree and the nature of his emotion. This is rhythm in its primordial purity, this is rhythm in the masterpieces of Negro art, especially sculpture. It is composed of a theme—sculptural form—which is set in opposition to a sister theme, as inhalation is to exhalation, and that is repeated. It is not the kind of symmetry that gives rise to monotony; rhythm is alive, it is free. . . . This is how rhythm affects what is least intellectual in us, tyrannically, to make us penetrate to the spirituality of the object; and that character of abandon which is ours is itself rhythmic.[7]

Had I read that right? I read it again with redoubled attention. From the opposite end of the white world a magical Negro culture was hailing me. Negro sculpture! I began to flush with pride. Was this our salvation?

Notes

1 Jean Lhermitte, *L'Image de notre corps* (Paris, Nouvelle Revue critique, 1939), p. 17.
2 Sir Alan Burns, *Colour Prejudice* (London, Allen and Unwin, 1948), p. 16.
3 *Anti-Semite and Jew* (New York, Grove Press, 1960), pp. 112–13.
4 *Ibid.*, p.115.
5 Jon Alfred Mjoen, "Harmonic and Disharmonic Race-crossings," The Second International Congress of Eugenics (1921), *Eugenics in Race and State,* vol. II, p. 60, quoted in Sir Alan Burns, *op. cit.,* p. 120.
6 In English in the original (Translator's note.)
7 "Ce que l'homme noir apporte," in Claude Nordey, *L'Homme de couleur* (Paris, Plon, 1939), pp. 309–10.

Chapter 38

Henry Louis Gates, Jr.

THE SIGNIFYING MONKEY AND THE LANGUAGE OF SIGNIFYIN(G)

Rhetorical difference and the orders of meaning

Building upon his research on a shared black cultural tradition, that of the playful, mediating "trickster" figure called in Nigerian Yoruba mythology Esu-Elegbara (but existing in many other indigenous belief systems throughout the world), Henry Louis Gates here examines the black American equivalent, the "Signifying Monkey" and the trope of Signifyin(g). Trickster, in diverse cultures, shares the trait of being a disruptive, trouble-making, powerful mythological figure, who at the same time brings about cultural development and change; he (she or it — trickster can cross genders) causes trouble between individuals or groups, but thereby he also brings about resolution, healing cultural divides. Trickster forms part of what Gates calls "black structures of meaning", something contributed to by Gates's original and timely scholarship in books such as *Figures in Black* (1987), *The Signifying Monkey* (1988), and *The Norton Anthology of African American Literature* (co-ed., 1997). Gates discusses the trope of Signifyin(g) in the first section of the extract, noting that Afro-American "Signification" exists in a parallel discursive world within white American cultural "signification". These words are homonyms—words spelt the same way, but having different meanings—distinguished by Gates with the capital "S" versus lower-case "s". The difference for Gates is that Signification works through a trickster discourse of repetition and difference, of politically charged rhetorical playfulness, a "chaos of ambiguity" which is quite different from white signification, made up of standard English, and the sign as mapped by Saussure (see Chapter 4). Saussure argued that society cannot change the coded meanings embodied by the signifier (sound image) and the signified (concept); Gates argues that the history of Afro-American slavery, and the counter-discursive aesthetics of Signifyin(g) which is revealed by the complex use of the vernacular (symbolized here by the oral dropping of the "g" in pronunciation of the word), does show that "the masses" can bring about changes in meaning. Charting this alternative Afro-American notion of the sign operating in the black vernacular, shows that Signifyin(g) is a "black act of (re)doubling" one which functions in analogous ways to Esu-Elegbara's trickster activities. The literary tales of the Signifying Monkey, then, act out Signifyin(g) as a "black trope of tropes", which means that it is a rhetorical schema upon and through which other instances of oppositional Afro-American aesthetics can be understood. Gates traces the Signifying Monkey tales back to slavery, and the production of narratives, poems, and music. In jazz, Signifyin(g) is illuminated through the techniques of revision, troping, pastiche, repetition and difference.

But rather than call Signifyin(g) a master trope (or "master's trope"), Gates calls the process a "slave's trope" since it subversively reverses the values of the colonial masters. Gates warns not to reduce Signifyin(g) to mere binary opposition: in the Signifying Monkey tales, there are usually three main actors: the Monkey, the Lion (his opponent), and the Elephant. The Monkey works through intermediaries, such as the Elephant, and he causes disruption followed by reconciliation; he hovers somewhere between being a mediating/anti-mediating force, one which is explored in a poetics of "daydreams", that is to say, Gates applies Freudian insights to argue that Signifying Monkey narratives are powerful daydreams of the "Black Other", whereby power reversals are complexly intertwined. Similarly, Signifyin(g) never simply overturns or frees itself from it symbiotic relationship with white discourse, since Gates's radical claim is that black and white discourses are co-constitutive, energetically bound to one another, creating in turn an American discourse that is founded on the slave's-trope, not on standard English.

> Some of the best dozens players were girls. . . . before you can signify you got to be able to rap. . . . Signifying allowed you a choice—you could either make a cat feel good or bad. If you had just destroyed someone or if they were down already, signifying could help them over. Signifying was also a way of expressing your own feelings. . . . Signifying at its best can be heard when the brothers are exchanging tales.
>
> H. Rap Brown

> And they asked me right at Christmas
> If my blackness, would it rub off?
> I said, ask your Mama.
>
> Langston Hughes

I

If Esu-Elegbara stands as the central figure of the Ifa system of interpretation, then his Afro-American relative, the Signifying Monkey, stands as the rhetorical principle in Afro-American vernacular discourse. Whereas my concern in Chapter 1 was with the elaboration of an indigenous black hermeneutical principle, my concern in this chapter is to define a carefully structured system of rhetoric, traditional Afro-American figures of signification, and then to show how a curious figure becomes the trope of literary revision itself. My movement, then, is from hermeneutics to rhetoric and semantics, only to return to hermeneutics once again.

Thinking about the black concept of Signifyin(g) is a bit like stumbling unaware into a hall of mirrors: the sign itself appears to be doubled, at the very least, and (re)doubled upon ever closer examination. It is not the sign itself, however, which has multiplied. If orientation prevails over madness, we soon realize that only the signifier has been doubled and (re)doubled, a signifier in this instance that is silent, a "sound-image" as Saussure defines the signifier, but a "sound-image" *sans* the sound. The difficulty that we experience when thinking about the nature of the visual (re)doubling at work in a hall of mirrors is analogous to the difficulty we shall encounter in relating the black linguistic sign, "Signification," to the standard English sign, "signification." This level of conceptual difficulty stems from—indeed, seems to have been intentionally inscribed within—the selection of the signifier "Signification" to represent a concept remarkably distinct from that concept represented by the standard English signifier, "signification." For the standard English word is a homonym of the Afro-American vernacular word. And, to compound the dizziness and the giddiness that we must experience in the vertiginous movement between these two "identical" signifiers, these two homonyms have everything to do with each other and, then again, absolutely nothing.[1]

In the extraordinarily complex relationship between the two homonyms, we both enact and recapitulate the received, classic confrontation between Afro-American culture and American culture. This confrontation is both political and metaphysical. We might profit somewhat by thinking of the curiously ironic relationship between these signifiers as a confrontation defined by the politics of semantics, semantics here defined as the study of the classification of changes in the signification of words, and more especially the relationships between theories of denotation and naming, as well as connotation and ambiguity. The relationship that black "Signification" bears to the English "signification" is, paradoxically, a relation of difference inscribed within a relation of identity. That, it seems to me, is inherent in the nature of metaphorical substitution and the pun, particularly those rhetorical tropes dependent on the repetition of a word with a change denoted by a difference in sound or in a letter (agnominatio), and in homonymic puns (antanaclasis). These tropes luxuriate in the chaos of ambiguity that repetition and difference (be that apparent difference centered in the signifier or in the signified, in the "sound-image" or in the concept) yield in either an aural or a visual pun.

This dreaded, if playful, condition of ambiguity would, of course, disappear in the instance at hand if the two signs under examination did not bear the same signifier. If the two signs were designated by two different signifiers, we could escape our sense of vertigo handily. We cannot, however, precisely because the antanaclasis that I am describing turns upon the very identity of these signifiers, and the play of differences generated by the unrelated concepts (the signifieds) for which they stand.

What we are privileged to witness here is the (political, semantic) confrontation between two parallel discursive universes: the black American linguistic circle and the white. We see here the most subtle and perhaps the most profound trace of an extended engagement between two separate and distinct yet profoundly—even inextricably—related orders of meaning dependent precisely as much for their confrontation on relations of identity, manifested in the signifier, as on their relations of difference, manifested at the level of the signified. We bear witness here to a protracted argument over the nature of the sign itself, with the black vernacular discourse proffering its critique of the sign as the difference that blackness makes within the larger political culture and its historical unconscious.

"Signification" and "signification" create a noisy disturbance in silence, at the level of the signifier. Derrida's neologism, "différance," in its relation to "difference," is a marvelous example of agnominatio, or repetition of a word with an alteration of both one letter and a sound. In this clever manner, Derrida's term resists reduction to self-identical meaning. The curiously suspended relationship between the French verbs *to differ* and *to defer* both defines Derrida's revision of Saussure's notion of language as a relation of differences and embodies his revision which "in its own unstable meaning [is] a graphic example of the process at work."[2]

I have encountered great difficulty in arriving at a suitably similar gesture. I have decided to signify the difference between these two signifiers by writing the black signifier in upper case ("Signification") and the white signifier in lower case ("signification"). Similarly, I have selected to write the black term with a bracketed final *g* ("Signifyin(g)") and the white term as "signifying." The bracketed *g* enables me to connote the fact that this word is, more often than not, spoken by black people without the final *g* as "signifyin'." This arbitrary and idiosyncratic convention also enables me to recall the fact that whatever historical community of Afro-Americans coined this usage did so in the vernacular as spoken, in contradistinction to the literate written usages of the standard English "shadowed" term. The bracketed or aurally erased *g,* like the discourse of black English and dialect poetry generally, stands as the trace of black difference in a remarkably sophisticated and fascinating (re)naming ritual graphically in evidence here. Perhaps replacing with a visual sign the *g* erased in the black vernacular shall, like Derrida's neologism, serve both to avoid confusion and the reduction of these two distinct sets of homonyms to a false identity and to stand as the sign of a (black) Signifyin(g) difference itself. The absent *g* is a figure for the Signifyin(g) black difference.

Let me attempt to account for the complexities of this (re)naming ritual, which apparently took place anonymously and unrecorded in antebellum America. Some black genius or a community of witty and sensitive speakers emptied the signifier "signification" of its received concepts and filled this empty signifier with their own concepts. By doing so, by supplanting the received, standard English concept associated by (white) convention with this particular signifier, they (un)wittingly disrupted the nature of the sign = *signified/signifier* equation itself. I bracket *wittingly* with a negation precisely because origins are always occasions for speculation. Nevertheless, I tend to think, or I wish to believe, that this guerrilla action occurred intentionally on this term, because of the very concept with which it is associated in standard English.

"Signification," in standard English, denotes the meaning that a term conveys, or is intended to convey. It is a fundamental term in the standard English semantic order. Since Saussure, at least, the three terms *signification, signifier, signified* have been fundamental to our thinking about general linguistics and, of late, about criticism specifically. These neologisms in the academic-critical community are homonyms of terms in the black vernacular tradition perhaps two centuries old. By supplanting the received term's associated concept, the black vernacular tradition created a homonymic pun of the profoundest sort, thereby marking its sense of difference from the rest of the English community of speakers. Their complex act of language Signifies upon both formal language use and its conventions, conventions established, at least officially, by middle-class white people.

This political offensive could have been mounted against all sorts of standard English terms – and, indeed, it was. I am thinking here of terms such as *down, nigger, baby,* and *cool,* which snobbishly tend to be written about as "dialect" words or "slang." There are scores of such revised words. But to revise the term *signification* is to select a term that represents the nature of the process of meaning-creation and its representation. Few other selections could have been so dramatic, or so meaningful. We are witnessing here a profound disruption at the level of the signifier, precisely because of the relationship of identity that obtains between the two apparently equivalent terms. This disturbance, of, course, has been effected at the level of the conceptual, or the signified. How accidental, unconscious, or unintentional (or any other code-word substitution for the absence of reason) could such a brilliant challenge at the semantic level be? To revise the received sign (quotient) literally accounted for in the relation represented by *signified/signifier* at its most apparently denotative level is to critique the nature of (white) meaning itself, to challenge through a literal critique of the sign the meaning of meaning. What did/do black people signify in a society in which they were intentionally introduced as the subjugated, as the enslaved cipher? Nothing on the *x* axis of white signification, and everything on the *y* axis of blackness.[3]

It is not sufficient merely to reveal that black people colonized a white sign. A level of meta-discourse is at work in this process. If the signifier stands disrupted by the shift in concepts denoted and connoted, then we are engaged at the level of meaning itself, at the semantic register. Black people vacated this signifier, then—incredibly—substituted as its concept a signified that stands for the system of rhetorical strategies peculiar to their own vernacular tradition. Rhetoric, then, has supplanted semantics in this most literal meta-confrontation within the structure of the sign. Some historical black community of speakers most certainly struck directly at the heart of the matter, on the ground of the referent itself, thereby demonstrating that even (or especially) the concepts signified by the signifier are themselves arbitrary. By an act of will, some historically nameless community of remarkably self-conscious speakers of English defined their ontological status as one of profound difference vis-à-vis the rest of society. What's more, they undertook this act of self-definition, implicit in a (re)naming ritual, within the process of signification that the English language had inscribed for itself. Contrary to an assertion that Saussure makes in his *Course*, "the masses" did indeed "have [a] voice in the matter" and replaced the sign "chosen by language." We shall return to Saussure's discussion of the "Immutability and Mutability of the Sign" below.[4]

Before critiquing Saussure's discussion of signification, however, perhaps I can help to clarify an inherently confusing discussion by representing the black critique of the sign, the replacement of the semantic register by the rhetorical, in Chart 1.

Whereas in standard English usage signification can be represented *signified/signifier* and that which is signified is a concept, or concepts, in the black homonym, this relation of semantics has been supplanted by a relation of rhetoric, wherein the signifier "Signification" is associated with a concept that stands for the rhetorical structures of the black vernacular, the trope of tropes that is Signifyin(g). Accordingly, if in standard English

$$\text{signification} = \frac{\text{signified}}{\text{signifier}} = \frac{\text{concept}}{\text{sound image}}$$

then in the black vernacular,

$$\text{Signification} = \frac{\text{rhetorical figures}}{\text{signifier}}$$

In other words, the relation of signification itself has been critiqued by a black act of (re) doubling. The black term of *Signifyin(g)* has as its associated concept all of the rhetorical figures subsumed in the term *Signify*. To Signify, in other words, is to engage in certain rhetorical games, which I shall define and then compare to standard Western figures . . .

It would be erroneous even to suggest that a concept can be erased from its relation to a signifier. A signifier is never, ultimately, able to escape its received meanings, or concepts, no matter how dramatically such concepts might change through time. In fact, homonymic

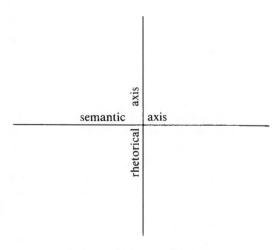

Chart 1. The Sign, "Signification"

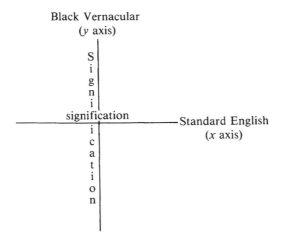

Chart 2. Black and Standard English

puns, antanaclasis, turn precisely upon received meanings and their deferral by a vertical substitution. All homonyms depend on the absent presence of received concepts associated with a signifier.

What does this mean in the instance of the black homonym *Signifyin*(g), the shadowy revision of the white term? It means, it seems to me, that the signifier "Signification" has remained identical in spelling to its white counterpart to demonstrate, first, that a simultaneous, but negated, parallel discursive (ontological, political) universe exists within the larger white discursive universe, like the matter-and-antimatter fabulations so common to science fiction. It also seems apparent that retaining the identical signifier argues strongly that the most poignant level of black-white differences is that of meaning, of "signification" in the most literal sense. The play of doubles here occurs precisely on the axes, on the threshold or at Esu's crossroads, where black and white semantic fields collide. We can imagine the relationship of these two discursive universes as depicted in Chart 2. Parallel universes, then, is an inappropriate metaphor; *perpendicular* universes is perhaps a more accurate visual description.

The English-language use of *signification* refers to the chain of signifiers that configure horizontally, on the syntagmatic axis. Whereas signification operates and can be represented on a syntagmatic or horizontal axis, Signifyin(g) operates and can be represented on a paradigmatic or vertical axis. Signifyin(g) concerns itself with that which is suspended, vertically: the chaos of what Saussure calls "associative relations," which we can represent as the playful puns on a word that occupy the paradigmatic axis of language and which a speaker draws on for figurative substitutions. These substitutions in Signifyin(g) tend to be humorous, or function to name a person or a situation in a telling manner. Whereas signification depends for order and coherence on the exclusion of unconscious associations which any given word yields at any given time, Signification luxuriates in the inclusion of the free play of these associative rhetorical and semantic relations. Jacques Lacan calls these vertically suspended associations "a whole articulation of relevant contexts," by which he means all of the associations that a signifier carries from other contexts, which must be deleted, ignored, or censored "for this signifier to be lined up with a signified to produce a specific meaning."[5] Everything that must be excluded for meaning to remain coherent and linear comes to bear in the process of Signifyin(g). As Anthony Easthope puts the matter in *Poetry as Discourse*,

> All of these absences and dependencies which have to be barred in order for meaning to take place constitute what Lacan designates as the *Other*. The presence of meaning along the syntagmatic chain necessarily depends upon the absence of the Other, the rest of language, from the syntagmatic chain.[6]

Signifyin(g), in Lacan's sense, is the Other of discourse; but it also constitutes the black Other's discourse as its rhetoric. Ironically, rather than a proclamation of emancipation from the white person's standard English, the symbiotic relationship between the black and white, between the syntagmatic and paradigmatic axes, between black vernacular discourse and standard English discourse, is underscored here, and signified, by the vertiginous relationship between the terms *signification* and *Signification,* each of which is dependent on the other. We can, then, think of American discourse as both the opposition between and the ironic identity of the movement, the very vertigo, that we encounter in a mental shift between the two terms.

The process of semantic appropriation in evidence in the relation of Signification to signification has been aptly described by Mikhail Bakhtin as a double-voiced word, that is, a word or utterance, in this context, decolonized for the black's purposes "by inserting a new semantic orientation into a word which already has—and retains—its own orientation." Although I shall return later in this chapter to a fuller consideration of this notion of double-voiced words and double-voiced discourse, Gary Saul Morson's elaboration on Bakhtin's concept helps to clarify what Bakhtin implies:

> The audience of a double-voiced word is therefore meant to hear both a version of the original utterance as the embodiment of its speaker's point of view (or "semantic position") *and* the second speaker's evaluation of that utterance from a different point of view. I find it helpful to picture a double-voiced word as a special sort of palimpsest in which the uppermost inscription is a commentary on the one beneath it, which the reader (or audience) can know only by reading through the commentary that obscures in the very process of evaluating.[7]

The motivated troping effect of the disruption of the semantic orientation of signification by the black vernacular depends on the homonymic relation of the white term to the black. The sign, in other words, has been demonstrated to be mutable.

Bakhtin's notion, then, implicitly critiques Saussure's position that

> the signifier . . . is fixed, not free, with respect to the linguistic community that uses it. The masses have no voice in the matter, and the signifier chosen by language could be replaced by no other. . . . [The] community itself cannot control so much as a single word; it is bound to the existing language.[8]

Saussure, of course, proceeds to account for "shift(s) in the relationship between the signified and the signifier," shifts in time that result directly from "the arbitrary nature of the sign." But, simultaneously, Saussure denies what he terms to be "arbitrary substitution": "A particular language-state is always the product of historical forces, and these forces explain why the sign is unchangeable, i.e. why it resists any arbitrary substitution." The double-voiced relation of the two terms under analysis here argues forcefully that "the masses," especially in a multiethnic society, draw on "arbitrary substitution" freely, to disrupt the signifier by displacing its signified in an intentional act of will. Signifyin(g) is black double-voicedness; because it always entails formal revision and an intertextual relation, and because of Esu's double-voiced representation in art, I find it an ideal metaphor for black literary criticism, for the formal manner in which texts seem concerned to address their antecedents. Repetition, with a signal difference, is fundamental to the nature of Signifying(g), as we shall see.[9]

II

The Poetry of Signification

The literature or tales of the Signifying Monkey and his peculiar language, Signifyin(g), is both extensive and polemical, involving as it does assertions and counterassertions about the relationship that Signifyin(g) bears to several other black tropes. I am not interested in either recapitulating or contributing to this highly specialized debate over whether or not speech act *x* is an example of this black trope or that. On the contrary, I wish to argue that Signifyin(g) is the black trope of tropes, the figure for black rhetorical figures. I wish to do so because this represents my understanding of the value assigned to Signifyin(g) by the members of the Afro-American speech community, of which I have been a signifier for quite some time. While the role of a certain aspect of linguistics study is to discern the shape and function of each tree that stands in the verbal terrain, my role as a critic, in this book at least, is to define the contours of the discursive forest or, perhaps more appropriately, of the jungle.[10]

Tales of the Signifying Monkey seem to have had their origins in slavery. Hundreds of these have been recorded since the early twentieth century. In black music, Jazz Gillum, Count Basie, Oscar Peterson, the Big Three Trio, Oscar Brown, Jr., Little Willie Dixon, Snatch and the Poontangs, Otis Redding, Wilson Pickett, Smokey Joe Whitfield, and Johnny Otis—among others—have recorded songs about either the Signifying Monkey or, simply, Signifyin(g). The theory of Signifyin(g) is arrived at by explicating these black cultural forms. Signifyin(g) in jazz performances and in the play of black language games is a mode of formal revision, it depends for its effects on troping, it is often characterized by pastiche, and, most crucially, it turns on repetition of formal structures and their differences. Learning how to Signify is often part of our adolescent education.

Of the many colorful figures that appear in black vernacular tales, perhaps only Tar Baby is as enigmatic and compelling as is that oxymoron, the Signifying Monkey.[11] The ironic reversal of a received racist image of the black as simianlike, the Signifying Monkey, he who dwells at the margins of discourse, ever punning, ever troping, ever embodying the ambiguities of language, is our trope for repetition and revision, indeed our trope of chiasmus, repeating and reversing simultaneously as he does in one deft discursive act. If Vico and Burke, or Nietzsche, de Man, and Bloom, are correct in identifying four and six "master tropes," then we might think of these as the "master's tropes," and of Signifyin(g) as the slave's trope, the trope of tropes, as Bloom characterizes metalepsis, "a trope-reversing trope, a figure of a figure." Signifyin(g) is a trope in which are subsumed several other rhetorical tropes, including metaphor, metonymy, synecdoche, and irony (the master tropes), and also hyperbole, litotes, and metalepsis (Bloom's supplement to Burke). To this list we could easily add aporia, chiasmus, and catechresis, all of which are used in the ritual of Signifyin(g).

Signifyin(g), it is clear, means in black discourse modes of figuration themselves. When one Signifies, as Kimberly W. Benston puns, one "tropes-a-dope." Indeed, the black tradition itself has its own subdivisions of Signifyin(g), which we could readily identify with the figures of signification received from classical and medieval rhetoric, as Bloom has done with his "map of misprision" and which we could, appropriately enough, label a "rap of misprision." The black rhetorical tropes, subsumed under Signifyin(g), would include marking, loud-talking, testifying, calling out (of one's name), sounding, rapping, playing the dozens, and so on.[12]

The Esu figures, among the Yoruba systems of thought in Benin and Nigeria, Brazil and Cuba, Haiti and New Orleans, are divine: they are gods who function in sacred myths, as do characters in a narrative. Esu's functional equivalent in Afro-American profane discourse is the Signifying Monkey, a figure who would seem to be distinctly Afro-American, probably derived from Cuban mythology which generally depicts Echu-Elegua with a monkey at his side. Unlike his Pan-African Esu cousins, the Signifying Monkey exists not primarily as a character in a narrative but rather as a vehicle for narration itself. Like Esu, however, the Signifying Monkey stands as the figure of an oral writing within black vernacular language rituals. It is from the corpus of mythological narratives that Signifyin(g) derives. The Afro-American rhetorical strategy of Signifyin(g) is a rhetorical practice that is not engaged in the game of information-giving, as Wittgenstein said of poetry. Signifyin(g) turns on the play and chain of signifiers, and not on some supposedly transcendent signified. As anthropologists demonstrate, the Signifying Monkey is often called the Signifier, he who wreaks havoc upon the Signified. One is signified upon by the signifier. He is indeed the "signifier as such," in Kristeva's phrase, "a presence that precedes the signification of object or emotion."

Alan Dundes's suggestion that the origins of Signifyin(g) could "lie in African rhetoric" is not as far-fetched as one might think. I have argued for a consideration of a line of descent for the Signifying Monkey from his Pan-African cousin, Esu-Elegbara. I have done so not because I have unearthed archeological evidence of a transmission process, but because of their functional equivalency as figures of rhetorical strategies and of interpretation. Esu, as I have attempted to show in Chapter 1, is the Yoruba figure of writing within an oral system. Like Esu, the Signifying Monkey exists, or is figured, in a densely structured discursive universe, one absolutely dependent on the play of differences. The poetry in which the Monkey's antics unfold is a signifying system: in marked contrast to the supposed transparency of normal speech, the poetry of these tales turns upon the free play of language itself, upon the displacement of meanings, precisely because it draws attention to its rhetorical structures and strategies and thereby draws attention to the force of the signifier.[13]

In opposition to the apparent transparency of speech, this poetry calls attention to itself as an extended linguistic sign, one composed of various forms of the signifiers peculiar to the black vernacular. Meaning, in these poems, is not proffered; it is deferred, and it is deferred because the relationship between intent and meaning, between the speech act and its comprehension, is skewed by the figures of rhetoric or signification of which these poems consist. This set of skewed relationships creates a measure of undecidability within the discourse, such that it must be interpreted or decoded by careful attention to its play of differences. Never can this interpretation be definitive, given the ambiguity at work in its rhetorical structures. The speech of the Monkey exists as a sequence of signifiers, effecting meanings through their differential relation and calling attention to itself by rhyming, repetition, and several of the rhetorical figures used in larger cultural language games. Signifyin(g) epitomizes all of the rhetorical play in the black vernacular. Its self-consciously open rhetorical status, then, functions as a kind of writing, wherein rhetoric is the writing of speech, of oral discourse. If Esu is the figure of writing in Ifa, the Signifying Monkey is the figure of a black rhetoric in the Afro-American speech community. He exists to embody the figures of speech characteristic to the black vernacular. He is the principle of self-consciousness in the black vernacular, the meta-figure itself. Given the play of doubles at work in the black appropriation of the English-language term that denotes relations of meaning, the Signifying Monkey and his language of Signifyin(g) are extraordinary conventions, with Signification standing as the term for black rhetoric, the obscuring of apparent meaning.

Scholars have for some time commented on the peculiar use of the word *Signifyin(g)* in black discourse. Though sharing some connotations with the standard English-language word, *Signifyin(g)* has rather unique definitions in black discourse. While we shall consider these definitions later in this chapter, it is useful to look briefly at one suggested by Roger D. Abrahams:

> Signifying seems to be a Negro term, in use if not in origin. It can mean any of a number of things; in the case of the toast about the signifying monkey, it certainly refers to the trickster's ability to talk with great innuendo, to carp, cajole, needle, and lie. It can mean in other instances the propensity to talk around a subject, never quite coming to the point. It can mean making fun of a person or situation. Also it can denote speaking with the hands and eyes, and in this respect encompasses a whole complex of expressions and gestures. Thus it is signifying to stir up a fight between neighbors by telling stories; it is signifying to make fun of a policeman by parodying his motions behind his back; it is signifying to ask for a piece of cake by saying, "my brother needs a piece a cake."[14]

Essentially, Abrahams continues, Signifyin(g) is a "*technique* of indirect argument or persuasion," "a language of implication," "to imply, goad, beg, boast, by *indirect* verbal or gestural means." "The name 'signifying,'" he concludes, "shows the monkey to be a trickster, signifying being the language of trickery, that set of words or gestures achieving Hamlet's 'direction through indirection.'" The Monkey, in short, is not only a master of technique, as Abrahams concludes; he *is* technique, or style, or the literariness of literary language; he is the great Signifier. In this sense, one does not signify something; rather, one signifies in *some way*.[15]

The Signifying Monkey poems, like the *ese* of the Yoruba *Odu*, reward careful explication; this sort of extensive practical criticism, however, is outside the scope of this book, as fascinating as it might be. The stanzaic form of this poetry can vary a great deal, as is readily apparent from the selections listed in this book's appendix. The most common structure is the rhyming couplet in an a-a-b-b pattern. Even within the same poem, however, this pattern can be modified, as in the stanzas cited below, where an a-a-b-c-b and an a-b-c-b pattern obtain (followed in the latter example by an a-b-a concluding "moral"). Rhyming is extraordinarily important in the production of the humorous effect that these poems have and has become the signal indication of expertise among the street poets who narrate them. The rhythm of the poems is also crucial to the desired effect, an effect in part reinforced by their quasi-musical nature of delivery.

The Monkey tales generally have been recorded from male poets, in predominantly male settings such as barrooms, pool halls, and street corners. Accordingly, given their nature as rituals of insult and naming, recorded versions have a phallocentric bias. As we shall see below, however, Signifyin(g) itself can be, and is, undertaken with equal facility and effect by women as well as men.[16] Whereas only a relatively small number of people are accomplished narrators of Signifying Monkey tales, a remarkably large number of Afro-Americans are familiar with, and practice, modes of Signifyin(g), defined in this instance as the rubric for various sorts of playful language games, some aimed at reconstituting the subject while others are aimed at demystifying a subject. The poems are of interest to my argument primarily in three ways: as the source of the rhetorical act of Signification, as examples of the black tropes subsumed within the trope of Signifyin(g), and, crucially, as evidence for the valorization of the signifier. One of these subsumed tropes is concerned with repetition and difference; it is this trope, that of naming, which I have drawn upon as a metaphor for black intertextuality and, therefore, for formal literary history. Before discussing this process of revision, however, it is useful to demonstrate the formulaic structure of the Monkey tales and then to compare several attempts by linguists to define the nature and function of Signifyin(g). While other scholars have interpreted the Monkey tales against the binary opposition between black and white in American society, to do so is to ignore the *trinary* forces of the Monkey, the Lion, and the Elephant. To read the Monkey tales as a simple allegory of the black's political oppression is to ignore the hulking presence of the Elephant, the crucial third term of the depicted action. To note this is not to argue that the tales are not allegorical or that their import is not political. Rather, this is to note that to reduce such complex structures of meaning to a simple two-term opposition (white versus black) is to fail to account for the strength of the Elephant.

There are many versions of the toasts of the Signifying Monkey, most of which commence with a variant of the following formulaic lines:

> Deep down in the jungle so they say
> There's a signifying monkey down the way
> There hadn't been no disturbin' in the jungle for quite a bit,
> For up jumped the monkey in the tree one day and laughed
> "I guess I'll start some shit."[17]

Endings, too, tend toward the formulaic, as in the following:

> "Monkey," said the Lion,
> Beat to his unbooted knees,
> "You and your signifying children
> Better stay up in the trees."
> Which is why today
> Monkey does his signifying
> *A-way-up* out of the way.[18]

In the narrative poems, the Signifying Monkey invariably repeats to his friend, the Lion, some insult purportedly generated by their mutual friend, the Elephant. The Monkey, however, speaks figuratively. The Lion, indignant and outraged, demands an apology of the Elephant, who refuses and then trounces the Lion. The Lion, realizing that his mistake was to take the Monkey literally, returns to trounce the Monkey. It is this relationship between the literal and the figurative, and the dire consequences of their confusion, which is the most striking repeated element of these tales. The Monkey's trick depends on the Lion's inability to mediate between these two poles of signification, of meaning. There is a profound lesson about reading here. While we cannot undertake a full reading of the poetry of the Signifying Monkey, we can, however, identify the implications for black vernacular discourse that are encoded in this poetic diction.

Signifyin(g) as a rhetorical strategy emanates directly from the Signifying Monkey tales. The relationship between these poems and the related, but independent, mode of formal language use must be made clear. The action represented in Monkey tales turns upon the action of three stock characters—the Monkey, the Lion, and the Elephant—who are bound together in a trinary relationship. The Monkey—a trickster figure, like Esu, who is full of guile, who tells lies,[19] and who is a rhetorical genius—is intent on demystifying the Lion's self-imposed status as King of the Jungle. The Monkey, clearly, is no match for the Lion's physical prowess; the Elephant is, however. The Monkey's task, then, is to trick the Lion into tangling with the Elephant, who is the true King of the Jungle for everyone else in the animal kingdom. This the Monkey does with a rhetorical trick, a trick of mediation. Indeed, the

Monkey is a term of (anti)mediation, as are all trickster figures, between two forces he seeks to oppose for his own contentious purposes, and then to reconcile.

The Monkey's trick of mediation—or, more properly, antimediation—is a play on language use. He succeeds in reversing the Lion's status by supposedly repeating a series of insults purportedly uttered by the Elephant about the Lion's closest relatives (his wife, his "mama," his "grandmama, too!"). These intimations of sexual use, abuse, and violation constitute one well-known and commonly used mode of Signifyin(g).[20] The Lion, who perceives his shaky, self-imposed status as having been challenged, rushes off in outrage to find the Elephant so that he might redress his grievances and preserve appearances. The self-confident but unassuming Elephant, after politely suggesting to the Lion that he must be mistaken, proceeds to trounce the Lion firmly. The Lion, clearly defeated and dethroned from his self-claimed title, returns to find the Monkey so that he can at the very least exact some sort of physical satisfaction and thereby restore his image somewhat as the impregnable fortress-in-waiting that he so urgently wishes to be. The Monkey, absolutely ecstatic at the success of his deception, commences to Signify upon the Lion, as in the following exchange:

> Now the Lion come back more dead than alive,
> that's when the Monkey started some more of his old signifying.
> He said, "King of the Jungles, ain't you a bitch,
> you look like someone with the seven-year itch."
> He said, "When you left [me earlier in the narrative] the lightnin' flashed and
>   the bells rung,
> you look like something been damn near hung."
> He said, "Whup! Motherfucker, don't you roar,
> I'll jump down on the ground and beat your funky ass some more."
> Say, "While I'm swinging around in my tree,"
> say, "I ought to swing over your chickenshit head and pee."
> Say, "Everytime me and my old lady be tryin' to get a little bit,
> here you come down through the jungle with that old 'Hi Ho' shit."[21]

This is a salient example of Signifying(g), wherein a verbal fusilade of insults spews forth in a structure of ritual rhetorical exchanges.

What happens next is also fascinating. The Monkey, at this point in the discourse deliriously pleased with himself, slips and falls to the ground:

> Now the little old Monkey was dancing all around
> his feet slipped and his ass must have hit the ground.

The startled Monkey, now vulnerable, seeks to repair his relationship with the Lion in the most urgent manner. So he begs initially:

> Like a streak of lightning and a bolt of white heat,
> the Lion was on the Monkey with all four feet.
> Monkey looks up with tears in his eyes,
> he says, "I'm sorry, brother Lion," say, "I apologize."
> The Lion says, "Apologize, shit," say, "I'm gonna stop you from your
>   signifyin'." (p. 165)

The Lion now turns on the Monkey (only, incidentally, to be tricked rhetorically again), not because he has been severely beaten but because he has been beaten, then Signified upon. Another text substitutes the following direct speech of the Lion for that quoted immediately above:

> [The Lion say], "I'm not gonna whip your ass 'cause that Elephant whipped mine,
> I'm gonna whip your ass for signifyin'." (p. 168)

The Monkey's trick of Signification has been to convince the hapless Lion that he has spoken literally, when all along he has spoken figuratively. The Lion, though slow-witted enough to repeat his misreading through the eternity of discourse, realizes that his status has been deflated, not because of the Elephant's brutal self-defense but because he fundamentally misunderstood the status of the Monkey's statements. As still another poem represents this moment of clarity:

> Said, "Monkey, I'm not kicking your ass for lyin',
> I'm kicking your hairy ass for *signifyin'*." (p. 172)[22]

The black term *to lie,* as J. L. Dillard, Sterling A. Brown, and Zora Neale Hurston amply demonstrate, signifies tale-telling and constitutes a signal form of Signifyin(g).[23] But it is the naming ritual, in which the Monkey speaks aloud his editorial recapitulation of the previous events and their import, which even the dense Lion recognizes to be his most crucial threat, and against which he must defend himself, especially since the Lion returns to the Monkey's tree initially, at least, to impose *his* interpretation on his interchange with the Elephant:

> Now the Lion looked up to the Monkey, "You know I didn't get beat."
> He said, "You're a lyin' motherfucker, I had a ringside seat."
> The Lion looked up out of his one good eye, said, "Lord, let that skinny bastard
> fall out of that tree before I die." (p. 172)

Which he, of course, does, only (in most cases) to escape once again, to return to Signify on another day:

> He said, "You might as well stop, there ain't no use tryin'
> because no motherfucker is gonna stop me from signifyin'." (p. 163)

While the insult aspect of the Monkey's discourse is important to the tales, linguists have often failed to recognize that insult is not at all central to the nature of Signifyin(g); it is merely one mode of a rhetorical strategy that has several other modes, all of which share the use of troping. They have, in other words, mistaken the trees for the forest. For Signifyin(g) constitutes all of the language games, the figurative substitutions, the free associations held in abeyance by Lacan's or Saussure's paradigmatic axis, which disturb the seemingly coherent linearity of the syntagmatic chain of signifiers, in a way analogous to Freud's notion of how the unconscious relates to the conscious. The black vernacular trope of Signifyin(g) exists on this vertical axis, wherein the materiality of the signifier (the use of words as things, in Freud's terms of the discourse of the unconscious) not only ceases to be disguised but comes to bear prominently as the dominant mode of discourse.

I do not cite Freud idly here. *Jokes and Their Relation to the Unconscious* and *The Interpretation of Dreams* have informed my reading of Signifyin(g), just as have Lacan's reading of Freud and Saussure, and Derrida's emphasis on the "graphematic" aspect of even oral discourse. Just as jokes often draw upon the sounds of words rather than their meanings, so do the poetry of the Signifying Monkey and his language of Signifyin(g). Directing, or redirecting, attention from the semantic to the rhetorical level defines the relationship, as we have seen, between signification and Signification. It is this redirection that allows us to bring the repressed meanings of a word, the meanings that lie in wait on the paradigmatic axis of discourse, to bear upon the syntagmatic axis. This redirection toward sound, without regard for the scrambling of sense that it entails, defines what is meant by the materiality of the signifier, its thingness. As Freud explained, there is nothing necessarily infantile about this, although infants, of course, engage in such paradigmatic substitutions gleefully. Similarly, there is absolutely nothing infantile about Signifyin(g) either, except perhaps that we learn to use language in this way in adolescence, despite the strangely compulsive repetition of this adjective as a pejorative in the writings of linguists about Signifyin(g).

If Freud's analysis of the joke mechanism is a useful analogue for Signifyin(g), then so too is his analysis of the "dream-work," which by now is so familiar as not to warrant summary here. The Signifying Monkey poems can usefully be thought of as quasi-dreams, or daydreams, dream narratives in which monkeys, lions, and elephants manifest their feelings in direct speech. Animals, of course, do not speak, except in dreams or in mythological discourse. As Freud puts it in *The Interpretation of Dreams*

> this symbolism is not peculiar to dreams, but is characteristic of unconscious ideation, in particular among the people, and it is to be found in *folklore,* and in popular myths, legends, *linguistic idioms,* proverbial wisdom and current jokes, to a *more complete extent* than in dreams.[24] (emphasis added)

The Signifying Monkey tales, in this sense, can be thought of as versions of daydreams, the Daydream of the Black Other, chiastic fantasies of reversal of power relationships. One of the traditional Signifying poems names this relationship explicitly:

> The Monkey laid up in a tree and he thought up a scheme,
> and thought he'd try one of his fantastic dreams. (p. 167)

To dream the fantastic is to dream the dream of the Other.

Because these tales originated in slavery, we do not have to seek very far to find typological analogues for these three terms of an allegorical structure. Since to do so, inescapably, is to be reductive, is to redirect attention away from the materiality of the signifier toward its supposed signified, I shall avoid repeating what other scholars have done at such great length. For the importance of the Signifying Monkey poems is their repeated stress on the sheer materiality, and the willful play, of the signifier itself.

Notes

1   Ferdinand de Saussure, *Course in General Linguistics,* ed. Charles Bally and Albert Sechehaye, trans. Wade Baskin (New York: McGraw-Hill, 1966), p. 66ff.

2   For a superbly lucid discussion, see Christopher Norris, *Deconstruction: Theory and Practice* (New York: Methuen, 1982), p. 32.

3   See my discussion of the word "down" in *Figures in Black: Words, Signs, and the Racial Self* (New York: Oxford University Press, 1986).

4   Saussure, *Course,* p. 71.

5   Jacques Lacan, *Ecrits: A Selection,* trans. Alan Sheridan (New York: Norton, 1977), p. 154.

6   Anthony Easthope, *Poetry as Discourse* (New York: Methuen, 1983), p. 37.

7   Quoted in Gary Saul Morson, *The Boundaries of Genre: Dostoevsky's "Diary of a Writer" and the Traditions of Literary Utopia* (Austin: University of Texas Press, 1981), p. 108.

8   Saussure, *Course,* p. 71.

9   Ibid., pp. 75, 72.

10   See, for example, Claudia Mitchell-Kernan, *Language Behavior in a Black Urban Community* (Monographs of the Language-Behavior Laboratory, University of California, Berkeley, No. 2), pp. 88–90; and Roger D. Abrahams, *Talking Black* (Rowley, Mass.: Newbury House Publishers, 1976), pp. 50–51.

11   On Tar Baby, see Ralph Ellison, "Hidden Name and Complex Fate: A Writer's Experience in the United States," *Shadow and Act* (New York: Random House, 1964), p. 147; and Toni Morrison, *Tar Baby* (New York: Knopf, 1981).

12   Geneva Smitherman defines these and other black tropes, then traces their use in several black texts. Smitherman's work, like that of Mitchell-Kernan and Abrahams, is especially significant for literary theory. See Geneva Smitherman, *Talkin and Testifyin: The Language of Black America* (Boston: Houghton Mifflin, 1977), pp. 101–67. And on signifying as a rhetorical trope, see Smitherman, *Talkin' and Testifyin'*, pp. 101–67; Thomas Kochman, *Rappin' and Stylin' Out: Communication in Urban Black America* (Urbana: University of Illinois Press, 1972); Thomas Kochman, "'Rappin' in the Black Ghetto," *Trans-Action* 6 (February 1969): 32; Alan Dundes, *Mother Wit from the Laughing Barrel: Readings in the Interpretation of Afro-American Folklore* (Englewood Cliffs: Prentice-Hall, 1973), p. 310; Ethen M. Albert, "'Rhetoric,' 'Logic,' and 'Poetics' in Burundi: Culture Patterning of Speech Behavior," in John J. Gumperz and Dell Hymes, eds., *The Ethnography of Communication, American Anthropologist* 66 (1964): 35–54. One example of signifying can be gleaned from the following anecdote. While writing this essay, I asked a colleague, Dwight Andrews, if he had heard of the Signifying Monkey as a child. "Why, no," he replied intently. "I never heard of the Signifying Monkey until I came to Yale and read about him in a book." I had been signified upon. If I had responded to Andrews, "I know what you mean; your Mama read to me from that same book the last time I was in Detroit," I would have signified upon him in return.

13   Julia Kristeva, *Desire in Language: A Semiotic Approach to Literature and Art* (New York: Columbia University Press, 1980), p. 31; Dundes, editor's note, *Mother Wit from the Laughing Barrel*, p. 310.

14   Roger D. Abrahams, *Deep Down in the Jungle: Negro Narrative Folklore from the Streets of Philadelphia* (Chicago: Aldine Publishing, 1970), pp. 51–52, 66–67, 264. Abrahams's awareness of the need to define uniquely black significations is exemplary. As early as 1964, when he published the first edition of *Deep Down in the Jungle*, he saw fit to add a glossary, as an appendix of "Unusual Terms and Expressions," a title which unfortunately suggests the social scientist's apologia.

15   Ibid., pp. 66–67, 264. (Emphasis added.)

16   Gloria Hall is a well-known professional storyteller, and she includes in her repertoire the Signifying Monkey poems.

17   Ibid., p. 113. In the second line of the stanza, "motherfucker" is often substituted for "monkey."

18   "The Signifying Monkey," *Book of Negro Folklore,* ed. Langston Hughes and Arna Bontemps (New York: Dodd, Mead, 1958), pp. 365–66.

19   *Lies* is a traditional Afro-American word for figurative discourse, tales, or stories.

20   Also known as "the dozens."

21   See Bruce Jackson, *"Get Your Ass in the Water and Swim Like Me": Narrative Poetry from the Black Oral Tradition* (Cambridge: Harvard University Press, 1974), esp. pp. 164–65. Subsequent references to tales collected by Jackson will be given in the text. Jackson's collection of "Toasts" is definitive.

22   A clear example of paradigmatic contiguity is the addition of the metonym "hairy" as an adjective for "ass" in the second quoted line.

23   J. L. Dillard, *Lexicon of Black English* (New York: Continuum, 1977), pp. 130–41; Zora Neale Hurston, *Mules and Men* (Philadelphia: J. B. Lippincott, 1935), p. 37; Sterling A. Brown, "Folk Literature," in *The Negro Caravan* (1941; New York: Arno, 1969) , p. 433.

24   Sigmund Freud, *The Interpretation of Dreams,* trans. James Strachey (1953; New York: Avon, 1965), p. 386.

Paul Gilroy

"NOT A STORY TO PASS ON"

Living memory and the slave sublime

Paul Gilroy ends his book on black modernity with a surprising topic: that of tradition. It is surprising because the previous five chapters explore the transitional and transnational diasporic spaces of the "Black Atlantic", that is to say, the physical and cultural routes between Africa, America and Europe, that produce a hybrid black aesthetic and double consciousness. "Tradition", however, is that which some thinkers oppose to such a black, hybrid modernity, so it needs re-examination in light of Gilroy's argument. Modernity generates such an aesthetic and cultural diversity that it appears a "maelstrom" which threatens a coherent and stable notion of black identity. Gilroy's aim is to develop a new notion of tradition, one which is not simply modernity's "polar opposite". This means that Afrocentrism—a way of tracing black identity back to African origins as they existed before colonialism and slavery, thereby "recovering" an authentic notion of self—also needs to be reconceptualized in the light of black modernist production. Previous groundbreaking work by Gilroy had focused on black British culture and racist state formations, in the books *The Empire Strikes Back: Race and Racism in 70s Britain* (ed., 1982) and *"There Ain't No Black In The Union Jack": The Cultural Politics of Race and Nation* (1987). In the extract from *The Black Atlantic*, Gilroy argues more broadly that Afrocentrism can lead to a downplaying, if not outright forgetting, of the experience and signification of slavery. Thus African "antiquity" meets contemporary black subjectivity, with the colonial experiences airbrushed from the picture. Gilroy critiques the linear conception of time apparent in Afrocentrism, in favour of decentred non-teleological (i.e., not end-goal oriented) notions of time and space, where slavery is not just a temporary and inconvenient "interruption", and neither is there a simple reversal of the white/black hierarchy. Perhaps Afrocentrism is really "Americocentricity" argues Gilroy, that is to say, the projecting of a bigger narrative of history and settlement, based upon some of the common tropes of the American dream, such as the primacy of family. Gilroy turns to Richard Wright, in this case his book *Black Power*, to develop a more complex notion of tradition and modernity, since Wright opposed the use of tradition if it meant a denial of democracy and the creative potential in black subject formation. Turning to the Afrocentric adoption of "traditional" African clothing and names, Gilroy notes both the positive and negative sides of a cultural reclaiming that is also a cultural invention, such as the alternative Afrocentric ritual for Christmas called "Kwanzaa" initiated by Dr. Maulana Ron Karenga in 1966. Such cultural reclaiming can also reinscribe outmoded gender values, or at the least, rigid notions of gender, race and the primacy of patriarchal family structures. Gilroy turns to another more fluid model of cultural reclaiming, articulated by contributors to the journal *Présence Africaine* (founded 1947), and especially at the second Congress of Negro Writers and Artists in Rome, 1959. The colonial experience of slavery and diaspora was regarded at the conference as contributing to racial identity, not as an experience to be forgotten or downplayed. In fact the conference developed a more nuanced notion of "diaspora time", one which included the experiences and technologies of modernity. Instead of a falsely unified fantasy of some originary authentic culture, this leads to a notion of "discontinuous and contemporary notions" of black Atlantic identity.

> Slavery was a terrible thing, but when black people in America finally got out from under that crushing system, they were stronger. They knew what it was to have your spirit crippled by people who are controlling your life. They were never going to let that happen again. I admire that kind of strength. People who have it take a stand and put their blood and soul into what they believe.
>
> Michael Jackson

> To articulate the past historically does not mean to recognise it "the way it really was." It means to seize hold of a memory as it flashes up in a moment of danger. Historical materialism wishes to retain that image of the past which unexpectedly appears to man singled out by history at a moment of danger. The danger affects both the content of the tradition and its receivers. The same threat hangs over both: that of becoming a tool of the ruling classes. In every era the attempt must be made anew to wrest tradition away from a conformism that is about to overpower it. The Messiah comes not only as the redeemer, he comes as the subduer of Antichrist. Only that historian will have the gift of fanning the spark of hope in the past who is firmly convinced that even the dead will not be safe from the enemy if he wins. And this enemy has not ceased to be victorious.
>
> Walter Benjamin

THE IDEA OF TRADITION HAS A STRANGE, mesmeric power in black political discourse. Considering its special force and usage seems an appropriate operation with which to begin the end of a book about blacks and modernity. Tradition crops up frequently in the cultural criticism that has cultivated a dialogue with black political discourse. It operates as a means to assert the close kinship of cultural forms and practices generated from the irrepressible diversity of black experience. This suggests that, in the hands of some black intellectuals and artists at least, the pursuit of social and political autonomy has turned away from the promise of modernity and found new expression in a complex term that is often understood to be modernity's antithesis. This can be explained partly through the threat which the maelstrom of modernity poses to the stability and coherence of the racial self. That self can be safely cultivated and remain secure behind the closed shutters of black particularity while the storms rage outside. We have already examined the work of several black writers who held out against this form of retreat and opted instead to embrace the fragmentation of self (doubling and splitting) which modernity seems to promote. However, this option is less fashionable these days. Appeals to the notion of purity as the basis of racial solidarity are more popular. These appeals are often anchored in ideas of invariant tradition and provisioned equally by positivistic certainty and an idea of politics as a therapeutic activity. The first aim of this chapter is to rethink the concept of tradition so that it can no longer function as modernity's polar opposite. This necessitates a brief discussion of the idea of Africentricity,[1] which may be useful in developing communal discipline and individual self-worth and even in galvanising black communities to resist the encroachments of crack cocaine, but which supplies a poor basis for the writing of cultural history and the calculation of political choices. The Africentric project has an absolute and perverse reliance on a model of the thinking, knowing racial subject which is a long way away from the double consciousness that fascinated black modernists. Its European, Cartesian outlines remain visible beneath a new lick of Kemetic paint: "Afrocentricity is African genius and African values created, recreated, reconstructed, and derived from our history and experiences in our best interests . . . It is an uncovering of one's true self, it is the pinpointing of one's centre, and it is the clarity and focus through which black people *must see* the world in order to escalate"[2] (emphasis added).

The idea of tradition gets understandably invoked to underscore the historical continuities, subcultural conversations, intertextual and intercultural cross-fertilisations which make the notion of a distinctive and self-conscious black culture appear plausible. This usage is important and inescapable because racisms work insidiously and consistently to deny both historicity and cultural integrity to the artistic and cultural fruits of black life. The discourse of tradition is thus frequently articulated within the critiques of modernity produced by blacks in the West. It is certainly audible inside the racialised countercultures to which modernity gave birth. However, the idea of tradition is often also the culmination, or centrepiece, of a rhetorical gesture that asserts the legitimacy of a black political culture locked in a defensive posture against the unjust powers of white supremacy. This gesture sets tradition and modernity against each other as simple polar alternatives as starkly differentiated and oppositional as the signs black and white. In these conditions, where obsessions with origin and myth can rule contemporary political concerns and the fine grain of history, the idea of tradition can constitute a refuge. It provides a temporary home in which shelter and consolation from the vicious forces that threaten the racial community (imagined or otherwise) can be found. It is interesting that in this understanding of the position of blacks in the modern, western world, the door to tradition remains wedged open not by the memory of modern racial slavery but in spite of it. Slavery is the site of black victimage and thus of tradition's intended erasure. When the emphasis shifts towards the elements of invariant tradition that heroically survive slavery, any desire to remember slavery itself becomes something of an obstacle. It seems as if the complexity of slavery and its location within modernity has to be actively forgotten if a clear orientation to tradition and thus to the present circumstances of blacks is to be acquired. Rebel MC's moving assertion in his track "Soul Rebel" that "there's more than just slavery to the history, we have dignity"[3] typifies the best of these revisionist impulses. However, there is a danger that, apart from the archaeology of traditional survivals, slavery becomes a cluster of negative associations that are best left behind. The history of the plantations and sugar mills supposedly offers little that is valuable when compared to the ornate conceptions of African antiquity against which they are unfavourably compared. Blacks are urged, if not to forget the slave experience which appears as an aberration from the story of greatness told in African history, then to replace it at the centre of our thinking with a mystical and ruthlessly positive notion of Africa that is indifferent to intraracial variation and is frozen at the point where blacks boarded the ships that would carry them into the woes and horrors of the middle passage. Asante dismisses the idea of racial identity as a locally specific, social, and historical construction by associating it with the outmoded and pejorative term "Negro":

> One cannot study Africans in the United States or Brazil or Jamaica without some appreciation for the historical and cultural significance of Africa as source and origin. A reactionary posture which claims Africology as "African Slave Studies" is rejected outright because it disconnects the African in America from

thousands of years of history and tradition. Thus, if one concentrates on studying Africans in the inner cities of the Northeast United States, which is reasonable, it must be done with the idea in the back of the mind that one is studying African people, not "made-in-America Negroes" without historical depth.[4]

Worse than this, black people are urged to find psychological and philosophical nourishment in the narrative of Africa expressed in rewritten accounts of civilisation's development from its African sources or the spurious security of knowing that our melanin provides us with a measure of biological superiority.[5]

Slavery, which is so deeply embedded in modernity, gets forgotten and the duration of a black civilisation anterior to modernity is invoked in its place: "Our anteriority is only significant because it re-affirms for us that if we once organized complex civilizations all over the continent of Africa, we can take those traditions and generate more advanced ideas."[6] This statement, also taken from the revised edition of *Afrocentricity,* is striking both for its tacit acceptance of the idea of progress and for the easy, instrumental relationship with tradition which it suggests. This gesture minimises the difficulties involved in locating tradition let alone transforming it. It is routinely complemented by the argument that the unique civilisation to which the West lays claim is itself the product of African civilisation. Cheik Anta Diop, George James, and others have demonstrated the power of these claims which even in their crudest form have the virtue of demystifying and rejecting "European particularism" dressed up "as universal."[7] A discussion of the extent to which these historiographical and linguistic claims can be substantiated would be a distraction here. The difficulties involved in projecting the typologies of modern racism back into a past where they are wholly irrelevant can be illustrated through the problems that arise in attempts to name the Egyptians black according to contemporary definitions rather than seeing them as one African people among many others. Martin Bernal's detailed reconstruction of the Hellenistic cults which articulated racism and anti-Semitism into nineteenth-century scholarship is a rare exception in a literature where some Africentric thinkers have come to share the historical assumptions and techniques of eighteenth-century racial metaphysics with their opponents.

Dealing equally with the significance of roots and routes, as I proposed in Chapter 1, should undermine the purified appeal of either Africentrism or the Eurocentrisme it struggles to answer. This book has been more concerned with the flows, exchanges, and in-between elements that call the very desire to be centred into question. By seeking to problematise the relationship between tradition and modernity, this chapter turns attention toward the particular conceptions of time that emerge in black political culture from Delany on. The desire to bring a new historicity into black political culture is more important than the vehicles that have been chosen to bring this end about.

The Africentric movement appears to rely upon a linear idea of time[8] that is enclosed at each end by the grand narrative of African advancement. This is momentarily interrupted by slavery and colonialism, which make no substantial impact upon African tradition or the capacity of black intellectuals to align themselves with it. The anteriority of African civilisation to western civilisation is asserted not in order to escape this linear time but in order to claim it and thus subordinate its narrative of civilisation to a different set of political interests without even attempting to change the terms themselves. The logic and categories of racial metaphysics are undisturbed but the relationship between the terms is inverted. Blacks become dominant by virtue of either biology or culture; whites are allocated a subordinate role. The desperate manner in which this inversion proceeds betrays it as merely another symptom of white supremacy's continuing power.

The idea of ready access to and command of tradition—sometimes ancient, always anti-modern—has become essential to the disciplinary mechanisms that today's stern traditionalists seek to exercise over diverse processes of black cultural production. Tradition provides the critical bond between the local attributes of cultural forms and styles and their African origins. The intervening history in which tradition and modernity come together, interact, and conflict is set aside along with the consequent implications of this process for the mediation of African purity. Tradition thus becomes the means to demonstrate the contiguity of selected contemporary phenomena with an African past that shaped them but which they no longer recognise and only slightly resemble. Africa is retained as one special measure of their authenticity. The enthusiasm for tradition therefore expresses not so much the ambivalence of blacks towards modernity, but the fallout from modernity's protracted ambivalence towards the blacks who haunt its dreams of ordered civilisation.

These features in the use of the term "tradition" take it outside of the erratic flows of history. In the work of some African-American writers, they sometimes sanction a crucial and regrettable slippage from the vernacular and the popular to the provincial and the parochial. In this sense what is known as Africentricity might be more properly called Americocentricity. Its proponents frequently struggle to place their histories onto a bigger diaspora web[9] but have no inhibitions about claiming a special status for their particular version of African culture.[10] It might be possible to demonstrate that the trope of family which is such a recurrent feature of their discourse is itself a characteristically American means for comprehending the limits and dynamics of racial community.[11]

In the light of these problems, this concluding chapter tries to integrate the *spatial* focus on the diaspora idea that has dominated earlier sections of this book with the diaspora temporality and historicity, memory and narrativity that are the articulating principles of the black political countercultures that grew inside modernity in a distinctive relationship of antagonistic indebtedness. It proceeds by querying the importance that has become attached to the idea of tradition in this area of cultural critique, history, and politics. In moving toward a different and more modest formulation of tradition, it asks initially whether the premium placed on duration and generation can itself be read as a response to the turbulent patterns of modern social life that have taken blacks from Africa via slavery into an incompletely realised democracy that racialises and thus frequently withholds the loudly proclaimed benefits of modern citizenship.

In the previous chapter, we encountered Richard Wright emphasising that tradition "is no longer a guide" for the creative aspirations of black artists. The idea that there might be a single, straight road from tradition to modernity was both repudiated and rehabilitated by Wright. His confusion is symptomatic of more than his own ambivalence towards modernity and the precise sense of modernity's aporias that we have already seen governing the radical political movements in which he located himself. For him, in America or Europe, modernity emerged at best as a fleeting respite from the barbarity that is endemic to human civilisation. This barbarity is underlined not only by slavery but by the brutal and unjust social order of the Jim Crow South where he grew up. However, as his grasp of the fatal complicity of technology and imperialism evolved in conjunction with his involvement with Africa and anti-colonial struggles, Wright's position shifted in that he grew to identify the forces of tradition explicitly as an enemy. They fetter black progress towards the limited, unjust, and incomplete democracy that may be the best outcome currently available. The West is bound to pursue new modes of unfreedom, and, recognising the dangers involved, Wright urged the "developing countries" to experiment with their history and autonomy and undertake a gamble against making the same catastrophic mistakes that had emerged from modernisation elsewhere. The open letter to Kwame Nkrumah which concludes his important and neglected book *Black Power* is a piece of writing that seems to re-engage with the issues of tradition and modernity that aroused his nineteenth-century predecessors. However, Wright's observations are made from an irreversibly post-colonial vantage point:

Above all feel free to improvise! The political cat can be skinned in many fashions; the building of that bridge between tribal man and the twentieth century can be done in a score of ways . . . AFRICAN LIFE MUST BE MILITARISED!

. . . not for war, but for peace; not for destruction but for service; not for aggression, but for production; not for despotism, but to free minds from mumbo jumbo.[12]

Similarly sceptical views of the value of the premodern can be glimpsed periodically in the work of the other writers, artists, and cultural activists whose work this book has cited or examined. But their distaste for the "mumbo jumbo" of traditional societies is complex and contradictory. Some nineteenth-century thinkers saw a means to redeem Africa through colonisation. Their love of English was profound and their ambivalence about the African's capacity for civilisation merits extended consideration. Some romanticised Africa as a homeland and a source of Negro sensibility, others didn't. Any scepticism born from their reflections on African barbarism can be matched precisely to the enthusiasms which other "new world" blacks have shown for the stable forms of social life that are identified with the image of the premodern African idyll. These responses to Africa transcode a debate about the value of western modernity that stretches down the years from Delany's railway-building schemes through Crummell's and Blyden's activities in Liberia via Du Bois and Wright in Ghana to contemporary disputes over the contending values of traditional and universal cultures.

In recent years the affirmative, pro-traditional side of this dispute has extended into the active reinvention of the rituals and rites of lost African traditions. African names are acquired and African garments are worn. It can be argued in support of these practices that the bodily fruits of imagined African sensibility can provide a bulwark against the corrosive effects of racism, poverty, and immiseration on individuals and communities. But it is deeply significant that ideas about masculinity, femininity, and sexuality are so prominent in this redemptive journey back to Africa. In a discussion of Kwanzaa, the invented traditional ritual substitute for Christmas, Dr. Maulana Karenga, an important architect of this political position, presents its value through the ideas of rescue and reconstruction: "As cultural nationalists, we believe that you must rescue and reconstruct African history and culture to re-vitalize African culture today . . . Kwanzaa became a way of doing just that. I wanted to stress the need for a reorientation of values, to borrow the collective life-affirming ones from our past and use them to enrich our present."[13]

This rescuing and reconstructive consciousness reaches it highest point of expression so far in Shahrazad Ali's best-selling book *The Blackmail's Guide to Understanding the Blackwoman*, where the reconstruction of an appropriately gendered self becomes the sine qua non of communal rehabilitation:

When the Blackwoman accepts her rightful place as queen of the universe and mother of civilization the Blackman will regenerate his powers that have been lost to him for over 400 years directly. The Blackwoman should not mimic the ideas and attitudes of Western civilization. The whiteman clearly understands that the preservation of the family order is what allows him to rule the world. This fact is not hidden knowledge. When the standards that preserve civilization are disregarded the result is a do-your-own-thing reckless and disorganized existence.[14]

Similar ideas about the interrelationship of time, generation, authenticity, and political authority animate the belief that the contemporary political and economic crises of blacks in

the West are basically crises of self-belief and racial identity. They can be rectified by therapeutic strategies that find their ready equivalent in Delany's proposals for racial uplift. These
crises are most intensely lived in the area of gender relations where the symbolic reconstruction of community is projected onto an image of the ideal heterosexual couple. The patriarchal family is the preferred institution capable of reproducing the traditional roles, cultures,
and sensibilities that can solve this state of affairs.[15] However, where it is not thought to be
reconstructable, the same ideas underpin controversial policy proposals like the demand for
special schools in which black boys, under the guidance of "positive male role models,"[16] can
receive the culturally appropriate forms of education that will equip them for life as
fine, upstanding specimens of black manhood, "the true backbone of the people," capable of
leading the community to its rightful position. The integrity of the race is thus made
interchangeable with the integrity of black masculinity, which must be regenerated at all
costs. This results in a situation where the social and economic crises of entire communities
become most easily intelligible to those they engulf as a protracted crisis of masculinity.[17]
Without wanting to undermine struggles over the meaning of black masculinity and its
sometimes destructive and anti-communitarian consequences, it seems important to reckon
with the limitations of a perspective which seeks to restore masculinity rather than work
carefully towards something like its transcendence. There is a notable though often inarticu-
late tension between therapeutic tactics like All's that are premised on the regeneration or
recovery of tradition and their global circulation through the most sophisticated means that
technological postmodernity can furnish. This is especially obvious where transnational
entertainment corporations unwittingly supply a vehicle for circulating these ideas in the
form of black popular music. These means of distribution are capable of dissolving distance
and creating new and unpredictable forms of identification and cultural affinity between
groups that dwell far apart. The transformation of cultural space and the subordination of
distance are only two factors that contribute to a parallel change in the significance of appeals
to tradition, time, and history. In particular, the invocation of tradition becomes both more
desperate and more politically charged as the sheer irrepressible heterology of black cultures
becomes harder to avoid.

For those of us endeavouring to make sense of these questions from black Atlantic rather
than African-American perspectives, it is particularly important that this problem of tradition, modernity, and their respective temporalities was directly confronted in the political
activities around the journal *Présence Africaine*. Its formation in 1947 was an important moment
in the developing awareness of the African diaspora as a transnational and intercultural multiplicity. The journal sought to synchronise the activities of Africanists and Africans with
blacks from the western hemisphere in a new and potent anti-imperialist configuration. It
was especially central to their second Congress of Negro Writers and Artists, held in Rome
in 1959 but planned and organised from Paris.[18] The central themes of this conference were
the unity of "Negro Culture" and the creative political responsibilities which fell upon the
caste of black intellectuals responsible for both demonstrating and reproducing that unity.
The proposed plan of the event (which bears Richard Wright's characteristic imprint) and its
published proceedings[19] demonstrate that the unity of culture was not thought to be guaranteed by the enduring force of a common African heritage. That heritage was to be acknowledged wherever it could be identified and is explored in the conference proceedings across a
number of different disciplines—from palaeontology to theology—but other discontinuous
and contemporary dimensions of the looked-for "racial" unity were also specified. The
"Colonial experience" was, for example, identified as an additional source of cultural synthesis and convergence. This key term was used broadly so as to include slavery, colonialism,
racial discrimination, and the rise of national(ist) consciousness(es) charged with colonialism's negation. Lastly, the technological economic, political, and cultural dynamics of

modernisation were identified by the conference planners as factors that were fostering the unity of black cultures by forcing them to conform to a particular rhythm of living.

Rough as it is, this threefold model seems to me to be significantly in advance of some of the contemporary approaches to the same problem of calculating the unity and diversity of black cultures. These days, the power of the African heritage is frequently asserted as if interpretation were unnecessary and translation redundant. The different flavour of the event in Rome was conveyed in the remarks given at its opening session by Alioune Diop, the Senegalese who is regularly identified as having initiated the *Présence Africaine* project. He began by exploring the significance of the congress's location for the meaning of the event:

> If it be true that we can bring out the features of our personality only through a dialogue with the West, what better representative spokesman for the West could we find than Paris or Rome? . . . These cities are responsible for that image of man which presided over the construction of the world; not necessarily man as he should be, but such as he is, portrayed in the beliefs of those who rule the world. It is according to definitions, principles and objectives of Western Culture that our lives are evaluated and controlled. We have every reason to pay attention to the evolution of Western Culture and to its inner laws. Ought we not then to seek, before the eyes of these cultural authorities, to uncover and set free the original outline and the inherent driving force of our personality?
>
> We are scattered over the four corners of the world, according to the dictates of Western hegemony . . . The effect of an African presence in the world will be to increase the wealth of human awareness and . . . to foster man's sensibility with richer and more human values, rhythms and themes . . .[20]

The ambivalence towards the West which these words convey is easier to bring into focus than the way that they communicate a tension around the teleology of black experience and the registering of time itself. Diaspora time is not, it would seem, African time. The words "original" and "inherent" belong to one cultural field while "evolution" and "scattered" operate in a different plane. Bringing them together requires a stereoscopic sensibility adequate to building a dialogue with the West: within and without.

Notes

1   "Africalogy is defined, therefore, as the Afrocentric study of phenomena, events, ideas and personalities related to Africa. The mere study of phenomena of Africa is not Africalogy but some other intellectual enterprise. The scholar who generates research questions based on the centrality of Africa is engaged in a very different research enquiry than one who imposes Western criteria on the phenomena . . . Afrocentric is perhaps the most important word in the above definition of Africalogy. Otherwise one could easily think that any study of African phenomena or people constitutes Africalogy." Molefi Kete Asante, *Kemet, Afrocentricity and Knowledge* (Trenton, N.J.: Africa World Press, 1990), p. 14.

2   Asante, *Afrocentricity*, rev. ed. (Trenton, N.J.: Africa World Press, 1989), p. viii. Asante suggests that Afrocentric psychological theories have close affinities with the work of Jung; see *Kemet*, pp. 180–83.

3   Rebel MC, "Soul Rebel," Desire Records, London, 1991.

4   Asante, *Kemet*, p. 15.

5   Frances Cress Welsing, *The Isis Papers: The Keys to the Colors* (Chicago: Third World Press, 1990); Richard King, *African Origin of Biological Psychiatry* (New York: Seymour Smith, 1990); Michael Eric Dyson, "A Struggle for the Black Mind: Melanin Madness," *Emerge* 3, no. 4 (February 1992).

6   Asante, *Afrocentricity*, pp. 106–7.

7   Ibid., p. 104.

8   I have found Julia Kristeva's remarks on different temporalities in "Women's Time" very helpful in framing this argument. Her essay appears in *Feminist Theory: A Critique of Ideology,* ed. Nannerl O. Keohane et al. (Brighton: Harvester Press, 1981), pp. 31–54. See also Homi K. Bhabha's adaptation of Kristeva's work to the post-colonial predicament in *Nation and Narration* (London: Routledge, 1990).

9   Asante's assertion that Fanon wrote "in the tradition established by Garvey and Du Bois" is one example of this; *Kemet,* p. 179. He also puzzles over the fact that black Americans are only 47 percent of new world blacks. All the "essential grounds" of his theory of Afrocentricity are drawn from African-American history; *see Afrocentricity,* pp. 1–30.

10   Kwame Anthony Appiah, *In My Father's House* (London: Methuen, 1992).

11   I attempt this in "It's a Family Affair," in Gina C. Dent, ed., *Black Popular Culture* (Seattle: Bay Press, 1992).

12   Bichard Wright, *Black Power: A Record of Reactions in a Land of Pathos* (New York: Harper and Brothers, 1954), pp. 346–47.

13   "A Dialogue with Karenga," *Emerge* 3, no. 3 (January 1992), p. 11.

14   Shahrazad Ali, *The Blackman's Guide to Understanding the Blackwoman* (Philadelphia: Civilized Publications, 1989), p. 40.

15   This evasive possibility was recently signified by its absence in the narratives of Clarence Thomas and Anita Hill, Mike Tyson and Desiree Washington.

16   "How Black Men Are Responding to the Black Male Crisis," *Ebony Man* (September 1991): 36.

17   "America, in the eighties was essentially about taking black men's jobs, lives—and souls. In fact, it was really a war about money and how it was used, a war about lies and how those lies were deployed to cover the strategy and tactics of the war makers." William Strickland, "Taking Our Souls," *Essence* 22, no. 7, 10th Annual Men's Issue (November 1991): 48.

18   The first congress had been held in the Amphitheatre Descartes at the Sorbonne in 1956.

19   *Présence Africaine,* no. 24–25 (February–May 1959).

20   Ibid., pp. 45–54.

Chapter 40

George Elliott Clarke

THE COMPLEX FACE OF
BLACK CANADA

George Elliott Clarke's review essay presents a personal and academic response to a key analytical report concerning black identity and community in Canada in the 1990s, beginning with his own existential account of interpellation in Kingston, Ontario. Like Fanon (see Chapter 37), whose identity is fixed by the child who exclaims when he sees him, calling out a racist name, Clarke is similarly fixed in place (*out of place* might be more accurate), when his skin colour is equated with the status of being a "foreigner". Clarke, Canada's leading professor of African-Canadian literary criticism and theory (as well as being an author and playwright), provides a personal genealogy across several generations to show the complexity of black Canadian—or African Canadian—identity, including his ancestral West Indian background and his ancestors' escape from slavery, in Virginia, by moving to Nova Scotia in 1813. As Clarke bluntly puts it, a Canadian Civil Liberties poll in the mid 1990s revealed "that 83 percent of Canadians did not know that slavery had been practised in pre-Confederation Canada." Clarke's existential and genealogical account of his own identity leads to the notion that African Canadian identity is not really accounted for by W.E.B. Du Bois's African American "double consciousness" (a split identity, between African and American; between racist stereotype and actual person; between African spirituality/myth and American materiality). Instead, Clarke posits a Canadian "poly consciousness", one which goes beyond binary oppositions, in favour of hybrid diversity. Yet this diversity also represents a statistical problem: that almost half of Canada's black citizens do not self-identify as such on census forms, for example, many black Haitians identify themselves as French, while a similar number of Jamaicans identity themselves as British. Clarke argues that people from "black-majority countries" often identify via class, and that it is only within a North American context that race becomes a primary identifier. More positively, however, such a response to census requests is indicative of ethnic and cultural diversity within black communities in Canada, even though the majority of African Canadians live in the large urban centres of Toronto and Montreal. Clarke also suggests that such self-identification with one's country of origin may be indicative of a common bond between more recent immigrants and Canadian-born blacks: that of experiencing, and developing shared strategies to resist widespread racism. To prove this point, Clarke details some of the key educational achievements of black Canadians, noting how academic attainment has not translated into job security or high-level appointments in government or industry. Gender differences in academic attainment may be accounted for by a stress on male achievement within an African context, different immigration policies (at one time favouring, for example, Caribbean women who were trained as domestics), and visiting students choosing to stay in Canada once they have graduated. Clarke stresses, however, that the bigger point to be made is that while black Canadians have the same levels of academic achievement as the Canadian population as a whole, they suffer more widespread unemployment; as he argues: "Systematic racism must lie behind these statistics". Throughout the essay Clarke provides a number of references to key fictional and historical African Canadian texts which both enrich his analysis of the report, and point the way towards a deeper understanding of race in Canada.

Review of *Diversity, Mobility and Change: The Dynamics of Black Communities in Canada*, by James L. Torczyner et al. [Montreal]: McGill Consortium for Ethnicity and Strategic Social Planning, 1997.

A FEW SUMMERS AGO, VIA RAIL offered an enticing 50 per cent fare reduction for foreign visitors to Canada, but did not advertise the bargain, suspecting that it would anger Canadians whose taxes subsidize the corporation. I learned about the scheme while purchasing a ticket in Kingston, Ontario. The agent asked, stealthily, for my passport. I was puzzled. 'What do you mean, my passport?' She then advised me about the discount for foreigners, specifying that my 'American accent' marked me as an eligible passenger. I informed the agent that (as the *trés* white beer commercial says) 'I AM CANADIAN.' But it's never been simple to be a black in Canada.

My bloodlines run deep in this country. My father's father was West Indian, but his mother's father came to Nova Scotia from Virginia in 1898. My mother's ancestors — slaves liberated by British forces during the War of 1812 — voyaged to Nova Scotia, from Chesapeake Bay, in 1813. I was born, raised, and educated in Nouvelle-Écosse. I went to Expo 67, I sang along with Ian and Sylvia and the Great Speckled Bird, I wanted Robert Stanfield to win in '72. Either I am Canadian, or the word means nothing.

Then again, the VIA Rail incident was not about accent. Because my colour distinguishes me from most Canadians, most assume that I hail from 'somewhere else.' When someone asks what island I'm from, I reply, 'Cape Breton.' Moreover, Canadians are abysmally ignorant about African-Canadian history. For instance, a Canadian Civil Liberties Association poll, conducted in 1995, found that 83 per cent of Canadians did not know that slavery had been practised in pre-Confederation Canada.

To be black in Canada is, then, an existential experience. A constant interrogation of our belonging inculcates within us, not just the 'double consciousness' that the superb African-American intellectual W.E.B. Du Bois (pronounced 'Do Boyce' in the U.S.) posited for Black Americans, but a 'poly consciousness.' For as our blackness ranges from ivory to indigo hues, our heritages, ethnic allegiances, religions, and languages are also varied. In fact, African Canada, in its gorgeous, explicit diversity, is a microcosm of Canada.

A McGill study published this year provides both the most current demographic information about Canada's black communities and several surprising findings. Although I prefer the terms *African-Canadian* or *Africadian* — they capture the experiences of those from the United States, Africa, and Caribbean — the authors sought to understand the 'black experience' and how blacks fare in Canadian society. *Diversity, Mobility and Change: The Dynamics of Black Communities in Canada* was written by McGill professor of social work James L. Torczyner, along with colleagues Wally Boxhill, Carl James, and Crystal Mulder.

The report is a response to one consequence of African-Canadian diversity: the fact that almost half of us do not identify ourselves as 'Black' on Canadian census documents. True: 43 per cent of African-heritage respondents to the 1991 census listed themselves as

French or British, or as Barbadian, Ethiopian, Ghanaian, Haitian, Somali, Jamaican, Guyanese, Trinidadian/Tobagonian, *et cetera*, leading to a serious undercounting of African-heritage Canadians. Boxhill, a former Statistics Canada employee, recast the numbers to count the above groups as black. This means that, as of 1991, there were 504,290 blacks in Canada, not 366,625 as formerly counted.

These figures entail consequences, but, before I discuss them, I want to tease out an issue that seems to have eluded the study's compilers, namely, the reason for the failure of so many African Canadians to call themselves 'Black.' As Boxhill tells us in a fine essay, 'about half of the respondents born in Haiti – and, in all likelihood black – reported that they were French. A similarly high proportion of persons born in Jamaica reported that they were British.' These self-identifications are neither shocking nor disturbing, if we understand that anti-Africanism, the social construct that turns human beings into 'black' and 'white' (in the U.S. and Canada), is not a potent source for identity in Haiti or in Jamaica, the two countries which have contributed the largest numbers of African-heritage immigrants to Canada in the past thirty years. (Torczyner reveals that 44.2 per cent of all black persons in Canada immigrated in the past twenty years.)

As Québec writer Dany Laferrière's 1985 satire *Comment faire l'amour avec un nègre sans se fatiguer* takes uproarious pains to point out, it is only on the North American mainland that a Haitian becomes 'black,' or is expected to subscribe, instantly, to the white-black angst that plagues the white (and white supremacist) majority in the United States and Canada. In black-majority countries, social divisions occur around class and less so around race (though colourism – discrimination by light-skinned blacks against darker-skinned blacks – is a problem). The Barbados-born, African-Canadian writer Austin Clarke, in 1973, described the 'West Indian writer' as 'a man from a society ostensibly free of the worst pathologies of racialism, a man from a society into which Black nationalism had to be imported from American Blacks.' Clarke's comments underline the weirdness of white-versus-black constructs for many Caribbean emigrés. (I will never forget the chaos that ensued when Haiti-born Jean Alfred, a *péquiste* MNA, told a meeting of the now-defunct National Black Coalition of Canada, in Toronto, in May 1979, that he cared more about the liberation of Québec than he did about 'national black unity.' Conference delegates felt that the black community and its needs should be paramount.)

What all this means is that Canadian blackness is a complex identity, rich with contradictions and fissures. Certainly, the danger in talking about 'Canadian Blacks' is that one can elide the real differences among, say, a Vancouver Rastafarian, an Anjou Sénégalaise, and a 'Scotian' African Baptist. The Torczyner study skirts this problem, but only barely. Torczyner recognizes, in his informative essay, that there are 'unique regional agendas for the various Canadian Black communities.' Still, he tends to take the immigrant black experience, especially in Ontario and Québec (where 86.9 per cent of all 'Blacks' live), as the norm, even arguing that 'Black immigration' will 'determine something of the collective identity of Black persons in Canada.' Yet, the centuries-old African-heritage populations in the Maritimes, Québec, and southwestern Ontario are jealously insisting upon recovering and rejoicing in their histories. Torczyner does state that 'in Halifax, with its long history of Black settlement, more than nine out of ten persons in the Black communities were born in Canada, and the "Caribbean influence" is comparatively low.' But this knowledge does not pervade the study.

Too, once black immigrants have been settled for a long enough period in Canada, they also begin to confront the barriers that white supremacism erects against black achievement in this society, barriers that indigenous African Canadians understand intimately. A Trinidad-born, black scholar-friend told me recently that in celebrating a recent success of his with several Euro-Canadian friends, one of them said, after a few drinks, 'Well, David, you may have won a grant, but I'm still a white man.'

How does the fact that so many blacks identify themselves with where they came from, and not their colour, affect Canada? I foresee a *rapprochement* in which immigrant African Canadians who identify with their homelands establish an affinity with Canadian-born blacks and exchange strategies of resistance to racism, a common denominator of *black* experience. (Black cultures in Canada are diverse, but all black peoples living in this racialized nation-state experience racism.) These strategies include arguing vociferously against injustices and organizing to reduce the incidence of poverty and illiteracy.

The African-Canadian communities, accounting for only 3 per cent of the Canadian population, will have a more difficult time achieving solidarity than African Americans, who comprise 13 per cent of the American population. In Canada, the increasing numbers of second-generation blacks, living now within a white-majority context, have more in common with the experiences of indigenous African Canadians than with an increasingly remote Caribbean 'homeland.' Two writers who wonderfully evoke this sensibility are Montrealer Robert Edison Sandiford, the son of Bajan immigrants, in his short story collection *Writer, Spring, Summer, Fall: Stories* (1995), and also Calgary's Suzette Mayr, the daughter of German and Caribbean immigrants, in her novel *Moon Honey* (1995), in which the protagonist changes – at least psychologically – from white to brown. According to Torczyner, 85 per cent of all African-Canadian children, *circa* 1991, were born in Canada. They are, all of them, *indigenous* African Canadians.

Canada's blacks are primarily an urban people living in Montréal and Toronto. Boxhill reports that some 240,940 blacks live in Toronto, representing 47.8 per cent of the African-Canadian population; another 101,390 blacks live in Montréal, accounting for another 20.1 per cent of the total. Nevertheless, rural black enclaves still exist in Nova Scotia, New Brunswick, southwestern Ontario, and in Alberta and Saskatchewan. Halifax and Vancouver (with its 3.1 per cent of the African-Canadian population, that is, 15,385 souls) are crucial centres in their own right.

Undeniably, the concentration of blacks in Canada's two largest cities grants these populations some political and economic clout. Not unexpectedly, then, Ontario has sent blacks, beginning with Lincoln Alexander, to the House of Commons in every election since 1968; in contrast, the first Africadian (Black Nova Scotian) to enter Parliament, Gordon Earle, was only elected this past spring in Halifax, a city containing just 2.1 per cent of the African-Canadian population (that is, 10,560 souls). Though it was possible to elect a black, Leonard Braithwaite, to the Ontario legislature in 1963, the feat could not be accomplished in the Nova Scotia legislature until 1993, when Wayne Adams won the constituency of Preston (the largest all-black community in Canada).

As well as stressing diversity, Torczyner's review of the census data says much about mobility and adds to knowledge of the social circumstances of African Canadians. His statistics portray relative black success, despite the community's well-founded complaints of job, school, and housing discrimination as well as its justified charges of police brutality *contra* black males. (Two *causes célèbres* include the shooting of Anthony Griffin in Montréal in 1987 and the suffocation of Robert Gentles in Kingston Penitentiary in 1993.)

However, black men fare better educationally and economically in Canada than they do in the United States. Torczyner finds that 'Black men have marginally higher levels of educational attainment than do all men, all women, or Black women in Canada.' The explanation for this fact is, I wager, the premium that Caribbean and African governments place upon education, especially technical and scientific instruction, particularly for males. Searching the National Library of Canada for literary texts by black authors, I have often found, instead, droves of dissertations, in the sciences, by African-born doctoral candidates. The point is well illustrated by St Vincent-born author H. Nigel Thomas in *Spirits in the Dark* (1993), his first novel, in which the male protagonist is groomed for scholastic achievement by male elders in his society. Some 3.5 per cent African-Canadian men have graduate degrees – slightly more than the average of 3.0 per cent for Canadian men as a whole.

Another explanation lies in Canadian immigration policy, which at first favoured admitting only Caribbean women, only as domestics, and only later permitted the admission of black men, but with a bias for professionals. (Torczyner's discovery that there are 20,000 more black women than men in Canada is attributable to federal immigration rules. This point also explains, in part, the higher number of female-led, single-parent households among African Canadians than among Canadians as a whole.)

Furthermore, some Africans who entered Canada as students chose to remain here after they had completed their education. Too, many of the Haitians who fled the Duvalier dictatorships in the 1960s and 1970s represented their nation's intelligentsia. While Torczyner states that 'Black persons in Montreal had the highest rates of educational attainment when compared to Toronto and Halifax,' he may be referring to that fact. Moroever, the Africans who fled apartheid in South Africa, civil wars in Somalia and Ethiopia, and dictatorships in Uganda, Nigeria, and elsewhere tended to be well-educated members of their nations. Canada has gained – deliberately – from an epochal brain drain. One in five African Canadians is enrolled in university or has a bachelor's degree – which, at 20 per cent, is on par with the Canadian population as a whole.

When one examines employment opportunities, a strange paradox emerges. Blacks are as well educated as the average Canadian but suffer higher unemployment (15 per cent compared to the Canadian average of 10 per cent in 1991). Even university education isn't a guarantee of mobility. One in six black persons with a university degree was poor in 1991. While 7 per cent of all Canadians with bachelor's degrees were poor, the statistic for blacks is 17 per cent – the same as Canadians without a university degree. Systemic racism must lie behind these statistics. African Canadians are nearly absent from higher-paying jobs and senior management positions.

Blacks are less likely to be self-employed or supported by investments. Also, there is the depressing summation that 'Black persons in Canada earn less money on average than the Canadian population as a whole' ($20,617 per year or 15 per cent less than the Canadian average of $24,001). These statistics point again to systemic racism. In this regard, I see that a recent Canadian Human Rights Commission report shows that the federal Government has not been as aggressive as the private sector in hiring visible minorities. Only 4.5 per cent of the public service workforce consists of visible minorities, as opposed to 8.8 per cent of the employees of federally regulated companies (such as airlines, banks, radio and television stations, and telephone companies).

Further, despite the positive educational and employment indicators, and the fact that 'members of the Black community are less likely to be dependent on public assistance . . .' than is the population as a whole (10.6 per cent compared to 11.4 per cent), almost a third of all African Canadians, some 31.5 per cent of the population, lived below the Canadian poverty line in 1991, including 40 per cent of all African-Canadian children. These rates are appalling. They cry out for remedial action from all levels of government and NGO institutions, but also from the African-Canadian communities themselves. Torczyner's call, in his conclusion, for 'community organizing strategies to promote access to entitlements,' to ensure that eligible families receive mandated public supports, is one place to start. Also valuable is Torczyner's advice that African Canadians develop a 'national Black consensus.' This is easier said than done in a country that must toil to find a consensus on anything. Nevertheless, his promotion of 'a parliament of Black communities in Canada' is intriguing.

Diversity, Mobility and Change begins to answer, for Canada, a challenge that Du Bois issued to American sociologists in 1898 to study the 'Negro problems.' His rhetoric (the language of the day) is problematic, but his insight is valid. We can only truly weld together an African-Canadian people by studying intensively our conditions, from coast to coast to coast, across five and one-half time zones, two official languages, and a hundred ethnicities. Torczyner, Boxhill, James, and Mulder have made a remarkable stride in that direction.

The report isn't perfect. I wish, for instance, that the brief survey of African-Canadian history had referenced a few more texts, including Robin W. Winks's *The Blacks in Canada: A History* (1971), despite its American liberal blindness toward the substantive Canadian difference from the United States, and James Walker's *The West Indians in Canada* (1984). I also wish that ampler precision had been granted figures and dates in the historical essay. (For example, 1,200, not 2,500, Black Loyalists left Nova Scotia for Sierra Leone in 1792.) Discussing Black Canadian economic stats, Torczyner could have referred to Adrienne Shadd's 1987 study of black male employment and wage rates in Ontario and Nova Scotia as well as to Agnes Calliste's 1995 essay on black families in Canada. Peccadilloes and omissions aside, the McGill group merits kudos for taking a nicely wide-angle snapshot of the state of African Canada.

Chapter 41

Dara N. Byrne

THE FUTURE OF (THE) "RACE"

Identity, discourse and the rise of computer-mediated public spheres

With the rise of web sites dedicated to specific ethnic groups, which occurred in the first major wave of internet social networking, new practices that engage in defining and articulating community consensus emerged, with a uniquely produced computer-mediated public sphere. While much larger social networking sites have dominated the second wave of internet development, ethnically dedicated sites are still highly functional and active, providing a technological modern day "hush harbor" (a term from the slavery era in the US, meaning a public place where slaves gathered to surreptitiously engage in dialogue and debate). Dara N. Byrne, a professor at The City University of New York, with specialisms in media and intercultural communication, focuses on the sites AsianAvenue, BlackPlanet and MiGente (a Latino site), and the critical "discursive exchanges" concerning race and ethnicity that form a part of these digital domains. Racial identity is regarded in the light of new technologies and poststructuralist theories of subjectivity as occurring where rhetorical articulations intersect. Byrne notes how researchers have moved from Sherry Turkle's notion of parallel virtual and real worlds, to that of Emily Noelle Ignacio's trope of "perpendicular" lives, i.e., both worlds create authentic realities for the participants. Social networking sites also facilitate a doubled state of involvement: as producer and consumer, thus as much as these sites facilitate community development, they also function as zones for targeted corporate marketing. Byrne suggests that they are reciprocal "gift economies" whereby users have given up certain commercial rights in exchange for community rights, and these have been used to great effect by black groups, such as Naijanet (a Nigerian site that facilitates "diasporan interconnectivity") and the site that helped coordinate the Million Woman March in the US in 1997. This digital meeting of minds retains, if not contributes, to what John Rawls calls "private interests", that which he argues need to be bracketed in favour of universal issues in the public domain; Byrne argues that his theory of consensus in the public sphere does not account for such ethnically dedicated web sites. To understand how race is articulated on these web sites, Byrne applies critical discourse analysis (CDA), which connects individual linguistic/semiotic expressions with the social, ideological backgrounds from which such expressions emerge. CDA examines power relations between groups, as well as the ways in which discursive formations create consensus concerning ethical, political and identity values. Using CDA, Byrne looks closely at listserv discussions concerning race or ethnicity, examining questions, discussion, and modes of labelling racial insiders/outsiders, as well as the process whereby participants learn "acceptable" racial behaviour from one another. The question of "essentialism" is key (certain universal attributes define racial identity), although as Byrne notes, it is highly performative, shifting as participants redefine "essences" revealing that they are in fact social constructs. Achieving communal consensus among participants does lead to dissenters being silenced or driven away from the listservs. Byrne's conclusion suggests, however, that even given her examples of public activism being supported by web sites, more needs to be done to convert the achievements of racial identity and social cohesion in the digital domain, converting to social change in the material world.

> Pretend you are a white person. Hmmm . . . Yahoo chat sites, Excite, Globe, noooo . . . I think I'll go to Asian Avenue. Why? Because I want to learn Asian culture, of course . . . How about the forums? The only thing a white person will contribute is a posting that will defend their position or undermine anything that would not be in their best interests, whether it helps Asians or not. Often they will appeal to an idealistic logic that has no basis in the real world. I think the minds and opinions of Asians are diverse enough to provide opposing views in all forums. So why are white people here? What do you think? My personal view is to let them hit on the girls. However, they should not be in the forums because they contribute NOTHING to the forum, except to taint the forums with their own self-serving ideas. Hell, they already got control of the media, is there any way for an Asian to express their [sic] ideas to other Asians without a white person corrupting the exchange of ideas?
>
> —Delpi[1]

The quotation above was taken from an April 2000 discussion thread on AsianAvenue.com, an Asian American Web site that serves as one of the most popular online social networks for the Asian diaspora. This polemical posting, contributed under the pseudonym "Delpi,"[2] though not unique in its subject matter, articulates Delpi's sense that AsianAvenue represents an Asian public sphere—an imaginary borderless place superimposed on "real" Web space. By questioning the motives of white participants, who are perceived as "corrupting the exchange of ideas," Delpi appeals to members of his community who, by virtue of being racial citizens, would likely share in the notion that this immaterial territory should be marked and defended. In fact, Delpi expresses a desire to ensure that the exchange of ideas remains pure, or at least racially honest and "authentic," by virtue of limiting the dialogue to its "real" citizens. Delpi's protective impulse is rather common in such discussion forums, where participation by racial others—particularly whites—is often viewed as an effort to thwart "nation" (and movement) building, identity formation, belonging, and ownership.

The forum is a locus of community vitality on such racially dedicated sites. Their discussion threads serve as relatively permanent recorded instances of discourse production, and they are central to public life as they offer members the unique opportunity to react and respond to a myriad of globally relevant and racially specific topics. Despite the popular claim that the Internet presents the possibility of a raceless space, participation on dedicated sites is growing exponentially. That just three of the most trafficked—AsianAvenue.com, Black-Planet.com, and MiGente.com—are home to more than 16 million subscribers[3] suggests that the dissolution of racial identification in cyberspace is neither possible nor *desirable*.

Theorizing about the ways in which dedicated sites serve as informal learning environments makes the case for studying them even more compelling, especially for minority youths. To understand more about what participants learn and teach each other about race and ethnicity online, this chapter focuses on the exchange of ideas, and public Discourse,[4] on dedicated Web sites. I explore prevailing views about race by analyzing the rhetorical dynamics of more than 3,000 discussion threads in the Heritage and Identity forums on AsianAvenue, BlackPlanet, and MiGente. Drawn from data accumulated over a seven-year period (August 1999 to August 2006), the analysis shows (1) how online communities are giving rise to new collective subjectivities unfolding across local, national, and international lines; (2) how real-world forces, such as the shift in racial tensions post-9/11, contribute to renewed commitments to racial identification and anti-imperialism; and (3) how these discourses accept and reject racial typologies. There are three parts to this chapter. The first part addresses the current impact of computer-mediated networks and new media on the development of dedicated public spheres online and youth participation therein. The second part presents an analysis of race-related discussion threads and is guided by a Critical Language Studies[5] framework, one that helps to illustrate the often hidden connections between language, power, and ideology.[6] The third part considers the role ongoing participation plays in the ways young people teach–learn about race and ethnicity.

When we consider the significant role played by online forums, listservs, and other computer-mediated social networks in the lives of minority youths, this phenomenon of dedicated sites takes on new meaning. This is especially pertinent given the desirability of youths as target markets for these Internet companies. Community Connect, Inc. (CCI), is the parent company of AsianAvenue, BlackPlanet, and MiGente. CCI's first site, AsianAvenue, was introduced in 1997, and in less than two years it became the leading Asian American Web site, garnering more than 2.2 million members by March 2002.[7] As a result of this success, BlackPlanet was launched in September 1999. In the first year, more than 1 million members joined BlackPlanet, and by April 2002 its community expanded to 5.3 million users.[8] Both AsianAvenue and BlackPlanet have consistently ranked among the highest trafficked sites for their respective ethnic markets. The third site, MiGente, was launched in October 2000, and is considered the most popular English-language community for Latinos. More than 500,000 members registered within the first two years.[9]

At the time of this writing, AsianAvenue had about 1.4 million members, BlackPlanet about 14.9 million, and MiGente about 2.5 million. Though the company does not release any statistics about its users, changes to platform design, special features, and advertisers over the years suggests that their interest is in appealing to a primarily sixteen-to twenty-four-year-old ethnic base. Advertisements and sponsorships have come from JCrew, Disney, Sony, Miramax Films, college preparation resource the Princeton Review, and the U.S. Army. Features have included dating subscription services, early career job searches in partnership with Monster.com, modeling discovery opportunities with Ford Models, and exclusive music content from singers like Janet Jackson, Mario Vasquez, and Enrique Iglesias, as well as rappers P. Diddy and Ludacris. Taking the largest share of the e-commerce pie among ethnic social networking companies, CCI expected to net about $20 million in revenues across all three sites in 2006, of which 15 percent was expected to come from its dating services, 50 percent from advertising, and 35 percent from job notices.[10]

As impressive as CCI's stake is in the young online ethnic market, some might consider participation in any one of the organization's sites a bit passé, given the current media and critical attention focused on the more recent crop of mainstream sites such MySpace, Friendster, and Facebook. Noted for their innovations in attracting mainstream youth, these more popular social networks have been so successful that any one of them has a membership base that is at least double the size of the three CCI sites combined. So marginalized is CCI from discussions on the impact of social networking on our youth, even on minority youth, that in a September 2006 BusinessWeek.com article, one media expert erroneously pegged CCI (launched in 1997) as at the forefront of the "second wave" of social networking sites, while naming Friendster (launched in 2002) as an example of a "first wave" site.[11] Admittedly, popularity and participation on the three CCI sites seemed to have peaked back in 2002. At that time, its largest site, BlackPlanet, had daily participation averaging in the millions. Today its figures are somewhere in the thousands of daily users. Likewise, the $20 million in revenues that places Community Connect in the top three of the social networking companies (based on sales) is all but a blip on NewsCorp/MySpace's $327-million radar. But when it comes to longevity, sustaining an interactive community, and the ability to continue recruiting younger participants over a seven-plus-year span, CCI seems to have figured out what some critics see as the real challenge facing those popular "first wave" sites.[12]

The ongoing Web presence in the lives of more than 16 million young Asian, black, and Latino users means that the CCI sites have become established pillars of their respective communities rather than the latest fads with unpredictable futures. These sites represent relatively stable homes for their target users; whether they are long-time members or are newly emerging voices, holding membership on at least one of the CCI sites is likely. This ongoing Web presence also means that these dedicated sites can serve as valuable resources for understanding the ways in which ethnic communities construct, stabilize, modify, and challenge individual and community senses of identity over a relatively long period of time. It must be noted that there are few other Web communities out there that can provide researchers with opportunities for exploring the ways in which sustained online interaction impacts a community's ideas about nation, culture, race, and ethnicity, much less those that are organized around youth expressions of these issues. In this sense, CCI sites bear as much relevance on these *au courant* discussions about youth participation on social networking sites as do MySpace and the others. Given that race and ethnicity are the principal features around which public life is organized on AsianAvenue, BlackPlanet, and MiGente, it is critical that scholarship begins to pay attention to the variety of ways young people publicly engage with concepts like these, especially with respect to the diasporic interconnectedness that such sites offer.

Ironically, the relative anonymity of dedicated sites like CCI's may be one of the key reasons they continue to thrive. Recent work by Vorris Nunley posits that unmonitored and unrestricted quasi-public places like African American barbershops and beauty salons, sites of what he calls African American hush harbor rhetoric, serve as important spaces for the production and exchange of community-centered knowledges.[13] Historically, the term *hush harbor* refers to the places where slaves gathered to participate in various aspects of public life, hidden, unnoticed, and especially inaudible to their white masters. As Nunley argues, the hushedness ensured the survival of this form of African American publicness and the rhetorical practices that serviced it.[14] Drawing loose parallels with Nunley's notion of hush harbor rhetoric, these little theorized dedicated sites that fly well below the mainstream radar have also, for years, been developing a sense of group cohesion and rhetorical practices that members perceive as being very valuable to their online lives because they are relatively free of *mass* participation by ethnic outsiders.

The importance of racially "pure" public spaces is an aspect of community life that CCI participants are especially not afraid to talk about. As Delpi so aptly describes in the posting quoted at the beginning of this chapter, the site is premised on an exchange of ideas in a specialized public sphere where racial identity serves as common ground for participants and as a primary determinant of one's right to participate. In this way, dedicated Web sites can be thought of as imaginary public spheres that overcome the complexities of real-world distancing by using computer-mediated technologies to cultivate critical spaces for discursive exchange.

Because this chapter proceeds from the perspective that discourse is governed by social practice, the primary concern of this study is analyzing the relationship between texts, processes, and social conditions as reflective of "both the immediate conditions of the situational context and the more remote conditions of institutional and social structures."[15] I believe that the application of a critical language theory is an essential tool for investigating the intersection between race, representation, and the production of social knowledge. Of equal importance are the ways in which online discourses intersect with young users, and addressing the dearth of research and critical analyses of the ways in which participants, the majority of whom are likely to be 16–24, articulate race and social interaction. The goal is to provide valuable insights into the disjunctures between local, national, and international identifications, which are essential for new thinking about intersections between globalization and diaspora cultures, and their relevance for youths of color.

Part I: new media publicness

> Latino, contrary to popular belief, is not a racial group. But yet, when referred to it is always put in comparison to racial groups such as whites, blacks, or asians [sic]. But Latinos come in all racial groups, from the average Negra in Santiago de Cuba to the indigenous peoples of Peru to its former Japanese President Fujimori. It seems every other day I get that annoying question: "What are you?" Well, human of course. My nationality? Well, American, born and raised. "No, I mean, really, what are you?" What question is really being asked here? Does the Spanish [sic] I speak change who I am? Does the cinnamon skin determine my personality or my capacity to learn and achieve? I am a mixture of many things, but I will always be me. So tell me, what are you really?—labellalatina1001[16]

For MiGente's labellalatina1001 (name changed), the fundamental question, "What are you?" is as personal as it is communal. The seemingly individual and self-reflective question, one that considers the relevance of race to her personality, also addresses the tensions between history, culture, nationhood, and identity formation. Notice that even though she is frustrated with the limitations of race as a means of grouping and categorizing others, she still begins her question by asserting its naturalness. As she explores the layers of her identity, labellalatina 1001 offers potential respondents an outline of the methodological implications of the question. In fact, by wondering about the connection between country and culture or skin color, personality and intelligence, labellalatina1001 articulates not only the richness of her racial identification but also its potential inadequateness. By structuring the question in this manner, the series of responses is inclined to engage with the history of (their) "race" and the interplay of dominant ideologies.

From the ongoing reverberations of Trujillo's reign in the Dominican Republic to the destructiveness of intraracial hate, respondents also present several theories about how the members of the community should conceptualize their race. Interestingly, most users' initial posts contextualize their personal experiences—signifying their degree of authenticity and authority—by describing their skin color, their bloodline, or their familiarity with back home (food, music, visiting every summer). In so doing, users rarely questioned another's right to contribute to the dialogue, whether or not they agreed with the one who thought "we are all African cuz [sic] we got the African blood," or whether they applauded the one who proclaimed, in all caps, "WE ARE [OUR] OWN RACE!!!!!"[17] In integrating various aspects of personal and community history, participants construct a framework for engaging with their Latinoness.[18] That this dialogue generated some forty-seven pages of threaded discussion and was sustained for more than a year, with members continually revising their definitions, indicates that their sense of Latinoness is neither bound to group consensus nor is it completely independent of it.

This dialogue is but one example of how online community forums serve as vital public spaces[19] for (re)thinking and (re)producing social knowledge and why new theorizing about new media publicness is necessary. Remarking on the relevance of poststructuralist theorists like Foucault, Lacan, Deleuze, and Guattari to digital media analysis, noted scholar Sherry Turkle observed that, as online interactions increasingly move us away from the computer's information-gathering purpose, the boundaries between real and virtual have become blurred, if not irrelevant.[20] Her study of Internet identity exemplifies what the French scholars named above meant when they argued that the self and other—fluid, unstable, and reflexive—are constituted in language. According to this position, language affects the character of human consciousness and conditions as it is conditioned by users' experiences.

So even when free to make up any identity online as Turkle discusses, the discourse that makes the characters real or "authentic" is inevitably structured by an interplay of sociocultural forces. As Lisa Nakamura shows, when white users play Asian characters in online games, they engage in a form of cyber tourism that is often guided by centuries-long Western fantasies of the exotic Oriental other.[21] In terms of poststructuralist theory, racial identity (or any form of identity, for that matter) is not a universal reality; rather, it is a sequence of intersecting rhetorics, each articulating some existing social knowledge. Like scripts, or what Stuart Hall describes as a "common sense" within culture, the ideologies undergirding such knowledge prescribe how users think, act, and function, the roles they play, the assumptions they make, and the ways in which they interpret and understand lived experiences.[22]

For more than fifteen years, a small group of academics has been writing about the intricacies of identity formation and community building online.[23] From Howard Rheingold's notion of the Internet as a virtual community to Anna Everett's early attention to the role networked connectivity might play for the black public sphere, this emerging discourse about race and ethnicity in online discourse questions how offline realities condition users online. But with the Internet and cyberlife now well into their teenage years, scholarship is increasingly faced with the implications of online realities conditioning users in the world offline. Waning in popularity is Sherry Turkle's view that users' online worlds are parallel with their offline worlds.[24] Some scholars, like Emily Noelle Ignacio, contend that Turkle's use of the term *parallel* gives the false impression that users engage in community and communication practices that are completely apart from their "real" lives, much like the way parallel lines in a diagram never touch one another.[25] Preferring the term *perpendicular* instead, Ignacio suggests that, because many Internet communities are also home to "real" offline communities[26]—as would clearly be the case for Asian-, black-, and Latino-targeted sites— these worlds are more likely to connect with each other than they are to be absolutely distinct. Serving as extensions of and intersections with each other, social and community-based interaction in both worlds play significant roles in shaping the identities of their users.

As we know well, the social and community-based dimension of the Internet has been flourishing for quite some time. From classmates.com (founded in 1995) to the MySpace boom in 2005, belonging to a social networking community has characterized much of the online experience, so much so that MySpace is known as "one of the major destinations on the Web" and has become a real competitor for the likes of MSN, Yahoo! and AOL.[27] When the site received more page views in 2005 than search engine giant Google, some bloggers humorously quipped that MySpace should launch its own record label and vie for world—aka media—domination.[28] In an almost prophetic turn later that year, MySpace, with Rupert Murdoch at the helm, announced its partnership with Interscope Records and the launch of a record label.[29] As MySpace CEO Chris Wolfe stated, "It's become a lot more than just a website. It's become a lifestyle brand."[30] Indeed, MySpace has become a lifestyle, with more than 80 million registered users and the resources to impact consumer and market interests alike. Further indicative of MySpace eclipsing a *mere* Web presence is its August 2006 partnership with Google. As Fox executives report, the typical reason users leave MySpace is to use a search engine, so by providing onsite googling capabilities, MySpace would be able to retain participation for longer periods of time and, of course, increase marketing potential. Evidently, there is immense value in sustaining online communities, as news of this deal drove both Google and NewsCorps market price up.[31]

In many ways, social networking sites like these straddle the debate between a viable youth-centered public sphere and a calculated corporate venture.[32] On the one hand, the popularity of these sites translates into vibrant communities with strong communications networks, especially through the use of tools such as instant messengers, chatrooms, Weblogs, and discussion boards that, among other things, increase the rapidity of discursive exchange. On the other hand, there are the commercial interests and the efforts to appeal to the broadest base of participants. When MySpace's Wolfe remarked that "radio has become less and less important,"[33] perhaps the only truism behind such a statement is that the decline in radio listenership is indicative of the audience's taste for real-time dialoguing and consumer-controlled content.

On social networking sites, community members serve both as producers and consumers, and have an equal ability to influence and to be heard. As Kollock notes, online participants are generally motivated by the anticipation of reciprocity, the opportunity to build their reputations and the reputations of the sites, and the sense that their contributions directly affect the pulse of the community.[34] Drawing on Rheingold's notion that the Internet is a gift economy,[35] Kollock explains that, in addition to the gratification of helping to build the site's culture, users are rewarded with full rights of access.[36] In this way, pride of membership is also about being an active producer as opposed to a passive or irrelevant consumer. But filling out demographic profiles, providing e-mail addresses, accepting cookies, and, in some cases, selecting from a list of potential advertisers (as is the case for joining BlackPlanet and MiGente), has become part and parcel of the gift exchange of this social experience. As the commercial stakes in online communities rise, so too will the interest in directing the attention of participants, or controlling the format of interaction, to suit the profit-making agendas of corporate partners. Nonetheless, the promise of new media publicness is compelling.

Functioning as vibrant public spaces—imagined territories developed by CCI made real in typed discursive exchanges—participants, who are stripped of their local exigencies, shape online communities to sometimes reflect, refine, reject, and reproduce social knowledge as informed by their offline experiences.[37] But new media publics also proffer well-defined discourse communities based around the sensibility of a purely online aesthetic with grammars of communication that dictate much more than when to use ROFL or LOL.[38] With the expectation of civic engagement and the de-centering of an absolute information source, the traditional sense of consensus is eroded, and is certainly not a prerequisite to community development. Aside from the obvious trend in establishing social communities, there is an additional effort toward sustaining them. First, sustaining refers to the effort to keep participants logged on and active for longer periods of time; this, in turn, increases the rate and quality of fresh content. Second, sustaining also refers to the longevity of the community on the whole. As noted before, some communities have maintained Web presences for more than ten years. While it may be too early to predict the material impact of these long-term Web cultures, the desire to carve out online niches, to territorialize Web space, and to commit to preserving them, speaks to the most basic need to stake out turf and plant roots.

More than a decade ago, some scholars were declaring that increasing trends toward globalization have dissolved territories,[39] that national borders have become immaterial, superfluous, or superseded;[40] that nationally organized politico-cultural identities are being "deterritorialised";[41] and that "supraterritorial" spaces based upon "distanceless, borderless interactions"[42] are de-centering the role of territorial and place-based socio-institutional forms. But this new media publicness and the overwhelming popularity of online communities is unequivocally tied to creating and defining borders, if only symbolically, and publicly laying claims to distinct identities. Signs of territory, and the accompanying rhetorics of "nation building," are more visible than ever.

My own recent experience lurking in a black chatroom on Yahoo! made it clear just how territorialized certain Web spheres have become. When a participant posted messages in Arabic, several members "shouted" (using a big font) to either stop or leave the chatroom because he had "no business speaking where you don't belong." Another remarked, "Why come online if no one can't understand you. Makes no since [sic]."[43] Angered over a breakdown in the exchange of ideas—the centerpiece of social networking—English-speaking members readily identified the poster as an outsider who likely had no real right to participate in that dialogue, and perhaps even on the English-language-dominated "World" Wide Web. That the poster could very well have been black did not seem to be important enough to grant him access, since—for these participants—a "real" community is clearly forged out of a common tongue. Though not deliberately intending to refer to a historically racialized term, the "tribal" impulse and the subsequent territorial responses exhibited here are difficult to ignore. As will be explored later in this chapter, instances where Asian, black, or Latino members vilify a common enemy—particularly white participants, as representatives of white power structures—are fairly prevalent on dedicated sites.

Though it can be tempting to reduce these discourses to reverse racism or to make the claim that participants on dedicated sites tend to be racist (as is sometimes the position held by outsiders), more careful analysis shows that participants are much more concerned with the ways outside voices can affect public dialogues than they are about these individuals having access to the sites. In fact, it is the outsider's motivation for contributing to this aspect of community life that is most scrutinized—treated with suspicion—because many see these discussions as intimately connected with the future of (the) race. As the analysis in Part II of this chapter shows, public life is organized around rich dialogues about the myriad of ways racial identity guides community life online. The effect of whiteness, ideologically and materially, is but a small part of it.

Everett's postulations about black public life online shows that, among other things, dedicated sites are being used to strengthen ties across national borders (as is exemplified in the Nigerian diaspora site Naijanet), and to support activist interests (as is demonstrated by the ways black women used the Internet to share information about the 1997 Million Woman's March within their on- and offline communities).[44] In this sense, black publics online are borne out of desires to deepen interconnectivity and to use new media, whether strategic or not, for their own community-building purposes. It is important to underscore Everett's examples here because they show that, while marginalized communities are creating spaces for interaction online, raced publics are not responses to that marginalization.

In fact, the connection between Internet technologies and diasporan interconnectivity, as can be evidenced by the popularity and ongoing presence of dedicated sites, lays challenge to the centrality of generalized publicness that philosophers like John Rawls tend to privilege. Rawls argues that, in order to participate in *the* public sphere, participants must strip themselves of their private interests so that they can come to some form of consensus about issues of general concern to all.[45] According to him, "comprehensive doctrines" (like race or religion, for instance), are private matters that impede upon our ability to have "overlapping consensus," because such doctrines inevitably influence our ability to think or act "rationally" about collective interests.[46] But, as shown in the examples offered by Everett, Naijanet, and the Million Woman March, in particular, participants' raced and ethnic identities are the common ground out of which a vibrant online public life emerges. Although these participants may very well be engaged in other publics, as in the case of some MiGente members who hold memberships on MySpace, their comprehensive doctrines are neither secondary nor completely separated.[47] Even though participants are not drawing clear lines between "public" and "private" in the way for which Rawls has argued, the strengthening of communication networks has nonetheless created new pathways for translating such public discourse into meaningful social action.

There are some indications that one of the consequences of an online race-centered public life—activism particularly around issues of social justice—is just on the horizon. Consider that in July 2006 a coalition of black gay bloggers launched a worldwide online campaign to protest the scheduled performances by Jamaican dancehall artists Beenie Man and TOK at LIFEbeat's annual HIV/AIDS fundraising conference in New York to benefit infected people in the Caribbean.[48] The concert was sponsored by music powerhouses Black Entertainment Television, *Vibe Magazine,* Music Choice, and New York-based radio station Power 105.1 FM. Outraged at scheduled performances by artists who have been criticized for lyrics that call for violence against gays, the coalition posted a series of blogs on the subject and e-mailed organizers, activists, media, loyal readers, and concert organizers. Within twenty-four hours, there was intense media coverage. A few days later, efforts included a news conference at LIFEbeat headquarters, protests by leading black LGBT figures in New York, and e-mails from black gay activists in London voicing their support. By July 12, LIFEbeat canceled the concert, citing fear of violence stemming from the pressures of "a select group of activists."[49]

LIFEbeat's response—canceling the concert, rather than canceling those particular performances—was an unintended, albeit serious, consequence of an effort aimed at addressing what protesters truly saw as the perpetuation of intracommunity intolerance of its gay members. LIFEbeat's decision to cancel the concert must be understood as an attempt to cast blame deliberately on these activists for speaking out and as evidence of the organization's refusal to enter into (perhaps be a catalyst for) serious community dialogue about these matters. That the outcome of LIFEbeat's discursive gatekeeping was a canceled benefit concert does not negate the significance of the coalition's using its online social networks to incite civic action and bring about community change. Likewise, this example shows how strategic organizing online, coupled with diasporic interconnectedness, can potentially translate into meaningful grassroots action in just a few days. After all, the protest came from the black American and British GLBT communities in response to performances by Jamaican dancehall artists at a benefit concert in New York for persons in the Caribbean living with HIV/AIDS.

Part II: heritage, identity, and discourses of racial authenticity

> I don't believe that the brother was implying that anyone "smiled" as the Towers came down. If he was thinking in the same sense as I was, he probably had "raised brows" that the "chickens had come home to roost." Our government doesn't have clean hands in [foreign] policies whatsoever. We have been playing the "dozens" for quite sometime now. And now, it's ironic, that the shoe is on the other foot. It's sad that when a black man or woman gets pulled over by a police officer, he or she doesn't know [whether] or not they are going to make it home alive. Depending on what city you live in, this is a reality. In Americas [sic] silent war against "the boyz in the hood," we all became victims. The movie Crash covered this magnificently. So to see that [the] script had been flipped, and know that the white male was now the "target" of profiling, the target of his own conception, was almost like poetic justice.—MinorityReporter[50]

This admission from BlackPlanet's pseudonymous MinorityReporter that he has very little sympathy for (white) Americans over the 9/11 attacks sparks a rather interesting debate about the community's place in American public life. His response, and the originating question "How do you feel about another black person who had no feelings about 9/11?" also represents a rather noticeable shift in discussions around this topic.[51] In 2001, participants on BlackPlanet (and all three CCI sites) expressed sympathy, fear, and a sense of allegiance with the United States. But today those expressions tend to ebb and flow between suspicion and disinterest. (In 2005, no threads on MiGente or BlackPlanet acknowledged 9/11.) When participants talk about 9/11, it is frequently the source of intense debate as to whether this really is "family business." Although some participants support the troops and were saddened by 9/11, many note that their empathy was heightened only as a result of being made aware of the deaths of "innocent black people." When ShugaSuga is incensed by the feeling that blacks are siding with "the terrorists" who "hate white America," she reminds them that "anyone of us could have died in that [terrorist] attack," and that mourning with the nation does not detract from "the knowledge of 'self' and the hardships in this society."[52] Her response is a useful counter to MinorityReporter's view that (black) family business is distinct from American business. ShugaSuga offers participants a way of intertwining them, especially given the longstanding contributions that African Americans have made. Furthermore, she cautions her family to be wary of siding with those who:

> don't care about what happened to us [during] slavery and [Jim Crow] . . . they don't care about Black [people] at all . . . they hate America . . . and as far as they are concerned we are part of America . . . they didn't send out a memo for all the Black people to stay home so that only whites got killed . . . they attacked our country and they are the enemy . . . period.[53]

Noting that there is a significant difference between being allies in the fight against social and economic problems blacks face and the killing of thousands of Americans who likely played no role in the injustice they suffer, ShugaSuga's post inevitably alters the tone of the discussion from one that was previously unsympathetic to one that encourages patriotism and sympathy, even in spite of the injustices done unto black people.

In the example above and the ones at the beginning of each section of this chapter, my analyses and observations are informed by critical theory, to underscore the intersection between the creation and dispersion of social knowledge about race and ethnicity online. In an environment where a fundamental component of online life for these young people is discourse about race, new knowledge is constituted both by individual and by institutional interpretations of these notions. In light of this complex discursive context, my recourse to Critical Discourse Analysis (CDA), a methodological tool in Critical Language Studies, is used to call attention to some of the often hidden connections between language, power, and ideology. In this way, the application of CDA allows us to interrogate further the intersection between online discursive events (or conversations) and participants' larger sociocultural positions. In so doing, one can better understand the ways in which communities pass along ideas about themselves and how they mask or make ideological norms more transparent.

Thus, there are two underlying theoretical assumptions at work when we approach texts from a CDA position. First, because online discursive interactions are also sites of social interaction, they must be understood as *reflections* of a "knowledge base" that reveals larger offline social structures, situations, and norms about language and language use. Second, these knowledge bases are sites for the *reproduction* of other social structures, situations, and norms about language and language use. In this sense, when members of an online community participate in the production of discourse, they negotiate meanings and form newer ones to suit their needs, but these discourses are never free from the cultural norms and histories to which participants are bound. As Potter and Wetherell note, critical analysis of a discursive event isn't as much about the content as it is about the interpretations of it.[54] Thus, a critical approach allows us to appreciate the development of new forms of discourse while still interrogating the conditions under which longstanding ideologies are reproduced and maintained throughout.

Norman Fairclough's approach to CDA is most instructive here, and provides clear and useful analytical strengths for understanding the power of dedicated sites for youths and the larger racialized online communities.[55] His is a three-step method that involves describing the linguistic features within the text, interpreting the relationships between the discursive processes and that of the text, and, finally, explaining the relationships between discursive processes and larger social processes.[56] Rather than explain and address each of the steps individually, as is fairly standard in CDA, this section presents some of the illustrative findings from my seven-year case study, so as to underscore the dominant rhetorical strategies and techniques, themes, and ideologies with which young people can expect to engage when they are in dialogue about race and ethnicity on dedicated sites. My research findings suggest that (1) there is a relationship between topic titles, participation rate, and age of participants in the Heritage and Identity forum; (2) race-based essentialism operates more as an implicit element in these dialogues and is rejected outright when made explicit; (3) knowledge of the community's history is used to establish one's authority and authenticity, and in many cases history is treated uncritically like the physical sciences (as immutably factual, objective, and free from interpretation); and (4) a healthy sense of racial identity is one of the key parameters based on which participants are judged.

To better understand the role that discussions of race and ethnicity play on these sites, samples of exchanges in the Heritage and Identity message board forums were used exclusively.[57] A total of 3,027 threaded forum messages were considered for this particular analysis. This accounted for 415 messages on Asian Avenue, 1,735 messages of BlackPlanet, and 877 messages on MiGente. All the data were analyzed over time according to CDA, with multiple critical readings over time for the purpose of identifying salient discursive patterns, structural features, and repetition of themes. The messages under analysis were taken from a larger pool gathered from random visits over a seven-year period.[58] Only those discussions that generated responses from more than five participants were considered in an effort to pay closer attention to dialogic characteristics of a particular issue. Threads with fewer than five participants did not yield as many exchanges. Rather, participants responded to the original posts without engaging with or building on the contributions of members before them. Some of these discussion threads had few participants, were flooded with advertisements, were repeat postings, or were off-topic exchanges between online friends. Similarly, because the sizes of these communities range in the millions, the volume of daily message board postings is quite considerable. Many discussion threads do not receive more than a few responses because there are so many new topics each day. In the case of current events, several threads may present the same issue, thus lowering participation across all of them.

Nonetheless, even when accounting for the participation issues described above, the Heritage and Identity forum is still the centerpiece of interaction on two of the sites. As the January 2007 screen capture from BlackPlanet shows (Figure 1), the 4,161 discussion topics located in this forum generated 46,033 responses. In comparison, the second- and third-ranked forums were Religion & Spirituality and Current Events, where the combined participation is comparable with Heritage and Identity.

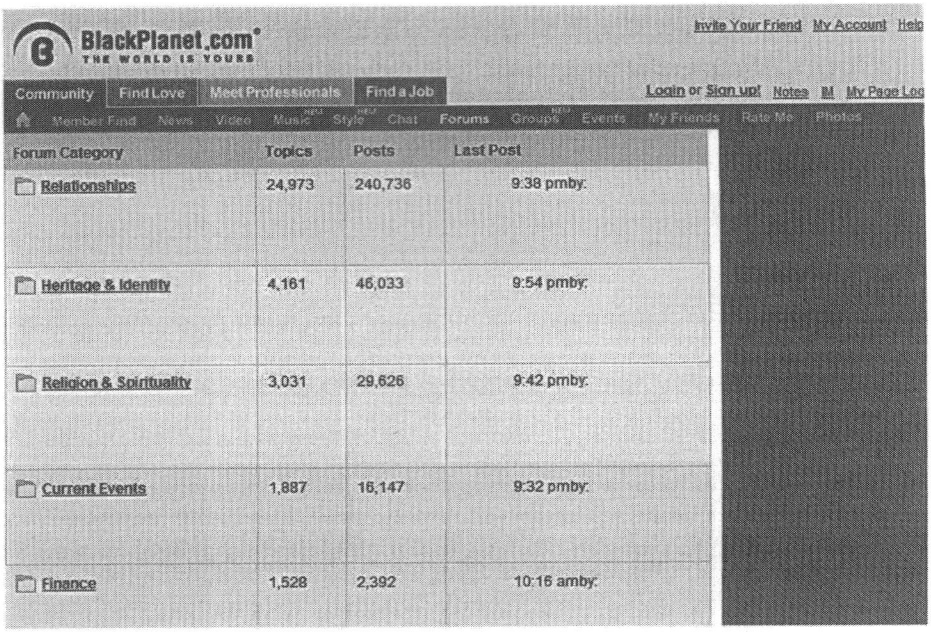

Figure 1

This pattern is fairly similar on MiGente (Figure 2). Whereas Religion & Spirituality currently has more topics and more responses than the others, Heritage and Identity has a comparable rate of participation per thread. For example, each of the 112 topics in Heritage and Identity that were still receiving posts in January 2007 had more than five participants.

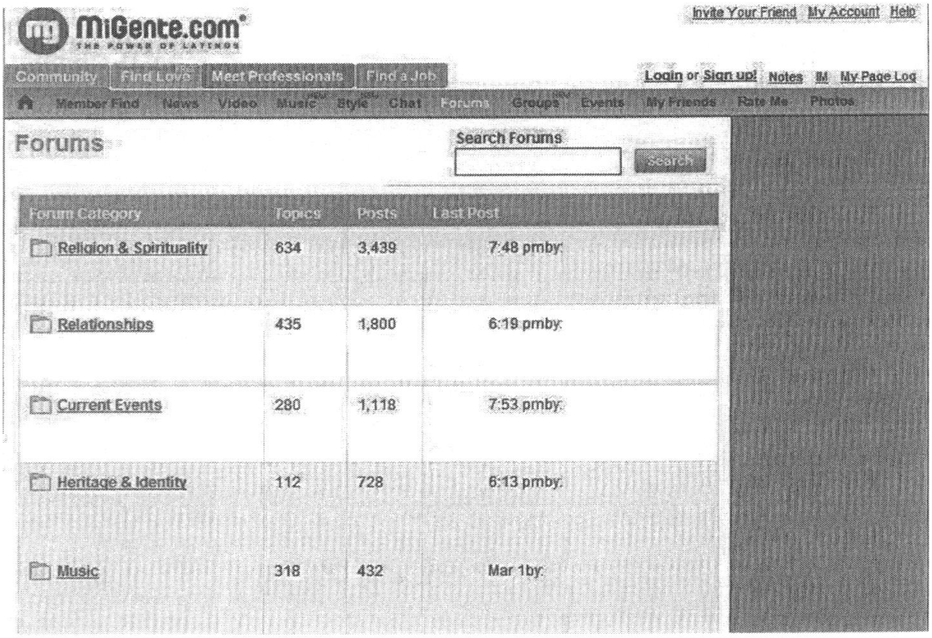

Figure 2

On the other hand, Religion & Spirituality had 634 topics, but many of them asked users similar questions over the course of the day or the week, and in those cases there were few or no responses.

It must be noted that AsianAvenue discontinued its message boards for reasons currently unknown to the author.[59] However, until 2005 (about the time it was removed), participation in the Heritage and Identity section also outnumbered that of the other forums, and was the site of participation from various ethnic groups. It is interesting to note that the Asian Avenue chatrooms, which are the only remaining places CCI provides for group interaction, separate members by ethnicity (Figure 3). For example, there is a chatroom for DESIs (i.e., South Asian descent), East Asians (i.e., Chinese, Japanese, etc.), and Filipinos. At the time of this writing, separation by ethnicity does not occur on either of the other two sites.

The most popular discussions in Heritage and Identity are those that explicitly ask questions about race or ethnicity. Appearing at least once a day, a post may ask members to relate how racial identity impacts their way of life. Not only are these threads most prevalent, but they also tend to rank highest in participation, especially when the race of the community or the group under discussion is mentioned in the thread title. For example, on BlackPlanet, when looking at two threads with the same topic like, "I'm Black and I Voted For Bush . . . Are U Crazy"[60] and "War,"[61] the originators of the threads asked essentially the same question about whether black people should support President Bush and the war in Iraq. However, forty-one people responded to the post in which race was noted, and only eight responded to the post in which it was not. Similarly, of the topics generated from May to June 2006 on MiGente, each of the most popular threads included the words *Brown, Puerto Rican, Taino, Latino,* or *Mexican.*[62] On AsianAvenue, threads like "Do U Consider Hmongs to be like us?"[63] "Filipinos: Latino or Asian?"[64] and "What makes DESIs Asians?"[65] were among the most popular, each receiving responses well into a year after they were started.

As of 2006, CCI has given participants the option of revealing their age in their profiles. When looking at the age of participants in the BlackPlanet and MiGente forums over a two-month span, there also seems to be a relationship between explicit use of race and age range of participants within discussion threads. Of those whose ages were visible, all were over the age of 30 in the "War" thread, while those in the "I'm Black and I Voted For Bush" thread had seven participants under 25. Likewise, "Blacks and the military" attracted participants ranging

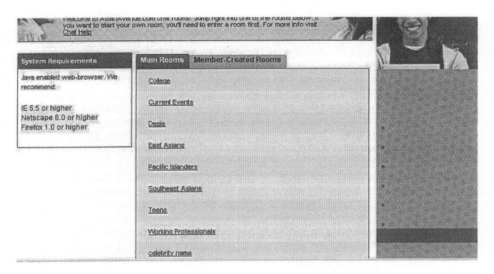

Figure 3

in age from 19 to 40, while the "9/11 and Bush" thread had fewer respondents and none who were younger than 35. In the MiGente threads "Race Confusion Among So-Called Latins"[66] and "If You Are Latino and Dont Speak Spanish Does This Make You Hispanic?"[67] the average age of the respondents was 22, with the youngest participants aged 17 and 16, respectively. However, in "your take on the war?"[68] much like on BlackPlanet, participants were, on average, eight years older, with the eldest contributor being age 45.

Years ago, it was typical for participants to claim their communities rhetorically by declaring their cultures or heritages before engaging with a particular question. As was described in the previous section, when members responded to labellalatina1001's question, "What are you," they frequently qualified their "Latinoness" as their rite of participation in the forum. As a rhetorical strategy, qualifying one's Latinoness makes one an authority and implies that one is a credible source of information about community issues. In this way, respondents make clear that racial proximity to community is tied to one's right to influence decision making. Today, however, this relationship seems to have gone underground. While race or ethnicity is still the benchmark for participation, very few members or users actually state who they are. In response to a question about whether speaking Spanish defines one's Latinoness, one respondent states, "The problem with Hispanics is that we don't network like [Jews], [Europeans] do,"[69] while another retorts, "No one should consider themselves [sic] Hispanic we are LATINO."[70]

Rather than provide evidence that either one is Hispanic or Latino, the use of the inclusive term *we* establishes that both participants are part of the dominant group and thus are capable of legitimately contributing to conversations about the community "problem." While this shift away from qualifying one's identity can be the result of ongoing interaction, the prevalence of this pattern may also suggest that the default assumption is that participants are indeed in dialogue with members of the dominant group, unless otherwise stated. Moreover, the presumption is that the site is more or less free from outsiders, and that being from the dominant CCI racial community group still determines one's right to weigh in, particularly when weighing in means being critical of that particular group.

So assumed is membership in the racial/ethnic dominant group that participants are shocked when CaseyCanada, the originator of the seventy-three-page thread (and counting) "How Do You Feel about 'Whites' on BP," reveals that she is white and participates in the site because she prefers "the company of blacks" over her own.[71] (Notice that this very popular thread names a race in the title.) Responses, which vary from, "You white?" to "What u doin on [here]?" to "Wow had no idea," show that even with a picture beside her name, most thought CaseyCanada was black because she had not stated otherwise.[72] Her use of "you" in the thread title shows that she, too, assumes that everyone else responding will be black. Ironically, the quotation marks around *whites* suggests that she is skeptical about race-based categorizing even when she proceeds to normalize her experiences, being "unwelcome" in several threads, as representative of black views on the whole. Though most simply acknowledge their surprise and continue to offer very candid responses, some abandon the question altogether and interrogate her connection to the community. Respondents try to understand her relational position as much as she feels compelled to explain and justify it. As is frequently the case with outsiders on these dedicated sites, signifiers of interpersonal relationships (i.e., "my best friend is," "I grew up near," or "my girl/boyfriend is") are offered as evidence of participants' alliances and intentions. For example, CaseyCanada posts:

> I joined BP to interact with people not to pretend to be something [I'm] not. My reasons for [preferring] the company of black people (over my own) is mostly because: I have spent my whole life living amongst black people its what I've come to be comfortable with. I feel "out of touch" when Im around my own as crazy as it sounds.[73]

Embedded in CaseyCanada's statement above is the understanding that not wanting to be among one's own is simply not normal, and that by "living amongst black people" and by becoming "comfortable with" them, she is "out of touch" with her natural state of being—an outsider among whites. Seemingly unaware of the implications of her statement, CaseyCanada fails to understand why respondents accuse her of being racist, no different from "others," and just another example of how white power manifests itself time and time again. Since she didn't "say" anything racist and rather "prefers" being around black people, Casey Canada deduces that this is yet another instance of how race is a "[delinquent] subject and one word out of context can cause havoc!"[74]

Members tend to scrutinize outsiders who present themselves as allies with much more rigor than they do explicitly racist ones. For example, when AryanNationPrincess created racist posts (before her account was deleted), participants humorously quipped that her hatred must have been the result of a sexual relationship gone bad, or that "massa" was just "pissed" that she now has to purchase natural black features in order to get attention from white men. AryanNationPrincess's post received a mere twenty-one responses from seven participants in total, none of them really analyzing it with the care and attention paid to CaseyCanada. It must be noted that respondents quickly establish that a romantic interest in the opposite sex is the primary motivation for both CaseyCanada and AryanNationPrincess to join BlackPlanet. This pattern appears on all three sites, whether respondents are critically engaging the poster or humorously dismissing him or her. The particular community's sexualized history frequently undergirds its discursive interactions with outsiders.

But simply belonging to any one of CCI's dominant racial or ethnic groups does not guarantee that participants' contributions to these sites are welcome either. Knowledge of community history (or the willingness to learn) is just as critical as knowledge of a participant's own genetic makeup. In fact, familiarity with the community's origins, how the "race" really came to be, and how it has developed are typically offered as historical "facts" that vouch for both the "authenticity" and the authority of the poster. When LiLing2K (age unknown) details her schoolyard experiences with Japanese racism in Seattle, Washington, and connects this with centuries of Japanese–Chinese conflict, respondents congratulate her for being a "good girl" and for keeping her eyes on "who she is," in spite of her American influences. It is assumed here that LiLing2K's ability to interpret these experiences stems from cultural pride, and by extension a healthy sense of racial identity. In this way, LiLing2K becomes the model citizen in the discussion thread because she is born Chinese and is also conscious of the "undeniable facts of our history" that distinguish her from others grouped under "Asian." This consciousness is then associated with racially, and often gender-, appropriate behaviors. While youth demographics are not specifically at issue here, I believe we can extrapolate that, in this informal learning context, youth will indeed learn which attitudes they must subscribe to in order to become full-fledged members of their on- and offline communities.

As is evidenced above, there is an underlying assumption in the rhetoric that there are essential properties to one's racial or ethnic identity. Although participants never seem to agree on what that essence is—food, music, geography, blood, slavery, white domination, disenfranchisement, and skin color are some of the frequently occurring themes—their responses imply that this essence of race and ethnicity exists nonetheless. Examples of the ways in which participants on all three sites engage with the notion of "mixed blood" will demonstrate this ideological belief. Responses can run the gamut from "since I am *only* half I don't know if I can say"[75] (emphasis added), "am Haifa and proud. The best of both bloods in me,"[76] or "I [don't] care what anybody says [I'm] black cuz I got half [black] blood."[77] These few statements show how simple words like "only half," "both bloods," and "half black blood" contribute to a prevailing ideology that being born into a particular race largely determines who you are. But when faced with more overt essentialist notions, participants typically reject them, noting instead that there is so "much diversity of our race [defining] us is impossible."[78] As the following illustrates, when AsianAvenue's LeeK asks why Asians try to act like "the inferior race" by speaking "ebonics"—is it the popularity of hip-hop culture or is it reflective of deeper reasons such as identity or cultural displacement—his extremist position is admonished by the group, he is labeled a racist, and worse yet, he is viewed as being no different from whites. Responses increasingly address the inappropriateness of his comment, the way it does not account for diversity, how it threatens peace within and across communities, and how, ironically, it reveals his self-hate, insecurity, and overall ignorance.[79] LeeK's desire to reduce all blacks to inferior "ebonics" speakers or to propose that Asians who speak it are "less" Asian, is vehemently opposed. In spite of this, most participants on other threads tend to agree that speaking another language changes them, and that to be real Asians means that they must speak their real languages.

The view that language is tied to *being* and identity is echoed on MiGente. When one poster asks why Latinos prefer Ebonics over Spanglish, a conversation that takes place in English on the English-speaking Latino site, many agree that it is because "[Latinos] are losing their way, have no pride, don't remember where [they] come from."[80] The premise of LeeK's post, that a community ought to speak its natural language, is understood, perhaps applauded. Whereas overt essentialism in LeeK's post is the focus of critical attention, a similar, albeit less obvious form, goes relatively unnoticed in the MiGente thread. Furthermore, those overt claims left LeeK open to charges of being ignorant and lacking in real self-worth, "Why else wouldn't [*sic*] you feel so threatened by blacks being on this site."[81] On MiGente, participants conclude that not to speak Spanish means that *those* Latinos are trying to be something they are not. The connection between speaking and *being* is a fairly recurring theme in the Heritage and Identity forum. Although several respondents on MiGente assert that Spanish is not the "natural language" of any Latino, such views are rarely the subject of intense dialogues. The more popular view supports the idea that Spanish is indeed a distinguishing feature of one's Latinoness.

Because consensus or group cohesion plays a large role in community life, it is fairly common for members to silence, modify, or limit the fullness of dissenting voices in favor of the dominant opinion within the thread. Even though some respondents in LeeK's thread remarked, "I hear what you're saying but you're going about it the wrong way," or "No comment," clearly indicating that they had alternative, perhaps even supportive, views, such sentiments were never elaborated upon.[82] Given that LeeK's question was not only met with unfavorable replies but was also used to determine that his was a self-esteem desperately in need of repair, it is no wonder that no one publicly sided with him. If we draw from these emotional issues and their consequences for young participants, we can see how easily dominant beliefs are passed on through the discourse, informing them that simply being born Asian, black, or Latino is not enough. Furthermore, there are opinions, views, and ways of acting online that are significant components of an authentic Asian, black, or Latino identity. Indeed, young participants on all three sites will learn which views will be applauded and which ones will be admonished. They will also learn that there are inherent discursive rules for *acting* or *being* online, and that these rules determine whether one has a healthy sense of racial pride, as well as whether one is a credible source of knowledge in the community.

As this discussion shows, discourse about race and ethnicity on social networking sites is rather complex. On the one hand, participants tend to object to the notion that they can be reduced to shared or essentialist racial or ethnic characteristics, frequently citing the diversity of personalities, appearances, and interests among their interpersonal networks as evidentiary. The most vehement opposition, though, comes about when they are faced with what is perceived as racist ideologies, particularly those that posters feel exemplify the continuation of white supremacist attitudes. On the other hand, participants also play active roles in reinforcing some of these prevailing notions, often inadvertently, by implying that there are definitive ways of being Asian, black, or Latino. Given that these forums are the centerpiece of public life for a cross-section of participants, particularly young people, there are profound implications when considering that what is said about race, and how it is said, determines how the community interprets the value of each participant's contribution.

Part III: the future of dedicated sites

As I have argued throughout this chapter, dialogues about race and ethnicity are purposeful discursive events taking place on dedicated sites. It must be reiterated that these conversations are not inevitable consequences of holding membership in such sites; rather, participants willingly contribute to race-based discussion topics out of the myriad of others available to them. The Heritage and Identity forums have consistently been loci of public life, and with the addition of the age feature, it appears that these forums attract a fair share of the sites' young members. As loci of public life for several years, these online forums are where ideologies are likely to be developed, promoted, contested, and institutionalized. Furthermore, for any participant who has a stake in the community, weighing in about race becomes a fundamental component of large-scale community engagement. That these conversations are likely to bring with them taken-for-granted beliefs is certainly nothing new. Demonstrating what critical language theorists mean when they say that discourse reflects the sociocultural material affecting producers of that discourse, some ideologies are so deeply embedded in the common sense of their cultures that participants inevitably reify values that, when otherwise made conscious of them, they would oppose.

But unlike other forms of media, participants in these online networks—many of whom are youth—are active producers of their content and exert a real sense of ownership over these spaces. It is much easier under these conditions to naturalize various ideological strains, because it appears as though what is circulated as discursive truths originate from the communities that utter (type) them. Because consensus in such peer-communities is inherently bound to community status and degree of racial pride, participants are also less likely to critique these truths, further allowing them to be upheld as the standard. As a result, becoming critical of and interrogating such below-the-radar ideologies is made more difficult (though not impossible), especially when adherence to them is the benchmark of identity, participation, and public life. This situation is further complicated because young people are more susceptible to the influence of their peers, whether positive or negative, and are participating in these communities at a time when their needs for acceptance, approval, and belonging are highest.

Given that these beliefs are produced and consumed—learned and taught—by those that have been troped by them underscores the need for theorizing about what young people consume as participants in these informal learning spaces, and for developing effective tools for helping them to engage with them more critically. Aside from learning the rules about initiating, structuring, and participating in large-scale discussions with others from around the world, members are constantly learning and teaching each other about the overall effect that the individualized act of voicing opinion has on collective thinking and action. The latter element could well be one of the most important discursive acts taking place on these sites. For those who may not yet be granted full access to the public sphere offline (if ever), participants have the opportunity to speak and be heard on what they see as more equal ground. By virtue of their contributions to public life, members learn the importance of consensus, as both a measure of collective reasoning and as a mechanism for silencing or ignoring those opinions that are out of favor with the majority. Informal citizenship schools with no prescribed curriculum so to speak, participants effectively learn and teach each other about which aspects of race and ethnicity are fundamental for public engagement. In learning how to speak about, listen to, or repress certain ideas about race and ethnicity, participants also forge a much deeper understanding of the connection between online politicking and offline social structures. Interaction on these sites becomes a fundamental aspect of relationship-building under conditions like mass participation, which inevitably teaches them about the complex ways in which racial identifications continue to serve as common ground, especially in an increasingly globalized, multicultural world. With so many members, millions dialoguing in larger conversations, participants not only learn to form community but they learn the different styles of communication within their respective diasporas.

For participants in these learning environments, online literacy skills will be useful tools in providing them with the ability to read and interpret texts of which they are both consumers *and* producers. Though much has been said about critical literacy skills elsewhere[83] and the ways in which such tools have been used historically to empower communities of color, we must also listen to the cautionary words of scholars like Adam Banks who argue that for a society in which racist ideologies run so deep, literacy skills alone cannot guarantee the kind of material, functional, experiential, and critical access that is needed for young users of color to see themselves as "users, producers, and even transformers" of the varying technologies informing their day-to-day lives.[84]

As ripe with potential as these online forums are—imagine the possibility of Malcolm X ushering a call to 16 million African Americans in 1960—there has yet to be any real hypothesizing or organizing around key issues that each community deems important to its offline life. By real hypothesizing or organizing, I mean that group discussions about issues like police profiling, discrimination in restaurants, improper translation of ballots, flying while Muslim, or driving while black do not include ways of translating this level of community consciousness into the type of collective action or decision making that is part and parcel of any public sphere. What is rarely heard or seen in seven years' worth of observations is the sense that "something can be done" to counter the varying forms of hegemonic control participants encounter offline. Although examples can be called upon where communities of color have deliberately used online networking to impact offline conditions (part II of this chapter provided just a few of them), public life for the more than 16 million participants on CCI's sites has yet to produce the kind of action consistent with the level of discourse about racism and social justice taking place. My most recent work on BlackPlanet has shown that, while youth are clearly engaged in conversations about issues of common concern to the larger black community, these discussions never moved beyond a discursive level of civic engagement. In fact, when I analyzed postings about Hurricane Katrina and genocide in Darfur, participants who suggested that the group should "do something" were either summarily dismissed, called "irrational," or placated with polite acknowledgments.[85]

Developing new ways to combat the pernicious effects of the "why bother" rhetoric I witnessed in these discussions is of chief importance because young participants must see that there is a fundamental relationship between collective voice and social change. Likewise, helping young people to see that such sites are public forums that are useful vehicles for civic engagement is necessary, especially for black and Latino communities, who continue to internalize the otherwise immobilizing rhetoric of the digital divide. Teaching them about the potential of such connective capabilities will have real consequences on how young people of color think about the possibilities of new media, and themselves, in bringing about material change.

Despite the range of challenges discussed above, for young people, participating in dedicated social networking sites is especially important because they can be useful vehicles for strengthening their cultural identities, for teaching them how to navigate both public and private dimensions of their racial lives, and for providing them access to a more globalized yet unfixed conversation about their community histories. Scores of contemporary research studies show how important cultivating intragroup cultural networks is to minority youth.[86] Much like the world offline, participating in online cultural communities will help them to develop a healthy sense of racial identity, what psychologists argue is necessary to resist the pernicious effects of racism. In likening a healthy cultural identity to a healthy psyche, Marcia suggests that without it, an individual is unable to adapt easily in more diverse environments.[87] These findings also underscore why minority youth must have access to dedicated online spaces, not just mainstream or "race neutral" ones. Seeking out and logging in to online communicative spaces is a central component of the lives of all young people today; however, participating in those that are more likely to value the raced experiences of minority youth not only teaches them that who they are offline bears as much relevance to who they are online, but it also teaches them that talking about this aspect of social life can help them redress the impact of racism.

Notes

1   Delpi, Why Are So Many Whites Here? *Asian Avenue*, April 9, 2000. Retrieved May 28, 2000. http://www.asianavenue.com/Members/Forums/FORUM=13501.

2   The names of CCI participants quoted in this chapter have been changed to protect their identities. Although the rules for conducting online research are not firm, I have followed some of the guidelines prescribed by Norman K. Denzin, Cybertalk and the Method of Instances, in *Doing Internet Research: Critical Issues and Methods for Examining the Net,* ed. Steve Jones (Thousand Oaks, CA: Sage, 1999), 107–26. Throughout this study, I have never interacted with any of the participants cited nor have I asked for permission to quote directly. Such practices are fairly common, given that all of the information included in this chapter is "public" and available to anyone who registers on the particular CCI site. Nonetheless, I have changed the participants' names and have not provided the URLs to their specific posts. Instead of URLs to the posting, I have included the URL for the thread, the site name, and date the post was created.

3   Because members are not restricted from opening multiple accounts, it is likely that the number of subscribers per site is not representative of the actual number of individual members. For example, in 2004, BlackPlanet boasted a whopping 18 million subscribers; in 2006 the number hovered around 14 million. Although users are worldwide, the majority are based in the United States. In 2004, Forrester Research estimated that Asian Americans, African Americans, and Latinos accounted for over 18 million Web users combined, and that in 2000, 3.8 million African American households were online. Nonetheless, the combined membership of these sites is still likely to be well in the millions.

4   Gee defines *Discourses* (with a capital D) as our ways of being in the world. Every Discourse has a "tacit theory" as to what determines a normal person within discourse, and this defines what is the right way for each person to speak, listen, act, value, and think. See James Paul Gee, *Social Linguistics and Literacies: Ideology in Discourses* (London: Taylor & Francis, 1999). According to Josephine Peyton Young, Discourse is like a "club with [implicit rules] about how [members] are [to] behave." See Boy Talk: Critical Literacy and Masculinities, *Reading Research Quarterly* 35, no. 3 (2000): 312. For example, BlackPlanet member BigWhiteBlob (name used with permission) posted a rather interesting response to a forum question that asked whether it is possible to "know" with certainty that someone is Black in cyberspace. He stated that "it isn't really the sprinkling of faces that are like your own, that is nice, but it is really about the content, I can tell by the expressions used on people's pages or the way they describe themselves that I am in my real community." Interestingly, BigWhiteBlob refers to the ways in which members speak (quite frankly type) as evidence of their insider/outsider positionalities. That seeing a picture of someone who looks like you is not enough suggests that some transference of real-world communicative modalities is necessary to gain full access. Discourses (and language choices) function as boundary markers, signs of proximity to territory, mapping who is inside or outside, what is authentic, and who belongs, as well as a host of historical, political, and epistemological understandings of realities, knowledge(s), texts, and selves.

5   According to Norman Fairclough, Critical Language Studies (CLS) analyzes "social interactions in a way which focuses upon their linguistic elements, and which sets out to show up their generally hidden determinants in the system of social relationships, as well as hidden effects they may have

upon that system." See *Language and power* (London: Longman, 1989), 5. With these postulations on the relationship of language and power, along with the contributions of Foucault, CLS becomes an "alternative orientation to language studies which implies a different demarcation of language study into approaches or branches, different relationships between them, and different orientations within each of them" (Ibid., 13).

6   Ibid., 5.

7   See Community Connect, Inc., "About us." Retrieved May 4, 2002. http://www.communityconnect.com/about.html.

8   Ibid.

9   Ibid.

10   John Gangemi, A MySpace That Speaks Your Language, *BusinessWeek.com,* September 2006, http://www.businessweek.com/smallbiz/content/sep2006/sb20060920_307149.htm?chan=search. Retrieved October 11, 2006.

11   Ibid.

12   In spite of the decline in daily participation on the CCI sites, the company has managed to maintain its foothold as the leading special-interest Web publisher for American ethnic groups, and remains in the top fifty of Web content publishers for the last eight years. Web trafficking sites like Alexa and comScore are useful resources for comparing the daily participation of these sites.

13   Vorris Nunley, Hush Harbors: Barbershops, Rhetorical Theory, and African American Expressive Culture (Doctoral dissertation, Pennsylvania State University, 2005), 1–19.

14   Ibid., 16.

15   Norman Fairclough, *Language and Power* (London: Longman, 1989), 26.

16   labellalatina1001, What Are You, *MiGente,* February 10, 2003, http://www.migente.com/Members/Forums/28392. Retrieved March 8, 2003.

17   OrelleAngelle, What Are You, *MiGente,* March 20, 2004, http://www.migente.com/Members/Forums/28392. Retrieved March 21, 2004.

18   *In Modernity and Self-Identity,* Anthony Giddens notes that "[a] person's identity is not to be found in behaviour, nor—important though this is—in the reactions of others, but in the capacity to keep a particular narrative going. The individual's biography, if she is to maintain regular interaction with others in the day-to-day world, cannot be wholly fictive. It must continually integrate events which occur in the external world, and sort them into the ongoing 'story' about the self." See *Modernity and Self-Identity: Self and Society in the Late Modern Age* (Palo Alto, CA: Stanford University Press, 1991), 54.

19   Habermas argues, through a Kantian analysis, that civil society allows man "to engage in a debate over the general rules of governing relations in the basically privatized but publicly relevant sphere of commodity exchange in social labor." See Jurgen Habermas, *The Structural Transformation of the Public Sphere,* trans. Thomas Burger (Cambridge, MA: MIT Press, 1989), 27. For Kant, civil society in Europe relied on the private man's public use of his reason. See Immanuel Kant, *Foundations of the Metaphysics of Morals and What Is Enlightenment,* trans. Lewis White Beck (New York: Macmillan, 1990). For a discussion on alternative public spheres, read Nancy Fraser, "Rethinking the Public Sphere: A Contribution to the Critique of Actually Existing Democracy," in *Habermas and the Public Sphere,* ed. Craig Calhoun (Cambridge, MA: MIT Press, 1992), 109–42.

20   Sherry Turkle, *Life on the Screen: Identity in the Age of the Internet* (New York: Simon & Schuster, 1997), 14–16.

21   Lisa Nakamura, *Cybertypes: Race, Ethnicity, and Identity on the Internet* (New York: Routledge, 2002), 102–23.

22   Stuart Hall, Culture, the Media and the "Ideological Effect," in *Mass Communication and Society,* ed. James Curran, Michael Gurevitch, and Janet Woolacott (London: Edward Arnold, 1977), 318–23.

23   The list of scholarship on identity and cyberculture is very extensive. Some recent publications on race or online communities include Darin Barney. *The Network Society* (Cambridge, UK: Polity Press, 2004); John Rodzvilla, ed., *We've Got Blog: How Weblogs Are Changing Our Culture* (Cambridge, MA: Perseus, 2002); Leah A. Lievrouw and Sonia Livingstone, eds, *Handbook of New Media: Social Shaping and Consequences of ICTs* (London: Sage, 2002); Manuel Castells, ed., *The Network Society: A Cross-cultural Perspective* (Northampton, MA: Elgar, 2004); K. Ann Renninger and Wesley Shumar, eds., *Building Virtual Communities: Learning and Change in Cyberspace* (New York: Cambridge University Press, 2002); Beth Kolko, Lisa Nakamura, and Gibert Rodman, *Race in Cyberspace* (London: Routledge, 2002); and Alondra Nelson, Thuy Linh N. Tu, and Alicia Headlam Hines, *Technicolor: Race, Technology, and Everyday Life* (New York: New York University Press, 2001).

24   Sherry Turkle, Constructions and Reconstructions of Self in Virtual Reality: Playing in the MUDS, *Mind, Culture and Activity* 1, no. 3 (1994): 158–67.

25 Emily Noelle Ignacio, E-scaping Boundaries: Bridging Cyberspace and Diaspora Studies through Nethnography, in *Critical Cyberculture Studies,* ed. David Silver and Adrienne Massanari (New York: New York University Press, 2006), 186–87.

26 Ibid., 187.

27 Steven Rosenbush, News Corp.'s Place in MySpace, *Businessweek,* July 19, 2005, http://www.businessweek.com/technology/content/jul2005/tc20050719_5427_tcll9.htm. Retrieved August 12, 2006.

28 Robert Young, Why Rupert Murdoch Really Bought MySpace? *GigaOM,* August 6, 2005, http://gigaom.com/2005/08/06/why-murdoch-bought-myspace/. Retrieved August 12, 2006.

29 News.com, MySpace.com Creates Own Record Label, *News.com,* November 2005, http://news.com.com/MySpace.com+creates+own+record+label/2100–1027_3–5930390.html?tag=nefd.top. Retrieved August 12, 2006.

30 Ibid.

31 GlobeandMail.com, Google, MySpace Ink Deal, *ReportOnBusiness,* August 8, 2006, http://www.theglobeandmail.com/servlet/story/RTGAM.20060807.wgoog0807/BNStory/Business. Retrieved August 12, 2006.

32 Benedict Anderson, When the Virtual Becomes the Real: A Talk with Benedict Anderson, http://www.nira.go.jp/pube/review/96spring/intervi.html. Retrieved August 18, 2006.

33 News.com, MySpace.com Creates Own Record Label.

34 Peter Kollock, The Economies of Online Cooperation: Gifts and Public Goods in Cyberspace, in *Communities in Cyberspace,* ed. Marc A. Smith and Peter Kollock (London: Routledge, 1999), 220–39.

35 Howard Rheingold, *The Virtual Community: Homesteading on the Electronic Frontier* (Reading, MA: Addison-Wesley, 1993), 57–58.

36 Kollock, 225–39.

37 For further discussion on imagined communities, see Benedict Anderson, *Imagined Communities* (London: Verso, 1991).

38 ROFL is netspeak for "rolling on the floor laughing"; LOL is netspeak for "laughing out loud."

39 John G. Ruggie, Territoriality and Beyond: Problematising Modernity in International Relations, *International Organization* 47 (1993): 139–74.

40 Kenichi Ohmae, *The End of the Nation State* (New York: Free Press, 1995).

41 Arjun Appadurai. *Modernity at Large: Cultural Dimensions of Globalization* (Minneapolis, MN: University of Minnesota Press, 1996).

42 Jan Aart Scholte, The Geography of Collective Identities in a Globalizing World, *Review of International Political Economy* 3 (1996): 565–608.

43 SK and NYCTony posting to African American Chat 261, *Yahoo!* August 1, 2006, http://www.yahoo.com/chatrooms. To access Yahoo! chat rooms, one must have a Yahoo! e-mail address and install Yahoo! Instant Messenger.

44 Anna Everett, The Revolution Will Be Digitized: Afrocentricity and the Digital Public Sphere, *Social Text* 20, no. 2 (2002): 131, 139.

45 John Rawls, *Political Liberalism* (New York: Columbia University Press, 1993), 4–44.

46 Ibid., 13–23.

47 I visited some of these MiGente members pages on MySpace and, in most cases, they reproduced their MiGente content.

48 Keith Boykin, Black Gay Bloggers Unite Against Homophobic Artists, *KeithBoykin* blog, July 11, 2006, http://www.keithboykin.com/arch/2006/07/11/black_gay.blogg; EURWeb, Black Gay Bloggers Launch Protest: Target Is Music Industry's Anti-Gay AIDS Concert, July 11, 2006, http://www.eurweb.com/story/eur27394.cfm. Retrieved August 15, 2006.

49 Fox News Online, NYC Reggae Concert Canceled after Protests, *FoxNews.com,* July 12, 2006, http://www.foxnews.com/wires/2006Jull2/0,4670,ReggaeProtest,00.html. Retrieved August 15, 2006.

50 BlackPlanet, 911 Response to Unsaddened Blacks, *BlackPlanet,* http://www.blackplanet.com/forums/thread.html?thread_id=18603. Retrieved August 21, 2006.

51 Ibid.

52 Ibid.

53 Ibid.

54 John Potter and Margaret Wetherell, *Discourse and Social Psychology: Beyond Attitudes and Behaviour* (London: Sage, 1987).

55 Norman Fairclough, *Critical Discourse Analysis* (London: Longman, 1995).

56 Ibid., 97.

57   In order to gain access to all of the features that each of these sites offer, participants must register and disclose their sex, age, level of education, and racial or ethnic characteristics. Interestingly, the identity categories and requirements differ on each site. Identity on AsianAvenue is denoted by one's ethnicity, with members choosing from among twenty-one ethnic groups. From 2000 to 2005, BlackPlanet members only had five choices available to account for their identities: Black, Asian, Latino, Native American, and White. By 2006, with its site redesign, members can choose "other" or type in a specific ethnicity. MiGente registrants can choose from among ethnic origin and race. There are twenty-five ethnic categories like Dominican, Cuban, and so forth and the same five racial categories available on BlackPlanet. Commenting on the click-box identity, Lisa Nakamura argues that the process of choosing identity in this way forces users into dominant notions of race. Arguably, the various changes to these categories in the site redesign may be indicative of an increased social awareness of the inadequateness of these categories. Nakamura, *Cybertypes.*

58   CCI has twice revamped its sites and, as a result of this, older threads and discussions that may have been brimming with meaning were deleted. The discussion forums were disabled during the time of the redesign, and in the case of AsianAvenue, discontinued altogether.

59   It appears as though AsianAvenue has undergone the most drastic modifications in comparison to the other two CCI sites. I suspect that these changes are in an effort to keep up with current social networking trends used on sites like MySpace. As such, there is no general public forum for the entire AsianAvenue community.

60   Blackplanet, I'm Black and I Voted For Bush . . . Are U Crazy, *BlackPlanet,* http://www.blackplanet. com/forums/thread.html?thread_id=1851. Retrieved June 9, 2006.

61   BlackPlanet, War, *BlackPlanet,* http://www.blackplanet.com/forums/thread.html?thread_ id=185. Retrieved June 9, 2006.

62   For example, on MiGente, see threads http://www.migente.com/forums/thread.html?thread_ id=2720; http://www.migente.com/forums/thread.html?thread_id=658; http://www.migente. com/forums/thread.html?thread_id=2511; http://www.migente.com/forums/thread.html?thread_ id=2200; http://www.migente.com/forums/thread.html?thread_id=373; and http://www. migente.com/forums/thread.html?thread_id=1567.

63   AsianAvenue, Do You Consider Hmongs To Be Like Us? *AsianAvenue,* http://www.asianavenue. com/Members/Forums/viewforum.html? VIEW=THREAD&PID=17036&RID=17036&FORUM =1011. Retrieved May 4, 2000.

64   AsianAvenue, Filipinos: Latino or Asian? *AsianAvenue,* http://www.asianavenue.com/Members/ Forums/viewforum.html?VIEW=THREAD&PID=18726&RID=18726&FORUM=1011. Retrieved May 4, 2000.

65   AsianAvenue, What Makes DESIs Asians? *AsianAvenue,* http://www.asianavenue.com/Members/ Forums/viewforum.html?VIEW=THREAD&PID=182340&RID=182340&FORUM=27375. Retrieved May 8, 2000.

66   MiGente, Race Confusion Among So-called Latins, *MiGente,* http://www.migente.com/forums/ thread.html?thread_id=619. Retrieved June 16, 2006.

67   MiGente, If You Are Latino and Dont Speak Spanish Does This Make You Hispanic? *MiGente,* http://www.migente.com/forums/thread.html?thread_id=1802. Retrieved June 16, 2006.

68   MiGente, Your Take on the War? *MiGente,* http://www.migente.com/forums/thread.html? thread_id=192. Retrieved June 16, 2006.

69   MiGente, If You Are Latino.

70   Ibid.

71   BlackPlanet, How Do You Feel About 'Whites' on BP? *BlackPlanet,* http://www.blackplanet.com/ forums/forum.html?forum_id=156. Retrieved February 1, 2007.

72   Ibid.

73   Ibid.

74   Ibid.

75   BlackPlanet,InterracialChaos,*BlackPlanet,*http://www.blackplanet.com/forums/thread.html? thread_id=2162. Retrieved August 18, 2006.

76   AsianAvenue, Haifas Identify [Yourselves], *AsianAvenue,* http://www.asianavenue.com/forums/ thread.html?threadJd=1910. Retrieved May 20, 2000.

77   MiGente, Blacarican? *MiGente,* http://www.blackplanet.com/forums/thread.html?thread_ id=1078. Retrieved July 9, 2006.

78   Ibid.

79   AsianAvenue, Chronic Ebonics, *AsianAvenue,* http://www.asianavenue.com/Members/Forums/ viewforum.html?VIEW=THREAD&PID=187034&RID=187034&FORUM=27375.Retrieved May 20, 2000.

80   MiGente, Spanish Spanglish English, *MiGente,* http://www.migente.com/Members/Forums/
      viewforum.html?VIEW=THREAD&PID=18575&RID=18575&FORUM=4377. Retrieved July 9,
      2006.

81   AsianAvenue, Chronic Ebonics.

82   Ibid.

83   See, e.g., Cynthia Selfe, *Technology and Literacy in the Twenty-first Century: The Importance of Paying
      Attention* (Carbondale, IL: Southern Illinois University Press, 1999); and Barbara Warnick, *Critical
      Literacy in a Digital Era* (Mahwah, NJ: Erlbaum, 2002).

84   Adam Banks, *Race, Rhetoric & Technology: Searching for Higher Ground* (Mahwah, NJ: Erlbaum, 2005),
      138.

85   Dara N. Byrne, Public Discourse, Community Concerns, and Its Relationship to Civic Engagement:
      Explaining Black Social Networking Traditions on BlackPlanet.com, *Journal of Computer Mediated
      Communication* 13 (2007), http://jcmc.indiana.edu.

86   Janet E. Helms, ed., *Black and White Racial Identity: Theory, Research and Practice* (New York:
      Greenwood, 1990); Harvey P. Oshman and Martin Manosevitz, The Impact of the Identity Crisis on
      the Adjustment of Late Adolescent Males, *Journal of Youth and Adolescence* 3 (1974): 207–16; Mary-
      Jane Rotheram-Borus, Ethnic Differences in Adolescents' Identity Status and Associated Behavioral
      Problems, *Journal of Adolescence* 12 (1989): 361–74; and James E. Marcia, Identity and Intervention,
      Journal of Adolescence 12 (1989): 401–10.

87   Marcia, Identity and Intervention, 401–10.

Chapter 42

Rebecca E. Karl

RACE, COLONIALISM AND HISTORY

China at the turn of the twentieth century

Two models of race in nineteenth- and twentieth-century China are contrasted by Rebecca E. Karl: essentialist racial differences that need to be effaced in the name of world unity (Kang), and race as an anti-colonial component or force within society. These models need to be understood in light of national and global transformations, in relation to which Chinese nationalism articulates a response to modernity (i.e., a space of transformation). Karl, a professor of East Asian Studies at New York University, and the author of books on the 1898 Reform Period in China, Chinese nationalism, and Mao Zedong and China, develops a new approach to race in the late-Qing era (1895–1911) by turning to Deleuze and Guatari's concept of "social subjection", that is to say, what occurs at a national level (here, notions of "race") is coded at a higher level, say, the globalized demands of capitalism. "Race", then, in turn-of-the-twentieth-century China, is overdetermined: multiple national and global discourses concerning Chinese identity, nationalism, colonialism, foreignness, unity, difference, and so on intersect with this one term. Of particular interest to Karl, following the work of Ann Laura Stoler, is the way in which this overdetermined notion of race can "unmask" historical regimes and hierarchies of power that have presented themselves as organic, or natural. The first of two main models of race examined in detail is that of Kang Youwei's (1858–1927) *Datong shu* or One World Philosophy articulated in his book *On Confucius as a Reformer* (1897). Kang reinterprets Confucianism in light of the demands of modern society, arguing that world unity is arrived at by dissolving boundaries such as that of class, race and sex. In terms of race, Kang argues for a melting pot approach, whereby racial differences would be eliminated through racial interbreeding, with the aim of reaching a "neutral" or white racial type. The inbuilt contradiction is that Kang's "aestheticism", or essentialist notion of race based upon surface differences, clashes with his notion of race as a malleable category. Race, conceived in this contradictory sense, is both a utopian possibility, and an essentialist *racism*. Karl then examines the genre called *wangguo shi* (or the history of "perished states") to look at another approach to race in China, here contributing to the anti-colonial revolution, such as the Boxer Rebellion (1900–1901), an attempt at expelling foreign powers from China. The *wangguo shi*—popular biographies of Chinese and foreign heroes—re-read world history as a way of offering a new perspective on Chinese dynastic state history, one which re-codifies nation and race in terms of colonization. In these narratives, race is about boundaries and differences, the state of the "foreigner" being applied to people who "colonize" China, either from within, or from overseas. Those who struggle against colonization are considered "same race" allies, and race here is part of a political project, rather than the essentialist and eugenicist approach as taken by Kang. Karl goes into considerable detail with individual narrative analysis, concluding that after the anti-colonial movements largely failed, the global approach to race was turned inwards to focus on the nation state and the vilification of the Manchu Qing; however, racialized discourses of colonialism were still firmly in place, and these were applied to those who were not Han Chinese. The fluidity of notions of race is here embodied by the switching between narratives of inclusion/exclusion, identity and unity, as well as the state and globalized political projects at the turn of the twentieth century.

HISTORICALLY, PHILOSOPHICAL REFLECTIONS ON 'race' in China are linked to the beginnings of nationalism as an articulated albeit highly contested theoretical and political topos at the turn of the twentieth century, during the late-Qing period (1895–1911). This was the time at which China's participation in global systems of signification and power relations – including 'race' and 'nation,' among others – came to be consciously recognized by Chinese intellectuals as at least incipient totalities.[1] As I elucidate below, these systems of signification and power were integrally incorporated into new understandings of history, through which China was constitutively linked to a modern world of flux and instability. This chapter thus argues, contrary to much that has been written recently on 'race' in China,[2] that a philosophy of race was initially elaborated not primarily to define 'others' as non-Chinese – that is, not merely as a permutation of previous systems of Sinocentric civilizational or blood-lineage significations – nor as a wholesale adoption of Spencerian Darwinism,[3] but rather as a politico-philosophical attempt by Chinese intellectuals to mark out an autonomous relationship to a violently invasive modernity, while simultaneously incorporating China into a new sense of globality. As such, despite clear and long-standing Chinese systems for signifying 'others' – for example, as those who stood outside the pale of a Confucian civilizational norm (*huawai*) expressed either in terms of 'raw' (*sheng*) and 'cooked' (*shu*) peoples,[4] or in the less culinary terms of 'barbarian' (*yi*) and 'civilized' (*wen*) – my contention is that these older signifying practices cannot be considered philosophies of 'race', if we take 'race' to be, at the very least, a system of signification that is, in Ato Sekyi-Otu's words, 'an order . . . made manifest in *space*'.[5]

On such a view, exclusive historiographical or ethnological attention to the temporally continuous contemptuous attitudes of (mostly Han) Chinese towards 'others', and the linking of these attitudes to putatively unchanging assumptions of centrality, must be modified by an account of how 'race' came to be elaborated in the late nineteenth and early twentieth centuries in explicitly global spatialized terms. These terms, as I understand them, referred to at least two spatialities simultaneously: to modernity, understood as a global space of transformation; and a newly conceptualized national space that was to be constituted through the reinvention of hierarchies of politics, economy, and culture – hierarchies that were at once demanded and yet also disallowed by the very nation project itself.[6] Dwelling on the second (internalist) aspect without elucidating the former (globalist) one, as much recent commentary does, is to miss the historical complexity of 'race' philosophy in China, and thereby to assimilate the concept too easily either into an unchanging (Han) Chinese culturalist–ethnic normativity or into a simple Western (or Japanese) derivativeness that strips the concept of its contradictions and political potentials.

To grasp the nature of these overlapping global and domestic spatialities and their inherent contradictions and potentials, it is helpful to think the problem of late-Qing race philosophies in terms of what Gilles Deleuze and Felix Guattari have called the process of social subjection.[7] According to Deleuze and Guattari, social subjection is the dominant mode of social coding in modernity, as that coding is pursued through the nation-state, which seeks to order social integration both through a national-level politics/economy and via the articulation of that configuration to the capitalist world.[8] Social subjection is thus a congeries of national and global processes; it is also simultaneously productive and reactive. As such, the process of social subjection is not merely repressive, but also opens onto a productive plane of immanence, through which it poses political (and other) possibilities not immediately derivable from the structure of its superficial logics.[9] Yet, as is clear for a globally subordinated place such as China, both the conditions for national integration as well as the possibilities for global equality through the non-isomorphic processes of social subjection are always illusory. They are illusory, not only because of suppressed strands in the narrative of nation (that is, not because 'nation' in the narrowest sense is an imposed statist narrative ideology or teleology) but at the very least because states – those seemingly bounded spaces – into which global capitalism makes inroads must, on the one hand, resist equality in internal socio-political-economic integration by reconfiguring older inequalities into new unequal formations able to cope with those inroads, while at the same time being forced to succumb to spatially articulated inequality enforced by differential power relations globally.

As a new philosophy in turn-of-the-century China, the multiple strands of 'race' figured and reflected this consciously grasped historical contradiction and modern condition of social subjection, without, however, necessarily resonating very well with existing popularly articulated systems of differentiation. The latter were perhaps more beholden to local regionalisms, language groups, and so on, and only later became racialized. As such, 'race' in late-Qing China reflected upon the intersections between global and national spaces, and many Chinese intellectuals – who themselves were increasingly able to negotiate those spaces both epistemologically and in experiential practice – appropriated the concept to name both national and global desires.[10] In the process of the constitution of the national desire, race and ethnos – with the latter understood initially as a people defined not by common lineage/culture, but by a putatively common commitment to the political project of overthrowing the Manchu Qing rulers[11] – quickly came to be socio-political synonyms; at the same time, however, as a form of immanentism, 'race' also named a desire for the revolutionary transformation of a newly-glimpsed global regime of temporal unity marked by constantly produced and reproduced global division and unevenness: that regime that can be named modernity.[12] This latter version, too, was linked to an imputed common political project: that of non-Western anti-colonial revolutions. In this mutuality, 'race' can be seen as the name of a History[13] that in part repudiated the modernist packaging indicated by nineteenth-century Western imperialist epistemologies – which attempted to codify differences among peoples across the globe in an essentialist way – and attempted to reposition modernity as an enabling political topos, not merely as a prison-house of language and form.[14]

In the sense I explore below, then, 'race' was not primarily a philosophy forged by those directly in the service of power although it was that, too; nor is it to be understood primarily as a lived experience.[15] Rather, I explore the philosophy of 'race,' borrowing Ann Laura Stoler's words, as it was 'embraced . . . by those unmasking the fiction of natural and legitimate rule'.[16] In the specific historical context of turn-of-the-century Chinese intellectual circles, the primary fictions unmasked were, on the one hand, the claims on 'China' made by the Manchu Qing dynasty, whose deposing of the Ming dynasty in the mid-seventeenth century was re-examined at the beginning of the twentieth century in the dual light of newly available discourses of 'race/ethnicity' and the newly grasped import of colonialism as a modern global historical trajectory of dominance and power; and, on the other, the incipient normalization of a modernist teleology derived from would-be hegemonic notions of modernization learned and observed from Western political philosophies and recent Western and Japanese historical experiences.[17]

That said, I should note that the provisional historical outcome of the contradictions introduced and reflected upon through a 'race' philosophy at the turn of the century was the victory of a culturalist philosophy of an essentially racialized ethnos embodied by the Han Chinese (projected as the political essence of the national people) over the more Utopian global transformative philosophy. This ethno-nationalist understanding restricted 'race' (and 'nation') to an ethnic normativity delimited by Han Chinese-ness. It was politically motivated by that version of the national project that sought to overthrow the Manchu Qing dynasty in order to restore the Han to their 'rightful' place as rulers of China. This over-determined outcome – over-determined both by changing configurations of political and economic power within China and between Chinese and non-Chinese, and by the posing of the modern question of 'nation' itself in terms of political divisions among 'national peoples' globally – was temporarily solidified by the successful deposing of the Qing dynasty in 1911 and the subsequent inscription of new Republican statist–culturalist discourses of race/ethnos (*minzu*) upon definitions of the Chinese people and of the Chinese nation (-state).[18] The following discussion is less concerned with this historical outcome – which I have treated at length elsewhere[19] – than with the conceptual relationship between 'race', 'colonialism' and 'history' at the turn of the twentieth century in those texts that produced this nexus as a cornerstone of analysis.

Erasing boundaries and a global utopia

As a point of departure, it is useful to examine one of the most explicitly global and Utopian expositions of 'race' in China: that included in Kang Youwei's *Datong shu* [One World Philosophy].[20] Around the turn of the century, Kang (1858–1927) was best known for his reinterpretation of Confucianism in his 1897 volume *Kongzi gaizhi kao* [On Confucius as a Reformer], which was essentially a reworking of the premises of the Song neo-Confucian imperial tradition – or, that version of Confucianism encoded by the civil service examinations that all would-be state officials were required to pass. Kang's Confucianism was thus an activist doctrine of practical statesmanship rather than a conservative doctrine of the status quo.[21] Indeed, Kang's radical (for the time) critique of imperial Confucianism, in addition to his strict focus on the needs of the global present and future, rather than on the glories of the Chinese past, earned him a reputation: those who admired his boldness sought to become his students; those who deplored his challenge set out to destroy him.[22]

Through his reinterpretation of Confucianism, which was heavily informed by his studies in Buddhism, Kang explicitly mobilized his 'sage-Bodhisattva's sense of mission', in Hao Chang's words,[23] to explore how, what he saw as the historically evolved 'boundaries' (*jie*) of the world could be eliminated so as to prepare the way for one-worldism. On Kang's reading of the contemporary global situation, it was precisely boundaries – of space and kind – that prevented the world (or, life in its broadest sense) from achieving its full potential. According to Kang, there were nine such primary boundaries: those of states, classes, race, sex, family, occupation (or property), disorder (or unjust laws), kind (or, species), and suffering (or, perpetuation of suffering). The goal of his quest to define and eliminate these boundaries was to arrive at a just and humane 'one world' (*datong:* unity) which would provide the condition of possibility for the overcoming of suffering (*ku*) and the achievement of happiness (*le*). Without going into the complex sources for Kang's particular Utopian vision, it is important to note, as does Hao Chang, that Kang's transcendental utopianism was firmly a this-world affair and had little to do with a dualism between this- and other-worldliness.[24] It is also important to point out that 'culture' was not a boundary for Kang:

that is, 'culture' neither defined division nor did cultures need to be abolished, or seemingly even addressed as such.

In his discussion of Kang's philosophy, Hao Chang emphasizes Kang's reliance upon the Confucian realm of *ren* (humane-ness) as an inner-world orientation that described and reflected Kang's desire to achieve a philosophically plausible moral unity between Heaven and the human world. It is with reference to this inner world of moral perfection that Chang places Kang's desire for one-world unity. However, in his concern to trace how indigenous patterns of thought were unsettled by and through China's modern crisis, where he carefully notes the selective incorporations of Western political and social philosophies (most notably, Social Darwinism and the startling turn to a unilinear progressive temporality), Chang under-emphasizes the crucial spatial turn that underpins Kang's philosophy, and, in consequence, the unstable relationship between space and globality assumed therein.[25]

Kang's specification of his current era was placed in the context of what he saw as a strong historical trend leading from 'division to unity'. This trend he elaborated through a whirlwind narrative of China's imperial unification; the unifications of India, Greece, and Rome; all the way to the more recent unifications of Germany and Italy in the mid-nineteenth century. Making clear that his concept of 'unity' was not limited to any necessary sense of contiguous territoriality but was spatially universalist, Kang further noted, for example, that more recently, France's taking of Annam (Vietnam) and Morocco; England's conquest of Egypt, India, and Burma; and the continental swallowing of whole swathes of North America by the United States (which, he surmised, was leading to a full unification of the Americas – North and South – under the USA), were all evidence of 'parts becoming joined', a trend that, Kang averred in the Social Darwinistic language of the time, was due to 'natural selection, the swallowing up by the strong and large and the extermination of the weak and small'. This trend, he noted, 'may be considered to presage One World'.[26]

It is clear that Kang fundamentally ignored the production of unevenness – internally and globally – in his understanding of the trend towards 'unity'. It thus appears that he was unconcerned with any historically specific explanation for dominance, or for modern colonialism/imperialism as the production of uneven global space. In this regard, what by the early 1900s many were despairingly calling 'imperialism' (*diguo zhuyi*), 'national expansionism' (*guojia pengzhang zhuyi*), or 'colonialism' (*zhimin zhuyi*) was for Kang not only a natural but a desirable move towards boundary elimination. By the same token, it is also clear that a sense of global space is crucial to Kang's Utopian formulation. Yet, that space was, for Kang, a continuous and purely immanent affair, marked and shaped by human activity, to be sure, but essentially blank. That is, for him, space was abstract, not particularistically performative,[27] and thus, globality was not one topos of an historically specific lifeworld enacted and actualized as a relationship, but an historically given condition of being. Kang's view therefore posits an abstract and decentred global condition and in this narrow sense, his Utopian vision is fully of his time. It could not have been articulated much earlier in China. It is also in this sense that Kang's view is basically ahistorical. For, as we shall see below, it was precisely with the recognition of 'space' and globality as a material and thus historical productivity *and* only in consequence of that productivity an immanence, and with the incorporation of this recognition into new modes of historical analysis, that the question of 'boundaries' and their relationship to 'race' was turned into something else altogether: explicitly spatialized systems of difference and signification that, in the global arena, were potentially politically unifying because of a shared anti-colonialism; and simultaneously in the domestic arena, an exclusionary culturalist ethnic system that rendered differences between Manchu and Han (among others) a cornerstone of nationalist praxis.

For the moment, suffice it to note that Kang's interpretive premise rests upon two primary units of socio-political analysis, neither of which is particularly problematized: *the world,* which stands as an abstract given space and a Utopian desire; and *the state,* whose territoriality was the concrete and historical form through which all other boundaries were instantiated and hence whose loosening from territoriality was the process through which all other boundaries could be dissolved.[28] In this regard, democracy – by which Kang mostly meant rule by law – was understood as the governing form that permitted contemporary interstate federations (the 'joinings') as well as the form of government that presented itself as the politically neutral substance of One Worldism.

In Kang's view, then, the current situation yielded two contradictory but potentially complementary movements: the union of divisive states into ever-larger territories, not necessarily understood 'nationally' or contiguously; and the continuing divisions produced within territorial states that spawned conflict among people, where conflict was understood as a temporal, or even temporary, condition, rather than as an historical spatial productivity. That is, for Kang, unity was constructed as a spatial aspiration devoid of conflict (and thus of historicity), and conflict a temporal problem shorn of productive spatiality. In consequence, the absolute conquest of time by space – which I take to be the core of Kang's Utopian vision – would spell not only the end to strife but, indeed, the end of history.[29] This quasi-modernist view of the potential Utopian reconciliation between space and time – or, the transcendence of time by space – can be likened to a type of *posthistoire,* as Lutz Niethammer has called such a vision, that presents itself as an 'overcoming of chaotic historicity', or, as an end of materiality itself.[30]

It is in this context of a globally spatially construed *posthistoire* magically shorn of any specific cultural meaning or centre that Kang's exposition on 'abolishing racial boundaries and amalgamating the races' can be placed. Many commentators treat this chapter of Kang's *Datong shu* with extreme skepticism – in large part because his solution to racial division is to 'smelt' the races into what he considers to be the only really neutral 'race' (white) through the encouragement of large-scale miscegenation and immigration.[31] Yet, despite Kang's jejune and patently crude equations of skin colour with a slightly modified environmental and biological determinism in his designations of racial essences, and despite his elevation of 'white' and 'yellow' above other colours, Kang's combination of a Utopian spatial universalism with a racialized particularism that is *not* tied to culture (understood as a productive spatiality) and that is thus transcendable offers insights into how 'race' became one pillar of a very different organizational philosophy of globality at the turn of the century.

In the 'race' chapter of *Datong shu* – the third section, after 'states' and 'classes' – Kang notes:

> inequality of creatures is a fact. Whenever we speak of equality, it is necessary that creatures have the capacity to be equal in abilities, knowledge, appearance and bodily characteristics before equality can be effected. If not, then even though it be enforced by state laws, constrained by a ruler's power, and led by universal principles, it still cannot be effected.[32]

Because 'difference' in appearance, in and of itself, leads to injustice and the irrational exercise of social and political power, in Kang's estimation, the racial boundary was perhaps the most pernicious as well as the most difficult of all to abolish.[33] As such, 'race' was specifiable as a particularity – an appearance – with consequences in the concreteness of all history, including in the period that would emerge as the threshold to one-worldism (after states had joined completely into spatio-political unity), and the residues of race could continue to structure inimically the achievement of one-worldism. Because of his focus on visible difference – rather than on the historical production of difference – Kang specifically articulated race in the language of aestheticism; he was emphatic that the 'races of India' are 'fierce and ugly', while Blacks (speaking of American Blacks) had 'iron faces, silver teeth, slanting jaws like a pig, front view like an ox, full breasts and long hair, their hands and feet dark black, stupid like sheep or swine'.[34] Yet, this aestheticism derived from a socio-philosophical concern with what he saw as the bases of social injustice, as power that was perpetrated and perpetuated through unchanging ways of seeing rather than historically-produced ways of being.

From today's vantage point, perhaps most remarkable about Kang's view is that he seems not even vaguely concerned with subjectivities and identities as constituted in and through race (or sex or nationality). This absence raises the question of 'culture' quite directly. Indeed, on Kang's view, one of the major obstacles to overcoming boundaries was to equalize civilization across the globe. Yet, his idea of 'civilization' (wenming not wenhua)[35] is curiously evacuated, or rather is emphatically not articulated in the culturalist vein usually connoted by the term wen.[36] Thus, while 'civilization' is articulated as a universalistically unbounded topos, it carries little content. Indeed, as Kang writes:

> When civilizations are equal, when they are the same in their [social] aspects, when [peoples] have become intermingled, [receiving] the same education and the same upbringing so that there is no natural division of the people into high and low, then equality [among men] will be near at hand, and the change will certainly be natural and easy.[37]

Kang's emphasis on civilization as a series of visible or tangible social indices of universal quotidian existence and not as historically constitutive of subjective cultural beings precisely shapes his understanding of 'race' as a both a malleable – indeed, erasable – and an essential category of human unity/division.

On this view, Kang's proposal for abolishing 'race' – along with class, gender and other divisions, which are also mostly articulated in terms of visible signs of inequality and injustice – can only be constructed as plausible if we understand 'race' in his terms: that is, as an abstract spatiality rather than historically specific productivity. For, it is only in this sense that for Kang 'race' could help constitute an understanding of current conflicts without posing an absolute barrier to a global unity envisioned as the erasure of visible bases for the exercise of power. It is hence Kang's contradictory combination of what we might today see as virulently racist and essentialist attitudes (towards Blacks, Indians, or non-whites and non-yellows in general) with the Utopian desire for one-world unity that marks not only a crucial global spatial turn in Chinese philosophy in general of the time, but also the possibility for 'race' to become important in such explorations. 'Race' was not a means to instrumentally rationalize the relevance of the outside world to China in contemporary historical terms, but, more important, it was Kang's way to reconceptualize that mutual incorporation as a transformative appropriation aimed at moving beyond the divisiveness of the contemporary world.

Several possible and ostensibly opposed trajectories are present in Kang's incipient philosophy of race and globality: the systematization of divisions in terms of an essentialized racialism combined with national territoriality as global spatial organizational topoi tied to a historically productive sense of spatiality; and, the further refinement of Utopian notions of globality. That Chinese 'race' philosophies went in both directions simultaneously at the turn of the century has much to do with the new relevance in Chinese historical consciousness of the modern category of colonialism after 1900 and the initial ways in which Chinese intellectuals came to link Chinese history and its contemporary situation to the world through this new category of analysis.

Colonialism, revolution, and race

At the same time as Kang was working out his one-world philosophy, which, as we have seen, attempted to think the world in a utopian-transformative fashion, other genres of historical writing that combined the world and China into a new unity also arose. Less abstract than Kang's version, one genre in particular, in part adapted from Japan, was the *wangguo shi,* or histories of perished states. These were narratives that largely concerned themselves with recounting the terminal fate of states that had either perished by being eaten up by stronger powers or declined and disappeared because of the fall into corruption of ruling elites. This fate of perishing – not understood as an abstract spatial 'joining' as with Kang but as the disappearance of cultural nations – was most often said to be traceable to a complacently 'enslaved' people, who were unwilling or unable to act to prevent either the swallowings or the corruptions. As such, *wangguo shi* could encompass such distantly past examples as the decline and fall of Babylonia and Rome, and such more recent examples as the 'perishing' of India, Vietnam, Ireland, and Poland, among many others.

Sociologists Hu Fengyang and Zhang Wenjian note that *wangguo shi* made their appearance in China most clearly after the allied occupation of Beijing during the Boxer Rebellion (1900–901).[38] Historian Yu Danshi has characterized them as 'important constituent parts of early twentieth-century Chinese patriotism',[39] because they were written and translated just as nationalist sentiment was stirring among intellectuals. The appearance of the *wangguo shi* as a distinct genre was thus connected to a dramatic increase at the time in journalistic writings and translated books (from the West and Japan) on the world, the latter often called comprehensive world histories (*shijie tongshi*), even though most of these so-called 'world histories', as the prominent journalist and intellectual Liang Qichao complained in 1899, actually were merely histories of Western countries.[40] *Wangguo shi* were hence also intimately connected to contemporaneous efforts being made by Liang Qichao and, from a different direction, Chen Fuchen, among others, to write new national histories of China that departed from the state-dominated dynastic chronicles prevalent in most official Chinese historiographical practice. Indeed, all these histories – the *wangguo shi,* ostensibly about other places and often other times, the 'world' histories and the attempts at national histories – explicitly aimed 'to look anew at China itself from the perspective of the world'.[41]

To grasp the novelty of *wangguo shi* as a genre, it is important to note that, as a term, *wangguo* had first had to be detached from its traditional connotation of the deposing of one dynasty by another. Indeed, by the turn of the twentieth century, *wangguo* had come to refer, not to internal dynastic replacement, but to the colonization of specific places by external powers, where colonization (or *wang*) was understood as more than the usurpation of state power. As Liang Qichao wrote in 1900, in reference to his observations on the colonization of Hawaii by the United States, 'Of old, in the perishing of a state [*wangguo*], the state alone was lost. Today it is different: when the state is destroyed, the race/people follows it [*guowang er zhong ji sui zhi*].'[42] As such, by the first decade of the twentieth century, the weight of the meaning of *wangguo* was decisively shifted from connoting an internal dynastic change to a centrally constitutive moment of modern world history tied to a complex, spatially produced globality. In this guise, the term was increasingly used interchangeably with the contemporaneous understandings of 'imperialism' (*diguo zhuyi*), 'expansionism' (*pengzhang zhuyi*), and 'colonialism' (*zhimin zhuyi*).[43] Moreover, in its compound conjoining with *wangzhong* (perishing of the race), as *wangguo wangzhong,* or as *wangguo nu* (slave of a perished state), it referred to the colonized transformation of whole peoples, including culture, language, organization of labour, and so on.

By the same token and at the same time, the concept used to denote 'revolution' – *geming* – also underwent a sea-change in meaning, in which *geming* provided the flipside to colonization. Previously, *geming* had denoted the withdrawal of the mandate of heaven from a given dynasty/emperor; it was thus, like the older notion of *wangguo,* tied to a paradigm of internal dynastic change and exclusively tied to the state. By the turn of the century, *geming* had taken on the meaning of socio-political revolution, understood both as anti-colonial action against an externalized conquering power – also known as *paiwai* (expelling outsiders/foreigners) – and, as in the case of the French (1789) or Persian (1908) revolutions, as the popular removal of a monarchy in favour of a republican arrangement.[44]

The combination of the popularization of the *wangguo shi,* Qing China's increasingly precipitous decline into social and political chaos, and contemporaneous revolutionary actions erupting throughout the colonized world turned colonialism into the dominant paradigm of historical analysis, while also rendering revolution one of the most hotly debated issues of the first decade of the twentieth century.[45] Of singular importance in constituting these paradigms was the specification of 'difference' and of boundaries; and, with the linked change in the historical connotations of *wangguo* and *geming* – as colonialism and revolution – came a turn in historical consciousness towards an understanding of a politically produced global space of transformative modernity that was to be animated by anti-colonial revolutions across the globe, all connected in global space by the co-temporality of their historical moment, even though each was led by different peoples/races and each sought to reinscribe local boundaries between 'nation' and 'world'.

This turn is noticeable in any number of essays, books, and publications of the time. Here, I wish to discuss briefly the proliferation of popular biographies written at the turn of the century on Chinese and foreign heroes, all of whom were designated heroes of anti-colonial revolutionism. In the first case, Chinese anti-dynastic figures from the past – who had had thriving afterlives in popular prose narratives and local dramatic works, but who were nowhere present as heroes in official histories – were turned into national patriots, with their single most noteworthy patriotic acts said to be their struggles against foreigners (Mongols, Manchus, *et al*, were now understood not as potentially Sinicized and thus legitimate rulers of the empire, but rather into racial outsiders, or colonizers). In this process of historical reinterpretation, many distant figures from the past came to the fore. These included Huang Zongxi, whose 1662 text *Mingyi daifang lu* [The Way of the Prince] was rediscovered in the late-Qing and promoted as paradigmatic of ethno-nationalism; the late-Ming scholar Wang Fuzhi, who was barely known in his time, yet became well known at the turn of the century 'with the upsurge in anti-Manchu revolutionism';[46] Gu Yanwu, another late-Ming scholar; Yue Fei, a Southern Song general who was executed in the twelfth century despite his struggle against Jurchen invaders, and who, in 1906 was dubbed 'the first Chinese anti-foreign nationalist';[47] and Zheng Chenggong, a.k.a., Koxinga, the Ming restorationist holdout on Taiwan against the Manchu Qing in the mid-seventeenth century;[48] among others.[49]

In the second case, foreign patriots, contemporaneous leaders of anti-colonial struggles across the globe – including the Filipinos Emiliano Aguinaldo and José Rizal; the Transvaal President and Afrikaaner leader in the Boer War, Paul Kruger; the deposed Hawaiian Queen Liliukalani, among others – were rendered not only into patriotic defenders of their people against colonizing outsiders, but, more interestingly, they were also rendered into *tongzhong* (same race) allies with Chinese would-be revolutionaries in the struggle against imperialist modernity. In naming these foreign revolutionaries and anti-colonial activists as racially 'same', 'race' came to signify a common global political project unconnected to skin colour, rather than, as in Kang's sense, a boundary only remedied by wiping away visible signs of difference. While the utopianism encoded in what might be called this incipient Third World solidarity was perhaps no less attainable or realistic than was Kang's Utopian vision of the elimination of all visible boundaries – and indeed the moment was quickly swamped by the realities of global revolutionary failure – by the same token, this common political project of 'race' as solidarity was no *posthistoire*. Rather, it was an attempt to imagine and mobilize a different history of modernity that was, however, completely structured and informed by the historicity of the modernist moment. As such, contemporary anti-colonial *paiwai* (expelling outsiders) activism – or, anti-colonial revolution – created an identifiable national/global praxis that could be immediately appropriated for a re-interpretation of the Chinese past and the contemporary historical task, both nationally and globally. In this sense, not only did the immediacy and contingency of global anti-colonial activity lend foreign 'heroes' and their specific spheres of activity contemporary cogency, but, by offering examples of 'patriotism' that were not over-determined by a teleology of completed state-building or by the functionality of symbolic mobilization by an existing state, these anti-colonial figures and resuscitated Chinese heroes were also imbued with a global racial significance informed by an optimistic reading of the dynamics of modern global politics.

For example, in early 1903, Tang Tiaoding [Erhe][50] wrote a series of linked studies of the recently failed Philippine Revolution against the United States. One study in particular focused on José Rizal, whom Vincent Raphael has called the 'first Filipino'[51] and whose novel, *Noli me Tangere,* forms the opening subject of Benedict Anderson's now classic study of nationalism.[52] Yet, while both Raphael and Anderson concentrate on how Rizal helped create a sense of the Philippine nation in the late nineteenth century for (elite) Filipinos through his rendering of a national-temporal homogeneity, Tang Tiaoding's purpose in introducing Rizal to Chinese readers was to help create a global solidarity amongst different peoples, who were ostensibly linked in contemporary political sympathy. As Tang writes, emphasizing Rizal's resonance not in the Philippines but in the global sphere:

> Alas! This superior talent who was so educated, this Tagalog man, was a great and fierce person of the yellow race [*huangren*]. Indeed, one unique characteristic of our yellow people is that we have a false reputation [in the world] for being primitive [*yeman zhi yuanming*]. Yet, had it not been for the primitive behaviour [*manxing*] of Spain, what would Rizal's contributions have been called? And who would have known [of them]?[53]

At one level, Tang appropriates 'this Tagolog man' for the yellow race, thus placing him in an intimate connection with Chinese, who, when they had written of the Philippines in the past, had generally dismissed Filipinos as uncivilized primitives. At another level, however, Tang's appropriation is not merely a familiarizing gesture or, at least, not a gesture aimed at assimilating the Filipinos into some already understood regime of 'yellowness' that the Chinese (or Japanese) represented. Tang's is, rather, an appropriative gesture aimed at seizing the definition of 'yellowness' away from imperialist epistemologies and their destructive production of the organizing structures of the modern world; and, more interestingly, an attempt to hitch China to this new powerful 'yellowness' represented by the formerly ignored Filipinos.

This point was reinforced, albeit in a different way, by another commentator, who wrote at the same time as Tang of the arms shipment scheme Chinese activists had organized to assist Filipino revolutionaries via Japanese intermediaries, a scheme that was betrayed by those very intermediaries:

> These ever-perfidous [*sic*] Japanese, who speak all the time of a same continent [*tongzhou*], same culture [*tongwen*], same race [*tongzhong*] Asian alliance, who say all the time that the Filipinos are related to them by blood;[54] these very Japanese nevertheless engage in immoral trickery and have forced the Filipinos into horse

and cow slavery forever. Alas! Heaven does not oppress yellow people; yellow people oppress each other! With such a race, I wish the world would no longer produce anything in the colour yellow![55]

To be sure, using the very epistemological constructions of racialization mobilized by colonial/imperialist discourses (whether Western or Japanese) in Asia only gets Chinese commentators so far. Nevertheless, the basis upon which Chinese and Filipinos are both 'yellow' (and, in the latter commentary, the basis upon which Japanese are to be excluded from 'yellowness' because of treachery) is understood to be not only the imperialist/colonial ideology of primitiveness that taints China and the Philippines equally in the global sphere, but the Filipinos' falsification of that ideology globally through their political-revolutionary activities.

In particular, in the latter regard, Tang Tiaoding mentions Rizal's 1887 novel, *Noli me Tangere* (whose title Tang translates as *Ru wuchu wo,* or *Don't you touch me!*):

> Although this book was written in the form of a prose narrative [*xiaoshuo*], it actually introduced the problem of the Philippines to the world. It described how the Spanish ruled the Philippines, and how this rule was clearly not designed for the benefit of the Filipinos. [Rizal] loudly protested the position of the Spanish friars in the Philippines and cast doubt upon their supposed righteousness.[56]

Having nothing at all to say about internal racial/class relations among Filipinos themselves – abundantly depicted in Rizal's novel in, for example, the interactions between Spanish-educated, lighter-skinned Filipinos and uneducated, darker-skinned ones; and/or between upper-class, urban Filipinos and rural peasants – Tang is able to concentrate his whole commentary about Rizal, and indeed about the whole revolutionary endeavour, upon the Philippines-in-the-world. This concentration, on the one hand, was most congenial to Tang, who, as with many Chinese elites of his time, was not much concerned with internal bases of social inequity in China (most, other than anarchists, deeming such inequity easily reversible once the global and internal political situations had been settled). Moreover, Tang almost certainly had not read *Noli me Tangere,* at most having heard of it through Filipinos in exile in Japan, where Tang resided briefly in 1902–3. Indeed, as Ma Junwu, another Chinese intellectual in Japan, noted in his translation of some of Rizal's poetry in 1903: 'Those of us living in Japan communicate with one another frequently; in the course of drinking together, we listened carefully to recitations of Rizal [by Filipino revolutionaries], so he became famous [among us].'[57]

Yet, on the other hand, Tang and other commentators' focus on the global production of racialist ideologies for imperialist/colonial purposes was also conditioned by the perceived similarity between the political anti-colonial projects which the Philippines and Chinese intellectuals such as Tang were engaged in fomenting. This latter focus is reinforced in Tang's biographical treatment of Emiliano Aguinaldo, then leader of the Philippine revolution against US colonial occupation. As Tang comments, bringing Paul Kruger of the Transvaal into the narrative at the same time:

> Since the waning years of ancient Greece, no one has resisted the world's strongest states in defence of their own people's independence from the space of a tiny state. The Transvaal's President Kruger is one man with this type of vigorous spirit and determination. Yet, there is another, not yet forty years old, who, from his tiny island no bigger than a grain afloat in the ocean, has led his

people in opposition to the world's biggest and wealthiest nation in order to gain his people's independence. Is this not Aguinaldo, the fellow from the Philippines? Although these two are separated by wide oceans and have never met, they have performed moving political dramas on the world stage at the end of the nineteenth century. They can be called jewels of the world.[58]

The contemporaneity of the revolutionary upheavals in the Transvaal – where the Boer War was dominantly understood as an anti-colonial war of independence against Britain – and the Philippines simultaneously creates their respective national and their common global 'stage' of politics. Both stages are racialized, insofar as each participant people separately and all together are engaged in the production of a new globality and a nationalism aimed in part at combatting the racialized primitivism ascribed to them all by imperialist epistemologies. As such, there is no doubt that the condition of possibility for this restructuration of political desire – whether on the national or global 'stage' – is the perceived monolithic production and reproduction of colonial/imperialist race philosophies that seemed to underpin the circulation of representations globally, with their local effectivities and instantiations understood as delimited to the denial of national independence and sovereignty.

Indeed, later in the biography, Tang Tiaoding ostensibly quotes Aguinaldo as declaring:

> if Americans approach our people with unjust arrogance, do not fear: we have shaken off the shackles of Spain and we are now prepared to go against heaven and earth . . . Descendants of Washington: try closing your eyes to examine your conscience! You should be ashamed! The Filipinos have united in order to protect their lives; they have drawn energy and lessons from the pitiful native people [*kelian zhi tumin*], endured battlefields raining with canonballs and gunsmoke, and have died in great numbers. Americans have long boasted of their history; I now beg to inquire: where has the great spirit of North America gone?[59]

Here, Tang, via Aguinaldo, is only too happy to conceal internal racial and class division through an appeal to global unevenness and global injustice, an appeal that is globally radical and yet locally blind to its own elitist bases. With this, it is possible to see both the potential and the inherent limitations in the racial formulation of global political solidarity, as this appeal was explicitly conjoined to colonial paradigms of modern history.

The challenge of 'race'?

By the time of the failures of the turn-of-the-century anti-colonial revolutionary wave – that is, by 1905 at the latest – historical and contemporary emphasis increasingly turned away from linked global solutions to the solving of local problems. In this turn, the newly adopted colonial paradigm of modern history was mobilized to vilify the Manchu Qing, as much for their Manchu-ness as for their corruption, political failures, and purported 'slavishness' towards the foreign powers. With the racialized understanding of colonialism now in place, Manchus were understood to be the real colonizers of China – rather than being seen as the latest rulers of the millennia-old empire – and the contemporary Chinese task was understood to be anti-colonial revolution aimed against the Manchus, as racially and ethnically 'other' than the Han Chinese. In a longer-term sense, the initial racialization/ethnicization of the Manchus in these years through a colonial paradigm of modernity contributed to the Republican era's proliferating racialization/ethnicization of all non-Han Chinese, inside and outside the borders of China. As a corollary, it also contributed to the racialization of the Han Chinese themselves, most evident in the Republican era turn (and the default return ever since) towards a discourse of a Chinese *minzu* (ethno-nation), whose contemporary historical task was to recapture the greatness of culturalist China's past.[60]

As is evident from the discussion above, 'race' philosophy in China, particularly at the moment of its initial introduction in the late Qing, was tied to a complex and shifting understanding of globality and spatiality. In its more optimistic instantiations, which have returned episodically during China's most revolutionary moments, 'race' was an inclusionist philosophy of defiance, and referred to a global political solidarity. In the language of the late Qing, it was a *tongzhong* (same race) unity, and in its episodic recurrence ever since, this unity was expressed as a shared experience of 'the oppressed peoples of the world' (*bei yapo renmin / minzu*). In its more localist, or narrowly nationalist instantiations, which have also often returned with a vengeance (most recently, in the current era), it was an exclusionist philosophy. Both versions emerged at the same time and have co-existed uneasily for the ensuing century. Yet, the act of remembering the globally radical version is a political challenge, as Ato Sekyo-Otu writes of remembering Fanon in the current moment: a challenge to remember both 'the fledgling promises and prospects' as well as the 'congenital errors and imminent tragedies'[61] of a world history understood as a spatial relationship among peoples brought into being violently and not yet fully confronted or resolved.

Notes

1   For more on this, see Rebecca E. Karl, 'Staging the World in Late-Qing China: Globe, Nation, and Race in a 1904 Beijing Opera', *Identities*, vol. 6, no. 4, 2000, pp. 551–606.

2   For this 'othering' approach to 'race', see Frank Dikötter, *The Discourse of Race in Modern China*, Stanford University Press, Stanford, CA, 1992; and the various essays on China in Dikötter (ed.), *The Construction of Racial Identities in China and Japan*, University of Hawaii Press, Honolulu, 1997.

3   This is James Pusey's argument, in *China and Charles Darwin*, Harvard University Press, Cambridge, MA, 1983.

4   For food metaphors in Chinese political and philosophical discourse, see Gang Yue, *The Mouth That Begs: Hunger, Cannibalism, and the Politics of Eating in Modern China*, Duke University Press, Durham, NC, 1999.

5   Ato Sekyi-Otu, *Fanon's Dialectic of Experience*, Harvard University Press, Cambridge, MA, 1996, p. 72. As Sekyi-Otu makes clear in an explicit argument against many postcolonial versions of Fanon, this spatialized system of radical irreciprocity cannot be accessed through analysis of the slippages in the language and discourse of colonial texts alone, but rather must be accessed through analyses of historical experience.

6   Clearly, there were also sub-national spatialities of region, district, language group, and so on, some of which were tied to divisions of labour within economic sectors and some to other historical factors. I will not be overtly concerned in this chapter with those issues, although my analyses are not antithetical to problems of sub-national 'race' – usually labelled 'ethnicity'.

7   Gilles Deleuze and Félix Guattari, *A Thousand Plateaus: Capitalism and Schizophrenia*, trans. Brian Massumi, University of Minnesota Press, Minneapolis, 1987, pp. 456–57.

8   Ibid., p. 456. For a slightly differently emphasized elaboration of this view of nationalism, see Rebecca E. Karl, *Staging the World: Chinese Nationalism at the Turn of the Twentieth Century*, Duke University Press, Durham, NC, 2002, Chapter 1.

9   For more on immanence and immanentism, see Deleuze and Guattari, *A Thousand Plateaus*, *passim*; also Michael Hardt and Antonio Negri, *Labour of Dionysus: A Critique of the State-Form*, University of Minnesota Press, Minneapolis, 1994, Chapter 7.

10 On 'appropriation' see Sekyi-Otu's discussion in *Fanon's Dialectic*, pp. 184–211 and *passim*:

> Appropriation . . . would be the activity of coming into one's own when there is no primal self to return to, no inviolate native essences to recapture; consequently, the enterprise of transforming into one's own tradition of possibilities an imposed order of practices and thereby overcoming their violence. (p. 184)

This meaning derives from Martin Heidegger.

On 'desire', Foucault figures it as a regulatory discourse (*History of Sexuality,* vol. 1, Vintage, New York, 1985). Yet, as Ann Laura Stoler points out, in a colonial context, 'desire' must also include its manufacture and not only its regulation and release (*Race and the Education of Desire: Foucault's History of Sexuality and the Colonial Order of Things,* Duke University Press, Durham, NC, 1995, p. 167). 'Desire' is here understood in the dialectical sense of what desire produces and what is productive of desire.

11   On 'ethnos' in Japan, see Naoki Sakai, *Translation and Subjectivity: On 'Japan' and Cultural Nationalism,* University of Minnesota Press, Minneapolis and London, 1997; for China, see Karl, *Staging the World,* Chapter 5. I take 'ethnos' to be different from 'ethnicity', insofar as 'ethnicity' — at least in the Chinese case — derives from a prior concept of the 'ethnos' and is thus rendered an instrumentalized category of differentiation. A different way of putting this might be that 'ethnicity' is about populations, whereas 'ethnos' is about peoples. For 'ethnicity' in China in its anthropological-sociological sense, see the various essays in Stevan Harrell (ed.), *Cultural Encounters on China's Ethnic Frontiers,* University of Washington Press, Seattle, 1995.

12   See Neil Lazarus, *Nationalism and Cultural Practice in the Postcolonial World,* Cambridge University Press, Cambridge, 1999, p. 25: '(capitalist) modernity is characterized by unevenness: that is, by the dynamics of development and underdevelopment, autocentricity and dependency, the production and entrenchment of localisms . . . within larger processes of globalization, incorporation, and homogenization'.

13   Here, I borrow Jacques Rancière's notion of 'names of history', as that which is 'the very disruption of the relations between names and states of affairs'. Rancière, *The Names of History: On the Poetics of Knowledge,* trans. Hassan Melehy, University of Minnesota Press, Minneapolis, MN, 1994, p. 93.

14   On 'packaging,' see Theodor W. Adorno, 'Bourgeois Opera', in *Sound Figures,* trans. Rodney Livingstone, Stanford University Press, Stanford, CA, 1999, p. 16. On language, see Fredric Jameson, *The Prison-House of Language,* Princeton University Press, Princeton, NJ, 1972.

15   It is clear that, in the context of overseas Chinese — in South-east Asia or elsewhere — or of Chinese intellectuals residing in Japan, or yet in the treaty ports, whose socio-political organization was based upon imperialist racialisms, 'race' was indeed a potent lived experience for many Chinese. Particularly in the latter context, it would be interesting to investigate the ways in which Manchu/Han separation in urban spatial design and Western/Chinese separation in urban treaty port design were similarly or differentially understood; these topics, however, fall outside the parameters of the current chapter.

16   Stoler, *Race and the Education of Desire,* pp. 68–69.

17   For the renarration of the Manchu Qing deposing of the Ming through a colonial paradigm, see Rebecca E. Karl, 'Creating Asia: China in the World at the Beginning of the Twentieth Century', *American Historical Review,* vol. 103, No. 4 (October 1998), pp. 1096–1118.

18   For a suggestive discussion of this issue for post-dynastic, pre-Communist China, see Joseph Levenson, *Revolution and Cosmopolitanism,* University of California Press, Berkeley, CA, 1971, pp. 6–11.

19   See Karl, *Staging the World.*

20   The title is also translated as *A Discourse on the Grand Unity.* Kang's book was written between 1884 and 1902. It began with the title *Universal Principles of Mankind* [*Renlei gongli*] and ended up as *One World Philosophy* [*Datong shu*]. The book was finished during Kang's sojourn in Darjeeling, India, where, among other places, he resided after being forced into exile after the 1898 reform movement. The book was only published in full after 1911. For more on the history of the book, a brief biographical sketch of Kang, and a full translation of the text, see Laurence G. Thompson, *The One World Philosophy of K'ang Yu-wei,* George Allen & Unwin, London, 1958.

21   See Lionel M. Jensen, *Manufacturing Confucianism: Chinese Traditions and Universal Civilization,* Duke University Press, Durham, NC, 1997, Chapter 3.

22   For more on Kang, see Hsiao Kung-ch'uan, *A Modern China and a New World: K'ang Yu-wei, Reformer and Utopian,* University of Washington Press, Seattle 1975; Tang Zhijun, *Kang Youwei yu wuxu bianfa* [Kang Youwei and the Wuxu Reforms], Zhonghua shuju, Beijing, 1984; Li Zehou, *Zhongguo jindai sixiangshi lun* [*Essays on Modern Chinese Intellectual History*], Renmin chubanshe, Beijing, 1986, pp. 92–181.

23   Hao Chang, *Chinese Intellectuals in Crisis: Search for Order and Meaning,* University of California Press, Berkeley, CA, 1987, p. 25.

24   Ibid., p. 57.

25   Ibid., pp. 56–65.

26   Thompson, trans., *The One World Philosophy of K'ang Yu-wei,* pp. 84–85.

27 On this distinction in a different context, see D.R. Howland, *Borders of Chinese Civilization: Geography and History at Empire's End,* Duke University Press, Durham, NC, 1996, pp. 4, 177.

28 As Hao Chang notes (*Chinese Intellectuals in Crisis,* p. 62), unlike many Utopias from both Chinese and other traditions, which 'feature the negation of government and authority as such, Kang's Utopia is a politically organized universal state'.

29 As Lutz Niethammer summarizes pre-Second World War notions of 'post-histoire' in European thought: 'these authors see themselves facing anonymous structural processes before which individuals feel so powerless that they endow them with omnipotence . . . These processes are endowed with . . . a capacity to dissolve cultural values in non-temporal randomness.' (*Posthistoire: Has History Come to an End?,* Verso, London, 1994, p. 57).

30 Niethammer, *Posthistoire,* p. 17. Niethammer adds, this type of posthistoire – characteristic of the European nineteenth century – 'did not contain the frustration of cultural pessimism, but rather the hope that the chaos of history . . . might finally be overcome' (p. 18).

31 As he notes, white and yellow peoples are more similar in colour and intelligence, and thus, the amalgamation of these is relatively easily accomplished, which leaves 'brown and black . . . [who are] so distant from the white people [that they] will be really difficult to amalgamate'. His solution is to encourage miscegenation between white women and coloured men – where women are understood as the bearers of race – so as to produce successive generations of lighter offspring; and to encourage blacks and browns to move to northern climes (for example, Africans to Sweden) where darker colours will, over time, naturally fade. See Thompson, trans., *The One World Philosophy of K'ang Yu-wei,* pp. 140–48. Dikötter (*The Discourse of Race in Modern China,* p. 90) asserts that Kang's racial assimilationism is merely a transformation of 'the traditional concept of cultural absorption into a vision of physical amalgamation'. This, it seems to me, is only a superficial reading.

32 Thompson, trans., *The One World Philosophy of K'ang Yu-wei,* p. 143.

33 The sex boundary between man and woman could be dealt with, according to Kang, by abolishing the institution of marriage and its links to private property, restructuring society so that all were equally responsible for the raising of children, and degendering clothing.

34 Thompson, trans., *The One World Philosophy of K'ang Yu-wei,* p. 144. Kang had been several times to the United States, where he had witnessed the treatment of black Americans in the West and the north-east; he also sojourned in India, the treaty ports of China, Hong Kong, and south-east Asia, where Indians served as soldiers and servants to British colonials and settlers.

35 *Wenming* in this period can be understood either as civilization as a behavioural norm or as modernity, or being modern. *Wenhua* is an older civilizational notion that carries with it a certain set of references to education in the classics and Confucian normativity; as a concept, it was also at just this time beginning to take on the meaning of 'national culture'. For more on the latter issue, see Lydia Liu, *Translingual Practice: Literature, National Culture, and Translated Modernity,* Stanford University Press, Stanford, CA, 1995, Chapter 9.

36 On *wen* as 'civilization' see Howland, *Borders of Chinese Civilization.* On 'civilizing missions' in China *vis-à-vis* non-Han peoples in the empire and on its fringes, see Stevan Harrell, 'Civilizing Projects and the Reaction to Them', in *Cultural Encounters on China's Ethnic Frontiers,* pp. 3–36.
    Kang was also, however, one of the major proponents of tying a formerly universalist Confucian civilizational topos to a national cultural realm, particularly in his later efforts to specify a religious content to Confucianism and to promote Confucianism as the religion of China. On this aspect, see Li Zehou, *Kang Youwei yu Tan Sitong sixiang yanjiu* [*A Study of the Thought of Kang Youwei and Tan Sitong*], in *Zhongguo jindai sixiangshi lun* [*Essays on Modern Chinese Intellectual History*], Renmin chubanshe, Beijing, 1986; also Jensen, *Manufacturing Confucianism,* Chapter 3.

37 Thompson, trans., *The One World Philosophy of K'ang Yu-wei,* pp. 140–41.

38 Hu Fengyang and Zhang Wenjian, *Zhongguo jindai shixue sichao yu liupai* [*Trends and Schools in Modem Chinese Historiography*], Huadong shida chubanshe, Shanghai, 1991, pp. 240–44.

39 Yu Danchu, 'Zhongguo jindai aiguo zhuyi de "*wangguo shijian*" chukao' ['Preliminary Investigation into Modern Chinese Patriotic "Mirrors on the History of Perished States"'], *Shijie lishi,* vol. 1, 1984, pp. 23–32; citation from p. 23.

40 Liang Qichao, 'Dongji yuedan' ['A Critique of Japanese Booklists'], in Liang Qichao, *Yinbingshi wenji* [*Collected Essays from the Ice-Drinker's Studio*], juan 4, p. 102.

41 Wu Tingjia, *Wuxu sichao zongheng lun* [A Complete Discussion of Intellectual Trends in the *wuxu* period], Renmin chubanshe, Beijing, 1988, p. 96. Liang's 1902 essay, *Xin shixue* [*New Historiography*], is generally considered the first attempt to write a national history of China; at the same time, Chen Fuchen [Jieshi], less a new-style journalist/intellectual (such as Liang) than an old-style scholar-literatus, also wrote an outline piece entitled *Dushi* [*Independent History*] that articulated guidelines for

a new type of historical practice. Liang's *Xin shixue* was published serially in the middle of 1902 in *Xinmin congbao* [*New People's Miscellany*]; Chen's *Dushi* was published at the end of 1902 in *Xinshijie xuebao* [*New World Scholarly Journal*].

42   Liang Qichao, 'Xiaweiyi youji' ['Diary of Travel to Hawaii'], *Yinbingshi zhuanji*, vol. 7, pp. 149–60; citation from p. 160.

43   With this turn, the previous instances of a non-Han dynasty taking over from a Han Chinese dynasty – for example, the Mongol Yuan over the Song, the Manchu Qing over the Ming – were reinterpreted as colonizations, rather than as changes in dynasty.

44   The American Revolution was understood as both anti-colonial and anti-monarchical. The Mexican Revolution, begun in 1910, was the first seen as a peasant revolution of a different type altogether. But, because China's Republican revolution erupted in 1911, commentaries on Mexico – which had been numerous in 1910 – ended; Mexico was brought up again only in the 1920s, when a new wave of revolutionary theorizing got under way in China.

45   Indeed, the paradigm of colonialism was extended backwards to stand in for all occurrences of dominance of one state over another people or state. For more on the specific revolutionary movements at the turn of the century and how they were interpreted and appropriated in China, see Karl, *Staging the World*.

46   Kauko Laitinen, *Chinese Nationalism in the late-Qing Dynasty: Zhang Binglin as Anti-Manchu Propagandist*, Curzon, London, 1990, p. 24.

47   Anon., 'Yue Fei Zhuan' ['Biography of Yue Fei'], *Jinye xunbao* [*The Struggle*], vols 5–7, 8–9 (1906 and 1907). Also see Anon., 'Zhongguo minzu zhuyi diyi ren Yuefei zhuan' ['Biography of China's First Ethno-nationalist, Yue Fei'], *Hubei xuesheng jie* [*Hubei Student World*], 4–5 (April–May 1903), among others.

48   See, for example, 'Zhongguo aiguozhe Zheng Chenggong zhuan' ['Biography of the Patriot, Zheng Chenggong'], *Zhejiang chao*, vol. 4 (1903); 'Zheng Chenggong zhuan' ['Biography of Zheng Chenggong'], *Jiangsu*, vol. 3 (1903).

49   For a list with publication details, see Yu Danchu, 'Xinhai geming shiqi de minzu yingxiong renwu shijian chukao' ['Preliminary Investigation on National Heroes, Personnages, and their Times during the Xinhai Revolutionary Period'], *Jindaishi yanjiu*, vol. 6 (1991), pp. 34–52.

50   Tang (1871–1940) came from mean circumstances, even though his father had been a lower-level official in the Qing bureaucracy; yet, after his father's death, Tang had been brought up by his poverty-stricken uncle in a rural town in Zhejiang province, and after years of informal schooling, only at age 22 did he begin to attend a formal school in Hangzhou. After the 1911 revolution and many years of study in Japan, Tang became a prominent medical scholar and co-founded several of China's first comprehensive medical schools; in the late 1930s, Tang worked in the fields of medicine and education with the Japanese occupation government in Peking. He died in 1940. For an exonerating biography by Tang's son, see [Tang] Yousong, *Tang Erhe xiansheng* [*Mr Tang Erhe*], Zhonghua shuju, Beijing, 1942.

51   Vincent Raphael, 'Nationalism, Imagery, and the Filipino Intelligentsia in the Nineteenth Century', *Critical Inquiry*, vol. 16 (Spring 1990), pp. 591–611.

52   Benedict Anderson, *Imagined Communities*, Verso, London, 1991.

53   Tang Tiaoding, 'Feilübin haojie zhuan' ['Biographies of Heroes of the Philippines'], *Xinshijie xuebao* [New World Scholarly Journal] vol. 10 (12 February 1903), p. 10.

54   There was a certain trend at the time in Japan to claim that the Filipinos and Japanese were related, because of the widespread intermarriage on certain of the Philippines islands to which a number of Japanese had previously emigrated. See Lydia N. Yu-Jose, *Japan Views the Philippines, 1900–1944*, Ateneo de Manila University Press, Manila, 1992.

55   Hansheng, 'Feilübin wangguo canzhuang jilue' ['A Brief Outline of the Tragic Colonization of the Philippines'], *Hubei Xuesheng jie* [*Hubei Student World*], vol. 7.

56   Tang, 'Feilübin haojie zhuan', p. 11. I should note in passing that it was only in these first years of the twentieth century that novels were beginning to be recognized by elite intellectuals as a viable form of writing. Indeed, only a few months earlier, in late 1902, Liang Qichao had called for the development of the political novel as a specific form of national literature in his *Xin xiaoshuo* [New Fiction]. This recognition of political novels was tied to the rise of political novels in Japan at the time. For more, see Xia Shaohong, *Jieshi yu chuanshi: Liang Qichao de wenxue daolu* [*Enlightenment and Eternity: Liang Qichao's Literary Path*], Renmin chubanshe, Shanghai, 1991.

57   Ma Junwu, 'Feilübin zhi aiguozhe' ['A Filipino Patriot'], *Xinmin congbao* [*New People's Miscellany*], vol. 27 (12 March 1903); reprint *Xinxuejie congbian* [*Compendium of New Learning*], vol. *8, juan 13*, part 2, 4b–5b. These recitations were almost certainly provided by Mariano Ponce, delegate from the

revolutionary Philippine Republican government to Japan, 1900–903. For more on the Chinese and Ponce in Japan, see Karl, *Staging the World,* Chapter 4.

58   Tang Tiaoding, 'Feilübin haojie zhuan', *Xinshijie xuebao,* vol. 10, p. 1.

59   Ibid., p. 6.

60   The People's Republic of China moved for four decades away from this *minzu* discourse to a more racially/ethnically neutral, albeit super-politically charged discourse of the *renmin* (the masses). However, since the 1980s, the *minzu* focus has become much more pronounced, in official and unofficial discourse alike.

61   Sekyi-Otu, *Fanon's Dialectic of Experience,* p. 11.

Chapter 43

Pamela Scully

RACE AND ETHNICITY IN WOMEN'S AND GENDER HISTORY IN GLOBAL PERSPECTIVE

Understanding "race" as a social construct can lead to a re-examination of historical narratives concerning racial and ethnic differences. Pamela Scully, professor of Women's Studies and African Studies at Emory University, and the author of two key books on gender and slave emancipation (1997 & 2005), argues that racial discrimination based upon skin colour is relatively recent, and that ancient cultures around the world, including Europe in the Middle Ages, did not discriminate upon this basis. From a women's studies perspective, "race" only makes sense as part of an intersecting cluster of discourses—including gender, sexuality, class and ethnicity—which are historically and culturally situated differently. Studied in this way, progressive or teleological (end-goal) oriented narratives of race (either histories of increasing racism or of a decline in racist aspects of society) are rejected, since race is defined through social and political *interaction*, which changes across time. Furthermore, since gender and sexualities are now studied from non-essentialist perspectives, it is important to note the consequences by re-reading "normalizing" positions on race, say, those of white women, in favour of cultural and ethnic diversity, and a "perspectivism" that reveals different notions of race from multiple viewpoints rather than the white/black binary hierarchy. However, quoting Higginbotham's work, Scully does point out that as a concept race is "Janus" faced, that is, it faces two ways simultaneously: towards oppression, and towards liberation. Even with the Janus image in mind, the history of "race" is situated in varying notions of the interaction of colonizers and slaves, starting with the fifteenth-century European colonizing of the American continent and of Southeast Asia. Whether scholars think that Eurocentric notions of race predated these experiences or were constituted by them, race became a European discourse used to "explain cultural difference." This was also a gendered discourse, with philosophers problematically equating whiteness and masculinity, and blackness, femininity and pathology. In other words, notions of racial primitivism, degeneracy and even disease, were tied-in with the category of the feminine. Complicating this discourse further were the complex sexual relations of slave-holders and their subjugated people; a sexual economy developed that was related to European notions of gender and power, although cultural differences, for example between Dutch, French and British slaveholders, were apparent. The production of monolithic European cultures, alongside economic productivity, were factors in colonial anxieties concerning racial hybridity and long-held allegiances, for example, between Canadian settlers and indigenous peoples in North America. Scully concludes by examining the convergence of nineteenth-century concerns over slavery and women's rights, especially in the area of suffrage (women and blacks were *not* allowed to vote). However, white women often regarded themselves as superior in cultural and ethnic terms, and in fact it was the black "self-help" organizations that Scully presents as being a more viable form of independent racial recognition. Beginning in the US, constituted through acts of racial exclusion, these organizations (churches, non-profits, and educational based) spread to other countries such as South Africa, playing a key role in recoding race and ethnic identity and achievements.

DIFFERENT SOCIETIES' UNDERSTANDINGS OF RACE, class, masculinity, and femininity critically affected and produced knowledge about appropriate behavior and aspirations of individuals at particular moments.[1] Historians are paying attention to how ideas of blackness or whiteness—or colonized or colonizer—were produced and reproduced in gender and women's history.[2] Race in particular is now seen not as a biological truth so much as a cultural classification resulting from cognition or perception.

Discrimination based upon differences in skin color or cultural affiliation is a relatively new phenomenon. In Ancient Egypt, for example, skin color or place of origin appears to have had little place in determining a person's social or economic position. Even by the European Middle Ages, when people increasingly made an association between whiteness and purity, racism as a way of excluding people solely because of their skin color did not exist. For example, people respected the legacies of scholars of African descent such as St. Augustine and Ptolemy.[3]

Likewise, when Christopher Columbus's expedition encountered the Taino of the Caribbean, race was not the category through which people understood the encounter. The Taino perhaps saw Columbus and his men as an ancestor or dead chief returning from the land of the dead across the sea rather than as a biologically different kind of person. Columbus understood his meeting with the Taino in terms of a variety of grids of understanding prevalent in the European Middle Ages. The views ranged from believing that the outer limits of the European world were populated by monsters to believing that the world was divided into the Christian world, China, and the uncivilized remainder.[4] Thus, although Columbus and his European contemporaries certainly held prejudices against indigenous people and feelings of superiority about European civilization, race as a biological category of difference was not the category through which they understood the Colombian encounter.

Some ten years earlier, across the Atlantic on the shores of Central West Africa, people of the Kongo Kingdom welcomed white spirits of the dead who emerged out of the sea near present-day Congo. The governor of the province of Soyo greeted the spirits as representatives of a new cult of the earth and water spirits and sought to be initiated into the cult.[5] The BaKongo were witnessing the first Portuguese exploration of the central African coast. They made sense of the pale men who spoke a different language not through the lens of race but through a framework of spiritual knowledge and explanation that fit with Kongo religion and cosmology.

Race, as a way of thinking about and classifying individuals by skin color and putative biology, is a product of particular historical interactions between Europe and indigenous societies around the globe, at least from the fifteenth century. A study of race and ethnicity as social historical constructs within women's and gender history thus only makes sense if one studies race, ethnicity, and gender as historically specific and within a comparative perspective. Even within Europe, the history of the idea of race as well as of the category *woman*, for example, have undergone many permutations and understandings.[6] Across time and geography, the history of women, perceptions of woman, and the intersection of race and gender are much more intricate and complex.

Ethnicity, too, has an uneasy history that spans many centuries. Forms of ethnic identification appear to have older roots than that of race. In Asia and Southeast Asia, for example, caste and ethnicity have long histories of cultural identification and exclusion. Indeed, it is sometimes difficult to distinguish clearly between ethnicity and race. In China and Japan, discrimination of ethnic minorities has long existed, with the bodies of women often being seen to represent the purity or impurity of a given ethnic group. Thus, for example, women of ethnic minorities were spared foot binding in nineteenth-century China because they were seen to be outside of the boundaries of Chinese civilization.

With the rise of a new wave of European imperialism from the 1880s, Europeans tended to perceive distinctions within putative racial groups through ethnicity. British colonialism in particular employed the concept of ethnicity, closely related to that of tribe, to accomplish rule over myriad societies within Africa, for example.[7] Ethnicity in America has been an important site of struggle in debates about immigration for well over a century. Throughout the 1920s nativists sought to limit or stop immigrants from Ireland and Southern Europe, arguing that certain ethnic groups were inferior to others. Thus the category *white* could be further subdivided into a gradation of racially coded ethnic groups.

Historiographies of race and racism

Historians of women's and gender history have inserted new dynamics into the historiography of race by establishing a methodology for studying race as a historical category linked to notions of gender and sexuality. In addition, they have sought to analyze race and ethnicity within Europe and the colonies, both in the Americas and in Southeast Asia, in the same frame. In so doing, feminist historians have shown that attempts are ill-advised to provide a rigid chronology for the rise of racial thinking that extends neatly across time and space. They have suggested that rather race and ethnic identities can be embraced and accentuated in one context and time period and can decline and become relatively unimportant social and economic markers in another. They have also called attention to ways in which women and men have experienced gendered racial identities as a source of empowerment and disenfranchisement in the political arena.

Historians have tended to see black identity as a synonym for race, with whiteness being "so natural, normative and unproblematic that racial identity" is seen as a "property only of the nonwhite."[8] Some historians have begun to analyze the politics of whiteness in white women's political lives, but that is a relatively new trend in women's history. During the Victorian era, women missionaries, teachers, explorers, and suffragists to some extent embraced whiteness as a way of creating a "positive female identity" for themselves "in a deeply misogynistic society."[9]

Historians of gender have shown that there is no essential womanhood to which historians and history can appeal. That has implications for the study of race in women's history, and Evelyn Brooks Higginbotham most powerfully calls for greater theorizing of race within that discipline.[10] Higginbotham charges that many white feminists have tended to conflate white woman with black womanliness and assume that all women are alike in identities and aspirations. Higginbotham argues against any kind of essentialist invocation of race. She also maintains that historians of African American women's history, by invoking concepts such as "black womenhood," are in danger of assuming that all black women are the same and somehow share the same feminine identity. Such a notion obscures differences of class experience, family experience, and geography that shape experiences of race and gender. Yet talking of black womanhood points to ways in which race and racism have powerfully affected black women's lives. It also alerts historians to how the experience of racial oppression can help create foundations for powerful identity politics.

Higginbotham instructs historians studying race and women's and gender history to understand how race was constructed or understood at different periods in history. It should not be assumed that people have always understood or recognized race. Higginbotham also advises grappling with race's power as a "metalanguage" or model that shapes concepts such as "gender, class, and sexuality."[11] By that she means seeing how ideas about blackness and whiteness operate in tandem, or in concert, with other ideas about manliness or femininity. Race, that is, cannot be examined in isolation from other categories that shape society and history. Finally, Higginbotham suggests trying to analyze the Janus face of race. It can, they say, be used as a tool of oppression and also serve as a vehicle or concept for liberation. Thus, we need to appreciate how race works in history and not naturalize race and its effects.

Other authors have also asserted the need to attend to the many sites of difference and identity within women's history. Elsa Barkley Brown argues that merely mentioning difference—that is, talking of white and black women in the same breath—does not itself constitute analysis of the discrete experiences of women. Brown suggests that historians write of women's various experiences through the idiom of jazz rather than classical music. This means that teachers and writers accept that there is no one universal historical score by which to write or teach history. "Race (and yes gender, too) is at once too simple an answer," Brown observes, "and at the same time a more complex answer than we have yet begun to make it."[12]

Part of the complexity of dealing with race lies precisely in confusion about how to account for the genesis of the concept. Historians tend to locate the rise of biological racism within the eighteenth century arising from a fifteenth-century backdrop of European colonization of the Americas and Southeast Asia. Historians of race in the Atlantic world in particular have long debated the causes of racial thinking. Winthrop Jordan argued in *White over Black* that Europeans, even before the rise of the slave trade, associated blackness with death and evil. Jordan therefore concluded that racism, or at least racial thinking, predated colonial slave systems. Settlers in the Americas enslaved Africans because they already saw them as inferior. Other historians, such as Eric Williams in *Capitalism and Slavery,* maintained instead that racism arose from the experience of slavery and the slave trade in the Americas.[13] The emergence of a system of slavery, with slaves being drawn almost exclusively from Africa, a geographical and cultural context different from that of slaveholders, gave rise to settlers' association of blackness and inferiority and the rise of formal legal racism.

More recently, scholars have again looked to Europe for explanations for the rise of race as an important marker of difference. Scholars of the Enlightenment argue that the era produced both hardened forms of gender inequality and new ideas about race. Men's increasing social and political liberty was in many instances formally dependent on their domination of women and children in the home. In addition, the rise of classification as a model for understanding the world helped produce racial thinking. The encyclopedic model of classifying things and people tied individuals to biology and the group in new ways. That fascination with categorization arose in part as away of mastering the new information about people, biology, and cultures that Europe confronted as a result of the discovery of the Americas from the fifteenth century. Race became a primary language through which European intellectual thought sought to explain cultural difference.

Racial explanations of difference also drew on contemporary notions of gender. During the late eighteenth and early nineteenth centuries philosophers such as Jean-Jacques Rousseau as well as scientists such as George Cuvier sought to account for what they perceived as the natural differences of men and women. Race and gender became linked to the extent that a description of whiteness invoked associations with masculinity. White male scientists as well as European popular culture increasingly came to see femininity as well as blackness as forms of pathology.[14]

Ideas about women as somehow marginal, and perhaps threatening to male society, thus mirrored and came to enhance in intricate ways white racist ideas about people of African descent. The invention of race thus drew on the experiences of slaveholders in the Atlantic slave colonies, where white men had almost total power over the bodies of black women. The idea of race, however, also was informed by longer negative male understandings, rooted in European history, of women.

Historians of gender and women's history argue that languages of race, gender, and sexuality emerged not so much in either Europe or the colonies but rather across the divide of metropole and colony. Colonialism depended on racial categories of inclusion and exclusion to maintain boundaries between colonized and colonizers. Sexuality and gender were essential pillars of the construction of racial discrimination and identities within the colonial setting. Who was allowed to marry whom—and which children were counted as children of the colonizers and which were not—helped secure colonial rule. But race as a category of knowledge changes across time and space. Children of settler men and indigenous women could at one time be included within the settler definition of "white" and at another be included in a category of "mixed race."[15] In early-eighteenth-century Louisiana, for example, French authorities were very concerned about relationships between French men and Indian women. At the same time in the Dutch Cape Colony, South Africa, and in the Dutch East Indies, authorities actually encouraged concubinage as a way of maintaining colonial rule. Similarly, early in the history of the Colony of Virginia slaveholders formed ideas about blackness being an inferior racial and sexualized category. In contrast, in the slaveholding Cape Colony, although women were regarded differently according to geographic origin, race as such does not appear to have been a salient organizing category until into the nineteenth century.

In Louisiana at the turn of the eighteenth century, French colonial authorities worried that settler men, many of whom came from Canada and had long interaction with Native American communities there, were becoming too involved with indigenous communities. French-speaking men both lived in Native American villages and established relationships with Indian women. Officials believed that such relationships "retard[ed] the growth" of Louisiana in that men were less likely to settle down and become farmers, thus rendering the colony stable and profitable. Officials also worried that settlers would be drawn into the fold of Indian communities and not reproduce French culture on American soil.[16]

Whereas the French actively encouraged French women to emigrate to Louisiana, including forcibly putting prostitutes onboard ships, the VOC (Dutch East India Company) for much of its tenure as an imperial power actively discouraged white women from emigrating. The VOC established a way station in the Cape Colony in 1652 for its boats en route to the Dutch East Indies. It also discouraged any kind of formal settlement, although it had to rescind the policy within a few years. The company did allow relationships between its employees and African women, however. At the Cape, one indigenous woman named Eva was able to marry into the higher echelons of the Dutch East India Company in Cape Town. She served as a linguistic and cultural translator between the Dutch and the indigenous Khoisan.[17]

The Dutch policy of encouraging sexual relationships between Dutch men and indigenous women, and the ambivalent acceptance of children of mixed-race, continued well into the nineteenth century in the Dutch East Indies. In Malaysia, the Dutch saw colonialism as dependent upon the same sort of sexual relationships. The VOC believed that European marriage would be so costly that it would draw Europeans down into a poorer white class and thus complicate the neat divides of wealthier whites and poorer local societies. That, too, changed, however, with the rise of eugenics and racial science in the twentieth century. Ann Stoler argues that colonial authority came to rest more clearly on "European-ness" and on more racially distinct populations.[18]

The creation of "knowledge" about race appears to have been in operation much earlier on in other societies, particularly in the Americas. Virginia's early colonial history people, for example, identified themselves with local communities, with kin groups, and, perhaps, with "nations" conceived as African, Indian, and English. Yet soon after the establishment of slavery, ideas of femininity and blackness became laden with pejorative associations within a context of slaveholding. The relative openness of both ethnicity and racial categories changed in the mid-seventeenth century with the consolidation of patriarchal colonial power. Racial categorization of blackness versus whiteness became the primary social, economic, and political identifier. Kathleen Brown shows that gender ideals about good, industrious wives versus wenches, concepts settlers imported from England, underwent changing gender and racial meanings. By the late seventeenth century, the "good wife," who had the connotation of being an industrious household worker, became increasingly a white category, at least in public discourse. Black women became wenches, sexual, licentious, and unruly. "Womanhood . . . began to take on a race-specific meaning in the colony."[19]

In contrast, race in the Cape Colony was not a central feature of company rule. Like Virginia in the early years, many different status and categories of origin existed, for example, French, German, Dutch, bastard, bastard hottentot, and hottentot. The categories referred to a person's geographic origin, sometimes to the status of their parents and sometimes to their putative nationality. A "bastard hottentot," for example, was the child of a slave man and a Khoi woman. Compared to Virginia, at the Cape before the arrival of the British in the nineteenth century the "respectability" of women was determined in part by baptism as by recognition of European heritage. The conflation of slaveholding status primarily with Europeans and Christians—and the facts that most Africans were not Christian and most slaves were denied baptism by their owners—helped establish possible foundations for a kind of racialized consciousness before the nineteenth century. Scholars, however, generally consider that race at the Cape only became a fully elaborated category of exclusion or self-definition in the nineteenth century.

The British, in contrast to the Dutch, actively sought to classify everyone into racial groupings. Given the confusion about status and origin, the British found it almost impossible to keep up with the categories created by the Dutch. Thus, over the course of the nineteenth century the category *coloured* enlarged to include people recognized neither as African nor as European. With the abolition of slavery in 1838, racial identities seem to have become the primary marker of status, and "colouredness" became a cultural category into which former slaves, freed in 1838, also were absorbed. Although some children of black descent had become part of the white population before slavery, after slavery their trajectory was much more likely to lie within the category *coloured*.[20]

There is no teleological story about race and ethnicity and the history of these categories does not move from liberalism to a more racist culture or the other way around. Nor can we easily argue that racism emerged in Europe and was exported to the colonies or vice versa. Historians have also shown how messy concepts of race were affected by (and helped shape) emergent ideas about class and femininity within European society during the nineteenth century. Analogies among the Irish, the working class, or prostitutes drew on a set of ideas of laziness, immorality, and degeneracy that coded the middle classes as the norm and others as deficient. It is clear that a "repertoire of racial and imperial metaphors were deployed to clarify class distinctions in Europe at a very early date."[21] Different regional literatures, however, including those of the United States, Latin America, the Caribbean, Africa, and Southeast Asia, have developed distinctive historiographies on race and ethnicity in women's and gender history.

Notes

1   For a good overview of the literature on women, class, and race, see Eileen Boris and Angelique Janssens, "Complicating Categories: An Introduction," in *Complicating Categories: Gender, Class, Race and Ethnicity,* ed. Eileen Boris and Angelique Janssens, supplement 7 of *International Review of Social History* (New York: Cambridge University Press, 1999).

2   Evelyn Brooks Higginbotham, "African-American Women's History and the Metalanguage of Race," *Signs* 17 (Winter 1992): 251–74; Ann Stoler "Rethinking Colonial Categories: European Communities and the Boundaries of Rule," *Comparative Studies in Society and History* 31 (Jan. 1989): 134–61. A major exception is Nancy Stepan, "Race and Gender: The Role of Analogy in Science," Isis 77 (June 1986): 261–77.

3   Martin Bernal, "Race in History," in *Global Convulsions: Race, Ethnicity, and Nationalism at the End of the Twentieth Century,* ed. Walter Van Home (Albany: State University of New York Press, 1997), 75–92.

4   Seymour Phillips, "The Outer World of the European Middle Ages," in *Implicit Understanding: Observing, Reporting, and Reflecting on the Encounters between Europeans and Other Peoples in the Early Modern Era,* ed. Stuart Schwartz (New York: Cambridge University Press, 1994), 23–63.

5   Wyatt MacGaffey, "Dialogues of the Deaf: Europeans on the Atlantic Coast of Africa," in *Implicit Understanding: Observing, Reporting, and Reflecting on the Encounters between Europeans and Other Peoples in the Early Modern Era,* ed. Stuart Schwartz (New York: Cambridge University Press, 1994), 249–67.

6   Denise Riley, *"Am I That Name?": Feminism and the Category of "Women" in History* (Minneapolis: University of Minnesota, 1988).

7   Leroy Vail, ed., *The Creation of Tribalism in Southern Africa* (Berkeley: University of California Press, 1989).

8   Ann duCille, "The Occult of True Black Womanhood: Critical Demeanor and Black Feminist Studies," *Signs* 19 (Spring 1994): 591–629, cited in Susan Stanford Friedman, "Beyond White and Other: Relationality and Narratives of Race in Feminist Discourse," *Signs* 21 (Autumn 1995): 1–49, quotation on 1.

9   Louise Michele Newman, *White Women's Rights: The Racial Origins of Feminism in the United States* (New York: Oxford University Press, 1999), 20.

10 Higginbotham, "African-American Women's History." This is also collected in an excellent collection edited by Darlene Clark Hine, Wilma King, and Linda Reed: *"We Specialize in the Wholly Impossible": A Reader in Black Women's History* (Brooklyn: Carlson, 1995). The volume covers the experience of black women in Africa, the Caribbean, and the United States. The first section includes some of the key theoretical pieces on race and women's history.

11 Higginbotham, "African-American Women's History," 252.

12 Elsa Barkley Brown, "'What Has Happened Here': The Politics of Women's History and Feminist Politics," in *"We Specialize in the Wholly Impossible": A Reader in Black Women's History,* ed. Clark Hine, Wilma King, and Linda Reed (Brooklyn: Carlson, 1995). 48.

13 Winthrop Jordan, *White over Black: American Attitudes toward the Negro, 1550–1812* (Chapel Hill: Published for the Omohundro Institute of Early American History and Culture at Williamsburg, Virginia, by the University of North Carolina Press, 1968); Eric Williams, *Capitalism and Slavery* (New York: Capricorn Books, 1944).

14 Stepan, "Race and Gender."

15 Ann Stoler, "Rethinking Colonial Categories: European Communities and the Boundaries of Rule," *Comparative Studies in Society and History* 31 (Jan. 1989): 134–61; Ann Stoler, "Making Empire Respectable: The Politics of Race and Sexual Morality in Twentieth-Century Colonial Cultures," *American Ethnologist* 16, no. 4 (1989): 634–60.

16 Jennifer Spear, "They Need Wives': Metissage and the Regulation of Sexuality in French Louisiana, 1699–1730," in *Sex, Love and Race: Crossing Boundaries in North American History,* ed. Martha Hodes (New York: New York University Press, 1999), 35.

17 Julia Wells, "Eva's Men: Gender and Power in the Establishment of the Cape of Good Hope, 1652–74," *Journal of African History* 39, no. 3 (1998): 417–37.

18   Ann Laura Staler, "Rethinking Colonial Categories: European Communities and the Boundaries of Rule," *Comparative Studies in Society and History* 31 (Jan. 1989): 134–61.

19   Kathleen Brown, *Good Wives, Nasty Wenches, Anxious Patriarchs: Gender, Race, and Power in Colonial Virginia* (Chapel Hill: Published for the Omohundro Institute of Early American History and Culture by University of North Carolina Press, 1996), 136.

20   Pamela Scully, *Liberating the Family? Gender and British Slave Emancipation in the Rural Western Cape, South Africa, 1823–1853* (Portsmouth: Heinemann, 1997).

21   Ann Staler, *Race and the Education of Desire: Foucault's History of Sexuality and the Colonial Order of Things* (Durham: Duke University Press, 1995), 123.

PART VII

Postcolonial studies

A HIGHLY COUNTER-DISCURSIVE CRITICAL approach within literary studies, the postcolonial is in many respects a "writing back" against the Eurocentric literary canon that was used by colonists (educators, missionaries, government functionaries, and so on) both during and after colonization of the Third World, to maintain European hegemony or dominance. Such "writing back" happens in myriad ways: through production of a deeply intertextual literature that creates internal debates and criticism concerning the canon, i.e., at the level of the very fabric of literary texts; through linguistic playfulness and creativity to produce an oppositional postcolonial English language; through deliberate rejection of European religions, symbols, allegories, standards, and values, in favour of indigenous cultures, practices, alternative histories, and belief systems (including indigenous foundational narratives and key indigenous characters or figures such as trickster). Colonialism, then, is not just a brute material force, but it also functions through its discursive formations, the power-knowledge semiotic networks and narratives that inculcate the ideology of the colonizer in and through colonized subjects. This process has been mapped most thoroughly—through what is called colonial discourse analysis—by Edward Said, in his books *Orientalism* (1978) and *Culture and Imperialism* (1993). Other critics have identified at the level of rhetoric one of the key tropes of colonial discourse: that of allegory, which works by finding a deeper spiritual or ethical meaning beneath the surface level of a text. For example, pondering the explorer Christopher Columbus's ritualistic act of imperial naming of the Caribbean islands—a naming choice based upon Biblical and Spanish dynastic figures—critic Stephen Slemon argues that such a "ritual" is "inalienably allegorical, for here Columbus 'reads' the site of otherness by reference to an anterior [previous] set of signs that is already situated within an overarching, supposedly universal, metaphysical and political master code of recognition."[1] Replicated across colonial society, allegory becomes a "technology of appropriation",[2] one that is productive of new colonial subjectivities, loyal to the Crown. More generally speaking, Slemon argues that allegory privileges Eurocentric "doctrine and metaphysical system at the expense of 'otherness'."[3] Thus the standard definition of allegory as an "other speaking" is better translated in a colonial/postcolonial context as "speaking *for*, the 'other'."[4] Slemon and others have expertly expanded upon this process, but what is of interest here is the postcolonial response, since allegory not only instils colonial values, but actively continues to reinforce and produce them. Allegory, in other words, is the site not just of colonial construction, but also when re-appropriated it can function as a postcolonial deconstruction: "Whatever its precise form or historical moment, allegorical writing is associated with 'a belief in the possibility of transformation'. This characteristic of allegory may have served the ideology of imperialism in legitimizing the transformation of the 'other' into colonial subject, and it may continue to underwrite neo-colonial codes. But by foregrounding the fact that history is not a set of immovable past achievements but a discourse, open, as are all discursive practices, to reinterpretation, post-colonial allegorical narratives show that allegorical transformation can also be an effective means of subverting imperial myths."[5] But this is to move too far ahead, and to gain an understanding of how postcolonial studies developed in literary critical terms, the story returns to a point much earlier than Said's groundbreaking texts or Slemon's later incisive criticism.

Literary critical postcolonial studies began in university departments with courses on what was known as Commonwealth,[6] New or World Literatures. One of the earliest of these courses was taught by A. Bruce Sutherland at Pennsylvania State University in 1942, called "English 70: The Literature of the British Dominions and Colonies."[7] Two main types of literature were often studied on these courses, written from within "the predominantly European settler communities" and from the perspective of peoples and nations "in the process of gaining independence from British rule, such as those from the African, Caribbean and South Asian nations."[8] Regardless of the types of literature studied, the prevailing critical norm was that of liberal humanism, or, the belief that great works of literature express universal (usually meaning "European") humanistic values. What this norm signified more practically was that Commonwealth Literature was often studied *comparatively* to see how it "measured up", so to speak, against the texts of the liberal humanist canon (Milton, Shakespeare, the Romantics, major modern novelists, and so on). Critics such as John McLeod have noted how this approach creates a space of serious study of other cultural texts and traditions within a university setting; yet at times this mode of study neutralizes or merely fails to focus on the cultural and political specificity of non-European writing. Critic Phillip Darby has noted how key African authors stress their cultural and political "responsibilities": "Chinua Achebe has written of his commitment 'to help [his] society regain its belief in itself and put away the complexes of the years of denigration and self-denigration'. Nuruddin Farah began writing, he once explained, 'in the hope of enabling the Somali child at least to characterize his otherness'. According to Ngugi wa Thiong'o, literature is 'a very important weapon . . . in the struggle for communal and individual self-definition', and for him this involves taking a stand against the imperialist tradition."[9] The crucial shift, then, from liberal humanism into postcolonialism, actually came about through the more widespread critique within universities of liberal humanism per se. Such a critique occurred quite aggressively with the rise of theory during the 1960s through to the 1980s as alternatives to universalizing critical methodologies, and it led to a more politicized approach to postcolonial literary criticism.

The relationship between the rise of theory and postcolonial studies is modelled in the Palestinian American critic Edward Said's intellectual trajectory, especially in his two more theoretical works: *Beginnings: Intention and Method* (1975) and *The World, the Text and the Critic* (1983). In the former book, drawing upon French theorist Michel Foucault among others, Said argues against a metaphysical universalizing and potentially liberal humanist notion of "origin" and for a secular, contingent, fictionalizing notion of "beginning"; in the latter book, Said argues for the importance of the socio-political context of texts, rejecting an overly formal application of literary theory.[10] In *Orientalism* (1978), Said drew upon Foucault and the social theorist Antonio Gramsci, to study the hegemonic discursive formation called "Orientalism", that is to say, the highly productive distributed power-knowledge network that simultaneously represents and subjugates the "Orient" (what would now be called the Middle East, a term which still betrays a Eurocentric or Western *position* if not perspective). Said's main task is to analyze the colonial discourses that make up Orientalism, which he does through close reading of the "dreams, images, and vocabularies"[11] found in myriad Orientalist texts, many of which take a comparative approach to reveal the "superiority" of the European mindset. As Said says, "Whether this comparative attitude is principally a scholarly necessity or whether it is disguised ethnocentric race prejudice, we cannot say with absolute certainty."[12] What is certain is that Said reveals that Orientalist discourse tells us more about nineteenth- and twentieth-century Western attitudes to the Other (enthusiasm, fear, racism, desire, self-aggrandizing, and so on) than it does about the peoples and places that such texts purportedly represent. In other words, Orientalism creates a shadow or mirror world, one which is "radically real" in the sense that if an Orientalist says something is real, then that becomes accepted, empirical data; it becomes reality for the European mindset.

In *Culture and Imperialism* (1993), Said embraces an even larger task: examining Western "imperial" discursive formations, and the intellectuals, activists and authors who resisted attempts at subjugating and denigrating their cultures, for example Frantz Fanon, Amilcar Cabral, C.L.R. James, Walter Rodney, Chinua Achebe, Ngugi wa Thiongo, Wole Soyinka, Salman Rushdie and Gabriel Garcia Márquez among others.[13] What Said calls the "great cultural archive" was precisely the "intellectual and aesthetic investments in overseas dominion",[14] and this reveals some surprising shifts of postcolonial critical focus, for example on Charles Dickens or Jane Austen, novelists whose works are among the many which were "part of the structure of an expanding imperialist venture."[15] And indeed Said does focus on the novel, in the case of Austen being that which "steadily, if unobtrusively, opens up a broad expanse of domestic imperialist culture without which Britain's subsequent acquisition of territory would not have been possible."[16]

Feminist approaches to postcolonial studies are profoundly indebted to the work of Gayatri Spivak; her essay "Can the Subaltern Speak? Speculations on Widow Sacrifice" (1985; first reprinted 1988), was one of the key theoretical texts during the 1980s; this essay was substantially revised by Spivak in her book *A Critique of Postcolonial Reason: Toward a History of the Vanishing Present* (1999). The Subaltern Studies Group set out to produce a non-elitist history of modern India which would express the "politics of the people",[17] i.e., the politics of the subaltern/people of inferior position rather than the viewpoint of the Raj, or of the Indian bourgeoisie who took over from the British after independence in 1947. The Subaltern Studies academics theorized that because the bourgeoisie controlled the production of historical narratives, there was a failure to even recognize or identify the active role of a vast class of mainly labouring people who make up a large part of Indian society, consequently leading to a "monistic" perspective of Indian history, that is to say, basing the entire historical project on a single principle of governance and cultural production by the elites. Rejecting the monistic perspective leads to a new understanding of postcolonial India, for example, the Subaltern Studies group reject the notion that colonization was based upon the "consent" of the people.[18] But even given the academically marginalized status of the early Subaltern Studies group, the question remains how these academics, who are themselves not labourers or peasants, claim to represent or recover the suppressed voices of the subaltern Other? In an earlier essay on the topic, "Subaltern Studies: Deconstructing Historiography" (1985), this is one of Spivak's main criticisms, with the additional suggestion that Subaltern Studies academics produce an essentialist account of subaltern subjectivity, one which is always defined in contrast to that of the ruling elites. Spivak argues that even more problematically, within Subaltern Studies the question of gender was initially minimized, thereby doubly effacing subaltern women's voices. In focusing on the subaltern, Spivak is making a wider point concerning postcolonial studies, that is to say, critics need to remember that postcolonial identities are heterogeneous (diverse, different, hybrid), and that for all the good intentions of critical approaches to the postcolonial, the entire methodology runs the risk of misrepresenting the Other. In her revised version of

"Can the Subaltern Speak?", this part of her argument is contextualized globally, and she also argues that a deconstructive approach is needed to maintain theoretical flexibility to avoid essentialism and re-appropriation of the Other.

A major theoretical strategy to avoid foreclosing the heterogeneity of postcolonial narratives and subjectivity has been to register and explore the concept of hybridity. As critics Ashcroft, Griffiths and Tiffin write in another groundbreaking text in the development of postcolonial studies, called *The Empire Writes Back: Theory and Practice in Post-Colonial Literatures* (1989), "The post-colonial text is always a complex and hybridized formation. It is inadequate to read it either as a reconstruction of pure traditional values or as simply foreign and intrusive."[19] "Hybridized" means that texts are constructed by drawing upon multiple traditions and modes of expression. The term "hybrid" does have a problematic provenance for some critics, since it is used in animal and plant breeding, and even more troublingly in the nineteenth-century Eugenics and related movements such as Nazism (attempting to selectively breed "criminal" or "defective" traits out of human populations). An alternative term that avoids some of these problems is "syncretist", a joining-together or fusion of otherwise separate traditions, yet one which still maintains internal differences and oppositional forces.[20] Both terms, hybridity and syncretist, imply processes, and this is another way to avoid negating the energies and resistances of postcoloniality, that is to say, to remain in process, simultaneously reaching back into indigenous traditions, and forwards to the reclaiming of these traditions in modern-day expressions of new postcolonial identities. This process is not based upon one particular world view, which is something that Ashcroft, Griffiths and Tiffin stress: "the syncretic and hybridized nature of post-colonial experience refutes the privileged position of a standard code in the language and any monocentric view of human experience."[21] But such a "nature" implies the need for ever-increasing theoretical complexity to explicate postcolonial sites of signification.

The theoretical turn in postcolonial studies is apparent in Homi K. Bhabha's theoretically dense writing throughout the 1980s and 1990s, collected in *The Location of Culture* (1994). Bhabha draws deeply upon psychoanalytical critics (particularly Freud and Lacan), poststructuralist theorists (Derrida, Foucault, and again Lacan), colonial discourse analysts and critics such as Frantz Fanon and Edward Said, and authors such as Toni Morrison, Salman Rushdie and Derek Walcott.[22] What Bhabha offers is a highly nuanced critique of binary thinking, especially where it is inadvertently reinscribed; for example, when the colonial masters are portrayed as being monolithic in culture and power. As critic Bart Moore-Gilbert writes: "Bhabha interprets the regime of stereotype as evidence not of the stability of the 'disciplinary' gaze of the colonizer, or security in his own conception of himself, but of the degree to which the colonizer's identity (and authority) is in fact fractured and destabilized by contradictory psychic responses to the colonized Other."[23] The colonizer needs to create a sense of his own identity through constantly negating the identity of the Other (using derogatory stereotypes); yet this leads to an unstable performativity (see Chapter 51), constantly needing to *repeat* the disavowal of the Other, but in reality being *constituted* by this relationship with the Other. Bhabha utilizes poststructuralist theory to analyze this "destabilized" relationship, self-reflexively observing the blindspots concerning race and ethnicity within theoretical discourse. So Bhabha's use of theory is doubled: at one level he utilizes theory to expand upon the complexities of postcolonialism, and at another level, he uses postcolonialism to critique theory![24] It is this doubled theoretical discourse that readers of Bhabha and other postcolonial critics find exhilarating or infuriating. A good example concerns Bhabha's theorizing of "hybridity". Rather than seeing colonialism as productive of authority per se, Bhabha argues that colonialism produces "hybridization",[25] which occurs in a number of ways: through the hollowness of authoritative discourse, the paranoiac and excessive fears/desires projected onto the submissive-yet-potentially-anarchic Other, or simply via the signs of colonial difference and Otherness.[26] Wanting to bolster its own identity and solidity through disavowing the Other, colonial discourse only partially succeeds; in other words, this partial success can be turned around and seen as the beginning of colonial fragmentation and destabilization. As Bhabha puts it: "the desire of colonial discourse *is* a splitting of hybridity that is *less than one and double*."[27] To get to this point Bhabha has drawn upon Freud, Lacan, Foucault, Fanon and Derrida, among others, to make the point that the colonizer's culture does not precede colonization in a purified and homogenous form, to which all colonial "reactions" can be measured; rather, it is *constituted* within the colonial context as a divided and doubled discourse, hybrid, split, and inherently unstable.

In Bhabha's later writing, there is a marked shift from analyzing colonial discourses and situations, to focusing on migrant or diasporic communities in the West. As Moore-Gilbert argues, this constitutes for Bhabha a "second phase of work" which "is primarily devoted to the problems posed by colonial history and inherited discourses, of race, nation and ethnicity, for contemporary cultures."[28] But it also involves a further postcolonial interrogation of theory: in this case, a postcolonial critique of postmodernism. Partly, this critique involves registering the fact that modernity is incomplete, because academics have never fully registered the role of non-Western peoples in the formation of modernity, and that the benefits of modernity— its rights and obligations—have not been applied by the West to indigenous peoples.[29] Postmodernism cannot therefore be a stable theory of the contemporary world if it is based upon a largely colonial notion of modernity, or that which it subsumes and replaces. Bhabha's critique, then, proceeds by a "reinscription of the repressed histories and social experiences of the historically marginalized"[30] a procedure undertaken most notably by Fanon.[31] What Bhabha finds in the process of reinscription is an irreducible presence within indigenous subjectivity, a "foreignness", from the perspective of the West, that postmodernism attempts to neutralize via ideologies of multiculturalism and diversity (i.e., multiple subjectivities, but usually with a core shared identity); for Bhabha, this irreducible presence works instead to deconstruct postmodernism, to reveal culture as always being at work in a "third space" of in-betweenness, an ambivalent and disruptive place of translation and creativity. As with translation, there is always some difference that remains, an untranslatable kernel, that means that the Other can never be effaced, however dispersed or apparently "integrated" into Western cultures.

Recognition of diasporic postcolonial subjects, and associated literatures throughout the world, has subsequently led to an expansion of the postcolonial canon, which as critic Deborah Madsen and others have pointed out, follows from the "desire to revise and expand the postcolonial paradigm to accommodate the contributions of such colonized peoples as Native Americans, Chicano/as, Afro-Hispanic and African-American peoples."[32] Madsen argues that "if we are to create an authentic post-colonial canon then we need to lift our critical sights higher than the restricted field of ex-British Commonwealth literatures."[33] Madsen writes in the context of authors who were once primarily read through the lens of American literature; yet these authors come from or represent people colonized within the USA, a situation which is found in Aboriginal writing in Australia, Maori writing in New Zealand, and First Nations, Métis, or Inuit writing in Canada. Arguments concerning multicultural American writing don't wash for Madsen: "Writers of colour, publishing in America, face precisely the problems of marginalization and cultural erasure that confront post-colonial writers of Africa and the Caribbean, and indigenous post-colonial writers of Canada and Australia and New Zealand."[34] Indigenous authors such as Cherokee Thomas King entirely reject, however, the postcolonial paradigm, arguing that it situates indigenous history and culture with a political transformation (the event of colonialism, or as King puts it, "the advent of Europeans in North America"[35]) that came long after the arrival of First Nations in Canada; furthermore, even after colonialism's demise, First Nations are still compared and contrasted with this event that they both resisted and have thoroughly critiqued. But King goes even further, arguing that postcolonialism suggests: a progressive movement (first, indigenous, then colonial, then postcolonial literatures) that simply is not the case; that all indigenous literatures are about the "struggle between guardian and ward"; and that it places a barrier between indigenous peoples and their traditions which were in place long before the arrival of Europeans.[36] Of course, rejecting the postcolonial label and all that it entails does not mean that indigenous writing somehow becomes isolated from the rest of the world; without wishing to homogenize real differences, critics continue to find valuable shared experiences and writing strategies between indigenous and marginalized groups, such as critic Gina Wisker's work on South African and Aboriginal women writers (see Chapter 49). Comparative work can register the impact of colonialism without entirely situating indigenous authors in a purely postcolonial framework, since it focuses on shared traits and values, here the "similarly powerful investment in the relationships between land and identity" or the choice of a writing strategies such as "polemical . . . semi-fictionalized autobiographical forms that utilize orally based structures and expressions."[37] Working across cultural boundaries that were artificially imposed by colonial powers, rejecting and removing intellectual and political borders that have been fiercely guarded, allows the critic to return to authentic, pre-colonial ways of being, as well as the forging of new artistic and intellectual communities.

Further reading: a selection

Said (1979), Spivak (1987) and Ashcroft, Griffiths and Tiffin (1989) are excellent places to start reading significant material from the 1970s and 1980s, with Spivak being the most theoretical critic in this list. Ashcroft, Griffiths and Tiffin (1989) cover "indigenous theory" in chapter 4, with subsections on Indian, African, and Caribbean theories, as well as those of the "settler colonies" of the US, Canada, Australia and New Zealand. As usual with theory, terminology and specialist language can be a challenge for beginning readers, but Ashcroft, Griffiths and Tiffin (1998) provide a concise guide to key theoretical concepts explaining terms such as diaspora, discourse, hybridity and syncretism. Lazarus brings together a series of accessible, comprehensive essays to give an overview of the topic, including intersections with globalization theory, poststructuralism, nationalism and feminism. Several authors in Lazarus examine the institutionalization or formation of postcolonial studies. Excellent introductions are written by McLeod and Loomba. Bhabha's edited and authored work is available in two main books, with Huddart providing a clearly written introduction, as does Sanders with his introduction to Spivak. Spivak's later book on postcolonialism examines the politics and philosophies of postcolonial thought. Key essays by leading critics are gathered in readers, for example those edited by Bayoumi and Rubin, Guha, Landry and MacLean, Williams and Chrisman. A variety of approaches are sampled here, including postcolonialism and: international relations (Darby), drama (Gilbert & Tompkins), expanding the new canon (Madsen 1999), native authenticity (Madsen 2010), process (Quayson) and counter-discourse (Thieme).

Ashcroft, Bill Gareth Griffiths and Helen Tiffin. *The Empire Writes Back: Theory and Practice in Post-Colonial Literatures.* London & New York: Routledge, 1989.
Ashcroft, Bill Gareth Griffiths and Helen Tiffin. *Key Concepts in Post-Colonial Studies.* London & New York: Routledge, 1998.
Bayoumi, Moustafa and Andrew Rubin, eds. *The Edward Said Reader.* New York: Vintage, 2000.
Bhabha, Homi K., ed. *Nation and Narration.* London & New York: Routledge, 1990.
Bhabha, Homi K. *The Location of Culture.* London & New York: Routledge, 1994.
Darby, Phillip. *The Fiction of Imperialism: Reading Between International Relations and Postcolonialism.* London and Washington: Cassell, 1998.
Gilbert, Helen and Joanne Tompkins. *Post-Colonial Drama: Theory, Practice, Politics.* London & New York: Routledge, 1996.
Guha, Ranajit ed. *A Subaltern Studies Reader, 1986–1995.* Minneapolis: University of Minnesota Press, 1997.

Huddart, David. *Homi K. Bhabha*. Abingdon, Oxon & New York: Routledge, 2000.

Landry, Donna and Gerald MacLean, eds. *The Spivak Reader*. London & New York: Routledge, 1996.

Lazarus, Neil, ed. *The Cambridge Companion to Postcolonial Literary Studies*. Cambridge: Cambridge University Press, 2004.

Loomba, Ania. *Colonialism/Postcolonialism*. London & New York: Routledge, 2005.

Madsen, Deborah L., ed. *Post-Colonial Literatures: Expanding the Canon*. London & Sterling, VA: Pluto, 1999.

Madsen, Deborah L., ed. *Native Authenticity: Transnational Perspectives on Native American Literary Studies*. Albany: State University of New York, 2010.

McLeod, John. *Beginning Postcolonialism*. Manchester & New York: Manchester University Press, 2000.

Moore-Gilbert, Bart. *Postcolonial Theory: Contexts, Practices, Politics*. London & New York: Verso, 2000.

Quayson, Ato. *Postcolonialism: Theory, Practice or Process?* Cambridge: Polity, 2000.

Said, Edward W. *Orientalism*. New York: Vintage, 1979.

Said, Edward W. *Culture and Imperialism*. New York: Vintage, 1993.

Sanders, Mark. *Gayatri Chakravorty Spivak: Live Theory*. London & New York: Continuum, 2006.

Spivak, Gayatri Chakravorty. *In Other Worlds: Essays in Cultural Politics*. London & New York: Routledge, 1987.

Spivak, Gayatri Chakravorty. *A Critique of Postcolonial Reason: Toward a History of the Vanishing Present*. Cambridge, MA: Harvard University Press, 1999.

Thieme, John. *Postcolonial Con-Texts: Writing Back to the Canon*. London & New York: Continuum, 2001.

Williams, Patrick and Laura Chrisman, eds. *Colonial Discourse and Post-Colonial Theory: A Reader*. New York: Columbia University Press, 1994.

Notes

1   Stephen Slemon, "Monuments of Empire: Allegory/Counter-Discourse/Post-Colonial Writing", *Kunapipi*, 9.3 (1987): 1–16, p.8.

2   Stephen Slemon, "Monuments of Empire: Allegory/Counter-Discourse/Post-Colonial Writing", p.8.

3   Stephen Slemon, "Post-Colonial Allegory and the Transformation of History", *The Journal of Commonwealth Literature* 23.1 (1988): 157–68, p.161.

4   Stephen Slemon, "Post-Colonial Allegory and the Transformation of History", p.161.

5   Stephen Slemon, "Post-Colonial Allegory and the Transformation of History", p.164.

6   Countries that were no longer colonies, but remained symbolically joined in organizational terms.

7   A.L. McLeod, ed., *The Commonwealth Pen: An Introduction to the Literature of the British Commonwealth*, Ithaca, NY: Cornell University Press, 1961, p.2; see, also, my discussion of Commonwealth and Postcolonial Literatures in chapter one of Richard J. Lane, *The Postcolonial Novel*, Cambridge: Polity, 2006.

8   John McLeod, *Beginning Postcolonialism*, Manchester & New York: Manchester University Press, 2000, pp.10–11.

9   Phillip Darby, *The Fiction of Imperialism: Reading Between International Relations and Postcolonialism*, London and Washington: Cassell, 1998, p.28.

10   See Richard J. Lane, "Edward Wadie Said (1935–2003)", in Richard J. Lane, *Fifty Key Literary Theorists*, London & New York: Routledge, 2006, 234–40, pp.234–35.

11   Edward W. Said, *Orientalism*, New York: Vintage, 1979, p.73.

12   Edward W. Said, *Orientalism*, p.149.

13   Edward W. Said, *Culture and Imperialism*, New York: Vintage, 1993, pp.xxi–xxii.

14   Edward W. Said, *Culture and Imperialism*, p.xxiii.

15   Edward W. Said, *Culture and Imperialism*, p.114.

16   Edward W. Said, *Culture and Imperialism*, p.114.

17   Ranajit Guha, "Introduction", in Ranajit Guha, ed., *A Subaltern Studies Reader, 1986–1995*, Minneapolis: University of Minnesota Press, 1997, ix–xxii, p.xiv.

18   Ranajit Guha, "Introduction", pp.xvii–xviii.

19   Bill Ashcroft, Gareth Griffiths and Helen Tiffin, *The Empire Writes Back: Theory and Practice in Post-Colonial Literatures*, London & New York: Routledge, 1989, p.110.

20   Bill Ashcroft, Gareth Griffiths and Helen Tiffin, *Key Concepts in Post-Colonial Studies*, London & New York: Routledge, 1998, p.229.

21   Bill Ashcroft, Gareth Griffiths and Helen Tiffin, *The Empire Writes Back: Theory and Practice in Post-Colonial Literatures*, p.41.

22   Richard J. Lane, *Fifty Key Literary Theorists*, pp.30–31.

23   Bart Moore-Gilbert, *Postcolonial Theory: Contexts, Practices, Politics*, London & New York: Verso, 2000, p.117.

24   Bart Moore-Gilbert, *Postcolonial Theory: Contexts, Practices, Politics*, p.118.

25   Homi K. Bhabha, *The Location of Culture*, London & New York: Routledge, 1994, p.112.

26   Homi K. Bhabha, *The Location of Culture*, pp.113–14.

27   Homi K. Bhabha, *The Location of Culture*, p.116.

28   Bart Moore-Gilbert, *Postcolonial Theory: Contexts, Practices, Politics*, p.121.

29   Bart Moore-Gilbert, *Postcolonial Theory: Contexts, Practices, Politics*, pp.122–23.

30   Bart Moore-Gilbert, *Postcolonial Theory: Contexts, Practices, Politics*, p.123.

31   Bart Moore-Gilbert, *Postcolonial Theory: Contexts, Practices, Politics*, p.124.

32   Deborah L. Madsen, "Beyond the Commonwealth: Post-Colonialism and American Literature", in Deborah L. Madsen, ed., *Post-Colonial Literatures: Expanding the Canon*, London & Sterling, VA: Pluto, 1999, 1–13, p.2.

33   Deborah L. Madsen, "Beyond the Commonwealth: Post-Colonialism and American Literature", p.3.

34   Deborah L. Madsen, "Beyond the Commonwealth: Post-Colonialism and American Literature", p.5.

35   Thomas King, "Godzilla vs Post-Colonial", in Ajay Heble, Donna Palmateer Pennee and J.R. (Tim) Struthers, eds., *New Contexts of Canadian Criticism*, Peterborough, ON: Broadview, 1997, 241–48, pp.242–43.

36   Thomas King, "Godzilla vs Post-Colonial", p.243.

37   Gina Wisker, "Locating and Celebrating Difference: Writing by South African and Aboriginal Women Writers", in Deborah L. Madsen, ed., *Post-Colonial Literatures: Expanding the Canon*, 72–87, p.73.

Chapter 44

Gautam Bhadra

THE MENTALITY OF SUBALTERNITY

Kantanama **or** Rajdharma

This key "subaltern studies" document, functioning within the wider field of postcolonialism, examines the tension between submissiveness and defiance in the "subaltern" consciousness (people of lower position or rank). Gautam Bhadra, the Tagore National Fellow at the National Library in Kolkata, closely analyzes a long poem by Dewan Manulla Mandal called *Kantanama* or *Rajdharma*, situating it culturally and historically, to comprehend how submission can also be a mechanism of resistance to one's rulers, leading to the restoration of justice and social order. Bhadra, one of the members of the Subaltern Studies group who explore non-elitist Indian cultural texts, also worked as a professor and director at the Centre for Studies in Social Sciences, Kolkata. Mandal's poem is precisely the sort of text that the Subaltern Studies group turn to to access a wide range of Indian cultural documents: written at a time of crisis, the poem blends Bengali "devotional" writing (*panchali*), with that of ballads (*mangal kavyas*) written to celebrate a deity. Steeped in oral culture, Bhadra notes how the Kathakata (storytellers) performances of Manulla's cultural world (in Dinajpur) were "popularized" morality tales that drew upon the value systems of the elites, yet they also were dynamic enough to include narrative elements that derived from "the lives of ordinary people". This two-way structural element is important because it reveals that cultural flows within hierarchical systems are not always simply "top down". On a larger scale, the intersections and crossings between "classical" and "popular" culture replicate this two-way structure. The colonial viewpoint of Dinajpur is of a place devoid of significant events, and thus devoid of history! But from Manulla's perspective, the opposite is the case, not only in the vitality and lives of the ordinary people, but through the ways in which their experiences can help with an understanding of larger socio-political structures. For example, Manulla reveals how "terror and coercion" play a role in the welfare or good governance of the people (known as *rajdharma*, which is the universal ethic or *dharma*, applied to society). Punishment (*danda*) is seen as a corrective of dharma, and rather than the top-down model, the subject who has rejected or transgressed the dharma (say, rebellion) is seen as responsible for the corrective. But just as the subject is individually responsible for his or her behaviour and, in effect, punishment, Manulla observes that "terror and coercion" are only acceptable correctives applied by the king in the name of universal justice (rajdharma), and once this is no longer the aim of correction, then the system has gone wrong. Manulla's analogy is that of the relationship between father and son, where there is a "duality of chastisement and protection". What is being mapped out here is not just the natural order, but the sacred duty of the ruler to maintain universal justice and the *social order*, i.e., the duty to look after the peasant class, but always in terms of the "mutual responsibility" between the classes. The subaltern, then, is a subject in process, and in a mutually binding relationship. Intriguingly, Bhadra ends by not only arguing that peasant resistance and rebellion is an assertion of rajdharma—the belief in a moral order that needs to be returned to, not a revolutionary overturning of that order—but also more radically that "abject submission" can represent an internalization of rajdharma, leading to defiance when the *rulers* deviate from its norms.

I **ATTEMPT IN THIS CHAPTER TO FOCUS ON** certain features of what may be called the subaltern mentality. It is well known that defiance is not the only characteristic of the behavior of subaltern classes. Submissiveness to authority in one context is as frequent as defiance in another. It is these two elements that together constitute the subaltern mentality. It is on account of this combination that the poor and the oppressed have, time and again, and in different histories, made voluntary sacrifices in favor of the rich and the dominant, at least as often as they have rebelled against the latter.

Certain assumptions made here need to be emphasized. First, the idioms of domination, subordination, and revolt, I believe, are often inextricably linked together; we separate them here only to facilitate analysis. If this is true, it follows that subordination or domination is seldom complete, if ever. The process is marked by struggle and resistance. The purpose of my analysis is precisely to highlight some of these tensions with reference to a particular text.

The text

The text under discussion is a long poem called *Kantanama* or *Rajdharma*. It was written by one Dewan Manulla Mandal, who lived in a village called Fakanda, now situated in Balurghat subdivision, West Dinajpur, West Bengal. The text was discovered in 1913 (1320 B.S. [Bengali era]) by the noted Bengali scholar Nalinikanta Bhattasali while he was engaged in a search for old Bengali manuscripts. The exact transcription of the manuscript, with all its typical spellings and local usages, was later published by the Dacca Sahitya Parishat. Bhattasali wrote an introduction and added notes to the text, which I have found useful.[1] Let us introduce the poet in his own words:

> Fakanda is the name of my village,
> Gurai Mandal that of my father,
> And I thus, humble fellow,
> Am his son,
> Dinachpur is my Sirasthan [Sudder area].
> Jobsa is the name of my pargana [revenue district],
> While my *chakala* [subdivision] is in Bhongra.[2]

The village of Fakanda lay in the zamindari of the famous Kasimbazar Raj. The area was named Kantanagar, after the founder of the house, Krishna Kanta Nandi. It was within five miles of Bairatnagar, a place of ancient legends and archaeological remains. Inquiries made by Bhattasali in Manulla Mandal's village revealed that Manulla had often worked as a copyist of texts such as *Mainamatir Punthi*. He also wrote a long narrative in verse about the old kingdom of Bairatnagar. Bhattasali was confident that the manuscript of the text of *Kantanama* that he had discovered was written in the author's own handwriting. The text runs to sixty pages and the date given on the last page is 1250 B.S. (1842–43), a couple of years before the zamindar Krishna Nath Nandi died. Krishna Nath figures very prominently in Mandal's book. It was during Krishna Nath's rule that Mandal felt the urge to write the book. Kantanama and Rajdharma were names given by the author himself; he referred to the text by these names, although more often by "Rajdharma" than by "Kantanama."[3]

From the text it is evident that the author was a member of the hereditary Mandal family; he refers to male ancestors of five generations. He belonged to a joint family. At the time of composition of the book he was an old man and was seemingly under severe personal stress. He had experienced economic distress because of a fire that destroyed his house and property. By the time he came to write the book, Mandal had lost all his relatives, including seven sons. "My seven sons have been taken away from me, hurting me greatly. What happiness can be there if sons die before the father?"[4] And again, "Yet another calamity befell me. My house and possessions were destroyed in a fire. And then God gave me a dream."[5]

It is necessary to underline here the social significance of the terms *mandal* and *dewan* in the context of the rural society of Dinajpur during the late eighteenth and nineteenth centuries. *Mandal* was the term for the head man of the rural community and referred to the family of the original settlers of the village. In the nineteenth century *patwaris* and mandals were gradually incorporated into the revenue system of the zamindars and became their salaried agents. It has been suggested, however, that in Dinajpur, where the zamindars were relatively less powerful, mandals retained some of their old autonomy and customary position. A mandal was the representative of his "community"; he was "one of the persons of the village who bear in the estimation of the community the highest character of responsibility and trustworthiness." He was an arbitrator of disputes and a spokesman who represented peasants to the authorities. He was not generally on the payroll of the zamindar but certainly enjoyed certain privileges at the time of revenue assessment.[6] In fact, many mandals in the area under discussion belonged to the *khudkasht* (resident husbandman cultivating his own land) category of peasants—prosperous and enjoying *sir* lands (in which the owner has exclusive rights) at concessional rates. This land was the mandal's *jot* (land in which owner has occupancy rights), which sometimes extended over a fairly large area. Most mandals were Muslims and were hereditary resident cultivators.[7]

Manulla also held the title of dewan. *Dewan* generally meant the principal officer of a big zamindari establishment.[8] But in Dinajpur and Rangpur *dewan* had a specific meaning. People who pleaded the case of peasants in court or to the zamindar and were well versed in laws and regulations of settlement were called dewans. Various settlement officers have commented on the influence these dewans exercised in the affairs of the village and their capacity to regulate the connection of the rural community with the outside world.[9] It is therefore not surprising that Manulla Mandal's connection to his own village should take on a particular significance in the text. Bhattasali had also witnessed how Manulla's descendants, engaged in cultivation and living in the same village, had a familiarity with the local court. Long residence in a particular village was characteristic of a khudkasht peasant. Being a mandal and a dewan, therefore, it is very likely that Manulla, in his long poem, spoke not only as a prosperous peasant but also as a leader of the village community to which he belonged.

Manulla wrote his poem within the tradition of the medieval Bengali *panchali* (devotional poems) or *mangal kavyas* (ballads celebrating the glory of a deity). Like all other poets in this tradition, he avers that he was asked to write by his destiny or fate (*bidbi*) or God (*niranjan*), at a time of intense personal and familial crisis. His sufferings, he later realized, were but a trial intended to prove his suitability for the task that fate had kept in store for him. As he wrote, "A purposeless existence in this world—such indeed must have been my destiny. Two-thirds of my life passed in happiness, the last one-third was to be full of sorrow. I stayed back [in the world] for a useless existence. I lost my way and became unhappy. The world became barren for me." In the context of this depiction of a sorry and fruitless life, he recounts:

> On hearing this Niranjan spoke,
> Cry not, he said, my blue-eyed boy.
> You can write off your brothers or sons as illusions.
> Only I can take you across
> [the ocean of existence] in your final days,
> I have judged your mind and found you pure,
> You are indeed dear to me.
> Why do you think your life is wasted?
> You will live in heaven,
> And I shall never forsake you.
>
> Go and write the story of the King—
> Your name will reign supreme in this world.[10]

Manulla repeats this story several times: that he received a divine order to write down in poetic form the exploits and glory of the zamindar. He sees his material and familial crises as following from this divinely appointed task:

> And the lord began to wonder how the deeds
> of the king could be propagated in the world.
> The narrator of the exploits of the virtuous
> king must pass the test of having his relatives
> killed by me.
>
> Only he who does not forget me even in suffering
> will qualify to write this story
> That will bring salvation [literally benefit]
> to the king's ancestors. . . .
>
> Helpless, I have to write down the words of God.
> O my fate,
> Your heart is made of stone,
> You have dealt me a severe blow
> And [thus] made me record the exploits of the King.[11]

This is a familiar theme within the medieval panchali. From Mukundaram to Manik Datta—the well-known writers of the *Chandi Mangal* and the *Manasa Mangal*—to the lesser-known writer of the poem *Gosain-mangal,* written in Coochbehar, medieval authors almost invariably cite divine inspiration as explanation of their reason for writing. This was characteristic of the particular mentality in which an individual's writing was not seen as the product of his own talent but as ordained by God, fate, or destiny. Chandi or Dharma or Manasa or Vishnu or Allah or Niranjan was the real actor, while the mortal author was merely an instrument of divine will. Manulla was thus communicating his own thoughts within a well-established tradition, using the forms of *lachari* and *dopadi*. His losses and sufferings were personal and his own experience was the basis of his poem; yet the author transcended his own experience by placing it in a wider framework of religion and divinity. Everything in that framework was predestined and expressed the work of Niranjan or Allah. To write *Kantanama* was a task to be performed, and through this Manulla would achieve the ultimate mission of his life.

At the same time, *Kantanama* was not merely a piece of literary self-fulfillment. Manulla intended to read it at the court of the zamindar, hoping to be materially rewarded for his effort. He thus thought of his spiritual future as well as of immediate material gain: "I write *Rajdharma* at the bidding of God. When shall I be able to read it before the king? God willing, I should read it before the king one day. Otherwise there is no security for me."[12] His expectations of the king are equally clearly stated: "The king began to think of all the sufferings of the writer who was writing about his deeds. If I give him an elephant loaded with wealth, he thought, even that will not compensate his sufferings."[13]

A historian has suggested that a local village official called Brajanath Hazra encouraged Manulla to write this poem, but there is no evidence to this effect.[14] Nor is it clear that Manulla really got an opportunity to read his poem before the zamindar. However, he also had a general audience in mind. A refrain in *Kantanama* or *Rajdharma* runs:

> The king, an incarnation of dharma,
> Never mentions *babat* [cess].
> Know this,
> O you, the community of *praja* [subjects]
> That God is merciful.[15]

Throughout his work Manulla Mandal never forgets this *prajar samaj*. His own experience, his social role, his own despair and hopes, are all expressed in a language and consciousness that is permeated with a religiosity meaningful to rural society. Its expression is perfectly in tune with the panchali tradition of medieval Bengali poetry. The following passage will ring familiar to any student of Bengali panchalis:

> With great care
> Shah Manulla has written this story
> As told to him in a dream.
> He who listens to it with devotion
> Will be saved from all misfortunes.
> He who plagiarizes this book
> Will have donkeys for parents,
> Will be born in poverty, and
> Will have his desires unfulfilled.
> Go to hell he will in the end
> And his family line will be terminated,
> While he who takes care of this book *Rajdharma*
> Will be rewarded with a place in the world of Baikuntha.[16]

The cultural world of Manulla

Fakanda is now an obscure village in Dinajpur. But it has its own culture, and Manulla was aware of that. There was a strong tradition of *pirism* among the peasants in Dinajpur, mostly Rajbangshis and Muslims. Many Rajbangshis had been converted to the *pir* variant of Islam and were called the *nasyas* (lower-caste men who converted to Islam).[17] The strength of this tradition made it difficult for the Farazis to penetrate this region in the nineteenth century.[18]

Even after their partial success in the early twentieth century, pirism thrived as before. It was noted by an acute observer in the early nineteenth century (1807) that there was hardly any village in this district that did not contain a *pirsthan* (place of worship).[19] Official statements of the 1930s confirm this impression. Along with this, Vaishnavism had spread among the Rajbangshis and survived the onslaught of a Kshatriya movement led by Rai Bahadur Panchanan Barman.[20] These two religious movements—Vaishnavism and pirism—have always overlapped, producing shifting and indeterminate boundaries. For both Satya Pir's song and Manasa's song the group of singers often remained the same; only the symbols and the dress changed.[21] In the two big locally held fairs, called Nek Marad and Gopinather *mela,* people of various communities participated without hesitation or inhibition.[22]

G. A. Grierson noted this development in his study of Rangpur and Dinajpur. He found illiterate minstrels roaming the countryside reciting to peasants the ballads of Mainamati and Gopichandra.[23] He also discovered in this area a ballad, adapted from the Bhagavat, that described the birth of Srikrishna. His comments are worth quoting:

> The third specimen is a song describing the birth of Krishna. It is by far the most popular song among the Hindus of the district. It is not extant complete but I have been able to collect many pieces and to repatch them into something like the original song which no doubt originally existed. I have been able to produce a pretty fair text; as there is hardly a line of which I have not obtained two or three copies. Considering the great distances from each other at which the places were whence I obtained the fragments, it is wonderful how they agree; especially as it is not customary for the reciters to possess written copies, or even to be able to read them if they did.[24]

The unity and similarity of the textual content of the songs current over a vast region of north Bengal indicate the existence of a vigorous oral tradition. The illiterate singers of villages have continued within that tradition, making improvisations but retaining the overall structure of the *pala* (drama or narrative poem).

Alongside these palas and songs there was also a tradition of Kathakata. Putatively of ancient origin, this tradition was popular in rural Bengal as late as the last decades of the nineteenth century. The *kathaks* (*katha* means tale; a *kathak* is a storyteller) recited Vaishnava stories before rural gatherings. It was a performing art requiring considerable histrionic skills on the part of the performer. The speaker told stories from the Puranas, always explaining their moral import, adapting them to suit the taste of the local audience but successfully delivering the moral contained in these stories.[25] It has been stated in official documents that high-caste Brahmans from various areas visited Dinajpur annually at a particular time of the year, and their presence, daily norms, and discourses created great excitement among various categories of people in Dinajpur.[26] A typical description of this type of art performed by the Brahmans is given by a person from another part of Bengal—from the Rarh area—where this art form was quite popular. In this case the narrator's mother arranged for the performance in order to keep a pledge she had made to the gods.

> A raised platform was erected at the Atchala and all the people of the village were invited to listen to a reading of the Ramayana. . . . In the evening the reader began to read the text. The village was small. About fifty to sixty men and thirty to forty women came and took their place in the audience. The *pathak* [reader] at first read out three or four verses from the Ramayana and then began to explain them. What a range of strategies he had for interpretation. Sometimes he would act, sometimes he would use a characteristically male language, on

other occasions he would begin to lament in the soft voice of a woman, and so
on and so forth. He thus performed for one and a half hours. The audience
listened with rapt attention. Every day this type of performance was put on. It
wasn't the same people who turned up every day to listen. . . . Few among the
audience were educated, and even for those who were their education stopped
at *pathsala* [village primary school] level. Yet they were able to grasp the sense
of the highly Sanskritized language used by the kathak. . . . The audience came
for two reasons. It was thought that listening to a recitation of the Ramayana
conferred *punya* [merit] on people; they used to come to earn such punya.
Second, if they did not come, my mother's vow would be broken and she would
become a sinner. They could not do that to her. For this reason also, they
attended the performance.[27]

Bankimchandra also once noted the role that "the dark and plump" *kathak thakur* (Brahman
kathak) played in preaching certain moral values among rural people:

The ploughman, the cotton-carder, the spinner, or even the person without
food—they all learned [from listening to the kathak]. They learned that *dharma*
was eternal and divinely ordained, that to be self-seeking was demeaning, that
there was a thing called *pap* [sin] and a thing called *punya* deserving punishment
and reward, and that life was not meant for one's self [i.e., for one's own
pleasures] but for others.[28]

Thus Kathakata performed certain distinct services. It popularized Brahmanical culture
through highly effective fables and stories, upholding certain standards of morality and values
derived essentially from the culture of the elite. However, within its framework there was
always ample scope for accommodating elements that emerged out of the lives of ordinary
people. Through twists and turns in the narrative, through varying emphases, through
additional commentaries, the kathak always made references to local affairs and incidents.
The text he used usually contained a variety of themes, ranging from Sanskritized moral tales
to erotic descriptions of prostitutes or humorous descriptions of different types of sweets.
His songs made up a mixed bag, containing Sanskrit verses as well as local Bengali songs. A
successful kathak was always responsive to the moods of the different types of audience he
encountered, for these could be, at times, highly sensitive and responsive to his performance.[29]
   Throughout the eighteenth and nineteenth centuries many local chieftains in their own
interest began to popularize various Vaishnava and Sanskrit texts in this region. The Raj
families of Coochbehar and Dinajpur took the initiative in this matter.[30] The panel of
sculptures at the famous temple at Kantanagar in Dinajpur, for example, contains a full
depiction of the life of Krishna.[31] In this cultural world we can probably discern the interaction
of two elements: the classical, or *marga,* with the popular, or *jana.* Through the Kathakata and
extensive translation of the various texts of the Puranas and the Bhagavat there could have
been a conscious attempt on the part of the local zamindari house to spread and uphold
certain kinds of values and moral frameworks among the lower orders. But this was an active
and two-way process. The popular and folk elements continuously changed and absorbed the
classical in their own way. Grierson describes the perception of the Bhagavat by the singers
themselves in the villages of north Bengal: "They have found them in songs, and it is not their
business to alter things written in the Satya-yuga. Sometimes they are unable to explain
whole passages, saying 'it is Satyayuger Katha, how are we to know it?' For other words they
have a traditional meaning."[32] Incomprehension, ambiguity, and tradition made the popular
reception of these classical tales quite distinct from the appreciation they received in the

shastric world. Many local versions of various incidents of these epics and of the Puranas were composed, catering to an altogether different rustic audience. *Angad's Raibar* (the story of Angad abusing Ravana), for example, was universally popular among the peasants. It was later expunged from the standard edition of Krittibas's Ramayana by its famous editor Dinesh Sen, as it was supposed to be vulgar.[33] This type of acceptance, adaptation, and rejection is mutual at both levels and is an expression of power relations between the dominant and the dominated. Thus, while one can discern certain "classical" (marga) elements in "popular" (jana) culture, the blending is never entirely harmonious.

As opposed to this vertical interaction between the classical and the popular elements of culture, another type of connection was horizontal, taking place among the various trends within popular culture itself. Here, many contiguous local and regional cultural groups overlapped with each other. In north Bengal the cult of Sona Rai was an example of this. He was, at one place, known as the protector of the field, while at another place he was the god of tigers. Somewhere else he was a Vaishnava saint who had saved the Koran from desecration, while at yet another place he was a pir and had saved the Hindu religious texts from a similar fate.[34]

It was almost impossible to distinguish Madari (a Muslim sect) *pirs* and the Naths (a sect of worshipers of Gorakhnath) in Dinajpur.[35] Here the Niranjan of the Naths and the Allah of the Madaris were almost interchangeable. There were, and still are, a large number of small ruined buildings in this area, and these are used both by the Burhana pirs and the Nath *jogis* (ascetics) for purposes of worship.[36] One of the major features of these types of cultural interaction is to be seen at the linguistic level. Here, recourse is often had to the consonance of sounds or images to transform one god into another, a procedure that appeals more to popular conceptions of godheads, as well as to popular responses to alliteration, rhyming, and other rhetorical devices, rather than to any elaborate structure of reason and argument. The following is a typical example of such transformation:

> Dharma has assumed the form of a *Yavan.*
> Sporting a black cap and wielding a bow and arrows
> He rides a powerful horse,
> And is a terror to the world.
> The formless Niranjan has become a heavenly avatar,
> The word *dam* constantly on his lips.
> Brahma became Muhammad,
> Vishnu, Paigambar, [and]
> the holder of the trident [i.e., Shiva]
> transformed into Adam.
> Ganesh changed into Ghazi
> Kartik into Kazi
> And the *munis* [hermits] all became fakirs.[37]

This particular type of transformation and mutuality between two cultures, Hindu and Muslim, has generally been hailed by liberal scholars as proof of the tolerance or "syncretism" practiced by Hindus and Muslims at the popular level. This, however, is not an entirely satisfactory formulation. It is true that these transformations do show a certain tendency to transgress the boundaries of official or formal Islam and Hinduism. There was a flexibility in these types of movements that may have made it comparatively easy for the lower orders to bypass the rigid and formal structures of elite culture in a feudal society.[38] In our area, Grierson provides an example. Side by side with the recitation of the Bhagavat and Puranic palas there existed a tradition of bawdy and satirical rhymes in which everything turned into its opposite, every action led to an unintended and unconventional end. This was a way of pointing out the inconsistencies of this world. Such songs were quite popular in the rural areas of north Bengal.[39] So, in this culture, there was a mixture of many things that cannot be formalized in accordance with a hierarchical principle and that could not be easily appropriated by elite culture. At the same time, this mutuality of Hindu and Muslim gods does not imply their fusion. Brahma becoming Muhammad and Ganesh becoming Ghazi did not mean that they had lost their separate identities. As gods they usually retained their separate significations. Nor does a bland theory of "tolerance" help much in understanding the acute intolerance and sectarianism that popular sects sometimes displayed toward one another.

The imprint of both popular and elite culture, that is, of both *jana* and *marga,* can be traced in Manulla Mandal's text. The author begins his poem with an invocation to Vishnu or Hari:

> Hari is the ultimate wealth [possession];
> He is the essence of everything.
> Without him there is no salvation.
> Ill-fated are those who do not know [the power of] Hari,
> For to hell they are eternally condemned.

But Hari is, at the same time, Niranjan, the symbol of the Naths and the Burhana *pirs.* Time and again Hari is replaced by Niranjan:

> Of forms he has none.
> Like the air, he is without color or shape.
> By the power of his *nur* [light]
> He created the world
> And nurtures it as a father.[40]

Manulla Mandal was aware of Puranic and Sanskritic traditions, and often cites instances from these. He describes Baikuntha, the abode of Hari, and mentions the Kalki avatar. He writes thus about the court pundits of Krishna Nath: "They know the Tantras, the Puranas and the great Bhagavat. They know even the Chaitanya-Charitamrita."[41] He adds, "Whatever I have written in this book has support in the Bhagavat Puran."[42] At the same time he was aware of the local tradition. He made a copy of Sukur Muhammad's *Gopichandrer Geet,* and wrote a poem about Bairatnagar that contained the ballad "Ghazi Kalu and Champavati."[43] It is not unnatural, therefore, that this Hari could be easily interchanged with Niranjan or Allah. In his book, God can easily say, "I am Ram, I am Rahim, and I am Hari."[44] Once again, the alliterative mechanism works, and the glory of Hari can easily be expressed in the *nur* of Allah.

Thus, Manulla's book stands at a symmetrical intersection of traditions where Baikuntha finds its counterpart in Behesht, where Hari and Niranjan reflect each other's forms. Manulla moves freely in both traditions and borrows images and arguments from both; at the same time, he changes them in the process. This gives the text flexibility and plasticity, and also helps Manulla fashion his stories and messages more effectively.

Dinajpur: its people and history

The history of the district of Dinajpur has been characterized by an official in very clear terms:

> With the breaking of the Dinajpur Raj (1800–808), the history of the district
> ceases to be of interest to the outside public. The old saying that "happy is the
> country that has no history" may fairly be applied to Dinajpur, in which no
> important events of political nature have occurred to disturb the even tenor of
> administration and material development.[45]

This is typical of the colonial view: "no important events of political nature," hence "no history." But Manulla's *Kantanama* is full of "events," events important for his life and village. His overall concern was with the Kasimbazar zamindari and its development, but he also wrote as a ryot who was concerned about zamindari demands, especially the extra cess, or *abwab*.

It has been argued recently that in this area there were a few big zamindaris and families who came from outside the district and who maintained control within it through zamindari *amlahs* (functionaries) and extensive establishments.[46] On the other hand, as a consequence of the breakdown of older zamindari houses like the Dinajpur Raj family, zamindari officials and substantial peasant proprietors reaped the maximum possible benefit. Through the *kuthkanidars* (undertenants) they established contact with the zamindar to pay revenue and transferred the burden of rent onto the tenants. This class provided the big *jotedars* (proprietors with large landholdings) of the later period. In areas where land was abundant it was these big farmers who organized cultivation, controlled capital and foodstock, and fought zamindars if the terms were not favorable to them. Buchanan-Hamilton has eloquently described their power: "Whenever one of them is discontented, he gives up his farm, and retires with all his dependants to some other estate, where there are waste lands which his stock enables him to clear. The village which he left is then for some years unoccupied, unless the landlord can find a fugitive of the same kind." This type of mandal peasant could create a lot of trouble for the zamindar, the *izaradar* (leaseholder) and the state; from time to time their threat to withdraw from cultivation would even take the more serious form of defiance.

The small peasants and tenants were, in many ways, forced to depend on them, to bow to their will. In another well-known passage Buchanan-Hamilton has underlined the nature of this dependence: "It is true, that these large farmers exact enormous profits for whatever they advance to their necessitious dependants but still they are of infinite use to these people, who without their assistance would be instantly reduced to the state of common labourers and often to beggary."[47] This mutuality of dominance and dependence has also been stressed by later writers. It has been said that ordinary ryots were extremely wary of dealing directly with outsiders.[48] For Europeans and native officials the mandals were often the only contact with the village people. It seems that collectors like Grierson and Sherwill were always associated with fresh measurements or tax, and as such were unwelcome visitors to the village. State officials and the amlahs of landlords were also considered "outsiders," a source of potential threat.[49] In this context of tension and distrust between the zamindari establishment and the peasant, the conciliatory ideology of *rajdharma* preached by Manulla Mandal in his *Kantanama* acquires special significance.

One of the major issues in the tension between landlord and peasant was the question of *abwab*. In general, abwab is considered by historians to have been an illegal cess and an extra burden on the peasants who, because of their helplessness and the superior political power of the landlords, had to pay up and suffer.[50] In Bengal there were three categories of these extra payments: abwab, a regular cess to be paid at regular intervals; *mathot* (from *matha,* or head), payment taken for official needs and purposes; and *kharcha*, a payment for the expenses on revenue collection.[51] In practice the distinctions often got blurred. Although the colonial government banned these in the late eighteenth century, the peasants still had to pay these cesses to the zamindars. A colonial historian has explained this in terms of the "mysterious passive sentiment" of the Bengali peasant.[52] In actual practice payments of abwab had much to do with the nature of the relationship between ryots and zamindars.

In many cases in Dinajpur, the ryots agreed to pay the abwab only as a gesture of compromise. In many areas the khudkasht peasants concealed the actual amount of land under cultivation, opposing any attempt on the part of the zamindar to measure the land afresh and to reassess the rent. The ryots agreed to pay some cess as "compensation" to the zamindar, provided he did not insist on fresh measurement.[53] In most of these cases, the imposition of abwabs and *mangans* (cess) was a tacit compromise between ryots and zamindars, not an easy victory for the landlords. The amount collected varied from estate to estate. There are several instances of estates where the landlord succeeded in completing a fresh measurement with the result that the peasants of that estate refused to pay any extra cess. In other estates, where the new measurement was not made, the ryots, without apparent protest, paid various dues as abwab, mangan, and kharcha. There are also reports of cases where the peasants themselves took the initiative in paying extra amounts to salvage the prestige of zamindaris in crisis.[54] At the same time, many zamindars did not hesitate to levy the cess from their ryots by using the threat of force. However, they also kept up the appearance of making all these impositions look like voluntary gifts from the peasants. They actually described these dues, in their local languages, as *bhiksha* or mangan (kinds of beggary) by the landlord from his subjects.[55]

Various other cases show the involvement of headmen or prosperous ryots in the collection of abwabs. On the occasion of a visit of a new zamindar to his estate, it was often these "big" ryots who collected dues from the poorer ryots and offered *nazar* (tribute) to the new master. In lieu of their services they received *siropa* (gifts) and concessions. The collection of abwabs often became a source of income and of authority for the bigger ryots.[56] However, in all these attempts there was a notion of justice grown out of custom, experience, historical dispute, and the actual agrarian situation of the area. Excessive collection or continuous imposition of the new abwabs or mathots might well lead to an explosive situation like the *dhing* (revolt) against Deby Singh in Rangpur in 1783. This point was stressed in a petition from the zamindars of Rangpur that underscores the role of custom in agrarian disputes:

> The ryots of this country objected to engaging for any certain quantity of land and to the revenue being fixed, on account of its being contrary to the custom of country and the lands never having been measured according to *ruckha bandi* [a measure of land], they paying revenue only according to the quantity of land actually cultivated by them after deducting *moojraee* of a certain part remitted to them as an engagement. . . . If the settlement be not made with them according to the established custom of the country, they desert. . . . If the *bundabasts* [settlements] be not concluded agreeably to the customs of the country, the collections will be endangered.[57]

When there were agrarian disturbances in Baharband against the zamindar of Kantanagar, the peasants, the zamindar, and the government alike referred to *kanoon* (rules) and *raj-ul-mulk* (laws of the kingdom) as the basis for their action.[58] What constituted the particular kanoon in question was ultimately decided through a process of struggle. The willingness or reluctance to pay abwab or to allow the landlord to measure the area under cultivation depended on the economic logic as well as the power equation as it existed between the landlord, the big ryots, and the lesser peasants. Specific instances of deference and defiance in such matters were determined by the specific context. But there was no legally defined limit to how much the landlord could demand of the peasant: there was nothing written or definitive about it. It was kept vague and judged by the nebulous boundaries of "custom": landlords and cultivators had each their own interpretation of kanoon. In some cases the payment of mathot or abwab was a compromise between two contending groups; in other cases it was a forced exaction but taken in the name of some freshly invented tradition; in still other cases it was paid voluntarily, owing to a kind of attachment that the peasant felt toward the overlord—a notion of duty to a landlord rightly or wrongly perceived to be in need of such service.

Abwabs became a contentious issue with the zamindari family of Kasimbazar. The case of Krishna Kanta Nandi, the *bania* (agent) of Warren Hastings, was typical. Through political connections, manipulations of *izara* (lease) contracts, and *benami* transactions (under false names), Krishna Kanta, starting in 1764, slowly built up his extensive landed property all over Bengal. He defeated Rani Bhawani in a series of legal and political games and consolidated his position in Dinajpur by buying the two most prosperous and contiguous parganas of Baharband and Bhitarband in Rangpur.[59] Thus came into being the zamindari of Kantanagar, with "an illegitimate origin in the obscure depths of eighteenth century politics and intrigues."[60] After the death of Krishna Kanta's son, Lokenath Nandi, the zamindari came under the management of the Court of Wards from 1804 to 1820, during the minority of Harinath Nandi. Harinath Nandi was involved in a prolonged lawsuit with his relatives and died shortly after becoming zamindar. Due to the minority of Krishna Nath Nandi, the Court of Wards took charge of the zamindari again in 1832 and administered it until 1840. The amlahs and managers who ran the administration on behalf of the Court of Wards also shared in the spoils, becoming izaradars themselves. The zamindari house was vertically split because of an unsavory tussle between Krishna Nath Nandi and his advisers, on one side, and Rani Susarmayi and Rani Hara Sundari, his mother and grandmother, on the other.[61] With two parallel administrations and "uncontrolled gatherings of the *Muffassil Umlahs*," the condition of the ryots became worse, and the income of the estate fell.[62] Even when Krishna Nath finally became zamindar in 1840, the situation did not much improve because of his intemperate behavior and reckless administration. Finally, in the face of a charge of willful murder, he committed suicide in 1844.

Thus there was no dearth of tension and conflict in this so-called peaceful district. The colonial government failed to recognize this reality because of its limited view; Manulla, however, did not fail to mention some of these events. *Kantanama* is intended to interpret rajdharma as well as to chronicle some of the events that marked the rule of the zamindars of the Kasimbazar house.

Rajdharma: the face of terror

One important source of rajdharma lies in terror and coercion. Manulla never forgot that he was a ryot, a subject, or that the Nandis were the zamindars. God had appeared in his dream and asked him to write the text, but as soon as he woke up he worried: "I am terribly afraid to write about the exploits of the King. Who knows, the King may dislike it. After all I am a subject and he is the King. He might be a sinner [i.e., one who ignores the words of God] and develop a dislike for me."[63] Manulla repeatedly reminds himself and his reader that he would not have written his book at his own initiative: "Helpless, I have to write down the words of God. . . ."

> The faith wavers,
> my mind is impure,
> I am narrating the deeds of the King,

As I have seen them in a dream,
. . . it is with great fear that I write,
I am terribly afraid.[64]

"It is with great fear that I write" is a sentence that recurs often in the first half of the poem. Manulla was also aware of the distance between the ruler and ruled: "Will the King understand my suffering? He will recognize his own work, but will he understand my pain [grief]?"[65] Thus his praise and eulogy of the "king" or landlord, all his protestations of loyalty and devotion, are evoked at least in part by fear of the zamindar's power. In all the praise addressed to the overlord, terror is the mark by which the subordinate differentiates himself from the superordinate, the expression of a cosmic helplessness by the author offering testimony of his very material, earthly terror.

The terrorizing power of the landlord is of course the subject of many volumes by colonial observers. Even in the remote area of Dinajpur, an official wrote:

> Every village has, it is true, an Officer attached to it called a *Kotwal*. . . . Besides the Kotwals, landholders entertain the *paiks* [footmen], but these men never quite reach the threshold of the zamindar's *sudder cutchery* during the night, and their duties by day are confined to seizing the *ryots* and committing all sorts of violence under the orders of their masters in the prosecution of most objectionable extortions and most cruel oppression. . . . The proportion of *paiks* entertained by the zamindar averages about one per village. . . . If a zamindar has twenty villages, he has but one cutchery; at the break of day he sends forth his twenty *paiks* to levy his rents, who towards the close of the day, return with the sums they may have collected, bringing also with them, all such, as either may not have been able to meet the suddenness of the demand, or who may have had courage enough to dispute the justness of the claim. This is the sum of the *paik's* "duty."[66]

Buchanan-Hamilton also gives a detailed description of the elaborate establishments by which the zamindar extorted rents and coerced defiant peasants. He comments in particular upon the power and authority of zamindari amlah necessary in Kantanagar.[67] On the same subject, Manulla says:

> Like the moon of the heaven sitting along with his stars, the zamindar sits with his amlahs.
> . . . He has a canopy over his head.
> . . . The Chief Diwan is Herkolots sahib.
> . . . The chief Nazir is Gangadhar Ghose, a name dear to god.
> . . . Durgacharan Babu is the head of the Cutchery, he is *sheristadar* [highest managerial officer] of the King.
> . . . Everybody is in his place, the king in his *darbar* [royal court] the whole Sabha is radiant.[68]

A peasant like Manulla, however prosperous, had to take cognizance of the power of this establishment, and deify it. This ritualized description, suggestive of a cosmology and a divine plan revealing itself in the physical arrangement of the royal court, was perhaps part of the strategy the peasant used to adjust himself to zamindari power. Subordination seems almost desirable by such a glorification of the source of oppression.

The capacity to punish has always been a signifier of royalty. It is through the exercise of such power (*danda*) that the king preserves the moral order of dharma. From the Manusamhita to the Mahabharata to the localized Puranas in medieval Bengal, the terrorizing power of rajdharma or danda is described in exalted terms.[69] In a typical passage of the Mahabharata, Arjuna, the legendary hero, says this of danda: "O King, Danda protects and rules the subjects. Even when everybody sleeps, Danda remains awake. The wise have described Danda as the principal dharma [*dandam dharmam bidurbhudha*]. Most sinners do not commit crimes for fear of *rajdanda*. It is the natural law of this world: Danda is the foundation of everything [*ebam samsidhiki loke sarvam danda pratisthitam*]."[70] As we can see from this, in the marga tradition, danda is fused with moral order. Disruption and withdrawal of danda mean the breakdown of social order, crisis in caste society, even a total reversal of the existing patterns of domination and subordination. Everybody is within the pale of danda; no subject is beyond it. The exercise of danda is natural and good; its suspension unnatural and bad. Danda and dharma thus became synonymous; "dandam dharmam bidurbhudha." This type of identity places rajdharma in the dual world of morality and terror, the one associated with the other in such a manner that it becomes impossible to draw a boundary between them.[71] This picture is present in the *Kantanama* but with a difference. We do not have the speech of heroes like Arjuna or Bhisma; rather, the peasant, the subject of terror, is given speech. The exercise of terror by the king is explained and depicted in the *Kantanama* through the behavior of the peasant, the object of danda rather than one who wields it.

The story begins with the terrorized subject. Krishna Kanta establishes his zamindari and his rule: "Kantababu became the King in the year seventy-two; he was declared the zamindar in [B.S.] 1772. God has favored him. . . . The two annas of the area have been given in the name of Kantababu. The Maharaja circulated his *parwana* [warrant] throughout his *bhum* [area] and named the Pargana Kantanagar after his own name."[72]

In this way Manulla describes the establishment of a new zamindari, the exercise of a new power through the parwanas, through the measure of renaming an old place. The success of the landlord showed he had the support of God because of the good deeds of his previous lives. If success was a reward for the inherent goodness and merit in a man, Kantababu, who had been able to establish his order (*dohai*) in this area, naturally deserved to be respected: "The pargana belongs to Kantababu. It bears his name. All the subjects recognize that and salute him." Again, "Kantababu became the ruler of the *Dowani* pargana. He has found it easy to collect rents from this area."[73]

Kantababu, however, following the proper norms, did not go beyond the limit imposed by *insaf* (justice): "He never demands abwab. All the subjects [*praja*] live in great happiness."[74] But there are erring prajas, people incapable of understanding the goodness of Dharmaraj Kantababu. They are bad and defiant subjects, while Manulla himself, by implication, conforms to the ideal: "The Raja has got a kingdom [*mulk*]. Its name is Baharband. The story of this area is puzzling [*dhandha*]. The country is wicked, its people are wicked. There, no one pays rent, no one accepts authority."[75]

The area of Baharband, even according to the official documents, was well known for its recursive tradition of rebellion. Mir Kasim as well as Rani Bhawani of Natore had their times of trouble in this pargana. When Krishna Kanta Nandi purchased the estate *benami* (under a fictitious name) on account of his influence over Hastings, he wanted to make his holdings lucrative by introducing "scientific administration." At this the dominant and prosperous khudkasht ryots of the area were up in arms. In a petition to the East India Company they talked of their customary rights; referred to the earlier history of the pargana, in which "bad" zamindars were often taught a lesson; and spoke in favor of "their ancient settlements" and "raj-ul-mulk." The zamindar, Lokenath Nandi, son of Krishna Kanta, gave his own interpretation. He upheld "the universal law of empire," as well as the absolute authority of the landlord over his ryots. He also rejected the complaints as a conspiracy of the big ryots to disguise the actual area of land under their own cultivation to avoid proper measurement, and to shift the burden of the rent onto the poor ryots. Failure in effecting a compromise led to a revolt of these "artful ryots" under the command of Hargovind Bakshi, Mohan Bakshi, and Maniram Hazra.[76] Forces led by Goodlad, the collector of Rangpur, eventually crushed the rebellion on behalf of Kasimbazar Raj.[77]

It is to this incident that Manulla alludes in his poem. His aim was to represent rajdharma. Baharband was a place where lived the wicked subjects, as opposed to good and loyal subjects elsewhere. Their rebellion arose not out of their misery and poverty or a sense of acute oppression, but on account of their wicked nature their innate desire to defy all authority. They were rich enough to possess elephants, yet they refused to pay because "it is a wicked [khal] kingdom, its subjects are also wicked" and "they do not accept the King and do not pay the revenue. In an organized way, they forbade everybody to pay revenue. They know nothing better than to cause trouble. They said to the Raja: 'We do not recognize you.'" Kanta Babu himself went to the pargana with his army, with the result that the ryots retreated and went into hiding:

> The King sent summons to the subjects.
> From a distant place, they sent back their reply:
> "We do not recognize you and we will not pay any revenue.
> Return to your own house for your own benefit [safety].
> If you apply much pressure, the consequence may be worse. Then you will not
>   be allowed to return to your house [country] alive."

In the eyes of Manulla, the king ought to be patient and kindhearted: "Even after hearing this, the king refused to be angry. He feels compassion toward his subjects." But his entreaties were repeatedly met with defiance. Ultimately, however, finding them to be "compulsive trouble-mongers" and having lived without provisions for twenty days, the king's patience ran out. He now gave a fitting reply to the strength of the organized peasantry, a reply known to everybody through the ages:

> Failing to get hold of any of the subjects,
> the king turned furious and set fire [to the villages].
> All the houses in the country were destroyed by fire.
> The prajas received what they deserved.
> One and all were punished in the right measure,
> The rent for three years being collected all at once.
> The king's authority was proclaimed all over the country.
> Pacified, the prajas returned to their houses.[78]

The burning of houses, the beating of people, the taking of all rents due in a single installment were the outcomes of the exercise of danda. In Manulla's opinion this was the only recourse open to Kanta Babu. If his subjects refused to obey, they transgressed the limits of prajadharma and violated the code of behavior sanctioned to subjects. In order to rectify this lapse the exercise of legal power was necessary, for without danda the bad praja cannot be restored to the right path. To establish authority is the beginning of rajdharma, and to punish the subject who deviates from his own dharma is its sacred duty. In the last resort, through the exercise of terror—danda—prajadharma was restored. Rajdharma's quality had thus been fully vindicated:

> Without objection, they accepted the King's judgment [and] paid rent, including
> cess on grazing land.

> The King, kindness personified, felt sorry for the subjects.
> In justice [insaf] he relinquished the cess for ever.
> It is thus that he collected the revenue,
> And named the pargana Kantanagar after himself.
> The pargana is Kantanagar, And the King is called Kantababu.
> The Prajas all accept this and salute the king.

He who did not understand the glory and significance of rajdharma is, according to Manulla, "a thoroughbred savage."[79]

Refusal to be terrorized by danda is equally a crime, for the danda of the king is not arbitrary or blind. Krishna Kanta gave his subjects the chance to correct themselves; he condoned their initial defiance. His exercise of power was tempered by kindness, limited by justice, or insaf. Hence, Manulla suggests that while the use of terror and coercion was legitimate and the ideal praja was expected to fear the king's power, the king, too, had the moral right to coerce only so long as the exercise of royal power was moored in the notion of insaf, or justice.

Limits to Rajdharma: the nature of Insaf

The institution of abwab illustrates well the notion of insaf as it was actually practiced. In the day-to-day existence of zamindari, the regular payment of rent is a point around which the relation between a landlord and his peasants revolves. To collect rent is the right of the zamindar, and, in the opinion of Manulla, the peasants are duty bound to pay. But to measure the land, to collect revenue, and then to ask for abwab and mathot are, according to him, clear instances of oppression, be-insaf, zulm. We have seen how the issue of land measurement vis-à-vis the collection of abwabs became a bone of contention between landlords and the substantial peasantry in Dinajpur and Rangpur in the early nineteenth century. In the late eighteenth century, Lokenath Nandi rejected the demand of his khudkasht ryots, who opposed measurement and instead offered a cess as compensation. The powerful ryots of Baharband and Gayabari fought the zamindars successfully for the most part of the nineteenth century, until they were defeated by Rani Swarnamayi. However, in other areas the khudkasht ryots were not so powerful; they lost ground on the issue of land measurement. Hence, the collection of abwabs gradually became a contentious issue. It is interesting to observe that Manulla's discussion of abwabs is significantly different in tone and content from his discussion of danda. The collection of abwabs involved the practice of insaf, and here Manulla often sees the zamindar as the offender. After praising Nal, Harischandra, Karna, Bali, and Yudhisthir, all well-known mythological kings, Manulla introduces a king called Srishchandra, his own creation: "Srishchandra was a king and a great archer. . . . No one was able to match him. . . . He passed his days happily [until] he became the victim of a bad intention after a long period." What was this bad intention? He began to take mathot for the *annaprasan* ceremony of his son, for mortuary rites in connection with his father's death, and for the marriage ceremony of his son. As a consequence, "God became angry with him, the peasants suffered much for the payment of abwab. God with his own hands made the King a sinner."[80] Srishchandra's name cannot be found in any Purana, and he is clearly created as a counterimage of good kings like Bali, Nal, and Yudhisthir. To collect mathot on all these ceremonies was clearly an act of oppression. Using the structure of Puranic tales, Manulla depicts the imagined experience of an oppressive landlord. At the same time he places Krishna Kanta and his successors within that Puranic tradition.

Kanta Babu followed the rules of rajdharma because "he does not even utter the word 'abwab,' he is dharmaraj [himself]." Under the reign of his son Lokenath, the subjects were very happy because "he never oppressed anyone in the name of abwab."[81] Krishna Nath also belonged to the same category. Yudhisthir in the *Mahabharata*, too, belongs to that tradition: "Yudhisthir was famous in this world for his truthfulness. He never uttered the word 'abwab.'"[82] There was, obviously, no discussion of abwabs in the *Mahabharata*, but Manulla's Yudhisthir is made in the image of a just zamindar at Dinajpur, the sign of that insaf being that he does not collect illegal cess and abwabs from peasants.

Manulla is not unique in pursuing this theme. It is also present in the ballads of Mainamati and Gopichandra, so popular with illiterate Muslim peasants, weavers, and the Yugis, agricultural laborers and lime-makers of north Bengal. Through the work of Sukur Muhammad, Manulla was familiar with these stories. In the kingdom of Manikchandra, "the great righteous king," the tax was levied per plow and everybody was prosperous. The images of prosperity in these stories are identical with those used by Manulla to describe the Baharband ryots. It was the bad amlah, usually an outsider, who urged the raja to extract abwabs. The condition of the whole estate deteriorated, and the ryots appealed to God, who advised them to curse the king. "The King became greedy for wealth [*dhana-kangali*]. Dharma Niranjan would judge it." Ultimately, the half-naked peasants wished death on him and thus caused his death. Throughout this ballad of Manikchandra, the anger against the dhana-kangali (greedy) reverberates like an echo.[83] On this point Manulla is close to Gopichandra's *git* rather than to any shastric literature.

In Manulla's *Kantanama* this oppression has been perpetrated by the officials of the zamindar. Their presence was immediate and real to the peasantry; the landlords were far away—in Kasimbazar and Calcutta. In the *mahals* (estates) the amlahs were all in all. During the king's minority and management by the Court of Wards, their oppression increased.[84] Manulla gives a typical description of the situation during the period of the minor Raja Harinath. His description may be paraphrased thus: The amlahs collected money from the ryots but showed it as their own borrowings from the latter, and thus the estate became a defaulter in the eyes of the government. "They gave a bad name to the ryots," says Manulla, "and became *izaradars* [themselves]. Inflicting losses on the king [i.e., the treasury], they laid the blame at the door of the ryots. They pleased the king by promising *daul* [rent collections] and obtained their izara at the court. Returning to the country, they ruined the pargana." According to Manulla, they imposed cesses under various names, such as *bandobust, daul, milani,* and so on. The pargana was plunged deep into chaos.

Manulla's descriptions are amply confirmed by official documents. Izaradar oppression was, perhaps, even greater. During the time of the minority of Krishna Nath, the izaradar had hold of the pargana; as Manulla puts it: "Krishna Nath, being a minor, was innocent [of the affairs of the estate]. The Sahibs now became the *mukhtiars* [representatives] for the king, [and] Shyamkishore made arrangements in the collectorate [for the izara]."[85] According to official documents, Shyamkishore was an active patron of a faction of local amlahs and was "a man of business [who was] well acquainted with and engages in speculations."[86] He was a typical product of the permanent settlement, a relentless pursuer of profit from rent and speculation in land. Manulla gives an eloquent description of this man and his activities:

> He speaks only the language of violence. Nobody dares to speak in his presence. Summons came [from him] declaring all current rents as arrears. It was as if the pargana trembled [in fear]. The order from the collectorate was for the arrears to be paid within three *years*. But he [Shyamkishore] collected it all in three months. Varieties of abwabs he took from the ryots. He sold their jewelery, even their pots and pans. He respects nothing, not even *hurumat* [honor].

The izaradar did not respect custom and cared nothing for natural calamity, and the invocation of *izzat* or hurumat cut no ice with him. Eventually the peasants ran away:

> No water, no cultivation, no prosperity in the household.
> The izaradar still exacts his dues under so many pretexts.
> The people desert and flee from the pargana.[87]

This was a part of "normal" life for the peasantry. There was nothing unusual about their having to sell their essentials in order to meet the excess demands of rapacious farmers and the agents of zamindars. Desertion was quite common, too. In the songs of Gopichandra, the singer says, "The peasants sell their plows, their yoke, and all their agricultural implements to meet the demand of rent; they even sell their own infants."[88]

Their actual experience of amlahs and izaradars made the peasants despise immediate authority and created in them the expectation of justice from a higher, distant authority.[89] Manulla makes this distinction throughout his writing: amlahs and izaradars are not synonymous with the king but are his (bad) agents because they do not conform to the dictates of honor, or hurumat. What was the way out of this misery? "Prayer" is Manulla's considered answer: "Those of us who cannot escape, think of God. How long before the king ascends the throne? Let the king grow up and take charge of the kingdom: this is what we, the subjects, pray for."[90]

But why is the king necessarily more just, more responsible, and kinder than the izaradar and the amlah? To answer this question, Manulla postulated a general principle that was central to his notion of rajdharma. To take abwab or not, to be generous or not, to obey the preceptor (guru) or not—these were merely outward expressions of a general principle of dharma. They were the specific signs of a general principle, and there could be numerous variations on these signs in a specific situation. Manulla explains the point:

> Like a father the king looks after his kingdom with care and attention.
> Others oppress with injustice for they know not any kindness.
> Without the father the son becomes helpless like the destitute [*kangal*] from
>   Nadia,
> An orphan, he has no one to turn to.
> Likewise, the praja is the son And the raja the father.
> [If] the father leaves his ward [*praja*]
> The praja becomes miserable.
> The father is both a preceptor and a friend.
> Know it for sure then
> [that] the father is the god Niranjan himself.
>
> The raja is for the praja as father is to son.
> Who else would value the praja as a son?[91]

The crucial feature of rajdharma is this relationship of father and son, through which the relationship between the king and his subject is viewed. It is a relationship, in colloquial language, of "ma-baap."[92] The father punishes and also looks after his son. This duality of chastisement and protection is the basis of rajdharma. The authority of the father and the submission of the son are matched by the helplessness of the son in the absence of the father. Manulla cites one example after another from the Puranas in support of his theory. Nal, Bali, Karna, and Yudhisthir were all rewarded in heaven precisely because they had conducted themselves in accordance with this ideal of rajdharma: "They looked after their subjects as sons [*putra bhave palan kaila*]."[93] Conversely, Srishchandra was rebuked by the messengers of Yama in hell for not behaving in a fatherly way toward his subjects.[94]

All the zamindars of the Kasimbazar Raj were made (by Manulla) in the model of these mythical heroes—their exact replicas. They treated their subjects as their own sons.[95] In this way, the Puranic kings and the zamindars of the Nandi family all became instances of dharmaraj, and a Puranic framework of time could be superimposed on a chronology that was local and specific. In the *Mahabharata* and the Puranas the same ideas and epithets are expressed to explain rajdharma as the relation between ruler and ruled.[96] In the Bhagavat, it has been said, the prajas, being sons, were even entitled to offer *pindas* (offerings to dead ancestors) after the death of the king. They remain before the king as "children before a father."[97]

In this notion, there was a fusion of the two opposing ideas of dominance and subordination. In the consciousness of the peasant, the king or the lord was duty bound to look after him. The authority of the father in a family is taken as "given" or "natural," so the lord's authority over his domain, by this analogy, becomes "natural" and "everlasting." This analogy from family to society and from society to the state comprehends various levels of authority and submission and makes these part of a whole order. Hence a particular landlord or king could be bad, but monarchy and landlordism were part of a "good and beneficial" arrangement. The king had certain duties toward the peasant, not as a part of the legal rights of the peasant but derived from a general moral and social order. The peasant had duties toward the king. Everybody in this hierarchical order accepts the chains of duty and moral obligation.

This was not just a figment of Manulla's imagination. We encounter the same theme in a petition that Rani Bhawani made to the East India Company against her izaradar in 1775:

> I am an old zamindar and not being able to see the griefs of my ryots, I agreed to take the country as farmer. . . . The high ground of Rarh yielded nothing for want of water and in Bhaturia, which is very low, the gentlemen [the officials of the company] took the *pool-bandi* [embankment] into their own hands and made the banks and in August 1773, the banks broke and the ryots' ground and their crops failed by being overflowed with water. I am a zamindar, so was obliged to keep the ryots from ruin and gave what ease to them I could by giving them time to make up their payments and requested the gentlemen would in same manner give me time when I would pay up the revenues but not crediting me, they were pleased to employ Dulal Roy as *Sejawal*. . . . The two men [Dulal Roy and Paran Bose] . . . have depopulated and destroyed the country. I am an old zamindar. I hope I have committed no fault. My country is plundered and the ryots are full of complaints. . . . For this reason I am ready [to offer the same amount] and will take care that the *sircar* suffers no loss.[98]

It is irrelevant to ask here whether the rani's sentiments were genuine or not. The language of the petition and what she has to say of her duty as an old zamindar are what interest us. In the history of the Dinajpur Raj, too, an anecdote expressing a similar kind of mutual responsibility between the landlord and his subjects has been reported. When Raja Radhanath was faced with the prospect of bankruptcy, the headmen of all the villages sought a meeting with the "king" to work out an arrangement whereby they could assist the landlord in this time of crisis. The king agreed, pitched a tent, arranged a "solemn ceremony," and dressed himself accordingly. The ceremony was in the end cancelled, as certain amlahs did not favor the idea, but the anecdote reflects the notion of mutuality of duties between the ruler and the ruled.[99] As a famous passage in the *Mahabharata* puts it: "The first body of the subject is the king, the subject is also like the body of the king. Without the king, there is no country, without the country there is no king."[100]

Thus, by relating the day-to-day experiences of the peasant to the traditions of the *smritis,* the Puranas, and the sayings of wise men, Manulla transforms the mundane into the heavenly, the natural into the supernatural. The personal and historical experiences of Manulla thus become generalized beyond his immediate space and time.[101]

Transgression of Rajdharma: the story of Harinath

Manulla also speaks of a rajdharma that might be interfered with by the ruler himself, and the consequences that would follow. Those who ruled according to rajdharma went to *baikuntha* (the abode of Hari, i.e., heaven) and those who violated his norms went to *narak* (hell): "If you do good, your place will be in baikuntha. If you do otherwise, you will be sent to narak." There is a clear distinction between the worlds of dharma and adharma, sin and merit: "The place in opposition to dharma is narak, the kingdom of Yama, riven with dissension, while Niranjan, the Lord, rules over baikuntha, the abode of dharma."[102] Srishchandra and Shyamkishore went to hell forever and were physically punished for their actions. From Yudhisthir to Lokenath, everybody who acted according to rajdharma was rewarded with a place in heaven.

The life of Harinath, the son of Lokenath Nandi and the father of Krishna Nath, was, however, not so simple. Harinath was a righteous king, but during the last days of life he deviated from the principles of rajdharma. This incident is crucial for the narrative of *Kantanama,* and Manulla describes the event at least twice. A peasant went to see Harinath and complained against the oppression of an izaradar. Harinath listened to the complaint but gave no decision. For thirteen days the peasant waited for a royal decision, but the king did not even attend his darbar. Reduced to poverty and despair, the peasant eventually managed to find the landlord sitting in his darbar. But, as Manulla says: "The doorkeeper did not allow him into the darbar. Being forbidden, he called out to the king. The king heard the cry but did not respond. . . . Being a king he refused to listen to the complaints of the subject. Nor would the sentry let him [the peasant] enter. The *praja* went away, wiping his tears." Thus Manulla brought two specific charges against Raja Harinath:

> Although a raja he does not attend the darbar everyday. Also unbecoming [of a king] is the fact that he does not listen to the complaints of the prajas. If the praja has to pay for food at the royal palace, or go without it altogether, this is yet another sin that attaches to the raja.

Harinath went to baikuntha all right, but he remained there in extreme discomfiture, for "Niranjan wrote *gunah* [sin] against the name of the righteous king."[103]

> No cool breeze soothes his person, which always burns [as though] from summer heat. Restless inside, with sweat running down all over his body, he finds [the situation] unbearable. "Oh, save me!" cries out his soul in desperation, and even though he is in Baikuntha itself, he still has to pray to God.

God eventually came in the disguise of a Brahman and explained the cause of his suffering. He also said that the suffering would last forever, for it was *bemiyadi,* without any time limit. The king pleaded for remission. Showing compassion for him, God said, "'Well, only a part may be remitted. Ten annas of your sin will remain for what you have done to your praja.' As soon as the Brahman uttered this, the king's suffering was lessened by six annas. The king now realized that this person [the Brahman] was none other than God himself."[104]

Pap and punya are the two most important themes of this discussion that goes on in baikuntha between the zamindar and God in the shape of a Brahman. Yet the peasant-poet's imagination shows all the signs of the political order in which the peasant lives. Just as the king was expected to respond kindly to petitions by the peasants and occasionally reduce their burden of rent, God, in response to Harinath's petition, did the same. The relation between landlord and peasant has been replicated in baikuntha as a relation between Hari and Harinath. Similarly, the punishments meted out in hell are reminiscent of the physical torture the peasants suffer at the zamindar's establishment.[105]

Manulla's heaven, by contrast, overflows with various items of food. For a peasantry used to hunger and physical deprivation, it was perhaps natural that "heaven" should represent all that was materially desirable:

> Rice was served with a variety of dishes. The plates were made of gold; so were the bowls and waterpots. . . . The king ate the meal with great relish—milk, curds, sweets, *khir,* and butter. The meal over, the king put some betel leaves in his mouth and was offered a golden hookah. He was now very pleased.[106]

Through this description of heaven and hell Manulla upholds the hierarchy of authority. To Niranjan every devotee is a ryot, a subject. "It is God, the master of all living beings," he writes, "who rules all men as his subjects and looks after them as a father."[107] The landlord in fact is shown to be afraid in the presence of God. Fearing punishment, "the king began to cry: alas I do not know what . . . calamity fate has decreed for me."[108]

But the lapses in this exercise of rajdharma are temporary. Stability and order are natural. And, in Manulla's narrative, the restoration of stability comes through sacrifices made by the subject. Harinath committed lapses because of his bad behavior with his praja; he suffered for that. His exculpation comes when God asks an ordinary praja, Manulla, to relate to others the story of the dynasty to which Harinath belongs. But in order to qualify for this noble task that God has entrusted, Manulla had to pass the test of suffering and thus lost everything—his family and his houses:

> The king's thoughts turned to the writer and the sufferings he had borne in order to document royal deeds. . . . "In narrating to the world the exploits of my dynasty [the king said], my subject has sacrificed his father and sons. For my exploits the writer suffers." Thus the king laments over the misfortune of the subject. . . . "Our exploits have been propagated in this world. For that my subject has lost his sons and brothers."[109]

But Manulla is duty bound to do this; any subject is duty bound to help his lord in times of distress. As God says to Manulla: "Do the work in the interest of the king. You can be sure that your work will be everlasting."[110]

Thus the initiative of the subject is recognized, but in favor of the lord, not against him. Manulla is here a successor of Kalu Dom, a model in medieval Bengali literature of old, trustworthy servants. Kalu sacrificed his life and made Lau Sen, his overlord, victorious in a battle. Manulla's worldly sufferings are given a similar meaning: it is because he passes the test of suffering that he qualifies to write the history of the raj. This alone can reduce the king's sufferings in hell. Manulla's sacrifices show his loyalty to the king and to the divine order that kingship represents. It was also, one might say, a clever, if unconscious, ploy to ensure that his sufferings were after all not in vain, that they brought him adequate rewards from the royal court. We do not know if the strategy worked.

God, the king, and the subject: the question of submission and autonomy

In *Kantanama,* God—the king or the landlord—and the subject—Manulla—interact in a manner that deserves to be treated separately. Manulla wished to please the landlord, so he wrote about the deeds of his family. But the text is not simply supplicatory in tone. In the first place, Manulla wasn't even sure that the text would please Krishna Nath Nandi. What if it only aroused his anger? The fear of a negative reaction terrorized Manulla so much that to bolster his self-confidence he often invoked God's support. God's authority is superior to that of the landlord. It is interesting to note Manulla's strategy for self-protection. It speaks of the fear that even a subject who is praising the landlord feels. But in this imagined, hierarchical community, one's superiors also had their superiors, and one could always appeal to—or in the name of—the higher authority.

And this gives Manulla a voice of his own, a certain degree of autonomy even when he is submissive. It is interesting that he manages even to abuse the very landlord whom he was supposed to please. If the landlord dared to treat him badly because he did not like Manulla's poem, he would show himself up as a "mean" person (*pamar*). Only a king who was a "thoroughbred fool" (as God would say, Manulla hastens to add) would be unable to sympathize with the heartfelt sorrow of the subject.[111] Thus, by counterposing the authority of God to that of the landlord, Manulla not only saved himself from the ire of the master but also issued a veiled threat to him in case his expectations were not fulfilled. Manulla in fact even goes beyond this. He makes Harinath, the landlord, suffer in baikuntha because of his lapses from dharma. His redemption is only possible through Manulla's act of writing the text, and in the narrative, Harinath is forced by God to recognize this. But again, the ultimate actor, as Manulla says, is God himself. Harinath was forced to commit lapses because Manulla was destined to write the book: "Niranjan has confused the king because of the need to have his exploits written."[112] Thus, all the acts of Manulla, according to the order of God, are not meant for his own liberation but for that of his master.

Through his act of writing Manulla was, thus, an agent of God, and was outside the pale of the landlord's judgment. His own decision was also irrelevant here. Manulla is "entrapped in religiosity." He has, as Marx would have said, either not yet found himself or has already lost himself again. All his initiative belongs to the other world; his supplication and protest have their source in other worlds. Religion here becomes the opium of the people. But it is also, as Marx himself recognized, the sigh of the oppressed. Manulla is caught up in an endless cycle of transference: he creates a god whom he believes to be his own creator.

Manulla is not really representative of poor, indigent peasants. He was a Mandal, a headman whose social world was that of the well-to-do peasant. How then does *Kantanama* help us to understand the culture of the subordinate classes? Is it not the mentality of the substantial ryot that *Kantanama* documents? There may have, of course, been interesting and important differences between the thoughts of a poor peasant and those of a Mandal, and we cannot make *Kantanama* stand in as a substitute for evidence reflecting more directly the thought world, say, of a sharecropper or a landless laborer. However, it seems to me that we would be erring in the opposite direction to think that there could be no exchange or sharing of ideals or ideas between classes, or that classes, even when they were in conflict, did not learn from each other. There is, prima facie, no reason to assume that classes, like scholars, are deaf to each other, that ideas cannot travel across the boundaries of class. The cognitive map that Manulla had of the world may easily have been shared, although not necessarily wholly, by a poor peasant.

There is yet another reason why Manulla's text may be thought to have a general significance. If we were to think of subordination not as a static and fixed property of particular classes but as a process and a relationship, which people could enter into or reproduce in different contexts of hierarchy, the relevance of Manulla's text becomes apparent. In his statement, we begin to see the different elements in the cultural repertoire of rural Bengal that are marshaled and arranged in order to communicate to his masters his feelings of loyalty and submission. Hence, Manulla's text is of interest to us not simply because it allows us to see a particular form in which a peasant may try to present his view of rajdharma to his landlord in order to get material benefit as well as merit. What makes the text rich are its contradictions and ambiguities—the fact that a text ostensibly written to please the landlord should carry within it its own moments of irony, fear, resistance, and resentment.

From recent researches it can be shown that, time and again, the subordinate classes have risen in rebellion because of their faith in some moral order, out of an urge to restore justice. Rajdharma can be seen to have played a similar role. The praja recognizes his first identity as praja (subject) against the raja (as king) in terms of rajdharma. He thus becomes conscious of the marks of his distinction. This is the first step of self-recognition, without which rebellion is impossible. The peasant's submission is not to a particular king or to a lord but to a universal law such as rajdharma. Even at the moment of abject submission he, in his own way, internalizes the principle of rajdharma, on whose basis he might recognize or challenge any violation of it. From the same belief structure, he can rationalize both defiance as well as submission. During the Rangpur rebellion of 1783, peasants raised slogans against Devi Singh, saying "Dine zalim kutha asht" (the religion of the oppressor is short). The religious message that teaches submission also forms the basis of rebellion. Again, at the very moment of insurrection, peasants are quite capable of accepting a theory of kingship such as rajdharma, while rebelling against a particular king. Thus collaboration and resistance, the two elements in the mentality of subalternity, merge and coalesce to make up a complex and contradictory consciousness. How this consciousness overcomes and transcends its contradictions is another question.

Notes

For specific references and detailed quotations, see the Bengali version of this article in *Anustup*, autumn, 1987. However, essential notes and references have been cited. All the translations are mine. I am grateful to Dipesh Chakrabarty, who has thoroughly edited this essay and helped me formulate my ideas. I thank Ranajit Guha, Partha Chatterjee, and Gayatri Chakravorty Spivak for their comments.

1   Dewan Manulla Mandal, *Kantanama* or *Rajdharma*, ed. Nalinikanta Bhattasali (Dacca Sahitya Parishat Granthabali, no. 8, 1320 B.S., Calcutta, 1913; cited hereafter as KN).

2   KN, p. 80.

3   Introduction by Bhattasali, ibid., pp. 14–19.

4   KN, p. 5.

5   Ibid., pp. 8, 16.

6   *Papers Regarding the Village of Rural Indigenous Agency Employed in Taking the Bengal Census of 1872* (Calcutta, 1873, Bengal Govt. selections, no. 47), pp. 27–28.

7   F. O. Bell, *Final Report on the Survey and Settlement Operations in the District of Dinajpur, 1934–40* (Calcutta, 1942), pp. 9–11, para. 42; p. 88, para. 72.

8   Francis Buchanan-Hamilton, *A Geographical, Statistical and Historical Description of the District or Zilla of Dinajpur* (Calcutta, 1833), p. 250.

9   Bell, *Final Report, Dinajpur,* p.16, para. 16; F. W. Strong, *Eastern Bengal District Gazetteer: Dinajpur* (Allahabad, 1912), pp. 33–34; F. Hartley, *Final Report on the Survey and Settlement Operations in Rangpur,* 1931–38 (Alipore, 1940), p. 45, para. 20.

10   KN, pp. 9–11.

11   Ibid., pp. 75–76.

12   Ibid., p. 82.

13   Ibid., p. 91.

14   S. C. Nandy, *History of the Cossimbazar Raj,* vol. 1 (Calcutta, 1986), p. 286.

15   NK, p. 105.

16   Ibid., pp. 106–7.

17   Strong, *Gazetteer: Dinajpur,* pp. 36–37. *Report on the Survey and Settlement of the Churaman Estate* (Calcutta, 1891), p. 9.

18   Bell, *Final Report, Dinajpur,* p. 11, para. 12.

19   Buchanan-Hamilton, *Description,* pp. 92–93, III.

20   Bell, *Final Report, Dinajpur,* pp. 9–13; Atulchandra Chakraborty, "Pashim Dinajpurer tin laukik debata," *Pratilipi,* Ashvin 1388, 3rd issue; Golam Saklaen, *Purba Pakistaner sufi sadhak* (Dacca, 1368 B.S.), pp. 63–68; Hartley, *Final Report, Rangpur,* pp. 84–87.

21   J. C. Sengupta, *West Bengal District Gazetteer, West Dinajpur* (1965), pp. 84–87.

22   Strong, p. 2.39; J. L. Sherwill, *Geographical and Statistical Report of the Dinajpur District* (Calcutta, 1863), p. 28.

23   G. A. Grierson, "The Song of Manik Chandra," *Journal of Asiatic Society of Bengal* 47 (1878): 35–238.

24   G. A. Grierson, "Notes on the Rangpur Dialect," *Journal of Asiatic Society of Bengal* 46 (1877): 201.

25   Dinesh Chandra Sen, *History of Bengali Language and Literature* (Calcutta, 1911), pp. 588–90; Sukumar Sen, "Kathakata," in *Bharatkosh,* vol. 2 (Calcutta, 1967), pp. 150–51. See also Bipinbihari Chakrabarti, *Khaturar itihas O Kushodvip kahini* (Calcutta, 1908).

26   W. K. Firminger, ed., *Bengal District Records: Dinajpur,* letter no. 194, dated 3 September 1787, vol. 2, 1786 (Calcutta, 1924).

27   Jogesh Chandra Roy Vidyanidhi, *Pauranik upakhyan* (Calcutta, 1361 B.S.), pp. 87–88. Cf. Dinendra Kumar Roy, *Sekaler smriti* (Calcutta, 1395 B.S.), pp. 42–43.

28   Bankimchandra Chattopadhyay, "Loksiksha," *Collected Works,* Samsad ed., vol. 2 (Calcutta, 1371 B.S.), p. 377.

29   Prankishor Goswami, *Kathakatar hatha* (Calcutta, 1375 B.S.), pp. 19–20; Haripada Chakraborty, "Kathakatar punthi," in Ashutosh Bhattacharya and Asit Bandyopadhyay, eds., *Subarnalekha* (Calcutta, 1974), pp. 580–92.

30   Sashi Bhusan Dasgupta, *A Descriptive Catalogue of Bengali Manuscripts Preserved in the State Library of Cooch-Behar* (Calcutta, 1948); Sukumar Sen, *Bangla sahityer itihas,* pt. 1 (Calcutta, 1975), pp. 427, 447.

31   Gauri Shankar De, "Temple of Kantanagar," in *Proceedings of Indian History Congress* (Burdwan, 1983), pp. 592–603.

32   Grierson, "Rangpur Dialect," p. 226.

33   Sukumar Sen, *Bangla sahityer itihas,* pp. 424–25; Dinesh Sen, ed., *Krittibasi Ramayan* (Calcutta, 1955), introduction.

34   Sarat Chandra Mitra, "On the Cult of Sonaraya in Eastern Bengal," *Journal of the Department of Letters* (Calcutta University) 8 (1922): 141–72, 173–206.

35   Abdul Wali, "Notes on the Faqirs of Balia-dighi in Dinajpur," *Proceedings, Journal of Asiatic Society of Bengal* 72 (1903): 100; J. M. Ghosh, *Sannyasi and Fakir Raiders in Bengal* (Calcutta, 1920). For detailed descriptions on the Nath-Panthis, see Kalyani Mallik, *Nath-sampradayer itihas: darshan O sadhan pranali* (Calcutta, 1950), pp. 14–15, 102, 181.

36   Abdul Kalam Muhammad Jakaria, ed., *Sukur Muhammader Gopichander sanyas* (Dacca: Bangla Academy, 1974), pp. 92–94.

37   Bhakti Madhav Chattopadhyay, ed., *Ramai panditer sunya puran* (Calcutta, 1977), p. 160. Along with Professor Muhammad Shahidullah, the editor says that this part is a later edition and has been composed, probably, in the eighteenth century.

38   Cf. Mikhail Bakhtin, *Rabelais and His World* (Cambridge, Mass., 1968), chap. 1.

39   Grierson, "Rangpur Dialect," pp. 196–97.

40   *KN,* pp. 1–3.

41   Ibid., p. 87.

42   Ibid., p. 105.

43   Introduction to *Kantanama,* pp. 3–5.

44   *KN,* p. 71.

45 Strong, *Gazetteer: Dinajpur,* p. 27.

46 For the process, see Ratnalekha Ray, *Change in Bengal Agrarian Society, 1960–1860* (New Delhi, 1979), chap. 8; S. Taniguchi, "Structure of Agrarian Society in Northern Bengal" (unpublished thesis, Calcutta University, 1977).

47 Buchanan-Hamilton, *Description,* pp. 23 5–6.

48 Sherwill, *Dinajpur District,* p. 9; Grierson, "Rangpur Dialect," pp. 187–88.

49 *Survey and Settlement on Churaman Estate,* p. 36; *Survey and Settlement on Maldwar Wards Estate* (1891), para. 78.

50 Irfan Habib, *The Agrarian System of Mughal India* (Bombay, 1963), pp. 247–48; John R. Mclane, "Land Revenue Transactions in Eighteenth Century West Bengal," *Bengal Past and Present* 104 (1985): 1–23.

51 James Grant, *Historical and Comparative Analysis of Finances in Bengal,* in W. K. Firminger, ed., *Affairs of the East India Company (The Fifth Report),* vol. 2, (reprint, New Delhi, 1984), pp. 205–31.

52 W. K. Firminger, *Historical Introduction to the Bengal Portion of the Fifth Report* (Calcutta, 1917; reprint, Calcutta, 1962), pp. 50–51.

53 Buchanan-Hamilton, *Description,* pp. 252–53.

54 T. Sisson, Judge and Magistrate of Rangpur, to Bayly, 2 April 1815, para. 35; Report of Mcleod on Crime, 30 September 1817, paras. 45–47, in E. G. Glazier, *Further Notes on Rungpore Records,* vol. 2 (Calcutta, 1876), appendix A, nos. 31–32.

55 T. Sisson to Bayly, 2 April 1915, para. 29.

56 Buchanan-Hamilton, *Description,* p. 236; J. H. Harrington's report to Charles Stewart on Pargana Swaruppore, 20 March 1790, Board of Revenue (BR), 22 March 1790, Proc. N0. 14/5, West Bengal State Archives (WBSA).

57 Petition of the Zamindars of Rungpur to Mr Purling, Ist of Aghoon, 1197, B.S., in Glazier, *Further Notes,* appendix G.

58 A petition from Zamindar of Baharband, Lokenath Nandi, BR, 16 June 1786, no. 30. Comm. of Revenue, 3 April 1786, Proc. no. 44 and 48, WBSA.

59 Somendra Chandra Nandy, *Life and Times of Cantoo Baboo,* vol. 1 (Calcutta, 1978), chaps. 2 and 4; vol. 2 (Calcutta, 1981).

60 Bell, *Final Report, Dinajpur,* p. 73, para. 55.

61 S. C. Nandy, *History of the Cassimbazar Raj in the Nineteenth Century,* vol. 1 (Calcutta, 1986), chap. 6.

62 J. W. Steer, 30 December 1835, Board of Revenue Wards (BRW), January 1836, no. 30, para. 30, WBSA.

63 KN, pp. 13–14.

64 Ibid., p. 17.

65 Ibid., p. 15.

66 T. Sisson, Magistrate Dinajpur to G. Dowdeswell, 11 July 1814, Judicial-Criminal, 19 August 1815, no. 1, paras. 2 to 4, WBSA.

67 Buchanan-Hamilton, *Description,* p. 252; Nandy, *Cassimbazar Raj,* vol. 1, pp. 44, 22.

68 *KN, pp.* 83–85.

69 Kaliprasanna Sinha, trans., *Mahabharat* (Bengali), Santi Parva (Basumati ed.), pp. 245, 253, 259; *The Mahabharatam* (Sanskrit, Arya Sastra ed.), p. 5999 (SI. 138), p. 6022 (SI. 16), p. 6037 (SI. 104); Bhutnath Saptatirtha, ed. and trans, *Manusmritir Medhatithi Bhasya* (Calcutta, 1361 B.S.), pp. 633–38, SI. 17–25; Panchanan Tarkaratna, ed. and trans., *Brihatdharma Puranam,* Uttar Khanda, 3, SI. 13–19.

70 Kaliprasanna Sinha, *Mahabharat,* chap. 15, pp. 182–83, *Mahabharatam,* p. 5846, SI. 6.

71 On rajdharma and danda, see Jan Gonda, *Ancient Indian Kingship from the Religious Point of View* (Leiden, 1966); Charles Drekmeir, *Kingship and Community in Early India* (Berkeley, 1962); and J. C. Heesterman, *The Inner Conflict of Tradition* (Delhi, 1985). I am most indebted to the classic work of P. V. Kane, *History of Dhar-masastras,* vol. 3 (Poona, 1946), pp. 3–6.

72 KN, pp. 29–33.

73 Ibid.

74 *KN,* p. 28.

75 Ibid., p. 29.

76 All the descriptions and quotations are taken from translations of a representation from the ryots of Baharband; translation of the answer of Lokenath Nandy; and the humble petition of Lokenath Nandy, Zamindar of Baharband, Committee of Revenue, 3 April 1786, Proc. no. 49. See also "Particulars of the Reasons for Hutabood in 1189 B.S.," BR, 16 June 1786, Proc. no. 30, WBSA. For the early history of the pargana, see E. G. Glazier, *A Report on the District of Rungpore* (Calcutta, 1873), pp. 27–28, 84; Glazier, *Further Notes,* appendix C.

77 Nikhil Nath Roy, *Murshidabad Kahini* (1903; reprint, Calcutta, 1978), pp. 271–22.

78 KN, pp. 30–33.

79   Ibid.

80   Ibid., pp. 21–23.

81   Ibid., pp. 30–34.

82   Ibid., p. 20.

83   Ashutosh Bhattacharya, ed., *Gopichandrer Gan* (Calcutta University, 1965), pp. 1–6.

84   KN, p. 37. Cf. Anderson to J. P. Wards, Bankura, 13 May 1816, BRW, 31 May 1816, no. 30; Nandy, *Cossimbazar Raj,* vol. 1, pp. 45–46.

85   KN, p. 77.

86   Nandy, *Cossimbazar Raj,* pp. 173–74; BRW, May 1836, no. 48, WBSA.

87   KN, p. 78.

88   *Gopichandrer Gan,* p. 2.

89   The Arzee of the ryots of Purgunnah Lushkerpore, Proc. of the Provincial Council of Revenue, Murshidabad, 26 June 1775; the petition of the ryots, Pargana Silberry, ibid., 9 October 1779, WBSA.

90   KN, pp. 35–37, 77–78.

91   Ibid., p. 36.

92   Cf. Dipesh Chakrabarty, "On Deifying and Defying Authority: Managers and Workers in the Jute Mills of Bengal, 1890–1940," *Past and Present,* no. 100 (August 1983): 130–32. It must be noted, however, that in the colonial situation, this certainly had undergone some distortions where coercion was probably more pronounced than protection.

93   KN, pp. 19–20.

94   Ibid., p. 24.

95   Ibid., pp. 33, 38, 106.

96   Cf. *Mahabharat,* Santi Parva, chap. 87, p. 281. *Brahmavaivarta Puranam,* Mathuranath Tarkaratna, ed. and trans., chap. 90, Srikrishna Janmakanda, SI. 6 (Calcutta, 1881–85); *Brihatdharma Puranam,* Uttar Khanda, chap. 3, SI. 11.

97   Taranath Kavyatirtha, ed. and trans., *The Srimat Bhagavat* (Calcutta, 1373 B.S.), *skanda* 1, chap. 11, and *skanda* 4, chap. 21, pp. 282, 283.

98   Petition by Rani Bhavani, March 1775, quoted in A. B. M. Mahmood, *Revenue Administration of Northern Bengal* (Dacca, 1970), pp. 84–85.

99   E. V. Westmacott, "The Dinajpore Raj," *Calcutta Review,* 1872, p. 223.

100 *The Mahabharatam,* Santi Parva, chap. 68, SI. 59.

101 Cf. R. Barthes, "Change the Object Itself," in *Image-Music-Text* (Glasgow, 1982), p. 165.

102 KN, pp. 18, 55, 59.

103 Ibid., pp. 55–59.

104 Ibid., pp. 63–67.

105 Ibid., pp. 23–24, for a description of *narak,* or hell. For similar descriptions of punishment for a revenue defaulter in the nawab's establishment, see "Madan Pala," quoted in Sukumar Sen, *Bangla sahityer itihas,* vol. 2, p. 487; for torture in the zamindar's establishment, see G. C. Dass, *Report on the Statistics of Rungpore for the Year 1872–73* (Calcutta, 1874).

106 KN, pp. 62–63.

107 Ibid., p. 4.

108 Ibid., p. 92.

109 Ibid., pp. 90–91.

110 Ibid., p. 12.

111 Ibid., p. 17.

112 Ibid., p. 56.

Chapter 45

Gayatri Chakravorty Spivak

"CAN THE SUBALTERN SPEAK?"

Another way of phrasing Gayatri Chakravorty Spivak's theoretically challenging question "can the subaltern speak?" might be: "who speaks for the subaltern and why?" Spivak's essay has functioned for many years as a central document in postcolonial studies, and this extract from her revised version adopts a number of strategies. First, it comments on and engages in dialogue with the work of the Subaltern Studies group (see Chapter 44); second, it performs a critique of Deleuze's and Foucault's notion that the subaltern can not only speak but "know" or understand their positions within society; and third, it situates the subaltern subject within the new globalized capitalist flows and structures of First/Third Worlds as they emerge from the more conventional realms of imperialism and colonialism. Embedded within these strategies is a core thesis that Spivak develops in the essay as a whole: that within the world of the subaltern, women are "doubly effaced". One of the leading North American postcolonial theorists, with major texts being *In Other Worlds: Essays in Cultural Politics* (1987), *Selected Subaltern Studies* (co-ed., 1988), and *The Spivak Reader* (1996), Spivak is also the translator of Derrida's *Of Grammatology* (trans. 1976), with her accompanying introduction being a key document in bringing deconstruction to an English-speaking audience. Spivak's language is at times very difficult, partly because of her self-reflective, hybrid theoretical approach, and partly with this extract because she is showing how subaltern subjects and their own voices are silenced, denied, foreclosed (expelled) or appropriated, even by those theorists most keen on facilitating their speech, be they First or Third World elites. Referring to the Subaltern Studies group, Spivak argues that this notion of autonomous speech is essential, especially as peasant "insurgencies" were a key part of Indian nation formation, the narrative of which is appropriated by colonial and "neo-colonial" elites. The complication is that the heterogenous nature of the subaltern classes is both a strength and a potential barrier to representation (i.e., any representation will replace diversity and difference with a reductive essentialism). Spivak also suugests a strange chiastic reversal: anti-essentialist poststructuralist theories end up essentializing the subaltern, whereas apparently essentialist Subaltern Studies approaches lead to more dynamic "radical textual" practices of "difference." So the Subaltern Studies approach looks at gaps between social classes, the fissures of undefinable spaces and voices, leading to a methodology that is closer to Marx, suggests Spivak, than Deleuze and Foucault. Spivak also teases out the notion that there is a "pure form of consciousness" that commentators on the subaltern ultimately theorize or work with in the background, although she argues that the Subaltern Studies group need to do more work in this area, just as the female subaltern subject, doubly effaced without history or speech, similarly needs to be brought out from this "shadow". The history of capitalism (imperial, colonial and globalized processes of appropriation and maintenance of a low-paid peasant or working class) is introduced, partly to situate local politics with that of larger global elites and new social formations dependent upon a new proletariat. Spivak also uses this history to critique Deleuze and Foucault and the general "reinscription" of Third World subjects as a limited and limiting "Other" (i.e., those who have access to First World societies and marketplaces, or what Spivak calls "the migrant struggles in Northern countries"). Spivak suggests that Derrida's work escapes such "ethnocentrism" and his analyses of Western crises of representation per se (writing conceived within a colonial context) brings Spivak to the act of foreclosure, or the imperial expelling of native subjects/ systems which is also constitutive of First World identity.

LET US NOW MOVE TO CONSIDER the margins (one can just as well say the silent, silenced center) of the circuit marked out by this epistemic violence, men and women among the illiterate peasantry, Aboriginals, and the lowest strata of the urban subproletariat. According to Foucault and Deleuze (in the First World, under the standardization and regimentation of socialized capital, though they do not seem to recognize this) and mutatis mutandis the metropolitan "third world feminist" only interested in resistance within capital logic, the oppressed, if given the chance (the problem of representation cannot be bypassed here), and on the way to solidarity through alliance politics (a Marxist thematic is at work here) *can speak and know their conditions.* We must now confront the following question: On the other side of the international division of labor from socialized capital, inside *and* outside the circuit of the epistemic violence of imperialist law and education supplementing an earlier economic text, *can the subaltern speak?*

We have already considered the possibility that, given the exigencies of the inauguration of colonial records, the instrumental woman (the Rani of Sirmur) is not fully written.

Antonio Gramsci's work on the "subaltern classes" extends the class-position/class-consciousness argument isolated in *The Eighteenth Brumaire.* Perhaps because Gramsci criticizes the vanguardistic position of the Leninist intellectual, he is concerned with the intellectual's rôle in the subaltern's cultural and political movement into the hegemony. This movement must be made to determine the production of history as narrative (of truth). In texts such as *The Southern Question,* Gramsci considers the movement of historical-political economy in Italy within what can be seen as an allegory of reading taken from or prefiguring an international division of labor.[1] Yet an account of the phased development of the subaltern is thrown out of joint when his cultural macrology is operated, however remotely, by the epistemic interference with legal and disciplinary definitions accompanying the imperialist project. When I move, at the end of this essay, to the question of woman as subaltern, I will suggest that the possibility of collectivity itself is persistently foreclosed through the manipulation of female agency.

The first part of my proposition—that the phased development of the subaltern is complicated by the imperialist project—is confronted by the "Subaltern Studies" group. They *must* ask, Can the subaltern speak? Here we are within Foucault's own discipline of history and with people who acknowledge his influence. Their project is to rethink Indian colonial historiography from the perspective of the discontinuous chain of peasant insurgencies during the colonial occupation. This is indeed the problem of "the permission to narrate" discussed by Said.[2] As Ranajit Guha, the founding editor of the collective, argues,

> The historiography of Indian nationalism has for a long time been dominated by elitism—colonialist elitism and bourgeois-nationalist elitism . . . shar[ing] the prejudice that the making of the Indian nation and the development of the consciousness—nationalism—which confirmed this process were exclusively or predominantly elite achievements. In the colonialist and neo-colonialist historiographies these achievements are credited to British colonial rulers, administrators, policies, institutions, and culture; in the nationalist and neo-nationalist writings—to Indian elite personalities, institutions, activities and ideas.[3]

Certain members of the Indian elite are of course native informants for first-world intellectuals interested in the voice of the Other. But one must nevertheless insist that the colonized subaltern *subject* is irretrievably heterogeneous.

Against the indigenous elite we may set what Guha calls "the *politics* of the people," both outside ("this was an *autonomous* domain, for it neither originated from elite politics nor did its existence depend on the latter") and inside ("it continued to operate vigorously in spite of [colonialism], adjusting itself to the conditions prevailing under the Raj and in many respects developing entirely new strains in both form and content") the circuit of colonial production. I cannot entirely endorse this insistence of determinate vigor and full autonomy, for practical historiographic exigencies will not allow such endorsements to privilege subaltern consciousness. Against the possible charge that his approach is essentialist, Guha constructs a definition of the people (the place of that essence) that can be only an identity-in-differential. He proposes a dynamic stratification grid describing colonial social production at large. Even the third group on the list, the buffer group, as it were, between the people and the great macrostructural dominant groups, is itself defined as a place of in-betweenness. The classification falls into: "dominant foreign groups," and "dominant indigenous groups at the all-India and at the regional and local levels" representing the elite; and "[t]he social groups and elements included in [the terms 'people' and 'subaltern classes'] represent[ing] *the demographic difference between the total Indian population and all those whom we have described as the 'elite.'*"[4]

"The task of research" projected here is "to investigate, identify and measure the *specific* nature and degree of the *deviation* of [the] elements [constituting item 3] from the ideal and situate it historically." "Investigate, identify, and measure the specific": a program could hardly be more essentialist and taxonomic. Yet a curious methodological imperative is at work. I have argued that, in the Foucault-Deleuze conversation, a postrepresentationalist vocabulary hides an essentialist agenda. In subaltern studies, because of the violence of imperialist epistemic, social, and disciplinary inscription, a project understood in essentialist terms must traffic in a radical textual practice of differences. The object of the group's investigation, in this case not even of the people as such but of the floating buffer zone of the regional elite—is a *deviation* from an *ideal*—the people or subaltern—which is itself defined as a difference from the elite. It is toward this structure that the research is oriented, a predicament rather different from the self-diagnosed transparency of the first-world radical intellectual. What taxonomy can fix such a space? Whether or not they themselves perceive it—in fact Guha sees his definition of "the people" within the master-slave dialectic—their text articulates the difficult task of rewriting its own conditions of impossibility as the conditions of its possibility. "At the regional and local levels [the dominant indigenous groups] . . . if belonging to social strata hierarchically inferior to those of the dominant all-Indian groups *acted in the interests of the latter and not in conformity to interests corresponding truly to their own social being.*"[5] When these writers speak, in their essentializing language, of a gap between interest and action in the intermediate group, their conclusions are closer to Marx than to the self-conscious naivete of Deleuze's pronouncement on the issue. Guha, like Marx, speaks of interest in terms of the social rather than the libidinal being.

The Name-of-the-Father imagery in *The Eighteenth Brumaire* can help to emphasize that, on the level of class or group action, "true correspondence to own being" is as artificial or social as the patronymic.

It is to this intermediate group that the second woman in this chapter belongs. The pattern of domination is here determined mainly by gender rather than class. The subordinated gender following the dominant within the challenge of nationalism while remaining caught within gender oppression is not an unknown story.

For the (gender-unspecified) "true" subaltern group, whose identity is its difference, there is no unrepresentable subaltern subject that can know and speak itself; the intellectual's solution is not to abstain from representation. The problem is that the subject's itinerary has not been left traced so as to offer an object of seduction to the representing intellectual. In the slightly dated language of the Indian group, the question becomes, How can we touch the consciousness of the people, even as we investigate their politics? With what voice-consciousness can the subaltern speak?

My question about how to earn the "secret encounter" with the contemporary hill women of Sirmur is a practical version of this. The woman of whom I will speak in this section was not a "true" subaltern, but a metropolitan middle-class girl. Further, the effort she made to write or speak her body was in the accents of accountable reason, the instrument of self-conscious responsibility. Still her Speech Act was refused. She was made to unspeak herself posthumously, by other women. In an earlier version of this chapter, I had summarized this historical indifference and its results as: the subaltern cannot speak.

The critique by Ajit K. Chaudhury, a West Bengali Marxist, of Guha's search for the subaltern consciousness can be taken as representative of a moment of the production process that includes the subaltern.[6] Chaudhury's perception that the Marxist view of the transformation of consciousness involves the knowledge of social relations seems, in principle, astute. Yet the heritage of the positivist ideology that has appropriated orthodox Marxism obliges him to add this rider: "This is not to belittle the importance of understanding peasants' consciousness or workers' consciousness *in its pure form*. This enriches our knowledge of the peasant and the worker and, possibly, throws light on how a particular mode takes on different forms in different regions, *which is considered a problem of second order importance in classical Marxism.*"[7]

This variety of "internationalist Marxism," which believes in a pure, retrievable form of consciousness only to dismiss it, thus closing off what in Marx remain moments of productive bafflement, can at once be the occasion for Foucault's and Deleuze's rejection of Marxism *and* the source of the critical motivation of the subaltern studies groups. All three are united in the assumption that there *is* a pure form of consciousness. On the French scene, there is a shuffling of signifiers: "the unconscious" or "the subject-in-oppression" clandestinely fills the space of "the pure form of consciousness." In orthodox "internationalist" intellectual Marxism, whether in the First World or the Third, the pure form of consciousness remains, paradoxically, a material effect, and therefore a second-order problem. This often earns it the reputation of racism and sexism. In the subaltern studies group it needs development according to the unacknowledged terms of its own articulation.

Within the effaced itinerary of the subaltern subject, the track of sexual difference is doubly effaced.[8] The question is not of female participation in insurgency, or the ground rules of the sexual division of labor, for both of which there is "evidence." It is, rather, that, both as object of colonialist historiography and as subject of insurgency, the ideological construction of gender keeps the male dominant. If, in the contest of colonial production, the subaltern has no history and cannot speak, the subaltern as female is even more deeply in shadow.

In the first part of this chapter we meditate upon an elusive female figure called into the service of colonialism. In the last part we will look at a comparable figure in anti-colonialist nationalism. The regulative psychobiography of widow self-immolation will be pertinent in both cases. In the interest of the invaginated spaces of this book, let us remind ourselves of the gradual emergence of the new subaltern in the New World Order.

The contemporary international division of labor is a displacement of the divided field of nineteenth-century territorial imperialism. Put in the abstractions of capital logic, in the wake of industrial capitalism and mercantile conquest, a group of countries, generally first-world, were in the position of investing capital; another group, generally third-world, provided the field for investment, both through the subordinate indigenous capitalists and through their ill-protected and shifting labor force. In the interest of maintaining the circulation and growth of industrial capital (and of the concomitant task of administration within nineteenth-century territorial imperialism), transportation, law, and standardized education systems were developed—even as local industries were destroyed or restructured, land distribution was rearranged, and raw material was transferred to the colonizing country. With so-called decolonization, the growth of multinational capital, and the relief of the administrative charge, "development" did not now involve wholesale state-level legislation and establishing education *systems* in a comparable way. This impedes the growth of consumerism in the former colonies. With modern telecommunications and the emergence of advanced capitalist economies at the two edges of Asia, maintaining the international division of labor serves to keep the supply of cheap labor in the periphery. The implosion of the Soviet Union in 1989 has smoothed a way to the financialization of the globe. Already in the mid-seventies, the newly electronified stock exchanges added to the growth of telecommunication, which allowed global capitalism to emerge through export-based subcontracting and postfordism. "Under this strategy, manufacturers based in developed countries subcontract the most labor intensive stages of production, for example, sewing or assembly, to the Third World nations where labor is cheap. Once assembled, the multinational re-imports the goods—under generous tariff exemptions—to the developed country *instead of selling them to the local market.*" Here the link to training in consumerism is almost snapped. "While global recession has markedly slowed trade and investment worldwide since 1979, international subcontracting has boomed. . . . In these cases, multinationals are freer to resist militant workers, revolutionary upheavals, and even economic downturns."[9]

Human labor is not, of course, intrinsically "cheap" or "expensive." An absence of labor laws (or a discriminatory enforcement of them), a totalitarian state (often entailed by development and modernization in the periphery), and minimal subsistence requirements on the part of the worker will ensure "cheapness." To keep this crucial item intact, the urban proletariat in what is now called the "developing" nations must not be systematically trained in the ideology of consumerism (parading as the philosophy of a classless society) that, against all odds, prepares the ground for resistance through the coalition politics Foucault mentions (*FD* 216). This separation from the ideology of consumerism is increasingly exacerbated by the proliferating phenomena of international subcontracting.

In the post-Soviet world, the Bretton Woods organizations, together with the United Nations, are beginning to legislate for a monstrous North/South global state, which is coming into being as micrologically as the trade-controlled colonial state that was mentioned earlier. If Macaulay had spoken of a class of persons, Indian in blood and colour, but English in taste, in opinions, in morals, and in intellect; and Marx of the capitalist as *Faust's* "mechanical man," there is now an impersonal "Economic Citizen," site of authority and legitimation, lodged in finance capital markets and transnational companies.[10] And if under postfordism and international subcontracting, unorganized or permanently casual female labor was already becoming the mainstay of world trade, in contemporary globalization, the mechanism of "aid" is supported by the poorest women of the South, who form the base of what I have elsewhere called globe-girdling struggles (ecology, resistance to "population *control*"), where the boundary between global and local becomes indeterminate. This is the ground of the emergence of the new subaltern—rather different from the nationalist example we will consider later. To confront this group is not only to represent (*vertreten*) them globally in the absence of infrastructural support, but also to learn to represent (*darstellen*) ourselves. This argument would take us into a critique of a disciplinary anthropology and the relationship between elementary pedagogy and disciplinary formation. It would also question the implicit demand, made by intellectuals who choose the "naturally articulate" subject of oppression, that such a subject come through a history that is a foreshortened mode-of-production narrative.

Not surprisingly, some members of *indigenous dominant* groups in the "developing" countries, members of the local bourgeoisie, find the language of alliance politics attractive. Identifying with forms of resistance plausible in advanced capitalist countries is often of a piece with that elitist bent of bourgeois historiography described by Ranajit Guha.

Belief in the plausibility of global alliance politics is increasingly prevalent among women of dominant social groups interested in "international feminism" in the "developing" nations as well as among well-placed Southern diasporics in the North. At the other end of the scale, those most separated from any possibility of an alliance among "women, prisoners, conscripted soldiers, hospital patients, and homosexuals" (*FD* 216) are the females of the urban subproletariat. In their case, the denial and withholding of consumerism and the structure of exploitation is compounded by patriarchal social relations.

That Deleuze and Foucault ignored both the epistemic violence of imperialism and the international division of labor would matter less if they did not, in closing, touch on third-world issues. In France it is impossible to ignore the problem of their *tiers monde,* the inhabitants of the erstwhile French African colonies. Deleuze limits his consideration of the Third World to these old local and regional indigenous elite who are, ideally, subaltern. In this context, references to the maintenance of the surplus army of labor fall into reverse-ethnic sentimentality. Since he is speaking of the heritage of nineteenth-century territorial imperialism, his reference is to the nation-state rather than the globalizing center:

> French capitalism needs greatly a floating signifier of unemployment. In this perspective, we begin to see the unity of the forms of repression: restrictions on immigration, once it is acknowledged that the most difficult and thankless jobs go to immigrant workers; repression in the factories, because the French must reacquire the "taste" for increasingly harder work; the struggle against youth and the repression of the educational system. (*FD* 211–12)

This is certainly an acceptable analysis. Yet it shows again that the Third World can enter the resistance program of an alliance politics directed against a "*unified* repression" only when it is confined to the third-world groups that are directly accessible to the First World.[11] This benevolent first-world appropriation and reinscription of the Third World as an Other is the founding characteristic of much third-worldism in the U.S. human sciences today.

Foucault continues the critique of Marxism by invoking geographical discontinuity. The real mark of "geographical (geopolitcal) discontinuity" is the international division of labor. But Foucault uses the term to distinguish between exploitation (extraction and appropriation of surplus value; read, the field of Marxist analysis) and domination ("power" studies) and to suggest the latter's greater potential for resistance based on alliance politics. He cannot acknowledge that such a monist and unified access to a conception of "power" (methodologically presupposing a Subject-of-power) is made possible by a certain stage in exploitation, for his vision of geographical discontinuity is geopolitically specific to the First World:

> This geographical discontinuity of which you speak might mean perhaps the following: as soon as we struggle against *exploitation,* the proletariat not only leads the struggle but also defines its targets, its methods, its places and its instruments; and to ally oneself with the proletariat is to consolidate with its positions, its ideology, it is to take up again the motives for their combat. This means total immersion [in the Marxist project]. But if it is against *power* that one struggles, then all those who acknowledge it as intolerable can begin the struggle wherever they find themselves and in terms of their own activity (or passivity). In engaging in this struggle that is *their own,* whose objectives they clearly understand and whose methods they can determine, they enter into the revolutionary process. As allies of the proletariat, to be sure, because power is exercised the way it is in order to maintain capitalist exploitation. They genuinely serve the cause of the proletariat by fighting in those places where they find themselves oppressed. Women, prisoners, conscripted soldiers, hospital patients, and homosexuals have now begun a specific struggle against the particular form of power, the constraints and controls, that are exercised over them. (FD 216)

This is an admirable program of localized resistance. Where possible, this model of resistance is not an alternative to, but can complement, macrological struggles along "Marxist" lines. Yet if its situation is universalized, it accommodates unacknowledged privileging of the subject. Without a theory of ideology, it can lead to a dangerous utopianism. And, if confined to migrant struggles in Northern countries, it can work against global social justice.

The topographical reinscription of imperialism never specifically informed Foucault's presuppositions. Notice the omission of the fact, in the following passage, that the new mechanism of power in the seventeenth and eighteenth centuries (the extraction of surplus value without extra-economic coercion is its marxist description) is secured *by means of* territorial imperialism—the Earth and its products—"elsewhere." The representation of sovereignty is crucial in these theaters: "In the seventeenth and eighteenth centuries, we have the production of an important phenomenon, the emergence, or rather the invention, of a new mechanism of power possessed of highly specific procedural techniques . . . which is also, I believe, absolutely incompatible with the relations of sovereignty. This new mechanism of power is more dependent upon bodies and what they do than the Earth and its products" (*PK* 104).

Sometimes it seems as if the very brilliance of Foucault's analysis of the centuries of European imperialism produces a miniature version of that heterogeneous phenomenon: management of space—but by doctors; development of administrations—but in asylums; considerations of the periphery—but in terms of the insane, prisoners, and children. The clinic, the asylum, the prison, the university—all seem to be screen-allegories that foreclose a reading of the broader narratives of imperialism. (One could open a similar discussion of the ferocious motif of "deterritorialization" in Deleuze and Guattari.) "One can perfecdy well not talk about something because one doesn't know about it," Foucault might murmur (*PK* 66). Yet we have already spoken of the sanctioned ignorance that every critic of imperialism must chart.

By contrast, the early Derrida seemed aware of ethnocentrism in the production of knowledge.[12] (We have seen this in his comments on Kant quoted in Chapter 1. Like "empirical investigation, . . . tak[ing] shelter in the field of grammatological knowledge" obliges "operat[ing] through 'examples,'" *OG* 75.)

The examples Derrida lays out—to show the limits of grammatology as a positive science—come from the appropriate ideological self-justification of an imperialist project. In the European seventeenth century, he writes, there were three kinds of "prejudices" operating in histories of writing which constituted a "symptom of the crisis of European consciousness" (*OG* 75): the "theological prejudice," the "Chinese prejudice," and the "hieroglyphist prejudice." The first can be indexed as: God wrote a primordial or natural script: Hebrew or Greek. The second: Chinese is a perfect *blueprint* for philosophical writing, but it is only a blueprint. True philosophical writing is "independen[t] with regard to history" (*OG* 79) and will sublate Chinese into an easy-to-learn script that will supersede actual Chinese. The third: that the Egyptian script is too sublime to be deciphered.

The first prejudice preserves the "actuality" of Hebrew or Greek; the last two ("rational" and "mystical," respectively) collude to support the first, where the center of the logos is seen as the Judaeo-Christian God (the appropriation of the Hellenic Other through assimilation is an earlier story)—a "prejudice" still sustained in efforts to give the cartography of the Judaeo-Christian myth the status of geopolitical history:

> The concept of Chinese writing thus functioned as a sort of *European hallucination*. . . . This functioning obeyed a rigorous necessity. . . . It was not disturbed by the knowledge of Chinese script . . . which was then available. . . . A "*hieroglyphist prejudice*" had produced the same effect of *interested blindness*. Far from proceeding . . . from ethnocentric scorn, the occultation takes the form of an hyperbolical admiration. We have not finished demonstrating the necessity of this pattern. Our century is not free from it; each time that ethnocentrism is precipitately and ostentatiously reversed, some effort silently hides behind all the spectacular effects to *consolidate an inside* and to draw from it some domestic benefit. (*OG* 80; Derrida italicizes only "hieroglyphist prejudice")

This pattern operates the culturalist excuse for Development encountered, for example, in John Rawls's *Political Liberalism,* as it does all unexamined metropolitan hybridism.[13]

Derrida closes the chapter by showing again that the project of grammatology is obliged to develop *within* the discourse of presence. It is not just a critique of presence but an awareness of the itinerary of the discourse of presence in one's *own* critique, a vigilance precisely against too great a claim for transparency. The word "writing" as the name of the object and model of grammatology is a practice "only within the *historical* closure, that is to say within the limits of science and philosophy" (*OG* 93).

Derrida calls the ethnocentrism of the European science of writing in the late seventeenth and early eighteenth centuries a symptom of the general crisis of European consciousness. It is, of course, part of a larger symptom, or perhaps the crisis itself, the slow turn from feudalism to capitalism via the first waves of capitalist imperialism. The itinerary of recognition through assimilation of the Other can be more interestingly traced, it seems to me, in the imperialist constitution of the colonial subject and the foreclosure of the figure of the "native informant."

Abbreviations

FD = Michel Foucault, *Language, Counter-Memory, Practice: Selected Essays and Interviews*, tr. Donald Bouchard and Sherry Simon (Ithaca: Cornell University Press, 1977), pp. 205–17.

OG = Jacques Derrida, *Of Grammatology*, trans. Gayatri Chakravorty Spivak (Baltimore: The Johns Hopkins University Press, 1976).

PK = Michel Foucault, "On Popular Justice: A Discussion with Maoists," in *Power/Knowledge: Selected Interviews and Other Writings, 1972–1977*, ed. Colin Gordon (New York: Pantheon, 1980).

Notes

1   Antonio Gramsci, *The Southern Question,* tr. Pasquale Verdicchio (West Lafayette, Ind.: Bordighera, Inc., 1995). As usual, I am using "allegory of reading" in the sense suggested by Paul de Man.
2   Edward W. Said, "Permission to Narrate," *London Review of Books* (16 Feb. 1984).
3   Guha, *Subaltern Studies,* (Delhi: Oxford Univ. Press, 1982), 1:1.
4   Ibid., pp. 4, 8. The usefulness of this tightly defined term was largely lost when *Selected Subaltern Studies* was launched in the United States under Spivak's initiative (New York: Oxford Univ. Press, 1988). Guha, ed., *A Subaltern Studies Reader* (Minneapolis: Univ. of Minnesota Press, 1997) is now a corrective. In the now generalized usage, it is precisely this notion of the subaltern inhabiting a space of difference that is lost in statements such as the following: "The subaltern is force-fed into appropriating the master's culture" (Emily Apter, "French Colonial Studies and Postcolonial Theory," *Sub-Stance* 76/77, vol. 24, nos. 1–2 [1995]: 178); or worse still, Jameson's curious definition of subalternity as "the experience of inferiority" ("Marx's Purloined Letter," *New Left Review* 209 [1994]: 95).
5   Guha, *Subaltern Studies,* 1:1.
6   Since then, in the disciplinary fallout after the serious electoral and terrorist augmentation of Hindu nationalism in India, more alarming charges have been leveled at the group. See Aijaz Ahmad, *In Theory: Classes, Nations, Literatures* (New York: Verso, 1992), pp. 68, 194, 207–11; and Sumit Sarkar, "The Fascism of the Sangh Parivar," *Economic and Political Weekly,* 30 Jan. 1993, pp. 163–67.
7   Ajit K. Chaudhury, "New Wave Social Science," *Frontier* 16–24 (28 Jan. 1984), p. 10. Emphasis mine.
8   I do not believe that the recent trend of romanticizing anything written by the Aboriginal or outcaste ("dalit" = oppressed) intellectual has lifted the effacement.
9   "Contracting Poverty," *Multinational Monitor* 4.8 (Aug. 1983):8. This report was contributed by John Cavanagh and Joy Hackel, who work on the International Corporations Project at the Institute for Policy Studies. Emphasis mine.
10 Saskia Sassen, "On Economic Citizenship," in *Losing Control? Sovereignty in An Age of Globalization* (New York: Columbia Univ. Press, 1996), pp. 31–58.
11 The mechanics of the invention of the Third World as signifier are susceptible to the type of analysis directed at the constitution of race as a signifier in Carby, *Empire*. In the contemprary conjuncture, in response to the augmentation of Eurocentric migration as the demographic fallout of postcoloniality, neocolonialism, end of the Soviet Union, and global financialization, the South (the Third World of yore, with shifting bits of the old Second World thrown in) is being reinvented as the South-in-the-North. Even so brilliant a book as Etienne Balibar and Immanuel Wallerstein, *Race, Nation, Class: Ambiguous Identities,* tr. Chris Turner (New York: Verso, 1991) starts from this invention as unquestioned premise.
12 Subsequently, as I indicate at length elsewhere (*Outside,* pp. 113–15; "Ghostwriting," pp. 69–71, 82) his work in these areas has speculated with the tendencies of computing migrancy or displacement as an origin (see page 17); in the figure of the absolute *arrivant,* of the marrano, and, most recently, in his seminars, hospitality. He would figure the indigenous subaltern, from the perspective of the metropolitan hybrid, as a correlative of cultural conservatism, topological archaism, ontopological nostalgia (*Specters,* p. 82). Here, too, he speculates with already existing tendencies. Just as pedigreed Marxists have been told, by Derrida among others, that Marx must be read in Marx's way, *as if* the reader were haunted by Marx's ghost; so might one deconstruct deconstruction (as Klein Freuded Freud): do not accuse, do not excuse, make it "your own," turn it around and use—with no guarantees—except that this formula too will become useless tomorrow—or in the moment of its saying: "each time that ethnocentrism is precipitately and ostentatiously reversed, some effort silently hides behind all the spectacular effects to consolidate an inside and to draw from it some domestic benefit."
13 John Rawls, *Political Liberalism* (New York: Columbia Univ. Press, 1993).

Chapter 46

Edward Said

ORIENTALISM NOW

Edward Said's theory of Orientalism is that it is a hegemonic discursive formation, or, actively used body of knowledge about the Orient (a term coming into use in the eighteenth century which from a European perspective signifies the Middle East). What this means—following Gramsci and Foucault—is that such a body of knowledge produces real, material effects in the world, in this case, the creation of colonial space. Said is one of the founders of postcolonial studies, and in a later publication, *Culture and Imperialism* (1993), he addresses the intellectuals and activists who resisted colonial domination. In the extract, Said is exploring the mechanisms whereby colonial space is formed, and he suggests that this act of creation can be seen in the shift from Orientalism as a "textual and contemplative" activity (creating theories and writing books about the Orient) to one that is "administrative, economic and military" (literally, building the British, German and French empires). Or to put this another way, Said suggests that textual Orientalism is about mapping "alien" space whereas the engagement with and creation of an actuality—colonized countries—*is* an engagement with "colonial" space. Said opens his chapter from *Orientalism* with a useful summary of his book up to this point, before arguing that textual Orientalism has a "cumulative and corporate identity", that is to say, it exists in the individual *and* group research outputs produced, managed and regulated as a wider discursive field. Such a formation is primarily subjective—Said compares it to Nietzsche's famous dictum about language being "a mobile army of metaphors"—since it is primarily semiotic (or a system of linguistic signs), but it is one that is political in its intent and force. Orientalism isn't just an academic discourse, then, it is one that functions through military, economic, political and state intervention. But what such a formation lacks in terms of objectivity, it makes up for in terms of sheer productivity, seen in the huge imbalance between Orientalist texts and those written from an Eastern perspective looking back at the West. Said suggests that this is a particularly "aggressive" Western will-to-knowledge and power, representing an imbalance of power between the East and the West. Even more troubling is the fact that the Orientalist discursive formation became normalized as a coherent and accepted body of knowledge that needed no evaluation or critique; rather it simply functioned as a substrate upon which more Orientalist notions could be developed. Such a substrate is called by Said "latent Orientalism" while individual texts or utterances made by Orientalists are called "manifest Orientalism". One of the issues with this stable and unexamined substrate is that it conveys problematic values, such as that of now outmoded Eugenicist ideas (certain racial and class groups are inherently weak, criminal, etc.), or the patriarchal and gendered notion that Oriental peoples are effeminate. Latent Orientalism, then, is based upon a lack of direct experiencing of the Orient, but when that does occur, leading to a qualitative change in Orientalist discourse, it is one based upon the Western desire to invade and colonize the Orient, not understand it more authentically. Said notes that this leads to a transformation of the Orientalist notion of "geographical space" and further analysis of how that space had been colonized by the British or the French. In other words, the Orientalist project gains a closer understanding of its own administrative systems, not one of the actual people who have been colonized.

Latent and manifest orientalism

In Chapter One, I tried to indicate the scope of thought and action covered by the word *Orientalism,* using as privileged types the British and French experiences of and with the Near Orient, Islam, and the Arabs. In those experiences I discerned an intimate, perhaps even the most intimate, and rich relationship between Occident and Orient. Those experiences were part of a much wider European or Western relationship with the Orient, but what seems to have influenced Orientalism most was a fairly constant sense of confrontation felt by Westerners dealing with the East. The boundary notion of East and West, the varying degrees of projected inferiority and strength, the range of work done, the kinds of characteristic features ascribed to the Orient: all these testify to a willed imaginative and geographic division made between East and West, and lived through during many centuries. In Chapter Two my focus narrowed a good deal. I was interested in the earliest phases of what I call modern Orientalism, which began during the latter part of the eighteenth century and the early years of the nineteenth. Since I did not intend my study to become a narrative chronicle of the development of Oriental studies in the modern West, I proposed instead an account of the rise, development, and institutions of Orientalism as they were formed against a background of intellectual, cultural, and political history until about 1870 or 1880. Although my interest in Orientalism there included a decently ample variety of scholars and imaginative writers, I cannot claim by any means to have presented more than a portrait of the typical structures (and their ideological tendencies) constituting the field, its associations with other fields, and the work of some of its most influential scholars. My principal operating assumptions were—and continue to be—that fields of learning, as much as the works of even the most eccentric artist, are constrained and acted upon by society, by cultural traditions, by worldly circumstance, and by stabilizing influences like schools, libraries, and governments; moreover, that both learned and imaginative writing are never free, but are limited in their imagery, assumptions, and intentions; and finally, that the advances made by a "science" like Orientalism in its academic form are less objectively true than we often like to think. In short, my study hitherto has tried to describe the *economy* that makes Orientalism a coherent subject matter, even while allowing that as an idea, concept, or image the word *Orient* has a considerable and interesting cultural resonance in the West.

I realize that such assumptions are not without their controversial side. Most of us assume in a general way that learning and scholarship move forward; they get better, we feel, as time passes and as more information is accumulated, methods are refined, and later generations of scholars improve upon earlier ones. In addition, we entertain a mythology of creation, in which it is believed that artistic genius, an original talent, or a powerful intellect can leap beyond the confines of its own time and place in order to put before the world a new work. It would be pointless to deny that such ideas as these carry some truth. Nevertheless the possibilities for work present in the culture to a great and original mind are never unlimited, just as it is also true that a great talent has a very healthy respect for what others have done before it and for what the field already contains. The work of predecessors, the institutional life of a scholarly field, the collective nature of any learned enterprise: these, to say nothing of economic and social circumstances, tend to diminish the effects of the individual scholar's production. A field like Orientalism has a cumulative and corporate identity, one that is particularly strong given its associations with traditional learning (the classics, the Bible, philology), public institutions (governments, trading companies, geographical societies, universities), and generically determined writing (travel books, books of exploration, fantasy, exotic description). The result for Orientalism has been a sort of consensus: certain things, certain types of statement, certain types of work have seemed for the Orientalist correct. He has built his work and research upon them, and they in turn have pressed hard upon new writers and scholars. Orientalism can thus be regarded as a manner of regularized (or Orientalized) writing, vision, and study, dominated by imperatives, perspectives, and ideological biases ostensibly suited to the Orient. The Orient is taught, researched, administered, and pronounced upon in certain discrete ways.

The Orient that appears in Orientalism, then, is a system of representations framed by a whole set of forces that brought the Orient into Western learning, Western consciousness, and later, Western empire. If this definition of Orientalism seems more political than not, that is simply because I think Orientalism was itself a product of certain political forces and activities. Orientalism is a school of interpretation whose material happens to be the Orient, its civilizations, peoples, and localities. Its objective discoveries—the work of innumerable devoted scholars who edited texts and translated them, codified grammars, wrote dictionaries, reconstructed dead epochs, produced positivistically verifiable learning—are and always have been conditioned by the fact that its truths, like any truths delivered by language, are embodied in language, and what is the truth of language, Nietzsche once said, but

> a mobile army of metaphors, metonyms, and anthropomorphisms—in short, a sum of human relations, which have been enhanced, transposed, and embellished poetically and rhetorically, and which after long use seem firm, canonical, and obligatory to a people: truths are illusions about which one has forgotten that this is what they are.[1]

Perhaps such a view as Nietzsche's will strike us as too nihilistic, but at least it will draw attention to the fact that so far as it existed in the West's awareness, the Orient was a word which later accrued to it a wide field of meanings, associations, and connotations, and that these did not necessarily refer to the real Orient but to the field surrounding the word.

Thus Orientalism is not only a positive doctrine about the Orient that exists at any one time in the West; it is also an influential academic tradition (when one refers to an academic specialist who is called an Orientalist), as well as an area of concern defined by travelers, commercial enterprises, governments, military expeditions, readers of novels and accounts of exotic adventure, natural historians, and pilgrims to whom the Orient is a specific kind of knowledge about specific places, peoples, and civilizations. For the Orient idioms became frequent, and these idioms took firm hold in European discourse. Beneath the idioms there was a layer of doctrine about the Orient; this doctrine was fashioned out of the experiences of many Europeans, all of them converging upon such essential aspects of the Orient as the Oriental character, Oriental despotism, Oriental sensuality, and the like. For any European during the nineteenth century—and I think one can say this almost without qualification—Orientalism was such a system of truths, truths in Nietzsche's sense of the word. It is therefore correct that every European, in what he could say about the Orient, was consequently a racist, an imperialist, and almost totally ethnocentric. Some of the immediate sting will be taken out of these labels if we recall additionally that human societies, at least the more advanced cultures, have rarely offered the individual anything but imperialism, racism, and ethnocentrism for dealing with "other" cultures. So Orientalism aided and was aided by general cultural pressures that tended to make more rigid the sense of difference between the European and Asiatic parts of the world. My contention is that Orientalism is fundamentally a political doctrine willed over the Orient because the Orient was weaker than the West, which elided the Orient's difference with its weakness.

This proposition was introduced early in Chapter One, and nearly everything in the pages that followed was intended in part as a corroboration of it. The very presence of a "field" such as Orientalism, with no corresponding equivalent in the Orient itself, suggests the relative strength of Orient and Occident. A vast number of pages on the Orient exist, and they of course signify a degree and quantity of interaction with the Orient that are quite formidable; but the crucial index of Western strength is that there is no possibility of comparing the movement of Westerners eastwards (since the end of the eighteenth century) with the movement of Easterners westwards. Leaving aside the fact that Western armies, consular corps, merchants, and scientific and archaeological expeditions were always going East, the number of travelers from the Islamic East to Europe between 1800 and 1900 is minuscule when compared with the number in the other direction.[2] Moreover, the Eastern travelers in the West were there to learn from and to gape at an advanced culture; the purposes of the Western travelers in the Orient were, as we have seen, of quite a different order. In addition, it has been estimated that around 60,000 books dealing with the Near Orient were written between 1800 and 1950; there is no remotely comparable figure for Oriental books about the West. As a cultural apparatus Orientalism is all aggression, activity, judgment, will-to-truth, and knowledge. The Orient existed for the West, or so it seemed to countless Orientalists, whose attitude to what they worked on was either paternalistic or candidly condescending—unless, of course, they were antiquarians, in which case the "classical" Orient was a credit to *them* and not to the lamentable modern Orient. And then, beefing up the Western scholars' work, there were numerous agencies and institutions with no parallels in Oriental society.

Such an imbalance between East and West is obviously a function of changing historical patterns. During its political and military heyday from the eighth century to the sixteenth, Islam dominated both East and West. Then the center of power shifted westwards, and now in the late twentieth century it seems to be directing itself back towards the East again. My account of nineteenth-century Orientalism in Chapter Two stopped at a particularly charged period in the latter part of the century, when the often dilatory, abstract, and projective aspects of Orientalism were about to take on a new sense of worldly mission in the service of formal colonialism. It is this project and this moment that I want now to describe, especially since it will furnish us with some important background for the twentieth-century crises of Orientalism and the resurgence of political and cultural strength in the East.

On several occasions I have alluded to the connections between Orientalism as a body of ideas, beliefs, clichés, or learning about the East, and other schools of thought at large in the culture. Now one of the important developments in nineteenth-century Orientalism was the distillation of essential ideas about the Orient—its sensuality, its tendency to despotism, its aberrant mentality, its habits of inaccuracy, its backwardness—into a separate and unchallenged coherence; thus for a writer to use the word *Oriental* was a reference for the reader sufficient to identify a specific body of information about the Orient. This information seemed to be morally neutral and objectively valid; it seemed to have an epistemological status equal to that of historical chronology or geographical location. In its most basic form, then, Oriental material could not really be violated by anyone's discoveries, nor did it seem ever to be revaluated completely. Instead, the work of various nineteenth-century scholars and of imaginative writers made this essential body of knowledge more clear, more detailed, more substantial—and more distinct from "Occidentalism." Yet Orientalist ideas could enter into alliance with general philosophical theories (such as those about the history of mankind and civilization) and diffuse world-hypotheses, as philosophers sometimes call them; and in many ways the professional contributors to Oriental knowledge were anxious to couch their formulations and ideas, their scholarly work, their considered contemporary observations, in language and terminology whose cultural validity derived from other sciences and systems of thought.

The distinction I am making is really between an almost unconscious (and certainly an untouchable) positivity, which I shall call *latent* Orientalism, and the various stated views about Oriental society, languages, literatures, history, sociology, and so forth, which I shall call *manifest* Orientalism. Whatever change occurs in knowledge of the Orient is found almost exclusively in manifest Orientalism; the unanimity, stability, and durability of latent Orientalism are more or less constant. In the nineteenth-century writers I analyzed in Chapter Two, the differences in their ideas about the Orient can be characterized as exclusively manifest differences, differences in form and personal style, rarely in basic content. Every one of them kept intact the separateness of the Orient, its eccentricity, its backwardness, its silent indifference, its feminine penetrability, its supine malleability; this is why every writer on the Orient, from Renan to Marx (ideologically speaking), or from the most rigorous scholars (Lane and Sacy) to the most powerful imaginations (Flaubert and Nerval), saw the Orient as a locale requiring Western attention, reconstruction, even redemption. The Orient existed as a place isolated from the mainstream of European progress in the sciences, arts, and commerce. Thus whatever good or bad values were imputed to the Orient appeared to be functions of some highly specialized Western interest in the Orient. This was the situation from about the 1870s on through the early part of the twentieth century—but let me give some examples that illustrate what I mean.

Theses of Oriental backwardness, degeneracy, and inequality with the West most easily associated themselves early in the nineteenth century with ideas about the biological bases of racial inequality. Thus the racial classifications found in Cuvier's *Le Règne animal,* Gobineau's *Essai sur l'inégalité des races humaines,* and Robert Knox's *The Races of Man* found a willing partner in latent Orientalism. To these ideas was added second-order Darwinism, which seemed to accentuate the "scientific" validity of the division of races into advanced and backward, or European-Aryan and Oriental-African. Thus the whole question of imperialism, as it was debated in the late nineteenth century by pro-imperialists and anti-imperialists alike, carried forward the binary typology of advanced and backward (or subject) races, cultures, and societies. John Westlake's *Chapters on the Principles of International Law* (1894) argues, for example, that regions of the earth designated as "uncivilized" (a word carrying the freight of Orientalist assumptions, among others) ought to be annexed or occupied by advanced powers. Similarly, the ideas of such writers as Carl Peters, Leopold de Saussure, and Charles Temple draw on the advanced/backward binarism[3] so centrally advocated in late-nineteenth-century Orientalism.

Along with all other peoples variously designated as backward, degenerate, uncivilized, and retarded, the Orientals were viewed in a framework constructed out of biological determinism and moral-political admonishment. The Oriental was linked thus to elements in Western society (delinquents, the insane, women, the poor) having in common an identity best described as lamentably alien. Orientals were rarely seen or looked at; they were seen through, analyzed not as citizens, or even people, but as problems to be solved or confined or—as the colonial powers openly coveted their territory—taken over. The point is that the very designation of something as Oriental involved an already pronounced evaluative judgment, and in the case of the peoples inhabiting the decayed Ottoman Empire, an implicit program of action. Since the Oriental was a member of a subject race, he had to be subjected: it was that simple. The *locus classicus* for such judgment and action is to be found in Gustave Le Bon's *Les Lois psychologiques de l'évolution des peuples* (1894).

But there were other uses for latent Orientalism. If that group of ideas allowed one to separate Orientals from advanced, civilizing powers, and if the "classical" Orient served to justify both the Orientalist and his disregard of modern Orientals, latent Orientalism also encouraged a peculiarly (not to say invidiously) male conception of the world. I have already referred to this in passing during my discussion of Renan. The Oriental male was considered in isolation from the total community in which he lived and which many Orientalists, following Lane, have viewed with something resembling contempt and fear. Orientalism itself, furthermore, was an exclusively male province; like so many professional guilds during the modern period, it viewed itself and its subject matter with sexist blinders. This is especially evident in the writing of travelers and novelists: women are usually the creatures of a male power-fantasy. They express unlimited sensuality, they are more or less stupid, and above all they are willing. Flaubert's Kuchuk Hanem is the prototype of such caricatures, which were common enough in pornographic novels (e.g., Pierre Louÿs's *Aphrodite*) whose novelty draws on the Orient for their interest. Moreover the male conception of the world, in its effect upon the practicing Orientalist, tends to be static, frozen, fixed eternally. The very possibility of development, transformation, human movement—in the deepest sense of the word—is denied the Orient and the Oriental. As a known and ultimately an immobilized or unproductive quality, they come to be identified with a bad sort of eternality: hence, when the Orient is being approved, such phrases as "the wisdom of the East."

Transferred from an implicit social evaluation to a grandly cultural one, this static male Orientalism took on a variety of forms in the late nineteenth century, especially when Islam was being discussed. General cultural historians as respected as Leopold von Ranke and Jacob Burckhardt assailed Islam as if they were dealing not so much with an anthropomorphic abstraction as with a religio-political culture about which deep generalizations were possible and warranted: in his *Weltgeschichte* (1881–88) Ranke spoke of Islam as defeated by the Germanic-Romanic peoples, and in his "Historische Fragmente" (unpublished notes, 1893) Burckhardt spoke of Islam as wretched, bare, and trivial.[4] Such intellectual operations were carried out with considerably more flair and enthusiasm by Oswald Spengler, whose ideas about a Magian personality (typified by the Muslim Oriental) infuse *Der Untergang des Abendlandes* (1918–22) and the "morphology" of cultures it advocates.

What these widely diffused notions of the Orient depended on was the almost total absence in contemporary Western culture of the Orient as a genuinely felt and experienced force. For a number of evident reasons the Orient was always in the position both of outsider and of incorporated weak partner for the West. To the extent that Western scholars were aware of contemporary Orientals or Oriental movements of thought and culture, these were perceived either as silent shadows to be animated by the Orientalist, brought into reality by him, or as a kind of cultural and intellectual proletariat useful for the Orientalist's grander interpretative activity, necessary for his performance as superior judge, learned man, powerful cultural will. I mean to say that in discussions of the Orient, the Orient is all absence, whereas one feels the Orientalist and what he says as presence; yet we must not forget that the Orientalist's presence is enabled by the Orient's effective absence. This fact of substitution and displacement, as we must call it, clearly places on the Orientalist himself a certain pressure to reduce the Orient in his work, even after he has devoted a good deal of time to elucidating and exposing it. How else can one explain major scholarly production of the type we associate with Julius Wellhausen and Theodor Nöldeke and, overriding it, those bare, sweeping statements that almost totally denigrate their chosen subject matter? Thus Nöldeke could declare in 1887 that the sum total of his work as an Orientalist was to confirm his "low opinion" of the Eastern peoples.[5] And like Carl Becker, Nöldeke was a philhellenist, who showed his love of Greece curiously by displaying a positive dislike of the Orient, which after all was what he studied as a scholar.

A very valuable and intelligent study of Orientalism—Jacques Waardenburg's *L'Islam dans le miroir de l'Occident*—examines five important experts as makers of an image of Islam. Waardenburg's mirror-image metaphor for late-nineteenth- and early-twentieth-century Orientalism is apt. In the work of each of his eminent Orientalists there is a highly tendentious—in four cases out of the five, even hostile—vision of Islam, as if each man saw Islam as a reflection of his own chosen weakness. Each scholar was profoundly learned, and the style of his contribution was unique. The five Orientalists among them exemplify what was best and strongest in the tradition during the period roughly from the 1880s to the inter-war years. Yet Ignaz Goldziher's appreciation of Islam's tolerance towards other religions was undercut by his dislike of Mohammed's anthropomorphisms and Islam's too-exterior theology and jurisprudence; Duncan Black Macdonald's interest in Islamic piety and ortho-doxy was vitiated by his perception of what he considered Islam's heretical Christianity; Carl Becker's understanding of Islamic civilization made him see it as a sadly undeveloped one; C. Snouck Hurgronje's highly refined studies of Islamic mysticism (which he considered the essential part of Islam) led him to a harsh judgment of its crippling limitations; and Louis Massignon's extraordinary identification with Muslim theology, mystical passion, and poetic art kept him curiously unforgiving to Islam for what he regarded as its unregenerate revolt against the idea of incarnation. The manifest differences in their methods emerge as less important than their Orientalist consensus on Islam: latent inferiority.[6]

Waardenburg's study has the additional virtue of showing how these five scholars shared a common intellectual and methodological tradition whose unity was truly international. Ever since the first Orientalist congress in 1873, scholars in the field have known each other's work and felt each other's presence very directly. What Waardenburg does not stress enough is that most of the late-nineteenth-century Orientalists were bound to each other politically as well. Snouck Hurgronje went directly from his studies of Islam to being an adviser to the Dutch government on handling its Muslim Indonesian colonies; Macdonald and Massignon were widely sought after as experts on Islamic matters by colonial administrators from North Africa to Pakistan; and, as Waardenburg says (all too briefly) at one point, all five scholars shaped a coherent vision of Islam that had a wide influence on government circles throughout the Western world.[7] What we must add to Waardenburg's observation is that these scholars were completing, bringing to an ultimate concrete refinement, the tendency since the six-teenth and seventeenth centuries to treat the Orient not only as a vague literary problem but—according to Masson-Oursel—as "un ferme propos d'assimiler adéquatement la valeur des langues pour pénétrer les moeurs et les pensées, pour forcer même des secrets de l'histoire."[8]

I spoke earlier of incorporation and assimilation of the Orient, as these activities were practiced by writers as different from each other as Dante and d'Herbelot. Clearly there is a difference between those efforts and what, by the end of the nineteenth century, had become a truly formidable European cultural, political, and material enterprise. The nineteenth-century colonial "scramble for Africa" was by no means limited to Africa, of course. Neither was the penetration of the Orient entirely a sudden, dramatic afterthought following years of scholarly study of Asia. What we must reckon with is a long and slow process of appropriation by which Europe, or the European awareness of the Orient, transformed itself from being textual and contemplative into being administrative, economic, and even military. The fundamental change was a spatial and geographical one, or rather it was a change in the quality of geographical and spatial apprehension so far as the Orient was concerned. The centuries-old designation of geographical space to the east of Europe as "Oriental" was partly political, partly doctrinal, and partly imaginative; it implied no necessary connection between actual experience of the Orient and knowledge of what is Oriental, and certainly Dante and d'Herbelot made no claims about their Oriental ideas except that they were corroborated by a long *learned* (and not existential) tradition. But when Lane, Renan, Burton, and the many hundreds of nineteenth-century European travelers and scholars discuss the Orient, we can immediately note a far more intimate and even proprietary attitude towards the Orient and things Oriental. In the classical and often temporally remote form in which it was reconstructed by the Orientalist, in the precisely actual form in which the modern Orient was lived in, studied, or imagined, the *geographical space* of the Orient was penetrated, worked over, taken hold of. The cumulative effect of decades of so sovereign a Western handling turned the Orient from alien into colonial space. What was important in the latter nineteenth century was not *whether* the West had penetrated and possessed the Orient, but rather *how* the British and French felt that they had done it.

The British writer on the Orient, and even more so the British colonial administrator, was dealing with territory about which there could be no doubt that English power was truly in the ascendant, even if the natives were on the face of it attracted to France and French modes of thought. So far as the actual space of the Orient was concerned, however, England was really there, France was not, except as a flighty temptress of the Oriental yokels. There is no better indication of this qualitative difference in spatial attitudes than to look at what Lord Cromer had to say on the subject, one that was especially dear to his heart:

> The reasons why French civilisation presents a special degree of attraction to Asiatics and Levantines are plain. It is, as a matter of fact, more attractive than the civilisations of England and Germany, and, moreover, it is more easy of imitation. Compare the undemonstrative, shy Englishman, with his social exclusiveness and insular habits, with the vivacious and cosmopolitan Frenchman, who does not know what the word shyness means, and who in ten minutes is apparently on terms of intimate friendship with any casual acquaintance he may chance to make. The semi-educated Oriental does not recognise that the former has, at all events, the merit of sincerity, whilst the latter is often merely acting a part. He looks coldly on the Englishman, and rushes into the arms of the Frenchman.

The sexual innuendoes develop more or less naturally thereafter. The Frenchman is all smiles, wit, grace, and fashion; the Englishman is plodding, industrious, Baconian, precise. Cromer's case is of course based on British solidity as opposed to a French seductiveness without any real presence in Egyptian reality.

> Can it be any matter for surprise [Cromer continues] that the Egyptian, with his light intellectual ballast, fails to see that some fallacy often lies at the bottom of the Frenchman's reasoning, or that he prefers the rather superficial brilliancy of the Frenchman to the plodding, unattractive industry of the Englishman or the German? Look, again, at the theoretical perfection of French administrative systems, at their elaborate detail, and at the provision which is apparently made to meet every possible contingency which may arise. Compare these features with the Englishman's practical systems, which lay down rules as to a few main points, and leave a mass of detail to individual discretion. The half-educated Egyptian naturally prefers the Frenchman's system, for it is to all outward appearance more perfect and more easy of application. He fails, moreover, to see that the Englishman desires to elaborate a system which will suit the facts with which he has to deal, whereas the main objection to applying French

administrative procedures to Egypt is that the facts have but too often to conform
to the ready-made system.

Since there is a real British presence in Egypt, and since that presence—according to
Cromer—is there not so much to train the Egyptian's mind as to "form his character," it
follows therefore that the ephemeral attractions of the French are those of a pretty damsel
with "somewhat artificial charms," whereas those of the British belong to "a sober, elderly
matron of perhaps somewhat greater moral worth, but of less pleasing outward appearance."[9]

Underlying Cromer's contrast between the solid British nanny and the French coquette
is the sheer privilege of British emplacement in the Orient. "The facts with which he
[the Englishman] has to deal" are altogether more complex and interesting, by virtue of their
possession by England, than anything the mercurial French could point to. Two years
after the publication of his *Modern Egypt* (1908), Cromer expatiated philosophically in
Ancient and Modern Imperialism. Compared with Roman imperialism, with its frankly assimila-
tionist, exploitative, and repressive policies, British imperialism seemed to Cromer to be
preferable, if somewhat more wishy-washy. On certain points, however, the British were
clear enough, even if "after a rather dim, slipshod, but characteristically Anglo-Saxon
fashion," their Empire seemed undecided between "one of two bases—an extensive military
occupation or the principle of nationality [for subject races]." But this indecision was academic finally, for in practice Cromer and Britain itself had opted against "the principle of
nationality." And then there were other things to be noted. One point was that the Empire
was not going to be given up. Another was that intermarriage between natives and English
men and women was undesirable. Third—and most important, I think—Cromer conceived
of British imperial presence in the Eastern colonies as having had a lasting, not to say cataclys-
mic, effect on the minds and societies of the East. His metaphor for expressing this effect
is almost theological, so powerful in Cromer's mind was the idea of Western penetration
of Oriental expanses. "The country," he says, "over which the breath of the West, heavily
charged with scientific thought, has once passed, and has, in passing, left an enduring mark,
can never be the same as it was before."[10]

In such respects as these, nonetheless, Cromer's was far from an original intelligence.
What he saw and how he expressed it were common currency among his colleagues both in
the imperial Establishment and in the intellectual community. This consensus is notably true
in the case of Cromer's viceregal colleagues, Curzon, Swettenham, and Lugard. Lord Curzon
in particular always spoke the imperial lingua franca, and more obtrusively even than Cromer
he delineated the relationship between Britain and the Orient in terms of possession, in terms
of a large geographical space wholly owned by an efficient colonial master. For him, he said
on one occasion, the Empire was not an "object of ambition" but "first and foremost, a great
historical and political and sociological fact." In 1909 he reminded delegates to the Imperial
Press Conference meeting at Oxford that "we train here and we send out to you your
governors and administrators and judges, your teachers and preachers and lawyers." And this
almost pedagogical view of empire had, for Curzon, a specific setting in Asia, which as he
once put it, made "one pause and think."

> I sometimes like to picture to myself this great Imperial fabric as a huge structure
> like some Tennysonian "Palace of Art," of which the foundations are in this
> country, where they have been laid and must be maintained by British hands, but
> of which the Colonies are the pillars, and high above all floats the vastness of an
> Asiatic dome.[11]

Notes

1   Friedrich Nietzsche, "On Truth and Lie in an Extra-Moral Sense," in *The Portable Nietzsche,* ed. and trans. Walter Kaufmann (New York: Viking Press, 1954), pp. 46–47.

2   The number of Arab travelers to the West is estimated and considered by Ibrahim Abu-Lughod in *Arab Rediscovery of Europe: A Study in Cultural Encounters* (Princeton, N.J.: Princeton University Press, 1963), pp. 75–76 and passim.

3   See Philip D. Curtin, ed., *Imperialism: The Documentary History of Western Civilization* (New York: Walker & Co., 1972), pp. 73–105.

4   See Johann W. Fück, "Islam as an Historical Problem in European Historiography since 1800," in *Historians of the Middle East,* ed. Bernard Lewis and P. M. Holt (London: Oxford University Press, 1962), p. 307.

5   Ibid., p. 309.

6   See Jacques Waardenburg, *L'Islam dans le miroir de l'Occident* (The Hague: Mouton & Co., 1963).

7   Ibid., p. 311.

8   P. Masson-Oursel, "La Connaissance scientifique de l'Asie en France depuis 1900 et les variétés de l'Orientalisme," *Revue Philosophique* 143, nos. 7–9 (July–September 1953): 345.

9   Evelyn Baring, Lord Cromer, *Modern Egypt* (New York: Macmillan Co., 1908), 2: 237–38.

10   Evelyn Baring, Lord Cromer, *Ancient and Modern Imperialism* (London: John Murray, 1910), pp. 118, 120.

11   George Nathaniel Curzon, *Subjects of the Day: Being a Selection of Speeches and Writings* (London: George Allen & Unwin, 1915), pp. 4–5, 10, 28.

Chapter 47

Homi K. Bhabha

OF MIMICRY AND MAN

The ambivalence of colonial discourse

The comprador class within colonialism is usually made up of indigenous peoples who have been trained to not only run local colonial administrative affairs but who are also expected to replicate the national and ethnic attitudes and values of the colonizers. Embedded in the Latin etymology of the word "comprador" is in fact two revealing terms: to purchase and to prepare. Another word for these expectations held of the comprador class is one that Homi Bhabha uses: "mimicry"—putting on the dress, adopting the mannerisms, laws and rituals of, say, the British, yet never quite becoming the same, what later in his essay Bhabha calls being "almost but not quite", or, "not quite/not white". This indeterminacy fascinates Bhabha from a theoretical and cultural perspective, and bringing together a wide range of poststructuralist theory with postcolonial insights is a signature of Bhabha's work in his collection of influential essays, *The Location of Culture* (1994). In the extract, what Bhabha shows is that the representational strategies of the colonial authorities, attempting that is to reinforce notions of whole, unified, white subjectivity, alongside the universal truths encoded in the Bible, are deconstructed by the indeterminacy and "double articulation" of mimicry. The problem with mimicry is that it is *not representational* of something (here, British identity); rather, it is what Bhabha calls a "metonymy of presence", or, something that literally stands *adjacent to* British identity, appearing to reproduce it, but always failing, undercutting, or ironically parodying Britishness through markers of difference. Mimicry is the sign of the Other's "reform" (casting aside indigenous values in favour of British values, for example), making the Other "recognizable" as Bhabha puts it, but it is also the sign that this process of reformation is underway, and necessarily fails. What is strange about mimicry is that it creates an uncanny double, where the uncanniness is the sign of an irreducible difference, say, black skin (as Fanon suggests). Worse still, is mimicry's excess: copying mannerisms such as upper-class English speech patterns to such an exaggerated extent that it comes across as a parody. Mimicry, then, is what Bhabha calls "the sign of a double articulation", where powerful regulation of the native subject meets an evasive, slippery signifier of repetition and difference. In other words, this reveals that "mimicry" and "mockery" go hand-in-hand, seen in Bhabha's examples of slavery, and evangelical reform of character in India, as well as in the literary examples that he mentions in passing. Bhabha stresses that mimicry is not a psychological "mask" concealing some essentialist true identity underneath; rather it is a doubling, creating "part-objects" of colonial "command" and "desire"; colonial power-knowledge mechanisms can only partially "see" or fix such part-objects; thus such surveillance is incomplete. Furthermore, if there is no "essence" behind the mask, and if what is seen is what is fantasized and desired, then in effect the colonial subject becomes like the signifier, impossible to constrain or control, at the precise point at which an interdiction or regulatory structure is applied. The colonial subject, then, ambivalently crosses from being constituted by the regulatory, desiring gaze, to being *constitutive* of that gaze, not only turned back upon it, but also questioning its apparently stable or universal values, institutions and texts.

> Mimicry reveals something in so far as it is distinct from what might be called an itself that is behind. The effect of mimicry is camouflage. . . . It is not a question of harmonizing with the background, but against a mottled background, of becoming mottled — exactly like the technique of camouflage practised in human warfare.
>
> Jacques Lacan, 'The line and light', *Of the Gaze.*[1]

> It is out of season to question at this time of day, the original policy of a conferring on every colony of the British Empire a mimic representation of the British Constitution. But if the creature so endowed has sometimes forgotten its real significance and under the fancied importance of speakers and maces, and all the paraphernalia and ceremonies of the imperial legislature, has dared to defy the mother country, she has to thank herself for the folly of conferring such privileges on a condition of society that has no earthly claim to so exalted a position. A fundamental principle appears to have been forgotten or overlooked in our system of colonial policy — that of colonial dependence. To give to a colony the forms of independence is a mockery; she would not be a colony for a single hour if she could maintain an independent station.
>
> Sir Edward Cust, 'Reflections on West African affairs . . . addressed to the Colonial Office', Hatchard, London 1839

The discourse of post-Enlightenment English colonialism often speaks in a tongue that is forked, not false. If colonialism takes power in the name of history, it repeatedly exercises its authority through the figures of farce. For the epic intention of the civilizing mission, 'human and not wholly human' in the famous words of Lord Rosebery, 'writ by the finger of the Divine'[2] often produces a text rich in the traditions of *trompe-l'œil,* irony, mimicry and repetition. In this comic turn from the high ideals of the colonial imagination to its low mimetic literary effects mimicry emerges as one of the most elusive and effective strategies of colonial power and knowledge.

Within that conflictual economy of colonial discourse which Edward Said[3] describes as the tension between the synchronic panoptical vision of domination — the demand for identity, stasis — and the counter-pressure of the diachrony of history — change, difference — mimicry represents an *ironic* compromise. If I may adapt Samuel Weber's formulation of the marginalizing vision of castration,[4] then colonial mimicry is the desire for a reformed, recognizable Other, *as a subject of a difference that is almost the same, but not quite.* Which is to say, that the discourse of mimicry is constructed around an *ambivalence;* in order to be effective, mimicry must continually produce its slippage, its excess, its difference. The authority of that mode of colonial discourse that I called mimicry is therefore stricken by an indeterminacy: mimicry emerges as the representation of a difference that is itself a process of disavowal. Mimicry is, thus the sign of a double articulation; a complex strategy of reform, regulation and discipline, which 'appropriates' the Other as it visualizes power.

Mimicry is also the sign of the inappropriate, however, a difference or recalcitrance which coheres the dominant strategic function of colonial power, intensifies surveillance, and poses an immanent threat to both 'normalized' knowledges and disciplinary powers.

The effect of mimicry on the authority of colonial discourse is profound and disturbing. For in 'normalizing' the colonial state or subject, the dream of post-Enlightenment civility alienates its own language of liberty and produces another knowledge of its norms. The ambivalence which thus informs this strategy is discernible, for example, in Locke's Second Treatise which *splits* to reveal the limitations of liberty in his double use of the word 'slave': first simply, descriptively as the locus of a legitimate form of ownership, then as the trope for an intolerable, illegitimate exercise of power. What is articulated in that distance between the two uses is the absolute, imagined difference between the 'Colonial' State of Carolina and the Original State of Nature.

It is from this area between mimicry and mockery, where the reforming, civilizing mission is threatened by the displacing gaze of its disciplinary double, that my instances of colonial imitation come. What they all share is a discursive process by which the excess or slippage produced by the *ambivalence* of mimicry (almost the same, *but not quite*) does not merely 'rupture' the discourse, but becomes transformed into an uncertainty which fixes the colonial subject as a 'partial' presence. By 'partial' I mean both 'incomplete' and 'virtual'. It is as if the very emergence of the 'colonial' is dependent for its representation upon some strategic limitation or prohibition *within* the authoritative discourse itself. The success of colonial appropriation depends on a proliferation of inappropriate objects that ensure its strategic failure, so that mimicry is at once resemblance and menace.

A classic text of such partiality is Charles Grant's 'Observations on the state of society among the Asiatic subjects of Great Britain' (1792)[5] which was only superseded by James Mills's *History of India* as the most influential early nineteenth-century account of Indian manners and morals. Grant's dream of an evangelical system of mission education conducted uncompromisingly in the English language, was partly a belief in political reform along Christian lines and partly an awareness that the expansion of company rule in India required a system of subject formation – a reform of manners, as Grant put it – that would provide the colonial with 'a sense of personal identity as we know it'. Caught between the desire for religious reform and the fear that the Indians might become turbulent for liberty, Grant paradoxically implies that it is the 'partial' diffusion of Christianity, and the 'partial' influence of moral improvements which will construct a particularly appropriate form of colonial subjectivity. What is suggested is a process of reform through which Christian doctrines might collude with divisive caste practices to prevent dangerous political alliances. Inadvertently, Grant produces a knowledge of Christianity as a form of social control which conflicts with the enunciatory assumptions that authorize his discourse. In suggesting, finally, that 'partial reform' will produce an empty form of 'the *imitation* [my emphasis] of English manners which will induce them [the colonial subjects] to remain under our protection'.[6] Grant mocks his moral project and violates the Evidence of Christianity – a central missionary tenet – which forbade any tolerance of heathen faiths.

The absurd extravagance of Macaulay's 'Minute' (1835) – deeply influenced by Charles Grant's 'Observations' – makes a mockery of Oriental learning until faced with the challenge of conceiving of a 'reformed' colonial subject. Then, the great tradition of European humanism seems capable only of ironizing itself. At the intersection of European learning and colonial power, Macaulay can conceive of nothing other than 'a class of interpreters between us and the millions whom we govern – a class of persons Indian in blood and colour, but English in tastes, in opinions, in morals and in intellect'[7] – in other words a mimic man raised 'through our English School', as a missionary educationist wrote in 1819, 'to form a corps of translators and be employed in different departments of Labour'.[8] The line of descent of the mimic man can be traced through the works of Kipling, Forster, Orwell, Naipaul, and to his emergence, most recently, in Benedict Anderson's excellent work on nationalism, as the anomalous Bipin Chandra Pal.[9] He is the effect of a flawed colonial mimesis, in which to be Anglicized is *emphatically* not to be English.

The figure of mimicry is locatable within what Anderson describes as 'the inner compatibility of empire and nation'.[10] It problematizes the signs of racial and cultural priority, so that the 'national' is no longer naturalizable. What emerges between mimesis and mimicry is a *uniting,* a mode of representation, that marginalizes the monumentality of history, quite simply mocks its power to be a model, that power which supposedly makes it imitable. Mimicry *repeats* rather than *re-presents* and in that diminishing perspective emerges Decoud's displaced European vision of Sulaco in Conrad's *Nostromo* as:

> the endlessness of civil strife where folly seemed even harder to bear than its ignominy . . . the lawlessness of a populace of all colours and races, barbarism, irremediable tyranny. . . . America is ungovernable.[11]

Or Ralph Singh's apostasy in Naipaul's *The Mimic Men:*

> We pretended to be real, to be learning, to be preparing ourselves for life, we mimic men of the New World, one unknown corner of it, with all its reminders of the corruption that came so quickly to the new.[12]

Both Decoud and Singh, and in their different ways Grant and Macaulay, are the parodists of history. Despite their intentions and invocations they inscribe the colonial text erratically, eccentrically across a body politic that refuses to be representative, in a narrative that refuses to be representational. The desire to emerge as 'authentic' through mimicry – through a process of writing and repetition – is the final irony of partial representation.

What I have called mimicry is not the familiar exercise of *dependent* colonial relations through narcissistic identification so that, as Fanon has observed,[13] the black man stops being an actional person for only the white man can represent his self-esteem. Mimicry conceals no presence or identity behind its mask: it is not what Césaire describes as 'colonization-thingification'[14] behind which there stands the essence of the *présence Africaine.* The *menace* of mimicry is its *double* vision which in disclosing the ambivalence of colonial discourse also disrupts its authority. And it is a double vision that is a result of what I've described as the partial representation/recognition of the colonial object. Grant's colonial as partial imitator, Macaulay's translator, Naipaul's colonial politician as play-actor, Decoud as the scene setter of the *opéra bouffe* of the New World, these are the appropriate objects of a colonialist chain of command, authorized versions of otherness. But they are also, as I have shown, the figures of a doubling, the part-objects of a metonymy of colonial desire which alienates the modality and normality of those dominant discourses in which they emerge as 'inappropriate' colonial subjects. A desire that, through the repetition of *partial presence,* which is the basis of mimicry, articulates those disturbances of cultural, racial and historical difference that menace the narcissistic demand of colonial authority. It is a desire that reverses 'in part' the colonial appropriation by now producing a partial vision of the colonizer's presence; a gaze of otherness, that shares the acuity of the genealogical gaze which, as Foucault describes it, liberates marginal elements and shatters the unity of man's being through which he extends his sovereignty.[15]

I want to turn to this process by which the look of surveillance returns as the displacing gaze of the disciplined, where the observer becomes the observed and 'partial' representation rearticulates the whole notion of *identity* and alienates it from essence. But not before observing that even an exemplary history like Eric Stokes's *The English Utilitarians and India* acknowledges the anomalous gaze of otherness but finally disavows it in a contradictory utterance:

> Certainly India played *no* central part in fashioning the distinctive qualities of English civilisation. In many ways it acted as a disturbing force, a magnetic power placed at the periphery tending to distort the natural development of Britain's character.[16] (My emphasis)

What is the nature of the hidden threat of the partial gaze? How does mimicry emerge as the subject of the scopic drive and the object of colonial surveillance? How is desire disciplined, authority displaced?

If we turn to a Freudian figure to address these issues of colonial textuality, that form of difference that is mimicry – *almost the same but not quite* – will become clear. Writing of the partial nature of fantasy, caught *inappropriately*, between the unconscious and the preconscious, making problematic, like mimicry, the very notion of 'origins', Freud has this to say:

> Their mixed and split origin is what decides their fate. We may compare them with individuals of mixed race who taken all round resemble white men but who betray their coloured descent by some striking feature or other and on that account are excluded from society and enjoy none of the privileges.[17]

Almost the same but not white: the visibility of mimicry is always produced at the site of interdiction. It is a form of colonial discourse that is uttered *inter dicta*: a discourse at the crossroads of what is known and permissible and that which though known must be kept concealed; a discourse uttered between the lines and as such both against the rules and within them. The question of the representation of difference is therefore always also a problem of authority. The 'desire' of mimicry, which is Freud's 'striking feature' that reveals so little but makes such a big difference, is not merely that impossibility of the Other which repeatedly resists signification. The desire of colonial mimicry – an interdictory desire – may not have an object, but it has strategic objectives which I shall call the *metonymy of presence*.

Those inappropriate signifiers of colonial discourse – the difference between being English and being Anglicized; the identity between stereotypes which, through repetition, also become different; the discriminatory identities constructed across traditional cultural norms and classifications, the Simian Black, the Lying Asiatic – all these are *metonymies* of presence. They are strategies of desire in discourse that make the anomalous representation of the colonized something other than a process of 'the return of the repressed', what Fanon unsatisfactorily characterized as collective catharsis.[18] These instances of metonymy are the non-repressive productions of contradictory and multiple belief. They cross the boundaries of the culture of enunciation through a strategic confusion of the metaphoric and metonymic axes of the cultural production of meaning.

In mimicry, the representation of identity and meaning is rearticulated along the axis of metonymy. As Lacan reminds us, mimicry is like camouflage, not a harmonization of repression or repression of difference, but a form of resemblance, that differs from or defends presence by displaying it in part, metonymically. Its threat, I would add, comes from the prodigious and strategic production of conflictual, fantastic, discriminatory 'identity effects' in the play of a power that is elusive because it hides no essence, no 'itself'. And that form of *resemblance* is the most terrifying thing to behold, as Edward Long testifies in his *History of Jamaica* (1774). At the end of a tortured, negrophobic passage, that shifts anxiously between piety, prevarication and perversion, the text finally confronts its fear; nothing other than the repetition of its resemblance 'in part': '[Negroes] are represented by all authors as the vilest of human kind, to which they have little more pretension of resemblance *than what arises from their exterior forms*' (my emphasis).[19]

From such a colonial encounter between the white presence and its black semblance, there emerges the question of the ambivalence of mimicry as a problematic of colonial subjection. For if Sade's scandalous theatricalization of language repeatedly reminds us that discourse can claim 'no priority', then the work of Edward Said will not let us forget that the 'ethnocentric and erratic will to power from which texts can spring'[20] is itself a theatre of war. Mimicry, as the metonymy of presence is, indeed, such an erratic, eccentric strategy of authority in colonial discourse. Mimicry does not merely destroy narcissistic authority through the repetitious slippage of difference and desire. It is the process of the *fixation* of the colonial as a form of cross-classificatory, discriminatory knowledge within an interdictory discourse, and therefore necessarily raises the question of the *authorization* of colonial representations; a question of authority that goes beyond the subject's lack of priority (castration) to a historical crisis in the conceptuality of colonial man as an *object* of regulatory power, as the subject of racial, cultural, national representation.

'This culture . . . fixed in its colonial status', Fanon suggests, '[is] both present and mummified, it testified against its members. It defines them in fact without appeal.'[21] The ambivalence of mimicry – almost but not quite – suggests that the fetishized colonial culture is potentially and strategically an insurgent counter-appeal. What I have called its 'identity-effects' are always crucially *split*. Under cover of camouflage, mimicry, like the fetish, is a part-object that radically revalues the normative knowledges of the priority of race, writing, history. For the fetish mimes the forms of authority at the point at which it deauthorizes them. Similarly, mimicry rearticulates presence in terms of its 'otherness', that which it disavows. There is a crucial difference between this *colonial* articulation of man and his doubles and that which Foucault describes as 'thinking the unthought'[22] which, for nineteenth-century Europe, is the ending of man's alienation by reconciling him with his essence. The colonial discourse that articulates an *interdictory* otherness is precisely the 'other scene' of this nineteenth-century European desire for an authentic historical consciousness.

The 'unthought' across which colonial man is articulated is that process of classificatory confusion that I have described as the metonymy of the substitutive chain of ethical and cultural discourse. This results in the *splitting* of colonial discourse so that two attitudes towards external reality persist; one takes reality into consideration while the other disavows it and replaces it by a product of desire that repeats, rearticulates 'reality' as mimicry.

So Edward Long can say with authority, quoting variously Hume, Eastwick and Bishop Warburton in his support, that: 'Ludicrous as the opinion may seem I do not think that an orangutang husband would be any dishonour to a Hottentot female.'[23]

Such contradictory articulations of reality and desire – seen in racist stereotypes, statements, jokes, myths – are not caught in the doubtful circle of the return of the repressed. They are the effects of a disavowal that denies the differences of the other but produces in its stead forms of authority and multiple belief that alienate the assumptions of 'civil' discourse. If, for a while, the ruse of desire is calculable for the uses of discipline soon the repetition of guilt, justification, pseudo-scientific theories, superstition, spurious authorities, and classifications can be seen as the desperate effort to 'normalize' *formally* the disturbance of a discourse of splitting that violates the rational, enlightened claims of its enunciatory modality. The ambivalence of colonial authority repeatedly turns from *mimicry* – a difference that is almost nothing but not quite – to *menace* – a difference that is almost total but not quite. And in that other scene of colonial power, where history turns to farce and presence to 'a part' can be seen the twin figures of narcissism and paranoia that repeat furiously, uncontrollably.

In the ambivalent world of the 'not quite/not white', on the margins of metropolitan desire, the *founding objects* of the Western world become the erratic, eccentric, accidental *objets trouvés* of the colonial discourse – the part-objects of presence. It is then that the body and the book lose their part-objects of presence. It is then that the body and the book lose their representational authority. Black skin splits under the racist gaze, displaced into signs of bestiality, genitalia, grotesquerie, which reveal the phobic myth of the undifferentiated whole white body. And the holiest of books – the Bible – bearing both the standard of the cross and the standard of empire finds itself strangely dismembered. In May 1817 a missionary wrote from Bengal:

> Still everyone would gladly receive a Bible. And why? – that he may lay it up as a curiosity for a few pice; or use it for waste paper. Such it is well known has been the common fate of these copies of the Bible. . . . Some have been bartered in the markets, others have been thrown in snuff shops and used as wrapping paper.[24]

Notes

1   J. Lacan, 'The line and the light', in his *The Four Fundamental Concepts of Psychoanalysis,* Alan Sheridan (trans.) (London: The Hogarth Press and the Institute of Psycho-Analysis, 1977), p. 99.
2   Cited in E. Stokes, *The Political Ideas of English Imperialism* (Oxford: Oxford University Press, 1960), pp. 17–18.
3   E. Said, *Orientalism* (New York: Pantheon Books, 1978), p. 240.
4   S. Weber, 'The sideshow, or: remarks on a canny moment', *Modern Language Notes,* vol. 88, no. 6 (1973), p. 112.
5   C. Grant, 'Observations on the state of society among the Asiatic subjects of Great Britain', *Sessional Papers of the East India Company,* vol. X, no. 282 (1812–13).
6   ibid., ch. 4, p. 104.
7   T. B. Macaulay, 'Minute on education', in W. Theodore de Bary (ed.) *Sources of Indian Tradition,* vol. II (New York: Columbia University Press, 1958), p. 49.
8   Mr Thomason's communication to the Church Missionary Society, 5 September 1819, in *The Missionary Register,* 1821, pp. 54–55.
9   B. Anderson, *Imagined Communities* (London: Verso, 1983), p. 88.
10   ibid., pp. 88–89.
11   J. Conrad, *Nostromo* (London: Penguin, 1979), p. 161.
12   V. S. Naipaul, *The Mimic Men* (London: Penguin, 1967), p. 146.
13   F. Fanon, *Black Skin, White Masks* (London: Paladin, 1970), p. 109.
14   A Césaire, *Discourse on Colonialism* (New York: Monthly Review Press, 1972), p. 21.
15   M. Foucault, 'Nietzche, genealogy, history', in his *Language, Counter-Memory, Practice,* D. F. Bouchard and S. Simon (trans.) (Ithaca: Cornell University Press, 1977), p. 153.
16   E. Stokes, *The English Utilitarians and India* (Oxford: Oxford University Press, 1959), p. xi.
17   S. Freud, 'The unconscious' (1915), *SE,* XIV, pp. 190–91.
18   Fanon, *Black Skin, White Masks,* p. 103.
19   E. Long, *A History of Jamaica,* 1774, vol. II, p. 353.
20   E. Said, 'The Text, the world, the critic', in J. V. Harari (ed.) *Textual Strategies* (Ithaca: Cornell University Press, 1979), p. 184.
21   F. Fanon, 'Racism and culture', in his *Toward the African Revolution,* H. Chevalier (trans.) (London: Pelican, 1967), p. 44.
22   M. Foucault, *The Order of Things* (New York: Pantheon Books, 1971), part II, ch. 9.
23   Long, *History of Jamaica,* p. 364.
24   *The Missionary Register,* May 1817, p. 186.

Chapter 48

Chinua Achebe

THE AFRICAN WRITER AND
THE ENGLISH LANGUAGE

One of the challenges of postcolonial studies involves approaching a *broad* field of study with specific analyses of *local* cultures and their particular aesthetic objects (art, texts, song, oral stories, and so on). To put this another way, postcoloniality is a complex cultural, historical, and political state of being, involving the localized trauma of colonialism, the imposition of foreign languages, modes of education and existence, as well as abrupt religious or spiritual transformation (economic colonization usually went hand-in-hand with, or was preceded by, Christian missionary work). Chinua Achebe, internationally famous for his postcolonial novel *Things Fall Apart* (1958), and his influential literary criticism, meditates upon these issues by exploring questions of national versus local literary identity, and that of globalized versus indigenous languages. In attempting to define "African literature", numerous questions are raised, including those of place, theme and language. Ambiguities arise, especially when terms such as "authentically handled" African settings are applied: Achebe is amused to find that following this criteria, the Polish novelist Joseph Conrad is an "African" novelist because he wrote *Heart of Darkness*. Achebe's preferred definition of African literature is that it is "the sum total of all the *national* and *ethnic* literatures of Africa." For Achebe, Professor of Africana Studies at Brown University (as well as holding the David and Marianna Fisher University Chair), this means that to meet the "national" criteria, the author has to use what he calls the "*national* language" (*sic*) of English, "ethnic" literatures being written according to Achebe in local languages. This somewhat controversial claim—English being of course one of the main languages of colonization—is also prophetic, since globalized postcolonial literatures are often written in English today, regardless of the country of origin. Achebe also argues that to think of "Africa" as a homogenous entity is reductive and simplistic: "Africa" is made up of heterogenous ethnic and national groups, states, and languages. Just as one should not "exclude North Africa" from this debate, neither should one simplify "Black Africa" into one homogenous mass. Achebe argues that having a "national" language, even if it was one that served colonialism, can be a positive communication tool, without eliding local differences and particularities. As an example, Achebe notes that he can appreciate the poetry of Kenyan poet Joseph Kariuki because he writes in English, whereas he cannot even read the Swahili poet Shabaan Robert. Achebe's pragmatic approach is open to the possibility that in a future postcolonial environment, English may simply not dominate. For the moment, he regards

English as globally important, and the vehicle for "a new voice coming out of Africa" essentially "speaking of African experience". Does this mean that the African writer has to adapt to standard English? Achebe argues for a balance: maintaining a universally understandable mode of English expression, but adapted and expressive of African experiences, concerns, and idioms. Quoting from his own novel *Arrow of God*, Achebe demonstrates his theory by rewriting a passage expressive of indigenous character, in a more formal style. In this way Achebe argues for a "new" English, one which is still debated among postcolonial authors and critics today.

IN JUNE 1952, THERE WAS A WRITERS'** gathering at Makerere, impressively styled: "A Conference of African Writers of English Expression." Despite this sonorous and rather solemn title, it turned out to be a very lively affair and a very exciting and useful experience for many of us. But there was something which we tried to do and failed—that was to define "African literature" satisfactorily.

Was it literature produced *in* Africa or *about* Africa? Could African literature be on any subject, or must it have an African theme? Should it embrace the whole continent or south of the Sahara, or just *Black* Africa? And then the question of language. Should it be in indigenous African languages or should it include Arabic, English, French, Portuguese, Afrikaans, et cetera?

In the end we gave up trying to find an answer, partly—I should admit—on my own instigation. Perhaps we should not have given up so easily. It seems to me from some of the things I have since heard and read that we may have given the impression of not knowing what we were doing, or worse, not daring to look too closely at it.

A Nigerian critic, Obi Wali, writing in *Transition 10* said: "Perhaps the most important achievement of the conference . . . is that African literature as now defined and understood leads nowhere."

I am sure that Obi Wali must have felt triumphantly vindicated when he saw the report of a different kind of conference held later at Fourah Bay to discuss African literature and the University curriculum. This conference produced a tentative definition of African literature as follows: "Creative writing in which an African setting is authentically handled or to which experiences originating in Africa are integral." We are told specifically that Conrad's *Heart of Darkness* qualifies as African literature while Graham Greene's *Heart of the Matter* fails because it could have been set anywhere outside Africa.

A number of interesting speculations issue from this definition which admittedly is only an interim formulation designed to produce an indisputably desirable end, namely, to introduce African students to literature set in their environment. But I could not help being amused by the curious circumstance in which Conrad, a Pole, writing in English could produce African literature while Peter Abrahams would be ineligible should he write a novel based on his experiences in the West Indies.

What all this suggests to me is that you cannot cram African literature into a small, neat definition. I do not see African literature as one unit but as a group of associated units—in fact the sum total of all the *national* and *ethnic* literatures of Africa.

A national literature is one that takes the whole nation for its province and has a realized or potential audience throughout its territory. In other words a literature that is written in the *national* language. An ethnic literature is one which is available only to one ethnic group within the nation. If you take Nigeria as an example, the national literature, as I see it, is the literature written in English; and the ethnic literatures are in Hausa, Ibo, Yoruba, Efik, Edo, Ijaw, etc., etc.

Any attempt to define African literature in terms which overlook the complexities of the African scene at the material time is doomed to failure. After the elimination of white rule shall have been completed, the single most important fact in Africa in the second half of the twentieth century will appear to be the rise of individual nation-states. I believe that African literature will follow the same pattern.

What we tend to do today is to think of African literature as a newborn infant. But in fact what we have is a whole generation of newborn infants. Of course, if you only look cursorily, one infant is pretty much like another; but in reality each is already set on its own separate journey. Of course, you may group them together on the basis of anything you choose—the color of their hair, for instance. Or you may group them together on the basis of the language they will speak or the religion of their fathers. Those would all be valid distinctions; but they could not begin to account fully for each individual person carrying, as it were, his own little, unique lodestar of genes.

Those who in talking about African literature want to exclude North Africa because it belongs to a different tradition surely do not suggest that Black Africa is anything like homogeneous. What does Shabaan Robert have in common with Christopher Okigbo or Awoonor-Williams? Or Mongo Beti of Cameroun and Paris with Nzekwu of Nigeria? What does the champagne-drinking upper-class Creole society described by Easmon of Sierra Leone have in common with the rural folk and fishermen of J. P. Clark's plays? Of course, some of these differences could be accounted for on individual rather than national grounds, but a good deal of it is also environmental.

I have indicated somewhat offhandedly that the national literature of Nigeria and of many other countries of Africa is, or will be, written in English. This may sound like a controversial statement, but it isn't. All I have done has been to look at the reality of present-day Africa. This "reality" may change as a result of deliberate, e.g., political, action. If it does, an entirely new situation will arise, and there will be plenty of time to examine it. At present it may be more profitable to look at the scene as it is.

What are the factors which have conspired to place English in the position of national language in many parts of Africa? Quite simply the reason is that these nations were created in the first place by the intervention of the British which, I hasten to add, is not saying that the peoples comprising these nations were invented by the British.

The country which we know as Nigeria today began not so very long ago as the arbitrary creation of the British. It is true, as William Fagg says in his excellent new book, *Nigerian Images,* that this arbitrary action has proved as lucky in terms of African art history as any enterprise of the fortunate Princess of Serendip. And I believe that in political and economic terms too this arbitrary creation called Nigeria holds out great prospects. Yet the fact remains that Nigeria was created by the British—for their own ends. Let us give the devil his due: colonialism in Africa disrupted many things, but it did create big political units where there were small, scattered ones before. Nigeria had hundreds of autonomous communities ranging in size from the vast Fulani Empire founded by Usman dan Fodio in the north to tiny village entities in the east. Today it is one country.

Of course there are areas of Africa where colonialism divided up a single ethnic group among two or even three powers. But on the whole it did bring together many peoples that had hitherto gone their several ways. And it gave them a language with which to talk to one another. If it failed to give them a song, it at least gave them a tongue, for sighing. There are not many countries in Africa today where you could abolish the language of the erstwhile colonial powers and still retain the facility for mutual communication. Therefore those African writers who have chosen to write in English or French are not unpatriotic smart alecks with an eye on the main chance—outside their own countries. They are by-products of the same process that made the new nation-states of Africa.

You can take this argument a stage further to include other countries of Africa. The only reason why we can even talk about African unity is that when we get together we can have a manageable number of languages to talk in—English, French, Arabic.

The other day I had a visit from Joseph Kariuki of Kenya. Although I had read some of his poems and he had read my novels, we had not met before. But it didn't seem to matter. In fact I had met him through his poems, especially through his love poem, *Come Away My Love,* in which he captures in so few words the trials and tensions of an African in love with a white girl in Britain:

> Come away, my love, from streets
> Where unkind eyes divide
> And shop windows reflect our difference.

By contrast, when in 1960 I was traveling in East Africa and went to the home of the late Shabaan Robert, the Swahili poet of Tanganyika, things had been different. We spent some time talking about writing, but there was no real contact. I knew from all accounts that I was talking to an important writer, but of the nature of his work I had no idea. He gave me two books of his poems which I treasure but cannot read—until I have learned Swahili.

And there are scores of languages I would want to learn if it were possible. Where am I to find the time to learn the half dozen or so Nigerian languages, each of which can sustain a literature? I am afraid it cannot be done. These languages will just have to develop as tributaries to feed the one central language enjoying nationwide currency. Today, for good or ill, that language is English. Tomorrow it may be something else, although I very much doubt it.

Those of us who have inherited the English language may not be in a position to appreciate the value of the inheritance. Or we may go on resenting it because it came as part of a package deal which included many other items of doubtful value and the positive atrocity of racial arrogance and prejudice which may yet set the world on fire. But let us not in rejecting the evil throw out the good with it.

Some time last year I was traveling in Brazil meeting Brazilian writers and artists. A number of the writers I spoke to were concerned about the restrictions imposed on them by their use of the Portuguese language. I remember a woman poet saying she had given serious thought to writing in French! And yet their problem is not half as difficult as ours. Portuguese may not have the universal currency of English or French but at least it is the national language of Brazil with her eighty million or so people, to say nothing of the people of Portugal, Angola, Mozambique, etc.

Of Brazilian authors I have only read, in translation, one novel by Jorge Amado, who is not only Brazil's leading novelist but one of the most important writers in the world. From that one novel, *Gabriella,* I was able to glimpse something of the exciting Afro-Latin culture which is the pride of Brazil and is quite unlike any other culture. Jorge Amado is only one of the many writers Brazil has produced. At their national writers' festival there were literally hundreds of them. But the work of the vast majority will be closed to the rest of the world forever, including no doubt the work of some excellent writers. There is certainly a great advantage to writing in a world language.

I think I have said enough to give an indication of my thinking on the importance of the world language which history has forced down our throats. Now let us look at some of the most serious handicaps. And let me say straightaway that one of the most serious handicaps is *not* the one people talk about most often, namely, that it is impossible for anyone ever to use a second language as effectively as his first. This assertion is compounded of half truth and half bogus mystique. Of course, it is true that the vast majority of people are happier with their first language than with any other. But then the majority of people are not writers. We do have enough examples of writers who have performed the feat of writing effectively in a second language. And I am not thinking of the obvious names like Conrad. It would be more germane to our subject to choose African examples.

The first name that comes to my mind is Olauda Equiano, better known as Gustavus Vassa, the African. Equiano was an Ibo, I believe from the village of Iseke in the Orlu division of Eastern Nigeria. He was sold as a slave at a very early age and transported to America. Later he bought his freedom and lived in England. In 1789 he published his life story, a beautifully written document which, among other things, set down for the Europe of his time something of the life and habit of his people in Africa, in an attempt to counteract the lies and slander invented by some Europeans to justify the slave trade.

Coming nearer to our times, we may recall the attempts in the first quarter of this century by West African nationalists to come together and press for a greater say in the management of their own affairs. One of the most eloquent of that band was the Honorable Casely Hayford of the Gold Coast. His presidential address to the National Congress of British West Africa in 1925 was memorable not only for its sound common sense but as a fine example of elegant prose. The governor of Nigeria at the time was compelled to take notice and he did so in characteristic style: he called Hayford's Congress "a self-selected and self-appointed congregation of educated African gentlemen." We may derive some amusement from the fact that British colonial administrators learned very little in the following quarter of a century. But at least they *did* learn in the end—which is more than one can say for some others.

It is when we come to what is commonly called creative literature that most doubt seems to arise. Obi Wali, whose article "Dead End of African Literature" I referred to, has this to say:

> " . . . until these writers and their Western midwives accept the fact that any true African literature must be written in African languages, they would be merely pursuing a dead end, which can only lead to sterility, uncreativity and frustration."

But far from leading to sterility, the work of many new African writers is full of the most exciting possibilities. Take this from Christopher Okigbo's *Limits:*

> Suddenly becoming talkative
> like weaverbird
> Summoned at offside of
> dream remembered
> Between sleep and waking
> I hand up my egg-shells
> To you of palm grove,
> Upon whose bamboo towers hang
> Dripping with yesterupwine
> A tiger mask and nude spear. . . .
>
> Queen of the damp half light,
> I have had my cleansing.
> Emigrant with air-borne nose,
> The he-goat-on-heat.

Or take the poem, *Night Rain,* in which J. P. Clark captures so well the fear and wonder felt by a child as rain clamors on the thatch roof at night and his mother, walking about in the dark, moves her simple belongings

> Out of the run of water
> That like ants filing out of the wood
> Will scatter and gain possession
> Of the floor. . . .

I think that the picture of water spreading on the floor "like ants filing out of the wood" is beautiful. Of course if you had never made fire with faggots, you may miss it. But Clark's inspiration derives from the same source which gave birth to the saying that a man who brings home ant-ridden faggots must be ready for the visit of lizards.

I do not see any signs of sterility anywhere here. What I do see is a new voice coming out of Africa, speaking of African experience in a world-wide language. So my answer to the question *Can an African ever learn English well enough to be able to use it effectively in creative writing?* is certainly yes. If on the other hand you ask: *Can he ever learn to use it like a native speaker?* I should say, I hope not. It is neither necessary nor desirable for him to be able to do so. The price a world language must be prepared to pay is submission to many different kinds of use. The African writer should aim to use English in a way that brings out his message best without altering the language to the extent that its value as a medium of international exchange will be lost. He should aim at fashioning out an English which is at once universal and able to carry his peculiar experience. I have in mind here the writer who has something new, something different to say. The nondescript writer has little to tell us, anyway, so he might as well tell it in conventional language and get it over with. If I may use an extravagant simile, he is like a man offering a small, nondescript routine sacrifice for which a chick, or less, will do. A serious writer must look for an animal whose blood can match the power of his offering.

In this respect Amos Tutola is a natural. A good instinct has turned his apparent limitation in language into a weapon of great strength—a half-strange dialect that serves him perfectly in the evocation of his bizarre world. His last book, and to my mind, his finest, is proof enough that one can make even an imperfectly learned second language do amazing things. In this book, *The Feather Woman of the Jungle,* Tutola's superb storytelling is at last cast in the episodic form which he handles best instead of being painfully stretched on the rack of the novel.

From a natural to a conscious artist: myself, in fact. Allow me to quote a small example from *Arrow of God,* which may give some idea of how I approach the use of English. The Chief Priest in the story is telling one of his sons why it is necessary to send him to church:

> I want one of my sons to join these people and be my eyes there. If there is nothing in it you will come back. But if there is something there you will bring home my share. The world is like a Mask, dancing. If you want to see it well you do not stand in one place. My spirit tells me that those who do not be-friend the white man today will be saying *had we known* tomorrow.

Now supposing I had put it another way. Like this for instance:

> I am sending you as my representative among these people—just to be on the safe side in case the new religion develops. One has to move with the times or else one is left behind. I have a hunch that those who fail to come to terms with the white man may well regret their lack of foresight.

The material is the same. But the form of the one is *in character* and the other is not. It is largely a matter of instinct, but judgment comes into it too.

You read quite often nowadays of the problems of the African writer having first to think in his mother tongue and then to translate what he has thought into English. If it were such a simple, mechanical process, I would agree that it was pointless—the kind of eccentric pursuit you might expect to see in a modern Academy of Lagado; and such a process could not possibly produce some of the exciting poetry and prose which is already appearing.

One final point remains for me to make. The real question is not whether Africans *could* write in English but whether they *ought to*. Is it right that a man should abandon his mother tongue for someone else's? It looks like a dreadful betrayal and produces a guilty feeling.

But for me there is no other choice. I have been given this language and I intend to use it. I hope, though, that there always will be men, like the late Chief Fagunwa, who will choose to write in their native tongue and insure that our ethnic literature will flourish side by side with the national ones. For those of us who opt for English, there is much work ahead and much excitement.

Writing in the London *Observer* recently, James Baldwin said:

> My quarrel with the English language has been that the language reflected none of my experience. But now I began to see the matter another way. . . . Perhaps the language was not my own because I had never attempted to use it, had only learned to imitate it. If this were so, then it might be made to bear the burden of my experience if I could find the stamina to challenge it, and me, to such a test.

I recognize, of course, that Baldwin's problem is not exactly mine, but I feel that the English language will be able to carry the weight of my African experience. But it will have to be a new English, still in full communion with its ancestral home but altered to suit its new African surroundings.

Chapter 49

Gina Wisker

LOCATING AND CELEBRATING DIFFERENCE

Writing by South African and Aboriginal women writers

In comparing writing strategies developed by South African and Aboriginal women authors, Gina Wisker observes some shared features that function to resist the tripartite oppression of "gender, race and class". South African and Aboriginal women authors resist colonization and the "silencing" that they have been subject to, through: reinterpretation (of constricting stereotypical labels); reinvestment (i.e., being in relationship with the land); recognition of identity (being anchored in place and context); and relating identity to the colonial structures of displacement and effacement (South African apartheid and the Australian genocide of Aboriginal peoples). At the level of genre, both groups utilize a hybrid form—semi-fictionalized autobiography—which enables an inscription of the rhythms and community-based performances of oral cultures in a writing that has "polemical" force. Furthermore, this genre enables both groups to reject colonial notions of the relationships between indigenous peoples and place, re-inscribing non-colonial and postcolonial community/land relationships. Wisker argues that this also leads to a rejection of the postmodern conception of the subject, with stress instead upon individual particularity of experience and self-present identity. The trope of "locating" enables critics to approach the writing of South African and Aboriginal women authors from a postcolonial perspective that does *not* re-inscribe the colonial acts of "naming and labelling" which were mechanisms of oppression and effacement. Semi-fictionalized autobiography facilitates the intersection of personal and community "testifying", helps reveal how constructed identities worked to make such women invisible, and recovers an authentic notion of a re-empowered self. In two sections of her essay—"Representation and Writing" and "Bessie Head"—Wisker, author of *Key Concepts in Postcolonial Studies* (2007) and *Teaching African American Women's Writing* (2010), examines specific authors and writing strategies, starting with the Aboriginal project to "dispel myths" about indigenous peoples, while asserting their experiences of "the truth about racism and sexism". Parallels in the two sections offer insightful analysis of the "dichotomies" that both groups of writers face and articulate, such as the related strategy taken in an American context by author Toni Morrison, where "fictionalizing" enables the author to reach deeper into individual and community truth claims; for example, the fictionalized "I" draws upon oral stories that themselves make sense of actual cultural and historical events and experiences. In Bessie Head's writing, and that of other South African women authors, the parallel is made whereby semi-fictionalized autobiography both records and documents factual details while rearticulating these through creativity and imagination, which Wisker calls suggesting "that life could be other". Wisker concludes with the dichotomies that these two groups encounter, exist within, and re-articulate as part of their politics of resistance and rewriting. These dichotomies tend to involve suspended choices or lived contradictions, such as home being a place of exile. Both groups share the desire to reclaim location, through renaming, and the articulation of a relational site of place and identity.

> Here they [women] are, returning, arriving over and again, because the unconscious is impregnable. They have wandered around in circles, confined to the narrow room in which they've been given a deadly brainwashing. You can incarcerate them, slow them down, get away with the old Apartheid routine, but for a time only. At the same time as they're taught their name, they can be taught that their territory is black: because you are Africa, you are black . . . we have internalized this horror of the dark.
>
> (Cixous, 1981, pp. 247–48)

Women and women's bodies, notes Cixous, are consistently expressed as sites ripe for oppression or liberation. 'Otherized' triply because of gender race and class, for black women silence and subordination is often a seemingly inescapable state. It would be naive to insist that the experiences of South African and Aboriginal women are identical, but there are similarities, both in that continued state of oppression and silence and in the power of articulation, through which arises expression of identity, a claiming of community and power.

The literary and feminist literary critical theories and practices of African-American women writers such as Toni Morrison, Alice Walker and bell hooks have provided both a stimulus and a framework in relation to which many emergent black women writers have developed their writing practices, and more particularly through which we can start to read their work. Distinctive feminist literary critical practices have, however, also grown up in Australia and South Africa and these too can influence reading of African-American texts. Through semi-fictionalized autobiographical forms South African and Aboriginal women write out against such colonization and silencing. They reinterpret labellings and constrictions, and reinvest relationships between land, community and individual. Aboriginal writers consistently stress land title, and the right to claim self as well as land, recognizing identity as formed and located in relation to cultural, geographical and historical context. South African writers, often in exile, also relate identity to the problematized constructed space of South Africa that so often, under apartheid, attempted to erase them.

The dangers of homogenizing the writing of black women writers are ever present when making critical comparisons between the writing of women from different locations. Indeed, the histories of many of our relationships with, and representations of, the people of previously colonized countries and their writings have suffered from such an accidental or deliberate erasure of their differences, their specificity and individual worth. But there are also many similarities and fascinating comparisons to be made, particularly between the writings of Aboriginal and black South African women. These arise, I would argue, from their very location in contested, colonially appropriated southern spaces and the vital interest in linking location and identity evident in their work. Land is important in the work of both groups of writers, because it relates to placing and locating identity in oneself and one's community:

> Aboriginality means to me that you come from the land. It's your land, Australia, the trees, the grass, the seas, the deserts, the rain forests, are all linked with ourself. It's something nobody can take away from you. (Whitlock and Carter, 1992, p. 99)

South African and Aboriginal women writers make a similarly powerful investment in the relationships between land and identity, and challenge the renaming and appropriating of their lands and identities by northern imperial invaders and settlers. Both South African and Aboriginal women, writing of identity and location, choose polemical, often semi-fictionalized autobiographical forms that utilize orally based structures and expressions. Such works articulate and embody their assertion of different readings, different interpretations, and different selves, challenging northern or Eurocentric imperatives of relationships with the land. Linked to this, there is another challenge, to postmodernism's denial of the subject. They assert a renewed recognition and expression of identity. Of Bessie Head, the South African writer, Craig Mackenzie notes that apartheid effectively prevented identification with African communities. But she became connected through her move across the border to Botswana: 'The sense of Botswana's almost uninterrupted African history had an immediate and profound influence on her, a victim of almost total deracination in the land of her birth' (Head, 1990, p. xvii).

The title of this chapter suggests several areas of argument that I wish to develop. Locating indicates relationships between people and their location – the place from which they speak – more than just context, and also a placing and naming. Historically, for both South African and, more particularly, for Aboriginal peoples, naming and labelling has been a dangerous, destructive act. It erased their land ownership rights and erased them along with it. Misnaming and renaming have taken difference as a first stage in relationships of hierarchy in which indigenous peoples are always subordinated, categorized and devalued in the terms of white European culture. I wish to indicate some of the difficulties in actually locating texts by South African and Aboriginal women writers, although this lessens with time as publishers seek to recuperate and publish lost texts, opening their categorization systems as well as their minds to the recognition of different kinds of writing which often evade canonical labels.

Semi-fictionalized autobiography

> Why is it that just at the moment when so many of us who have been silenced begin to demand the right to name ourselves to act as subjects rather than objects of history, that just then the concept of subjecthood becomes problematical? . . . Our nonbeing was the condition and being of the One, the center, the taken-for-granted ability of one small segment of the population to speak for all . . . we need . . . to develop an account of the world which treats our perspective not as subjugated or disrupted knowledge, but as primitive and constitutive of a different world. (Harstock, 1990, pp. 163, 171)

Aboriginal and South African women writers have in common their expression through semi-fictionalized autobiography, a form favoured by women writers, but often treated by postmodernist critics as critically dubious because of its assertion of a fixed subject position.

Autobiography is a form of testifying and in the hands of South African and Aboriginal women writers it enables not only the establishment of individual identity but an expression of the identity and experiences of a people, a community for whom the individual speaks. Both Aboriginal and South African women are recuperating versions of their past lives through the explorations and expressions of autobiography:

> Telling our stories, using the 'self as subject', shows the intersection between the individual and the larger forces of our history. In telling our stories we

attempt to understand both intellectually and emotionally. We each have a story to tell, in its uniqueness and commonalty [*sic*], but also in its constructedness. In remembering in the present, we begin to realise that parts of our past are waiting to be reclaimed, re-visioned and told as we view the past through the lens of the present, weaving an inter-textual narrative. (Govinden, 1995, pp. 170–83)

Women writers in post-apartheid South Africa testify to a history of suffering and silencing, forming versions of a lived, shared history that can be communicated to others. The autobiographical project for both groups of women writers enables this kind of recognition, and expression of the self and the community in history, a reinscription of women's lives into the location from which they spring which has largely, historically, erased them at least in terms of their recognition by a wider audience. It would be a culturally arrogant mistake to assume that their stories have been unheard in a largely oral culture, clearly they have, but the time has come, they seem to say, through publication, to share their experiences with wider groups of readers. As they shape versions of their own lives they shape expressions of their shared histories, of experience. Critically, this is set against the postmodernist project that attempts to reject the expression of a constructed subject and subject position, aware of the constructedness of 'self' and 'reality'. In a time when self and reality need to be recognized and expressed, the postmodern project is clearly out of place. As André Brink puts it, 'it is too artificial, too controlled and then too conservative' (Brink, 1998, p. 18).

Autobiography enables the reclamation of voice, empowerment, and a choice over forms of representation by the writers themselves in the face of misrepresentation through the discourses of colonial power. Autobiography becomes a form that enables first steps to be made in establishing, sharing and expressing cultural identities.

Bessie Head and Zoë Wicomb use semi-fictionalized autobiographies. For them and the COSAW (Congress of South African Writers Collective) and Lesotho writing groups, forms of autobiography provide particularly authentic first-person testimony of history and experiences otherwise rendered secondhand through other written versions, including journalism. As with the early slave narratives, testifying to one's experience has always had strength and authenticity for Black communities. When allied with the need to frame, control and make sense of experience rather than merely record it, and to construct an 'I' figure, a fictionalized version of the self, an awareness of the problematic, a constructed status of this authentic voice emerges. Bessie Head and Zoë Wicomb's semi-fictionalized autobiographies are both authentic *and* constructed, interpreted; they represent the self and the community.

Noni Jabavu (1960; 1963) and Bessie Head (1969; 1974) led the way in South African fictionalized autobiography. Under apartheid, Black women's fiction was often banned. Miriam Tlali's *Muriel at the Metropolitan* (1975) reacted against oppression and subordination, and was banned. This was followed by *Amandla* (1980), and *Soweto Stories* (1989). Lauretta Ngcobo's *Cross of Gold* (1981) was banned in South Africa. Agnes Sam wrote *Jesus is Indian and Other Stories* (1989); Jayapraga Reddy, *On the Fringe of Dream-Time and Other Stories* (1987). Zoë Wicomb published her short story sequence/novel *You Can't Get Lost in Cape Town* (1987). All relate identity to location.

Cultural contexts affect, condition, encourage and prevent forms of reading as they do forms of writing. South Africa is in the exciting, challenging, often contradictory process of reinventing itself. Women's autobiographies are dialogues between an oppressive and silencing present and a resisting, culturally generated, self-creating individual voice.

The fictionalized autobiographical works of Bessie Head, Zoë Wicomb, Lauretta Ngcobo, Ellen Kuzwayo and women of the COSAW collective (*Like a House on Fire,* 1994 and Kendall, *Basali!,* 1995) represent different versions, from different South(ern) African contexts, of the wish to reconstruct, and represent the self in the face of silencing social, political and textual colonial master narratives. 'It is not the raw truth, the raw events of our embittered days of violence. Essentially writing is about the truth contemplated through the crucible of the imagination, and therefore truth becomes art' (Ngcobo, 1994, p. 2).

South African Ellen Kuzwayo (*Call Me Woman,* 1988) writes both as the individual 'I' and as a member of the collective community 'we'. Her autobiography 'puts aside the rhinoceros hide, to reveal a people with a delicate nervous balance like everyone else' (Head, 1990, p. 89):

> [O]ne feels as if a shadow history of South Africa has been written; there is a sense of triumph, of hope in this achievement and that one has read the true history of the land, a history that vibrates with human compassion and goodness. (Kuzwayo, in Head, 1990, p. 89)

The record of her life is a testament of suffering, and hope.

Autobiographical and semi-autobiographical works also belong to a long tradition of Aboriginal creative response:

> The widespread use of biography and autobiography by Aboriginal writers can be linked to a cultural tradition in which verse or song would detail the lives of dreaming ancestors . . . It remains to be seen, if this tradition was used to detail the lives of ordinary people . . . It may have been so. (Narogin, 1985, p. 2)

Historically, Aboriginal women were subject to misrepresentation and sexual abuse: 'Black women were viewed by white males as being founts of insatiable libidinal desire' (Narogin, 1985, p. 18). Misunderstood and appropriated by white men, they were stolen, raped, owned, forced into servitude, abandoned, dehumanized on stations and throughout Australia while genocide wiped out Aboriginal people, reducing them in Queensland from 120,000 in the 1820s to less than 20,000 by the 1920s. Discourse is power. Dehumanizing language underwrote dehumanizing treatment. Aboriginal women, 'gins', 'stud gins', 'black velvet', were hunted, captured, mustered and kept for sexual and domestic chores on stations. Prostitutes and homestead girls were paid in bad drink and bad opium, then discarded. Venereal disease spread, starvation and exposure followed, the birth-rate fell, and kin alienation resulted, aided later by the mass removal of black children into adoption or into Mission upbringing, and the blurring of racial lines by mixed race relationships.

Representation and writing

Set against this history of disempowerment and translation, Aboriginal women write of their lives, and those of family and community to describe and so pass on the tenor of the everyday in these very different contexts. By doing so they dispel myths about Aboriginal peoples – for example, that they are always lazy and drunk – and tell the truth about racism and sexism. They also write of the difficulties of recognizing blackness and identity in a racist community.

Growing out of the oral tradition, many works are life stories, some co-authored, some semi-fictionalized. Autobiographies include Evonne Goolagong's *Evonne! On the Move* (1973), and work by Margaret Tucker, Theresa Clemens and Shirley C. Smith who, with the assistance of Bobbi Sykes, wrote *Mumshirl: An Autobiography* (1981). Marnie Kennedy's *Born a Half Caste* (1985), and Sally Morgan's *My Place* (1987), Glenyse Ward's *Wandering Girl* (1988), and

Ruby Langford's *Don't Take Your Love to Town* (1988) followed. The very first novels, which have a great deal of autobiographical content, are Faith Bandler's *Wacvie* (1977), and Monica Clare's *Karobran* (1978). Recent works include Melissa Lucashenko's *Steam Pigs* (1997), and Alexis Wright's *Plains of Promise* (1997).

Without partnership and cultural translation, Aboriginal women are now writing for themselves and their communities: 'A new phenomenon of contemporary Aboriginal writing is emerging whereby women writers have the double advantage of relating their history in literally black and white terms, and simultaneously transcending and cutting across cultural boundaries' (Huggins, 1987/8, p. 22). The scripting of oral story-telling and oral histories has its losses as well as its gains, and only the sensitive Aboriginal author can retain and build upon the cadences and the spiralling forms of the traditional modes of story and life tales. What can be lost in the written recording of oral history or oral literature is a 'different voice': 'Its rhythms, its spiral not linear chronology, its moods of non-verbal communication, its humour, and its withholding of information. Many of these things will be untranslatable to the printed page' (Ferrier, 1991, p. 135). Mudrooroo Narogin, among others, has questioned both the authenticity and the right of some Aboriginal writers to speak of their lives and those of their families, particularly if this involves white ghost writing, or the 'battler' genre, a largely white Australian mode.

Gillian Whitlock, collecting a variety of versions of autobiographical writings notes: 'The issue of who is authorised to speak, and who is not is complex and has attracted a good deal of critical attention of late, these debates draw our attention to the mechanics of the autobiographical text, the details of language, structure and point of view' (Whitlock, 1996, p. xvi). But, as Carole Ferrier argues, in a context where withholding of knowledge, and particularly that of the traditional elders, is seen as properly upholding cultural traditions, nonetheless speaking out is also empowering. Daisy, in Sally Morgan's *My Place* (1987), tells some parts of her history and withholds others, taking them to her grave.

> 'I got secrets, Sally. I don't want anyone to know.'
> 'Everything can't be a secret: You dunno what a secret is.'
> 'I don't like secrets. Not when thems the sort of secrets you could use to help
>   your own people.'
> 'It wouldn't make no difference.'
> 'That's what everyone says. No one will talk, don't you see, Nan, someone's
>   got to tell.
> Otherwise things will stay the same, they won't get any better.' (Morgan,
>   1987, p. 319)

Arthur, her uncle, says Daisy misunderstands history when she retains these secrets – so there is a tussle between telling to establish a history, and retaining to maintain the secret which is itself an act of power. This is a very different interpretation for readers whose Eurocentric or American-oriented reading practices always favour speaking out. Jan Labarlestier comments on this debate of empowerment and silence: 'Aboriginality has been constructed in dominant "white" discourses. In contemporary Australian society "Living black" and writing about it can be seen as a process of confrontation' (Labarlestier, 1991, p. 90). This confrontation some avoid.

The debate about the relative value of various forms of expression in the literary and Aboriginal community is highly politicized and problematic. 'Merely' recording black life has been a criticism levelled at Toni Morrison, who has seen herself as rising above this to produce fiction, creative, experimental, an art form, while fictionalizing itself might be a form of truth. Morrison addresses this problem in her essay 'The Site of Memory' (1987, p. 161), by arguing that her fictionalizing forms gain access to a deeper truth beyond the mere recording of facts. This recognition can inform our reading of both Aboriginal and South African women's fictionalized autobiographies, records of facts and experiences, individual and community, and fictional in their formats, constructing a speaking 'I', retelling tales which themselves grow from various cultural and myth genres.

Aboriginal women writers are aware of the disempowerment of remaining absent and silent, and of the reality of appropriation, of being misrepresented in any transaction which offers their works wider dissemination. Sally Morgan's My *Place* (1987) is a record of the lives of her family and her people, like Glenyse Ward's *Wandering Girl* (1988). The style of the latter is realistic, wryly humorous, a testimony to the ability to survive bigotry and racism, showing the survival tactics of this lively, outspoken, self-aware woman to speak out for others such as herself, brought up in a Mission away from her family then employed for basic wages in domestic labour. Unnamed in her work for Mrs Bigelow, Glenyse deliberately enjoys freedom, eating what she wishes in her employer's absence, and enters the dining room to present herself to guests, insisting that she has a name, much to her employer's embarrassment. She is speaking out and speaking back, and speaking for others also brought up in Missions away from their families, expected to be erased in the white households where they worked. Alexis Wright (1997) also speaks of the alienation of Mission upbringing.

My Place (1987) locates Sally Morgan and her family as Aboriginal people, their history and lifestyles devalued in a racist white society. Part of the book focuses on cultural identification. Sally's family hid their origins to escape abuse, and on realizing she was Aboriginal rather than Indian, Sally's identity confusions and locations clamour together. No positive representations of Aboriginals aid her search for points of contact with her origins:

> The kids at school had also begun asking us what country we came from. This puzzled me because, up until then I'd thought we were the same as them. If we insisted that we came from Australia, they'd reply, 'Yeah, but what about ya parents, bet they didn't come from Australia.'
> One day I tackled mum about it as she washed the dishes.
> 'What do you mean, where do we come from?'
> 'I mean, what country, the kids at school want to know what country we come from. They reckon we're not Aussies. Are we Aussies, Mum?' (Morgan, 1987, p. 38)

Sally's artwork is the key to the expression of difference. It is laughed at at school, but clearly grows from an innately different way of seeing; one aligned with the Aboriginal forms in which Nan, her grandmother, draws in the sand. Nan's silences and anger indicate her own internalized response to everyday racism. One symbolic moment sees Nan hoarding Australian coins which are about to be devalued: a symbol of her precious hold on Aboriginal values which, ironically, the contemporary political world constantly denies and devalues like the coins. Nan's artwork and values, unknowingly inherited by Sally, enrich and unite the family (but are socially denied and devalued): 'Nan punched. She lifted up her arm and thumped her clenched fist hard on the kitchen table. "You bloody kids don't want me, you want a bloody white grandmother, I'm black. Do you hear, I'm black, black, black!"' (Morgan, 1987, p. 97). Sally and her sister find few positive representations with which to relate and friends disappear:

> 'Don't Abos feel close to the earth and all that stuff?'
> 'God, I don't know. All I know is none of my friends like them'. (Morgan, 1987, p. 98)

Nan and Arthur speak their stories to Sally and these, deriving from 'battler' genres recorded as part of her work, make it a semi-fictionalized community-linked autobiography, witty, ironic, and proud to identify with Aboriginal identity.

The writing of Faith Bandler, Glenyse Ward and Sally Morgan is based on particularly women-oriented forms, the diary and personal reminiscence, interwoven with the rhythms, patterns and cadences of traditional Aboriginal story-telling. Like Toni Morrison's recovery of lost periods of African-American history, they are speaking out powerfully against racism, and silence.

As black or 'coloured', mixed race women writing under apartheid, South Africans Bessie Head and Zoë Wicomb seek to explore their own histories, their identities, and to represent marginalized, silenced subjects. In so doing, they and other South African women writers choosing fictionalized autobiography as their form – Lauretta Ngcobo, COSAW, Ellen Kuzwayo and others – both creatively utilize and subvert the master narratives which would seek to subjugate their experience and prevent its expression.

Bessie Head

> If all my living experience could be summarised I would call it knowledge of evil, knowledge of its sources, of its true face and the misery and suffering it inflicts on human life . . . What has driven me is a feeling that human destiny ought not to proceed along tragic lines, with every effort and every new-born civilisation throttling itself in destruction with wrong ideas and wrong ways of living. (Head, 1990, p. 63)

Head's own life story is fraught with the constrictions of the Immorality Act which, accompanied by the incarceration of her mother in a mental asylum for bearing a child from a relationship with a Zulu stable boy, inscribed on Bessie the horrors of apartheid. Her own silenced mother can be heard through her work which recuperates a lost past, like Alice Walker's *In Search of Our Mothers' Gardens* (1983). As Jayapraga Reddy comments of history in the written and oral expression transaction: 'Our writing tradition and culture can only be strongly built if we have a sense of the foundations on which we are building' (Reddy, 1994, p. 74). Head sought exile and a new life in Botswana, closer to African land, traditions and continuities. And it is through a creative relationship with the land, the Motabeng project of vegetable growing, that her protagonist, Elizabeth, moves on from her oppression-induced breakdown into health. Her work defies silence, working to recognize and express self.

In her letters, Bessie Head refuses the master narrative and literally recreates herself as a version of her mother, speaking for her. She creates an identity from this version of her mother in letters and narratives. Bessie spent her adolescence in an orphanage, married journalist Harold Head, had one son, Howard, divorced, and in 1964 left the restrictions of South Africa for neighbouring Botswana on an exit permit. When Botswana became independent in 1966, bureaucracy 'Otherized' South African refugees, denying Bessie citizenship. In 1979, her international literary reputation persuaded the authorities that she was worth claiming as a Botswanan writer. Citizenship enabled her to travel to conferences and sign books abroad. Head's early work appeared in *The New Africa,* with Lewis Nkosi and Eskia Mphahele. Her writing for *Drum* was more personal and 'apolitical' rather than the sensational journalism of her colleagues. She refused political activism and was sceptical about religion, although equating the idea of 'unholy places' with those that are clearly intolerant and oppressive – notably the South Africa of her youth.

In Botswana her writing flourished, but first she had to work through expressing and exploring her own breakdown, which took place in 1969. Of *A Question of Power* (1974), Bessie Head says:

> I had such an intensely personal and private dialogue that I can hardly place it in the context of the more social and outward-looking work I had done. It was a private philosophical journey to the source of evil. (Head, 1990, p. 69)

A Question of Power expresses the protagonist Elizabeth's restless struggle to find a sense of identity and belonging. Her daytime productive and creative work on the land with crops in the experimental utopian community of Motabeng contrasts with the engulfment she experiences in her waking nightmares, peopled by mythical figures – two awful men, Sello and Dan – warped, highly sexualized, oppressive versions of village men. Familiar, they turn terrifyingly into seductive, sexually perverse and patriarchal figures, products of her imaginative revolt against her own internalized sense of social and political, sexual and racial contradiction. Increasingly invading and disabling her days, their struggle for power almost destroys her.

Head transmutes the painful material of her alienation, isolation and mental breakdown in Botswana into Elizabeth's story in realistic/surrealistic detail both particular (one woman's breakdown) and representative of the effects of internalizing oppressions of race and gender under apartheid. Amidst his mother's breakdown, her son's normality and everyday demands help to restore her balance.

Startling events in the fictionalized autobiography parallel reality. Head pasted notices outside the Post Office in Serowe, accusing Sir Seretse Khama (Sello, in the book) of obscenity and cannibalism. This latter act helped to confirm her breakdown. Her hospital confinements led eventually to her stabilization, aided by writing of her experiences in *A Question of Power*, the novel *Maru* (1971) and, to a lesser extent, the works also featuring Serowe – *When Rain Clouds Gather* (1969) and *Serowe, Village of the Rain Winds* (1981). About her life, these also record the harshness of life in Southern Africa and the potential for utopian change. Racism and oppression have overwhelmed Elizabeth:

> In spite of her inability to like or to understand political ideologies, she had lived the back-breaking life of all black peoples in South Africa. It was like living with permanent nervous tension, because you did not know why white people there had to go out of their way to hate you or to loathe you . . . there wasn't any life to the heart, just this vehement vicious struggle between two sets of people with different looks. (Head, 1974, p. 19)

and: 'I perceived the ease with which one could become evil and I associated evil in my mind with the acquisition of power' (Head, 1974, p. 77).

'She felt herself to be part of a soul drama, a new act of the eternal conflict between good and evil. She believed her strange birth and destiny to be part of a large pattern of things' (Stead Eilerson, 1995, p. 129). The narrative gives a controlling shape to what is initially perceived and experienced as pure evil:

> Her first drafts of *A Question of Power*, when she still called it *Summer Flowers*, were hardly to be distinguished from some of the descriptions of her own life she had given friends. She saw herself singled out for an incomprehensible assault of evil. She had come to the conclusions that it was necessary for the clearing of a lot of junk out of the soul. (Stead Eilerson, 1995, p. 149)

Bessie Head wrote through some of these feelings in *Maru* where Margaret the Masarwa or Bushman is ostracized by the village, considered the lowest of the low because of her racial origins. In 1969 this internalization of racism was tortuously real to Bessie. *Maru* was published in 1971.

Jolly and Attridge note of Boehmer's argument (1995), comparing autobiography and fiction, that:

> The unbearable reality of the apartheid world, she suggests, resists the novelistic imagination. There are some periods, it would seem, in which the task of imagining difference – temporally speaking and with regard to the other – is less possible than at other times. (Attridge and Jolly, 1998, p. 8)

It is important that we recognize in South African writing the ability to record detail and to document, and still to suggest that life could be other; thus harnessing both the realistic detail and the creative imaginative leap, positing another world.

Location, geography and identity

South African women writers combine often dichotomous responses and forms to a creative imaginative end. They do this most particularly when investigating and embodying the shifting relationships between identity and self, and place and location. Miriam Tlali's characters in *Soweto Stories* (1989) seek homes in crowded rooms, are dominated by bed bugs in transit hotels, terrorized out of temporary apartments and find solace working in enclosed spaces. Zoë Wicomb's sense of place in *You Can't Get Lost in Cape Town* (1987) returns her to home and to the recognition of new versions of identity, based on memory and imaginative exploration, linked to Cape Town's exclusions and space regulations.

Basali!: Stories by and about Women in Lesotho (Kendall, 1995) collects semi-fictionalized autobiographies of women's lives in South Africa, Lesotho and Swaziland (the borderlands), evidencing the brutality of living under apartheid from which several authors escaped. 'Escape to Manzini' by Nomakhosi Mntuyedwa charts her escape, from Soweto, to a Swaziland convent. Hiding from South African cars at the border,

> We were alerted by the grind of gears that a vehicle of sorts was approaching us. It was coming from the South African side of the border. There was no place to hide. The alternative was to lie down flat in the veld and hope that our city clothes blended in well with the bush. Baba Mzimande had told us to dress plainly for the trip. (Mntuyedwa, in Kendall, 1995, p. 100)

Produced in writing seminars where they read Toni Morrison, Alice Walker and Ngugi wa Thiong'o and 'intrigued by the notion of creating a variant English as West Africa and African-American writers have done, which would be unique to Lesotho and therefore, in a sense, their own and not the colonisers' English' (Kendall, 1995, p. x), many tales are only tellable in multiple languages, 'a bridge, perhaps, between orature and literature' (Kendall, 1995, pp. xi–xii).

In the work of Miriam Tlali, Bessie Head, and Zoë Wicomb, imagery enabling exploration of the ideas of identity and hope for creative change in the future recurs as imagery of location, of the house and home space, and of journeying. The familiarity of spaces, the accommodation of difference in a place (usually outside apartheid South Africa) which allows you to expand and be yourself is a crucial stimulus to the writer, and nurtures engaged, imaginative works.

Spaces of Australia and Africa in colonial discourse and representation are figured as dangerous, different, to be renamed, and appropriated. J. M. Coetzee comments on this phenomenon in twentieth-century white South African poetry, arguing that:

> In all the poetry commemorating meetings with the silence and emptiness of Africa . . . it is hard not to read a certain historical will to see as silent and empty a land that has been, if not full of human figures, not empty of them either. (Coetzee, 1989, p. 101)

Emptying the spaces of indigenous people in order to fill them with your own people and with your own representations is a popular stance for the colonizer. Imperial and colonial texts reinscribed southern landscapes as if they were women: dangerous, rich, fertile, to be possessed. Renaming, insisting on the importance of location and identity is a shared cultural project for Aboriginal and South African women writers. It is through the identity and voice enabled by fictionalized autobiography that Aboriginal and South African women writers express their own versions of the relation between identity and location, celebrating difference.

Works cited

Attridge, Derek and Rosemary Jolly (eds), 1998. *Writing South Africa,* Cambridge: Cambridge University Press.

Bandler, Faith, 1977. *Wacvie,* Adelaide: Rigby.

Boehmer, Elleke, 1995. *Colonial and Post-Colonial Literature,* Oxford: Oxford University Press.

Brink, André, 1998. 'Interrogating Silence', in Attridge and Jolly (eds), *Writing South Africa,* Cambridge: Cambridge University Press, pp. 14–29.

Cixous, Hélène, 1981. 'The Laugh of the Medusa', trans. Keith Cohen and Paula Cohen, in Elaine Marks and Isabelle de Courtivron (eds), *New French Feminisms, an Anthology,* New York: Schocken, pp. 245–64.

Clare, Monica, 1978. *Karobran: The Story of an Aboriginal Girl,* Sydney: APCOL.

Clemens, Theresa, Shirley S. Smith (Mumshirl) and Bobbi Sykes, 1981. *Mumshirl: An Autobiography with the Assistance of Bobbi Sykes,* Richmond: Heinemann Educational.

Coetzee, J. M., 1989. *White Writing: The culture of Letters in South Africa,* New Haven, CT: Yale University Press.

COSAW (Congress of South African Writers Collective), 1994. *Like a House on Fire: Contemporary Women's Writing from South Africa,* Johannesburg: COSAW Publishing.

Ferrier, Carole (ed.), 1985. 'Aboriginal Women's Narratives', in Carole Ferrier (ed.), *Gender, Politics and Fiction,* Brisbane: University of Queensland Press, pp. 200–219.

Ferrier, Carole, 1991. 'Resisting Authority', *Hecate,* vol. 16, no. 1–2, pp. 135ff.

Goolagong, Evonne, 1973. *Evonne! On the Move,* Sydney: Dutton.

Govinden, Betty, 1995. 'Learning Myself Anew', *Alternation,* vol. 2, no. 2, pp. 170–84.

Harstock, Nancy, 1990. 'Foucault on power: a theory for women?', in Joyce Nicholson (ed.), *Feminism/Post-Modernism,* New York: Routledge, pp.163–71.

Head, Bessie, 1969. *When Rain Clouds Gather,* Oxford: Heinemann.

Head, Bessie, 1971. *Maru,* Oxford: Heinemann.

Head, Bessie, 1974. *A Question of Power,* Oxford: Heinemann.

Head, Bessie, 1981. *Serowe, Village of the Rain Winds,* Oxford: Heinemann.

Head, Bessie, 1990. *A Woman Alone, Autobiographical Writings,* ed. Craig Mackenzie, Oxford: Heinemann.

hooks, bell, 1981. *Ain't I A Woman: Black Women and Feminism,* London: Pluto Press, 1986.

Huggins, Jackie, 1987/8. 'Firing on the Mind: Aboriginal Women Domestic Servants in the Inter-War Years', *Hecate,* vol. 13, no. 2, pp. 5–23.

Jabavu, Noni, 1960. *Drawn in Colour,* London: John Murray.

Jabavu, Noni, 1963. *The Ochre People,* London: John Murray.

Kendall, K. Limakatso, 1995. *Basali!: Stories by and about women in Lesotho,* Durban: University of Natal Press.

Kennedy, Marnie, 1985. *Born a Half Caste,* Canberra: AIAS.

Kuzwayo, Ellen, 1988. *Call Me Woman,* London: The Women's Press.

Labarlestier, Jan, 1991. 'Through Their Own Eyes: An Interpretation of Aboriginal Women's Writing', in Gill Bottomley (ed.), *Intersections: Gender/Class/Culture/Ethnicity,* London: Allen and Unwin, pp. 77–90.

Langford, Ruby, 1988. *Don't Take Your Love to Town,* Sydney: Penguin.

Lucashenko, Melissa, 1997. *Steam Pigs,* Brisbane: University of Queensland Press.

Morgan, Sally, 1987. *My Place,* Fremantle: Fremantle Arts Centre Press.

Morrison, Toni, 1987. *Beloved,* London: Chatto & Windus.

Narogin, Mudrooroo, 1985. Cited in J. Davis and B. Hodge (eds), *Aboriginal Writing Today,* Canberra: AIAS.

Ngcobo, Lauretta, 1981. *Cross of Gold,* London: Longman.

Ngcobo, Lauretta, 1994. Introduction to *Like a House on Fire: Contemporary Women's Writing from South Africa,* Johannesburg: COSAW Publishing, pp. 1–2.

Reddy, Jayapraga, 1987. *On the Fringe of Dream-time and Other Stories,* Johannesburg: Skotaville.

Reddy, Jayapraga, 1994. 'The Unbending Reed', in *Like a House on Fire: Contemporary Women's Writing from South Africa,* Johannesburg: COSAW Publishing, pp. 75–81.

Sam, Agnes, 1989. *Jesus is Indian and Other Stories,* Denmark: Dangaroo Press.

Smith, Shirley C. and Bobbi Sykes, 1981. *Mumshirl: An Autobiography,* Richmond, Victoria: Heinemann.

Stead Eilerson, Gillian, 1995. *Thunder Behind Her Ears,* Cape Town: David Philip.

Tlali, Miriam, 1975. *Muriel at the Metropolitan,* Johannesburg: Ravan.

Tlali, Miriam, 1980. *Amandla,* Johannesburg: Ravan.

Tlali, Miriam, 1989. *Soweto Stories,* London: Pandora.

Walker, Alice, 1983. *In Search of our Mothers' Gardens,* London: The Women's Press.

Ward, Glenyse, 1988. *Wandering Girl,* Broome: Magabala Books Aboriginal Corporation.

Whitlock, Gillian, 1996. *Disobedient Subjects,* Brisbane: University of Queensland Press.

Whitlock, Gillian E. and David Carter (eds), 1992. *Images of Australia,* Brisbane: University of Queensland Press.

Wicomb, Zoë, 1987. *You Can't Get Lost in Cape Town,* London: Virago.

Wright, Alexis, 1997. *Plains of Promise,* Brisbane: University of Queensland Press.

Chapter 50

Thomas King

GODZILLA VS. POST-COLONIAL

Writing from an indigenous perspective, the prolific Native author, radio dramatist, critic and professor Thomas King (Cheroke) entirely rejects the postcolonial paradigm as applied to Native literatures, because it implies that Native cultures only begin to make sense with the advent of colonialism, as well as in relation to its impact and aftermath. Native cultures existed orally *before* the arrival of European invader-settlers, and for King there is no intrinsic connection between them and colonial existence. At an even deeper level, King is rejecting the concept of "progress" embedded in the colonial–postcolonial narrative, that is to say, even though postcoloniality is about the *resistances* to colonialism, and moving on in positive ways from colonialism, this still implies "progress and improvement". For indigenous peoples around the world, not only was colonialism catastrophic, but their identities, argues King, are already anchored in their own traditions, one which many Native peoples argue have existed since time immemorial. In other words, indigenous peoples have, against all the odds, not only maintained their traditions, but they continue to autonomously develop them. The postcolonial paradigm, then, is something which is held "hostage to nationalism"; writing from Canada, King is aware of the term "First Nations", meaning indigenous peoples who existed before the British and French forged a new nation with alien traditions, laws and religious denominations. King posits alternative literary critical terms to replace that of the "postcolonial": the terms tribal, interfusional, polemical, and associational. Tribal literature is Native community or tribe based, usually written in an indigenous language. Polemical literature is about the clash of Native and non-Native cultures, or, asserts the benefits of indigenous ways of being. Interfusional literature blends oral and written narratives. Associational literature is primarily focused on indigenous life, utilizing a flat narrative style (a steady tone, similar to that of postmodern writing) which gives equal value to community members. King argues that these terms are not hierarchical or "progressive" in the sense of anthropological notions of developing cultures ("primitivism gives way to sophistication"); rather, they represent a *continuum* of Native being. For example, tribal literature is usually not accessible to those outside the language group within which it was written; yet given that certain aspects of indigenous narratives are sacred or transmit important cultural secrets, this offers advantages for cultural integrity. Polemical literature often asserts not just Native resistance, but also autonomy, so even though it is taught on postcolonial courses, it usually rejects any mode of non-Native labelling or categorization.

Interfusional literature may be written in English, but it is a way of reworking the English language via the rhythms, patterns and dynamic structures of oral cultures. Associational literature deliberately avoids overtly conflictual narrative and focuses instead on daily life, and in the process, a Native worldview emerges which reveals the community-based values of indigenous cultures. In each of these cases, King suggests that the theoretical terms used represent merely a perspective, a different way of seeing the heterogeneity of Native cultures, while not privileging any particular activity or value.

I GREW UP IN NORTHERN CALIFORNIA, and I grew up fast. I don't mean that I was raised in a tough part of town where you had to fight to survive. I was raised in a small town in the foothills, quite pastoral in fact. I mean I grew up all at once. By my first year of high school, I already had my full height, while most of my friends were just beginning to grow.

We had a basketball team at the high school and a basketball coach who considered himself somewhat of an authority on the subject of talent. He could spot it, he said. And he spotted me. He told me I had a talent for the game, and that I should come out for the team. With my size, he said, I would be a natural player. I was flattered.

I wish I could tell you that I excelled at basketball, that I was an all-star, that college coaches came to see me play. But the truth of the matter is, I wasn't even mediocre. Had I not been so very young and so very serious, I might have laughed at my attempts to run and bounce a ball at the same time. Certainly most everyone who saw me play did.

Now before you think that my embarrassment in basketball was the fault of an overzealous coach, you have to remember that we both made more or less the same assumption. The coach assumed that because I was tall, I would be a good player. And once the coach called my height to my attention and encouraged me, I assumed the same thing. We spent the rest of our time together trying to figure out why I was so bad.

Just before the first game of my second season, I tore my knee, mercifully ending my basketball career. My experience taught me little about basketball, but it did teach me a great deal about assumptions.

Assumptions are a dangerous thing. They are especially dangerous when we do not even see that the premise from which we start a discussion is not the hard fact that we thought it was, but one of the fancies we churn out of our imaginations to help us get from the beginning of an idea to the end.

Which brings me, albeit by a circuitous route, to post-colonial literature. I am not a theorist. It's not an apology, but it is a fact. So I cannot talk to the internal structure of the theory itself, how it works, or what it tells us about the art of language and the art of literature. Nor can I participate to any great extent in what Linda Hutcheon calls "the de-doxifying project of postmodernism."

But having played basketball, I can talk about the assumptions that the term post-colonial makes. It is, first of all, part of a triumvirate. In order to get to "post," we have to wend our way through no small amount of literary history, acknowledging the existence of its antecedents, pre-colonial and colonial. In the case of Native literature, we can say that pre-colonial literature was that literature, oral in nature, that was in existence prior to European contact, a literature that existed exclusively within specific cultural communities.

Post-colonial literature, then, must be the literature produced by Native people sometime after colonization, a literature that arises in large part out of the experience that is colonization. These particular terms allow us to talk about Native literature as a literature that can be counterpoint to Canadian literature, a new voice, if you will, a different voice in the literary amphitheatre. I rather like the idea of post-colonial literature, because it promises to set me apart from the masses and suggests that what I have to offer is new and exciting. But then again, I rather liked the idea of playing basketball, too.

I said at the beginning that I was not a theorist and was not going to concern myself with how post-colonialism operates as a critical method. But I am concerned with what the term says about Natives and Native literature and the initial assumptions it makes about us and our cultures.

When I made that rather simplistic comparison between pre-colonial and post-colonial, I left out one of the players, rather like talking about pre-pubescence and post-pubescence without mentioning puberty. My apologies. It was a trick to make you think I was going to say something profound, when, in fact, I was going to make the rather simple observation that in the case of pre- and post-pubescence and pre- and post-colonial, the pivot around which we move is puberty and colonialism. But here, I'm lying again. Another trick, I'm afraid, for in puberty's case, the precedent, the root, and the antecedent are, at least, all part of a whole, whereas in the case of colonialism – within a discussion of Native literature – the term has little to do with the literature itself. It is both separate from and antithetical to what came before and what came after.

Pre-colonial literature, as we use the term in North America, has no relationship whatsoever to colonial literature. The two are neither part of a biological or natural cycle nor does the one anticipate the other, while the full complement of terms – pre-colonial, colonial, and post-colonial – reeks of unabashed ethnocentrism and well-meaning dismissal, and they point to a deep-seated assumption that is at the heart of most well-intentioned studies of Native literatures.

While post-colonialism purports to be a method by which we can begin to look at those literatures which are formed out of the struggle of the oppressed against the oppressor, the colonized and the colonizer, the term itself assumes that the starting point for that discussion is the advent of Europeans in North America. At the same time, the term organizes the literature progressively suggesting that there is both progress and improvement. No less distressing, it also assumes that the struggle between guardian and ward is the catalyst for contemporary Native literature, providing those of us who write with method and topic. And, worst of all, the idea of post-colonial writing effectively cuts us off from our traditions, traditions that were in place before colonialism ever became a question, traditions which have come down to us through our cultures in spite of colonization, and it supposes that contemporary Native writing is largely a construct of oppression. Ironically, while the term itself – post-colonial – strives to escape to find new centres, it remains, in the end, a hostage to nationalism.

As a contemporary Native writer, I am quite unwilling to make these assumptions, and I am quite unwilling to use these terms.

A friend of mine cautioned me about this stridency and pointed out that post-colonial is a perfectly good term to use for that literature which is, in fact, a reaction to the historical impositions of colonialization. She suggested I look at Maria Campbell's *Halfbreed* and Beatrice Culleton's *In Search of April Raintree* as examples of works for which the term is appropriate. She further suggested that post-colonial was not such a simple thing, that much of what I was concerned with – centres, difference, totalizing, hegemony, margins – was being addressed by post-colonial methodology. If this is true, then it is unfortunate that the method has such an albatross – as the term – hanging around its neck. But I must admit that I remain sceptical that such a term could describe a non-centred, non-nationalistic method.

If we are to use terms to describe the various stages or changes in Native literature as it has become written, while at the same time remaining oral, and as it has expanded from a specific language base to a multiple language base, we need to find descriptors which do not invoke the cant of progress and which are not joined at the hip with nationalism. Post-colonial might be an excellent term to use to describe Canadian literature, but it will not do to describe Native literature.

As a Native writer, I lean towards terms such as tribal, interfusional, polemical, and associational to describe the range of Native writing. I prefer these terms for a variety of reasons: they tend to be less centred and do not, within the terms themselves, privilege one culture over another; they avoid the sense of progress in which primitivism gives way to sophistication, suggesting as it does that such movement is both natural and desirable; they identify points on a cultural and literary continuum for Native literature which do not depend on anomalies such as the arrival of Europeans in North America or the advent of non-Native literature in this hemisphere, what Marie Baker likes to call "settler litter." At the same time, these terms are not "bags" into which we can collect and store the whole of Native literature. They are, more properly, vantage points from which we can see a particular literary landscape.

Two of these terms are self-apparent: tribal and polemical. Tribal refers to that literature which exists primarily within a tribe or a community, literature that is shared almost exclusively by members of that community, and literature that is presented and retained in a Native language. It is virtually invisible outside its community, partly because of the barrier of language and partly because it has little interest in making itself available to an outside audience. In some cases, tribes – the Hopi come to mind – take great pains in limiting access to parts of their literature only to members of their immediate community. Polemical refers to that literature either in a Native language or in English, French, etc. that concerns itself with the clash of Native and non-Native cultures or with the championing of Native values over non-Native values. Like Beatrice Culleton's *In Search of April Raintree,* Maria Campbell's *Halfbreed,* D'Arcy McNickle's *The Surrounded* and *Wind from an Enemy Sky,* and Howard Adams' *Prison of Grass,* polemical literature chronicles the imposition of non-Native expectations and insistences (political, social, scientific) on Native communities and the methods of resistance employed by Native people in order to maintain both their communities and cultures.

The terms interfusional and associational are not as readily apparent. I'm using interfusional to describe that part of Native literature which is a blending of oral literature and written literature. While there are contemporary examples that *suggest* the nature of interfusional literature – some of the translations of Dennis Tedlock and Dell Hymes work along with those of Howard Norman in *The Wishing Bone Cycle* – the only complete example we have of interfusional literature is Harry Robinson's *Write It on Your Heart.*

The stories in Robinson's collection are told in English and written in English, but the patterns, metaphors, structures as well as the themes and characters come primarily from oral literature. More than this, Robinson, within the confines of written language, is successful in creating an oral voice. He does this in a rather ingenious way. He develops what we might want to call an oral syntax that defeats readers' efforts to read the stories silently to themselves, a syntax that encourages readers to read the stories out loud.

The common complaint that we make of oral literature that has been translated into English is that we lose the voice of the storyteller, the gestures, the music, and the interaction between storyteller and audience. But by forcing the reader to read aloud, Robinson's prose, to a large extent, avoids this loss, re-creating at once the storyteller and the performance.

> Yeah, I'll tell you "Cat With the Boots On."
> Riding boots on.
> That's the stories, the first stories.
> There was a big ranch, not around here.
> That's someplace in European.
> Overseas.
> That's a long time, shortly after the "imbellable" stories.
> But this is part "imbellable" stories.
> It's not Indian stories.

This is white people stories,
because I learned this from the white people.
Not the white man.
The white man tell his son,
that's Allison – John Fall Allison.
White man.
He is the one that tell the stories to his son.
His son, Bert Allison.
His son was a half Indian and a half white,
because his mother was an Indian.
And his father was a white man.
So his father told him these stories.
But he told me – Bert Allison.
So he told me,
"This is not Indian stories.
White man stories."
You understand that?

This metamorphosis – written to oral, reader to speaker – is no mean trick, one that Robinson accomplishes with relative ease. More important, his prose has become a source of inspiration and influence for other Native writers such as Jeannette Armstrong and myself.

Associational literature is the body of literature that has been created, for the most part, by contemporary Native writers. While no one set of criteria will do to describe it fully, it possesses a series of attributes that help to give it form.

Associational literature, most often, describes a Native community. While it may also describe a non-Native community, it avoids centring the story on the non-Native community or on a conflict between the two cultures, concentrating instead on the daily activities and intricacies of Native life and organizing the elements of plot along a rather flat narrative line that ignores the ubiquitous climaxes and resolutions that are so valued in non-Native literature. In addition to this flat narrative line, associational literature leans towards the group rather than the single, isolated character, creating a fiction that de-values heroes and villains in favour of the members of a community, a fiction which eschews judgements and conclusions.

For the non-Native reader, this literature provides a limited and particular access to a Native world, allowing the reader to associate with that world without being encouraged to feel a part of it. It does not pander to non-Native expectations concerning the glamour and/or horror of Native life, and it especially avoids those media phantasms – glitzy ceremonies, yuppie shamanism, diet philosophies (literary tourism as one critic called them) – that writers such as Carlos Castenada and Lynn Andrews have conjured up for the current generation of gullible readers.

For the Native reader, associational literature helps to remind us of the continuing values of our cultures, and it reinforces the notion that, in addition to the usable past that the concurrence of oral literature and traditional history provides us with, we also have an active present marked by cultural tenacity and a viable future which may well organize itself around major revivals of language, philosophy, and spiritualism.

Two of the better examples of associational literature are Basil H. Johnston's *Indian School Days* and Ruby Slipperjack's *Honour the Sun*. Each creates an Indian community, Johnston at a Jesuit boarding school, Slipperjack in northern Ontario. The novels themselves describe daily activities and the interaction of the community itself, and, aside from the first-person narrator, no one character is given preference over another.

Because *Indian School Days* is about a boarding school, we might well expect to see a
sustained attack on this particularly colonial institution, and, while Johnston does on occasion
criticize the expectations that the Jesuits have for their Native wards, he defuses most of the
conflicts by refusing to make easy judgements and by granting responsibility and choice to
both the Jesuits and the Native boys. The boys are not portrayed as hapless victims, and the
Jesuits are not cast as uncaring jailers. Particularly telling are the concerted efforts made by
the clerics and the students to care for the very young students, "babies" as Johnston calls
them, who "seldom laughed or smiled and often cried and whimpered during the day and at
night." While the older boys tried to act "as guardians or as big brothers," the burden of care
"fell on the young scholastics, who had a much more fatherly air than the senior boys in
Grades 7 and 8."

Ruby Slipperjack concerns herself with an isolated Native community in northern
Ontario. Written in the form of a diary, the book follows the everyday life of an extended
family. The book has no pretense at plot nor is there a desire to glorify traditional Native life.
The story is told in simple and unassuming prose that focuses on relationships:

> There are seven of us in the family, four girls and three boys. My oldest brother
> got married and went away a long time ago. My other brother, Wess, spends
> most of his time at the cabin on our old trapline. The rest of us girls are all here.
> We live in a one-room cabin our father built before he died. Mom got someone
> to make a small addition at the back a couple of years ago. That's where she
> sleeps with our little brother, Brian. Brian was just a little baby when my father
> died and he's about six years old now. The rest of us sleep in the main room on
> two double beds and a bunk bed.
>
> Three other kids live with us. Mom looks after them because their parents
> left their home. I guess three more doesn't make much difference aside from the
> fact the food and clothes have to stretch a little further. The father came to see
> them once. I heard Mom say that she has never gotten a penny for their keep.
> Their mother has never come. Actually, I am closer to them than to my own
> sisters, since mine are gone all winter. Maggie and Jane have become my regular
> sisters and Vera and Annie are my special sisters when they are home in the
> summer.

Within the novel, the narrator neither posits the superiority of Native culture over non-
Native culture nor suggests that the ills that beset the community come from outside it. Her
brother's tuberculosis, John Bull's violent rampages, and the mother's eventual alcoholism
are mentioned and lamented, but they are presented in a non-judgemental fashion and do not
provide an occasion for accusation and blame either of non-Native culture at large or the
Native community itself.

Both books provide access to a Native world, but the access is not unlimited. It is, in
fact, remarkably limited access. While Johnston hints at some of the reasons why Indian
parents allow their children to be placed at St. Peter Claver's, he does not elaborate on the
complex cultural dynamics that have helped to maintain these schools. Much of this is hidden,
as are the Native communities outside the school from which the students come. While
Slipperjack appears more forthright in her description of the family and the community, she
refuses to share with us the reasons for the narrator's mother's alcoholism, the cause of John
Bull's violent behaviour, and the reasons for the narrator's leaving the community. In the
end, what is most apparent in these two books is not the information received but the silences
that each writer maintains. Non-Natives may, as readers, come to an association with these
communities, but they remain, always, outsiders.

Now it goes without saying that creating terms simply to replace other terms is, in most instances, a solipsistic exercise, and I do not offer these terms as replacements for the term post-colonial so much as to demonstrate the difficulties that the people and the literature for which the term was, in part, created have with the assumptions that the term embodies.

Unlike post-colonial, the terms tribal, interfusional, polemical, and associational do not establish a chronological order nor do they open and close literary frontiers. They avoid a nationalistic centre, and they do not depend on the arrival of Europeans for their *raison d'être*.

At the same time, for all the range they cover, they do not comfortably contain the work of such Native writers as Gerald Vizenor and Craig Kee Strete. Vizenor's postmodern novels *Darkness in St. Louis Bearheart* and *Griever: An American Monkey King in China* and Strete's short story collections of surreal and speculative fiction *The Bleeding Man* and *If All Else Fails* cross the lines that definitions – no matter how loose – create.

And it may be that these terms will not do in the end at all. Yet I cannot let post-colonial stand – particularly as a term – for, at its heart, it is an act of imagination and an act of imperialism that demands that I imagine myself as something I did not choose to be, as something I would not choose to become.

PART VIII

Gender and queer theory

S EXUALITY, DECLARES CRITIC JEFFREY WEEKS, "is a 'fictional unity', that once did not exist, and at some time in the future may not exist again."[1] This statement is a useful entry point into the study of gender and queer theory since it indicates three possibilities: (1) that how society understands sexuality and gender was once radically different from how society understands it today; (2) that over time new conceptions of sexuality and gender were constructed and eventually stabilized; and (3) that these conceptions may pass on to some other understanding in the future. "Fictional unity" is also a very striking term for readers who are used to thinking of sexuality and gender from a biological or anatomical perspective: that is to say, empirically proven (not "fictional") physiological differences in reproductive organs, usually associated with a primarily heterosexual notion of the function of sex. From this biological perspective, sexuality is anchored in pre-ordained, consistent male and female behaviours that are considered normal especially when expressed in terms of heterosexual relations. But even the language used here fails to maintain such anchoring in an essentialist notion of human sex: "behaviours" vary considerably from this norm, and "relations" may function quite differently. Still, by asserting a heterosexual norm and then measuring all other sexual behaviour in relation to that norm (which is considered primary or original), variations and differences can be categorized as "deviant", "dangerous" or from a religious perspective "sinful".

Biological essentialism came under attack from a number of quarters during the mid-twentieth century, including John Money's research on human hermaphroditism undertaken at Harvard University in the 1940s and 1950s,[2] and the more widely known Kinsey Reports (1948 and 1953), which examined sexual behaviour in the US, discovering at a time of apparent social uniformity—the stereotypical suburban heterosexual family with two children, the father at work, and the mother at home—immense diversity in everyday sexual practices. While there are limitations to the sample groups utilized, the Kinsey reports presented a body of statistical evidence that began to question previously held notions of sexual norms, especially by placing heterosexual and homosexual activity upon a continuum, rather than presenting them as binary opposites.[3] What this means is that people had reported a range of heterosexual and homosexual experiences at different stages in their lives, and so these sexual experiences could no longer be considered antithetical.

In 1968, sociologist Mary McIntosh published "The Homosexual Role", which triggered radically new approaches to the study of sexuality. McIntosh argued that labelling homosexuals from a socially normative perspective as "deviant" was a mode of "social control" (183).[4] In other words, regarding homosexuality as a medical "condition" just like any other illness means that the humans in question are fixed as being outside of "normal" life and in need of a cure. McIntosh replaces the concept of "condition" with that of "role" to register the discrepancy between stereotypes and actual sexual practices. She also argues that the concept of a "role" enables investigators to examine not just society's ideas about homosexuality, but also what she called its "institutional arrangements" that construct and regulate sexuality, including: ". . . all the forms of heterosexual activity, courtship, and marriage as well as the labelling processes — gossip, ridicule, psychiatric diagnosis, criminal conviction — and the groups and networks of the homosexual subculture."[5] McIntosh's essay covers a lot of ground: she examines different societies where homosexuality is *not* registered as a deviant mode of behaviour, and she focuses historically on Britain, and the emergence in the seventeenth century of a homosexual subculture, based in certain taverns such as the "Mollies' Club" in London ("Molly" is slang for an effeminate man). McIntosh makes the acute observation that historical surveys of homosexual subcultures need to be flexible enough to register *historical differences* in sexual categorization; for example in the seventeenth century, homosexuality and transvestism were not regarded as separate modes of sexual expression, as they are today.

An alternative chronology of the genealogy of sexuality to that proposed by McIntosh, although with obvious analogous exploration of the social mechanisms of personal and institutional construction and regulation of the self, is that of Michel Foucault's *The History of Sexuality* (French 1976; first English trans. 1978), followed by two more volumes in 1984: *The Use of Pleasure* and *The Care of the Self* (English trans. 1985 & 1986). Critics have noted how Foucault's history is "widely celebrated as the first detailed articulation of the social construction of homosexuality",[6] one in which Foucault rejects the theory of sexual repression (the "repressive hypothesis") which supposedly began in the seventeenth century, taking hold until the Victorian age, and then being progressively rejected by a more liberal — and sexually liberated — society. Instead, Foucault continues his lifelong project of understanding society through its discursive formations, where a discourse is a set of articulations and practices that define human subjects in relation to knowledge and power (e.g., medicine, law, disciplinary codes, and so on). Foucault argues that it is in the nineteenth century that a new discursive formation concerning sexuality emerges, one based upon pseudo-scientific observation and analysis in new academic fields such as psychoanalysis, forming in the process notions of deviant subjects and associated transgressive, if not criminalized, behaviour. While Foucault's four volumes on this topic (the fourth remains unpublished) are historically and philosophically exhaustive, Foucault's aim was to not only understand how sexuality is constituted, but also to grapple with the fact that sexuality is consistently presented in different eras as an "object of moral preoccupation."[7] In other words, while it may be obvious that religious notions of sexuality are deeply moralistic, it is also true that other conceptions carry their own ethical charge. For example, while psychoanalysis might have opened up previously taboo topics such as childhood sexuality, or same sex relations, this liberated discourse is in the service of "returning" the patient back to "normality", be that "normality" defined as health, heterosexuality, patriarchal family life, and so on. As Foucault puts it, Freudianism attempted "to ground sexuality in the law — the law of alliance, tabooed consanguinity, and the Sovereign Father", which he summarizes as "all the trappings of the old order of power."[8]

Decoupling sexuality from essentialism and an ethical understanding leads to the conundrum that if society does not believe that "anything goes" (sex with minors, abusive modes of sexuality, etc.), then as Weeks puts it, "how do we determine appropriate and inappropriate behaviour?"[9] In other words, if theories of desire — say the human subject as a "desiring machine" (Deleuze and Guattari) — are based upon a cybernetic/mechanistic scientific understanding concerning humanity, then how is a new sexual ethics to be built from this position? As Weeks suggests, "The trouble is that this 'scientific knowledge' is, as we know, full of divisions and contradictions about what the self is, what desire may be, and even whether there is such a thing as 'the unconscious'. Yet if we reject these guidelines, is there anything else?"[10] Weeks suggests that a potential answer is found in the methodological indirectness of the second and third volumes of Foucault's *History*, which appear on the surface to be "simple exegeses of ancient Greek and Latin texts on how people should live."[11] However, Foucault is also revealing parallels between the classical age and our own postmodern age, that is to say, "the task of elaborating an ethic that was not founded in religion or any other *a priori* justification, least of all science."[12] In rejecting a strict codification of sexuality and ethics, the Greeks and Romans instead charted a middle ground, one in which different modes of sexuality co-existed; for Foucault this is what the contemporary age needs, "not a transcendent truth, but ways of coping with a multiplicity of truths. We need not so much a morality based upon absolute values, but an ethics and politics which will enable us to cope with a variety of choices."[13]

Foucault's power-knowledge analysis revealed the importance of a political understanding of sexuality, one which had been developing for decades. In fact just one year after McIntosh's article was published, a more visceral response to the "institutional arrangements" which regulated sexuality erupted in the form of the Stonewall riots, at a gay bar called the Stonewall Inn, in Greenwich Village, New York. For five days, the patrons of the bar resisted police intrusion into their lives by rioting and demonstrating against attempts by the state to criminalize and suppress gay subcultures. "Stonewall" as it is often simply known, was not the only act of gay resistance to the state, but it symbolizes a turning point, registered the following month by the formation of the activist Gay Liberation Front in New York. However, for all of its reaching out to other resistance networks, based on race, class or alternative lifestyles, the Gay Liberation Front did primarily focus on gay men. For example, recounting his experiences in London, Keith Birch notes that "The people who came to GLF were overwhelmingly male, white, young and appeared independent of family and other restrictions."[14] As historians have rightly pointed out, gay liberation movements did not begin with Stonewall, and they did not end with the eventual demise of the GLF. Furthermore, a more politicized approach to sexualities cannot function comprehensively alongside an internalized repression or marginalization of other sexual groups, especially since such groups also have a unique history of autonomous activism. Another consideration triggered by the question of "history" concerns the power/knowledge nexus of sexual categorization and historical "evidence", or, to put this more clearly in terms of the lesbian narratives elided by the term "gay" in the acronym GLF, this is a question of recovering marginalized narratives from a wider range of sources than those suggested by restrictive or hostile notions of lesbians as overly "masculine" or "aggressive" women. Thus, women who played a major role in the gaining of the right to vote ("suffrage"), for example, were attacked on grounds other than their political beliefs, as a way of undermining their legitimacy. In her article "Compulsory Heterosexuality and Lesbian Existence" (1980), Adrienne Rich advocated the use of the broader terms "lesbian existence" and "lesbian continuum" to open up areas of lesbian subjectivity and history that had previously been ignored by scholars; thus women who resisted heterosexuality could be welcomed into a complex genealogy of lesbianism, which can be seen in the fact that Rich's lesbian continuum included "the Beguines of medieval Europe, devout women who lived collectively outside the institutions of both marriage and the convent; African women who formed secret sororities and economic networks; and Chinese marriage resisters."[15] To better reflect the diversity of anti-heterosexual resistances, the word "lesbian" became an essential marker in discussion of "gay and lesbian" movements. However, as Marinucci notes, this opens up the question of other alternative modes of sexuality, such as "bisexuality": "Given the popular misconception that bisexuality is a temporary identity that people eventually overcome, either by fully committing to homosexuality or by fully committing to heterosexuality, it is especially important to assert bisexuality as a sexual identity distinct from both . . . GLB was introduced to refer to gay, lesbian, and bisexual identities."[16] Transgender identities are also added to this abbreviation, as well as a re-positioning of lesbians in the order of description, to make LGBT, or, adding Questioning/Other to this list, to make LGBTQ or LGBTO. The category of "Other" can also be thought of as "Open": not just to exploration, but to further ways of practising and conceiving of sexuality, such as "intersex". In many ways, the open categories of Questioning/Other are a supplement that deconstructs the entire list. In other words, they are indicative of an active resistance to any fixed mode of categorization or hierarchical distribution of names, however well intentioned and meaningful.

Another issue with the well-intentioned decisions concerning the acronym LGBTQ/O is that it leads to the false impression of a unified approach to non-heterosexual identities; at the University of California, Santa Cruz in 1990, such an impression was unsettled by the first "queer theory" conference, which was organized by Teresa de Lauretis, creating shock waves with this more formal, academic use of a potentially "gay-affirmative" word that came from the vernacular world of activism and street culture.[17] Critic David Halperin notes that de Lauretis "wanted specifically to unsettle the complacency of 'lesbian and gay studies' . . . which implied that the relation of lesbian to gay male topics in this emerging field was equitable, perfectly balanced, and completely understood—as if everyone knew exactly how lesbian studies and gay male studies connected to each other and why it was necessary or important that they should evolve together."[18] The word "queer" implicitly undermines any attempt at a false synthesis of identities because as Jagose notes: "Broadly speaking, queer describes those gestures or analytical models which dramatize incoherencies in the allegedly stable relations between chromosomal sex, gender and sexual desire."[19] This fluid definition emphasizes performativity and theatricality as well as foregrounding the instability of previously held universal truths (e.g., heterosexuality being a norm that precedes homosexuality). Sedgwick defines "queer" as "a continuing moment, movement, motive – recurrent, eddying . . . it is relational and strange."[20] This also implies connections with poststructuralist theories that assert new modes of subjectivity: always in process, composed of energy flows, intensities, and temporary or ongoing performances that are often countercultural, working across the grain, traversing normative understanding of identity and being. Two groundbreaking studies published the same year as the queer theory conference, Judith Butler's *Gender Trouble: Feminism and the Subversion of Identity* (1990; anniversary edition 1999), and Eve Kosofsky Sedgwick's *The Epistemology of the Closet* (1990), provide a comprehensive intellectual, critical framework for these new approaches to subjectivity (see Chapters 51 and 54).

In her preface to the 1999 edition of *Gender Trouble*, Butler traces some of the influences and roots of her project: poststructuralist theory, feminism, psychoanalysis and debates concerning the social construction of gender; more specifically she foregrounds the work on "drag, sexuality, and kinship" by Gayle Rubin (especially her essay "The Traffic in Women"), and the theory and fiction of Monique Wittig.[21] Butler summarizes one of the main questions of *Gender Trouble*: "how do non-normative sexual practices call into question the stability of gender as a category of analysis?"[22] "Call into question" is perhaps a mild phrase for the powerful deconstructive demonstration that follows in the book, which Sedgwick also undertakes through the deconstructive "strand" in her text, that is to say the "analytic move"[23] that rejects hierarchical binary gender oppositions (heterosexual/homosexual), arguing instead that they "actually subsist in a more unsettled and dynamic tacit relation."[24] Sedgwick provides a useful schema here, where the category "heterosexual" is term "A" and "homosexual" is term "B": "first, term B is not symmetrical with but subordinated to term A; but, second, the ontologically valorized term A actually depends for its meaning on the simultaneous subsumption and exclusion of term B; hence, third, the question of priority between the supposed central and the supposed marginal category of each dyad is irresolvably unstable, an instability caused by the fact that term B is constituted as at once internal and external to term A."[25] This long sentence is worth re-reading, because it maps out a core queer theory concept: that not only are alternative gender performances *not* secondary to heterosexual ones, but that heterosexual gender performances depend upon the act of excluding and marginalizing homosexual ones. Further, as Butler argues, this process of constitution-through-exclusion does not happen once-and-for-all; instead, heterosexual gender performances are inherently unstable and must therefore continue to repeatedly exclude and assert identity. Or as she puts it in a more punchy phrase: "gay is to straight *not* as copy is to original, but, rather, as copy is to copy."[26] Sedgwick argues that for this maxim to be revealed, political and aesthetic acts need to be brought out of the closet in "risky and affirming acts of the most explicit self-identification";[27] furthermore, this applies to the literary canon as well, especially "with the re-creation of minority gay canons from currently noncanonical material."[28] Such a process cannot be too prescriptive since this would be to foreclose queer possibilities found within the canon as it stands, and within the new canon(s) that are currently being constructed. Butler examines gender performances via the aesthetics and practices of gender parody in drag, cross-dressing and butch/femme roles.[29] Her core thesis here is that "In imitating gender, drag implicitly reveals the imitative structure of gender itself—as well as its contingency."[30] Performance, in other words, is no longer regarded as mere re-presentation of some normative original, instead, it reveals how notions of "the original" are in themselves simply performances, powerfully unsettling the primary/secondary binary hierarchy.

Queer theory, following Butler and Sedgwick, is about asserting an identity-through-performance, i.e., through repetition, while at the same time such repetition subverts notions of normativity and sameness. Queer theory is not about being secondary, different from a norm, it is about "asserting difference as such."[31] This means that with queer theory there is a sense of identity politics, yet it is always one that thinks identity differently in positive ways (if it was always reacting to a norm, it would be a negative identity). For some queer theorists, this leads to a desire to move entirely beyond identity politics, into the realm of pure positivities, such as a new queer aesthetics or multiple modes of sexuality and being. Colebrook maps out some of the questions that arise from specific situations: "Rather than seeing gay marriage, trans-gendering or gay parenting as compromised manoeuvres in which the queer self repeats and distorts given norms, we need to look at the positivity of each encounter. How do bodies establish relations in each case, and what powers are opened (or closed) to further encounters and modifications?"[32] Colebrook and other critics suggest that the work of Gilles Deleuze offers possible theoretical answers to questions such as these, especially with the notion that human beings can be reconfigured as intensities (energy, desire, production) which "precede" symbolic systems, such as the law of patriarchy. Queer theory is open, then, to anarchic and creative new intensities, ones which cannot be mapped in advance, and in fact they may not even be recognized by heteronormative society as even existing once they come into being, since they may partake of the realm of the symbiotic post-human (cybernetics, quantum systems, information networks, animal–human crossovers).

Nigianni argues that the task for queer theory is "to imagine, form and actualise new forms of political agency: instead of communities of an identitarian logic, machinic assemblages, instead of the individual, a 'crowd' ... instead of identities, singularities; instead of representations, expressions; instead of interpretations, codings through mappings; instead of signifiers, signs 'which flash across the interval of a difference'."[33] Other critics assert that it is not entirely clear how sexualities are reconfigured in everyday encounters or situations: are such reconfigurations triggered by extreme or intense events, such as trauma, or are such reconfigurations more gradual, caused by more gentle changes such as a job relocation, or other ways of being plunged into new social and sexual environments?[34] Conjoining queer theory with Deleuzian theory is, arguably, a way of moving beyond social coding, but such a "beyond" is often shared by particular new group formations, or assemblages. Rather than seeing this process as a contradiction, it is more accurate to regard such new group formations/assemblages as being deliberately unstable and constantly open to change. Pondering such an open process in relation to "Becoming-Lesbian", Nigianni charts what an anti-Oedipal, Deleuzian "schizo-analysis" of lesbian desire looks like: "a desire free from fixed subjectivity and complete-object representations, which is positive and productive (rather than reproductive) by producing 'anarchic multiplicities', myriad partial-object connections, unnatural relations of an 'estranged sameness' that defy dialectic alterity; a desire that is not constituted by lack and negation (for example, the trauma of castration) but by positivity and affirmation."[35] Queer theory takes the reader into new territory, new detours through sexualities, literary and other texts, among myriad other domains of expression, and yet the challenge is to not then anchor a new notion of "queer" to one site or experience of intensity. Perhaps the biggest challenge for queer theory is to remain entirely open to the next move, one which may or may not be oppositional, but one which will undoubtedly involve powerful acts of creativity.

Further reading: a selection

Two starting points are the clearly written and comprehensive overviews by Hall (on queer theories) and Weeks (on sexualities). Hall keeps the student reader in mind at every stage, including some suggested actions beyond reading and theorising, put forward in the last chapter called "A Final Query"; Weeks provides historical, ethical, and social coverage in a compelling discourse of critical questioning and openness to other possibilities and differences. Selected "classic" texts in gender and queer theory in this list include Butler, De Lauretis, Foucault and Sedgwick. Butler's theories of camp can be usefully read alongside De Lauretis (who focuses on film), in a section of her book called "Lesbianism and the Theory of Spectatorship"; both Butler and De Lauretis perform radical re-readings of psychoanalytical and poststructuralist theory, in Butler's case deconstructing Kristeva, Foucault, and Lacan, in De Lauretis's case deconstructing Freud and French feminists such as Irigaray. Sedgwick (in *Between Men*) approaches homosexuality and the canon from a feminist perspective, critiquing and applying a new approach to the "erotic triangle" or "mimetic desire" theorized by Rene Girard to a wide range of literary texts including Shakespeare, the gothic, and Victorian poetry; *The Epistemology of the Closet* looks at Melville, Proust, Wilde, James, Nietzsche, legal and biblical text among many others. Winders also examines Nietzsche (in chapter 6), as well as Descartes, Marx, Freud and Flaubert. The first volume of Foucault's three-volume set is the most useful for beginner readers since he explores his rejection of previous understandings of sexuality and offers new theses and genealogies. Marinucci, Weed and Schor bring together feminism and queer theory to examine the interrelations and differences between these theories; Turner does this in chapter 3 of his genealogy or history of queer theory. The wide-ranging essays in Hanson focus on film, while Cant and Hemmings provide useful historical documentation about gay and lesbian liberation movements.

Butler, Judith. *Gender Trouble: Feminism and the Subversion of Identity*. London & New York: Routledge, 1990. Anniversary Edition 1999.

Butler, Judith. *Bodies that Matter: On the Discursive Limits of "Sex"*. London & New York: Routledge, 1993.

Cant, Bob and Susan Hemmings, eds. *Radical Records: Thirty Years of Lesbian and Gay History, 1957–1987*. London & New York: Routledge, 2010.

De Lauretis, Teresa. *The Practice of Love: Lesbian Sexuality and Perverse Desire*. Bloomington, IN: Indiana University Press, 1994.

Foucault, Michel. *The History of Sexuality, Volume 1: An Introduction*. Trans. Robert Hurley. New York: Vintage, 1990.

Foucault, Michel. *The History of Sexuality, Volume 2: The Use of Pleasure*. Trans. Robert Hurley. New York: Vintage, 1990.

Foucault, Michel. *The History of Sexuality, Volume 3: The Care of the Self*. Trans. Robert Hurley. New York: Vintage, 1986.

Hall, Donald E. *Queer Theories*. Houndmills, Basingstoke & New York: Palgrave Macmillan, 2003.

Hanson, Ellis, ed. *Out Takes: Essays on Queer Theory and Film*. Durham, NC: Duke University Press, 1999.

Marinucci, Mimi. *Feminism Is Queer*. London & New York: Zed Books, 2010.

Nigianni, Chrysanthi and Merl Storr, eds. *Deleuze and Queer Theory*. Edinburgh: Edinburgh University Press, 2009.

Sedgwick, Eve Kosofsky. *Between Men: English Literature and Male Homosocial Desire*. New York: Columbia University Press, 1985.

Sedgwick, Eve Kosofsky. *The Epistemology of the Closet*. Berkeley & Los Angeles: University of California Press, 1990.

Sullivan, Nikki. *A Critical Introduction to Queer Theory*. New York: New York University Press, 2003.

Turner, William B. *A Genealogy of Queer Theory*. Philadelphia: Temple University Press, 2000.

Weed, Elizabeth and Naomi Schor, eds. *Feminism Meets Queer Theory*. Bloomington, IN: Indiana University Press, 1997.

Weeks, Jeffrey. *Sexuality*. Third Edition. Abingdon, Oxon & New York: Routledge, 2010.

Winders, James A. *Gender, Theory, and the Canon*. Madison: the University of Wisconsin Press, 1991.

Notes

1   Jeffrey Weeks, *Sexuality*, Third Edition, Abingdon, Oxon & New York: Routledge, 2010, p.7.
2   Jennifer Germon, *Gender: A Genealogy of An Idea*, New York: Palgrave Macmillan, 2009. p.2.
3   Mimi Marinucci, *Feminism is Queer*, London & New York: Zed Books, 2010, p.5.
4   Mary McIntosh, "The Homosexual Role", *Social Problems*, 16.2 (Autumn 1968): 182–92, p.189.
5   Mary McIntosh, "The Homosexual Role", p.189.
6   Mimi Marinucci, *Feminism is Queer*, p.17.
7   Didier Eribon, *Michel Foucault*, trans. Betsy Wing, Cambridge, MA: Harvard University Press, 1991, p.320.
8   Michel Foucault, *The History of Sexuality, Volume 1: An Introduction*, trans. Robert Hurley, New York: Vintage, 1990, p.150.
9   Jeffrey Weeks, *Sexuality*, p.143.
10   Jeffrey Weeks, *Sexuality*, p.143.
11   Jeffrey Weeks, *Sexuality*, p.143.
12   Jeffrey Weeks, *Sexuality*, p.143.
13   Jeffrey Weeks, *Sexuality*, p.144.
14   Keith Birch, "A Community of Interests", in *Radical Records: Thirty Years of Lesbian and Gay History, 1957–1987*, ed. Bob Cant and Susan Hemmings, London & New York: Routledge, 2010, 32–37, p.33.
15   Bonnie Zimmerman, ed., *Lesbian Histories and Cultures*, New York: Garland, 2000, p.369.
16   Mimi Marinucci, *Feminism is Queer*, p.31.
17   Mimi Marinucci, *Feminism is Queer*, p.33.
18   David M. Halperin, "The Normalization of Queer Theory", *Journal of Homosexuality*, 45.2/3/4 (2003): 339–43; p.340.
19   Quoted in Mimi Marinucci, *Feminism is Queer*, p.33.
20   Quoted in Donald E. Hall, *Queer Theories*, Houndmills, Basingstoke & New York: Palgrave Macmillan, 2003, p.12.

21   Judith Butler, *Gender Trouble: Feminism and the Subversion of Identity*, London & New York: Routledge, 1999, p.x.

22   Judith Butler, *Gender Trouble: Feminism and the Subversion of Identity*, p.xi.

23   Eve Kosofsky Sedgwick, *The Epistemology of the Closet*, Berkeley & Los Angeles: University of California Press, 1990, p.9.

24   Eve Kosofsky Sedgwick, *The Epistemology of the Closet*, p.10.

25   Eve Kosofsky Sedgwick, *The Epistemology of the Closet*, p.10.

26   Judith Butler, *Gender Trouble: Feminism and the Subversion of Identity*, p.41.

27   Eve Kosofsky Sedgwick, *The Epistemology of the Closet*, p.58.

28   Eve Kosofsky Sedgwick, *The Epistemology of the Closet*, p.58.

29   Judith Butler, *Gender Trouble: Feminism and the Subversion of Identity*, p.174.

30   Judith Butler, *Gender Trouble: Feminism and the Subversion of Identity*, p.175.

31   Claire Colebrook, "On the Very Possibility of Queer Theory", in *Deleuze and Queer Theory*, ed. Chrysanthi Nigianni and Merl Storr, Edinburgh: Edinburgh University Press, 2009, 11–23, p.15.

32   Claire Colebrook, "On the Very Possibility of Queer Theory", p.21.

33   Chrysanthi Nigianni, ". . . so as to know 'us' better Deleuze and Queer Theory: two theories, one concept – one book, many authors . . .", in *Deleuze and Queer Theory*, ed. Chrysanthi Nigianni and Merl Storr, Edinburgh: Edinburgh University Press, 2009, 1–10, p.7.

34   Donald E. Hall, *Queer Theories*, pp.181–3.

35   Chrysanthi Nigianni, "Butterfly Kiss: The Contagious Kiss of Becoming-Lesbian", in *Deleuze and Queer Theory*, ed. Chrysanthi Nigianni and Merl Storr, Edinburgh: Edinburgh University Press, 2009, 168–82, p.170.

Chapter 51

Judith Butler

FROM INTERIORITY TO GENDER PERFORMATIVES

Surprisingly, Judith Butler begins this key extract from her book on gender with Michel Foucault's notion that the "soul" is punitively inscribed on the material body by those who hold power. These surface signs indicate what the subject lacks—the soul—and thus it is brought into being not as a liberating internal essence or attribute, but more as an external imprisonment or effect of power and subjection. Butler, a leading theorist of gender, subjectivity and performativity, begins here because her argument is that the gendered body utilizes semiotic and material signs ("words, acts, gestures, and desire") to similarly create what appears to be an interiority, which she calls "the effect of an internal core or substance." This in turn becomes a new prison within which human subjects are trapped. Gender, then, is a "disciplinary production" one which in most societies follows what Butler calls "compulsory" and "normative" heterosexuality. Butler's wider argument begins with two prohibitions that all people are subject to: (1) the taboo against homosexuality, and (2) the incest taboo. For Butler, this leads to a "false stabilization of gender" which is necessary when the goal of society is one of regulated, reproductive sexuality. Put more simply, then, gender is stabilized by the construction of a norm—heterosexuality—against which all other gender constructions are measured and found wanting. This norm may be stabilized, but it is not fixed. It constantly needs to be re-performed since it is constituted by its "acts", not by some essentiality. These acts are performed within the public domain, and take on social and political significance (as well as contributing to the wider discursive formation of normative behaviour). Here, Butler is suggesting that to shift focus to a purely psychoanalytical understanding of gender differences is to evade or even foreclose the political realities through which gender is produced. Other gender performances— here, drag—create a "dissonance" that parodies the notion of an originary heterosexuality. Drag foregrounds the complex interrelationships between what Butler calls the "three contingent dimensions of significant corporeality", which are "anatomical sex, gender identity, and gender performance." Further, these interrelationships reveal the deficiencies in arguing that there is an "original" versus secondary genders. To put this another way, drag, as complex gender imitation, parody, and pastiche, reveals that even heterosexual normativity is an "imitation" of an absent original. If there is no essential normative subjectivity, then the key to the maintenance of heterosexuality is a *repetition* of its performance. Such a repetition means that gender exists temporally, in process, rather than being located in one site or event of subject formation. Gender is a style, rather than a substance, and styles are subject to change—they are fundamentally unstable, in need of further theatrical performance and public consensus concerning their importance. Butler argue that all of the norms produced by gender performances on the material surface of the body/society are ultimately arbitrary, constructed, and "phantasmatic", thus subject to deformation, breakdown, and change. In this vision of human identity, essentialism is entirely rejected and shown to be the ultimate illusion of human subjectivity.

I N *DISCIPLINE AND PUNISH* FOUCAULT challenges the language of internalization as it operates in the service of the disciplinary regime of the subjection and subjectivation of criminals.[1] Although Foucault objected to what he understood to be the psychoanalytic belief in the "inner" truth of sex in *The History of Sexuality,* he turns to a criticism of the doctrine of internalization for separate purposes in the context of his history of criminology. In a sense, *Discipline and Punish* can be read as Foucault's effort to rewrite Nietzsche's doctrine of internalization in *On the Genealogy of Morals* on the model of *inscription.* In the context of prisoners, Foucault writes, the strategy has been not to enforce a repression of their desires, but to compel their bodies to signify the prohibitive law as their very essence, style, and necessity. That law is not literally internalized, but incorporated, with the consequence that bodies are produced which signify that law on and through the body; there the law is manifest as the essence of their selves, the meaning of their soul, their conscience, the law of their desire. In effect, the law is at once fully manifest and fully latent, for it never appears as external to the bodies it subjects and subjectivates. Foucault writes:

> It would be wrong to say that the soul is an illusion, or an ideological effect. On the contrary, it exists, it has a reality, it is produced permanently *around, on, within,* the body by the functioning of a power that is exercised on those that are punished. (my emphasis)[2]

The figure of the interior soul understood as "within" the body is signified through its inscription *on* the body, even though its primary mode of signification is through its very absence, its potent invisibility. The effect of a structuring inner space is produced through the signification of a body as a vital and sacred enclosure. The soul is precisely what the body lacks; hence, the body presents itself as a signifying lack. That lack which *is* the body signifies the soul as that which cannot show. In this sense, then, the soul is a surface signification that contests and displaces the inner/outer distinction itself, a figure of interior psychic space inscribed *on* the body as a social signification that perpetually renounces itself as such. In Foucault's terms, the soul is not imprisoned by or within the body, as some Christian imagery would suggest, but "the soul is the prison of the body."[3]

The redescription of intrapsychic processes in terms of the surface politics of the body implies a corollary redescription of gender as the disciplinary production of the figures of fantasy through the play of presence and absence on the body's surface, the construction of the gendered body through a series of exclusions and denials, signifying absences. But what determines the manifest and latent text of the body politic? What is the prohibitive law that generates the corporeal stylization of gender, the fantasied and fantastic figuration of the body? We have already considered the incest taboo and the prior taboo against homosexuality as the generative moments of gender identity, the prohibitions that produce identity along the culturally intelligible grids of an idealized and compulsory heterosexuality. That disciplinary production of gender effects a false stabilization of gender in the interests of the heterosexual construction and regulation of sexuality within the reproductive domain. The construction of coherence conceals the gender discontinuities that run rampant within heterosexual, bisexual, and gay and lesbian contexts in which gender does not necessarily follow from sex, and desire, or sexuality generally, does not seem to follow from gender—indeed, where none of these dimensions of significant corporeality express or reflect one another. When the disorganization and disaggregation of the field of bodies disrupt the regulatory fiction of heterosexual coherence, it seems that the expressive model loses its descriptive force. That regulatory ideal is then exposed as a norm and a fiction that disguises itself as a developmental law regulating the sexual field that it purports to describe.

According to the understanding of identification as an enacted fantasy or incorporation, however, it is clear that coherence is desired, wished for, idealized, and that this idealization is an effect of a corporeal signification. In other words, acts, gestures, and desire produce the effect of an internal core or substance, but produce this *on the surface* of the body, through the play of signifying absences that suggest, but never reveal, the organizing principle of identity as a cause. Such acts, gestures, enactments, generally construed, are *performative* in the sense that the essence or identity that they otherwise purport to express are *fabrications* manufactured and sustained through corporeal signs and other discursive means. That the gendered body is performative suggests that it has no ontological status apart from the various acts which constitute its reality. This also suggests that if that reality is fabricated as an interior essence, that very interiority is an effect and function of a decidedly public and social discourse, the public regulation of fantasy through the surface politics of the body, the gender border control that differentiates inner from outer, and so institutes the "integrity" of the subject. In other words, acts and gestures, articulated and enacted desires create the illusion of an interior and organizing gender core, an illusion discursively maintained for the purposes of the regulation of sexuality within the obligatory frame of reproductive heterosexuality. If the "cause" of desire, gesture, and act can be localized within the "self" of the actor, then the political regulations and disciplinary practices which produce that ostensibly coherent gender are effectively displaced from view. The displacement of a political and discursive origin of gender identity onto a psychological "core" precludes an analysis of the political constitution of the gendered subject and its fabricated notions about the ineffable interiority of its sex or of its true identity.

If the inner truth of gender is a fabrication and if a true gender is a fantasy instituted and inscribed on the surface of bodies, then it seems that genders can be neither true nor false, but are only produced as the truth effects of a discourse of primary and stable identity. In *Mother Camp: Female Impersonators in America,* anthropologist Esther Newton suggests that the structure of impersonation reveals one of the key fabricating mechanisms through which the social construction of gender takes place.[4] I would suggest as well that drag fully subverts the distinction between inner and outer psychic space and effectively mocks both the expressive model of gender and the notion of a true gender identity. Newton writes:

> At its most complex, [drag] is a double inversion that says, "appearance is an illusion." Drag says [Newton's curious personification] "my 'outside' appearance is feminine, but my essence 'inside' [the body] is masculine." At the same time it symbolizes the opposite inversion; "my appearance 'outside' [my body, my gender] is masculine but my essence 'inside' [myself] is feminine."[5]

Both claims to truth contradict one another and so displace the entire enactment of gender significations from the discourse of truth and falsity.

The notion of an original or primary gender identity is often parodied within the cultural practices of drag, cross-dressing, and the sexual stylization of butch/femme identities. Within feminist theory, such parodic identities have been understood to be either degrading to women, in the case of drag and cross-dressing, or an uncritical appropriation of sex-role stereotyping from within the practice of heterosexuality, especially in the case of butch/ femme lesbian identities. But the relation between the "imitation" and the "original" is, I think, more complicated than that critique generally allows. Moreover, it gives us a clue to the way in which the relationship between primary identification—that is, the original meanings accorded to gender—and subsequent gender experience might be reframed. The performance of drag plays upon the distinction between the anatomy of the performer and the gender that is being performed. But we are actually in the presence of three contingent dimensions of significant corporeality: anatomical sex, gender identity, and gender performance. If the anatomy of the performer is already distinct from the gender of the performer, and both of those are distinct from the gender of the performance, then the performance suggests a dissonance not only between sex and performance, but sex and gender, and gender and performance. As much as drag creates a unified picture of "woman" (what its critics often oppose), it also reveals the distinctness of those aspects of gendered experience which are falsely naturalized as a unity through the regulatory fiction of heterosexual coherence. *In imitating gender, drag implicitly reveals the imitative structure of gender itself—as well as its contingency*. Indeed, part of the pleasure, the giddiness of the performance is in the recognition of a radical contingency in the relation between sex and gender in the face of cultural configurations of causal unities that are regularly assumed to be natural and necessary. In the place of the law of heterosexual coherence, we see sex and gender denaturalized by means of a performance which avows their distinctness and dramatizes the cultural mechanism of their fabricated unity.

The notion of gender parody defended here does not assume that there is an original which such parodic identities imitate. Indeed, the parody is *of* the very notion of an original; just as the psychoanalytic notion of gender identification is constituted by a fantasy of a fantasy, the transfiguration of an Other who is always already a "figure" in that double sense, so gender parody reveals that the original identity after which gender fashions itself is an imitation without an origin. To be more precise, it is a production which, in effect—that is, in its effect—postures as an imitation. This perpetual displacement constitutes a fluidity of identities that suggests an openness to resignification and recontextualization; parodic proliferation deprives hegemonic culture and its critics of the claim to naturalized or essentialist gender identities. Although the gender meanings taken up in these parodic styles are clearly part of hegemonic, misogynist culture, they are nevertheless denaturalized and mobilized through their parodic recontextualization. As imitations which effectively displace the meaning of the original, they imitate the myth of originality itself. In the place of an original identification which serves as a determining cause, gender identity might be reconceived as a personal/cultural history of received meanings subject to a set of imitative practices which refer laterally to other imitations and which, jointly, construct the illusion of a primary and interior gendered self or parody the mechanism of that construction.

According to Fredric Jameson's "Postmodernism and Consumer Society," the imitation that mocks the notion of an original is characteristic of pastiche rather than parody:

> Pastiche is, like parody, the imitation of a peculiar or unique style, the wearing of a stylistic mask, speech in a dead language: but it is a neutral practice of mimicry, without parody's ulterior motive, without the satirical impulse, without laughter, without that still latent feeling that there exists something *normal* compared to which what is being imitated is rather comic. Pastiche is blank parody, parody that has lost it humor.[6]

The loss of the sense of "the normal," however, can be its own occasion for laughter, especially when "the normal," "the original" is revealed to be a copy, and an inevitably failed one, an ideal that no one *can* embody. In this sense, laughter emerges in the realization that all along the original was derived.

Parody by itself is not subversive, and there must be a way to understand what makes certain kinds of parodic repetitions effectively disruptive, truly troubling, and which repetitions become domesticated and recirculated as instruments of cultural hegemony. A typology of actions would clearly not suffice, for parodic displacement, indeed, parodic laughter, depends on a context and reception in which subversive confusions can be fostered. What performance where will invert the inner/outer distinction and compel a radical rethinking of the psychological presuppositions of gender identity and sexuality? What performance where will compel a reconsideration of the *place* and stability of the masculine and the feminine? And what kind of gender performance will enact and reveal the performativity of gender itself in a way that destabilizes the naturalized categories of identity and desire.

If the body is not a "being," but a variable boundary, a surface whose permeability is politically regulated, a signifying practice within a cultural field of gender hierarchy and compulsory heterosexuality, then what language is left for understanding this corporeal enactment, gender, that constitutes its "interior" signification on its surface? Sartre would perhaps have called this act "a style of being," Foucault, "a stylistics of existence." And in my earlier reading of Beauvoir, I suggest that gendered bodies are so many "styles of the flesh." These styles all never fully self-styled, for styles have a history, and those histories condition and limit the possibilities. Consider gender, for instance, as *a corporeal style,* an "act," as it were, which is both intentional and performative, where *"performative"* suggests a dramatic and contingent construction of meaning.

Wittig understands gender as the workings of "sex," where "sex" is an obligatory injunction for the body to become a cultural sign, to materialize itself in obedience to a historically delimited possibility, and to do this, not once or twice, but as a sustained and repeated corporeal project. The notion of a "project," however, suggests the originating force of a radical will, and because gender is a project which has cultural survival as its end, the term *strategy* better suggests the situation of duress under which gender performance always and variously occurs. Hence, as a strategy of survival within compulsory systems, gender is a performance with clearly punitive consequences. Discrete genders are part of what "humanizes" individuals within contemporary culture; indeed, we regularly punish those who fail to do their gender right. Because there is neither an "essence" that gender expresses or externalizes nor an objective ideal to which gender aspires, and because gender is not a fact, the various acts of gender create the idea of gender, and without those acts, there would be no gender at all. Gender is, thus, a construction that regularly conceals its genesis; the tacit collective agreement to perform, produce, and sustain discrete and polar genders as cultural fictions is obscured by the credibility of those productions—and the punishments that attend not agreeing to believe in them; the construction "compels" our belief in its necessity and naturalness. The historical possibilities materialized through various corporeal styles are nothing other than those punitively regulated cultural fictions alternately embodied and deflected under duress.

Consider that a sedimentation of gender norms produces the peculiar phenomenon of a "natural sex" or a "real woman" or any number of prevalent and compelling social fictions, and that this is a sedimentation that over time has produced a set of corporeal styles which, in reified form, appear as the natural configuration of bodies into sexes existing in a binary relation to one another. If these styles are enacted, and if they produce the coherent gendered subjects who pose as their originators, what kind of performance might reveal this ostensible "cause" to be an "effect"?

In what senses, then, is gender an act? As in other ritual social dramas, the action of gender requires a performance that is *repeated.* This repetition is at once a reenactment and reexperiencing of a set of meanings already socially established; and it is the mundane and ritualized form of their legitimation.[7] Although there are individual bodies that enact these significations by becoming stylized into gendered modes, this "action" is a public action. There are temporal and collective dimensions to these actions, and their public character is not inconsequential; indeed, the performance is effected with the strategic aim of maintaining gender within its binary frame—an aim that cannot be attributed to a subject, but, rather, must be understood to found and consolidate the subject.

Gender ought not to be construed as a stable identity or locus of agency from which various acts follow; rather, gender is an identity tenuously constituted in time, instituted in an exterior space through a *stylized repetition of acts*. The effect of gender is produced through the stylization of the body and, hence, must be understood as the mundane way in which bodily gestures, movements, and styles of various kinds constitute the illusion of an abiding gendered self. This formulation moves the conception of gender off the ground of a substantial model of identity to one that requires a conception of gender as a constituted *social temporality*. Significantly, if gender is instituted through acts which are internally discontinuous, then the *appearance of substance* is precisely that, a constructed identity, a performative accomplishment which the mundane social audience, including the actors themselves, come to believe and to perform in the mode of belief. Gender is also a norm that can never be fully internalized; "the internal" is a surface signification, and gender norms are finally phantasmatic, impossible to embody. If the ground of gender identity is the stylized repetition of acts through time and not a seemingly seamless identity, then the spatial metaphor of a "ground" will be displaced and revealed as a stylized configuration, indeed, a gendered corporealization of time. The abiding gendered self will then be shown to be structured by repeated acts that seek to approximate the ideal of a substantial ground of identity, but which, in their occasional *discontinuity*, reveal the temporal and contingent groundlessness of this "ground." The possibilities of gender transformation are to be found precisely in the arbitrary relation between such acts, in the possibility of a failure to repeat, a de-formity, or a parodic repetition that exposes the phantasmatic effect of abiding identity as a politically tenuous construction.

If gender attributes, however, are not expressive but performative then these attributes effectively constitute the identity they are said to express or reveal. The distinction between expression and performativeness is crucial. If gender attributes and acts, the various ways in which a body shows or produces its cultural signification, are performative, then there is no preexisting identity by which an act or attribute might be measured; there would be no true or false, real or distorted acts of gender, and the postulation of a true gender identity would be revealed as a regulatory fiction. That gender reality is created through sustained social performances means that the very notions of an essential sex and a true or abiding masculinity or femininity are also constituted as part of the strategy that conceals gender's performative character and the performative possibilities for proliferating gender configurations outside the restricting frames of masculinist domination and compulsory heterosexuality.

Genders can be neither true nor false, neither real nor apparent, neither original nor derived. As credible bearers of those attributes, however, genders can also be rendered thoroughly and radically *incredible*.

Notes

1   Parts of the following discussion were published in two different contexts, in my "Gender Trouble, Feminist Theory, and Psychoanalytic Discourse," in *Feminism/Postmodernism,* ed. Linda J. Nicholson (New York: Routledge, 1989) and "Performative Acts and Gender Constitution: An Essay in Phenomenology and Feminist Theory," *Theatre Journal,* Vol. 20, No. 3, Winter 1988.

2   Michel Foucault, *Discipline and Punish: the Birth of the Prison,* trans. Alan Sheridan (New York: Vintage, 1979), p. 29.

3   Ibid., p. 30.

4   See the chapter "Role Models" in Esther Newton, *Mother Camp: Female Impersonators in America* (Chicago: University of Chicago Press, 1972).

5   Ibid., p. 103.

6   Fredric Jameson, "Postmodernism and Consumer Society," in *The Anti-Aesthetic: Essays on Postmodern Culture,* ed. Hal Foster (Port Townsend, WA.: Bay Press, 1983), p. 114.

7   See Victor Turner, *Dramas, Fields and Metaphors* (Ithaca: Cornell University Press, 1974). See also Clifford Geertz, "Blurred Genres: The Refiguration of Thought," in *Local Knowledge, Further Essays in Interpretive Anthropology* (New York: Basic Books, 1983).

Chapter 52

Slavoj Žižek

THE MELANCHOLIC DOUBLE BIND

In dialogue here with the work of Judith Butler (see Chapter 51), Slavoj Žižek engages at a deeply philosophical level, in part based upon his own readings of the philosopher Hegel who stands behind Butler and Žižek himself. Another key thinker brought into play is Lacan (see Chapters 25 and 26), especially in relation to his re-reading of Freud. Butler's theories of gender performance intrigue Žižek, in part because he wishes to counteract Butler's theories about gender with Lacanian theories concerning sexuality, but also as part of a bigger project in which Žižek has been intellectually engaging with the key nineteenth- and twentieth-century thinkers in philosophy and the arts. Beginning with Butler's Freudian move — her argument that human beings "foreclose" (expel/drive away, becoming constituted in the process) their innate homosexuality or "attachment to Sameness" to enter the Symbolic realm of law, language, and society — Žižek notes that this precedes the incest taboo, which implies a heterosexual normativity, and even more radically, such homosexuality was foreclosed per se, or as Butler articulates it, "proscribed from the start". After exploring the apparent paradoxes of this procedure, Žižek locates what he calls the "key ambiguity" of Butler's gender theory, that is to say, the difference between foreclosing a desire for sameness, and a desire for difference. To put this into concrete terms, Žižek asks if straight or heterosexual subjectivity is a process of melancholic incorporation of the foreclosed identity, or, a psychically defensive manoeuvre, whereby one resists adopting the position of being a woman. For Žižek, this ambiguity proves that melancholic foreclosure, is not foreclosure of an originary homosexuality, but that of a stable sexuality that partakes of the Symbolic order. In other words, it is sexual difference that "forever eludes" being normative. In this way, Žižek replaces Butler's Freudianism with that of Lacan's theories of psyche and sexuality, especially the notion that sexual difference is not about binary opposition, but rather a process of loss, impossibility, and symbolic castration. In other words, there is an internal psychic split not because of an external sexual difference (Žižek's reference here is to the title of a best-selling book *Men are from Mars, Women are from Venus*), but because of a sexual difference which is already "within" men and women. For Žižek, then, Butler's equation of sexual difference with a heterosexual normativity in itself forecloses the possibility that there is in reality no such thing as a stable, symbolized sexuality against which all other gender performances are measured, but rather a "gap" between the symbolic ideal of sexuality, so to speak, and the *actuality* of a whole range of diverse sexual/gender performances and practices. For Žižek, sexual difference partakes of an "enigmatic domain" that is somewhere between the biological or physiological and the constructed realm of gender performances; this domain is not collapsible into one or the other, instead it is the Real in the Lacanian sense of being beyond symbolization, and not open to direct access; any "mode" of symbolization—what Butler would call a gender performance—is thus temporary, "contingent", and always already destabilized from within.

IN RECENT YEARS, BUTLER HAS endeavoured to supplement her early 'constructionist' criticism of psychoanalysis by a 'positive' account of the formation of (masculine or feminine) sexual identity, which draws on the Freudian mechanism of mourning and melancholy. She relies here on the old Freudian distinction between foreclosure and repression: repression is an act performed by the subject, an act by means of which a subject (who is already there as an agent) represses part of his psychic content; while foreclosure is a negative gesture of exclusion which grounds the subject, a gesture on which the very consistency of the subject's identity hinges: this gesture cannot be 'assumed' by the subject, since such an assumption would involve the subject's disintegration.

Butler links this primordial and constitutive foreclosure to homosexuality: it is the foreclosure of the passionate attachment to Sameness (to the parent of the same sex) which has to be sacrificed if the subject is to enter the space of the socio-symbolic Order and acquire an identity in it. This leads to the melancholy constitutive of the subject, including the reflexive turn which defines subjectivity: one represses the primordial attachment – that is, one starts to hate to love the same-sex parent; then, in a gesture of reflexive reversal proper, this 'hate to love' turns around into 'love to hate' – one 'loves to hate' those who remind one of the primordially lost objects of love (gays). . . . Butler's logic is impeccable in its very simplicity: Freud insists that the result of the loss of a libidinal object – the way to overcome the melancholy apropos of this loss – is identification with the lost object: does this not also hold for our sexual identities? Is not the 'normal' heterosexual identity the result of successfully overcoming melancholy by identifying with the lost object of the same sex, while the homosexual is the one who refuses fully to come to terms with this loss, and continues to cling to the lost object? Butler's first result is thus that the primordial Foreclosure is not the prohibition of incest: the prohibition of incest already presupposes the predominance of the heterosexual norm (the repressed incestuous wish is for the parent of the opposite sex), and this norm itself came into place through the foreclosure of the homosexual attachment:

> The oedipal conflict presumes that heterosexual desire has already been *accomplished*, that the distinction between heterosexual and homosexual has been enforced . . .; in this sense, the prohibition on incest presupposes the prohibition on homosexuality, for it presumes the heterosexualization of desire.[1]

The primordial 'passionate attachment' to the same sex is thus posited as not only repressed but foreclosed in the radical sense of something which never positively existed, since it was excluded from the very start: 'To the extent that homosexual attachments remain unacknowledged within normative heterosexuality, they are not merely constituted as desires which emerge and subsequently become prohibited; rather, these desires are proscribed from the start.' So, paradoxically, it is the very excessive and compulsive 'straight' identification which – if we take into account the fact that, for Freud, identification relies on the melancholic incorporation of the lost object – demonstrates that the primordial attachment was homosexual:

> In this sense, the 'truest' lesbian melancholic is the strictly straight woman, and the 'truest' gay male melancholic is the strictly straight man. . . . The straight man *becomes* (mimes, cites, appropriates, assumes the status of) the man he 'never' loved and 'never' grieved; the straight woman *becomes* the woman she 'never' loved and 'never' grieved.[2]

Here Butler seems to get involved in a kind of Jungianism *à l'envers*: a man is longing not for his complementary feminine counterpart (*animus* for *anima*, etc.), but for sameness – it is not sameness which 'represses' difference, it is (the desire for) difference which forecloses (the desire for) sameness. . . . However, what about the fact, quoted by Butler herself, that the man, in remaining attached to the compulsive male identification, fears being put in the 'passive' position of femininity as the one who desires (another) man? What we have here is the obverse of the melancholic incorporation: if, in the latter, one *becomes* what one was compelled to give up – *desiring as an object* (a man), then, in the first case, one *desires as an object* what one is afraid to *become* (a woman): a man 'wants the woman he would never be. He wouldn't be caught dead being her: therefore he wants her. . . . Indeed, he will not identify with her, and he will not desire another man. That refusal to desire, that sacrifice of desire under the force of prohibition, will incorporate homosexuality as an identification with masculinity.'[3] Here we encounter the key ambiguity of Butler's argument, an ambiguity which also affects the inconclusive character of her important discussion of transsexual drag dressing: her definition of the foreclosed primordial 'passionate attachment' oscillates between two subjective positions *from which* one desires another man – is it that one desires another man *as a man*, or that one desires to be *a woman* desired by (and desiring) another man? In other words, is my straight masculine identification the melancholic incorporation of my foreclosed attachment to another man, or a defence against assuming the subjective position of a woman (desiring a man)? Butler herself touches upon this ambiguity later in the text, when she asks:

> Does it follow that if one desires a woman, one is desiring from a masculine disposition, or is that disposition retroactively attributed to the desiring position as a way of retaining heterosexuality as the way of understanding the separateness or alterity that conditions desire?[4]

This question, of course, is rhetorical – that is, Butler clearly opts for the second choice. In that case, however, why does she, in the quoted passage, identify desiring another man with assuming a feminine disposition, as if a man 'wouldn't be caught dead being her', since this would mean that he desires another man? Does not all this indicate that the primordial loss constitutive of subjectivity cannot be defined in terms of the foreclosure of a *homosexual* attachment? In other words, *why* does a man fear becoming a woman; why 'wouldn't [he] be caught dead being her'? Is it only because, as such, he would desire (and be desired by) another man? Let us recall Neil Jordan's *The Crying Game*, a film in which we have a passionate love between two men, structured as a heterosexual affair: the black transsexual Dil is a man who desires another man *as a woman*. It thus seems more productive to posit as the central enigma that of sexual difference – *not* as the already established symbolic difference (heterosexual normativity) but, precisely, as that which forever eludes the grasp of normative symbolization.

Butler is right in opposing the Platonic-Jungian notion that the loss involved in sexuation is the loss of the other sex (the notion which opens up the path to various obscurantist androgynous myths of the two halves, feminine and masculine, joined in a complete human being): it is wrong 'to assume from the outset that we only and always lose the other sex, for it is as often the case that we are often in the melancholic bind of *having lost our own sex in order, paradoxically, to become it*'.[5] In short, what the Platonic–Jungian myth fails to take into account is that the obstacle or loss is strictly *inherent*, not external: the loss a woman has to assume in order to become one is not the renunciation of masculinity but, paradoxically, the loss of something which, precisely, forever prevents her from fully becoming a woman – 'femininity' is a masquerade, a mask supplementing a failure to become a woman. Or – to put it in Laclau's terms – sexual difference is the Real of an antagonism, not the Symbolic of a differential opposition: sexual difference is not the opposition allocating to each of the two sexes its positive identity defined in opposition to the other sex (so that woman is what man is not, and vice versa), but a common Loss on account of which woman is never fully a woman and man is never fully a man – 'masculine' and 'feminine' positions are merely two modes of coping with this inherent obstacle/loss.

For that reason, the paradox of 'having lost our own sex in order to become it' holds even more for sexual difference: what one has to lose in order to assume sexual difference *qua* the established set of symbolic oppositions that define the complementary roles of 'man' and 'woman' is sexual difference itself *qua* impossible/real. This dialectical paradox of how an entity can *become* X only in so far as it has to renounce directly *being* X is precisely what Lacan calls 'symbolic castration': the gap between the symbolic place and the element which fills it, the gap on account of which an element can *fill* its place in the structure only in so far as it *is not* directly this place.

Notes

1   Butler, *The Psychic Life of Power, p.* 135.
2   Ibid., pp. 147, 146–47.
3   Ibid., pp. 137–38.
4   Ibid., p. 165.
5   Ibid., p. 166.

Chapter 53

Michel Foucault

SCIENTIA SEXUALIS

If scholars in the West are under the impression that two centuries of discussion concerning human sexuality has led to an understanding and a language capable of communicating the heterogenous nature of sex, then Michel Foucault suggests this is merely part of the "screen-discourse" that functions in quite the opposite way: it masks or conceals the fact that Western discourse concerning sexuality is fundamentally evasive. Discursive formations claim to tell the truth about a topic since they constitute the very framework within which topics may be delineated and articulated; Foucault suggests that many non-Western countries—he lists China, Japan, India, Rome [*sic*], the "Arabo-Moslem [*sic*] societies"—approach sexuality as an "*ars erotica*", literally an "erotic art", one that foregrounds pleasure and its performances. The West, on the other hand, approaches sexuality via a "*scientia sexualis*", not a "science" concerning sexuality, but literally, in Latin, "knowledge" of sexuality. Foucault is famous for exploring the relationships between power and knowledge in highly influential texts such as *Madness and Civilization* (1954), *The Birth of the Clinic* (1963) and *The Order of Things* (1966); this project is continued in *The History of Sexuality*, here with two modes of *scientia sexualis*: the religious "confessional" and the "multiple localization" of confession since the nineteenth century under the remit of a "scientific discourse"—not just psychoanalysis, but all modes of interrogating subjects about sex, receiving in turn different types of confessions/ reports from those subjects. From the Middle Ages to the present day, Foucault argues that "confession" in all its guises is one of the most common ways of producing "truth", not simply in a religious environment, but also with legal, medical, and aesthetic practices. "Truth" is regarded as something interior which needs to be "extracted" in the confessional act, and sex is the primary topic of that act, but the power-knowledge dynamic leads to the subject both speaking and being the site of that truth. Put simply, one confesses to the person or authority who will be judging one's actions in return. For Foucault, the transition from religious to scientific confession begins with the downplaying of ritualistic performances in the Reformation (and what followed), as well as the shift from confessing to "reconstructing" the truth about sex, i.e., the narrative form utilized by psychoanalysis and others. Ironically, by the nineteenth century this created a surfeit of knowledge about sex, with the narrative form transgressively dominating. Foucault argues that the transition from this surfeit to a more regulated, scientific discourse took place via five mechanisms. First, the confession itself becomes "clinically" or scientifically codified, so that it follows empirical procedures, creating data sets ready for analysis. Second, sexuality is regarded as a universal causal factor. Third, hidden sins are replaced by interiorized zones of subjectivity that can only be accessed by experts. Fourth, a sort of psychoanalytical peer review has to take place, with one's confessions being regarded as provisional and incomplete until interpreted by experts. And fifth, another codification of confession is necessary to reinscribe the entire procedure as being therapeutic, imposing in the process overarching labels such as the normative versus the pathological.

I SUPPOSE THAT THE FIRST TWO POINTS will be granted me; I imagine that people will accept my saying that, for two centuries now, the discourse on sex has been multiplied rather than rarefied; and that if it has carried with it taboos and prohibitions, it has also, in a more fundamental way, ensured the solidification and implantation of an entire sexual mosaic. Yet the impression remains that all this has by and large played only a defensive role. By speaking about it so much, by discovering it multiplied, partitioned off, and specified precisely where one had placed it, what one was seeking essentially was simply to conceal sex: a screen-discourse, a dispersion-avoidance. Until Freud at least, the discourse on sex—the discourse of scholars and theoreticians—never ceased to hide the thing it was speaking about. We could take all these things that were said, the painstaking precautions and detailed analyses, as so many procedures meant to evade the unbearable, too hazardous truth of sex. And the mere fact that one claimed to be speaking about it from the rarefied and neutral viewpoint of a science is in itself significant. This was in fact a science made up of evasions since, given its inability or refusal to speak of sex itself, it concerned itself primarily with aberrations, perversions, exceptional oddities, pathological abatements, and morbid aggravations. It was by the same token a science subordinated in the main to the imperatives of a morality whose divisions it reiterated under the guise of the medical norm. Claiming to speak the truth, it stirred up people's fears; to the least oscillations of sexuality, it ascribed an imaginary dynasty of evils destined to be passed on for generations; it declared the furtive customs of the timid, and the most solitary of petty manias, dangerous for the whole society; strange pleasures, it warned, would eventually result in nothing short of death: that of individuals, generations, the species itself.

It thus became associated with an insistent and indiscreet medical practice, glibly proclaiming its aversions, quick to run to the rescue of law and public opinion, more servile with respect to the powers of order than amenable to the requirements of truth. Involuntarily naïve in the best of cases, more often intentionally mendacious, in complicity with what it denounced, haughty and coquettish, it established an entire pornography of the morbid, which was characteristic of the *fin de siècle* society. In France, doctors like Garnier, Pouillet, and Ladoucette were its unglorified scribes and Rollinat its poet. But beyond these troubled pleasures, it assumed other powers; it set itself up as the supreme authority in matters of hygienic necessity, taking up the old fears of venereal affliction and combining them with the new themes of asepsis, and the great evolutionist myths with the recent institutions of public health; it claimed to ensure the physical vigor and the moral cleanliness of the social body; it promised to eliminate defective individuals, degenerate and bastardized populations. In the name of a biological and historical urgency, it justified the racisms of the state, which at the time were on the horizon. It grounded them in "truth."

When we compare these discourses on human sexuality with what was known at the time about the physiology of animal and plant reproduction, we are struck by the incongruity. Their feeble content from the standpoint of elementary rationality, not to mention scientificity, earns them a place apart in the history of knowledge. They form a strangely muddled zone. Throughout the nineteenth century, sex seems to have been incorporated into two very distinct orders of knowledge: a biology of reproduction, which developed continuously according to a general scientific normativity, and a medicine of sex conforming to quite different rules of formation. From one to the other, there was no real exchange, no reciprocal structuration; the role of the first with respect to the second was scarcely more than as a distant and quite fictitious guarantee: a blanket guarantee under cover of which moral obstacles, economic or political options, and traditional fears could be recast in a scientific-sounding vocabulary. It is as if a fundamental resistance blocked the development of a rationally formed discourse concerning human sex, its correlations, and its effects. A disparity of this sort would indicate that the aim of such a discourse was not to state the truth but to prevent its very emergence. Underlying the difference between the physiology of reproduction and the medical theories of sexuality, we would have to see something other and something more than an uneven scientific development or a disparity in the forms of rationality; the one would partake of that immense will to knowledge which has sustained the establishment of scientific discourse in the West, whereas the other would derive from a stubborn will to nonknowledge.

This much is undeniable: the learned discourse on sex that was pronounced in the nineteenth century was imbued with age-old delusions, but also with systematic blindnesses: a refusal to see and to understand; but further—and this is the crucial point—a refusal concerning the very thing that was brought to light and whose formulation was urgently solicited. For there can be no misunderstanding that is not based on a fundamental relation to truth. Evading this truth, barring access to it, masking it: these were so many local tactics which, as if by superimposition and through a last-minute detour, gave a paradoxical form to a fundamental petition to know. Choosing not to recognize was yet another vagary of the will to truth. Let Charcot's Salpêtrière serve as an example in this regard: it was an enormous apparatus for observation, with its examinations, interrogations, and experiments, but it was also a machinery for incitement, with its public presentations, its theater of ritual crises, carefully staged with the help of ether or amyl nitrate, its interplay of dialogues, palpations, laying on of hands, postures which the doctors elicited or obliterated with a gesture or a word, its hierarchy of personnel who kept watch, organized, provoked, monitored, and reported, and who accumulated an immense pyramid of observations and dossiers. It is in the context of this continuous incitement to discourse and to truth that the real mechanisms of misunderstanding (méconnaissance) operated: thus Charcot's gesture interrupting a public consultation where it began to be too manifestly a question of "that"; and the more frequent practice of deleting from the succession of dossiers what had been said and demonstrated by the patients regarding sex, but also what had been seen, provoked, solicited by the doctors themselves, things that were almost entirely omitted from the published observations.[1] The important thing, in this affair, is not that these men shut their eyes or stopped their ears, or that they were mistaken; it is rather that they constructed around and apropos of sex an immense apparatus for producing truth, even if this truth was to be masked at the last moment. The essential point is that sex was not only a matter of sensation and pleasure, of law and taboo, but also of truth and falsehood, that the truth of sex became something fundamental, useful, or dangerous, precious or formidable: in short, that sex was constituted as a problem of truth. What needs to be situated, therefore, is not the threshold of a new rationality whose discovery was marked by Freud—or someone else—but the progressive formation (and also the transformations) of that "interplay of truth and sex" which was bequeathed to us by the nineteenth century, and which we may have modified, but, lacking evidence to the contrary, have not rid ourselves of. Misunderstandings, avoidances, and evasions were only possible, and only had their effects, against the background of this strange endeavor: to tell the truth of sex. An endeavor that does not date from the nineteenth century, even if it was then that a nascent science lent it a singular form. It was the basis of all the aberrant, naïve, and cunning discourses where knowledge of sex seems to have strayed for such a long time.

Historically, there have been two great procedures for producing the truth of sex.

On the one hand, the societies—and they are numerous: China, Japan, India, Rome, the Arabo-Moslem societies—which endowed themselves with an *ars erotica*. In the erotic art, truth is drawn from pleasure itself, understood as a practice and accumulated as experience; pleasure is not considered in relation to an absolute law of the permitted and the forbidden, nor by reference to a criterion of utility, but first and foremost in relation to itself; it is experienced as pleasure, evaluated in terms of its intensity, its specific quality, its duration, its reverberations in the body and the soul. Moreover, this knowledge must be deflected back into the sexual practice itself, in order to shape it as though from within and amplify its effects. In this way, there is formed a knowledge that must remain secret, not because of an element of infamy that might attach to its object, but because of the need to hold it in the greatest reserve, since, according to tradition, it would lose its effectiveness and its virtue by being divulged. Consequently, the relationship to the master who holds the secrets is of paramount importance; only he, working alone, can transmit this art in an esoteric manner and as the culmination of an initiation in which he guides the disciple's progress with unfailing skill and severity. The effects of this masterful art, which are considerably more generous than the spareness of its prescriptions would lead one to imagine, are said to transfigure the one fortunate enough to receive its privileges: an absolute mastery of the body, a singular bliss, obliviousness to time and limits, the elixir of life, the exile of death and its threats.

On the face of it at least, our civilization possesses no *ars erotica*. In return, it is undoubtedly the only civilization to practice a *scientia sexualis;* or rather, the only civilization to have developed over the centuries procedures for telling the truth of sex which are geared to a form of knowledge-power strictly opposed to the art of initiations and the masterful secret: I have in mind the confession.

Since the Middle Ages at least, Western societies have established the confession as one of the main rituals we rely on for the production of truth: the codification of the sacrament of penance by the Lateran Council in 1215, with the resulting development of confessional techniques, the declining importance of accusatory procedures in criminal justice, the abandonment of tests of guilt (sworn statements, duels, judgments of God) and the development of methods of interrogation and inquest, the increased participation of the royal administration in the prosecution of infractions, at the expense of proceedings leading to private settlements, the setting up of tribunals of Inquisition: all this helped to give the confession a central role in the order of civil and religious powers. The evolution of the word *avowal* and of the legal function it designated is itself emblematic of this development: from being a guarantee of the status, identity, and value granted to one person by another, it came to signify someone's acknowledgment of his own actions and thoughts. For a long time, the individual was vouched for by the reference of others and the demonstration of his ties to the commonweal (family, allegiance, protection); then he was authenticated by the discourse of truth he was able or obliged to pronounce concerning himself. The truthful confession was inscribed at the heart of the procedures of individualization by power.

In any case, next to the testing rituals, next to the testimony of witnesses, and the learned methods of observation and demonstration, the confession became one of the West's most highly valued techniques for producing truth. We have since become a singularly confessing society. The confession has spread its effects far and wide. It plays a part in justice, medicine, education, family relationships, and love relations, in the most ordinary affairs of everyday life, and in the most solemn rites; one confesses one's crimes, one's sins, one's thoughts and desires, one's illnesses and troubles; one goes about telling, with the greatest precision, whatever is most difficult to tell. One confesses in public and in private, to one's parents, one's educators, one's doctor, to those one loves; one admits to oneself, in pleasure and in pain, things it would be impossible to tell to anyone else, the things people write books about. One confesses—or is forced to confess. When it is not spontaneous or dictated by some internal imperative, the confession is wrung from a person by violence or threat; it is driven from its hiding place in the soul, or extracted from the body. Since the Middle Ages, torture has accompanied it like a shadow, and supported it when it could go no further: the dark twins.[2] The most defenseless tenderness and the bloodiest of powers have a similar need of confession. Western man has become a confessing animal.

Whence a metamorphosis in literature: we have passed from a pleasure to be recounted and heard, centering on the heroic or marvelous narration of "trials" of bravery or sainthood, to a literature ordered according to the infinite task of extracting from the depths of oneself, in between the words, a truth which the very form of the confession holds out like a shimmering mirage. Whence too this new way of philosophizing: seeking the fundamental relation to the true, not simply in oneself—in some forgotten knowledge, or in a certain primal trace—but in the self-examination that yields, through a multitude of fleeting impressions, the basic certainties of consciousness. The obligation to confess is now relayed through so many different points, is so deeply ingrained in us, that we no longer perceive it as the effect of a power that constrains us; on the contrary, it seems to us that truth, lodged in our most secret nature, "demands" only to surface; that if it fails to do so, this is because a constraint holds it in place, the violence of a power weighs it down, and it can finally be articulated only at the price of a kind of liberation. Confession frees, but power reduces one to silence; truth does not belong to the order of power, but shares an original affinity with freedom: traditional themes in philosophy, which a "political history of truth" would have to overturn by showing that truth is not by nature free—nor error servile—but that its production is thoroughly imbued with relations of power. The confession is an example of this.

One has to be completely taken in by this internal ruse of confession in order to attribute a fundamental role to censorship, to taboos regarding speaking and thinking; one has to have an inverted image of power in order to believe that all these voices which have spoken so long in our civilization—repeating the formidable injunction to tell what one is and what one does, what one recollects and what one has forgotten, what one is thinking and what one thinks he is not thinking—are speaking to us of freedom. An immense labor to which the West has submitted generations in order to produce—while other forms of work ensured the accumulation of capital—men's subjection: their constitution as subjects in both senses of the word. Imagine how exorbitant must have seemed the order given to all Christians at the beginning of the thirteenth century, to kneel at least once a year and confess to all their transgressions, without omitting a single one. And think of that obscure partisan, seven centuries later, who had come to rejoin the Serbian resistance deep in the mountains; his superiors asked him to write his life story; and when he brought them a few miserable pages, scribbled in the night, they did not look at them but only said to him, "Start over, and tell the truth." Should those much-discussed language taboos make us forget this millennial yoke of confession?

From the Christian penance to the present day, sex was a privileged theme of confession. A thing that was hidden, we are told. But what if, on the contrary, it was what, in a quite particular way, one confessed? Suppose the obligation to conceal it was but another aspect of the duty to admit to it (concealing it all the more and with greater care as the confession of it was more important, requiring a stricter ritual and promising more decisive effects)? What if sex in our society, on a scale of several centuries, was something that was placed within an unrelenting system of confession? The transformation of sex into discourse, which I spoke of earlier, the dissemination and reinforcement of heterogeneous sexualities, are perhaps two elements of the same deployment: they are linked together with the help of the central element of a confession that compels individuals to articulate their sexual peculiarity—no matter how extreme. In Greece, truth and sex were linked, in the form of pedagogy, by the transmission of a precious knowledge from one body to another; sex served as a medium for initiations into learning. For us, it is in the confession that truth and sex are joined, through the obligatory and exhaustive expression of an individual secret. But this time it is truth that serves as a medium for sex and its manifestations.

The confession is a ritual of discourse in which the speaking subject is also the subject of the statement; it is also a ritual that unfolds within a power relationship, for one does not confess without the presence (or virtual presence) of a partner who is not simply the interlocutor but the authority who requires the confession, prescribes and appreciates it, and intervenes in order to judge, punish, forgive, console, and reconcile; a ritual in which the truth is corroborated by the obstacles and resistances it has had to surmount in order to be formulated; and finally, a ritual in which the expression alone, independently of its external consequences, produces intrinsic modifications in the person who articulates it: it exonerates, redeems, and purifies him; it unburdens him of his wrongs, liberates him, and promises him salvation. For centuries, the truth of sex was, at least for the most part, caught up in this discursive form. Moreover, this form was not the same as that of education (sexual education confined itself to general principles and rules of prudence); nor was it that of initiation (which remained essentially a silent practice, which the act of sexual enlightenment or deflowering merely rendered laughable or violent). As we have seen, it is a form that is far removed from the one governing the "erotic art." By virtue of the power structure immanent in it, the confessional discourse cannot come from above, as in the *ars erotica,* through the sovereign will of a master, but rather from below, as an obligatory act of speech which, under some imperious compulsion, breaks the bonds of discretion or forgetfulness. What secrecy it presupposes is not owing to the high price of what it has to say and the small number of those who are worthy of its benefits, but to its obscure familiarity and its general baseness. Its veracity is not guaranteed by the lofty authority of the magistery, nor by the tradition it transmits, but by the bond, the basic intimacy in discourse, between the one who speaks and what he is speaking about. On the other hand, the agency of domination does not reside in the one who speaks (for it is he who is constrained), but in the one who listens and says nothing; not in the one who knows and answers, but in the one who questions and is not supposed to know. And this discourse of truth finally takes effect, not in the one who receives it, but in the one from whom it is wrested. With these confessed truths, we are a long way from the learned initiations into pleasure, with their technique and their mystery. On the other hand, we belong to a society which has ordered sex's difficult knowledge, not according to the transmission of secrets, but around the slow surfacing of confidential statements.

The confession was, and still remains, the general standard governing the production of the true discourse on sex. It has undergone a considerable transformation, however. For a long time, it remained firmly entrenched in the practice of penance. But with the rise of Protestantism, the Counter Reformation, eighteenth-century pedagogy, and nineteenth-century medicine, it gradually lost its ritualistic and exclusive localization; it spread; it has been employed in a whole series of relationships: children and parents, students and educators, patients and psychiatrists, delinquents and experts. The motivations and effects it is expected to produce have varied, as have the forms it has taken: interrogations, consultations, autobiographical narratives, letters; they have been recorded, transcribed, assembled into dossiers, published, and commented on. But more important, the confession lends itself, if not to other domains, at least to new ways of exploring the existing ones. It is no longer a question simply of saying what was done—the sexual act—and how it was done; but of reconstructing, in and around the act, the thoughts that recapitulated it, the obsessions that accompanied it, the images, desires, modulations, and quality of the pleasure that animated it. For the first time no doubt, a society has taken upon itself to solicit and hear the imparting of individual pleasures.

A dissemination, then, of procedures of confession, a multiple localization of their constraint, a widening of their domain: a great archive of the pleasures of sex was gradually constituted. For a long time this archive dematerialized as it was formed. It regularly disappeared without a trace (thus suiting the purposes of the Christian pastoral) until medicine, psychiatry, and pedagogy began to solidify it: Campe, Salzmann, and especially Kaan, Krafft-Ebing, Tardieu, Molle, and Havelock Ellis carefully assembled this whole pitiful, lyrical outpouring from the sexual mosaic. Western societies thus began to keep an indefinite record of these people's pleasures. They made up a herbal of them and established a system of classification. They described their everyday deficiencies as well as their oddities or exasperations. This was an important time. It is easy to make light of these nineteenth-century psychiatrists, who made a point of apologizing for the horrors they were about to let speak, evoking "immoral behavior" or "aberrations of the genetic senses," but I am more inclined to applaud their seriousness: they had a feeling for momentous events. It was a time when the most singular pleasures were called upon to pronounce a discourse of truth concerning themselves, a discourse which had to model itself after that which spoke, not of sin and salvation, but of bodies and life processes—the discourse of science. It was enough to make one's voice tremble, for an improbable thing was then taking shape: a confessional science, a science which relied on a many-sided extortion, and took for its object what was unmentionable but admitted to nonetheless. The scientific discourse was scandalized, or in any case repelled, when it had to take charge of this whole discourse from below. It was also faced with a theoretical and methodological paradox: the long discussions concerning the possibility of constituting a science of the subject, the validity of introspection, lived experience as evidence, or the presence of consciousness to itself were responses to this problem that is inherent in the functioning of truth in our society: can one articulate the production of truth according to the old juridico-religious model of confession, and the extortion of confidential evidence according to the rules of scientific discourse? Those who believe that sex was more rigorously elided in the nineteenth century than ever before, through a formidable mechanism of blockage and a deficiency of discourse, can say what they please. There was no deficiency, but rather an excess, a redoubling, too much rather than not enough discourse, in any case an interference between two modes of production of truth: procedures of confession, and scientific discursivity.

And instead of adding up the errors, naïvetés, and moralisms that plagued the nineteenth-century discourse of truth concerning sex, we would do better to locate the procedures by which that will to knowledge regarding sex, which characterizes the modern Occident, caused the rituals of confession to function within the norms of scientific regularity: how did this immense and traditional extortion of the sexual confession come to be constituted in scientific terms?

1. *Through a clinical codification of the inducement to speak.* Combining confession with examination, the personal history with the deployment of a set of decipherable signs and symptoms; the interrogation, the exacting questionnaire, and hypnosis, with the recollection of memories and free association: all were ways of reinscribing the procedure of confession in a field of scientifically acceptable observations.

2. *Through the postulate of a general and diffuse causality.* Having to tell everything, being able to pose questions about everything, found their justification in the principle that endowed sex with an inexhaustible and polymorphous causal power. The most discrete event in one's sexual behavior—whether an accident or a deviation, a deficit or an excess—was deemed

capable of entailing the most varied consequences throughout one's existence; there was scarcely a malady or physical disturbance to which the nineteenth century did not impute at least some degree of sexual etiology. From the bad habits of children to the phthises of adults, the apoplexies of old people, nervous maladies, and the degenerations of the race, the medicine of that era wove an entire network of sexual causality to explain them. This may well appear fantastic to us, but the principle of sex as a "cause of any and everything" was the theoretical underside of a confession that had to be thorough, meticulous, and constant, and at the same time operate within a scientific type of practice. The limitless dangers that sex carried with it justified the exhaustive character of the inquisition to which it was subjected.

3.   *Through the principle of a latency intrinsic to sexuality.* If it was necessary to extract the truth of sex through the technique of confession, this was not simply because it was difficult to tell, or stricken by the taboos of decency, but because the ways of sex were obscure; it was elusive by nature; its energy and its mechanisms escaped observation, and its causal power was partly clandestine. By integrating it into the beginnings of a scientific discourse, the nineteenth century altered the scope of the confession; it tended no longer to be concerned solely with what the subject wished to hide, but with what was hidden from himself, being incapable of coming to light except gradually and through the labor of a confession in which the questioner and the questioned each had a part to play. The principle of a latency essential to sexuality made it possible to link the forcing of a difficult confession to a scientific practice. It had to be exacted, by force, since it involved something that tried to stay hidden.

4.   *Through the method of interpretation.* If one had to confess, this was not merely because the person to whom one confessed had the power to forgive, console, and direct, but because the work of producing the truth was obliged to pass through this relationship if it was to be scientifically validated. The truth did not reside solely in the subject who, by confessing, would reveal it wholly formed. It was constituted in two stages: present but incomplete, blind to itself, in the one who spoke, it could only reach completion in the one who assimilated and recorded it. It was the latter's function to verify this obscure truth: the revelation of confession had to be coupled with the decipherment of what it said. The one who listened was not simply the forgiving master, the judge who condemned or acquitted; he was the master of truth. His was a hermaneutic function. With regard to the confession, his power was not only to demand it before it was made, or decide what was to follow after it, but also to constitute a discourse of truth on the basis of its decipherment. By no longer making the confession a test, but rather a sign, and by making sexuality something to be interpreted, the nineteenth century gave itself the possibility of causing the procedures of confession to operate within the regular formation of a scientific discourse.

5.   *Through the medicalization of the effects of confession.* The obtaining of the confession and its effects were recodified as therapeutic operations. Which meant first of all that the sexual domain was no longer accounted for simply by the notions of error or sin, excess or transgression, but was placed under the rule of the normal and the pathological (which, for that matter, were the transposition of the former categories); a characteristic sexual morbidity was defined for the first time; sex appeared as an extremely unstable pathological field: a surface of repercussion for other ailments, but also the focus of a specific nosography, that of instincts, tendencies, images, pleasure, and conduct. This implied furthermore that sex would derive its meaning and its necessity from medical interventions: it would be required by the doctor, necessary for diagnosis, and effective by nature in the cure. Spoken in time, to the proper party, and by the person who was both the bearer of it and the one responsible for it, the truth healed.

Notes

1   Cf., for example, Désiré Bourneville, *Iconographie photographique de la Salpêtrière* (1878–81), pp. 110 ff. The unpublished documents dealing with the lessons of Charcot, which can still be found at the Salpêtrière, are again more explicit on this point than the published texts. The interplay of incitement and elision is clearly evident in them. A handwritten note gives an account of the session of November 25, 1877. The subject exhibits hysterical spasms; Charcot suspends an attack by placing first his hand, then the end of a baton, on the woman's ovaries. He withdraws the baton, and there is a fresh attack, which he accelerates by administering inhalations of amyl nitrate. The afflicted woman then cries out for the sex-baton in words that are devoid of any metaphor: "G. is taken away and her delirium continues."

2   Greek law had already coupled torture and confession, at least where slaves were concerned, and Imperial Roman law had widened the practice.

Chapter 54

Eve Kosofsky Sedgwick

EPISTEMOLOGY OF THE CLOSET

The *Oxford English Dictionary's* etymology of the word "closet" that precedes Eve Kosofsky Sedgwick's extract, has a usage from 1612 to 1615: "There are stage-sins and there are closet-sins". In mapping the legal responses to the act of "coming out" of the closet (publically revealing one's homosexuality), Sedgwick, one of the founders of queer theory with key books being *Between Men* (1985) and *Epistemology of the Closet* (1990), shows how the trope of being inside/outside of the closet is not necessarily a simple binary opposition, and that both phrases can be used as "evidence" against homosexuals. In other words, echoes of the 1612–15 usage still prevail today, leading Sedgwick to caution *against* regarding the "epistemology of the closet" as something which—in a progressive liberal society—is now outmoded. Arguing instead for the closet's centrality, Sedgwick suggests that as a practice and trope, the experience of the closet has been historically productive. As proof of the non-binary epistemology of the closet, Sedgwick explores a number of court cases that reveal the inconsistencies concerning attitudes towards sexual orientation, not only in law, but within society. In *Acanfora*, the plaintiff found, through two cases, that he had paradoxically disclosed both too much and not enough knowledge concerning his sexuality, leading to loss of a teaching position; in *Rowland v. Mad River Local School District*, unlike Ancanfora's public disclosure being considered at first protected speech (i.e., the First Amendment), a bisexual counsellor's coming-out was *not* awarded such consideration and protection. With these two cases alone, competing definitions of private/public space, discourse and disclosure, become unstable and contradictory in the daily lives of gays, lesbians and transgendered people. As Sedgwick suggests, the question of "coming out" intersects with the epistemology of the closet to such an extent that the two are in many respects inseparable. Sedgwick argues that this intersection can also be seen with "coming out" used as a metaphor for other categorizations, such as race and ethnicity, or body shape/size; in other words, crises of "definition" also reveal the structuring oppositions of culture in general. To elide sexualities in the more general use of "coming out" may be to unwittingly reproduce homophobic attitudes. Turning to Foucault's first volume of *The History of Sexuality*, Sedgwick suggests parallels between the Enlightenment conception of knowledge, and knowledge of sexuality; in other words, the desire to "know" is always already the desire to know about sex. While initially this was articulated via same-sex desire, Sedgwick argues that repressive forces throughout the eighteenth and nineteenth centuries led to a "refusal" and an interiorization within psychoanalytical discourse of same-sex desire. Again, this is not a dated notion: Sedgwick refers to the court case *Bowers v. Hardwick,* which argued in 1986 that "sodomy" was illegal. Subversively, and given the dissenting opinions of some of the judges, Sedgwick imaginatively reconstructs the case in relation to closeted/out subjects, creatively questioning how the case could have proceeded differently from that of the majority/ heterosexually normative and oppressive decision, one that was not overruled until 2003. Returning also to the question of other "coming out" parallels, Sedgwick follows Proust in exploring the Book of Esther in relation to Jewish "self-identification" and "revelation of identity".

Closet

From the OED:

Closet sb. [a. OF. *closet,* dim. of *clos* :-L. *clausun*]

1. A room for privacy or retirement; a private room; an inner chamber; formerly often = *bower*; in later use always a small room.

    1370 A slepe hym toke In hys closet.

    1586 We doe call the most secret place in the house appropriate unto our owne private studies . . . a Closet.

    1611 Let the bridegroome goe forth of his chamber, and the bride out of her closet.

    1750 A sudden intruder into the closet of an author.

    b. *esp.* Such a room as the place of private devotion (with allusion to 1611 version of Matt. vi.6). *arch.*

    c. As the place of private study or secluded speculation; *esp.* in reference to mere theories as opposed to practical measures.

    1746 The knowledge of the world is only to be acquired in the world, and not in the Closet.

2. The private apartment of a monarch or potentate.

3. a. A private repository of valuables or (*esp.* in later use) curiosities; a cabinet. *arch.* or *Obs.*

    b. A small side-room or recess for storing utensils, provisions, etc.; a cupboard.

    c. *Skeleton in the closet* (or *cupboard*): a private or concealed trouble in one's house or circumstances, ever present, and ever liable to come into view.

4. With special reference to size: Any small room: especially one belonging to or communicating with a larger.

5. *fig.* The den or lair of a wild beast. *Obs.*

6. a. *transf.* That which affords retirement like a private chamber, or which encloses like a cabinet; a hidden or secret place, retreat, recess.

    1450–1530 Went the sonne of god oute of the pryuy closet of the maydens wombe.

    1594 This skinne . . . is also called the little closet of the heart.

7. Short for 'Closet of ease,' 'water-closet'

    1662 A Closet of ease.

9. A sewer. *Sc. Obs.*

    [Translating L. *cloaca*: origin doubtful; there is nothing like it in French.]

10. *attrib.,* as, . . . a place . . . of private study and speculation, as *closet- lucubration, -philosopher, -politician, -speculation, -student, -study,* etc.

1649 Reasons, why he should rather pray by the officiating mouth of a
       Closet-chaplain.
1649 They knew the King . . . to have suckt from them and their
       Closetwork all his impotent principles of Tyrannie and
       Superstition.
1612–15 There are stage-sins and there are closet-sins.

Epistemology of the closet

> The lie, the perfect lie, about people we know, about the relations we have had
> with them, about our motive for some action, formulated in totally different
> terms, the lie as to what we are, whom we love, what we feel with regard to
> people who love us . . . —that lie is one of the few things in the world that can
> open windows for us on to what is new and unknown, that can awaken in us
> sleeping senses for the contemplation of universes that otherwise we should
> never have known.
>
> Proust, *The Captive*

The epistemology of the closet is not a dated subject or a superseded regime of knowing.
While the events of June, 1969, and later vitally reinvigorated many people's sense of the
potency, magnetism, and promise of gay self-disclosure, nevertheless the reign of the telling
secret was scarcely overturned with Stonewall. Quite the opposite, in some ways. To the fine
antennae of public attention the freshness of every drama of (especially involuntary) gay
uncovering seems if anything heightened in surprise and delectability, rather than staled, by
the increasingly intense atmosphere of public articulations of and about the love that is famous
for daring not speak its name. So resilient and productive a structure of narrative will not
readily surrender its hold on important forms of social meaning. As D. A. Miller points out
in an aegis-creating essay, secrecy can function as

> the subjective practice in which the oppositions of private/public, inside/
> outside, subject/object are established, and the sanctity of their first term kept
> inviolate. And the phenomenon of the "open secret" does not, as one might
> think, bring about the collapse of those binarisms and their ideological effects,
> but rather attests to their fantasmatic recovery.[1]

Even at an individual level, there are remarkably few of even the most openly gay people who
are not deliberately in the closet with someone personally or economically or institutionally
important to them. Furthermore, the deadly elasticity of heterosexist presumption means
that, like Wendy in *Peter Pan*, people find new walls springing up around them even as they
drowse: every encounter with a new classful of students, to say nothing of a new boss, social
worker, loan officer, landlord, doctor, erects new closets whose fraught and characteristic
laws of optics and physics exact from at least gay people new surveys, new calculations, new
draughts and requisitions of secrecy or disclosure. Even an out gay person deals daily with
interlocutors about whom she doesn't know whether they know or not; it is equally difficult
to guess for any given interlocutor whether, if they did know, the knowledge would seem
very important. Nor—at the most basic level—is it unaccountable that someone who
wanted a job, custody or visiting rights, insurance, protection from violence, from "therapy,"
from distorting stereotype, from insulting scrutiny, from simple insult, from forcible
interpretation of their bodily product, could deliberately choose to remain in or to reenter

the closet in some or all segments of their life. The gay closet is not a feature only of the lives of gay people. But for many gay people it is still the fundamental feature of social life; and there can be few gay people, however courageous and forthright by habit, however fortunate in the support of their immediate communities, in whose lives the closet is not still a shaping presence.

To say, as I will be saying here, that the epistemology of the closet has given an overarching consistency to gay culture and identity throughout this century is not to deny that crucial possibilities around and outside the closet have been subject to most consequential change, for gay people. There are risks in making salient the continuity and centrality of the closet, in a historical narrative that does not have as a fulcrum a saving vision—whether located in past or future—of its apocalyptic rupture. A meditation that lacks that particular Utopian organization will risk glamorizing the closet itself, if only by default; will risk presenting as inevitable or somehow valuable its exactions, its deformations, its disempowerment and sheer pain. If these risks are worth running, it is partly because the nonutopian traditions of gay writing, thought, and culture have remained so inexhaustibly and gorgeously productive for later gay thinkers, in the absence of a rationalizing or often even of a forgiving reading of their politics. The epistemology of the closet has also been, however, on a far vaster scale and with a less honorific inflection, inexhaustibly productive of modern Western culture and history at large. While that may be reason enough for taking it as a subject of interrogation, it should not be reason enough for focusing scrutiny on those who inhabit the closet (however equivocally) to the exclusion of those in the ambient heterosexist culture who enjoin it and whose intimate representational needs it serves in a way less extortionate to themselves.

I scarcely know at this stage a consistent alternative proceeding, however; and it may well be that, for reasons to be discussed, no such consistency is possible. At least to enlarge the circumference of scrutiny and to vary by some new assays of saltation the angle of its address will be among the methodological projects of this discussion.

***

In Montgomery County, Maryland, in 1973, an eighth-grade earth science teacher named Acanfora was transferred to a nonteaching position by the Board of Education when they learned he was gay. When Acanfora spoke to news media, such as "60 Minutes" and the Public Broadcasting System, about his situation, he was refused a new contract entirely. Acanfora sued. The federal district court that first heard his case supported the action and rationale of the Board of Education, holding that Acanfora's recourse to the media had brought undue attention to himself and his sexuality, to a degree that would be deleterious to the educational process. The Fourth Circuit Court of Appeals disagreed. They considered Acanfora's public disclosures to be protected speech under the First Amendment. Although they overruled the lower court's rationale, however, the appellate court affirmed its decision not to allow Acanfora to return to teaching. Indeed, they denied his standing to bring the suit in the first place, on the grounds that he had failed to note on his original employment application that he had been, in college, an officer of a student homophile organization—a notation that would, as school officials admitted in court, have prevented his ever being hired. The rationale for keeping Acanfora out of his classroom was thus no longer that he had disclosed too much about his homosexuality, but quite the opposite, that he had not disclosed enough.[2] The Supreme Court declined to entertain an appeal.

It is striking that each of the two rulings in *Acanfora* emphasized that the teacher's homosexuality "itself" would not have provided an acceptable ground for denying him employment. Each of the courts relied in its decision on an implicit distinction between the supposedly protected and bracketable fact of Acanfora's homosexuality proper, on the one hand, and on the other hand his highly vulnerable management of information about it. So very vulnerable does this latter exercise prove to be, however, and vulnerable to such a contradictory array of interdictions, that the space for simply existing as a gay person who is a teacher is in fact bayonetted through and through, from both sides, by the vectors of a disclosure at once compulsory and forbidden.

A related incoherence couched in the resonant terms of the distinction of *public* from *private* riddles the contemporary legal space of gay being. When it refused in 1985 to consider an appeal in *Rowland v. Mad River Local School District*, the U.S. Supreme Court let stand the firing of a bisexual guidance counselor for coming out to some of her colleagues; the act of coming out was judged not to be highly protected under the First Amendment because it does not constitute speech on a matter "of public concern." It was, of course, only eighteen months later that the same U.S. Supreme Court ruled, in response to Michael Hardwick's contention that it's nobody's business if he do, that it ain't: if homosexuality is not, however densely adjudicated, to be considered a matter of *public* concern, neither in the Supreme Court's binding opinion does it subsist under the mantle of the *private*.[3]

The most obvious fact about this history of judicial formulations is that it codifies an excruciating system of double binds, systematically oppressing gay people, identities, and acts by undermining through contradictory constraints on discourse the grounds of their very being. That immediately political recognition may be supplemented, however, by a historical hypothesis that goes in the other direction. I want to argue that a lot of the energy of attention and demarcation that has swirled around issues of homosexuality since the end of the nineteenth century, in Europe and the United States, has been impelled by the distinctively indicative relation of homosexuality to wider mappings of secrecy and disclosure, and of the private and the public, that were and are critically problematical for the gender, sexual, and economic structures of the heterosexist culture at large, mappings whose enabling but dangerous incoherence has become oppressively, durably condensed in certain figures of homosexuality. "The closet" and "coming out," now verging on all-purpose phrases for the potent crossing and recrossing of almost any politically changed lines of representation, have been the gravest and most magnetic of those figures.

The closet is the defining structure for gay oppression in this century. The legal couching, by civil liberties lawyers, of *Bowers v. Hardwick* as an issue in the first place of a Constitutional right to privacy, and the liberal focus in the aftermath of that decision on the image of the *bedroom invaded by policemen*—"Letting the Cops Back into Michael Hardwick's Bedroom," the *Native* headlined[4]—as though political empowerment were a matter of getting the cops back on the street where they belong and sexuality back into the impermeable space where *it* belongs, are among other things extensions of, and testimony to the power of, the image of the closet. The durability of the image is perpetuated even as its intelligibility is challenged in antihomophobic responses like the following, to *Hardwick*, addressed to gay readers:

> What can you do—alone? The answer is obvious. You're *not* alone, and you can't afford to try to be. That closet door—never very secure as protection—is even more dangerous now. You must come out, for your own sake and for the sake of all of us.[5]

The image of coming out regularly interfaces the image of the closet, and its seemingly unambivalent public siting can be counterposed as a salvational epistemologic certainty against the very equivocal privacy afforded by the closet: "If every gay person came out to his or her family," the same article goes on, "a hundred million Americans could be brought to our side. Employers and straight friends could mean a hundred million more." And yet the Mad River School District's refusal to hear a woman's coming out as an authentically public speech act is echoed in the frigid response given many acts of coming out: "That's fine, but why did you think I'd want to know about it?"

Gay thinkers of this century have, as we'll see, never been blind to the damaging contradictions of this compromised metaphor of *in* and *out* of the closet of privacy. But its origins in European culture are, as the writings of Foucault have shown, so ramified—and its relation to the "larger," i.e., ostensibly nongay-related, topologies of privacy in the culture is, as the figure of Foucault dramatized, so critical, so enfolding, so representational—that the simple vesting of some alternative metaphor has never, either, been a true possibility.

I recently heard someone on National Public Radio refer to the sixties as the decade when Black people came out of the closet. For that matter, I recently gave an MLA talk purporting to explain how it's possible to come out of the closet as a fat woman. The apparent floating free from its gay origins of that phrase "coming out of the closet" in recent usage might suggest that the trope of the closet is so close to the heart of some modern preoccupations that it could be, or has been, evacuated of its historical gay specificity. But I hypothesize that exactly the opposite is true. I think that a whole cluster of the most crucial sites for the contestation of meaning in twentieth-century Western culture are consequentially and quite indelibly marked with the historical specificity of homosocial/ homosexual definition, notably but not exclusively male, from around the turn of the century.[6] Among those sites are, as I have indicated, the pairings secrecy/disclosure and private/public. Along with and sometimes through these epistemologically charged pairings, condensed in the figures of "the closet" and "coming out," this very specific crisis of definition has then ineffaceably marked other pairings as basic to modern cultural organization as masculine/feminine, majority/minority, innocence/initiation, natural/artificial, new/old, growth/decadence, urbane/provincial, health/illness, same/different, cognition/paranoia, art/kitsch, sincerity/sentimentality, and voluntarity/addiction. So permeative has the suffusing stain of homo/heterosexual crisis been that to discuss any of these indices in any context, in the absence of an antihomophobic analysis, must perhaps be to perpetuate unknowingly compulsions implicit in each.

For any modern question of sexuality, knowledge/ignorance is more than merely one in a metonymic chain of such binarisms. The process, narrowly bordered at first in European culture but sharply broadened and accelerated after the late eighteenth century, by which "knowledge" and "sex" become conceptually inseparable from one another—so that knowledge means in the first place sexual knowledge; ignorance, sexual ignorance; and epistemological pressure of any sort seems a force increasingly saturated with sexual impulsion—was sketched in Volume I of Foucault's *History of Sexuality*. In a sense, this was a process, protracted almost to retardation, of exfoliating the biblical genesis by which what we now know as sexuality is fruit—apparently the only fruit—to be plucked from the tree of knowledge. Cognition itself, sexuality itself, and transgression itself have always been ready in Western culture to be magnetized into an unyielding though not an unfissured alignment with one another, and the period initiated by Romanticism accomplished this disposition through a remarkably broad confluence of different languages and institutions.

In some texts, such as Diderot's *La Religieuse*, that were influential early in this process, the desire that represents sexuality per se, and hence sexual knowledge and knowledge per se, is a same-sex desire.[7] This possibility, however, was repressed with increasing energy, and hence increasing visibility, as the nineteenth-century culture of the individual proceeded to elaborate a version of knowledge/sexuality increasingly structured by its pointed cognitive *refusal* of sexuality between women, between men. The gradually reifying effect of this refusal[8] meant that by the end of the nineteenth century, when it had become fully current— as obvious to Queen Victoria as to Freud—that knowledge meant sexual knowledge, and secrets sexual secrets, there had in fact developed one particular sexuality that was distinctively constituted *as* secrecy: the perfect object for the by now insatiably exacerbated epistemological/sexual anxiety of the turn-of-the-century subject. Again, it was a long chain of originally scriptural identifications of a sexuality with a particular cognitive positioning (in this case, St. Paul's routinely reproduced and reworked denomination of sodomy as the crime whose name is not to be uttered, hence whose accessibility to knowledge is uniquely preterited) that culminated in Lord Alfred Douglas's epochal public utterance, in 1894, "*I am* the Love that dare not speak its name."[9] In such texts as *Billy Budd* and *Dorian Gray* and through their influence, the subject—the thematics—of knowledge and ignorance themselves, of innocence and initiation, of secrecy and disclosure, became not contingently but integrally infused with one particular object of cognition: no longer sexuality as a whole but even more specifically, now, the homosexual topic. And the condensation of the world of possibilities surrounding same-sex sexuality—including, shall we say, both gay desires and the most rabid phobias against them—the condensation of this plurality to *the homosexual topic* that now formed the accusative case of modern processes of personal knowing, was not the least infliction of the turn-of-the-century crisis of sexual definition.

To explore the differences it makes when secrecy itself becomes manifest as *this* secret, let me begin by twining together in a short anachronistic braid a variety of exemplary narratives—literary, biographical, imaginary—that begin with the moment on July 1, 1986, when the decision in *Bowers v. Hardwick* was announced, a moment which, sandwiched between a weekend of Gay Pride parades nationwide, the announcement of a vengeful new AIDS policy by the Justice Department, and an upcoming media-riveting long weekend of hilarity or hysteria focused on the national fetishization in a huge hollow blind spike-headed female body of the abstraction Liberty, and occurring in an ambient medium for gay men and their families and friends of wave on wave of renewed loss, mourning, and refreshed personal fear, left many people feeling as if at any rate one's own particular car had finally let go forever of the tracks of the roller coaster.

In many discussions I heard or participated in immediately after the Supreme Court ruling in *Bowers v. Hardwick,* antihomophobic or gay women and men speculated—more or less empathetically or venomously—about the sexuality of the people most involved with the decision. The question kept coming up, in different tones, of what it could have felt like to be a closeted gay court assistant, or clerk, or justice, who might have had some degree, even a very high one, of instrumentality in conceiving or formulating or "refining" or logistically facilitating this ruling, these ignominious majority opinions, the assaultive sentences in which they were framed.

That train of painful imaginings was fraught with the epistemological distinctiveness of gay identity and gay situation in our culture. Vibrantly resonant as the image of the closet is for many modern oppressions, it is indicative for homophobia *in a way it cannot be for other oppressions.* Racism, for instance, is based on a stigma that is visible in all but exceptional cases (cases that are neither rare nor irrelevant, but that delineate the outlines rather than coloring the center of racial experience); so are the oppressions based on gender, age, size, physical handicap. Ethnic/cultural/religious oppressions such as anti-Semitism are more analogous in that the stigmatized individual has at least notionally some discretion—although, importantly, it is never to be taken for granted how much—over other people's knowledge of her or his membership in the group: one could "come out as" a Jew or Gypsy, in a heterogeneous urbanized society, much more intelligibly than one could typically "come out as," say, female, Black, old, a wheelchair user, or fat. A (for instance) Jewish or Gypsy identity, and hence a Jewish or Gypsy secrecy or closet, would nonetheless differ again from the distinctive gay versions of these things in its clear ancestral linearity and answerability, in the roots (however tortuous and ambivalent) of cultural identification through each individual's originary culture of (at a minimum) the family.

Proust, in fact, insistently suggests as a sort of limit-case of one kind of coming out precisely the drama of Jewish self-identification, embodied in the Book of Esther and in Racine's recasting of it that is quoted throughout the "Sodom and Gomorrah" books of *A la recherche*. The story of Esther seems a model for a certain simplified but highly potent imagining of coming out and its transformative potential. In concealing her Judaism from her husband, King Assuérus (Ahasuerus), Esther the Queen feels she is concealing, simply, her identity: "The King is to this day unaware who I am."[10] Esther's deception is made necessary by the powerful ideology that makes Assuérus categorize her people as unclean ("cette source impure" [1039]) and an abomination against nature ("Il nous croit en horreur à toute la nature" [174]). The sincere, relatively abstract Jew-hatred of this fuddled but omnipotent king undergoes constant stimulation from the grandiose cynicism of his advisor Aman (Haman), who dreams of an entire planet exemplarily cleansed of the perverse element.

I want it said one day in awestruck centuries:
"There once used to be Jews, there was an insolent race;
widespread, they used to cover the whole face of the earth;
a single one dared draw on himself the wrath of Aman,
at once they disappeared, every one, from the earth."

(476–80)

The king acquiesces in Aman's genocidal plot, and Esther is told by her cousin, guardian, and Jewish conscience Mardochée (Mordecai) that the time for her revelation has come; at this moment the particular operation of suspense around her would be recognizable to any gay person who has inched toward coming out to homophobic parents. "And if I perish, I perish," she says in the Bible (Esther 4:16). That the avowal of her secret identity will have an immense potency is clear, is the premise of the story. All that remains to be seen is whether under its explosive pressure the king's "political" animus against her kind will demolish his "personal" love for her, or vice versa: will he declare her as good as, or better, dead? Or will he soon be found at a neighborhood bookstore, hoping not to be recognized by the salesperson who is ringing up his copy of *Loving Someone Jewish*?

The biblical story and Racinian play, bearable to read in their balance of the holocaustal with the intimate only because one knows how the story will end,[11] are enactments of a particular dream or fantasy of coming out. Esther's eloquence, in the event, is resisted by only five lines of her husband's demurral or shock: essentially at the instant she names herself, both her ruler and Aman see that the anti-Semites are lost ("*AMAN, tout bas*: Je tremble" [1033]). Revelation of identity in the space of intimate love effortlessly overturns an entire public systematics of the natural and the unnatural, the pure and the impure. The peculiar strike that the story makes to the heart is that Esther's small, individual ability to risk losing the love and countenance of her master has the power to save not only her own space in life but her people.

It would not be hard to imagine a version of *Esther* set in the Supreme Court in the days immediately before the decision in *Bowers v. Hardwick*. Cast as the ingenue in the title role a hypothetical closeted gay clerk, as Assuérus a hypothetical Justice of the same gender who is about to make a majority of five in support of the Georgia law. The Justice has grown fond of the clerk, oddly fonder than s/he is used to being of clerks, and . . . In our compulsive recursions to the question of the sexualities of court personnel, such a scenario was close to the minds of my friends and me in many forms. In the passionate dissenting opinions, were there not the traces of others' comings-out already performed; could even the dissents themselves represent such performances, Justice coming out to Justice? With the blood-let tatters of what risky comings-out achieved and then overridden—friends', clerks', employees', children's—was the imperious prose of the majority opinions lined? More painful and frequent were thoughts of all the coming out that had not happened, of the women and men who had not in some more modern idiom said, with Esther,

> I dare to beg you, both for my own life
> and the sad days of an ill-fated people
> that you have condemned to perish with me.

(1029–31)

What was lost in the absence of such scenes was not, either, the opportunity to evoke with eloquence a perhaps demeaning pathos like Esther's. It was something much more precious: evocation, articulation, of the dumb Assuérus in all his imperial ineloquent bathos of unknowing: "A périr? Vous? Quel peuple?" ("To perish? You? What people?" [1032]). "What people?" indeed—why, as it oddly happens, the very people whose eradication he personally is just on the point of effecting. But only with the utterance of these blank syllables, making the weight of Assuérus's powerful ignorance suddenly audible—not least to him—in the same register as the weight of Esther's and Mardochée's private knowledge, can any open flow of power become possible. It is here that Aman begins to tremble.

Just so with coming out: it can bring about the revelation of a powerful unknowing *as* unknowing, not as a vacuum or as the blank it can pretend to be but as a weighty and occupied and consequential epistemological space. Esther's avowal allows Assuérus to make visible two such spaces at once: "You?" "What people?" He has been blindly presuming about herself,[12] and simply blind to the race to whose extinction he has pledged himself. What? *you're* one of *those*? Huh? *you're* a *what*? This frightening thunder can also, however, be the sound of manna falling.

Notes

1   D. A. Miller, "Secret Subjects, Open Secrets," in his *The Novel and the Police*, p. 207.
2   On this case see Michael W. La Morte, "Legal Rights and Responsibilities of Homosexuals in Public Education," *Journal of Law and Education* 4, no. 23 (July 1975): 449–67, esp. 450–53; and Jeanne La Borde Scholz, "Comment: Out of the Closet, Out of a Job: Due Process in Teacher Disqualification," *Hastings Law Quarterly* 6 (Winter 1979): 663–717, esp. 682–84.
3   Nan Hunter, director of the ACLU's Lesbian and Gay Rights Project, analyzed *Rowland* in "Homophobia and Academic Freedom," a talk at the 1986 Modern Language Association National Convention. There is an interesting analysis of the limitations, for gay-rights purposes, of both the right of privacy and the First Amendment guarantee of free speech, whether considered separately or in tandem, in "Notes: The Constitutional Status of Sexual Orientation: Homosexuality as a Suspect Classification," *Harvard Law Review* 98 (April 1985): 1285–1307, esp. 1288–97. For a discussion of related legal issues that is strikingly apropos of, and useful for, the argument made in *Epistemology of the Closet*, see Janet E. Halley, "The Politics of the Closet: Towards Equal Protection for Gay, Lesbian, and Bisexual Identity," *UCLA Law Review* 36 (1989): 915–76.
4   *New York Native*, no. 169 (July 14, 1986): 11.
5   Philip Bockman, "A Fine Day," *New York Native*, no. 175 (August 25, 1986): 13.
6   A reminder that "the closet" retains (at least the chronic potential of) its gay semantic specification: a media flap in June, 1989, when a Republican National Committee memo calling for House Majority Leader Thomas Foley to "come out of the liberal closet" and comparing his voting record with that of an openly gay Congressman, Barney Frank, was widely perceived (and condemned) as insinuating that Foley himself is gay. The committee's misjudgment about whether it could maintain deniability for the insinuation is an interesting index to how unpredictably full or empty of gay specificity this locution may be perceived to be.
7   On this, see my "Privilege of Unknowing."
8   On this, see *Between Men*.

9   Lord Alfred Douglas, "Two Loves," *The Chameleon* 1 (1894): 28 (emphasis added).

10   Jean Racine, *Esther,* ed. H. R. Roach (London: George G. Harrap, 1949), line 89; my translation. Further citations of this play will be noted by line number in the text.

11   It is worth remembering, of course, that the biblical story still ends with mass slaughter: while Racine's king *revokes* his orders (1197), the biblical king *reverses* his (Esther 8:5), licensing the Jews' killing of "seventy and five thousand" (9:16) of their enemies, including children and women (8:11).

12   In Voltaire's words, "un roi insensé qui a passé six mois avec sa femme sans savoir, sans s'informer même qui elle est" (in Racine, *Esther*, pp. 83–84).

Chapter 55

Chrysanthi Nigianni

BUTTERFLY KISS

The contagious kiss of becoming-lesbian

Beginning with an overview of Deleuze and Guattari's "schizoanalysis" (see Chapter 28) Chrysanthi Nigianni adopts the "schizoanalytic framework" of desiring machines, energy flows, intensities, couplings and uncouplings, to create a non-normative engagement with the presentation of lesbianism. Nigianni's work in this area includes co-editorship of a special edition of *New Formations* on the "turn to Deleuze" (vol. 68), and the co-edited book *Deleuze and Queer Theory* (2009). What Deleuze and Guattari's anti-Oedipal approach offers queer theory is a rejection of "master" signifiers, such as the law-of-the-father/the phallus (Lacanian psychoanalysis), castration/taboos (Freudian psychoanalysis), or the logos (transcendent or religious knowledge/law/language). Instead of these stabilized, humanistic and hetero-normative notions of being—often based upon the notion that lesbianism is negatively brought about via some kind of "lack"—Nigianni adopts an anti-Oedipal approach to reveal a "becoming-lesbian", i.e., a *resisting subjectivity* that is always in dialogue and process, creating a new erotic ontology which describes the productivity of a "virtual body" in the sense of a body which is always open to potentiality and the unknown. But to move beyond a hierarchical semiotics involves a schizoanalytic rejection of the normative thought processes of "analogy, comparison, resemblance and identity". This is partly an anti-Capitalist process, since commodification (of the body, the subject, of sexuality) involves definable and stabilized subjectivities. It is also a process that involves replacing logical and commodifying systems with creativity and poetic expression. Nigianna suggests that Deleuze's concept of the "time-image"—that is to say a cinematic/virtual, non-representational image—facilitates the production of "becoming-lesbian". Subsequently, this is illuminated by Nigianna through her "cine-schizoanalysis" of the film *Butterfly Kiss* (dir. Winterbottom, 1995), facilitating an erotic/poetic *mapping* of lesbianism, rather than an appropriation or reduction of becoming, subsumed thereby into hierarchical being. This notion of the cinematic as affect-based replaces the Oedipal transition into the law of a fully symbolized semiotics. In other words, thinking Nigianni's argument through from a Kristevan perspective (see Chapter 13) the rhythms and patterns prior to symbolic, patriarchal ordering, remain intensities that disruptively recur, and in this case, can replace that ordering. It also replaces the single, apparently objective voice with a multitude or heterogenous collective of different voices, none of them claiming to transcend any other point of view. In the section "'I' for Invisibility", the essay switches into a performative, schizo-mode of writing, deliberately falling "short of the rules" to remain mobile and to present differing intensities, strategically missing "goals, orientations, end points" to replace the singular with the relational. Whole objects are replaced by part-objects, ordered linear conceptions of subjectivity are replaced by anarchic "differentiations", and cultural codes used to normatively eroticize parts of the body are deconstructed. Deleuze and Guattari suggest that new "organs" can arise, here re-appropriated for a lesbian conception of the body. Nigianni also rejects a subjectivity based upon the Judeo-Christian notion of "the face", i.e., the ethical point of recognizing the Other in the work of Levinas, as well as notions of sacrificial redemption. Instead, "cine-schizoanalysis" allows for an exploration of the body-without-organs, that is to say, letting go of a hierarchical Judeo-Christian concept of the body in favour of becoming-woman and becoming-lesbian.

> Art is never an end in itself. It is only an instrument for tracing lines of lives, that is to say, all these real becomings that are not simply produced in art, all these active flights that do not consist in fleeing into art . . . but rather sweep it away with them toward the realms of the asignifying, the asubjective . . . (Deleuze and Guattari 2003: 187)

This essay will attempt to conduct a twofold experiment: on the one hand, it will attempt to make the shift from a psychoanalytic thinking about lesbianism as identity corresponding to a certain psycho-social mode of 'being a lesbian', to a schizoanalytic thinking that conceives of it as a becoming-lesbian, a schizophrenic process that constitutes 'a rupture, an eruption, a break-through which smashes the continuity of personality and takes it on a kind of trip through "more reality"' (Deleuze 2006: 27). The essay will thus argue for a 'schizophrenic' lesbian desire not in its clinical but in its critical meaning: an 'anoedipal, schizoid, included, and inclusive' desire whose excess (rather than lack) violates strict definitions and exceeds linguistic meaning and signifiers; a desire whose 'meaning' can be nothing else than its forces and effects.

Deleuze's use of medical terms in philosophy resonates with his belief that philosophy, art and science, although distinct and autonomous, necessarily enter into relations of mutual resonance and exchange.[1] Thus, Deleuze and Guattari depart from a clinical concept so as to open it up and reveal intensities of becomings that lurk underneath 'normal' bodies and 'healthy' subjectivities, to shed light on migrations that are under way on an affective rather than perceptive or cognitive level; in other words, to trace lines of becomings:

> *I feel* that I am becoming woman, *I feel* that I am becoming God, that I am becoming clairvoyant, that I am becoming pure matter . . . (Deleuze 2006: 22)

Rather than restricting schizophrenia to narrowly defined psychological characteristics and medical symptoms, Deleuze and Guattari conceive of it in broader social, cultural, libidinal and material terms. More precisely, schizophrenia constitutes a dynamic both produced and repressed by capitalism: a revolutionary code-breaking force, a process of constant erasure of stable meanings and beliefs, an intensification which leads to an a-logical explosion of signs that in turn end up losing their (common) sense or meaning. In other words, schizophrenia as a process disrupts the static structures of signification, by initiating a frenzied process of endless re-signification; a process which ends up producing 'a properly schizophrenic non-sense' (Deleuze 2006: 22).

Thus, schizophrenia for Deleuze and Guattari is a form of 'unlimited semiosis', both psychical and social, which the system has to control and constrain for its own survival through the promotion of a counter-dynamic, what they call 'paranoia' (with the schizophrenic as a medical case being produced by the repression caused by paranoia):

> Whereas schizophrenia designates the affirmation of the signifying process itself
> without stable codes or familiar meaning, in paranoia not only is everything
> coded and meaningful, but it all means the same thing – whatever the terrifying
> god or despot says it means. (Deleuze and Guattari 2004: 192–94)

Hence, while schizophrenia is related to a free, immanent, (a-)signifying process of auto-creation that produces new meanings, which overturn established truths, paranoia is a process of submission under one dominant, transcendent signifier; hence, a controlled production of equivalences that supports and enhances the established order of things. Consequently, for Deleuze, any description of schizophrenia in negative terms like those of 'dissociation', 'autism' and 'loss of reality' is convenient and politically useful for those who wish to silence schizophrenics and deprive them of their 'ability' to disrupt the political economy of capitalism; an economy developed upon acts of axiomatisation, capture and appropriation, which in turn engender a reality of static molarities, frozen categories and suffocating identities, all subsuming to a superior signifier (to name but a few, the phallus, the-name-of-the-Father, logos, the capital, discourse, etc.). Hence, what is threatening about the schizophrenic is his/her inherent instability, his/her stubborn resistance against any form of identity, his/her allergic reaction to processes of coding and overcoding, his/her 'incapacity' to conform to any category of 'being', even that of the self. And it is precisely these 'incapacities' that provide the schizophrenic with a revolutionary force, with active lines of flight that escape the 'normality' of a system based on codification and subjectification:

> Unlike the paranoid whose delirium consists of restoring codes and reinventing
> territories, the schizophrenic never ceases to go one more step in a movement
> of self-decoding and self-deterritorialisation (this is the schizophrenic break-
> through, the voyage or trip, the process). The schizophrenic is like the limit
> of our society but an abhorred, always suppressed, always cast out. (Deleuze
> 2006: 28)

Thus, by turning the focus on schizophrenia as a positive and revolutionary breakthrough (and not a breakdown), 'not only [as] a human fact but also a possibility for thought' (Deleuze 2004: 185), Deleuze and Guattari develop a counter to the psychoanalytic form of analysis which is non-transferential, non-interpretative but instead inventive (Guattari 1995): schizoanalysis, which aims at a reconceptualisation of both desire and body in non-psychoanalytic terms. More precisely, schizoanalysis argues for a desire which is anoedipal, spontaneous, free from social coding (what they call 'desiring machines' conceived of as 'endless connections, nonexclusive disjunctions, non-specific conjunctions, partial objects and flows' (Deleuze and Guattari 2004: 61)) while it re-posits the body in terms of the concept of the 'Body without Organs'; that is, the body seen primarily as a potentiality, free from the restraints of the organism and the hierarchical organisation of (signified) organs.

Consequently, approaching lesbianism through a schizoanalytic framework means a de-oedipalization of lesbian desire: a desire free from fixed subjectivity and complete-object representations, which is positive and productive (rather than reproductive) by producing 'anarchic multiplicities',[2] myriad partial-object connections, unnatural relations of an 'estranged sameness'[3] that defy dialectic alterity; a desire that is not constituted by lack and negation (for example, the trauma of castration) but by positivity and affirmation. No longer an issue of an either/or identification, an either/or object-choice or orientation, lesbian desire is no longer considered to be springing from an originary loss (the maternal body) or lack (the phallus), but constitutes instead one among other expressions of the desire to become-woman-other that leads to a process of serial differentiations: a differentiation emerging from productive (non-)sameness, from a monstrous auto-affection. In other words, it leads to the multiplication of the potentialities of the female body: a body in which the sexual investments of specific organs and erotogenic zones (that is, signified differences that are produced by a devaluing process of othering) give way to zones of intensity, affective lines that sketch out the Body without Organs (BwO).[4] A body in absolute nakedness (disinvested from fantasies, social significations and cultural codes), an intensive raw materiality, an organless body inhabited by impersonal and de-facialised organs[5] of an infinite nature that lack nothing: 'a' breast, 'a' mouth, 'a' hand, whose connections eschew interpretations and thus become a-signifying. Connections between 'a' mouth and 'a' breast, 'a' nose and 'a' rose, 'a' finger and 'a' cunt, which produce new intensities and unknown sensations, and enhance a desire that desires only its own expansion and proliferation. Within this new economy, organs acquire new meanings intrinsically tied to the temporality and the singularity of the machinic connection they are part of, so that:

> the fingers become flowers, become silver become torture instruments . . . these bodily relations are not anonymous, quick encounters, but rather a relation to a singularity or particularity, always specific never generalisable. Neither anonymous nor yet entirely personal, they are still an intimacy of encounter, a pleasure/unpleasure always of and for themselves. (Grosz 1995:182–83)

It is through this molecular revolution, through the eruption of 'new' organs produced by micro-affections, that the virtual body is born: no longer a 'possible' body that is realised in pre-determined choices of 'straightness', 'gayness', 'lesbianism', but the 'unknown' body of a becoming (-lesbian) as the overcoming of closure and permanence in bodily connections and desiring encounters, as the loss of faith in dominant signifiers and the structures of signification. Hence, becoming-lesbian constitutes the woman's becoming-woman process; that is, the experiencing and exploration of the creative and experimental potentialities of a minoritarian nature, which lead to the opening and expansion of the economy of the Woman, the Subject, the Human. As a result, a lesbian body emerges – conceived of as a desiring surface of an unlimited semiosis that overturns stable, fixed patterns of connections – which enables an anarchic 'erotics of connection' (Shildrick 2004) and effectuates ontological transformations into the field of sex acts.

However, the concepts of the schizophrenic lesbian desire and body, in order to be conceived, require a new image of thought, or better, a thinking-image that is able to move beyond the semiotic perspective, since the latter blocks schizophrenia's expressivity by restricting thinking to processes of analogy, comparison, resemblance and identity (Grosz 1994). Such a new thinking-image is to be found (though not exclusively) in the Deleuzian concept of the cinematic 'time-image'.[6] According to Deleuze, time-image signals the passage from the image of resemblance and the possible to the image of the simulacrum and the virtual; an image that no longer depicts, reflects, represents but becomes-other-in-time, producing thus a schizophrenic narrative. This new thinking-image will be sought in the cinematic event of 'Butterfly Kiss' (1995) directed by Michael Winterbottom; a film which, in my opinion, manages to incarnate (rather than merely present) in a rather explicit and violent way the links between madness, sexuality, identity, selfhood, desire, and thus constitutes a journey of schizophrenisation as the process of going through more reality; a process, which provokes an earthquake in the ontological grounds of our reality and our sense of 'being'.

Hence, the second experimental move of this paper is related to the field that is generally known as film analysis, and consists of its distancing from established and dominant linguistic/semiological paradigmatic frameworks of reading/analysing films (the Saussurian,

Althusserian or Lacanian approach). More specifically, it will attempt the shift from 'cine-psychoanalysis' to 'cine-schizoanalysis',[7] so as to draw a new cartography of lesbian subjectivity, by highlighting the traces a butterfly's kiss leaves behind: a contagious kiss that spreads and takes us over, forcing our thinking to move from the 'paranoia of being' to the 'schizophrenia of becoming-lesbian'.

More specifically, the turn from cine-psychoanalysis to cineschizoanalysis requires the replacement of an 'interpretation of texts' with the 'mapping of territories'. A shift that in turn requires a parallel shift in language: apart from the traditional analytic discourse, a poetic writing should be included as well, that will be able to 'sketch the diagrams'[8] of the schizophrenic body and desire; or even more radically, it will be able to actually produce the schizophrenic body and desire (rather than simply depict or sketch them, since the schizo cannot be represented, only continually produced). This is mainly due to poetic language's intrinsic capacity to bring form and matter together.

In addition, thinking cinema through schizoanalysis requires the forgetting of the grand theatre of the Oedipal drama, so as to connect with a virtual heterogeneity that cannot fit into the narrative of Oedipus. It thus signals the move from the figure of subjectivity as a molar, oedipal entity, a representation of some wholeness endowed with a subjective articulation, to the figuration of a 'machinic'[9] character as the carrier of a collective enunciation. Or even better, the move towards what I call the 'cinematic persona' as the 'intercessor'[10] between thinking and feeling, perception and the percept, affection and the affect: a shady existence of undecidability, which rather than following and doubling its actual body (the filmic character), complements and expands it through contradictions and deviations produced by the act of dialoguing. A dialogue consisting of asymptomatic monologues that set adrift schizophrenia's unlimited semiosis and thus enable a thought of the multiple to be reached. Hence, the produced schizophrenic dialogical delirium[11] will not consist of clearly distinguished interlocutors (how could it be in any case?). On the contrary, the individual voices will often be confused by a third term – the intervention of an indirect discourse – that will set off the transition from 'a personal expression [of the filmic character] to a demonic possession [of the cinematic persona]' (Massumi 1992: 28, parentheses added); the move from a personal voice to the howling of the pack that articulates a 'properly schizophrenic nonsense' of an unconscious agency. A nonsense which,

> Rather than look(ing) at schizophrenics as people who are paralysed inside their own body and need tutelage, [. . .] seeks to map (and not interpret) how they function in the social domain in which they struggle, and what are the transversal, diagrammatic questions they address to us. (Guattari 1984: 172)

Thus, the collective, heterogeneous voice of the cinematic persona produces new utterances and thus introduces another kind of movement into image; a movement in thought that gives rise to new pre-signified concepts and a-subjective affects and percepts. Concepts that do not require interpretation but are linked to a limit-experience, producing thus a stammering effect in language and the structures of signification.

A schizoanalytic experimentation with films will thus aim at revealing the voices of abstract figurations; an abstraction that denotes the figure's de-facialisation and impersonalisation, so as to achieve the distancing from organising structures of subjectification, enabling thus a polyphony to be heard. Rather than aiming at a supposed purification of ideas and concepts, the abstraction of the figurative aspires to magnify the character's speeds and affects, its intensities, giving voice to the mute delirium of becoming-schizophrenic-minoritarian within one's own language, thus allowing the orgasmic sound of the becoming-lesbian (trapped within the organism) to come out.

'I' for invisibility

Repeating 'Butterfly Kiss' differently

'U'[12] for Good Victory

> Look at us.
> It's me.
> Here I am![13]

An 'I' that moves constantly and desperately, in an attempt to find its place, to be self-defined, located and positioned, determined by being spatialised, solidified and stabilised: an 'I' that insists on moving to a 'here and now' position (to an 'am'), on lines of becoming-actual, becoming visible.

> Look at us – it's me.
> Here I am.
> Look at us!
> Look at us!
> It's me.
> Here I am!

The call for a gaze that will take her out of her invisibility, that will make her an 'I' by pushing her forward from a 'she' to an 'I' position, by reducing the distance from the self to the Other. The desire for a gaze of the invisible that will reflect back an 'us', a multiplicity, a pack, by inducing and embracing the non-visible, the imperceptible, the imageless: the other-within-herself. A cry for the other, a cry against the other that occupies her place, substitutes her, forgets her, and condemns her to invisibility.

> You don't see enough of me.
> I was trying to kill her – but she still wouldn't look at me.

> Look at us – it's me.
> It's me!

A visible invisibility, a mute delirium, a soundless musicality, a failed declaration of localities, an unsuccessful statement of missing 'I's: a performativity that fell short of the rules, that forgot its lines, that missed the gestures, appearing thus discordant within a harmonious whole. No it's not a failed mimicry, a sad parody, a playful imitation of the 'I', of U-the-other. It's just my incapacity to find the way, to reach 'being', to read maps, to reach ends.

> I always get lost. And I always end up in the wood.
> Déjà vu.
> Over and over again.

An orphan faith, a stray desire, a nomadic movement, a roaming body, a wild howling:

> They've forgotten,
> God has forgotten me.

> God's forgotten me.
> God's forgotten me.

Is it vain? Shall 'I' insist on believing without God, existing without her, living without home, being without U? Can 'I' endure her absence? Keep on searching? Keep on moving? Where are You? 'I' the enemy, 'U' the good victory. Vanity becomes stubbornness, rage, persistence, despair . . . loss becomes fulfilment, absence becomes affirmation: 'I' has to keep moving. Looking for her is a life goal, not finding her the impossibility of my reaching a point of stillness, the condition of my becoming.

> I've looked all these roads.
> Looked for what?
> I don't know someone to love me I suppose.

Lines of a lost highway: molar lines, molecular lines, lines of life and death, abstract lines, cracking lines, composing lines, lines of love . . . they all intermingle. Lines that meet, collide, connect, disconnect changing the map, transforming the landscape, getting me lost. Where am I? 'I': one line among others, one movement among movements, a different speed along speeds. 'I' becomes you, she, it, they. 'I' becomes anything, everything. Falling short of the 'superior race' of humanity, of the majoritarian subject, 'I' becomes the world.

> I am everyone and anyone.

And this is hard, painful, it hurts. You have to become a stranger to the self, stranger to perception and (re)cognition . . . 'I' has become a stranger to my inner feeling, alienated from interiority, an outsider to exteriority: an un-recognisable, imperceptible (non)being. 'I' becomes the world by losing the face, taking off the skin and thus destroying the affective bridges between 'I' and 'not-I'; bridges that bring I and U together in their distance. I am thus becoming-indiscernible, -imperceptible, invisible. I am

> no longer anything more than an abstract line,
> or a piece in a puzzle
> that is itself abstract.
>   (Deleuze and Guattari 2003: 280)

No, she can't search for her inside . . . where is my soul? Nor outside . . . where is the world? Neither up . . . where is God? Nor down . . . where are U? Everything becomes her, she becomes *with* everything, she becomes *with* the world. Her journey seems motionless – am I moving at all? Yet it feels shaky, overwhelming, devastating.

> I'm a human bomb today.

The goal is different now: to miss goals, orientations, end points . . . to move around, to draw new maps, to make diagrams, to expand not to develop, to fly not to make steps, to create not to predetermine, to forget not to remember. They say forgetting is wrong, immoral, a sin, a violation: forgetting is the violation of what is forgotten.

> I know the song . . . but I cannot remember how it's called.

> It's a love song . . . it goes tatatatatatata . . .

it's not really a love song;
it's a song *about* love.

Is forgetting it a violation of love?

'Cause people when nobody loves them,
They end up killing someone . . .
Even if it's only themselves.

I must find it. I need to remember it. But it's there in me . . . I'm sure. Its music echoes inside me, expands my life-lines, detonates my body. What I cannot remember is how to name it, to articulate it, to put it in words. Does it have a name? No, it can't have a name. Every time a name appears, the music vanishes. Naming destroys everything, kills hope, reaffirms vanity, confirms absence. Only love songs have names; songs about love have feelings, affects: a fleeting existence below and above cognition, beyond naming.

'*Don't take away my power to love . . .*'
    (Deleuze and Guattari 2003: 187)

I must find it, find her. I must find love,
I must find Judith.

You're not Judith!
. . .
You've got to find somebody to love You.
. . . they end up killing someone
even if it's only themselves.
. . . when nobody loves them . . .
You're not Judith.
Are you Judith?
What's your name then?

Judith will not come.
She is not here.
She doesn't see me.
Where are U?

Look at me!
. . .
You've got to find somebody to love you.
People, they end up killing someone . . .
. . . somebody to love you
Haven't you?
Now I have to do it again.
I kill people
And nothing happens.
Look at me!
Now I have to do it again.

Where everyone could see.

. . .

. . . somebody to love You.

Love is a war machine . . . life becomes death becomes life. Production becomes destruction becomes production. Being becomes becoming, becomes imperceptible, becomes non-being . . . a circular game of sameness, a vicious circle of differentiation(s). No assurance for the outcome . . . the war is still on: either incompatible, broken lines, unable to connect, or else creative lines, lines of love: lines of reconstitution, composition; lines of writing, musicality, pictorialism through which 'I' become(s)-animal-demon, U becomes-child, -woman, Us becomes-imperceptible.

'Us' as uncoupling, the escape of conjugality; 'us' as the doubling of sameness, the differentiation of doubles, the non-reflective mirrorings, the production of serial differences, auto-affection's monstrous child.

Either 'I' or 'U' . . . or . . . or . . .

We're no longer one, two, three . . . numbers fail us. We have always been more: a band, a pack, a peopling that 'mates' through contagion rather than reproduction: the spread of migrations, the explosion of dangerous nomadic desires, the burst of lethal diseases, the unnatural eclectic coming together of multiplicities.

'I' the enemy, 'U' the good victory.

How does 'I' love U? How does 'I' come closer to U? 'I' the periphery, the Loner, the Demon. U the centre, the heart of the pack. I must become lines, veins to reach U by keeping the distance, by running the distance, by experiencing it. 'Cause I still have to come back here, be on the sidelines to protect the pact, be at the front to lead the pact: I am the skin of this new landscape. I am the holes. I am the entries and the exits.

Take off the face and kiss you perhaps? That's what keeps us lonely, isolated, individual: the face.

> The face, what a horror . . .
> (Deleuze and Guattari 2003: 190)

How do I take off the face? Do I have to forget the face?
They say forgetting is violation . . . is violation the means to forget then?
A process towards oblivion?

> We must forget in order to remain present,
> forget in order not to die,
> forget in order to remain 'faithful'.
> (Augé 2004: xii)

My body is in chains. My body is in pain, my body desires pain, my body hurts. My body wants to be forgotten. Violating the body is the desire to forget it; leave the organism behind, put organs into oblivion, so as to let them be born anew and find a new body to inhabit. A violated body that wishes to become a body without organs, without face, without memory; an amnesiac body which dares to ask:

> Why not walk on your head, sing with your sinuses,
> see through your skin, breathe with your belly?
> (Deleuze and Guattari 2003: 149–50)

My body screams:

> They've made me an organism!
> They've wrongfully folded me!
> They've stolen my body!
> (Deleuze and Guattari 2003: 159)

> That's what I really want: someone to kill me.

I'm looking for someone to get me rid of my body, render my organs orphans, kill me so that I become-other, release me from my self, from my sex, so that a sexless 'I' encounters the organs for the first time. Look at them! You are not Me any more; you are not mine and I am not yours. Who are you? Are you my breast? Are you her eye? Are you her hand? Are you my mouth? How do we connect now? How can 'I' kiss 'U'? I forgot how to kiss . . . is it with the lips? Why not with the hands or the eyes?

> . . . no longer to look at or into the eyes but to swim through them . . .
> (Deleuze and Guattari 2003: 187)

A faceless, non-human kiss . . . an animal kiss perhaps? Almost like a butterfly kiss: another touch, a strange sensation spreading through the body. 'I' swims through the eyes; 'I' leaves the body and swims through U to an unknown landscape, an unknown sea . . . 'I' becomes fluid, runs inside you, becomes with you.

I have to forget the organism so that 'I' becomes; that's the battle. I the enemy, U the Good Victory.

Tell me what you forget, and I'll tell you who you are, who you are not, what you become, what you will never be.

> I will be a victim,
> A sacrificial victim,
> A present to God.

But God does not see me. He does not see me. Neither does he see U.

> God's forgotten me.
> God's forgotten me.
> He doesn't see me.

> I kill people
> And nothing happens.

> Look at us!
> It's me.
> Here I am!

He doesn't listen. He can't hear.

The face is a veritable megaphone.
   (Deleuze and Guattari 2003: 179)

Without the face I am mute. I am invisible. He doesn't see me. Do I have to be Christianised, facialised again? Do I have to be like Him? Like the White Man face, the face of the Christ?

> Jesus died at the cross for you.
> He died at the cross for me.
> He died so the whole wide world
> could see that only his love is true.

Does he love me though? Does he love U? Why do I feel alone then?

> Look at us!
> . . . *only* his love is true
> only *his* love is true . . .

Is my love to U true? Am I capable of love? I'm evil . . .
. . . because since you do it then it's done.
'I' killed him.
   My desire for U killed him. 'I' fell short of the face, short of the standard, short of the norm. 'I' lost the face by taking it off, and then

> It's done. You are finished.
> You can't go back and undone it.
> Nobody will forgive it.

I killed him to save me from the face of Christ, from the Universal Man face . . . or did he kill Me first? 'I' the Evil, U the Good. U told me once:

> I'll do it for you. To save you.

'U' has always been like me: evil.
'Us' has always been beyond God.

> All my selves have reached this stage
> because as far as I am concerned
> I'm not listening to you.
>   (Artaud 1995: 75)

I am not listening to you! I am not listening to Him. I can do what I like.

> Where is my face? Where is my body?
> 'I' for Impossibility. U for hope.
> Incapable of loving a Face, capable of loving *without* a face.
> That's my love.
> It's not *his* love anymore.
> It's *my* love, a love *to* U.[14]

> I have become capable of loving
> by abandoning love and self
>> (Deleuze and Guattari 2003: 199)

'I' is the gift to U. 'I' is a victim of forgetfulness, the sacrifice of memory, the killing of the enemy. 'I' has become

> Defenceless
> Helpless
> Sinless
> I deserve to be hurt.

Becoming-organless, faceless, subjectless, living in pieces. That's my present to U: pieces of my self, fragments of my realities, breaks of my ego.

> That's my victory: I am crossed by U, traversed by U.
> I feel that I am becoming with You,
> 'I' becoming-U,
> The becoming-U of the non-I.
> I have always been You after all.
> 'I' has always been 'U'.
>> *I feel* that I am becoming woman,
>> *I feel* that I am becoming God,
>> that I am becoming clairvoyant,
>> that I am becoming pure matter . . .
>>> (Deleuze 2006: 22)

I feel that I am becoming-lesbian.
That's my victory.

Notes

1   'The critical (in the literary sense) and the clinical (in the medical sense) may be destined to enter into a new relationship of mutual learning' (Deleuze 1991:14).

2   'A pure and dispersed anarchic multiplicity, without unity or totality, whose elements are welded and pasted together by the real distinction or the very absence of a link' (Deleuze and Guattari 2004: 324).

3   'As they [lesbians] are not two they are always and already one and more than one, an unnatural alliance because two singularities together are not dialectic and yet not the same' (MacCormack, this volume).

4   'The BwO is what remains when you take everything away. What you take away is precisely the fantasy, the significances, and the subjectifications as a whole. Psychoanalysis does the opposite: it translates everything into phantasies, it converts everything into phantasy, it retains the phantasy' (Deleuze and Guattari 2003: 150).

5   'Hand, breast, stomach, penis and vagina, thigh, leg and foot, all come to be facialized . . . It is not a question at all of taking a part of the body and making it resemble a face . . . Facialization operates not by resemblance but by an order of reasons . . . in which the role of the face is not as a model or an image, but as an overcoding of all the decoded parts' (Deleuze and Guattari 2003: 170).

6   Time-image could be described as a prolific serialisation of images that aim at their own limit and not at the constitution of a closed narrative; by giving time an ontological priority, time-image produces provisional truths which falsify established truths: 'time as becoming questions every formal model of truth' (Deleuze, cited in Rodowick 1997: 15).

7   It is only through the schizoanalytic lenses of the unlimited semiosis that time-image, as an a-signifying narrativity of singular creation, brings out the fullest of its potentialities. Any other (post-)structuralist analysis drains image from its temporal, transformative movement.

8   'In writing poems, I sketch diagrams, I find the words which will allow a new stage in my thinking' (Irigaray 2004: 29).

9   'The machinic for Deleuze is yet another figuration that expresses the non-unitary, radically materialist and dynamic structure of subjectivity. It expresses the subject's capacity for multiple, non-linear and outward-bound inter-connections with a number of external forces and others' (Braidotti 2006).

10   'Whether real or imaginary, animate or inanimate, you have to form your intercessors. It's a series. If you're not in some series, you're lost. I need my intercessors to express myself, and they'd never express themselves without me: you're always working in a group, even when you seem to be on your own' (Deleuze 1995: 125).

11   'Delirium can serve as a weapon against analytic formalism' (René Girard, 'Delirium as a system', trans. Paisley N. Livingston and Tobin Siebers).

12   The letter 'U' here is used in its written representation so as to denote three things simultaneously: the meaning of the word 'you', the sound U as the shortening of the name Eunice that is the main character's name (a biblical name that also means 'good victory'), as well as the shape of the womb, given by the iconic representation of the letter 'U'. Hence, it is a play of doubles between the 'I' and the 'You' which forms the same person: Eunice. A war of opposites that leads to the 'good victory', a relation of sameness-in-difference, the coming together of singularities through the mediation of a She-the-body, she-the-affect, she-the-Other, she-the-lover.

13   All the written parts put in the middle of the page are quotes from the actual film, though playful repetitions and rearrangements of the order of words and phrases are added by me.

14   '*I love to you* means I maintain a relation of indirection to you. I do not subjugate you or consume you. I respect you (as irreducible)' (Irigaray 1996: 109).

References

Artaud, A. (1995), *Watchfiends & Rack Screams,* ed. and trans. C. Eshleman with Bernard Bador, Boston: Exact Change (E).

Augé, M. (2004), *Oblivion,* Minneapolis: University of Minnesota Press.

Braidotti, R. (2006), 'Affirming the Affirmative: On Nomadic Affectivity', *Rhizomes 11/12,* http://www.rhizomes.net/issuell/braidotti.html [Retrieved 9 January 2007]

Deleuze, G. (1991), 'Coldness and Cruelty', in *Masochism,* New York: Zone Books.

Deleuze, G. (1995), *Negotiations – 1972–1990,* New York: Columbia University Press.

Deleuze, G. (2004), *Difference and Repetition,* London and New York: Continuum.

Deleuze, G. (2006), *Two Regimes of Madness,* New York and Los Angeles: Semiotext(e).

Deleuze, G. and Guattari, F. (2003), *A Thousand Plateaus – Capitalism and Schizophrenia,* London and New York: Continuum.

Deleuze, G. and Guattari, F. (2004), *Anti-Oedipus,* London and New York: Continuum.

Girard, R. (2001), 'Delirium as a system' in *Deleuze and Guattari: critical assessments of leading philosophers,* ed. Gary Genosko, Vol. 2, Guattari, London: Routledge.

Grosz, E. (1994), *Volatile Bodies,* Bloomington and Indianapolis: Indiana University Press.

Grosz, E. (1995), *Space, Time and Perversion,* London and New York: Routledge.

Guattari, F. (1984), *The Molecular Revolution,* London: Penguin Books.

Guattari, F. (1995), *Chaosmosis,* Bloomington and Indianapolis: Indiana University Press.

Irigaray, L. (1996), *I Love to You,* New York and London: Routledge.

Irigaray, L. (2004), *Everyday prayers,* University of Nottingham and Paris: Maisonneuve and Larose.

MacCormack, P. (2007), 'Unnatural Alliances.' In *Deleuze and Queer Theory,* Chrysanthi Nigianni and Merl Storr (eds), Edinburgh: Edinburgh University Press.

Massumi, B. (1992), *A User's Guide to Capitalism and Schizophrenia, Deviations from Deleuze and Guattari,* Cambridge, MA: MIT Press.

Rodowick, D. N. (1997), *Gilles Deleuze's Time Machine,* Durham and London: Duke University Press.

Shildrick, M. (2004), 'Queering Performativity: Disability after Deleuze', *SCAN: Journal of Media Arts* 1.3 www.scan.net.au/scan/journal

Chapter 56

K. L. Walters, T. Evans-Campbell, J. M. Simoni, T. Ronquillo and R. Bhuyan

"MY SPIRIT IN MY HEART"

Identity experiences and challenges among American Indian two-spirit women

Rejecting colonial notions of sex and gender differences based upon heterosexual norms, in 1990 lesbian, gay, bisexual and transgender (LGBT) Natives in the US agreed to the alternative term: "two-spirit". Karina L. Walters et al. note that various offensive and reductive labels had previously been proposed by colonists in North America, including "third gender", "*berdache*" (derived from a word for homosexual sex slaves), "women-men" and "men-women". But even contemporary terminology is an uncomfortable fit for indigenous peoples, especially in relation to a search for non-binary language. Through extensive interviews with Native women, the authors gain a sense of what the term "two-spirit" means from an indigenous, activist perspective, focusing in this extract on five core attributes: 1. spirituality; 2. community; 3. counter-discourse; 4. collective identity and social mobilization; and 5. coming out vs. becoming. The term "two-spirit" in itself connects sexuality and spirituality in ways quite different from the Western emphasis upon bodily, material practices of pleasure/transgression; put succinctly, two-spirit women claim an interrelatedness of body and spirit. Similarly, rather than being considered outside the "normative" community, two-spirit women argue that they are part of the wider indigenous community, not just in the sense of sacred rituals which traditionally offer a significant place for two-spirit peoples, but also in more recent roles such as political/legal activism on behalf of the entire community. The term "two-spirit" also registers Native difference from the white, western LBGT communities; yet while this is counter-discursive (building indigenous narratives of sexuality) it is non-hostile and can accommodate dialogue. Further, the indigenous women interviewed report a different agenda to that of white, middle-class lesbian-feminist politics, such as the importance of maintaining good relations between two-spirit Native women and Native men. In this sense, "two-spirit" as a term registers the need within white, middle-class lesbian politics to accommodate differences of race and class. Native women who identify as two-spirit, then, regard it as a unifying term, one which accommodates indigenous world-views and differences, and thereby provides coherence for Native political resistance and "mobilization". Walters et al. are careful to point out that from an indigenous perspective, "unifying" does not necessarily mean "homogenous", since Native belief systems privilege community as a collection of diverse peoples and nations, as well as iterative processes (repeated/developed oral stories, for example) rather than linear, logical systems thinking. The term "two-spirit" is sometimes thought of as "a momentary construct" which facilitates indigenous modes of becoming, rather than fixing identity in one time and place using western notions of being. This provisionality is embedded in the term itself, and is perhaps better articulated as a "becoming out", which replaces western terms such as "in the closet"/"coming out" with an indigenous notion of homecoming, spiritual createdness, and an essentialism that is at odds with whitestream LBGT ideology. "Two-spirit", then, conveys a self-sufficient culture, which does not need whites to tell Native peoples how to identify, and thus be, themselves.

> I feel as though being a queer Indian is the hardest job in the world . . . you have
> a colonized situation and dissolution of traditional ways—it's hard to be queer
> and Indian. (Maxine, a two-spirit Native activist)

Historically, Native societies incorporated gender roles beyond *male* and *female* (Brown, 1997; Lang, 1998; Little Crow, Wright, & Brown, 1997). Individuals embracing these genders may have dressed; assumed social, spiritual and cultural roles; or engaged in sexual and other behaviors not typically associated with members of their biological sex. From the community's perspective, the fulfillment of social or ceremonial roles and responsibilities was a more important defining feature of gender than sexual behavior or identity. Although there were exceptions, many of the individuals who embodied *alternative* gender roles or sexual identities were integrated within their community, often occupying highly respected social and ceremonial roles.

Western colonization and Christianization of Native cultures, however, attacked traditional Native conceptions of gender and sexual identity. The colonizing process succeeded in undermining traditional ceremonial and social roles for two-spirits within many tribal communities, replacing traditional acceptance and inclusivity with shaming condemnation (Tinker, 1993).

From within the academy, anthropologists have sought—unsuccessfully—to understand the historical status of indigenous peoples who lived with more fluid gender and sexual expressions (Farrer, 1997). As Blackwood (1997, p. 285) explained, "The critical importance of biology to Western constructs of gender meant that White scholars were rarely able to separate biology from gender successfully." The label of *third gender* they proposed is based on the Western binary system of gender and diminishes the complexity of multi-gendered statuses and expressions. The term *berdache* is offensive because of its colonial origins and purely sexual connotations: it is a non-Native word of Arabic origin (i.e., *berdaj*), which refers to male slaves who served as anally receptive prostitutes (Jacobs, Thomas, and Lang, 1997; Thomas & Jacobs, 1999). More contemporary anthropologists created the terms *women-men* and *men-women,* which are similarly deficient (Lang, 1998).

Native activists emerged with a term of their own—*two-spirit*. Adopted in 1990 at the third annual spiritual gathering of lesbian, gay, bisexual, and transgender (LGBT) Natives, the expression derives from the Northern Algonquin word *niizh manitoag,* meaning *two spirits,* and refers to the inclusion of both feminine and masculine components within one individual (Anguksuar, 1997). The term *two-spirit* is used currently to reconnect with tribal traditions related to sexuality and gender identity; to transcend the Eurocentric binary categorizations of homosexual vs. heterosexual or male vs. female; to signal the fluidity and non-linearity of identity processes; and, to counteract heterosexism in Native communities and racism in LGBT communities (Walters, 1997; Walters et al., 2001).

Blackwood (1997) suggested moving beyond labeling and classifying two-spirits to considering two-spirits as part of lived, contemporary human culture, situated within social relations that are negotiated and contested by family, community, and historical interpretations. She further recommended that extending the analysis of two-spirit gender into the realm of social relations and asking how two-spirit people position themselves in relation to other Natives as well as to White LGBT groups and individuals.

Toward these ends, we present in this paper experiences, perceptions, and challenges regarding the adoption of a two-spirit identity among Native women based on data from a large-scale national study of two-spirit health (i.e., the HONOR Project). Working in concert with local and regional two-spirit communities and Native agencies, HONOR Project staff conducted over 60 in-depth interviews with two-spirit leaders and activists covering topics from identity to community strengths to health concerns. Consistent with narrative and indigenist research methods, the qualitative interviews provided opportunity for two-spirit leaders to give their *testimonios*, a type of oral history and life story as two-spirit leaders and women (Bishop, 2005; McMahon & Rogers, 1994; Tuhiwai Smith, 2005). Interviewers did not focus on eliciting factual historical data; rather, they aimed to uncover the meanings that familial, spiritual, communal, and historical events have in shaping identity and quality of life for two-spirit women. The five two-spirit women whose narratives we review here range in age from late 20s through late 50s and represent considerable tribal diversity. To protect confidentiality, pseudonyms are used and limited tribal and other socio-demographic information is provided. Many of the quotes presented here were edited for readability and grammatical correctness.

"It's on a more deeper spiritual level": de-centering sexuality and centering spirituality in two-spirit identity

For Native persons, indigenous worldviews, including the centrality of spirituality, and ways of relating form the core of any behavioral expression. Indigenous traditional worldviews recognize the interdependency among humans and nature, the physical and spiritual worlds, the ancestors and future generations—connections that bind all living beings in spiritual ways. It is not surprising then that the term *two-spirit* is connected to traditional spiritual values and extends beyond the mainstream focus of sexual orientation as rooted in sexuality. Alex Wilson (1996), a two-spirit woman activist and educator, wrote that the term two-spirit "proclaims a sexuality deeply rooted in our own cultures. Two-spirit identity affirms the interrelatedness of all aspects of identity, including sexuality, gender, culture, community, and spirituality" (p. 303). The women in our study concurred with this perspective.

> Being two-spirited, kind of goes beyond my sexuality. I am attracted to women, prefer to be with a woman, but it also is more about who I am as a person . . . there's a spiritual side to it . . . there is a spiritual side that I just can't find words for. (Sandy)
>
> For me, I look at the word and I hear the word two-spirit, I look at the spiritual component of that, and I have to really say if I use this, what does this mean to me on a spiritual level, what is my identity to this on a spiritual level? . . . I say I'm a spiritual woman walking a spiritual way of life. You know, that's how I really want to be seen, that's how I really want to be known. Not as necessarily the two-spirit woman, but a woman who's walking the spiritual path and struggling on that spiritual path but learning to walk it and to embrace it and be a spiritual kind of woman, but it's not gender specified . . . so anyways, so yeah. (Roberta)

"Being responsible to the people": two-spirit identity means serving the community

Indigenism values familial, communal, and ancestral roles and responsibilities. Indeed, all of the two-spirit women talked about the general importance of their roles as community caregivers.

> I just feel like I have this responsibility to community that I have to fulfill and that's just a part of me and I feel like I'm—that's just something I naturally gravitate to, even if I consciously don't feel like I want to do that, you know, it's like I've gone through periods where I needed to take care of myself and I need to do this and work at this job or go to school or whatever, but it's like this community always seems like it takes priority to me, that I need to be something no matter how small it is . . . (Winona)

Additionally, many connected their fulfillment of these roles specifically to their identity as two-spirit women.

> I believe that there have always been roles and I believe that each nation has had names for people like us. And it was just a way of life. There was no—my belief is that we didn't have to explain who we were, we didn't have to justify our existence, we were just who we were, part of our community and part of our village and those roles that we took on were just a natural aspect of who we were . . . And within myself today I see it happening. I don't have to think about it, I just fall into some role. I don't say—yeah, I'll do that! You know? It just happens to be. I might be there at the right time, the right place. I always believe that there have been roles for us. And those roles, either spoken or unspoken, [involve] just naturally filling in those gaps. (Roberta)

The traditional sacred ceremonial roles for two-spirit women have expanded in contemporary space to include political organizing and engaging in legal battles for indigenous sovereignty. As Maxine indicates, these roles often are perceived as a central organizing component of two-spirit identity.

> I feel like the gift that I can try and give back to the Native community is um speaking out and saying things I've said and the work that I've done for treaty rights. And, of course, I'm one of many, many people. I mean it's not like I'm center of anything. I'm just doing what I see to do . . . that's where my heart is, you know, in trying to do that kind of work and make people's lives easier. Like I said, sending stuff to the rez and you know. . . . I don't have any traditional knowledge, I can't speak my language fluently, I'm not a very useful Indian [laughs] for Indians except for what I can do you know to help people who have less than myself so that's kind of what my center is.

Overall, this approach to conceptualizing a two-spirit identity is similar to how the women view their Native identity: multifaceted, involving spirituality, and manifesting in socially sanctioned behavior.

> My great-grandfather said to me once that being Indian isn't being on a piece of paper; it's spirit. So I don't think for me that's what it's always been about.

> My identity isn't on a piece of paper, isn't on a tribal card, isn't a number—it's me and my spirit in my heart and the way I choose to live my life. So that keeps me grounded in what I do. (Roberta)

"We needed to kind of develop our own identity": countering oppressive dominant discourses with a two-spirit identity

Many of the women spoke of how the term two-spirit emphasizes the importance of indigenous worldviews, histories, and experiences in the face of White hegemony in the mainstream LBGT community. Winona commented on how the two-spirit term has come to represent a form of indigenous resistance:

> I usually use the term two-spirit . . . most people felt a lot of alienation from the White gay/lesbian community and really—I don't want to make it seem like it was reactionary to that—it really felt like we needed to kind of develop our own identity outside of that prejudice and I think the term two-spirit came out of that, of trying to have that identity outside of, you know, the prejudice from the Native community and the prejudice from the White gay-lesbian community or non-Indian gay-lesbian community.

The homogenizing effect of lesbian feminism, with its identity movement, positioned itself as "the expression of the aspirations of all women" (Stein, 1992: p. 558). The lesbian movement from the 1970s through the 1980s privileged White middle-class women for whom lesbianism represented a sexual object choice and political identity in opposition to white-male dominated systems. Lorde (1985) noted that lesbian women of color and white working-class lesbians were compelled by the privileged White middle-class majority to assimilate to their political agenda and identity politics, making this hegemonic lesbian identity their primary identity. This assimilation required a marginalization of race and class issues paramount in the lives of lesbian women of color and white working-class lesbians. As Roberta lamented:

> How can one separate themselves from being two-spirit to being an Indian? So, I mean, to me it's a very hard concept to say that I am this or that. I'm all of that. Yes, I'm a Native woman, I'm two-spirit . . . it's all those things and encompassing and being, and for me to say I'm only this over here is not healthy because I'm not only this, I'm a multitude of things.

In response to the hegemonic identity politics of the White middle-class majority, many women of color challenged the notion of lesbian identity as organized around a fight against patriarchal influences and oppression and pushed for a more "diffuse notion of power and resistance" (Stein, 1992, p. 561). The women in our study were particularly uncomfortable with the anti-male separatism that is a core principle in some lesbian communities.

> I have to thank the White gay and lesbian community for that because of their separatist issues. . . . I refuse to go into that little box, shutting every [man] out, because they're an important part of all creation and you know they're going to be there. (Sandy)

For Native women, embracing men was a way to fortify defenses against White oppression.

> A lot of times in the White community, lesbians will say, you know, 'I just don't like men.' Actually, I think that identifying as two-spirit, I have more of an alliance with Native men . . . because they're Native men and they have experienced a lot of similar racist attitudes as well as homophobic attitudes on the reservation that I have. Um, we seem to bond together better, the male and the female sides sort of complement one another. I have difficulty explaining it to White lesbians who would say, 'Well, why would you want gay men at an event?' Because Native gay men are not gay men, they're my two-spirit brothers. (Sandy)

Just as two-spirit women value women and men in the Native community, they embrace the feminine and masculine in their own two-spirit identity. Wilson (1996) noted that the balance of feminine and masculine qualities, of male and female spirits, embodied in persons is often emphasized in traditional Native communities. Indeed, many Native origin stories speak to the balance of male and female, the importance of harmony between opposites as a way of wellness and wholeness. For many of the two-spirit women, reconnecting with this sense of wholeness meant also reconnecting with both the masculine and feminine aspects of their spirit.

> When we had pow wows at the two-spirit gatherings, there were men who danced traditional women's dances and I think that's definitely something that is a two-spirit thing that is important to those men and like I haven't seen any women dance traditional men's but, you know, when I was younger it was very important to me to not–to be able to have that male side of my personality come out and that was very repressed and I think especially younger women really need to have that option of being able to have that part of your personality. (Winona)

> It's definitely a balance in understanding assets of both genders. (Sandy)

It is no wonder that the term two-spirit emerged in the late 1980s, given the emergence of race and class-based ideological shifts to de-center the lesbian feminist model of identity during this time. For many of the two-spirit women, the lesbian feminist movement first served as an initial haven in which to share and bond with other lesbian women. However, it later became a community whose underlying ideology about men and gender relations failed to connect with indigenous women's realities and solidarity with Native men in the fight against colonialism and racist oppression.

Sadly, the term created by Natives for Natives, in their effort to secure their own identity free from oppressive influences, in part has been appropriated by the very forces they were struggling against. Consequently, the term *two-spirit* has acquired metaphoric power, becoming synonymous with spiritual power and ceremonial practices in an inaccurate and misappropriated fashion (Wilson, 1996). The metaphoric power associated with the term has led to romanticization and objectification of indigenous peoples who are two-spirit, in yet another example of colonial oppression.

> It's confusing sometimes because a lot of White people have started to identify as two-spirit and they don't get it, that it's not appropriate, you know. (Janis)

> I don't mean that, you know, that every gay Native person is, you know, a shaman or a guru, you know. That's the way White people want to see us . . . (Sandy)

"A unifying name to start to have a community": two-spirit as a collective identity to spur social mobilization

Two-spirit identity served not only to push away White dominance but to pull together the Native community with a collective identity in the struggle against racism, heterosexism, and internalized oppression. Many of the women described a two-spirit identity as a unifying construct that allows them to join with other Natives to explore their sexuality and gender from an indigenist perspective. As Winona remarked:

> People are acting like it [the two-spirit label] has been around forever, it has this deep meaning and all of this, which it has come to have more meaning to different people but to me it was just something that was—something we needed at that time . . . it was just . . . important to have kind of a unifying name to start to have a community of some common kind of things . . . we always knew everybody had their own traditions and communities we needed to go back to, but as far as having support, it's not always realistic for people to expect to be able to have support from other two-spirit people in their own community . . . that name I think to unify people and to have a place where people can go and be safe and talk about being two-spirit.

The increasing acceptance of the two-spirit identity among Natives facilitated national and international gatherings that served to create a safe space for identity exploration and development and to mobilize the community.

> I don't feel like I have to divide myself up so much anymore because I went to a lot of [two-spirit] gatherings in the early years . . . so I have a lot of two-spirit friends . . . At the [two-spirit gathering] there was a lake there and it was just nice, and we laughed . . . it was a space where you could be normal, a week out of the year, and so just that in itself I guess is what kept me going back to the gatherings—even today where things are so much better, it's like you just can't go anyplace and not feel like you have to protect somebody or alter your identity or whatever. (Winona)

> In general, the two-spirit gatherings every year are really helpful to me because it feels like that's the only time in the year I get to be my whole self in one place . . . to me it's healing. (Maxine)

The problem with a unifying term is that, although it is necessary for political mobilization, it simultaneously privileges a single experience of identity and diminishes within-group heterogeneity (Melucci, 1989). As the Native women had observed in the White LGBT community, unifying terms tend to privilege within-group dominant discourses and marginalize other voices, a process antithetical to the original intent of the term *two-spirit*. Indeed, social movement theorists have elaborated upon the ways in which the U.S. political environment makes stable collective identities both necessary and damaging (Gamson, 1998).

However, indigenous worldviews tend to embrace ambiguity, complexity, and non-linearity—processes that run counter to group mobilization for a singular unifying construct. Perhaps, then, this is why some of the two-spirit women noted the ambiguity in the construct of two-spirit. Instead of embracing a singular definition of the construct, they were comfortable with having it be a placeholder, a momentary construct that is readily contested and negotiated within Native communities and two-spirit spaces until a word is created that captures the fluidity of gender and sexual identity and the interconnectedness and inseparability of identity with spirituality and traditional worldviews.

> You know, even the word two-spirit as you may know is really just a contemporary marker . . . for lack of a yet-to-be-found better word. (Sandy)

> So even today, I probably would acknowledge myself more as two-spirit than anything else. Because it fits me better and it's not the name in our language that says it all, but it's probably about the best fit I can find right now and that's how I consider myself to be-two-spirit. (Roberta)

> I'm still kind of trying to figure out um, you know, what is the term for myself. (Janis)

"They come out into this world like that": coming out vs. becoming

From two-spirits' perspective, coming out to self and others might be better thought of as *becoming out* in the sense that this process of identity acquisition is really a process of becoming who they were meant to be–a process of coming home or coming in, as opposed to coming out or leaving an old identity behind to embrace a new one. Wilson (1996, p. 310) captured this experience: "We become self-actualized when we become what we've always been . . . " A two-spirit woman's assertion that she's "been this way from birth," conveys her understanding of how the Creator brought her into this world, this life, in a certain way that is directly connected to the ancestors and future generations in what might be called spiritual essentialism. This stands in contrast to the biological essentialism of mainstream lesbian discourses evoked by the same phrase, which alludes to genetic make-up or biological determinism. Hall's description of "warrior" women exemplifies this idea of spiritual essentialism.

> They are just being, that is the way the Great Mystery made them. They come out into this world like that. And they are living their lives . . . they were just manifesting what they were. And how they lived. It was something given to them by Spirit-this way of living. (Hall, 1999, p. 274)

This process of becoming can be misread or missed by non-Natives, because two-spirits might not be out in ways that are consistent with LGBT politics or anthropological paradigms. For example, the following incident illustrates how two-spirit behavior can be misinterpreted when viewed through a Western lens.

> When [an anthropologist] came to do her fieldwork, she said she wanted to meet some "warrior women," so I told her, "O.K., come to the reservation, I'll introduce you to some warrior women." But [she] came back . . . and she said, "You know, they're just the kind of women I am looking for but they do not know who they are." Well, it is not that they do not know who they are, just because they do not know the label anthropologists have put on them—because they are just who they are. (Hall, 1999, p. 274).

References

Anguksuar [LaFortune, R] (1997). A postcolonial perspective on Western [mis]conceptions of the cosmos and the restoration of indigenous taxonomies. In S. E. Jacobs, W. Thomas & S. Lang (Eds.), *Two-spirit people: Native American gender identity, sexuality, and spirituality* (pp. 217–22). Chicago: University of Illinois Press.

Balsam, K.F., Huang, B., Fieland, K.C., Simoni, J.M. & Walters, K.L. (2004). Culture, trauma, and wellness: A comparison of heterosexual, lesbian, gay, bisexual, and two-spirit Native Americans. *Cultural Diversity and Ethnic Minority Psychology 10*(3), 287–301.

Bishop, R. (2005). Freeing ourselves from neocolonial domination in research: A Kaupapa Maori approach to creating knowledge. In N. Denzin and Y.S. Lincoln (Eds.), *The SAGE handbook of qualitative research, 3rd edition* (pp. 109–38). Thousand Oaks, CA: Sage.

Blackwood, E. (1997). Native American genders and sexualities: Beyond anthropological models and misrepresentations. In S. E. Jacobs, W. Thomas & S. Lang (Eds.). *Two-spirit people: Native American gender identity, sexuality, and spirituality* (pp. 284–94). Chicago: University of Illinois Press.

Brown, L. B. (1997). Women and men, not-men and not-women, lesbians and gays: American Indian gender style alternatives. *Journal of Gay & Lesbian Social Services*, *6*(2), 5–20.

Falco, K. (1991). *Psychotherapy with lesbian clients: Theory into practice.* New York: Brunner/Mazel.

Farrer, C.A. (1997). Dealing with homophobia in everyday life. In S.E. Jacobs, W.T. Thomas, & S. Lang (Eds.), *Two-spirit people: Native American gender identity, sexuality, and spirituality* (pp. 297–317). Chicago: University of Illinois Press.

Gamson, J. (1998). Must identity movements self-destruct? A queer dilemma. In P.M. Nardi & B.E. Schneider (Eds.), *Social Perspectives in Lesbian and Gay Studies: A Reader* (pp. 589–604). New York: Routledge.

Garnets, L. & Kimmel, D. (1991). Lesbian and gay male dimensions in the psychological study of human diversity. In J. Goodchilds (Ed.), *Psychological perspectives on human diversity: Masters lecturers* (pp. 143–89). Washington, DC: American Psychological Association.

Gongaware, T.B. (2003). Collective memories and collective identities: Maintaining unity in Native American educational social movements. *Journal of Contemporary Ethnography 32*(5), 483–520.

Hall, C.M. (1997). You anthropologists make sure you get your words right. In S. E. Jacobs, W. Thomas & S. Lang (Eds.), *Two-spirit people: Native American gender identity, sexuality, and spirituality* (pp. 272–75). Chicago: University of Illinois Press.

Jacob, S.E., Thomas, W., & Lang, S. Introduction. In S. E. Jacobs, W. Thomas & S. Lang (Eds.), *Two-spirit people: Native American gender identity, sexuality, and spirituality* (pp. 1–18). Chicago: University of Illinois Press.

Lang, S. (1998). *Men as women, women as men: Changing gender in Native American cultures* (J. L. Vantine, Trans.). Austin: University of Texas Press.

Little Crow, Wright, J. A. & Brown, L. A. (1997). Gender selection in two American Indian tribes. *Journal of Gay & Lesbian Social Services*, *6*(2), 21–28.

Lorde, A. (1985). *I am your sister: Black women organizing across sexualities.* New York: Kitchen Table Women of Color Press.

McMahon, E. & Rogers, K.L. (Eds.) (1994). *Interactive oral history interviewing.* Hillsdale, NJ: Lawrence Erlbaum.

Melucci, A. (1989). *Nomads of the present: Social movements and individual needs in contemporary society.* Philadelphia: Temple University Press.

Morales, E. (1989). Ethnic minority families and minority gays and lesbians. *Marriage & Family Review*, *14*, 217–39.

Red Earth, M. (1997). Traditional influences on a contemporary gay-identified Sisseton Dakota. In S. E. Jacobs, W. Thomas & S. Lang (Eds.), *Two-spirit people: Native American gender identity, sexuality, and spirituality* (pp. 210–16). Chicago: University of Illinois Press.

Ross, R. (1992). *Dancing with a ghost: Exploring Indian reality.* Markham, Ontario: Octopus.

Stein, A. (1992). Sisters and queers: The decentering of lesbian feminism. In P.M. Nardi & B.E. Schneider (Eds.). *Social Perspectives in Lesbian and Gay Studies: A Reader* (pp.553–63). New York: Routledge.

Thomas, W., & Jacobs, S. E. (1999). ". . . And we are still here": From *berdache* to two-spirit people. *American Indian Culture and Research Journal, 23*(2), 91–107.

Tinker, G. E. (1993). *Missionary conquest: The gospel and Native American cultural genocide.* Minneapolis: Fortress Press.

Tuhiwai Smith, L. (2005). On tricky ground: Researching the Native in the age of uncertainty. In N. Denzin and Y.S. Lincoln (Eds.), *The SAGE handbook of qualitative research, 3rd edition* (pp. 85–107). Thousand Oaks, CA: Sage.

Walters, K.L. (1997). Urban lesbian and gay American Indian identity: Implications for mental health service delivery. In L.B. Brown (Ed.), *Two spirit people: American Indian lesbian women and gay men* (pp. 43–65). Binghamton, NY: Haworth Press, Inc.

Walters, K.L. & Simoni, J.M. (2002). Reconceptualizing Native women's health: An "Indigenist" stress-coping model. *American Journal of Public Health, 92*(4), 520–24.

Walters, K. L., Simoni, J. M. & Horwath, P. F. (2001). Sexual orientation bias experiences and service needs of gay, lesbian, bisexual, transgender, and two-spirited American Indians. *Journal of Gay & Lesbian Social Services, 13*, 113–49.

Wilson, A. (1996). How we find ourselves: Identity development and Two-Spirit people. *Harvard Educational Review, 66*(2), 303–17.

PART IX

Feminism

In 1792 a groundbreaking feminist manifesto was published, which continues to resonate today: called *A Vindication of the Rights of Woman*, written by Mary Wollstonecraft, the manifesto argues that rather than being naturally passive, inferior, or emotional, women are *taught* to adopt and express these qualities within a patriarchal society; thus women can actively resist being educated into and reduced to the state of mere "creatures of innocence."[1] Wollstonecraft's Enlightenment vision of women stresses the importance and primacy of rationality, and how social, political and pedagogic pressures lead to gender differences, not some inherent natural or biological division of men and women. This message was later amplified in aesthetic form in Wollstonecraft's novel *The Wrongs of Woman, or Maria* (1798). It would take many years of political transformation before women began to gain the rights that Wollstonecraft adumbrates, years of uneven development (the gaining of suffrage, or the right to vote; gaining financial and legal autonomy within marriage, anti-slavery legislation in the US, etc.) in terms of the implementation of government policies, national and international law, emerging from what has become known as the first phase of feminism.

In North America women reformers in the first phase were often radicalized through their involvement in the temperance movements (anti-alcohol consumption), eventually becoming key activists in the quest for universal suffrage. In Canada, for example, sisters Lillian Beynon (President of the Manitoba Political Equality League) and Francis Marion Beynon (journalist, political reporter and novelist) helped with the passage of the suffrage bill in Manitoba in 1916; Francis's anti-war writing would lead to her being driven out of journalism.[2] In the US, anti-slavery campaigner Elizabeth Cady Stanton wrote a "Declaration of Sentiments" for a women's rights convention that met at Seneca Falls in 1848; Stanton also co-authored the 1876 "Declaration of Rights of the Women of the United States" and with Susan B. Anthony, founded the National Woman Suffrage Association.[3] In the UK, the suffrage achievement had been long in the making, with the first National Association for Women's Suffrage formed in Manchester in 1865. J.S. Mill had "... presented a motion to Parliament to include female suffrage in the 1867 Reform Bill, but he was defeated by 196 votes against 73."[4] There followed a further series of bills in the House of Commons which were all crushingly defeated; however, the suffrage movement developed a new, more confrontational approach, which began towards the end of the nineteenth century. This new militancy led to direct action and public demonstrations with powerful leaders such as Emmeline Pankhurst (1858–1928) directing events in coordination with other activists. The British Establishment responded with even more violence, out of proportion to the demonstrators' so-called "crimes", culminating in "Black Friday" on the 18th November 1910, when a Westminster demonstration was ". . . met with unprecedented violence and indecent assault."[5] In the US, the establishment of universal suffrage with the passing of the Nineteenth Amendment to the Constitution enshrined this right in law, and is widely regarded as bringing the first phase or wave of feminism to a close.

As Castle notes, "Not all feminist movements involved political activism in this early period."[6] A major aesthetic movement that occurred in the first phase of feminism was modernism, with practitioners being deeply involved in innovative work, such as Vanessa Bell's post-Impressionist paintings, her sister Virginia Woolf's experimental novels and short stories, or the poetry of H.D. (Hilda Doolittle). Woolf also produced a landmark in early feminist criticism, with her book *A Room of One's Own* (1929), a "work in which representations of women by male authors are roundly criticized and a new model for female identity and agency is proffered."[7] Woolf's criticism of society and sexism, especially the fact that during her era women were not educated to the same level as men, led her to posit androgyny as an ideal, a suggestion that still generates debate today. Woolf's diaries and correspondence (1897–1941) also provide a wealth of material from the first phase of feminism, combining commentary on aesthetics, politics, sexuality, biographical observations of leading women and men within British society, autobiographical narrative, and cultural analysis. However, some critics have argued that to understand Woolf's project in her meticulous detailing of everyday life involves turning to contemporary feminist theory, especially the concept of *écriture feminine*, which is an intertwining of critical and creative language open to the Other, embracing the maternal, the female body, and any subject excluded or oppressed by patriarchy (see below).[8]

It would be a mistake to see the second major phase (or second "wave") of feminism (the 1960s to the late 1970s) as being completely isolated from the first, even though there was a long period of consolidation and transformation of women's working and social conditions during the First and Second World Wars, building upon the achievements of first phase feminism, for example, with women taking on traditional "male" jobs, and being actively engaged in military support and service. Yet for all that had changed, some things also remained the same: domesticity was regarded as a woman's realm, the sanctity of marriage and reproduction was still a social ideal, and modes of sexual, artistic and political freedom remained limited for women in general. Such a constraining environment was explored in a key text that "bridges" the first and second phases of feminism: Simone de Beauvoir's *The Second Sex* (1949; English translation 1953).[9] De Beauvoir's text is a hybrid of autobiography, existentialism and philosophizing about the history of sexuality, gender and the patriarchal oppression of women, opening with a Hegelian analysis of gender, where women are seen within patriarchy as "defined and differentiated with reference to man", making women "the incidental, the inessential as opposed to the essential."[10] Man is the subject per se, the "Absolute" (sticking with the Hegelian terminology), and woman is the object, or the "Other".[11] In other words, woman has been made a "second" sex, and it is the historical and social process that led to such a construction that de Beauvoir uncovers and critiques. For example, de Beauvoir argues that marriage is an oppressive and constraining institution, an "exploitative economic arrangement, which reinforces sexual inequality, and binds women to domesticity."[12] De Beauvoir utilizes an existential philosophy to undercut biological essentialism—the notion that woman are born into their secondary status, and cannot overcome inherent characteristics— in favour of her argument that one "becomes" a woman, which Judith Butler picks up on at a later date, suggesting that this "formulation distinguishes sex from gender and suggests that gender is an aspect of identity gradually acquired."[13]

Second phase feminists in the 1960s and 1970s returned to, and worked through, the implications of first phase feminism; for example, even if feminists rejected Woolf's notion of androgyny, or de Beauvoir's existentialist approach, they still found much of value to constructively critique and build upon. Woolf became an icon during the second phase, and beyond, her name and work becoming an overdetermined symbol of the potential of feminist studies, but also the cultural resistances and anxieties to such transformations in the arts and humanities.[14] De Beauvoir's social construction theory was developed in multiple ways. For example Kate Millett's *Sexual Politics* (1969) examines the way in which men construct female identity through literary texts; her study includes exceptionally strong criticism of D.H. Lawrence, Henry Miller, Norman Mailer, and Jean Genet, as well as the founding father of psychoanalysis, Sigmund Freud. While Millett rejects Freud, especially his theory of penis-envy and the Oedipus Conflict, Juliet Mitchell, in *Psychoanalysis and Feminism* (1974), provides a recuperation of Freudian concepts that could contribute to feminist analysis. Millett's methodology became known as "phallocentric criticism" and it was adopted by feminists such as Germaine Greer, in *The Female Eunuch* (1970). But a backlash against this approach soon formed, partly because, ironically, men remained the main subject of study, and partly because as a methodology, there was little sense of how a feminist tradition had *already* developed, either critically or aesthetically.

The development of "gynocriticism", as Elaine Showalter termed it, set about to rectify the weaknesses in phallocentric criticism, with a shift of focus to a female and/or feminist tradition, perspective, and innovative modes of expression; as Fiona Tolan observes, it also brought practical changes in the study of literature by printing, or re-printing, women authors: "Virago Press was instrumental in both of these processes. Established in 1973, its intention was to publish only female authors, and in 1978, it published Antonia White's *Frost in May*, the first in the Virago Modern Classics series that republished books by women that were no longer easily available."[15] Three key critical texts published were Ellen Moers' *Literary Women* (1976), Elaine Showalter's *A Literature of Their Own* (1977), and Sandra Gilbert and Susan Gubar's *The Madwoman in the Attic* (1979). Moers drew inspiration from another key book that had appeared between the two phases—Betty Freidan's *The Feminine Mystique* (1963)—especially Freidan's notion that women needed to be treated as a separate group, not merged into the general culture.[16] This pioneering work by Moer, provided plot summaries, biographies, and a feminist-humanist female literary history, that would be built upon by later, more theoretically astute critics.[17] More radical and alternative canon-forming is Showalter's study, foregrounding not just women's experiences and literary representations, but developing in the process a more powerful understanding of feminist literary history, divided into three epochs: the Feminine (1840–80), the Feminist (1880–1920) and the Female (1920 – the present). Showalter researched and brought to light women writers who had been ignored or forgotten by mainstream literary critics, as well as charting thematic and conceptual concerns shared by diverse authors. Gilbert and Gubar, however, provide the most exhaustive survey of nineteenth-century womens' writing, rejecting the patriarchal anxiety-of-influence theory of Harold Bloom (see Chapter 59), in favour of celebration of the feminist subcultures that are the new site of female creativity and artistic achievement. Gilbert and Gubar suggest, in other words, that women experience not a patriarchal or male-centric anxiety of influence, but an "anxiety of authorship": a rejection of the way in which patriarchy constitutes female (mis)identity. In conclusion, the second phase of feminism combined political and social activism with a transformation in artistic and critical practices, which Showalter calls "The Feminist Critical Revolution", in which she argues "Whether concerned with the literary representations of sexual difference, with the ways that literary genres have been shaped by masculine or feminine values, or with the exclusion of the female voice from the institutions of literature, criticism, and theory, feminist criticism has established gender as a fundamental category of literary analysis."[18] What brought about the shift to the third phase of feminism, however, was both a desire for an increasingly theoretical sophistication, and a sense in which the first and second phases of feminism had assumed too much about female subject positions, those of white, heterosexual, middle-class women being monolithically prevalent.

A key theoretical assault on second phase feminism was published in 1985: Toril Moi's *Sexual/Textual Politics: Feminist Literary Theory*. In her introduction on Virginia Woolf, Moi deconstructs those feminists whom she considers liberal humanists in disguise, arguing "that current [second phase] Anglo-American feminist criticism tends to read Woolf through traditional aesthetic categories, relying largely on a liberal-humanist version of . . . aesthetics."[19] After reviewing and critiquing key second phase literary critics and theorists, Moi moves to a study of French feminist theory focusing on three figures: Hélène Cixous, Luce Irigaray and Julia Kristeva. Alongside a shift towards more militant, Marxist theory underway in the UK and the US during the late 1960s and the 1970s, and developing in France via the political upheavals of 1968, French theory and French feminism influenced a discursive and intellectual shift in Anglo-American feminism in general, one which moves away from essentialism/biologism, phallocentric or gynocentric criticism, feminist literary history and biography, and instead theorizes more radically—and at times abstractly—the constructedness, performativity, and strategic politics of identity. As Moi notes, ". . . French feminist critics have preferred to work on problems of textual, linguistic, semiotic or psychoanalytic theory, or to produce texts where poetry and theory intermingle in a challenge to established demarcations of genre."[20] This sometimes led in the third phase to an uneasy truce between Anglo-American and French theory, since the French feminists often drew deeply upon the patriarchal canon, "particularly the exclusively male pantheon of French modernism from Lautréamont to Artaud or Bataille."[21]

Anglo-American feminists were much more active in challenging and dismantling the male-centric canon, and naturally this led to some suspicion of an overdependence upon male French thinkers such as psychoanalyst Jacques Lacan, or deconstructionist Jacques Derrida. What these male thinkers did provide was methodological tools that could be divorced from their own projects and put into the service of feminist criticism. In the case of Lacan, his theory of three symbolic orders of subjectivity and subject formation—the Imaginary, the Symbolic, and the Real—was useful because the Imaginary exists before the subject's entry into language, and the law of the Father/the phallus, that creates and orders the Symbolic through linguistic constraints and rules. Feminist critics not only re-conceive female writing at the level of the Imaginary, but they also create a new mode of resistance to the Symbolic (what Kristeva calls "signifiance") or the continual deconstruction of the Symbolic by a female "semiotic". Perhaps the main manifestation of this semiotic is the concept of *écriture feminine*—literally "feminine writing", which Hélène Cixous devised as a bisexual and deconstructive mode of writing that is predicated upon a total openness to the Other, "not just to hear the Other, but to facilitate the coming-into-being of other or different modes of expression."[22] *Écriture feminine* is playful and experimental (where patriarchal language is considered closed and rule-bound), and it evades being anchored by the symbolic phallus or law-of-the-father by constantly and dynamically being on-the-move. Collaborative and creative work exemplifies *écriture feminine* so it is apt that Cixous explores this writing process in collaboration with Catherine Clément, in *La Jeune Née* (1975, Engl. trans. 1986 as *The Newly Born Woman*). Cixous and Clément resist binary thinking, where one side of the binary is always subsumed and placed under the privileged other side (e.g., feminine subsumed under the privileged masculine, or black under the privileged white), by deconstructively rejecting binary hierarchies, and recuperating the importance of the female and maternal body (in terms of symbolism, tropes and materiality), as well as the intense pleasures of creative thought (the *jouissance* of *écriture feminine*). Cixous and Clément's work has been critiqued—for example most of Cixous's examples of *écriture feminine* are texts by men, from Shakespeare to James Joyce—but also developed, as with the work of French

Canadian theorist and author Nicole Brossard (b.1943), who modified the concept to produce the term *écriture au feminine*, literally "writing in the feminine". A more radical rejection of male-centric epistemologies is found in Irigaray's work, especially her thesis *Speculum of the Other Woman* published in 1974 (English trans. 1985), where she rejects and critiques phallocentric psychoanalytic theory by utilizing it against itself. Irigaray argues that Freudian and Lacanian psychoanalysis posits subjectivity (what she calls the "Selfsame subject") upon theories of castration anxiety, the male-centred Oedipal complex, and a specular or mirror-stage process that is structured by phallic symbolization. Her feminist alternative involves a deconstructive re-reading of the foundational texts of patriarchal speculative knowledge.

For some feminists, the ever-increasing theoretical sophistication of third phase feminism actually detracts from its viability, either because it no longer represents women of colour, of working class, or of different sexualities (bisexuality, lesbianism, transgendered, etc.), or because it appears to offer transformation and revolution but not at the level of normal everyday life, especially for women outside of the Developed World. Critic Margaret Homans argues that highly theoretical feminism is in effect a "poststructuralist disembodiment" of women, particularly black women.[23] Third phase feminism underwent profound changes due to these criticisms, becoming far more diverse in its voices and perspectives. Key interventions occurred in postcolonial studies, especially with the work of Gayatri Chakravorty Spivak, in particular her essay "Can the Subaltern Speak? Speculations on Widow Sacrifice" (1985; first reprinted 1988), revised by Spivak in her book *A Critique of Postcolonial Reason: Toward a History of the Vanishing Present* (1999). Spivak raises the question of how postcolonial feminists and others potentially co-opt indigenous and oppressed voices, such as Third World women who do not have entry to mechanisms of representation. In Black American studies, the critic bell hooks argues in *Ain't I a Woman: Black Women and Feminism* (1981) that race and racism should be central to feminism, as well as a re-positioning of feminist perspectives from the margins, explored in her *Feminist Theory: From Margin to Center* (1984). Alice Walker's *In Search of Our Mothers' Gardens: Womanist Prose* (1983) reveals that a Black American feminist aesthetic is radically different to that of Whites, with autobiographical narratives that merge the personal and the theoretical in story-based form, as does Gloria Anzaldúa in her *Borderlands/La Frontera: The New Mestiza* (1987). However not all criticisms of third phase feminism suggest rejecting "high" French theory. In the case of Judith Butler, her influential concept of gender performance derives from a grounding in the phenomenological philosophy of Hegel. In her book *Gender Trouble: Feminism and the Subversion of Identity* (1990), Butler argues that transgender performances such as drag acts reveal not an aberration or state of exception but instead the mechanism whereby gender functions in general; she argues that there is no such thing as a normative or "originary" heterosexuality, against which other-gendered subjects are measured, but instead there is a continual gender "imitation"; that is to say, an endless re-performance of gendered states that are always subject to destabilization and transformation.

Further reading: a selection

There are different routes through this short selection of texts, for example a chronological study can be done starting with early phase/wave materials, such as Millett, Showalter (1977), Gilbert and Gubar, hooks, Walker and Moi. Fallaize edits a range of essays on Simone de Beauvoir, including Butler's "Sex and Gender in Simone de Beauvoir's Second Sex" and Moi's "'Independent Women' and 'Narratives of Liberation'". Key figures, events and concepts in feminism are found in Kowaleski-Wallace, for example, entries on adolescence, black feminist criticism, British feminism, feminist jurisprudence, jouissance, socialist feminism, and subaltern studies, to list just a few of the many terms covered in some depth. Rooney collects longer essays on feminism and feminist literary theory, and this text is highly recommended for its range of critical applications. More theoretical feminisms are explored by Ives, who is careful to explore the "poetics" of French feminism, i.e., the importance of hybrid, creative and experimental poetic form. Lee also collects a series of essays on Virginia Woolf, with contributions on topics such as language, modernism, politics, feminism and psychoanalysis. Primary theoretical texts in translation are Kristeva and Irigaray (1985), with key American theory from Butler (1990 and 1993), Harraway, and Showalter (1985); Salih's text on Butler, and Sellers' on Cixous are two of the many excellent introductions to feminist theory and key theorists that are now available in series such as the Routledge Critical Thinkers. A classic of "border" studies, liminality and hybridity is Anzaldúa (Anniversary Edition, 2007).

Anzaldúa, Gloria. *Borderlands/La Frontera: The New Mestiza*. San Francisco: Aunt Lute Books, 2007. Anniversary Edition.

Butler, Judith. *Gender Trouble: Feminism and the Subversion of Identity*. London & New York: Routledge, 1990. Anniversary Edition, 1999.

Butler, Judith. *Bodies that Matter: On the Discursive Limits of Sex*. London & New York: Routledge, 1993.

Fallaize, Elizabeth, ed. *Simone de Beauvoir: A Critical Reader*. London & New York: Routledge, 1998.

Gilbert, Sandra Mortola and Susan David Gubar. *The Madwoman in the Attic: The Woman Writer and the Nineteenth-Century Literary Imagination*. New Haven, CT & London. Yale University Press, 1979.

Harraway, Donna. *Simians, Cyborgs, and Women: The Reinvention of Nature*. London & New York: Routledge, 1991.

hooks, bell. *Ain't I a Woman: Black Women and Feminism*. London: Pluto, 1981.

Irigaray, Luce. *Speculum of the Other Woman*. Trans. Gillian G. Gill. Ithaca, NY: Cornell University Press, 1985.

Irigaray, Luce. *The Sex Which Is Not One*. Trans. Catherine Porter. Ithaca, NY: Cornell University Press, 1985.

Ives, Kelly. *Cixous, Irigaray, Kristeva: The Jouissance of French Feminism*. Kidderminster: Crescent Moon, 1996.

Kowaleski-Wallace, Elizabeth, ed. *Encyclopedia of Feminist Literary Theory*. New York & London: Garland, 1997.

Kristeva, Julia. *Desire in Language: A Semiotic Approach to Literature and Art*. Trans. Thomas Gora, Alice Jardine and Leon Roudiez. New York: Columbia University Press, 1980.

Lee, Hermione, ed. *The Cambridge Companion to Virginia Woolf*. Cambridge: Cambridge University Press, 2000.

Millett, Kate. *Sexual Politics*. London: Virago, 1971.

Moi, Toril. *Sexual/Textual Politics: Feminist Literary Theory*. London & New York: Routledge, 1989.

Rooney, Ellen, ed. *The Cambridge Companion to Feminist Literature*. Cambridge: Cambridge University Press, 2006.

Salih, Sara. *Judith Butler*. London & New York: Routledge, 2002.

Sellers, Susan. *Hélène Cixous: Authorship, Autobiography and Love*. London: Polity, 1996.

Showalter, Elaine. *A Literature of Their Own: British Women Novelists from Brontë to Lessing*. Princeton, NJ: Princeton University Press, 1977.

Showalter, Elaine, ed. *The New Feminist Criticism: Essays on Women, Literature and Theory*, New York: Pantheon, 1985.

Showalter, Elaine. *The Female Malady: Women, Madness and English Culture, 1830–1980*. New York: Pantheon, 1985.

Spivak, Gayatri Chakravorty. *A Critique of Postcolonial Reason: Toward a History of the Vanishing Present*. Cambridge, MA: Harvard University Press, 1999.

Walker, Alice. *In Search of Our Mothers' Gardens: Womanist Prose*. San Diego, CA: Harcourt Brace Jovanovich, 1983.

Notes

1   Michelle L. Deal, "Wollstonecraft, Mary", in Elizabeth Kowaleski-Wallace, ed., *Encyclopedia of Feminist Literary Theory*, New York & London: Garland, 1997, pp.429–30. See, also, Timothy J. Reiss, "Revolution in Bounds: Wollstonecraft, Women, and Reason", in Linda Kauffman, ed., *Gender and Theory: Dialogues on Feminist Criticism*, Oxford & New York: Basil Blackwell, 1989, pp.11–50.

2   Richard J. Lane, *The Routledge Concise History of Canadian Literature*, London & New York: Routledge, 2011, p.85.

3   Gregory Castle, *The Blackwell Guide to Literary Theory*, Oxford: Blackwell, 2007, pp.94–95.

4   Claire Buck, ed., *Bloomsbury Guide to Women's Literature*, London: Bloomsbury, 1992, p.1054.

5   Jane Goldman, *The Feminist Aesthetics of Virginia Woolf: Modernism, Post-Impressionism and the Politics of the Visual* (Cambridge: Cambridge University Press, 1998), p.81.

6   Gregory Castle, *The Blackwell Guide to Literary Theory*, p.95.

7   Gregory Castle, *The Blackwell Guide to Literary Theory*, p.95.

8   Susan Sellers, "Virginia Woolf's diaries and letters", in Hermione Lee, ed., *The Cambridge Companion to Virginia Woolf*, Cambridge: Cambridge University Press, 2000, pp.109–26.

9   See Fiona Tolan, "Feminisms", in Patricia Waugh, ed., *Literary Theory and Criticism*, Oxford: Oxford University Press, 2006, pp.319–39, p.319.

10   Simone de Beauvoir, *The Second Sex*, trans. H.M. Parshley, New York: Alfred A. Knopf, 1968, p.xvi.

11   Simone de Beauvoir, *The Second Sex*, p.xvi.

12   Fiona Tolan, "Feminisms", in Patricia Waugh, ed., *Literary Theory and Criticism*, p.321.

13   Judith Butler, "Sex and Gender in Simone De Beauvoir's *Second Sex*", in Elizabeth Fallaize, ed., *Simone de Beauvoir: A Critical Reader*, London & New York: Routledge, 1998, pp.29–42, p.30; see also, Richard J. Lane, "Simone De Beauvoir (1908–86)", in *Fifty Key Literary Theorists*, pp.58–62.

14   See Brenda R. Silver, *Virginia Woolf Icon*, Chicago & London: University of Chicago Press, 1999.

15   Fiona Tolan, "Feminisms", in Patricia Waugh, ed., *Literary Theory and Criticism*, p.328.

16   Toril Moi, *Sexual/Textual Politics: Feminist Literary Theory*, London & New York: Routledge, 1989, p.53.

17   Toril Moi, *Sexual/Textual Politics: Feminist Literary Theory*, pp.53–55.

18   Elaine Showalter, ed., *The New Feminist Criticism: Essays on Women, Literature and Theory*, New York: Pantheon, 1985, p.3.

19   Toril Moi, *Sexual/Textual Politics: Feminist Literary Theory*, p.17.

20   Toril Moi, *Sexual/Textual Politics: Feminist Literary Theory*, p.97.

21   Toril Moi, *Sexual/Textual Politics: Feminist Literary Theory*, p.97.

22   Richard J. Lane, "Glossary of terms", *The Routledge Concise History of Canadian Literature*, London & New York: Routledge, 2011, pp.211–12.

23   Margaret Homans, " 'Women of Colour': Writers and Feminist Theory", *New Literary History*, 25.1 (Winter 1994): 73–94, p.87.

Chapter 57

Luce Irigaray

THE BLIND SPOT OF AN OLD DREAM

To deconstruct patriarchal psychoanalytical discourses, Luce Irigaray goes back to the beginnings of the subject with her interrogation of Sigmund Freud. Irigaray argues that for Freud (bearing in mind that he stands in for patriarchal psychoanalysis as a whole, as the originator and symbolic father of its discourse), women are a "riddle", one which remains murky and troubling. In fact Irigaray uses the term "logogriph" which is a complex riddle or puzzle composed of linguistic and poetic word games. This word in turn provides a clue for how to read Irigaray: she will try to solve the enigma, not of "woman" but of Freud's reductive, if not subtractive, account of female sexuality and subjectivity, one which depends upon key linguistic or semiotic moves in a complex patriarchal game of denigration and disappearance. Here Irigaray develops a methodological intervention based upon what she calls a "reopening" of the key concepts/figures of philosophical discourse, deconstructing from within, through utilizing a psychoanalytical discourse, published in a large number of texts, including not only *Speculum of the Other Woman* (1973) but also *The Sex Which Is Not One* (1977), *The Marine Lover of Friedrich Nietzsche* (1980), and *The Forgetting of Air in Martin Heidegger* (1983), among many others. In the extract, through weaving together a series of key statements made by Freud on female sexuality, Irigaray occupies and re-codes key terms, starting with "distinction" (distinguishing between men and women through mere visual knowledge), which becomes "discrimination" (in all senses of the word). "Disposition" is interrogated in the section on anatomy, where Irigaray notes that Freud's argument concerning the common biological origins of male and female reproductive systems leads to the notion of bisexuality, which then has to be denied; the mysterious "disposition" is replaced with an even more undecipherable "unknown characteristic". Similarly, Irigaray deconstructs the active/passive binary opposition that is so important in Freud's sexual universe, especially with Freud's example of active "breast-feeding", which Irigaray argues causes him more problems than really offering any simple solution. Another realm of "activity" that Irigaray strategically examines is what Freud calls "the suppression of women's aggressiveness"; this might initially appear to offer some analysis of social and psychic constriction, but again the evidence is sorely lacking; Irigaray argues that instead Freud quickly re-imposes a series of limits: female aggression is internalized, and is thus seen as self-destructive; yet it is simultaneously a sign of "masculinity", in which case it both fixes an identity and displaces it at the same time. The patriarchal mystification at work thus posits an originary difference, or otherness: women are always under the sign of this difference—"Sexuality, Difference, Phallus, etc."—since it is what "lifts" up the masculine side of the equation. Put another way, it is precisely the downplaying of the female side of this series of binary oppositions that marks the importance of the masculine. Female sexuality, for Freud, is therefore always already "male sexuality", which suggests a process of effacement or subtraction leading to this position. Men "are" (masculine Being), while for Freud, women "become" (feminine *becoming*, finding a way out of childhood bisexuality); for Irigaray this means that women are always engaging with the series of negations through which masculine subjectivity is constituted (her reference is to the philosopher Hegel, in which case this is a dialectical process in need of halting); women are "Off-stage, off-side, beyond representation, beyond selfhood." Irigaray turns the tables and utilizes Freud's subtractive "logic" on the question of masculinity, but the weight of patriarchal psychoanalytical discourse counters the parody; instead, Irigaray turns to childhood feminine sexuality and discovers that for Freud it is a case that even before a woman's role in the "sexual economy" has been reached, her subjectivity has already been negated.

Woman, science's unknown

"Ladies and Gentlemen . . . Throughout history people have knocked their heads against the riddle of the nature of femininity— . . . Nor will *you* have escaped worrying over this problem—those of you who are men; to those of you who are women this will not apply— you are yourselves the problem."[1]

So it would be a case of you men speaking among yourselves about woman, who cannot be involved in hearing or producing a discourse that concerns the *riddle,* the logogriph she represents for you. The enigma that *is* woman will therefore constitute the *target,* the *object,* the *stake,* of a masculine discourse, of a debate among men, which would not consult her, would not concern her. Which, ultimately, she is not supposed to know anything about.

How can they immediately be so sure?

"When you meet a human being," he says, they say, first of all, "the first distinction you make is 'male or female?' and you are accustomed to making the distinction with unhesitating certainty" (p. 113). How? This remains implicit and seems to require no remark among yourselves. Silence, then, on the subject of that extreme assurance which keeps you from being mistaken *at first sight* about the sex of the person you run across. The important point, it seems, is for you to be without possible hesitation, that you cannot be in error, that there is no ambiguity possible. That culture (?) assures you, reassures you—or once did so—of an infallible discrimination.

The anatomical model

"Anatomical science shares your certainty at one point and not much further. The male sexual product, the spermatozoon, and its vehicle are male; the ovum and the organism that harbours it are female. In both sexes organs have been formed which serve exclusively for the sexual functions; they were probably developed from the same [innate] disposition into two different forms" (p. 113). Which disposition? It must surely be concluded that up to this point the element defined as both specific to each and common to both sexes involves nothing but a process of *reproduction and production*. And that it is as a function of the way they participate in this economy that one will with certainty label some male and others female. So-called scientific objectivity can be decisive in the matter only after inspection, under the microscope, of the difference between reproductive cells. Unless that objectivity equally recognizes the (anatomico-physiological) evidence of the *product* of copulation. Everything else, in fact, appears too murky for science to risk—as you risk—making a judgment, coming to a differentiated verdict.

For of course "the other organs, the bodily shapes and tissues, show the influence of the individual's sex, but this is inconstant and its amount variable" (p. 113). And should you happen carelessly to rely on such secondary sexual characteristics, science is honor-bound to put you on your guard. In fact, science "tells you something that runs counter to your expectations and is probably calculated to confuse your [and its?] feelings. It draws your attention to the fact that portions of the male sexual apparatus also appear in women's bodies though in atrophied state and vice versa in the alternative case" (p. 114). Science thus forces you to see in this objective fact "the indications of *bisexuality* [Freud's italics], as though an individual is not a man or a woman but always both" (p. 114). You are then man and woman. Man, or woman. Yet—you may be assured, reassured—one character always prevails over the other. But all the same you are asked to make yourselves familiar with the idea that "the proportion in which masculine and feminine are mixed in an individual is subject to quite considerable fluctuations" (p. 114). It is fitting therefore to display some caution before claiming to belong to one sex or the other. Nonetheless, let us be serious and get back to scientific certainties, "only one kind of sexual *product*—ova or semen—is nevertheless present in one person." Apart, alas, from "the very rarest of cases" (p. 114).

All this, certainly, is very embarrassing and you are going to be led to conclude that "what constitutes masculinity or femininity is an *unknown* characteristic which anatomy cannot lay hold of" (p. 114). It is, thus, the expectation of the discovery of an unknown that arrests and obstructs the objectivity of scientific or at least anatomical discourse, as far as sex difference is concerned.

A science that still cannot make up its mind

Can psychology lay hold of this unknown characteristic? Can it resolve the problem of attributing some value to the unknown variable(s)? It seems that you have been accustomed to "*transfer* the notion of bisexuality to mental life" and that you speak, hence, of the same person "behaving" in a more masculine or a more feminine way. But in doing so, your so-called psychological discourse has simply "given way to anatomy and convention" (p. 114). In other words, the distinction is not of a psychological nature. Moreover, in general, you take the term "masculine" to connote "active," the term "feminine" to connote "passive," and "it is true that a relation of the kind exists." For "the male sex cell is actively mobile and searches out the female one and the latter, the ovum, is immobile and waits passively" (p. 114). And I, Freud, am here to tell you that the "behaviour of the *elementary* sexual organisms is indeed a model for the conduct of sexual individuals during intercourse" (p. 114). My way of envisaging things, these "things," would there fore imply that the psychic is prescribed by the anatomical according to a *mimetic order,* with anatomical science imposing the truth of its model upon "psychological behaviour." In intercourse, man and woman *mime* the type of relationship between sperm and ovum. "The male pursues the female for the purpose of sexual union, seizes hold of her and penetrates into her" (p. 114). But "by this you have precisely reduced the characteristic of masculinity to the factor of aggressiveness as far as psychology is concerned" (pp. 114–15). As for the characteristic of femininity, I, you, we . . . let's say nothing about it. On the other hand, *you* have in this demonstration, or testimony, lent "desire" to the sperm in its race toward the ovum.

But let us return to this somewhat unfavorable determination of the psychic character of masculinity. It is now zoology that invites you to be cautious in your univocal attribution of aggressivity to the male alone. Zoology reminds you, in fact, that "in some classes of animals, the females are the stronger and more aggressive" (p. 115). Remember, to take one example, the sexual behavior of the *spider!*

Moreover, zoology casts doubt on the idea that "rearing and caring for the young" are specifically female functions. "In quite *high* species we find that the sexes share the task of caring for the young between them or even that the male alone devotes himself to it" (p. 115). Is the necessary conclusion, then, that such animals are more able than you, than we, to distinguish between the sexual function and the parental function? And notably that they at least notice the distinction between female and maternal, between female sexuality and mothering, a distinction that "culture" might perhaps have effaced?

A question of method

But the reminder, or exemplary appeal, of the zoological in this matter will be ill attended to and perhaps worse understood. For it is nonetheless the mother "in the sphere of human sexual life" that will now serve as *paradigm* for the female in the debate about the relations between the masculine/feminine and the active/passive pairings. In fact, Freud goes on, "you soon see how inadequate it is to make masculine behaviour coincide with activity and femininity with passivity. *A mother is active in every sense* towards her child" (p. 115). The example of breast-feeding that is immediately adduced in evidence, is, of course, questionable; it is difficult to see how the verb "to breast-feed" can be simply reduced to an activity by the mother unless by virtue of purely grammatical criteria (as an active, transitive verb, etc.). And in any case, such criteria become immediately questionable when opposed to the verb "to suck," for then the mother finds herself the object of the infant's "activity." Unless of course breast-feeding—and we've been here before—is assimilated to the fabrication in concert (?) of a *product?* One might have assumed *milk* was the one single product that is incontestably attributed to the female—the mother—and, moreover, one that she makes alone.

Any consideration of pleasure in breast-feeding seems here to be excluded, misunderstood, under silent ban. That factor would certainly introduce a little shading to statements such as these last. But it really seems that at stake here is the *monopoly of productive "activity,"* the distribution of a *"phallic" power.* Obviously, the way this is announced in relation to breast-feeding is dubious, though not perhaps as dubious as the identification of the female with the maternal—an identification whose impact, impasse, and prescriptions are still hard to measure. Yet the Freudian discourse does not stop here, but goes on to pursue its strange gynecology, leaving behind in mid-air an image of a (woman) mother *actively* breast-feeding her child.

All this leaves our gentlemen perplexed in their discussion of the criteria of sexual difference. But the text goes on. . . . Apparently without a problem, a rupture. Yet on this occasion as on so many others, particularly when it is a question of woman, the text will have surreptitiously broken the thread of its reasoning, its logic. Striking off on another path that will no doubt intersect with the previous one, will in some way take up where it had left off, but in a zigzag fashion that defies all resumption of a linear discourse and all forms of rigor as measured in terms of the law of excluded middle. Here the unconscious is speaking. And how could it be otherwise? Above all when it speaks of sexual difference.

So you will now hear that "the further you go from the narrow sexual sphere"—constitutable then as a regional activity? compartmentalized? specialized? but in regard to what generality? totality? capital?—"the more obvious will the 'error of super imposition' become" (p. 115) (an error to which recourse has been and will be made almost continuously, even as an effort is made to dissuade you yourselves from having recourse to it). "For certain women, with whom only men capable of showing themselves passively docile can manage to get along [?], may display, in many domains, tremendous activity."[2] The important thing here is the way certain terms mediate the statement, suggesting that in the case of these women, it must be a question of activism exerting itself by gracious permission of the submissive docility of the male. A curious choice of example for bisexuality. . . . In any case, the essential activity would still be allotted to the male: that during intercourse. You will remember, in fact, that this is the pattern of behavior with certain animals: "in some classes of animals, the females are the stronger and more aggressive and the male is *active* only in *the single act of sexual union*" (p.115). And yet, if you stand by the conviction that passivity is equivalent to femininity and activity with masculinity, "I advise you against it" and "it seems to serve no useful purpose and adds nothing to our knowledge" (p. 115). So what now?

What is involved in (re)production, and how it aids and abets the phallic order

Let us begin again, or rather let us continue to listen, without impatience. "One might consider characterizing femininity psychologically as giving preference to *passive aims*. This is not, of course, the same thing as passivity; to achieve passive aims may call for a large amount of activity. It is perhaps the case that in a woman, on the basis of her share in the *sexual function*, a preference for passive behaviour and passive aims is carried over into her life to a greater or lesser extent, in proportion to the limits, restricted or far-reaching, within which her sexual life thus serves as a model" (pp. 115–16). Thus, now that it has been decreed that the active/passive opposition is not pertinent to the characterization of the male/female difference, an attempt is to be made to save what is at stake in that opposition by bringing in the difficult notion of "passive aims." Not that such a notion is lacking in interest and would not merit more extensive commentary, but what does it involve but a complication of the economy of active/passive relationships? By giving them authority to function within each of the two poles of masculine and feminine but in differentiated and in some way complementary times and tenses. The "roles" are being cast in such a way that, yet again and in all instances, passivity is required of woman at the moment of intercourse by reason of its usefulness in sexual functioning. A certain tendency to activity may, on the other hand, be recognized in woman insofar as that activity prepares for sexual functioning and is rigorously regulated in proportion to the so-called sexual life's involvement as model.

The reproductive function is not explicitly named, but passages before and after, as well as reference to other texts,[3] indicate clearly that when it comes to sexual function and its model-value, the reproductive function alone is being referred to. The point being that man is *the* procreator, that sexual *production-reproduction* is referable to his "activity" alone, to his "project" alone. Woman is nothing but the receptacle that passively receives his *product,* even if sometimes, by the display of her passively aimed instincts, she has pleaded, facilitated, even demanded that it be placed within her. Matrix—womb, earth, factory, bank—to which the seed capital is entrusted so that it may germinate, produce, grow fruitful, without woman being able to lay claim to either capital or interest since she has only submitted "passively" to reproduction. Herself held in receivership as a certified means of (re)production.[4]

One may agree that it is difficult to decide between what is activity and what passivity in the economy of sexual reproduction. But this in no way prevents us from wishing to interpret correctly the appeal to a (supposedly) other economy which claims (*a*) to cure indecision or to suspend the undecidable that is set in play by such a question, (*b*) to resolve the question by attributing "activity" to man in the process of generation, in other words, to settle the question in terms of the active/passive opposition.

Moreover, this recourse to an "other" order intervenes at this point in Freud's argument in an unforeseeable and inexplicit fashion. As it were in parentheses, and in a curiously injunctive form: "But we must beware in this of underestimating the influence of social customs, which *similarly* force women into passive situations" (p. 116). Of which social customs must we beware of understanding the influence? What influence is capable of forcing women to remain in "passive situations"? What is meant by "similarly"? An enumeration of concurrent factors? But might one not envisage the possibility that the one might prescribe "the other," that is to say by legitimating, even by producing the discourse, the ideology, which determine it as a factor? The question would doubtless be unavoidable were it not that these "social customs" are left in an evocative imprecision so general, so devoid of commitment, as to lose all impact. The only pertinence is to be found, so it would seem, in the almost compulsory recall of a problem that butts in, insists, harps back, but whose data appear to escape the "lecturer." He admits that "all this is *far from being cleared up*." As obscure, as black, perhaps, as the *dark* continent of femininity?

He continues, nonetheless; "There is one particularly constant relation between femininity and instinctual life which we do not want to overlook. The suppression of women's aggressiveness which is prescribed for them constitutionally [whatever that means] and imposed upon them socially [by what mechanisms?] favours the development of powerful masochistic impulses" (p. 116). Somehow, there seems to be no permitted mode of female aggression. But, once again, the mobilization of arguments as heterogeneous as "constitution" and "social pressure" raises questions as to how the said pressure might have prescriptive power over the representation of the said constitution, how the former might have a vested interest in becoming the prop, the accomplice in such an estimation of "the female constitution." Must one see here proof that customs and indeed Freud's own text, which finds support in them, evaluate all aggressiveness by the yardstick of *masculine homosexuality?* Since competitiveness and rivalry in commerce, notably sexual commerce, can be practiced only by males? Whence these redoubled prohibitions on female aggression? And with the result that woman, on pain of infringing the laws of both social custom and constitution, develops strongly masochistic tendencies which succeed in eroticizing destructive tendencies that are directed "inward." For it is equally necessary to assign her a role in the function of the inside/outside pairing that turns up here in some way to intersect and sustain the active/passive opposition. As far as the "inside" goes—her own, of course—woman will thus tend to be destructive, since nothing authorizes her aggression or activity toward another "inside" or toward the outside. (One might bring up the "activity" of breast-feeding, but that has been left hanging in mid-air some where.) If activity or aggression there be in woman, it will hence be given the connotation of "masculine" or "destructive." "Thus masochism, *as people say,* is truly feminine" (p. 116). And as I, Freud, say again. "But if, as happens so often, you meet with masochism in men, what is left to you but to say that these men exhibit very plain feminine traits?" (p. 116). This seems sufficiently vexatious to break off the line of argument, move on to the next paragraph, and conclude that:

"And now you are already prepared to hear that psychology too is unable to solve the riddle of femininity". Who has managed to follow the links in the chain of this argument except he who gets some bonus of pleasure out of it? A pleasure which gives it a force that cannot easily be defrayed. For, in fact, once bisexuality has been admitted, why cut short its implications, notably with regard to masculine masochism? The riddle—the mysteria/ hysteria?—might perhaps concern not only femininity, even in this lecture on the problem of femininity. Why, in that case, wish to reserve the mystery to women? As if, for the argument to be possible, "male sexuality" at the very least had to impose itself as clearly defined, definable, even practicable.

So psychology does not offer us the key to the mystery of femininity—that black box, strongbox, earth-abyss that remains outside the sphere of its investigations: *light* must no doubt come from elsewhere (p.116). (One cannot give up so soon, when so much energy has been invested in a metaphoricity dominated by the photological.) But the illumination "cannot come till we have learnt how in general the differentiation of living organisms into two sexes came about. We know nothing about it . . ." (p. 116). So you can be assured that the explanation is not immediately available. But understand, however, that you are once more being referred to science in order to understand "the mystery of femininity."

Unless you interpret this statement as meaning that as far as the differentiation into two sexes is concerned, we can know something certain about only one of the terms of the difference. Ultimately this alone would be envisaged as the variable factor in a re-marking of sexuality—but which one?—through its own process. In other words, for light to be or be spoken in the matter of (so-called) female sexuality, we can assume that difference is always already in operation although no acknowledgment is made of it (perhaps because its character is only representable with difficulty?). Out of this difference will be lifted one of the two terms—but determined in relation to what?—and this one term will be constituted as "origin," as that by whose differentiation the other may be engendered and brought to light. *The same re-marking itself*—more or less—would thus produce the other, whose function in the differentiation would be neglected, forgotten. Or else carried back into mere extrapolation, into the infinity of some capital letter: Sexuality, Difference, Phallus, etc. Up to now, therefore, nothing can be clearly articulated but the history of the practice of "male sexuality" with regard to Sexuality.

A difference not taken into account

"Yet the existence of two sexes is a most striking characteristic of organic life which distinguishes it sharply from inanimate nature" (p. 116). Could this not be a difference thus clearly cut out in the service of argument? Once the heterogeneous is found to be reduced in sexual practice, would we not observe a proliferation of differences, a compulsion to differentiate, either to retain the pleasure, or calm the anguish of indifference, at least in the art or science of dialectic?

Whereas "we find enough to study in those human individuals who, through the possession of female genitals, are characterized as manifestly or predominantly feminine. In conformity with its peculiar nature, psycho-analysis does not try to describe what a woman is—that would be a task scarcely performable—but sets about enquiring how she comes into being, how a woman develops out of a child with a bisexual disposition" (p. 116). One can only agree in passing that it is impossible exhaustively to represent what woman might be, given that a certain economy of representation—inadequately perceived by psychoanalysis, at least in the "scientific discourse" that it speaks—functions through a tribute to woman that is never paid or even assessed. The whole problematic of Being has been elaborated thanks to that loan. It is thus, in all exactitude, unrealizable to *describe the being* of woman. As for how "a woman develops out of a child with a bisexual disposition," one might begin by being surprised, being suspicious, that it should be necessary to *become* a woman—and a "normal" woman to boot—and that this evolution should be "more difficult and more complicated" than becoming a man. This is again a question that arises out of an economy—and again an economy of representation—to which Freud has recourse without criticism, without sufficient questioning: this is an organized system whose meaning is regulated by paradigms and units of value that are in turn determined by male subjects. Therefore, the feminine must be deciphered as inter-dict: within the signs or between them, between the realized meanings, between the lines . . . and as a function of the (re)productive necessities of an intentionally phallic currency, which, for lack of the collaboration of a (potentially female) other, can immediately be assumed to need *its* other, a sort of inverted or negative alter ego—"black" too, like a photographic negative. Inverse, contrary, contradictory even, necessary if the male subject's process of specul(ariz)ation is to be raised and sublated. This is an intervention required of *those* effects of negation that result from or are set in motion through a censure of the feminine, though the feminine will be allowed and even obliged to return in such oppositions as: be/*become,* have/*not have* sex (organ), phallic/*non-phallic,* penis/*clitoris* or else penis/*vagina,* plus/*minus,* clearly representable/*dark continent,* logos/*silence* or idle chatter, desire for the mother/*desire to be the mother,* etc. All these are interpretive modalities of the female function rigorously postulated by the pursuit of a certain game for which she will always find herself signed up without having begun to play. Set between—at least—two, or two half, men. A hinge bending according to their exchanges. A reserve supply of *negativity* sustaining the articulation of their moves, or refusals to move, in a partly fictional progress toward the mastery of power. Of knowledge. In which she will have no part. Off-stage, off-side, beyond representation, beyond selfhood. A power in reserve for the dialectical operations to come. We shall come back to this.

But as far as "becoming woman" is concerned—and the task will consist mainly in recognizing and accepting her atrophied member—one might stress in passing that in the elaboration of analytic theory there will be little question of reducing bisexual tendencies in men. Doubtless a more delicate matter than in the case of the aforementioned female sexuality. For what male "organ" will be set forth in derision like the clitoris?—that penis too tiny for comparison to entail anything but total devaluation, complete decathexization. Of course, there are the breasts. But they are to be classed among the *secondary*, or so-called secondary, characteristics. Which no doubt justifies the fact that there is so little questioning of the effects of breast atrophy in the male. Wrongly, of course. Let us recall all the perplexity about the criteria of sexual difference entailed by the question of breast-feeding. But it seems, all the same, that one might be able to interpret the fact of being deprived of a womb as the most intolerable deprivation of man, since his contribution to gestation—his function with regard to the origin of reproduction—is hence asserted as less than evident, as open to doubt. An indecision to be attenuated both by man's "active" role in intercourse and by the fact that he will mark the product of copulation with *his own name.* Thereby woman, whose intervention in the work of engendering the child can hardly be questioned, becomes the anonymous worker, the machine in the service of a master-proprietor who will put his trademark upon the finished product. It does not seem exaggerated, incidentally, to understand quite a few products, and notably cultural products, as a counterpart or a search for equivalents to woman's function in maternity. And the desire that men here displays to determine for himself what is constituted by "origin," and thereby eternally and ever to reproduce him (as) self, is a far from negligible indication of the same thing.

There is, therefore, for man no prohibition upon substitutes that permit the realization of bisexual tendencies, provided that these have been historically valorized. (This is not the case, you will recall, with masochism. Nor, one might add, with passive homosexuality, which is doubtless too close to the function required of woman in intercourse.) Whereas a repression of the so-called phallic desires is supposed to have held woman back from a potential participation in the elaboration of the symbolic. Such participation is still liable to provoke suspicion and irony on the part of psychoanalysts. Thus, for example: "In recent times we have begun to learn a little about this, thanks to the circumstance that several of our excellent [?] women colleagues in analysis have begun to work at the question." So, *their practice* has brought us some information that elucidates *our theory*. "The discussion of this has gained special attractiveness from the distinction between the sexes. For the ladies, whenever some comparison seemed to turn out unfavourable to their sex, were able to utter a suspicion that we, the male analysts, had been unable to overcome certain deeply-rooted prejudices against what was feminine, and that this was being paid for in the partiality of our researches. We, on the other hand, standing on the ground of bisexuality, had no difficulty in avoiding impoliteness [?]. We had only to say: 'This doesn't apply to *you* [Freud's italics]. You're the exception; on this point you're *more masculine than feminine*'" (pp. 116–17). So, in order to avoid all impoliteness toward our excellent "female colleagues," who are capable of affording a few insights on fragmentary aspects of our theory, it was/is sufficient to treat them explicitly as *male colleagues,* thus preventing any parallelism that would necessarily be unfavorable to their sex. Sic. . . .

The labor "to become a woman"

"We approach the investigation of the sexual development of women with two expectations. The first is that here once more the constitution will not adapt itself to its function without struggle" (p. 117). A statement that is in itself somewhat enigmatic since it has just been asserted that "woman's own constitution" demanded she repress all signs of aggressivity—a repression encouraged by "social custom" and certainly also by the "sexual function" that we recognize in or attribute to her. How, therefore, is this proposition to be understood? As a result of the section that follows? That is, the section explaining that certain precocious abilities observed in the little girl—an earlier control of her excretory functions, a greater, more lively intelligence, a better disposition toward the external world—will yield only with a struggle to the sexual function she will have to fulfill? This is a possible reading, though one hesitates to assert it. In any case, these leads in development recognized in the little girl are immediately explained away as "greater dependency," "pliancy," "a greater need to be shown affection," or again are said to be outweighed by the fact that she forms "stronger object-cathexes." Her precociousness in the controlled production of feces, of language, of social relationships—whose relation to the production and circulation of currency you will be familiar with—would thus be envisaged as merely the effect of her desire to function, herself, as "merchandise." Her childish superiority would be motivated simply by the desire to appear the most attractive of all negotiable assets.

Yet, and even if the preceding remarks concerning the advantages of the little girl do not seem confirmed "by exact observations," it remains true that "girls cannot be described as intellectually *backward*"! But, he goes on, "these sexual differences are not of great consequence: they can be outweighed by individual variations. For our immediate purpose they can be disregarded" (p. 117). Let us, then, forget the troublesome question that might be raised by the incidental precociousness of the little girl, and the problem of what may *become of it,* so that we can keep to the heart of the matter, to the capital, that is to say.

The second point to be noted in our study of sexuality consists in the fact that "the decisive turning points will already have been prepared for or completed before puberty" (p. 117). This second observation and claim are no more supported than the first. At any rate, at the point when the claim is made. One may, of course, consider the whole of the text—the whole of the Freudian corpus—as a demonstration of its relevance: the role of the castration complex in the "becoming (of) a woman" intervenes well before puberty. Yet it is not perhaps vain to express surprise that the game should be played out, or at any rate the rules agreed upon, before reproduction—whose implicit or explicit precedence in this theory of sexuality has already been hinted at—can be effectively possible, materially fulfilled. It must be concluded, once again, that this preeminence finds its rationality elsewhere or otherwise. In any case, the culturally, socially, economically valorized female characteristics are correlated with maternity and motherhood: with breast-feeding the child, restoring the man. According to a certain dominant ideology, the little girl can thus have *no value* before puberty. Moreover, by Freud's own assertion, at the age at which the castration complex would be stressed by the little girl, "the truly female vagina is still undiscovered" (p. 118). This is to say, then, that everything concerning woman's allotted role and the representations of that role proposed or lent to her would be decided even before the socially recognized specificity of her intervention in the sexual economy is practicable, and before she has had access to a particular "essential feminine pleasure." It is hardly surprising, then, that she seems as a result to be "lacking in," "deprived of," "envious of," "jealous of" . . . But of what?

Notes

1   Sigmund Freud, "Femininity," in *New Lectures on Psycho-analysis.* The choice of this text—a fictional lecture—can be justified by its late date in Freud's work. It groups, thus, a fair number of statements' developed in other essays that I shall in fact be referring to. Except where otherwise stated, it is I who have italicized Freud's remarks in one way or another. I shall also have occasion to modify the translation somewhat, to complete it in certain cases where fragments of statements in the original have been omitted. But the most meticulous translation would not have changed much of the significance of this speech on "femininity."

    (All quotations from Freud, unless otherwise noted, are from *The Standard Edition of the Complete Psychological Works of Sigmund Freud,* under the general editorship of James Strachey, 24 vols. [London: Hogarth Press, 1953–74], henceforth referred to as *SE.* The essay "Femininity" can be found in *SE* XXII 112–35. The quotation above is from p. 113, and the italics are Strachey's. Henceforth page numbers will be given in the text. In LI's French text, page references are given only a few times in footnotes, but here the more comprehensive citation policy usual in English has been followed. The *Standard Edition* text is unaltered, except for the addition of LI's italics.—Tr.)

2   (Here the French translation of Freud differs significantly from the Strachey translation, and I have had to give an English version of the French version of the German. The *Standard Edition* text runs: "Women can display great activity in various directions, men are not able to live in company with their own kind unless they develop a large amount of passive adaptibility" [p. 115]—Tr.)

3   Cf. the *Three Essays on the Theory of Sexuality, SE,* VII.

4   A very old point of contention, whose different transformations can be followed throughout the history of philosophy.

Chapter 58

Hélène Cixous and Catherine Clément

SORTIES

Out and out: attacks/ways out/forays

A number of targets are addressed here by Hélène Cixous and Catherine Clément, including: binary hierarchical thinking; patriarchal systems that assign women to passive modes of non-existence; Hegelian dialectical logic; and phallocentric discourses, i.e., psychoanalytical, linguistic, semiotic, etc., systems that are centred upon the primacy of the symbolic "phallus" or father/master. Cixous and Clément's critique of these interrelated gendered ways of seeing the world is in turn playfully and creatively written, in a genre called *écriture feminine*, a term translated by critic Susan Sellers (1996) as "an/other writing", meaning a generous intertwining of critical and creative language open to the other, embracing the maternal, the female body, and any subject excluded or oppressed by patriarchy. Collaboration between Cixous and Clément comes as no surprise as both are intellectuals, theorists, feminists, and prolific authors of fiction; *The Newly Born Woman* (1975) is considered one of the key texts of French feminism. Much of the section of the book extracted is devoted to unweaving or deconstructing binaries such as Logos/Pathos, or Parole/Écriture; "logos" is considered a Judeo-Christian concept, meaning knowledge, wisdom and even Christ, all of the concepts clustered together in the "parole" or self-present speech utterances. In such a system, "écriture" is seen in a derogatory sense as absence, writing, death, that is to say, writing divorced from patriarchal self-presence and mastery. Cixous and Clément note that from a gender perspective, this logocentric system is not only organized by hierarchy, but always implicates the values of activity/passivity on either side of the binaries, where woman is either "passive or she does not exist." An extreme but representative case is Mallarmé's short story "For Anatolé's Tomb", where the Father replaces the Mother/woman entirely. Another example is James Joyce's modernist novel *Ulysses*, where the character of Molly Bloom passively dreams and exists as a bodily, sexual presence. Women are also exiled by the notion of their subjectivity being a "dark continent", a racist phrase once used for Africa during the colonial period, meaning mysterious, unknowable, primitive, and racially black. Cixous and Clément reject this label, although they note that in relation to literary and mythological narratives, women are situated "between two terrifying myths", that of an abyssal nothingness or the classical image of the Medusa, a woman who turns men who look at her into stone. Rejecting all of these patriarchal discourses, Cixous and Clément argue that women are not "castrated" (the basis of female sexuality for Freud and Lacan), and that they are returning from this zone of passivity and exclusion through writing (*écriture feminine*), rejecting the male myths and fears, the racism and the colonialism. In an autobiographical section, Cixous reminds her readers that she comes from a Sephardic Jewish and Austro-German background, living in Algeria under the French occupation. Seeing the worse side of French colonialism, Cixous rejects one of the most central components of the Hegelian dialectic, that of the master/slave episode, which she aligns with the colonial process of claiming two "races" in a "distribution of violence". It is here that Cixous also notes how patriarchy depends upon the violently excluded other, that the exclusion itself is how the dialectic works. And so she retreats into a re-imagining of patriarchy, one in which a powerful creativity looks for those subjects who share her "rebellion" and her "hope".

Where is she?
Activity/passivity
Sun/Moon
Culture/Nature
Day/Night

Father/Mother
Head/Heart
Intelligible/Palpable
Logos/Pathos.
Form, convex, step, advance, semen, progress.
Matter, concave, ground – where steps are taken, holding- and dumping-ground.
Man
Woman

Always the same metaphor: we follow it, it carries us, beneath all its figures, wherever discourse is organized. If we read or speak, the same thread or double braid is leading us throughout literature, philosophy, criticism, centuries of representation and reflection.
Thought has always worked through opposition,
Speaking/Writing
Parole/Écriture
High/Low

Through dual, hierarchical oppositions. Superior/Inferior, Myths, legends, books. Philosophical systems. Everywhere (where) ordering intervenes, where a law organizes what is thinkable by oppositions (dual, irreconcilable; or sublatable, dialectical). And all these pairs of oppositions are *couples*. Does that mean something? Is the fact that Logocentrism subjects thought – all concepts, codes and values – to a binary system, related to "the" couple, man/woman?

Nature/History
Nature/Art
Nature/Mind
Passion/Action

Theory of culture, theory of society, symbolic systems in general – art, religion, family, language – it is all developed while bringing the same schemes to light. And the movement whereby each opposition is set up to make sense is the movement through which the couple is destroyed. A universal battlefield. Each time, a war is let loose. Death is always at work.

Father/son Relations of authority, privilege, force.

The Word/Writing Relations: opposition, conflict, sublation, return.

Master/slave Violence. Repression.

We see that "victory" always comes down to the same thing: things get hierarchical. Organization by hierarchy makes all conceptual organization subject to man. Male privilege, shown in the opposition between *activity* and *passivity,* which he uses to sustain himself. Traditionally, the question of sexual difference is treated by coupling it with the opposition: activity/passivity.

There are repercussions. Consulting the history of philosophy — since philosophical discourse both orders and reproduces all thought — one notices[1] that it is marked by an absolute *constant* which orders values and which is precisely this opposition, activity/passivity.

Moreover, woman is always associated with passivity in philosophy. Whenever it is a question of woman, when one examines kinship structures, when a family model is brought into play. In fact, as soon as the question of ontology raises its head, as soon as one asks oneself "what is it?," as soon as there is intended meaning. Intention: desire, authority—examine them and you are led right back . . . to the father. It is even possible not to notice that there is no place whatsoever for woman in the calculations. Ultimately the world of "being" can function while precluding the mother. No need for a mother, as long as there is some motherliness: and it is the father, then, who acts the part, who is the mother. Either woman is passive or she does not exist. What is left of her is unthinkable, unthought. Which certainly means that she is not thought, that she does not enter into the oppositions, that she does not make a couple with the father (who makes a couple with the son).

There is Mallarmé's tragic dream,[2] that father's lamentation on the mystery of paternity, that wrenches from the poet *the* mourning, the mourning of mournings, the death of the cherished son: this dream of marriage between father and son. — And there's no mother then. A man's dream when faced with death. Which always threatens him differently than it threatens a woman.

"a union
a marriage, splendid   And dreams of filiation
—and with life   that is masculine, dreams
still in me   of God the father
I shall use it   issuing from himself
for . . .   in his son — and
so not mother then?"   no mother then

She does not exist, she can not-be; but there has to be something of her. He keeps, then, of the woman on whom he is no longer dependent, only this space, always virginal, as matter to be subjected to the desire he wishes to impart.

And if we consult literary history, it is the same story. It all comes back to man — to *his* torment, his desire to be (at) the origin. Back to the father. There is an intrinsic connection between the philosophical and the literary (to the extent that it conveys meaning, literature is under the command of the philosophical) and the phallocentric. Philosophy is constructed on the premise of woman's abasement. Subordination of the feminine to the masculine order, which gives the appearance of being the condition for the machinery's functioning.

Now it has become rather urgent to question this solidarity between logocentrism and phallocentrism — bringing to light the fate dealt to woman, her burial — to threaten the stability of the masculine structure that passed itself off as eternal-natural, by conjuring up from femininity the reflections and hypotheses that are necessarily ruinous for the stronghold still in possession of authority. What would happen to logocentrism, to the great philosophical systems, to the order of the world in general if the rock upon which they founded this church should crumble?

If some fine day it suddenly came out that the logocentric plan had always, inadmissibly, been to create a foundation for (to found and fund) phallocentrism, to guarantee the masculine order a rationale equal to history itself.

So all the history, all the stories would be there to retell differently; the future would be incalculable; the historic forces would and will change hands and change body – another thought which is yet unthinkable – will transform the functioning of all society. We are living in an age where the conceptual foundation of an ancient culture is in the process of being undermined by millions of a species of mole (Topoi, ground mines) never known before.

When they wake up from among the dead, from among words, from among laws.

Once upon a time . . .

One cannot yet say of the following history "it's just a story." It's a tale still true today. Most women who have awakened remember having slept, *having been put to sleep.*

Once upon a time . . . once . . . and once again.

Beauties slept in their woods, waiting for princes to come and wake them up. In their beds, in their glass coffins, in their childhood forests like dead women. Beautiful, but passive; hence desirable: all mystery emanates from them. It is men who like to play dolls. As we have known since Pygmalion. Their old dream: to be god the mother. The best mother, the second mother, the one who gives the second birth.

She sleeps, she is intact, eternal, absolutely powerless. He has no doubt that she has been waiting for him forever.

The secret of her beauty, kept for him: she has the perfection of something finished. Or not begun. However, she is breathing. Just enough life – and not too much. Then he will kiss her. So that when she opens her eyes she will see only *him;* him in place of everything, all-him.[3]

– This dream is so satisfying! Whose is it? What desire gets something out of it?

He leans over her . . . Cut. The tale is finished. Curtain. Once awake (him or her), it would be an entirely different story. Then there would be two people, perhaps. You never know with women. And the voluptuous simplicity of the preliminaries would no longer take place.

Harmony, desire, exploit, search – all these movements are preconditions – of woman's arrival. Preconditions, more precisely, of her *arising.* She is lying down, he stands up. She arises – end of the dream – what follows is sociocultural: he makes her lots of babies, she spends her youth in labor; from bed to bed, until the age at which the thing isn't "woman" for him anymore.

"Bridebed, childbed, bed of death": thus woman's trajectory is traced as she inscribes herself from bed to bed in Joyce's *Ulysses.* The voyage of Ulysses with Bloom standing constantly at the helm as he navigates Dublin. Walking, exploring. The voyage of Penelope – Every woman: a bed of pain in which the mother is never done with dying, a hospital bed on which there is no end to Mrs. Purefoy's labor, the bed framing endless erotic daydreams, where Molly, wife and adulteress, voyages in her memories. She wanders, but lying down. In dream. Ruminates. Talks to herself. Woman's voyage: as a *body.* As if she were destined – in the distribution established by men (separated from the world where cultural exchanges are made and kept in the wings of the social stage when it is a case of History) – to be the nonsocial, nonpolitical, nonhuman half of the living structure. On nature's side of this structure, of course, tirelessly listening to what goes on inside – inside her belly, inside her "house." In direct contact with her appetites, her affects.

And, whereas he takes (after a fashion) the risk and responsibility of being an agent, a bit of the public scene where transformations are played out, she represents indifference or resistance to this active tempo; she is the principle of consistency, always somehow the same, everyday and eternal.

Man's dream: I love her – absent, hence desirable, a dependent nonentity, hence adorable. Because she isn't there where she is. As long as she isn't where she is. How he looks at her then! When her eyes are closed, when he completely understands her, when he catches on and she is no more than this shape made for him: a body caught in his gaze.

Or woman's dream? It's only a dream. I am sleeping. If I weren't asleep, he wouldn't look for me, he wouldn't cross his good lands and my badlands to get to me. Above all, don't wake me up! What anguish! If I have to be entombed to attract him. And suppose he kissed me? How can I will this kiss? Am I willing?

What does she want? To sleep, perchance to dream, to be loved in a dream, to be approached, touched, almost, to almost come (*jouir*). But not to come: or else she would wake up. But she came in a dream, once upon a time.

And once again upon a time, it is the same story repeating woman's destiny in love across the centuries with the cruel hoax of its plot. And each story, each myth says to her: "There is no place for your desire in our affairs of State." Love is threshold business. For us men, who are made to succeed, to climb the social ladder, temptation that encourages us, drives us, and feeds our ambitions is good. But carrying it out is dangerous. Desire must not disappear. You women represent the eternal threat, the anticulture for us. We don't stay in your houses; we are not going to remain in your beds. We wander. Entice us, get us worked up – that is what we want from you. Don't make us stretch out, soft and feminine, without a care for time or money. Your kind of love is death for us. A threshold affair:[4] it's all in the suspense, in what will soon be, always differed. On the other side is the fall: enslavement for the one and for the other, domestication, confinement in family and in social function.

By dint of reading this story-that-ends-well, she learns the paths that take her to the "loss" that is her fate. Turn around and he's gone! A kiss, and he goes. His desire, fragile and kept alive by lack, is maintained by absence: man pursues. As if he couldn't have what he has. Where is she, where is woman in all the spaces he surveys, in all the scenes he stages within the literary enclosure?

We know the answers and there are plenty: she is to the shadow. In the shadow he throws on her; the shadow she is.

Night to his day – that has forever been the fantasy. Black to his white. Shut out of his system's space, she is the repressed that ensures the system's functioning.

Kept at a distance so that he can enjoy the ambiguous advantages of the distance, so that she, who is distance and postponement, will keep alive the enigma, the dangerous delight of seduction, in suspense, in the role of "eloper." she is Helen, somehow "outside." But she cannot appropriate this "outside" (it is rare that she even wants it); it is his outside: outside on the condition that it not be entirely outside, the unfamiliar stranger that would escape him. So she stays inside a domesticated outside.

Eloper: carried away with herself and carried off from herself.

–Not only is she the portion of strangeness – *inside* his universe where she revives his restlessness and desire. Within his economy, she is the strangeness he likes to appropriate. Moreover, the "dark continent" trick has been pulled on her: she has been kept at a distance from herself, she has been made to see (= not-see) woman on the basis of what man wants to see of her, which is to say, almost nothing. She has been forbidden the possibility of the proud "inscription above my door" marking the threshold of The Gay Science. She could never have exclaimed:

> The house I live in is my own,
> I never copied anyone . . .

She has not been able to live in her "own" house, her very body. She can be incarcerated, slowed down appallingly and tricked into apartheid for too long a time — but still only for a time. One can teach her, as soon as she begins to speak, at the same time as she is taught her name, that hers is the dark region: because you are Africa, you are black. Your continent is dark. Dark is dangerous. You can't see anything in the dark, you are afraid. Don't move, you might fall. Above all, don't go into the forest. And we have internalized this fear of the dark. Women haven't had eyes for themselves. They haven't gone exploring in their house. Their sex still frightens them. Their bodies, which they haven't dared enjoy, have been colonized. Woman is disgusted by woman and fears her.

They have committed the greatest crime against women: insidiously and violently, they have led them to hate women, to be their own enemies, to mobilize their immense power against themselves, to do the male's dirty work.

They have committed an antinarcissism in her! A narcissism that only loves itself if it makes itself loved for what is lacking! They have created the loathsome logic of antilove.

The "Dark Continent" is neither dark nor unexplorable: It is still unexplored only because we have been made to believe that it was too dark to be explored. Because they want to make us believe that what interests us is the white continent, with its monuments to Lack. And we believed. We have been frozen in our place between two terrifying myths: between the Medusa and the abyss. It would be enough to make half the world break out laughing, if it were not still going on. For the phallo-logocentric *aufhebung* is there, and it is militant, the reproducer of old schemes, anchored in the dogma of castration. They haven't changed a thing: they have theorized their desire as reality. Let them tremble, those priests: we are going to *show* them our *sexts!*

Too bad for them if they collapse on discovering that women aren't men, or that the mother doesn't have one. But doesn't this fear suit them fine? Wouldn't the worst thing be — isn't the worst thing that, really, woman is not castrated, that all one has to do is not listen to the sirens (because the sirens were men) for history to change its sense, its direction? All you have to do to see the Medusa is look her in the face: and she isn't deadly. She is beautiful and she laughs.

They say there are two things that cannot be represented: death and the female sex. Because they need femininity to be associated with death: they get a hard-on when you scare their pants off! For their own sake they need to be afraid of us. Look at the trembling Perseuses, with their advance, armor-clad in apotropes as they back toward us! Pretty backs. There's not a minute to lose. Let's get out of here.

They, the feminine ones, are coming back from far away, from forever, from "outside," from the heaths where witches stay alive; from underneath, from the near side of "culture;" *from their childhoods,* which men have so much trouble making women forget, and which they condemn to the *in-pace.* Walled in — those little girls with their "bad-mannered" bodies. Preserved, safe from themselves and intact, on ice, Frigified. But the signs of unrest down there! How hard the sex cops have to work, always having to start over, to block women's threatening return. So many forces have been deployed on both sides that the struggle has been stuck for centuries, balanced in a shaky standstill.

We, coming early to culture, repressed and choked by it, our beautiful mouths stopped up with gags, pollen, and short breaths; we the labyrinths, we the ladders, we the trampled spaces; the stolen and the flights — we are "black" *and* we are beautiful.

A Woman's Coming to Writing:
Who
Invisible, foreign, secret, hidden, mysterious, black, forbidden
Am I . . .
Is this me, this no-body that is dressed up, wrapped in veils, carefully kept distant, pushed to the side of History and change, nullified, kept out of the way, on the edge of the stage, on the kitchen side, the bedside?
For you?
Is that me, a phantom doll, the cause of sufferings and wars, the pretext, "because of her beautiful eyes," for what men do, says Freud, for their divine illusions, their conquests, their havoc? Not for the sake of "me," of course. But for my "eyes," so that I will look at you, so that he will be looked at, so that he will see himself seen as he wants to be. Or as he fears he is not. Me, nobody, therefore, or else the mother that the Eternal Male always returns to when seeking admiration.

Men say that it is for her that the Greeks launched a thousand ships, destroyed, killed, waged a fabulous war for ten-times-ten years — among men! For the sake of her, yonder, the idol, carried off, hidden, lost. Because it is for-her and without-her that they live it up at the celebration of death that they call their life.
Murder of the Other:
I come, biographically, from a rebellion, from a violent and anguished direct refusal to accept what is happening on the stage on whose edge I find I am placed, as a result of the combined accidents of History. I had this strange "luck": a couple of rolls of the dice, a meeting between two trajectories of the diaspora,[5] and, at the end of these routes of expulsion and dispersion that mark the functioning of western History through the displacements of Jews, I fall. — I am born — right in the middle of a scene that is the perfect example, the naked model, the raw idea of this very process: I learned to read, to write, to scream, and to vomit in Algeria. Today I know from experience that one cannot imagine what an Algerian French girl was; you have to have been it, to have gone through it. To have seen "Frenchmen" at the "height" of imperialist blindness, behaving in a country that was inhabited by humans as if it were peopled by nonbeings, born-slaves. I learned everything from this first spectacle: I saw how the white (French), superior, plutocratic, civilized world founded its power on the repression of populations who had suddenly become "invisible," like proletarians, immigrant workers, minorities who are not the right "color." Women.[6] Invisible as humans. But, of course, perceived as tools — dirty, stupid, lazy, underhanded, etc. Thanks to some annihilating dialectical magic. I saw that the great, noble, "advanced" countries established themselves by expelling what was "strange"; excluding it but not dismissing it; enslaving it. A commonplace gesture of History: there have to be *two* races — the masters and the slaves.

We know the implied irony in the master/slave dialectic: the *body* of what is strange must not disappear, but its force must be conquered and returned to the master. Both the appropriate and the inappropriate must exist: the clean, hence the dirty; the rich, hence the poor; etc.

So I am three or four years old and the first thing I see in the street is that the world is divided in half, organized hierarchically, and that it maintains this distribution through violence. I see that there are those who beg, who die of hunger, misery, and despair, and that there are offenders who die of wealth and pride, who stuff themselves, who crush and humiliate. Who kill. And who walk around in a stolen country as if they had had the eyes of their souls put out. Without seeing that the others are alive.

Already I know all about the "reality" that supports History's progress: everything throughout the centuries depends on the distinction between the Selfsame, the ownself (– what is mine, hence what is good) and that which limits it: so now what menaces my-own-good (good never being anything other than what is good-for-me) is the "other." What is the "Other"? If it is truly the "other," there is nothing to say: it cannot be theorized. The "other" escapes me. It is elsewhere, outside: absolutely other. It doesn't settle down. But in History, of course, what is called "other" is an alterity that does settle down, that falls into the dialectical circle. It is the other in a hierarchically organized relationship in which the same is what rules, names, defines, and assigns "its" other. With the dreadful simplicity that orders the movement Hegel erected as a system, society trots along before my eyes reproducing to perfection the mechanism of the death struggle: the reduction of a "person" to a "nobody" to the position of "other" – the inexorable plot of racism. There has to be some "other" – no master without a slave, no economico-political power without exploitation, no dominant class without cattle under the yoke, no "Frenchmen" without wogs, no Nazis without Jews, no property without exclusion – an exclusion that has its limits and is part of the dialectic. If there were no other, one would invent it. Besides, that is what masters do: they have their slaves made to order. Line for line. They assemble the machine and keep the alternator supplied so that it reproduces all the oppositions that make economy and thought run.

The paradox of otherness is that, of course, at no moment in History is it tolerated or possible as such. The other is there only to be reappropriated, recaptured, and dest-royed as other. Even the exclusion is not an exclusion. Algeria was not France, but it was "French."

Me too. The routine "our ancestors, the Gauls" was pulled on me. But I was born in Algeria, and my ancestors lived in Spain, Morocco, Austria, Hungary, Czechoslovakia, Germany; my brothers by birth are Arab. So where are we in history? I side with those who are injured, trespassed upon, colonized. I am (not) Arab. Who am I? I am "doing" French history. I am a Jewish woman. In which ghetto was I penned up during your wars and your revolutions? I want to fight. What is my name? I want to change life. Who is this "I"? Where is my place? I am looking. I search everywhere. I read, I ask. I begin to speak. Which language is mine? French? German? Arabic? Who spoke for me throughout the generations'? It's my luck. What an accident! Being born in Algeria, not in France, not in Germany: a little earlier and, like some members of my family, I would not be writing today. I would anonymiserate eternally from Auschwitz. Luck: if I had been born a hundred years earlier, I told myself, I would have been part of the Commune. How? – you? Where are my battles? my fellow soldiers? What am I saying . . . the comrades, women, my companions-in-arms?

I am looking everywhere. A daughter of chance. One year earlier. A miracle. I know it; I hate it: I might never have been anything but dead. Yesterday, what could I have been? Can I imagine my elsewhere?

– I live all of my childhood in this knowledge: several times I have miraculously survived. In the previous generation. I would not have existed. And I live in this rebellion: it is impossible for me to live, to breathe, to eat in a world where my people don't breathe, don't eat, are crushed and humiliated. My people: all those that I am, whose same I am. History's condemned, the exiled, colonized, and burned.

Yes, Algeria is unliveable. Not to mention France.
Germany! Europe the accomplice! . . .

– There has to be somewhere else, I tell myself. And everyone knows that to go somewhere else there are routes, signs, "maps" – for an exploration, a trip – That's what books are. Everyone knows that a place exists which is not economically or politically indebted to all the vileness and compromise. That is not obliged to reproduce the system. That is writing. If there is a somewhere else that can escape the infernal repetition, it lies in that direction, where *it* writes itself, where *it* dreams, where *it* invents new worlds.

And that is where I go. I take books; I leave the real, colonial space: I go away. Often I go read in a tree. Far from the ground and the shit. I don't go and readjust to read, to forget – No! Not to shut myself up in some imaginary paradise. I am searching: somewhere there must be people who are like me in their rebellion and in their hope. Because I don't despair: if I myself shout in disgust, if I can't be alive without being angry, there must be others like me. I don't know who, but when I am big, I'll find them and I'll join them, I don't yet know where. While waiting, I want to have only my true ancestors for company (and even at that I forgive the Gauls a great deal, thanks to their defeat; they, too, were alienated, deceived, enslaved, it's true) – my true allies, my true "race." Not this comical, repulsive species that exercises power in the place where I was born.

And naturally I focused on all the texts in which there is struggle. Warlike texts; rebellious texts. For a long time I read, I lived, in a territory made of spaces taken from all the countries to which I had access through fiction, an antiland (I can never say the word "patrie," "fatherland," even if it is provided with an "anti-") where distinctions of races, classes, and origins would not be put to use without someone's rebelling. Where there are people who are ready for anything – to live, to die for the sake of ideas that are right and *just*. And where it was not impossible or pathetic to be generous. I knew, I have always known, what I hated. I located the enemy and all his destructive figures: authority, repression, censorship, the unquenchable thirst for wealth and power. The ceaseless work of death – the constant of evil. But that couldn't last. Death had to be destroyed. I saw that reality, history, was a series of struggles, without which we would have long ago been dead. And in my mental voyage, I gave great importance to battlefields, conflicts, the confrontation between the forces of death and the forces of life, between wrong ideas and right ideas. Actually, I have always wanted war; I did not believe that changes would be made except through revolutionary movements. I saw the enormity of power every day. Nazism, colonialism, centuries of violent inequality, the massacre of peoples, religious wars. Only one answer – struggle. And without theorizing any of that, of course – I forged through the texts where there was struggle.

I questioned might – its use, its value; through a world of fiction and myths. I followed closely those who had it and who used it. I asked everywhere: where does your strength come from? What have you done with your power? What cause have you served? I watched the "masters" especially closely – the kings, chiefs, judges, leaders, all those who I thought could have changed society; and then the "heroes": that is to say, the persons endowed with an individual strength but without authority, those who were isolated, eccentric, the intruders: great, undaunted, sturdy beings, who were at odds with the Law.

I have not read the Bible: I took short cuts, I lingered with Saul and with David. The rise and fall of men spoiled by power.

I liked Hercules very much, because he did not put his muscles to work for death, until the day I began to discover he was not a revolutionary but a gullible policeman.

I fought the Trojan war my own way: on neither one side nor the other. I loathed the chiefs' stupid, petty, and sanctifying mentality. What did they serve? A narcissistic glory. What did they love? Their royal image. The masculine code, squared: not only the masculine value but the essence of virility as well, that is undisputed power. Now onto the stage comes the species of men-kings. Vile patterns. Villainous bosses. Wily. Guilty consciences. The Agamemnon type. I despised the species.

And I pushed ahead into all the mythical and historical times.

And what would I have been then? Who? — A question that didn't come to me until later. The day when suddenly I felt bad in every skin I had ever worn.

Indeed, in Homeric times I was Achilles. I know why. I was the antiking. And I was passion. I had fits of rage that made History difficult. I didn't give a damn for hierarchy, for command, and I know how to love. I greatly loved women and men. I knew the value of a unique person, the beauty, the sweetness. I didn't ask myself any petty questions, I was unaware of limits. I enjoyed my bisexuality without anxiety: that both kinds harmonized within me seemed perfectly natural to me. I never even thought it could be otherwise. Had I not lived among women for a long time? And among men I gave up nothing of the tender, feminine intensities. Prohibition didn't come near me. I was far above stupid superstitions, sterile divisions. And I always loved wholly: I adored Patroclus with all my might; as a woman I was his sister, his lover, his mother; as a man, his brother, his husband, and himself. And I knew better than any man how to love women because of having been their companion and their sister for so long. I loved and I loved love. I never went back on love.

But sometimes I was ashamed: I was afraid of being Ulysses, and wasn't I sometimes? As Achilles I was uncompromising. But when I changed weapons? When I used the weapons of the crafty one, the one who knew too much about mediocrity and human weakness and not enough about true unbending strength — ? "Silence, exile and cunning" are the tools of the young man-artist with which Stephen Dedalus arms himself to organize his series of tactical retreats while he works out in "the smithy of his soul the uncreated conscience of his race." A help to a loner, of course. But I didn't like to catch myself being Ulysses, the artist of flight. The Winner: the one who was saved, the homecoming man! Always returning to himself — in spite of the most fantastic detours. The Loaner: loaning himself to women and never giving himself except to the ideal image of Ulysses, bringing his inalterable resistance home to his hot-shot little phallic rock, where, as the crowning act of the *nostos* — the return, which was so similar, I said to myself, to the Jewish fantasy (next year in Jerusalem) — he produced a remarkable show of force. I didn't analyze the bowshot, of course, but I did suspect it contained some "male" symbolic values that made it repugnant to me. How banal! To resist the Sirens, he ties himself up! to a mast! a little phallus and a big phallus too. . . . Later on Ulysses becomes a radical socialist. Noteworthy. I was bitter for a long time about having believed I was this resourceful man when I tried to get out of threatening situations by lying or subterfuge (which happened two or three times in my childhood). I was furious that I had been on the defensive. And, at that time, I didn't have the knowledge, the intellectual means that would have allowed me to understand and forgive myself. Thus from hero to hero went my armor, my sword, my shield.

Then the day comes — rather late for that matter — when I leave childhood. My anger is unmollified. The Algerian war approaches. Societies falter, I feel — the smell of my blood, too, is changing — a real war is coming, coming to a boil. And I quit being a child who is neuter, an angry bundle of nerves, a me seething with violent dreams, meditating widespread revenge, the overthrow of idols, the triumph of the oppressed.

No longer can I identify myself simply and directly with Samson or inhabit my glorious characters. My body is no longer innocently useful to my plans, (breasts) I am a woman.

Then everything gets complicated. I don't give up on war. That would be suicide: struggle is more necessary than ever. For in reality, the offense is also against me, as a woman, and the enemy is all over the place: not only are there class enemies, colonialists, racists, bourgeois, and antisemites against me — "men" are added to them. Or rather, the enemy becomes twice as formidable and more hated. But the worst of it is that among my brothers, in my own imaginary camp, some aggressors appear who are as narrow-minded, crude, and frightening as the ones confronting me. In some way I always knew, always saw this glaring, sexual brutishness surrounding me. But it never becomes intolerable to me until it hurts me as it passes through my own body and drags me into this spot of insoluble contradictions, impossible to overcome, this place I have never been able to get out of since: the friend is also the enemy. All women have lived that, are living it, as I continue to live it. "We" struggle together, yes, but, who is this "we"? A man and beside him a thing, somebody – (a woman: always in her parenthesis, always repressed or invalidated as a woman, tolerated as a non-woman, "accepted"!) – someone you are not conscious of, unless she effaces herself, acts the man, speaks and thinks that way. For a woman, what I am saying is trite. It has often been said. It is that experience that launched the front line of the feminist struggle in the U.S. and in France: discovering discrimination, the fundamental unconscious masculine racism in places where, theoretically, it should not exist! A political irony: imagine fighting against racism with militants who *are* racist!

I, revolt, rages, where am I to stand? What is my place if I am a woman? I look for myself throughout the centuries and don't see myself anywhere. I know now that my fighters are masculine and that their value almost inevitably is limited: they are great in the eyes of men and for each other. But only on the condition that a woman not appear and make blind and grotesque tyrants of them, marred by all the flaws that I want them to be free of – exposing them to be miserly, inhuman, small, fearful . . .

Where to stand? Who to be? Who, in the long continuing episodes of their misfortune – woman's abundance always repaid by abandonment? Beginning Medea's story all over again, less and less violently, repeating more and more tenderly, sadly, the gift, the fervor, the passion, the alienation, the stunning discovery of the worst (which isn't death): that total love has been used by the loved one for his base ambitions. "The one who was everything for me, I know only too well, my husband has become the worst of men." (Euripides, *Medea*).

Vast – this procession of mistreated, deceived, devastated, rejected, patient women, dolls, cattle, cash, Stolen swarms. Exploited and plundered to such an extent. They give everything. That, doubtless, is their offense. For example – Ariadne, without calculating, without hesitating, but believing, taking everything as far as it goes, giving everything, renouncing all security – spending without a return – the anti-Ulysses – never looking back, knowing how to break off, how to leave, advancing into emptiness, into the unknown. But as for Theseus, he ties himself tightly to the line the woman holds fast to make him secure. While she, she takes her leap without a line. I read the *Life of Theseus* in Plutarch.

Notes

1   All Derrida's work traversing-detecting the history of philosophy is devoted to bringing this to light. In Plato, Hegel, and Nietzsche, the same process continues: repression, repudiation, distancing of woman; a murder that is mixed up with history as the manifestation and representation of masculine power.

2   "For Anatole's Tomb" (Seuil, 1961, p. 138). This is the tomb in which Mallarmé keeps his son from death and watches over him as his mother.

3   "She only awakens at love's touch and before that moment she is only a dream. But in this dream existence one can distinguish two stages: first love dreams of her, then she dreams of love." Thus Kierkegaard's *Seducer* dreams.

4   The pleasure is preliminary, Freud says. This is a "truth" but only a partial one. It is a point of view, in fact, coming from and upheld by the masculine Imaginary, to the extent that the masculine Imaginary is shaped by the threat of castration.

5   My father, Sephardic – Spain – Morocco – Algeria – my mother, Ashkenazy – Austria – Hungary – Czechoslovakia (her father) and Spain (her mother) passing by chance through a Paris that was short-lived.

6   Women: at that time I wasn't thinking about them. At first, occupying the stage in a way that I could plainly see, the battle to death was the battle pitting colonial power against its victims. Beyond that I perceived that it was the imperialist result of capitalist structure and that it intensified the class struggle by deepening it and making it more monstrous and inhuman: the exploited were not even "workers" but, with racism's assistance, something worse – subhuman; and the universe could pretend to obey "natural" laws. War was on the horizon, partially concealed from me. I wasn't in France. I didn't see betrayal and collaboration with my own eyes. We were living under Vichy: I perceived its effects without knowing their causes. I had to guess why my father couldn't do his work, why I couldn't go to school, et cetera. And I had to guess why, as a little white girl informed me, "all Jews are liars."

Chapter 59

Sandra M. Gilbert and Susan D. Gubar

INFECTION IN THE SENTENCE

The woman writer and the anxiety of authorship

Sandra M. Gilbert and Susan D. Gubar's approach to the conundrum of finding a woman's authorial voice in a patriarchal culture involves here rejecting a key critical paradigm, that of Bloom's "anxiety of influence" theory, whereby new literary writers need to overcome their canonical forefathers. As leading North American feminist critics, Gilbert and Gubar have produced extensive readings of traditional and new female canons, explored in their groundbreaking *The Madwoman in the Attic* (1979), focusing on nineteenth-century writing, and three volumes of *No Man's Land* (1988, 1989 and 1994), turning to the twentieth-century. Gilbert and Gubar argue that the notion of overcoming one's canonical forefathers is essentially a "paternal" metaphor: the child is thereby engaged in an Oedipal struggle for dominance with the father. Ironically, this is also seen as an acute observation on the part of Bloom, because while Gilbert and Gubar reject his overarching agonistic vision of literary history, they agree that he has correctly revealed the *patriarchal structure* of literary history. Female authors, then, can be analyzed in terms of their different responses to the male-centric anxiety of influence paradigm, not just their reaction to patriarchal literary authority, but also their *rejection of* that authority for defining female aesthetic identity. This leads not so much to an anxiety concerning a struggle with the great chain of literary inheritance, but to the notion that under specifically male terms and conditions, a female author cannot even enter this chain by generating a maternal line; in Gilbert and Gubar's phrase, "she can never become a 'precursor'". "Self-creation" which is the stuff of the Romantic poets and beyond, needs to be wrested from the control of the literary patriarchs, through a female revisionary "swerve" which both seeks a female tradition and embodies the loneliness of the embattled artist as one of the by-products of "inferiorization". This doubled state of subjectivity offers insights into how women can articulate a rejection of patriarchy and yet simultaneously engage in modes of "inferiorization". Gilbert and Gubar celebrate the feminist subcultures that are the new site of female creativity and artistic achievement, in comparison with the exhausted survivors of the patriarchal battlefield. Gilbert and Gubar suggest, then, that women experience not an anxiety of influence, but an "anxiety of authorship": a rejection of the way in which patriarchy constitutes female (mis)identity. This anxiety can be debilitating, "infecting" women's discourses, making the writing act appear an act of imprisonment or fever. Gilbert and Gubar link this process with a wider point, that "patriarchal socialization" can lead to illness, for example with reference to studies that link negative stereotyping of women's bodies with the resulting teenage anorexia. In the nineteenth century, women were constructed in an ideal sense as being permanently in a state of psychological and physiological illness, in other words, as a sign of "femininity", leading to the "cult of female invalidism". Too much reading or creative writing was regarded as particularly problematic and liable to lead to breakdown; the "rest cure" during the nineteenth century, being an enforced exile from creative expression, can be seen as a patriarchally expected outcome of creative female subjectivity, what Gilbert and Gubar call the "goals" of Victorian training for proper (i.e., male-centric notions of) female decorum.

The man who does not know sick women does not know women.
                                                  —S. Weir Mitchell

I try to describe this long limitation, hoping that with such power as is now mine, and such use of language as is within that power, this will convince anyone who cares about it that this "living" of mine had been done under a heavy handicap. . . .
                                                  —Charlotte Perkins Gilman

A Word dropped careless on a Page
May stimulate an eye
When folded in perpetual seam
The Wrinkled Maker lie
Infection in the sentence breeds
We may inhale Despair
At distances of Centuries
From the Malaria—

                              —Emily Dickinson

I stand in the ring
in the dead city
and tie on the red shoes
. . . .
They are not mine,
they are my mother's,
her mother's before,
handed down like an heirloom
but hidden like shameful letters.
                              —Anne Sexton

What does it mean to be a woman writer in a culture whose fundamental definitions of literary authority are, as we have seen, both overtly and covertly patriarchal? If the vexed and vexing polarities of angel and monster, sweet dumb Snow White and fierce mad Queen, are major images literary tradition offers women, how does such imagery influence the ways in which women attempt the pen? If the Queen's looking glass speaks with the King's voice, how do its perpetual kingly admonitions affect the Queen's own voice? Since his is the chief voice she hears, does the Queen try to sound like the King, imitating his tone, his inflections, his phrasing, his point of view? Or does she "talk back" to him in her own vocabulary, her own timbre, insisting on her own viewpoint? We believe these are basic questions feminist literary criticism—both theoretical and practical—must answer, and consequently they are questions to which we shall turn again and again, not only in this chapter but in all our readings of nineteenth-century literature by women.

That writers assimilate and then consciously or unconsciously affirm or deny the achievements of their predecessors is, of course, a central fact of literary history, a fact whose aesthetic and metaphysical implications have been discussed in detail by theorists as diverse as T. S. Eliot, M. H. Abrams, Erich Auerbach, and Frank Kermode.[1] More recently, some literary theorists have begun to explore what we might call the psychology of literary history—the tensions and anxieties, hostilities and inadequacies writers feel when they confront not only the achievements of their predecessors but the traditions of genre, style, and metaphor that they inherit from such "forefathers." Increasingly, these critics study the ways in which, as J. Hillis Miller has put it, a literary text "is inhabited . . . by a long chain of parasitical presences, echoes, allusions, guests, ghosts of previous texts."[2]

As Miller himself also notes, the first and foremost student of such literary psychohistory has been Harold Bloom. Applying Freudian structures to literary genealogies, Bloom has postulated that the dynamics of literary history arise from the artist's "anxiety of influence," his fear that he is not his own creator and that the works of his predecessors, existing before and beyond him, assume essential priority over his own writings. In fact, as we pointed out in our discussion of the metaphor of literary paternity, Bloom's paradigm of the sequential historical relationship between literary artists is the relationship of father and son, specifically that relationship as it was defined by Freud. Thus Bloom explains that a "strong poet" must engage in heroic warfare with his "precursor," for, involved as he is in a literary Oedipal struggle, a man can only become a poet by somehow invalidating his poetic father.[3]

Bloom's model of literary history is intensely (even exclusively) male, and necessarily patriarchal. For this reason it has seemed, and no doubt will continue to seem, offensively sexist to some feminist critics. Not only, after all, does Bloom describe literary history as the crucial warfare of fathers and sons, he sees Milton's fiercely masculine fallen Satan as *the* type of the poet in our culture, and he metaphorically defines the poetic process as a sexual encounter between a male poet and his female muse. Where, then, does the female poet fit in? Does she want to annihilate a "forefather" or a "foremother"? What if she can find no models, no precursors? Does she have a muse, and what is its sex? Such questions are inevitable in any female consideration of Bloomian poetics. And yet, from a feminist perspective, their inevitability may be just the point; it may, that is, call our attention not to what is wrong about Bloom's conceptualization of the dynamics of Western literary history, but to what is right (or at least suggestive) about his theory.

For Western literary history *is* overwhelmingly male—or, more accurately, patriarchal—and Bloom analyzes and explains this fact, while other theorists have ignored it, precisely, one supposes, because they assumed literature had to be male. Like Freud, whose psychoanalytic postulates permeate Bloom's literary psychoanalyses of the "anxiety of influence," Bloom has defined processes of interaction that his predecessors did not bother to consider because, among other reasons, they were themselves so caught up in such processes. Like Freud, too, Bloom has insisted on bringing to consciousness assumptions readers and writers do not ordinarily examine. In doing so, he has clarified the implications of the psychosexual and sociosexual contexts by which every literary text is surrounded, and thus the meanings of the "guests" and "ghosts" which inhabit texts themselves. Speaking of Freud, the feminist theorist Juliet Mitchell has remarked that "psychoanalysis is not a recommendation *for* a patriarchal society, but an analysis of one."[4] The same sort of statement could be made about Bloom's model of literary history, which is not a recommendation for but an analysis of the patriarchal poetics (and attendant anxieties) which underlie our culture's chief literary movements.

For our purposes here, however, Bloom's historical construct is useful not only because it helps identify and define the patriarchal psychosexual context in which so much Western literature was authored, but also because it can help us distinguish the anxieties and achievements of female writers from those of male writers. If we return to the question we asked earlier—where does a woman writer "fit in" to the overwhelmingly and essentially male literary history Bloom describes?—we find we have to answer that a woman writer does *not* "fit in." At first glance, indeed, she seems to be anomalous, indefinable, alienated, a freakish outsider. Just as in Freud's theories of male and female psychosexual development there is no symmetry between a boy's growth and a girl's (with, say, the male "Oedipus complex" balanced by a female "Electra complex") so Bloom's male-oriented theory of the "anxiety of influence" cannot be simply reversed or inverted in order to account for the situation of the woman writer.

Certainly if we acquiesce in the patriarchal Bloomian model, we can be sure that the female poet does not experience the "anxiety of influence" in the same way that her male counterpart would, for the simple reason that she must confront precursors who are almost exclusively male, and therefore significantly different from her. Not only do these precursors incarnate patriarchal authority (as our discussion of the metaphor of literary paternity argued), they attempt to enclose her in definitions of her person and her potential which, by reducing her to extreme stereotypes (angel, monster) drastically conflict with her own sense of her self—that is, of her subjectivity, her autonomy, her creativity. On the one hand, therefore, the woman writer's male precursors symbolize authority; on the other hand, despite their authority, they fail to define the ways in which she experiences her own identity as a writer. More, the masculine authority with which they construct their literary personae, as well as the fierce power struggles in which they engage in their efforts of self-creation, seem to the woman writer directly to contradict the terms of her own gender definition. Thus the "anxiety of influence" that a male poet experiences is felt by a female poet as an even more primary "anxiety of authorship"—a radical fear that she cannot create, that because she can never become a "precursor" the act of writing will isolate or destroy her.

This anxiety is, of course, exacerbated by her fear that not only can she not fight a male precursor on "his" terms and win, she cannot "beget" art upon the (female) body of the muse. As Juliet Mitchell notes, in a concise summary of the implications Freud's theory of psychosexual development has for women, both a boy and a girl, "as they learn to speak and live within society, want to take the father's [in Bloom's terminology the precursor's] place, and *only the boy will one day be allowed to do so.* Furthermore both sexes are born into the desire of the mother, and as, through cultural heritage, what the mother desires is the phallus-turned-baby, *both* children desire to be the phallus for the mother. Again, *only the boy can fully recognize himself in his mother's desire.* Thus *both* sexes repudiate the implications of femininity," but the girl learns (in relation to her father) "that her subjugation to the law of the father entails her becoming the representative of 'nature' and 'sexuality,' a chaos of spontaneous, intuitive creativity."[5]

Unlike her male counterpart, then, the female artist must first struggle against the effects of a socialization which makes conflict with the will of her (male) precursors seem inexpressibly absurd, futile, or even—as in the case of the Queen in "Little Snow White"—self-annihilating. And just as the male artist's struggle against his precursor takes the form of what Bloom calls revisionary swerves, flights, misreadings, so the female writer's battle for self-creation involves her in a revisionary process. Her battle, however, is not against her (male) precursor's reading of the world but against his reading of *her.* In order to define herself as an author she must redefine the terms of her socialization. Her revisionary struggle, therefore, often becomes a struggle for what Adrienne Rich has called "Revision—the act of looking back, of seeing with fresh eyes, of entering an old text from a new critical direction . . . an act of survival."[6] Frequently, moreover, she can begin such a struggle only by actively seeking a *female* precursor who, far from representing a threatening force to be denied or killed, proves by example that a revolt against patriarchal literary authority is possible.

For this reason, as well as for the sound psychoanalytic reasons Mitchell and others give, it would be foolish to lock the woman artist into an Electra pattern matching the Oedipal structure Bloom proposes for male writers. The woman writer—and we shall see women doing this over and over again—searches for a female model not because she wants dutifully to comply with male definitions of her "femininity" but because she must legitimize her own rebellious endeavors. At the same time, like most women in patriarchal society, the woman writer does experience her gender as a painful obstacle, or even a debilitating inadequacy; like most patriarchally conditioned women, in other words, she is victimized by what Mitchell calls "the inferiorized and 'alternative' (second sex) psychology of women under patriarchy."[7] Thus the loneliness of the female artist, her feelings of alienation from male predecessors coupled with her need for sisterly precursors and successors, her urgent sense of her need for a female audience together with her fear of the antagonism of male readers, her culturally conditioned timidity about self-dramatization, her dread of the patriarchal authority of art, her anxiety about the impropriety of female invention—all these phenomena of "inferiorization" mark the woman writer's struggle for artistic self-definition and differentiate her efforts at self-creation from those of her male counterpart.

As we shall see, such sociosexual differentiation means that, as Elaine Showalter has suggested, women writers participate in a quite different literary subculture from that inhabited by male writers, a subculture which has its own distinctive literary traditions, even—though it defines itself *in relation to* the "main," male-dominated, literary culture—a distinctive history.[8] At best, the separateness of this female subculture has been exhilarating for women. In recent years, for instance, while male writers seem increasingly to have felt exhausted by the need for revisionism which Bloom's theory of the "anxiety of influence" accurately describes, women writers have seen themselves as pioneers in a creativity so intense that their male counterparts have probably not experienced its analog since the Renaissance, or at least since the Romantic era. The son of many fathers, today's male writer feels hopelessly belated; the daughter of too few mothers, today's female writer feels that she is helping to create a viable tradition which is at last definitively emerging.

There is a darker side of this female literary subculture, however, especially when women's struggles for literary self-creation are seen in the psychosexual context described by Bloom's Freudian theories of patrilineal literary inheritance. As we noted above, for an "anxiety of influence" the woman writer substitutes what we have called an "anxiety of authorship," an anxiety built from complex and often only barely conscious fears of that authority which seems to the female artist to be by definition inappropriate to her sex. Because it is based on the woman's socially determined sense of her own biology, this anxiety of authorship is quite distinct from the anxiety about creativity that could be traced in such male writers as Hawthorne or Dostoevsky. Indeed, to the extent that it forms one of the unique bonds that link women in what we might call the secret sisterhood of their literary subculture, such anxiety in itself constitutes a crucial mark of that subculture.

In comparison to the "male" tradition of strong, father-son combat, however, this female anxiety of authorship is profoundly debilitating. Handed down not from one woman to another but from the stern literary "fathers" of patriarchy to all their "inferiorized" female descendants, it is in many ways the germ of a dis-ease or, at any rate, a disaffection, a disturbance, a distrust, that spreads like a stain throughout the style and structure of much literature by women, especially—as we shall see in this study—throughout literature by women before the twentieth century. For if contemporary women do now attempt the pen with energy and authority, they are able to do so only because their eighteenth- and nineteenth-century foremothers struggled in isolation that felt like illness, alienation that felt like madness, obscurity that felt like paralysis to overcome the anxiety of authorship that was endemic to their literary subculture. Thus, while the recent feminist emphasis on positive role models has undoubtedly helped many women, it should not keep us from realizing the terrible odds against which a creative female subculture was established. Far from reinforcing socially oppressive sexual stereotyping, only a full consideration of such problems can reveal the extraordinary strength of women's literary accomplishments in the eighteenth and nineteenth centuries.

Emily Dickinson's acute observations about "infection in the sentence," quoted in our epigraphs, resonate in a number of different ways, then, for women writers, given the literary woman's special concept of her place in literary psychohistory. To begin with, the words seem to indicate Dickinson's keen consciousness that, in the purest Bloomian or Millerian sense, pernicious "guests" and "ghosts" inhabit all literary texts. For any reader, but especially for a reader who is also a writer, every text can become a "sentence" or weapon in a kind of metaphorical germ warfare. Beyond this, however, the fact that "infection in the sentence *breeds*" suggests Dickinson's recognition that literary texts are coercive, imprisoning, fever-inducing; that, since literature usurps a reader's interiority, it is an invasion of privacy. Moreover, given Dickinson's own gender definition, the sexual ambiguity of her poem's "Wrinkled Maker" is significant. For while, on the one hand, "we" meaning especially women writers "may inhale Despair" from all those patriarchal texts which seek to deny female autonomy and authority, on the other hand "we" meaning especially women writers "may inhale Despair" from all those "foremothers" who have both overtly and covertly conveyed their traditional authorship anxiety to their bewildered female descendants. Finally, such traditional, metaphorically matrilineal anxiety ensures that even the maker of a text, when she is a woman, may feel imprisoned within texts—folded and "wrinkled" by their pages and thus trapped in their "perpetual seam[s]" which perpetually tell her how she *seems*.

Although contemporary women writers are relatively free of the infection of this "Despair" Dickinson defines (at least in comparison to their nineteenth-century precursors), an anecdote recently related by the American poet and essayist Annie Gottlieb summarizes our point about the ways in which, for all women, "Infection in the sentence breeds":

> When I began to enjoy my powers as a writer, I dreamt that my mother had me sterilized! (Even in dreams we still blame our mothers for the punitive choices our culture forces on us.) I went after the mother-figure in my dream, brandishing a large knife; on its blade was writing. I cried, "Do you know what you are doing? You are destroying my femaleness, my *female power,* which is important to me *because of you!*"[9]

Seeking motherly precursors, says Gottlieb, as if echoing Dickinson, the woman writer may find only infection, debilitation. Yet still she must seek, not seek to subvert, her *"female power, which is important"* to her because of her lost literary matrilineage. In this connection, Dickinson's own words about mothers are revealing, for she alternately claimed that "I never had a mother," that "I always ran Home to Awe as a child. . . . He was an awful Mother but I liked him better than none," and that "a mother [was] a miracle."[10] Yet, as we shall see, her own anxiety of authorship was a "Despair" inhaled not only from the infections suffered by her own ailing physical mother, and her many tormented literary mothers, but from the literary fathers who spoke to her—even "lied" to her—sometimes near at hand, sometimes "at distances of Centuries," from the censorious looking glasses of literary texts.

It is debilitating to be *any* woman in a society where women are warned that if they do not behave like angels they must be monsters. Recently, in fact, social scientists and social historians like Jessie Bernard, Phyllis Chesler, Naomi Weisstein, and Pauline Bart have begun to study the ways in which patriarchal socialization literally makes women sick, both physically and mentally.[11] Hysteria, the disease with which Freud so famously began his investigations into the dynamic connections between *psyche* and *soma,* is by definition a "female disease," not so much because it takes its name from the Greek word for womb, *hyster* (the organ which was in the nineteenth century supposed to "cause" this emotional disturbance), but because hysteria did occur mainly among women in turn-of-the-century Vienna, and because throughout the nineteenth century this mental illness, like many other nervous disorders, was thought to be caused by the female reproductive system, as if to elaborate upon Aristotle's notion that femaleness was in and of itself a deformity.[12] And, indeed, such diseases of maladjustment to the physical and social environment as anorexia and agoraphobia did and do strike a disproportionate number of women. Sufferers from anorexia—loss of appetite, self-starvation—are primarily adolescent girls. Sufferers from agoraphobia—fear of open or "public" places—are usually female, most frequently middle-aged housewives, as are sufferers from crippling rheumatoid arthritis.[13]

   Such diseases are caused by patriarchal socialization in several ways. Most obviously, of course, any young girl, but especially a lively or imaginative one, is likely to experience her education in docility, submissiveness, self-lessness as in some sense sickening. To be trained in renunciation is almost necessarily to be trained to ill health, since the human animal's first and strongest urge is to his/her *own* survival, pleasure, assertion. In addition, each of the "subjects" in which a young girl is educated may be sickening in a specific way. Learning to become a beautiful object, the girl learns anxiety about – perhaps even loathing of—her own flesh. Peering obsessively into the real as well as metaphoric looking glasses that surround her, she desires literally to "reduce" her own body. In the nineteenth century as we noted earlier, this desire to be beautiful and "frail" led to tight-lacing and vinegar-drinking. In our own era it has spawned innumerable diets and "controlled" fasts, as well as the extraordinary phenomenon of teenage anorexia.[14] Similarly, it seems inevitable that women reared for, and conditioned to, lives of privacy, reticence domesticity, might develop pathological fears of public places and unconfined spaces. Like the comb, stay-laces, and apple which the Queen in "Little Snow White" uses as weapons against her hated stepdaughter, such afflictions as anorexia and agoraphobia simply carry patriarchal definitions of "femininity" to absurd extremes, and thus function as essential or at least inescapable parodies of social prescriptions.

   In the nineteenth century, however, the complex of social prescriptions these diseases parody did not merely urge women to act in ways which would cause them to become ill; nineteenth-century culture seems to have actually admonished women to *be* ill. In other words the "female diseases" from which Victorian women suffered were not always byproducts of their training in femininity; they were the goals of such training. As Barbara Ehrenreich and Deirdre English have shown, throughout much of the nineteenth century "Upper-and upper-middle-class women were [defined as] 'sick' [frail ill]; working class women were [defined as] 'sickening' [infectious, diseased]". Speaking of the "lady," they go on to point out that "Society agreed that she was frail and sickly," and consequently a "cult of female invalidism" developed in England and America. For the products of such a cult, it was, as Dr. Mary Putnam Jacobi wrote in 1895, "considered natural and almost laudable to break down under all conceivable varieties of strain—a winter dissipation, a houseful of servants, a quarrel with a female friend, not to speak of more legitimate reasons. . . . Constantly considering their nerves, urged to consider them by well-intentioned but short-sighted advisors, [women] pretty soon become nothing but a bundle of nerves."[15]

Notes

Epigraphs: Doctor on Patient (Philadelphia: Lippincott, 1888), quoted in Ilza Veith, *Hysteria: The History of a Disease* (Chicago: University of Chicago Press, 1965), pp. 219–20; *The Living of Charlotte Perkins Gilman* (New York: Harper & Row, 1975; first published 1935), p. 104; J. 1261 in *The Poems of Emily Dickinson,* ed. Thomas Johnson, 3 vols. (Cambridge, Mass.: The Belknap Press of Harvard University Press, 1955: all subsequent references are to this edition); "The Red Shoes," *The Book of Folly* (Boston: Houghton Mifflin, 1972), pp. 28–29.

1   In "Tradition and the Individual Talent," T. S. Eliot of course considers these matters. In addition, in *Mimesis* Erich Auerbach traces the ways in which the realist includes what has been previously excluded from art in the name of ever-larger slices of life. Similarly, in *The Sense of an Ending* Frank Kermode shows how poets and novelists lay bare the literariness of their predecessors' forms in order to explore the dissonance between fiction and reality, paradigmatic (inherited) forms and contingency.

2   J. Hillis Miller, "The Limits of Pluralism, III: The Critic as Host," *Critical Inquiry* (Spring 1977): 446.

3   See Harold Bloom, *The Anxiety of Influence.*

4   Juliet Mitchell, *Psychoanalysis and Feminism* (New York: Vintage, 1975), p. xiii.

5   Ibid., pp. 404–5.

6   Adrienne Rich, "When We Dead Awaken: Writing as Re-Vision," in *Adrienne Rich's Poetry,* ed. Barbara Charlesworth Gelpi and Albert Gelpi (New York: Norton, 1975), p. 90.

7   Mitchell, *Psychoanalysis and Feminism,* p. 402.

8   See Elaine Showalter, *A Literature of Their Own* (Princeton: Princeton University Press, 1977).

9   Annie Gottlieb, "Feminists Look at Motherhood," *Mother Jones* (November 1976):53.

10   *The Letters of Emily Dickinson,* ed. Thomas Johnson, 3 vols. (Cambridge, Mass.: The Belknap Press of Harvard University Press, 1958), 2:475; 2:518.

11   See Jessie Bernard, "The Paradox of the Happy Marriage," Pauline B. Bart, "Depression in Middle-Aged Women," and Naomi Weisstein, "Psychology Constructs the Female," all in Vivian Gornick and Barbara K. Moran, ed., *Woman in Sexist Society* (New York: Basic Books, 1971). See also Phyllis Chesler, *Women and Madness* (New York: Doubleday, 1972), and—for a summary of all these matters—Barbara Ehrenreich and Deirdre English, *Complaints and Disorders: The Sexual Politics of Sickness* (Old Westbury: The Feminist Press, 1973).

12   In *Hints on Insanity* (1861) John Millar wrote that "Mental derangement frequently occurs in young females from Amenorrhoea, especially in those who have any strong hereditary predisposition to insanity," adding that "an occasional warm hipbath or leeches to the pubis will . . . be followed by complete mental recovery." In 1873, Henry Mauldsey wrote in *Body and Mind* that "the monthly activity of the ovaries . . . has a notable effect upon the mind and body; wherefore it may become an important cause of mental and physical derangement." See especially the medical opinions of John Millar, Henry Maudsley, and Andrew Wynter in *Madness and Morals: Ideas on Insanity in the Nineteenth Century,* ed. Vieda Skultans (London and Boston: Routledge & Kegan Paul, 1975), pp. 230–35.

13   See Marlene Boskind-Lodahl, "Cinderella's Stepsisters: A Feminist Perspective on Anorexia Nervosa and Bulimia," *Signs* 2, no. 2 (Winter 1976): 342–56; Walter Blum, "The Thirteenth Guest," (on agoraphobia), in *California Living, The San Francisco Sunday Examiner and Chronicle* (17 April 1977): 8–12; Joan Arehart-Treichel, "Can Your Personality Kill You?" (on female rheumatoid arthritis, among other diseases), *New York* 10, no. 48 (28 November 1977) :45: "According to studies conducted in recent years, four out of five rheumatoid victims are women, and for good reason: The disease appears to arise in those unhappy with the traditional female-sex role."

14   More recent discussions of the etiology and treatment of anorexia are offered in Hilde Bruch, M. D., *The Golden Cage: The Enigma of Anorexia Nervosa* (Cambridge, Mass.: Harvard University Press, 1978), and in Salvador Minuchin, Bernice L. Rosman, and Lester Baker, *Psychosomatic Families: Anorexia Nervosa in Context* (Cambridge: Harvard University Press, 1978).

15   Quoted by Ehrenreich and English, *Complaints and Disorders,* p. 19.

Chapter 60

Margaret Homans

"WOMEN OF COLOUR"

Writers and feminist theory

The location of "women of colour" in contemporary feminist theory is the central concern of feminist critic and queer theorist Margaret Homans's essay, whereby she additionally analyzes and articulates the role and function of these misplaced and (mis)represented subjects. Homans, professor of English and Women's, Gender, and Sexuality Studies at Yale University, frames her essay with a narrative by Alice Walker to explore racially inflected differences in theorizing, that is to say, theorizing through story, "riddles and proverbs". The problematic alignment in popular and academic discourses of black women with corporeal or bodily subjectivity (especially compared with that of white subjects being aligned with "mind") leads to the recognition that in much white theoretical writing, black women function to re-embody the otherwise dematerialized conceptual theoretical text or argument. An example from Toril Moi is shocking in that it implies an absent presence in her text, whereby black women are regarded as identical to white women, and thus their voices do not need articulating within a theoretical feminist context. But even more problematic is when black women do appear—if the minimal use of their voices can be articulated in this way—as exemplary subjects in white theoretical texts. For example, in Haraway's "A Manifesto for Cyborgs" (1985), "women of colour" are represented as ideal postmodern subjects, being culturally and linguistically hybrid, embodying perhaps a free-floating semiotic world of non-essentialist signs. Elsewhere, Haraway adds to this through her theorizing of Sojourner Truth as a dematerialized cyborg body or subject. Homans argues that this representational analysis reveals a wider problematic: that black women are used by white poststructuralist and postmodernist feminists to function as an "alibi" for a "dematerializing" agenda, aimed specifically at a dematerializing of the female body. Revisiting a key book for Haraway, Cherrie Moraga's *Loving in the War Years*, Homans reads instead of a postmodern free-floating hybridity, a subject who is passionately aware of racially inflected corporeality, and an intense mother–daughter connection which is a key component of Moraga's lesbian identity. Homans compares this text to Gloria Anzaldúa's *Borderlands/La Frontera*, which models ambivalent subjectivity such as that which is also found in Moraga's narrative. Metaphors of liminality and difference are related by Anzaldúa to a quest for cultural and spiritual recovery and healing, rather than postmodern celebration of the endless play of difference. Judith Butler's use of Aretha Franklin in *Gender Trouble* is explored by Homans as another instance of a black woman appearing as an exemplary figure in a text which deconstructs identity in favour of process and performance; in this instance, Homans does not entirely reject Butler's reading, but she does argue that yet again it is a black woman who embodies the critique of the bodily! Homans sketches the wider black feminist response to such theorizing, arguing that the reclamation of individual black experiences is key, or, as Diana Fuss puts it in her *Essentially Speaking*, there is a "political necessity" to "the strategic use of essentialism", that is to say, in creating a coherent and corporate difference which can also express a shared identity, one which does not serve the aims of a particular white mode of high theory.

ALICE WALKER'S 1983 VOLUME *In Search of Our Mothers' Gardens* ends with the autobiographical narrative/essay, "Beauty: When the Other Dancer is the Self." Haunted in adulthood by self-doubt because of an eye blinded and scarred in childhood by a brother's BB-gun shot, Walker narrates in this essay the story of her healing, first surgical, then, in time, psychological. The essay ends in this way: looking steadily into her eyes one day at naptime, and recalling a televised image of the earth from outer space, Walker's three-year-old daughter says to her, "Mommy, there's a *world* in your eye." Rushing to a mirror while her daughter naps, Walker confirms the insight her daughter has given her: that her blemished eye is indeed lovable and integral to her identity or, as she puts it, "deeply suitable to my personality, and even characteristic of me." She notes that her two eyes operate independently of each other, the blind eye drifting in fatigue or boredom, or "bearing witness" in excitement. The final paragraph recounts a dream Walker has that night. She is dancing, "happier than I've ever been in my life." She is joined by another joyous dancer, and "we dance and kiss and hold each other through the night." This other dancer, the essay concludes, is "beautiful, whole and free. And she is also me."[1]

Barbara Christian writes in her 1987 essay "The Race for Theory," "people of color have always theorized—but in forms quite different from the Western form of abstract logic. . . . our theorizing . . . is often in narrative forms, in the stories we create, in riddles and proverbs . . . since dynamic rather than fixed ideas seem more to our liking. . . . My folk [she says punningly] have always been a race for theory."[2] If Christian is right, Walker's moving narrative is also doing the work of theory, and I believe it is. What *is*, then, the theoretical work that a scene like Walker's is doing? Before attempting to answer that question, I would like to frame it in the context of debates about black and white feminisms and poststructuralist theory, debates that might either authorize my endorsement of Christian's claim or invalidate it, or do both in different ways.

Toni Morrison has recently been writing about the cultural work whites have required of blacks in this country, long after the end of slavery. In *Playing in the Dark,* her 1992 essays on the ways in which whiteness has been constructed in and as American literature by means of the repression of what she calls the "Africanist presence," she argues that the "Africanist character" has been used as "surrogate and enabler," "the vehicle by which the American self knows itself as not enslaved, but free; not repulsive, but desirable; not helpless, but licensed and powerful."[3] More recently and specifically, she has focused her anger on the requirement that black persons signify the body so that mind can be white. Writing about Clarence Thomas in her Introduction to the essays she collected on the Hill/Thomas controversy, she calls attention to the *New York Times's* "curious spotlight on his body"—mention of his accomplishments as a weight lifter—in their initial story, before Hill's allegations became public.[4] Morrison writes: "a reference to a black person's body is de rigueur in white discourse. Like the unswerving focus on the female body (whether the woman is a judge, an actress, a scholar, or a waitress), the black man's body is voluptuously dwelled upon in biographies about them, journalism on them, remarks about them. 'I wanted to find out,' said Senator Pete Domenici, 'as best I could what his life—from outhouse to the White

House . . . has been like'" (xiv). Although Morrison also discusses the equally over determined construction of Anita Hill as a black woman as "contradiction itself, irrationality in the flesh" (xvi), it is odd that when she writes about the requirement that certain groups serve as white culture's body she uses the timeworn analogy between black men and all women, for she of all people is attuned to the specificity of black women's subjection to this cultural work. And indeed some of the essays she collected make exactly this point about Hill even if Morrison herself does not.[5]

Setting aside the specifics of the Hill/Thomas controversy, it is possible that, even more than black men or than all women taken together, black women have been required to do the cultural work of embodying the body for white culture. Or so Valerie Smith had been arguing long before October 1991. In her 1989 essay "Black Feminist Theory and the Representation of the 'Other'" Smith calls attention to what she finds a disturbing trend: the use of black women writers by white feminists (as well as black men) to represent the ground of experience, or as Smith puts it, "to rematerialize the subject of their theoretical positions."[6] Smith writes:

> That the black woman appears in all of these texts as a historicizing presence testifies to the power of the insistent voices of black feminist literary and cultural critics. Yet it is striking that at precisely the moment when Anglo-American feminists and male Afro-Americanists begin to reconsider the material ground of their enterprise, they demonstrate their return to earth, as it were, by invoking the specific experiences of black women and the writings of black women. This association of black women with reembodiment resembles rather closely the association, in classic Western philosophy and in nineteenth-century cultural constructions of womanhood, of women of color with the body and therefore with animal passions and slave labor. (45)

Smith is referring here to writing by Elizabeth Meese and Teresa de Lauretis. Meese, Smith points out, illustrates her argument for a politicized deconstructive practice with readings of Walker and Hurston, and de Lauretis uses Flo Kennedy and Hortense Spillers to argue for grounding feminism in "'a politics of everyday life'" (44–45). But Meese and de Lauretis are not alone in performing this kind of gesture. And this is why I would be hesitant to say right away what theoretical work I think Walker's essay is doing: you would have to think that I am doing just what bothers Smith—using a black woman writer as an example of white feminist theory.

Toril Moi, to choose an example more safely remote than myself, in 1985 notoriously and bluntly asserted a position that could hardly be articulated now: "Some feminists might wonder why I have said nothing about black or lesbian (or black-lesbian) feminist criticism in America in this survey. The answer is simple: this book purports to deal with the theoretical aspects of feminist criticism. So far, lesbian and/or black feminist criticism have presented exactly the same *methodological* and *theoretical* problems as the rest of Anglo-American feminist criticism."[7] If it is the same theory, one wonders on reading this passage, why not use some black or lesbian writers to evoke it? Part of what is shocking about this statement is Moi's assumption that without offering readings of work by women of color she can nonetheless expect us to believe her that none of it would alter her definition of feminist theory. Her theory, while purporting to be race-neutral, derives only from white writers and excludes whatever women of color might have to say that differs from the white model. But my point in quoting this embarrassing passage is to call attention to its assumption that whites provide the theory whereas black women could only provide more examples. Moi's failure to invoke the writings of black women is thus of a piece with Meese's and de

Lauretis's flawed invocations of them, in Valerie Smith's view: in each case, in a world view that binarizes into theory and examples, or mind and body, the black woman equals the body or the example.[8]

At this point I want to discuss the ways in which three more white women theorists, whose writings are currently of much greater importance to feminism than are Moi's, construct African American women, and in some cases Chicana women, as grounds of embodiment in the context of theoretical abstractions.[9] I want to emphasize that my reason for discussing these theorists—Donna Haraway, Judith Butler, and Diana Fuss—is their inescapable importance for anyone thinking about feminist theory today. What I want to uncover is a cultural problematic in some of their most influential writings, a problematic that does not lessen the very great value of their work but that none of them has fully articulated herself. (My critique applies only to the texts I will discuss here, and is not intended to be generalized to more recent writing; Butler's new book reached me too late to be considered here.[10]) The problem I see here could be viewed both as a problem of race relations in the academy and as part of the widespread debate over the uses of postmodernist theory for feminist political practice.[11] What does it mean to identify "women of color" with the body in a postmodern context; and what is the status of *any* body in that context?

In her pathbreaking essay "A Manifesto for Cyborgs," which appeared in the same year as Moi's *Sexual/Textual Politics* (1985), Donna Haraway uses some African American and Chicana writers, together with the generic grouping "women of color," to render concrete her extremely and deliberately abstruse account of the cyborg. One of her reiterated points about the cyborg as a model for feminism is its praiseworthy demystification of biological origins. Because it has none, no mother specifically, the cyborg would prevent feminists from romanticizing nature or the notion of woman's essence. Because "it skips the step of original unity," it teaches us to avoid the illusions perpetrated by both liberal and essentialist feminisms, illusions that would reinstall feminism in the patriarchal myth of bounded identity.[12] Haraway underscores the cyborgs' unnaturalness when she describes them as "floating signifiers" (MC 71) or as "ether, quintessence" (MC 70). The cyborg is, if not precisely disembodied, all surface, no depth—ironic, related to others by affinity, not blood; as abstract as a microelectronic signal.[13]

Near the start of her manifesto, Haraway cites a claim made by Chicana writer (and her student at the time) Chela Sandoval, that "women of color" negate the possibility of an essential identity of "woman" and thus that women of color are paradigmatically postmodern because cyborgian: "no 'she', no singularity, but a sea of differences among U.S. women who have affirmed their historical identity as U.S. women of color" (MC 73). "Women of color," like cyborgs, unite through affinity rather than through blood, because their blood identity is, happily, impossible to establish.[14] Toward the end of the essay—and it is generally at the ends of white women's essays or chapters that black and other "of color" women writers turn up—Cherrie Moraga and Audre Lorde, along with some women science fiction writers including Octavia Butler, are invoked as rather different paradigms of cyborg identity. Here Haraway fleshes out her claim that "women of color" are cyborgs by offering brief accounts of Audre Lorde's figure of the "Sister Outsider" and of Cherrie Moraga's book *Loving in the War Years*. "Sister Outsider" is a cyborg because she sounds like the "offshore women" who do the labor of the integrated circuit, like the young Korean women Haraway has discussed earlier. Never mind that, in the context in which Lorde invented this figure in *Zami*, "Sister Outsider" refers specifically and concretely to the ambiguous position of the black lesbian in the 1950s Greenwich white gay-girl scene: here she floats offshore in the ether of microelectronic signaling.

Haraway celebrates Moraga for the linguistic dislocations of her bilingual book—written in Spanish and English, it cannot be tied down to one linguistic identity—and for her reclaiming of the story of La Malinche, the cyborg equivalent to Eve, the anti-mother-figure who originates not through legitimate birth but through cross-cultural betrayal and bastardy. Haraway writes: "Moraga's writing, her superb literacy, is presented in her poetry as the same kind of violation as Malinche's mastery of the conqueror's language—a violation, an illegitimate production, that allows survival" (MC 94). Her "superb literacy"? Haraway intends a compliment to Moraga's mastery of languages through her violation of their boundaries, but I cannot get away from the condescension of the phrase, however ironic. Moreover, the word "literacy," alluding to the remarkableness of Moraga's being literate at all under conditions of racism and poverty, calls to mind the legally enforced illiteracy of African Americans under slavery. The cyborg, according to Julia Erhardt, frighteningly resembles the African American slave as depicted in Hortense Spillers's "Mama's Baby, Papa's Maybe"—deprived of a maternal origin through the enforced separation of parents from children, a hybrid (part animal, part machine), a bastard. Is slavery what Haraway celebrates when she celebrates the cyborg?[15] I do not want to diminish the historical specificity of slavery by generalizing it, but certainly there is an uncomfortable similarity between what Valerie Smith objects to in white feminists and Haraway's rhetorical practice. As Erhardt writes, "Haraway's move of employing [what Spillers calls] 'the body of the black woman in her material and abstract phase as a resource of metaphor' [see MB 66] is precisely the practice of rhetorical domination Spillers denounces in her piece" (AI 5). Haraway's women of color work for her—they do the work of her theory.

Haraway does much the same thing with Sojourner Truth in a more recent essay, in which she makes Sojourner Truth into the successor to Jesus Christ, the "figure" of the "suffering servant" as trickster, who represents universal "humanity."[16] Haraway is aware of just the dangers I am pointing to now, insisting that her use of Sojourner Truth "resist[s] representation, resist[s] literal figuration" (86). Instead, Truth can be seen to "refigure a nongeneric, nonoriginal humanity after the breakup of the discourses of Eurocentric humanism" (96) because of Haraway's attention to the particularity of her situation as a northern former slave and speaker of Afro-Dutch English. But it would seem impossible for Haraway to use her as a figure of Trinh Minh-ha's "inappropriate/d other" without appropriating her and the referential spectacle of her body in just the way that Erhardt's critique of the cyborg as slave would predict. Contrast Alice Walker's brief essay "A Name Is Sometimes an Ancestor Saying Hi, I'm with You," in which she claims, simply, to be Sojourner Truth: "She smiles within my smile. That irrepressible great heart rises in my chest. Every experience that roused her passion against injustice in her lifetime shines from my eyes."[17] Like Haraway, Walker connects Sojourner Truth with Jesus Christ, but she understands Christ's and Truth's representational status differently from Haraway: "the transformation required of us is not simply to be 'like' Christ, but to be Christ" (AN 98). Whereas Haraway delicately eschews "literal figuration," Walker openly embraces a literal and bodily identification that, if it is appropriative (and I would not deny that the essay is arrogant), is at least based on "this name Sojourner Truth and I share" (she has pointed out that a Sojourner is a Walker and that Alice means truth) and thus on a personal identification rather than on generalizations about Truth's representative qualities, however evasive and tricksterlike Truth (and "the truth of representation") has become.

Valerie Smith's argument both applies and applies differently, then, to what Haraway and some other white poststructuralist feminists are doing with certain African American and Chicana women writers and with the category "women of color." Haraway would seem to be using Lorde and Moraga to lend concreteness to her anti-essential argument, but what she is really doing is using them as an alibi for dematerializing the female body. The text of Moraga's *Loving in the War Years* does not quite bear out Haraway's emphasis on the cyborg aspects of Moraga's self representation and of La Malinche's heritage. For one thing, skin color—a physical fact—matters a great deal. Moraga dwells on her love for her mother's darkness and explores the complexity of living a Chicana life with a white skin. Moraga sees race as having been both a cyborgian choice for her (because, with a white father, she can pass) and also not a choice: she refers again and again to "the women of my race."[18] Secondly, she romanticizes the physicality of her mother's body (*L* 94) and she links her lesbianism directly to her love for her mother, her darkness, and her smell. In Moraga's cyborgian, lesbian critique of the family, she nonetheless holds on to the value of blood bonds, especially the blood tie to the mother, precisely that which Haraway's cyborg rejects. Moraga writes of "finding familia among friends where blood ties are formed through suffering and celebration shared" (*L* 111). The notion of forming blood ties makes Moraga inhabit ambiguously both a cyborgian ideology and an older, more romantic one. Similarly ambiguous is her memorable chapter title, "From a Long Line of Vendidas" (or sexual sellouts): this long line is both cultural—her descent, as a traitor to Chicano ideas about women's subservience, from La Malinche—and, at the same time, biological: her descent from her mother, who, because she married a white man and bore racial bastards, was, like La Malinche, a *vendida*. When Haraway makes Moraga into a cocelebrant of the tradition of La Malinche and defines that tradition entirely through its postmodern antinaturalness, she overlooks Moraga's insistence on biological inheritance and her persistent, somatic nostalgias for her own blood mother's body.

Thinking about Haraway's use of Moraga, I was also reminded of Gloria Anzaldúa, whose autobiographical and multilingual *Borderlands/La Frontera* constructs a subject that tropes itself simultaneously through conventions of identity—words like *inner life, the self deep core, integrity*—and as a shifting borderland, simultaneously geographic, linguistic, cultural, racial, and sexual, never stably occupied by one culture or another but by many, where home is "this thin edge of/barbwire."[19] In her important early essay, "Speaking in Tongues," Anzaldúa encompasses what to white feminist theory might appear a paradox: "The act of writing is the act of making soul, alchemy. It is the quest for the self, for the center of the self, which we women of color have come to think as 'other.'"[20] Anzaldúa here equates *making* soul—constructing an identity—with *discovering* the self, an act that would seem to presume the prior existence of what is, in the first sentence, in the process of being made. Clearly, finding that that preexistent self is other—a situation a cyborg might enjoy—is represented here as a rift to be healed, not celebrated.

So Haraway has it both ways: perhaps because Moraga really does celebrate bodily identity, she grounds Haraway's argument by providing an example, and therefore, as in Valerie Smith's critique, she works for the white woman to represent reembodiment. But the argument she is serving is, self-contradictorily, an argument against embodiment— against biological definitions of woman and against nostalgia for biological origins, an argument that forgets the very body that allows Moraga to work as an example in the first place. Haraway's brief for postmodernism leads her to highlight only the cyborg aspects of Moraga's text and to downplay her ambivalence.

Virtually the same pattern as in Haraway appears in Judith Butler's use of a black woman—in this case not a writer but a singer—in her 1989 essay "Gendering the Body: Beauvoir's Philosophical Contribution," in the Introduction to her 1990 book *Gender Trouble,* and again in her 1991 essay "Imitation and Gender Insubordination."[21] I will focus here on *Gender Trouble,* the most widely influential of these three texts. Butler argues (with great philosophical rigor) that there is no such thing as essential or even stable identity, that all identities are constructs or effects of discourses, rather than, as common sense is thought to tell us, that identity is the origin and cause of everything else. She is skeptical of the value to feminism even of strategic essentialism and identity politics, because she believes they are founded on the dangerous illusion of stable identity. Butler has been the subject of the same kind of controversy within feminism that has surrounded Haraway: while her deconstruction of identity unquestionably holds out emancipatory promises, some feminists worry about both the status of the body in her theory ("is there a body in this text?" queries Susan Bordo [*UW* 38]) and its political utility. Time and again, discussions of postmodern feminist politics founder on the question of how to act politically without using totalizing categories such as "women."

Just as Haraway initially and briefly uses Chela Sandoval to make the analogy between cyborgs and "women of color" that she will concretize later on, Butler implicitly invokes the generic category of women of color briefly at the beginning of *Gender Trouble* as part of what authorizes her critique of identity. In her Introduction, she offers this rationale for putting her poststructuralist understanding of identity at the center of feminist theory: "it may be time to entertain a radical critique that seeks to free feminist theory from the necessity of having to construct a single or abiding ground which is invariably contested by those identity positions or anti-identity positions that it invariably excludes. Do the exclusionary practices that ground feminist theory in a notion of 'women' as subject paradoxically undercut feminist goals to extend its claims to 'representation'?" (*GT* 5). That is, Butler argues, "identity" is a category that imposes a false and coercive unity, just as white, middleclass, Western feminism itself has been accused of imposing one interpretive grid on the multiplicity of female lives by privileging the category "woman" over those of race, ethnicity, class, nationality, age, and so on. Identity, like some kinds of white feminism, must be done away with because of what it excludes. Historically it was from "women of color"—chiefly African Americans—that these accusations against white, middle-class feminism initially and most effectively came, and thus Butler, although without referring to anyone in particular, uses a generic allusion to this group (while, like Haraway, seeking precisely not to totalize it as a group) to justify her anti-identity poststructuralism.

She makes it clear that this point refers to the general category of women of color, in her 1992 essay "Contingent Foundations," when she defends postmodern feminism in this way: "There is the refrain that, just now, when women are beginning to assume the place of subjects, postmodern positions come along to announce that the subject is dead. . . . Some see this as a conspiracy against women and other disenfranchised groups who are now only beginning to speak on their own behalf. But what precisely is meant by this, and how do we account for the very strong criticisms of the subject as an instrument of Western imperialist hegemony theorized by Gloria Anzaldúa, Gayatri Spivak, and various theorists of postcoloniality?"[22] Butler would seem to be characterizing my own criticism, in her reference to this anti-postmodern "refrain," and refuting it. But as I suggested in discussing Haraway, this use of Anzaldúa to justify an anti-identity position, fleeting as it is—Butler supplies a footnote to Anzaldúa's entire book, not to any particular passage—does not do justice to Anzaldúa's careful positioning on both sides of the debate. Nor does the use of Anzaldúa, Spivak, and "various theorists of postcoloniality," to stand for grievances that have come largely from African American women, do justice to the specificity of any of these positions. And to turn Anzaldúa into a one-dimensional figure for anything at all is to do precisely what I have been arguing feminist theorists should be wary of doing.

Toward the end of the Introduction to *Gender Trouble,* Butler cites the example of Aretha Franklin singing "You Make Me Feel Like a Natural Woman" (*GT* 22) in support of her anti-identity position. In a footnote Butler explains how: "'Like a natural woman' is a phrase that suggests that 'naturalness' is only accomplished through analogy or metaphor. In other words, 'You make me feel like a metaphor of the natural,' and without 'you', some denaturalized ground would be revealed" (*GT* 154–55). And then Butler compares what she calls "Aretha's claim" to Beauvoir's claim that "one is not born, but rather becomes a woman."[23] Or as Butler clarifies the point in "Imitation and Gender Insubordination," "[a]lthough Aretha appears to be all too glad to have her naturalness confirmed, she also seems fully and paradoxically mindful that that confirmation is never guaranteed, that the effect of naturalness is only achieved as a consequence of that moment of heterosexual recognition. After all, Aretha sings, you make me feel *like* a natural woman, suggesting that this is a kind of metaphorical substitution, an act of imposture, a kind of sublime and momentary participation in an ontological illusion produced by the mundane operation of heterosexual drag" (IGI 27–28). There are very few examples of anything in *Gender Trouble,* in "Gendering the Body," or in "Imitation and Gender Insubordination." Although Butler uses Aretha Franklin as an example of her poststructuralist critique of identity, her very uniqueness as an example and the fact that Butler uses her three times (and does not come up with other examples for the same point) suggest that she is also an example of exemplariness itself. And it matters that we are more likely to conjure up a physical image of the singer performing in her body than we are to conjure up similar images of the white European writers whose theories Franklin exemplifies—Lacan or Beauvoir, even Wittig or Foucault.

Thus, like Haraway, Butler uses a "woman of color" as a form of embodiment—an example, a body—who nonetheless justifies a critique of bodily or biologically based theories of gender, a critique of identity even more severe than Haraway's. This is not to say that I necessarily disagree with Butler's reading of the song. But like Butler's allusion to Anzaldúa, it goes by too fast, for all the times it is repeated. Lines from the body of the song would suggest that the singer is less clearly on the poststructuralist side of the identity debate than Butler wants her to be. "When my soul was in the lost and found / You came along to claim it"[24] suggests, like the passage from Anzaldúa about both questing for and making the soul, that the soul (the natural woman?) already exists even if it is now alienated from its owner. The line Butler cites in support of her anti-identity position is the song's refrain, and that is exactly the term she uses to denote and disparage the pro-identity position in the passage quoted above from "Contingent Foundations." Reading these essays together, with the 1992 essay (which does not use Aretha Franklin but does use the word *refrain*) seen as a gloss upon the texts from 1989, 1990, and 1991 (the ones that do use Aretha Franklin), one could conclude that Butler's 1992 text, in its choice of the word *refrain,* knows that Franklin's refrain coincides with a pro-identity position (the naive feminists' refrain) as much as it does with her own anti-identity position. It is also worth mentioning that Franklin sings not her own words but those of Carole King (born Carol Klein, in Brooklyn), another way perhaps in which a black woman enacts or embodies a white woman's words, and a situation that calls to mind the political context of Aretha Franklin's success; through the 1960s, African Americans were allowed to succeed only in those arenas—such as sports, music, and dance— that whites could imagine as being reducible to bodily performance. I like Aretha Franklin's singing, but it makes me think too unhappily about the ways black women have always done this country's work of embodiment to feel happy about Butler's use of her.

There is something odd about both Haraway's and Butler's invoking African American, Chicana, and other "women of color" to justify the use of postmodernist or poststructuralist theory in feminism given that many black women critics, like Barbara Christian and Joyce Ann Joyce, have recently argued exactly the opposite: the elitist irrelevance of theory to black women's lives. Christian's "The Race for Theory" attacks theory, or what she calls the New Philosophy, as hegemonic, an instrument for egoistic career advancement, disembodied, and replicating the mind/body split exclusively in favor of abstraction. She writes that feminist theorists fail to "take into account the complexity of life—that women are of many races and ethnic backgrounds [and classes] with different histories and cultures. . . . Seldom do they note these distinctions, because if they did they could not articulate a theory" (RT 233). Presupposing that theory depends on categorical distinctions and cannot deal with concrete particulars, and preferring the concrete to the abstract, Christian could in a sense be said to share Toril Moi's view that feminist theory and black women's writing have little to do with each other.

In some ways Christian's position resembles that taken by a larger group of black feminists. The writers with whom Christian speaks in concert have tended to claim experience rather than its supposed opposite, abstract categories, as the ground from which any criticism and theory should be generated. Early in the history of black feminism, its defining practitioners—such as Mary Helen Washington, Deborah McDowell, and Barbara Smith—embraced what we would now term essentialism and posited that the function of black feminist criticism was to establish a correct representation of black women and that such criticism could only be practiced by women who were themselves black. Similarly, from the same period, the Combahee River Collective's "Black Feminist Statement" has been construed by most readers as defining "identity politics" to mean that you act according to who you are and that identity precedes culture and politics.[25] More recently, in the same year that Christian's essay came out, Joyce Ann Joyce published a highly controversial attack on the use of white European theory (chiefly deconstruction) by black theorists such as Henry Louis Gates, Jr. and Houston Baker, an attack that, like Christian's, seeks to recall black theory to its experiential and sensual roots.[26] Patricia Hill Collins, publishing in *Signs* in 1989, wrote that "living life as an African American woman is a necessary prerequisite for producing black feminist thought."[27] In 1990, bell hooks reported a "resistance on the part of most black folks to hearing about real connection between postmodernism and black experience" (*Y* 25).

Although a number of black feminists have also been writing in eurocentric theoretical modes, and hooks discusses this "resistance" in order to "interrogate" it, in 1989 it was still possible for Diana Fuss (in her book *Essentially Speaking*) to point out, and to call "disturbing," the "relative absence of Afro-American *feminist* poststructuralism. With the exception of the recent work of Hazel Carby and Hortense Spillers, black feminist critics have been reluctant to renounce essentialist critical positions and humanist literary practices."[28] She asks why so many women of color "resist" joining "the race for theory" and thus risk being accused of conservatism, as Joyce is by Baker (*ES* 95). She proposes that the answer lies in "political necessity," in the strategic use of essentialism for the aims of political solidarity within an embattled group (*ES* 95).

It is disturbing (to use Fuss's word) to think about how closely this apologetic, conciliatory account resembles Toril Moi's blunt statement about the lack of theoretical innovation in black women critics. In thinking she needs to apologize at all, and in focusing on what black feminists don't do, Fuss is listening as inattentively as Moi is to what African American feminists are saying. Even though one aim of her book is to defamiliarize poststructuralism and to encourage tolerance for apparently essentialist positions, here her standards for what constitutes the category of the disturbing do not derive from the group of which she speaks but rather from a standpoint where poststructuralism is intrinsically good. Fuss's chapter on race is unique in her feminist book in focusing almost exclusively on men: all the blacks are men, to borrow that unhappily still appropriate phrase, just as in the other chapters nearly all the women are white.

But the important point for my argument is that Fuss, like Butler and Haraway, closes her text with black women who are simultaneously identified with the body, retrograde notions of identity, and essentialism—doing the work of embodiment—and used to justify poststructuralism; or rather, what she sees as the majority of untheoretical black women are used for the one purpose, while Spillers and Carby are singled out for praise as endorsing poststructuralism, just as Aretha Franklin, Anzaldúa, and Moraga are by Butler and Haraway. But as in the case of Moraga, a closer reading of the writers being deployed here suggests that the picture is more complex. Yes, Spillers and Carby are associated with "theory," but neither of them celebrates disembodiment as wholeheartedly as the whites I have been discussing. There are specific historical reasons why bodily definitions of the human should appeal to some black feminists at just the moment when they are anathema to white poststructuralists.

Spillers's essay "Mama's Baby, Papa's Maybe" after all argues for reclaiming gender identities violently expropriated by slavery, specifically that of the black mother, quantified, commodified, unsexed by the slave trade. To quote again from Erhardt's paper, arguing that the cyborg sounds ominously like the black slave, "For Haraway a genderless cyborg world represents a world without end; for Spillers, a culture inhabited by hermaphrodite bestial bastard hybrids (in this case, one which was historically realized) represents the end of the world" (AI 4). With a logic that recalls Nancy K. Miller's "[o]nly those who have it can play with not having it,"[29] Spillers writes at the start of her essay:

> At a time when current critical discourses appear to compel us more and more decidedly toward gender "undecidability," it would appear reactionary, if not dumb, to insist on the integrity of female/male gender. But undressing these conflations of meaning, as they appear under the rule of dominance, would restore, as figurative possibility, not only Power to the Female (for Maternity), but also Power to the Male (for Paternity). We would gain, in short, the *potential* for gender differentiation as it might express itself along a range of stress points, including human biology in its intersection with the project of culture. (MB 66)

While Spillers is often careful to define gender as a social category, she also has a lot to say about the flesh: "only the female stands *in the flesh,* both mother and mother-dispossessed" (MB 80), she writes in the last paragraph of the essay.

In a related fashion, Hazel Carby, in the important statement on black feminist theory that introduces her book *Reconstructing Womanhood,* denounces reliance on the category of "experience" as "essentialist and ahistorical" because "experience" assumes that the infinitude of human experiences can be totalized.[30] But she also recuperates much that has traditionally made part of the category of experience by defining her approach as "materialist," an analysis of the impact of the concrete material conditions of production on the works of black women writers. Had Fuss been able to take into consideration bell hooks's 1990 essay "Postmodern Blackness," that essay's critiques of those in the black community who disdain theory and postmodernism would have supported my point about Carby and Spillers. Arguing against those who would retain the category of (black) identity as essence, she nonetheless insists on the compatibility of the postmodern critique of identity and the retention of "the authority of experience" (Y 29) as a useful political category: the postmodern "critique allows us to affirm multiple black identities, varied black experience" (Y 28).[31]

What I am suggesting, then, to summarize, is that Valerie Smith's critique of the use of black women writers by white feminists, valid though it is, needs to be inflected by two additional considerations. First—and for specific historical reasons, not naïveté—at least some black feminist critics are using black women writers in something like the way that Valerie Smith says whites are using them. Writers like Christian and Collins use black women to represent experience, sensuality, emotion, matter, practice as opposed to theory, and survival. When Smith turns from white to black feminisms, she discusses the ways in which Carby, Spillers, and others focus on the specific "material circumstances" of black women. Although her point is to differentiate between the "totalizing" use to which white feminists put black women to represent embodiment and the specificity of Carby et al's attention to particular material experiences, I would argue that this shift amounts to a change of emphasis rather than an absolute difference. But in any case, whether or not white and black feminisms are using black women in the same way, there is an overriding difference: because of the history of slavery, whether an African American woman works for herself or for a white woman is freighted with political and cultural meanings.

As a way of dramatizing the ambiguity that can arise from this situation, let me return briefly to Aretha Franklin. Some pages back I argued that Franklin's singing of "Natural Woman" may not be so deconstructive as Butler claims and, at the same time, that Butler relies on Franklin's "naturalness," her status as a visualizable popular icon, to make an antinatural point. (This could also serve as a summary of my argument about Moraga and Haraway's use of her.) The relation between these potentially contradictory arguments might be clarified by saying that while I would defend Franklin's partisanship for the naturalness of womanhood—as I would defend those black feminist critics who, for whatever reasons, continue to construct the body and/or black female identity as natural—I would object to a white philosopher's making use of this very gesture.[32] A recent news item about Franklin in *Newsweek* features a photograph of her over the caption "Whole Lot of Shaking Going On."[33] The three-sentence report concerns Franklin's bravura singing at a concert, but the news is her body: "During a vigorous rendition of 'This Old Heart of Mine,' Aretha came dangerously close to overflowing her low-cut beaded bustier—and proving that she is every ounce a Natural Woman" (49). This news item demonstrates at once, and contradictorily, the unlikeliness that "ordinary" readers would hear Franklin's line as Butler does—of course most listeners hear only her valorization of the natural—and the distastefulness (to say the least) of having her "naturalness" displayed, photographically and textually, as a joke for a white audience. Her performances of "Natural Woman" may articulate as much enthusiasm for the natural as *Newsweek*'s report attributes to her, but the report does so from a point of view that is not Franklin's own and thus constitutes a use of her body that offends because it is not her own.

The second consideration with which we would need to inflect Smith's critique is this: when at least some prominent white feminist poststructuralist theorists—Fuss, Butler, and Haraway—use black or, in the case of Moraga and Anzaldúa, Chicana women, they do so not simply to make them do the work of embodiment or identification but also to make their embodiment at the same time an alibi for poststructuralist disembodiment or the deconstructing of identity. (It is not just that Butler uses Franklin, but that she uses her in this particular way.) This second usage of "women of color" would seem opposite to, and therefore the antidote to, the usage decried in Smith's critique, and attractive on those grounds; but it is problematic because the usage decried by Smith is authorized by some "women of color" themselves and also because the political utility of arguments that dissociate feminism from the body has yet to be decided. It is problematic also because the status of a figure of embodiment in an argument against embodied identity must finally be that of excluded other: even though these figures are enlisted in the cause of poststructuralism, they must finally be left out of it. They define it by their difference from it. The woman of color as deployed by Haraway et al is still a figure, a figure for something—a bounded identity—serving a larger cause. And enlisting black women as figureheads for poststructuralism does not yet make a convincing case for its utility for women of color. That is, there certainly are poststructuralist black feminisms, but we would not know that from the texts I have discussed.

Let me stop focusing on the white theorists, for whose self-contradictory arguments the embodied black woman tends to become part of the machinery for validating disembodiment, to say something about the uses to which black women have been putting figures of their own embodiment. I would like to return to Christian's claim that her folk theorize in narrative forms and to turn specifically to a narrative essay by Patricia Williams together with the autobiographical story by Alice Walker with which I began. Continuing the line of argument

I began with my brief discussions of Moraga and Anzaldúa, I wish to suggest that when Williams and Walker image their own bodies, they set up a constructive dialogue between poststructuralist and humanist views of identity rather than either reducing the black woman's body to sheer ground or matter or, to the contrary, using that body to validate disembodiment. I realize that in turning to black women's narrativized self-embodiments, I am open to the accusation that I am using women of color in just the ways I have been objecting to, as "examples" following a discussion of "theory." But I would justify this practice in two ways. First, not to give African American women writers' theories the same kind of close scrutiny I have just given to white feminists would leave me open to the opposite danger, the one that befell Toril Moi. Second, because I will be talking about figures that these authors have already encapsulated and embodied as figures, my practice follows and is authorized by theirs. Thus they are working—doing cultural and psychological work—for themselves at least as much as for me.[34] Perhaps it could even be said that I am working for them.

The link that Erhardt demonstrates between the cyborg and Spillers's enslaved women can help us see that Patricia Williams's self-presentation includes many of the cyborg's hallmarks too. Spillers opens her essay by describing herself as a hybrid and a construct: listing the names a black woman academic can be called, from "Brown Sugar" to "Black Woman at the Podium," Spillers writes: "I describe a locus of confounded identities, a meeting ground of investments and privations in the national treasury of rhetorical wealth. My country needs me, and if I were not here, I would have to be invented" (MB 65). Very similarly, Patricia Williams opens "Owning the Self in a Disowned World" with what she calls her "disintegration into senselessness," which is making her crazy and giving her a headache.[35] She describes herself as caught between conflicting expectations or, as Spillers puts it, "confounded identities" (MB 65). She reflects on Derek Bell's "Chronicle of the Twenty-Seventh Year Syndrome," the disease afflicting only young black professional women: "if they are not married to, or have not yet received a marriage proposal from, a black man by their twenty-seventh year, they fall into a deep coma from which they awaken only after several weeks, physically intact but having lost all their professional skills" (191). This leads Williams to tell the story of Judge Maxine Thomas, who suffered a terminal nervous breakdown in her chambers and whose life was dissected in the media according to conflicting demands: "A woman who was too individualistic. . . . A woman who couldn't think for herself. . . . A woman who had the perfect marriage. . . . A woman who had no marriage at all" (193). A woman who was too professional, too unfeeling; a woman who wasn't professional enough, too emotional. Reflecting on her own and her mother's morning rituals of self-construction—clothes, makeup, jewelry—Williams herself feels "very close to being Maxine. When I am fully dressed, my face is hung with contradictions" (196). The fine line between herself and Maxine Thomas is that "I try not to wear all my contradictions at the same time. I pick and choose among them; like jewelry" (196). Maxine Thomas "split at the seams," but Williams will not, quite yet anyway.

At the close of the essay, Williams presents a figure that may recall Butler's use of Aretha Franklin. Here, it is a dream of Williams herself. In the dream, there are two of her: one self who is "creeping" around the back wall of an amphitheater, the other who is on stage, magnificently performing. She is wearing outrageously feminine hair and clothing from her unprofessional youth (a beehive and a sequined, lowcut red dress). Here are the final two paragraphs of the essay:

> The me-that-is-on-stage is laughing loudly and long. She is extremely vivacious, the center of attention. She is, just as I have always dreamed of being, fascinating: showy yet deeply intelligent. She is not beautiful in any traditional sense, as I am not in real life—her mouth and teeth are very large, her nose very long, like a

claymation model of myself—but her features are riveting. And she is radiantly, splendidly good-natured. She is lovely in the oddest possible combination of ways. I sit down in the small circle of friends-around-myself, to watch myself, this sparkling homely woman, dressed like a moment lost in time. I hear myself speaking: *Voices lost in the chasm speak from the slow eloquent fact of the chasm. They speak and speak, like flowing water.*

From this dream, into a complicated world, a propagation of me's awakens, strong, single-hearted, and completely refreshed. (201)

This dream seems to cure the headache with which Williams begins the essay. Donna Haraway ends her manifesto, "I would rather be a cyborg than a goddess" (MC 101); but both Williams and Spillers already know what it is to be a cyborg, better than Haraway— by her own admission—can ever do, and they know that being a cyborg gives them a headache. Even Barbara Christian, for all her alleged "resistance" to theory (Fuss's term), sometimes feels like a cyborg too, and she doesn't like it either; it makes her tired: "I, for one, am tired of being asked to produce a black feminist literary theory as if I were a mechanical man" (RT 227). How does the dream relieve Williams of the headache, the fatigue, of being a cyborg?

The dream both celebrates a post-Lacanian, cyborgian, split subjectivity and perceives that split as something painful, in need of healing. For example, there are two Williamses but they collaborate to make possible the pleasure of voyeurism. The self in the sequined dress may represent the stressful requirement for black professional women to be "feminine," but this performer's intelligence integrates the professional and the woman, for her charm is characterized by "the oddest possible combination." Her "femininity" is both a costume— heterosexual drag—and her deep identity. The dream produces "a propagation of me's," but somehow they are, collectively, "single-hearted" too. Williams wants to have it both ways— to be whole and split, to be single and multiple, to have a self and to deconstruct the notion of self, to be practical and theoretical—and this dream represents that wish in a way that Williams seems to find satisfying. It does not just embody a theory: it does for her the work of a cure.

Williams's dream-figure is both like and unlike Butler's Aretha Franklin, whose words suggest both the desire to be a natural woman and the greater recognition that there is no such thing. Both dream-women link embodiment and identity on the one hand to the denaturalizing of identity on the other. But the difference is that while Butler explicitly— even, we might say, coercively—turns that ambiguity toward justification of her denaturalizing project and privileges the poststructuralist reading of Aretha Franklin's song over the natural gender one, Williams leaves the two possibilities open, and lets her sequined self work for the better health and pleasure of her own body: her "me's" awake "refreshed." Williams's dream-figure may constitute a recognition that cyborg identity is unavoidable for a professional black woman, but it makes that recognition in the form that, as we have seen, identifies the black woman with her body: an example at the end of an essay. Williams celebrates embodiment as the only salve for a self wounded by the demands of life as a cyborg. And so I might legitimate my own turning to Williams as an example by her own celebratory practice of doing so—but only because I am using her as a figure for her own effective and pragmatic ambivalence (perhaps, one might say, her strategic ambivalence), not, as Haraway or Butler might, as a figure for a philosophically pure but deconcretized position.

The same point might also justify my returning now to the Alice Walker essay with which I began. As you will remember, Walker, like Williams, ends with a celebratory dream of herself as two selves, a dream that resolves an anxiety, in this case about her appearance and by extension about her value in the world. Walker's account of her dream involves and ends by emphasizing the same ambiguity as Williams's, between split and whole, between a Lacanian-poststructuralist cyborg self and a liberal humanist self. Walker becomes two dancers, but they kiss and hold each other. There are two dancers, but the other dancer is "whole. . . . And she is also me." Possibly there is a third, since the fear of blindness has been safely projected onto Stevie Wonder, to whose music she dances. Like Williams's "propagation of me's," Walker devises a collective self that is both one and many. As in Williams's essay, this doubled, divided dream-self answers the emotionally and politically strategic need to say "I" without falling into the trap of reduplicating an invidious humanism or the phallocentric oneness of form. If Walker, like Williams, has suffered from having a divided self—as figured synecdochally by her having two eyes (I's) that operate independently of each other—then she can also turn that division to her advantage in avoiding an imprisoning self-identity.

Walker and Williams both write of their selves as unstable constructions provisionally made up of different and continuously shifting elements and especially of different languages. At the same time, they keep in mind practical considerations about living and acting politically in this world. As for hooks writing on postmodernism, it is crucial to them that a deconstructive understanding of the self not militate against political activism, as it is often thought to do. Walker's split or fragmented self is a touchstone of Lacanian psychology and therefore of poststructuralism, but she does not derive it from that source. It is a *world* that her eye resembles, the body understood as politicized even in that intensely personal and physical moment in her daughter's bedroom: the eye or I is founded not on the notion of a core self but rather on the global village (a concept that is central to the "Manifesto for Cyborgs," although in the affectively different form of the international integrated circuit).

Living by the Word, Walker's more recent essay collection, extends this notion of the multiple self and extends this representation of it too as historicized and politicized, its origins traceable to non-Western cultures rather than to Western theory. The doubled self that ends the first essay collection reappears at the start of the next one in a brief journal entry about a dream of a woman with two heads who dispenses advice: "what I realized in the dream is that two-headedness was at one time an actual physical condition and that two-headed people were considered wise. . . . [T]wo-headed people, like blacks, lesbians, Indians, 'witches,' have been suppressed, and, in their case, suppressed out of existence. . . . For surely two-headed people have existed. And it is only among blacks (to my knowledge) that a trace of their existence is left in the language. Rootworkers, healers, wise people with 'second sight' are called 'twoheaded' people."[36] Perhaps a two-headed woman could have done something for Patricia Williams's headache. This distinctively non-Western wise woman—who exists simultaneously as a real referential being and as a cyborgian effect of language—grounds Walker's experiments with nonunitary selves in the politics of postcolonial culture and aligns that experimentation not with the white middle class domain of pure, theoretical poststructuralist psychoanalysis but with the historical fact of Walker's varied ancestry instead. As in Moraga's "From a Long Line of Vendidas," blood ancestry matters along with cyborgian affinity. The identity "black" in Walker's case means being descended not only from African slaves but from a Cherokee great-great-grandmother and also from a white slave owner and rapist, all of whom, later in the volume, she animates as living voices in her head, experienced somatically as well as psychically, competing noisily to be heard by her. Walker's ancestors politicize the female body and construct its identity pragmatically as a contentious argument, not a stable and timeless unity, and always as a body. Walker, we might say, has a headache, too, to go along with her eye-strain—the headache of slavery's cyborg "confounded identities"—and she cures it by listening to all the voices in her head and then channeling them into aesthetic wholes signed with the unmistakable signature of

Alice Walker. For the other distinctive feature of the journal entry about the two-headed woman is its insistence on Walker's name as an identity and as a form of concerted action. The entry ends:

> When I asked her what I/we could/should do, she took up her walking stick and walked expressively and purposefully across the room. Dipping a bit from side to side.
> She said: Live by the Word and keep walking. (2)

Notes

1   Alice Walker, "Beauty: When the Other Dancer is the Self," in her *In Search of Our Mothers' Gardens: Womanist Prose* (San Diego, 1983), p. 393.

2   Barbara Christian, "The Race for Theory" (1987), rpt. in *Gender and Theory: Dialogues in Feminist Criticism,* ed. Linda Kaufmann (Oxford, 1989), p. 226; hereafter cited in text as RT.

3   Toni Morrison, *Playing in the Dark: Whiteness and the Literary Imagination* (Cambridge, Mass., 1992), pp. 51–52.

4   Toni Morrison, Introduction, *Race-ing Justice, En-Gendering Power: Essays on Anita Hill, Clarence Thomas, and the Construction of Social Reality,* ed. Toni Morrison (Cambridge, Mass., 1992); p. xiii; hereafter cited in text.

5   Kimberlé Crenshaw points out that Hill was appropriated by white feminists to tell a story about sexual harassment that did not take into account black women's historical experience of their bodies' legal expropriation under slavery, a story that—because it seemed to be a white woman's story—allowed Thomas to cast himself as "the victim of racial discrimination with Hill as the perpetrator" ("Whose Story Is It, Anyway? Feminist and Antiracist Appropriations of Anita Hill," in *Race-ing Justice, En-Gendering Power,* p. 415).

6   Valerie Smith, "Black Feminist Theory and the Representation of the 'Other,'" in *Changing Our Own Words: Essays on Criticism, Theory, and Writing by Black Women,* ed. Cheryl A. Wall (New Brunswick, N.J., 1989), p. 44; hereafter cited in text.

7   Toril Moi, *Sexual/Textual Politics: Feminist Literary Theory* (London, 1985), p. 86.

8   It is for this reason that I use the terms *black* and *white* in this paper, despite the danger that such usage perpetuates the very phenomenon of racism: these terms name a historical reality. On the political need for these terms in continuing to recognize racism, see bell hooks, *Yearning: Race, Gender, and Cultural Politics* (Boston, 1990), p. 52; hereafter cited in text as Y.

9   My project thus parallels Elizabeth Abel's recent critique of white feminists who write on African American writers (Barbara Johnson and myself), although the nature and direction of her critique differs from mine. See Elizabeth Abel, "Black Writing, White Reading: Race and the Politics of Feminist Interpretation," *Critical Inquiry,* 19 (1993), 470–98.

10   Judith Butler, *Bodies that Matter: On the Discursive Limits of "Sex"* (New York, 1993).

11   Although Haraway certainly identifies herself with postmodern theory, while Butler and Fuss more distinctly align themselves with deconstructive poststructuralism (which overlaps with but is not coextensive with postmodern theory), I allude here to the sort of questions asked again and again in such a volume as *Feminism/Postmodernism,* ed. Linda Nicholson (New York, 1990)—questions in regard to which the kind of poststructuralism practiced by Butler and Fuss could certainly be subsumed within postmodern theory.

12   Donna Haraway, "A Manifesto for Cyborgs: Science, Technology, and Socialist Feminism in the 1990s," *Socialist Review,* 15, no. 80 (Mar.–Apr. 1985), 67; hereafter cited in text as MC.

13   It is still a matter of contention among feminist intellectuals what the political utility of such a concept is, or what it might constitute as a practice involving actual female bodies. While Haraway's postmodern project has for good reason galvanized the feminist community, some have expressed measured skepticism. Susan Squier, writing about Haraway's enthusiasm for postmodern fragmentation in another context, comments that while "cyborgization . . . may *metaphorically* embody the emancipatory possibility of escaping the unitary, gendered and bounded construction of the human subject, on the level of scientific and medical practice such concepts continue the narrative of sadism and masculine usurpation of female procreative power that Haraway has previously documented." Susan Squier, rev. of *Gender and Genius* by Christine Battersby and *Primitive Visions* by Donna Haraway, *The Minnesota Review,* ns 37 (Spring 1992), 155. Susan Bordo puts

her worry more succinctly: "the postmodern body is no body at all." Susan Bordo, *Unbearable Weight: Feminism, Western Culture, and The Body* (Berkeley, 1993), p. 229; hereafter cited in text as *UW*.

14   As Bordo points out (*UW*, p. 229), "women of color" is a problematic term because it totalizes exactly the individuals who are being used to demonstrate the failure of totalization. By initially using quotation marks, Haraway acknowledges this problem, but after a first usage she drops them. I thank Diana Paulin (in conversation at the University of Washington, Seattle) for pointing out, in response to an earlier version of this paper, that my own use of the term "women of color" unintentionally replicated the usage I criticize in Haraway and others. I have since tried to defamiliarize this term by using quotation marks when referring to others' use of it or to substitute more specific referents.

15   See Julia Erhardt, "Am I (Black or) Blue?: A Critique of Cyborg Feminism," unpublished paper, Yale University, 1992, hereafter cited in text as AI; Hortense Spillers, "Mama's Baby, Papa's Maybe: An American Grammar Book," *Diacritics*, 17, no. 2 (Summer 1987), 65–81; hereafter cited in text as MB.

16   See Donna Haraway, "Ecce Homo, Ain't (Ar'n't) I a Woman, and Inappropriate/d Others: The Human in a Post-Humanist Landscape," in *Feminists Theorize the Political*, ed. Judith Butler and Joan W. Scott (New York, 1992), pp. 86–100; hereafter cited in text. Haraway's title refers to Trinh T. Minh-ha's "She, The Inappropriate/d Other," *Discourse*, 8 (1986–87) (cited in Haraway, p. 91).

17   Alice Walker, "A Name Is Sometimes an Ancestor Saying Hi, I'm with You," in *Living By the Word: Selected Writings 1973–1987* (San Diego, 1988), p. 98; hereafter cited in text as AN.

18   Cherríe Moraga, *Loving in the War Years* (Boston, 1983), p. 140; hereafter cited in text as L.

19   Gloria Anzaldúa, *Borderlands/La Frontera: The New Mestiza* (San Francisco, 1987), p. 3.

20   Gloria Anzaldúa, "Speaking in Tongues: A Letter to Third World Women Writers," in *This Bridge Called My Back: Writings by Radical Women of Color*, ed. Cherríe Moraga and Gloria Anzaldúa (Watertown, Mass., 1981), p. 169.

21   Judith Butler, "Gendering the Body: Beauvoir's Philosophical Contribution," in *Women, Knowledge, and Reality: Explorations in Feminist Philosophy*, ed. Ann Garry and Marilyn Pearsall (Boston, 1989), pp. 253–62; *Gender Trouble: Feminism and the Subversion of Identity* (New York, 1990), hereafter cited as *GT*; and "Imitation and Gender Insubordination," in *Inside/Out: Lesbian Theories, Gay Theories*, ed. Diana Fuss (New York, 1991), hereafter cited as IGI.

22   Judith Butler, "Contingent Foundations: Feminism and the Question of 'Postmodernism,'" in *Feminists Theorize the Political*, p. 14.

23   Simone de Beauvoir, *The Second Sex*, tr. H. M. Parshley (New York, 1974), p. 30, qtd. in *GT*, p. 155; see also Butler, "Gendering the Body," p. 254.

24   Aretha Franklin, "(You Make Me Feel Like) A Natural Woman," by Goffin, Wexler, and King (Screen Gems-EMI Music, BMI), on *The Best of Aretha Franklin*, Atlantic, CS 81280–84–Y, 1984.

25   Combahee River Collective, "Black Feminist Statement," in *This Bridge Called My Back*, pp. 210–18.

26   Joyce Ann Joyce, "The Black Canon: Reconstructing Black American Literary Criticism" and "'Who the Cap Fit': Unconsciousness and Unconscionableness in the Criticism of Houston A. Baker, Jr. and Henry Louis Gates, Jr.," in *New Literary History*, 18 (1987), 335–44 and 371–84.

27   Patricia Hill Collins, "The Social Construction of Black Feminist Thought," *Signs*, 14 (1989), 745–73.

28   Diana Fuss, *Essentially Speaking: Feminism, Nature, and Difference* (New York, 1989), pp. 94–95; hereafter cited in text as ES.

29   Nancy K. Miller, "The Text's Heroine: A Feminist Critic and Her Fictions," *Diacritics*, 12, no. 2 (Summer 1982), 53.

30   Hazel V. Carby, *Reconstructing Womanhood: The Emergence of the Afro-American Woman Novelist* (New York, 1987), p. 16.

31   Susan Bordo argues on the basis of her reading of Audre Lorde and Luce Irigaray for an "embodied postmodernism," one that acknowledges not an essence of the body or identity but the "historically located body" (*UW*, pp. 40–41), so that, with bell hooks, it would still be possible to speak of "black identity" and "experiences" as historically constituted. I would identify my own position with this one.

32   See Jay Clayton's discussion of the difference made by the pragmatic situation of a writer: no matter how sensitive or imaginative, "a work by a white writer cannot function in the same way as a work by a black. . . . To speak from a position of marginality is to engage listeners in a different social relation from that of the dominant culture." Jay Clayton, "The Narrative Turn in Recent Minority Fiction," *American Literary History*, 2 (1989), 389.

33   Jean Seligman with Jennifer Boeth, "Whole Lot of Shaking Going On," *Newsweek*, 10 May 1993, p. 49; hereafter cited in text.

34   In accord with Donna Haraway's notion of "situated knowledges" (see her *Simians, Cyborgs, and Women: The Reinvention of Nature* [New York, 1991], pp. 183–201), I recognize that my reading of Walker and Williams is symptomatic of my critical positioning as a feminist scholar, raised on deconstruction but deeply invested in the practical politics of feminism and women's studies, and also as a women's studies teacher often assailed from both sides, by students who find poststructuralist feminism hopelessly arid and alien to their experience and by other, equally impassioned students who find identity-based feminisms hopelessly naive.

35   Patricia J. Williams, "Owning the Self in a Disowned World," in her *The Alchemy of Race and Rights* (Cambridge, Mass., 1991), p. 183; hereafter cited in text.

36   Alice Walker, "Journal (April 17th, 1984)," in *Living By the Word*, pp. 1–2; hereafter cited in text.

Chapter 61

Sonia Shah

SLAYING THE DRAGON LADY

Toward an Asian American feminism

Rather than being another book representing Asian American women per se, investigative international journalist and critic Sonia Shah is careful to point out in her introduction that a politically inflected, truly unifying force, for this ethnic group will of necessity be feminist and activist, bringing together subdivisions such as class and professional status. This is a shift away from notions of shared Asian American women's experiences, which are of course diverse, to how such women encounter and engage with what Shah calls "three major driving forces in U.S. society": racism, patriarchy and "imperial aggression against Asia." In other words, Shah is interested in the biopolitical subjectivity of Asian American women, or, how they are constructed, excluded, stereotyped, or degraded by intersecting social and political forces, such as immigration policies, societal racism, or gender relations within Asian American communities (Shah has also investigated the biopolitics of disease and the global pharmaceutical industry). In her account of the term "dragon ladies"—one which by the end of the essay has been reclaimed and recodified—Shah notes the discrepancy between the stereotype of the "reptilian" aggressive and evil woman, and the actual Asian women who immigrated to the US during the mid nineteenth century, who were disempowered, poor, and often forced to work in the sex industry. Asian women were regarded as abject, potentially capable of "infecting" whites (physically or morally), and thus subjects in need of saving by religious whites. Shah also observes that as Asian immigration changed over time, it was US labour needs that drove immigration policy, i.e., women needed for cheap labour. A low point in this history was the internment of Japanese Americans during the Second World War, in which women were once again dispossessed and subject to abusive labour practices. Asian American resistance and protest groups in the 1960s did not always lead to a recognition of women's perspectives and differences within such activist movements. Other factors that fragmented oppositional Asian American women were the rise of economic opportunities and associated professional organizations, as well as the new social narrative of the "model minority", whereby Asians and others where portrayed as being successful and exemplary minorities within a multicultural society that had deep divisions among whites and African Americans. Shah calls this vision of liberal white America a "feel-good fantasy", one which depended upon docile bodies. But a transition to a less vibrant labour market and declining economic opportunities among other factors has once again resulted in labour inequalities and abuses of Asian American women workers. For Shah this directly links to the newfound energy and growth of Asian American labour movements, and she provides an interesting case study: a campaign against a fashion designer led by the Asian Immigrant Women Advocates, that successfully countered the legal cutouts that have previously offered legal protection to the companies which use sewing shops and cheap labour without providing adequate recompense to the workers. For Shah, the newly unified and activist movements that have arisen in more recent years, can lead to a new sense of shared essentially, and necessarily *feminist*, activist histories and strategies among Asian American women.

WHY PUBLISH A BOOK ON Asian American feminism? Many fine works on Asian American women have been published in recent years, from anthologies such as the recently released *Making More Waves, Our Feet Walk the Sky,* and *The Very Inside* to literary collections, such as *The Forbidden Stitch, The Politics of Life,* and *Unbroken Thread,*[1] to name just a few.

But this book is fundamentally different. It focuses explicitly on the political perspectives of Asian American women, describing a growing social movement and an emerging way of looking at the world: Asian American feminism. As I argue below, an Asian American feminist perspective—more than being Asian American or a woman—can animate and unite Asian American women into a lasting and fruitful social movement.

Works on Asian American women often take as their focal point their experiences, tacitly assuming *something* is similar or unifying in Asian American women's experiences, despite the obligatory disclaimers to the contrary.[2] As critics and scholars have long pointed out, the experiences of Asian American women are fantastically diverse. We are a group of people with different nationalities, languages, religions, ethnicities, classes, and immigration status. I agree that there *is* something unifying in women's varying experiences. But in works on Asian American women, that something is left undefined—it is vaguely referred to, if at all, as something about being from Asia, or about stereotypes, foods, and career choices.

All of the above similarities do exist, to varying degrees. But, I think, in the end, that those similarities are only skin-deep, not enough to make relations between different Asian American women any more likely than relations between Asian women and any other group of people. Indeed, the differences are at times much bigger, more real, more visceral and emotionally laden than the similarities, which are so often abstract.

To critics who would then say, well then, how does it make sense to talk about Asian American women at all? I would respond: it makes as much sense as it does to talk about white people or black people or Latinos. These racial groups admit just as much, if not more, diversity within their ranks than they have similarities. In the end, they are historical constructs, kept in place by social and political institutions, in service of a hierarchical, racially biased society. White people include poor Irish Catholic illegal immigrants, rich WASPS, and Jewish intellectuals. They are at least as different as they are similar. But it makes sense to talk about them as a group because they all share the same rung on the racial hierarchy, which, in many areas of life, is the most significant determinant of their social status in the United States. More than their shared language, ethnic heritage, or class, their *whiteness* determines who they live with, who they go to school with, what kind of jobs they get, how much money they make, and with whom they start families.

Similarly, the reason to talk about Asian American women as a single group is because we all share the same rung on the racial hierarchy *and* on the gender hierarchy. It is not that our lives are so similar in substance, but that our lives are all monumentally shaped by three major driving forces in U.S. society: racism and patriarchy most immediately, and ultimately, imperial aggression against Asia as well. As long as those systems of distributing and exercising power continue to exist, it will continue to make sense to talk about Asian American women as a group (as well as other racial and gender groups.)

Explicitly defining this book as one *not* about Asian American women, but rather exploring the topic of Asian American feminism, is the embodiment of the above point. There is no *political* point in just talking about Asian American women's experiences, even as the very question rests upon the years of vital scholarship and creative work done on detailing that experience. What it makes *political* sense to talk about is how the forces of racism, patriarchy, and imperialism specifically affect Asian American women. And, most importantly, how Asian American women counter resistance to those forces. In other words, about a racially conscious, international feminism: Asian American feminism.

Dragon ladies: a brief political history

Empress Tsu-hsi ruled China from 1898 to 1908 from the Dragon Throne. The *New York Times* described her as "the wicked witch of the East, a reptilian dragon lady who had arranged the poisoning, strangling, beheading, or forced suicide of anyone who had ever challenged her autocratic rule."[3] Decades later, scholars such as Sterling Seagrave attempted to balance this self-servingly racist caricature of Empress Tsu-hsi. But the shadow of the Dragon Lady— with her cruel, perverse, and inhuman ways—continued to darken encounters between Asian women and the West they flocked to for refuge: the 1996 Meriam Webster dictionary describes a dragon lady as "an overbearing or tyrannical woman."

Far from being predatory, many of the first Asian women to come to the United States in the mid-1800s were disadvantaged Chinese women, who were tricked, kidnaped, or smuggled into the country to serve the predominantly male Chinese community as prostitutes.[4] The impression that *all* Asian women were prostitutes, born at that time, "colored the public perception of, attitude toward, and action against all Chinese women for almost a century," writes historian Sucheng Chan. Police and legislators singled out Chinese women for special restrictions and opprobriums, "not so much because they were prostitutes as such (since there were also many white prostitutes around plying their trade) but because— as Chinese—they allegedly brought in especially virulent strains of venereal diseases introduced opium addiction, and enticed white boys to a life of sin."[5] While Chinese men bought Chinese women's sex and displayed their bound feet to curious Americans (at the St. Louis World's Fair, for example),[6] white women took to "saving" their disadvantaged sisters. Protestant missionary women brought policemen with hatchets to brothels to round up Chinese women into Mission Homes, where everything from personal mail to suitors was overseen by the missionary women.[7] Chinese women who were not prostitutes ended up bearing the brunt of the Chinese exclusion laws that passed in the late-1800s, engendered by the missionaries' and other anti-Chinese campaigns.

During these years, Japanese immigration stepped up, and with it, a reactionary anti-Japanese movement joined established anti-Chinese sentiment. During the early 1900s, Japanese numbered less than 3 percent of the total population in California, but nevertheless encountered virulent and sometimes violent racism. The "picture brides" from Japan who emigrated to join their husbands in the United States were, to racist Californians, "another example of Oriental treachery," according to historian Roger Daniels.[8]

U.S. immigration policy towards Asians has in large part been shaped by its perceived labor needs. Early Chinese and Japanese immigrants were actively recruited from the poorer classes to work as manual laborers on the railroads and elsewhere. As has been widely noted, before the immigration laws were radically changed in 1965, few Asian women emigrated to the United States. But it bears noting that despite the fact that they weren't in the country, Asian women shouldered much of the cost of subsidizing Asian men's labor. U.S. employers didn't have to pay Asian men as much as other laborers who had families to support, since Asian women in Asia bore the costs of rearing children and taking care of the older generation.[9]

Asian women who did emigrate here in the pre-1960s years were also usually employed as cheap laborers. In the pre-World War II years, close to half of all Japanese American women were employed as servants or laundresses in the San Francisco area.[10] The World War II internment of Japanese Americans made them especially easy to exploit: they had lost their homes, possessions, and savings when forcibly interned at the camps. Yet, in order to leave, they had to prove they had jobs and homes.[11] U.S. government officials thoughtfully arranged for their employment by fielding requests, most of which were for servants.

The 1965 immigration act brought in a huge influx of immigrants from Asia to fill primarily professional positions in the United States. Asian engineers, physicians, students and other professionals flocked to the country, drastically altering the face of Asian America and Asian American politics.

Making waves, big and small

The first wave of Asian women's organizing formed out of the Asian American movement of the 1960s, which in turn was inspired by the civil rights movement and the anti-Vietnam War movement. While many Asian American women are quick to note that women's issues are the same as men's issues—i.e. social justice, equity, human rights—history shows that Asian American men have not necessarily felt the same way. Leftist Asian women in Yellow Power and other Asian American groups often found themselves left out of the decision making process and their ideas and concerns relegated to "women's auxiliary" groups that were marginal to the larger projects at hand. Some Asian male activists rationalized this by

> pointing to their own oppression, arguing that they had a "right" to the sexual
> services of "their" women, after years when Asian women were excluded from
> the country. Moreover, they saw services from women as "just compensation"
> for the sacrifices they were making on behalf of the "people."[12]

As Asian American scholar Gary Okihiro notes, "Europe's feminization of Asia, its taking possession, working over, and penetration of Asia, was preceded and paralleled by Asian men's subjugation of Asian women."[13] Asian women naturally gravitated together in response to men's patronizing attitudes and some formed ambitious, radical political projects. Eager to advance "the correct line," most of these early groups petered out over sectarian conflicts. They were unable to inspire large numbers of Asian or other women or to hammer out unity amongst themselves.

While earnest, hardworking, and vital, these early Asian women radicals couldn't compete with the growing reality that for many Asian American women, there was money to be made. The highly educated and affluent Asian immigrants who came to the United States after 1965 were eager to be incorporated into the U.S. economy, and could be treated as a sort of second-tier professional class by U.S. employers. Not surprisingly, large organizations of primarily middle-class East Asian women, such as Asian Women United and the Organization of Asian Women, flourished during these years. These groups devoted themselves to educational and service projects, rather than to directly resisting social injustices.[14] Their popularity was at least partly affected by the fact that they helped professional Asian American women, in various ways, get and keep better jobs. The National Network of Asian and Pacific Women, founded in 1982 under the auspices of a federal grant, provides a case in point. As William Wei writes:

> It has been castigated for catering to middle-class women who are mainly interested in enhancing their employment opportunities. . . . [The Network believes that] it will be the professionals, rather than the workers, who will be in the vanguard of social change in the United States. Besides, its leaders claim, when it organizes activities that focus mainly on middle-class women, it is merely responding to the wishes of the majority of its members.[15]

Whatever oppositional sparks organizers of these groups may have had were easily squelched by the triple pressure created by the growing model minority myth and multiculturalism's identity politics. Conservative and mainstream institutions who wanted to advance racialized theories supported model minority myth-making because it implied there was a "good" minority in tacit opposition to the "bad" minorities—African Americans and Latinos. At the same time, the model minority myth helped countless struggling Asian Americans start businesses and send their kids to Ivy League schools, and was thus consciously upheld by Asian American community leaders. The ongoing condemnation of white supremacy by African Americans and others was answered by liberals with the benign image of multiculturalism: a scenario in which white people don't exploit black people, but white, brown, yellow, black, and red live together harmoniously. White feminists and other liberals advanced this feel-good fantasy with celebrations of Asian American culture and people. The result was a triple pressure on Asian women to conform to the docile, warm, upwardly mobile stereotype liberals, conservatives, and their own community members all wanted to promote.

The political context of the 1990s is significantly different, and likewise colors Asian women's organizing in this decade. Today, Asian immigrant professionals are less vital to the labor market and are thus, in a familiar cycle, being forced down the status ladder.[16] Affirmative action policies that benefited them are being dismantled. Laws that restrict their access to public assistance and legal rights have been enacted.[17] China and Japan are once again being invoked as evil empires—due now to their financial strength—as a new Yellow Peril is sweeping the country.[18]

At the same time, Asian immigration laws have changed such that the new Asian immigrant is not educated and professional but working-class or poor. Trade agreements such as NAFTA and GATT have broken down protections for workers and the environment in order to secure a free-wheeling capitalist global economy, and Asian workers in Asia and in the United States, especially women, are suffering the worst of it—laboring under worse working conditions and being forced to compete for the most degraded, worst-paying jobs.[19] As Miriam Ching Louie points out, the U.S. workforce is "increasingly female, minority, and immigrant." For example, in San Francisco's garment industry—its largest manufacturing sector—90 percent of the workers are women: 80 percent of those are Chinese speaking, and less than 8 percent are unionized.[20]

Activists have responded to these new changes with a renewed labor movement and new worker campaigns that cross borders and industries. Asian women organizers have been at the forefront of these campaigns. Most significant among these is the groundbreaking campaign by Asian Immigrant Women Advocates (AIWA) to organize Asian seamstresses against a powerful fashion designer, Jessica McClintock. AIWA's Garment Workers Justice Campaign was launched in May 1992 to secure $15,000 in back wages for Asian immigrant seamstresses who had been stiffed by their employer, Lucky Sewing Company. Instead of going after the sewing shop, which had declared bankruptcy, AIWA aimed its campaign directly at the designer who used the shop's labor. (This was a vital strategic move, as manufacturers often seek to immunize themselves against workers' grievances by subcontracting with shops for whose working conditions they don't take responsibility.) Not only did this campaign, which in the end secured a generous settlement for the seamstresses, establish a vital precedent for labor organizing, it politicized hundreds of young Asian American women across the country. AIWA staff inspired the seamstresses to outrage by showing them McClintock's fancy boutiques and organized Asian American women college students to stage protests at McClintock stores nationwide.[21]

With worker campaigns such as AIWA's, new issue-oriented organizations such as the National Women's Health Organization, and rejuvenated Asian battered women's organizations, a new generation of activists is springing up. They are uncovering the hidden history of previous generations of Asian women activists. With fewer and fewer class interests to divide them, they are shaping a new movement, one that goes beyond just agitating for our little piece of the ever-shrinking pie. They are putting poor immigrant and refugee Asian women at the forefront of their organizing, they are thinking globally, and they are making the connections among the politics of labor, health, environment, culture, nationalism, racism, and patriarchy: connections that have in the past eluded left activists.

An Asian American feminist movement is *the only movement* that will consistently represent Asian American women's interests. As the chapters in this book illustrate, neither the feminist movement nor the Asian American movement have taken Asian American women's interests into consideration on their agendas. But it's much more than that. An Asian American feminist movement is vital for the larger project of uncovering the social structure, with its built-in injustices and inequities, that affect us all. In today's global economy, in which nothing is certain for anyone save the most elite of the elite, this is a project that vitally concerns the majority.

My goal in publishing this book is to describe, expand, and nurture the growing resistance of Asian American women. I hope this book will provide a common ground for Asian women and girls and their allies. In so doing, it provides a set of issues, terms, ideas, and stories for folks to talk about—whether it is to debunk and decry them or to transform them into an agenda for action. As the pieces in this book show, Asian American women are already making their movement happen. A different sort of Dragon Lady is emerging—not a cold-blooded reptile, but a creature who breathes fire.

Notes

1   Kim, Elaine H., Lilia V. Villanueva, and Asian Women United, ed. *Making More Waves: New Writing by Asian American Women.* Boston: Beacon Press, 1997; Women of South Asian Descent Collective, ed. *Our Feet Walk the Sky: Women of the South Asian Diaspora.* San Francisco: Aunt Lute Books, 1994; Lim-Hing, Sharon, ed. *The Very Inside: An Anthology of Writing by Asian and Pacific Islander Lesbian and Bisexual Women.* Toronto: Sister Vision, 1994; Lim, Shirley Geok-Lin, ed. *The Forbidden Stitch: An Asian American Women's Anthology.* Corvallis, OR: Calyx Books, 1989; Houston, Velina Hasu, ed. *The Politics of Life: Four Plays by Asian American Women.* Philadelphia, Temple University Press, 1993; Uno, Roberta, ed. *Unbroken Thread: An Anthology of Plays by Asian American Women.* Amherst: University of Massachusetts Press, 1993.

2   Lim, in her introduction to *The Forbidden Stitch,* describes Asian American women's cultural and other diversity, but then points to Asian American women's "plural singularity," as their unifying principle. *The Forbidden Stitch* was the first anthology of Asian American women's writings to appear in the United States. In the 1997 anthology *Making More Waves,* the editors' preface states that they "wanted . . . to go beyond simply representing the various Asian ethnic groups." Still, their book is a celebration of diversity—"an attempt to weave history and memory with desire and possibility in

such a way that multiple identities emerge as irregularities and discontinuities, beautiful and unpredictable, in the pattern."

3   Seagrave, Sterling. *Dragon Lady: the Life and Legend of the Last Empress of China.* New York: Knopf Books, 1992.

4   In 1860, over 80 percent of the Chinese women in San Francisco were prostitutes. Yung, Judy. "The Social Awakening of Chinese American Women." Ed. Ruiz, Vicki L., and Ellen Carol DuBois. *Unequal Sisters: A Multicultural Reader in U.S. Women's History.* New York: Routledge, 1990. 247–48.

5   Sucheng, Chan. "The Exclusion of Chinese Women, 1870–1943." *Entry Denied: Exclusion and the Chinese Community in America, 1882–1943.* Ed. Sucheng Chan. Philadelphia: Temple University Press, 1991. 97–99, 138.

6   Yung 248–49.

7   Pascoe, Peggy. "Gender Systems in Conflict: The Marriages of Mission-Educated Chinese American Women, 1874–1939." Ed. Ruiz, Vicki L., and Ellen Carol DuBois. *Unequal Sisters: A Multicultural Reader in U.S. Women's History.* New York: Routledge, 1990. 142–45.

8   Daniels, Roger. *The Politics of Prejudice: The Anti-Japanese Movement in California and the Struggle for Japanese Exclusion.* New York: Atheneum and the University of California Press, 1973. 1, 44.

9   Bonacich, Edna, and Lucie Cheng, eds. *Labor Immigration Under Capitalism: Asian Workers in the United States before World War II.* University of California Press, 1984. 5–34.

10   Glenn, Evelyn Nakano. "From Servitude to Service Work." Eds. Ruiz, Vicki L., and Ellen Carol DuBois. *Unequal Sisters: A Multicultural Reader in U.S. Women's History.* New York: Routledge, 1990. 408–10.

11   Glenn 413.

12   Wei, William. *The Asian American Movement.* Philadelphia: Temple University Press, 1993. 76.

13   Okihiro, Gary. *Margins and Mainstreams: Asians in American History and Culture.* Seattle: University of Washington Press, 1994. 68.

14   Wei 72–100.

15   Wei 98.

16   Zamichow, Nora. "Education Fails Some Immigrants: Professionals in Other Countries Often Forced into Menial Positions." *The Boston Globe.* 28 May 1996.

17   "Actions by States Hold Keys to Welfare Law's Future." *The New York Times.* 1 October 1996: A22.

18   Conservative writer William Safire summed it up when he responded to campaign fundraising scandals allegedly involving illegal contributions from Asian nationals. Safire decried "the penetration of the White House by Asian interests" and "the Asian connection," calling Asians and Asian Americans "aliens" and "favor-hungry foreigners" who "shell out." Safire, William. "Absence of Outrage." Op-ed. *The New York Times.* 10 October 1996: A33.

19   Brecher, Jeremy, and Tim Costello, *Global Village or Global Pillage: Economic Reconstruction from the Bottom Up.* Boston: South End Press, 1994.

20   Louie, Miriam Ching. "Immigrant Asian Women in Bay Area Garment Sweatshops: 'After Sewing, Laundry, Cleaning, and Cooking, I Have No Breath Left to Sing.'" *Amerasia Journal* 18.1 (1992): 1–26.

21   Delgado, Gary. "How the Empress Gets Her Clothes: Asian Immigrant Women Fight Fashion Designer Jessica McClintock." Ed. Anner, John. *Beyond Identity Politics: Emerging Social Justice Movements in Communities of Color.* Boston: South End Press, 1996. 81–94.

Chapter 62

Gwendolyn Mikell

AFRICAN FEMINISM

Toward a new politics of representation

Exploring the resistances to the concept of "feminism" within an African context enables Gwendolyn Mikell to both observe how African women perceive their traditional and emerging roles in society, and why they have more recently shifted to a more activist feminist agenda in the Western sense of the word. Mikell, a professor of Anthropology and Foreign Service at Georgetown University, and author of *African Feminism: The Politics of Survival in Sub-Saharan Africa* (1997), argues that with the reinvention of the postcolonial African "states" during the 1990s there also came a concomitant reshaping of African feminism, which previously had been suspicious of Western feminism, if not entirely rejecting it. Mikell suggests that this rejection was partly to do with the suspicion of Western "extreme individualism" from heterogenous, but fundamentally community oriented African perspectives, alongside a rejection of Western feminists' sustained critique of patriarchy and subsequent "hostility to males". Mikell also argues that diversity among African women activists includes a whole host of traditional and modern approaches, an "African continuum" of intervention and action that does not overlap with Western feminism, which would tend to reject "traditional" heteronormative values or experiences. The binary divide between urban/educated and rural/traditional women also is not so marked within an African context. However, even if feminist issues in Africa are perceived as being about human subjects rather than primarily gendered and sexual subjects, Mikell does observe a "new consensus" for African feminism which is clustered around notions of oppression and politics. African women, who were so crucial to the shift from colonialism to postcolonial autonomy, were often subsequently excluded from the political machinery dominated by men, but this is not to say that women's political organizations disappeared—in fact the opposite is the case, with groups actively lobbying for a larger role in political decision making. Furthermore, national political crises have facilitated a loosening of otherwise static patriarchal political systems, presenting opportunities for women to intervene and participate in a "new political space" of mobilization. Such a space is not just political, but legal, symbolic, and dynamic in its processes; crises also free up space for dialogue concerning gender, and thus a re-codifying of the components of such space. It is important to recognize that from an African perspective, such re-codifying includes fairly conventional paradigms, such as marriage and heterosexual families. But what Mikell observes is that if an anti-discriminatory agenda is developed, it will function across the entire spectrum of gendered experiences, regardless of indigenous frameworks of understanding. After a series of detailed case studies, Mikell observes that African feminism has emerged from indigenous necessities and understanding, one suspicious of individualism and therefore cautious in its critique of tradition and community-based society. Intriguingly, Mikell concludes by arguing that African feminism is less about the female "body" (i.e., contemporary Western feminist theory), or an attack upon heterosexual marriage institutions, and more about gender equality and how this is to be achieved via indirect and direct political engagement.

I AM CONVINCED THAT I AM observing the birth of feminism on the African continent—a feminism that is political, pragmatic, reflexive, and group oriented.[1] These observations have grown out of my work in various parts of West Africa, in the 1970s and 1980s, and in South Africa, in 1992; out of my dialogues with women from Kenya and other parts of the continent; and most recently out of workshops on women and legal change that I conducted in Liberia, Sierra Leone, and Nigeria during May 1994. My research and involvement with Africa goes back to the early 1970s, when the charismatic energy of nationalist leaders like Kwame Nkrumah and Julius Nyerere had faded, the disillusionment with modernization and the capitalist economy was strong, and a rash of military coups marked the emergence of a new crisis orientation. In the nationalist phase, women had played crucial roles, but their importance in politics had waned by 1971 when I began research on cocoa farmers in Ghana and visited many West African countries. I have watched the episodic rise of women's movements during the United Nations Decade of Women (1975–85) and during the difficult economic crises and structural adjustment program experiments of the 1980s, but I see the peaking of a new feminism now as African states reinvent themselves in the 1990s.

This recognition of an emerging African feminism has been met with unanticipated enthusiasm by some of my Japanese, female, African studies colleagues who pursue autonomy within their own unique cultural environment, with ambivalence by some colleagues who work in Africa, and with amused tolerance on the part of many Western feminists who saw it as a moot point which I had (fortunately) resolved in the affirmative. There were relatively few African women who used the term "feminism" prior to the 1990s, and those who do so now are explicit in acknowledging the breadth that appears within it. For me, the recognition of a new African feminism represents a gargantuan change, because previously I was unwilling, for several reasons, to apply the feminist label to the African women's movement.

First, there was the recurring issue of hegemony. To a large extent I responded to the anger many African women have felt toward what they perceived as attempts by Western academics and activists to co-opt them into a movement defined by extreme individualism, by militant opposition to patriarchy, and, ultimately, by a hostility to males. This has been reflected most cogently in the reaction of African women writers, such as Buchi Emecheta, to the persistent questions from Western audiences about why they refused to call themselves feminists. Certainly, the writings of sociologist/novelist Buchi Emecheta (such as *The Bride Price*) portray both traditional and modern African women searching for fulfillment while attempting to overcome oppression by familial and patriarchal elements within their own cultures. In Emecheta's book *Head above Water*, we see that her own life also reflects such struggles. However, when asked about the feminist label in 1994, Emecheta's heated response was: "I have never called myself a feminist. Now if you choose to call me a feminist, that is your business; but I don't subscribe to the feminist idea that all men are brutal and repressive and we must reject them. Some of these men are my brothers and fathers and sons. Am I to reject them too?"[2]

Second, I was exercising caution born of my knowledge that what we called the African women's "movement" actually consisted of a broad continuum. The Nigerian researcher and writer Nina Mba, in her *Nigerian Women Mobilized* (1982), has shown that separate-gender, "dual-sex" organizing has generated the emergence of a broad spectrum of women's associations. This continuum includes women's associations with largely traditional frames of reference, the organizations and activities of educated women who were often engaged in overtly political or advocacy work, as well as the activities of urban women whose realities straddle these cultural worlds. Neither end of the African continuum aligns with the Western feminist continuum, but it does reflect African realities, as Florence Abena Dolphyne, the Ghanaian linguist and women's development organizer, points out in her 1991 book, *The Emancipation of Women: An African Perspective*.[3]

Third, I was resisting the projection of a dichotomy on to this continuum, with educated and elite women seen as ideologically far more advanced (and therefore feminist) and rural/ ordinary African women seen as parochial and prefeminist. Class differences do exist in the positions that African women have taken, as well as in their degrees of radicalism and types of activism, but collaboration between classes still occurs. It has been my position that an ideological dichotomy is largely negated by African cultural traditions which legitimate female organizations and collective actions by women in the interest of women,[4] an awareness shared by women at all points along the continuum. This continuum appears to be grounded in African communal, historical, symbolic, and experiential constructs, rather than in cultural constructs based on Western individualism and competition.

The strategic consensus that I see emerging among African women in many parts of the continent is an impressive one. The consensus, which many label "feminist" given the new meanings with which they are endowing the term, is reflected in Filomina Steady's description of African feminism as "dealing with multiple oppressions" and as dealing with women first and foremost as human, rather than sexual beings.[5] However, I point out that as new subtleties in African women's realities surface, politics is becoming the central point around which a new feminist consensus is emerging. I believe that the pragmatics of women's political representation in the 1990s are shaping the emerging African women's movement.

In the early part of this century, women's declining political status was directly related to the oppressive control of the colonial regime. African women took strength from the fact that their participation was essential if their countries were to end the colonial experience and achieve independence. However, after independence, male suppression of African women's political autonomy increased, despite the contributions women had made to nationalist politics and despite state claims to equitable approaches in education, policies, and laws. Given this, much scholarly discussion has been focused on understanding why African women eschewed an explicitly woman-oriented politics, while being victimized by military regimes and oppressed by males in both public and private life.

The results of such questioning have been greater insights into state and gender interactions, but we have little information on women's ideological and practical configurations.[6] I have for some time observed women's groups in West Africa (Ghana, Côte d'Ivoire, Nigeria), where women's organizations and associations have a long history, and I have followed the interactions of African women with the courts, constitutional issues, and new family laws.[7] I have been disturbed by the obstacles that formerly prevented the construction of national woman-oriented social agendas under whatever label. Now women are striving to overcome these obstacles. The growth of active women in development legal programs, of assertive women's movements in a number of countries, especially in Kenya prior to the 1992 elections, and of the African National Congress (ANC) Women's League's demands for greater female political representation in South Africa are positive signs of this feminist emergence.

I suspect that the greater willingness of African women to embrace feminist politics and gender representation in the 1990s is traceable to the current national crises and political transitions[8] which have been occurring throughout the continent over the past fifteen decades. Political transitions (whether in the traditional or the modern system) are always fraught with tensions because they represent points at which there is a change in the persona of the sovereign, the renewal or revision of a preexisting political compact, or the possibilities of potential challenges to the actual sovereignty of the polity.[9] It is to these societally specific compacts and experiences that we must look to understand the ideological assumptions that shape the "culture of feminine politics" which influenced women's behavior in the past and still exerts influences on African women's behavior today. But it is at these crisis/transition points that the disjuncture between the existing sociocultural compacts and modern political realities becomes most visible, and the audible discourse about gender roles alerts us to the subterranean conflicts that are occurring within the society. The heightening of contradictions and gender discourse may actually open up space for the emergence of a new configuration in the various African women's movements.

The 1990s post-cold war environment provides the first chance that most Africans—in particular, women of different ethnic and religious communities—have had to participate in a serious way in deciding the legal and constitutional rights of people in their own countries and the desired forms of government. During the past two decades, the crisis-initiated space expanded, but African women were sometimes hesitant to move into it because they did not want self-interests to take precedence over state interests, they recognized the existence of increasingly complicated "identity politics" (to use Valentine M. Moghadam's term) occurring around them,[10] and they were primarily concerned with resisting what many saw as Western hegemony in the guise of international feminist support. In addition, those market women's groups or elite women's groups, which were the first to attempt to move into this political space, were in many cases ruthlessly crushed by the government or military forces.[11]

But the harsh pressures exerted by contemporary national economic crises and political failures have removed some of women's fears and much of their reluctance to seek public office. African women's psychic involvement with these national and local processes is more clearly visible, as is their desire for equitable change. They appear strengthened in their beliefs that women's performance can be no worse than those of earlier male politicians, and is likely to be considerably better. Many women are saying that more assertive female actions are necessary to ensure gender-balanced approaches in the aftermath of the 1980s' economic collapses, military coups, civil wars, refugee crises, feminization of poverty, and structural adjustment programs.

Women appear aware that the present climate of political experimentation and "democratization," whether resulting from Western pressures or internal shifts within cultural/religious communities, offers them unique political opportunities to alter their sociopolitical positions. Even in the Muslim communities of Nigeria and Sudan,[12] some women are making use of the new political spaces that national crises and elections have created in order to mobilize women to achieve increased status in many areas of life. They, like women in many other areas, are analyzing the ways in which the lack of legal and policy supports may have affected their ability to play roles in development and politics.[13] In addition, it has not escaped their attention that in 1995, the year of the long-anticipated UN Fourth World Conference on Women (the Beijing Conference), women may have a unique opportunity to formulate a feminist agenda which will be seriously discussed.

I often refer to these crisis-generated political spaces as "dialogue opportunities." In referring to the implicit potential to alter colonial and more recent legal inequities[14] and to sketch the outlines of new relationships, I often describe it as "an invitation to gender dialogue." This amuses some of my African women friends who understand that the invitation is often forced and seldom purely voluntary on the part of any state. Nor is this an easy invitation for African women to accept, because it often means taking a critical view of traditional/ethnic norms which may have structured gender relations in the past, and it sometimes means traversing a dangerous obstacle course between women's groups, the party, the military/government, and the courts. But as an anthropologist I recognize the existence of different types of normative systems which regulate gender relations and that legal notions readjust and change as emerging social relationships require.[15] In the process of constructing law, we create symbols for the new set of relationships we are seeking to institutionalize in a particular society, although this is never done in isolation from the "forces of the larger world by which [law] is surrounded."[16] The questions that now guide my inquiries concern whether African women perceive and pursue the possibilities of altering their structural position, the extent to which they are willing to work for changes in laws and other political structures which affect women,[17] and the extent to which African women see this as part of their essential "feminist agenda."[18]

Now, almost two decades after the beginning of the United Nations Decade of Women, the discourse of African women's activism displays considerable maturation because it contains more explicit gender-political critiques. It is more woman-action and national/global issue oriented. Still, it has retained some of the earlier focus on rectifying inequities in conjugality and domestic relations, particularly in defining women's rights within marriage.[19] There have always been a few self-proclaimed feminists like the Ghanaian writer Ama Ata Aidoo,[20] who assigns some of the responsibility for women's plight to Western hegemony and an embattled African political economy. However, most women activists still hesitate to use the term "feminism," although they are more willing to seek legal change, promote gender equity, and to label their persistent grievances as "human rights" ones. It has become clear that today, even more than in the 1980s, African women are searching for a new deal,[21] and are more willing to work for the eradication of discrimination against women in customary norms, modern law, and social conventions.[22]

Because of time and space considerations, I shall describe only a small part of the plethora of feminist activities in which I observed African women's involvement in 1994. The backdrop for these observations was my earlier experience observing and documenting the activities of women's groups in Ghana, particularly the National Council of Women and Development (1975–86); rural women's cooperatives and women's economic groups; the 31 December movement headed by Nana Konadu Agyeman Rawlings, wife of Ghana's head of state (1984 to present); and the operations of Ghanaian women's church groups during the 1992 presidential elections. I have also observed and analyzed women in family-related court cases in Ghana (1986–90) to assess women's position relative to laws and their implementation. In 1992 I had talked with ANC women involved in the Gender Advisory Committee of the CODESA II talks[23] during my preliminary research stay in Durban in South Africa. Such research experience had allowed me to debate which factors led women to mobilize, organize, and make political demands; to question whether first ladies were ideal leaders for such organizations; and to assess the appropriate organizational and ideological structures for presenting these demands. However, my comments here are more specific, focusing on women's politicolegal activities which are becoming more visible. I believe that these new activities mark the willingness of African women to engage in actions and dialogue with the goal of mediating gender differences and restoring women to valued roles and statuses through constitutional and legal means.

In May 1994 my workshops on sociolegal change in Monrovia (Liberia), Freetown (Sierra Leone), and in various parts of Nigeria offered me an opportunity to have a dialogue with women from a wide variety of groups—craftswomen, church-women, teachers, clerks, nongovernmental (NGO) representatives, professors, businesswomen, lawyers, judges, ministers, and first ladies.[24] This allowed me to assess whether they stated narrow social and economic goals or broader ones and to assess where they stood along the "feminist" continuum. I agreed to go to two areas in which I had not worked previously, in order to facilitate discussions among African women, as well as to deepen my understanding of gender dynamics in areas involved in some intense political crises such as civil war (Liberia), and governmental fragmentation/rebel actions (Sierra Leone). The venues varied from informal meetings in the evening at the women's craft center, to formal workshops at the American Cultural Center, or the state house, depending on the composition of the groups and their sizes.

In these workshops, I aimed to present a researcher's overview of some paramount sociolegal issues confronting African women across the continent, to encourage dialogue on the interaction between social and legal rights, and to elicit women's feelings about the correct approaches to the problems of gender and law. Perhaps not surprisingly, the African women I met were intrinsically pronatal, operating from shared assumptions that African women value marriage and motherhood. The major areas that women articulated as problematic were domestic relations (problems of marriage and spousal relationships given polygyny and lineage systems, as well as the monitoring of male responsibilities in the maintenance/custody of children),[25] women's rights of access to property and other resources,[26] and that controversial category called "privacy" rights (which includes many sexual and reproductive issues, as well as violence against women).[27]

One might have predicted that many women were interested in the status of American women's legal rights in these categories, but this time these topics occupied far less of our conversation than they have in the past. Instead, women were anxious to discuss the heightening of the above problems in direct correlation to the economic collapse, structural adjustment, constitutional/democratic stalemates, and war which had engulfed the African state. And they stressed that they would never be able to address them directly unless they stepped up to the challenge of direct self-representation and involvement in the political realm.

The word "feminism" was scarcely used, although some men jokingly called us feminists and other men angrily pinned the label on these workshops; in addition, the newspapers occasionally referred to the "feminist talks" taking place. However, the content of the women's discourse made it clear that they wanted change and were searching for ideas and strategies through which they could achieve it. The manner in which they discussed women's problems indicated their awareness of the decreased capacity of traditional systems to respond to their complaints and the absolute necessity for women's assertive actions in support of specific legal initiatives. In some cases, they reminded each other that modern laws which address their situation were on the books, although the social environment did not encourage use of legal remedies; and they discussed how such contradictions could be eliminated.

In Liberia, the ongoing civil war in the countryside and the trauma of displacement, torture, and starvation appeared to have defused many earlier distinctions and inequities among women[28] and radicalized and mobilized women. Although we think in terms of ethnic/religious differences (Americo-Liberians versus indigenous peoples) and class differences as separating Liberians, women sought to coalesce in ways that bypassed the ethnic rivalries implicit in the civil war. During 1994, Monrovia, the capital city, was protected by the military operations group of the Economic Community of West African States, as well as by the United Nations Interim Military forces in Liberia. So, it had been possible for women to set up shelters and job-training programs for women, such as My Sister's Place, as well as crafts and agricultural training projects, all of which tended to lessen the socioeconomic class distinctions between women who were involved. In addition to Concerned Women of Liberia, which was headed by Mrs. Vulate Tate (a former member of the Interim Legislative Assembly), there were other politically involved groups. The Liberian Women's Initiative, a woman's action network, had encouraged the warring parties and the interim government to go to the bargaining table, and the women had coordinated public demonstrations when it had appeared that agreements were not being kept. It would have been idealistic to expect that such a network could have resolved the civil war and the stalled negotiations, but the women intended that when peace was reached that there would be a national organization capable of assembling women to create a "national women's agenda" and to participate in elections and constitutional talks. In fact, the National Organization of Women Lawyers of Liberia was inaugurated two days prior to my arrival and was a likely group to play such an organizing role.

As Liberian women talked about rape of women by troops of all sides, and about the climate in which male violence against women was tolerated, they voiced something I was to hear repeated in each place: "Until the government makes an explicit commitment to the enforcement of basic human rights for women, our existing legal rights are irrelevant because men know that they do not need to respect them." Thus, women intended that one of the anticipated fruits of peace was also to be mechanisms that would protect them as they brought charges against assaulters, regardless of whether they were soldiers or husbands.

The challenges of competition *within* the women's movement were visible in Freetown, Sierra Leone, where the country struggled under a military government composed of relatively young, dissatisfied soldiers. Sierra Leone shared Liberia's history of Black settlers who provided for the elite, but this Creole group (Krio) was much smaller in size than Liberia's. Here, feminism was struggling to coalesce but could not do so easily because of divided class and ethnic interests. Educated women were concerned about the political fragmentation and rebel actions which existed throughout the country, a reality which dominated even their organizational meetings and contributed to a sense of helplessness.[29] Rural women, on the other hand, were concerned about violence and the absence of economic stability, both of which were decimating community life. However, thinking holistically in terms of what was good for Sierra Leonean women as a whole was difficult for women in Freetown because of the real social and class divides that were only being erased by the current political chaos. Elite women were open to some change in their legal status, but they were uncertain about whether it was desirable if such change challenged their status as married women by also benefiting men's rural polygynous wives and their "illegitimate" children.

Nevertheless, in a striking example of the new gender initiatives, the young wife of Sierra Leone's military head of state (Captain Valentine Strasser), pushed by an urban coterie of ministers' wives, had formed an embryonic women's movement called SILWODMO (Sierra Leonean Women's Development Movement), which was designed as a national NGO. Although they patterned it after the 31st December Organization, led by Ghana's first lady, their desire to have it gain greater legitimacy among women led them to organize a private meeting for me with first lady Gloria Strasser and SILWODMO officers, so that they could have a critical appraisal of their efforts and goals. It was clear to me that in the face of an emerging feminism, smart state and military leaders may attempt to co-opt or redirect women's movements, perhaps avoiding confrontations on legal, political, and economic issues where leaders anticipate a divide between gender rights, human rights, and national power. The role of first ladies in the emerging feminist politics is still being debated by African women across the continent.

Some of my most fruitful experiences took place in Nigeria, a formerly oil-rich country, the largest in West Africa, which has had a succession of military coups interspersed with short-lived electoral politics in the years since independence. Increasingly, political instability accompanied by economic restructuring and continued conflict with the United States over corruption and drugs has made Nigerians cynical about achieving democracy within African state structures. Within Nigeria, my most exciting discussions occurred in a workshop at the

Lakoja State House, in an area bordering Kaduna, where more than fifty women (rural and urban, educated and illiterate, Muslim and Christian) discussed specific problems of concern. Nigeria has a tradition of diverse public and private roles for women,[30] a history of women's activism in the south, and a growing involvement of women in public organizations in Muslim areas of the north, as Ayesha Imam indicates.[31] However, the sheer multicultural nature of the group forced greater clarity in how women defined and thought about the problems faced by different groups of Nigerian women, and it reinforced the important role of culture in advancing or retarding women's progress. Large numbers of Muslim women attended the workshop, and some confided that they were unwilling to speak in public because of their lack of fluency in English or because their support for "feminist causes" might be reported to husbands. But they vigorously nodded their heads in agreement with certain interpretations of women's problems, leaving no confusion about where they stood. A fascinating discussion ensued about how women's activism need not constitute a rejection of religion or culture (although women wanted to see gender equity introduced into particular aspects of community life and national life) and about how material or legal rights for women could influence the culture in more equitable ways.

Nigerian women repeated the comments I had heard voiced in Monrovia about the priority of explicit state recognition of human rights for women. They wanted to see Nigeria publicize its acceptance of the International Convention on Human Rights, its support for women's rights within the 1979 Lagos Plan of Action, and a national recognition of women's rights under law and constitution, which they think will reinforce other rights within the domestic, economic, and privacy categories outlined above. Then, they challenged each other to think of both legal and extralegal methods of addressing concerns such as forced child-marriages, vesico-vaginal fistulas among teenage mothers,[32] and women's rights to decision making about work and other economic activities. For northern Nigerian women, more than for any other group of women I encountered, gender liberation was symbolized in a woman's right to operate in public space—to determine for herself whether she would enter the work force or run for public office. They clearly stated that the economic decline had crystallized for them the fact that work outside the home could be a route out of poverty and that male refusal to allow wives to work was an attempt to oppress women.

But national politics was the minor theme to which these women kept returning and the backdrop against which these workshops occurred. Women were angry with Ibrahim Babangida, the former military president, for annulling the results of the 1993 elections and halting the return to a civilian government. They were cynical about the intentions of the military government of Sani Abatcha, who replaced Babangida. Therefore, many women scoffed at the upcoming Constitutional Conference in Nigeria (May 1994), because they wondered whether only hand-picked progovernment representatives would attend and whether support for government positions and prolonged military government rule was a foregone conclusion. In Lagos, most women—whether appointees to government commissions, students, journalists, teachers, businesswomen, clerks, or traders—wanted a return to electoral politics. However, there was no illusion that with elections women would simply vote their female representatives into power and inaugurate a feminist agenda. In fact, given the multiplicity of women's groups and would-be-leaders, the identity politics of the Muslim communities and the anger in southern communities, and government inroads into some women's groups, Nigerian women were skeptical that they would be able to agree on a "Nigerian women's agenda" to be presented at the Beijing Conference in 1995.

The emerging African feminism is intensely prodemocratic and supportive of some sort of rapprochement between the pure market economics and "justice economics." They, like their menfolk, believe that there is a link (implicit or explicit) between structural adjustment[33] and stalemated democratization and that recent verbalization of gender-equity goals might be another tool for internal control. Many male policymakers have been prone to criticize these "conditionalities" as the latest colonialism, and some are hostile to women's groups which pursue a "feminist" agenda. However, African women have increasingly mixed responses to this twin restructuring. Many Liberian, Nigerian, and Sierra Leonean women are beginning to believe that now may be the time to utilize the expanding political space to correct legal inequities related to the control of resources, which made them the paramount victims of the economic crises of the 1980s. Most African women are concerned that their governments see the link between support for women's rights and economic stability for women and the family.

Seen in this light, I understood that my presence created a number of less sensitive political spaces in which women's varying perceptions of their sociolegal realities could be aired, agreements or disagreements could be discussed, alternative strategies outlined, and potential alliances between leaders and groups could be acknowledged and perhaps later acted upon. By responding to invitations to discuss innocuous-sounding women's issues, rather than "politics," urban women could temporarily circumvent the political restrictions put in place by the military government.

It does not require the presence of an outsider to make nascent African feminist developments coalesce, but that presence does allow space for the ongoing discourse to be amplified. I found this to be true not just for feminist issues but also for issues of concern to cocoa farmers, when I worked among them in Brong-Ahafo, Ghana. However, during 1994, there had been a number of women's conferences and a workshop on women's issues in northern Nigeria. In fact, several organizations working on women's legal issues put copies of their publications into my hands during this latest visit. But these events have not received attention from the government or the media, so women across the country and abroad often do not know of them. To a large extent, much of the emerging feminist consciousness and the current movement toward feminist agendas in each country remains hidden—hidden first because the chaotic economic and political conditions there causes primary emphasis to be placed on survival issues. But they also remain hidden because governments allow political and economic events to monopolize national public media space and foreign attention, thus downplaying the cultural and gender developments which they sometimes find troublesome.

Overt and public feminism has its price, but women now seem willing to pay it. When African women's movements seize the space and command attention, they face ostracism and often severe reprisals. Kenyan women provide the most outstanding examples. Wangari Mathai's Green Belt movement began with issues of urban ecology and gradually taught women that they could become shapers of their own agroeconomic destinies. Led by Mathai, this was a grassroots movement among women to reclaim their environment, restore "green spaces" in which they could produce food, and revive women's agrarian strategies which had been of benefit to them and their communities. The movement helped to produce a large woman-oriented constituency for later politicians, but Mathai herself faced imprisonment, harassment, and victimization even as the movement grew. Other issues, such as the privileging of traditional law over modern law as a regulator of women's rights, have emerged in Kenya with the Wambui Otieno case.[34] However, with President Arap Moi's announcement of elections for December 29, 1992, the National Committee on the Status of Women (NCSW) became the beneficiary of Mathai's consciousness raising among women and helped women elect forty-five female civic leaders and six parliamentarians.[35] Despite the fact that women who stood for election faced ostracism and in some cases were raped as punishment, the successful NCSW is involved in planning systematic women's agendas for education, local government, and legal reform.

My point is that the emergence of African feminism has been in accordance with its own internal clock, evolving in dialogue with the cultural contexts from which it has sprung and only cautiously acknowledging individualism. After many years of observing, it is gratifying to see that an internally driven and aggressively democratic politics appears to be characteristic of the African feminism which is emerging across the continent. As one example, the Women's League of the African National Congress abandoned its former principle of "liberation before feminism," and through the protest activities of women it managed to extract from the ANC a promise of the appointment of women to 30 percent of political offices after the 1994 elections.

The ANC, as well as Black women, will have to work hard to bring such promises to fruition. However, Mamphela Ramphele has alerted us to some of the unique characteristics of this new Black feminism.[36] In the same vein, when I spoke with the newly elected Black parliamentarian Mavivi Manzini this past September, she proudly stated her feminist commitment to using democratic structures to bring about equity for South African women.[37]

In the search for gender equity, this African feminism has the ability to subject indigenous cultural norms, received legal notions, and new state laws to new scrutiny as it assesses whether they are in women's interest. Such behavior has led me to believe that in charting an African course, this will not be a feminism which will fixate on the female "body," champion woman's autonomy from man the "victimizer," or question the value of marriage and motherhood. Admittedly, the implications for female-male relationships remain to be seen. But feminism is to be judged by women's actions, so there seems little doubt that the emerging African feminism will generate positive changes in African political structures and contribute to greater gender equality before the law on the African continent.

Notes

1   Here, feminism is defined as approaches to addressing the unequal status of women relative to men, with the goal of mediating gender differences and providing women access to the repertoire of valued roles and statuses within society. Note that I have left the issue of various ideological currents within feminism unaddressed here, because this is primarily a Western, not an African, concern. Rosemarie Tong lists some of these approaches as liberal, Marxist, radical, psychoanalytic, socialist, existentialist, postmodern, although we might add structuralist, essentialist, and others to the above. See her *Feminist Thought: A Comprehensive Introduction* (Boulder: Westview Press, 1989).
2   Buchi Emecheta, giving a lecture at Georgetown University in Washington, D.C., on 8 Feb. 1994.
3   See Florence Abena Dolphyne, *The Emancipation of Women: An African Perspective* (Accra: Ghana University Press, 1991). Dolphyne reports that at the 1980 UN conference in Denmark, African women resisted the Western feminist insistence on abolishing female circumcision, and they also refused to abandon their position of criticizing apartheid in South Africa (x–xi).
4   I have written elsewhere about the existence of several traditional cultural models which structured the polity and gender relations and which contained coherent statements about what constitutes political identity, authority, and legitimacy. Briefly, these were the *corporate model,* which included women as intrinsic gender-defined members of family and other communal groups; a *dual-sex model,* which included autonomous women's structures that functioned as complementary to male structures, as well as a check on patriarchy or autocracy; and a superficial *gender-biased model,* which grew out of the challenges of state-consolidation as leaders attempted to centralize and restrict political access to males. See Gwendolyn Mikell, "Introduction," in "African Women: States of Crisis" (Philadelphia: University of Pennsylvania Press, forthcoming 1996).
5   Filomina Chioma Steady, "African Feminism: A Worldwide Perspective," in *Women in Africa and the African Diaspora,* ed. Rosalyn Terborg-Penn, Sharon Harley, and Andrea Benton Rushing (Washington, D.C.: Howard University Press, 1987), 4.
6   Iris Berger and Claire Robertson, *Women and Class in Africa* (New York: Africana Publishing, 1986).
7   Gwendolyn Mikell, "Pleas for Domestic Relief: Akan Women and Family Courts in Ghana," in *Poverty in the 1990s: The Situation of Urban Women,* ed. Fatima Meer (Geneva: UNESCO, 1994), 65–86.
8   Pearl Robinson's notion of the culture of politics (i.e., "political practice that is culturally legitimated and societally validated by local knowledge") meshes nicely with my notions of gender behavior

which grows out of preexisting cultural models as they have been elaborated over time. See Pearl Robinson, "Approaches to the Study of Democratization: Scripts in Search of Reality" (paper presented at the African Studies Association meeting in Boston, 5 Dec. 1993).

9   Gwendolyn Mikell and E.P. Skinner, "African Women and the Early State in West Africa" (Women in Development Series, Michigan State University, Working Paper, no. 190, 1989).

10   Valentine M. Moghadam, "Preface" in *Identity Politics and Women: Cultural Reassertions and Feminism in International Perspective,* ed. Valentine M. Moghadam (Boulder: Westview Press, 1993).

11   Ann Fraker and Barbara Harrell-Bond, "Rawlings and the 1979 Revolution" (American Field Service Committee Report, no. 4, 1980).

12   Ayesha Imam and Sonya Hale point out the changing configurations of gender within various Islamic cultural/religious constructs and how these respond to altered local circumstances and power relationships, as well as to national politics. Imam emphasizes the plurality of responses from women, with some Muslim women attempting to move toward a more secularist interpretation of women's roles, while others retain more orthodox interpretations of gender roles. Hale argues that different political ideologies have sought to strategically manipulate the image of woman, often conflating it to the essentialist "ideal woman as mother" stereotype in an attempt to further control women's actions. See Ayesha Imam, "Politics, Islam, and Women in Kano, Northern Nigeria" (123–44); and Sonya Hale, "Gender, Religious Identity, and Political Mobilization in Sudan," both in *Identity Politics and Women.*

13   "Women, Legal Reform, and Development in Sub-Saharan Africa," *Findings,* no. 20 (Africa Technical Department, World Bank, July 1994), 1.

14   Margaret Jean Hay and Marcia Wright, eds., *African Women and the Law: Historical Perspectives* (Boston: Boston University Papers on Africa, 7, 1982).

15   Bronislaw Malinowski (*Crime and Custom in Savage Society* [London: Routledge & Kegan Paul, 1926]) cautions that "the maintenance of law is . . . a dynamic process of constant struggle and readjustment" (p. 41). See also Leopold Pospisil, "Social Change and Primitive Law," *American Anthropologist* 60, no. 5 (1958): 832–37; Laura Nader, ed., *Law in Culture and Society* (Chicago: Aldine Publishing, 1969).

16   June Starr, *Law as Metaphor: From Islamic Courts to the Palace of Justice* (Albany: State University of New York Press, 1992); Sally Falk Moore, *Law as Process: An Anthropological Approach* (London: Routledge & Kegan Paul, 1978), 55.

17   See Katharine T. Barlett and Rosanne Kennedy, "Introduction" (1–14); and Wendy Wilson, "The Equality Crisis: Some Reflections on Culture, Courts, and Feminism" (15–34), both in *Feminist Legal Theory: Readings in Law and Gender,* ed. Katharine T. Barlett and Rosanne Kennedy (Boulder: Westview Press, 1991).

18   Catharine MacKinnon says that many of women's barriers to equality "exist at an interface between law and society (241), and achieving equality will require change not reflection-a new [feminist] jurisprudence" (249). See Catharine MacKinnon, *Towards a Feminist Theory of the State* (Boston: Harvard University Press, 1989).

19   See Dorothy Dee Vallenga, "Who Is a Wife? Expressions of Heterosexual Conflict in Ghana," in *Female and Male in West Africa,* ed. Christine Oppong (London: Allen & Unwin, 1983), 144–55. See also the case studies on Ghana and Kenya in *Law and the Status of Women: An International Symposium* (New York: Columbia University School of Law, 1977).

20   See Ama Ata Aidoo, "The African Woman Today," *Dissent,* summer 1992, pp. 319–25; and Ama Ata Aidoo, interview by Mary Mackay, in *belles lettres,* fall 1993, pp. 33–35.

21   Filomina Chioma Steady, "African Women at the End of the Decade," in *Africa Report* (March–April 1985): 4–8.

22   Although earlier our focus was on the contradictions involved in using received laws or "imposed law," whether derived from colonialism or global influences, the focus is shifting. African women recognize that global interaction is moving local realities in directions which sometimes cannot be adequately addressed by traditional legal norms and may require resorting to several legal levels or systems. Some important questions concern the nature of the syncretism or blending of legal ideas. See Leopold Pospisil, *Anthropology of Law: A Comparative Theory* (New York: Harper & Row, 1970), 97–126; and Richard Abel, "Western Courts in Non-Western Settings: Patterns of Court Use in Colonial and Neo-Colonial Africa," in *The Imposition of Law: Studies in Law and Social Control,* ed. Sandra Burman and Barbara Harrell-Bond (New York: Academic Press, 1979), 167–200.

23   CODESA is the Commission for a Democratic South Africa, a series of negotiations in 1992 involving the business community, political parties, and other representative groups in order to generate a process for moving toward democratic nonracial elections and a transitional structure for governance.

24   These activities were sponsored by the AMPART lecture program of the United States Information
        Agency. USIA has helped to support other women and development activities and workshops,
        particularly in Nigeria.

25   As one example, in terms of domestic rights, the rights of African women as wives and mothers vary
        depending upon the type of lineage, ethnic, and legal systems they participate in, that is, whether
        they are Christian, Muslim, or traditionalists, and the degrees of control that husbands acquire over
        wives and their activities. Of major concern to women were, first, the registration and equalization
        of marriages, whether they are under ordinance or statute, whether they are Mohammedan, or
        whether under customary law. Many women felt that one national law would uniformly entitle a
        wife to specified rights, including the right to make decisions about the conjugal family and residence,
        and the right to own conjugal or private property. Second, women are concerned about the equality
        of women in obtaining divorce and equality after divorce. Here, they voice their needs for some
        guarantees of male contributions to the maintenance and custody of children should the marriage not
        endure. They do not want men being given the privilege of ownership of the children but not having
        the legal responsibility to support the children if women are awarded custody.

26   In addition to clear economic rights to produce and own things of value, to inherit and to work,
        women want other social changes which support these economic rights. For example, equality of
        spouses, so that no husband "owns" his wife, despite payment of any brideprice; and no husband
        matters more before the law than the wife. In Nigeria, this concern is a strong one given that under
        traditional culture, brideprice provides a major incentive for families to give women in arranged
        marriage, often at a very young age, or to disrupt a girl's education so that she can marry. Many
        Nigerian women say equality of women will allow them to be equal as spouses. In addition, Nigerian
        women say they want recognition of the married couple as economic unit, which takes into
        consideration contributions the wife may have made to existing property that may be owned in the
        husband's name. They are concerned about situations in which husbands die, and the paternal families
        take everything including the domicile and its contents, leaving nothing for the wife and children.

27   Noteworthy is that the women did not even raise the issues of women's right to birth control.
        Although national women's groups often work on family planning and demographic issues, these
        issues were not even a part of the conversation of the cross-section of women attending these
        workshops. See Christine Oppong, *Marriage, Parenthood, and Fertility in West Africa* (Canberra:
        Australian National University Press, 1978). On the other hand, the issue of forced female
        circumcision and women's objections to it surfaced in Nigeria as a problem that even educated
        women and their children faced. Interestingly enough, women argued for private diplomatic
        interventions and the need to educate men about the hazards of clitoridectomy, so that their wives or
        daughters would face fewer communal pressures, rather than for legal suppression of female
        circumcision.

28   Jeanette Carter and Joyce Mends-Coles, *Liberian Women: Their Roles in Food Production and Their
        Educational and Legal Status* (Monrovia: University of Liberia, USAID: 1982). Also see Mary Moran,
        Civilized Women: Gender and Prestige in Southeast Liberia (Ithaca: Cornell University Press, 1990).

29   There have long been women's groups in Sierra Leone, but they were mostly urban Krio organizations
        of Christian teachers, churchwomen, lawyers, and so forth, who were quite distinct from the African
        women leaders and chiefs of ethnic and Muslim communities on the interior. See Adelaide M.
        Cromwell, *An African Victorian Feminist: The Life and Times of Adelaide Smith Casely-Hayford, 1868–1960*
        (Washington, D.C.: Howard University Press, 1992), 1–17.

30   Bolanle Awe, *Nigerian Women in Historical Perspective* (Lagos: Sankori/Bookcraft, 1992).

31   Imam, 123–44.

32   Particularly in the north, one by-product of economic crisis has been the increased marriage of
        underaged girls to obtain bridewealth or to lessen the numbers of mouths to feed in the family.
        Although the young girl has experienced menstruation, she is often physically unprepared for
        pregnancy and childbirth. In vesico-vaginal fistulas, the stress of pregnancy ruptures the bladder
        muscles, leaving the young mother unable to control urination. This frequently results in husbands
        or families abandoning these teenaged mothers and leads to destitution among young girls.

33   In the 1980s, in response to plummeting rural production, declining prices for African exports, and
        rising external debts, the International Monetary Fund and the World Bank devised a generic
        program of economic adjustment for African countries. Structural adjustment is designed to achieve
        sectorial balance within the economy by (1) devaluing currency to destroy parallel markets, moderate
        imports, and encourage diversified exports; (2) privatizing the economy by cutting subsidies for
        food, social services, such as education and health, and inputs for farming; (3) creating a legal and
        economic climate encouraging private investment; (4) liberalizing trade by removing import or
        producer taxes, thus allowing market principles to operate in setting agricultural and other prices;

and (5) trimming government bureaucracy, selling many state-owned enterprises, cutting wages, and retrenching government workers. Women were among the most adversely affected by these changes, particularly in the food, health, and education arenas. This was evident in the feminization of poverty during early phases of structural adjustment programs. But the question is whether many foreign assistance projects which incorporate "women and development" components truly aim to assist women economically or aim to gain greater control over domestic political and economic agendas.

34   In Kenya, the 1989 Wambui Otieno case created considerable concern because the widow was prevented from determining the disposition and burial of her husband's body by the claimed rights of the lineage and ethnic community. See Patricia Stamp, "Burying Otieno: Politics of Gender and Ethnicity in Kenya," *Signs* 16 (summer 1991): 808–45.

35   The National Committee on the Status of Women, headed by Maria Nzomo, held a national conference which drew Kenyan women from all walks of life and helped organize women's workshops and political training exercises all across the country. See Maria Nzomo, ed., *Women's Initiatives in Kenya's Democratization* (Nairobi: NCSW, 1993), and Maria Nzomo, ed., *Empowering Kenyan Women: Report of a Seminar on Post Election Women's Agenda-Forward Looking Strategies to 1997 and Beyond* (Nairobi: NCSW, 1993).

36   Mamphela Ramphele, "The Dynamics of Gender Politics in the Hostels of Cape Town: Another Legacy of the South African Migrant Labor System," *Journal of Southern African Studies* 15 (April 1989): 393.

37   On 25 Sept. 1994, in Washington, D.C., I conducted an interview with Mavivi Manzini, former ANC Women's League chairperson in Zambia, and now parliamentarian from a Johannesburg district, newly elected in the April 1994 democratic elections in South Africa. See also an earlier conversation with Manzini in Diana Russell's book, *Lives of Courage: Women for a New South Africa* (New York: Basic Books, 1989).

Chapter 63

Miriam Cooke

ARAB WOMEN'S LITERARY HISTORY

Impacted by colonialism and warfare, the emerging "literary negotiations" of Arab women have involved a different strategy to that of postcolonial allegorical counter-discourse; what Miriam Cooke imagines instead as the stones in a mosaic, where each piece of Arab women's writing thereby resonates "with those of the others." Cooke, professor of Asian and Middle East Studies at Duke University, and co-editor of the groundbreaking anthology of Arab feminist writing called *Opening the Gates* (second expanded edition 2004), sketches the development of Arab women's literary production, noting that there has been a shift from largely secular to Islamic concerns, with two main themes being foregrounded: war and emigration. Tracing this literary history from the late nineteenth century to the end of the twentieth century, Cooke shows how even though women were producing texts, they initially received very little critical attention until the 1960s and 1970s. One of the main factors that changed this situation was translation, with Cooke noting in particular the English translations of Hanan al-Shaykh's *The Story of Zahra* (1980) and Alifa Rifaat's *Distant View of a Minaret* (1986), as well as the production of an important bibliography in 1986, updated in 1999. Cooke also stresses the importance of anthology publication—especially in light of her mosaic metaphor—in which contextualization can reveal depth and breadth. The role of women as combatants has long been a concern of Arab women writers, since whether as physical or intellectual combatants, this reverses the notion of passivity and domesticity being the only legitimate domain of activity; further, political and aesthetic counter-discursivity is another form of "combat", one which is transcultural and transformative. As a powerful experience and case study in relation to the fluidity of this role, warfare is key for Cooke, be it civil war (Lebanon), anticolonial war (Algeria) or what can be called "conventional" war (the Gulf Wars); the first Gulf War is explored by Cooke in detail, from Kuwaiti and Iraqi perspectives.

BEFORE LOOKING AT THE MOST RECENT developments in Arab women's writings, which have moved from a generally secular focus to an increasingly Islamic orientation, it is necessary to situate these writings more broadly within their historical context. In this chapter I examine the ways in which some Arab women have used their stories to change conceptions of modern Arabic literature. There are many issues that have concerned Arab writers in the twentieth century, but two narratives have had a particular impact on the way in which Arab intellectuals shape their experience. The first is the War Story; the second is the story about the emigrant's experience after leaving the homeland.

It is not generally known that Arab women have been writing and publishing fiction since the end of the nineteenth century. Three Lebanese women, Zaynab Fawwaz (1860–1914), Labiba Hashim (1880–1947), and Mayy Ziyada (1886–1941), and in Egypt Aisha Taimuriyya (1840–1902), should be considered the pioneers of Arab women's literary history. The first half of the twentieth century witnessed more women taking up the pen, yet their works received so little notice that it was as though they had not written. It was only in the 1960s and 1970s that sporadic critical attention was paid to a few, like the Egyptian Nawal El Saadawi, the Lebanese Layla Baalbaki, and the Syrian Colette Khuri. During the 1980s, however, this situation changed as these women's fiction began to be translated. In 1986, at the first International Feminist Bookfair in London, two Arab women writers were introduced to the English-speaking world. The publishing house Quartet brought out in English the Lebanese Hanan al-Shaykh's controversial novel on the Lebanese civil war, *The Story of Zahra* (1980), and the Egyptian Alifa Rifaat's *Distant View of a Minaret* (1986), a collection of stories about lonely women in Cairo. Fourteen years later, Arab women writers are much better known at home and abroad.

Critical response

Recognition abroad is more than paralleled by an upsurge in creativity at home. Even in Saudi Arabia, where women's education was introduced in the 1960s only, women are publishing in growing numbers. In November 1999 I was invited to give the keynote address to the first conference of Saudi women writers. Drawing only from cities on the Red Sea coast, the conference nonetheless managed to assemble over sixty women. The critical response to this literary activity always takes time.

The first serious attempt to categorize and take stock of the productivity of Arab women writers came in 1986, when Joseph Zeidan published a bibliography of 486 women who wrote in Arabic between the 1880s and 1980s. Almost half of these women had published two or more books. Whereas during the first half of this century there were few women writing anywhere outside the literary centers of Cairo and Beirut, by the 1970s in every single Arab country women were beginning to write. Zeidan's staging of this process is revealing. Between the late nineteenth century and 1930, he found only twenty women who had written (some in magazines only), with about five women writing per decade. This number then doubled to ten between 1930 and 1940, and during the next decade fifteen women published. Between 1950 and 1960 their numbers more than doubled to thirty-three, and between 1960 and 1970 this last number almost tripled to ninety-six. By the next decade, the last to be covered by the bibliography, 129 women were writing, even in the countries of the Arabian Peninsula where education for women was new. In 1999 Zeidan published a revised version of the 1986 bibliography to extend it up to 1996. This updated bibliography contains information on an astounding 1,271 women. In other words, with the addition of only a few years at both ends he was able to almost triple the number of entries.

Over the past century, hundreds of women have been writing despite a meager critical response. Until recently, the few scholars who were at all interested framed Arab women's writings chronologically within totalizable stages each with its own sense of closure. In general, critics have noted development from personal preoccupations to sporadic expressions of political awareness as the writers' countries went through wars of independence from colonial rule. Some critics have praised evolution from the poor to the good; from imitation through identity formation to nationalist preoccupations; from the personal to the political. Modernization is good, and particularly for women (cf. Zeidan 1995).

A closer look at the texts, however, reveals that different things were happening in different places during a single time period; women's preoccupations fluctuated from one period to another, from one country to another, and even from one woman to another at various points during her life. Individual women writers might range across a spectrum of topics, so that sometimes they might write of themselves, at other times of what was happening to the men and women in their communities. Women, like men, think and write about more than one thing at the same time, and this is particularly true in the course of a career.

Women in the Arab world have long written about politics, if often indirectly, in ways that have been particularly revealing. Their literary negotiations with those in positions of domestic, local, and international power have highlighted the tensions that postcolonial societies confront as they deal with the legacies of colonialism while trying to find an honorable place in an unfriendly world. Each novel or short story rarely serves as an allegory but rather as a stone in a mosaic where its preoccupations resonate with those of others.

Arab women respond to each other, test local possibilities, plug into transcultural concerns. Their collective literary project can best be appreciated in anthologies, which provide the context that gives the individual piece of writing meaning and impact beyond itself. Anthologies of women's writings do more than contextualize; they ensure that the collective expression is not silenced with the elimination of one voice. Anthologies exemplify the Woolfian maxim that great works and writers do not emerge out of a void but rather out of a larger literary enterprise. When Yusuf al-Sharuni published *The Night After the 1001 Nights* in 1975, he introduced twenty Egyptian women writers into a literary world that had refused to acknowledge that women had been writing, except as oddities to be exceptionalized. His first words are, "Women's relationship with storytelling is ancient," and he predictably, in view of the title of his book, mentions Sheherezade, the legendary storyteller of *1001 Nights*. But he is not merely drawing on myth and folklore when he extols women's contributions to Arabic literature. He compares literary developments in the twentieth-century Arab world, which he calls "a radical transformation as astounding as the invention of the automobile," with socioeconomic changes in women's roles and rights (al-Sharuni 1975: 8). The stories al-Sharuni anthologizes focus on women's struggles against unfair expectations for women's behavior. Their collection in one volume with a large bibliography demonstrated for the first time how active women have been and for how long.

Another important anthology was Layla Muhammad Salih's *Women's Literature in the Arabian Peninsula and Gulf*. Its publication in 1982 revealed that despite the lack of widespread education in the region and general representations of radical segregation and therefore of public invisibility and political acquiescence, several women had been writing for a long time and in ways that were remarkably critical of their societies. Many of these women questioned the relevance of the term "women's literature," preferring to be counted with their male colleagues. Physical apartheid should at the very least be countered with literary integration.

My own writing, whether it takes the form of monograph or anthology, has consistently engaged Arab women's collective literary endeavors. *War's Other Voices* (1988) collects the testimony of women who had written about the Lebanese civil war between 1975 and 1982. I called these women the Beirut Decentrists in order to draw attention to them as a school of writers who had collectively contributed as women citizen-combatants to the literature on the war. Reading their texts together allowed me to discern a transformation in the writers' consciousness and self-representation. For the Beirut Decentrists the chaos could not be described as a revolution or as a just war pitting the good against the bad. It was a bad war fought for individual gain, and it destroyed the nation on whose behalf it was said to have been waged.

In *Women and the War Story* (1997), I analyzed the production of other groups of women who wrote about the Algerian war of independence, the Palestinian reactions to Israeli occupations in 1948 and then after 1967, and the Iran-Iraq War. Reading their writings *together* revealed a difference in self-perception between women who participated in the precolonial and colonial wars as opposed to postcolonial wars. Anticolonial women fighters saw themselves as doing what the men did. Cross-dressing did not change their perception of who they were and how the roles that they might play in the postbellum society might change. Women in the postcolonial wars, on the other hand, did not even have to take up arms to see themselves as combatants. They portrayed themselves as women combatants who were fighting not as men but specifically *because they were women,* sometimes directly targeted for harm. When they named what they had done "combat," they transformed their consciousness about themselves, as well as about their society. They came to understand that nations struggling to be free need all of their citizens to fight for them. When the previously excluded became combatants they changed not only the nature of the fighting, they also began to make a dent in the armor of the War Story.

The Gulf War story

Arab women have written a great deal about war because in many ways it has become part of many of their lives. The war may be civil as in Lebanon, anticolonial as in Algeria and all the countries that shook off colonial rule in the mid-twentieth century, or apparently conventional as was the Iran-Iraq War. Alternatively, it may be more metaphorical or spiritual even, as in the notion of jihad, or religious struggle against the current condition of ignorance and corruption. This awareness of the prevalence of violence, both organized and random, has arguably become a part of everyday lives. Technology has facilitated the generalization of war in postmodernity. States have sponsored and companies have created weapons that travel such great distances that the fiction of a place of fighting has become difficult to sustain. If there is no front and it is not clear who are the combatants, how are we to know when the fighting has begun in such a definitive way that it warrants the name of war? And if we do not have clear signals about the beginning of wars, how can we end what was never declared to have started? All of this uncertainty and its concomitant uncontrol is monitored by the mass media and then telecast into homes in the heart of New York City, the Borneo rain forest, and the Sahara Desert.

However, there is one war-related certainty: women are involved in postcolonial wars in a way that was never before so clear. Women may have always been with men in war as nurses, as camp followers, as cross-dressing soldiers, but they have not before fought *as women.* During anticolonial wars in Asia and Africa women were represented as guerrilla fighters, hijackers, and organizers of local resistance movements. More recently, as in the Palestinian popular uprising, women have fought as mothers, confronting the soldiers with their maternal bodies so as to disable conventional means of violence. Yet even when women do not choose to engage in combat, they may be forced into it because their bodies are officially designated military targets for rape or for bombs.

Arab women are telling many individual stories about their encounters with violence, both organized and disorganized. They are eloquent about the Gulf War, which has played such an influential role in Arab identity construction, particularly in the United States (see chapter 6). In 1991 the controversial, censored Kuwaiti poet-princess Su'ad al-Sabah published an anthology of ironic and bitter poetry on the Gulf War entitled *Will You Let Me Love My Country?* The poems delve into the spiritual crisis experienced by most Arab intellectuals, but most of all by the children, in the wake of the war. She evokes the dissonance between the rhetoric of Arab unity, learned from school-books, and the fragmented, fractured reality just lived in the Gulf (al-Sabah 1991: 97). Her anger at the Iraqi government does not extend to the people. As we shall see, Kuwaiti women writers understood that the Iraqi people are not to blame. She writes: "The great Iraqi people will remain in my heart forever, for they are certainly innocent" (112).

Iraqi and Kuwaiti women questioned grand narratives about medieval dictatorships confronting modern democracies, good Muslims opposing bad Muslims. These women's different stories need to be read as testimonials, a special kind of witness that allows others to glimpse another kind of reality that challenges the absoluteness of the Gulf War Story as it has been told by those in power, whether in the United States or in Iraq.

On January 17, 1991, the Gulf War broke out. Two weeks earlier, the French cultural critic Jean Baudrillard had published in the French newspaper *Libération* the first of three articles on the war. Convinced, as many of us were at the time, that the spectacle of preparations for war might dispense with the need for actual warfare, he declared his thesis: "The Gulf War will not take place." He was shortly proven wrong when in a remarkably traditional manner George Bush declared war on Iraq's Saddam Hussein. Undaunted, Baudrillard stuck to his guns. For three long weeks, the United States and its allies mercilessly bombed the Iraqis, but the inventor of hyperreality remained skeptical, asking in his second article: "The Gulf War: is it really taking place?" What, one might ask, was he questioning? The "really" or the "place"? Apparently, he could not tell if this was a war or just the "illusion of massacre" (Baudrillard 1995: 58). On March 29, 1991, he dealt the warness of the Gulf War his coup de grace: "The Gulf War did not take place." In this final essay, he writes that

> a war without victims does not seem like a real war but rather the prefiguration of an experimental, blank war, or a war even more inhuman because it is *without human losses*. No heroes on the other side either, where death was most often that of *sacrificed extras,* left as cover in the trenches of Kuwait, or civilians serving as bait and martyrs for the dirty war. . . . The minimal losses of the coalition pose a serious problem, which never arose in any earlier war. The paltry number of deaths may be cause for self-congratulation, but nothing will prevent this figure being paltry. (73)

At a time when we are all fascinated by the virtuality of our lives, it is more than ever critical that we hold on to their materiality also.

Was the Gulf War not a war for Baudrillard because there were so few *Western* losses and the massacre was of Iraqi *sacrificed extras?* I suspect that it was not a war for still another reason: it did not provide an "alibi" for savagery (76). Unlike World War II, it did not produce great war stories. Listen to the regret and nostalgia in the following passages: "Since this war was won in advance, we will never know what it would have been like had it existed. We will never know what an Iraqi taking part with a chance of fighting would have been like. We will never know what an American taking part with a chance of being beaten would have been like" (61). This illusion of massacre did not pit good against evil. It had lost its libidinal attraction: "[w]ar stripped of its passions, its phantasms, its finery, its veils, its violence, its images: war stripped bare by its technicians even, and then reclothed by them with all the artifices of electronics, as though with a second skin" (64). War as a woman, or rather a robot.

Baudrillard was not alone. The Gulf War was and remains for many in the West an event hard to frame in a story. Throughout the fall of 1990, the U.S. press was filled with debate about intervention in southwest Asia. After the outbreak of the air war, however, the media's patriotic hype silenced dissenting voices. What followed, behind the screen of clean weapons and surgical airstrikes, was confusion, friendly fire, and a brutality that the press did not cover. What we did hear about was "a global confrontation between humanity and bestiality, a battle between civilization and barbarism. This was a war to defend the principles of modernity and reason against the forces of darkness" (Aksoy and Robins 1992: 202).

The best version of the U.S. Gulf War Story was told by Richard Cheney, the U.S. secretary of defense. It took the form of a *Final Report of Congress: Conduct of the Persian Gulf War,* that "pursuant to Title V, Public Law 102–25 . . . discusses the conduct of hostilities in the Persian Gulf theater of operations" (xiii). In seventeen pages, the "Military Victory over Iraq" is loudly trumpeted. Like all good war stories, this one provided a blueprint for the next time around. The war in question began on January 17, when President George Bush launched the first strikes on Iraq. From August, when the U.S. buildup began, the war would not have provided such a neat model for the conduct of future wars. Restricted to the shorter period, it became a circumscribed *battle* as told by John Keegan in *The Face of Battle* (1976). This battle demonstrated how well the U.S. defense system works, since it could contend with the "fourth largest army in the world, *an army hardened in long years of combat against Iran*" (xiii, my emphasis). The war confirmed that funding to the Department of Defense must not be reduced: "If we fail to fund the training and high quality we have come to expect, we will end up with an organization that may still outwardly look like a military, but that simply will not function" (xxx). The Gulf War provided an unprecedented marketing opportunity for the Department of Defense, which could show off its "revolutionary new generation of high-technology weapons" (xviii), these wonderful weapons they were testing for the first time.

This U.S. Gulf War Story, like all war stories, promised that there would be more wars because good wars make you proud (Theweleit 1993). Pride is the single most important factor in the U.S. Gulf War Story; Cheney's parting paragraph goes as follows:

> America can be *proud* of its role in the Persian Gulf war. There were lessons to be learned and problems to be sure. But overall there was an outstanding victory. We can be *proud* of our conviction and international leadership. We can be *proud* of one of the most remarkable deployments in history. We can be *proud* of our partnership in arms with many nations. We can be *proud* of our technology and the wisdom of our leaders at all levels. But most of all we can be *proud* of those dedicated young Americans soldiers, sailors, airmen and marines who showed their skill, their commitment to what we stand for, and their bravery in the way they fought this war.

These "proud"s are followed by Cheney's *own signature.*

Throughout, Cheney waxes lyrical about the military leadership, which had been "outstanding," "unique," "exceptional," "smart," "superb," "excellent," "innovative," and that the whole operation which had succeeded through a "magnificent team effort" (xxv). Above all, these soldiers were not merely effective military personnel, they were deeply human, portraying "the best in American values." Cheney concludes melodramatically that the "world will not soon forget pictures of Iraqi soldiers kissing their captors' hands" (xxvi).

So why did the world forget those other Iraqis, the ones who were plowed into the sand? Because the U.S. government and media have modified the memory of this war in such a way that the United States and its allies have emerged clean and humane. This memory of innocence has erased the charred sculptures of horror that littered the Kuwait-Basra highway on February 25, the night of the Iraqi flight. Henry A. Giroux has described this "politics of innocence" as a U.S. invention, part of a worldwide neocolonial campaign that serves "to police and constrain the potentially subversive notions of memory and public culture" (1993: 87, 89). We were not shown the victims. What we saw was the image of American liberators borrowed from World War II films depicting American soldiers liberating the concentration camps. This insistent image should have drawn international attention to the victims, the Iraqi soldiers and civilians who were at the mercy of a ruthless dictator. What it achieved instead was the purge of U.S. war crimes, erasing the struggle over the legitimacy of the war.

Ironically, Saddam Hussein's insistent declaration of victory mirrored and complemented the U.S. government War Story. As late as January 28, in an interview in Baghdad with CNN's Peter Arnett, his words are full of bombast and confidence that America is suffering "internal defeat" and that it has "miscalculated." He talks patronizingly about the good American citizens who oppose "the hostile policy" (Bengio 1992: 174–88). On February 10 he broadcasts a speech about the need to look for victory inside "this great and immortal chapter of the time that has passed" (191). Six days before the end, he focuses on Israeli aggressions, on Arab treacheries, on the aerial bombing that exacerbates the sufferings caused by the international boycott. He ends: "Dignity, glory, and *victory* for the heroes of this path, the sons of our nation and mankind" (204). Even in retreat from Kuwait, he declares victory for his "valiant men, you fought the armies of thirty states and the capabilities of an even greater number of states which supplied them with the means of aggression and support" (212).

This is the other War Story, the one the loser tells to make it look as though he has not lost, buying time while he looks for another war that will prove that he did not lose. But did Saddam Hussein lose this war? Apparently not. On January 17, 1992, the world media reported on the parade through the streets of Baghdad held to celebrate the first anniversary of Iraq's great 1991 victory. Nor was this his last hurrah! On January 17, 1998, Saddam Hussein gave a speech in honor of the seventh anniversary of the start of Gulf War II. Describing himself as "the fearless defender of the Arabs and all poor nations against the American tyrant," he declared himself ready to launch a jihad to lift sanctions that the United Nations had imposed throughout the intervening years. Journalist Barbara Crossette reported that in the speech Saddam Hussein "seamlessly rewrote the history of January 17, 1991, by leaving out what had caused the war: his army's occupation of Kuwait five months earlier. . . . Iraq won that war, he said—still calling it 'the mother of all battles'—because 'Iraq refused to comply and surrender'" (Crossette 1998). Both sides declared and continue to declare victory.

What about those thousands of Iraqis who died? We have forgotten them because we have not heard the witnesses, those whose language "suggests the unimaginable of the real, that is, a hidden dimension that exceeds the strict limits of objective description" (Taminiaux 1993: 4–6). We must search for "the traces of the war so as to fight effectively its work of destruction" (17). Below are some traces of the unimaginable of the real that I have made out in the words of Iraqi and Kuwaiti women.

Gendering the Gulf War story

In November 1995 I spent a week in Kuwait with Layla al-'Uthman, Kuwait's leading woman writer. We toured the war "sites": the rusty bullet-riddled ship that had housed the Ramada Inn, the Kuwaiti National Museum, of which nothing remains but a burned-out shell. We drove past new buildings that had risen from the rubble. I heard about fires in the oil fields, and faces filmed over with black oil soot, months when it was always night, and electricity cuts, and then candles until they ran out of wax.

On the third evening Layla had a party. Everyone was singing and dancing. Around 3 A.M. the mood changed, became nostalgic, somber even. When I asked someone what was happening, he told me that the musicians had started to play Iraqi music. Everyone sat down and listened quietly. Soon they were gone. I had not noticed the change in the music. Next morning over coffee, Layla explained that the guests had become depressed because the music reminded them of the past and of what they had lost: "We were the same people: we shared music, food, and art as well as language—the southern Iraqi dialect is almost indistinguishable from the Kuwaiti."

But these neighbors had invaded. Journals I have received chronicle the war from the arrival of 100,000 Iraqi soldiers in Kuwait City on August 2, 1990, at 3 A.M. through January 17, 1991, the beginning of Desert Storm—a term the Kuwaitis also were using (al-Zibn 1993: 99)—until the Iraqi withdrawal on February 27. Communications were immediately cut, and the only contacts with the outside world were the international media, such as Reuters, BBC, and CNN. [Later, when the United States and its allies attacked, this would be true in Iraq also. The journalist Warid Badr al-Salim describes a night in Basra when the bombing was intense: "A night of constant broadcasts bringing news of the war blow by blow. The Allied planes kept on attacking various targets in Iraq and CNN." He then mentions Voice of America and Radio Monte Carlo, whose commercials for Mazola, fancy restaurants, and cars brought him a sense of well-being and even hope (1993: 48, 59).]

The Kuwaitis were in the war, yet like us halfway across the world, they knew it "only through the international media" (al-Zibn 1993: 117). The Iraqis quickly tightened their grip on the city, taking over the hospitals, surrounding the embassies, emptying the streets. Bread lines, hoarded food, public executions, arrests, house searches, expropriation of cars and apartments, water and power cuts, exploded oil wells, two million barrels of oil on the gulf. They even arrested members of the Red Crescent and stole their supplies. In November, "organized looting" began and civil registers were destroyed, as Kuwait became part of Iraq, and Kuwaitis had to submit a request for Iraqi identity cards. Men between the ages of seventeen and forty-five were arrested. Sports clubs were turned into prisons.

Despite the dangers, many Kuwaiti women stayed to endure the invasion while the men left. Moreover, they were the ones at the forefront of the resistance to the Iraqi invasion. Fatima Hussein, editor of the Kuwaiti daily newspaper *Al-Watan,* said that "the first anti-Iraq demonstration three days after the invasion was made up of only women and children. . . . Kuwaiti women played a major role in the Resistance." She compares their actions, which included smuggling arms and resistance documents, with those of Algerian women during their war of independence between 1954 and 1962: "they completely veiled themselves, which gave them a certain invisibility and enabled them to move quickly around the country more easily than men" (Goodwin 1995: 158–59). The Jordanian novelist Fadia Faqir writes of a woman whose vision of the receding skyline made her decide to stay in Kuwait. Regardless of the danger, she writes, "It is my country, where I belong, and where I should stay" (Faqir 1991: 81). What remains implicit in such a decision, but needs emphasis, is that there was a choice. Dalai Faysal Su'ud al-Zibn also realized that merely "staying in the country is a nationalist action for anyone who feels any sense of responsibility. . . . Whoever during times of trouble can think of something other than saving the nation does not deserve to live in a free state" (al-Zibn 1993: 128, 141). Here is the refrain from Arab women's writings on the wars they have experienced: When the country is in trouble, its citizens must stay.

The women who stayed in Kuwait throughout the fall of 1990 provided the needy with food, medical help, and logistical support in disposing of the dead and consoling the bereaved. They shared anger, grief, and the determination not to submit. In all that they did they risked imprisonment and even execution. Like the Lebanese, Palestinian, and Algerian women who stayed in their countries during their wars, these women constructed a "humanist nationalism" that interprets staying during a war as a form of combat—and combatants should be considered citizens with rights due to them (see Cooke 1997: 267–90). Some Kuwaiti women accused those who left of having "forgotten their compatriots who stayed" (al-Zibn 1993: 162). Those who have forgotten those who stayed are not worthy of being considered Kuwaiti citizens.

As had happened during the Lebanese civil war, the violence drove some women to the pen for the first time. Three weeks into the air war, al-Zibn sees herself as a "writer." From the perspective of this new identity, she considers her experiences to be peculiarly important, useful for others: "I recorded these experiences so as to hold on to scattered thoughts and time . . . [and to] express what it is like to live the dailiness of war. There are few such [chronicles] and I believe that what I write will be important in the future!" At night she hides the journal lest the Iraqis steal it (63, 98, 135). Her journal has become valuable, worth stealing. In closing, she dedicates what she has come to call "memoirs" to "those who remained loyal to their country and their people" (171). This small, personal journal has been transformed into a big book of memoirs, as the author feels her relationship with her text and her readers develop. Writing them has made her experiences important and has transformed her into a witness.

Whereas some wrote for the first time, others, like Layla al-'Uthman, already an established writer, were silenced. It was not until 1994, three years after the war was over, that she published *Black Barricades*. These short stories evoke the shock of the invasion, its brutalities, the rape of mothers witnessed by their sons, the small acts of resistance and defiance. But within the mayhem, she bears witness to the odd innocence of the disoriented young Iraqis. The collection ends with nine sections, each entitled "Barricade." In each "Barricade," the narrator converses with Iraqi soldiers. One is almost apologetic about his presence, assuring her, "I curse the hour my feet stepped on this ground!" When she asks him why he came, he replies, "Orders!" When she is surprised that he asks for a cigarette and is not afraid that it might be poisoned, he replies, "We have already drunk poison over there."

"Where's there?"
"During the Eight Year War" (referring to the Iran-Iraq War).
"So you came to participate in a new war of liberation!!"
"You didn't need anyone to liberate you. You were free and we were envious."
"Do you know the truth?"
"I know it very well . . . I wish . . . Ah . . . "
"What do you wish?"
"That *Iraq* might be liberated" (al-'Uthman 1994: 149–51).

Other Kuwaiti women confirmed that the Iraqi soldiers were not simply inhuman enemies but rather victims. They were, of course, barbarian criminals sometimes, but they were also, as al-Zibn writes, "Saddam's misled animals [who] ran away from their war with Iran into the streets of Kuwait" (1993: 65–66). Like a pendulum, she swings between anger, maternal concern for the terrorized and alienated soldiers, and contempt for the leader who wanted Kuwait as a consolation prize for his failure against Iran. Saddam Hussein is one thing and the miserable creatures who have found themselves far from home and performing unspeakable acts are quite another.

These are the witnesses to whom we should listen: Kuwaiti women whose journals distinguish between the Iraqi people and their leader. Even as they were being victimized, they recognized that these soldiers were themselves victims. The Iraqi writer 'Amir Badr Hassun reports a conversation with a Kuwaiti intellectual who said to him, "Had we paid attention to what was happening to you and your people we might have protected our homeland from Saddam's occupation" (Hassun n.d.: 13).

Works cited

Aksoy, Asu, and Kevin Robins. 1992. "Exterminating Angels: Morality, Violence, and Technology in the Gulf War," in Hamid Mowlana, George Gerbner, and Herbert I. Schiller, eds., *Triumph of the Image: The Media's War in the Persian Gulf: A Global Perspective.* Boulder, Colo.: Westview.

Baudrillard, Jean. 1995 (1991). *The Gulf War Did Not Take Place.* Bloomington, Ind.: Indiana University Press.

Bengio, Ofra. 1992. *Saddam Speaks on the Gulf Crisis: A Collection of Documents.* Tel Aviv: Shiloah Institute.

Cooke, Miriam. 1997. *Women and the War Story.* Berkeley: California University Press.

Crossette, Barbara. 1998. "Hussein Delivers a New Ultimatum to U.N. Inspectors." *New York Times,* Jan. 18.

Faqir, Fadia. 1991. "Tales of War: Arab Women in the Eye of the Storm," in *The Gulf Between Us: The Gulf War and Beyond.* London: Virago Press.

Giroux, Henry A. 1993. "Beyond the Politics of Innocence: Memory and Pedagogy in the 'Wonderful World of Disney.'" *Socialist Review* 2: 79–107.

Goodwin, Jan. 1995. *The Price of Honor: Muslim Women Lift the Veil of Silence of the Islamic World.* New York: Penguin.

Hassun, 'Amir Badr. n.d. *Kitab al-qaswa. Muhawala li ifsad ma tabaqqa min hayatikum* (The Book of Brutality: An Attempt to Spoil What Is Left of Your Lives), n.p.

al-Sharuni, Yusuf. 1975. *Al-layla al-thaniya ba'da al-alf* (The Night After the 1001 Nights: Selections from Women's Stories in Egypt), Cairo: al-Hay'a al-Misriya al-'Amma lil-Kitab.

Taminiaux, Jean Pierre. 1993. "La Guerre du Golfe ou l'histoire d'un monde sans temoin," in *Peuples Mediterranéens,* 64–65.

Theweleit, Klaus. 1993. "The Bomb's Womb," in Cooke and Woollacott.

al-'Uthman, Layla. 1994. *Al-hawajiz al-sawda'* (Black Barricades). Kuwait: al-Qabas al-Tijariya.

Zeidan, Joseph. 1995. *Arab Women Novelists: The Formative Years and Beyond.* New York: New York University Press.

al-Zibn, Dalai Faysal Su'ud. 1993. *Ayyam al-qahr al-kuwaytiya al-thani min aghustus 1990 hatta 27 fabrayir 1991* (Kuwaiti Days of Oppression August 2, 1990–February 27, 1991). Kuwait: Dar Su'ad al-Sabah.

PART X

New textualities

WRITING IN 2001, SOCIAL THEORISTS José López and Garry Potter assert in a striking phrase that "a new and different intellectual direction *must* come after postmodernism, simply because postmodernism is inadequate as an intellectual response to the times we live in."[1] Almost a decade later, critic Jens Zimmermann argues that "The malaise of postmodernity ... is its inability to provide us with a much-needed unified notion of rationality."[2] In fact Zimmermann goes even further than this, with reference to Marxist critic Terry Eagleton's attack upon postmodernism in *After Theory*: "According to Eagleton, postmodernity has rightly criticized naïve and oppressive notions of universal reason, but it has also left us without any common ground for a universal sense of human dignity."[3] In each of the above quotations, "postmodernism/postmodernity" can stand in for a broader term: that of "theory". In other words, "postmodernism/ postmodernity" are terms which represent what can be called the new orthodoxy of Western contemporary literary theory as a widespread discourse utilized far beyond literary criticism itself, but sharing many key assumptions about society, gender, race and language. Why turn, however, against a set of methodological procedures and concepts that for about four decades served scholars so well? Why turn from the very discourse that promised so much, and continues to argue that it is delivering so much?

López and Potter are writing in the context of a book of essays that offer a methodology "after postmodernism", in this case a methodology called "critical realism", an approach to knowledge which recognizes the material real, as well as our social constructions and interpretations of that real, and additionally argues that science is the most reliable mode of investigation and understanding of our world. As López and Potter suggest, "postmodernism is not able to explain why it is the case that science continues to produce useful knowledge."[4] The implications for literary critical understanding are immense, especially as critical realism incorporates both the lessons of the "linguistic turn" *and* argues for the reinstating "of the thing-in-itself"; thus "realism utilises a 'signification paradigm' (. . . a system of signifiers and signifieds) in understanding the production of meaning, but it also stresses the importance of the material reality referents."[5] Or as critic Philip Tew puts it more forcibly: "all thoughts, all theories, are about something. All perceptions are of something. All texts have referents. They exist independently of our perceptions, thoughts and theories."[6] In contrast to critical realists, Zimmermann is writing in the context of the religious turn, that is to say, a renewed interest among theorists, philosophers and humanists in the very religious discourses and universal truth-claims that theory had apparently deconstructed or permanently debunked. As Hent De Vries argues in the opening pages of *Philosophy and the Turn to Religion* (1999), "citations from religious traditions are more fundamental to the structure of language and experience than the genealogies, critiques, and transcendental reflections of the modern discourse that has deemed such citations obsolete and tended to reduce them to what they are not."[7] For Zimmermann, while postmodernism and high theory fail to have anything to say about the big, fundamental human questions, it is secular, scientific reason itself which is suffering from "exhaustion", in other words, widespread belief in "scientific objectivism" is no longer the case, and he argues that there has been a return to a fundamentally humanistic desire to understand those very facets of human life that science and high theory have failed to adequately or even partially explain, such as "religion, tradition, love, and ultimate questions."[8]

Eagleton argues that one of the biggest problems with theory is the translation of *political* questions into *cultural* questions, which, combined with a historical amnesia, leads to a celebration of all that is most shallow, narcissistic and at the service of (globalized) capitalism. Eagleton's searing wit and powerful sarcasm in *After Theory* is the vehicle he uses for undermining not just theoretical orthodoxies, but also the contemporary turn to religion and conservative beliefs, which he perceives to be a turn to "fundamentalisms". However, it is important to pay close attention to what exactly are the theoretical orthodoxies according to Eagleton, since he notes that "Structuralism, Marxism, post-structuralism" have given way to a focus on sexuality, the body, "sensationalist subjects", and popular culture, all of which are evidence of, or are subject to, trivialization.[9] This in turn is ironic, since as Eagleton argues "One of the towering achievements of cultural theory has been to establish gender and sexuality as legitimate objects of study, as well as matters of insistent political importance."[10] While Eagleton also speaks highly of postcolonial studies, he argues that a historical amnesia undermines its potential for achievement, or real political change and the subsequent transformation of people's lives. Similarly, the shift in postcolonial studies from "class and nation to ethnicity" leads to relatively benign Western identity politics, the rise of which "helped to depoliticize the question of post-colonialism, and inflate the role of culture within it, in ways which chimes with the new, post-revolutionary climate in the West itself."[11]

Most of Eagleton's bile is reserved for postmodernism, and the "creature who emerges from postmodern thought" which, like a cybernetic Frankenstein's monster, is "centreless, hedonistic, self-inventing, [and] ceaselessly adaptive."[12] This creature is a product not only of postmodernism, but of the rejection of universality, "absolute truth",[13] the idea of progress and, concomitantly, these notions expressed via "grand narratives".[14] Here humanity "finally breaks free of the restriction which is itself"[15] although Eagleton appears to find even this new creature less problematic than "the lethal self-righteousness"[16] of religious fundamentalists. In fact, throughout *After Theory*, Eagleton is acutely aware that his Marxist defense of the real (human beings, history, progress, dialectical argumentation which is based in a scientific world-view, and so on), is paralleled by religion's competing claims of relevance to real human lives and situations. Perhaps this is why religion becomes reduced to "fundamentalism" in Eagleton's hands, however much he abjures those who would "advance a version of religion which nobody in their right mind would subscribe to . . . [accepting] the sort of crude stereotypes of it that would no doubt horrify them in any other field of scholarly inquiry."[17] If postmodernists are monstrous creatures, then for Eagleton, fundamentalist religious people — be they followers of Islam, Judaism, or Christianity — are "frauds" to use just one of the negative categories assigned them in *After Theory*. Possibly Eagleton protests too much, or too satirically, since some of his most valuable insights in *After Theory* come from thinkers such as Saint Augustine. Eagleton's challenge — "to construct a version of religion which is actually *worth* rejecting"[18] — never really occurs in the book (although Eagleton could undoubtedly have produced this), possibly because a religion worth rejecting is also one worth following, but more likely because such a religion would also be one that does speak into and about precisely those areas that Zimmermann suggests are in need, once more, of a universal, ethical voice.

Each of these three powerful critiques of postmodernism offers an alternative worldview: critical realism; religion; Marxism. Each are dismissive, in different but related ways, of the failure of postmodern thought to address the big questions in people's lives, be they about science, politics, belief or ethics. Yet each critique also defends in some ways the gains made by theory, the lessons learnt that should not be unlearnt. For López and Potter, much of the insight produced by theory needs to be valued, but also re-evaluated and re-situated. They argue that critical realism "accepts": "that human society is much more like a language than a mechanical machine . . . the full significance of the manner in which theorising is socially located . . . the significance of the 'language-borne' nature of theory . . . [and] the socially constructed nature of knowledge."[19] But all this because "it is in fact those very peculiarities of the human condition which not only make it amenable to scientific study but actually make social life possible at all."[20] Eagleton is similarly pragmatic, arguing that lessons have been learnt, especially "If theory means a reasonable systematic reflection on our guiding assumptions",[21] and also where theory has led to taking more seriously "the everyday life of the common people."[22] But Eagleton also argues that those lessons came from the first wave of "high" theory, and that the post-theory phase has little to offer; thus via the thinkers of "high" theory "New concepts were forged and new methods elaborated"[23] whereas we are now a pale shadow of these big thinkers. Eagleton offers hope, but only if theory starts "thinking ambitiously once again",[24] which in light of *After Theory* really means thinking politically. Zimmermann also defends postmodern thought, since it "is in essence a criticism of Western rationality, including scientific objectivism, a critique with an ethical focus that tries to examine the very nature of reason and the self."[25] Furthermore, he argues that "We must not bypass but integrate the correctives of postmodernity's critique of reason into recovering a broader concept of human reason. . . . we should not forget that postmodernism is itself an important part of the history of the Logos."[26] To be "after theory", then, is to have learnt the lessons of theory, to have accepted that these were in and of themselves important, if not progress, but to also suggest that theory has the potential to lead into a blind alley, while the rest of the world is living in the surrounding city, asking challenging questions about ethics, literature, belief, politics and science, to name just a few, questions that theory cannot seem to begin to answer, or if it does, the answers no longer feel sufficient or relevant to many people. The problem with the phrase "after theory", however, is that it suggests a new awareness of theory's deficiencies; whereas in reality, this awareness paralleled the rise to dominance of theory in the humanities, and yet was deemed unorthodox enough to be shunted off into the sidings (to adjust metaphors slightly). A productive way to approach what has happened "after theory" is examination of these marginalized methodologies, especially at the points in which they re-emerge into mainstream critical awareness. This approach enables the reader to get a sense of what is being called here the "new textualities"; that is to say, areas of literary critical and theoretical studies that were once considered irrelevant or marginal from a highly theoretical perspective, as well as new fields that combine humanistic, technological and theoretical perspectives, such as the digital humanities.

In many respects, the new textualities share a sense of "the-thing-in-itself". In ecocriticism, for example, there is a rejection of the notion that the natural world is an entirely linguistic, social construct, and that furthermore the natural world powerfully "resists our narratives" as Rebecca Raglon and Marian Scholtmeijer put it.[27] As they argue, "The idea that language constructs reality, when pushed to its logical conclusion, reveals a disturbing human arrogance and one-sidedness."[28] Cheryll Glotfelty argues that the linguistic turn necessarily leads to our notions of world being entirely social, whereas ecocriticism begins with "the fundamental premise that human culture is connected to the physical world, affecting it and affected by it. [. . .] As a critical stance, it has one foot in literature and the other on the land; as a theoretical discourse, it negotiates between the human and the nonhuman."[29] Intriguingly, ecocriticism came of age at the height of the theory debates, in a period in which even the notion of something "outside the text" was being thoroughly rejected. In light of global environmental damage and destruction, including the rapid extinction of myriad species, a sense of urgency also drives ecocritical awareness; as Richard Kerridge notes, "Ecocritics worry that too much attention to nature as a cultural and ideological construct . . . will lead to neglect of nature as an objective, material, and vulnerable reality."[30] But this is not to say that ecocriticism is non-theoretical or somehow theoretically naïve. Ecocriticism, like many of the new textualities, is a *hybrid discourse*, for example, examining the ways in which society *has* constructed competing notions of Nature, while at the same time, *not* entirely reducing Nature to those constructs. Also, ecocritics look at intersections with other theories, such as gender studies, feminism, and postcolonialism; for example, Travis V. Mason's work on the representation of animals in literary texts that bridge ecocriticism and postcolonialism, thereby moving beyond the dominant ecocritical genre of realism.[31]

A similar hybrid approach, holding on to a sense of the material real—in this case individual lived experience—yet also being aware of the theoretical complexities of representing that lived experience, is "life writing" or auto/biography (the slash indicating a theoretical awareness of the paradoxical crossings of fact and fiction within this genre). As James Olney asks in one of the key early texts on life writing, *Autobiography: Essays Theoretical and Critical* (1980), "What do we mean by the self, or himself (*autos*)? What do we mean by life (*bios*)? What is the significance and the effect of transforming life or a life into a text?"[32] For Olney, these questions are important because a more sophisticated understanding of auto/biography moves from the traditional perspective of the auto/biographical text being seen as a mere reflection or secondary representation of a person's life, to being in many respects *constitutive*, creating one coherent narrative of a person's "unique psychic configuration."[33] While "high" theory was attacking and deconstructing traditional notions of authorship and intentionalism—for example Roland Barthes often-quoted essay from 1968 which advocated "The Death of the Author" and the rise of the reader—the study of life writing intensified in a parallel realm of inquiry that debated such tough theoretical claims.[34] As Jakki Spicer notes, "since its inception as a formalized field of study, autobiography studies has been preoccupied with whether an autobiographical text can communicate to its readers the reality of its author's experiences. One side of the debate— typified by theorists such as Paul de Man—has held that it is impossible for language ever to represent reality 'accurately,' even asserting that autobiography is theoretically impossible. The other side—elaborated by thinkers like James Olney—claims that the truth of unique individuals can be known through the autobiographies they write, even if language is not purely transparent and 'truth' is not the same thing as 'fact.'"[35] Some critics see these theoretical debates as initiating a new phase of auto/biography studies, which began with the sophisticated analyses of Philippe Lejeune's "Autobiographical Pact" (1975; English trans. 1982), and includes not only De Man's and Olney's work mentioned above, but also William Spengemann's *The Forms of Autobiography* (1980), and Paul John Eakin's *Fictions in Autobiography: Studies in the Art of Self-Invention* (1985).[36] In this phase, the study of auto/biographies written by women became synthesized with the rise of new feminist theory, to suggest fundamental gender differences in the genre. Thus, through feminist notions of auto/biography, the "sovereign, centred" male self is rejected in favour of a "dispersed and decentred subjectivity"; the autonomous male self is rejected in favour of a "dialogical conception of Selfhood"; and the disembodied male auto/biographical narrative that privileges intellectual and other abstract achievements, is rejected in favour of a return to the body as a key experience of "women's subjectivity."[37] Two key texts in the 1990s that explore feminist approaches to auto/biography are Leigh Gilmore's *Autobiographics: A Feminist Theory of Women's Self-Representation* (1994) and Laura Marcus's *Auto/biographical Discourse: Theory, Criticism, Practice* (1994). Gilmore's notion of the provisional status of auto/biographical "authority" sums up the hybrid nature of feminist auto/biographical discourse: "Whether and when autobiography emerges as an authoritative discourse of reality and identity, and any particular text appears to tell the truth, [this] has less to do with that text's presumed accuracy about what really happened than with its apprehended fit into culturally prevalent discourses of truth and identity."[38]

The complex dynamics of the "new textualities" can be seen in two apparently antithetical critical movements that have occurred "after" theory: the religious turn, and the rise (and rise) of the digital humanities. The religious turn is an interesting phenomenon, since some of the most influential theorists within this field have also driven theory's deconstruction of metaphysics and virtually all modes of transcendence and belief. Jacques Derrida's unremitting critique of a metaphysics of presence which is expressed via what theorists calls "logocentrism", would naturally lead to an expectation that he would never go near religious questions, but of course readers of Derrida know that the opposite is the case. Religious questions arise throughout Derrida's works, embedded in texts such as *Of Grammatology* (1967, Engl. trans. 1976), *Writing and Difference* (1967, Engl. trans. 1978), *The Post Card: From Socrates to Freud and Beyond* (1980, Engl. trans. 1987), and *Of Spirit: Heidegger and the Question* (1987, Engl. trans. 1989); more explicitly religion is the subject matter of "Des Tours de Babel" (1980, Engl. trans. 1985), "Force of Law: The 'Mystical Foundation of Authority'" (1990 French & Engl.); and "A Silkworm of One's Own (Points of View Stitched on the Other Veil)" (Engl. 1996, French version 1997). Writing in the introduction to Derrida's essay collection *Acts of Religion* (2002), Gil Anidjar argues that "when Derrida writes on religion, it is always on the Abrahamic", where "this ancient notion, the Abrahamic has been considered either the original and gathering root of the three major monotheistic faiths [Judaism, Islam, Christianity] or, more pervasively, as the (three) branches of one single faith."[39] Derrida's writing about religion is enormously influential, and while this dimension of his writing had been explored in the 1980s, by a number of key thinkers, such as Kevin Hart in *The Trespass of the Sign: Deconstruction, Theology and Philosophy* (1989), it was in the 1990s that more widespread engagement with religion and theory in relation to Derrida's work occurred. A notable contribution to this movement is the Religion and Postmodernism conferences (and ensuing publications) at Villanova University, US, beginning in 1997 with the theme of "God, The Gift, and Postmodernism", followed by "Questioning God" (1999), "Confessions" (2001), "Transcendence and Beyond" (2003), and "Athens and Jerusalem on the Polis" (2005). Derrida's presence at the first three of these conferences, as well as many leading theorists of the religion-theory intersection—including Richard Kearney, Mark C. Taylor, Kevin Hart, John D. Caputo, Geoffrey Bennington, Mark Vessey and Hent de Vries—led to important critical publications and debates, such as John D Caputo and Michael J. Scanlon's edited essay collection on *Augustine and Postmodernism: Confessions and Circumfession* (2005). Caputo and Scanlon introduce this text with reflections on the terrorist events of 9/11, as well as the religious turn: "In the last fifteen years or so of Continental philosophical reflection, God has been making a comeback among continental philosophers and, along with God . . . one of the West's most passionate and God-filled men, Augustine of Hippo."[40] Notable texts in this "comeback", shifting explicitly from the "Abrahamic" to the Christian, include Alain Badiou's *Saint Paul: The Foundation of Universalism* (1997, Engl. trans. 2003), Giorgio Agamben's *The Time That Remains: A Commentary on the Letter to the Romans* (2000, Engl. trans. 2005), and Slavoj Žižek's *The Puppet and The Dwarf: The Perverse Core of Christianity* (2003). What is intriguing about this triune is that each one of these theorists usually explores secular or atheistic theory, such as Badiou's philosophy of mathematical set-theory in *Being and Event* (1988, Engl. trans. 2005), Agamben's work on a key process of secularization, in *Profanations*

(2005, Engl. trans. 2007), and Žižek's exploration of Descartes, Hegel and Lacan in *The Ticklish Subject: The Absent Centre of Political Ontology* (1999). Both Badiou and Žižek are drawn to the Apostle Paul as a revolutionary figure; for the former, he "is a poet-thinker of the event, as well as one who practices and states the invariant traits of what can be called the militant figure";[41] for the latter, Paul is less a post-event thinker, and more a post-event organizer: "after confirming Jesus' death and resurrection, Paul goes on to his true Leninist business, that of organizing the new party called the Christian community."[42] Similarly, Agamben reads Paul's messianism (the "eschatological tension" or, the event has happened, the event is yet to come) via the materialist dialectics of Walter Benjamin.

Another major philosopher who has driven much of the religious turn in contemporary theory is Emmanuel Levinas, whose key essays in this area were collected in 1986 in the volume *Of God Who Comes To Mind* (Engl. trans. 1998). Levinas's ethical theories of the face of the Other draw deeply upon Judaism, even though he is a secular thinker; as Zimmermann notes, Levinas "calls for nothing less than recovering a concept of rationality that is intrinsically ethical, beyond any totalizing structures."[43] The tension between the secular and the transcendent runs throughout Levinas's great work: *Totality and Infinity: An Essay on Exteriority* (1961, Engl. trans. 1969). Here, the trace of the transcendent is found in the working out of human desire and responsibility, as one of the most prolific theorists of the religious turn, Richard Kearney, puts it in *The God Who May Be: A Hermeneutics of Religion* (2001).[44]

If the religious turn in theory brings together ancient and new texts, combining theories of transcendence with theories of immanence, the digital humanities analogously juxtaposes the entire gamut of humanist cultural memory (digitized medieval religious manuscripts; text analysis of canonical great thinkers and their works; new notions of hypertext and electronic reading) with that of cutting-edge computing and technology. The digital humanities has been called "an umbrella term" since it covers so many disciplinary practices, and of course the prioritizing of technology or of humanistic inquiry will dramatically change one's definition of the methodology.[45] With the former, critics argue that the digital humanities supports a capitalist, technologist re-invention of education, whereas with the latter, critics often argue from the perspective of identity politics and contemporary gender and race theory, suggesting that the digital humanities is too white, politically neutral, and suspiciously "nice" (i.e., it supports the study of culture, not politicized cultural studies). Divisions within the subject are more a question of focus, for example *digital humanism*, with the emphasis on "humanism", versus, say, *digital futurism*, with emphasis upon speculative (fantastic, gothic, cybernetic, etc) subjectivities. As the founder of the digital humanities, Father Roberto A. Busa suggests, "Humanities computing is precisely the automation of every possible analysis of human expression (therefore, it is exquisitely a 'humanistic' activity), in the widest sense of the word, from music to theatre, from design and painting to phonetics, but whose nucleus remains the discourse of written texts."[46] Busa's own extensive humanities computing project, his *Index Thomisticus*, was begun in 1949, using IBM punch-cards (one of the earliest ways of storing machine readable data), was transferred on to magnetic tape (completed 1980), printed in hard-copy form (1974), and then transferred onto CD-ROM format (1992). Busa's work quite remarkably spans the first three main phases of the digital humanities:[47] in the first phase (1949–70s), emphasis was upon using computers to assist in the creation of text concordances, as well as the analysis of texts using these tools; in the second phase (1970s to mid-1980s), a wide range of activities meant that the field matured—these activities included the establishment of the Oxford Text Archive in 1976, and the Association for Computers and the Humanities;[48] the third phase (mid-1980s to early 1990s) included the creation of the Text Encoding Initiative (2001), for a structured approach to text mark-up; there was also a shift away from mainframe computing to new modes of personal computing and electronic communication.[49] Susan Hockey, writing in *A Companion to Digital Humanities* (2004), argues that the invention of the internet ushered in a fourth phase (early 1990s to the present), especially in its graphical interface mode known initially as the World Wide Web: "the Web was a superb means of publication, not only for the results of . . . scholarly work, but also for promoting . . . activities among a much larger community of users."[50]

As Johanna Drucker suggests, the digital humanities "continues to evolve as the scope of online projects expands from creation of digital repositories to peer-reviewed publishing, the design of interpretive tools, and other humanities-specific activities. The encounter of texts and digital media has reinforced theoretical realizations that printed materials are not static, self-identical artifacts and that the act of reading and interpretation is a performative intervention in a textual field that is charged with potentiality."[51] This "encounter" involves a wide range of technologies and digital systems: "various kinds of computer-based educational technology, digital library collections, open access, digital or collaborative scholarship through the Internet and Web, digital institutional repositories, online (electronic) learning, digital preservation, and even online computer games, to name just a few."[52] Yet there is a sense in which, even with enormous advances in computer hardware, software and communication and archival/database systems, that many of the most critical debates are becoming more, not less urgent. Crudely put, as online resources and text analysis tools become more freely available, critical engagement intensifies. As Wernimont and Flanders put it in relation to the Brown University Women Writers Project, and the associated Women Writers Online (WWO), "we understand that an archive like the ever-growing WWO is a conduit through which to experiment with new modes of scholarly intervention—at the level of production as well as analysis—in ways that can make substantive changes to feminist, literary, and digital humanities scholarship."[53] This statement can be more widely applied, as the new digital textualities become ubiquitous.

Further reading: a selection

The texts below are just a small sample of the "new textualities", with the best place to start being Eagleton (1990 – with focus on his introduction and first chapter; & 2003). While the essays in López and Potter have not been extracted in this anthology, the critique of postmodernism in this text is extensive, and parts V (on gender) and VI (culture, criticism, literature) are key for literary theorists. For ecocriticism, one of the best places to start is Clark and Garrard, with many of the early major essays in the field in Glottfelty and Fromm. Thematic approaches to ecocriticism include DeLoughrey and Handley on postcolonial topics, and Fiamengo, on animals and Canadian literature. Anderson and Marcus provide accessible and wide-ranging introductions to auto/biography, with thematic focus in Grace and Wasserman (theatre/performance) and Moore-Gilbert (postcolonial studies). Extensive coverage of the digital humanities and humanities computing is found in Schreibman, Siemens and Unsworth, as well as Berry's comprehensive overview. Deegan and Sutherland examine text editing, with McGann theorizing editing and textuality; Drucker explores creativity and speculative computing. An extensive collection of essays in Gold, including blog posts and an electronic supplement, provides critique of the digital humanities, e.g., on gender, race, accessibility, and political aspects of the topic, among many other approaches and issues. Digital information and aesthetics are covered by the essays in Bartscherer and Coover; the text includes instructions for a related game. The debates with the religious turn in theory are deeply explored by De Vries, Kearney, and Zimmermann; key primary essays by Derrida are collected in Derrida. Focus on theory, theology and narrative can be found in Nelson, Szabo and Zimmermann, with focus on postmodernism and Augustine in Caputo and Scanlon. Three interrelated texts are Agamben, Badiou and Žižek, on Christianity, theory and the Apostle Paul.

Agamben, Giorgio. *The Time That Remains: A Commentary on the Letter to the Romans*. Trans. Patricia Dailey. Stanford, California: Stanford University Press, 2005.

Anderson, Linda. *Autobiography*. London & New York: Routledge, 2001.

Badiou, Alain. *Saint Paul: The Foundation of Universalism*. Trans. Ray Brassier. Stanford, California: Stanford University Press, 2003.

Bartscherer, Thomas and Roderick Coover, eds. *Switching Codes: Thinking Through Digital Technology in the Humanities and the Arts*. Chicago and London: University of Chicago Press, 2011.

Berry, David M. *Understanding Digital Humanities*. Houndmills, Basingstoke: Palgrave, 2012.

Caputo, John D. and Michael J. Scanlon, eds. *Augustine and Postmodernism: Confessions and Circumfession*. Bloomington and Indianapolis: Indiana University Press, 2005.

Clark, Timothy. *The Cambridge Introduction to Literature and the Environment*. Cambridge: Cambridge University Press, 2011.

De Vries, Hent. *Philosophy and the Turn to Religion*. Baltimore & London: the Johns Hopkins University Press, 1999.

Deegan, Marilyn and Kathryn Sutherland, eds. *Text Editing, Print and the Digital World*. Farnham, Surrey & Burlington, VT: Ashgate, 2009.

DeLoughrey, Elizabeth and George B. Handley, eds. *Postcolonial Ecologies: Literatures of the Environment*. Oxford: Oxford University Press, 2011.

Derrida, Jacques. *Difference in Translation*. Ed. Joseph F. Graham. Ithaca, NY: Cornell University Press, 1985.

Drucker, Johanna. *Speclab: Digital Aesthetics and Projects in Speculative Computing*. Chicago & London: University of Chicago Press, 2009.

Eagleton, Terry. *The Significance of Theory*. Oxford: Basil Blackwell, 1990.

Eagleton, Terry. *After Theory*. New York: Basic Books, 2003.

Fiamengo, Janice, ed. *Other Selves: Animals in the Canadian Literary Imagination*. Ottawa: University of Ottawa Press, 2007.

Garrard, Greg. *Ecocriticism*. London & New York, 2011.

Glotfelty, Cheryll and Harold Fromm, eds. *The Ecocriticism Reader: Landmarks in Literary Ecology*. Athens & London: University of Georgia Press, 1996.

Gold, Matthew K., ed. *Debates in the Digital Humanities*. Minneapolis: University of Minnesota Press, 2012.

Goody, Alex. *Technology, Literature and Culture*. Cambridge & Malden, MA: Polity, 2011.

Grace, Sherril and Jerry Wasserman, eds. *Theatre and AutoBiography: Writing and Performing Lives in Theory and Practice*. Vancouver, BC: Talon, 2006.

Kearney, Richard. *The God Who May Be: A Hermeneutics of Religion*. Bloomington and Indianapolis: Indiana University Press, 2001.

López, José and Garry Potter, eds. *After Postmodernism: An Introduction to Critical Realism*. London & New York: Athlone, 2001.

Marcus, Laura. *Auto/Biographical Discourses: Criticism, Theory, Practice*. Manchester & New York: Manchester University Press, 1999.

McGann, Jerome. *Radiant Textuality: Literature After The World Wide Web*. Basingstoke, Hampshire & New York: Palgrave, 2001.

Moore-Gilbert, Bart. *Postcolonial Life-Writing: Culture, Politics and Self-Representation*. Abingdon, Oxon & New York: Routledge, 2009.

Nelson, Holy Faith, Lynn R. Szabo and Jens Zimmermann, eds. *Through a Glass Darkly: Suffering, the Sacred, and the Sublime in Literature and Theory*. Waterloo, ON: Wilfrid Laurier University Press, 2010.

Schreibman, Susan, Ray Siemens and John Unsworth, eds. *A Companion to Digital Humanities*, Oxford: Blackwell, 2004.

Zimmermann, Jens. *Recovering Theological Hermeneutics: An Incarnational-Trinitarian Theory of Interpretation*. Grand Rapids, MI: Baker Academic, 2004.

Žižek, Slavoj. *The Puppet and The Dwarf: The Perverse Core of Christianity*. Cambridge, MA: MIT Press, 2003.

Notes

1   José López and Garry Potter, eds., "General Introduction", in *After Postmodernism: An Introduction to Critical Realism,* London & New York: Athlone, 2001, 3–16, p.4.

2   Jens Zimmermann, "Suffering Divine Things: Cruciform Reasoning or Incarnational Hermeneutics", in Holy Faith Nelson, Lynn R. Szabo and Jens Zimmermann, eds., *Through a Glass Darkly: Suffering, the Sacred, and the Sublime in Literature and Theory,* Waterloo, ON: Wilfrid Laurier University Press, 2010, pp.377–99, p.379.

3   Jens Zimmermann, "Suffering Divine Things: Cruciform Reasoning or Incarnational Hermeneutics", p.378.

4   José López and Garry Potter, eds., "Introduction", in *After Postmodernism: An Introduction to Critical Realism,* p.11.

5   José López and Garry Potter, eds., "General Introduction", in *After Postmodernism: An Introduction to Critical Realism,* p.182.

6   Philip Tew, "Reconsidering Literary Interpretation", in José López and Garry Potter, eds., *After Postmodernism: An Introduction to Critical Realism,* pp.196–205, p.202.

7   Hent De Vries, *Philosophy and the Turn to Religion,* Baltimore & London: the Johns Hopkins University Press, 1999, p.2.

8   Jens Zimmermann, "Suffering Divine Things: Cruciform Reasoning or Incarnational Hermeneutics", p.379.

9   Terry Eagleton, *After Theory,* New York: Basic Books, 2003, p.3.

10 Terry Eagleton, *After Theory,* p.3.

11 Terry Eagleton, *After Theory,* p.12.

12 Terry Eagleton, *After Theory,* p.190.

13 Terry Eagleton, *After Theory,* p.103.

14 Terry Eagleton, *After Theory,* p.179.

15 Terry Eagleton, *After Theory,* p.190.

16 Terry Eagleton, *After Theory,* p.191.

17 Terry Eagleton, *After Theory,* p.177.

18 Terry Eagleton, *After Theory,* p.177.

19 José López and Garry Potter, eds., "General Introduction", in *After Postmodernism: An Introduction to Critical Realism,* p.9.

20 José López and Garry Potter, eds., "General Introduction", in *After Postmodernism: An Introduction to Critical Realism,* p.9.

21 Terry Eagleton, *After Theory,* p.2.

22 Terry Eagleton, *After Theory,* p.4.

23 Terry Eagleton, *After Theory,* p.72.

24 Terry Eagleton, *After Theory,* p.73.

25 Jens Zimmermann, "Suffering Divine Things: Cruciform Reasoning or Incarnational Hermeneutics", p.383.

26 Jens Zimmermann, "Suffering Divine Things: Cruciform Reasoning or Incarnational Hermeneutics", p.382.

27 Rebecca Raglon and Marian Scholtmeijer, "Heading Off the Trail: Language, Literature, and Nature's Resistance to Narrative", in Karla Armbruster and Kathleen R. Wallace, eds., *Beyond Nature Writing: Expanding the Boundaries of Ecocriticism,* Charlottesville & London: University Press of Virginia, 2001, pp.248–62, p.248.

28 Rebecca Raglon and Marian Scholtmeijer, "Heading Off the Trail: Language, Literature, and Nature's Resistance to Narrative", p.251.

29 Cheryll Glotfelty, "Introduction: Literary Studies in an Age of Environmental Crisis", in Cheryll Glotfelty and Harold Fromm, eds., *The Ecocriticism Reader: Landmarks in Literary Ecology,* Athens & London: University of Georgia Press, 1996, pp.xv–xxxvii, p.xix.

30 Richard Kerridge, "Environmentalism and Ecocriticism", in Patricia Waugh, ed., *Literary Theory and Criticism,* Oxford: Oxford University Press, 2006, pp.530–43, p.531.

31 Travis V. Mason, "Lick Me, Bite Me, Hear Me, Write Me: Tracking Animals between Postcolonialism and Ecocriticism", in Janice Fiamengo, ed., *Other Selves: Animals in the Canadian Literary Imagination,* Ottawa: University of Ottawa Press, 2007, pp.100–124.

32   James Olney, "Autobiography and the Cultural Moment", in James Olney, ed., *Autobiography: Essays, Theoretical and Critical*, Princeton: Princeton University Press, 1980, pp.3–27, p.6.

33   James Olney, quoted in Jakki Spicer, "The Author Is Dead, Long Live the Author: Autobiography and the Fantasy of the Individual", *Criticism*, 47.3 (Summer 2005): 387–403, p.388.

34   Jakki Spicer, "The Author Is Dead, Long Live the Author: Autobiography and the Fantasy of the Individual", p.388.

35   Jakki Spicer, "The Author Is Dead, Long Live the Author: Autobiography and the Fantasy of the Individual", p.388.

36   For an excellent overview, see Bart Moore-Gilbert, *Postcolonial Life-Writing: Culture, Politics and Self-Representation*, Abingdon, Oxon & New York: Routledge, 2009, p.xiii.

37   Bart Moore-Gilbert, *Postcolonial Life-Writing: Culture, Politics and Self-Representation*, p.xvii.

38   Gilmore, quoted in Anne Nothof, "Resonant Lives: The Dramatic Self-Portraiture of Vincent and Emily", in Sherril Grace and Jerry Wasserman, eds., *Theatre and AutoBiography: Writing and Performing Lives in Theory and Practice*, Vancouver, BC: Talon, 2006, pp.37–151, p.138.

39   Gil Anidjar, "Introduction: 'Once More, Once More': Derrida, the Arab, the Jew", in Jacques Derrida, *Acts of Religion*, ed. by Gil Anidjar, London & New York: Routledge, 2002, pp.1–39, p.3.

40   John D. Caputo and Michael J. Scanlon, "Introduction: The Postmodern Augustine", in John D. Caputo and Michael J. Scanlon, eds., *Augustine and Postmodernism: Confessions and Circumfession*, Bloomington and Indianapolis: Indiana University Press, 2005, pp.1–15; pp.2–3.

41   Alain Badiou, *Saint Paul: The Foundation of Universalism*, trans. Ray Brassier, Stanford, CA: Stanford University Press, 2003, p.2.

42   Slavoj Žižek, *The Puppet and The Dwarf: The Perverse Core of Christianity*, Cambridge, MA: MIT Press, 2003, p.9.

43   Jens Zimmermann, "Suffering Divine Things: Cruciform Reasoning or Incarnational Hermeneutics", p.385.

44   Richard Kearney, *The God Who May Be: A Hermeneutics of Religion*, Bloomington and Indianapolis: Indiana University Press, 2001, pp.62–63.

45   Presner and Johanson quoted in Patrik Svensson, "The Digital Humanities as a Humanities Project", *Arts and Humanities in Higher Education*, 11.1–2 (2011): 42–60, p.45.

46   Roberto A. Busa, "Foreword: Perspectives on the Digital Humanities", in Susan Schreibman, Ray Siemens and John Unsworth, eds., *A Companion to Digital Humanities*, Oxford: Blackwell, 2004, pp.xvi–xxi; p.xvi.

47   Following the phases as delineated by Susan Hockey, in her essay "The History of Humanities Computing", in Susan Schreibman, Ray Siemens and John Unsworth, eds., *A Companion to Digital Humanities*, pp.3–19.

48   Susan Hockey, "The History of Humanities Computing", p.8.

49   Susan Hockey, "The History of Humanities Computing", pp.10–12.

50   Susan Hockey, "The History of Humanities Computing", p.13.

51   Johanna Drucker, *Speclab: Digital Aesthetics and Projects in Speculative Computing*, Chicago & London: University of Chicago Press, 2009, pp.8–9.

52   David Mattison, "The Digital Humanities Revolution", *Searcher*, 14.5 (2006): 25–34, p.25.

53   Jacqueline Wernimont and Julia Flanders, "Feminism in the Age of Digital Archives: The Women Writers Project", *Tulsa Studies in Women's Literature*, 29.2 (Fall 2010): 425–35, pp.425–26.

Chapter 64

Linda Hutcheon and Michael Hutcheon

WHY DISEASE AND OPERA?

Canada's leading theorist of postmodernism and literary theory, Linda Hutcheon, teams up in this book extract with her partner, Michael Hutcheon, M.D., a professor of medicine at The University of Toronto, to produce a lively and thoughtful synthesis of medical and humanistic discourses in their analysis of disease and opera. In the extract, the authors consider the social and political implications of the small number of diseases represented in opera, such as the plague, or tuberculosis, as well as tying these in to theories of desire and sexuality. A key operatic metaphor here—suffering—initially appears quite different from sudden death, but using contemporary medical knowledge in this area reveals suffering to be about a threat or disruption of personal identity. The dramatic narrative of pain and suffering is given additional force in the multimedia domain of opera, one which is focused on the embodied subject. The authors note that these bodies are gendered, and the question of sexuality—"that shorthand term for the social organization of sexual relations"—therefore becomes integrated with operatic representations of disease and death. Such a representation is complicated by historical transformations in knowledge concerning gender and sexuality, e.g., the shift into modern medical discourses, such as biology and physiology. The authors observe that many prevalent historical diseases rarely get performed in opera; shifting to some overdetermined diseases such as syphilis, cholera, and tuberculosis, there is clearly a link between disease and sexuality, especially where the disease is interpreted in a moral sense. Examples explored include Sophocles's play *Oedipus Rex*, and operatic versions such as Stravinsky's operatic version (1927), and George Enescu and Edmond Fleg's version called *Oedipe* (1936). Scapegoating in Oedipus reveals an ethical notion of disease, i.e., the plague brought about by personal impropriety, being interpreted thereby as a punishment or condemnation. In the extract, the authors compare Stravinsky's attempt to constrain the "chaos" of the immoral disease brought about by Oedipus's incestuous relationship with his mother, with Enescu and Fleg's focus on the tragic side of Oedipus's scapegoating. Disease is doubled: it is both biological and social event, i.e., affecting an individual, but also the society that can in turn be infected and destroyed. The example of Oedipus is important, because the societal response to "plague" is repeated in later times, even up to the present day with the moral notion of AIDS as a divine judgment or condemnation. This is an important observation, because the common notion of scientific and humanistic progress would appear to be undermined by such a response to a modern-day auto-immune disease. The authors explore, then, how "cultural concepts of disease work to help frame scientific theories", or, in other words, how complex artistic representations can shape our present-day understandings of disease. After a series of chapter summaries, the authors return to AIDS, and the way in which artistic representations of this disease does in fact differ from historical representations of other illnesses, namely a self-conscious or self-reflective attempt to resist and control moral interpretation and condemnation, through the production of a "countermythology", i.e., performative works created by gay men and women.

O PERA HAS ALWAYS BEEN AN ART FORM obsessed with death: Monteverdi's *La favola d'Orfeo* (1607) establishes a story pattern of love and loss that influences the staged representations of operatic death from the very start. In most nineteenth- and twentieth-century operas of the tragic variety, those obsessions and preoccupations with death continue to be associated with love, but the deaths are most frequently violent. There are stabbings: think of *Rigoletto, Pagliacci, Wozzeck, Tosca, Lucia di Lammermoor, Un ballo in maschera* (Boston setting). Then there are shootings: *Tosca* again, *Un ballo in maschera* (Stockholm setting), *Eurent Onegin*. Occasionally there are drownings: *Lady Macbeth of Mtsensk, Kátya Kabanová, Jenůfa*. Catherine Clément has suggested in *Opera, or The Undoing of Women*, that the victims are most frequently female.[1] Frequently they are, but by no means always, as the lists above suggest. In the name of love, women do often die at their own hands (Cio-Cio-San in *Madama Butterfly*), but so too do men (Edgar in *Lucia di Lammermoor*). In short, as we shall see, the gender question in opera is more complex than some people have suggested: it may be that for every Senta who leaps to her death (in *Der fliegende Holländer*) there is a Peter Grimes who rows out to sea to die. Indeed, as Michel Poizat notes in his "quick autopsy of the heaps of bodies strewn across the opera stage since the beginning," "male and female graves appear with equal frequency"—however "counterintuitive" that may seem.[2] Nevertheless, it is clear that opera has many ways of configuring death for both sexes in conjunction with love and desire, many of them violent.

Here we will look at what happens when an opera forgoes the obvious dramatic power of such sudden and violent final action in favor of a differently structured story of illness and suffering leading to death. As the testimony of works like *La Bohème* suggests, giving up the shock of violent death does not mean depriving the audience of tragic catharsis or emotional satisfaction. What is gained is the narrative power of an individual's struggle with illness. Recent medical thinking about suffering suggests that bodily pain is not the only element to be considered.[3] Suffering is said to occur when one's personal identity is threatened or disrupted. Of all the art forms, perhaps only opera is so thoroughly dependent on suffering in general as a narrative and emotional staple. The *body*, the singing body, gives voice to the drama of the suffering *person*—in this case the sick person; in the process it also gives meaning to both the disease and the one who suffers from it, meaning that includes but *supplements* the medical understanding of bodily pain.

In *The Body in Pain*, Elaine Scarry has argued that physical pain resists language. It "has no voice," she claims, but adds: "When it at last finds a voice, it begins to tell a story."[4] David B. Morris, in *The Culture of Pain*, specifies the form that story takes: for him it is in the action of staged tragedy that pain and the suffering it entails can be seen and heard. King *Lear* and *Oedipus the King* present "the ruined human body and the sound of suffering."[5] But imagine for a moment staged tragedy amplified by the emotional power of music—in other words, imagine opera—and you have an even more effective representation of the suffering person. It is also one that, through the music, would go a long way toward eliminating Lessing's famous nineteenth-century aesthetic worries about the negative effect of having someone scream on stage—that this sign of physical pain would offend the ears and eyes of the audience and arouse only pity or compassion.[6] But that may be the whole point, as chapter 3 will argue. Through the aural and visible staged manifestations of his physical pain and psychological suffering, the character of Amfortas, in Wagner's *Parsifal,* has to arouse precisely such compassion (and the word for compassion in German, *Mitleid,* literally and significantly means "with suffering")—both in his redeemer, Parsifal, and in the audience.

Bodies, however, are unavoidably gendered, and with gender enters sex: in opera, in fact, questions of gender turn out to be inseparable from representations of not only love and desire but also "sexuality," that shorthand term for the social organization of sexual relations. This is why gender is more complicated in opera than Clément and others have suggested. It is only relatively recently that sexuality has come to be thought of as an important part of our understanding of the dynamics between the individual and the social, both in the present and in the past, and especially where moral judgments are concerned.[7] At the point where we begin, in the nineteenth century, it has been argued that there was a major shift in how people in the West thought about sex and sexuality: Lawrence Kramer writes, "What had been physical became biological; what had been moral became physiological."[8] This was a shift to a medicalized focus on sexuality as potentially pathological or aberrant, and certainly in need of regulation. Because sexuality cannot be separated from desire—in theory or in practice—one of the consequences of this new psychobiological model was that sexual identity and desire became basic to how people thought of themselves as human. This complicated immensely that connection between disease (or pathology) and any aspects of sexuality that fell outside the narrow confines of nineteenth-century bourgeois societal norms.

Given the obvious importance of desire and death to opera plots, then, this book is a study of the operatic representations of disease in conjunction with sexuality and its increasing medicalization over the past two centuries. Such a focus offers a way to look at the historically different ways people have constructed notions of themselves and their societies, in part through the prevailing concepts of love and death, but also through those of disease and health—social as well as individual.[9] We were curious because there are no major operas we know of about yellow fever, typhus, or influenza; there seems to be little sung on stage about diphtheria or polio or cancer. When so many women died of childbirth in earlier years, why did this so rarely make it onto the stage? Debussy's Mélisande in *Pelléas et Mélisande* seems one of the few even to give birth, and her death as presented in the opera could well be the result more of her love than of childbirth. Wagner's Sieglinde dies offstage somewhere between *Die Walküre* and *Siegfried* (in *Der Ring des Nibelungen*), but we are hard pressed to think of others.

For a disease to appear as a significant thematic element or plot device in opera, it seems that it must have strong cultural associations beyond its medical meaning and physical signs. The cultural clichés it has to draw on seem all to involve desire—that much discussed but vaguely defined term in cultural theory todays.[10] On the opera stage, however, desire (especially if linked to suffering and disease) always means specifically sexual desire, perhaps because that is a time-tested way "to score a direct hit at the spectator's sensibility."[11] But it almost always also means sexual anxiety. And so we find syphilis, not surprisingly, but also cholera and tuberculosis. Such a linking of sexuality and disease goes far back in Western culture, of course. *Oedipus the King* is the story of parricide, but also of incest and the resultant plague. As we shall see in the epilogue as well, "plague" is a word newly revived in discussions of AIDS. It is emotionally charged, for good historical reasons. Unlike a word like "epidemic," "plague" (be it in literature or in historical accounts) has always connoted moral blame. The idea of an incurable and devastating illness suddenly attacking an entire society has long been read as a divine scourge, a punishment for godlessness, evil, or sometimes a specific sin. This has always been seen as an affliction with a moral purpose, and so it has been available, from the Bible and before, as a metaphoric domain for matters of sexual transgression.[12]

Framed as it is by the Florentine plague of 1348 that killed over 100,000 people, Boccaccio's *Decameron* articulates forcefully the view that God sent the plague to punish evil ways and cleanse the city of filth. The clinical horrors of this scourge are rehearsed in gruesome detail; so too is its terrifying contagiousness—for this is what drives the seven young women and three men to flee the city for the safer countryside where they would tell their famous stories.[13] No doubt the panic of mass death, the sight of the plague cart passing through the streets hourly, and the physical horrors of the disease itself all made the city a place of personal as well as public terror—as they had done since the Athens of Thucydides and would continue to do through Pepys's London and Camus's Oran.[14] When religious or medical authorities failed to halt a plague, George Deux reports, societies "were tempted in their disillusionment and despair to find cause in the malevolence of men: witches and poisoners who, for whatever reason, were killing them."[15] They often blamed specific people, scapegoating the powerless (the poor, witches, Jews, and so on). Or they sought the phantom poisoner who was believed to be working among them.[16] As we shall see, this conjunction, in one form or another, of sexual worries with some sense of a pestilential divine scourge, scapegoating, and poisoning offers a particular configuration of plague that operatic narratives (like literary ones) have used to powerful ends in operas that vary from Wagner's *Parsifal* to Benjamin Britten/Myfanwy Piper's *Death in Venice*.

As European cultures learned from the Black Death, plagues have emotional and aesthetic power not only because of their moral or sexual associations but also because they are both "a personal affliction and a social calamity."[17] in a sense any disease can be seen as double: "as a *biological event* that infects our bodies and as a *social event* to which a variety of meanings are attached by the choices we make in response to disease."[18] Plagues seem to be dual, in this sense, in a particularly significant way. Though a disease that affects individual people, plague also affects the whole society: rich and poor, evil and good, all can die from it. Social hierarchies are ignored, transgressed, and then abolished; political and religious authority collapses. The physical breakdown of the body becomes the model for the pathological breakdown of the culture.[19] The plague's threat to the community and to the very existence of a communal social life is as terrifying as its power over individual death. It is these parallels between the social and the physical body that give the plague much of its dramatic potential and, as chapter 5 will explore, its metaphoric value in the political arena.

This is the terror of anarchy and social chaos that Stravinsky's opera *Oedipus Rex* (1927) explicitly draws on. The opera relies on the power of the familiar, ancient story and the associations of plague in conjunction with forbidden sexuality to better dramatize its composer's theory of the power of music's form. This is the power of form and order to restrain the imagination—or, in Greek mythic terms (as made popular by Nietzsche), to curb the riot of Dionysus with the control of Apollo. In Stravinsky's words: "Music is given to us to establish an order in things; to order the chaotic and the personal into something perfectly controlled, conscious and capable of lasting vitality."[20] Rejecting what he saw as the easy emotionalism of nineteenth-century psychological music drama but still wanting a plot with power, Stravinsky chose what he called a "universally known tragedy," the Oedipus story, with its focus on plague.[21] He asked Jean Cocteau to provide a French libretto of the Greek play, which he then had translated into Latin—a dead language he felt was devoid of triviality but dense with associations of artifice and control. He inserted a plot-narrating speaker between the audience and the stage action, such as it was: he made his characters stand like living statues in a kind of operatic still life.[22] The music of what he called this "opera-oratorio" was composed to stand aloof from the words and narrative action, not emotionally reinforcing either.

This is, in a way, "opera in a straightjacket."[23] But it is nonetheless a powerful opera, one whose subject—illicit sexuality and plague—represents the chaos to be restrained by that straitjacket. It opens violently, with the chorus and orchestra "attacking the downbeat together in a gesture of panic and despair."[24] The curtain rises on the chorus and Oedipus, both of whom obsessively, ritualistically repeat the word "plague." It appears six times in the first eight lines of the work, always in conjunction with the fate of the city, Thebes. The chorus begins

Caedit nos pestis,	*The* plague *falls on us,*
Theba peste *moritur.*	*Thebes is dying of* plague.
E peste *serva nos*	*From the* plague *preserve us*
qua Theba moritur.	*for Thebes is dying.*
Oedipus, adest pestis;	*Oedipus, the* plague *has come,*
e peste *libera urbem,*	*free our city from* plague,
urbem serva morientem.	*preserve our dying city.*

To this Oedipus responds, "Citizens, I shall free you from the *plague*" ("Liberi, vos liberabo a *peste*"). Throughout the opera, as in the play, the plague is directly linked to moral guilt, to one individual's murder and incest; but it is the city, the suffering society, that must be purged of its stain if the god who has infected it with plague is to be appeased.

George Enescu and Edmond Fleg's opera *Oedipe* (1936) focuses more on Oedipus as a tragic figure, for whom the plague is but the culmination of the horrors to be confronted. But act 3 opens with a funeral procession in the background and loud crowd lamentations about the deaths of the wealthy, the virtuous, the virginal, and the innocent. Three times the chorus begs Oedipus to heed their laments and moans ("nos pleurs et nos gémissements") and to deliver them from what the High Priest calls the plague with the fiery teeth that is devouring the city ("La Peste aux dents de feu dévore ta Cité"). In his tragically ironic innocence, Oedipus calls on the gods to find the cause, the scapegoat, on whom the physical horrors of the plague should be made to fall: "May the Plague, with its rotting teeth, devour his bones" ("Et que la Peste, aux dents de pourriture, dévore ses os"). Incest and parricide, as the opera makes clear, are sexual and social transgressions that carry a heavy price, for societies as well as individuals.

As these operas show, the meanings that have accrued to plague in Western culture go well beyond its medical meanings to include those notions of the attribution of divine wrath and punishment, scapegoating, and the threat of social chaos. As we shall see, all these elements recur in the representations of other diseases that are also made to involve sexuality in some way or other: syphilis, cholera, and most recently, AIDS. Even tuberculosis was dubbed the "white plague." The act of representing these diseases *on stage* in singing bodies is what so forcefully calls up and calls upon such a wealth of cultural associations. Our argument is that the act of paying critical attention to these diseases can bring into focus different aspects of the narrative and the text—and even the music. Details that previously went unnoticed now become significant. New perspectives allow new interpretations of operas.

But it is not only the interpretation of operas that can change. These same cultural concepts of disease work to help frame scientific theories. Sander Gilman and others argue for a two-way communication between culture and medicine.[25] Art creates images of disease based on history, popular belief, and medical science; these images in turn often provide the models for that same science to understand and articulate its own goals. Art's images of the sick, they argue, become images of the disease itself. Repeated representations can work to bring about social and scientific reality. These representations and the complex and dynamic interaction between medical and cultural meanings in European opera in the past two centuries form the core of this book.[26]

Notes

1   For relevant and related analyses of representations of death and women in Western culture, see Elisabeth Bronfen, *Over Her Dead Body: Death, Femininity and the Aesthetic* (New York: Routledge, 1992), and for opera in particular, Michel Poizat, *The Angel's Cry: Beyond the Pleasure Principle in Opera*, trans. Arthur Denner (Ithaca: Cornell University Press, 1992). Poizat's focus is on voice and the powerful emotional response to it that he associates with both the erotic and the divine, connecting the two in the image of woman suffering and dying.

2   Poizat, *Angel's Cry*, 134.

3   See Howard Brody, *Stories of Sickness* (New Haven: Yale University Press, 1987); Arthur Kleinman, *The Illness Narratives: Suffering, Healing, and the Human Condition* (New York: Basic Books, 1988); Eric Cassell, *The Nature of Suffering and the Goals of Medicine* (New York: Oxford University Press, 1991).

4   Elaine Scarry, *The Body in Pain: The Making and Unmaking of the World* (New York: Oxford University Press, 1985), 3.

5   David B. Morris, *The Culture of Pain* (Berkeley: University of California Press, 1991), 248.

6   Gottfried Ephraim Lessing, *Werke in drei Bänden*, ed. Herbert G. Göpfert (München: Carl Hanser, 1982), 31: "Zudem ist der körperliche Schmerz überhaupt des Mitleidens nicht fähig, welches andere Übel erwecken."

7   See Jeffrey Weeks, "AIDS and the Regulation of Sexuality," in *AIDS and Contemporary History*, ed. Virginia Berridge and Philip Strong (Cambridge: Cambridge University Press, 1993), 18–19.

8   Kramer, *Music as Cultural Practice*, 136.

9   For more on the debate over sexuality and its social construction, see Edward Stein, ed., *Forms of Desire: Sexual Orientation and the Social Constructionist Controversy* (New York: Routledge, 1992).

10   On the complex (and often confused) meanings given to "desire," see the special issue of *Textual Practice* 7, 3 (1994), and Jay Clayton's detailed survey in "Narrative and Theories of Desire," *Critical Inquiry* 16 (1989): 33–53.

11   Mosco Carner, *Puccini; A Critical biography*, 2d ed. (London: Duckworth, 1974), 258, where he is writing of *verismo* opera's "uninhibited inflation of every dramatic and emotional moment": "Characters are presented over-life-size and are swept along in a whirlwind of passions in which sex becomes the driving force. Erotic desire is always thwarted and thus leads to acts of insensate jealousy and savage revenge." See also Peter Conrad, *Song*, 13, where he calls opera the realm of "emotional atavism," the "empire of irresistible, coercive impulse," where the libido rules. His chapter "Eros" (42–54), expands on this hedonistic, sensual drive in opera. Realist opera, he argues, is the domain of "pathological desire" (191).

12   See Julien S. Murphy, "The AIDS Epidemic: A Phenomenological Analysis of the Infectious Body," in *The Meaning of AIDS: Implications for Medical Science, Clinical Practice, and Public Health Policy*, ed. Eric T. Juengst and Barbara A. Koenig (New York: Praeger, 1989), 55; Brian Inglis, *The Diseases of Civilization* (London: Hodder and Stoughton, 1981), 150; Owsei Temkin, *"The Double Face of Janus" and Other Essays in the History of Medicine* (Baltimore: Johns Hopkins University Press, 1977), 460.

13   See Giovanni Boccaccio, *Il Decamerone* (1353; Milano: Ulrico Hoepli, 1965), 5–12. The operetta *Boccaccio* by Franz Suppé/F. Zell and Richard Genée omits the plague frame completely and concentrates on the stories of amorous intrigue told by the young people.

14   For an extended analysis, see David Steele, "Plague Writing: From Boccaccio to Camus," *Journal of European Studies* 11 (1981): 88–110.

15   George Deaux, *The Black Death 1347* (London: Hamish Hamilton, 1969), 6.

16   Günter B. Risse, "Epidemics and History: Ecological Perspectives and Social Responses," in Fee and Fox, *AIDS: The Burdens of History*, 40; Johannes Hohl, *The Black Death: A Chronicle of the Plague*, trans. C. H. Clarke (London: Allen and Unwin, 1926), chapter 8, "Persecution of the Jews," 181–206; Deaux, *Black Death*, 22.

17   Paul Slack, *The Impact of Plague in Tudor and Stuart England* (London: Routledge and Kegan Paul, 1985), 3.

18   Murphy, "AIDS Epidemic," 52.

19   René Girard, "The Plague in Literature and Myth," *Texas Studies in Literature and Language* 15, 5 (1974): 846.

20   Igor Stravinsky, cited in Roman Vlad, *Stravinsky,* trans. Frederick Fuller, 3d ed. (Oxford: Oxford University Press, 1978), 113.

21   Stravinsky, in Robert Craft, ed., *Stravinsky; Selected Correspondence* (London: Faber and Faber, 1982), 1:94.

22   See Eric Walter White, *Stravinsky: The Composer and His Works,* 2d ed. (Berkeley: University of California Press, 1979), 329.

23   Conrad, *Song,* 76.

24   Stephen Walsh, *Stravinsky: Oedipus Rex* (Cambridge: Cambridge University Press, 1993), 34.

25   Gilman, *Disease and Representation,* 7; Elizabeth Fee, "Sin versus Science: Venereal Disease in Twentieth-Century Baltimore," in Fee and Fox, *AIDS: The Burdens of History,* 121.

26   There has recently been considerable interest in the intersection of medicine and opera, though most of it is on the level of thematic concerns (doctor figures in opera) or the causes of death of either composers or famous singers. See, for a particularly germane example, the special issue of the *Tribuna Médica: Revista Latinoamericana de Educación Médica Continuada* 88, 6 (December 1993). On the relation of music to medicine and the idea of music's therapeutic functions, see A. Markoff, *La Musique, les musiciens, la fonction musicale: Essai thérapeutique, anthropologique, anatomo-clinique* (Toulouse: Université de Toulouse, 1937); Erhard Völkel, *Die spekulative Musiktherapie zur Zeit der Romantik: Ihre Tradition uni ihr Fortwirken* (Düsseldorf: Triltsch, 1979); Raoul Blondel, *Propos variés de musique et de médecine* (Paris: Editions d'Art et de Médecine, n.d.); Simin Baradaran-Chassemi, *"Der musikalische Arzt" von Peter Lichtenthal* (Düsseldorf: Medizinischen Akademie, 1965); Dorothy M. Schullian and Max Schön, eds. *Music and Medicine* (New York: Henry Schuman, 1948).

Chapter 65

Sherrill Grace

THEATRE AND THE
AUTOBIOGRAPHICAL PACT

Reflecting on the contemporary approach to "auto/biography" signalled by the slash in this word (or the capitals in "AutoBiography"), Sherrill Grace draws in part upon her expertise as an internationally significant scholar of Malcolm Lowry—including her transcription and editing of his correspondence—a literary author who bridges modernist and postmodernist conceptions of self and subjectivity; she also draws upon considerable expertise in Canadian literature, aesthetics and culture. Auto/biography is a post-theory approach to the more traditional genres of biography and autobiography; that is to say, it brings together humanistic, theoretical, and post-humanist notions of subjectivity and life-writing. In the extract, Grace introduces an essay collection that examines auto/biography within the context of the theatre, although Grace also points out that auto/biography is immensely popular in a wide range of media, such as reality TV, blogs, and photography. Grace argues that even if the proliferation of auto/biographical texts emerges from a shallow and egocentric (as well as voyeuristic) culture, used more thoughtfully, the genre still has the ability to humanize an inhuman world, offer a democratic space for self-expression, create a voice for oppressed minorities, and become "a crucial site for inscribing and preserving cultural memory." Auto/biographical plays are also sites of intense self-reflectivity, i.e., self-consciously revealing or sharing the performative nature of subjectivity, as well as engaging in philosophical and ethical questions about selfhood and subject formation. Literally "staging processes of identity formation" such plays engage in an intersubjective meditation between actor and audience on the critical and creative processes of writing/performing a life. Grace refers to the "autobiographical pact" theorized by Philippe Lejeune, that is to say, the suspension of disbelief leading to the notion that in autobiography we are engaging (as readers or audience) in "real life" while simultaneously being aware that we are actually experiencing an artistic representation. This pact is further exaggerated by the literal embodiment of the auto/biographical narrative on stage. Again this leads to the self-reflective notion of a "performance of performance", foregrounding at the same time a dramatic actuality and aesthetic, one which resists erasure and oppression, thus aligning with many of the shared concerns of feminist criticism and activism. Grace notes that contemporary auto/biography thus recovers lost lives and provides a space for marginalized, "minor" or oppressed peoples. Post-theoretical reflection on this genre is necessarily sceptical and self-aware (having learnt the lessons of postmodernism, the "fictional" basis of all discourses, the arbitrary sign, and so on), as well as having a focus on theories of narrative and memory.

I

If "acting and autobiography go hand in hand," as Evelyn Hinz suggests (200), can we also think of playwriting and AutoBiography, or more specifically of the playwright and the auto/biographer, as doppelgängers? Hinz's proposal and my question raise a host of further questions and open up enticing possibilities, many of which are explored in this book. Our collective purposes in *Theatre and AutoBiography* is to identify, analyse, and debate the issues that arise when contemporary drama meets biography and autobiography on stage or page because variations on these relationships (one set of which is signalled by the double capitalization in AutoBiography or by the slash in auto/biographical to indicate the interdependence of the who genres) seem extraordinarily popular amongst today's artists, theatre practitioners, readers, and audiences. Something is going on out there in front of the lights; someone's *real* life story is being staged, performed, revealed, or re-discovered, and we have been invited to watch, participate in, and discuss the show.

But just what are these so-called *real* life stories? Why are they popping up so frequently? How do these stories, when created in a play and presented in live performance, differ from the many other forms of contemporary life writing that enjoy such immense popularity today, at least in Western culture? How does the playwright function as an auto/biographer and what challenge does the auto/biographical playwright create for his or her own biographer? And where, in all this life-storying, does the theorist, theatre historian, or critic fit in? In this brief introduction I cannot hope to answer these questions or even identify all the issue—that is the work of the following chapters. What I can do, to some small degree, is set the stage, move a few key props into position, and provide you with a quick cue-to-cue.

That both autobiography and biography have acquired a position of unprecedented importance over the past thirty years is now obvious (see, for example, Gilmore 2001, 1, and Alpern et al. 5). Less obvious, or less often examined, are the reasons for this phenomenon. Theorists and students of AutoBiography, a research subject now viewed as respectable in academic circles, have mapped the contours and shifting parameters of the autobiographical and, to a lesser degree, the biographical processes, thereby contributing to the profile and stature of both. This collection contributes to current debates in both Theatre and AutoBiography Studies by clarifying the role of AutoBiography in the theatre. For me, the most exciting contribution these chapters make to our thinking about AutoBiography lies in their critical attention to the creative conjunction of theatre and the auto/biographical; not only is this critique fairly new and innovative (certainly in such a sustained and multifaceted manner), but, I believe, theatre enables us to investigate the current appetite for AutoBiography from new angles and, therefore, to gain fresh insight into the underlying reasons for its popularity. There is something about the live performance of a play before a witnessing, reacting, participating audience that accentuates what is crucial in life stories *and* unique to theatre. And there is something fundamental to the life and work of an actor or playwright that foregrounds the performance of living and thereby complicates the biographical recreation of that life.

In general terms, AutoBiography—whether as prose memoir, biography, feature film or documentary life story (another hugely popular form in Europe and North America at present), portraiture, photography, "reality TV" programs, online diaries (blogs), performance arts, and auto/biographical plays—appeals to audiences because we live in a culture of *me* or I at a time when access to this cultural production is easy. But there are other much more interesting and complex explanations for our obsession with the personal. Auto/Biographies satisfy our desire for story at the same time as they promise to give us *truths* (if not Truth), to provide meaning, identity, and possibly even order, in an otherwise incoherent, arbitrary, and often violent world. They seem to put a human face on the abstract, impersonal forces of globalization, terrorism, and the corporatism of our so-called post-national condition. (Just reflect for a moment on the box-office success of films like *Supersize Me* or *Fahrenheit 9/11.*) They are, moreover, more democratic than many other forms of communication, and this is especially true of autobiography. While it is not accurate to claim that *anyone* can write a memoir or keep a diary or create a blog or stage a performance piece on their life (economics, access, and education are not equally available), the autobiographical voice and eye/I are available to minorities and to groups, such as women, who have been excluded from the dominant discourse and whose stories have been dismissed as worthless. With the post-postmodern return of the author and the waning of a deep-seated anti-humanism associated, in Western culture, with modernist ideology and aesthetics, a desire for agency, voice, visibility, and subjectivity has surfaced, clamouring for attention and seeking ways to create meaningful identity (personal and public, individual and communal) in the face of contemporary dehumanization, fragmentation, trauma, and commodification. While this predilection for AutoBiography no doubt satisfies a basic voyeuristic impulse (and does well in the marketplace), it also represents a crucial site for inscribing and preserving cultural memory. Indeed, AutoBiography and memory are inextricable, no matter what genre or medium is doing the auto/biographical work.

It is my contention, shared by the contributors to this volume, that the relationship between AutoBiography and Theatre Studies is a highly productive one and that over the past thirty years, at least in the English-speaking world, we have seen a proliferation of plays and performance works that take biography and autobiography as their subjects. From Michael Frayn's *Copenhagen* and *Democracy* or Pam Gem's *Stanley* to several plays by Adrienne Kennedy and Michel Tremblay to Edward Albee's *Three Tall Women* or Sharon Pollock's *Doc* and *Moving Pictures,* major playwrights have put the lives of real people or aspects of their own life stories on stage. Or perhaps I should say that they have *created* life stories about themselves and others that portray familiar historical figures or explore personal identity within a wider socio-historical context that resonates with audiences. To be sure, playwrights have written auto/biographical plays before—*The Glass Menagerie* (1945), *Long Day's Journey into Night* (1956), *Krapp's Last Tape* (1958), *After the Fall* (1964), and *Betrayal* (1978) are all, to varying degrees, just such plays. However, Samuel Beckett and Arthur Miller would reject this categorization of their plays, no matter how nuanced and carefully argued the claim.[1] The more contemporary playwrights whom I have mentioned, along with many others who are discussed in the following chapters, are less likely to reject, or even resist, the notion. While they will dismiss narrow labels and express concern over reductive analogs, they know they are working with life stories, creating biographical fictions, openly exploring auto/biographical concerns, and often inventing new ways of presenting biography within autobiography, of dramatizing autobiography through biography, or of illustrating how the performance of a life story can constitute, as well as represent, the life-as-lived.

When performed, these auto/biographical plays become what Elin Diamond has called "the site in which concealed or dissimulated conventions might be investigated" (5). In Jill Dolan's phrase, they often "*reveal* performativity" (431), and by doing so they examine a number of intertwined contemporary questions about identity, subjectivity, truth, and memory. At their best, auto/biographical plays are profoundly philosophical; they probe and weigh what it means to claim a personal or national identity—to use the first person pronoun and assert I (or even *not I*)—make ethical choices that affect, or have affected the actual lives of other real people, and they challenge the social construction or identity by staging processes of identity formation that invite audiences to see themselves and others as able to recreate identity and to reassert personal agency. At their best, these plays use the facts of a personal story to make us rethink the concept of *self* and the relationship of *self* to other.[2] That they can do all this while also remembering individual and collective pasts or giving voice and embodiment to marginalized, forgotten, or devalued lives only adds to their significance.

And, at their best, these plays are deeply engaging (for readers and audiences); they entertain, as theatre must do, and they are often funny as well as, at times, harrowing.

In trying to understand how auto/biographical plays work and where to locate the source of their wide appeal, I return to Philippe Lejeune's concept of the autobiographical pact with which a reader, viewer, or participant must comply (1989, 124–26). As Lejeune explains, when we sign on to this pact we expect to be told the truth about someone's life, we believe that the people we encounter are *real,* that they live outside the text and go to the bank and grocery store as we do, and we bring this expectation to autobiography and biography (as to portraiture, documentary film, blogs, and family photograph albums) *despite our realization that we are engaged with art, not life.* Furthermore, additional expectations arise when the AutoBiography takes place on stage because the identities being performed live are inescapably embodied and performative, as several recent theatre theorists engaged in the performance/performativity debate have demonstrated.[3] It is surely no coincidence that so much of the recent theory in both AutoBiography and Theatre Studies has been feminist in orientation, even when it can be usefully applied to non-feminist issues and texts, because such an approach recognizes the erasure of certain identities, voices, and bodies and exposes the interpellation, within a dominant Western ideology, of all identity—to the advantage of some and the great disadvantage of others. But this is precisely where auto/biographical plays, at least in performance, hold out such promise: if Diamond, Dolan, and Geraldine Harris are correct (as I believe they are), then what Harris calls the "performativity of performance" (23) facilitates change by identifying essentialized and constructed conditions of self production, by *playing* with these conditions and, in the process of performance, by recreating identities. While some performance work may have "a basis in autobiography" (37) and therefore, as Harris argues, be *especially* responsive to performative reconfigurations of the self, I believe that many auto/biographical plays *also* invite us to re-think who we are and how we come to see ourselves—and others—as changing human beings with some degree of agency and the capacity to remember.

But just as playwrights find innovative ways to dramatize life stories and, in the process, question the nature of identity, so too are contemporary biographers and autobiographers reinventing genres that have been around in Western culture for a very long time, in fact, since Augustine with his auto/biographical *Confessions* or Agnellus, a Roman biographer who proudly claimed of his biographees, "I invented lives for them and I do not believe them to be false" (quoted in Gould and Staley 90). Biography is simply not written as it was in Dr. Johnson's day, or even in Virginia Woolf's, although her *Orlando* would have satisfied Agnellus. Today, biographies are not restricted to famous male politicians, military leaders, or artists, and they no longer presume to capture and fix the unchanging essence of their subject any more than they impose rigid teleologies on the shifting sands of a life story. Some of the best biographies are of minor figures within a larger cultural scene, and the remembering of that scene is as important as the individual life. Playwright-biographer Ken Mitchell goes so far as to insist that the lesser known the figure, the safer (indeed, more free) the playwright is when constructing a successful *drama* from the facts, and the more conventional and flawed, or basically human, the subject is, the more appealing and culturally resonant his or her dramatic recreation will be (265–72). As yet, the *art* of biography has been less studied and theorized than the art of autobiography, but the two genres have never existed entirely independently; any biographer worth her salt knows the importance (and the seductive dangers) of autobiographical materials like letters, diaries, journals, and personal memoirs.[4] And no autobiographer can tell his personal story without infringing on the biographies of others, without, in fact, tacitly acknowledging what Paul John Eakin calls the relationality of identity (43–44)· Thus, to a significant degree, the theory of autobiography informs the biographer's task, and the constraints on the biographer (even the playwright-biographer) highlight the fabrications and the fictional process (of selected detail, repressed facts, tricks of memory, a created voice) of the autobiographer, who, after all, should never be trusted entirely.

Underlying and informing all AutoBiography, then, are two basic tools that are also deep-seated needs: story and memory. Narrative desire both motivates and structures life writing, so it is not surprising to find a great deal of critical attention paid to the narratology of all life writing (see Bal, Caruth, Eakin, Lejeune, Gilmore 1994, Marcus, Nadel, and Olney). Narrative has the capacity to reveal, organize, and create meaning. To speak of culture without story is a contradiction. It is through stories that we isolate facts, build histories, and contextualize events; it is through story that we strive to make sense of experience, discover what we accept as truths, and come to know ourselves and others (insofar as we ever do that). But without memory we cannot have recognizable narrative, stories that cohere, and contemporary Western culture strikes me as virtually obsessed with memory and acts of remembering.[5] This wide-spread obsession with memory surfaces in the private, public, local, and national attention to commemorative and physical sites of memory; recent cultural work on the First and Second World Wars in plays, films, books, art exhibitions, television programs, memorial buildings, and museums is a case in point. It is apparent in the prominence and resources granted to medical research on the brain and on the neurochemistry and physiology of memory, research no doubt spurred on by the prevalence of diseases like Alzheimer's. If we judge (and I do) by the current interest in prose memoirs, films depicting cultural memory, trauma narratives, and auto/biographical memory plays, then we are, right now, in Europe and North America, experiencing a crisis of remembering.

Various generic parallels for AutoBiography have been posited in attempts to contain what often seems like a scurrilous monster with a dubious genealogy and spurious claims to legitimacy. The most common comparison for both forms is with the novel, although historiography and portraiture are invoked by some theorists, but I am less convinced by these analogies than by the one with drama because, for a start, AutoBiography, like a play, demands a dramatic plot even when the facts must be rearranged to achieve that end. Evelyn Hinz, with whom I began this introduction, calls "drama the 'sister-art'" (196) of AutoBiography because in both endeavours it is the unfolding story *as lived,* embodied, and enacted by individuals (including actors), communities, and nations that draws us in and holds our attention. Moreover, the drama of living, much like the actual performance of a life on stage, *is a process,* subject to the vagaries of memory, scripted and experienced relationally by many participants. The play, like all auto/biographical activity, is reproducible but always different, always open to reinterpretation, at least until the final curtain ends the life. To speak this way of theatre performance, of course, is to speak in metaphors. But when such metaphors are grounded in auto/biographical plays, then they underscore the theatre's representation of what I call performative autobiographics: the creation of identities that exist in performance, that challenge fixed notions of the *self* and *of subjectivity,* and that are new each time the life story is performed.

Notes

1   Miller was especially hostile to descriptions *of After the Fall* as autobiographical; see Gottfried 345, 352–71. See also Knowlson on Beckett, 406–7.

2   This relationality is central to Eakin's thinking about autobiography and identity, and he does not see relationality as an exclusively feminist or feminine condition; see chapter 2 of *How Our Lives Become Stories*. See also Egan, and Smith and Watson.

3   See the arguments made by Claycombe, Diamond, Dolan, Harris, Holledge and Tompkins Postlewait, Sidnell, and Worthen. In *Interfaces,* Smith and Watson explore issues of performance and performativity, but not in terms of theatre; for them, "the autobiographical is a performative site"

(11), but this formulation ignores the discipline of theatre performance by merging it in a broader concept of performance.

4   A small number of studies of biography have appeared to date, but the theorizing of biography still lags behind that of autobiography. See Alpern et al., Epstein, Gould and Staley, Pachter, Rhiel and Suchoff, and Wagner-Martin.

5   Paul Fussell may have sparked this academic interest in memory and culture but numerous critical studies, explicitly on memory, have appeared since 1975 when *The Great War and Modern Memory* was published. One of the more comprehensive is Peter Middleton and Tim Wood's *Literatures of Memory*, but most recent work in autobiography theory deals centrally with the connections among trauma, memory, and identity; see also Malkin, Marcus, and Sturkin. Several recent novels, plays, and films might well be described as memory·texts due to the structural and thematic stress placed on memory, or on the loss or disruption of memory films like *Rosenstrasse* (2003), *A Very Long Engagement* (2004), and *Mémoires affectives* (2004) come immediately to mind.

6   I have discussed my concept of performative autobiographics in "Performing the Auto/biographical Pact." The term "autobiographics" is Gilmore's and I have adapted it to identify how the self is expressed and articulated—in short, *performed* in an auto/biographical play. However, the debate about performance and performativity has been closely addressed by feminist theatre specialists such as Harris, Diamond, and Dolan, and I am indebted to their analyses.

Works cited

Abbott, H. Porter. *Beckett Writing Beckett: The Author in the Autograph.* Ithaca: Cornell University Press, 1996.

Alpern, Sara, and Joyce Antler, Elizabeth Isreals Perry, and Ingrid Winther Scobie, eds. *The Challenge of Feminist Biography: Writing the Lives of Modern American Women.* Urbana and Chicago: University of Illinois Press, 1992.

Bal, Mieke. "Memories in the Museum: Preposterous Histories for Today." In *Acts of Memory: Cultural Recall in the Present,* ed. Mieke Bal, Jonathan Crewe, and Leo Spitzer. Hanover, N.H.: University Press of New England, 1999. 171–90.

Caruth, Cathy. *Unclaimed Experience: Trauma, Narrative, and History.* Baltimore: Johns Hopkins University Press, 1996.

Cavell, Richard. "Architectural Memory and Acoustic Space." *Architecture in Canada* 29, nos. 1–2 (2004): 59–66.

Claycomb, Ryan. "Playing at Lives: Biography and Contemporary Feminist Drama." *Modern Drama* 47, no. 3 (2004): 525–45.

Coghill, Joy. *Song of This Place.* Toronto: Playwrights Canada, 2003.

Diamond, Elin. *Performance and Cultural Politics.* London and New York: Routledge, 1996.

Dolan, Jill. "Geographies of Learning: Theatre Studies, Performance, and the 'Performative.'" *Theatre Journal* 45, no. 4 (1993): 417–41.

Eakin, Paul John. *How Our Lives Become Stories: Making Selves.* Ithaca: Cornell University Press, 1999.

Egan, Susanna. *Mirror Talk: Genres of Crisis in Contemporary Autobiography.* Chapel Hill: University of North Carolina Press, 1999.

Epstein, William, ed. *Contesting the Subject: Essays in the Postmodern Theory and Practice of Biography and Biographical Criticism.* West Lafayette: Indiana University Press, *1991.*

Filewod, Alan. *Performing Canada: The Nation Enacted in the Imagined Theatre.* Kamloops, B.C.: Textual Studies in Canada, 2002.

Fussell, Paul. *The Great War and Modern Memory.* New York and London: Oxford University Press, 1975·

Gale, Lorena. *Je me souviens.* Vancouver: Talonbooks, 2001.

Gilmore, Leigh. *Autobiographics: A Feminist Theory of Women's Self-Representation.* Ithaca: Cornell University Press, 1994.

——. *The Limits of Autobiography: Trauma and Testimony*. Ithaca: Cornell University Press, 2001.

Gottfried, Martin. *Arthur Miller: His Life and Work*. Cambridge, Mass.: Da Capo, 2003.

Gould, Warwick and Thomas E. Staley, eds. *Writing the Lives of Writers*. New York: St. Martin's, 1998.

Grace, Sherrill. "Performing the Auto/biographical Pact: Towards a Theory of Identity in Performance." In *Tracing the Autobiographical*, ed. Marlene Kadar, Linda Warley, Jeanne Perreault, and Susanna Egan. Waterloo: Wilfrid Laurier University Press, 2005. 65–79.

Griffiths, Linda. *Alien Creature*. Toronto: Playwrights Canada, 2000.

Harris, Geraldine. *Staging Femininities: Performance and Performativity*. Manchester: Manchester University Press, 1999.

Hinz, Evelyn. "Mimesis: The Dramatic Lineage of Auto/Biography." In *Essays on Life Writing: From Genre to Critical Practice*, ed. Marlene Kadar. Toronto: University of Toronto Press, 1992. 195–212.

Hirsch, Marianne. *Family Frames: Photography, Narrative, and Postmemory*. Cambridge: Harvard University Press, 1997.

Holledge, Julie and Joanne Tompkins. *Women's Intercultural Performance*. London and New York: Routledge, 2000.

Jeunet, Jean-Pierre, dir. *A Very Long Engagement*. Warner Brothers, France/U.S.A., 2004.

Knowlson, James. *Damned to Fame: The Life of Samuel Beckett*. London: Bloomsbury, 1996.

Leclerc, Francis, dir. *Mémoires affectives*. Montreal: Palomar, 2004.

Lejeune, Philippe. "The Autobiographical Pact (bis)." In *On Autobiography*, ed. Paul John Eakin, trans. Katherine Leavy. Minneapolis: University of Minnesota Press, 1989. 119–37.

Malkin, Jeanette R. *Memory-Theatre and Postmodern Drama*. Ann Arbor: University of Michigan Press, 1999.

Marcus, Laura. *Auto/biographical Discourse: Theory, Criticism, Practice*. Manchester: University of Manchester Press, 1994.

Middleton, Peter and Tim Woods. *Literatures of Memory: History, Time and Space in Postwar Writing*. Manchester: Manchester University Press, 2000.

Mitchell, Ken. "Between the Lines: Biography, Drama, and N. F. Davin." In *Biography and Autobiography: Essays on Irish and Canadian History and Literature*, ed. James Noonan. Ottawa: Carleton University Press, 1993. 263–72.

Nadel, Ira. "Biography and Theory, or Beckett in the Bath." In *Biography and Autobiography: Essays on Irish and Canadian History and Literature*, ed. James Noonan. Ottawa: Carleton University Press, 1993. 9–17·

Olney, James. *Memory and Narrative: The Weave of Life Writing*. Chicago: University of Chicago Press, 1998.

Pachter, Marc, ed. *Telling Lives: The Biographer's Art*. Philadelphia: University of Pennsylvania Press, 1985.

Postlewait, Thomas. "Autobiography and Theatre History." In *Interpreting the Theatrical Past: Essays in the Historiography of Performance*, ed. Thomas Postlewait and Bruce A. McConachie. Iowa City: University of Iowa Press, 1989. 248–72.

Rhiel, Mary and David Suchoff, eds. *The Seductions of Biography*. New York and London: Routledge, 1996.

Sidnell, Michael. "Authorizations of the Performative: Whose Performances of What, and for Whom?" In *The Performance Text*, ed. Domenico Pietropaolo. New York, Ottawa, and Toronto: LEGAS, 1999. 97–112.

Smith, Sidonie, and Julia Watson, eds. *Interfaces: Women, Autobiography, Image, Performance*. Ann Arbor: University of Michigan Press, 2002.

Sturken, Marita. "Personal Stories and National Meanings: Memory, Reenactment, and the Image." In *The Seductions of Biography*, ed. Mary Rhiel and David Suchoff. New York and London: Routledge, 1996. 31–41.

Thiessen, Vern. *Einstein's Gift*. Toronto: Playwrights Canada, 2003.

Thomson, R. H. *The Lost Boys: Letters from the Sons in Two Acts 1914–23*. Toronto: Playwrights Canada, 2002.

Verdecchia, Guillermo. *Fronteras Americanas* (American Borders). Vancouver: Talonbooks, 1997.

Von Trotta, Margarethe, dir. *Rosenstrasse*. Los Angeles: Samuel Goldwyn Films, 2003.

Wagner-Martin, Linda. *Telling Women's Lives: The New Biography*. New Brunswick, N.J.: Rutgers University Press, 1994.

Worthen, W. B. "Drama, Performativity, and Performance." *PMLA* 113, no. 5 (1998): 1093–1107.

Young, James E. *At Memory's Edge: After-images of the Holocaust in Contemporary Art and Architecture*. New Haven and London: Yale University Press, 2000.

Patrick Holland and Graham Huggan

TRAVEL WRITING AT THE MILLENNIUM

Exploring why travel writing has increased since the modernist assertion that the genre was coming to an end, author, travel writer and critic Patrick Holland joins forces with the travel and postcolonial critic Graham Huggan, to argue that three aspects of contemporary travel writing provide some answers: these are "commodification, specialization, and nostalgic parody." Ironically, the transformation of place into a travel industry commodity is inadvertently contributed to by more intellectual or critical travel writing, even that which attempts to resist, or critiques, commodification. Oppositional travel writing, such as postcolonial or ecological writing, leads to literary "specialization", contributing in turn to the proliferation of the genre as a whole, even if the specialised travel text appears unique. Further, traditional colonial or "English imperial" travel writing does not end through these processes—on the contrary, this mode continues in a parodic form. Writing their study as the world approached the millennium, Holland and Huggan note that this event heightened the sense among critics of travel writing that the genre was again at a point of transformation (the end/the new beginning; intensified apocalyptic claims; increasingly stark binary oppositions such as "East against West" and so on). In a debate in the *Guardian Weekly*, critics bemoan the negatives of travel and travel writing, such as Catherine Bennett's attack on travel to oppressive regimes, or Robyn Davidson's notion of the travel writer being "a cultural 'invader'." Ian Sansom and other critics reject the concept of travel entirely, indicating a millennial "exhaustion", which leads to the advice to simply stay at home and read . . . a travel book! For Holland and Huggan, such advice reinscribes the notion of travel writing as a higher level activity than the debased act of being a tourist/travelling per se, leading to a paradoxical re-affirmation of the "authentic" travel writing genre at the moment of its apparent millennial demise. Other critics give travel writing canonical status, shifting it even further away from a debased inauthentic experience into high literary culture, where "writing is 'better' than experience." In opposition to postmodern millennial exhaustion and the fetishization of the travel text are journalistic travelogues and guide books, offering advice or "instruction" for those about to embark on fresh new journeys. Such texts could be called "post-touristic" being both meta-textual commentary on outmoded and clichéd forms of tourism and travel as well as offering new modes of more "authentic" travel experiences. More serious "post-touristic" texts are explored in some detail, such as those by Robert D. Kaplan, where there is insightful political analysis, as well as constant mobility and grappling with alternative perspectives, which leads to a "replenishment" of the genre. Holland and Huggan suggest that in this replenishment, the travel writer, on the verge of the millennium, is situated in a deeply "ambivalent" site of intersecting criticisms and claims whereby commodification is an uneasy bedfellow with processes of defamiliarization and openness to difference or otherness. Travel writing, then, continues because of, not in spite of, this paradoxical and productive tension between industry and art.

THIS STUDY BEGAN WITH EVELYN WAUGH'S apocalyptic—if wry—1946 announcement that the end of travel writing, and of real travel itself, was drawing nigh. Waugh's announcement, echoed by Lévi-Strauss, later elegized by Fussell, was very much part of late—specifically postwar English—modernist anxiety. Bureaucratic impersonality; progressive means of transportation allied to a sophisticated travel infrastructure; the monstrous rise of tourism—all of these struck Waugh as symptoms of the modern (male) adventurer's decline. But as we have seen, Waugh's sense of crisis—of belatedness and approaching impotence—was a component of the traveler's anxiety rather than its baleful diagnosis. Travels multiplied exponentially; and travelogues also flourished, impelled like their guidebook counterparts by an ever-expanding tourist industry. Whatever losses the crisis of modernism precipitated, travel and its adjunct, the travel book, have hardly been among them. But why not? How is it that travel writing has continued to flourish, only gaining in prestige? This study has sought to reflect on these compelling questions. Summarizing those reflections, we have suggested that contemporary travel writing has answered Waugh's challenge by invoking a number of late-capitalist cultural possibilities. Three of these are notable, and can be briefly recapitulated here: commodification, specialization, and nostalgic parody.

The inexorable cultural mechanism of commodification works symbiotically with textuality: with writing, as with a whole host of other media forms (film, video, computer graphics, artistic and photographic images, and so forth). However strenuously the travel text might attempt to decommodify travel—to recuperate its "authenticity"—it presents itself to a world that the travel industry has played a major role in referencing to the global. The global field emerges not so much as a two-dimensional, chartable surface but rather as a set of interlocking—specialized but also readily accessible—spaces: exotic zones, adventure terrains, hedonistic playgrounds, interactive museums, political mazes, "new" frontiers, and so on. The late-capitalist process of hypercommodification involves the production of commodities that are commodifying in their turn—such as travel and the travel book. Many travel books, of course, are little more than advertising vehicles, commodifying their respective terrains as a means of selling their second-level products. But even those books— and there are also many—that seek to disrupt the flow of the market invariably show their complicity with it (as might also be said, of course, of this particular study!). This is not a call for dismissal, but rather an invitation to analysis—an analysis that takes account of the resilience of travel texts. Such resilience can be seen, for example, in the appeal to specialized kinds of travelers. Among those we have identified in this book are (postcolonial) countertravelers, resisting the history and cultural myths of Eurocentrism; women travelers, subverting the male traveler's traditional values and privileges; gay male travelers, either seeking liberatory spaces or flouting heterosexual travel codes; and ecological travelers, reacting against the environmental damage that they most frequently associate with tourists. Such special-interest groups generally locate themselves in opposition to "conventional" modes of travel, particularly tourism; this oppositional stance provides a further alibi for travel writing while still depending on its traditions and its—not least, commercial—cachet. Together with the invention of new models for the traveler (the postmodern nomad, the virtual traveler) and the traveled world (the global village, hyperreality), these guises—or, more accurately, *dis*guises—have produced a spawn of recent travel narratives while conveying the illusion of all but endless travel/writing possibilities. In invoking a specialized mission, these writers often appeal to the reader's yearning for a kind of countertravel to assuage their heightened (Western, postmodern) guilt. Countertravel, of one sort or another, has certainly energized travel writing and, increasingly, travel theory in the decades since the war. Yet such oppositional narratives cannot escape being haunted by an array of hoary tropes and clichés (originary, primitivist, exotic, etc.), any more than they can hope to distill "authentic" encounters from their commodified sources.

Specialization, the several forms of countertravel, might have been expected to put Waugh's old-fashioned travel adventurism out of business. But it has not done so. On the contrary, English imperial questing—or more or less self-conscious parodies of it—continues to form the basis of many a recent traveler's tale. In such tales, as we have seen, a surface gesture to self-parody barely conceals a deep nostalgia for obsolete empires and manly discoverer-explorers. This, it seems, is a subgenre that lends itself to endless replication. Many readers continue to find exercises of even the most basic kind (say, Newby's) hilariously funny, as parodies of any developed genre can often prove to be; but even writers aiming for some more complex response than the belly laugh tend to produce moments of parody and self-indulgence, perhaps to disarm that shifting line known to all travelers who *tell*: the line where recounted episode sinks into repeated cliché. But then repeated cliché sometimes appears to be the stuff of travel writing, a commodity that cries out to be purchased and consumed and purchased again. It is as if this cycle of production, consumption, and reproduction were at the genre's core; and as if repetition were the paradoxical gesture that both marked and warded off the risk of its demise.

It is hardly surprising, then, that Waugh's postwar premonitions about travel and writing are currently being repeated on the edge of the third millennium. Countless writers—from erudite scholars to sensation-seeking journalists—seem to assume that the world is poised at a crucial, epoch-making moment. This moment is spatial, as well as temporal, the product of boundary marking; confusion over where exactly to place the millennial moment reflects the shifting borders of the contemporary political world. Similarly, the times through which we are moving, whether with hope or in despair, carry no essential dates, no definitively demarcating stages. The world's millennial moment cannot be revealed as if by magic; the world is less in progress (or in regress) than it is in process.

Millennial discourses usually invoke two registers. On the one hand, there is the register of decisive ends and beginnings: the "end of history" (Fukuyama); the beginning of "global culture." On the other, there is the register of process: of emergence and rise, of fall and exhaustion. Both registers, however much they reference postwar/postmodern intellectual trends (the paradigm shifts of Thomas Kuhn, for example, or the world-systems theory of Immanuel Wallerstein), seem to risk miring the traveler in the well-worn tracks of Western thought, with past matched against future, East against West, center against margins, atavistic tribalism against progressive globalism, apocalyptic dread against millennial optimism, and so on. And it is within these all-too-familiar, frequently stereotypical parameters that the current debates surrounding travel and travel writing are often placed.

A glance, for instance, at the relevant *Guardian Weekly* files from the midnineties reveals a startling unanimity among British travelers, travel writers, and reviewers on the subject of travel. It might seem inherently silly to ask a question like "where is travel/travel writing going?" But asked the question is and, increasingly, answered: "nowhere; don't move; just stay at home." While the general (postmodern) malaise of belatedness encourages inertia, the specific forms it takes—political resistance, postcolonial guilt, antitouristic distaste—can produce something stronger: a revulsion from travel. Catherine Bennett, for example, one of the contributors to the *Guardian Weekly* debate, seeks an explanation for "[w]hy the right people choose to stay at home" by excoriating the travel industry itself. For Bennett, the industry's glossy brochures strike all the right exotic chords, inviting clients, say, to indulge their postimperial fantasies in Burma (Myanmar) from the insulated space of the appropriately fabular cruise ship *The Road to Mandalay*. These brochures say nothing, of course, about child exploitation, forced labor, the torture of dissidents, and the persecution of opposition leaders in countries like Myanmar. And although some guidebooks (in trendy series like Lonely Planet) do refer to such unsavory features, they tend to do so in what Bennett calls inappropriately "jaunty" terms. The Lonely Planet "Myanmar," for instance, mentions "hav[ing] heard tell [there] of a smorgasbord of dictators, anti-government rebels, guerrillas, insurgents, and assorted malcontents"—an unruly hodgepodge of troublemakers that merely makes travel in that country more compelling. Bennett quotes tellingly from the guidebook: "[Myanmar] offers a glimpse of an incredibly Orwellian society. . . . We believe—now more than ever— that the positives of travel to Myanmar outweigh the negatives" (qtd. in Bennett 30).

Bennett avoids the usual classificatory markers—group/individual tourist, "alternative" backpacker, and so on—that might allow her to justify a superior kind of travel; instead, she blames the increasing thirst for travel in "difficult and bewildering territory" on the romantic travelogues of writers like Thubron, Chatwin, and Raban, correctly if uncharacteristically acknowledging the link between "high literary" travel narratives and their "lowly" counterparts, the guidebook and the tourist brochure. Rounding off her brief commentary, Bennett offers the caustic judgment that "most travelers bring back nothing more useful than tarnished jewellery from their expeditions into the lands of contrast. It seems like a small justification for . . . callous curiosity" (30). And, collapsing travel with travel writing, she goes on to quote from Robyn Davidson: "I think perhaps the whole genre needs to close. . . . We all carry a lot of cultural prejudices, and I just don't feel comfortable with it" (30). It seems to have escaped Bennett's attention, though, that Davidson is making a different point; for while the former is implying that travelers should embargo such territories as Myanmar and Iran as a form of political dissociation, the latter is caught up in something quite distinct, a version of liberal cultural guilt. Bennett's high-handed dismissal overlooks the fact that travel to "other" countries opens up, at least potentially, an opportunity for considered self-reflection—it offers a chance, that is, to interrogate and negotiate, if not eliminate, both the traveler's cultural prejudices and those of the peoples he or she encounters.

In her own contribution to the *Guardian Weekly* debate, Davidson, respected author of *Tracks* and *Desert Places* (see chap. 3), recounts how she came to see herself as a cultural "invader." Davidson's confession fails, however, into some of the usual traps. She endorses the myth that tourists are, by definition, people who "impose home environments on a foreign place"—as if, by implication, travelers do not—but she does express some sympathy, that rare commodity, for the tourist: "It's a bit much to ask people who have three weeks holiday a year to spend it struggling with the confusions of an alien place, or to put up with discomforts when what they have earned is rest" (27). Is Davidson, with perverse magnanimity, doing herself out of a job here? Apparently not, for the solution she offers to the tourist's quandary is the travel *book:*

> If literature was a compensation for the problems created by civilisation, then perhaps books provide us with a way out. Reading is like taking a journey. It's an entry into another world, another consciousness. It can satisfy curiosity, educate, excite imagination. There are too many of us: there are too many books. Ergo, stay home and read (27).

However frankly Davidson might disabuse herself of some of the recurrent myths of travel— the one, for instance, that leads the lonely, enterprising, hardship-enduring pioneer to wax self-righteous on encountering signs of others' invasions—she leaves herself at the end with the travel writer's standard escape clause: namely, she will continue to travel and to produce further literary journeys in order to satisfy that most insatiable (and most convenient) of consumers, the "armchair traveler."

Ian Sansom, another contributor to the *Guardian Weekly* symposium, produces a similarly double-edged review of a recent anthology of travel fictions. Such travel stories, Sansom suggests, might be taken along as holiday reading, but then again "the mass-market middlebrow paperback . . . is the modern *vade mecum* for a journey" (28). Sansom's skepticism about travel targets the figure of the traveler himself/herself, a figure who is always liable to return from trips arrogant and wasted. At best, according to Sansom, travel is futile, unduly bothersome:

> Travel, etymologically, is identical with "travail"; they share a common root in the Latin *trepaliare*, meaning "to torture with a *trepalium*, a three-staked instrument of torture." There's no denying it, travel is a pain—you're better off staying at home, reading. (28)

Tongue similarly in cheek, Veronica Horwell, also a reviewer for *Guardian Weekly*, acidly observes that "we lost an empire and gained The Traveller's Bookshop" (28).

Sansom, discounting the potential of travel to diffuse (and also defuse?) the traveling subject, underlines the "terrible truth that confronts any travel writer": "you can run but you can't hide; you can pretend to be someone else, but you can't escape yourself; you may be moving through a landscape, but it's still you who's moving through it" (28). An obvious but still interesting theorem, one that the travel books of Paul Theroux might confirm; and one that Sansom, as in his comments on travel as travail and pain, raises without inflection, with no apparent connection to issues of postcoloniality, postmodernity, or even "post-tourism" (Feifer). Sansom's theorem, nonetheless, usefully suggests the topos of *exhaustion*. There is literal exhaustion, of course, where the traveler runs out of steam or the destination is crowded out. But an end-of-century and, especially, an end-of-millennium view is more likely to indicate less literal forms of exhaustion, to point to the ways in which travel and travel writing participate in hypertextual exhaustions, where both subject and world are construed as postcolonial, postmodern, "posthistoric." Significantly, though, the *Guardian Weekly* writers cited above (with the possible exception of Catherine Bennett) take care to reserve a last place for travel writing—and thus for travel writers. Their collective advice is to stay home, because there is nowhere left to go, because travel is essentially futile, because "correct" people do not travel. But they then displace travel itself onto the travel book, which apparently—or so they see it—offers a "purer" form of journey. In this way they manage, in spite of themselves, to reinstate some threadbare distinctions: between the traveler and the tourist, between both of these and the travel writer. Travel writing's value as commodity rises as that of travel itself falls.

Sallie Tisdale, whose personal perspective on pornography, *Talk Dirty to Me: An Intimate Philosophy of Sex* (1994), gained her some notoriety, has recently recommended that even travel writers are best off staying home. Tisdale's long piece in *Harper's*, "Never Let the Locals See Your Map," purports to be a review article covering eight travel books, but the article soon turns into a wide-ranging discussion of travel writing that canvasses a number of issues currently under debate. The article exhibits ambivalent attitudes. On the one hand, Tisdale follows Evelyn Waugh, Paul Fussell, and others in lamenting the exhausted possibility for "genuine" travel and the sad decline of the travel book: whereas "[t]ravel books were [once] shiny with promise—informing and diverting in good measure," now, in contrast, although "travel literature is booming," "good travel writers are few and far between" (66). Since her travelers of promise turn out to include such household favorites as Robert Byron and Eric Newby, Tisdale alerts us to the link between the notion of exhaustion and the barely concealed motivation for a good deal of travel writing: nostalgia. Decrying a cult of personal idiosyncrasy in the travel writer, Tisdale decides that "[t]oday, true travel writing—the lyrical account of an adventure marked by curiosity and courage rather than showmanship— scarcely exists" (67). As if neither Byron nor Newby enlists idiosyncrasy or showmanship in his narratives! It is worth noting again (see the introduction) that this type of lament for "true" travel writing can be used to *promote*, rather than discourage, the circulation of contemporary travel narratives.

Tisdale falls short, however, of simply endorsing Fussell, whose second major thesis is the necessity of distinguishing the "true" traveler from the tourist. While she agrees that "a particular distinction between travel and tourism marks modern travel writing," it is a fine distinction, and "all travel writers think they know where it is—far from themselves" (67). One function the contemporary travel book serves, then, is to flatter readers who "wish to separate [themselves] from the rabble," to identify themselves as bona fide travelers, not vulgar tourists. In dismantling this distinction, Tisdale makes an ingenious move: she argues that the traveler's professed desire to "pass" is fundamentally dishonest, because he or she is also yearning to be noticed, to stand out: "Travelers dissociate themselves from tourists not because tourists are noticed but because they are *not*. . . . tourists are the least intrusive travelers of all" (72). For Tisdale, it is not tourists who give offense but contemporary travel writers, who strive (seemingly in panic) to purvey "authentic" experience. Travel narratives, Tisdale concludes, may well discourage not only tourists but also "purer" travelers. Marred though her essay is by its nostalgic appeal to a history of "true" travel, Tisdale's association of exhaustion with the commodification of the dream of "authentic experience" needs to be taken seriously. It is hardly surprising, in this context, that a number of recent travel books make their pitch to the "traveler [who] grows ever more desperate for pure experience, something *authentic*" (72); nor is it surprising that this ideal traveler is more likely to be a reader.[1]

This quest for "authenticity" is, as will be clear by now, curiously fraught. It seeks to engage further frontiers that are, by definition, exotic. These frontiers are at extremities: of the map; of the Western, metropolitan world; of historical regimes; of fully grounded worldly experience.[2] There is seldom any doubt, though, that the frontier is out there somewhere: as one writer puts it, "beyond the last tollbooth on the last scrap of potholed pavement at the very end of the turnpike" (Millman 239). The frontier exists in the future, beckoning, enticing, seducing. Yet it is also chimerical, vanishing, already extinguished as soon as reached (see discussion of the exotic travel zone in chapter 2). Tisdale formulates the conundrum neatly: the traveler "wanders the back roads, then writes his book so that everyone will know what matters most: not to be the first to see remote lands, but to be the last to see the land remote" (72). The traveler-writer attests to having been there last, and to having turned out the lights on leaving. All the lights but one: the bedside lamp that allows the reader to accompany the author into the always-receding territory of the exotic. While there is nothing intrinsically harmful in the transactions between traveler, writer, and reader that satisfy individual fantasies of discovery, exploration, and exotic experience, the relationship of such fantasies to collective geopolitical practices of control, exploitation, and subjugation is problematic at best.

The end-of-millennium commentary just examined illustrates the dilemma. This commentary, offered through a series of book reviews and articles, makes clear that it is the genre itself, rather than the work of any individual writer, that is at stake. For, as Tisdale says, travel writing has proliferated as "travel has burgeoned" within a global, media-driven economy (72); as the genre has "become . . . a way of life, a way of seeing the world" (67); and as it has begun to formulate its protocols, to shape a canon for itself. No doubt Paul Fussell's study *Abroad* has been instrumental in suggesting not only criteria for a serious canon but also individual "landmark" works. Evidence of a travel-writing canon, and of its importance to the marketing of travel books as both supplementary to and an alternative form of travel, can be seen in the recent establishment of the "Picador Travel Classics." This is a series that partly announces the classic status—the canonicity—of its volumes through their hardback covers, their introductions, and their numbering—they are intended to form a library.[3] This canonizing impulse is foreshadowed in Ian Pearson's article in *Destinations*, the travel section of the Toronto *Globe and Mail* (November 1992): "Around the World in 6,000 Pages. A Guide to the Ultimate in Armchair Journeys." Pearson is unsure whether classic travel writing is literary privilege or salvage mission, its primary function being to "preserve" the "truly great journeys" in books, even while the "serendipitous adventure is becoming harder and harder to achieve as the juggernaut of massive tourism levels the planet" (15). But whether they are mandarins of a superior order or merely last-ditch rescuers, the mainly British, postwar "club" members all find themselves represented: Byron, Leigh Fermor, Lewis, Thesiger, Newby, O'Hanlon, Raban, Theroux, Chatwin—and one woman, Dervla Murphy.[4] Literary credentials are strengthened by the inclusion of such older works as Kinglake's *Eothen* (1844), Twain's *The Innocents Abroad* (1869), and Stevenson's *Travels with a Donkey* (1879). Pearson leaves the reader in little doubt that travel writing is a consolidated genre, with its acknowledged classics—its founding monuments—and its rapidly expanding membership; and that it has achieved respectability as a (Western) cultural product by moving off the beaten paths of travel into the rarefied sphere of "high" literature. Henceforth— or so the formula runs—every ambitious travel narrative will have to situate itself in relation to its literary precursors even before it gets to the starting line. The tacit message here is that travel is a primarily textual activity; and that in an age of depletion and exhaustion, writing is "better" then experience.

To publish, or retrospectively place, an individual writer's book within a named series already gestures toward the canonical by proclaiming the work's affiliation with a supposedly identifiable, and already validated, group. (The Picador Classics imprint assumes both the patent existence of the "travel classic" and the purchaser's automatic assent to the volumes' "classic" status.) Some readers of travelogues might be predisposed to favor certain imprints or series, knowing, like seasoned travelers perhaps, what kind of thing they want. The dust jackets and back covers of travel books are also witness to the process and function of canon formation. You can see the "club" at work as established authors write blurbs congratulating one another, or signaling a probationary acceptance for lesser-known writers. One of these latter might be hailed as a "true successor" to Redmond O'Hanlon, another as a "stylish descendant" of Robert Byron, a third as an "eagle-eyed observer" of the absurd, like Paul Theroux.[5] The blurb industry, an indispensable agent in moving books off the store table and into consumers' hands, always risks discrediting itself; after all, some readers are more likely to see blurbs as revealing, not the candid opinions of experts, but the interested gestures, insider friendships, and mutual puffery of a handful of card-carrying club members.[6] At this point, prestigious literary prizes (like the Thomas Cook Award) become useful supports, supplying the travel-writing business with a regulated set of "impartial" endorsements. As with other elements in the travel-writing infrastructure, such prizes validate not only the single, notable instance but the genre as a whole, which emerges worthily as a stable yet expanding entity.

The expansion of travel writing as genre, particularly in the cities for urban audiences, arguably serves to counteract the discourse of exhaustion. The travel sections of major newspapers, as well as journals like *Granta* and *Condé Nast*, work continuously to recuperate and reinvigorate travel in a format that blurs the distinction between activity and text and (even when it seems to invoke it) between traveler and tourist. These travel sections offer practical instruction for those who seek to be "active"; responding to inquiries about equipment for "tramping" New Zealand wildernesses or about the cheapest way to Tibet, they rehearse the travelogue in personal profiles of particular places or, playing up the travel-as-literature angle, they include brief reviews of travel books. A quick survey of the substantial "Travel Books" column in the "Travel" section of the *Toronto Globe and Mail* over a period of some weeks in 1996 confirms that travel can be marketed as replenishment and innovation, whether in guidebooks, travel narratives, or anthologies of shorter travel accounts. Laszlo Buhasz, for example, recommends Jim Haynes's *People to People* "guides to eastern European countries," which are "directories of people . . . who speak English or another western European language, are from professions ranging from medicine to engineering, and who are willing to house, guide or help visitors to their countries"; Haynes, effuses Buhasz, "is trying to transform tourists into travellers. Good for him" (August 14, 1996). Buhasz also notes that *Arthur Frommer's New World of Travel* "deals with a rapidly growing demand for alternative ideas by spirited, intellectually curious travellers tired of mass-produced vacation packages," and quotes from Frommer's preface: "After 30 years of writing standard travel guide books, I began to see that most of the vacation journeys undertaken by Americans were trivial and bland, devoid of important content, cheaply commercial, and unworthy of our better instincts and ideals" (March 23, 1996). Anthologies, too, seek to recuperate and reinvigorate travel. Buhasz commends the Travelers' Tales series (edited by James O'Reilly and Larry Habegger) for their "articulate explanation of the difference between travel guides and travel literature," a difference apparently marked by the latter's emphasis on experience and story. According to O'Reilly and Habegger, travelers need to be prepared, "with feelings and fears, hopes and dreams, goals. . . . Nothing can replace listening to the experience of others, to the war stories that come out after a few drinks, to the memories that linger and beguile" (February 10, 1996). The *Travelers' Tales* editors clearly throw their pitch to those who plan to use travel texts as an overture to travel, as a preparation for the real thing.

As suggested throughout this study, neither travel itself nor the travel book exists in isolation; in the symbiosis between them, it is less a matter of seeing one as "superior" than of seeing each as a supplement to the other: the travel account as a companion to actual travel, the travel itinerary as supplementary to its texts. Eric Korn, in a recent *TLS* article, suggests that supplementarity can take positions of "before," "after," and "instead":

> I went to Marrakech because I read *The Alleys of Marrakech*; I went to Cannery Row because I read *Cannery Row*. . . . On the other hand I returned from Haiti late in Papa Doc's time, read *The Comedians* and discovered . . . just where I'd been, who had been sitting in my chair, sleeping in my bed, floating in my swimming-pool. In retrospect (the best way to enjoy abroad), a deeper tint of danger coloured my rather placid trip. . . . On the third hand, I didn't go to Borneo . . . and have given the Yanomami a wide berth, because I read Redmond O'Hanlon. (36)

Various mechanisms continue to enforce a distinction between actual, degraded, "post-touristic" travel and "purer" forms of travel, not of course as a means of actively discouraging travel, but rather of replenishing it by appealing to untainted motivations and higher ideals. The material continuity between higher and lower forms of travel is evident in most bookstores, where the shelves filled with travel guides are adjacent to those, almost as many, carrying travelogues. The Lonely Planet imprint, among others, has begun to exploit this overlap by establishing a sister series, Lonely Planet Journeys, which converts the raw material of travel guides into more "literary" travel accounts. This travelogue series, like its guidebook counterpart, is clearly aimed at the lifestyle and mindset of self-styled "offbeat" travelers and "irreverent" backpackers. The following summary, for instance, is taken from the cover of the first in the series, Sean Condon's *Sean and David's Long Drive* (1996):

Sean Condon is young, urban and a connoisseur of hair-wax. He can't drive, and he doesn't really travel well.

So when Sean and his friend set out to explore Australia in a duck-egg blue 1966 Ford Falcon, the result is a decidedly offbeat look at life on the road. Over 14,000 death-defying kilometers, our heroes check out the re-runs on TV, get fabulously drunk, listen to Neil Young and wonder why they ever left home.

Sean and David's Long Drive mixes sharp insights with deadpan humour and outright lies. Crank it up and read it out loud.

Another in the series, Annie Caulfield's *Kingdom of the Film Stars* (1997), takes the reader (according to a brief newspaper notice) "through a jolly romp through contemporary Jordan. As you'd expect from a long-time television comedy-script writer . . ., Caulfield always sees the funny side of things. And there's plenty to laugh at: struggling with her toilette in the middle of the Jordanian desert, dealing with the 'Marlboro Boys' and their horses at the foot of the ruins at Petra." Aficionados of the popular Lonely Planet "Travel Survival Kit" series will be familiar with the travelogues' jocular, wryly self-ingratiating tone. But the publishers also acknowledge a more significant point, namely that the transparent "fictions" of travelogues are closely intertwined with the guidebook's hard "facts." Their spaces overlap; you can stay home with the Lonely Planet "Australia" kit or you can "overland" with Sean and David— both books serve as facilitators of the actual process of travel while locating the traveler fair and square within a set of (Western) travel myths.[7]

Clearly, the culture and media industries are continuing to mobilize travel in its widest sense, both activating and responding to mainstream, overwhelmingly metropolitan avidity to experience—or, rather, purchase—the greatest range of global commodities. Among those commodities are, of course, the ideologies and collective fantasies of the West, in particular America, Britain, the white diaspora in Canada, Australia, New Zealand, and South Africa, parts of Europe and, increasingly—though in a different form—the countries of the Pacific Rim. As the millennium approaches, the fetishizing of the moment in terms of "end of and "dawn of," of (pessimistic) apocalypticism and (optimistic) global progress, is ubiquitous. Some travel writing, particularly the strand that crosses over into political journalism, seems well attuned to geopolitical hysteria, the obverse of global optimism. The work of the American writer Robert D. Kaplan—*Balkan Ghosts* (1993), "The Coming Anarchy" (1994), and, most recently, *The Ends of the Earth: A Journey at the Dawn of the 20th Century* (1996)—is worth considering at some length here because of the eagerness with which many readers have embraced his vision of the Balkans and the Third World. A blurb for the paperback edition acclaims *The Ends of the Earth* as "a terrifying journey around what is both the rim and the center of the world," a journey that "describes, in haunting detail, the abyss on which so much of the world teeters." Where Kaplan's Balkan chronicle had specified a local instance of breakdown, and his *Atlantic Monthly* article had generalized the terrain and deepened the despair, the last item in his trilogy fits in somewhere between, with the journey moving from Africa through Central Asia and ending up in the Indian subcontinent and Indochina, and with Kaplan attempting to balance a sense of the abyss with tentative hope. Overall though, Kaplan's work evokes "The Second Coming" in its remorseless apocalyptic gloom, and it seems likely that the title of his article "The Coming Anarchy" was intended to stir an echo of Yeats's famously doom-laden poem.

Kaplan himself labels *The Ends of the Earth* a "travel book," "a premodern generalist's book that mixes history and other subjects in with travel," and is written "in the style of John Gunther, not Paul Theroux" (preface, n.p.). Using Gunther and Theroux to represent opposing extremes of the travel book seems at first to be a useful move: Gunther's "*Inside . . .*" series establishes these "insides" through an accumulation of facts and statistics, largely erasing any sense of a traveling, perceiving subject, whereas Theroux foregrounds a subject who constitutes place precisely through his unstable "outsider" presence. But the distinction is hardly that simple, and Kaplan's narrative, far from locking on factual details, floats between alternative means of recording and registering cultural difference. At one point, Kaplan claims that, to optimize knowledge of the "other," the traveler should go on foot:

> In an air-conditioned four-wheel-drive Toyota Land Cruiser—the medium through which senior diplomats and top Western relief officials often encounter Africa—suspended high above the road and looking out through closed windows, your forehead and underarms comfortably dry, you may learn something about Africa. Traveling in a crowded public bus, flesh pressed upon wet, sour flesh, you learn more; and in a "bush taxi," or "mammy wagon," where there are not even windows, you learn even more still. But it is on foot that you learn the most. You are on the ground, on the same level with Africans rather than looking down at them. You are no longer protected by speed or air-conditioning or thick glass. The sweat pours from you, and your shirt sticks to your body. This is how you learn. (25)

Kaplan's apparent aim is to move through Africa on the level, presenting a sequence of experiential encounters whose "authenticity" is guaranteed by the rejection of insulating media (speed, windows, air conditioning, etc.). Yet this smacks (as it so often does in this type of narrative) of disingenuousness; as a seasoned American journalist moving freely on the international circuit, Kaplan frequently capitalizes on reliable and expensive transport, on comfortable, protected lodging and, especially, on the kind of personal contacts only available to the privileged Westerner.

In spite of distancing himself from the kind of self-absorbed travel associated with Theroux, Kaplan, in his account, makes use of several similar materials and techniques. For example, like Theroux, Kaplan works up the personal encounter or interview. When a man approaches him on the road, inviting recognition, Kaplan has to think hard before he recalls having met him the previous day. Kaplan remembers that the man, seeing him without change, had offered to pay for his Coke: "Though I had thanked him profusely only yesterday, today he was at first glance just another black face, another of my statistics" (26). Here, however, a major difference between Theroux and Kaplan emerges, for where the former would likely disarm the episode of sentimental potential, the latter makes it stand, somewhat improbably, for universal prospects: "To see individuals, I realized, was to see possibilities and, thus, more hopeful scenarios" (26).

Kaplan also shares with Theroux—and with a great many other contemporary travel writers—an impulse to keep (inter)textual layers between himself and what he is reporting. Kaplan's citations range from C. P. Cavafy to the Lonely Planet series, from Thomas Malthus to Thomas Mann, from Joseph Conrad to Barry Lopez, from Richard Burton to Bruce Chatwin.[8] It seems as if Kaplan has less confidence in what observation and interaction can achieve than his comments about traveling on foot might suggest. He confesses, at any rate, that he "read a lot" in preparation for his various tours (95). And then, surprisingly, he enlists such reading to distance himself from tourists: "In an age of mass tourism, adventure becomes increasingly an inner matter, where reading can transport you to places that others only a few feet away will never see" (96). It also suggests the achievement of an existential authenticity: "The more I read about a place and about issues that affect it, the more I feel I am traveling alone" (95).

While Kaplan's dense allusiveness and cultivated sensitivity align his travel with Theroux's, his anxiety to assign causes to the various regional malaises he witnesses links his work more closely with Gunther's.[9] Here, encounter narrative yields to data and written history. But neither of these can satisfy Kaplan's relentless search for causes, and his narrative returns addictively to—largely undeveloped—general theories. Africa is trapped in atavism (Kaplan entitles the section, "Back to the Dawn?") and enervation. "Nature," Kaplan observes, "appeared far too prolific in this heat, and much of what she created spoiled quickly" (19). Africa is a place of "passivity, fatalistic and defeated" (24), racked by overpopulation and disease, and lost in a kind of "premodern formlessness" (45). Even climate and geography point to violence and atrophy: "When you read the history of Sierra Leone you cannot help but realize how much the past was decreed by geography and climate" (48). The travel account swerves into disaster journalism. "Causes" become too "natural" ("blood," "heat," "tribalism," "the forest") or too pseudoscientific (overpopulation, disease, boundary problems) to engage. Such "causes" work against the production of useful analysis. The constant deployment of vivid metaphor, in which such natural phenomena as seeds, eruptions, and conflagrations produce cultural effects, occludes both historical terms and the consideration of economics and politics: those of the states and territories themselves, and those of powerful international interests and institutions.

In "explaining" what he sees in the Third World, Kaplan returns obsessively to a key formula. "Geography is destiny" (130) is not only Kaplan's personal motto; it is also a kind of shorthand for Western traveler-observers whose accounts of the countries through which they move substitute easy myths for hard analysis. Kaplan's speculations about Iran in *The Ends of the Earth* are symptomatic:

> [W]ere more of Iran—rather than just its north and northwest border provinces—graced by the moist and moderating influences of the Caspian, then perhaps the history and character of the Iranian people would have been very different, and the transformation of an airplane cabin into a veritable mosque would never have occurred. (176)

But geography's edicts are complicated by other universalizing structures, which lead Kaplan in turn to a number of portentous statements and questions: "The story of man is the story of nomadism" (130); "rural poverty is age-old and consistent with an ever-turning planet" (107); and, most egregiously perhaps, "the condition of a country's public toilets—or the lack of them—says something about its progress toward civil society" (274)! On the other hand, as Kaplan admits, "No-one can foresee the precise direction of history, and no nation and people is safe from its wrath" (438). Harmonizing such a cacophony of explanation is no easy matter. What is the relation between the human "story of nomadism" and "progress toward civil society"? How can we protect "a country's public toilets" from the wrathful judgment of an implacable history? In Freetown, Kaplan says, "I wished I had been younger and more naive, and that I was not addicted to political analysis" (43). Yet it is precisely firm political analysis, from any perspective, that seems to be missing, as Kaplan's text repeatedly entraps itself in a kind of apocalyptic banality:

> The end was nigh in the failed battle, fought valiantly by the liberal West, to equalize cultures around the world. The differences between some cultures and others (regarding the ability to produce exportable material wealth) appeared to be growing rather than diminishing. (54)

Platitudes like these render statements such as "Africa . . . has to be confronted" (25) opaque to the point of futility.

Kaplan's title phrase, "the ends of the earth," is oddly anachronistic, belying the awareness he otherwise shows of global shrinkage; while the subtitle, "a journey at the dawn of the 21st century," hints at an exploration of newness that flies in the face of the text's tired stereotypes and despair at the possibility of prediction. Kaplan's stated aim is to "map the future, perhaps the 'deep future,' by ignoring what was legally and officially there and, instead, touching, feeling, and smelling what was really *there*" (6); but his conclusion is that "the effect of culture was more of a mystery to me near the end of my planetary journey than at the beginning" (425). Kaplan's journey of political travel ends in all kinds of exhaustion: the exhaustion of the traveler, of the terrains and cultures he has traversed, of the textual effects of travel—and, perhaps, of the reader. Such a journey might perhaps more accurately be described as a "midnight" (of the twentieth century) than as a "dawn" (of the twenty-first).[10]

Notes

1   For other comments on Tisdale's provocative article, see Krotz, 183–84.
2   Variations on this theme include Millman, *Last Places* (1990); Middleton, *The Last Disco in Outer Mongolia* (1992); Winchester, *Outposts* (1985); and Iyer, *Falling Off the Map* (1993).
3   Robert Byron's *The Road to Oxiana*, volume 2 in the series, carries an introduction by Chatwin; the founding volume is Apsley Cherry-Garrard's *The Worst Journey in the World*.
4   The omission of women's texts from Pearson's selection seems to bear out Tisdale's observation about the classic travel book, that it is "a little bit sacred and masculine. It despises the masses and loves the unbeaten track, the self-imposed but public exile" (67). See chapter 3 of this book for an extended discussion of masculine models and paradigms in travel writing.
5   The phenomenon is so widespread that it seems pointless to provide specific examples.
6   The practice among leading writers of introducing their colleagues or friends, and then staging encounters with them in their travelogues, is surely an elaboration of the courtesies of the blurb.
7   Lonely Planet is apparently expanding in all directions. Another newspaper article observes, "They're on the Internet, of course, and now on our television screens. . . . You can't help but like [the presenter] Ian Wright. He's a great Lonely Planet man. Try anything once. And perfect for Alaska which, as Wright told us, is a wild place. Full of moose, the cause of some rather manufactured anxiety for Wright" (*New Zealand Herald,* February 19, 1997, B10). Even the newspaper plug assumes the flippant Lonely Planet tone.
8   The chapter on Africa makes considerable use of Joseph Conrad and Graham Greene, though not, surprisingly, of V. S. Naipaul. However, it clearly "reads" Africa from within the Conrad-Naipaul tradition (see Nixon, *London Calling*; also chap. 2 of this book).
9   Kaplan protests that "mine would be an unsentimental journey [unlike that of Laurence Sterne]. My impressions might be the 'wrong' ones to have, but they would be based on what I saw" (11); later, he asserts that he is "a time traveler, but not necessarily a romantic one. . . . I chart places where a literary tourist would rarely go" (131). *The Ends of the Earth*, nonetheless, is saturated with literary references; despite his attempts to provide alibis, Kaplan ultimately invites recognition as sentimental traveler, literary tourist, and adventurer-precisely the models of the traveler he wishes to disclaim.
10 For a recent, coruscating critique of Kaplan's work, which sees its "prognoses of disintegration" as possibly "testing conservative waters for the depths of a reemergent positivist racism," see Brennan, *At Home in the World*, 125–27. As Brennan argues, Kaplan's "rhetoric of fear and loathing" is "entirely at odds with mainstream humanities discourse" (126). But as will be clear from this book, it is not at odds with a certain strand of "political" travel writing, which uses the genre to justify—although also, in some cases, to ironize—xenophobic sentiments and cultural myths. Sophisticated examples of this form of political travelogue are the "African" and "Indian" works of V. S. Naipaul (see chaps. 1 and 2).

Works cited

Ascherson. Neil *Black Sea: The Birthplare of Civilisation and Barbarism*. London: Vintage. 1996.

Bennett. Catherine. "Why the Right People Choose to Stay at Home" *Guardian Weekly*. June 23. 1996. 30.

Bourke. Chris. "Have Imagination. Will Travel Jonathan Raban: The Studious Englishman Abroad." *New Zealand Listener*, April 12–18, 1997. 46–47.

Brennan. Timothy. *St Home in the World: Cosmopolitanism Now. Cambridge*. Mass: Harvard University Press, 19997.

Buhasz. Laszlo. "An Introspective South Pacific Voyage." *Toronto Globe and Mail*. June 27. 1992. n.p.

Byron. Robert. *The Road to Oxiana* 1937. London: Picador Travel Classics. 1994. Cahill. Tim. *Jaguars Ripped My Flesh*. New York: Vintage, 1996.

Carrington. Dorothy. *The Dream Hunters of Corsica*. London: Weidenfeld and Nicolson. 1995.

Caulfield. Annie. *Kingdom of the Film Stars*. Melbourne: Lonely Planet. 1997.

Cherry-Garrard. Apsley. *The Warst Journey in the World*. London: Constable, 1922.

Condon, Sean. *Sean and David's Long Drive*. Melbourne: Lonely Planet, 1996.

Davidson. Robyn. *Desert Places*. New York: Viking. 1996.

—. "Walk on the Wild Side." *Guardian Weekly*. August 4, 1996. n.p.

Feifer. Maxine. *Going Places: The Ways of the Tourist from Imperial Rome to the Present Day*. London: Macmillan, 1985.

Fukuyama. Francis. *The End of Hist and the Last Man*. New York: Free Press. 1992.

Fussell. Paul *Abroad: British Literary Traveling between the Wars*. Oxford: Oxford University Press. 1980.

Horwell. Veronica. "Sensibility on a Grand Tour." *Guardian Weekly,* July 14, 1996.

Iyer. Pico. *Falling Off the Map: Some Lonely Places of the World*. Toronto: Knopf Canada. 1993.

Kaplan. Robert D. *Balkan Ghosts: A Journey through History*. New York: St, Martin's Press. 1993.

—. "The Coming Anarchy: How Seareity. Crime. Overpopulation. Tribalism. and Disease Are Rapidly Destroying the Social Fabne of Our Planet" *Atlantic Monthly*. February 1994. 44–76.

—. *The end of the Earth: A Journey at the Dawn of 20th Century*. New York: Random House. 1996.

Kinglake. Alexander. *Eothen*. 1844 Evanston. III Marlboro Press 1996.

Korn. Fric. "Shelf-Travelling." *Times Literary Supplement*. July 26. 1996. 36.

Krotz, Larry. *Tourists: How Our Fastest Growing Industry Is Changing the World*. London: Faber and Faber. 1996.

Lampedusa. Giuseppe. *The Leopard* 1957. Trans Archibald Colquhoun. New York: Knopf. 1991.

Middleton. Nick. *The Last Disco in Outer Mongolia*. London: Sinclair-Stevenson, 1992.

Millman. Lawrence. *Last Places: A Journey in the North*. Boston: Houghton Mifflin. 1990.

Nixon, Rob. *London Calling: V. S. Naipaul. Postcolonial Mandarin*. Oxford: Oxford University Press. 1992.

Pearson, Ian. "Around the World in 6,000 Pages: A Guide to the Ultimate in Arm-chair Journeys." *Toronto Globe and Mail Destinations*. November 1992, 15–24.

Robb. Peter. *Midnight in Sicily*. Point Potts. New South Wales: Duncan and Snell-grove. 1996.

Sansom. lan. "Travel's Essential Futility." *Guardian Weekly*. June 16, 1996, 28.

Stevenson. Robert Louis. "The Beach of Falesa." *Dr Jekyll and Mr Hyde and Other Stories*. London: Penguin. 1979. 99–170

—. *Travels with a Donkey*. 1879. New York: Limited Editions, 1957.

Tisdale. Sallie. "Never Let the Locals See Your Map: Why Most Travel Writers Should Stay Home." *Harper's*. September 1995, 66 74.

—. *Talk Dirty to Me: An Intimate Philosophy of Sex*. New York: Doubleday, 1994.

Twain, Mark. *The Innocents Abroad* 1869. Oxford: Oxford University Press. 1996.

Winchester. Simon. *Outpasts*. London: Hodder and Stoughton. 1985.

Chapter 67

Rebecca Raglon and Marian Scholtmeijer

HEADING OFF THE TRAIL

Language, literature, and nature's resistance to narrative

One of the clearest expressions of a post-theory perspective is Rebecca Raglon and Marian Scholtmeijer's rejection of the poststructuralist and postmodernist notion that reality is entirely a linguistic construct. For Raglon and Scholtmeijer, the linguistic turn led to a reductive approach to writing about the natural world, one where historically situated human paradigms impose an understanding upon that which is fundamentally autonomous and independent of human existence or control. The natural world, then, "resists" human narratives, especially poorly written narratives that exist to express human ideas or ideals, rather than recognizing or at least acknowledging "nature's incandescent strangeness." In fact a binary opposition structures this extract: language versus literature. Language is world-forming, whereas literature is responsive to other worlds, making "countervailing gestures" or oppositional statements that counter anthropomorphism (everything becomes an image of mankind, or at least an expression of human desires or belief systems). Literature, then, can "redress" the balance, away from a human-centred perspective to one where nature is autonomous and self-expressive. Quoting poet Seamus Heaney, Raglon and Scholtmeijer return to the notion that literary texts may offer glimpses of alternative non-human-centric worlds—an area that Scholtmeijer explores in her book *Animal Victims in Modern Fiction* (1993). Intriguingly, the overall argument is partly dependent upon a notion of good versus lower quality literature, where the latter is defined as polemical or political writing, such as propaganda. Such lower quality writing is too close to human cares and concerns, in the sense that society becomes a filter through which all other subjects are represented (i.e., are constructed). Good literature, on the other hand, is "revivifying" and "renewing" through redressing the balance of power between humans and nature, and through expression of nature's resistances to the imposition of human constructs. Raglon and Scholtmeijer call the latter "strong narratives" of nature's "resistance", examining four main authors who exemplify this approach: Henry David Thoreau, Nadine Gordimer, Russell Holban, and Franz Kafka. Thoreau spent a lifetime searching for a form that would allow nature to speak for itself, deciding that mythology was the most suitable vehicle to do so; in Gordimer's work, nature is represented as "the originating experience" from which meaning emerges, rather than human agency and ideas being imposed upon nature; in Holban's fiction, animals are not bound by the thoughts of human characters; and in Kafka's oeuvre, animals are more accurately represented through their individuality rather than standing in, allegorically or metaphorically, for some other wider, usually human-centred, lesson or moral. Raglon and Scholtmeijer conclude that good nature writing remains open to nature's enigmatic, ambiguous and resistant state; as much as humans intervene in nature and reshape it, ignore it, or destroy it, still nature remains self-expressive and resistant to human interpretation or meaning. Reading even more literally in a post-theory sense, the creaturely life of nature is akin to a wild animal that escapes captivity, and Raglon and Scholtmeijer argue that their exemplary authors manage to reveal such creatures, rather than capturing and recodifying them.

THE ASSUMPTION THAT LANGUAGE PLAYS AN important role in constructing reality has achieved the status of a truism: something so obvious that it is well on its way to becoming the invisible underpinning of all literary discussion. To think otherwise is to be either naive or ironic, for references to nature should never be thought of as literal or unproblematic. According to this viewpoint, language is a powerful force that directs our perceptions, shaping it into coherent forms, or categories (Nadeau 5). Nature itself is such a category, and according to the most extreme expression of this point of view, nature does not exist apart from our language. This makes nature a thoroughly human product, much like soap, cars, and computers, for nature, "like everything else we talk about, is first and foremost an artifact of language" (Cawley and Chaloupka 5).

Accompanying this preoccupation with language is a sociological strain of criticism that concentrates on language's culpability in creating categories that are in turn responsible for a variety of social and environmental ills. What these viewpoints share is the idea that literature, language, and culture have much to answer for when faced with environmental catastrophe and human misery. Because language and literature direct our perceptions, they are guilty participants in the destruction of the world.

But does language only imprison us in concepts of our creation? Is literature really a culpable part of what we term an "environmental crisis"? Or is there another role that language and, in particular, literature can play in helping us negotiate changes in our relationship with the natural world? As set out below, this essay looks at the contemporary preoccupation with language, but it extends this absorption to include examples of literature that begin to gesture toward the rediscovery of a powerful natural word, one that resists our narratives. This essay thus takes the position that literature not only imposes categories on the natural world but can also be a flexible and vibrant agent of change.

Under the uncompromising instruction of the natural world, literature is capable of making amends for past mistakes. We are able to create new stories and fresh meanings. The modern era is replete with examples showing us that many of our past stories of nature were misguided. The silence of extinction, for example, provides us with a corrective to beliefs that nature is forever abundant and immutable—that great story of nature we told ourselves for centuries, almost as if we were in a collective trance. We convinced ourselves that nature was forever abundant as we beat the last passenger pigeons from their roosts, and then we were faced with nature's uncompromising answer—a terrible and profound silence. When we get our stories wrong in this way, we are given incentives—by nature—to correct our beliefs, to make redress, to confront nature's resistance to our impositions.

This essay will first look at the idea of literature's ability to make these adjustments, and then we present three examples we draw from twentieth-century writers who employ nature's resistance within their narratives. We discuss the implications of this resistance, and we conclude by suggesting that while contemporary critical preoccupations with language provide a necessary caution, in terms of our relationship to the world, it is in the far corners of certain stories that we can find moments when nature's incandescent strangeness is made available to us again.

Literary balancing acts

In one of the more interesting recent reassessments of the role of literature in society, Seamus Heaney looks at poetry not as something that contributes to oppression but, in a more refreshing way, as a "balancing act," a form of redress, or countervailing gesture. That is, while literary critics may be correct in their belief that language to some extent molds our impressions of reality to conform to existing oppressive tendencies, the best literature is simultaneously at work forming countervailing gestures that frustrate the inclination to be content with common expectations and complacency. Heaney writes, "This redressing effect of poetry comes from its being a glimpsed alternative, a revelation of potential that is denied or constantly threatened by circumstances" (4).

Heaney takes it for granted that poetry not only operates through a "self-delighting inventiveness" but, in addition, works to represent things in the world (5). In discussing one of John Clare's sonnets, for example, Heaney makes the point that in Clare's evocation of a butterfly "rarely has the butteriness of butterfly been so available" (71). Good writing can make available what formerly might have been masked, hidden, or constructed by less adept or clumsier uses of language such as propaganda or polemic. It is frank acknowledgment of the differences between good literature and literature of a lesser quality that is lacking in most postmodern criticism. Heaney emphasizes the vital distinction that must be made between good writing and writing that somehow misses the mark. It is less talented authors who expose the clumsy underpinnings of language and who impose a linguistic experience on the world. Others, more skillful, can do the opposite by revivifying and renewing our experience of the world.

In an earlier study of the relationship of language to reality (or nature), C. K. Stead suggests that any piece of literature must be viewed as existing within a tension among a writer, his or her audience, and reality (11–12). If a writer, for example, has a relationship that is too close to his or her audience, and too far from reality, the result is a literature that will appear stifled, or strangely distorted, to succeeding generations. Stead's concerns are with imperialist, propagandistic poetry written before the First World War, but his comments could apply to any period of piety and orthodoxy, including our own.

Discussions such as Stead's and Heaney's, which make distinctions between literature of the first rank and literature that is of a lesser quality, comprise a positive first step in clarifying literature's role in society, as well as its relationship to a broader reality. Writing that is about nature offers a special case in these discussions since genres such as nature writing so clearly have their roots in modern scientific observation, which holds a privileged role in its ability to describe reality. Here we would like to proffer a caution and point out that much writing that is ostensibly about the natural world—primarily nonfictionalized accounts such as nature writing—can display the same foibles as any other genre if literary concerns are submerged by the polemical needs of the moment. Early in the twentieth century, the nature study advocate Neltje Blanchan Doubleday, for example, writes that the American goshawk is a "villain of the deepest dye," a "murderer," the "most destructive creature on wings . . . bloodthirsty, delighting in killing what it often cannot eat" (Strom 65). Doubleday's contemporary reader is left to marvel not at the murderous goshawk but at the human preconceptions that inform her 1903 accounts about the bird. Writing at a later date (1954), and in a far more scientist vein, Fred Bodsworth, a noted Canadian journalist keenly interested in the natural world, describes the Eskimo curlew's dramatic bipolar flight but is careful to tell readers that the bird's "instinctive behavior code, planted deep in his brain by the genes of countless generations, told him only what to do, without telling him why. His behavior was controlled not by mental decisions but by instinctive responses to the stimuli around him" (36). While there is no villain here, the allusion to an "instinctive behavior code" in retrospect appears as unidimensional as the attribution of anthropomorphic claims. Neither example functions to redress harmful human conceptions of nature. Both examples demonstrate a relationship that is too close to an intended audience: moralistic on one hand, scientistic on the other. From a distance, it is possible to see how both examples have dated, absorbing the textures of their times, so that the nature presented is hardly recognizable to today's readers. Language, rather than imposing a hegemonic view on the world, here seems to have preserved these interpretations as if they were so many curios in a cabinet.

The idea that language constructs reality, when pushed to its logical conclusion, reveals a disturbing human arrogance and one-sidedness. What seems more productive is to view Doubleday's failure as a striking example of how nature evades human attempts to construct reality. Clearly, the living goshawk—the bird that is still available to us today—resists Doubleday's narrative. That we recognize Doubleday's villainous bird as little more than an early-twentieth-century construction speaks to the fact that not only does language attempt to impose on nature but that nature has the power to resist this imposition. In this case, far from shaping reality, the use of this type of language reveals its failure to impose its logic on the world and thus its failure to construct reality or to exist solely as a mental artifact. Such failures are far from providing evidence of the power of language, and they speak instead to nature's powerful resistance to our narratives.

Furthermore, such resistance can manifest itself not only when we glance back at what we have here termed "failures" but also expresses itself in the best writing—although in a different way. The difference between such failures as Doubleday's and writing that can help redress the terrible imbalance in the human relationship to the world exists in the fact that the best writing about nature builds into its narrative allusions to nature's resistance. That is, rather than merely giving nature symbolic or metaphoric roles, something literature of all eras has done, we believe that the best stories about nature are those that have sensed the power of nature to resist, or question, or evade the meanings we attempt to impose on the natural world.

Looking for the literature of nature

We are perhaps being too literal-minded if we believe that the answer to Henry David Thoreau's question, "Where is the literature which gives expression to Nature?" ("Walking" 120) is to be found primarily in nature writing, or in realistic descriptive passages, or even nature poetry. "He would be a poet who could impress the winds and streams into his service, to speak for him; who nailed words to their primitive senses," Thoreau muses, concluding that little in English literature gives adequate expression to the subject (120). Thoreau spent a lifetime pressing metaphor into expressing his sense of the wild, bending language almost as far as it can be bent, in order to adequately express nature. Thoreau's tastes led him to believe mythology came closer than any other genre to expressing the original vigor of nature.

That a literature that gives expression to nature might not fit neatly defined genres nor follow along narrative trails human desires have laid down for the order and control of nature seems obvious. As such, some of the best narratives about nature emerge in rather unexpected places. It is not just in nature writing, or nature poetry, or descriptive prose where examples of redress, or resistance, are found. Many different narratives convey the strangeness of life and the elusiveness of nature—and often with far more precision than do works that are more ostensibly about nature (that is, nonfiction nature writing, field guides, first person essays, and semi-scientific accounts). Weak narratives of nature, such as Doubleday's, reveal nature's resistance in retrospect, but strong narratives, such as Thoreau's, incorporate the idea of resistance into the narrative. Any literature that alludes to a natural order that exists apart from human control contains within it the elements of a strong narrative of nature, and it is less likely to display the weaknesses we associate with more overt and superficial constructions of the natural world. This fact can invert our expectations: some strong, fanciful narratives can provide insights into the natural world, while others, claiming to have science on their side, can appear to be a species of weak fiction. Thoreau makes a similar point when he remarks in his journal that he is finding the language of science restrictive, and that he prefers the skill of ancient writers who "left a more lively and lifelike account of the gorgon than modern writers give us of real animals" (*Journal 12* 18 February 1860).

Stories can, of course, turn the tables and show nature rebelling against human dominance. There are enough movies of this "revolt-of-nature" (Newman) variety to indicate a fondness in Western culture for witnessing a scripted assault on humankind by the natural world. Worms, reptiles, birds, sharks, bears, tornadoes, earthquakes, comets, and even vegetation rise up to attack us, and we enjoy watching. These days, it is not even necessary that humankind triumph in the end. We feel sufficient guilt over our relations with the environment that a victory for nature now and again is not only tolerable but welcome. As narratives, however, stories in the revolt-of-nature mode follow the usual path: escalating assaults, a crisis, and then some sort of resolution. The narrative line is left unaffected by the presence of natural phenomena, and we are not really obliged to think about the natural world except as it temporarily impinges on the continual quest for human happiness.

Similarly, writers can incorporate elements of the natural world in their work without really expressing much in terms of nature's resistance. John Hawkes's *The Frog* is a case in point. In the novel, a frog climbs out of a lily pond and into a boy's mouth and lives inside the boy's stomach for the remainder of the boy's life. As the boy Pascal grows to manhood, the frog emerges to give Pascal's father a fatal heart attack and to pleasure numerous women. At the end of the story, it turns out that all of the inmates in the asylum where Pascal has lived have acquired frogs of their own. A novel such as *The Frog*, while interestingly murky, has more to do with psychoanalysis than with nature. Once the frog-penis connection occurs, the only strangeness with which the reader is left to cope is how Pascal's penis manages to fly across the room or how even the female inmates of the asylum can possess frogs. A reader is not required, ultimately, to ponder the nature of literal frogs.

The genre of nature writing has tended to show nature eluding human control by minimizing the human presence and focusing attention on the nonhuman world. Works of fiction that successfully integrate nature and natural phenomena into human stories, however, are of greater interest to contemporary readers because they allow nature to change the shape, direction, and outcome of the narrative. The South African novelist Nadine Gordimer's "The Termitary" ends with the narrator's contemplation of her mother's power, and yet nature controls the story. If one is looking for a story with the "earth clinging to its roots" (Thoreau, "Walking" 120), "The Termitary" is a fine example. Indeed, when the woman who tells the story recalls her nine-year-old self coming home to find the floor beneath the Axminster rug in her family's parlor ripped up and the earth below exposed, we are all reminded that our solid, secure houses are built on the good earth. "The thought of that hollow, earth-breaking dark always beneath our Axminster thrilled me," the speaker says (115).

Workmen have ripped up the floor of her home because termites are destroying it. The workmen are earthy: "All had the red earth of underground clinging to their clothes and skin and hair. . . . These men themselves appeared to have been dug up, raw from that clinging earth entombed beneath buildings" (117). The work of the three exterminators throws into chaos both home and daily routine. This home is one of those attempts by the British to import British rules and values into colonized South Africa—a home containing an Axminster rug and a Steinway piano, a home where tea is served in china cups and children are taught proper deportment, and where the mother complains of her husband in that familiar Western manner of the 1930s to 1950s: "I haven't got a husband like other women's. . . . I haven't got a home like other women" (115). The three earthy workers intimidate this English woman who is queen of the household.

The object of the excavation is the queen of the termite colony, mother of all the termite thousands, the one who must be eradicated in order to destroy the colony. Gordimer gives us a brief nature lesson: "[T]he queen cannot move, she is blind; whether she is underground, the tyrannical prisoner of her subjects who would not have been born and cannot live without her, or whether she is captured and borne away in a shoe-box, she is helpless to evade the consequences of her power" (119). Gordimer reminds us that not only the earth but other kingdoms exist beneath our homes. As the speaker's mother is doing that most motherly of chores, mixing a cake, the workers come in bearing the termite queen in a shoe box. The children are fascinated and horrified. "We all gazed at an obese, helpless white creature, five inches long, with the tiny, shiny-visored head of an ant at one end. The body was a sort of dropsical sac attached to this head; it had no legs that could be seen, neither could it propel itself by peristaltic action, like a slug or worm. The queen. The queen whose domain, we had seen for ourselves in the galleries and passages that had been uncovered beneath our house, was as big as ours" (118).

The termitary is an impressive domain, chambered, dotted with food fungus, composed of "tunnels for conveying water from as much as forty feet underground [and an] elaborate defence and communications system" (120). Once the queen is removed from her domain, the termites abandon the termitary. "We lived on, above the ruin" (120), the narrator observes. Human-British order reasserts itself.

Now it is easy enough to read the termite queen and the termites as symbolic, to take the queen as symbol of bloated, powerful-powerless white South Africa and the termites as African people compelled to serve the colonizers—caught in some weirdly symbiotic colonial relationship. Since the story ends with the observation that the mother of the household, many years later, is dead and "the secret passages, the inner chamber in which she was our queen and prisoner are sealed up, empty," one can also take the termite queen as a symbol of the mother in her children's minds and memories, and the termitary as a metaphor for their socialization. Certainly, the idea of breaking through the artificial niceties of daily life and exposing the dim, chaotic underground has a symbolic, psychoanalytical quality. The implication that the termite queen the workers display might well be a fake, simply the same termite queen conveyed from house to house and triumphantly shown to the home owner, also lends itself to ironic interpretation. Perhaps the mother has the same iconic significance.

Regardless of the conclusions one might make about the correspondence between the human situation and life in the termitary, the point is that the originating experience is the termitary and not the human situation. In Western culture, we have sought in nature analogies to the human state; in "The Termitary," however, the exposure of the termites' underground world provides the inspiration, the reason, for contemplation of humanity, not vice versa. The termitary renders the corresponding human relationships deep, freighted with mystery. Without it, the mother and the home are merely cultural stereotypes.

Because the termitary thrills the narrator, and because it has had an impact on the mind of the author, the narrative takes an original shape. In a way, it is more of a meditation than a narrative. The ambiguity surrounding the authenticity of the termite queen leaves the possibility open that the termitary might still be intact, unconquered—despite the fact that the termites abandon it. The termitary remains a living place in the imagination. Decades are summed up in the last paragraph of the story, all with the one episode of breaking open the termitary as their foundation in memory. The narrator considers herself free; her memories are more spacious than her mother's. "Why should I remember? I, who—shuddering to look back at those five rooms behind the bow-window eyes and the front-door mouth—have oceans, continents, snowed-in capitals, islands where turtles swim, cathedrals, theatres, palace gardens where people kiss and tramps drink wine—all these to remember" (120). While the sense of liberty she expresses appears to cast the termitary in the symbolic negative, the idea of breaking out is initiated by the revelation of the termite's labyrinthine dominion existing under her childhood home. All of these features: the time frame, ambiguities, various possibilities in symbolic reading, and naturalistic information—preserve the termitary as a potent place that cannot be subsumed by the narrative. Here we find an example not of literature's culpability but of a gesture of redress toward the natural world.

Another example of narrative that acknowledges nature's ultimate resistance to our stories is *Turtle Diary* by Russell Hoban, an American-born, British-based author. The conventional view of turtles has little to do with freedom; one is inclined to think of tortoises, land turtles, burdened with heavy shells and achingly slow of movement. The graceful underwater flight of the swimming turtle may come to mind for people who watch nature programs, but turtles have been constructed socially in Western culture as models of ponderous deliberation and vulnerability—the proverbial sitting ducks. Perhaps it is this convention that renders the power and grace of the swimming turtle a thing of beauty. There can be little doubt that Hoban took inspiration from the freedom of marine turtles for his novel. Indeed, one could speculate that in *Turtle Diary* Hoban has transferred to three characters his desire to liberate turtles from a zoo, and he has used fiction as the means to satisfy that desire.

In some respects, *Turtle Diary* is a conventional narrative. Plotlines converge to move steadily toward the release of the turtles, the turtles are released, and then the two characters who have performed the deed go their separate ways and deliver the denouement. William G. and Neara H., who alternate as narrators throughout the story, have other experiences besides the central one with the turtles. Nevertheless, the narrative exists to enable contemplation of human relations with the natural world.

Following the release of the turtles, Neara observes: "The sea was wherever it was, and the turtles. It could not be done again. Of those who did the launching there were no survivors" (157). She is feeling the bleakness of life, the radically coincidental nature of all the world's phenomena. More than that, her observation that there were no survivors suggests that her narrative has been vacated with the launching of the turtles. Once Neara and William have served their purpose as the means of the turtles' release, the aimlessness of their lives becomes apparent to them. They lack the purposiveness that the turtles possess. The zookeeper who has abetted William and Neara comments, "'Nothing to be done really about animals. Anything you do looks foolish. The answer isn't in us. It's almost as if we're put here on earth to show how silly they aren't'" (158). "The answer isn't in us"—this could well be the ultimate finding of *Turtle Diary*.

Perhaps some of the observations about turtles and other animals could have been made in a piece of nature writing. Nevertheless, because *Turtle Diary* is a fictional narrative, and particularly a first-person narrative with two narrators, all thoughts on nature are conditional and contested rather than final and authoritative, as they might be in other genres. The expectation we bring to nature writing as a genre is that it can give us information, and it can tell us the facts. We might put up with an amusing or obstreperous nature writer—but even with the loosest of definitions, our expectation of nature writing does not allow a writer, a writer's emotions, or a writer's conflict with meaning to become our main concern. We bring different expectations to fiction, however. In the novel, Neara is free to imagine herself as another being and to pass judgment on her confessional musing. "What I do is not as good as what an oyster-catcher does. Writing and illustrating books for children is not as good as walking orange-eyed, orange-billed in the distance on the river, on the beaches of the ocean, finding shellfish" (49). Neara is free to wonder, on contemplating a water beetle in an aquarium, "If someone were to buy me, have me shipped in a tin with air-holes, what would I be a specimen of?" (76).

Granted, when William notes the "[t]housands of miles in [the turtles'] speechless eyes [and] submarine skies in their flipper wings," a nature writer might have said the same. It takes the added dimension of a fictional character, however, to give primacy to the emotional sense of lostness that William discovers in himself when he realizes that the turtles are not lost. "Could I abolish the human condition? Could I swim, experience swimming, finding, navigating, fearlessness, unlostness? Could I come back with an answer? The unlostness itself would be the answer. I shouldn't need to come back" (72).

William continues with the theme as he drives the van with the three turtles in their crates toward the coast:

> Looking at them I couldn't think there was any expectation in them. When they felt themselves once more in ocean they would simply do what turtles do in the ocean, their readiness was whole and undiminished in them. If permitted to live they would navigate by the sun, by chemical traces in the water, by the imprint in their genes of an ancient continent sundered. They were compacted of finding, finding was embodied in them (134).

The turtles' story, whatever it might be, is separate from the human story. And although a reader does become involved in the stories of William G. and Neara H., Hoban's technique of alternating between them means that no one human story in this novel determines the meaning of the release of the turtles. The openness of the two narrators to considering that nature points up the unreality of human life is repeated in the structure of the novel. The turtles can be free because all we have before us are the thoughts of two people. These people may be wrong, or they may be right. We may find their ideas congenial, or we may not. But both in themselves and in the way they are presented, the thoughts of these characters do not bind the turtles. Hoban's awareness that nature does not conform to our narratives necessitates the dual narrators because, as he writes, "The answer isn't in us."

A final example demonstrating nature's resistance comes from Franz Kafka. Much inclined to experiment with the world in stories such as "The Metamorphosis" and "The Hunger Artist," Kafka again turns the tables on our expectations in "A Report to an Academy." In the story, an ape, who by his own account has become human, observes human acrobats at a variety show. "What a mockery of holy Mother Nature! Were the apes to see such a spectacle, no theater walls could stand the shock of their laughter" (253). Given that Kafka's general theme is often humankind's lack of freedom, there is irony in the liberties he takes with the world, regularly employing phenomena of the natural world to destabilize the idea of humanity. In the process, Kafka compels his reader to think about nature.

Although rarely recognized in critical assessments of his work, the natural world is foundational to Kafka's stories. A vegetarian who felt empathy for animals, particularly animals held in zoos, Kafka suffered under a tyrannical father who called his son enough animal names so that Franz was obliged to wrestle with the idea of his own animality. All of Kafka's stories are strange, and so one cannot argue that nature alone is the force that caused him to produce enigmatic narratives—unless one means nature in the abstract. Nevertheless, when natural elements—usually animals—appear in his works, Kafka's habitual eccentricity reinforces the awareness that nature does not conform to our constructions.

"A Report to an Academy" is among the more intelligible of Kafka's stories. The frame for "A Report to an Academy" is a meeting of presumably learned men and women, although they are given no voice as the speaker tells his tale. The speaker is Red Peter, a chimpanzee who has become human and who solemnly tells his learned audience how he went about achieving this conversion. According to Red Peter, when he found himself in a tiny cage in the cargo hold of ship, his only way out of the cage was to become human. "There was nothing else for me to do, provided always that freedom was not to be my choice" (258). Becoming human means mastering a series of tricks: drinking schnapps, smoking a pipe, uttering words, and acquiring information about European culture. While clearly a commentary on the human condition, Red Peter's story also makes one think of how apparent successes in teaching apes to manipulate our semiotic systems convince some biologists that they are our kin.

Nature's invasion of culture could not be more thorough than it is in "A Report to an Academy." Kafka does not allow the assembled academics to question Red Peter's assertions. What do they see when they look at him? A performing chimpanzee, however talented? A squat, hairy raconteur? Either way, Red Peter has seized control of this story. Although he denies that choice was involved in his decision to become human—or to mimic humanity—it is clear that through Red Peter, nature and Kafka deconstruct the human image. Red Peter is "not appealing for any man's verdict." "I have only made a report," he says at the close of his speech (259). In an odd and ironic way, Kafka's chimpanzee is more himself ontologically than chimpanzees in other stories. Red Peter is not allegorical or metaphorical; he is not separate from ourselves, as are "natural" chimpanzees; and yet he remains immune to human construction. We have seen a situation like this, one that Gordimer creates with her termitary and its termite queen: the relationship between the natural phenomenon and human culture defies explanation.

Granted, one will not find in Kafka's stories what one is used to in conventional nature writing. Mice who sing, or appreciate singing, or what seems to them to be singing ("Josephine the Singer, or the Mouse Folk"); a dog who speculates that his species might be the only real entity in the world ("Investigations of a Dog"); a paranoid burrow dweller, possibly a badger, who is plagued by an invisible, whistling enemy ("The Burrow"); and a traveling salesman transformed into a gigantic cockroach ("The Metamorphosis")—little of this is recognizable as nature. Where are the trees and lakes? Where are the insouciant animals and their curious habits? Why are we not learning about bioregions? The least that can be said is that Kafka shakes us out of our customary ways of thinking about life, and this, we think, is the redress literature can offer us in the face of an environmental crisis. These are the kinds of stories that lead us to something that is, finally, "beyond nature writing."

Conclusion

Gordimer, Hoban, and Kafka place nature in the domain of the imponderable. They open up the narrative form so that nature can remain ambiguous, enigmatic, and resistant to the imposition of human meaning-making exercises. They accomplish this by constructing narratives that allude to nature's ultimate resistance to the human. This is not to say that nature is hostile to humanity but that it exists on its own terms. This fact alone can challenge our most dearly held beliefs, and contemporary authors have been quick to explore it.

We began our discussion by noting that much literary criticism is informed by the idea that language molds our perceptions of the world. This is a corrective to earlier concepts that held that certain unproblematic correlations existed between the natural world and language. Unfortunately, this insight has been distorted by those who are willing to proclaim that there is no relationship between language and the world and that all meaning is human meaning.

If we are to find creative responses to what we call an environmental crisis, we suggest it is important to keep our minds open to other possibilities. Tired slogans and old cliches (how tedious it is to hear for the one hundredth time that "man is a part of nature"?), while perhaps having served their purpose in an earlier period, are not what is needed now. Thinking and writing about nature and the environment is a grown-up task, and it requires all the subtlety, complexity, and sophistication writers can muster.

As a way to illustrate these points, we have examined three writers who have used some aspect of nature in their work. In the process, each writer has confronted something that is resistant to human meaning. While we might attempt to make a symbol of Gordimer's termite queen, or Hoban's turtle, or Kafka's chimpanzee, ultimately each of these creatures eludes capture by the author. While each story can work on a symbolic, metaphoric, or psychological level, for our purposes we have found that in each story's deepest level all such meanings fall away, and we are left to contemplate the unknowable, mysterious aspect of termite, turtle, or chimpanzee.

It is at this point that we recognize nature's resistance to our stories, and this recognition calls into question all the constructs we have built in our attempts to cement over the living earth. That fiction might be better situated to accomplish this than other genres is also something we have tentatively proposed. Our sense is that the environmental crisis is a crisis of meaning, and to recover what we have lost we need new stories about nature. As we continue to probe and manipulate all facets of the natural world, it is a timely moment to remind ourselves of that ultimate mystery of which we, too, are a part. Good stories, we believe, are able to do just that.

Works cited

Bodsworth, Fred. *Last of the Curlews*. 1954. Toronto: McClelland and Stewart, 1963.

Cawley, R. McGreggor, and William Chaloupka. "The Great Wild Hope." *In the Nature of Things*. Ed. Jane Bennett and William Chaloupka. Minneapolis: U of Minnesota P, 1993. 3–23.

Doubleday, Neltje Blanchan. "How to Attract the Birds and Other Talks about Bird Neighbors." 1903. Strom 52–66.

Gordimer, Nadine. "The Termitary." *A Soldier's Embrace: Stories by Nadine Gordimer*.

Harmondsworth, Middlesex: Penguin, 1980.113–20.

Hawkes, John. *The Frog*. New York: Penguin, 1996.

Heaney, Seamus. *The Redress of Poetry*. London: Faber and Faber, 1995.

Hoban, Russell. *Turtle Diary*. London: Pan, 1977.

Kafka, Franz. "A Report to an Academy." 1917. Trans. Willa Muir and Edwin Muir. *Franz Kafka: The Complete Stories*. Ed. Nahum N. Glatzer. New York: Schocken, 1971. 250–59·

Nadeau, Robert. *Readings from the Book of Nature*. Amherst: U of Massachusetts P, 1981.

Newman, Kim. *Nightmare Movies: A Critical History of the Horror Film, 1968–1988*. London: Bloomsbury, 1988.

Ragion, Rebecca, and Marian Scholtmeijer. "Shifting Ground: Metanarratives, Epistemology, and the Stories of Nature." *Environmental Ethics* (spring 1996): 19–38.

Stead, C. K. *The New Poetic: Yeats to Eliot*. London: Hutchinson & Co., 1964.

Strom, Deborah, ed. *Birdwatching with American Women*. New York: Norton, 1986.

Thoreau, Henry David. "Walking." *The Natural History Essays*. Salt Lake City: Peregrine Smith, 1980. 93–136.

—. *Journal 12*. Ed. Bradford Torry. Boston: Houghton Mifflin, 1906.

Chapter 68

Jacques Derrida

DES TOURS DE BABEL

As the founder of the methodology known as deconstruction, Derrida has had a profound and enduring impact upon literary criticism and poststructuralist theory. In this extract, Derrida creatively—and deconstructively—misreads Genesis 11:1–9, the story of Babel, in which humanity, unified through a single language, attempts to build a tower that will reach heaven; God's response is to scatter the people throughout the world, giving them in the process a multiplicity of languages. It is important to understand that Derrida uses a very unusual translation of the Old Testament, by the Algerian scholar André Chouraqi, in which he translates Genesis 11:9, "therefore is the name of it called Babel" (KJV), as "Over which he proclaims his name Babel, Confusion." This is important for Derrrida's deconstructive argument: that even in the Bible, the transcendent signified, God, is a proper name which can also signify "Babel, Confusion." In other words, the signified which is supposed to anchor the entire system of meaning, is revealed to be instead a "signifier"; that is to say, an arbitrary sign that may mean different things, depending upon its position within a fluid or mobile network of other signs. Derrida therefore opens by arguing that Babel signifies not just "the irreducible multiplicity of tongues" but also "an incompletion, the impossibility of finishing, of totalizing, of saturating, of completing something . . .". In many respects, this sentence is an incredibly condensed summary of Derrida's "Structure, Sign and Play" essay, but here Derrida will also apply this idea to theories of translation, and to theology. In fact this essay is one of the key documents in a series of texts by Derrida on religion, usually discussing Old Testament concepts and narratives, such as the Akedah or sacrifice of Isaac. The deconstructive riddle in this extract is that as a proper name, "Babel" should rise above the confusion of languages, and thus it should resist translation; as a common noun, meaning confusion, "Babel" is precisely what stands in need of translation. To complicate things further, although it is worth the work reading the intertext in question here, Derrida turns to Walter Benjamin's essay "The Task of the Translator" (1923), in which Benjamin argues that translation is not about communication or imparting some information to a reader; instead, a translation meditates upon the impossibility of translation, while creating a new transformational text that is the "afterlife" of the original, or, the original work's "survival". Derrida brings Benjamin in to confound simple, non-deconstructive theories of language and translation, and to deconstruct Benjamin, because the guarantee behind all successful translation, for Benjamin, is God. And we have already seen that

"God" can also mean "Confusion" or the dissemination that is known as Babel/a babel of languages. This proper name, which is also a common noun, is not the origin of languages, but it is the non-grounded ground, or the condition of possibility, of language itself. What Benjamin calls "pure language" (sacred, mysterious, messianic and redemptive), Derrida deconstructs and calls "différance", that is to say, a structure without origin or end, through which the play of linguistic differences takes place.

"B ABEL": FIRST A PROPER NAME, GRANTED. But when we say "Babel" today, do we know what we are naming? Do we know whom? If we consider the survival of a text that is a legacy, the narrative or the myth of the tower of Babel, it does not constitute just one figure among others. Telling at least of the inadequation of one tongue to another, of one place in the encyclopedia to another, of language to itself and to meaning, and so forth, it also tells of the need for figuration, for myth, for tropes, for twists and turns, for translation inadequate to compensate for that which multiplicity denies us. In this sense it would be the myth of the origin of myth, the metaphor of metaphor, the narrative of narrative, the translation of translation, and so on. It would not be the only structure hollowing itself out like that, but it would do so in its own way (itself *almost* untranslatable, like a proper name), and its idiom would have to be saved.

The "tower of Babel" does not merely figure the irreducible multiplicity of tongues; it exhibits an incompletion, the impossibility of finishing, of totalizing, of saturating, of completing something on the order of edification, architectural construction, system and architectonics. What the multiplicity of idioms actually limits is not only a "true" translation, a transparent and adequate interexpression, it is also a structural order, a coherence of construct. There is then (let us translate) something like an internal limit to formalization, an incompleteness of the con-structure. It would be easy and up to a certain point justified to see there the translation of a system in deconstruction.

One should never pass over in silence the question of the tongue in which the question of the tongue is raised and into which a discourse on translation is translated.

First: in what tongue was the tower of Babel constructed and deconstructed? In a tongue within which the proper name of Babel could also, by confusion, be translated by "confusion." The proper name Babel, as a proper name, should remain untranslatable, but, by a kind of associative confusion that a unique tongue rendered possible, one thought it translated in that very tongue, by a common noun signifying what we translate as confusion. Voltaire showed his astonishment in his *Dictionnaire philosophique*, at the *Babel* article:

> I do not know why it is said in *Genesis* that Babel signifies confusion, for *Ba* signifies father in the Oriental tongues, and *Bel* signifies God; Babel signifies the city of God, the holy city. The Ancients gave this name to all their capitals. But it is incontestable that Babel means confusion, either because the architects were con-founded after having raised their work up to eighty-one thousand Jewish feet, or because the tongues were then confounded; and it is obviously from that time on that the Germans no longer understand the Chinese; for it is clear, according to the scholar Bochart, that Chinese is originally the same tongue as High German.

The calm irony of Voltaire means that Babel means: it is not only a proper name, the reference of a pure signifier to a single being—and for this reason untranslatable—but a common noun related to the generality of a meaning. This common noun means, and means not only confusion, even though "confusion" has at least two meanings, as Voltaire is aware, the confusion of tongues, but also the state of confusion in which the architects find themselves with the structure interrupted, so that a certain confusion has already begun to affect the two meanings of the word "confusion." The signification of "confusion" is confused, at least double. But Voltaire suggests something else again: Babel means not only confusion in the double sense of the word, but also the name of the father, more precisely and more commonly, the name of God as name of father. The city would bear the name of God the father and of the father of the city that is called confusion. God, the God, would have marked with his patronym a communal space, that city where understanding is no longer possible. And understanding is no longer possible when there are only proper names, and understanding is no longer possible when there are no longer proper names. In giving his name, a name of his choice, in giving all names, the father would be at the origin of language, and that power would belong by right to God the father. And the name of God the father would be the name of that origin of tongues. But it is also that God who, in the action of his anger (like the God of Böhme or of Hegel, he who leaves himself, determines himself in his finitude and thus produces history), annuls the gift of tongues, or at least embroils it, sows confusion among his sons, and poisons the present (*Gift*-gift). This is also the origin of tongues, of the multiplicity of idioms, of what in other words are usually called mother tongues. For this entire history deploys filiations, generations and genealogies: all Semitic. Before the deconstruction of Babel, the great Semitic family was establishing its empire, which it wanted universal, and its tongue, which it also attempts to impose on the universe. The moment of this project immediately precedes the deconstruction of the tower. I cite two French translations. The first translator stays away from what one would want to call "literality", in other words, from the Hebrew figure of speech for "tongue," where the second, more concerned about literality (metaphoric, or rather metonymic), says "lip," since in Hebrew "lip" designates what we call, in another metonymy, "tongue." One will have to say multiplicity of lips and not of tongues to name the Babelian confusion. The first translator, then, Louis Segond, author of the Segond Bible, published in 1910, writes this:

> Those are the sons of Sem, according to their families, their tongues, their countries, their nations. Such are the families of the sons of Noah, according to their generations, their nations. And it is from them that emerged the nations which spread over the earth after the flood. All the earth had a single tongue and the same words. As they had left the origin they found a plain in the country of Schinear, and they dwelt there. They said to one another: Come! Let us make bricks, and bake them in the fire. And brick served them as stone, and tar served as cement. Again they said: Come! Let us build ourselves a city and a tower whose summit touches the heavens, and let us make ourselves a name, so that we not be scattered over the face of all the earth.

I do not know just how to interpret this allusion to the substitution or the transmutation of materials, brick becoming stone and tar serving as mortar. That already resembles a translation, a translation of translation. But let us leave it and substitute a second translation for the first. It is that of Chouraqui. It is recent and wants to be more literal, almost verbum pro verbo, as Cicero said should not be done in one of those first recommendations to the translator which can be read in his *Libellus de Optimo Genera Oratorum*. Here it is:

> Here are the sons of Shem
> for their clans, for their tongues,
> in their lands, for their peoples.
> Here are the clans of the sons of Noah for their exploits, in their peoples:
> from the latter divide the peoples on earth, after the flood.

> And it is all the earth: a single lip, one speech.
> And it is at their departure from the Orient: they find a canyon,
> in the land of Shine'ar.
> They settle there.
> They say, each to his like:
> "Come, let us brick some bricks.
> Let us fire them in the fire."
> The brick becomes for them stone, the tar, mortar.
> They say:
> "Come, let us build ourselves a city and a tower.
> Its head: in the heavens.
> Let us make ourselves a name,
> that we not be scattered over the face of all the earth."

What happens to them? In other words, for what does God punish them in giving his name, or rather, since he gives it to nothing and to no one, in proclaiming his name, the proper name of "confusion" which will be his mark and his seal? Does he punish them for having wanted to build as high as the heavens? For having wanted to accede to the highest, up to the Most High? Perhaps for that too, no doubt, but incontestably for having wanted thus to make a name for themselves, to give themselves the name, to construct for and by themselves their own name, to gather themselves there ("that we no longer be scattered"), as in the unity of a place which is at once a tongue and a tower, the one as well as the other, the one as the other. He punishes them for having thus wanted to assure themselves, by themselves, a unique and universal genealogy. For the text of Genesis proceeds immediately, as if it were all a matter of the same design: raising a tower, constructing a city, making a name for oneself in a universal tongue which would also be an idiom, and gathering a filiation:

> They say:
> "Come, let us build ourselves a city and a tower.
> Its head: in the heavens.
> Let us make ourselves a name,
> that we not be scattered over the face of all the earth."
> YHWH descends to see the city and the tower
> that the sons of man have built.
> YHWH says:
> "Yes! A single people, a single lip for all:
> that is what they begin to do! . . .
> Come! Let us descend! Let us confound their lips,
> man will no longer understand the lip of his neighbor."

Then he disseminates the Sem, and dissemination is here deconstruction:

> YHWH disperses them from here over the face of all the earth.
> They cease to build the city.
> Over which he proclaims his name: Bavel, Confusion,
> for there, YHWH confounds the lip of all the earth,
> and from there YHWH disperses them over the face of all the earth.

Can we not, then, speak of God's jealousy? Out of resentment against that unique name and lip of men, he imposes his name, his name of father; and with this violent imposition he opens the deconstruction of the tower, as of the universal language; he scatters the genealogical filiation. He breaks the lineage. He *at the same time* imposes and forbids translation. He imposes it and forbids it, constrains, but as if to failure, the children who henceforth *will bear* his name, the name that *he* gives to the city. It is from a proper name of God, come from God, descended from God or from the father (and it is indeed said that YHWH, an unpronounceable name, *descends* toward the tower) and by him that tongues are scattered, confounded or multiplied, according to a descendance that in its very dispersion remains sealed by the only name that will have been the strongest, by the only idiom that will have triumphed. Now, this idiom bears within itself the mark of confusion, it improperly means the improper, to wit: Bavel, confusion. Translation then becomes necessary and impossible, like the effect of a struggle for the appropriation of the name, necessary and forbidden in the interval between two absolutely proper names. And the proper name of God (given by God) is divided enough in the tongue, already, to signify also, confusedly, "confusion." And the war that he declares has first raged within his name: divided, bifid, ambivalent, polysemic: God deconstructing. "And he war," one reads in *Finnegans Wake*, and we could follow this whole story from the side of Shem and Shaun. The "he war" does not only, in this place, tie together an incalculable number of phonic and semantic threads, in the immediate context and throughout this Babelian book; it says the declaration of war (in English) of the One who says I am the one who am, and who thus was (*war*); it renders itself untranslatable in its very performance, *at least in* the fact that it is enunciated in more than one language at a time, at least English and German. If even an infinite translation exhausted its semantic stock, it would still translate into *one* language and would lose the multiplicity of "he war." Let us leave for another time a less hastily interrupted reading of this "he war," and let us note one of the limits of theories of translation: all too often they treat the passing from one language to another and do not sufficiently consider the possibility for languages to be implicated *more than* two in a text. How is a text written in several languages at a time to be translated? How is the effect of plurality to be "rendered"? And what of translating with several languages at a time, will that be called translating?

Babel: today we take it as a proper name. Indeed, but the proper name of what and of whom? At times that of a narrative text recounting a story (mythical, symbolic, allegorical; it matters little for the moment), a story in which the proper name, which is then no longer the title of the narrative, names a tower or a city but a tower or a city that receives its name from an event during which YHWH "proclaims his name." Now, this proper name, which already names at least three times and three different things, also has, this is the whole point, as proper name the function of a common noun. This story recounts, among other things, the origin of the confusion of tongues, the irreducible multiplicity of idioms, the necessary and impossible task of translation, its necessity as impossibility. Now, in general one pays little attention to this fact: it is in translation that we most often read this narrative. And in this translation, the proper name retains a singular destiny, since it is not translated in its appearance as proper name. Now, a proper name as such remains forever untranslatable, a fact that may lead one to conclude that it does not strictly belong, for the same reason as the other words, to the language, to the system of the language, be it translated or translating. And yet "Babel," an event in a single tongue, the one in which it appears so as to form a "text," also has a common meaning, a conceptual generality. That it be by way of a pun or a confused association matters little: "Babel" could be understood in one language as meaning "confusion." And from then on, just as Babel is at once proper name and common noun, confusion also becomes proper name and common noun, the one as the homonym of the other, the synonym as well, but not the equivalent, because there could be no question of confusing them in their value. It has for the translator no satisfactory solution. Recourse to apposition and capitalization ("Over which he proclaims his name: Bavel, Confusion") is not translating from one tongue into another. It comments, explains, paraphrases, but does not translate. At best it reproduces approximately and by dividing the equivocation into two words there where confusion gathered in potential, in all its potential, in the internal translation, if one can say that, which works the word in the so-called original tongue. For in the very tongue of the original narrative there is a translation, a sort of transfer, that gives immediately (by some confusion) the semantic equivalent of the proper name which, by itself, as a pure proper name, it would not have. As a matter of fact, this intralinguistic translation operates immediately; it is not even an operation in the strict sense. Nevertheless, someone who speaks the language of Genesis could be attentive to the effect of the proper name in effacing the conceptual equivalent (like *pierre* [rock] in *Pierre* [Peter], and these are two absolutely heterogeneous values or functions); one would then be tempted to say *first* that a proper name, in the proper sense, does not properly belong to the language; it does not belong there, *although and because* its call makes the language possible (what would a language be without the possibility of calling by a proper name?); consequently it can properly inscribe itself in a language only by allowing itself to be translated therein, in other words, *interpreted* by its semantic equivalent: from this moment it can no longer be taken as proper name. The noun *pierre* belongs to the French language, and its translation into a foreign language should in principle transport its meaning. This is not the case with *Pierre*, whose inclusion in the French language is not assured and is in any case not of the same type. "Peter" in this sense is not a *translation* of *Pierre*, any more than *Londres* is a translation of "London," and so forth. And second, anyone whose so-called mother tongue was the tongue of *Genesis* could indeed understand Babel as "confusion"; that person then effects a *confused* translation of the proper name by its common equivalent without having need for another word. It is as if there were two words there, two homonyms, one of which has the value of proper name and the other that of common noun: between the two, a translation which one can evaluate quite diversely. Does it belong to the kind that Jakobson calls intralingual translation or rewording? I do not think so: "rewording" concerns the relations of transformation between common nouns and ordinary phrases. The essay *On Translation* (1959) distinguishes three forms of translation. *Intralingual* translation interprets linguistic signs by means of other signs of the *same* language. This obviously presupposes that one can know in the final analysis how to determine rigorously the unity and identity of a language, the decidable form of its limits. There would then be what Jakobson neatly calls translation "proper," *interlingual* translation, which interprets linguistic signs by means of some other language—this appeals to the same presupposition as intralingual translation. Finally there would be intersemiotic translation or *transmutation*, which interprets linguistic signs by means of systems of nonlinguistic signs. For the two forms of translation which would not be translations "proper," Jakobson proposes a definitional equivalent and another word. The first he translates, so to speak, by another word: intralingual translation or *rewording*. The third likewise: *intersemiotic* translation or *transmutation*. In these two cases, the translation of "translation" is a definitional interpretation. But in the case of translation "proper," translation in the ordinary sense, interlinguistic and post-Babelian, Jakobson does not translate; he repeats the same word: "interlingual translation or translation proper." He supposes that it is not necessary to translate; everyone understands what that means because everyone has experienced it, everyone is expected to know what is a language, the relation of one language to another and especially identity or difference in fact of language. If there is a transparency that Babel would not have impaired, this is surely it, the experience of the multiplicity of tongues and the "proper" sense of the word "translation." In relation to this word, when it is a question of translation "proper," the other uses of the word "translation" would be in a position of intralingual and inadequate translation, like metaphors, in short, like twists or turns of translation in the proper sense. There would thus be a translation in the proper sense and a translation in the figurative sense. And in order to translate the one into the other, within the same tongue or from one tongue to another, in the figurative or in the proper sense, one would engage upon a course that would quickly reveal how this reassuring tripartition can be problematic. Very quickly: at the very moment when pronouncing "Babel" we sense the impossibility of deciding whether this name belongs, properly and simply, to one tongue. And it matters that this undecidability is at work in a struggle for the proper name within a scene of genealogical indebtedness. In seeking to "make a name for themselves," to found at the same time a universal tongue and a unique genealogy, the Semites want to bring the world to reason, and this reason can signify simultaneously a colonial violence (since they would thus universalize their idiom) and a peaceful transparency of the human community. Inversely, when God imposes and opposes his name, he ruptures the rational transparency but interrupts also the colonial violence or the linguistic imperialism. He destines them to translation, he subjects them to the law of a translation both necessary and impossible; in a stroke with his translatable-untranslatable name he delivers a universal reason (it will no longer be subject to the rule of a particular nation), but he simultaneously limits its very universality: forbidden transparency, impossible univocity. Translation becomes law, duty and debt, but the debt one can no longer discharge. Such insolvency is found marked in the very name of Babel: which at once translates and does not translate itself, belongs without belonging to a language and indebts itself to itself for an insolvent debt, to itself as if other. Such would be the Babelian performance.

This singular example, at once archetypical and allegorical, could serve as an introduction to all the so-called theoretical problems of translation. But no theorization, inasmuch as it is produced in a language, will be able to dominate the Babelian performance. This is one of the reasons why I prefer here, instead of treating it in the theoretical mode, to attempt to translate in my own way the translation of another text on translation. The preceding ought to have led me instead to an early text by Walter Benjamin, "On Language as Such and on the Language of Man" (1916), translated by Maurice de Gandillac (*Mythe et Violence*, Paris: Denoël, 1971). Reference to Babel is explicit there and is accompanied by a discourse on the proper name and on translation. But given the, in my view, overly enigmatic character of that essay, its wealth and its overdeterminations, I have had to postpone that reading and limit myself to "The Task of the Translator" (also translated by Maurice de Gandillac in the same volume). Its difficulty is no doubt no less, but its unity remains more apparent, better centered around its theme. And this text on translation is also the preface to a translation of the *Tableaux parisiens* by Baudelaire, and I refer first to the French translation that Maurice de Gandillac gives us. And yet, translation—is it only a theme for this text, and especially its primary theme?

The title also says, from its first word, the task (*Aufgabe*), the mission to which one is destined (always by the other), the commitment, the duty, the debt, the responsibility. Already at stake is a law, an injunction for which the translator has to be responsible. He *must* also acquit himself, and of something that implies perhaps a fault, a fall, an error and perhaps a crime. The essay has as horizon, it will be seen, a "reconciliation." And all that in a discourse multiplying genealogical motifs and allusions—more or less than metaphorical—to the transmission of a family seed. The translator is indebted, he appears to himself as translator in a situation of debt; and his task is to *render*, to render that which must have been given. Among the words that correspond to Benjamin's title (*Aufgabe*, duty, mission, task, problem, that which is assigned, given to be done, given to render), there are, from the beginning, *Wiedergabe, Sinnwiedergabe*, restitution, restitution of meaning. How is such a restitution, or even such an acquittance, to be understood? Is it only to be restitution of meaning, and what of meaning in this domain?

For the moment let us retain this vocabulary of gift and debt, and a debt which could well declare itself insolvent, whence a sort of "transference," love and hate, on the part of whoever is in a position to translate, is summoned to translate, with regard to the text to be translated (I do not say with regard to the signatory or the author of the original), to the language and the writing, to the bond and the love which seal the marriage between the author of the "original" and his own language. At the center of the essay, Benjamin says of the restitution that it could very well be impossible: insolvent debt within a genealogical scene. One of the essential themes of the text is the "kinship" of languages in a sense that is no longer tributary of nineteenth-century historical linguistics without being totally foreign to it. Perhaps it is here proposed that we think the very possibility of a historical linguistics.

Benjamin has just quoted Mallarmé, he quotes him in French, after having left in his own sentence a Latin word, which Maurice de Gandillac has reproduced at the bottom of the page to indicate that by "genius" he was not translating from German but from the Latin (*ingenium*). But of course he could not do the same with the third language of this essay, the French of Mallarmé, whose untranslatability Benjamin had measured. Once again: how is a text written in several languages at a time to be translated? Here is the passage on the insolvent (I quote as always the French translation, being content to include here or there the German word that supports my point):

> Philosophy and translation are not futile, however, as sentimental artists allege. For there exists a philosophical genius, whose most proper characteristic is the nostalgia for that language which manifests itself in translation.
>
> Les langues imparfaites en cela que plusieurs, manque la suprême: penser étant écrire sans accessoires ni chuchotement, mais tacite encore l'immortelle parole, la diversité, sur terre, des idiomes empêche personne de proférer les mots qui, sinon, se trouveraient, par une frappe unique, elle même matériellement la vérité.
>
> If the reality that these words of Mallarmé evoke is applicable, in full rigor, to the philosopher, translation, with the seeds [*Keimen*] that it carries within itself of such a language, is situated midway between literary creation and theory. Its work has lower relief, but it impresses itself just as profoundly on history. If the task of the translator appears in this light, the paths of its accomplishment risk becomming obscure in an all the more impenetrable way. Let us say more: of this task that consists, in the translation, in ripening the seed of a pure language ["den Samen reiner Sprache zur Reife zu bringen"], it seems impossible ever to acquit onself ["diese Aufgabe . . . scheint niemals lösbar"]; it seems that no solution would permit defining it ["in keiner Lösung bestimmbar"]. Does not one deprive it of any basis if rendering meaning ceases to be the standard?

Benjamin has, first of all, forgone translating the Mallarmé; he has left it shining in his text like the medallion of a proper name; but this proper name is not totally insignificant; it is merely welded to that whose meaning does not allow transport without damage into another language or into another tongue (and *Sprache* is not translated without loss by either word). And in the text of Mallarmé, the effect of being proper and thus untranslatable is tied less to any name or to any truth of adequation than to the unique occurrence of a performative force. Then the question is posed: does not the ground of translation finally recede as soon as the restitution of meaning ("Wiedergabe des Sinnes") ceases to provide the measure? It is the ordinary concept of translation that becomes problematic: it implied this process of restitution, the task (*Aufgabe*) was finally to render (*wiedergeben*) what was first given, and what was given was, one thought, the meaning. Now, things become obscure when one tries to accord this value of restitution with that of maturation. On what ground, in what ground will the maturation take place if the restitution of the meaning given is for it no longer the rule?

The allusion to the maturation of a seed could resemble a vitalist or geneticist metaphor; it would come, then, in support of the genealogical and parental code which seems to dominate this text. In fact it seems necessary here to invert this order and recognize what I have elsewhere proposed to call the "metaphoric catastrophe": far from knowing first what "life" or "family" mean whenever we use these familiar values to talk about language and translation; it is rather starting from the notion of a language and its "sur-vival" in translation that we could have access to the notion of what life and family mean. This reversal is operated expressly by Benjamin. His preface (for let us not forget: this essay is a preface) circulates without cease among the values of seed, life, and especially "sur-vival." (*Überleben* has an essential relation with *Übersetzen*). Now, very near the beginning, Benjamin seems to propose a simile or a metaphor—it opens with "just as . . . "—and right away everything moves in and about *Übersetzen, Übertragen, Überleben*:

> Just as the manifestations of life are intimately connected with the living, without signifying anything for it, a translation proceeds from the original. Indeed not so much from its life as from its survival [*Überleben*]. For a translation comes after the original and, for the important works that never find their predestined translator at the time of their birth, it characterizes the stage of their survival [*Fortleben*, this time, sur-vival as continuation of life rather than as life *post mortem*]. Now, it is in this simple reality, without any metaphor ["in völlig unmetaphorischer Sachlichkeit"], that it is necessary to conceive the ideas of life and survival [*Fortleben*] for works of art.

And according to a scheme that appears Hegelian, in a very circumscribed passage, Benjamin calls us to think life, starting from spirit or history and not from "organic corporeality" alone. There is life at the moment when "sur-vival" (spirit, history, works) exceeds biological life and death: "It is rather in recognizing for everything of which there is history and which is not merely the setting for history that one does justice to this concept of life. For it is starting from history, not from nature . . ., that the domain of life must finally be circumscribed. So is born for the philosopher the task [*Aufgabe*] of comprehending all natural life starting from this life, of much vaster extension, that is the life of history."

From the very title—and for the moment I stay with it—Benjamin situates the *problem*, in the sense of that which is precisely *before oneself* as a task, as the problem of the translator and not that of translation (nor, be it said in passing, and the question is not negligible, that of the translatoress). Benjamin does not say the task or the problem of translation. He names the subject of translation, as an indebted subject, obligated by a duty, already in the position of heir, entered as survivor in a genealogy, as survivor or agent of sur-vival. The sur-vival of works, not authors. Perhaps the sur-vival of authors' names and of signatures, but not of authors.

Such sur-vival gives more of life, more than a surviving. The work does not simply live longer, it lives more and better, beyond the means of its author. Would the translator then be an indebted receiver, subject to the gift and to the given of an original? By no means. For several reasons, including the following: the bond or obligation of the debt does not pass between a donor and a donee but between two texts (two "productions" or two "creations"). This is understood from the opening of the preface, and if one wanted to isolate theses, here are a few, as brutally as in any sampling:

1. The task of the translator does not announce itself or follow from a *reception*. The theory of translation does not depend for the essential on any theory of reception, even though it can inversely contribute to the elaboration and explanation of such a theory.

2. Translation does not have as essential mission any *communication*. No more than the original, and Benjamin maintains, secure from all danger of dispute, the strict duality between the original and the version, the translated and the translating, even though he shifts their relation. And he is interested in the translation of poetic or sacred texts, which would here yield the essence of translation. The entire essay extends between the poetic and the sacred, returning from the first to the second, the one that indicates the ideal of all translation, the purely transferable: the intralinear version of the sacred text, the model or ideal (*Urbild*) of any translation at all possible. Now, this is the second thesis: for a poetic text or a sacred text, communication is not the essential. This putting into question does not directly concern the communicative structure of language but rather the hypothesis of a communicable content that could be strictly distinguished from the linguistic act of communication. In 1916, the critique of semiotism and of the "bourgeois conception" of language was already directed against that distribution: means, object, addressee. "There is no content of language." What language first communicates is its "communicability" ("On Language as Such," trans. M. de Gandillac, 85). Will it be said that an opening is thus made toward the performative dimension of utterances? In any case this warns us against precipitation: isolating the contents and theses in "The Task of the Translator" and translating it otherwise than as the signature of a kind of proper name destined to ensure its sur-vival as a work.

3. If there is indeed between the translated text and the translating text a relation of "original" to version, it could not be *representative* or *reproductive*. Translation is neither an image nor a copy.

These three precautions now taken (neither reception, nor communication, nor representation), how are constituted the debt and the genealogy of the translator? Or first, how those of that which is *to-be-translated*, of the to-be-translated?

Let us follow the thread of life or sur-vival wherever it communicates with the movement of kinship. When Benjamin challenges the viewpoint of reception, it is not to deny it all pertinence, and he will undoubtedly have done much to prepare for a theory of reception in literature. But he wants first to return to the authority of what he still calls "the original," not insofar as it produces its receiver or its translators, but insofar as it requires, mandates, demands or commands them in establishing the law. And it is the structure of this demand that here appears most unusual. Through what does it pass? In a literary—more strictly speaking in this case, "poetic"—text it does not pass through the said, the uttered, the communicated, the content or the theme. And when, in this context, Benjamin still says "communication" or "enunciation" (*Mitteilung, Aussage*), it is not about the act but about the content that he visibly speaks: "But what does a literary work [*Dichtung*] 'say'? What does it communicate? Very little to those who understand it. What it has that is essential is not communication, not enunciation."

The demand seems thus to pass, indeed to be formulated, through the form. "Translation is a form," and the law of this form has its first place in the original. This law first establishes itself, let us repeat, as a demand in the strong sense, a requirement that delegates, mandates, prescribes, assigns. And as for this law as demand, two questions can arise; they are different in essence. First question: in the sum total of its readers, can the work always find the translator who is, as it were, capable? Second question and, says Benjamin, "more properly" (as if this question made the preceding more appropriate, whereas, we shall see, it does something quite different): "by its essence does it [the work] bear translation and if so—in line with the signification of this form—does it require translation?"

The answers to these two questions could not be of the same nature or the same mode. *Problematic* in the first case, not necessary (the translator capable of the work may appear or not appear, but even if he does not appear, that changes nothing in the demand or in the structure of the injunction that comes from the work), the answer is properly *apodictic* in the second case; necessary, a priori, demonstrable, absolute because it comes from the internal law of the original. The original requires translation even if no translator is there, fit to respond to this injunction, which is at the same time demand and desire in the very structure of the original. This structure is the relation of life to sur-vival. This requirement of the other as translator, Benjamin compares it to some unforgettable instant of life: it is lived as unforgettable, it is unforgettable even if in fact forgetting finally wins out. It will have been unforgettable—there is its essential significance, its apodictic essence; forgetting happens to this unforgettableness only by accident. The requirement of the unforgettable—which is here constitutive—is not in the least impaired by the finitude of memory. Likewise the requirement of translation in no way suffers from not being satisfied, at least it does not suffer in so far as it is the very structure of the work. In this sense the *surviving* dimension is an *a priori*—and death would not change it at all. No more than it would change the requirement (*Forderung*) that runs through the original work and to which only "a thought of God" can respond or correspond (*entsprechen*). Translation, the desire for translation, is not thinkable without this *correspondence* with a thought of God. In the text of 1916, which already accorded the task of the translator, his Aufgabe, with the response made to the gift of tongues and the gift of names ("Gabe der Sprache," "Gebung des Namens"), Benjamin named God at this point, that of a correspondence authorizing, making possible or guaranteeing the correspondence between the languages engaged in translation. In this narrow context, there was also the matter of the relations between language of things and language of men, between the silent and the speaking, the anonymous and the nameable, but the axiom held, no doubt, for all translation: "the objectivity of this translation is guaranteed in God" (trans. M. de Gandillac, 91). The debt, in the beginning, is fashioned in the hollow of this "thought of God."

Strange debt, which does not bind anyone to anyone. If the structure of the work is "sur-vival," the debt does not engage in relation to a hypothetical subject-author of the original text—dead or mortal, the dead man, or "dummy," of the text—but to something else that represents the formal law in the immanence of the original text. Then the debt does not involve restitution of a copy or a good image, a faithful representation of the original: the latter, the survivor, is itself in the process of transformation. The original gives itself in modifying itself; this gift is not an object given; it lives and lives on in mutation: "For in its survival, which would not merit the name if it were not mutation and renewal of something living, the original is modified. Even for words that are solidified there is still a postmaturation."

Postmaturation (*Nachreife*) of a living organism or a seed: this is not simply a metaphor, either, for the reasons already indicated. In its very essence, the history of this language is determined as "growth," "holy growth of languages."

4. If the debt of the translator commits him neither with regard to the author (dead insofar as his text has a structure of survival even if he is living) nor with regard to a model which must be reproduced or represented, to what or to whom is he committed? How is this to be named, this what or who? What is the proper name if not that of the author finite, dead or mortal of the text? And who is the translator who is thus committed, who perhaps finds himself *committed* by the other before having committed himself? Since the translator finds himself, as to the survival of the text, in the same situation as its finite and mortal producer

(its "author"), it is not he, not he himself as a finite and mortal being, who is committed. Then who? It is he, of course, but in the name of whom or what? The question of proper names is essential here. Where the act of the living mortal seems to count less than the sur-vival of the text in the *translation*—translated and translating—it is quite necessary that the signature of the proper noun be distinguished and not be so easily effaced from the contract or from the debt. Let us not forget that Babel names a struggle for the sur-vival of the name, the tongue or the lips.

From its height Babel at every instant supervises and surprises my reading: I translate, I translate the translation by Maurice de Gandillac of a text by Benjamin who, prefacing a translation, takes it as a pretext to say to what and in what way every translator is committed— and notes in passing, an essential part of his demonstration, that there could be no translation of translation. This will have to be remembered.

Recalling this strange situation, I do not wish only or essentially to reduce my role to that of a passer or passerby. Nothing is more serious than a translation. I rather wished to mark the fact that every translator is in a position to speak about translation, in a place which is more than any not second or secondary. For if the structure of the original is marked by the requirement to be translated, it is that in laying down the law the original begins by indebting itself *as well* with regard to the translator. The original is the first debtor, the first petitioner; it begins by lacking and by pleading for translation. This demand is not only on the side of the constructors of the tower who want to make a name for themselves and to found a universal tongue translating itself by itself; it also constrains the deconstructor of the tower: in giving his name, God also appealed to translation, not only between the tongues that had suddenly become multiple and confused, but first *of his name*, of the name he had proclaimed, given, and which should be translated as confusion to be understood, hence to let it be understood that it is difficult to translate and so to understand. At the moment when he imposes and opposes his law to that of the tribe, he is also a petitioner for translation. He is also indebted. He has not finished pleading for the translation of his name even though he forbids it. For Babel is untranslatable. God weeps over his name. His text is the most sacred, the most poetic, the most originary, since he creates a name and gives it to himself, but he is left no less destitute in his force and even in his wealth; he pleads for a translator. As in *La Folie du jour* by Maurice Blanchot, the law does not command without demanding to be read, deciphered, translated. It demands transference (*Übertragung* and *Übersetzung* and *Überleben*). The *double bind* is in the law. Even in God, and it is necessary to follow rigorously the consequence: *in his name.*

Insolvent on both sides, the double indebtedness passes between names. It surpasses a priori the bearers of the name, if by that is understood the mortal bodies which disappear behind the sur-vival of the name. Now, a proper noun does and does not belong, we said, to the language, not even, let us make it precise now, to the corpus of the text to be translated, of the to-be-translated.

The debt does not involve living subjects but names at the edge of the language or, more rigorously, the trait which contracts the relation of the aforementioned living subject to his name, insofar as the latter keeps to the edge of the language. And this trait would be that of the to-be-translated from one language to the other, from this edge to the other of the proper name. This language contract among several languages is absolutely singular. First of all, it is not what is generally called a language contract: that which guarantees the institution of *one* language, the unity of its system, and the social contract which binds a community in this regard. On the other hand, it is generally supposed that in order to be valid or to institute anything at all, a contract must take place in a single language or appeal (for example, in the case of diplomatic or commercial treaties) to a transferability already given and without remainder: there the multiplicity of tongues must be absolutely dominated. Here, on the contrary, a contract between two foreign languages as such engages to render possible a translation which *subsequently* will authorize every sort of contract in the originary sense. The signature of this singular contract needs no written document or record: it nevertheless takes place as trace or as trait, and this place takes place even if its space comes under no empirical or mathematical objectivity.

The topos of this contract is exceptional, unique, and practically impossible to think under the ordinary category of contract: in a classical code it would have been called transcendental, since in truth it renders possible every contract in general, starting with what is called the language contract within the limits of a single idiom. Another name, perhaps, for the origin of tongues. Not the origin of language but of languages—before language, languages.

The translation contract, in this transcendental sense, would be the contract itself, the absolute contract, the contract form of the contract, that which allows a contract to be what it is.

Will one say that the kinship among languages presupposes this contract or that the kinship provides a first occasion for the contract? One recognizes here a classic circle. It has always begun to turn whenever one asks oneself about the origin of languages or society. Benjamin, who often talks about the kinship among languages, never does so as a comparatist or as a historian of languages. He is interested less in families of languages than in a more essential and more enigmatic connection, an affinity which is not sure to precede the trait or the contract of the to-be-translated. Perhaps even this kinship, this affinity (*Verwandschaft*), is like an alliance, by the contract of translation, to the extent that the sur-vivals which it associates are not natural lives, blood ties, or empirical symbioses.

> This development, like that of a life original and elevated, is determined by a finality original and elevated. Life and finality—their correlation apparently evident, yet almost beyond the grasp of knowledge, only reveals itself when the goal, in view of which all singular finalities of life act, is not sought in the proper domain of that life but rather at a level more elevated. All finalized vital phenomena, like their very finality, are, after all, finalized not toward life but toward the expression of its essence, toward the representation [*Darstellung*] of its signification. Thus translation has finally as goal to express the most intimate relation among languages.

A translation would not seek to say this or that, to transport this or that content, to communicate such a charge of meaning, but to re-mark the affinity among the languages, to exhibit its own possibility. And that, which holds for the literary text or the sacred text, perhaps defines the very essence of the literary and the sacred, at their common root. I said "re-mark" the affinity among the language to name the strangeness of an "expression" ("to express the most intimate relation among the languages"), which is neither a simple "presentation" nor simply anything else. In a mode that is solely anticipatory, annunciatory, almost prophetic, translation renders *present* an affinity that is never present in this presentation. One thinks of the way in which Kant at times defines the relation to the sublime: a presentation inadequate to that which is nevertheless presented. Here Benjamin's discourse proceeds in twists and turns:

> It is impossible that it [the translation] be able to reveal this hidden relation itself, that it be able to restitute [*herstellen*] it; but translation can represent [*darstellen*] that relation in actualizing it in its seed or in its intensity. And this representation of a signified ["*Darstellung eines Bedeuteten*"] by the endeavor, by

the seed of its restitution, is an entirely original mode of representation, which has hardly any equivalent in the domain of nonlinguistic life. For the latter has, in analogies and signs, types of reference [*Hindeutung*] other than the intensive, that is to say anticipatory, annunciatory [*vorgreifende, andeutende*] actualization. But the relation we are thinking of, this very intimate relation among the languages, is that of an original convergence. It consists in this: the languages are not foreign to one another, but, a priori and abstracted from all historical relations, are related to one another in what they mean.

The entire enigma of that kinship is concentrated here. What is meant by "what they mean"? And what about this presentation in which nothing is presented in the ordinary mode of presence?

At stake here are the name, the symbol, the truth, the letter.

One of the basic foundations of the essay, as well as of the 1916 text, is a theory of the name. Language is determined starting from the word and the privilege of naming. This is, in passing, a very strong if not very conclusive assertion: "the originary element of the translator" is the word and not the sentence, the syntactic articulation. As food for thought, Benjamin offers a curious "image": the sentence (*Satz*) would be "the wall in front of the language of the original," whereas the word, the word for word, literality (*Wörtlichkeit*), would be its "arcade." Whereas the wall braces while concealing (it is *in front of* the original), the arcade supports while letting light pass and the original show (we are not far from the Parisian passages). This privilege of the word obviously supports that of the name and with it what is proper to the proper name, the stakes and the very possibility of the translation contract. It opens onto the *economic* problem of translation, whether it be a matter of economy as the law of the proper or of economy as a quantitative relation (is it translating to transpose a proper name into several words, into a phrase or into a description, and so forth?).

There is some to-be-translated. From both sides it assigns and makes contracts. It commits not so much authors as proper names at the edge of the language, it essentially commits neither to communicate nor to represent, nor to keep an already signed commitment, but rather to draw up the contract and to give birth to the pact, in other words to the *symbolon*, in a sense that Benjamin does not designate by this term but suggests, no doubt with the metaphor of the amphora, let us say, since from the start we have suspected the ordinary sense of metaphor with the *ammetaphor*.

If the translator neither restitutes nor copies an original, it is because the original lives on and transforms itself. The translation will truly be a moment in the growth of the original, which will complete itself in enlarging itself. Now, it has indeed to be, and it is in this that the "seminal" logic must have imposed itself on Benjamin, that growth not give rise to just any form in just any direction. Growth must accomplish, fill, complete (*Ergänzung* is here the most frequent term). And if the original calls for a complement, it is because at the origin it was not there without fault, full, complete, total, identical to itself. From the origin of the original to be translated there is fall and exile. The translator must redeem (*erlösen*), absolve, resolve, in trying to absolve himself of his own debt, which is at bottom the same—and bottomless. "To redeem in his own tongue that pure language exiled in the foreign tongue, to liberate by transposing this pure language captive in the work, such is the task of the translator." Translation is a poetic transposition (*Umdichtung*). We will have to examine the essence of the "pure language" that it liberates. But let us note for the moment that this liberation itself presupposes a freedom of the translator, which is itself none other than relation to that "pure language"; and the liberation that it operates, eventually in transgressing the limits of the translating language, in transforming it in turn, must extend, enlarge, and make language grow. As this growth comes also to complete, as it is *symbolon*, it does not reproduce: it adjoins in adding.

Hence this double simile (*Vergleich*), all these turns and metaphoric supplements: (1) "Just as the tangent touches the circle only in a fleeting manner and at a single point, and just as it is this contact, not the point, that assigns to the tangent the law according to which it pursues to infinity its course in a straight line, so the translation touches the original in a fleeting manner and only at an infinitely small point of meaning, to follow henceforth its proper course, according to the law of fidelity in the liberty of language movement." Each time that he talks about the contact (*Berührung*) between the bodies of the two texts in the process of translation, Benjamin calls it "fleeting" (*flüchtig*). On at least three occasions, this "fleeting" character is emphasized, and always in order to situate the contact with meaning, the infinitely small point of meaning which the languages barely brush ("The harmony between the languages is so profound here [in the translations of Sophocles by Hölderlin] that the meaning is only touched by the wind of language in the manner of an Eolian lyre"). What can an infinitely small point of meaning be? What is the measure to evaluate it? The metaphor itself is at once the question and the answer. And here is the other metaphor, the metamphora, which no longer concerns extension in a straight and infinite line but enlargement by adjoining along the broken lines of a fragment. (2) "For, just as the fragments of the amphora, if one is to be able to reconstitute the whole, must be contiguous in the smallest details, but not identical to each other, so instead of rendering itself similar to the meaning of the original, the translation should rather, in a movement of love and in full detail, pass into its own language the mode of intention of the original: thus, just as the debris become recognizable as fragments of the same amphora, original and translations become recognizable as fragments of a larger language."

Let us accompany this movement of love, the gesture of this loving one (*liebend*) that is at work in the translation. It does not reproduce, does not restitute, does not represent; as to the essential, it does not render the meaning of the original except at that point of contact or caress, the infinitely small of meaning. It extends the body of languages, it puts languages into symbolic expansion, and symbolic here means that, however little restitution there be to accomplish, the larger, the new vaster aggregate, has still to *reconstitute* something. It is perhaps not a whole, but it is an aggregate in which openness should not contradict unity. Like the urn which lends its poetic topos to so many meditations on word and thing, from Holderlin to Rilke and Heidegger, the amphora is one with itself though opening itself to the outside—and this openness opens the unity, renders it possible, and forbids it totality. Its openness allows receiving and giving. If the growth of language must also reconstitute without representing, if that is the symbol, can translation lay claim to the truth? Truth—will that still be the name of that which still lays down the law for a translation?

Here we touch—at a point no doubt infinitely small—the limit of translation. The pure untranslatable and the pure transferable here pass one into the other—and it is the truth, "itself materially."

The word "truth" appears more than once in "The Task of the Translator." We must not rush to lay hold of it. It is not a matter of truth for a translation in so far as it might conform or be faithful to its model, the original. Nor any more a matter, either for the original or even for the translation, of some adequation of the language to meaning or to reality, nor indeed of the representation to something. Then what is it that goes under the name of truth? And will it be that new?

Let us start again from the "symbolic." Let us remember the metaphor, or the ammeta-phor: a translation espouses the original when the two adjoined fragments, as different as they can be, complete each other so as to form a larger tongue in the course of a sur-vival that changes them both. For the native tongue of the translator, as we have noted, is altered as well. Such at least is my interpretation—my translation, my "task of the translator." It is what I have called the translation contract: hymen or marriage contract with the promise to produce a child whose seed will give rise to history and growth. A marriage contract in the form of a seminar. Benjamin says as much, in the translation the original becomes larger; it grows rather than reproduces itself—and I will add: like a child, its own, no doubt, but with the power to speak on its own which makes of a child something other than a product subjected to the law of reproduction. This promise signals a kingdom which is at once "promised and forbidden where the languages will be reconciled and fulfilled." This is the most Babelian note in an analysis of sacred writing as the model and the limit of all writing, in any case of all Dichtung in its being-to-be-translated. The sacred and the being-to-be-translated do not lend themselves to thought one without the other. They produce each other at the edge of the same limit.

This kingdom is never reached, touched, trodden by translation. There is something untouchable, and in this sense the reconciliation is only promised. But a promise is not nothing, it is not simply marked by what it lacks to be fulfilled. As a promise, translation is already an event, and the decisive signature of a contract. Whether or not it be honored does not prevent the commitment from taking place and from bequeathing its record. A translation that manages, that manages to promise reconciliation, to talk about it, to desire it or make it desirable—such a translation is a rare and notable event.

Translator's note

Translation is an art of compromise, if only because the problems of translation have no one solution and none that is fully satisfactory. The best translation is merely better than the worst to some extent, more or less. Compromise also precludes consistency. It would have been possible, and it once seemed plausible, to maintain regular equivalents at least for those terms that figure prominently in the argument. But the result was not worth the sacrifice. There was consolation for so much effort to so little effect in that whatever we did, we were bound to exhibit the true principles of translation announced in our text. And so this translation is exemplary to that extent. To the extent that we were guided in translation, the principles were also those found in the text. Accordingly, a silhouette of the original appears for effect in many words and phrases of the translation.

Publication of the French text is also significant in telling of our situation. Among the many differences in this translation, a few appear already in the original.

The quotations from Walter Benjamin are translated from the French, not the German. The biblical passages are also translated from their French versions, since Derrida works from translations in both cases.

Here are some of the problems for which I found solutions least satisfactory:

"Des Tours de Babel." The title can be read in various ways. *Des* means "some"; but it also means "of the," "from the," or "about the." *Tours* could be towers, twists, tricks, turns, or tropes, as in a "turn" of phrase. Taken together, *des* and *tours* have the same sound as *détour*, the word for detour. To mark that economy in language the title has not been changed.

langue/langage. It is difficult to mark this difference in English where "language" covers both. Whenever possible, "tongue" has been used for *langue*, and "language" only in those cases that are clearly specific rather than generic. *Langage* is then translated as "language" in the singular and without modifier, though not always. The German *Sprache* introduces further complications.

survie. The word means "survival" as well as "afterlife"; its use in the text also brings out the subliminal sense of more life and more than life. The hyphenation of "sur-vival" is an admitted cheat.

performance. The French has not the primarily dramatic connotation of the English but rather the sense of prowess and success; its use here also relates to the "performative" of speech acts.

pas-de-sens. With this expression Derrida combines the *pas* of negation with the *pas* of step in a most curious figure. My English suggested a skip.

De ce droit à la vérité quel est le rapport? This sentence could be translated by any and all of the following: What is the relation between this law and the truth? What is the gain from this law to the truth? What is the relation between this right to the truth and all the rest?

Chapter 69

Hent De Vries

HYPERTHEOLOGY

The basic premise explored by De Vries is that deconstruction *appears to be* analogous to the *via negativa*, or a system of thinking known as "negative theology", which argues that we can only approach God indirectly because God totally transcends our limited human perspective. Deconstruction and negative theology therefore share the quality of being "apophatic"; that is to say, both are methods of gaining knowledge and insight "by way of negation" (*OED*). The conundrum here is that because deconstruction *does* function through a mode of saying what we cannot say (language works through absence, not presence; meaning is always deferred; systems always have blind spots or aporias; all meaning depends upon undecidables such as the trace, the pharmakon, *différance*; etc.), then we cannot positively say that deconstruction is (or is not) a negative theology. De Vries, who is a Professor holding the Russ Family Chair in the Humanities at Johns Hopkins University, suggests that we cannot even decide whether deconstruction is a secularized, modern-day negative theology stripped bare of its religiosity, or, if negative theology is some secret inner sanctum of deconstruction. Derrida would appear to support this ambiguity; for example, he notes that any argument that proceeds by a series of apophatic statements is thereby already speaking about God, whether this was intended or not. So even when deconstruction denies the possibility of a transcendent signified, it does so via apophatic statements that adumbrate precisely that which was denied. To put this another way, the absent name of God is spoken whenever a series of negatives are produced. The impossibility of breaking free from this double bind, whereby the denial creates the conditions for shared identity (between deconstruction and negative theology), also means that this relationship can never be finally clarified. In other words, just as there cannot be a final, totalizing statement that rises above the humanly possible knowledge of God, neither can there be a final, certain division of deconstruction and other procedures that function via negation. Such a promised end (the final statement . . .) is always undercut by performativity, i.e., the desired ultimate description (of meaning; of God) is undercut by performative language (language that doesn't *describe*, but instead *acts*): the *via negativa* and deconstruction do not deal in what Austin calls "constatives" (provable statements), but instead they make all concepts performatives (conditional, arbitrary, dependent upon an action or a condition and a context). As De Vries notes, deconstruction undermines any contextual knowledge available to make sense of performatives, and even the concept of the "absolute" is thereby destabilized in terms of the impossibility of making any positive statements about it. Derrida renames this notion of the performative, the "perverformative", which De Vries intimates is an originary perversion of the performative found in the notion that it is God himself who generates the contradictions and ambiguities encountered in this torturous approach to knowledge. So Derrida turns to Heidegger to make sense of all this, especially Heidegger's notion that we do not need to turn to Being to understand God, even though it is in Being that we experience God; Derrida focuses on the German phrase *Offenbarung* (revelation), which he interprets as the opening or possibility of revelation, sidestepping his own reference to Luther to argue that this opening is the opening of that which is not, rather than an incarnational moment.

I N THE MODERN PERIOD, DERRIDA NOTES, the term *negative* theology no longer exclusively refers to a historically articulated doctrine, but has more and more "come to designate a certain typical attitude toward language, and within it, in the act of definition or attribution, an attitude toward semantic or conceptual determination" (HAS 4/536). It is by a process of increasing formalization of the *via negativa*—a progressive "kenosis" of discourse that tends to abstract from dogmatic content, as well as from its so-called secular reinscriptions—that the range of a diacritical deployment of this figure (and thereby of its possible practical effects) has also been vastly expanded. For the best and for the worst, since the figure in question provides the key to the problem of evil—to *radical evil* as Derrida puts it, following Kant—no less than to that of justice, not to distributive justice, to be sure, but to justice in the emphatic and excessive, Benjaminian or, rather, Levinasian sense of the word.

But then again, was there ever a substance that allowed us—in retrospect—to measure the distance between the mystic injunction as a pure performative, on the one hand, and a dogmatic content or context from which it sets itself apart? Derrida doesn't say so, but suggests that this presupposition may always have been the illusion—a transcendental illusion of sorts—without which no kenotic attitude toward language can come into its own. Yet stripped of this canonical or heterodox substance, the supposedly negative operation of apophatics was stretched to its limit, and this to the point of becoming virtually indistinguishable from any other purely formal discursive strategy. The *via negativa* thus seemed to have become the privileged "nonsynonymous substitution" for all negative operations, whether philosophical, aesthetic, literary, psychoanalytic, ethico-political, or even existential. God, the notion "God," it would seem, delivered the key to the understanding of the nothing (the *Nichts*) and the particular negative operation (the *Nichten*) of which Heidegger speaks with so much fervor.

Against this backdrop, Derrida proposes a thought experiment based on a possible analogy or family resemblance between an extremely formalized, one might say consistent, negative theology and any responsible thought of the trace or of *différance:*

> Suppose, by a provisional hypothesis, that negative theology consists of considering that every predicative language is inadequate to the essence, in truth to the hyperessentiality (the being beyond Being) of God; consequently only a negative ("apophatic") attribution can claim to approach God, and to prepare us for a silent intuition of God. By *a more or less tenable analogy,* one would thus recognize some traits, the *family resemblance* of negative theology, in every discourse that seems to return in a regular and insistent manner to this rhetoric of negative determination, endlessly multiplying the defenses and the apophatic warnings: this, which is called X (for example, text, writing, the trace, *différance,* the hymen, the supplement, the pharmakon, the parergon, etc.) "is" neither this nor that, neither sensible nor intelligible, neither positive nor negative, neither

inside nor outside, neither superior nor inferior, neither active nor passive, neither present nor absent, not even neutral, not even subject to a dialectic with a third moment, without any possible sublation ("Aufhebung"). Despite appearances, then, this X is neither a concept nor even a name; it does lend itself to a series of names, but calls for another syntax, and exceeds even the order and the structure of predicative discourse. It "is" not and does not say what "is." It is written completely otherwise. (HAS 4/536; emphasis added)

The seemingly metaphysical concept of analogy and the more Wittgensteinian notion of the family resemblance serve as technical terms, chosen here to illuminate a mode of comparison, of interleaving, of intersection, and of resonance that goes well beyond that of a merely accidental, contingent, or purely empirical, some would say ontic, association. An indelible interplay and co-implication of *chance* and *necessity* (of *tuchē* and *anankē*) is at work here, one that draws on an even older archive, which seems now out of reach; and this, I would venture to say, not only for the strategic or provisional use of such concepts as "analogy" or "family resemblance" (marked as they are by Aristotelian, scholastic, and pragmatic overtones respectively), but also, in the final analysis, for the very idea of transcendental historicity, which comes closest to being the key to the problem of hand.

But the invocation of *la Chance* and *la Nécessité* does not dispel the obvious difficulty of determining whether the given examples of the nonsynonymous substitutions mentioned above should be seen either as so many radical transformative reversals of an ancient paradigm, stripped of its overtly theological connotations, or as that paradigm's secret prolongation. This uncertainty functions as the silent axiom and central theme, if there is one (or just one), of Derrida's "How To Avoid Speaking" and sheds light on its dealing with the question of language, the tropes of space and place, and the oblique discussion of apophatic anthropology. "For essential reasons one is never certain of being able to attribute to anyone a project of negative theology as such," Derrida observes (HAS 3–4/535–36).

The least one can say is that in recent forms of critical and post-structuralist theory—for example, deconstruction—the persistence of the negative mode of predication—of denials and denegations, evasions and ellipses—seems as inevitable as its always possible confusion with religious apophatics. In Derrida's own words:

From the moment a proposition takes a negative form, the negativity that manifests itself need only to be pushed to the limit, and it at least resembles an apophatic theology. Every time I say: X is neither this nor that, neither the simple neutralization of this nor of that with which is *has nothing in common,* being absolutely heterogeneous to or incommensurable with them, I would start to speak of God, under this name or another. God's name would then be the hyperbolic effect of that negativity or of all negativity that is consistent in its discourse. (HAS 6/538)

All negative predication would somehow "produce divinity" (HAS 6/538), infinitely substituting the name (rather than the concept) of God or of whatever comes to take His place. All genuine or radical negativity could be said to be "haunted" by the ghost of "God" and thus to be responsive to a spectral figure—that of the *à dieu*—that is neither identifiable with a full presence nor reducible to the latter's mere abstract negation. Every thought deserving of the name would be faithful to this promise, to the putting forth of this figure (saying *adieu* and speaking *à dieu,* apophatically and cataphatically) and, in so doing, to putting *itself* before this very figure as well. What is more, it would have to promise to do so, not conditionally, but regardless of the future to come, in *any* future to come.

Conversely, divinity is not only "produced" but "productive"—or promising—in its turn. Put otherwise, "God," under this name or another, is not just the ineffable *telos* of every old and new *via negativa,* but also its very origin, its *archē,* or rather *an-archē,* and, in that sense, its first and last word:

> "God" would name *that without which* one would not know how to account for any negativity: grammatical or logical negation, illness, evil, and finally neurosis, which, far from permitting psychoanalysis to reduce religion to a symptom, would obligate it to recognize in the symptom the negative manifestation of God. Without saying that there must be at least as much "reality" in the cause as in the effect [the classic premise of the so-called cosmological argument for the existence of God-HdV], and that the "existence" of God has need of any proof other than the religious symptomatics, one would see on the contrary—in the negation or suspension of the predicate, even of the thesis of "existence"—the first mark of respect for a divine cause which does not even need to "be."[1]

If deconstruction is seen as the most consistent apophatic discourse, Derrida continues, one could indeed always choose to consider it simply "a symptom of modern or postmodern nihilism," or, on the contrary, "recognize in it the last testimony—not to say the martyrdom—of faith in the present *fin de siècle.* This reading will always be possible" (HAS 7/539).

However, to say this is not to deny that the purported analogy between deconstruction and negative theology remains, in a way, also arbitrary, provisional, problematic, hypothetical and even questionable: a begging of the very question of each of these two radically distinct discursive models, which are different in terms of their historical resources and aspirations. Or so it seems. For it should be clear from what we have found so far that the confessed analogy or family resemblance is by no means a simple retraction of Derrida's earlier statements that the thought of *différance* and the *via negativa* of apophatic theology differ in many crucial respects. If anything, these statements are now qualified or nuanced: *insofar* as negative theology still presupposes a trajectory that is proposition "and privileges not only the indestructible unity of the word but also the authority of the name" (HAS 7/539); *insofar,* moreover, as negative theology "seems to reserve beyond all positive predication, beyond all negation, even beyond Being, some hyperessentiality, a being beyond Being" (HAS 7–8/540); and *insofar,* finally, as negative theology stands and falls with the assumption (or the promise) of an ultimate intuition, a *visio* and *unio mystica*—*insofar,* then, as each of these deconstructible assumptions or postulates still seem to apply to what is called "negative theology," the latter remains to be sharply distinguished from what has come to be known as deconstruction. The latter, it seems, is analogous only to the most heterodox or the most orthodox—in any case, the most rigorous—apophatic theologies, not to those that go only halfway, leaving many presuppositions intact. However, to the extent that these presuppositions are unavoidable—that is to say, cannot be prevented from returning, but continue to be legible, visible, audible, or otherwise perceptible and intuitable under the marks of their erasure (and, in the era of metaphysics and its simple reversals that happens at every moment, everywhere), the confusion and, indeed, conflation of deconstruction with negative theology will persist, just as much as their radical distinction also remains necessary. Therefore, as Heidegger makes clear, both the ontotheological and the radically heterodox heritages of the *via negativa* cast their shadows indiscriminately well beyond modern attempts to illuminate their premises and implications.[2]

This said, it is clear that Derrida's attempts to reassess the question of "How to avoid speaking"—viewed here according to its form, regardless of whether it speaks of God or of Being—cannot and do not pretend to do justice to either apophatics or deconstruction, or cannot do so without testifying to their seeming confusion, that is to say, to their apparent substitutability. Nor is it clear how speaking of apophatics, how speaking apophatically—but also how speaking of deconstruction or speaking deconstructively—could simply be avoided in this day and age and at least for some time to come.

As a consequence, the question of how to avoid speaking of "God," of Being, and of whatever comes to take their place or adopts their name can no longer be assigned a proper place, whether in the discourse of apophatics or in the practice of deconstruction. Nor can one hope to approach this question meta-theoretically, empirically, or historically without immediately being drawn into the equation. Speaking of one, we may well be speaking—in the place or in the name—of the other, or vice versa. It is impossible to tell the difference.

Clarification of the relationship between deconstruction and apophatics is in the end nothing but an unfulfillable promise, and one that threatens to blur all the necessary distinctions at that. In other words, the result of any attempt to disentangle all the relevant threads and overlaps, intersections and overtones, remains for ever pending, not for lack of rigor, but because this is the precise answer we must expect. What is intelligible is only that there is a certain unintelligibility here. "One can never decide whether deferring, as such, brings about precisely that which it defers and alters [*diffère*]," Derrida says. "It is not certain that I am keeping my promise today; nor is it certain that in further delaying I have not, nevertheless, already kept it" (HAS 13/546).

As so often, Derrida's analysis performs here what it seeks to circumscribe, speaking of negative theology, not just in terms of a promise or with reference to the promise, but also, paradoxically, *within the promise* (HAS 14/547; emphasis added). It is only consequent that he indicates a little later in a similar vein: "I thus decided *not to speak* of negativity or of apophatic movements in, for example, the Jewish or Islamic traditions. To leave this immense place empty, . . . to remain thus on the threshold—was this not the most consistent possible apophasis?"[3]

It is precisely this moment of suspense—an *epochē* of sorts—that accounts for the fact that Derrida's reading of negative theology in its traditional and most unexpected modern guises not only mimics or mirrors the structure and privileged figures of the apophatic way but runs the risk of becoming its parody and, indeed, its most severe betrayal. The analysis of apophatics proposed here—which appears as an apophatics of deconstruction no less than as a deconstruction of apophatics, or as both at once—could therefore just as well be a form of ultimate respect as a sign of its opposite, that is to say, of blasphemy and idolatry. Again, the difference between these two extremes would be virtually impossible to tell. It gives itself to be seen only to those who are willing and are able to see and to testify to it; and this means, paradoxically, only to those who are willing and able to pass through the trial of this uncertainty. If anywhere, it is here that we would touch upon the heart of the apophatic anthropology that accompanies the tradition of negative theology and leaves its mark on Derrida's writing as well.

As long as complete silence is impossible—and even silence speaks (or can be telling enough) where it turns away from a particular "saying" or "said" or even "contradicts" the virtual totality of all that is said or can be said—apophatic discourse will always simultaneously say too little and too much. Again, the difference between these two seemingly opposite possibilities or extremes is almost impossible to discern. Each of them is inappropriate and therefore blasphemous, idolatrous, with the respect to the referent (whether God, a hyperessence, the trace, or some "nonsynonymous substitute"). In extremis, they converge to the point of becoming at least formally interchangeable. Saying too much or too little, as one cannot but do when one speaks—and one cannot but speak—the difference matters little. The only way out of this impasse, therefore, seems to be the one Jean-Luc Marion takes from Pascal's *Pensées:* only "God can well speak of God."[4] Everything else, every attempt to speak well—one way or another—is vanity, hypocrisy, idolatry.

Yet can we allow God this very possibility, as Pascal and Marion think we should and indeed must? Does God not already contradict Himself, as Derrida claims, following Jabès? Is God, the name or the concept, but also the "positive reality" and "presence" of God, in its very existence or essence, in and for itself, any more stable than anything else? Can God, for Himself, address Himself, without missing the point, without speaking already, as it were, off the mark?

True, the very notion of God implies and demands a full presence of Himself to Himself, an adequate self-reference, self-representation, or auto-affection, in addition to all divine names, epithets, and predicates, which the tradition of philosophical theology has investigated with indefatigable inventiveness, to the point where there is almost nothing to say that has not already been said. Even a superficial reading of Pseudo-Dionysius's *The Divine Names* and *The Mystical Theology,* to which I turn below, reveals that almost all thinkable categories and adjectives are carefully recited and reassessed, only to be found wanting to a greater or lesser degree. Nonetheless, they are never discarded, but remain in place as necessary stepping-stones on the way that leads upward and then downward, upward by leading downward, and vice versa. Dionysius's usage of these so-called divine names is—anachronistically speaking—marked by a certain performativity, and thereby repetition, that is far more pertinent than any search for the one appropriate and holy name. This is hardly an accident, but obeys a certain historical logic of traditionality, indeed, of transcendental historicity. A similar motif can be found in Heidegger's insistence, in his early courses on the phenomenology of religion, on the New Testament—indeed, Pauline—temporality of the *again of the already,* to which I turn in the next chapter. This structure captures the very dynamics and rhythm of Heidegger's formally indicative method, which, in turn, forms the heart of the procedure of ontological correction.

The Unavoidable

Aspiring to rehearse the apophatic gesture and keep its distance at the same time, Derrida's "How to Avoid Speaking" can, in the end, only present us with a "fabulous narration" (*narration fabuleuse*) (HAS 30/ 562; see also 60/ 592). In Derrida's vocabulary, informed as it is by both Francis Ponge's "Fable" (compare the opening pages of Derrida's *Psyché*)[5] and Michel de Certeau's *La Fable mystique,* the word *fable* does not so much stand for the Active or the literary (let alone for a merely aesthetic mode of presentation), as for the "condition of possibility" of these respective genres: a certain "fictionality" or "literacity" that both fiction and literature (as well as the aesthetic) share in principle with the philosophical, the ontological, and the theological. This fabulosity is precisely what qualifies the central meaning, often noted, of what Derrida calls the quasi-transcendental.

Much more is at stake here, however, than a "condition of possibility," or a redefinition of the concept of the transcendental. Derrida's more recent writings—and, again, this is most notable in his interrogations of the religious and the theological—are increasingly concerned with a singular structure of singularity that seems to absolve itself from the logic of the possible as such, from the thinking of "possibilization," and this at least as much as it outwits the conditions that are commonly defined as ontico-ontological, empirical, semantic, pragmatic or symbolic. It seems as if the law of the possible is increasingly suspected of being indebted to a metaphysical tradition that Derrida describes as a "logic of presupposition." Of the latter no clearer example can be found than in Heidegger's fundamental ontology and existential analytic, which for all its modification and radicalization continues to be a foundationalism, a possibilism, and even a humanism in disguise. In the two following chapters, I shall provide some of the most important reasons that enable Derrida to make this far-reaching claim.

In the writings that interest us here, Derrida's attention is focused on the testimonial, the confessional, and the secret, all of which relate to the question of autobiography. What is more, they each in their singular way redraw the lines of the debate that has come to dominate the reception of J. L. Austin's *How to Do Things With Words,* in speech-act theory as well as in contemporary cultural analysis: the distinction between the constative and the performative, the place of the first person singular and plural, the structure of the promise, the nature of repetition, or rather reiteration (or, as Derrida's *Limited Inc.* has it, of iterability), and so on. But the often implicit revisiting of these terms leaves none of them untouched or intact. And this relegation of these basic terms to the metaphysics of presence (in the case of the constative and the prominence of the first person singular), as well as its exposure to or reinscription into the language of religion or apophatics (in the case of the performative and the promise), makes room for—and, indeed, gestures toward—a quite different experience of words and things, one that escapes, not only the parameters of speech-act theory originally or commonly defined, but also the premises of its redeployments in current cultural theory.

Once again, this redescription leaves nothing intact. And the performativity around which Derrida's analyses of the apophatic and religion "at large" revolve is therefore at once that of a performative called absolute (or ab-solute) and one that undercuts the very concept and theory of performatives. It is no accident that in *The Postcard,* in the section entitled "Envois," Derrida speaks, if only in passing, of the "perverformative."[6] Yet it is precisely in this intrinsic instability or aporetics that the performativity of which we speak here can be said to border upon the most salient features of the *via negativa* and, indeed, of mystic speech. There is no better example of the meaning of the "performative" than the dictum that guides this entire discussion: "God already contradicts himself." It both captures the singular structure of performativity that interest us here—a performative contradiction or performative aporetics of sorts—and reminds us that this structure cannot adequately be described *in abstracto* but should, perhaps, best be seen in terms of a certain historico-theological overdetermination for which "God" is still the best and the most economical name. Hegel was right, then, albeit for other reasons than those the *Wissenschaft der Logik* provides: "und das unbestrittenste Recht hätte *Gott,* dass mit ihm der Anfang gemacht werde" ("and *God* would have the absolutely undisputed right that the beginning be made with him").[7]

The study of Jewish and Arab esoteric thought, a paradigm in our cultural heritage that approaches the apophatic—and thus, by analogy, deconstruction—even more closely than the Greco-Christian tradition, might enable us to grasp this better, Derrida suggests in "How to Avoid Speaking," but this path is not taken there. Discussions of Plato, Pseudo-Dionysius, Eckhart, Marion, Levinas, and Wittgenstein have a prominent place, but references to Jewish and Arabic mystics are absent or remain implicit. Derrida speaks of them—perhaps from within them, away from them, and toward them, apophatically and emphatically, as it were—but without speaking *about* them, at least not directly.

Instead, he turns to yet another apophatics, one that is neither simply Greek and Christian nor Jewish or Arab, but that may nonetheless very well "resemble the most questioning legacy, both the most audacious and most liberated repetition" (HAS 53/584) of Greco-Christian apophatics, to wit, Heidegger's questioning of Western metaphysics. Having questioned the Greek and Christian paradigms, he extends his analysis to the inquiry into "a few landmarks" (HAS 53/584) on Heidegger's path of thinking. These landmarks help to measure the degree to which the thought of Being, in its destruction of ontotheology, can itself, in turn, be shown to touch upon the theological, and to do so, moreover, in ways that Heidegger is generally at great pains to *avoid.* As is perhaps nowhere clearer than in

Heidegger's texts, the apophatic lets itself neither be bracketed (phenomenologically or otherwise) nor be crossed out. Citing one of Heidegges's "landmarks," Derrida writes:

> [Heidegger says:] "Faith has no need for the thinking of Being." As he often recalls, Christians ought to allow themselves to be inspired by Luther's lucidity on this subject. Indeed, even if Being is "neither the foundation nor the essence of God [*Grund und Wesen von Gott*]," the experience of God (*die Erfahrung Gottes*)— that is, the experience of revelation—"occurs in the dimension of Being [*in der Dimention des Seins sich ereignet*]." This revelation is not that *(Offenbarung)* of which the religions speak, but the possibility of this revelation, the opening for this manifestation . . . [the] *Offenbarkeit* . . . in which an *Offenbarung* can take place and man can encounter God. Although God is not and need not be thought from Being as His essence or foundation, the *dimension of Being* opens up access to the advent, the experience, the encounter with this God who nevertheless is not. The word *dimension*—which is also difference—here gives a measure while giving place. One could sketch a singular chiasmus. The anguished experience of the Nothing discloses Being. Here, the dimension of Being discloses the experience of God, who is not or whose Being is neither the essence nor the foundation.
>
> How not to think of this? This dimension of disclosure, this place that gives place without being either essence or foundation—would not this step or passage, this threshold that gives access to God, yet be the "parvis" *(vorbürge)* of which Meister Eckhart spoke? "When we apprehend God in Being, we apprehend Him in His outer sanctuary [*parvis*], for Being is the *parvis* in which He resides." Is this a theological, an onto-theological, tradition? A theological tradition? Would Heidegger adopt it? Would he disown it? Would he deny it? (HAS 58–59/591–92)

Derrida does not answer these questions in any direct or decisive way. And for good reason. For not only do we touch here upon an undecidable debate, the one that goes on and on, indefinitely, between Heidegger and the Christian theologians (as is suggested in an almost comical way by the closing argument and the last few pages of *Of Spirit*); these questions reflect on the status of Derrida's own position as well. In both cases, they testify to the difficulty one will always have in establishing a proper domain for the question of Being or the philosophical as such, in contradistinction to that of the theological, the apophatic, and the religion of which (on the basis or in view of which) they speak, irresistibly, unavoidably, yet always in vain.[8]

Abbreviations

HAS Jacques Derrida, "How to Avoid Speaking: Denials," in *Languages of the Unsayable: The Play of Negativity in Literature and Literary Theory*, ed., Sanford Budick and Wolfgang Iser (New York: Columbia University Press, 1989), 3–70; translation by Ken Frieden of "comment ne pas parler: Dénégations," in *Psyché: Inventions de l'autre* (Paris: Galilée, 1987), 535–95.

Notes

1   HAS 7/538–39. Up to certain point, "God" would occupy the same place as the Nothing, the *Nichts*, that gives itself in the grounding experience *(Grunderfahrung)* of anxiety, or Angst, and of which

Heidegger speaks compellingly in "Was ist Metaphysik?" (in *Wegmarken*, *103–21*,110, trans. as "What Is Metaphysics?" in *Pathmarks*, ed. McNeill, 82–96, 87). By contrast (although there is no real opposition here), the experience of "God" would resemble "our joy in the presence of the Dasein—and not simply the person—of a human being who we love" ("die Freude an der Gegenwart des Daseins—nicht der blossen Person—eines geliebten Menschen"), of which Heidegger speaks here.

2   It is no accident that, from the introduction to *Being and Time* on, Heidegger uses a notion of *Aufklärung* and, more generally, the metaphor of light and darkness in order to point the path from preontological to ontological understanding of the phenomena at hand. This should not be confused with mere repetition or continuation of the so-called project of modern Enlightenment but is not quite separable from it either.

3   HAS 53/584. "How to speak suitably of negative theology?" Derrida asks. "Is there a negative theology? A single one? A regulative model for the others? Can one adopt a discourse to it? Is there some discourse that measures up to it? Is one not compelled to speak of negative theology according to the modes of negative theology, in a way that is at once impotent, exhausting, and inexhaustible? Is there ever anything other than a 'negative theology' of 'negative theology'?" (HAS 13/546)

4   Blaise Pascal, *Pensées,* ed. Brunschvicq, no. 799, trans. A. J. Krailsheimer (New York: Penguin Books, 1966), 123. The Pascal of the *Pensées* is a thinker "in whom one could at times discern the genius or the machine of apophatic dialectics," Derrida observes in *Sauf le nom (Post-Scripte)* (Paris: Galilée, 1993), 88, trans. John P. Leavey, Jr., in *On the Name,* ed. Thomas Dutoit (Stanford: Stanford University Press, 1995), 72 (hereafter cited parenthetically in the text as SN, followed by the English and French page numbers).

5   Francis Ponge, "Fable," in *Proêmes,* 1: *Natare piscem doces* (Paris: Gallimard, 1948) and *Tome premier* (Paris: Gallimard, 1965). See also Derrida, *Psyché,* 18–19, and *Signéponge/Signsponge,* trans. Richard Rand, bilingual edition (New York: Columbia University Press, 1984), 102–3.

6   Jacques Derrida, *La Carte postale: De Socrate à Freud et au-delà* (Paris: Flammarion, 1980), 148, trans. Alan Bass as *The Postcard: From Socrates to Freud and Beyond* (Chicago: University of Chicago Press, 1987), 136.

7   G. W. F. Hegel, *Wissenschaft der logik* (Frankfurt a./M.: Suhrkamp: 1986), 1: 79, trans. A. V. Miller as *Hegel's Science of Logic* (Atlantic Highlands, N.J.: Humanities Press International, 1969), 78; trans, modified.

8   In *La Dette impensée: Heidegger et l'héritage hebraïque* (Paris: Éditions du Seuil, 1990), her sequel to *Heidegger et les paroles de l'origine* (Paris: Vrin, 1986), a book prefaced and inspired by Levinas, Marlène Zarader finds in Derrida's *De l'esprit: Heidegger et la question* (Paris: Galilee, 1987), trans. Geoffrey Bennington and Rachel Bowlby as *Of Spirit: Heidegger and the Question* (Chicago: Chicago University Press, 1989), a partial confirmation of her own reading of Heidegger's evasion and reinscription of the religious tradition, notably the one that precedes the Greek and Roman features of Christianity in its determination of *pneuma* and *spiritus* and that is epitomized by the Hebrew notion of *ruah*. She also suggests that Heidegger avoids ordenegates the structural resemblance between his ultimate interpretation of *Geist* (spirit) as *Flamme* (flame) in *Unterwegs zur Sprache* (Pfullingen: Neske, 1990), trans. Peter D. Hertz as *On the Way to Language* (New York: Harper, 1971). But she disagrees with Derrida's conclusion that we do in fact find ourselves here in an implicit, virtual debate whose main characteristic is that Heidegger and "the theologians" attempt to outbid each other in their quest for the originary. Following a line of interpretation that we encountered earlier in the work of Gasché, but that must result, perhaps, from any *philosophically* oriented reading of Derrida's writing, Zarader claims that *Of Spirit* seems finally to side with Heidegger. In maintaining that the meaning of *Geist* as flame must, indeed, be thought of as more originary than the meaning of either *ruah, pneuma,* or *spiritus* that it makes possible, Derrida would thus endorse what *Aporias* calls Heidegger's "logic of presupposition" and this regardless of his obvious displacement of the existential analytic (or fundamental ontology) in the direction of the quasi-transcendental thinking of *différance*.

But the gesture that turns Derrida's undertaking, here and elsewhere, into much more than the retrieval of the unthought Hebrew heritage—of the forgotten, avoided, negated, and denegated notions of *yet another spirit in flames*, of *ruah*—is precisely the fact that in his reading, this tradition is *just as much* originated by *Geist* (as *Flamme,* in Heidegger's sense) as the other way around. Each reveals and conceals the other; each is, in a sense, the "unthought debt" of the other. As a consequence, Derrida goes further than stating, as Zarader does, that Heidegger's thought ought to be situated in what it claims to make possible and that it even fails to mention as one of its most significant historical instances. For Derrida seems to insists on a certain co-originarity of the structural (formal or even quasi-ontological) on the one hand, and the concretely historical or traditional, on the other. What is more, the very distinction between the two, philosophically necessary as it may be, is in the end impossible to determine rigorously or once and for all. In Derrida's reading, a certain logic of the undecidable must therefore displace a certain logic of presupposition and its corresponding demarcation of the primary and the derivative, the a priori and the a posteriori, the proper and the impure.

Indeed, Heidegger forgets or avoids speaking of the Hebrew heritage and its understanding of *ruah* and the role the latter may or may not have played in the historical emergence of *pneuma*, of *spiritus*, and, who knows, of *Geist*. Yet the exact reason for Zarader's disagreement with Derrida can be found in the fact that she construes an alternative or dilemma where for Derrida there is none: "In the final analysis, there are only two coherent gestures: either one ignores, as Heidegger does, the Hebraic dimension (and thus chases from history that which exceeds the Greek dawn), or one takes it into account, as Derrida does, one restores it in history—something that necessarily leads to showing, not only the limits of the Heideggerian conception of historicality [*historialité*], but, by the same token [*du même coup*], *the already historical character of what Heidegger presented as pre-originary*" (*Dette impensée*, 197, trans. HdV). Immediately following this statement, Zarader recapitulates the general rule that seems to govern Heidegger's avoidance of the Hebrew tradition, and this not only in the few places, highlighted by Derrida, where he speaks of spirit. It is in this second, more general, assessment of Heidegger's itinerary that Zarader comes closest to Derrida's reading of the religious heritage in Heidegger's work and that of others, including his own: "Instead of privileging one gesture rather than another . . . , ought one not attempt to grasp them *together* [*ensemble*], like to the two faces of one and the same act? And of grasping them together, not only with regard to a particular question (that of spirit), but as characteristics of the Heideggerian questioning as such? . . . How can one think the singular articulation that reveals itself there: the thinker who has, more deeply [*plus amplement*] than any other, *restored* to Western thought the central determinations of the Hebraic universe is precisely the one who has never said anything about the Hebraic as such, who has—more massively than any other—effaced it from thought and, more extensively, from the West?" (ibid., trans. HdV).

Mutatis mutandis, this quotation anticipates the central thesis I defend throughout this book: *the task—and, indeed, conceptual necessity—of being at once at the furthest remove from and as close as possible to the tradition called religious.* This being said, Zarader assumes on the whole a far greater fidelity with respect to Heidegger's thinking on Derrida's part than, I think, is warranted by even the last three pages of *De l'esprit*, on which she bases her critical discussion, let alone by the many other relevant writings I am attempting to read in a different light in this study. As I have suggested already, Derrida's reservations vis-à-vis Heidegger are perhaps nowhere clearer than in his rereading of the latter's avoidance of the conflation or even intersection of philosophy or thought, on the one hand, and theology or religion, on the other. For Derrida's interpretation of Heidegger's assessment of spirituality and Christianity, as well as the former's reservations with regard to the overhasty attempt to "theologize" fundamental ontology and the thought of Being, see *Of Spirit*, 107ff./176ff.

Chapter 70

Jens Zimmermann

WESTERN IDENTITY, THE EXHAUSTION OF SECULAR REASON, AND THE RETURN OF RELIGION

The conundrum explored by Jens Zimmermann is that in becoming suspicious of universal experiences, concepts, and narratives, contemporary Western thought has deprived itself of the ability to articulate the big questions concerning human existence. For Zimmermann, who holds a Canada Research Chair in Interpretation, Religion, and Culture at Trinity Western University, BC, this means that Western culture is incapable of defending its own values at a time when other global cultures are strongly articulating—and acting out—their own; concomitantly, there is no clear goal towards which educators can work to teach foundational Western values. One of the problems is that two key Western narratives—that of Enlightenment rationality and Christian faith—are no longer considered viable approaches to foundational values. The "exhaustion" of secular reason and the waning of its grand narrative which sketched out the ideals and expectations of the Enlightenment, meet with the collapse of organized Christian religion in the postmodern era. Zimmermann points out that the subsequent *post-Christian* culture is also one that is equally sceptical of scientific solutions, or, in other words, is also *post-secular*. The ensuing "identity crisis of the West" leads to a renewed engagement with religion, either in the form of a recognition of the West's "Christian roots" or in more specific philosophical and intellectual debates, such as the one that occurred between Pope Benedict XVI and the German philosopher Jürgen Habermas. Zimmermann's core thesis, which he explores via this debate, is that Pope Benedict XVI's formula for humanism (a "synthesis of faith and reason"), also needs the critique of deep thinkers such as Habermas, for the West to arrive at a nuanced understanding of the turn to religion and its role in a new, more comprehensive humanism. Zimmermann turns to Nietzsche, Heidegger, Levinas and Derrida to show how these exemplary critics of logocentric thought also re-ignite debate about "the divine Logos and the humanistic tradition." Starting with Nietzsche and Heidegger, who appear to turn away from what they thought of as the *disastrous* synthesis of faith and reason, their overturning of metaphysics clears the way to re-think being and philosophy as a "participatory" process, leading to Heidegger's important *Letter on Humanism*, which asserts the central role of poetry in understanding being. Zimmermann turns to Levinas's critique of Heidegger, focusing on the argument that Heidegger's foregrounding of ontology is at the expense of human corporate "dignity"; that is to say, social and ethical processes need to be prioritized in the understanding of "being and reasoning". The trauma of always being exposed to the Other, however, is a high price, and Zimmermann also notes Levinas's anxieties concerning aesthetics; Zimmermann suggests that the Incarnation is thus needed within such a system. Turning to Derrida, Zimmermann argues that his deconstruction of "logocentrism" leads him to similar territory to that of Heidegger and Levinas, in effect unable "to say anything universally substantive about human nature, ethics, or justice." Zimmermann rearticulates this territory via the concepts of immanence and transcendence, examining how we fear both a restriction of particular human identities as well as generalizations that fail to articulate the big questions for actual individuals; rather than Richard Kearney's "hermeneutical middle way", which Zimmermann gently critiques, Zimmermann argues for an Incarnational solution, one which has a human "face" yet also transcends mere humanity.

W ESTERN CULTURE NEEDS TO COME TO TERMS with two crucial losses: first, with a loss of identity accompanied by the consequent failure to mount a convincing defence of its values in light of current global developments; second, with the loss of a clear goal for the education of its citizens. Terry Eagleton's voice is representative of other cultural critics, intellectuals, and politicians in his assessment that global political pressures, including religious confrontations, force the West "more and more to reflect on the foundations of its own civilization" at a time when we have lost the ability to think deeply.[1] According to Eagleton, postmodernity has rightly criticized naive and oppressive notions of universal reason, but it has also left us without any common ground for a universal sense of human dignity. Postmodern cultural theory has taught us to dislike universal truth claims and feel "embarrassed by fundamentals."[2] Yet world events require that we discuss human nature in terms of universal purpose and ask once again, in all seriousness, "What is the function of human beings? What are human beings for?"[3]

This loss of common ground has also affected Western educational ideals and their institutions. In his book *Simulacra and Simulation,* Jean Baudrillard, an important postmodern cultural critic, writes about the loss of purpose in university education and the consequent fragmentation of the disciplines. Designating the contemporary culture of knowledge as a "spiraling cadaver," he concludes that "the university is in ruins; nonfunctional in the social arenas of the market and employment, lacking cultural substance or an end purpose of knowledge."[4] He argues that since we have lost an ultimate unifying reason for knowledge, especially for knowledge of seemingly impractical values such as truth, justice, goodness, and beauty, we no longer know why we should invest real work in knowledge. The value of a university education and graduate certificates is no longer connected to any real ultimate content, and so we have a kind of inflation: university degrees are still valuable to get us someplace in society, a kind of job requirement, but they are actually increasingly worthless in themselves.[5]

In case you suspect that only a crazy French intellectual could come up with such a depressing view of higher education, a recent article in the *National Post* entitled "Hollow Halls of Academe" confirms Baudrillard's judgment almost verbatim. The modern Canadian university is a place "where students are more interested in the piece of paper they get at the end of their programs than in the intellectual journey along the way, where professors are cowed into watering down courses and bumping up grades, and where universities are run like corporations hawking mass-produced *degrees which are increasingly in demand but increasingly meaningless.*"[6]

Uncertainties about the essence of human nature, the loss of cultural identity, and the purpose of knowledge are all rooted in one basic problem: the exhaustion of secular reason. Precipitated by postmodernity, what Charles Taylor asserted decades ago has now trickled down fully into the public cultural arena: the malaise of modernity is that we have lost horizons of significance. The malaise of postmodernity, on the other hand, is its inability to provide us with a much-needed unified notion of rationality.

By the exhaustion of secular reason, I mean the breakdown of scientific objectivism. Following a fascination with the pristine clarity of mathematical certainty and geometrical purity which promised to transcend the murkiness of shifting historical circumstances and the emotionally unstable quality of religious truth, academics and, later, popular culture identified the rational with the scientific method. This test-tube epistemology makes short shrift of any human knowledge which does not show up under the microscope. Since religion, tradition, love, and ultimate questions concerning our humanity usually do not appear in a test tube, they do not count as real knowledge. It is no wonder that the human sciences have taken a back seat to the supposedly more practical rational or scientific disciplines such as the natural sciences, economics, or whatever else we count as conforming to the ideal of verifiable and calculable knowledge.

Thankfully, however, for a number of reasons we cannot enumerate here, scientific objectivism as the secular common sense idea of truth has run its course. We live not only in a post-*Christian* world but also in a *post-secular* one. Atheism and secular humanism, both in substance and rhetoric, depend on scientific objectivism, the very idea of truth as a neutral fact-finding mission that has failed. It has failed because scientific objectivism cannot generate by itself the values and interpretive frameworks that sustain its own scientific enterprise and which we require for a human way of being. It no longer is, because it never was, an adequate source for human self-understanding.

The identity crisis of the West, and the exhaustion of secular reason, has a number of philosophers and politicians calling for a return of religion into the heart of the academy and public policy. Especially in Europe, politicians and public intellectuals are recognizing the dependence of Western culture on Christian roots. The Italian statesman Marcello Pera, for example, proclaims specifically the Incarnation as the root of human rights, solidarity, equality, compassion, and the institutions shaped through them.[7]

Closer to home, North American academics are beginning to realize the importance of religion for keeping alive the distinction between nature and humanity, a crucial and foundational difference for any research. The historian John Sommerville explains in *The Decline of the Secular University* that "if the point of the secular university was to eliminate the religious dimension, it will eventually find that it has eliminated the human distinction as well, and be unable to make sense of any of its intellectual and professional disciplines."[8] Sommerville warns that, in light of the returning interest in religion, universities will completely lose touch with society unless they can adopt "an intellectual framework that is religiously suggestive."[9]

Many of us may also recall Stanley Fish's announcement several years ago in the *Chronicle of Higher Education* that religion will form the next research focus in North American literature departments, even in the university as a whole. The reason, Fish argues, is that one of the things 9/11 has taught us is that most people in the world are in fact religious. The time has now come for the small secular elite governing the overall outlook of university curricula to reinstitute religion as a real "candidate for the truth."[10] We find ourselves in a cultural situation where the weakening of secularism, in part effected by the postmodern critique of scientific objectivism, opens up space for less narrow conceptions of rationality that include religion.

A paradigmatic example of this new openness toward religion is the exchange between the current champion of recovering the Christian roots of reason, Joseph Ratzinger, Pope Benedict XVI, and the grey eminence of the Frankfurt school of social philosophy, Jürgen Habermas.[11] Benedict, both in his public debate with Habermas and later in his Regensburg address, calls for recovering a wider notion of human rationality that includes religion and offers the Christian model of reason that takes up, elevates, and transforms the Greek logos into the Christian incarnate Logos. Standing in the tradition of Augustine, Benedict argues that the concrete historical tie of the divine to the suffering and self-giving god-man of love ensures that religious reason is nonviolent, and he calls for the "co-rationality of reason and faith, reason and religion, which are destined to reciprocal cleansing and healing, and which need one another and have to recognize this need."[12]

While he fully admits that secular reason cannot provide of itself the ultimate transcendent values to make human life worth living, Habermas still refuses to buy into Benedict's all too easy return to a Thomistic merger of faith and reason. Habermas is not quite so ready to rush into the embrace of Queen Theology and asks whether her rational subjects did not have good reason to revolt. The very intellectual developments Benedict cites as detrimental to a healthy relationship between faith and reason Habermas regards as positive achievements of secular rationality: "The step taken by Duns Scotus toward Nominalism did not lead only to the Protestant God of voluntarism but also paved the way for modern natural science. Kant's critical turn not only dismantled proofs of God's existence but also led to the modern concept of autonomy which shaped our modern understanding of rights and democracy. Nor does historicism lead necessarily to a relativistic self-denial of reason, but . . . sensitizes us to cultural differences and protects us from generalizing judgments which depend on concrete historical contexts."[13]

It is safe to say that Habermas's warning not to ignore this secular legacy of reason is uttered with an eye to U.S. politics and political Islamic jihad. Yet as Benedict has pointed out, pathological developments have occurred in secular reason as well as in religion. And, surely, he is correct in identifying Western intellectual history as the fruitful correlation of faith and reason. Tracing this synthesis from the emergence of the Christian church to the present shows just how much this is a history of reason and self-understanding.

At the deepest conceptual level, the intellectual history of the West and its cultural identity is the story of reason. Western intellectual history is to a great part the history of logos, of rationality and its social implications. Human culture and its institutions are the expression both consciously and unconsciously of what is considered most rational and therefore most human. In the West, the question of human identity *is* the question of rationality. This Western ethos of rational human identity is most easily traced in the concept of humanism. Humanism in its broadest sense is the rational creature's question "Who am I?" or "What makes me most fully human?"[14]

Western rationality and identity have been shaped profoundly by the synthesis of Greek and Judeo-Christian ideals. The Delphic oracle's demand "know thyself," this ancient desire for self-knowledge, was taken up by Christianity and answered by elevating and transforming the Greek logos into the eternal Word of God and its incarnation in Jesus. This synthesis so closely knit together the question of reason, words, language, meaning, and human identity that in the West, try as we might, we cannot talk about any of these things without talking about Christianity, nor can we do so without talking about humanism.

It is equally true that this humanism was preoccupied with self-understanding. We do not need a modern humanist such as Hans-Georg Gadamer to tell us that "in the final analysis, *all* human understanding is self-understanding."[15] The Italian humanist Giambattista Vico summarized the humanist tradition in his orations on humanism when he announced to prospective students that "knowledge of oneself is for everyone the greatest incentive to acquire the universe of learning in the shortest possible time."[16] Yet this knowledge is by no means interior or private only. Even in the opening of the very first lecture, Vico makes an immediate connection between humanistic learning and the political life. Professors like him must convince the students "to take up the studies of liberal arts and sciences, which can be acquired only with strong dedication of the mind, with long and late hours of application, with sweat, with persistent discipline, and with punctilious discipline" because "our peaceful society" and its fruits are "for the most part based on the cultivation of these studies."[17]

For the classical humanists, studying the texts of the great orators, poets, and historians trained students in "breadth of learning and grace of style," and acquainted them with religion and "our duties in the world."[18] Reading of texts, learning of languages, and knowing how to argue and express oneself were eminently practical in producing good citizens—"the complete human being"—whose interest was the common weal of their society and of humanity.

At bottom, however, the humanistic ideal derives from a neo-Platonic view of reason transformed by Christianity into learning as reflection of and participation in the image of God. Vico writes, "As God is known by those things that have been created and are contained within this universe, so the spirit is recognized as divine by reason, in which it is pre-eminent, and by its sagacity, ability, memory, and ingenuity. The spirit is the most manifest image of God."[19] Such a universal notion of reason, let alone a participatory one, has been renounced by postmodern philosophers, who emphasize the particular over the universal and subscribe to the general argument that universal reason is an oppressive metaphysical construct favouring—mostly male—power brokers.

Given the historical development of rationality from Greek and Christian thought, Benedict is right in defining the Western intellectual ethos as a humanistic synthesis of faith and reason, but Habermas is equally correct in pointing out its problems. We must not bypass but integrate the correctives of postmodernity's critique of reason into recovering a broader concept of human reason. While many offer up silent prayers of thanksgiving that postmodernity and deconstruction seem to fade from prominence, we should not forget that postmodernism is itself an important part of the history of the Logos. Postmodernism is in essence a criticism of Western rationality, including scientific objectivism, a critique with an ethical focus that tries to examine the very nature of reason and the self. Let us take, for example, Nietzsche, Heidegger, Levinas, and Derrida. All four want to recall us to the historical dimensions of truth, reason, and the self, and all four understand that we cannot talk about reason and self-understanding without also always talking about the divine Logos and the humanistic tradition.

For example, Nietzsche's philosophy may be read as the overcoming of Platonic idealism. Instead of a direct interface or a "Vulcan mind-meld" with eternal forms that bypass life and body, Nietzsche suggests an anti-metaphysical approach to truth motivated by the highest value of the will to power. Heidegger certainly reads Nietzsche this way and derives from this impulse his own version of Western intellectual history as the departure from a dynamic and holistic way of thinking in which man thought of himself as embedded into a greater horizon of being toward the reductive, modern attitude of human-centered thinking. Heidegger regards the humanistic synthesis of faith and reason as a disaster, and Christianity is much to blame because it combined the Greek idea of logos with God: "logos in the New Testament does not, as in Heraclitus, mean the being of the beings, the gathering together of the conflicting; it means *one* particular being, namely the son of God [. . . .] a whole world separates all this from Heraclitus."[20] With this move, God turned into a metaphysical concept, the God of ontotheology; logos became logic; a more original unity between existence and thought was severed; and an opposition between logos and being was inscribed into Western thought.

From this misinterpretation of logos as reason, as meaning, even as word, stem all humanisms as a kind of Platonic disease that turns knowledge into objectification and splits thinking from being. Being and experience become objective, while thinking becomes subjective. For Heidegger, this split is responsible for the alienation of modern man from himself and the world. Only a philosophy that recognizes how reasoning works within and through history can heal this alienation by recovering the original meaning of logos as "the primal gathering principle." Only with this recovery can we overcome the separation of existence and thinking. Why? Because the human being, as the only truly reflective being, is in fact the place where the gathering logos appears. The really real, the *essent* of being, makes itself known through human being. This is why Heidegger can say, "Apprehension is not a function that man has as an attribute, but rather the other way around: apprehension is the happening that has man."[21]

Heidegger knows all about Faust's desire to combine being and knowing and he gets thinking on the right track by presenting a possible *participatory* model of reason. Rationality, historical being-in-the-world, and the question of human identity or self-understanding all come together. He writes, "[O]nly as a questioning, historical being does man come to himself; only as such is he a self. Man's selfhood means this: he must transform the being that discloses itself to him into history and bring himself to stand in it. Selfhood does not mean he is primarily an 'ego' and an individual. This he is no more than he is a we, a community. . . . Because man as a historical being is himself, the question about his own being must be reformulated. Rather than 'what is man,' we should say 'who is man?'"[22]

Heidegger answers this question in his *Letter on Humanism,* which aspires to a new humanism by designating human beings, poets in particular (especially German philosopher poets who read Trakl, Hölderlin, and Rilke), as shepherds of being. However fuzzy in substance, Heidegger's *Letter on Humanism* directly answers the questions of identity, reason, and self-understanding. All three are, or at least *seem,* radically and hermeneutically open: "We do not learn who man is by learned definitions; we learn it only when man contends with the essent, striving to bring it into its being, i.e. into limit and form, that is to say when he projects something new (not yet present), when he creates original poetry, when he builds poetically."[23] While a student may not understand the comment on his paper, "C+; not enough striving with the *Being* of being," Heidegger nonetheless offers an important justification for reading poetry and literature.[24] Literature and poetry are portals to self-understanding which move thinking closer to the perennial human questions of purpose and identity.

Heidegger is a central thinker for our discussion because he anticipates the postmodern demands on rationality and religion. By bringing together existence and reflection, Heidegger saves poetry and the humanities from disappearing in the dualistic abyss of opposing experiential and intellectual knowledge. In contrast to all forms of philosophical idealism, Heidegger's hermeneutic ontology valiantly struggles against subjectivism and calls for some kind of participation in being itself. The negative effect of this participation—at least according to the Jewish philosopher Emmanuel Levinas, one of Heidegger's severest critics—is that Heidegger's supposed openness to Being poses a threat to human dignity.

We cannot overlook in Heidegger a certain disdain, in the name of Being, not only for subjectivism, rationalism, and individualism, but also for community. We are neither fundamentally an *I* nor a *we* but the ears and mouthpiece of being. Levinas noticed this problem too. Since Heidegger's ontology is participation in an impersonal pagan notion of Being, which is rather flexible in its ethics, human dignity gets sold to the highest paid interpreter of what Being discloses to us. To forestall this disaster, Levinas argues that ethics has to be more primordial than ontology. He reintroduces the social and ethical categories of encounter and responsibility into human reason. The primary category of the human is the mode of revelation of address by another.

Moreover, Levinas does not accept Heidegger's openness toward Being as transcendence, but accuses him of creating yet other totalities. Levinas thus issues a fundamental challenge to interpretation because he realizes that the hermeneutical circle of understanding implies a totality: self-understanding always requires a whole, at least an anticipation of a prior whole in light of which we continue to develop our understanding of who we are. In other words, hermeneutics, contrary to Heidegger's claim, is not radically open but lacks transcendence because in its encounter with texts and with other people, it will never be able to have them fully appear on their own terms. Heidegger can talk about ethics as little as he can talk about God.[25]

Levinas, this philosophical Moses, holds up the command "thou shall not kill" as the ethical imposition by the other who founds my human identity with this call. He calls for nothing less than recovering a concept of rationality that is intrinsically ethical, beyond any totalizing structures, a "humanism of the other" configured primarily as responsibility for the other.[26] It is true what Levinas claims – namely, that he has no need of the Incarnation. God shows up in history through my ethical response to the other. Yet I would argue that Levinas does need the Incarnation, not least to relieve the traumatic experience of the ethical call. Some maybe drawn to this concept of the open wound of subjectivity, constantly exposed to the trauma of substitution, of being taken hostage to the other, as wholesome, but I find it too hard.[27]

Moreover, Levinas also leaves us with a fear of the ontological as that which tends to objectify and distort human dignity. It is no surprise that Levinas, despite his own frequent use of literary texts, can never quite shake off an intrinsic fear that writing and artwork is less a source of otherness than an ethical death trap, a form of idolatry which obscures the face of the other by freezing it into literary or artistic timelessness.

Another postmodern thinker who takes up Heidegger's questions concerning ontology and human rationality is Jacques Derrida, whose life's work constitutes a sweeping critique of Western rationality. Derrida's central argument is that Western philosophy has always defined human understanding with the Greeks as "sameness." We define understanding as participating in a common logos, in terms of familiarity and likeness, therefore suppressing difference. Derrida's observations on the abusive potential of defining "logos" in the West as immediate presence chide Heidegger for his belief in unified meaning and Levinas for his fear of mediated truth within ontology.[28] Yet somehow his criticism of rationality as logocentric lands him in a similar place as Heidegger and Levinas. All three long to escape rationalism and seek to recover a more human way of being and reasoning, but their fear of unifying and objectifying statements does not allow them to say anything universally substantive about human nature, ethics, or justice.

When we understand the rejection of metaphysics by postmodern critics in the light of their critique of Western rationality, two main and contrary emphases come to light: (a) the historical dimension of reason's unfolding in its linguistic and social determination, and (b) the ethical issue of sameness and difference. The first issue is the question of philosophical hermeneutics and the nature of reason: How does universal reason unfold in the cultural particularities of language and interpretation without becoming relativistic? How can we ever reach a universally acknowledged sense of who we are and what we live for? The second emphasis is the ethical question of identity and difference: how can we have a unified, universal ideal of reason and humanity which recognizes cultural and individual differences as intrinsic to self-understanding? This basic question of identity and difference is also the source for the common prejudice we mentioned earlier: that religious conviction necessarily results in intolerance and violence. According to this prejudice, religion stands for certain self-knowledge and identity, which inevitably creates the desire to make both God and others in the image of our particular interpretation of religion.

At the deepest and most abstract philosophical level, all of these questions boil down to the balance between immanence and transcendence. When all is said and done in postmodern theory, we are left with an emphasis on historicity on the one hand and ineffable transcendent otherness that cannot say anything substantive about ethics and justice on the other. The problem of exaggerated particularity is confirmed by Terry Eagleton's claim in *After Theory* that postmodern cultural theory has little to say about ultimate values and the big topics such as morality, metaphysics, love, biology, religion, revolution, evil, death, suffering, essences, and universal foundations. This, as he concludes, is indeed "on any estimate a rather large slice of human existence to fall down on."[29] As Richard Kearney has shown so convincingly in *Strangers, Gods, and Monsters,* on the other hand, when postmodern thinkers try to come up with ethics, radical otherness or alterity tends to lose all human contours. In the white, unspeakable space of transcendence, there is little difference between the monstrous and the divine. Even Levinas, who reintroduces Hebraic categories of personal transcendence into the project of self-understanding, overemphasizes this ethical transcendence so much that he renders it more traumatic, resorting to the hyperbolic expression of being taken hostage by the other. Too much transcendence can be a bad thing, because while it correctly limits human reason from colonizing the other, it leaves us still in opposition to the other; it traumatizes us with a sublime from on high which seems to prohibit real communion. Benedict affirmed the same problem for religious views of transcendence in his Regensburg lecture. If God transcends our human sense of reason, justice, and goodness absolutely, then violence may indeed be commanded in the name of God.[30] As a foundation for truly human dialogue, I must be able to know whether the other, whether human or divine, is intrinsically good and well disposed toward me.

What we need, in other words, is an ethical measure of our humanity and reason in which we participate ontologically and which unfolds hermeneutically but also transcends time, history, and culture. And this measure must have a face, preferably a human face. Reason should be intrinsically human and yet it cannot be fabricated by us. Where do we find such a concept? We could go to the work of Richard Kearney, who has written three books that chart a hermeneutical middle way between idolatrous views of religion and humanity and radical otherness. Kearney is an incarnational thinker who recognizes the human need for divine epiphanies, but he also knows the danger of truth-possession, hence his effort in establishing an eschatological hermeneutic of possibility, of the God who may be, and who becomes God when we "recreate the world for God."[31] Without question, Kearney is currently one of the most lucid, mediating philosophers of religion in the continental tradition, who combines the best of Levinas, Marion, and especially Ricoeur by emphasizing a narrative conception of the self and the realization of the divine in concrete human action.

The reason, however, I will not end with Kearney's eschatological hermeneutic of possibility is that his work is still too uneasy about God's presence. God is only real in this world, if we help God be God by helping "the least of these." Kearney touches here on the deep truth which applies to all human knowing, namely, that faith unfolds only in action. Yet his hermeneutic does not take full account of participation in the divine. To put it bluntly, it is not clear what role the institutional, visible church and its traditions have in Kearney's hermeneutic, and yet the incarnation demands a communal body, the church as the body of Christ, and the embryonic new humanity.[32]

This criticism of Kearney is not born from the usual academic need to save one's professional honour by finding fault in another's work. On the contrary, I am so impressed by Kearney's ability and desire to bring the transcendent into the human imagination, into human works and hence into literature, that I couldn't explain a feeling of unease in reading his work. It was not until Kearney clearly expressed his fundamental conviction in a CBC interview that the problem became clearer. Kearney opens the interview with this sentence: "In the beginning is hermeneuein – interpretation. In the beginning is the word. Not a stone, not a certitude. . . . In the beginning is the *word*; and as we know words are dialogical and you've got to listen and to respond."[33]

This primordial importance of interpretation frightens the fundamentalist evangelical. Yet after teaching for years in the climate of North American evangelicalism, I have come to understand that the evangelical may actually merely distort a fundamentally correct hermeneutical insight: his desire to reduce religion to absolute propositions is the survival instinct of the self, the *correct* desire for *having*, for *possessing*, an identity. Self-understanding as a hermeneutical process requires indeed, as Heidegger and later Gadamer have pointed out, a participation in universal reason, the ultimate whole of the hermeneutic circle by which we understand the penultimate part. Withholding this whole in the name of hermeneutics is not only cruel but self-defeating. Yet neither do we want this whole to turn into a totality by which we assimilate the other.

To emphasize a hermeneutical self, a narrative self that always develops and whose identity can only be deduced from what remains constant throughout this journey of the self, does not satisfy the human desire for identity but sacrifices it on the altar of hermeneutics to appease the idol of fundamentalism. We need a hermeneutic whole which grants us self-identity and in so doing—that is, in its very being—structures identity ontologically in its humanity as hermeneutical, ethical, and transcendent. This becomes possible when we change Kearney's sentence slightly from "in the beginning was interpretation" to "in the beginning was communion," or community. It is of course true that "in the beginning was the Word," but we cannot forget that the same text also tells us that "the Word was *with* God."

An incarnational hermeneutic must begin with this Trinitarian communal dimension at the heart of ontology; incarnational thinking proceeds from the realized communion of God with his people, the Incarnation of God in the church as the first Eucharist. It is from this first communion that all other Eucharistic acts, all other incarnations of the Divine into the lives of others, flow. No one makes this clearer than the Apostle Paul, whose advice to Christians is always "become what you already are." Possibility becomes actual only because of the actual already realized in Christ. But does not this view regress into sectarianism and triumphalism, into the hived-off "us" from the rest of humanity? This depends on our theology. By defining human identity Christologically, the Christian self is linked to the rest of humanity not "merely" as fellow creature, but also as a participant in the Christ event, which ensures that one's very being is shaped as "being-for-the-other."

Notes

1   Terry Eagleton, *After Theory* (London: Allen Lane; New York: Basic Books, 2003) 15, 73.
2   Ibid., 72.
3   Ibid., 123, 120.
4   Jean Baudrillard, *Simulacra and Simulation,* trans. Sheila Faria Glaser (Ann Arbor: University of Michigan Press, 2004) 149. His words are "le cadavre en spirale."
5   "The values of the university (diplomas, etc.) will proliferate and continue to circulate, a bit like floating capital or Eurodollars, they will spiral without referential criteria, completely devalorized in the end, but that is unimportant: their circulation alone is enough to create a social horizon of value, and the ghostly presence of the phantom value will even be greater, even when its reference point (its use value, its exchange value, the academic 'work force' that the university recoups) is lost. Terror of value without equivalence" (Baudrillard, *Simulacra and Simulation*, 155).
6   *National Post*, 28 Apr. 2007: A1; italics mine.
7   Pera recognizes the centrality of the Incarnation for Western liberal humanism when he writes, "[I]t is true that almost all of the achievements that we consider most laudable are derived from Christianity or were influenced by Christianity, by the message of God become Man. In truth without this message, which has transformed all human beings into persons in the image of God, individuals would have no dignity. In truth our values, rights, and duties of equality, tolerance, respect, solidarity, and compassion are born from God's sacrifice. In truth, our attitude toward others, toward all others, whatever their condition, class, appearance or culture is shaped by the Christian revolution. In truth, even our institutions are inspired by Christianity, including the secular institutions of government that render unto Caesar that which is Caesar's" (Joseph Ratzinger [Pope Benedict XVI] and Marcello Pera, *Without Roots: The West, Relativism, Christianity, Islam,* trans. Michael F. Moore [New York: Basic Books, 2006] 36–37).

8   John Sommerville *The Decline of the Secular University* (Oxford: Oxford University Press, 2006) 38.

9   Ibid., 26.

10   Stanley Fish, "One University under God?" *Chronicle of Higher Education,* 7 Jan. 2005, http://chronicle.com/article/One-University-Under-God-/45077.

11   Hereafter, Joseph Ratzinger, Pope Benedict XVI, will be identified in the body of the essay as Benedict.

12   Jürgen Habermas and Joseph Ratzinger (Pope Benedict XVI), *Dialektik der Säkularisierung: Über Vernunft und Religion,* ed. Florian Schuller (Freiburg: Herder, 2005) 57; unless otherwise noted, all translations from the German are mine.

13   Ibid., 4.

14   For example, the humanist Erasmus of Rotterdam writes, "And what is it that properly belongeth unto man? Verily, to live according to reason, and for that is called a reasonable creature and divided from those that cannot speak" (qtd. in Joanna Martindale, ed. *English Humanism: Wyatt to Cowley* [London: Croom Helm, 1985] 59). Also, the Reformers were united on this point, continuing the tradition of Augustine and Aquinas, who saw reason as part of the image of God in man, and made reason, any good reasoning or discovery of truth, dependent on divine illumination. Like Augustine before and John Calvin after him, Luther believed that even the achievements of the ungodly are witnesses to the divine likeness in human beings. Reason and culture generally point to God because, in contrast with the animals, humanity enjoys not merely a natural awareness but, by virtue of his divine likeness, also the light of reason: "but man *(der Mensch)* is especially gifted with the glorious light of reason and understanding. That human beings thought up and invented so many noble arts, be it wisdom, dexterity, or skilfulness, all this derives from this light, or from this Word, which was the life of humanity. In such a way this life, Christ, is not only a light to himself, but illumines all human beings with this light, so that all understanding, cleverness and skilfulness, as far as they are not demonic and demonic, flow from this light as Wisdom of the eternal father" ("Auslegung über den Evangelisten Johannes" in Martin Luther's *Sämtliche Schriften,* Band 7, ed. Johann G. Walch [Groß Oesingen, Ger.: Verlag der Lutherischen Buchhandlung Heinrich Harms, 1986], S. 1567. Also found in *Sermons on the Gospel of St. John: Chapters 1–4, Luther's Works,* gen. ed. J. J. Pelikan, vol. 22 [St. Louis, MO: Concordia Publishing House, 1956], 30). Clearly Jesus is here equated with logos, the word of God with reason.

15   Hans-Georg Gadamer, *Philosophical Hermeneutics,* ed. and trans. David E. Linge (Berkeley: University of California Press, 1976) 55; see also *Gesammelte Werke,* vol. 2 (Tübingen, Ger.: J.C.B. Mohr, 1985), 40–41; hereafter *Gesammelte Werke* will be abbreviated *GW.*

16   Giambattista Vico, *On Humanistic Education (Six Inaugural Orations, 1699–1707),* trans. Giorgio A. Pinto and Arthur W. Shippee (Ithaca, NY: Cornell University Press, 1993) 37–38.

17   Ibid., 35.

18   William Harrison Woodward, *Vittonno Da Feltre and Other Humanist Educators,* Renaissance Society of America Reprint Texts Series 5 (Toronto: University of Toronto Press; New York: Renaissance Society of America, 1996) 133.

19   Vico, *On Humanistic Education,* 41.

20   Martin Heidegger, *An Introduction to Metaphysics,* trans. Ralph Manheim (New Haven, CT: Yale University Press, 1987) 134–35.

21   Ibid., 141.

22   Ibid., 143–44.

23   Ibid., 144.

24   Gadamer in principle adopts Heidegger's model of reason but tones down the theological mysticism of Being to a more sober Greek idea of logos participation in suggesting the "mid-world" of language and the universality of interpretation on account of our existence in language as an expression of rationality; "understanding is inseparably tied to language *(sprachgebunden)*; that is how one should understand the universal claim of the hermeneutical dimension" (G W2.231). This is summarized in his well-known motto: "Being that can be expressed is language."

25   His former student Gadamer revealed in his last substantial interview that Mitsein and the other were concessions by Heidegger rather than intrinsic elements of his philosophy: "Mitsein is a concession for Heidegger that he had to make but which he didn't really believe in. Already back then when he developed this notion [of Mitsein], he really was not talking about the other. It can be said that Mit-sein is a statement about Dasein which, of course, has to allow for the existence of Mitsein. . . . His notion of 'Care' *(Sorge)* is always care about one's own being, and Mit-sein is in truth a very weak thought of the other, indicating more a 'letting the other be' than a being-turned-toward-the-other" (Hans-Georg Gadamer, *Die Lektion des Jahrhunderts* [Münster: Lit Verlag, 2002] 26). Gadamer adds that Heidegger recognized this difference: "He acknowledged that I associated more with the thought

about the other than he did with his Mit-sein. Mit-sein is a weak expression because it leaves open the 'with,' that the other is also a Dasein; 'this also' then becomes, so to speak, his justification for his conscience" (ibid., 27).

26 Emmanuel Levinas, *Humanismus des anderen Menschen,* ed. Ludwig Wenzler and Christoph von Wolzogen, Philosophische Bibliothek (Hamburg: F. Meiner, 2005) 90.

27 See Simon Critchley's description of this trauma and its need for sublimation: "Levinas seems to be describing ethical responsibility as the maintenance of a permanent state of Trauma." Critchley finds the necessary sublimation of this trauma in the discourse of philosophy, a return to ontology and reflection, but now to a same that had been altered through the ethical encounter. However, this depends on the nature of philosophy, and reflection here remains the constant ontological menace that threatens to ossify the saying in the said (Simon Critchley, *Ethics, Politics, Subjectivity: Essays on Derrida, Levinas and Contemporary French Thought* [London: Verso, 1999] 205–6).

28 While Levinas can still tie this notion of difference to a radically transcendent biblical God, Derrida can only talk about difference as such. His work constitutes, again, an examination of the nature of reason. All of humanity, says Derrida, is plagued by the desire for immediacy, for unmediated knowledge through the inner voice. In Western philosophy from Plato onward, this desire has expressed itself through the definition of reason, or the logos, as pure unmediated communication between minds or the full presence of truth. Hence his term "Logocentrism," which, to add to our problems, was largely defined in favour of male rationality, so that we end up with phallo-logo-centrism. Derrida thus becomes an inverted Platonist, driven by the fear of immediate presence which objectifies. Derrida leaves us with the fear of presence, and many have taken up his misunderstanding of presence as objectitification into the discussion of religion. Presence becomes equated with assimilation, with foreshortening interpretive possibilities, even with violence. Theologically, this fear of ontological participation is the soil from which sprout the gods without being (Jean-Luc Marion) and the gods who may be (Richard Kearney).

29 Eagleton, *After Theory,* 102.

30 Ratzinger, Joseph (Pope Benedict XVI), *Der Glaube ist Einfach! Ansprachen, Meditationen, Predigten während des Besuches in Bayern* (Leipzig: St. Benno Verlag, 2006) 112.

31 Richard Kearney, *The God Who May Be: A Hermeneutics of Religion,* Indiana Series in the Philosophy of Religion (Bloomington: Indiana University Press, 2001) 110.

32 There are statements in which Kearney specifies that his emphasis is a correction to excessive focus on God as substance: "It is my wager in this chapter that one of the main ways in which the infinite comes to be experienced and imagined by finite minds is as *possibility – that* is, as *the ability to be.* Even, and especially, when such possibility seems impossible to us. I am not saying this is the only way . . . just that it is a very telling way, and one that has been largely neglected in the history of Western metaphysics and theology in favor of categories such as substance, cause, actuality, absolute spirit, and sufficient reason" (Richard Kearney, "Hermeneutics of the Possible God," *Givenness and God: Questions of Jean-Luc Marion,* ed. Ian Leask and Eoin Cassidy [New York: Fordham University Press, 2005] 220).

33 Richard Kearney, "The God Who May Be," conversation with David Cayley, *Ideas,* CBC Radio, 20 Feb., 27 Feb., and 6 Mar. 2006 (*Ideas* Transcripts ID 2964).

Chapter 71

Slavoj Žižek

SUBTRACTION, JEWISH AND CHRISTIAN

What would our understanding of Biblical text be, if we avoided all allegorizing interpretations and instead read the text directly or literally? Slavoj Žižek sets out to do this with reference first to the Song of Songs, a deeply erotic part of the Old Testament, that is usually read metaphorically and allegorically (a physical act stands in for, or really means something moral, spiritual, theological, etc.). Žižek argues that read directly, the Song of Songs would reveal the spiritual dimension of human sexuality, rather than sexuality being denied or effaced through allegory, in an attempt to find a higher spiritual meaning in human relationships. But then a bigger question is posed by Žižek: is it possible to reach a "full identity" of humanity and spirituality within a Judaic context? The answer for Žižek, a Lacanian theorist, is "no", but it is a possibility, he suggests, for Christianity (in other words, the Incarnation, whereby God became fully human). Žižek argues that two Judaic factors—the trauma of the law (which we can never match up to), and the love expressed in God's everlasting covenant—remain "metaphorical" or "mitigating", that is to say, making less traumatic the encounter with the Divine Real (God/the Absolute/Judgment, etc.). Turning to the Old Testament character called Job, Žižek argues that here the transition to Christianity is most clear, not just because Job endures immense suffering, but because his story reveals God's "impotence" through a final display of "pure boasting" or "farcical spectacle" as Žižek puts it. Job's notion that his own suffering is ultimately meaningless is then a critique of ideology, or, a laying bare of the ultimately pointless repression of ideological structures. Similarly, God's "impotence" is given heightened form in his own sacrifice on the cross; Žižek argues that Christ "forsaken" is not calling out to an omnipotent God, but rather a revealing of the impotence of God. Job, then, prefigures Christ, and both reveal that it is God who is "on trial". The logic here is that of total revelation: while Judaism has many interpretive texts and layers of theological understanding, for Žižek, Christianity lays all bare, in the open, with no secret or hidden meanings to uncover. So the ongoing fascination with movements such as Gnosticism (there is a secret truth that Gnosticism will reveal to initiates, or readers of the latest best-selling book on this topic will discover, etc.) misses the fact that Christianity *has already publicly said it all*. The concept of the "chosen people" is thus reconfigured by the event of Christ's redemptive sacrifice, and instead of religion being a compensation or cover for an originary trauma (i.e., Freud's reading of Judaism in *Moses and Monotheism*), the trauma is out in the open, creating a new sense of inclusive community on the basis of what it has already achieved. Žižek turns to two German-Jewish thinkers for support: Franz Rosenzweig and Walter Benjamin, with emphasis upon the latter, in particular his notion of "now time", that is to say, the revolutionary moment or actuality, which achieves what no end of gradual progressive building-up-to can ever succeed in bringing about. The "now time" of Christianity is unlike the deferred Judaic Messianic arrival; in Christianity, the arrival has happened, and the Messiah was rejected and sacrificed. So the task becomes how to live "after the event", not one of living under the shadow of an originary trauma, still waiting for the redemptive moment. In parallel, Žižek explores the concept of "authentic revolution", which similarly needs the "now time" of action, while the real work is what comes after the revolution, i.e., living up to its ideals back in the time of the mundane. In both cases, this is a human task, since the transcendent force (God, or the overturning of society) is revealed to be impotent.

W HEN THEY ARE DEALING WITH AN EROTIC-RELIGIOUS text like the Song of Songs, commentators hasten to warn us that its extreme and explicit erotic imagery is to be read allegorically, as a metaphor: when, for instance, the lover kisses the woman's lips, this "really means" that He imparts to the Jews the Ten Commandments. In short, what appears to be a description of a "purely human" sexual encounter symbolically conveys the spiritual communion of God and the Jewish people. However, the most perspicacious Bible scholars themselves are the first to emphasize the limits of such a metaphorical reading that dismisses the sexual content as "only a simile": it is precisely such a "symbolic" reading that is "purely human," that is to say, that persists in the external opposition of the symbol and its meaning, clumsily attaching a "deeper meaning" to the explosive sexual content. The literal reading (say, of the Song of Songs as almost pornographic eroticism) and the allegorical reading are two sides of the same operation: what they share is the common presupposition that "real" sexuality is "purely human," with no discernible divine dimension. (Of course, a question arises here: if sexuality is just a metaphor, why do we need this problematic detour in the first place? Why do we not convey the true spiritual content directly? Because, due to the limitations of our sensual finite nature, this content is not directly accessible to us?) What, however, if the Song of Songs is to be read not as an allegory but, much more literally, as the description of purely sensual erotic play? What if the "deeper" spiritual dimension is already operative in the passionate sexual interaction itself? The true task is thus not to reduce sexuality to a mere allegory, but to unearth the inherent "spiritual" dimension that forever separates human sexuality from animal coupling. Is it, however, possible to accomplish this step from allegory to full identity in Judaism? Is this not what Christianity is about, with its assertion of the direct identity of God and man?[1]

There is a further problem with the Song of Songs. The standard defense of "psychoanalytic Judaism" against Christianity involves two claims: first, it is only in Judaism that we encounter the anxiety of the traumatic Real of the Law, of the abyss of the Other's desire ("What do you want?"); Christianity covers up this abyss with love, that is, the imaginary reconciliation of God and humanity, in which the anxiety-provoking encounter with the Real is mitigated: now we know what the Other wants from us—God loves us, Christ's sacrifice is the ultimate proof of it. Second claim: do not texts like the Song of Songs demonstrate that Judaism, far from being (only) a religion of anxiety, is also and above all the religion of love, an even more intense love than Christianity? Is not the covenant between God and the Jewish people a supreme act of love? As I have just indicated, however, this Jewish love remains "metaphorical"; as such, it is itself the imaginary reconciliation of God and humanity in which the anxiety-provoking encounter with the Real is mitigated. Or—to put it in a direct and brutal way—is not the Song of Songs ideology at its purest, insofar as we conceive of ideology as the imaginary mitigating of a traumatic Real, as "the Real of the divine encounter with a human face"?

How, then, do we go from here to Christianity proper? The key to Christ is provided by the figure of Job, whose suffering prefigures that of Christ. What makes the Book of Job so provocative is not simply the presence of multiple perspectives without a clear resolution of their tension (the fact that Job's suffering involves a different perspective than that of religious reliance on God); Job's perplexity stems from the fact that he experiences God as an impenetrable Thing: he is uncertain what He wants from him in inflicting the ordeals to which he is submitted (the Lacanian "*Che vuoi?*"), and, consequently, he—Job—is unable to ascertain how he fits into the overall divine order, unable to recognize his place in it.

The almost unbearable impact of the Book of Job derives not so much from its narrative frame (the Devil appears as a conversational partner of God, and the two engage in a rather cruel experiment in order to test Job's faith), but in its final outcome. Far from providing some kind of satisfactory account of Job's undeserved suffering, God's appearance at the end ultimately amounts to pure boasting, a horror show with elements of farcical spectacle—a pure argument of authority grounded in a breathtaking display of power: "You see all that I can do? Can *you* do this? Who are you, then, to complain?" So what we get is neither the good God letting Job know that his suffering was just an ordeal destined to test his faith, nor a dark God beyond Law, the God of pure caprice, but, rather, a God who acts like someone caught in a moment of impotence—or, at the very least, weakness—and tries to escape His predicament by empty boasting. What we get at the end is a kind of cheap Hollywood horror show with lots of special effects—no wonder many commentators tend to dismiss Job's story as a remainder of the previous pagan mythology, which should have been excluded from the Bible.

Against this temptation, we should precisely locate the true greatness of Job: contrary to the usual notion of Job, he is not a patient sufferer, enduring his ordeal with a firm faith in God—on the contrary, he complains all the time, rejecting his fate (like Oedipus at Colonus, who is also usually misperceived as a patient victim resigned to his fate). When the three theologians-friends visit him, their line of argumentation is the standard ideological sophistry (if you are suffering, you must by definition have done something wrong, since God is just). Their argumentation, however, is not confined to the claim that Job must somehow be guilty: what is at stake on a more radical level is the meaning (lessness) of Job's suffering. Like Oedipus at Colonus, Job insists on the utter *meaninglessness* of his suffering—as the title of Job 27 says: "Job Maintains His Integrity."[2] In this way, the Book of Job provides what is perhaps the first exemplary case of the critique of ideology in human history, laying bare the basic discursive strategies of legitimizing suffering: Job's properly ethical dignity lies in the way he persistently rejects the notion that his suffering can have any meaning, either punishment for his past sins or the trial of his faith, against the three theologians who bombard him with possible meanings—and, surprisingly, God takes his side at the end, claiming that every word Job spoke was true, while every word the three theologians spoke was false.[3]

And it is in the context of this assertion of the meaninglessness of Job's suffering that we should insist on the parallel between Job and Christ, on Job's suffering announcing the Way of the Cross: Christ's suffering is also meaningless, not an act of meaningful exchange. The difference, of course, is that, in the case of Christ, the gap that separates the suffering, desperate man (Job) from God is transposed into God Himself, as His own radical splitting or, rather, self-abandonment. This means that we should risk a much more radical reading of Christ's "Father, why hast thou forsaken me?" than the usual one: since we are dealing here not with the gap between man and God, but with the split in God Himself, the solution cannot be for God to (re)appear in all His majesty, revealing to Christ the deeper meaning of his suffering (that he was the Innocent sacrificed to redeem humanity). Christ's "Father, why hast thou forsaken me?" is not a complaint to the *omnipotent* capricious God-Father whose ways are indecipherable to us, mortal humans, but a complaint that hints at an *impotent* God:

it is rather like a child who, having believed in his father's powerfulness, discovers with horror that his father cannot help him. (To evoke an example from recent history: at the moment of Christ's Crucifixion, God-the-Father is in a position somewhat similar to that of the Bosnian father, made to witness the gang-rape of his own daughter, and to endure the ultimate trauma of her compassionate-reproachful gaze: "Father, why did you forsake me?" In short, with this "Father, why hast thou forsaken me?," it is God-the-Father who, in effect, dies, revealing His utter impotence, and thereupon rises from the dead in the guise of the Holy Spirit.)

Why did Job keep his silence after the boastful appearance of God? Is not this ridiculous boasting (the pompous battery of "Were you there when . . . " rhetorical questions: "Who is this whose ignorant words / Smear my design with darkness? / Were you there when I planned the earth, / Tell me, if you are so wise?" (Job 38:2–5)) the very mode of appearance of its opposite, to which one can answer by simply saying: "OK, if you can do all this, *why did you let me suffer in such a meaningless way?*" Do not God's thundering words make his silence, the absence of an answer, all the more palpable? What, then, if this was what Job perceived, and what kept him silent: he remained silent neither because he was crushed by God's overwhelming presence, nor because he wanted thereby to indicate his continuous resistance, that is, the fact that God avoided answering Job's question, but because, in a gesture of silent solidarity, he perceived the divine impotence. God is neither just nor unjust, simply impotent. What Job suddenly understood was that it *was not him, but God Himself, who was actually on trial in Job's calamities*, and He failed the test miserably. Even more pointedly, I am tempted to risk a radical anachronistic reading: Job foresaw God's own future suffering—"Today it's me, tomorrow it will be your own son, and there will be no one to intercede for *him*. What you see in me now is the prefiguration of your own Passion!"[4]

Since the function of the obscene superego supplement of the (divine) Law is to mask this impotence of the big Other, and since Christianity reveals this impotence, it is, quite logically, the first (and only) religion radically to leave behind the split between the official/public text and its obscene initiatory supplement: there is no hidden, untold story in it. In this precise sense, Christianity is the religion of Revelation: everything is revealed in it, no obscene superego supplement accompanies its public message. In Ancient Greek and Roman religions, the public text was always supplemented by secret initiatory rituals and orgies; on the other hand, all attempts to treat Christianity in the same way (to uncover Christ's "secret teaching" somehow encoded in the New Testament or found in apocryphal Gospels) amounts to its heretical reinscription into the pagan Gnostic tradition.

Apropos of Christianity as "revealed religion," we should thus ask the inevitable stupid question: what is actually revealed in it? That is to say: is it not a fact that *all* religions reveal some mystery through the prophets, who carry the divine message to humankind; even those who insist on the impenetrability of the *dieu obscur* imply that there is some secret that resists revelation, and in the Gnostic versions, this mystery is revealed to the select few in some initiatory ceremony. Significantly, Gnostic reinscriptions of Christianity insist precisely on the presence of such a hidden message to be deciphered in the official Christian text. So what is revealed in Christianity is not just the entire content, but, more specifically, that *there is nothing—no secret—behind it to be revealed*. To paraphrase Hegel's famous formula from *Phenomenology*: behind the curtain of the public text, there is only what we put there. Or—to formulate it even more pointedly, in more pathetic terms—what God reveals is not His hidden power, only His impotence as such.

Where, then, does Judaism stand with regard to this opposition? Is it not true that God's final appearance in the Job story, in which He boasts about the miracles and monsters He has generated, is precisely such an obscene fantasmatic spectacle destined to conceal this impotence? Here, however, matters are more complex. In his discussion of the Freudian figure of Moses, Eric Santner introduces the key distinction between symbolic history (the set of explicit mythical narratives and ideologico-ethical prescriptions that constitute the tradition of a community—what Hegel would have called its "ethical substance") and its obscene Other, the unacknowledgeable "spectral," fantasmatic secret history that actually sustains the explicit symbolic tradition, but has to remain foreclosed if it is to be operative.[5] What Freud endeavors to reconstitute in *Moses and Monotheism* (the story of the murder of Moses, etc.) is such a spectral history that haunts the space of Jewish religious tradition. One becomes a full member of a community not simply by identifying with its explicit symbolic tradition, but only when one also assumes the spectral dimension that sustains this tradition, the undead ghosts that haunt the living, the secret history of traumatic fantasies transmitted "between the lines," through the lacks and distortions of the explicit symbolic tradition—as Fernando Pessoa puts it: "Every dead man is probably still alive somewhere." Judaism's stubborn attachment to the unacknowledged violent founding gesture that haunts the public legal order as its spectral supplement enabled the Jews to persist and survive for thousands of years without land or a common institutional tradition: they refused to give up their ghost, to cut off the link to their secret, disavowed tradition. The paradox of Judaism is that it maintains fidelity to the founding violent Event precisely by *not* confessing, symbolizing it: this "repressed" status of the Event is what gives Judaism its unprecedented vitality.

Does this mean, however, that the split between the "official" texts of the Law, with their abstract legal asexual character (Torah—the Old Testament; Mishna—the formulation of the Laws; and Talmud—the commentary on the Laws, all of them supposed to be part of the divine Revelation on Mount Sinai), and Kabbalah (that set of deeply sexualized obscure insights, to be kept secret—take for instance, the notorious passages about the vaginal juices), reproduces within Judaism the tension between the pure symbolic Law and its superego supplement, the secret initiatory knowledge? A crucial line of separation is to be drawn here between the Jewish fidelity to the disavowed ghosts and the pagan obscene initiatory wisdom accompanying public ritual: the disavowed Jewish spectral narrative does not tell the obscene story of God's impenetrable omnipotence, but its exact opposite: the story of His *impotence* concealed by the standard pagan obscene supplements. The secret to which the Jews remain faithful is the horror of the divine impotence—and it is this secret that is "revealed" in Christianity. This is why Christianity could occur only after Judaism: it reveals the horror first confronted by the Jews. Thus it is only through taking this line of separation between paganism and Judaism into account that we can properly grasp the Christian breakthrough itself.

This means that Judaism in forcing us to face the abyss of the Other's desire (in the guise of the impenetrable God), in refusing to cover up this abyss with a determinate fantasmatic scenario (articulated in the obscene initiatic myth), confronts us for the first time with the paradox of human freedom. There is no freedom outside the traumatic encounter with the opacity of the Other's desire: freedom does not mean that I simply get rid of the Other's desire—I am, as it were, thrown into my freedom when I confront this opacity as such, deprived of the fantasmatic cover that tells me what the Other wants from me. In this difficult predicament, full of anxiety, when I know *that* the Other wants something from me, without knowing *what* this desire is, I am thrown back into myself, compelled to assume the risk of freely determining the coordinates of my desire.

According to Rosenzweig, the difference between Jewish and Christian believers is not that the latter experience no anxiety, but that the focus of anxiety is displaced: Christians experience anxiety in the intimacy of their contact with God (like Abraham?), while for Jews, anxiety arises at the level of the Jews as a collective entity without a proper land, its very existence threatened.[6] And perhaps we should establish a link here with the weak point of Heidegger's *Being and Time* (the "illegitimate" passage from individual being-toward-death, and assuming one's contingent fate, to the historicity of a collective): it is *only* in the case of the Jewish people that such a passage from individual to collective level would have been "legitimate."

How, then, does the Christian community differ from the Jewish one? Saint Paul conceives of the Christian community as the new incarnation of the chosen people: it is Christians who are the true "children of Abraham." What was, in its first incarnation, a distinct ethnic group is now a community of free believers that suspends all ethnic divisions (or, rather, cuts a line of separation within each ethnic group)—the chosen people are those who have faith in Christ. Thus we have a kind of *"transubstantiation" of the chosen people:* God kept his promise of redemption to the Jewish people, but, in the process itself, he changed the identity of the chosen people.[7] The theoretical (and political) interest of this notion of community is that it provides the first example of a collective that is not formed and held together through the mechanism described by Freud in *Totem and Taboo* and *Moses and Monotheism* (the shared guilt of the parricide)—are not further examples of this same collective the revolutionary party and the psychoanalytic society? "Holy Spirit" designates a new collective held together not by a Master-Signifier, but by fidelity to a Cause, by the effort to draw a new line of separation that runs "beyond Good and Evil," that is to say, that runs across and suspends the distinctions of the existing social body. The key dimension of Paul's gesture is thus his break with any form of communitarianism: his universe is no longer that of the multitude of groups that want to "find their voice," and assert their particular identity, their "way of life," but that of a fighting collective grounded in the reference to an unconditional universalism.

How, then, does the Christian subtraction relate to the Jewish one? That is to say: is not a kind of subtraction inscribed into the very Jewish identity? Is this not why the Nazis wanted to kill all Jews: because, among all the nations, the Jews are "the part that is no part," not simply a nation among nations, but a remainder, that which has no proper place in the "order of nations"? And, of course, that is the structural problem of the State of Israel: can one form, out of this remainder, a State like the others? It was Rosenzweig who made this point:

> But Judaism, and it alone in all the world, maintains itself by subtraction, by contraction, by the formation of ever new remnants. . . . In Judaism, man is always somehow a survivor, an inner something, whose exterior was seized by the current of the world and carried off while he himself, what is left of him, remains standing on the shore. Something within him is waiting.[8]

Thus the Jews are a remainder in a double sense: not only the remainder with regard to the other set of "normal" nations, but also, in addition, a remainder with regard to themselves, a remainder in and of themselves—the rest, that which remains and persists after all the persecutions and annihilations. These two dimensions are strictly correlated: if the Jews were to be a remainder only in the first (external) sense, they would simply constitute another self-identical ethnic group. So when the Jews are conceived of as a remainder, we should be very precise in defining this with regard to what they are a remainder of: of themselves, of course, *but also of humanity as such,* insofar as it was abandoned by God. It is as such, as "out of place," that the Jews hold the place of universal humanity as such. And it is only against this background that the Pauline "transubstantiation" of the Chosen People (no longer only Jews—a particular ethnic group—but anyone, irrespective of his or her origins, who recognizes himself or herself in Christ) can be properly understood: Paul, as it were, just switches back to the universality—that is, for him, the Christians are the remainder of humanity. *We all, the whole of humanity, considered as redeemed, constitute a remainder*—of what?

Here, we should return to the Hegelian point that every universal Whole is divided into its Part (particular species) and its Remainder. The Part (particular as opposed to universal) is the obscene element of existence—on the level of the law, for example, the obscene unwritten supplement that sustains the actual existence of universal Law, Law as an operative power. Take the tension between universal and particular in the use of the term "special": when we say "We have special funds!," it means illegal, or at least secret funds, not just a special section of public funds; when a sexual partner says "Do you want something special?," it means a non-standard "perverted" practice; when a policeman or journalist refers to "special measures in interrogation," it means torture or other similar illegal pressures. (And were not the units in the Nazi concentration camps that were kept apart, and used for the most horrifying job of killing and cremating thousands, and disposing of the bodies, called *Sonderkommando*, special units?) In Cuba, the difficult period after the disintegration of the Eastern European Communist regimes is referred to as the "special period."

Along the same lines, we should celebrate the genius of Walter Benjamin, which shines through in the very title of his early essay "On Language in General and Human Language in Particular." The point here is not that human language is a species of some universal language "as such," which also comprises other species (the language of gods and angels? animal language? the language of some other intelligent beings out there in space? computer language? the language of DNA?): there is no actually existing language other than human language—but, in order to comprehend this "particular" language, one has to introduce a minimal difference, conceiving it with regard to the gap which separates it from language "as such" (the pure structure of language deprived of the insignia of human finitude, of erotic passions and mortality, of struggles for domination and the obscenity of power). The particular language is thus the "really existing language," language as the series of actually uttered statements, in contrast to formal linguistic structure. This Benjaminian lesson is the lesson missed by Habermas: what Habermas does is precisely what one should not do—he posits the ideal "language in general" (the pragmatic universal) directly as the norm of actually existing language. So, along the lines of Benjamin's title, one should describe the basic constellation of the social law as that of the "Law in general and its obscene superego underside in particular." . . . The "Part" as such is thus the "sinful" unredeemed and unredeemable aspect of the Universal—to put it in actual political terms, every politics which grounds itself in the reference to some substantial (ethnic, religious, sexual, lifestyle . . .) particularity is by definition reactionary. Consequently, the division introduced and sustained by the emancipatory ("class") struggle is not the one between the two particular classes of the Whole, but the one between the Whole-in-its-parts and its Remainder which, within the Particulars, stands for the Universal, for the Whole "as such," as opposed to its parts.

Or, to put it in yet another way, we should bear in mind here the two aspects of the notion of remnant: the rest or remainder as what remains after subtraction of all particular content (elements, specific parts of the Whole), and the rest or remainder as the ultimate result of the subdivision of the Whole into its parts, when, in the final act of subdivision, we no longer get two particular parts or elements, two Somethings, but a Something (the Rest) and a Nothing. In this precise sense, we should say that, from the perspective of Redemption (of the "Last Judgment"), the unredeemed part is irrevocably lost, thrown into nothingness—all that remains is precisely the Remainder itself. This, perhaps, is how we should read the motto of the proletarian revolution "We were nothing, we want to become All"—from the perspective of Redemption, that which, within the established order, counts as nothing, the remainder of this order, its part of no part, will become All. . . .

The structural homology between the old Jewish or Pauline messianic time and the logic of the revolutionary process is crucial here: "The future is no future without this anticipation and the inner compulsion for it, without this 'wish to bring about the Messiah before his time' and the temptation to 'coerce the kingdom of God into being'; without these, it is only a past distended endlessly and projected forward."[9] Do not these words fit perfectly Rosa Luxemburg's description of the necessary illusion which pertains to a revolutionary act? As she emphasizes against the revisionists, if we wait for the "right moment" to start a revolution, this moment will never come—we have to take the risk, and precipitate ourselves into revolutionary attempt, since it is only through a series of "premature" attempts (and their failure) that the (subjective) conditions for the "right" moment are created.[10]

Agamben maintains that Saint Paul became readable only in the twentieth century, through Walter Benjamin's "Messianic Marxism": the clue to Paul's emergency of the "end of time" approaching is provided by the revolutionary state of emergency. This state of emergency is to be strictly opposed to today's liberal-totalitarian emergency of the "war on terror": when a state institution proclaims a state of emergency, it does so by definition as part of a desperate strategy to avoid the true emergency, and return to the "normal course of things." Recall a feature of all reactionary proclamations of the "state of emergency": they were all directed against popular unrest ("confusion"), and presented as a decision to restore normalcy. In Argentina, in Brazil, in Greece, in Chile, in Turkey, the military proclaimed the state of emergency in order to curb the "chaos" of overall politicization: "This madness must stop, people should return to their everyday jobs, work must go on!"

In some sense, we can in fact argue that, today, we are approaching a kind of "end of time": the self-propelling explosive spiral of global capitalism does seem to point toward a moment of (social, ecological, even subjective) collapse, in which total dynamism, frantic activity, will coincide with a deeper immobility. History will be abolished in the eternal present of multiple narrativizations; nature will be abolished when it becomes subject to biogenetic manipulation; the very permanent transgression of the norm will assert itself as the unconditional norm. . . . However, the question "When does ordinary time get caught in the messianic twist?" is a misleading one: we cannot deduce the emergence of messianic time through an "objective" analysis of historical process. "Messianic time" ultimately stands for the intrusion of subjectivity irreducible to the "objective" historical process, which means that things can take a messianic turn, time can become "dense," *at any point.*

The time of the Event is not another time beyond and above the "normal" historical time, but a kind of inner loop within this time. Consider one of the standard plots of time-travel narratives: the hero travels into the past in order to intervene in it, and thus change the present; afterward, he discovers that the emergence of the present he wanted to change was triggered precisely *through* his intervention—his time travel was already included in the run of things. What we have here, in this radical closure, is thus not simply complete determinism, but a kind of absolute determinism which includes our free act in advance. When we observe the process from a distant vantage point, it appears to unfold in a straight line; what we lose from sight, however, are the subjective inner loops which sustain this "objective" straight line. This is why the question "In what circumstances does the condensed time of the Event emerge?" is a false one: it involves the reinscription of the Event back into the positive historical process. That is to say: we cannot establish the time of the explosion of the Event through a close "objective" historical analysis (in the style of "when objective contradictions reach such and such a level, things will explode"): there is no Event outside the engaged subjective decision which creates it—if we wait for the time to become ripe for the Event, the Event will never occur. Recall the October Revolution: the moment when its authentic revolutionary urgency was exhausted was precisely the moment when, in theoretical discussion, the topic of different stages of socialism, of the transition from the lower to a higher stage, took over—at this point, revolutionary time proper was reinscribed into linear "objective" historical time, with its phases and transitions between phases.

Authentic revolution, in contrast, always occurs in an absolute Present, in the unconditional urgency of a Now.

It is in this precise sense that, in an authentic revolution, predestination overlaps with radical responsibility: the real hard work awaits us on the morning after, once the enthusiastic revolutionary explosion is over, and we are confronted with the task of translating this explosion into a new Order of Things, of drawing the consequences from it, of remaining faithful to it. In other words, the truly difficult work is not that of silent preparation, of creating the conditions for the Event of the revolutionary explosion; the earnest work begins *after* the Event, when we ascertain that "it is accomplished."[11]

The shift from Judaism to Christianity with regard to the Event is best encapsulated in terms of the status of the Messiah: in contrast to Jewish messianic expectation, the basic Christian stance is that *the expected Messiah has already arrived*, that is, that we are already redeemed: the time of nervous expectation, of rushing precipitately toward the expected Arrival, is over; *we live in the aftermath of the Event: everything—the Big Thing—has already happened.*[12] Paradoxically of course, the result of this Event is not atavism ("It has already happened, we are redeemed, so let us just rest and wait . . ."), but, on the contrary, an extreme urge to act: it has happened, *so now we have to bear the almost unbearable burden of living up to it, of drawing the consequences of the Act.* . . . "Man proposes, God disposes"—man is incessantly active, intervening, but it is the divine act which decides the outcome. With Christianity, it is the reverse—not "God proposes, man disposes," but the order is inverted: "God (first) disposes, (and then) man proposes." It is waiting for the arrival of the Messiah which constrains us to the passive stance of, precisely, waiting, while the arrival functions as a signal which triggers activity.

This means that the usual logic of the "cunning of reason" (we act, intervene, yet we can never be sure of the true meaning and ultimate outcome of our acts, since it is the decentered big Other, the substantial symbolic Order, which decides) is also strangely turned around—to put it in Lacanian terms, it is humanity, not God, which is the big Other here. It was God Himself who made a Pascalian wager: by dying on the Cross, He made a risky gesture with no guaranteed final outcome, that is, He provided us—humanity—with the empty S_1, Master-Signifier, and it is up to humanity to supplement it with the chain of S_2. Far from providing the conclusive dot on the i, the divine act stands, rather, for the openness of a New Beginning, and it is up to humanity to live up to it, to decide its meaning, to make something of it. It is as in Predestination, which condemns us to frantic activity: the Event is a pure-empty sign, and we have to work to generate its meaning. "The Messiah is here"—this summarizes the terrible risk of Revelation: what "Revelation" means is that God took upon Himself the risk of putting everything at stake, of fully "existentially engaging Himself" by, as it were, stepping into His own picture, becoming part of creation, exposing Himself to the utter contingency of existence. Here I am tempted to refer to the Hegelian-Marxian opposition of formal and material subsumption: through the Event (of Christ), we are *formally* redeemed, subsumed under Redemption, and we have to engage in the difficult work of actualizing it. The true Openness is not that of undecidability, but that of living in the aftermath of the Event, of drawing out the consequences—of what? Precisely of the new space opened up by the Event.

What this means, in theological terms, is that it is not we, humans, who can rely on the help of God—on the contrary, *we must help God*. It was Hans Jonas who developed this notion, referring to the diaries of Etty Hillesum, a young Jewish woman who, in 1942, voluntarily reported to a concentration camp in order to be of help there, and share the fate of her people: "Only this one thing becomes more and more clear to me: that you cannot help us, but that we must help you, and in so doing we ultimately help ourselves. . . . I demand no account from you; you will later call us to account."[13] Jonas links this stance to the radical idea that God is not omnipotent—the only way, according to him, to explain how God could have allowed things like Auschwitz to happen. The very notion of creation implies God's self-contraction: God had first to withdraw into Himself, constrain his omnipresence, in order first to create the Nothing out of which he then created the universe. By creating the universe, He set it free, let it go on its own, renouncing the power of intervening in it: this self-limitation is equivalent to a proper act of creation. In the face of horrors like Auschwitz, God is thus the tragic impotent observer—the only way for Him to intervene in history was precisely to "fall into it," to appear in it in the guise of His son.

Notes

1   Is not Catholic celibacy (the prohibition of marriage for priests and nuns) ultimately anti-Christian, a remainder of pagan attitudes? Is it not based on the pagan notion that those who sacrifice earthly sexual pleasures thereby gain access to divine *jouissance*?

2   According to Jung, in the conscious suffering of Christ, God atones for the suffering of Job: "for, just as man must suffer from God, so God must suffer from man. Otherwise there can be no reconciliation between the two" (C. G. Jung, *Answer to Job* [Princeton: Bollingen, 1958, p. 39]). The framework here is still that of exchange: one suffering for the other.

3   The interest of Milton's *Paradise Regained* lies in the fact that Satan in this poem is a completely different character from Satan in *Paradise Lost*: no longer the heroic fallen Angel, but a simple agent of temptation—if anything, it is Christ himself who is the counterpart to Satan in *Paradise lost* here. The topic of both poems is the same; how to resist temptation; and Christ succeeds where Satan fails. Christ is thus not so much the "second Adam" as the *second Satan*: he succeeds where Satan failed. This focus on the topic of fidelity and resisting temptation also links *Paradise Regained* to the Book of Job: not only is Christ's resistance to temptation parallel to Job's; one can also claim that Satan in *Paradise Regained* is a new version of the theological friends who come to comfort Job—the arguments of these "friends" are strictly correlative to Satan's four temptations: those of worldly pleasures, wealth, power, and false religious sacrifice itself (precisely sacrifice as an act of exchange, as "paying the price" for sins). In short, temptation is inherent to religion: Satan's realm is fake theology itself, theology as ideology. Just as the friends offer Job the four basic versions of ideological legitimization, Satan tempts Christ with four versions of ideology.

4   In the context of the "Jewish exception," I am tempted to risk a radical rereading of Freud, who attributed to the Jews the disavowal of the primordial crime (the parricide of Moses): what if even alternative Freudian readings, which propose the hypothesis of a displaced crime (in effect, it was Moses himself who was guilty of the "parricide," killing the Pharaoh), are wrong? What if Moses' true crime was not the murder, but the *humiliation* of the Pharaoh, the public display of his impotence? Is this not worse than a straightforward killing: after the killing, the father returns as the ideal agency of the Law, while the humiliated father merely survives as a ridiculous impotent excrement? What if this humiliation of the father was the precondition for establishing Judaism as the first great religion that, originally and most of the time, was not a state religion, but the religion of a group without a state identity? Furthermore, what if this is what makes the idea of the State of Israel problematic?

5   See Eric Santner, "Traumatic Revelations: Freud's Moses and the Origins of Anti-Semitism," in *Sexuation*, ed. Renata Salecl (Durham: Duke University Press, 2000).

6   See Franz Rosenzweig, *The Star of Redemption* (Notre Dame: University of Notre Dame Press, 1985).

7   See David Horell, *An Introduction to the Study of Paul* (New York and London: Continuum, 2000), p. 82.

8   Rosenzweig, *The Star of Redemption*, pp. 404–5. Of course, I owe this quote to Eric Santner, who developed this notion of Jewish identity in detail in his outstanding *On the Psychotheology of Everyday Life* (Chicago: University of Chicago Press, 2001). Interestingly, this notion of being a remainder is also part of the traditional Slovene national identity; the traumatic cut in Slovene history is the Counter-Reformation offensive in the late sixteenth century, as a result of which a third of all Slovenes were killed, a third emigrated to Germany in order to remain Protestants, and the remainder, the scum who compromised their fidelity, are the present-day Slovenes.

9   Rosenzweig, *The Star of Redemption*, p. 227.

10   And does not Martin Luther King make the same point in his "Letter from Birmingham Jail" (1963)?

We know through painful experience that freedom is never voluntarily given by the oppressor; it must be demanded by the oppressed. Frankly, I have never yet engaged in a direct-action movement that was "well timed" according to the timetable of those who have not suffered unduly from the disease of segregation. For years now I have heard the word "wait." It rings in the ear of every Negro with a piercing familiarity. This "wait" has almost always meant "never." It has been a tranquilizing thalidomide, relieving the emotional stress for a moment, only to give birth to an ill-formed infant of frustration. We must come to see with the distinguished jurist of yesterday that "justice too long delayed is justice denied." We have waited for more than three hundred and forty years for our God-given and constitutional rights. The nations of Asia and Africa are moving with jetlike speed toward the goal of political independence, and we still creep at horse-and-buggy pace toward the gaining of a cup of coffee at a lunch counter. I guess it is easy for those who have never felt the stinging darts of segregation to say "wait." But when you have seen vicious mobs lynch your mothers and fathers at will and drown your sisters and brothers at whim; when you have seen hate-filled policemen curse, kick, brutalize, and even kill your black brothers and sisters with impunity; when you see the vast majority of your twenty million Negro brothers smothering in an airtight cage of poverty in the midst of an affluent society; when you suddenly find your tongue twisted and your speech stammering as you seek to explain to your six-year-old daughter why she cannot go to the public amusement park that has just been advertised on television, and see tears welling up in her little eyes when she is told that Funtown is closed to colored children, and see the depressing clouds of inferiority begin to form in her little mental sky, and see her begin to distort her little personality by unconsciously developing a bitterness toward white people; when you have to concoct an answer for a five-year-old son asking in agonizing pathos, "Daddy, why do white people treat colored people so mean?"; when you take a cross-country drive and find it necessary to sleep night after night in the uncomfortable corners of your automobile because no motel will accept you; when you are humiliated day in and day out by nagging signs reading "white" and "colored"; when your first name becomes "nigger" and your middle name becomes "boy" (however old you are) and your last name becomes "John," and when your wife and mother are never given the respected title "Mrs."; when you are harried by day and haunted by night by the fact that you are a Negro, living constantly at tiptoe stance, never knowing what to expect next, and plagued with inner fears and outer resentments; when you are forever fighting a degenerating sense of "nobodyness"—then you will understand why we find it difficult to wait. There comes a time when the cup of endurance runs over and men are no longer willing to be plunged into an abyss of injustice where they experience the bleakness of corroding despair. I hope, sirs, you can understand our legitimate and unavoidable impatience.

11   And it is perhaps on this level that we should also approach the old question, which seems to have regained its relevance recently, of the line of separation between animal and man: at the level of positive being, there is no difference, man is just an animal with specific properties and abilities; it is only from the engaged position of being caught up in the process that the difference becomes palpable.

12   Perhaps the most succinct answer to Christianity, to the Christian notion that the Messiah is already here, was provided by Kafka's claim that the Messiah will definitely arrive, but too late, when humanity is already tired of waiting for him, and his arrival will no longer matter, and will leave people indifferent.

13   Quoted from Han Jonas, *Mortality and Morality* (Evanston: Northwestern University Press, 1996), p. 192.

Chapter 72

Johanna Drucker

DIGITAL HUMANITIES AND ELECTRONIC TEXTS

In exploring the differences between the digital humanities and speculative computing, Johanna Drucker's extract provides a good introduction to both. She argues that while speculative computing (an open-ended, subjective, playful and fundamentally creative approach to digital projects in the humanities) is grounded in the digital humanities, it also tries to resist the ensuing interpretive strictures of computer science-based approaches to aesthetic texts, which Drucker calls "mathesis" or the quest to understand and represent the "formal logic" of artistic expression. The digital humanities, according to Drucker, are about *disambiguation*, that is to say, taking deeply ambiguous artefacts, such as literary texts, and digitizing, transposing, and interpreting them in ways that facilitate their computational analysis, thus removing (or at the least re-codifying) inherent signs of ambiguity. Drucker, who is the Martin and Bernard Breslauer Professor in the Graduate School of Education and Information Studies, at the University of California, discusses both the history of the digital humanities—such as the foundational work of Father Roberto Busa (1913–2011), who worked with IBM to create his *Index Thomisticus* (begun in 1949; online version 2005)—and the basic procedures, tools and interpretive models that drive the discipline, such as digitization, coding with meta-data, and complex text analysis. For Drucker, these disciplinary processes are about creating authority over the text, i.e., the authority that is concomitant with applying a mark-up language to a text, which can be thought of as artificially restricting the text's breadth of meaning. Drucker contrasts such processes with those of speculative computing, which is "a set of principles" designed to resist, question and undermine the "cultural authority" of mathesis. In other words, speculative computing embraces deconstructive and postmodern theories developed in the late twentieth century, which would otherwise be subject to what Drucker calls "the normalizing pressures of digital protocols." An early form of interaction between high theory and digital worlds occurred with the creation of hyperlinked texts, for example, applying the theories of Deleuze and Guattari (such as the rhizomatic network). While these approaches are now less enthusiastically embraced by contemporary digital humanists, Drucker argues that they were an important stage in speculative computing. However, equally powerful has been the creation of mainly invisible hierarchies and power structures which are part-and-parcel of digitization processes, in other words, meta-data, tagging, style sheets, and so on, are all necessary coding components which remain largely hidden to the average user of digitized materials. For Drucker, all of these processes are interpretive, and thus it is important to foreground and critique them. An example is given in the section on "Metalanguages and Metatexts", namely, the ways in which "metadata schemes" are "models of knowledge" or "discursive instruments" that are constitutive, not passive reflectors of what they are describing. Drucker examines HTML and XML with the example of a tag that flags-up "flirtation" in a piece of textual dialogue. The undecidability involved makes Drucker's point: it is not clear where such a tag would be inserted or even how such a decision can be made, recoiling back upon all such tagging decisions. Critical analysis, then, is needed to understand the power-knowledge implications and effects of what might appear to be neutral coding.

From digital humanities to speculative computing

Our activities in speculative computing were built on the foundation of digital humanities. The community at the University of Virginia which these activities flourished was largely, though not exclusively, concerned with what could be done with texts in electronic form. Early on, it became clear that aggregation of information, access to surrogates of primary materials, and the manipulation of texts and images in virtual space all provided breakthrough research tools. Projects in visualization were sometimes part of first-generation digital humanities, but the textual inclination of digital humanities was nurtured in part by links to computational linguistics whose analyses were well served by statistical methods. (Sheer practicality played a part as well. Keyboarded entry of texts may raise all kinds of not so obvious issues, but no equivalent for "entering" images exists – a point, as it turns out, that bears on my arguments about materiality.) Some literary or historical scholars involved in critical editing and bibliographical studies found the flexibility of digital instruments advantageous.[1] But these environments also gave rise to theoretical and critical questions that prompted innovative reflections on traditional scholarship.

The early character of digital humanities was formed by concessions to the exigencies of computational disciplines.[2] Humanists played by the rules of computer science and its formal logic, at least at the outset. Part of the excitement was learning new languages through which to rethink our habits of work. The impulse to challenge the cultural authority of computational methods in their received form came later, after a period of infatuation with the power of digital technology and the mythic ideal of *mathesis* it seemed to embody. That period of infatuation (a replay of a long tradition) promoted the idea that formal logic might be able to represent human thought as a set of primitives and principles, and that digital representation might be the key to unlocking its mysteries. Naïve as this may appear in some circles, the Utopian ideal of a world fully governed by logical procedures is an ongoing dream for many who believe rationality provides an absolute basis for knowledge, judgment, and action.[3] The linguistic turn in philosophy in the early decades of the twentieth century was fostered in part by the development of formalist approaches that aspired to the reconciliation of natural and mathematical languages. The intellectual premises of British analytic philosophy and those of the Vienna Circle, for instance, were not anomalies but mainstream contributions to a tradition of mathesis that continued to find champions in structural linguistics and its legacy throughout the twentieth century.[4] The popular-culture image of the brain as a type of computer turns these analogies between thought and processing into familiar clichés.[5] Casual reference to nerve synapses as logic gates or behaviors as programs promotes an unexamined but readily consumed idea whose ideal is a total analysis of human thought processes, as if they could be ordered according to formal logic.[6] Science fiction writers have exploited these ideas endlessly, as have futurologists and pundits given to hyperbole, but widespread receptiveness to their ideas shows how deeply rooted the mythology of mathesis is in the culture at large.[7]

Digital humanists, however, were interested, not in analogies between organic bodies and logical systems, but in the intellectual power of information structures and processes. The task of designing content models or conceptual frameworks within which to order and organize information, as well as the requirements of data types and formats at the level of code or file management, forged a pragmatic connection between humanities research and information processing. The power of metalanguages expressed as classification systems and nomenclature was attractive, especially when combined with the intellectual discipline imposed by the parameters and stringencies of working in a digital environment. A magical allure attached to the idea that imaginative artifacts might yield their mysteries to the traction of formal analyses, or that the character of artistic expressions might be revealed by their place within logical systems. The distinction between managing or ordering texts and images with metadata or classification schemes and the interpretation of their essence as creative works was always clear. But still, certain assumptions linked the formal logic of computational processes to the representation of human expressions (in visual as well as textual form), and the playful idea that one might have a "reveal codes" function that would expose the compositional protocols of an aesthetic work had a compelling appeal. At first glance, the ability of formal processing to manage complex expressions either by modeling or manipulation appeared to be mere expediency. But computational methods are not simply a means to an end. They are a powerful change agent setting the terms of a cultural shift.

By contrast, speculative computing is not just a game played to create projects with uncertain outcomes, but a set of principles through which to push back on the cultural authority by which computational methods instrumentalize their effects across many disciplines. The villain, if such a simplistic character must be brought on stage, is not formal logic or computational protocols, but the way the terms of such operations are used to justify decisions about administration and management of cultural and imaginative life based on the presumption of objectivity.[8] The terms on which digital humanities had been established, while essential for the realization of projects and goals, needed to be scrutinized with an eye to the discipline's alignment with such managerial methods. As in any ideological formation, unexamined assumptions are able to pass as natural. We defined speculative computing to push subjective and probabilistic concepts of knowledge as experience (partial, situated, and subjective) against objective and mechanistic claims for knowledge as information (total, managed, and externalized).

If digital humanities activity were reduced to a single precept, it would be the requirement to disambiguate knowledge representation so that it operates within the codes of computational processing. This requirement has the benefit of causing humanist scholars to become acutely self-conscious about the assumptions under which we work, but also to concede many aspects of ambiguity for the sake of workable solutions. Basic decisions about the information or substantive value of any document rendered in a digital surrogate—whether a text will be keyboarded into ASCII, stripping away the formatting of the original, or how a file will be categorized—are fraught with theoretical implications. Is *The Confessions* of Jean Jacques Rousseau a novel? The document of an era? A biographical portrait? A memoir and first-person narrative? Or a historical fiction? Should the small, glyphic figures in William Blake's handwriting that appear within his lines of poetry be considered part of the text, or simply disregarded because they cannot be rendered as ASCII symbols?[9] At every stage of development, digital instruments require such decisions. And through these decisions, and the interpretive acts they entail, our digital cultural legacy is shaped.

Because of this intense engagement with interpretation and epistemological questions, the field of digital humanities extends the theoretical questions that came into focus in deconstruction, postmodern theory, critical and cultural studies, and other theoretical inquiries of recent decades. Basic concerns about the ways processes of interpretation constitute their objects within cultural and historical fields of inquiry are raised again, and with another level of historical baggage and cultural charge attached. What does it mean to create ordering systems, models of knowledge and use, or environments for aggregation or consensus? Who will determine how knowledge is classified in digital representations? The next phase of cultural power struggles will be embodied in digital instruments that model what we think we know and what we can imagine.

Digital humanities is an applied field as well as a theoretical one, and the task of applying these metaconsiderations puts humanists' assumptions to a different set of tests. It also raises the stakes with regard to outcomes.[10] Theoretical insight is constituted in this field in large part through encounters with application. The statistical analysis of texts, creation of structured data, and design of information architecture are the basic elements of digital humanities. Representation and display are integral aspects of these activities, but they are often premised on an approach influenced by engineering, grounded in a conviction that transparency or accuracy in the presentation of data is the best solution. Blindness to the rhetorical effects of design *as a form of mediation* (not of transmission or delivery) is an aspect of the cultural authority of mathesis that plagues the digital humanities community. Expediency is the name under which this authority exercises its control, and in its shadow grow the convictions that resolution and disambiguation are virtues, and that "well-formed" data behaves in ways that eliminate the contradictions tolerated by (traditionally self-indulgent) humanists. The attitude that objectivity-defined in many cases as anything that can be accommodated to formal logical processes – is a virtue, and the supposedly fuzzy quality of subjectivity implicitly a vice, pervades the computation community. As a result, I frequently saw the triumph of computer culture over humanistic values.[11]

Humanists are skilled at complexity and ambiguity. Computers, as is well known, are not. The distinction amounts to a clash of value systems, in which fundamental epistemological and ideological differences arise. Digital projects are usually defined in highly pragmatic terms: creating a searchable corpus, making primary materials for historical work available, or linking such materials to an interactive map and timeline capable of displaying data selectively. Theoretical issues that arise are, therefore, intimately bound to practical tasks, and all the lessons of deconstruction and poststructuralism – the extensive critiques of reason and grand narratives, the recognition that presumptions of objectivity are merely cultural assertions of a particular, historical formation – threaten to disappear under the normalizing pressures of digital protocols. This realization drove SpecLab's thought experiments and design projects, pushing us to envision and realize alternative possibilities.

Digital humanities and electronic texts

Digital humanities is not defined entirely by textual projects, though insofar as the community in which I was involved focused largely on text-based issues, its practices mirrored the logocentric habits endemic to the academic establishment.[12] Even so, many of my own convictions regarding visual knowledge production were formulated in dialogue with that community. Understanding the premises on which work in the arena of digital humanities was conceived is important as background for our design work at SpecLab – and to heading off the facile binarisms that arise so easily, pitting visual works against texts or analog modes against digital ones, thus posing obstacles to more complex thought.

Textual studies met computational methods on several different fields of engagement. Some of these were methods of manipulation, such as word processing, hypertext, or codework (a term usually reserved for creative productions made by setting algorithmic procedures in play).[13] Others were tools for bibliographical studies, critical editing and collation, stylometrics, or linguistic analysis. Another, mentioned briefly above, was the confluence of philosophical and mathematical approaches to the study of language that shared an enthusiasm for formal methods. The history of programming languages and their relation to modes of thought, as well as their contrast with natural languages, is yet another. All of these have a bearing on digital humanities, either directly (as tools taken up by the field) or indirectly (as elements of the larger cultural condition within which digital instruments operate effectively and gain their authority).

Twenty years ago a giddy excitement about what Michael Heim termed "electric language" turned the heads of humanists and writers. Literary scholars influenced by deconstruction saw in digital texts a condition of mutability that seemed to put the idea of differential "play" into practice.[14] The linking, browsing, combinatoric possibilities of hypertext provided a rush to authorial imagination. Suddenly it seemed that conventions of "linearity" were being exploded. New media offered new manipulative possibilities. Rhizomatic networks undercut the apparent stasis of the printed page. Text seemed fluid, mobile, dynamically charged. Since then, habits of use have reduced the once dizzying concept of links and the magic of being able to rework texts on the screen to the business of everyday life. But as the "wow" factor of those early encounters has evaporated, a deeper potential for interrogating what a text is and how it works has come into view within the specialized practices of electronic scholarship and criticism. In particular, a new order of metatexts has come into being that encodes (and thus exposes) attitudes toward textuality.

Early digital humanities is generally traced to the work of Father Roberto Busa, whose *Index Thomisticus* was begun in 1949. Busa's scholarship involved statistical processing (the creation of concordances, word lists, and studies of frequency), repetitive tasks that were dramatically speeded by the automation enabled by computers. Other developments followed in stylometrics (quantitative analysis of characteristics of style for attribution and other purposes), string searches (matching specific sequences of alphanumeric characters), and processing of the semantic content of texts (context sensitive analysis, the semantic web, etc.).[15] More recently, scholars involved in the creation of electronic archives and collections have established conventions for metadata (the Dublin Core Metadata Initiative), markup (the Text Encoding Initiative), and other elements of digital text processing and presentation.[16] This process continues to evolve as the scope of online projects expands from creation of digital repositories to peer-reviewed publishing, the design of interpretative tools, and other humanities-specific activities. The encounter of texts and digital media has reinforced theoretical realizations that printed materials are not static, self-identical artifacts and that the act of reading and interpretation is a performative intervention in a textual field that is charged with potentiality.[17] One of the challenges we set ourselves was to envision ways to *show* this dramatically rather than simply to assert it as a critical insight.

The processes involved in these activities are not simply mechanical manipulations of texts. So-called technical operations always involve interpretation, often structured into the shape of the metadata, markup, search design, or presentation and expressed in graphic display. The gridlike structures and frames in Web browsers express an interpretive organization of elements and their relations, though not in anything like an isomorphic mirroring of data structures. Features such as sidebars, hot links, menus, and tabs have become so rapidly conventionalized that their character as representations has become invisible. Under scrutiny, the structural hierarchy of information coded into buttons, bars, windows, and other elements of the interface reveals the rhetoric of display. Viewing the source code – the electronic equivalent of looking under the hood – shows an additional level of information structure. But this still doesn't provide access to or reading knowledge of the metadata, database structures, programming protocols, markup tags, or style sheets that underlie the display. Because these various metatexts actively structure a domain of knowledge production in digital projects, they are crucial instruments in the creation of the next generation of our cultural legacy. Arguably, few other textual forms will have greater impact on the way we read, receive, search, access, use, and engage with the primary materials of humanities studies than the metadata structures that organize and present that knowledge in digital form.[18]

Digital humanities can be described in terms of its basic elements: statistical processing, structured data, metadata, and information structures. Migrating traditional texts into electronic form allows certain things to be done with them that are difficult, if not impossible, with print texts. Automating the act of string searching allows the creation of concordances and other statistical information about a text, which in turn supports stylometrics. The capacity to search large quantities of text also facilitates discourse analysis, particularly the sort based on reading a word, term, or name in all its many contexts across a corpus of texts.

Many of the questions that can be asked using these methods are well served by automation. Finding every instance of a word or name in a large body of work is tedious and repetitive; without computers, the basic grunt work—like that performed by Father Busa—takes so long that analysis may be deferred for years. Automating narrowly defined tasks creates enormous amounts of statistical data quickly. The data then suggest other approaches to the study at hand. The use of pronouns versus proper names, the use of first person plural versus singular, the reduction or expansion of vocabulary, the use of Latinate versus Germanic forms—these are basic elements of linguistic analysis in textual studies that give rise to interesting speculation and scholarly projects.[19] Seeing patterns across data is a powerful effect of aggregation. Such basic automated searching and analysis can be performed on any text that has been put into electronic form.

In the last decade the processes for statistical analysis have grown dramatically more sophisticated. String searches on ASCII (keyboarded) text have been superceded by folksonomies and tag clouds generated automatically by tracking patterns of use. Search engines and analytic tools no longer rely exclusively on the tedious work of human agents as part of the computational procedure. And data mining allows context-dependent and context-independent variables to be put into play in ways that would have required elaborate coding in an earlier era of digital work.[20] The value of any computational analysis hangs, however, on deciding what can be expressed in terms of quantitative or otherwise standard parameters. The terms of the metric according to which any search or analytic process is carried out are framed with particular assumptions about the nature of data. What is considered data—that is, what is available for analysis—is as substantive a consideration as what is revealed by its analysis. I am not making a simple distinction between what is discrete and can be measured easily (such as counting the number of *e*'s in a document) and what cannot (quantifying the white space that surrounds them). Far more important is the difference between what we think can be measured and what is *outside that conception* entirely (e.g., the history of the design of any particular *e* as expressed or repressed in its form). The critique that poststructuralism posed to structuralist formalisms exposed assumptions based in cultural value systems but expressed as epistemological categories. The very notion of a standard metric is ideological. (The history of any *e* is a complicated story indeed.) The distinction between what can be parameterized and what cannot is not the same as the difference between analog and digital systems, but that between complex, culturally situated approaches to knowledge and totalized, systematic ones.[21]

Metalanguages and metatexts

The automated processing of textual information is fundamental to digital humanities, but so is the creation and use of metatexts, which describe and enhance information but also serve as performative instruments. As readers and writers we are habituated to language and, to some extent, to the "idea of the text" or "textuality." Insights into the new functions of digital metatexts build on arguments that have been in play for twenty years or more in bibliographic, textual, and critical studies.[22] Metalanguages have a fascinating power, carrying a suggestion of higher-order capabilities.[23] As texts that describes a language, naming and articulating its structures, forms, and functions, they seem to trump languages that are used merely for composition or expression. A metatext is a subset of metalanguage, one that is applied to a specific task, domain, or situation. Digital metatexts are not merely commentaries on a set of texts. In many cases they contain protocols that enable dynamic procedures of analysis, search, and selection, as well as display. Even more importantly, metatexts express models of the field of knowledge in which they operate. The structure and grouping of elements (what elements are included in the metadata for a title, publication information, or physical description of an artifact?) and the terms a metadata scheme contains (are graphical forms reproduced, and if so in what media and format, or just described?) have a powerful effect. Indeed, metadata schemes must be read as models of knowledge, as discursive instruments that bring the object of their inquiry into being, shaping the fields in which they operate by defining quite explicitly what can and cannot be said about the objects in a particular collection or online environment. Analysis of metadata and content models, then, is an essential part of the critical apparatus of digital humanities.

One tenet of faith in the field of digital humanities is that engaging with the constraints of electronic texts provides insight into traditional text formats.[24] Making explicit much that might elsewhere be left implicit is a necessity in a digital environment: computers, as we are often reminded, cannot tolerate the ambiguity typical of humanities texts and interpretative methods. Because digital metatexts are designed to *do* something to texts (divide elements by content, type, or behavior) or to do something as metatexts (in databases, markup languages, metadata) they are performative.

The term *structured data* applies to any information on which a formalized language of analysis has been imposed. In textual work in digital humanities, the most common mechanism for structuring data is known as markup language. "Markup" simply refers to the act of putting tags into a stream of alphanumeric characters. The most familiar markup language is HTML (HyperText Markup Language), which consists of a set of tags for instructing browsers how to display information. HTML tags identify format features—a < header > is labeled and displayed differently than a < br > (break) between paragraphs or text sections. While this may seem simplistic, and obvious, the implications for interpretation are complex. HMTL tags are content-neutral. They describe formal features, not types of information:

< italic >This, says the HTML tag, should be rendered in italics. < /italic >

But the italics used for a title and those used for emphasis are not the same. Likewise a "header" is not the same as a "title"—they belong to different classification schemes, one graphical and the other bibliographical. While graphic features—bold type, italics, fonts varying in scale and size—have semantic value, their semiotic code is vague and insubstantial.

XML (Extensible Markup Language), in contrast, uses tags that describe and model *content*. Instead of identifying "headers," "paragraphs," and other physical or graphical elements, XML tags identify titles, subtitles, author's names or pseudonyms, places of publication, dates of editions, and so on:

> < conversation >
>> < directquote > "Really, is that what XML does?" < /directquote > she asked. < directquote > "Yes," < /directquote > he replied, graciously, trying to catch her gaze.
> < /conversation >

All this seems straightforward enough until we pause to consider that perhaps this exchange should take a < flirtation > tag, given the phrases the follow:

> [or perhaps < flirtation > starts here?]
> < conversation >
>> < directquote > "Really, is that what XML does?" < /directquote > she asked. < directquote > "Yes," < /directquote > he replied, graciously, [or should < flirtation > start here?] trying to catch her gaze.
> < /conversation >
> < flirtation > [or start here?]
> His glance showed how much he appreciated the intellectual interest—and the way it was expressed by her large blue eyes, which she suddenly dropped, blushing. < directquote > "Can you show me?" < /directquote > < /flirtation >

Can we say with certainty where < flirtation > begins and ends? Before or after the first exchange? Or in the middle of it? The importance of defining tag sets and of placing individual tags becomes obvious very quickly. XML tags may describe formal features of works such as stanzas, footnotes, cross-outs, or other changes in a text. XML tags are based on domain- and discipline-specific conventions. The tags used in marking up legal or medical documents are very different from those appropriate to the study of literature, history, or biography. Even when tags are standardized in a field or within a research group, making decisions about which tags to use in a given situation involves a judgment call and relies on considerable extratextual knowledge. In the example above, the concept of < flirtation > is far more elastic than that of < conversation > .

XML documents are always structured as nested hierarchies, or tree structures, with parent and child nodes and all that such rigid organization implies. The implications of this rigidity brought the tensions between mathesis and aesthesis to the fore in what serves as an exemplary case. The hierarchical structure of XML was reflected in a discussion of what was called the OHCO thesis. OHCO stands for "ordered hierarchy of content objects." The requirements of XML were such that only a single hierarchy could be imposed on (actually inserted into) a document. This meant that scholars migrating materials into electronic form frequently faced the problem of choosing between categories or types of information to be tagged. One recurring conflict was between marking the graphic features and the bibliographic features of an original document. Did one chunk a text into chapters or into pages? One could not do both, since one chapter might end and another begin on the same page, in which case the two systems would conflict with each other. Such decisions might seem trivial, hairsplitting, but not if attention to material features of a text is considered important.

Returning to the example above, imagine trying to sort out, not only where < flirtation > begins and ends, but how it overlaps with other systems of content (technical advice, < XML queries > , < social behavior >). The formal constraints of XML simply do not match the linguistic complexity of aesthetic artifacts.[25] Even saying that texts *could be considered* ordered hierarchies for the sake of markup, rather than saying that they *are* structured in modular chunks, registers a distinction that qualifies the claims of the formal system. But despite these philosophical quarrels and challenges, the process of tagging goes on and is widely accepted as necessary for pragmatic work.[26]

Because XML schemes can be extremely elaborate, a need for standardization within professional communities quickly became apparent. Even the relatively simply task of standardizing nomenclature—such that a "short title" is always < short title > , not < ShortTitle > or < ShtTtl > —requires that tags be agreed upon. Creating significant digital collections would require consensus and regulation, so an organization called the Text Encoding Initiative was established. TEI, as Matt Kirschenbaum once wittily remarked, is a shadow world government. He was right of course. An organization setting standards for knowledge representation, especially standards that are essentially invisible to the average reader, is indeed a powerful entity. Protocols and practices that require conformity are the subtle, often insidious, means by which computational culture infiltrates humanist communities and assumes an authority over its operations. One can shrug off a monopoly hold on nomenclature as a smoothing of the way, akin to standard-gauge rails, or suggest that perhaps transportation and interpretation involve similar power struggles. But standards are powerful ideological instruments.

Discussion of tags is a bit of a red herring, as they may disappear into historical obsolescence, replaced by sophisticated search engines and other analytic tools. But the problem raised by XML tags, or any other system of classifying and categorizing information, will remain: they exercise rhetorical and ideological force. If < flirtation > is not a tag or recognized category then it cannot be searched. Think of the implications for concepts like < terror > or < democracy > . A set of tags for structuring data is a powerful interpretative grid imposed on innately complex and ambiguous human expression. Extend the above example to texts analyzed for policy analysis in a political crisis and the costs of conformity rise. Orwell's dark imaginings are readily realized in such a system of explicit exclusions and controls.

Paranoia aside, the advantages of structured data are enormous. Their character and content make digital archives and repositories different in scale and character from static websites and will enable next-generation design features to aggregate and absorb patterns of use into flexible systems. Websites built in HTML hold and display information in one fixed form, like objects in a display case or shop window. You can read it in whatever order you like, but you can't repurpose the data, aggregate it, or process it. A website might contain, for instance, a collection of book covers, hundreds of images that you can access through an index. If it has an underlying database, you might be able to search for information across various fields. But an archive, like Holly Shulman's Dolley Madison letters, contains fully searchable text.[27] That archive contains thousands of letters, and the ASCII text transcription of each is tagged, marked up, structured. Information about Madison's social and political life can be gleaned in a way that would be impossible in a simple website.

Through the combined force of its descriptive and performative powers, a digital metatext embodies and reinforces assumptions about the nature of knowledge in a particular field. But the metatext is only as good as the model of knowledge it encodes. It is built on a critical analysis of a field and expresses that understanding in its organization and the functions it can perform. The intellectual challenge comes from thinking through the ways the critical understanding of a field should be shaped or what should comprise the basic elements of a graphical system to represent temporality in humanities documents. The technical task of translating this analysis into a digital metatext is trivial by contrast to the compelling exercise of creating the intellectual model.

Notes

1   See the publications of the Association for Computational Linguistics (http://www.aclweb.org). PioneeringProjects include the William Blake Archive (http://www.blakearchive.org/blake/main.html), Perseus Digital Library (http://www.perseus.tufts.edu/hopper/), the Rossetti Archive, http://www.rossettiarchive.org, the Canterbury Tales Project (http://www.canterburytalesproject.org/CTPresources.html), the Piers Plowman Electronic Archive (http://www.iath.virginia.edu/piers), and the Brown University Women Writers Project and other work of the Scholarly Technology Group (http://www.stg.brown.edu).

2   Kathryne Sutherland (ed.), *Electronic Text* (Oxford: Clarendon Press, 1997).

3   See, for instance, William J. Mitchell, *City of Bits: Space, Place, and the Infobahn* (Cambridge: MIT Press, 1995).

4   Bertrand Russell, Alfred North Whitehead, young Ludwig Wittgenstein, Rudolf Carnap Gottlub Frege, and W. V. Quine are the outstanding figures in this tradition. See Robert J. Stainton, *Philosophical Perspectives on Language* (Peterborough, Ontario: Broadview Press, 1996); W. G. Lycan, *Philosophy of Language: A Contemporary Introduction.* (New York: Routledge, 2000).

5   Edmund C. Berkeley, *Giant Brains: Or Machines That Think* (New York: Wiley, 1950), is a classic in this genre.

6   For some of the early systematic thinking, see Marvin Minsky, *The Society of Mind* (New York: Simon and Schuster, 1986); Minsky with Seymour Papert, *Artificial Intelligence* (Eugene: Oregon State System of Higher Education, 1973); Herbert Simon, *Representation and Meaning: Experiments with Information Processing Systems* (Englewood Cliffs, NJ: Prentice Hall, 1972); Terry Winograd, *Artificial Intelligence and Language Comprehension* (Washington, DC: U.S. Department of Health, Education, and Welfare, National Institute of Education, 1976); Hubert Dreyfus, *What Computers Can't Do* (New York: Harper and Row, 1979); and even Richard Powers, *Galatea 2.2* (New York: Farrar, Straus, and Giroux, 1995). Daniel Crevier, *AI: The Tumultuous History of the Search for Artificial Intelligence* (New York: Basic Books, 1993), is still a useful introduction to the emergence of crucial fault lines in this area.

7   For a range of imaginings on this topic, see Philip K. Dick, *Do Androids Dream of Electric Sheep* (Garden City, NY: Doubleday, 1968); Rudy Rucker, *Software* (New York: Eos/HarperCollins, 1987); Bill Joy, "Why the Future Doesn't Need Us," http://www.wired.eom/wired/archive/8.04/joy.html; Donna Haraway, *Simians, Cyborgs, and Women* (New York: Routledge, 1991); and Chris Habels Gray and Steven Mentor, *The Cyborg Handbook* (New York: Routledge, 1995).

8   For an extreme view, see Arthur Kroker, *Digital Delirium* (New York: St. Martin's Press, 1997); Chun, *Control and Freedom,* offers a more tempered assessment. The writings of Critical Art Ensemble, at http://www.critical-art.net, synthesize critical philosophy and digital culture studies.

9   See Howard Besser's published works and online references, including "Digital Libraries, Standards, Metadata, and Longevity Activities," http://besser.tsoa.nyu.edu/howard/#standards.

10   For an overview of the field from varying perspectives, see Susan Schreibman, Ray Siemens, and John Unsworth (eds.), *Companion to Digital Humanities* (Oxford: Blackwell, 2004).

11   The EText Center at University of Virginia is a useful example: http://etext.virginia.edu.

12   Barbara Stafford, *Good Looking* (Cambridge: MIT Press, 1996), provides a striking demonstration of the extent to which logocentrism prevails in academic work. Her arguments, from the point of view of artists, art historians, or practitioners of visual knowledge production, seem so obvious as to be unnecessary, and yet, for textual scholars, they seemed to challenge basic assumptions, at least in some quarters. See also Franco Moretti, "Graphs, Maps, and Trees," *New Left Review,* no. 24, November-December 2003 (first of three articles, http://www.newleftreview.net/Issue24.asp?Article = 05).

13   On codework, see the exchanges between Rita Raley and John Cayley in Raley, "Interferences: [Net.Writing] and the Practice of Codework" (http://www.electron-icbookreview.com/thread/electropoetics/net.writing), and the discussions of digital poetry at http://www.poemsthatgo.com/ideas.htm.

14   Michael Heim, *Electric Language* (New Haven: Yale University Press, 1987); George Landow, *Hypertext* (Baltimore: Johns Hopkins University Press, 1992); J. David Bolter, *Writing Space* (Matwah, NJ: L. Erlbaum Associates, 1991).

15   Susan Hockey, *Electronic Texts in the Humanities* (Oxford: Oxford University Press, 2000) is an extremely useful, objective introduction to the field and its history. In addition see: Schreibman, Siemens, and Unsworth, *Companion to Digital Humanities;* McCarty, *Humanities Computing* (Hampshire:

Palgrave, 2005); and Elizabeth Bergmann Loizeaux and Neil Fraistat, *Reimagining Textuality* (Madison: University of Wisconsin Press, 2002).

16   For information on metadata standards, see http://dublincore.org; http://www.tei-c.org.

17   Jerome McGann, "Texts in N-Dimensions and Interpretation in a New Key," expands this list in a broader discussion that summarizes our work at SpecLab from his perspective (http://www. humanities.mcmaster.ca/~texttech/pdf/vol2_2_02.pdf).

18   Michael Day, "Metadata for Digital Preservation: A Review of Recent Development" (http://www. ukoln.ac.uk/metadata/presentations/ecdl2001-day/paper.html), and the discussion of metadata at http://digitalarchive.oclc.org/da/ViewObjectMain.jsp provide useful starting points.

19   Henry Kucera and Nelson Francis of *Computational Analysis of Present-Day American English* in 1967 is considered a turning point for this field. For current work in this area, see *Studies in Corpus Linguistics*, Elena Tognini-Bonelli, general editor, and the professional journal publications *Corpora,* and *Studies in Corpus Linguistics.*

20   Adam Mathes, "Folksonomies—Cooperative Classification and Communication through Shared Metadata,"http://www.adammatches.com/academic/computer-mediated-communication/ folksonomies.html; overview of search engines, http://jamesthornton.com/search-engine-research; updates on data mining, http://dataminingresearch.blogspot.com.

21   This distinction, more than any other, differentiates natural and formal languages and, not surprisingly, demarcates work in the fields of artificial intelligence from that in cognitive studies, for instance. The shift in the attitudes with which Ludwig Wittgenstein approached the study of language in his *Tractatus* and, later, in *Philosophical Investigations* registers the recognition that the project of totalized, objectified, formalistic approaches to language was a failure and the subsequent realization that only use, situated and specific, could provide insight into the signifying capabilities of languages.

22   JeromeMcGann, *The Critique of Modern Textual Criticism* (Chicago: University of Chicago Press, 1983) and *Black riders: The Visible Language of Modernism* (Princeton: Princepton University Press, 1993); Randall McLeod, lectures on "Material Narratives" (http://www.sas.upenn.edu/~traister/ pennsem.html); Steve McCaffery and bp nichol, *Rational Geomancy* (Vancouver: Talonbooks, 1992); Johanna Drucker, *The Visible Word: Experimental Typography and Modern Art, 1909–1923* (Chicago: University of Chicago press, 1994); and essays by McLeod, Nick Frankel, Peter Robinson, Manuel Portela, et al. in *Marking the Text,* ed. Joe Bray, Miriam Handley, and Anne C. Henry (Aldershot: Ashgate, 2000).

23   Joëlle Despeyroux and Robert Harper, "Logical Frameworks and Metalanguage," *Journal of Functional Programming* 13 (2003): 257–60.

24   Jerome McGann, *Radiant Textuality: Literature after the World Wide Web* (New York and Basingstoke: Palgrave, 2001), esp. chap. 5, "Rethinking Textuality," 137–66.

25   Allen Renear, "Out of Praxis: Three (Meta) Theories of Textuality," in Sutherland, *Electronic Text,* 107–26; Allen Renear, Steve De Rose, David G. Durand, and Elli Mylonas, "What Is Text, Really?" *Journal of Computing in Higher Education* 2, no. 1 (Winter 1990): 3–26.

26   Probably the most significant critique of markup, Dino Buzzetti's paper "Text Representation and Textual Models" (http://www.iath.virginia.edu/ach-allc.99/proceedings/buzzetti.html), brought much of that debate to a close by pointing out another important issue—that the insertion of tags directly into the text created a conflict between the text as a representation at the level of discourse (to use the classic terms of structuralist linguistics) and at the level of reference. Putting content markers into the plane of discourse (a tag that identifies the semantic value of a text relies on reference, even though it is put directly into the character string) *as if* they are marking the plane of reference is a flawed practice. Markup, in its very basis, embodies a contradiction. It collapses two distinct orders of linguistic operation in a confused and messy way. Buzzetti's argument demonstrated that XML itself is built on this confused model of textuality. Thus the foundation of metatextual activity was itself the expression of a model, even as the metatexts embodied in markup schemes model the semantic content of text documents.

27   Holly Shulman, ed., Dolley Madison Digital Edition, University of Virginia Press, http://www. upress.virginia.edu/books/shulman.html.

Chapter 73

Raymond Siemens

IMAGINING THE MANUSCRIPT AND PRINTED BOOK IN A DIGITAL AGE

Resisting the urge to re-imagine the eBook as a purely speculative digital component of a science fiction-based virtual reality, Raymond Siemens, Canada Research Chair in Humanities Computing at the University of Victoria, argues instead that a humanist understanding of the relationships between people and traditional books can be more productive in charting and comprehending current technological developments in electronic reading. Such a humanist approach involves re-examining the historical tradition of the codex (or bound manuscript with covers that we simply call a "book"), in particular the transition from handwritten manuscripts to printed texts following the invention of the mechanical printing press. Siemens observes that the physicality of the reading process is usually only foregrounded when the object itself presents itself in unusual ways, and this is also true of the early phase of manuscript production, which was undertaken by hand. Siemens notes that this period of book production necessarily led to a more intimate relationship between the materiality of the book and the physiological processes involved in producing, reading and interpreting such texts. But this also occurs historically at a time when marks inscribed upon a manuscript resonate with analogous "marks" or "inscriptions" such as those of Christian martyrdom. In other words, there is a homology between the physical and spiritual realms that is accentuated through the closer relationship between the scribe, the content, and the form of the text (say, a copy of the Bible or a book of selected Scriptural verses or commentaries). Siemens explores these homologies through a series of key images, such as that of a fresco from the Cathedral of Saint Cécile, in Albi, France, in which the human beings present at the Last Judgment have open books over their hearts, or the young man holding a heart-shaped book in the Master of the View of Saint Gudule. Another image-text explored in more depth by Siemens is that of the seventeenth-century poem by George Herbert called "Easter Wings". This is a poem shaped like two wings, which must be rotated to be read; content and form are in a complex interplay, one which is not just playful, but serious, given that this is a devotional poem. Siemens suggests that the physiological or phenomenological engagement with this text mimics and facilitates the religious practices the poem calls for; in other words the text's form is more than a passive reflection on what the content wants to bring into being; rather, the text's form is integral to the understanding of the very religious practices being brought about. In the final image, Siemens examines a page from the "scriptorium" (a room for copying manuscripts) of Peter Lombard, the Bishop of

Paris, upon which bodily and intellectual marginal commentary and interpretation is illuminated through a playful drawing of the human figure—an embodiment as such of the materiality of textual-physiological-intellectual interactions. Siemens argues that, with examples such as these, examining the transition to mechanical reproduction of texts offers a framework for the more recent transition to electronic reproduction, that is to say, as and through human embodiment, rather than disembodiment.

ONE OF THE MOST INTRIGUING IMAGININGS of the book and manuscript codex occurs when we endow it with human characteristics, when the book is something we perceive to have a body and a mind, a heart and a soul. Over time, we have both pleasurably noted and marvelled that the book at once *is embodied by us*—that is, we give it a physical shape, form, and content—and *is an embodiment of us*—acting, say, as our surrogate, across place and time. When we speak of the new and evolving electronic manifestation of the book today, however, we typically steer away from consideration of its more human characteristics. Instead, we have an awkward pattern of veering toward a characterisation of bookish manifestations that are quite foreign to us, focusing on the notion of an object that lacks recognizable physical form: disembodied texts, the ether of that which can be transmitted over computer networks, and so on. All told, this trend gestures more to the stuff of the grotesque and the futurist than that of the humanist, whose influence will surely be as strong in guiding the development of the book's current and emerging electronic manifestations as it has impacted, for centuries, the evolution of the manuscript and printed book. In our thinking about this, we need to chart a new course, one away from the futurist and the grotesque, and rather strongly toward that of the ongoing humanistic tradition of engagement with the codex form. Perhaps this should begin with a clearer understanding of our human relationship with the book itself.

The electronic representation of the codex—a book with no covers, as is said, perhaps with no immediately apparent physical form, lacking in assured fixity, and potentially with no beginning and no ending—can benefit from an understanding of the way in which aspects of the book have been figured variously across a number of centuries, centuries which we widely acknowledge to have seen two paradigm shifts: the first, from a culture that saw transmission of the codex via scribal copying to a culture that embraced the mechanical processes of the printing press, and the second, which is currently well along its way in seeing transmission shifting from the mechanical processes of the printing press to that of computer-assisted forms enabled by electronic media and the internet. My entry will be via several vignettelike imaginings of the codex form alongside its human producers and consumers, imaginings that imbue the book and manuscript with a reflected humanity and personality that is, realistically, denied by its physical limitations but are suggestive of the relationship between physical form and intellectual content, between presence and meaning, in both the physical book form and its electronic counterparts.

A context for theorising the codex

Our attention to the physical elements of books and reading is omnipresent, though often taken for granted. Indeed, many of us only consciously engage the physical form of the book when we encounter a form that somehow challenges our expectations; to list a few examples: the young child's first encounter with the book, which most likely involves the sense of taste at least as much as sight; the paperback that has permanently-bent pages and, thus it sits awkwardly; the book that is, say, circular in shape (rather than rectangular), or with a fold-out cover; and the book which has a page layout or font that is unique, such that our reading may be thrown off-balance for the first few minutes. Such encounters we have with books provide ample evidence of our engagement with the codex as a physical object as much as one housing intellectual content, and this separation of the codex's physical and intellectual attributes is something that has seen remark, exploration, and even good exploitation for some time.

Inscription and the human codex

Beyond the anecdotal, one finds this exemplified well in early manuscript culture: where the connection of the book with the physicality of its production, inscription, and use is much closer than it could possibly be in an age of comparatively hands-off mechanical reproduction—and even closer than it might be in early print culture, which adopted aspects of the scribal codex form at the same time as it sought new formal expressions, ones at times made more convenient or possible by the technologies of mechanical reproduction. Specific to my purpose here is the notion of inscription as it relates to that time, to the manuscript, and to the body. When we say, today, that we've inscribed something, we most likely mean that we've put pen or pencil to paper and written, yet an earlier interpretation of inscription would have the potential to be much more allusive.[1] Beyond the marks of the scribe on the page, one might equally consider the inscription left by one's feet on the ground, or, by way of further example, the marks of violence inflicted on a martyr (Plate 1). The footprint and the wound are each a type of inscription that have clear association with the marks on a scribe's page. Each of the inscribed media, if you will—the earth, the skin of Christ, and the prepared skin of the animal out of which most medieval manuscripts are made—bears the mark of the inscriber, in an act associated as much with the consequence of making that mark (walking, infliction of life-threatening wounds, or writing) as with what the mark suggests and represents (perhaps flight, martyrdom, or the word of God).

   The codex was a bodily entity for the early reader, one might say, and the acts of reading and writing were as much dominated by intellectual activity as by conscious sensual experience, even at times depicted as sexual. For those who produce it and for those who consume it, the book is an object very much associated with the humanity and human desire that is analogically imbued via its creation and use. The book's physical form and sensuality is seen to resemble ours, the content with which we imbue it is wholly ours, and the actions associated with its creation and use are human as well.

Content and meaning inscribing book form: the book of the heart

Ideas associated with the notion of the *book of the heart* illuminate this further, one of the best-known exemplifications of this seen in a fresco from the Cathedral of Albi (c. 1490, see Plate 2), depicting the last judgement with human figures in which their hearts are represented as opening like books.[2] Founded on the idea that one's innermost thoughts and personal history could be considered as inscribed within us, this tradition sees depiction across several millennia as a scroll rolled up in one's heart, a wax tablet which could be wiped clean by conversion to Christianity and, in the codex form, as a metaphoric reference to one's life record, connoting also intellectual capacity to recall, comprehend, and enact one's moral sense. Consider, for example, the personal associations of the heart-shaped book in the much-copied work by the Master of the View of Saint Gudule (Plate 3). While the physical form of the heart materially reflects an essential intellectual frame of reference, it is not the physicality of the book that is of paramount importance here; rather, form here readily depicts for us content, such that we can begin to understand content via observation of form. Our body here is represented by its most significant element privileged by this tradition.

Formal presence, illuminating meaning and practice: Herbert's "Easter Wings"

While textual theory of the past several decades has taught us not to ignore the importance of form, most will concur that form is rarely an end in itself and that medium is not exclusively the message, as much as medium may have everything to do with its conveyance. Rather, form and content, meaning and presence, are correlative, each informing the other. The seventeenth-century English devotional poet George Herbert illustrates such a relationship in his poem "Easter Wings", which has captured the professional imagination of those involved in textual studies, and editing, for over a century. The poem resists a traditional pattern of reading in its early printed form, in the first instance because one has to change the orientation of the text in order to begin to engage its textual content. Plate 4 (showing the second edition) depicts the text as it appears when one holds the book in the traditional manner. It must be re-oriented for the text to be read in normal fashion. Should one choose not to turn the book, one treats the content graphically rather than textually and appreciates the image of a pair of wings suggested by the correctly-oriented title. If one does choose to turn the book after recognising the shape, one can engage it textually and, in doing so, might note that the poem is connected as the title suggests to the church calendar and treats, among other things, the ascension of Christ and all that it symbolises.

In changing the orientation of the book, one also realises via its content that "Easter Wings" is a poem the form of which plays a very important role beyond that of the wing shape resembled by the text. Each ten-line stanza represents a decline and an elevation, with the decline emphasised in the shortening of the poetic lines, which move towards the phrases "most thin" and "most poor" in the middle of each stanza. The rise is indicated by increasing line lengths from the centre of each stanza to its end. When those expert in Herbert's thought discuss "Easter Wings", most work towards discussion of the notion expressed in the second-last line of page 35—"if I imp my wing on thine"—and treat it as a plea of the speaker, who presents the poem as a prayer for his own rise with Christ's ascension.

This pattern of interpretation is significant, to be sure, but its significance is increased by a clearer understanding of the full richness of interaction between presence and meaning in this text. It is generally accepted that each of the stanzas have association by their first word with, respectively, the speaker (on page 35 of the original; the first to be read in Figure 3) and (on page 34; the second to be read) the Lord, and it is considered that the poem is a prayer that can be intended for actual use, as are others in Herbert's collection of *The Temple* that houses them. Further, it has been suggested that devotional practices in Herbert's time would see a set prayer (such as this one, perhaps) read, silently alone or aloud to a group, followed by a time of silent deliberation in which the prayer book would likely be closed. Noting these points when exploring the relationship of form and meaning makes available to us some pertinent considerations. The first is that the reading process encourages holding the book in a specific manner, making it necessary to turn the volume in such a way that the poem can be read, and requiring both hands to be on the volume; one on each page and cover. The second is that, after the poem is read, the book would likely be returned to its more usual alignment and then, with two hands still on the pages and covers, the volume would be closed. The third takes place at the closure of the text—an act that many say brings the greatest formal significance to the content of the piece, because in closing the book in the manner that many believe it would have been closed, two very important events take place: one is that the two wings on opposite pages—that associated chiefly with the speaker and that with the Lord—are "imped", are brought together, in the way called for by the prayer; the other is that the most natural position of the closed hands on the volume as the book is closed is that resembling the position of prayer. Ingeniously, form encourages action and reading practice in ways central to that which is treated by content.

Multiplicity of intellectual presence and its formal representation: a comment on Peter Lombard's commentary

Without engagement of the poem's form, in the case of "Easter Wings" the reader cannot even begin to engage the textual content; but, once engaged, it is clear that form and content serve each other cleverly. Academic tradition might hold that the more salient of the two— that associated with form and physical presence and that associated with content and meaning—is intellectual content, but this example and others suggest the importance of remaining cognisant of the salient strength of form and presence. When the book, which can be figured as an extension of ourselves, speaks for us and encourages us to act, formal concerns manifest at least as importantly as that which form can hold and communicate for us. In this regard, one last print-oriented artefact to consider is presented in Plate 5, a page originating in the scriptorium of Peter Lombard, Bishop of Paris, exemplifying a contribution to the tradition of representing the complexly-interwoven commentary associated with the Epistles.

Here, in a method which serves as a recognisable foundation for that employed in scholarly editions today, extensive commentary is arranged to surround one small section of one epistle, the formal considerations of the page mimicking and augmenting, visually, aspects of the intellectual engagement by those whose expertise is rendered in the commentary on the section residing at the page's centre. The composite authorial form is provided by a line that runs almost the full vertical length of the inscribed page's right side, from head to feet of the human representation, at times marked with indications relating original text to the originators of the commentary (Jerome, Augustine, Ambrose) that provides the intellectual context for the reader's consideration. The visual image both identifies those providing the commentary and suggests clearly the composite, corporal nature of commentary in relation to the central author's body of work; the visualised body represents the composite sum of its constituent, intellectual parts—much as the way in which the material on the page is comprised of the original text itself plus that which tradition has deemed essential toward the understanding of this original text.

Presence and meaning, in the absence of physical form

Turning from argumentative preface to the matter of the collection, it is worth noting that one important trend in what is increasingly being called e-science and e-humanities research is not such an exponential leap forward in impacted disciplines that one cannot understand the future of disciplinary endeavour as anything other than a forward progression built on the progression of past advances, extending extant intellectual tradition. For all the radical rhetoric which surrounds the move from print to electronic media, even this paradigm shift isn't so radical that history and tradition are fully erased or rendered wholly irrelevant. Indeed, a valuable perspective for understanding our current paradigm shift is via the lens provided by that of the movement from manuscript culture to print culture, from scribal reproduction to mechanical. Our adoption and understanding of electronic media in those book-related activities that we carry out professionally and personally is best informed, explicitly and analogically, by our understanding of a past that presents valuable perspectives on and prospective solutions to concerns arising as part of our engagement of electronic media, specifically with reference to the patterns of physical and cognitive representation and the transmission, as well as the interaction, that they facilitate.

One does not have to look beyond the contents of this volume, and its resonance into all corners of the fields drawn upon and reflected among its papers, to see a very clear recognition that humanities-derived textual technologies and methodologies drawn from the age of manuscript and print have ready application to our understanding of the evolving new media culture in which we live, in the e-humanities, and even in emerging e-sciences. Examples abound, in the pages of this collection and well-beyond, the most striking along these lines perhaps being the adoption of techniques associated with complex textual collation by those doing string-based analysis of DNA; equally striking is the connection between twelfth century attempts at rendering detailed, human-associated commentary with that of our own evolving implementations of commentary in social computing environments that very clearly connect our own contributions to argument and discussion with visual self-representations, and the way in which we are beginning to imagine our human relationship to the form and style of the physical computer as well as its on-screen interface—particularly in increasingly ubiquitous devices such as laptop computers, iphones, and emerging micro-computers and reading tablets.

As with the book over time, so, too, with these devices. The devices that we embody by giving shape, form, and content continue to act as embodiments of us. Study of the multiple-authored disembodied text as represented by Lombard offers an important starting point in such considerations, as does our understanding of Herbert's method in manipulating physical form to augment significantly the reader's devotional experience, as does engaging the book of the heart tradition and the nature of the form-content relationship there—and, I would urge overall, as does our consideration of the relationship we have had, over time, with the book's physical form. Indeed, whatever the book might be—in manuscript, print, or some electronic manifestation—its connection is at least as much with us as humans as it is with the technologies associated with its production and dissemination, and surely more. Its sensuality is seen to resemble ours, the content with which we imbue it is ours, and the originating actions associated with the creation and use of the book are ours as well.

Nevertheless, even working in a tradition that understands the relationship between content and form, meaning and presence, we are often surprised when the results of our technological translation from print to digital representation yields unexpected results—largely, I would argue, based on a seemingly unconscious extension of our print expectations to the electronic medium and, further, by our tradition's valuation of intellectual content over physical form. A focus in our attention, now, on what is lost in that media-technological translation, on what from manuscript and print culture cannot yet be readily rendered and modelled in electronic media, provides us with a crucial foundation for research endeavour that gets to the heart of the paradigm shift and encourages an awareness of the way in which the electronic medium reconfigures our relationship to text at all levels. Examination of this crux requires exactly what is championed by the work represented in this volume: a firm grounding in the traditions associated with textual history and its culture coupled with the intellectual dexterity and interdisciplinary foresight to imagine how such a history can be extended into the world of electronic media. Chief among pertinent concerns here are issues of representation and re-presentation—and a focus on the maintenance of the conjoint importance of form and content, of presence and meaning, and the creative patterns that we have brought and continue to bring to our design and our intellectual engagement of the textual artefacts that show no sign of wavering in their centrality.

Plate 1: dead Christ lamented by Mary, St John and Joseph of Arimathea (?).

Plate 2: fresco depicting the Last Judgment, the Cathedral of Saint Cécile, Albi, France.

Plate 3: young man holding a heart-shaped book, Master of the View of Saint Gudule.

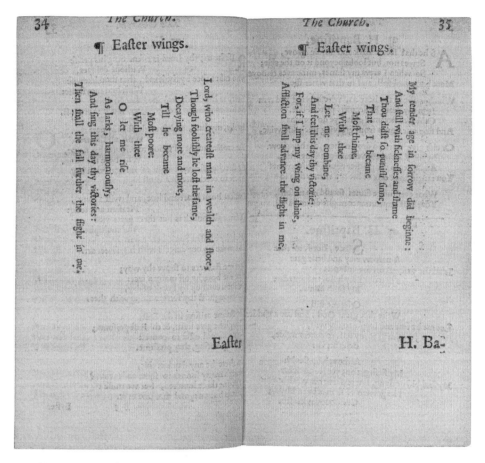

Plate 4: image of part of the seventeenth-century poem "Easter Wings", George Herbert.

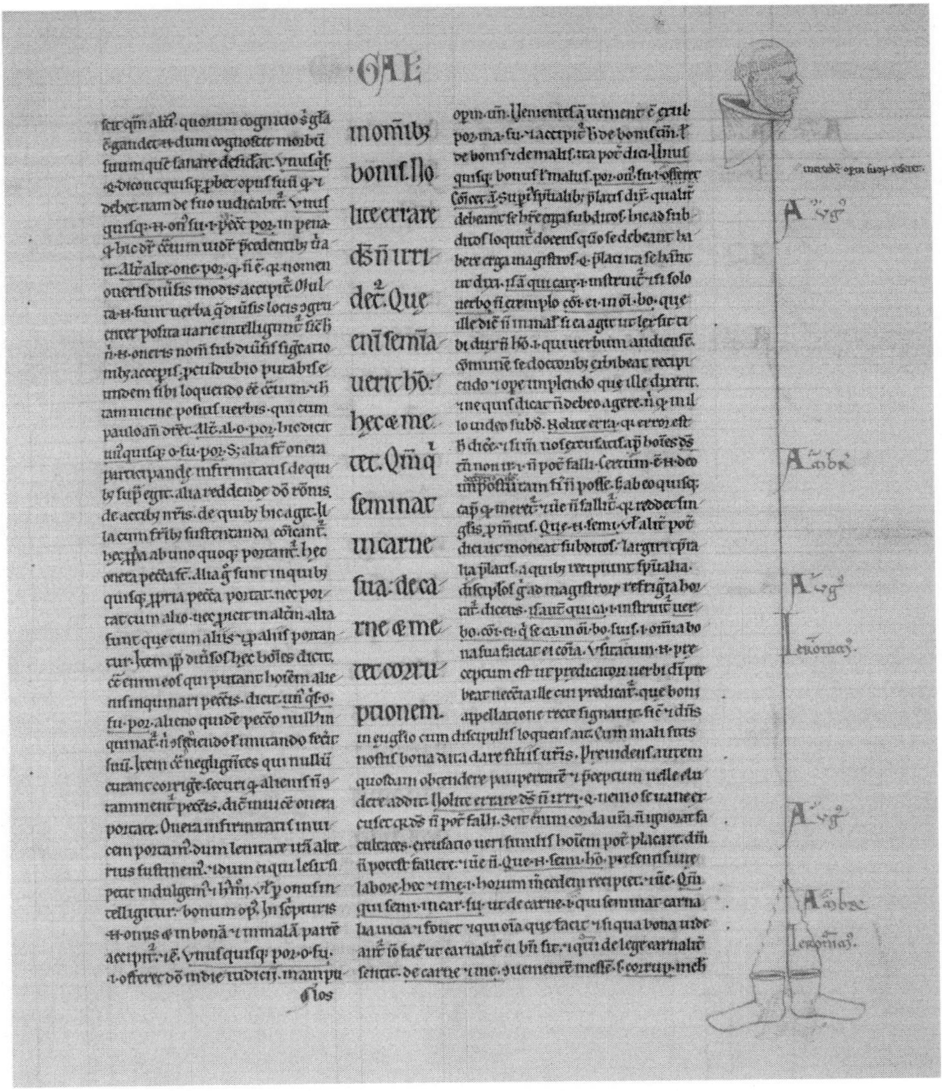

Plate 5: page from the scriptorium of Peter Lombard, Bishop of Paris.

Notes

1   Following, here and below, Frese and O'Keefe, Carruthers, Camille, and others.
2   Following Jager and others, here and below. Scroll depiction by Origen (ca. 250). Wax tablet as per
     St. Basil (ca. 329–79).

References

Camille, Michael, 'The book as flesh and fetish in Richard de Bury's *Philobiblon*', in Warwick
     Frese and O'Brien O'Keefe (eds), 34–77.
Carruthers, Mary, 'Reading with attitude, remembering the book', in Warwick Frese and
     O'Brien O'Keefe (eds), 1–33.
Jager, Eric, *Reading the book of the heart from the Middle Ages to the twenty-first century* (Chicago,
     2002).
Muri, Alison, 'The electronic page. Body/spirit, the virtual-digital and the real-tactile', in
     Architectures, ideologies, and materials of the page (Saskatoon, 2002).
Warwick Frese, Dolores, and Katherine O'Brien O'Keefe (eds), *The book and the body* (Notre
     Dame, 1997).
——, 'Introduction', in Warwick Frese and O'Brien O'Keefe (eds), ix–xviii.

Chapter 74

Liu Kang

THE INTERNET IN CHINA

Emergent cultural formations and contradictions

Hardly a week goes by without a news story about the internet in China, be it to do with debates about censorship, the implications of the rise of a vast internal internet user base, or stories about the clash of values between communist and capitalist ideologies. Kang Liu, professor of Chinese Studies and Director of the China Research Center at Duke University, explores the rise of the internet in China in the late twentieth century within the context of globalization and the transformation of the nation's economy. Three new domains are examined by Kang, being the internet: 1. as a new Chinese press; 2. as a "virtual public sphere" that exists alongside state-sanctioned and controlled media; and 3. as a site for new literary production (and reproduction/circulation). Rather than following a model of passive national acceptance of global ideas and technologies, Kang instead maps the intricate interrelations between internal and external shifts in national identity. For example, examining the internet as a new Chinese press, Kang notes how China has been engaged with its own "economic reform and opening-up"; that is to say, China is part of the globalized economy not simply subject to it. However, there are tensions which are played out in this new press, which tends to side with global, free-market values; while Kang argues that the state functions within a socialist model, leading to clashes of purpose and practice. Political control of internet news goes against the technological and informational flows generated in real time; censorship involves slowing-down news broadcasts and intervening in democratic reporting via cumbersome and not always very successful internet filters. Kang notes that as a political forum, the internet became more important with the rise of overseas-educated students and their viewpoints coinciding with those of the Tiananmen Square protestors. The example of the student-developed *China News Digest*, being published electronically from Canada, is explored and critiqued by Kang, mainly for its Western perspective on Chinese society, although the rise of internet chatrooms and forums has provided a myriad of alternative, dialogic news sources and alternative modes of debate. Kang also critiques a Western bias in new literary expression made possible by the internet, in particular where there is a foregrounding of hedonistic lifestyles rather than deep political commitment. However, Kang also recognizes the crucial fact that the internet is a new "interface" for exploration of new identities, in particular for the emerging urban youth cultures described here as the "New Humanity" or the "Newer, New Humanity." The internet offers a site of experimentation and publicity for new authors, and while Kang remains highly critical of much of the initial output in the 1990s, the importance of satirical and linguistically creative new fiction is also acknowledged. Kang also argues that while the internet often appears hedonistic and shallow, it does still offer spaces for more serious political engagement and expression. The main example explored is the interactive web-based dialogue surrounding the production of Zhang Guantian's play *Che Guevara*, which brings together Chinese and Western dramatic experimentation. Kang looks at the web-based publicity and discussion that surrounded and enhanced widespread engagement in this production. Finally, while Kang agrees that the internet has been powerful in "dismantling" hegemonic power structures, there is caution concerning whether much has been built as a worthwhile replacement.

SINCE THE MID-1990S, HUNDREDS AND THOUSANDS of Chinese-language Internet websites emerged in China, and the number of Internet users has increased dramatically. The Internet has become a dynamic force in China's cultural landscape. It is an important aspect of globalization, and plays an increasingly active role in China's transformation from its Maoist past to a post-revolutionary, post-socialist society. Globalization not only brings China closer than ever to the capitalist world economic system and market, but also generates new forms of culture and social interaction. The Internet has provided a new impetus to this process of transformation. Internet communication and global media have become central components of globalization processes. Given that the United States and Western Europe now dominate both technological developments and contents in global communications, the flow of information on the Internet promotes triumphant ideologies and values of capitalism across the world. China confronts these ideologies daily as it irreversibly moves toward globalization. It has sought to find new values and beliefs that can provide social cohesion and identities to its diversifying population. The state, of course, desperately needs an ideology, whether explicit or implicit, to ensure its legitimacy.

The Internet emerges in the midst of serious political and ideological changes. Can the Internet open up a new public sphere that will foster democracy for the Chinese people? To what extent will Internet communication erode the social and cultural fabrics and affect Chinese society negatively? Along with the technological and economic potential and promise it brings, the Internet will surely subject China to the ideologies of global capitalism under the various guises of "cultural imperialism," post-colonialism, and consumerism. What are the ideological impacts of global capitalism on Chinese culture and society? These questions cannot be answered with certainty; around the world people have been scrambling to find explanations for the sea changes in social life under globalization. But what the Internet can do in China is of critical importance to those aspiring to build a more democratic public life across the world, as well as those determined to amass unimaginable profit and power.

Communication technologies in the world at large provoke high hopes and anxieties primarily in technological and economic sectors. In China, the self-styled "largest developing country," technological and economic developments are set as its utmost priority. Ironically, however, rather than in the economic sector, the Internet has ignited a social engine mainly in the political, ideological, and cultural arenas. This chapter examines three distinct aspects of Internet development in China. First, the Internet creates a new press, which links to the global communication network. It trespasses the boundaries between the state-owned, centralized press and commercially-oriented local press, and between international press and national press. This new press inevitably affects Chinese media structures and practices, and will have profound implications not only on the Chinese media but also on the future of China's state ideological apparatuses. Second, the Internet provides an alternative public forum for political and intellectual debates that are rarely allowed in state-owned media. It appears as a virtual public sphere where the most politically sensitive issues—such as reforming the one-party system, fallacies of the past and present state and the communist bureaucracies—are being heatedly debated. As the Internet has become a site of fierce ideological and political contention, what will eventually transpire remains unknown. But the Internet political forum will undoubtedly alter the structure of public discourse in the political and ideological arenas, and will significantly affect China's political future. Third, an Internet literature has emerged, serving as the aesthetic representation of the urban youth generation, largely born in the 1970s and 1980s. As today's urban youth culture has largely been shaped by television and other digitally-based communication systems, Chinese young urbanites find the Internet a favorite channel for voicing their concerns and yearnings. Thriving literary activities in cyberspace have become a noticeable trend, while public interest in "serious" literature is eroded by the entertainment industry and consumer popular culture. Internet literary expressions of the urban youth are sharply divided. While commercialism nurtures sensuous indulgence and pleasure-seeking, some new experimental theaters are using the Internet to revive idealism and heroism reminiscent of the revolutionary past.

Globalization, the Internet, and new media

Globalization coincides with China's economic reform and opening-up, which constitutes the historical condition for the appearance of a new media. The Internet not only provides technological means to the new media but also brings to China ideologies and values from the newly developing global media system. The Internet stems largely from the US-based media conglomerates and transnational corporations, and, according to Edward Herman and Robert McChesney, serves as a "new missionary of global capitalism" to spread the gospel of market and profit (1). Such an ideological mission and "thoroughgoing commercialism" of the global media, Herman and McChesnye continue, threatens to undermine democratic participation of citizens and endanger the public sphere in the West. Meanwhile, Herman and McChesney concede that "media globalization" has its positive effects, by "carrying across borders some of the fundamental values of the West, such as individualism, skepticism of authority, and, to a degree, the rights of women and minorities," which can "help serve humane causes and disturb authoritarian governments and repressive traditional rules." (8) This self-contradictory view reflects, however, a deep-rooted conceptual dichotomy of the democratic West and undemocratic non-West, as though that "evils" are different—commercialism in the West, and authoritarianism in the non-West.

By abandoning its revolutionary tradition that was adamantly opposed to capitalist ideologies, and embracing a developmentalism to build a free market and a capitalist economy, China's case defies those simple West/East dichotomies. Deng Xiaoping's developmentalism is premised on economic marketization and corporatization, whereas the political order still rests on the ideological legitimation of socialism. The ideology of socialism still promises socio-economic equality to all citizens, and as such, is fundamentally at odds with the objectives of global capitalism to maximize profit at all costs. The paramount problem that China faces is the incommensurability between socialist ideologies and economic capitalism, which inevitably results in a legitimation crisis.

The media and the press are at the forefront of political and ideological change. The media in Mao's era served as a mouthpiece for the Chinese Communist Party (CCP), which was instrumental in the formation and dissemination of revolutionary ideologies and values. Since the reform, media not only have followed the directives of the Party, but have increasingly been compelled to adapt to the marketization trend that demands a service-oriented, more pragmatic and less politically preaching press. Jaime A. FlorCruz,

Time magazine's Beijing bureau chief, observes, "The vibrancy, diversity, and enterprise of newspapers, magazines and television shows reflect growing pluralism . . . and Beijing's inability to control it." (43)

The Internet has dramatically accelerated the pluralization of media in China. Since the mid-1990s, the Internet has created new media in cyberspace. China began developing the Internet in 1994, as the US federal government announced its agenda of constructing information superhighway [*sic*]. On 20 December 1995, *China Trade Daily* became the first Chinese news medium to have an online version on the Internet. By the end of 1995, only seven Chinese news media had an online service. Beginning in 1996, however, China's Internet development soared. By the end of that year, there were 100,000 Internet users, but by the end of 1998, the number of Internet users reached 2.1 million. One year later, that figure doubled, reaching more than 4 million in December 1999 (Xu). According to the statistics issued by the China Internet Information Center (CNNIC) in December 2000, the number of Internet users in China had leap-frogged to more than 20 million, a phenomenal growth of the cyberspace by any standard (*Beijing Youth Daily*). In a survey released in April 2002, Nielson Net Ratings, a US media research firm, states that "China has taken second place in the race for the world's largest at-home Internet population," as China becomes "the largest Internet in the Asia Pacific region, and the second largest worldwide after the US." According to the survey, in March 2002 there were "56.6 million people living in households with Internet connections" (Chan, Steyn). CNNIC's report on 21 July 2003 indicates that by 30 June 2003, Chinese Internet users reached 68 million.

The news media were among the first in China to develop Internet websites. By mid-1999, of 2,053 newspapers about 300 newspapers and presses had online publications, or about 14.6%. Major national newspapers began to set up online news centers. The Chinese government allocated substantial funds to the five major websites of the state presses: *People's Daily,* Xinhua News Agency, the English-language *China Daily,* China International Broadcasting Service, and China International News Center of the Internet *(Qiaobao).* China Central Television (CCTV), the national television network with eleven channels, also has a website compatible to these five presses in terms of its resources and audience. These websites have apparently learned formal and technical aspects from the major global media's websites, such as CNN, *New York Times,* and the Reuters, and have integrated the latest multimedia technology in online news reporting.

Although the contents of these websites remain largely identical to their print or electronic counterparts, changes have gradually taken place. First, the online international news coverage is quicker and more open to global media system than the print and electronic media. Online news is an around-the-clock, fast-tracking operation, which makes censorship by higher authorities much more cumbersome and often impossible, particularly when live reporting is called for. Chinese media today still must submit any news report on significant and politically sensitive events (such as the US Congress votes on China-related issues, US air-strikes against Iraq, etc.) to censorship agencies before it can be aired.[1] This normally causes a considerable delay in hours, even days. Live television news coverage is still a rarity in China. However, on the CCTV and *People's Daily* websites international news now appears almost simultaneously with those from CNN, the Reuters, etc. The CCTV online news is often broadcast faster than its TV news programs. The censorship mechanism apparently cannot catch up with the online news program's striving for ever faster headlines.

A significant change is the online interactive journalism and commentaries that major presses have experimented with in a variety of forms such as bulletin boards, chat rooms, online polls, and online opinion columns. The most important is the *People's Daily* online chat room *Qiangguo luntan* ("Strong Power Forum," literally, "strengthening the nation forum.") The chat room was set up in the wake of NATO's 1999 bombing of the Chinese embassy in

Belgrade. It has since grown into one of the hottest public political forums, allowing a blend of public debates, news stories, and letters of opinion that cover a wide range of issues. Some are politically highly contentious and sensitive, which can hardly be published by the print and electronic media. The creation of a chat room for public political debate in the most important mouthpiece of the ruling Communist Party indicates the significance of the Internet. The US media, of course, rushed to describe it as an avenue for political dissent in the cracks of the Communist authoritarian rule. The American media's politicizing and sensationalizing penchant aside, the Strong Power Forum of the *People's Daily* website shows that the press is caught between its traditional role as the bastion of the communist ideology and its current role to serve the CCP, which now promotes economic and technological development.

In the meantime, the major Internet portal companies such as Sina.com Netease.com, and Sohu.com, all established online news websites, with news reported by their own news crews rather than by the official Xinhua News Agency or by other state-owned media. This caused considerable alarm to the government. Since 1949, the Chinese media have always been controlled by the state, and all editorial members and journalists have been selected and trained through an established process that ensured conformity to a standard of journalism. The new commercial website news crews, however, have no institutional bond to the state-owned press and thus are under no obligation to conform to the state criteria. They choose to emulate either Western (mainly) American-style journalism or Taiwan-Hong Kong journalistic practices (the latter largely adopt Western journalism in Chinese language). Lacking Western-style professional training, and free from Chinese-style media control, the online novices, mostly in their twenties, face daunting difficulties in news reporting: they have yet to learn how to tell rumors and libels from real news, and how to verify the news sources and report first-hand news rather than relying on indirect news reports.

Although the government remains ambivalent about the online public debates and loose censorship on the websites of state-owned and semi-state-owned presses, the emergence of new media outside the existing media institutions and organizations was viewed as reaching over the limit. The National People's Congress (China's legislative body) issued in November, 2000, a regulation concerning the Internet and information security. The regulation is comprehensive, covering the potential Internet infringement of national security, as well as Internet violations and crimes in commercial and technological sectors and the news media. It prohibits Internet portal companies from using news reports written by unauthorized press sources, and requires general portal sites to obtain permission to use news from foreign media and to meet strict editorial conditions when using their own crew's news reports (AP).

The US media reacted with scorn for the "Chinese communist regime's dilemma," asserting: "Chinese leaders have been ambivalent about the Internet since its first explosive growth in China in the mid-1990s. They want to harness it for business and education while preventing it from becoming a tool of political discontent. The difficulty over managing bulletin boards is one of many dilemmas China faces in its effort to police the Internet, which the communist leadership has accepted as a necessary but awkward tool for modernizing the economy." (AP) It is true that the Chinese government is wary of the "the political discontent" that the Internet might bring, a worry that US media often reinforce by celebrating the political and ideological empowerment that the global media system can effect in China. Thomas Friedman, a *New York Times* neo-liberal media pundit, prescribes an emancipatory mission for the Internet in China: "Deep down, the leadership here [in China] knows that you can't have the knowledge that China needs from the Internet without letting all sorts of other information into the country, and without empowering more and more Chinese to communicate horizontally and create political communities. In the long run this will only give more tools to the forces here pushing for political pluralism" (A2).

Friedman and his cohorts are hopeful that the Internet will push for the kind of "political communities" that they preach every day to the "authoritarian" countries via the *New York Times,* CNN, *USA Today,* and so on. Their discourse reflects the dilemma that China faces, but not in the way they describe. The political communities and pluralism that the global media try to help create in China may serve a variety of purposes, which are not necessarily democratic or inherently good. Recent critical reassessments of "civil society" caution us not to automatically associate "civil society" and "pluralism" with democracy and equality in political and economic life. A civil society for democratic participation depends much on the state, which provides legal protection and resources and which implements an economic policy that aims at equality and justice for the majority (Ehrenberg, Cohen and Arato). China, in its transition from a highly centralized political system and a planned economic system to a market-oriented society, faces a dilemma: on the one hand, there is an imperative to further the process of decentralization; on the other, there is the danger of total social disintegration and fragmentation. Hence, some critics argue that what China needs now, first and foremost, is a state-rebuilding to re-establish an effective government system, in order to implement and reinforce law and to oversee democratic political participation (Ding). Ideological legitimation is a crucial aspect of state-rebuilding and social reconstruction. By issuing a series of laws of Internet media in order to establish normative regulation over the arena of ideology and values, the Chinese government faces ever increasing challenge from the pluralization and diversification of information channels brought about by the Internet and global media system, with uncertain, yet significant consequences to the society.

The Internet news media have attracted a growing audience, especially among the young and educated population. A June 2000 study shows that in the US, daily Internet news consumers consist largely of males (61%) less than fifty years old (75%), and college-educated (47%) (Pew). In comparison, a April 1999 survey of Beijing residents indicates that 25% of the residents, who are among the most educated in all Chinese cities, get international news from the Internet, whereas 48.6% relied on CCTV's National Evening News *(Beijing Youth Daily).* To be sure, China's modernization will depend largely on the generations younger than age 50 to achieve its preliminary goals in the first quarter of the twenty-first century. The younger Chinese are undoubtedly attuned to the Internet and global media for information and news. Although media pluralism and diversity may spawn more and more fragmentation and specialization of audience, the sheer number of the Chinese population to be affected by the Internet poses formidable problems for building social cohesion and consensus. Diversity without basic societal consensus and cohesion means no democracy but chaos, especially when each of the fragmented, segregated groups amounts to tens of millions of disenfranchised individuals. However, with the collapse of the revolutionary hegemony that once held together—by both ruthless coercion and massive consent—800 million people in Mao's era, the compelling need to rebuild a social consensus clashes with the imperative of pluralization. This contradiction is especially visible on websites dedicated to political debates.

Internet political forums: a virtual public sphere or a hotbed for antagonism?

It can be said that the Internet has served as a political forum for the Chinese since its inception. The development of the Internet in its earlier forms (the ARPAnet, NSFnet, usenet, bitnet, etc.) and email, in the late 1980s, coincided with a period of political and social unrest across the world, especially in the so-called "really existing socialist countries," including China. Apart from the fall of the Berlin Wall that signaled the demise of communism in the Soviet bloc, the events at Tiananmen Square in 1989 are generally perceived by the Western media as a turning point in China's political life (a perception which is nonetheless sharply disputed among the Chinese).

By 1989, there was a large contingent of Chinese students (more than 100,000) studying primarily natural sciences and engineering in the US. These students were, on the whole, sympathetic with the demonstrators in Beijing and outraged by the government's bloody crackdown. As the prominent activists in the demonstrations fled to the West and converged with the existing students there, a new alliance of political dissent was forged, thanks to the fast and convenient links of email.

The first Internet magazine in both English and Chinese, *China News Digest (CND)* <http://www.cnd.org> and *Hua Xia Wen Zhai (China Digest)* <http://www.cnd.org/HXWZ> , appeared at this juncture. *China News Digest,* an English web magazine, was created in March 1989 in Canada, by two Chinese students. They claimed that their purpose was to serve the "need for information exchange on the network among Chinese students and scholars" and "to evade the pressure from the Chinese consulate in Canada, which had a higher degree of control on Chinese students than their US counterparts" (Bo). At first, according to its creators, the CND had about 400 readers in Canada. The Tiananmen events gave the magazine a huge boost. By September 1989 it set up listserver accounts at Arizona State University and Kent State University, serving about 4,000 subscribers in the US and Canada. Then the CND became a full-fledged daily electronic newspaper, having several columns and services, such as Book Reviews, Market Watch, and special packages concerning the Olympic Games, the Most Favored Nation trade status, and Chinese students' permanent residency status. In 1991 the first electronic Chinese-language weekly magazine, *Hua Xia Wen Zhai,* was published by the CND. The CND's initial publication in March 1989 was only less than two years from the first ever web newspaper, *San Jose Mercury News* in California, which was launched in 1987. With the introduction of the World Wide Web in the mid-1990s, the CND rapidly expanded its service and audience. By March 1998, CND claimed that its homepage "receives about 17,000 visits a day, while the *Hua Xia Wen Zhai* sub-homepage is visited by an average of 18,000 times a day." By 1995 CND moved to Maryland and was "officially registered as a non-profit organization, as China News Digest International, Inc." And "on May 9, 1996, CND obtained its tax exemption status as approved by the IRS," according to the same account (Bo).

One may wonder, however, what kind of status (taxational, legal, and financial) the CND had actually had between the years, and one may question the purported nature of it as "a community-based, free news and information service provided by volunteers."[2] But its enormous popularity among the Chinese student communities in North America and in Western European countries was beyond any doubt, especially before the World Wide Web was launched in the mid-1990s.

CND was attractive to the students not only because it was cost-free and convenient, but also because it was available to most Chinese students who spent days and nights working on their computers in engineering laboratories, toiling over projects assigned by their American academic advisors and lab supervisors. It struck an emotional chord, and offered practical assistance to tens of thousands of Chinese students deeply estranged from the Chinese government, and determined to seek long-term career and personal development in the West. Students were particularly enamored of *Hua Xia Wen Zhai* because it publishes anecdotes, memoirs, stories, prose essays and investigative reports that are free from political cliches. *Hua Xia Wen Zhai* was, for a considerable period of time, an indispensable resource for tens and thousands of Chinese students in the US, providing news and useful information concerning immigration status, job opportunities, leisure, and entertainment.

But make it no mistake that the foremost objective of the CND *and Hua Xia Wen Zhai* is political and ideological, despite its editorial disclaimer to the contrary. Its editorial policy echoes most of the mainstream Western media in terms of "independent," "impartial," "balanced," and "unbiased" news and analysis. Its contents also resemble much of the Western mainstream news media in covering China-related news and in commenting on China's affairs. CND's editorial policies and orientation largely represent the overseas Chinese political dissident groups, aggregated mostly in the US.

Take one issue of *Hua Xia Wen Zhai,* No. 507 (15 December 2000), for example. There was no particular "newsworthy" event during the week in which the issue was published, and there was no special occasion marked during the week either. The issue consists of nine sections, which begins with the weekly news summary, and ends with a table of contents for its special issues on the Cultural Revolution. The other seven sections are journalistic and literary essays. The news section is divided into Chinese news and international news. The Chinese news section contains sixteen brief news items, of which five items concern "human rights abuses" (the alleged "government persecution of the Falun Gong members," US Congressman's accusation of China's "worsening human rights conditions," etc.); four about disasters and crimes, two about Hong Kong's legal battle with mainland illegal residents, two about Taiwan independence, the rest of the section about China's negotiation with the WTO (1); China's president Jiang Zemin's congratulations to George W. Bush for his US presidency (1); China's corruption trials (1), and so on. These news briefs are apparently either translations of the mainstream US media or headlines taken from Taiwan media. Its ratio of news categories corresponds to US media coverage of China, too: "human rights" news about 25–35%, crimes and disasters about 25%, and Sino-US relationship 10–15%, Taiwan and Hong Kong about 20%, and the rest (China's politics, economics, science and technology, social and cultural events, etc.) about 10–15%.

News categories thematize and frame worldly events according to certain agenda setting. In the early 1990s, as most overseas Chinese students were still caught in the anger and frustration of the "post-Tiananmen syndrome", *Hua Xia Wen Zhai's* agenda setting was in tune with this general mode. However, as China's reality has evolved in the mid-1990s beyond the politics of Tiananmen, and, in the meantime, the tension between China and the US has steadily risen, the mood of the overseas Chinese communities altered significantly. By the end of the 1990s, CND and *Hua Xiao Wen Zhai* no longer enjoyed the almost monopolizing power it once had among overseas Chinese students. Part of the reason is that booming Chinese-language websites offered more options. The fact that CND refuses to move beyond the "post-Tiananmen syndrome" is the primary cause of its loss of popularity among overseas Chinese readers.

By the late 1990s, new online Chinese-language forums and chat rooms began to boom. The most dramatic of these is unquestionably the Strong Power Forum, or *Qiangguo luntan, People's Daily* online chat room < http = //www.peopledaily.com.cn> . *The New York Times* report asserts that "For the government, the Internet has been, at times, a useful tool: after the embassy bombing in Belgrade, for example, chat rooms gave Chinese an outlet for their anger. But it is clearly a double-edged sword" *(New York Times).* The report continues that "In early May, for example, most of the entries were attacks on the United States, NATO and President Clinton, reflecting the widespread view that the Chinese Embassy had been deliberately chosen as a target. But by the end of the month, the anniversary of the June 4, 1989, crackdown in Tiananmen Square was fast approaching. Along with thousands of patriotic entries, a few more controversial thoughts occasionally made their way online—if only for a few minutes. On the chat room Netease, which was devoted to the embassy bombing, one person ventured: 'June 4 is coming. What do you think?' The events of June

1989, during which tanks moved into central Beijing, killing hundreds of civilians, are among China's ultimate political taboos."

The New York Times report catches the obvious timing of the tenth anniversary of the June 4, 1989 Tiananmen events, which by coincidence was only one month away from the May 7, 1999 embassy bombing that led to the launch of Strong Power Forum. But it misses the irony there. In ten years, icons about China have changed from a universalist symbol—the Goddess of Democracy at Tiananmen Square in 1989—to a set of particularistic images in the spring of 1999 in Beijing. There were crying mothers of the victims of the NATO's embassy bombing, which only appeared in the Chinese media. By contrast, the predominant image in the US media was the sullen face of James Sasser, the US ambassador to China, looking out from the broken window of the American embassy in Beijing, damaged by angry student demonstrators. Deliberately or unwittingly, the US media created (or excluded) these images to reaffirm certain ideological messages, but the irony is that the discourses used to narrativize the Beijing student demonstrations that took place in both 1989 and 1999 had to effect a thorough about-face. In 1989, at the triumphant moment of globalizing and universalizing ideologies of freedom and democracy, the US media touted the Chinese students as young heroes and heroines embracing the pro-American symbol of white-woman-as liberty. Only a decade later, the same kind of Chinese students from the same universities was portrayed by the same US media as mobsters, mobilized by the Communist regime for an anti-American, ultra-nationalistic, and xenophobic cause. What is absent in the 1999 discourse of the US media, though, is the universal and idealist claims of freedom and democracy, the individual plights of the bombing victims and the emotional reactions of the Chinese public. Much accentuated, instead, is equally particularistic, and nationalistic assertions by the US media of the "threat to American interests by Chinese mobsters" and the "rising tide of Chinese nationalism." In hindsight, one can now discern in the 1989 universalizing discourse of freedom and democracy the particularistic, Cold War ideological agenda to end communism, and to bring China under the geopolitical order set forth by the United States as the only remaining superpower.

Just as the particular American geopolitical motive to overthrow communism was largely concealed under the universalizing symbolism of freedom and democracy in the Tiananmen events, the truly universalist concerns of the Chinese people for progressive and democratic life in modernization and globalization become submerged in clamorous particularistic and nationalist rhetoric, derived from both Western censures against the alleged "upsurges of Chinese nationalism" and radical anti-Western forces, and the official versions of "patriotism" within China at the turn of the century.

These dialectic twists and turns constitute the context in which Strong Power Forum emerged, and the debates in the forum encompass the full complexity and contradictions of China's historical conjuncture. The universalizing, globalizing, and local, particularistic discourses of China's modernity and globalization, China's domestic politics and Sino-US relations, China's economic marketization and capitalist world system, China's state rebuilding, social and cultural reconstruction and global geopolitics, are all deeply entangled. Complex as they are, the discussions attract a great deal of participants. On its first day, 9 May 2000, one day after NATO warplanes bombed the Chinese embassy in Belgrade, Strong Power Forum had 50,000 visitors within 24 hours. It now averages 70,000 page views a day, primarily among people ages 19 to 35.

Apart from its regular chat room BBS which posts hundreds and thousands of messages daily, the forum has several special sections. One is the interactive live forum, which invites scholars, specialists, government officials and celebrities to "chat" online with the audience on certain topics. The other is a section of "In-depth Discussion," where contents of the messages are screened by editors with more rigor, and tend to be more focused. The third section is the "Forum Digest," which is broken down into 80 to 90 subcategories, ranging from "Taiwan Strait issues," "Political Democracy and Political Reform," "China's Military Buildup," to "Anti-Corruption," "Sovereignty and Human Rights," "China and Olympic Games," "Humors and Jokes," "Stock Market," and "Marriage and Law." Selected messages are posted and reposted in the "Digest" section, which resembles the size of a US Sunday newspaper, only without advertisement.

A random browse at one day's contents will illustrate the diversity of messages. The selective section of "In-depth Discussion" on 21 December 2000 (an uneventful, "normal" day) contains 114 messages. The first ten messages are as follows: (1) "Jiang Zemin spoke out!!!!!"; (2) "In 15 years Japan's second economic power status will be replaced by China and India—if we believe this we'll be utterly deceived"; (3) "This morning China launched its last satellite in this century"; (4) "National college entry examination frauds reflect China's social reality—what kind of 'stability' do we need?"; (5) "Attention to our peasant brothers (I)—who treats peasants as human beings?"; (6) "Attention to our peasant brothers (II)—how are the 'rogues' singled out among peasants?"; (7) "Attention to our peasant brothers (III)—the peasant problem is China's central problem"; (8) "China's old friends are vampires sucking Chinese blood!"; (9) "the key to China's economic problems is political reform"; and (10) "On advantages of public ownership of property."

Not only the issues vary a great deal, so do the forms and contents. Some messages are news stories taken from news media. Message 3 on satellite launch is a report from China News Agency (a state-owned media service catering to the international community). News from US, Western, Taiwan and Hong Kong media often sneak in as messages attached with comments. This kind of news reports or analyses do not appear even in *Reference News (Cankao xiaoxi)*, China's largest newspaper carrying translated news from foreign presses, edited by Xinhua News Agency. Although Chinese readers can usually see websites of *New York Times* and other Western presses by dodging the official Internet blockade, the news stories that appear in Strong Power Forum in Chinese translations give readers a more direct access. Apart from news, there are long essays in several segments, such as Messages 5 to 7 on "peasant problems," which are written in serious academic style, backed by considerable research. Some are very brief, perfunctory remarks, such as Messages 2 and 8.

A long essay (about 7,000 words), posted on 2 December 2000 by Zhou Xincheng and Chen Xiankui, warns the ideological and cultural infiltration of the "Western antagonistic forces." To emphasize their seriousness, the authors use their real names rather than nicknames used by most chat room participants. The essay lists seven major ways by which "the Western forces" infiltrate Chinese cultural and ideological domains, which include forcing China to accept "international and global standards" set up primarily by the US, "dismembering socialist China through globalization," and "spreading Western ideologies and values through high tech means, such as the Internet and information superhighway." The essay calls forth "opposing both 'leftist' and rightist trends," asserting that "under the current condition or globalization, we should remain vigilant primarily against rightist trends as we must fight peaceful evolution and ideological infiltration in dealing with Western countries" (Zhou and Chen). The essay apparently reflects the views of old communist ideologues, who have lost most of their political power but nonetheless still have considerable influence in the ideological domain, simply because institutionally and structurally that domain has been, and still is, the least touched estate during Deng Xiaoping's reform.

Not only has the *People's Daily* to pay some tribute to the old guards of communism in the Strong Power Forum, important media such as the People's Liberation Army (PLA)'s newspaper, *PLA Daily,* echo their concerns in their editorials. *PLA Daily* warns that the "information colonialism" is a real threat to national security and the cultural, ideological values of many developing countries, as most information in the global information network, the Internet in particular, comes from English-speaking nations, primarily the United States. The editorial demands that China establish its own information network by making use of technological innovations, and by "studying rigorously the strategies of the people's war in the information era" (*PLA Daily*). On the one hand, the concerns for national security and "information colonialism" is not unwarranted, given the US domination of the global information network and geopolitical assertions of the United States in the cultural and ideological domains. Joseph Nye, former assistant secretary of defense and Dean of Harvard Kennedy School of Government, argues in the major US media that exercising "soft power" in the ideological and cultural arena is critical in consolidating US interests globally (Nye). On the other hand, vigilance for security can readily become an excuse for suppressing free exchange of ideas on the Internet. Moreover, any slightest sign of the Chinese government's interference in ideological and cultural domains will inevitably invoke criticism and protests. This in turn will give the leftist old guards more ammunition to fire at "bourgeois liberalization" and "peaceful evolution." The vicious circle spins from there, and the authorities cannot effectively stop it. The government seems to have adopted a low-key, ambiguous tactic when tensions between the left and the right are on the rise, at least in the Internet forums, allowing both camps to air their grudges against each other without tipping the balance.

The contents of Strong Power Forum indicate the extent to which the Chinese Communist leaders are willing to tolerate, if not to endorse, this free flow of ideas in cyberspace. Yet the existence of the forum itself cannot testify whether it is a true public sphere for democratic participation, or simply a hotbed for antagonistic ideas spawning more cleavages. Under the present circumstances when laws of news press are non-existent, and the traditional censorship mechanism is increasingly ineffective and outdated, no one knows where the Internet forums in the state-owned media are heading.

The state-owned media, of course, no longer have the monopoly in China today. Many independent websites have mushroomed in recent years, and are dedicated to social and political debates. Some websites gain popularity in intellectual circles by their controversial standpoints, and some by extensive coverage of debates. Visions and Thoughts (Sixiang de jingjie <http://www.sixiang.com>) was a website produced by Li Yonggang, a lecturer at Nanjing University's Department of Political Science and Administration. It includes essays authored by some 50 scholars, covering the major issues of intellectual debates. The scholars represent a broad spectrum of views, from neo-liberalist, the New Left, to neo-conservative, and debate among themselves on a wide range of issues, such as China's modernity, political reform, economic developments, and social problems. Authors also include some exiled intellectuals known for their dissident politics, such as the journalist Dai Qing. The website was created in September 1999, and closed down in October 2000. This caused considerable stir in the media outside China. Some overseas Chinese media were quick to accuse the government of forcing the website to shut down, saying that "it again showed that there is no legitimate space in China for moderate, rational, gradualist, and open debates about reform as long as political issues are touched" (Chinese News Network). Inundated by hundreds of inquires immediately after the closing of the website was announced, the owner of the website had to send a long public statement to clarify that his decision to close it down "has nothing to do with the government and politics, and it's entirely my personal decision, for private reasons" (Li Yonggang). The essays of this website, however, reappear in many other websites as Internet forums and journals continue to grow.

These semi-independent or independent Internet forums are quite explicit in their political and ideological orientations and are sharply divided. Culture China (*Wenhua zhongguo*, <http://www.202.106.168.89/ ~culturechina >) is owned by Yu Shicun, editor-in-chief of *Strategy and Management* (*Zhanlue yu guangli*), a well-known journal with some military backgrounds, which often publishes controversial articles in social sciences and humanities. The website is not, however, an online version of the journal. It carries articles with poignant views critiquing social ills, moral and ethical problems that China faces from "secular and humanistic viewpoints." Recently a few websites with strong New Left inclinations have attracted a lot of attention. Shibo Forum (Shibo luntan, <http://www.pen123.net.cn>) carries mostly articles authored by scholars affiliated with the New Left or nationalist camps, and it also opens a section publishing articles by neo-liberalists, debating intensely over the issues of free market, liberalism, socialism, economic inequality and injustice, and authoritarianism. Most authors that publish in Internet forums and journals are well-known activists in China's intellectual debates now, and some are Chinese scholars residing in the US and Western Europe. They invariably take an active part in the Internet forums and journals, and are eager to disseminate their views first on the Internet. Apart from the China-based websites, there are many Chinese-language websites in North America and elsewhere, which participate in the heated online debates. Huayue Forum (Huayue luntan, <http://www.huayue.org>) is a popular US-based forum and chat room, which resembles Strong Power Forum in its format and content, with much less editorial constraints. China and the World (Zhongguo yu shijie, <http://www.chinabulletin.com>) is a well-known US-based website that is divided into an online journal, a historical archive and a chat room. The website has an ostensible leftist orientation, criticizing the neo-liberalist free market ideologies and Deng Xiaoping's developmentalism.

The Internet offers a major venue for China's political, ideological, and intellectual debates, with little and largely ineffective censorship or official interference. Hence, it can be viewed as a rare space for almost unrestrained free speech that hardly exists in China's mainland. Despite the sporadic tightening-up and crack-downs, and contrary to the reports of the Western media, the Chinese government in general has kept a low-profile and ambiguous gesture towards the Internet forums, tolerating their growth as long as no one publicly advocates the overthrow of the current regime. It is safe to predict that the Internet political forums in China will continue to grow and play more significant roles in China's social life. But what remains to be seen is whether the Internet political forums will lead to a democratic public sphere or a nursery for social antagonism.

Literature in cyberspace: urban youth's search for aesthetic expressions

Apart from having access to news and participating in political debates, interests in literature, or rather, in literary self-expressions have become another major attractive facet of the Internet among the Chinese net users. According to the estimates by the Internet Information Center of China, 80% of China's net users live in urban areas, and have a high school education or above. A significant portion (about 45%) of these urban net users are between 20 to 30 years old, or were born in the 1970s or later (Li Xiguang). This generation in a way is the main beneficiary of the reform in terms of material and economic prosperity, but it also bears the brunt of the transitional time in terms of the confusion and loss of values and ethical norms, as revolutionary idealism clashes head on with consumerism and egotism. As the turn of the century marks the coming of age of this new generation, a distinct urban youth culture is taking shape. Nurtured largely by an electronically-based consumer culture, this youth culture is the embodiment of globalization: it draws its icons, styles, images, and values mainly from the "global" (read: Western) consumer cultural production and entertainment industry. In the meantime, they have a much stronger desire than the "Mao's children" born in the 1950s, who have now become parents of the 1970s and 1980s generation, for a distinct cultural identity that marks their local, regional, ethnic and national differences.

Compared with their parents or their older siblings, this urban youth generation by and large seems much less interested in political debates. Rather, they are more drawn to pleasure-seeking, sensuous, or aesthetically-pleasing life-styles and expressions. The Internet hence provides the techno-savvy youth with a much freer and trendier (or "cooler") venue for self-expression in artistic and literary forms. The recent proliferation of e-fiction sites and the rise of several "e-fiction star writers," whose writings were published first as Internet literature, and later turned into bestsellers in print, have constituted a thriving cyberspace literary field. Not surprisingly, the Internet literature arouses both suspicion and enthusiasm from established writers and literary critics, but it will be too simplistic to brush it aside as merely a high-tech offspring of consumer culture. While the predominant mode of the Internet literature is that of pleasure-seeking and romanticizing, one also witnesses a recent surge of interests in revolutionary idealism in new experimental theaters and their websites, particularly the play of *Che Guevara* (2000) that has toured the country in recent months with remarkable success. The Internet has been most active in disseminating the information and debates about the play, creating an interface between theatrical performances and online discussions.

In a more general sense, the Internet also serves as an interface for the self-identities of the urban youth, consumer culture, global fashions and cultural trends. The urban youth often identify themselves as the New Humanity *(Xin renlei),* or the "Newer, New Humanity" *(Xin xin renlei).* The term was coined first in Taiwan in the mid-1990s, and reached the mainland China quickly. The Newer, New Humanity is said to have the inclination to "chase anything new, fashionable, vanguard, love cartoons, tattoos, disco, etc., and they are crazy about new life-styles, new technology and freedom. . . . They are the generation of information technology and the Internet. Their shared language is a cryptic 'digital slang' and 'Internet slang'" *(China Youth Daily).* A self-styled manifesto claims that "the Newer, New Humanity is born at the age of globalization and techno-logical innovation," and "they consist of middle-class Internet and e-commerce specialists, cartoon- and disco-loving generation, McDonalds, CocaCola, tele-marketing, independent workers, avant-garde artists. They are transforming the old values of life and relation-ships with their own life-styles, in order to fulfill the goal of more humane and self-pleasing existence" (Ye Niu). While the goal of this generation is both vague ("more humane") and pleasure-oriented ("self-pleasing existence"), it is clearly linked with the global (Western) trend.

The Chinese Newer, New Humanity embraces the Internet as the new literary starlet. A click on search engines of Sohu.com and Chinese Yahoo.com, two major Chinese-language website search engines, produces more than 200 websites dedicated to literature. Taking advantage of the virtual non-existence of online copyright laws, a majority of these websites simply put online published literary works from canonical classics to latest best-selling martial arts fiction (a popular genre analogous in its status to science fiction in the US) for free download or browsing. Still, a significant number of websites are devoted to original online literary writings, providing a venue for literary aspirants to freely publish their writings without the editorial screening and sifting of print presses and magazines. The Newer, New Humanity can practically experiment all sorts of writing styles and techniques, using interactive chat room to "collectively" produce literary works and creating "Internet slang" as a "cool," special kind of self-expression among the group.

Although the bulk of Internet literature looks largely like sophomoric composition, outstanding works have emerged, and several Internet writers have become consumer culture stars ever since. In the fall of 1999, Netease.com, a leading portal company, and Under the Banyan (Rongshuxia) <http://www.rongshu.com>, a website dedicated to Internet literature, organized separately two Internet Literature Contests. Rongshuxia received 7,000 e-fiction and e-prose essay submissions, and 50,000 readers participated in the two-month contest. The Contest Committee, composed of a host of China's most famous writers such as Wang Anyi, Jia Pingwa, Yu Hua, and Wang Shuo, selected 18 pieces for awards. Netease.com also asked such literary luminaries as Wang Meng and Liu Xinwu to select 30 winners among 3,000 submissions (Rongshuxia). And apart from the fanfare and pomp of these contests which smack of strong commercial calculation, a number of e-fiction writers have indeed gained widespread popularity.

In 1999, an e-fiction writer with a pen-name Long Yin (Dragon Singing) produces a new genre of "literary knight fiction" *(wenxia xiaoshuo)*, as a parody-travesty of the popular, traditional genre of martial arts fiction or "knight-errant" fiction. He published in the literary website, Great Tang Dynasty Chinese (*Da Tang Zhongwen*) <http://www.dtnets.com>, a trilogy, *Wise Sage Donfang Shuo (Zhisheng Dong Fangshuo)*. The trilogy is based on the legends of Dongfang Shuo (154 BC–93 BC), an off-beat humorist and court-entertainer during Western Han Dynasty. The hero's satirical discourse and quick wit are often described as a counter-weight to the stern, heavily didactic, moralistic Confucian literary canons in Chinese literary history.

Wise Sage Dongfang Shuo is filled with satire and humor, parodying the literary convention of martial art fiction and its hackneyed character types and stereotypes. The author is apparently well-versed in martial arts fictional styles and narrative techniques, and adaptable to the fad of "rewriting/dramatizing history" in the 1990s. A deluge of popular fiction, TV soap operas about emperors and their concubines, mistresses and romantic affairs of politicians, warriors, and writers in China's imperial past prevailed China's consumer culture scene. The e-fiction *Wise Sage Dongfang Shuo* adroitly gets on the bandwagon of romanticizers of the imperial glory, and wins the sentiment of the reading public instantaneously. The traditional print press immediately took note. In the spring of 2000, Writers Press (Zuojia chubanshe), one of the most prestigious literary presses in China, decided to publish the trilogy, and in less than a month about 10,000 copies were sold out, making the trilogy a first e-fiction-turned-into-bestseller. CCTVs TV Series Studio, China's largest TV soap-opera syndicate, bought the TV adaptation rights before the print books were on the market (Da Tang).

The commercial success of *Wise Sage Dongfang Shuo* in both cyberspace and traditional print book forms creates a new literary market in China. Many traditional presses follow suit, publishing popular e-novels and stories as bestsellers. Under the Banyan claims that it has signed contracts with 23 presses since the spring of 2000, and published 56 books of fiction, poetry or prose essay, which were all first published online, and the print books of e-literature by March 2001 already sold over 1,240,000 copies (*Da Tang,* 22 March 2001). The "e-fiction" label adds much to the appeal of this newly-cooked popular genre. It becomes a popular genre in commercial culture, along with other popular genres, such as the fiction of "beauty-baby authors." The "beauty-baby authors" are a group of young female writers, represented by Wei Hui, a Shanghai-based, Newer, New Humanity freelance writer. Wei Hui's novel, *Shanghai Baby (Shanghai baobei,* 2000), gained her popularity or notoriety for its graphic and allegedly "pornographic" depiction of sex, lust and drugs of Shanghai young women with leisure and money, made possible by high-pay jobs at transnational corporations and contacts with their Western executives and businessmen.[3] Not surprisingly, the Internet literary websites play a very active role in promoting the "beauty-baby authors" by publishing online all their works, some of which, including *Shanghai Baby,* are banned publicly because of their alleged obscenity.

Despite the alarms and warnings of parents and moralists, the Newer, New Humanity are determined to pursue their happiness in romantic adventures and sensuous experiences. E-fiction writers, who are most audacious and trendy, capture the emotions of the pleasure-seeking, desire-driven youth in their works, and are thereby made into stars by both the Internet and publishing industry. Of a dozen or so e-literary stars Bum Cai (Pizi Cai) is arguably the best known. Bum Cai is the pen-name of Cai Zhiheng, a 30-year-old Taiwanese who was working on his doctoral degree in hydraulic engineering in Taiwan in the spring of 2001 (no further information available concerning Cai's academic study). As a graduate student, Bum Cai was said to have played on the keyboard of his computer hours after hours, surfing the net and chatting, while working in the engineering lab, like most other "net worms" (*wangchong*—a nickname coined by net users) of his age. Then he was said to begin writing down his fantasies about romantic adventures through the Internet, thus the making of his first novel about Internet love, *The First Intimate Touch* (*Di yici qinmin jiechu*).

The impact *The First Intimate Touch* has on mainland readers is phenomenal. Sina.com, which publishes the e-novel on the mainland, asserts that the novel is the first landmark Internet novel in Chinese and that it "makes the underground Internet literature emerge above the ground" (Sina.com). Lest that any political connotations with "underground" be invoked, the novel actually has nothing whatsoever to do with politics, literally or metaphorically. It is a cyberspace romance populated by the Newer, New Humanity, embodied by the first-person narrator-protagonist Bum Cai—identical to the pen-name of the author. And the protagonist Bum Cai himself resembles the actual Bum Cai the author in the real world. The hero Bum Cai is an engineering graduate student in Taiwan, who buries himself in endless lab works and mathematical calculations in front of his computer. Often bored by the mechanical and repetitive work, he fantasizes about romantic encounters with beautiful girls, and finds the Internet chat room the best venue to share his fantasies with other net users who use pseudo-names and make up their gender and age at will. It is a unique way of fantasizing sexual encounters by remaining anonymous and sharing the private, intimate thoughts and desires with an equally anonymous other.

What makes the novel so attractive to the Newer, New Humanity is obviously not psychological (or psychoanalytical) intricacies about the Self/Other, absence/presence binary oppositions. Quite on the contrary, there is hardly any sign of such intellectual and linguistic plays that inhabit many post-modern or neo-avant-garde fiction. The novel's primary appeal lies in its language. The narrative discourse is mostly simple and straightforward, casual and conversational, akin to that of most popular fiction on the market. However, it creates freely Internet slang and neologism out of the Mandarin Chinese urban dialects, mixing English acronyms with Chinese short-hands, swear-words and even obscenity with high-tech jargon. The profuse usage and coinage of new slang in depicting cyberspace romance—anonymous "Internet lovers" who use very graphic and intimate languages to each other in reference to their bodies, innermost desires, sexual fantasies and habits—tend to have a liberating effect not only on the subject of the novel, i.e. romantic love and sexual anxiety, but also on the discourse about sex and desire. In other words, the Newer, New Humanity find Bum Cai's Internet slang a new, exciting discourse to articulate their "liberated" experience. Bum Cai's slang and stock phrases such as "beautiful brow" for "girls" (a homonym for "sister" or *meimei*), "dinosaur" *(konglong)* for "men in cyberspace," and "I love you ten thousand years," have created a mesmerizing appeal to the Newer, New Humanity who are nurtured by TV commercials and the MTV culture, and are long accustomed to the short-hand, yet "cute" and "cool" phrases articulated by the starlets.

The liberating effect of Bum Cai's Internet slang can be highlighted by contrasting it with the language of two bestselling novelists in China today: first, that of Hong Kong-based Jin Yong, China's foremost martial art author, and second, Wang Shuo, whose Beijing-dialect novels have won him the title of "the master of hooligan literature." Unlike Jin Yong who insists on an elegant literary style and Wang Shuo who relies much of his appeal on his superb reproduction of contemporary Beijing dialect and slang, Bum Cai's discourse neutralizes the vernacular, dialectal aspects of Chinese language, while globalizes the Chinese by mixing the "coolest" American English slang of the US "yetties" directly with the idioms of Chinese techno-savvy urbanites. It is an online linguistic hybridity, an incipient "globalized" Chinese favored by the Newer, New Humanity.

The literary devices and techniques that Bum Cai uses in his e-novels, however, are nothing innovative. The novel largely adopts rather worn-out formulae of melodramatic plots and "comedy of errors." Furthermore, its carefree depiction of love, sex, and human relationship is couched in technological and scientific jargon, in order to give its naked pursuit of sensual gratification an educated and high-tech facade. It can, however, hardly conceal its uncritical endorsement of pleasure-oriented, individualistic values and beliefs. It is hence disturbing to see that the Chinese urban youth culture is grounded on such an ideology of global consumerism and egotism. The consumer culture's tireless promotion of the ideology of unbridled individualism and consumerism severely obfuscates the social conditions of China today, and is detrimental to its social reconstruction, which calls forth social commitment and dedication of its citizenry.

The Internet has yet to become totally penetrated and dominated by consumer culture, and it offers opportunities to other alternative and radical aesthetic and literary expressions. A number of websites have appeared recently. They are dedicated to literary and artistic experiments that try to revive radical revolutionary idealism. These websites often collaborate with other groups, such as artists, musicians, dramatists, historians and literary critics who contribute frequently to the websites, or are website makers themselves. Together with the political and intellectual online forums and chat rooms, these literary and artistic websites have constituted a New Left presence with considerable constituents among the net users. A noticeable case is the interactive website discussion, dissemination and theatrical experimentation of *Che Guevara*.

Che Guevara is collectively written and directed by Beijing-based musician Zhang Guantian. It debuted as a small-theater, experimental play in Beijing in the spring of 2000. The crew members are not affiliated with any state-owned dramatic troupes or institutes and are financially self-supporting and artistically independent. They are professionals who work for the play part time. Except Zhang Guangtian who was born in 1966, other members of the *Che Guevara* team were mostly born in the 1970s, that is, the generation of the Newer, New Humanity. The *Che Guevara* team runs in a similar way to China's rock star Cui Jian and his team, who are largely independent of the state institutions. Yet, the ideologies of *Che Guevara* team and Cui Jian's rockers are visibly different. While Cui Jian draws on the protest songs of the 1960s and the American rock 'n' roll tradition as a way to renounce and satirize China's revolutionary legacy, the *Che Guevara* team wants to reinvigorate the revolutionary spirit, incarnated by the legendary Argentinian guerrilla leader, in order to wage new campaigns against social injustice and corruption in contemporary China and the world. The play is a medley of music, dance, mime and drama, poetry recitation and chorus singing. It is an experimental, non-realistic play with few state settings and props, drawing apparently on Chinese experimental theater of the 1980s and Western experimental theaters of Brecht and Beckett. The protagonist Che Guevara never appears on stage, only his voice is heard off-stage. The plot has two parallel lines, one tracing Che's revolutionary journey from the Cuban revolution to his final destiny in Bolivian guerrilla warfare in 1967, the other presenting contemporary, post-Cold War, post-revolutionary reflections on the revolution and its meaning in the face of rampant corruption and social injustice in China and the world. The two story lines are juxtaposed and intertwined, punctuated by sometimes solemn, and sometimes rueful, songs and dances. The message of the play is fairly explicit: calling for a revival of revolutionary idealism to right the wrongs in this materialistic, consumer-oriented, yet unjust and undemocratic world. The play is also a strong critique, cast in poignant satirical tone, of the current social ills in China and the lopsided official ideology of economic determinism and developmentalism.

The Internet websites Blackboard Literature and Arts (Heibanbao wenyi, a reference to Maoist practice of "culture of the masses") <http://www.heibanbao.com>, Music Big Character Posters (Yinyue dazibao, a reference to the Cultural Revolution's "big character posters") <http://www.person.zj.cninfo.net/~dazibao>, and Sina.com covered the tours and staging of the play extensively. They also launched a continous publicity campaign for the play. The director Zhang Guantian and a major playwright Huan Jisu published a number of theoretical and critical essays expounding their aesthetic views, and a number of online discussion panels were organized by these websites. The play's success owed significantly to the dissemination and publicity of the Internet websites as a much faster and alternative medium (the state-owned media remained somewhat ambiguous and largely silent on the play because of its critical stance on the official ideologies and policies). By the same token, the Internet websites involved in the play received a big boost, thanks to the success of the play.

Yet, does *Che Guevara's* radical revolutionary rhetoric reawaken a sense of social commitment among the young generation? Or does it reproduce a nostalgic feeling that merely valorizes the aesthetic dimension of the revolution? Che's decision to sacrifice himself in guerrilla battlefields may elicit a quasi-religious sense of the sublime among the post-revolutionary urban youth, but it hardly constitutes a viable alternative to the hegemony of global capitalism and its ideologies.

The Internet in the global information and media system embodies the dialectic tension and contradiction of globalization in terms of its democratic potentials for the disempowered majority, and its instrumental capacity in the service of global capitalism. And its double-edged capability is shown clearly in China today. The more specific or local issue in China can be seen as tensions between needs for normative regulation, state-rebuilding and social reconstruction on the one hand, and democratic participation of its vast population in a public sphere sustained by strong societal commitment on the other. In the three critical areas of ideology and values, namely the news media, the public political forum, and literature and the arts, the Internet has become one of the most dynamic driving forces. The Internet has been active in dismantling the discursive, institutional infrastructures of the revolutionary hegemony, and in disseminating global consumer culture to the Chinese urban youth. However, it has yet to vindicate itself in terms of its constructive potential in reinventing an ideological consensus conducive to China's social reconstruction. For the majority of the public this entails not only local (Chinese) restructure and reinvention, but resistance to global consumer culture and the political and economic hegemony of global capitalism.

The Internet holds out the promise of a new democracy and equality by nurturing a creative and constructive literacy and egalitarian social consciousness. Yet the promise can only be delivered by ceaseless and concerted efforts of the state and individual citizens. The Internet's constructive role in China depends on the social and cultural reconstruction, and as such, it is also an integral and constitutive part of the reconstruction. Under the condition of globalization, there are equally concerted but much more powerful efforts of global capitalism and its political agencies (IBM, Microsoft, Hollywood, etc.), and the governments and state institutions, to consolidate its global domination. And the Internet is a critical arena in which new forms of domination, inequality, and exclusion fight with forces for democracy and justice. Such a battle is thoroughly deterritorialized and China is no exception.

Notes

1   Media censorship in China is conducted by the Propaganda Departments of the Communist Party at various levels, from the county to municipal, provincial, and national (the highest being the Central Committee's Propaganda Department). Significant domestic and international news, such as Sino-American relations, a serious plane crash, and so on, must be approved by the Central Committee's censorship group.

2   A web source on *Huayue luntan* (a US-based Chinese-language online forum/chat room) reveals that the National Endowment for Democracy (NED) in the US funds several dozens of Chinese political dissident groups, including the CND and *Hua Xia Wen Zhai*. The source charges that the CIA is actually the underwriter of the NED (though the evidence of this allegation is not yet verified). *Huayue luntan,* January 14, 2001, http://huayue.org.

3   For a story of the "beauty-baby authors" told from the American media perspective, see Craig Smith.

References

"Bejing Residents and International News" (Beijing shimin yu guoji xinwen) *Beijing Youth Daily (Beijing qingnian bao)*, 12 April 1999

Associate Press (AP) "China to Tighten Web Regulation" *The New York Times*, 5 December 2000

Bo Xiong "The Making of 'China News Digest" In CND special issue, "CND Enters 10th Years of Internet Publishing, March 6, 1998" <http//www cnd org/CNDhistory html>

Chan, Eliza and Sten, Peter "China Takes Prize for World's Second Largest At Home Internet Population as Numbers Reach 56 6 Million" Nielson Net Rating Survey, 22 April 2002 <http//www nielson netratings com>

The China Press (Qiaobao) "The Case of 'people com cn' Observing the News Websites in China" (Cong renmin wang kan dalu xinwen wangzhan zouxiang) Special Report 11 December 2000 B12

China Youth Daily (Zhongguo qingnian bao) "A Profile of the Newer, New Humanity" 2 February 2001

Chinese News Network (Duowei xinwen wang). "Mainland China Visions and Thoughts Website Forced to Shut Down" (Zhongguo dalu sixiang de jingjie beipo guanbi). 14 October 2000. <http://www.chinesenewsnet.com>

Cohen, Jean and Arato, Andrew. *Civil Society and Political Theory*. Cambridge, MA: MIT Press, 1992.

Ding Xueliang. "Law and Order in Transitional Societies — the Russian Phenomenon" ("Zhuanxing sheheui de fa yu zhixu — eluosi xianxiang"). *Tsinghua Review of Sociology (Tsinghua shehuixie pinlun)*, No. 2, 2000.

Ding Xueliang. *The Decline of Communism in China: Legitimacy Crisis, 1978–1989*. Cambridge: Cambridge University Press, 1994.

Ehrenberg, John. *Civil Society: The Critical History of an Idea*. New York: New York University Press, 1999.

FlorCruz, Jaime a. "Chinese Media in Flux." *Media Studies Journal,* Special Issue: *Covering China,* Vol. 13, No. 1 (Winter 1999): 32–48.

Herman, Edward and McChesney, Robert. *The Global Media: The New Missionaries of Global Capitalism*. London: Cassele, 1977.

Li Xiguang. "Future to the New Humanity and Online Journalists" (Weilai shuyu xin renlei he wangluo jizhe). In Li Xiguang ed., *Online Journalists* (Wangluo jizhe). Beijing: Zhongguo sanxia chubanshe, 2000. 298.

Li Yonggang. "To Friends of My Website Again" (Zai zhi gewei guanxin benzhan de pengyou). 14 October 2000. <http://www.sixiang.com>

Nye, Joseph. "Hard Power, Soft Power," *Boston Globe*, 6 August 1999; "The Power We Must Not Squander," *The New York Times,* 3 January 2000.

People's Liberation Army (PLA) Daily (Jiefangjun bao). "Noting the Phenomenon of Information Colonialism" (Guanzhu xinxi zhiminzhuyi xianxiang), editorial. 8 February 2000.

Pew Research Center. "The People and Press Poll on New Media Trends." April–May, 2000. <http://www.people-press.org>

Sina.com News. "The Internet Literature's Standard-bearer Bum Cai Will Have His First Intimate Touch with the Mainland" (Wangluo wenxue qishou Pizi Cai jiang diyici quinmi jiechu zuguo dalu). 25 September 2000. <00/9/25"http://edu.sina.com.cn/news2000/9/25. html>

Smith, Craig. "Sex, Lust, Drugs: Her Novel's too Much for China." *New York Times.* 11 May 2000.

The New York Times. "Internet: A Double-Edged Sword in China." 23 December 1999.

Under the Banyan (Rongshuxia). "*Literature Gazette* Holds the Conference on Internet Literature" (Wenxue bao juban wangluo wenxue yantaohui). 23 January 2000. <http://www. rongshu.com>.

Xu Rongsheng ed. *Internet media* (Wangluo Meiti). Beijing: Wuzhou chuanbo chubanshe, 1999. 7–11.

Ye Niu (Boar). "The New Humanity — the Mainstream in Modernized China" (Xin renlei — Zhongguo qiandahou de zhuliu shehui). China University Campus Network — Newer, New Humanity (Zhongguo xiaoyan wang — xin xin renlei), 12 December 2000. <http:// www.54youth.com.cn./gb/paper107/zt/xyzt>

Zhou Xincheng and Chen Xiaokui. "Remaining Vigilant Against Western Antagonistic Forces' Infiltration in Ideological and Cultural Domains" (Jingti xifang didui shili de sixiag wenhua shentou). Strong Power Forum, *People's Daily*, 12 December 2000. <http://202.99.23. 237.cgi.bbs.>

PART XI

Globalization and global studies

WHILE THE RISE OF THEORY IN the late twentieth century was concurrent with global decolonization (as discussed in the introduction), this period was also one in which globalization became a new transforming force.[1] Historically, global trade and communication networks have always existed, and immensely powerful global empires such as the Roman Empire have come and gone. But "globalization" is a process that many thinkers regard as a new phenomenon, belonging to the world of post-industrial global flows of money, new high-speed technologies that offer near-instantaneous data communications, and the global distribution of ideas, brands, and ideologies (be this through the dominance of "Western capitalism", "Americanism", religious "fundamentalism(s)", and so on). The *Oxford English Dictionary* (third edition) offers a concise definition of "globalization": "The action, process, or fact of making global; *esp.* (in later use) the process by which businesses or other organizations develop international influence or start operating on an international scale, widely considered to be at the expense of national identity." The bland "making global" here is rapidly modified by the potential anxiety expressed in the phrase "at the expense of national identity"; in other words, when a business or a non-profit is globalized, it becomes more than an organization which simply functions "overseas"; rather, it has "influence" or more literally, "power", and not only does such influence/power have the potential to be beyond any one nation's control, but it also has the potential to impact and transform *local identity*. Critics might regard this as an adverse impact; for example, a Western product (such as a brand-named drink) is consumed in the non-Western world at the expense of a local product (such as locally produced tea) that was once seen as an important component of local identity. On the other hand, advocates might regard this local impact as being beneficial, say a product such as the cell phone, which offers up-to-date text-message-based market prices helping farmers in Africa negotiate in an informed way to get a better price for their crops. The positive perspective is seen in the *Oxford English Dictionary*'s example of the earliest usage of the word "globalization" (in 1930); intriguingly, this usage was in a book concerning education, and the quotation concerns the "keywords of the new education view of mind", which are "Wholeness . . . integration, globalization" (*OED*, "globalization"). Another positive usage is the next one given by the *Oxford English Dictionary* from the *Chicago Defender* (1944): "We stand in danger . . . of losing the otherwise beneficial aspects of the globalization of our problems" (*OED*, "globalization"). The word soon expressed a broader range of feelings about the diverse, although related, processes and systems that it stood in for. However, even though the word became more commonly used in the early 1960s, it was not until the 1980s that it entered academic discourse, and even then it was subject to what Mark Kesselman calls "a scholarly division of labor in the way that globalization is studied"; as he continues, "Economists tend to focus on the activities of transnational corporations, technological change, international trade and investment, and financial flows across borders; political scientists often focus on the role of international organizations such as the United Nations or International Monetary Fund; and sociologists and anthropologists tend to analyze the diffusion of culture and forms of popular resistance to economic and political globalization."[2] A key question here is how literary theorists have studied—or "focused"—on globalization, and how this has transformed understanding of self-reflexive critical activities. For Suman Gupta, this is a two-way process, whereby theorists need to "not only ... consider the relevance of globalization *within* literary studies ... but also to discern the locations/relocations/dislocations of literary studies *within* globalization."[3]

Three related working definitions of globalization offer a starting point for attempting the two-way process whereby globalization and theory not only intersect but begin to transform one another; the definitions are by Giddens; Robertson; and Tilly:

> Globalisation can ... be defined as the intensification of world-wide social relations which link distant localities in such a way that local happenings are shaped by events occurring many miles away and vice versa. This is a dialectical process because such local happenings may move in an obverse direction from the very distanciated relations that shape them. Local transformation is as much a part of globalisation as the lateral extension of social connections across time and space.[4]

> Globalization as a concept refers both to the compression of the world and the intensificaton of consciousness of the world as a whole ... both concrete global interdependence and consciousness of the global whole.[5]

> [G]lobalization means an increase in the geographic range of locally consequential social interactions, especially when that increase stretches a significant proportion of all interactions across international or intercontinental limits.[6]

Theory's global flows (global origins, crossing geographical borders, shifts via translation from one culture to another) are equally matched by an intensification of dialogical and shared discourses, interpretive strategies and potentially transgressive methodologies. Instead of the early model of literary critical humanism, whereby ideas from the European "centre" flowed outwards to the "colonies", within globalization the "lateral" movement and rapidly disseminated locally generated ideas, leads to a networked model, close to McLuhan's notion of the "global village" (see Chapter 15). From a political perspective, this discursive network can function in ways analogous to "grassroots globalization" or "globalization from below" where "a series of social forms has emerged to contest, interrogate, and reverse these developments [Western, corporate, political and intellectual control of global finance, society, knowledge, etc.] and to create forms of knowledge transfer and social mobilization that proceed independently of the actions of corporate capital and the nation-state system."[7] While some obvious examples leap to mind—subaltern studies, indigenous/postcolonial theory, the dislodging of "English" literature from literary studies, in favour of world literatures—this is also a cultural shift, from a liberal humanist vision of the function of the imagination, to one which is more politically astute, and representative of heterogenous values. As Appadurai argues, the "role of the imagination in social life" has undergone a profound transformation within globalization: "The imagination is no longer a matter of individual genius, escapism from everyday life, or just a dimension of aesthetics. It is a faculty that informs the daily lives of ordinary people in myriad ways: It allows people to consider migration, resist state violence, seek social redress, and design new forms of civic association and collaboration, often across national boundaries."[8] Critic Robert Young makes a similar argument for postcolonial studies, suggesting that it has the potential to not only focus "on forces of oppression and coercive domination that operate in the contemporary world" but also "to develop new forms of engaged theoretical work that contributes to the development of dynamic ideological and social transformation."[9] What these ideas may suggest to some is that this sort of theoretical work only happens in, say, postcolonial studies, or race and ethnicity studies, especially when such work focuses on the Other (elsewhere, possibly overseas or located at an unspecified *distance* from the academy). What globalization has revealed is that this work needs to happen as much "at home" as "elsewhere", as much in relation to one's locality as one's "globalized" network. Critic Herb Wyile makes this point in relation to globalization's impact upon Atlantic Canada: "one of the immediate effects of economic globalization has been increased pressure on workers and governments in the so-called developed world ... It has also led to much more vigorous and vocal pressure to cut back on the size of government, particularly on the scope of social programs in the welfare states of the developed world."[10] In terms of Wyile's specific focus he argues that "Atlantic Canadians are much more likely to experience the downside of globalization."[11] Globalization leads away from simple binaries (East/West; Developing versus Developed World, etc), and instead functions through "disjunctive flows",[12] but that is not to say that such "disjunctive" being is only experienced outside of the West, instead it becomes a primary experience for all peoples, at all locations.

A sceptical approach to what is revealed by the intersections of globalization and theory focuses not so intensely upon their shared transgressive, political "disjunctive" effects, but rather the ways in which both globalization studies and theory replace previous modes of knowledge production and political action. Of course such scepticism also necessitates depth and breadth of historical awareness and understanding on the part of the critic making the argument, which can be one of the positive outcomes of tracing the effaced or forgotten roots of globalization studies and theory. More programmatically, recovering such a history becomes a project in and of itself, and much research in this area is underway, leading to "a potential rethinking of world history as 'global history', which in turn contributes to the remaking of global education, escaping the parochial confines of nineteenth-century inspired nationalism and national historic narratives and mythologies."[13] This is a way beyond simply registering that a text expresses "Eurocentric" values, and actually replacing them with something else: "the strategy of going global by historicizing globalization offers opportunities to decentre Europe by situating European experience in the larger context of world history."[14] Yet as Bentley points out, as soon as that "larger context" is expressed in a coherent, unified manner, it paints a picture that appears to have the status of a "metanarrative"—and even moving beyond the limitations of postmodernism (in the "post theory" realm, or as Eagleton puts it, being "after theory"), the suspicion or "incredulity towards metanarratives" remains. Bentley carefully distinguishes between metanarratives and "larger human stories" or "contexts" which he argues "can serve as useful frameworks for analyzing the global past and historicizing globalization."[15] The examples that Bentley gives are important in recovering a sense of shared experiences:

> More specifically, the global stories of rising human population, expanding technological capacity and increasing interaction between peoples of different societies have profoundly shaped the experience of almost all human societies and,

furthermore, have worked collectively like a triple helix to reinforce one another with powerful effects throughout history . . . This approach to the global past . . . does not authorize rigid theoretical positions or teleological narratives, but rather emphasizes shifting patterns of cross-cultural connections, relationships, networks, interactions and exchanges. This approach maintains that the world has never been the site of discrete, unconnected communities, that cross-cultural interactions and exchanges have taken place since the earliest days of human existence on planet Earth, that Europe has not always been a unique or privileged site of dynamism and progress, that identities have always been multiple and malleable . . . [16]

Globalization studies and theory can therefore be re-situated within this "triple helix", and a number of critics have been working to achieve this. One of the most notable instances is Brennan's work on "postcolonial studies and globalization theory" where the essential thesis is that these methodologies are a forgetting of the political realms from which they emerge, standing in for relatively recent radical approaches which are foreclosed, namely those of the anti-imperialist/anticolonial intellectuals of the mid- to late twentieth century such as Nehru, Mao, Fanon, Lumumba, Guevara, and Ho Chi Minh.[17] Brennan argues that such an active forgetting is a "characteristic feature of contemporary capitalist societies" since they are essentially "*presentist* – that is, viewing each moment as the only reality while expunging the past in a gesture of calculated *anti*-historicism."[18] Returning then to his list of anti-imperialist/anticolonial intellectuals, a broader overview would include: "resistance intellectuals from Latin America throughout the nineteenth century, China of the 1920s, India of the 1940s, Algeria of the 1950s, Vietnam of the 1960s, Central America of the 1970s, and so on."[19] A "presentist" course on globalization and/or postcolonial studies will likely offer coverage of none of these periods, places, or precursors. Brennan observes that postcolonial theory was initially heavily influenced by poststructuralism, and thereby the foreclosure (of the past) is managed, leading the field into becoming "an intellectual movement driven by a critique of Eurocentrism and patriarchy"[20] which may have laudable emancipatory aims, but rarely gets the results of, say, one of the anticolonial activists fighting on the ground. As Brennan observes, even the term "postcolonial" is a euphemism for "harsher terms like imperialism or racism."[21] The point here is that even if Western intellectuals "believed the fight over the independence of sovereign states (over which the colonial struggle had once been fought) was no longer the issue",[22] by bringing together globalization and postcolonial theory, new forms of imperialism come into view, and these similarly need to be overthrown.

Further reading: a selection

The Very Short Introduction series is one of the best places to start studying a topic, which in this instance means turning to Steger. Gupta and Connell and Marsh raise a whole host of important questions concerning the relationship(s) between globalization and literature. There are numerous readers on the topic of globalization, often with essays or sections on culture, literature and aesthetics: recommendations here include Beynon and Dunkerley, Lechner and Boli, and with a focus on politics, Kesselman. Bauman and Appadurai both produce in-depth academic critiques of globalization (there are many popular anti-globalization books). An extensive area of study is the relationship between globalization and postcolonial studies; significant examples here include Acheraïou, Deckard, some of the essays in Lazarus, and Young. Key tropes include trade in Sebek and Deng, history in Gills and Thompson, travel in Huggan, transnationalism in Jay, and borders in Sadowski-Smith. Morar creates a new category that comes in an age of "late" globalization, called "cosmodernism". Two textual applications are Wyile on Atlantic Canada, and Taberner on contemporary German literature.

Acheraïou, Amar. *Questioning Hybridity, Postcolonialism and Globalization.* Houndmills, Basingstoke: Palgrave, 2011.

Appadurai, Arjun ed. *Globalization.* Durham, NC: Duke University Press, 2001.

Bauman, Zygmunt. *Globalization: The Human Consequences.* New York: Columbia University Press, 1998.

Beynon, John and David Dunkerley, eds. *Globalization: The Reader.* New York: Routledge, 2000.

Connell, Liam and Nicky Marsh, eds. *Literature and Globalization: A Reader.* Abingdon, Oxon & New York: Routledge, 2010.

Deckard, Sharae. *Paradise Discourse, Imperialism, and Globalization: Exploiting Eden.* Abingdon, Oxon & New York: Routledge, 2010.

Gills, Barry K. and William R. Thompson, eds. *Globalization and Global History.* Abingdon, Oxon & New York: Routledge, 2006.

Gupta, Suman. *Globalization and Literature.* Cambridge: Polity, 2009.

Huggan, Graham. *Extreme Pursuits: Travel/Writing in an Age of Globalization.* Ann Arbor, MI: University of Michigan Press, 2009.

Jay, Paul. *Global Matters: The Transnational Literary Turn in Literary Studies.* Ithaca, NY: Cornell University Press, 2010.

Kesselman, Mark ed. *The Politics of Globalization: A Reader.* Boston & New York: Houghton Mifflin, 2007.

Lazarus, Neil, ed. *The Cambridge Companion to Postcolonial Literary Studies.* Cambridge: Cambridge University Press, 2004.

Lechner, Frank J. and John Boli, eds. *The Globalization Reader.* Oxford: Blackwell, 2004.

Moraru, Christian. *Cosmodernism: American Narrative, Late Globalization, and the New Cultural Imaginary.* Ann Arbor, MI: University of Michigan Press, 2010.

Sadowski-Smith, Claudia. *Border Fictions: Globalization, Empire, and Writing at the Boundaries of the United States.* Charlottesville, VA: University of Virginia Press, 2008.

Sebek, Barbara and Stephen Deng, eds. *Global Traffic: Discourses and Practices of Trade in English Literature and Culture from 1550 to 1700.* Basingstoke: Palgrave, 2008.

Steger, Manfred. *Globalization: A Very Short Introduction.* Oxford: Oxford University Press, 2009.

Taberner, Stuart. *German Literature in the Age of Globalization.* London: Continuum, 2004.

Wyile, Herb. *Anne of Tim Hortons: Globalization and the Reshaping of Atlantic-Canadian Literature.* Waterloo, ON: Wilfrid Laurier University Press, 2011.

Young, Robert. *Postcolonialism: An Historical Introduction.* Oxford: Blackwell, 2001.

Notes

1   "A new era of globalization can be identified as beginning in the 1980s." Mark Kesselman, "Introduction", in Mark Kesselman, ed., *The Politics of Globalization: A Reader*, Boston & New York: Houghton Mifflin, 2007, p.4.

2   Mark Kesselman, "Introduction", *The Politics of Globalization: A Reader*, p.4.

3   Suman Gupta, *Globalization and Literature*, p.64.

4   Giddens, quoted in Malcolm Waters, *Globalization*, London & New York: Routledge, 2001 (second edition), p.4; quotation modified by Waters.

5   Robertson, quoted in Malcolm Waters, *Globalization*, p.4.

6   Tilly, quoted in Mark Kesselman, "Introduction", *The Politics of Globalization: A Reader*, p.2.

7   Arjun Appadurai, "Grassroots Globalization and the Research Imagination", in Arjun Appadurai, ed., *Globalization*, Durham, NC: Duke University Press, 2001, pp.1–21, p.3.

8   Arjun Appadurai, "Grassroots Globalization and the Research Imagination", p.6.

9   Robert Young, *Postcolonialism: An Historical Introduction*, Oxford: Blackwell, 2001, p.11.

10   Herb Wyile, *Anne of Tim Hortons: Globalization and the Reshaping of Atlantic-Canadian Literature*, Waterloo, ON: Wilfrid Laurier University Press, 2011, p.17.

11   Herb Wyile, *Anne of Tim Hortons: Globalization and the Reshaping of Atlantic-Canadian Literature*, p.19.

12   Arjun Appadurai, "Grassroots Globalization and the Research Imagination", p.6.

13   Barry K. Gills and William R. Thompson, "Globalizations, Global Histories and Historical Globalities", in Barry K. Gills and William R. Thompson, eds., *Globalization and Global History*, Abingdon, Oxon & New York: Routledge, 2006, pp.1–17, p.5.

14   Jerry H. Bentley, "Globalizing History and Historicizing Globalization", in Barry K. Gills and William R. Thompson, eds., *Globalization and Global History*, pp.18–32, p.27.

15   Jerry H. Bentley, "Globalizing History and Historicizing Globalization", p.28.

16   Jerry H. Bentley, "Globalizing History and Historicizing Globalization", pp.28–29.

17   Timothy Brennan, "From development to globalization: postcolonial studies and globalization theory", p.21.

18   Timothy Brennan, "From development to globalization: postcolonial studies and globalization theory", p.122.

19   Timothy Brennan, "From development to globalization: postcolonial studies and globalization theory", p.131.

20   Timothy Brennan, "From development to globalization: postcolonial studies and globalization theory", p.132.

21   Timothy Brennan, "From development to globalization: postcolonial studies and globalization theory", p.132.

22   Timothy Brennan, "From development to globalization: postcolonial studies and globalization theory", p.132.

Chapter 75

Suman Gupta

LITERARY STUDIES
AND GLOBALIZATION

Globalization is inherently narrative in its expression and realization, so, as Suman Gupta points out via an opening quotation by critics Susie O'Brien and Imre Szeman, the study of globalization and literature does *not* simply mean identifying and analyzing global themes, but rather understanding how there is a formative "entanglement" between literature and globalization. In other words, globalization and literature are not separate platforms from which to view the other, because they are fundamentally interconnected and implicated in shared ways of understanding and manifestation. As Principal Coordinator of the Globalization, Identity Politics, and Social Conflict project, with collaborators from the UK, India, Nigeria, China, Iran, Morocco and Bulgaria, Gupta is uniquely positioned to map out and analyze these interconnections, demonstrated in this extract through a close reading of the quotation by O'Brien and Szeman, examining its performativity, its strategies of reading and assertion, in particular the foregrounding of the importance of globalization's "narrative forms", that is to say, its discursive, fictionalizing methods of interpolating or identifying the Other. Gupta lists three main reading strategies that "tame" socio-economic approaches to globalization for the literary-critical reader: 1. "broad abstractions" that lead to an alignment of globalization and literary postcolonial studies; 2. the linguistic turn, i.e., all material global processes are read as discursive constructs; and 3. non-self-reflexive argumentation that effaces the literariness of the critics own writing, giving it an objectivity that it might not otherwise have. On a broader scale, Gupta considers six methodological procedures for bringing together literary studies and globalization: 1. thematic approaches; 2. globalized literature regarded as supporting evidence for non-literary arguments; 3. areas of terminological common ground; 4. areas of methodological common ground (e.g., postcolonial studies aligning with globalization studies); 5. how literary studies are part of globalization; and 6. alignments between literary and global industries. To elucidate further the differences between taking a thematic versus a co-constitutive approach to literary studies and globalization, Gupta compares and contrasts two substantial academic monographs: Michael Valdez Moses' *The Novel and the Globalization of Culture* (1995) and James Annesley's *Fictions of Globalization* (2006). In Moses' text, Gupta argues that the globalization theme within a number of literary texts is used as evidence to support Francis Fukuyama's "end of history" thesis from his influential book *The End of History and the Last Man* (1992), that is to say, the Cold War global standoff was resolved with the triumph of free market globalized capitalism as the culmination of different forms of socio-economic life. Literature is used here as "evidence" or proof that globalization has moved in a particular direction, and while there is value in such a methodology, it tends to disregard what is distinctive about "the literary." In Annesley's text, while globalization is also a literary theme, it is approached quite differently, in the sense of literature representing "ways of knowing"; that is, ways of knowing differently, what globalization can mean, and how it functions. Literature is not a passive reflection of globalization, or "instrumental" (evidence; proof), but rather it is part of globalization's discursive field. The model here is one of dispersal, of networked, integrated textual registers, whereby intervening in our understanding of globalized literature is also an intervention in key globalized mechanisms.

Literary entanglements

In introducing a special issue of the *South Atlantic Quarterly* (2001) on 'The Globalization of Fiction/The Fiction of Globalization', Susie O'Brien and Imre Szeman present the question underlying the various contributions as follows:

> [This special issue] seeks to understand a [. . .] fundamental entanglement between literature and the phenomena most commonly associated with globalization – transculturation, the various forms (from cultural to economic) and periods (from the time of Columbus to the present) of imperialism and colonialism, the violent and uneven impact of socio-cultural and economic systems on one another as they came into contact, the eclipse of traditional ways of life, the temporal (modernization) and spatial (nationalism-internationalism-transnationalism) demands of European modernity, the global spread of capitalism and Western liberalism, and so on. To [address this] is to think not just about how globalization is reflected thematically in fiction, for example, but also about literature's role in the narrative construction of the numerous discourses or 'fictions' of globalization. One of the first things to realize about globalization is that its significance can only be grasped through its realization in a variety of narrative forms, spanning the range from accounts of the triumphalist coming-into-being of global democracy to laments about the end of nature; literature no doubt has a role to play in how we produce these often contradictory narratives about globalization. (O'Brien and Szeman 2001, 604)

The quotation makes a move in precisely the direction in which I hope to take the present study at this juncture, away from consideration of 'how globalization is reflected thematically in fiction' and towards understanding a 'fundamental entanglement' between literature and globalization. Interestingly the quotation not only *states* an approach for making this move, but also *performs* that approach. In considering that conjunction of stating and performing, some of the imperatives underlying the approach of this study to the 'fundamental entanglement' are clarified.

At the level of statement, O'Brien and Szeman assume that (perceivably or constitutionally) literature and globalization do not have an immediately self-evident relationship (apart from globalization being thematized in literature in various ways). Literature and globalization are not, evidently, fields that are obviously implicated in each other, are not understood as being fields that feed into each other or contain each other in given ways. That is why any 'fundamental entanglement' has yet to be understood, is opened to question here. In making this explicit O'Brien and Szeman are doing no more than noting a given institutional disposition which certainly obtained at the time, and still obtains: 'globalization' as a term, and as connoting a cluster of concepts, has been located primarily in social studies disciplines and, until recently, relatively neglected in the humanities disciplines (especially in literature and art). At the level of statement, too, O'Brien and Szeman chart a particular way in which literature and globalization may be considered as being entangled. They insist that the significance of globalization 'can only be grasped through its realization in a variety of narrative forms', in 'the narrative construction of the numerous discourses or "fictions" of globalization'. By highlighting this aspect of globalization – its narrativizations, its discourses, its 'fictions' – an obvious link with the concerns of literature is discerned. It is, of course, understood that terms such as 'narrative' and 'discourse', not to mention 'fictions', are of the discipline of literature in a given institutionally recognizable way.

The emphasis on 'narratives of globalization' is, however, not really a matter of highlighting an important aspect of the phenomenon of globalization which is relevant to literature – and that's where the performative aspect of the quotation comes in. What happens in the quotation is not really the identification of an aspect of globalization (apart from as a theme) that is arguably entangled with literature; rather O'Brien and Szeman perform a literary taming (so to speak) of globalization and translate globalization into a register that is literary and is amenable to literature. This involves several implicit steps. First, there is an ostensible registering of the complexity of the 'phenomena most commonly associated with globalization'. The listing of some of these phenomena that follow, from which closure is carefully withheld, is heavily weighted towards directions with which literature students would be comfortable. The contextual specificities of the term 'globalization' are elided in precisely the way charted in chapter 1. The concrete economic and political nuances of that term's travels and accrual of meaning are underplayed in favour of broad abstractions such as 'transculturation' and 'spatial and temporal demands of European modernism', which are well ensconced in literary theory and criticism. The extension of a retrospective embrace for the term to incorporate histories of colonialism and imperialism (a field where 'globalization' would have been largely meaningless before the 1980s) is overplayed because, obviously, of the central institutional position that postcolonial theory enjoys in the literary academy. The advantages of these almost off-hand manoeuvres are evidenced in the essays in the special issue the quotation introduces. Second, in identifying narratives or discourses or 'fictions' of globalization as key, O'Brien and Szeman do something that few economists or sociologists or political scientists would recognize as being relevant to the area. They assume, in other words, that globalization is constituted in how it is talked about or narrated rather than in, say, material and technological and social processes and arrangements. By presenting 'narratives of globalization' as globalization, O'Brien and Szeman manage to bring globalization *within* the ken of literature (some might argue that regarding *all* narratives as being entangled with literature over-endows the ken of literature anyway).

The third, and perhaps most significant, step in the performance whereby globalization is tamed for the approach from literature is in O'Brien and Szeman's inattention to their own discourse. The above steps are taken silently, without elucidation of their presumptions, without explication of their context and location. These steps are performed *within* literature and *for* literature. O'Brien and Szeman speak where literature is a given and understood field; literature, that is, speaking to itself. Their observations issue and are recorded within that distinctive part of literature where literature institutionally speaks itself and perpetuates and reproduces itself even while addressing things outside itself – usually demarcated as the institutional practice of academic literary studies, literary theory and criticism, and text editing and bibliography.

In this and the next chapter, I look at the entanglement of literature and globalization insofar as it figures in or is relevant to this distinctive area of academic literary studies. Unlike

O'Brien and Szeman, I do not feel that this is an entanglement which can be engaged by simply rendering globalization amenable to the existing proclivities and institutional comfort zones of literary studies. Both the meeting points and the departures between globalization as an area of study and literature as an area of study, the fissures and overlaps between their institutional and disciplinary and discursive constructions, the amenabilities and discomforts involved in examining literature and globalization in relation to each other, need to be registered. This cannot simply be a matter of seeing how far debates about globalization are relevant to debates in literary studies, or how far existing ideas of interest in literary studies can be fitted with notions of globalization. This has also to take account of unexpected, or at least relatively unfamiliar, directions that are opened up for literary studies in coming to grips with debates about globalization. In other words, this entails taking account of the directions that literary studies may be pushed resistantly towards. That means that in this discussion I attempt not only to consider the relevance of globalization *within* literary studies, by performing a literary discourse, but also to discern the locations/relocations/dislocations of literary studies *within* globalization, by putting some of the discourse of literary studies and its presumptions into perspective. What that involves becomes, I hope, clearer as this chapter progresses.

Turning to literary studies

By way of approaching literature and globalization within literary studies, some stocktaking of the ways in which literary studies has evoked globalization provides a useful platform for the following discussion. There are several broad directions discernible here. First, the kind of exercise that has been conducted in the previous two chapters, and described in the above quotation as 'about how globalization is reflected thematically in fiction', represents one of the significant ways in which literary studies has engaged globalization. Second, in a related fashion, occasionally literary texts and the interpretation thereof have been recruited to support or elucidate conceptual positions taken by political and social theorists about globalization. Third, there have been some attempts to find accommodations between terms and formulations (such as 'text', 'culture', 'identity') in literary studies and in globalization studies (or discussions of the political, economic and cultural processes of globalization). Fourth, a number of studies have attempted – like O'Brien and Szeman above – to fit ideas of globalization with developed and familiar fields of literary studies. In particular postcolonial and postmodern literature and literary theory have proved fruitful ground for literary scholars to seek to embrace or draw in discussions of globalization. Fifth, noteworthy attempts have been made to understand globalization as a process that implicates the institutional or disciplinary pursuit (particularly at the level of pedagogy) of literary studies itself. This is available in some of the rethinking to which the disciplines of English studies and comparative literature have been exposed. And finally, sixth, some scholarly attention has been devoted to the industries that mediate the production, circulation and consumption of literature outside academic precincts, or more broadly in the buying and selling of books in the world. These industries – which implicate particularly the publishing and media industries – are at present understandably as subject to globalization processes as any industrial sector. The impact of globalization on these industries has considerable knock-on effects on literature and literary studies, which have also received some scholarly attention.

These six broad areas in which literary studies has evoked globalization suggests a structure for the remainder of this study. So far, in the previous two chapters I have examined some contemporary British and American fiction in which different aspects of globalization processes and debates are thematized or represented. Insofar as this chapter turns to *literary studies*, a retrospective look at what the exercise conducted in the previous two chapters implies in terms of literary criticism is called for – it is incumbent upon me not just to *do* literary interpretation but to explore my practice in doing that in a literary critical spirit. This retrospection can be usefully informed by reference to other criticism in a similar direction. The first two of the six areas just mentioned would be effectively covered in this. That in turn, puts this study in a position to undertake what I have stated above as an ambition: not only to consider the relevance of globalization *within* literary studies but also to discern the locations/relocations/dislocations of literary studies *within* globalization. That is appropriately attempted with reference to the four remaining areas remarked above, and best begun with the third. This has to do with formulations which occur in both globalization and literary studies. The latter part of this chapter is accordingly devoted to this – especially to exploring notions of 'text', 'identity' and 'culture'. In the following two chapters I pick up the next two areas in question: i.e. chapter 5 discusses globalization in relation to postcolonial and postmodern literature and literary theory, and chapter 6 examines globalization in relation to the institutional spaces of English studies and comparative literature. The final chapter focuses on the globalization of industries implicated in the production, circulation and consumption of literature.

To keep sight of specific literary texts within a discussion that might otherwise feel rather abstract at times, this and the following chapter will often (but not exclusively) revolve around two literary texts. James Joyce's *Ulysses* (1921) and Salman Rushdie's *Midnight's Children* (1981) offer some peculiar advantages for this study. These two texts have been at the heart of most significant literary critical debates and movements in and since the twentieth century.

Globalization thematized

The kind of exercise to which the previous two chapters have been devoted is not without precedent. Two books which, in similar ways, have tried to approach ideas of globalization through fiction are *The Novel and the Globalization of Culture* (1995) by Michael Valdez Moses and James Annesley's *Fictions of Globalization* (2006). Moses's book recruits a selection of European and Third World fiction to intervene in a contextually specific political debate about globalization, while Annesley's is an attempt at examining a range of issues associated with globalization through contemporary American novels. The decade that separates the two has something to do with the difference in approach. Examination of these two approaches can inform a retrospection of the previous two chapters.

Moses's book is a literary intervention in a debate conducted primarily by political theorists and sociologists in the early 1990s, arising from Francis Fukuyama's *The End of History and the Last Man* (1992). The latter wedded a strand of Hegel's philosophy to comparative democracy studies to argue that a global convergence on liberal democracy is in progress, and that a future of global political, social and cultural homogenization could be foreseen which would effectively be an end of history. In this instance the idea that history would end does not imply that human beings would cease to exist, but that the manner in which history has been conceived so far, the manner in which we are accustomed to thinking about history, would cease to apply. According to this argument, at the bottom of our current thinking lies that notion that history has a progressive direction or is teleological, and that this direction is maintained through conflicts and contradictions of various sorts within and between societies. Hegel envisaged an idealistic direction for history, whereby what he regarded as increasing degrees of 'self-consciousness' would be manifested in increasingly rational social organization through history, and could lead to an end of history where world society would have achieved complete 'self-consciousness'. Hegel's *Phenomenology of Spirit* ([1807] 1977) conceptualized this process, and his posthumously published lectures on the *Philosophy of History* ([1837] 1956) attempted a factual fleshing out of the idea by presenting a world history which ostensibly charts different levels of self-consciousness in different societies. Fukuyama recalled Hegel's view of history's direction and culmination, sieved through the work of philosopher Alexander Kojeve, significantly *in the early 1990s*. This period is now indelibly associated with what is regarded as the end of the Cold War. Fukuyama's declaration of an imminent Hegelian 'end of history' couldn't but have been received as the crowing of victorious North American capitalism and an announcement of its global ambition. To some extent the conceptual generality and argumentative quality of Fukuyama's book raised it above the level of a party-political manifesto. And yet, Fukuyama's inspiration from the Cold War-rooted comparative democratization studies, the unquestioning complacency with which he assumed that capitalism and democracy (as *a priori* good) are coeval, and his own Republican political allegiances in the United States placed the book fairly clearly for his audiences. A debate on the nuances of the book followed: neoconservatives and neoliberals were suspiciously congratulatory of the book; liberals of various other hues were uneasy about its universalist assertion; political realists observed that liberal democracy is not without debilitating contradictions; leftists worried about the impetus thus given to North American neocolonial ambitions (passing as globalization); and those with investments in neonationalisms and identity politics observed that the post-Cold War period is marked more by fragmentation than homogenization. In many ways, this debate encapsulated the myriad conceptual positions and ideas that have come to be associated with globalization – that have both constructed and interrogated globalization – in the course of the 1990s. Much more than the content of Fukuyama's book, it is the specific debate surrounding it that connects it to globalization. Moses's book is a somewhat unusual intervention in that debate, and needs to be placed accordingly.

Moses starts off by proclaiming himself persuaded by something like Fukuyama's Hegel-Kojeve inspired 'end of history' thesis, and by seeking to persuade his reader of it by distancing it from controversies:

> A less controversial way of stating that history has come to an end is to suggest that a homogenizing worldwide process of modernization has become irreversible. All human communities are gradually but inexorably coming to resemble one another, exhibiting the same salient characteristics of a modern society. [. . .] A modern society accepts and exploits the technological achievements of modern natural sciences, [. . .] Modern society is consequently one that at least implicitly embraces the secularization of human society. [. . .] Intimately connected to the spread of modern sciences and the secularization of society is the simultaneous advance of trade and commerce. The market economy, especially the advantages it produces from the division of labour, leads to an ever-increasing accumulation of capital. (Moses 1995, 6)

Even this briefest of quotations checks the markers of Fukuyama's thinking: it carries a recognizable sense of an autonomous agency-free process in human history. This process has a direction (modernization), it is understood as evidenced in the present and as being progressive in a normatively positive sense, and it consists in universal acceptance of liberal democratic political and advanced capitalist economic arrangements. To underline the plausibility of this perception, Moses covers the Hegel–Kojeve–Fukuyama ground in some detail, thus emphasizing the philosophical basis of his argument and leaving the sociological and political empirical evidence that is usually cited in support of that argument aside. Instead of the latter kind of evidence, Moses, interestingly, chooses to use works of literary fiction to a similar purpose. He picks up two works of European fiction (Thomas Hardy's *Mayor of Casterbridge,* 1886, and Joseph Conrad's *Lord Jim,* 1900), as representing moves towards social and political values that are espoused in the globally dominant West, and novels by two authors from the so-called Third World (Chinua Achebe's *Things Fall Apart,* 1958, and *No Longer at Ease,* 1960, and Mario Vargas Llosa's *The War at the End of the World,* 1981) representing views from the periphery. His reading of these is meant to demonstrate that, irrespective of their geopolitical origins and concerns, these chart a uniform vision of what modernity consists in, and what human aspirations should be. Having done this to his satisfaction, Moses observes modestly that the conformity of a handful of novels to an 'end of history' direction can hardly be regarded as proof of that thesis, examines some of the objections that have been raised to that thesis, and concludes by reiterating that the global homogenization that portends an 'end of history' advances despite evidence of exacerbated nationalism, religious communalism and particularist ideologies.

The point here is not to examine the extent to which Moses's readings of the chosen novels confirm an 'end of history' view. Rather, what is of interest here is the thinking underlying his methodology. In this methodology, clearly, literature and literary criticism are *instrumentalized* in the service of a debate of political and sociological and philosophical moment. The debate rages out there irrespective of literature, disregardful of literature, and Moses pushes his way in unexpectedly by drawing upon his literary resources – to take a position in the debate. It is a modest position, mainly giving the thumbs up to proponents of the 'end of history' without affecting the contours of the debate particularly. Nor does it specifically impinge upon the practice of literature and the pursuit of literary criticism: the range of literary reference is too limited. Using some literary fiction as exemplary for a general ideological position does not allow for reflection on the literary to a sufficient degree to feed back into literature and literary criticism. And yet there is a grain of an interesting idea in there. It is in the presumption that literary fictional texts can serve as evidence in a similar fashion as empirically based political or social observations. It is presumed that the processes represented within and implicit around fictional works, which can be discerned by a reader or interpreter, convey a reality or veracity about their geopolitical locations that is as germane as, say, statistical data or sociological field work or political reports. Moses obviously believes that, if one is looking for evidence to support a socio-political theory, one may call upon literature.

Appearing a decade later, James Annesley's *Fictions of Globalization* (2006) also treats globalization as a theme in a range of contemporary American fiction – touching on works by Don DeLillo, Paul Beatty, Chuck Palahniuk, Sandra Cisneros, Dave Eggers, Brett Easton Ellis, William Gibson, Jhumpa Lahiri and Bharati Mukherjee. Annesley's approach to this task and methodology are, however, substantially different from that of Moses, reflecting shifts in the connotations of 'globalization' in the interim. Annesley introduces his project in the following manner:

> The aim [of the book] is not [. . .] to read these novels in terms that evidence the reality of globalization, or to present them as homological expressions of the specifics of these material conditions, but to use the analysis of different texts to refine ways of knowing globalization's discourses. [. . .] The suggestion is that the examination of recent American fiction and a consideration of the ways in which globalization's processes are represented offers an insight into the shape and character of concerns that have a key bearing on the interpretation of contemporary culture, social and political life. In these terms the aim is neither to celebrate nor condemn globalization, but to finds ways in which it might be

possible to read contemporary fiction in terms that add to knowledge about, and understanding of, its discourses. (Annesley 2006, 6)

The idea here is not to instrumentalize literature to be able to contribute to an ongoing debate about globalization, but to become part and parcel with a more dispersed (than a specific debate) and familiar set of narratives of globalization. The latter implies that acts of literary reading will both register globalization's appearances as literary theme and seek to develop or extend narratives of globalization. Debates about globalization and literature, thus, are not held apart with merely the possibility of the latter being able to represent something of the former, but are meshed together so that they merge in a conjoined field that processes globalization in literature and the literariness of globalization.

Again, the point here is to examine not how far Annesley succeeds but the presumptions of his methodology in relation to that of Moses. Annesley's mid-2000s context, and the now somewhat different sense of the term 'globalization', is material. I had observed in chapter 1 that by the turn of the millennium the term had become almost ideologically neutral, and was gradually abstracted from specific histories and cultures, as a markedly protean and thickly connotative word. These shifts indicated a move from a disciplinary axis for 'globalization' in sociology, economics, politics, culture and media studies to application with regard to issues or topics relevant to almost any disciplinary frame. Something of this move is marked in the difference between the two authors' attitude to the term. For Moses globalization is primarily a conceptual matter, to do with a debate that is usually perceived as non-literary, a debate that is in the process of unfolding, and moreover one that is inevitably ideologically loaded. Moses could only intervene from outside, as it were, to take a definite position within the debate. For Annesley, however, the positions in this debate are already largely thrashed out (which doesn't mean they have been resolved – far from it), and the ideological commitments invested in debating globalization are not pressing. In fact he deliberately decides 'neither to celebrate nor condemn globalization', but to treat it as ideologically neutral. And this is possible for Annesley because globalization is not merely a conceptual field, but one that is manifest in a widely dispersed fashion in a range of issues or topics which are as literary as they are political or sociological or philosophical, etc., issues which *include* the 'globalization debate' itself: he addresses, in his words, 'the connections that tie ethnicity, identity and consumption together; the representation of globalization and the globalization debate; dreams of escape from, and rebellion against, consumer society and the forces of globalization; and the impact and consequences of tourism and migration' (Annesley 2006, 8). Consequently Annesley's engagement of globalization in fiction draws upon something like Moses's conviction in literature's ability to give access to contextually concrete reality and veracity. But, pace Moses, fictional texts are not instrumentalized as sociological evidence for globalization debates. Rather, Annesley reads his chosen texts as giving access to a field which constitutes the processes of globalization, and which can therefore inform ongoing discussion about globalization, inform its narratives. As he says at the end of his book:

> It is the understanding that globalization must be read in relation to the ordinary transactions of ordinary people that underpins this analysis of the representation of leisure, technology, consumer-culture, the market *and* migration in recent American fiction. [. . .] Instead of asking what the understanding of globalization can do for literary studies, this book has asked what the study of literature can do for the understanding of globalization. (Annesley 2006, 163)

The thematization of globalization that I have attempted in the previous two chapters is close in spirit to that in Annesley's book. That is, it is close in methodological approach and intention, rather than in themes addressed – which are obviously different. And, in contrast to Annesley's work, the previous chapters come with no attempt at maintaining an ideology-free attitude towards the term and its connotations. Ideological baggage and normative proclivities have accrued in a variegated fashion among the connotations of the term and cannot really be overlooked. Any treatment of themes associated with globalization in literature inevitably releases ideological nuances which are impossible to be neutral about, which immediately provoke evaluative attitudes. This is, I think, self-evident in the treatment of the fictional themes of globalization in the previous two chapters.

Timothy Brennan

FROM DEVELOPMENT
TO GLOBALIZATION

Postcolonial studies and globalization theory

Halfway through this extract, Timothy Brennan makes a key assertion, that "debates over globalization are discursive", and that these discourses in turn follow one of five basic moves through which globalization is registered as: 1. a political ideal; 2. a utopia or dystopia generated by free trade; 3. a technological, capitalist Americanization; 4. the contemporary version of Western imperialism; and 5. being purely speculative (or as Brennan puts it succinctly, globalization "does not exist"). What these at times overlapping, at other times contradictory moves reinforce, is Brennan's opening statement that globalization theory is notoriously difficult to pin down, and in comparing the parallels and crossings between globalization and postcolonial theory this elusiveness (which applies to both methodologies), is problematic. Brennan specializes in examining from a postcolonial perspective the intersections of global literatures in English, as well as diasporic music, cosmopolitanism, and cultural politics; in the extract he draws upon this knowledge to examine the histories of globalization and postcolonial studies to make more sense of their contemporary manifestations; he rapidly sketches the key thinkers and ideological movements that form these histories, before concluding that modernity breaks with the past, and functions in a permanent state of the current moment, or now, what is known as being "presentist"—therefore these histories are usually ignored or forgotten about. In this presentist state, there is a constant disavowal of the importance of any prior knowledge or process, and thus globalization and postcolonial studies are necessarily divorced from their intellectual and practical precursors, in an endless celebration of the new. Globalization theory disavows the past while functioning through a series of tensions, if not fundamental contradictions. Brennan notes that the idealistic, politically utopian vision of globalization is countered by a corporate, imperial vision that is its polar opposite. Even more problematically, it is not even clear if globalization theory is about "process" (societal changes, e.g., new technologies) or "policy" (societal projections, e.g., new ways of being). Brennan also asks whether globalization is open to the Other, or is in fact a way of imposing Western norms upon the Other. Such questions, he suggests, are not usually asked by globalization theory, which usually non-reflexively adopts or advocates one of the perspectives or moves stated above. Perhaps globalization, some critics argue, is moving too rapidly for academics to keep up with and account for: global flows of capital and new technologies, just to name two processes, are beyond individual or even state control. One of the main theorists of the new "anarchic" processes of globalization is sociologist Anthony Giddens, and Brennan gives a brief overview of his notion of chaotic, apocalyptic processes within globalization that leads to society having to deal with all-pervasive "risk", trusting systems (for example, banking systems) that are far too complex for human control. Brennan points out later in the extract that proponents of such anarchic globalization tend to be idealists or utopian thinkers, while those who are threatened by globalization sketch out far more structured organizational and ideological patterns of development and control. These two perspectives are, once more, not only at odds, but deeply contradictory. Common ground can be found, and Brennan lists these as the concepts of: modernity; the West; space/place; cosmopolitanism; and neoliberalism.

NEITHER "GLOBALIZATION THEORY" NOR "postcolonial studies" are terms that easily reveal their meanings. The areas of knowledge to which they refer are not what they seem, and a great deal of confusion surrounds their uses. Readers would be forgiven for thinking that "globalization theory" denoted an emergent body of writing called forth by inexorable recent developments in technology and communications, as well as radical shifts in the world economy and in geopolitics, all of them presaging the rise of a truly global culture – the obliteration of state sovereignty in a world marked by fluidity and border-crossing. In turn, these readers might suppose that "postcolonial studies" referred to an inaugural critique of Eurocentrism prompted by a new diasporic wave of intellectuals from the former colonies resident in metropolitan centers who – informed by postwar theories of language and representation – began in the late 1970s to cast older versions of "Western Man" in doubt in an act of writing back to Empire.

Actually, neither is the case. One has to begin by distinguishing between the study of global issues or colonial pasts *per se* and the fairly recent creation of schools of thought that retrospectively appropriate the more general cases fleetingly echoed in their names. When invoked in European or North American universities since the beginning of the 1990s, globalization theory and postcolonial studies turn out to be very specialized discursive formations passing for older and more varied types of enquiry. This slippage between connotation and code is one of the first things to understand about the conjunction of the two terms.

There have been many earlier traditions of investigating, on the one hand, globalizing features of world history and human societies and, on the other, colonial practices and anticolonial challenges in the cultural field. Indeed, these now separate foci were in earlier periods conjoined. The ancestors of both, as unified phenomena, include systemic analyses of colonization dating from the early years of the European conquest in the sixteenth century (Las Casas 1992; Raleigh 1997; Montaigne 1991), Enlightenment tracts protesting the ravages of imperial intervention in the late seventeenth, eighteenth, and early nineteenth centuries (Raynal 1991; Smith 1910; Bentham 1995; Voltaire 2001), studies in the nineteenth and early twentieth centuries of the origins and dynamics of capitalism as a global phenomenon (Marx and Engels 1988; Marx 1991; Melville 1988; Hobson 1902), comprehensive economic critiques of the division of the globe at the apex of European colonization prior to the First World War (Graham 1896; Morris 1901; Kautsky 1970; Lenin 1975), new forms of global or broadly regional historiographies associated with the *annales* school and other historical schools after the Second World War (Braudel 1992; McNeill 1963; Hodgson 1974), Marxist historiography based on the initiatives of the anticolonial movements (Kiernan 1969; Stavrianos 1981; Wolf 1982), dependency theory (Frank 1967; Rodney 1972; Santos 1978), and particularly – and very directly – world systems theory (Cox 1959, 1962, 1964; Wallerstein 1974; Samir Amin 1976). We will look at some of these efforts in more detail below.

In spite of reaching back several centuries, and despite being well developed, extensively documented, and self-conscious, these multiple and varied intellectual movements, with their own canons of texts and scholarly pantheons, are frequently discounted in contemporary globalization theory even as they are quietly accessed without acknowledgment. In a similar way, postcolonial studies – although in part resting on these same foundations – draws on more immediate precursors, especially the anticolonial intellectuals of the 1950s and 1960s, whose work was anticipated by, and directly inherited, interwar Marxist networks of anti-imperialism (Nehru 1946; Mao 1953; Fanon 1968; Lumumba 1972; Guevara 1969; Ho Chi Minh 1967; see Parry 2002; Brennan 2002b). Motifs of cultural difference, epistemological othering, colonial subjectivity, and social contradiction – all common in later postcolonial studies – were inaugurated by that earlier generation of politically engaged intellectuals, who were often members of actual governments following formal independence. These "independence intellectuals," if one can call them that, were in turn the inheritors of a tradition forged by intellectuals from Africa, Asia, and Latin America resident in Europe between the world wars, who in the communist milieux of those years had begun to forge a rhetorical and theoretical apparatus for studying colonialism as a comprehensive phenomenon, and even more importantly as a morally corrupt system of economic enrichment that could be defeated by organized counter-activity in which intellectuals from the colonies would play a prominent role.

The tendency of contemporary intellectual trends to supplant predecessors by erasing the history of their own making is not a chance occurrence, nor is it simply the work of uncharitable scholars. It is rather a characteristic feature of contemporary capitalist societies, which are at once *presentist* – that is, viewing each moment as the only reality while expunging the past in a gesture of calculated *anti*-historicism – and *modernist* in the technical sense of needing to judge every current discovery as an utterly new departure, an absolute rupture with all that went before. This intellectual reflex is, in fact, a central feature both of what globalization theory argues the world has become, and of what that theory unwittingly demonstrates about itself.

Contemporary modernism celebrates what earlier modernists greeted with suspicion or disparagement (as in those writers of the early twentieth century like Franz Kafka, Marcel Proust, or William Butler Yeats, who despised mass culture and the decline of the aristocratic sensibility of the refined patron of the arts). Today, by contrast, mass culture is enshrined in terms of obscure and refined aesthetic pleasure with populist pretensions that form the bedrock ideology of the most wealthy and the most privileged. Both versions are modernist in that they cast the new as the never-before-seen: in the first case, as a heroically constructed, formal experimentalism that preserves the unsurpassed intelligence and insight of the chosen few of the past, serving as a bulwark against the vulgarity of the masses; in the second case, as a radical break with a history considered to be heading in an unpredictable direction which is, then, valorized precisely for that reason. Although one speaks of *post*modernism today, the "post" does not connote a time after, but rather a heightening. What is meant by the term is less the supersession of modernity than *ultra*-modernity. The modernist does not merely express a neutral belief in the "year zero" of the now, as though dispassionately describing a fundamental historical fissure that evidence had forced him or her to accept. Instead, modernism (including its postmodern variant) is normative. The "now" is the new, and the new is rapturously and exuberantly embraced. Without ever questioning the fundamental self-contradiction of the move, the modernist then vigorously urges on a future that *should* unfold (because it is good) while simultaneously arguing that it *must* unfold (because it is inevitable). This style of thinking informs both globalization theory and postcolonial studies, and is another of the major links between them. Let us now develop in more detail the arguments outlined above.

Globalization theory: five possible positions

As a term, "globalization" is marked by a fundamental ambiguity. On the one hand, it holds out hope for the creation of new communities and unforeseen solidarities; on the other hand, it appears merely to euphemize corporatization and imperial expansion. At its base, in other words, lies a tension between *process* and *policy*. Is globalization theory about describing a "process": that is, an amalgam of material shifts, spatial re-orderings, anonymous developments and movements, the inexorable concatenation of changes in communication, transportation, demographics, and the environment? Or does it describe a "policy" (and is it a part of that policy): that is, a myth-making operation whose purpose is to project a world order that a small group of national and/or financial interests ardently desires to be the future for the rest of us – a future that has happily not yet arrived? There is, as well, a normative dimension to this tension. Does globalization presage a new openness to the foreign and the out-of-reach, or is it rather (and paradoxically) just the opposite: a veiled way of alluding to the Americanization of foreignness in a world dominated by US power following the fall of the Soviet Union (Bourdieu 2001; Foster 2002; Friedman 1999)? As expected, given our observations above, a similar ambiguity – structurally identical, in fact – marks postcolonial studies, where various critics have wondered aloud whether assaults on "imperial discourse" or the "epistemic violence" of colonial mentalities are, as their authors claim, a more sophisticated way of battling Eurocentrism or merely a rendering of earlier radical positions of dissent in a form more accommodating to power by a professional diaspora to the imperial centers (Appiah 1991; Dirlik 1997; Huggan 2001). Questions such as these interrogate globalization, but are already outside "globalization theory," which does not typically open itself up to this kind of self-questioning. In particular, it would consider raising the issue of the *interestedness* of academic knowledge as being impertinent, for reasons we will describe.

Current globalization theory, in its restricted sense, cannot logically doubt itself in the manner I have suggested because it does not merely claim that economic or cultural integration is occurring on a global scale. The import of what is being said goes significantly beyond that. The intended point is rather that the world is being reconstituted *as a single social space*. One might interpret this to mean that the world is becoming more homogenized, that we are seeing the creation of a single, albeit hybridized, world culture whose pace of life, tastes, and customs – conditioned by a similar regime of commodities consisting of cars, computers, and cellular phones – has increasingly fewer local variations. It could also be taken to mean that we are on the road to global political integration. It is worth recognizing, however, that it does not necessarily stipulate either of these positions. To say "a single social space" still allows for complex and dynamic internal variations across an interconnected system of localities and regions. The key component is that there be a governing logic or social tendency that brings all these localities and regions into a unity unknown before.

The idea is further posited that globalization has become its own explanation: that is, not only has space/time been "distanciated" as a result of analyzable causal forces (that is, distances are less relevant to one's particular experience given the instant availability of images, objects, and information from afar); what is being claimed is rather that social theory itself has undergone a spatio-temporal reformulation in which the earlier modes of analysis are no longer tenable. Class antagonisms, geopolitical rivalries, the entrenched defense of privileges, imperial designs, the blunt arguments of war and profit-making – all of the earlier mechanisms of historical causation are, in globalization theory, implicitly downgraded into second-order explanations.

As these are cast as vestiges of a vanishing social logic, globalization theory looks rather to a "new" dynamic forged by the happy chaos of an infinitely mobile citizenry, a constantly self-defined subjectivity, a terrain of virtual space consisting of multi-faceted niches of an always malleable and morphing freedom. As such (the argument goes) the mandate of reliable definitions crumbles away; the researcher, in order not to be left behind, sprints frantically after a reality vastly more innovative on its own than earlier utopias had been in the imagination. Social sense-making is no longer determined by students of history or the organizers of thought known as philosophers; in the view of the globalization theorist, their structures of understanding only impede their ability to recognize the future unfolding before their eyes, which is being created by investors, technologists, managers, and organizers, not – thankfully not – working according to plan, but swept along in a process that is anarchic and autopoetic (Bauman 1998; Giddens 1991; Agamben 1993).

The paradigmatic tone and style of globalization theory is perhaps provided best by the sociologist, Anthony Giddens, who gives a clear indication of the type of argument found in the field in our restrictive sense. For Giddens, people in ultra-modernity live apocalyptically, experiencing levels of risk unknown before. As social institutions become more and more complex, they operate (and force us to operate) at increasing levels of abstraction, now built into the fabric of individual life. As a result, the subject is forced to *trust*, since abstract systems tend to "disembed" the subject from immediate experience, transforming intimacy from the previously anchored criteria of kinship and obligation to a "life politics" based on controlling one's own body. As deskilling renders most of us utterly dependent on expert systems whose functioning we simply have to trust, this bio-political control becomes more important as a response to the "runaway world" of modernity, and the unitary framework of experience of which we are constantly reminded. Doubt as a pervasive feature of modern critical reason now permeates everyday life, becoming part of its existential dimension. Time and space are separable and controllable by way of the technologies of clock and map. Although aspects of this vision sound threatening at first, our initial impressions are deliberately confounded by Giddens's jubilant conclusions. For him, our ability in ultra-modernity to outgrow providential reason produces an increasingly secular understanding of the nature of things, and so intrinsically leads to a safer and more rewarding existence (Giddens 1991).

Such an account is obviously at odds with a systematic account of financial forces or the impure motives of privileged agencies. By taking these conflicting approaches into consideration, one comes to recognize that globalization is not waiting to be found, discrete and safe, in the world of living social communities. There are no facts to be rehearsed in order to determine either whether the term "globalization" is merited, or whether (if so) this *thing* has not existed for many centuries without it being accompanied by the heraldic futuristic utterances that are now widely evident (utterances that often have the ring of a campaign). By themselves the facts, such as they are, are mute: for instance, the ownership patterns of transnational corporations (TNCs), the explosive rise in internet traffic, the radical breakdown of treaties governing international law, the increasing recourse to off-shore banking, the orchestrated planning imposed by the Bretton Woods institutions (International Monetary Fund, World Bank), or the flows of migrant labor in Southeast Asia.

To this extent, it is vital to grasp that debates over globalization are discursive. That is, they are debates over *theory*: over which explanatory mechanism makes the most sense given a body of (usually implicit) ethical and political objectives. The ensemble of theories of globalization invoked at the outset of this chapter – centuries-old critiques of capitalism, Enlightenment protests against colonial excesses, conscious attempts since 1945 to write a fully world history, and the more recent exuberant "globalization theory" that characterizes both poststructuralism and neoliberalism (often in similar terms) – all of these taken together have yielded five basic positions which again and again arise in various guises in the now massive literature on globalization. Heuristically, it might be useful to spell them out at this point.

The first position argues that globalization – however much it is the unintended result of economic logics, technical discoveries, and population growth – finds its only real significance as a *political promise.* Here, finally, the great Enlightenment program of Immanuel Kant for a single world government under universal law is perhaps realizable (Kant 1963 [1795], 1991 [1784]; Toulmin 1990; Kristeva 1993). Possibilities at last exist for either world citizenship under a single governmental entity (a new world state), or some flexible federalist structure allowing significant local autonomy. It is an exciting and welcome development, taking us beyond the petty factionalism, ethnic rivalries, and bloodletting of the past, associated with the ancient, premodern, and modern nationalist eras. Globalization, in this view, is welcome (Falk and Strauss 2000, 2001).

By contrast, the second position argues that globalization is not so much a matter of formal political outcomes as the development of *trade* and of *finance,* in which the pure freedom of exchange revolutionizes human contact along with the potential for understanding, leisure, and cultural sampling. It is not political actors but transnational corporations that are responsible for globalization, and therefore what is happening is happening deliberately *outside* political structures, and even in opposition to them (Sklair 1991). There is no clear local, or national, beneficiary of globalization since the TNCs are indifferent to nations (they are, after all, technically owned by people from many countries), and hostile to them (they naturally desire the permeability of borders). They supersede nations, which have therefore become obsolete. In this variant, globalization can be considered either welcome or unwelcome. A theorist such as Jagdish Bhagwati, for instance – an economist at Columbia University who celebrates capitalism – considers these developments the fruit of the marvelous rationality of market forces, while Félix Guattari and Toni Negri (post-Marxist intellectuals who describe themselves as "communists") share much the same view, considering the runaway market as unleashing powerful utopian energies (Bhagwati 2001; Guattari and Negri 1990). By contrast, the billionaire financier, George Soros, deems the unrestricted mobility of finance to be a human catastrophe (Soros 1998).

The third position combines the emphasis on politics and trade while shifting the criterion to *geopolitical motive.* In this variant, globalization is the result of developments in technology, transportation, and financial/corporate restructuring working in concert with an underlying *ideology* that is basically American (Valladao 1998; Bauman 1998). Thus globalization, although undoubtedly permeating the rest of the world and in some ways benefiting actors in several countries, is structurally American. It is the United States that primarily benefits, not only directly as a specific nation-state, but in the more ambitious sense that the United States is a mini-model of the future world – the world as it will appear when globalized. Were we to examine this recognizably American ideology as the dynamic contemporary expression of capitalism (the argument goes), we would see how important it has been in facilitating technological developments in media, travel, fashion, and entertainment in a wild and intrepid search for novelty without any thought for the consequences. In a more localized sense, however, it is the American twist on capitalism that has made globalization seem desirable, and has done so by making the following concepts widely believed in, either because they are thought inexorable or because they are thought attractive (the fusing of the two qualities, again, is paradigmatic): pragmatism, pluralism, individualism, and suspicion towards the "state." Here globalization can, again, be thought either good or bad, with Thomas Friedman offering perhaps the most outspoken and extreme views on behalf of an irrepressible American genius and beneficence, and Paul Krugman, the economist and op-ed columnist for *The New York Times,* tirelessly exposing the emptiness of neoliberal ideology, and the rampant corruption and cronyism at the heart of American profit-making (Friedman 1999; Krugman 1997).

A fourth variant is less evolutionary than the third while retaining its focus on the United States. It explicitly ties globalization to the problematics of the colonizing "West." Here, globalization is basically the form that imperialism takes in the late twentieth century (Lapham 1998; Blaut 1993; Samir Amin *et al.* 1990; Bourdieu 2001). It is a shibboleth whose emergence as a master-term coincided exactly with the fall of the Soviet Union and the Eastern bloc – that period, in other words, in which the last credible adversaries to US global hegemony were removed. Most of the features said to characterize globalization are American, and they are coercively imposed on others as a universal norm. Rather than the hybridity that is widely acclaimed as being on the rise, we are instead seeing the violent incorporation of global difference into a single national project that is importantly, even vitally, not perceived as such. Although the forms and styles of this imperialism are crucially different from those of the past, the intentions and effects are identical (conquest, occupation, and the stealing of resources continue, and enrich distinct national entities, but they are now performed not under the sign of "civilization" or "God" or "Britain" but in the name of "globalization" or simply the "new," which universalizes the interests of that distinct national entity). This analysis presents globalization as a largely fictive enterprise, either cynical or guilty of wishful thinking. Here, globalization is seen as a threat.

The fifth position is the most distinctive. It avers that globalization does not exist. Although it concedes that travel and communication are much easier and more accessible than previously, and although it readily agrees that this increased human contact has had profound effects on the way people see the world, nothing qualitatively has changed. The nation-state structure is still the international norm; ethnic, linguistic, and religious divisions have only intensified; most of the world's people are entirely localized, provincial, traditional, and cut-off from others, not only living outside this supposedly new globalized world, but outside modernity itself. Globalization is therefore not a description, but a projection; or more properly, it is a projection that passes itself off as a description. Once again, this is a mixed view, with globalization being thought either good or bad. As the self-styled Metternich of the late twentieth century, for instance, Henry Kissinger is not particularly happy to observe that globalization is an overweening fiction (Kissinger 1994). With grim pragmatism, therefore, he counsels his readers to be wary of obstacles still remaining to American supremacy, wishing in fact that globalization were more real than it is. In both Immanuel Wallerstein and Janet Abu-Lughod, by contrast, globalization collapses as a concept not because of wishful thinking, but from want of scholarship (Wallerstein 1984; Abu-Lughod 1989). An investigation of material relations makes it vain, in their opinion, to distinguish our own time from the high Renaissance (or even earlier); both eras are "global" in more or less the same ways, just as both equally fail to approximate the complete integration fancifully described in globalization theory.

These representative positions display more than different diagnoses or emphases; they are methodologically at odds as well. For instance, in his own primer on globalization, Anthony McGrew assumes that the claims to "global society" are uncontroversially real, seeking to introduce the topic only by discussing the conflicting explanations for this reality given by major voices in the field. He does not mention the fact, but his discussion reveals a paradox (McGrew 1996). His own argument is representative of only one of two major methodologies – which can be found throughout globalization discourse – that emerge as perfect dialectical opposites. A seesawing between the multiple and the unitary is highlighted in both, but the two elements play very different roles in each. On the one hand, the proponents of the view of an already achieved "global village" (McGrew's position combines the second and third variants above) often tend to see a multiplicity, randomness, and disconnectedness at the heart of an overall, fortuitous unity portrayed as the result of a progressive telos. By contrast, some of the critics of globalization – both those skeptical of its desirability and those doubtful of its presence – see behind "globalization" an underlying, comprehensive set of motives and related processes working on behalf of limited and localized interests: a symmetrically inverted position. Theirs is a *total* explanation based on the repetition of patterns of power-brokering from capitalism's past, whereas the former's is, as a matter of taste and principle, individual, separable, and "federal," if you will, at the same time that it resists the suggestion of familiarity.

The concept of "totality" employed by some critics of globalization theory is reminiscent of that theory, but, again, inverts it. It does not merely stipulate a unity, but suggests that any contingent or local problem is only clearly seen as being conditioned by its place in a total relationship of objects and events, all governed by a dominant logic. So, for example, the idea presented by a globalization enthusiast like McGrew that Immanuel Wallerstein, James Rosenau, and Robert Gilpin pose incompatible views on globalization because Wallerstein emphasizes historical capitalism, Rosenau the shift from industrial to postindustrial order, and Gilpin the power and legitimacy of a hegemonic liberal state would, from the vantage point of totality, be a crude way of seeing the matter. A theory that conceives of society as a totality would tend not to separate the economic, the political, the social, and the aesthetic in this way. These modes of societal interaction all devolve from interests and material conditionings such that, say, the preferred goals of historical capitalism could be said to *demand* at a certain point precisely a "hegemonic liberal state" to oversee its concerns, managing the vast division of labor that involves moving basic industry to the Third World while drawing on the highly trained citizens of the wealthier countries to set up information- and service-based businesses (the "postindustrial" ones). Capitalism is the logic in each phase of this operation, and there are not three explanations, but one.

In all of its variants, globalization theory presumes a knowledge of the following key terms.

- *Modernity* – apart from suggesting widely available technologies associated with "modern life" (televisions, cars, high-rises, computers), modernity more generally refers to a cast of mind, an attitude, and an approach to problems as much as to a period. Modernity begins with the Enlightenment and never ends (we are still in "modernity"). It centrally involves the idea of the "new," the break, the departure. Earlier, intellectuals (church clerics, for example) tended to base their arguments on Aristotle, Scripture, or the like. In modernity, legitimacy and authority are no longer based on principles derived from the past. Rather in modernity, the questioner (of law, of right, of religion, of truth) offers his/her own justification. Modernity means to create one's own normativity out of oneself.

- *The West* – a historical rather than a geographical construct. It means developed, industrialized, urbanized, capitalist, secular, and modern. Any society that shares these features is usually thought of as existing in the orbit of the "West". Derived originally from the division of the Roman Empire, and later by the division of the Christian churches in the eleventh century, it took on a new, ideological, coloring in the era of the Crusades, when the "Orient" (which referred at first only to Islam) was then allowed to stand in for everything east of it as well (China, India, Persia, and so on). In the Cold War, a new binary opposition arose using the terms "East" and "West" with a slightly altered (but fundamentally similar) geopolitical significance (Lazarus 1991, 2002; Coronil 1997; Said 1993).

- *Space/Place* – the significance of the turn to space/place in globalization theory lies, first of all, in the overcoming of temporality. Time is supplanted by Space in a worldview that: a) perceives the conflicts of history as being decisively decided in favor of one of the warring parties; or (for exactly opposite reasons): b) allergically recoils from the Hegelian notion of a progressive telos to history, and is therefore drawn methodologically to a synchronic analysis, expressed in metaphors of spatiality (we identified these opposed, but complementary, features of globalization theory above in the terms "neoliberalism" and "post-structuralism"). In harmony with the assumption that globalization is an irrepressible unfolding, the logical issue is no longer what will happen, but when it will extend itself over a vast but finite territory. The optic logically shifts from pace to scale, and from the chronometric to the cartographic. As a matter of theory, the dual expression "space/place" means to suggest that a struggle over value is embedded in the way one thinks about spatiality (Sassen 1998). "Space" is more abstract and ubiquitous: it connotes capital, history, and activity, and gestures towards the meaningless of distance in a world of instantaneous communication and "virtuality"; "place" connotes, by contrast, the kernel or center of one's memory and experience – a dwelling, a familiar park or city street, one's family or community. An ambiguity of value is obviously contained in the pairing, since the former is both bloodless and forward-looking while the latter is both personally vital and static.

- *Cosmopolitanism* – colloquially associated with broad fellow-feeling, world-travel, openness to cultural otherness, and so on, cosmopolitanism discursively accompanies globalization as the political ethic of the humanities intellectual. It both describes and endorses (endorses *as* it describes) the creation of a singularity out of newness, a blending and merging of differences becoming one entity. Furthermore, it stipulates a theory of world government and world citizenship in which the term's cultural meaning is carried over to its political one. In that sense, it is distinct from internationalism, which sets out to establish a global network of respect and cooperation based on differences of polity as well as culture. Cosmopolitanism sprouts from an already existing culture of intellectuals and middle-class travelers, researchers, and businessmen. Internationalism, on the other hand – although based no less than cosmopolitanism on the facts of global interpenetration, the homogenization brought about by capitalist mass culture, and the cultural consequences of mass migration – is an ideology of the domestically restricted, the recently relocated, the exiled, and the temporarily weak (Hannerz 1990; Nussbaum 1996; Brennan 1997, 2002a).

- *Neoliberalism* – a position that became prominent in policy-making circles (and later in journalism and the academy) following the conservative electoral victories of Margaret Thatcher in Britain and Ronald Reagan in the United States. With the goal of dismantling the welfare state, neo-liberalism argues that an unrestrained market logic, freed from governmental constraints, will cure social ills and lead to general prosperity. As Pierre Bourdieu explains, it

> is not a discourse like others. Like psychiatric discourse in the asylum, as described by Erving Goffman, it is a 'strong discourse,' which is so strong and so hard to fight because it has behind it all the powers of a world of power relations which it helps to make as it is, in particular by orienting the economic choices of those who dominate economic relations and so adding its own – specifically symbolic – force to those power relations.

> (1998: 95)

It is a faith, rather than an analysis, which creates its own truth by imposing itself on the supposedly free agents of economic choice.

References

Abu-Lughod, Janet 1989. "On the Remaking of History: How to Reinvent the Past." *Remaking History*. Ed. Barbara Kruger and Phil Mariani. Seattle: Bay Press, 111-29.

Agamben, Giorgio 1993. *The Coming Community*. Trans. Michael Hardt. Minneapolis and London: University of Minnesota Press.

Amin, Samir 1976. *Unequal Development: An Essay on the Social Formations of Peripheral Capitalism*. New York: Monthly Review Press.

Amin, Samir, Giovanni Arrighi, Andre Gunder Frank, and Immanuel Wallerstein 1990. *Transforming the Revolution: Social Movements and the World-System*. New York: Monthly Review Press.

Appiah, Kwame Anthony 1991. "Is the Post- in Postmodernism the Post- in Postcolonial?" *Critical Inquiry* 17: 336–51.

Bauman, Zygmunt 1998. *Globalization: The Human Consequences*. New York: Columbia University Press.

Bentham, Jeremy 1995. *Colonies, Commerce, and Constitutional Law. "Rid yourselves of Ultramaria" and other Writings on Spain and Spanish America* [1822]. Ed. Philip Schofield. Oxford: Clarendon Press.

Bhagwati, Jagdish 2001. "Why Globalization is Good." *Items & Issues* 2.3–4: 7–8.

Blaut, J. M. 1993. *The Colonizer's Model of the World: Geographical Diffusionism and Eurocentric History*. New York and London: Guildford.

Bourdieu, Pierre 1998. *Acts of Resistance: Against the New Myths of Our Time*. Trans. Richard Nice. Oxford: Polity.

———2001. "Uniting to Better Dominate." *Items & Issues* 2.3–4: 1–6.

Braudel, Fernand 1992. "Economies in Space: The World Economies" and "By Way of a Conclusion: Past and Present." *Civilization and Capitalism: 15th–18th Century*. Vol. III of *The Perspective of the World*. [1979]. Trans. Siân Reynolds. Berkeley and Los Angeles: University of California Press, 21–45, 617–32.

Brennan, Timothy 1997. *At Home in the World: Cosmopolitanism Now*. Cambridge: Harvard University Press.

———2002a. "Cosmo-Theory." *South Atlantic Quarterly* 100.3: 657–89.

———2002b. "Postcolonial Studies between the European Wars: An Intellectual History." *Marxism, Modernity and Postcolonial Studies*. Ed. Crystal Bartolovich and Neil Lazarus. Cambridge: Cambridge University Press, 185–203.

Coronil, Fernando 1997. *The Magical State: Nature, Money, and Modernity in Venezuela*. Chicago: University of Chicago Press.

Cox, Oliver C. 1959. *The Foundations of Capitalism*. New York: Philosophical Library.

———1962. *Capitalism and American Leadership*. New York: Philosophical Library.

———1964. *Capitalism as a System*. New York: Monthly Review Press.

Dirlik, Arif 1997. *The Postcolonial Aura: Third World Criticism in the Age of Global Capitalism*. Boulder: Westview Press.

Falk, Richard, and Andrew Strauss 2000. "On the Creation of a Global People's Assembly: Legitimacy and Power of Popular Sovereignty." *Stanford Journal of International Law* 36.2: 191–219.

———2001. "Toward a Global Parliament." *Foreign Affairs* 80.1: 212–20.

Fanon, Frantz 1968. *The Wretched of the Earth* [1961]. Trans. Constance Farrington. New York: Grove Press.

Foster, John Bellamy 2002. "The Rediscovery of Imperialism." *Monthly Review* 54.6: 1–16.

Frank, Andre Gunder 1967. *Capitalism and Underdevelopment in Latin America*. New York: Monthly Review Press.

Friedman, Thomas 1999. *The Lexus and the Olive Tree*. New York: Farrar, Strauss and Giroux.

Giddens, Anthony 1991. "The Contours of High Modernity." *Modernity and Self-Identity: Self and Society in the Late Modern Age*. Cambridge: Polity, 10–34.

Graham, R. B. Cunninghame 1896. *The Imperial Kailyard: Being a Biting Satire on English Colonisation*. London: the Twentieth Century Press.

Guattari, Félix, and Toni Negri 1990. *Communists Like Us: New Spaces of Liberty, New Lines of Alliance* [1985]. Trans. Michael Ryan. New York: Semiotext(e).

Guevara, Ernesto "Che" 1969. *Guerrilla Warfare* [1961]. Trans. J. P. Morray, New York: Vintage Books.

Hannerz, Ulf 1990. "Cosmopolitans and Locals in World Culture." *Global Culture: Nationalism, Globalization and Modernity*. Ed. Mike Featherstone. London: Sage, 237–51.

Hobson, J. A. 1902. *Imperialism: A Study*. London: Allen & Unwin.

Ho Chi Minh 1967. *On Revolution: Selected Writings, 1920–66*. Ed. Bernard B. Fall. London: Pall Mall Press.

Hodgson, Marshall 1974. *The Venture of Islam: Conscience and History in a World Civilization*. Chicago: University of Chicago Press.

Huggan, Graham 2001. *The Postcolonial Exotic: Marketing the Margins*. London and New York: Routledge.

Kant, Immanuel 1963. "Perpetual Peace" [1795]. *On History*. Trans. and ed. Lewis White Beck. New York: Bobbs-Merrill, 85–135.

———1991. "Idea for a Universal History with a Cosmopolitan Standpoint" [1784]. *Political Writings*. Trans. H. B. Nisbet. Ed. Hans Reiss. Cambridge: Cambridge University Press, 41–53.

Kautsky, Karl 1970. "Ultra-imperialism" [1914]. *New Left Review* 59: 41–46.

Kiernan, V. G. 1969. *The Lords of Human Kind: European Attitudes to the Outside World in the Imperial Age*. London: Weidenfeld and Nicolson.

Kissinger, Henry 1994. *Diplomacy*. New York: Simon & Schuster.

Kristeva, Julia 1993. *Nations Without Nationalism*. Trans. Leon S. Roudiez. New York: Columbia University Press.

Krugman, Paul R. 1997. *The Age of Diminished Expectations: US Economic Policy in the 1990s*. Cambridge, MA: MIT Press.

Lapham, Lewis H. 1998. *The Agony of Mammon: The Imperial World Economy Explains Itself to the Membership in Davos, Switzerland*. London and New York: Verso.

Las Casas, Bartolomé de 1992. *A Short Account of the Destruction of the Indies* [1542]. Trans. and ed. Nigel Griffin. London: Penguin.

Lazarus, Neil 1991. "Doubting the New World Order: Marxism and Postmodernist Social Theory." *differences* 3.3: 94–138.

———2002. "The Fetish of 'the West' in Postcolonial Theory." *Marxism, Modernity and Postcolonial Studies*. Ed. Crystal Bartolovich and Neil Lazarus. Cambridge: Cambridge University Press, 43–64.

Lenin, Vladimir 1975. *Imperialism: The Highest Stage of Capitalism* [1917]. London: New Left Books.

Lumumba, Patrice 1972. *Lumumba Speaks: The Speeches and Writings of Patrice Lumumba*. Trans. Helen R. Lane. Ed. Jean van Lierde. Boston: Little, Brown.

Mao Zedong 1953. *On Contradiction*. New York: International Publishers.

Marx, Karl 1976. *Capital: A Critique of Political Economy* [1894]. Vol. III. Trans. David Fernbach. London: Penguin.

Marx, Karl, and Frederick Engels 1988. *Manifesto of the Communist Party* [1848]. Beijing: Foreign Languages Press.

McGrew, Anthony 1996. "A Global Society?" *Modernity: An Introduction to Modern Societies*. Ed. Stuart Hall, David Held, Don Hubert, and Kenneth Thompson. Oxford: Blackwell, 466–503.

McNeill, William 1963. *The Rise of the West: A History of the Human Community*. Chicago and London: University of Chicago Press.

Melville, Herman 1988. *Moby-Dick* [1851]. Oxford and New York: Oxford University Press.

Montaigne, Michel de 1991. "On the Cannibals" [1578–80]. *The Complete Essays*. Trans. and ed. M. A. Screech. London: Penguin, 228–41.

Morris, William 1901. *News from Nowhere: Or, An Epoch of Rest, Being some Chapters from a Utopian Romance*. New York: Longmans, Green.

Nehru, Jawaharlal 1946. *The Discovery of India*. New York: The John Day Company.

Nussbaum, Martha C., with respondents from 1996. *For Love of Country: Debating the Limits of Patriotism*. Ed. Joshua Cohen. Boston: Beacon.

Parry, Benita 2002. "Liberation Theory: Variations on Themes of Marxism and Modernity." *Marxism, Modernity and Postcolonial Studies*. Ed. Crystal Bartolovich and Neil Lazarus. Cambridge: Cambridge University Press, 125–49.

Raleigh, Walter, Sir 1997. *The Discoverie of the Large, Rich, and Bewtiful Empyre of Guiana* [1596]. Ed. Neil L. Whitehead. Manchester: Manchester University Press.

Raynal, Abbé (Guillaume-Thomas-François) 1991. *Histoire philosophique et politique des établissements et du commerce des européens dans les deux Indes* [1667]. Oxford: Voltaire Foundation at the Taylor Institution.

Rodney, Walter 1972. *How Europe Underdeveloped Africa*. London: Bogle L'Ouverture Publications; Dar-es-Salaam: Tanzania Publishing House.

Said, Edward W. 1993. *Culture and Imperialism*. New York: Alfred A. Knopf.

Santos, Theotonio dos 1978. *Imperialismo y dependencia*. Mexico City: Ediciones Era.

Sassen, Saskia 1998. *Globalization and Its Discontents*. New York: New Press.

Sklair, Leslie 1991. *Sociology of the Global System*. Brighton: Harvester Wheatsheaf.

Smith, Adam 1910. *The Wealth of Nations* [1776]. 2 vols. Ed. E. R. A. Seligman. London: Dent.

Soros, George 1998. *The Crisis of Global Capitalism: Open Society Endangered*. New York: Public Affairs.

Stavrianos, Leften Stavros 1981. *Global Rift: The Third World Comes of Age*. New York: Morrow.

Toulmin, Stephen Edelston 1990. *Cosmopolis: The Hidden Agenda of Modernity*. New York: Free Press.

Valladao, Alfredo 1998. *The Twenty-First Century Will be American*. Trans. John Howe. London and New York: Verso.

Voltaire 2001. *Candide: ou l'optimisme* [1759]. Paris: Maisonneuve et Larose.

Wallerstein, Immanuel 1974. *The Modern World-System: Capitalist Agriculture and the Origins of the European World Economy in the Sixteenth Century*. New York: Academic Press.

——1984. *The Politics of the World Economy: The States, the Movements, and the Civilizations*. Cambridge and New York: Cambridge University Press.

Wolf, Eric R. 1982. *Europe and the People Without History*. Berkeley: University of California Press.

Chapter 77

Shaobo Xie

IS THE WORLD DECENTRED?

A postcolonial perspective on globalization

One of the central conundrums that Shaobo Xie explores is how it is possible for globalization to simultaneously decentre and recentre cultures, technologies and economies. These opposing forces appear to generate different understandings of globalization, be they celebratory or critical, capitalist or Marxist. Xie's extract is largely critical of globalization, suggesting that it is another name for the capitalist Americanization of the world, so this structural conundrum needs to be accounted for to enable further investigation into how globalization functions in an oppressive or at the least problematical sense. Xie, who has published research on the cultural politics of resistance as well as neo-Marxism, globalization, and Chinese and Chinese-Canadian cultures, argues that such conundrums function dialectically, alongside others, such as the fact that globalization simultaneously homogenizes diverse peoples and celebrates, if not encourages, differences. As a dialectic, then, such apparently contradictory processes necessarily lead to a desired or planned outcome, which Xie argues can be revealed by adding to the equation Raymond Williams' concept of the "dominant aspect", here, the overall effect of recentring upon American capitalist values, ownership or simply profit. The dialectical approach also has the advantage of accounting for competing "grand narratives" concerning globalization, such as Fukuyama's "end of history" narrative, or Hardt and Negri's notion of the "end of capitalism." Xie argues that Hardt and Negri, while offering a vision beyond capitalism, fail to account for globalization's Americanization, and furthermore, their critique of postcolonialism as an ineffective discourse, is equally problematic. To prove that globalization is doing something unique (i.e., a contemporary version of American imperialism), Xie turns to China, examining cultural differences and a historical turning away from global influence. Xie also looks at the outsourcing of US manufacturing, global warfare designed to protect fossil fuel energy sources (in this case, the second Gulf War with Iraq), and cultural dominance (films, food, lifestyles), drawing upon Marxist analyses by critics such as Noam Chomsky and Fredric Jameson. Returning to the critique of postcolonialism, Xie argues that it is an important methodology for uncovering the true situation of affairs concerning globalization's postmodern imperialism (one which is dispersed, but centralizing; as much cultural as material, and so on). Postcolonialism is presented as a "counter-hegemonic" discourse which does engage in the material conditions of globalization, not just intellectual debate among academics in the developed world. Tied-in with a fairly standard Marxist account of global economics, these methodological approaches lead to Xie's thesis that "what is being globalized today in the day of global capitalism is capitalism itself." But if this postmodern imperialism is also a neo-colonialism, then it becomes imperative for postcolonialism "to theorize and mobilize new forms of decolonizing agency." In other words, postcolonialism also needs to adopt the strategies of globalization to counter neo-colonialism; for example, through a "mobile" criticism that can function in multiple ways, across multiple sites, such as the heterogenous global anti-capitalism movements. Xie also argues that postcolonialism needs to return more markedly to its Marxist roots, in part because of the rise of a new global proletariat due to the overseas outsourcing of Western manufacturing. Finally, Xie argues that diverse counter-hegemonic movements should join forces to create "an historic bloc", one which can mobilize and resist capitalism in all its forms.

THE POST-COLD WAR WORLD has witnessed many grand narratives of what is called New World Order or global capitalism emerging from both the Right and Left camps. From the Far Right, for example, Francis Fukuyama stands out as the most devout apologist of late capitalism, his Hegelian declaration of Americanist capitalism as the end-stage of history powerfully counterpoised on the far Left by Michael Hardt and Antonio Negri's Hegelian mapping of postmodern capitalism. In some important aspects, these two attempts to define the age of global capitalism are quite comparable, though their parallels ultimately reveal more of their political and ideological divergences than similarities. For, as Étienne Balibar remarks, both Hardt and Negri's *Empire* and Fukuyama's *The End of History and the Last Man* share "a kojevian notion of global market as post-history,"[1] though Hardt and Negri apocalyptically prophesy a global revolution beyond global capitalism. Hardt, Negri and Fukuyama fervently celebrate Americanism, and quote Hegel as an apologist of Americanism. But here their similarities end. For while Hardt and Negri's *Empire* has been widely acclaimed as a postmodern version of the Communist Manifesto, Fukuyama's *The End of History* can best be read as a postmodern manifesto of capitalism.

Fukuyama argues that history has completed its course of evolution in the age of global capitalism — has reached its end-stage with the triumph throughout the world of the political system of democracy. The universal triumph of democracy ensures the universal institution of democratic societies characterized by universal and equal recognition, which satisfies the individuals' desire for recognition as equals. Fukuyama's theory of history is built on two premises: economic motivation (profit and efficiency) and *thymos* (desire for recognition), or on two logics: the logic of modern natural sciences which leads to capitalism, and the logic of desire for recognition which leads to democracy. As a champion of capitalist democracy and an advocate of Americanism, Fukuyama, with his declaration of the end of history, aims at subsuming the world's different nations and societies under the singular orbit of American capitalism, defending free-market and capitalist democracy as the end-stage of human historical evolution.

In their magisterial *Empire*, Hardt and Negri optimistically forecast an impending collapse of capitalism while fully acknowledging the global order of capital as irresistible and irreversible, "permeat[ing] every pore of our social lives, the most intimate of spheres."[2] Their vision is a supersession of both the devout and unshakably triumphalist celebrations of capitalism from the Right and the bleakly pessimistic diagnoses of capitalism from the Left. From the vantage of a Hegelian–Marxian dialectic, they perceive subversive potential revolutionary agency in the fragmented, hybridized, mobile, violated multitude who prove to be irreconcilably antagonistic and rebellious to Empire. Indeed, *Empire* brings good news to all those powerless who are struggling for bodily survival in the global system of capital, for, in its geopolitical mapping of a New Global Order, the passage to Empire is also a passage to Revolution. In this sense, *Empire* stands as an inspiring counterbalance to *The End of History*. However, despite its profound insights and incisive analysis of the system as a whole, Hardt's and Negri's totalizing narrative does not fail to provoke serious doubts and questions. In their theorizing, for example, Empire or global capitalism is "a *decentered* and *deterritorializing* apparatus of rule," which "establishes no territorial center of power."[3] While unabashedly celebrating Americanism, they bluntly defend the USA against charges of imperialism:

> *The United States does not, and indeed no nation-state can today, form the center of an imperialist project.* Imperialism is over. No nation will be world leader in the way modern European nations were. (xiv)

Equally dubious is their argument that postcolonialist theory and criticism are not only "entirely insufficient for theorizing contemporary global power" (146) but also coincide with and reinforce new Empire's strategies of rule, on the grounds that both postcolonialism and Empire celebrate and deploy difference in the form of hybridity, circulation, mobility, diversity, and mixture. Capitalism feeds on difference; every difference opens an opportunity; postcolonialism helps capitalism because it celebrates difference.[4]

It is these conclusions that I find unacceptable and contestable. For, if imperialism is a story of the past, then how is one to account for all the recent happenings in the Gulf and Africa? How is one to define the actual processes of globalization or Americanization? If global capitalism establishes or endorses no territorial centre of power, then where do transnational corporations come from and who reaps the lion's share of market profit? No nation forms the centre of an imperialist project?! Then how did the latest war on Iraq happen? Has capitalism changed apparatuses of rule? Is global capitalism breeding difference or levelling difference? Does post-Fordism or Toyotism really prove postcolonialism deficient and complicitous in reinforcing capitalism? Do global capitalism and postcolonialism embrace or celebrate the same kind of difference? These are the questions I propose to address in investigating the issues of globalization, imperialism, neocolonization, and postcolonial resistance to global capitalism. I will show that, although technological revolution, transnational corporations and global restructuring of capitalism have made the world increasingly interdependent and interconnected, radically altering our concepts of time, space, politics, and relations, this has in no way changed the fundamental fact that the West still poses or imposes itself as the centre of the world. The mythology of a world already de-centred politically, culturally, economically, and ideologically papers over the lived global power-relations between the developed West and the underdeveloped Rest. On the one hand, multinational capital with its hegemonic ideology and technology is globally spreading and celebrating Americanism in economics, political institutions, and cultural productions, reinforcing the five-hundred-years-old colonial capitalism that established the West as the world's geopolitical, economic, cultural, and intellectual centre. On the other hand, the underdeveloped and premodernized of the earth, having hardly broken with old eurocentrism, are all of a sudden sucked into the processes of globalization, unabashedly and unhesitatingly celebrating American life-styles, fashions, values, and conveniences, all glorified and romanticized by Hollywood films. To back up my position on global capitalism's strategic differentiation, I will cite examples from contemporary China. Lastly, I will call for a relaunching of the postcolonial critique of colonialism and imperialism in deconstructing new figurations of West-centrism in the age of globalism.

There have been many attempts to define globalization. Some critics describe it as an interconnected and interdependent networked world which enables "proliferation of the logic of capital [. . . and] the spread of democracy in information, finance, investing, and the diffusion of technology";[5] others see it as an integrated international system which spreads "free-market capitalism to virtually every country in the world."[6] In most cases, however, the term is used in ways that seem surprisingly to neglect the question of agency: that is, who globalizes what? Let us take a look at the verb 'to globalize': according to *Random House Webster's College Dictionary*, 'to globalize' means "to extend to other or all parts of the globe; to make worldwide."[7] If the objects to be extended to the whole globe are markets, goods, capital, technology, spheres of influence, ideas, values, and life-styles, then the term 'globalization' applies only to historical imperialist nation-states or the contemporary West – more precisely, the USA. Non-Western countries, namely, were and are still incapable of such extension, even though some of them might wish to acquire these powers. Perhaps a comparison of 'globalization' with terms such as 'modernization' or 'democratization' will help illustrate this point. The latter terms also imply a question of agency, but they apply to almost all countries including developing or previous Third World countries, for all people have embarked on modernization projects, regardless of the result, and many non-Western countries claim to have made efforts to democratize their societies. China, for example, is obviously perceived by the West as an undemocratic society, but the Chinese regimes at different times in modern history have always proclaimed that they uphold and practise democracy, except that theirs is different from that of the West. In 1966, Mao Zedong even challenged the whole world to democratize social life to the fullest by means of cultural revolution. However, never in history has China or any other Third World country been the subject of globalization. In the time of the Ming Dynasty, before Columbus discovered America in 1492, China was capable of building huge ships, far larger than any being built in the rest of the world, but instead of continuing what they had started by sending out fleets and people to such far-flung areas as the east coast of Africa to 'globalize' Chinese culture, sociopolitical institutions, and Confucianism, it burned hundreds of its ocean-going ships, the major technological means of globalization at that time, for what the Chinese were centrally concerned with at that time was how to perpetuate the inherited imperial system with its Confucianist fabric of socio-economic life and political institutions within its borders instead of beyond. At present the Chinese government, politicians, technocrats, and capitalists all wield the rhetoric of globalization to serve their respective interests, although often at the cost of ordinary people, but they never consider themselves economically and technologically powerful enough to globalize or impose their ideas, values, life-styles and cultural products upon the rest of the world. Instead, they call upon the Chinese people to "merge rails with the world or the global system"; so who globalizes what? The answer to this question is closely related to the question of the centre/periphery structure of the world today.

In *Globalization Unmasked*, James Petras and Henry Veltmeyer provide a rich, rigorous and illuminating exploration of the ideology of globalization and the free-market imperialism it defends and promotes. While capital and goods flow across national boundaries, Petras and Veltmeyer point out, they nonetheless remain centred in specific nation-states.[8] In other words,

> the expansion of capital flows and commodity trade via unequal relations in the contemporary period is a continuation of the imperialist relations of the past. The subjects of globalization – the principal traders, investors and renters of services–have interests antagonistic to those of the objects of their policies – the workers, peasants, and national producers in the targeted countries [. . .] the major economic units are owned and operated in large part by stockholders in the imperial countries; and profits, royalties, rents and interest payments flow upward and outward in an asymmetrical fashion [. . . .] the imperial countries wield disproportionate or decisive influence. [. . .] Hence the concept of imperialism fits the realities much better than globalization. (29–30)

To Petras and Veltmeyer, globalization is both an empirical reality and an ideology which serves to gloss over inequality between imperial centres and dominated peripheries. In this sense, globalization is a euphemistic respelling of imperialism. In their view, globalization legitimates "the domination and exploitation by imperial states and multinational corporations and banks of less-developed states and labouring classes" (30). Global capitalism has transformed whole areas of Asia, Africa and Latin America into labour-intensive manufacturing bases controlled by "an elite of high-paid executives in the imperial *centres*" (41; my emphasis). This is a continuation of the nineteenth- and early-twentieth-century "international division of labour, between mining and agricultural workers in the Third World and manufacturing and service workers in the imperial countries" (41). As for international efforts to maintain peace, stability, and prosperity, the flow of intervention has always been

> unidirectional, from the imperial *centres* to the dominated countries. There is no mutual penetration of military commands, but only the extension of military missions from the imperial *centre* to the dominated countries. (31; my emphases)

The biggest imperial centre is none other than the US A, whose economic power increasingly controls the world. According to a recent survey, the US accounts for 244 of the 500 biggest companies in the world, followed by Japan with 46, and Germany with 23.[9] Of the largest 25 firms whose capitalization exceeds $86 billion (US) over 70 percent are US; of the top 100 companies, 61 percent are US. The entire Third World accounts for 26 of the 500 leading companies – only five percent. Today, the USA champions, argues Tariq Ali in his timely book *The Clash of Fundamentalisms,* "the most powerful imperialism [. . .] Its defence budget for 2000 was $267.2 billion, an amount greater than the combined military budgets of China, Russia, India, Germany and France"; it "has a military presence in 100 countries."[10] For the year 2002, US defence spending was $300 billion; even the post-9/11 increment in US defence spending proposed by the Bush administration is larger than the *entire* defence budget of Britain.[11] All this is part of imperialist logic. According to Thomas Friedman, one of the most fervent apologists of Americanism,

> The hidden hand of the market will never work without a hidden fist. McDonald's cannot flourish without McDonnell–Douglas, the designer of the F-15, and the hidden fist that keeps the world safe for Silicon Valley's technology is called the United States Army, Air Force, Navy and Marine Corps.[12]

The latest American war on Iraq is the best proof of this logic. The official reasons the Bush administration gave for the war were to destroy weapons of massive destruction and to start a model of democracy in the Middle East, while everyone knows their real purpose was to control the world's largest source of oil – the Persian Gulf.

The USA dominates the world economically, politically, militarily, and culturally. It is from some of the staunchest advocates of Americanism that we learn the bluntest truths about globalization. Fukuyama, for example, wrote recently that, in creating a stronger and more autonomous international trade and investment regime, "Americans benefit strongly from and indeed dominate the global economy, which is why globalization bears a 'made in USA' label."[13] Henry Kissinger admits that "globalisation is really another name for the dominant role of the United States."[14] Robert Cooper, a former advisor to Tony Blair, recently called for a "new imperialism [. . .] which, like all imperialism, aims to bring order and organization but which rests today on the voluntary principle."[15] In *The War Over Iraq,* William Kristol and Lawrence F. Kaplan write:

> The mission begins in Baghdad, but it does not end there. [. . .] We stand at the cusp of a new historical era. [. . .] This is a decisive moment. [. . .] It is so clearly about more than Iraq. It's about more even than the future of the Middle East and the war on terror. It is about what sort of role the United States intends to play in the twenty-first century.[16]

Noam Chomsky is certainly correct in insisting that "There can't be a War on Terror. It's a logical impossibility. The US is one of the leading terrorist states in the world."[17]

All these facts persuade us that the US government and American transnational capitalists and big firms are major agents of globalization, while all Third World countries are the wretched objects of that same process, and that the USA is imposing itself and actually operating as the new centre of the globe. The new global system is not only a centred empire, but it is more global and more omnipresent than ever. The White House, the American transnational capitalists, big firms, and state intellectuals all aim to build a truly global empire: an American Empire, reducing the rest of the world to the status of its provinces or manufacturing bases and markets. Contrary to the rhetoric of global balances between the different nation-states and between nation-states and world markets, we are confronted with the gaping reality of global imbalances between 'core' (First World) and 'periphery' (Third World) nations in trade, finance, and the flow of information and technology. The binary relations between parts of the new global empire are increasingly intensified instead of attenuated.[18] This is true not only economically and technologically, but also culturally. As Fredric Jameson remarks, in this day of global capitalism, the distinction between economics and culture has disappeared, for "commodification today is also an aestheticization" and "the entertainment business itself [is] one of the greatest and most profitable exports of the United States (along with weapons and food)."[19] Jameson sees globalization as synonymous with americanization:

> The standardization of world culture, with local popular or traditional forms driven out or dumped down to make way for American television, American music, food, clothes and films, has been seen by many as the very heart of globalization.[20]

In Europe, of the top 100 films in 1993, 88 were American, with France's *Les Visiteurs* as the highest-ranking foreign feature film on place 27. Shows such as *Beverly Hills 90210, Santa Barbara, Rescue 911* and *Dynasty* ranked among the top television shows in the Czech Republic, Poland and Russia.[21] In some African countries, 90 percent of all films shown are Hollywood-made. In South America as in the rest of the Third World, cultural imperialism manipulates and westernizes the psychology of the indigenous populations, controlling their psyche to ensure fertile markets for Western commodities. The glorification of Western life-styles by Hollywood films and other Western mass media has "made people all over South America turn against their own cultural roots and being indigenous is now generally looked on as old-fashioned and inferior."[22] The Chinese case is just as gloomy. In 1995, "more than 70 domestic Chinese films were shelved without any chance of being shown in theaters" because of the invasion of Hollywood and and the rental chain Blockbusters, which have caused a general crisis of home-grown films. In 1994, ten imported films, including *The Fugitive, The Lion King, Speed, Forrest Gump* and *True Lies*, occupied 70 percent of the Chinese market, leaving the remaining thirty percent for a hundred-odd, home-grown feature films.[23] McDonald's, Pizza Hut, KFC, Coca-Cola, Starbucks, rock 'n' roll, Hollywood films, and Blockbuster are emerging in increasing numbers in China. Every college student in China has some American Dream structuring his or her life, everyone approves of globalization as a passage to Americanization, and everyone, old or young, wants to possess some American goods to "smell [. . .] America," to borrow a term from Arjun Appadurai.[24] To Appadurai's list of things created by electronic media and migration, I should add an 'imagined America' in China and other developing and Third World countries. My own frequent returns to China over the past fifteen years have acquainted me with the widely shared romanticized West or America – a land of freedom, equality, democracy, consumerist pleasures and conveniences, and "cool" life-styles. Such an imagined modernity or romanticized 'elsewhere', I am afraid, is something mainly created by Western or American culture machines.

Undeniably, the world today is a global empire with the USA and all its economic, political, cultural and ideological apparatuses of rule at the centre and at the top. But to make this argument is not to ignore the fact that the world in some aspects is becoming increasingly decentred as well. As previously mentioned, digital telecommunications have thoroughly deterritorialized and decentred our geographical sense of the globe; electronic media and migrations have created vast numbers of borderless, transnational communities: diasporic, mobile and uncontrollable. Global flows of commodity, information, finance, and the world-wide diffusion of technology have made metropolises lose their previous centrality.[25] Perhaps a more enabling way of theorizing the world today is to acknowledge decentering and recentering as two dialectically related aspects of globalization, in parallel with the homogenization and differentiation that define the globalized world today. And in order to render a more objective geopolitical mapping of the contemporary world, one needs to introduce the term 'dominant' which Raymond Williams uses in examining the multiplicity of writing and different modes of culture.[26] Given that both decentering and recentering are characteristics of globalization, I argue that recentering is the dominant aspect. What 'centre' signifies, according to dictionary definitions, is an organizing or structuring principle, universal norm or source of authority, influence, decision or action. In this sense, the USA indisputably acts as the center or 'epicentre' from which capitalist imperialism dominates the world "via freedom of the market."[27] The spectre of Americanism is looming on every individual's and nation's horizon. What Edward Said wrote ten years ago can still serve as a beacon to us: "[We Americans] are number one, we are bound to lead, we stand for freedom and order, and so on. No American has been immune from this structure of feeling."[28] The way the USA runs the world via institutions such as IMF, GAAT, and WTO, the way it overlords the UN, the way American cultural imperialism embodied by Hollywood invades every part of the world, means that Imperial America thinks of itself as "the source of the world's significant action and life"; in its imperialist view, "the outlying regions of the world have no life, history, or culture to speak of, no independence or integrity worth representing without the West."[29]

If the world remains centred and filled with stories of imperialism in our day, then one would have to agree that, in contrast to Hardt and Negri's verdict, postcolonialism is not only good for reading history, it is just as useful for reading the present. There have been objections to the terms 'postcolonial' and 'postcolonialism', which were launched from a different perspective from Hardt and Negri's. Critics such as Ella Shohat, Anne McClintock, and Arif Dirlik distrust the terms for papering over contemporary global power-relations and for their suspected premature celebration of the pastness of colonialism. I have negotiated with these critics elsewhere.[30] In the light of the past two decades' textual practices categorized under the rubric of postcolonialism, the term 'postcolonialism' does not point to the demise or pastness of coloniality. Actually, it more often than not alerts us to a colonial past that remains to be investigated and interrogated, and to a postmodern wave of imperialism. Postcolonialism owes its emergence to neocolonialism, which is a rejuvenation of older European colonialism through West-centered transnational corporations and hegemonizing Western economy, technology, and ideology. Postcoloniality points to a world that has done with direct-rule colonies, but remains caught up in the neo-imperial global system of capitalism.[31] Postcolonialism as a counter-hegemonic discourse in the day of global capitalism

> admits an indebtedness to the past and a responsibility to the future; it [. . .] clear[s] the ground of older colonialism in order to resist neocolonialism. It is more formal and symbolic yet more thorough and subversive in addressing colonialism than anticolonialism has been.[32]

As Robert Young has recently pointed out, postcolonialism examines "the material and epistemological conditions of [the] postcoloniality and seeks to combat the continuing, often covert, operation of an imperialist system of economic, political and cultural domination."[33] Postcolonialism should in no way be taken as an "endorsement of the new world system," for it is a "radical response to its conditions."[34] True, postcolonialism, like any other critical enterprise whose name ends in '-ism', tends to point to a homogenous ideology, theoretical perspective, and political agenda; as such its name contradicts its divergent actual critical practices. However, despite its discursive and theoretical multiplicity and heterogeneity, all critical practices that go under the name of postcolonialism, one can argue, are urged (by an anxiety to undo various colonial structures of power) to deconstruct the West as the normative centre of the world, to move beyond West-centred historicism, beyond imperial binary structures of self/Other and centre/periphery, and ultimately beyond any form of imperialism.

Hardt's and Negri's objections to postcolonialism are based on the argument that it, ironically, ends up coinciding with and reinforcing the new Empire's strategies of rule, for both postcolonialism and global capitalism celebrate and deploy protean difference in the varied forms of hybridity, mobility, diversity and mixture. This indeed has the appeal of a strong argument to those who take difference not as an historically and politically situated experience, but as a Kantian entity. However, a closer look at the political, discursive motivations behind the strategies of differentiation deployed by global capitalism and postcolonialism respectively will show that the position of Hardt and Negri derives from an inadequate understanding of the concept of difference, and from a misunderstanding of the postcolonial deployment of difference. Postcolonialism's vindication of difference is to assert the equality of being on behalf of the previous and present colonized. For non-Western peoples to assert their equality of being is to confirm the West's colonization of the non-West and its imperial rule as unjust, illegitimate and condemnable. The West regarded the different Rest as inferior and backward, for its social organization, cultural life and aesthetic production did not conform or measure up to modern Western norms. The West's advanced science, technology and military might established the hegemony of its civilization, which perceived other civilizations as uncivilized and which achieved control over nations differently developed in science and technology.[35] Western civilization or modernity proclaims and propagates itself as universal, although its alleged universality ultimately indicates a masquerading particularity. History richly documents how the victor or colonizer has imposed, in the guise of 'universal values', culture-specific institutions, standards, and modes of production and representation upon the defeated or colonized, subsuming and homogenizing differential cultures and values within a singular orbit of normality. This is how imperialist hegemony asserts particularity in the name of universality. In investigating and interrogating colonialism and imperialism, postcolonialism must and does celebrate ethnic and cultural difference, deconstructing ideologies of universality. Only by legitimating and valorizing ethnic and racial difference, namely, can the dominated and marginalized peoples achieve recognition as equals and justify that equality, despite their insufficient degree of technological and infrastructural modernization.

The celebration and deployment of difference by multinational capitalism is an entirely different story. Global capitalism feeds on difference to create sameness at the other end. To say that capitalism feeds on difference is to say that capitalism grants areas, nation-states, and communities of different races, cultural practices and ethnic traditions uniform membership in the capitalist club, to subsume them under the global Empire of capital, and ultimately to integrate plural trajectories of modernity along a single route of development. When I talk about capitalism feeding on difference, I am referring to those concrete strategies and practices of customizing commodities to suit local preferences and tastes, of building Chevrolets, Toyotas, BMWs, Boeings, Airbuses, Toshiba lap-top computers and refrigerators, NECs, computer software, to meet local needs and likes, of fostering capitalists and technocrats with different racial features, wearing different ethnic costumes, and eating different ethnic foods, of creating an America-centred structure of feeling and commodity-fetishism in Nigeria, Ethiopia, Saudi Arabia, Tibet, Taiwan, Indonesia, Canada, Colombia, and the former Yugoslavia. True, postmodern differences also assume the form of mobile, deterritorialized, diasporic solidarities of experience, opinion, taste and pleasure, which are trans- or postnational in kind, uncontainable by nation-states and subversive to totalizing powers. But, if critics like Fredric Jameson and Wim Wenders are correct in arguing that capitalism in its global stage colonizes nature and the unconscious or the human psyche,[36] then should we not say that even those mobile diasporic, transnational communities risk living with cancelled or emasculated differences?

The point here is that capitalism feeds on difference and even breeds difference in varied forms, but it is all to serve its purpose of converting lands into territories of the global Empire, peoples into its appendages, cultures into commodities. Capital has to incorporate and reflect differences in order to "maintain its global position," and "in the end, the differences do not matter."[37] Nowadays so many CEOs or TNC representatives travel to China, where they learn to speak Chinese, observe Chinese table manners and rituals while having a business dinner with their local counterparts, and they even wear Chinese-style clothes. Capitalism, ever inventive, sees no humiliation in speaking indigenous languages so long as the overseas market is rewarding. It is expert in localizing its globality to disarm resistance. For example, when Coca Cola and Pepsi were first imported to China, few people liked them, for they taste so different from Chinese tea, which has been China's national soft drink for over two thousand years. Then transnational capitalists had Coca Cola and Pepsi transliterated into "*Kekou Kele*" and "*Baishi Kele*," which respectively mean in Chinese 'good taste and great joy' and 'all enjoyable'. Then they quickly became popular in China, because the Chinese set great store by sounds and names of things – what Western cultural critics call 'symbolic wish-fulfilment'. All such adaptations to a differential locality are, again, strategies of globalization invented to open the door to the Chinese market.

Over the past two decades, East and Southeast Asia have become manufacturing bases for all kinds of transnational corporations. Economic globalization drives Western firms to tap the lost-cost factors of production in developing countries. Saturating the Western stores and supermarkets are goods made in such places as China, Indonesia, Malaysia, Thailand, and Vietnam. But stories behind them are mostly unknown to their Western consumers. There are numerous factories in China, for example, which, as a recent research report shows, "produce for international garment and footwear companies, including Nike, Adidas, Disney, JanSport and Wal-Mart."[38] But workers there are forced to work overtime – twelve to fourteen hours a day, seven days a week, although Chinese labour law restricts normal working-hours to forty hours a week. They are paid about $30–$75 US per month. The working conditions and safety measures are extremely poor in those factories, with barred or locked gates. In a tragic accident in Southern China nine years ago, eighty-seven workers were killed in a fire in a factory making toys for Chicco, because all the gates were locked. In two Disney factories in Macao, workers mostly from Mainland China were forced to work overtime or overnight under very poor working conditions.[39] Those factories run by transnational corporations prefer rural migrants to urban workers, for they are "cheaper, harder-working and more willing to work overtime."[40] In many factories, most workers are single young women aged between sixteen and twenty-five. They often have to tolerate body searches by male guards lest they steal materials from the factories. After 11 September 2001, some American firms put in huge orders for American flags, and Chinese women in China were working night and day for lousy wages to meet this demand.[41] All these examples further document global capitalism's strategies of differentiation. MNCs and transnational corporations not only customize or modify their products to suit local needs and preferences, but also 'customize' or localize labour law to make maximum profits. Capitalism sets different wage standards,[42] different working-hour limits, and different treatments of the human body for different areas of the world. The implicit justification for such discriminations even has a humanitarian ring: we are providing job opportunities to the Third World jobless and the impoverished migrant, and the local workers at least are making more than before, though far less than their American or European counterparts. Indeed, these differential strategies work in China because there are 60 to 80 million Chinese peasants "surging out of poor regions in search of jobs"[43] and because the unemployment rates in many Chinese cities have soared between twenty and thirty percent. At present, the number of urban unemployed in China has reached 15 million in total. One 1997 World Bank estimate said that between 1992 and 1996 in Shanghai alone 220,000 of local textile positions were eliminated.[44] Such increasing unemployment rates are the consequence of economic globalization.

To obtain a full picture of capitalism feeding on difference, one should say that capitalism has always relied on differentiating strategies, creating and exploiting difference everywhere. Capitalism creates the capitalist class and the working class; it engenders widening gaps between the poor and the rich; it divides the world into unequally developed areas; it creates and exploits gender and racial difference as well as social difference in its designation of differential wage and employment standards. However, all these differences are deployed to serve capitalism's global project of converting all populations into its wage labourers. Capitalism may be apparelled in different ethnic costumes, speak different languages, differentiate the class structure at different points in history, employ different mechanisms to contain opposition, but none of these changes the basic fact, which is that capitalism, as Adorno warned thirty-five years ago, remains the same as it was 150 years ago – production for the sake of profit.[45] Anywhere it sets foot, capitalism disseminates alienation, exploitation, commodification, and consumerist sense and sensibility, threatening to ultimately colonize everyone's unconscious or psyche. The train of capitalism, to extend a metaphor from Fukuyama, will take along all populations as its passengers. All this was best described by Marx and Engels 150 years ago: "In one word, [capitalism] creates a whole world after its own image."[46] So what is being globalized in the day of global capitalism is capitalism itself with all its social relations, consumerist cultures, and structures of feeling. Such unification of the world by capitalism indeed logically results in what Michael Hardt and Antonio Negri call a new empire, a transnational, deterritorialized, interconnected empire of capital. But unlike the empire described by Hardt and Negri, the actual, lived Global Empire has never been decentred, and global capital is still "centered in the West, and it always speaks English."[47] If, as I have discussed earlier, the world is undergoing decentering, this occurs only to recentre the world with a vengeance. Whether a recentred, transnational, deterritorialized world is either an antinomy or a sheer contradiction, it can be best seen as a symptom of global capitalism. This world is full of antinomies or contradictions, and to force a contradictory social reality into a coherent theoretical model is another, pathological symptom of neurotic anxieties about fitting violated history into theory.

As we have seen, global capitalism is much more thorough in both differentiating and homogenizing our social life than critics like Hardt and Negri realize. While creating and feeding on differences, global capitalism's ultimate goal is to erase and destroy all differential social, ethnic and ideological legacies. As Marx and Engels pointed out in the mid-nineteenth century,

> The need for a constantly expanding market chases the bourgeoisie over the whole surface of the globe. It must settle everywhere, establish connexions everywhere. [. . .] The bourgeoisie has through its exploitation of the world market given a cosmopolitan character to production and consumption in every country. (46–47)

Capitalism as such tends to eliminate all times and spaces of Otherness. In pursuing expansionist policies to gain markets and resources, it resorts to militaristic and violent means wherever it is stopped and challenged. The Opium War on China of 1840–42, the Scramble for Africa in the 1880s, the Vietnam War of the 1960s, and the two Gulf Wars, including the latest invasion of Iraq, to cite only a few examples, are all landmarks in the expansionist history of capitalist imperialism. Indeed, capitalism and imperialism are essentially one aggressive process with two faces. If recent economic crises and political turbulence caused nations and peoples to question the free-market neoliberal utopianism which seized the world after the collapse of the Soviet Union and the Eastern European socialist bloc and the Chinese government's veiled capitulation to capitalism, then the recent barbaric bombarding of Afghanistan and Iraq has convinced the world that imperialism has returned – indeed, never disappeared. Capitalist imperialism or globalization constantly revolutionizes itself by the means of production and the rhetoric of colonization, and it keeps shifting its geopolitical centres. After the Second World War, the globalization process began to be centred on the USA, which sees itself

> as a beacon of freedom, individual rights, and democracy in a troubled world, as a model society to which everyone aspired, as a "shining city on the hill" doing battle, as Ronald Reagan framed it, with an "Evil Empire" of communism, as well as with the dark forces of ignorance, superstition, and irrationality.[48]

The actual reality of the contemporary global empire not only questions various grand narratives of globalization (Fukuyama, Huntington, Friedman, and Hardt and Negri), but also dares postcolonialism itself to think of effective strategies for resisting and interrogating neoimperialism. Apart from valorizing and emphasizing cultural and ethnic differences to counter West- or America-centrism, postcolonialism should fight all kinds of (neo) colonization. If colonization has been one of the most active terms applied to all kinds of oppression in the past few decades, then we should form an historic bloc of resistance against all kinds of colonization.

One major challenge confronting postcolonialism, as I see it, is how to theorize and mobilize new forms of decolonizing agency in opposition to neocolonizing global capitalism. Since the free market depends on state power and state institutions, the nation-state and its functionaries and indigenous capitalists are increasingly in collusion with TNCs, often at the cost of many indigenous peoples. Owing to this changed relationship between indigenous nation-states and Western nation-states and TNCs, indigenous nation-states no longer play a major role in anti-imperialist movements as they did previously, such as was manifested by Nehru's Indian government and Mao's Chinese government in the 1950s and 1960s. Rather, most contemporary indigenous governments have, one way or another, become agents of global capitalism. Therefore, nationalism has often lost its true counter-hegemonic energy and thrust and, if deployed at the collective national level, is used to consolidate the nation-state's power or to cover up or divert public attention from domestic crises, as is the case with countries like China. Postcolonialism as a counter-neocolonial discourse must fight a transnational, mobile battle on a global scale. In order to devise an enabling theoretical framework for investigating and interrogating neocolonialism, it is necessary for postcolonialism to take up the Marxist questions of capitalism and class domination while fighting new and old forms of colonization and imperialism, This is not only because it is hugely indebted to Marxism, owing its discursive formation to its non-Western Marxist beginnings,[49] but because the developed West and the underdeveloped non-West today are once more engaged in the relationship of capital and labor and previously colonized peoples are becoming the lumpenproletariat. In rewriting the labour/capital opposition in terms of the West and the Rest, and the colonized/colonizer confrontation in terms of the global rich and the global dispossessed, postcolonialism will hopefully renew its discursive energy and prove its legitimacy as an empowering neo-Gramscian counter-hegemonic discourse against neo-imperialism that goes by the name of globalization.

Western or American culture and ideology are neocolonizing geopolitical peripheries, erasing indigenous traditions, non-capitalist values and psychological habits as capitalism eradicated pre-capitalist traditions, cultures and sensibilities in eighteenth- and nineteenth-century Europe. Postcolonialism should form an historic bloc with all other counter-hegemonic forces against the common enemy – global capitalism – and identify all those forces working in collaboration with TNCs as functionaries and territories of the global empire. The most appealing rhetoric of neoconservatives and ultra-rightists served up to media-controlled populations is that capitalism is inevitable; there is no alternative. Postcolonialism must theorize against such rhetoric and imagine alternatives to American democracy and free-market capitalism. In forming a global united front against global capitalism in the age of electronic media and migration, perhaps we should indeed advocate and realize a "globalization-from-below" of resistance to the "globalization-from-above of corporate capitalism."[50] Over the past twenty years or so, alongside an explosion of varied insurgent discourses in the domains of cultural and sociopolitical thought and representation, there have emerged hundreds of anti-capitalist and anti-globalization movements on various scales. From Seattle, Prague, Genoa, Göteborg to Mexico City, Porto Alegre, Manila, and Daqing, the wretched and disinherited of the earth are fighting local battles against the global system. In forging global resistance to global capitalism, it is of the utmost importance to define commonalities by means of which to translate among disparate, divergent discursive and political forces of resistance.[51] This is how we can effectively withstand and weaken global capitalism. For, as David Harvey remarks, unless we resort to translation, "collective forms of action [are] impossible" and "all potential for an alternative politics disappears."[52] In pursuing this goal, it is to be hoped that a genuine global postcolonial resistance to global neocolonialism as championed by US imperialism will emerge. The global-resistance front includes all kinds of counter-hegemonic heterotopias,[53] fighting guerrilla wars against the total system of the New Empire. This project contests hegemonic centres of power, working towards a truly decentred, de-imperialized world. It looks imaginatively forward to a future when imperialism will truly be a story of the past, and when postcolonialism itself will likewise be past history.

Notes

1   The quotation is from Étienne Balibar's review of *Empire*. See Harvard UP Online Reviews of *Empire* (26 June 2003) www.hup.harvard.edu/reviews/HAREMI_R.html

2   Slavoj Žižek, *Revolution at the Gates* (London: Verso, 2002): 331.

3   Michael Hardt & Antonio Negri, *Empire* (Cambridge MA: Harvard UP, 2000):

4   Hardt and Negri, *Empire*, 138, 152.

5   Douglas Kellner, "Theorizing Globalization" (26 June 2003) www.gseis.ucla.edu/faculty/kellner/papers/theoryglob.htm

6   Thomas Friedman, *The Lexus and the Olive Tree* (New York: Farrar, Straus & Giroux, 1999): 8.

7   *Random House Webster's College Dictionary* (New York: Random House, 1995): 568.

8   James Petras & Henry Veltmeyer, *Globalization Unmasked: Imperialism in the 21st Century* (Halifax, N.S.: Fernword, 2001): 29.

9   See *Financial Times* (28 January 1999). Quoted in Petras & Veltmeyer, *Globalization Unmasked,* 62–63.

10   Tariq Ali, *The Clash of Fundamentalisms: Crusades, Jihads and Modernity* (London: Verso, 2002): 276–77.

11   See Francis Fukuyama, "Has History Restarted Since September 11?" The Nineteenth Annual John Bonython Lecture at the Grand Ballroom, the Grand Hyatt, Melbourne. 8 August 2002 (26 June 2003) www.cis.org.au/Events/JBL/JBL02.html

12   Thomas Friedman, "A Manifesto for the Fast World," *New York Times* (28 March 1999): 96.

13   Fukuyama, "Has History Restarted since September 11?"

14   See Henry Kissinger, "Globalization and World Order," Independent Newspapers Annual Lecture, Trinity College Dublin (12 October 1999).

15   Quoted in Lance Selfa, "A New Colonial Age of Empire?" *International Socialist Review* May-June 2002; *Third World Traveller*, 26 June 2003 thirdworldtraveler.com/American_Empire/New_Colonial_Age_Empire.html

16   This passage, taken from William Kristol & Lawrence F. Kaplan's *The War Over Iraq*, is quoted in Robert Dreyfuss, "Just the Beginning: Is Iraq the Opening Salvo in a War to Remake the World?" *American Prospect Magazine* (April 2003); *Third World Traveller*, 25 June 2003 thirdworldtraveler.com/American_Empire/Iraq_Just_Beginning?html

17   See Mark Thomas, "Interview with Chomsky," *ZNET,* 26 June 2003 www.zmag.org/cntent/print_article.cfm?itemID = 2804&sectionID = 15

18   Fredric Jameson, Preface in *The Cultures of Globalization*, ed. Fredric Jameson & Masao Miyoshi (Durham NC: Duke UP, 1998): xii.

19   Fredric Jameson, "Globalization and Political Strategy," *New Left Review* 4 (July–August 2000): 53.

20   Jameson, "Globalization and Political Strategy," 51.

21   See ReseAnne Sims, "The United States vs. The World: A Theoretical Look at Cultural Imperialism." 26 June 2003 www.mediaguide.hu/book/bookID11.html

22   Peter Woodman, "Cultural Imperialism in Columbia" (26 June 2003) www.columbiasolidarity.org.uk/Solidarity%208/culturalimperialism.html

23   "Domestic Movies under the Shadow of Hollywood?" (25 June 2003) china.com.cn/english/2002/Apr/30289.htm

24   Arjun Appadurai, *Modernity at Large: Cultural Dimensions of Globalization* (Minneapolis: U of Minnesota P, 1996): 1.

25   See Appadurai, *Modernity at Large,* 1–23.

26   See Raymond Williams, *Marxism and Literature* (Oxford: Oxford UP, 1977): 121–27.

27   David Harvey, *Spaces of Hope* (Berkeley: U of California , 2000): 192.

28   Edward Said, *Culture and Imperialism* (New York: Vintage, 1993): xvii.

29   Said, *Culture and Imperialism*, xix.

30   Shaobo Xie, "Rethinking the Problem of Postcolonialism," *New Literary History* 28 (1997): 7–19.

31   In his recent book *The Postcolonial Exotic: Marketing the Margins,* Graham Huggan also distinguishes between 'postcoloniality' and 'postcolonialism,' taking the former as pointing to a regime of "global processes of commodification" and defining the latter as a resistance politics "in obvious opposition" to those processes, although at the same time he calls attention to the danger of "postcolonialism and its rhetoric of resistance" themselves becoming "consumer products" (7; quoted in Chris Prentice, "Riding the Whale? Postcolonialism and Globalization in *Whale Rider*"; see this volume, xx – xx).

32   Xie, "Rethinking the Problem of Postcolonialism," 15.

33   Robert Young, *Postcolonialism: An Historical Introduction* (Oxford: Blackwell, 2001): 58.

34   Young, *Postcolonialism: An Historical Introduction,* 59.

35   See Simon During, "Postmodernism or Post-Colonialism Today?" in *Postmodernism: A Reader*, ed. Thomas Docherty (New York: Columbia UP, 1993): 455.

36   See Fredric Jameson, *The Ideology of Theory*, vol. 2: *Syntax of History* (Minneapolis: U of Minnesota Press, 1988): 47; Wim Wenders, *The Logic of Images: Essays and Conversations,* tr. Michael Hoffman (Frankfurt am Main: Verlag der Autoren, 1988; tr. London: Faber & Faber, 1991): 98.

37   Stuart Hall, "The Local and the Global," in *Dangerous Liaisons: Gender, Nation, and Postcolonial Perspectives,* ed. Anne McClintock, Aamir Mufti & Ella Shohat (Minneapolis: U of Minnesota P, 1997): 182.

38   Alice Kwan, "An Interview with Alice Kwan," 26 June 2003 multinational monitor.org/ mm2000/00may/interview.html, 3.

39   Alice Kwan, "An Interview with Alice Kwan," 5.

40   "The Unemployment Dilemma in China: A Side Effect of Globalization and the Remedy," 26 June 2003 www.lilywu.com/Unemployment%20Dilemma%20in%20China.pdf, 9.

41   This information comes from the Vancouver-based writer Rita Wong's unpublished paper "Resounding Dissent in a Time and Space of Imperial Delirium," presented at the Fred Wah Conference, University of Calgary, Alberta, Canada. May 2003.

42   According to Anita Chan, "the enormous wage gap between the minimum wages in the United States and that of developing countries in Asia and Central America [stands] at an order of at least 20 times." See Anita Chan, "Globalization and China's 'Race to the Bottom' in Labour Standards," 25 June 2003 coombs.anu.edu.au/~niap/morrison_trans.pdf, 3.

43   Anita Chan, "Globalization and China's 'Race to the Bottom' in Labour Standards," 12.

44   "The Unemployment Dilemma in China," 4.

45   Theodor Adorno, "Late Capitalism or Industrial Society?" Opening Address to the 16th German Sociological Congress, 1968, tr. Dennis Redmond, 2001 (26 August 2003) www.efn.org/~dredmond/AdornoSozAddr.PDF, 5.

46   Karl Marx & Friedrich Engels, *Manifesto of the Communist Party (Manifest der Kommunistischen Partei;* London, 1848; tr. Moscow: Progress, 1952): 47.

47   Stuart Hall, "The Local and the Global," 179.

48   David Harvey, *Spaces of Hope,* 192.

49   See Young, *Postcolonialism,* 57–59.

50   Douglas Kellner, "Theorizing Globalization" (26 June 2003). www.gseis.ucla.edu/faculty/kellner/papers/theoryglob. htm

51   For such commonalities, see David Harvey's suggested short-list of universal rights in *Spaces of Hope* (Berkeley: U of California P, 2000): 248–52.

52   Harvey, *Spaces of Hope,* 245.

53   The term 'heterotopia' is used here in a modified Foucauldian sense. See Harvey, *Spaces of Hope,* 183–85. According to Harvey, the Foucauldian term of heterotopia is best explained by K. Hetherington, who notes that the concept of heterotopia refers to "spaces of alternate ordering. Heterotopia organize a bit of the social world in a way different to that which surrounds them. That alternate ordering marks them out as Other and allows them to be seen as an example of an alternative way of doing things" (quoted in *Spaces of Hope*, 184). For further discussion of the concept of heterotopia, see Michel Foucault, "Of Other Spaces," *Diacritics* 16.1 (1986): 22–27.

Chapter 78

Akbar S. Ahmed and Hastings Donnan

ISLAM IN THE AGE OF POSTMODERNITY

Rejecting the colonial discourse analyses of Edward Said and other postcolonialists critical of what Said called "Orientalism", Akbar S. Ahmed and Hastings Donnan argue that because of contemporary globalization and interrelated transformations in the lives of many Muslims, a reassessment of Islamic studies is called for. Ahmed, the Ibn Khaldun Chair of Islamic Studies at the American University in Washington DC, and Donnan, Professor of Social Anthropology at Queen's University, Belfast, examine five main topics via which such a reassessment can take place: globalization; diaspora; global politics; the media; and postmodernism. The remainder of the extract surveys the essays in the ensuing book which this extract introduces. Ahmed and Donnan open with globalization in the sense of the global village—whereby through new communication and travel technologies the world becomes temporally and spatially closer—and the ways in which this impacts Islam, such as the speed with which the Muslim world reacted to the Rushdie Affair (in the UK this involved the burning of Salman Rushdie's book *The Satanic Verses* (1988) for blasphemy, and in 1989 the Ayatollah Khomeini ruled in a *fatwa* that Rushdie should be sentenced to death). Furthermore, the Rushdie Affair rapidly gained global commentary, throughout every media format imaginable, and popular media quickly introduced Islamic language into the vernacular. While Ahmed and Donnan recognize the historical roots of Islam–West relations, they argue that globalized cultural flows have become more important, and the threat of cultural homogenization should be taken seriously. But it is not just information that circulates in a globalized environment: it is people, too, thus Ahmed and Donnan stress the importance of an awareness of the Muslim diaspora, literally dispersal of peoples around the globe. Given permanent settlement "abroad" this reconfigures questions of location, and even categories of home/abroad; Ahmed and Donnan argue that not only does the Muslim diaspora transform notions of the "local", it also makes the Orientalist critique initiated by Edward Said less relevant to contemporary Muslim life. For diasporic Muslim subjects, the writings of Muslim "Orientalists" have become an important source of cultural knowledge. The heterogeneity of Muslim diasporic cultures also leads to a need for more negotiation between adherents of different sects and traditions. The hardening of positions is also apparent, for example, with the "detachment" of identity and place, an increased liberalism or fundamentalism may be the polarized outcome, especially where with the latter, traditional values become more, not less, important for diasporic individuals. Global political changes on the world stage are also crucial, such as the plight of Muslims during the Bosnia war, or Islamic support of Saddam Hussein during the Gulf Wars, and this ties in directly, according to Ahmed and Donnan, with the role of the global media. What appears to Muslim communities as media-based persecution may simply be a result of the need for sensationalism: two competing examples are explored. Finally, taking the line that postmodernism is merely a more recent variant of the modern, Ahmed and Donnan recognize a qualitative shift in the "intellectual milieu" in the globalized 1980s, one which can be summarized as being an incredulity towards tradition; this shift is important for the understanding of Islam and Islamic studies, as well as the contexts, as sketched above, in which cultural signs and discourses circulate and are consumed.

I SLAMIC STUDIES – OR THE STUDY OF MUSLIM groups and their religion Islam – has been changing dramatically in the last decades. Until recently, Islamic studies was largely the exotic focus of a relatively small group of academics who wrote books about it mainly for one another's consumption. Many of these intellectuals were based in the West, and few of these were Muslims. The Muslim voice itself was seldom heard outside the Muslim world. This has been changing, partly in response to the fact that the lives of many ordinary Muslims have been changing, and partly as a reflection of the equally dramatic changes taking place in the world more generally. Many factors can explain this, and this book sets out to trace both their impact on Muslims and the latter's responses to them.

Globalization

Firstly, we consider the phenomenon sometimes referred to as globalization. Since it is not always clear that people mean the same thing when they talk about globalization – some talk about globalization theory, others about a global process defined with varying degrees of precision (see Robertson 1987; 1990: 19–20) – it is as well to be clear at the outset about how the term is used here. By globalization we principally refer to the rapid developments in communications technology, transport and information which bring the remotest parts of the world within easy reach (cf. Giddens 1990: 64). For instance, today if a development takes place in New York it can be relayed instantly across the world to Cairo or Karachi. A good example of this process of globalization is the controversy surrounding Salman Rushdie which began in the late 1980s in the United Kingdom with the publication of *The Satanic Verses*. Within hours, developments in the United Kingdom – in Bradford and London – provoked responses in Islamabad and Bombay. Indeed, people died as they protested against the book. Government pronouncements, media chat shows, editorials, vigils and protests reflected the heated debate. Never before in history had such developments taken place in this manner and at such speed.

One consequence of the globalization process is the necessity to look at Islamic studies not as an esoteric or marginal exercise but as something that concerns the global community. We are thus forced to look at Muslims in different parts of the world not as the preserve of specialist scholars but as an ever-present and ubiquitous reality that relates to non-Muslims in the street. And let us not forget the truly global nature of Muslim society which totals something like one billion people living in about 50 countries with significantly some ten to fifteen million living in the USA and Europe. Issues of migration arise from this reality. Here Muslims face major problems as immigrants, including racism.

Owing to the developments in and around Islam, words such as *fatwa* (a sermon), *jihad* (struggle, including armed effort), *ayatollah* (highly learned scholar and cleric) are now common in the West. The tabloids have popularized these words and they have entered the

English language. This again is a consequence of the Western media using or misusing words and adopting and adapting them to the local usage. It also reflects the interplay and interchange of ideas between Islam and the West. An earlier example of borrowing is the word *mughal*, which signified the great Mughal emperors and dynasty of India and is now used for any powerful person, and particularly to refer to business tycoons ('moguls'). Another earlier example is harem, which in Arabic designates a female sanctuary to which only close male relatives have access but which in English often suggests only the voluptuous and licentious exploitation of women. It is clear, then, that borrowing of this kind has been going on for some time. Indeed, the process of globalization itself might be said to have a long history, even if the term is of fairly recent currency.

Like much of the rest of the world, Muslims and the West have long been interconnected through international trade and economic exchange (or exploitation), locked together in what has been referred to as the 'economic world-system' (Wallerstein 1974; 1984). An embryonic form of late twentieth century globalization might thus be discerned in the collaborations between the representatives of colonial power and the indigenous élites who helped them to rule. Indeed, there are those who consider this period of human history to be one stage – and not necessarily the first stage – in the development of what we now call globalization. For example, it has been suggested that the historical path to current global complexity has passed through five phases, beginning in the early fifteenth century (Robertson 1990: 26–27). Globalization is thus not necessarily the wholly novel phenomenon, unique to the latter half of this century, that some commentators appear to imply. As a process it is of considerable historical depth, and as a theory it exhibits all the notions of 'system' and 'stages of growth' which distinguish its forerunner, world-systems theory. Nevertheless, and most commentators appear to agree, late twentieth-century globalization does seem different from earlier forms in certain important respects (see Appadurai 1990: 1–5).

For one thing, the historical connections between nations have generally been previously understood largely in terms of an *economic* world-system. The economic content of international contact has thus been emphasized at the expense of the *cultural* flows which were obviously also taking place alongside the material exchanges; indeed, the place of 'culture' in analyses of global interconnections such as world-systems theory is a matter of some disagreement, with some alleging that it has mostly been left out (see Hannerz 1989a: 204; Wallerstein 1990; Boyne 1990; Worsley 1990). But there are obviously many examples of collaborations between colonials and locals which involved much more than just political and economic co-operation; thus when the values of gentlemanly behaviour and fair play arrived in India as a cultural export from Victorian and Edwardian England, they were quickly adopted by those – such as the Parsis (see Luhrmann 1994) – who wished to please their then colonial masters. But while these cultural flows clearly existed in the past, they never seem to have been an end in themselves, and they have usually been of less interest to scholars than the material realities which underpinned them.

Today the emphasis has shifted and it is the cultural flows between nations which above all else seem to typify the contemporary globalization process (or its current phase) (cf. Robertson 1987: 24). These cultural flows are not, of course, detached from economic and political realities. Because of their origins, some flows – mainly those in 'the West' – have more force than others and so reach a wider audience. Accordingly, there has been much discussion about the possible homogenization of culture – the move towards a 'global culture' in which everyone will drink the same soft drinks, smoke Marlboro cigarettes, and emulate JR. Such an homogenization of culture has been questioned from a number of perspectives, and the situation is certainly more complex than is sometimes supposed. Firstly, the notion of a hegemonic global cultural centre dispensing its products to the world's peripheries is more often assumed than described; and even if there is such a thing, it is not clear that its exports have any more significance to those they reach than its exports of a generation or two ago (Parkin 1993: 85–86). Secondly, even though the same cultural 'message' may be received in different places, it is domesticated by being interpreted and incorporated according to local values (see Featherstone 1990: 10). And finally, cultural flows do not necessarily map directly on to economic and political relationships, which means that the flow of cultural traffic can often be in many different directions simultaneously. We shall return to these points later.[1]

The globalization process today is also marked by the accelerated pace at which informational and cultural exchanges take place, and by the scale and complexity of these exchanges (on the latter, see Appadurai 1990: 6). Facilitated by the new technologies, it is the sheer speed, extent and volume of these exchanges that have engaged popular imagination, and that seem to have led to globalization being so often represented, if perhaps a little glibly, by the VCR. Cheater (1993: 3–4) lists an impressive array of such technologies from electronic mail to the satellite dish, and although these are clearly not accessible to all, they have obviously been directly or indirectly responsible for exposing many different sorts of people to new influences. Such technologies are able to uncouple culture from its territorial base so that, detached and unanchored, it pulsates through the airwaves to all those with the means to receive it.

Whatever the ultimate outcome might be — greater homogeneity or heterogeneity of culture — and this is hotly disputed, the contemporary phase of globalization has thus resulted in more people than ever before becoming involved with more than one culture (cf. Featherstone 1990: 8). It is perhaps this which above all else captures the sense in which the term is used here.

Diaspora

Of course, it is not just technologies which carry culture across national boundaries; people clearly do as well, and the twentieth century has witnessed dramatic developments in the ease with which people cross from one state to another. Moreover, unlike the population movements of the past, these post-industrial diasporas occur in a world where even the old 'geographical and territorial certainties seem increasingly fragile'; thus today's diasporas seem much less likely to have 'stable points of origin, clear and final destinations and coherent group identities' (Breckenridge and Appadurai 1989: i; see also Malkki 1992: 24).

These changes have resulted in diasporas of various kinds: that of the cosmopolitan academic parodied by Lodge (1985) in a book whose very title — *Small World* — plays on the sense of compressed global space characteristic of globalization, that of the international business/management/design consultant, and that of the migrant labourer and refugee. The former — who are always on the move — have given rise to the so-called 'third cultures', while the latter — often in search of a new home — have resulted in the linguistically, culturally and socially heterogeneous communities now typical of many parts of the globe.[2] Muslims are represented in all these groups, and this volume tries to deal with each: peripatetic intellectuals as well as labour migrants. Several of the contributors thus address directly the question of how people manage the cultural uncertainties typical of such poly-ethnic situations and of how Islam is moulded to 'foreign' settings (Gerholm, Antoun, Werbner, this volume).[3]

It has often been noted that Islam explicitly encourages and even enjoins certain forms of travel, and that the movement of Muslims from one part of the world to another, whatever the purpose, resonates with the historical foundations of their religion (Eickelman and Piscatori 1990: 5; Donnan and Werbner 1991: 9–10). But here too globalization seems to have greatly encouraged this willingness to move, and has added a dimension to it.

Transformations of the world economy brought about by the globalization of markets and labour under late capitalism – or 'disorganized capitalism' as it has been called by Lash and Urry (1987) – have resulted in enormous numbers of people moving round the globe in search of work. Muslims constitute a large proportion of this population movement. It is in this manner that Muslim societies have today become part and parcel of Western countries. Muslim doctors and engineers live as American or British citizens. Their children have no intention of going back to their place of origin. The study of this Muslim diaspora raises both empirical and conceptual issues.[4]

Since the bulk of Muslim migrant labour has settled abroad on a permanent basis, it is important to now look at these societies as local, as indigenous not as the other, the exotic or the Oriental, pace Edward Said (1978). Thus Said's Orientalism is dated in this new theoretical frame and we need to move beyond its position. Although pointing to something important – that is, the imbalance or asymmetry between Islam and the West and the continuing prejudice, stereotypes and caricatures created of Islam by the West – Said's position has created serious intellectual problems, principally because of the manner in which it has been received and applied. It has led to a cul-de-sac. 'Orientalism' itself has become a cliché, and third world literature is now replete with accusations and labels of Orientalism being hurled at critics and at one author by another at the slightest excuse. This has had a stultifying affect on the dispassionate evaluation of scholarship. Thus, for example, in the passion generated by the debate what has been missed out is the great contribution of many Orientalist scholars. The writings of Ibn Khaldun, Ibn Battuta, or the Mughal emperor Babar come to us only through the painstaking scholarship of Orientalists who spent a life-time deciphering notes in Asian languages and sitting in remote libraries. For them it was a labour of love. To dismiss their work as simply Orientalism or as an attempt to suppress or subjugate Muslim peoples denies an important truth. Unfortunately, after Edward Said, that is how many Muslim writers do see the work of the Orientalists. If research on contemporary Muslim societies is not to be similarly dismissed as the most recent manifestation of Orientalism, it is clearly imperative to introduce conceptual innovations which both surmount the limitations of Islamic studies as identified by Said, and transcend the shortcomings of his own analysis. This would seem to be possible only by contextualizing local versions of Islam within global structures.

Sensitive and innovative research seems particularly critical for understanding the Muslim diaspora. The diaspora has led to the oft-remarked quest for identity and authenticity, particularly for those who find themselves abroad but also, to some extent, for those who remain behind and who now find that their culture, transported to new settings, is being defined and practised in novel and sometimes disturbing ways. The empirical issues raised by diaspora thus chiefly revolve around questions of identity and the vulnerability of having to redefine the self in a world which seems constantly on the move. The hyphen of hyphenated identities like that of British-Muslim or American-Muslim, for example, both reflects and obscures the necessary conjunction of disparate cultural traces brought together in the act of 're-membering' and 're-creating', to borrow Fischer and Abedi's terms (1990: 253).

In the liminal zone of the culturally displaced, Muslims in the diaspora experience a range of practical, psychological and pragmatic difficulties, some of which are examined in this volume. These include the problems of establishing enduring relationships with the opposite sex, of contracting acceptable marriages, and of adapting religion to a new life (Antoun, Gerholm, Werbner). But they also include the problems of negotiating with other Muslims and agreeing with them on the meaning of Islam on foreign soil (Werbner). After all, Muslims who migrate are not only often in a minority in their place of destination, where they must encounter the cultures of the majority, but they also come from different sectarian and cultural traditions themselves. In some cases, as with Turkish Alevis in Germany for example, residence abroad may permit a greater freedom of religious expression. Thus the diaspora has released these Alevis from what they see as Sunni hegemony in Turkey, as well as enabling them to substantially reverse their hierarchically subordinate position to Sunni Turks based in Germany (Mandel 1990: 163, 166).

But the diaspora raises issues of identity and direction at 'home' too, among those faced with the fantasy if not the reality of moving (cf. Gardner 1993), and among those who now find their 'local cultures less pervasive, less to be taken for granted, less clearly bounded toward the outside' than they perhaps once were (Hannerz 1990: 249). Migrants return to their place of origin not only with novel versions of the world which challenge the views of those who never left (see Antoun, this volume), but also on occasion with fossilized and outmoded versions of what they left behind: ways of dressing, behaving, believing and so forth which have been developed and reshaped in their absence but which they have lovingly and carefully preserved intact while abroad. Either way, old certainties are challenged. To draw again on Fischer and Abedi writing about Iran, but to slightly modify their focus, the Muslim world and the Muslim habitations abroad 'mirror each other at acute or oblique angles, mutually affecting each other's representations, setting off mutating variations' (1990: 255). The very elasticity of the diasporic tie thus ensures the reciprocal redefinition of identity at both ends of the migratory chain as elements of culture rebound first this way and then that. Renewed attempts to define proper behaviour for Muslim women in Cairo and Lahore (Watson and Weiss respectively, this volume), and to establish an Islamic basis for the state in Malaysia (Nagata, this volume) might thus be interpreted as a search for identity which is at least partially stimulated by the Muslim diaspora.

The detachment of culture from territory which is entailed by diaspora, with its generation of cultures with no clear anchorage in any one space (Hannerz 1990: 237), has unleashed powerful forces which affect us all and not just those most directly involved. According to Appadurai (1990: 11), for example, it is this deterritorialization which is 'now at the core of a variety of global fundamentalisms, including Islamic and Hindu fundamentalism'. The 'problems of cultural reproduction for Hindus abroad' Appadurai suggests, have become 'tied to the politics of Hindu fundamentalism at home' (1990: 11). The same could easily and realistically be said of the Muslim diaspora, with the added complication that, unlike the Hindus, Muslims abroad do not even share a common homeland. It is in this sense that the new Islamic movements in the Arab world described by Bagader (this volume) must be seen in the context of the Muslim diaspora. Indeed, the politics of all Muslim countries in this postmodern age must similarly be seen within a global frame.

Global politics

New political developments have increased this awareness of the need to study Muslim societies in a global context. The recent events in Bosnia have created a sharp awareness of Muslims as a world community, both in the West and among Muslims themselves. Bosnia has become a rallying point for Muslims throughout the Muslim world, much in the manner of the Palestinians. The case of Bosnia is even used in *khutbas* (sermons) in a closed society like Saudi Arabia to attack the monarchy for not doing enough. The sub-text is that the élite are far too much under the sway of the West. In the West itself, Bosnia has driven home the point that Muslims tend to see the world through Islamic spectacles and interpret the suffering of the Bosnian Muslims as brought about by a West indifferent to the plight of ordinary Muslims: the feeling is that had they been Jews or Christians, the Western response would have been very different.

This in itself colours and affects how Muslim scholarship is seen or is to be seen in the current time. It tends to polarize tensions between Muslims and non-Muslims. For instance, many Muslims now argue that although the Bosnians were Europeanized – they drank alcohol, ate pork, married non-Muslims and so on – nonetheless, when the killings began, these secularized Muslims were the first victims of the Serbs. In short, there is no compromise and sooner or later the enemies of Islam will victimize Muslims whatever they do. It is thus best to rally round Islam. Bosnia has created and sharpened the sense of polarization and radicalization in Muslim societies, while at the same time increasing the sense of being a Muslim.

This too was the effect of the publication of Rushdie's *Satanic Verses*, and of the Gulf War, when the political symbolism of Islam readily mobilized the ordinary Muslim in the street. But if, in the case of the Gulf War, Muslims almost everywhere seemed to rally round Saddam Hussein, they did so in complex ways and not in some monolithic stance of Islam against the West. Muslim responses to the war certainly reflected suspicion of the West's motives, but they also drew on local political circumstances and on the long-standing unpopularity of the Gulf monarchies among Muslims living outside the Arabian Peninsula (cf. Piscatori 1991: 12–13). Furthermore, the response in one Muslim nation depended in important ways on the reaction in others, with sometimes surprising outcomes. Thus, for example, the Jamaat-i-Islami in Pakistan, who were long-time supporters of the Saudi Arabian government and who before the war had described Saddam Hussein as 'an enemy of Islam', took an aggressively anti-Saudi stance during the war itself. What seems to have contributed to this apparent volte-face were the Jamaat's growing contacts and identifications with Islamic movements elsewhere, and particularly with 'the anti-American and anti-Saudi orientations of the movements in Jordan . . . and in the Gaza strip' (Ahmad 1991: 174). Such connections again underline the significance of the web of global linkages.

Similar interactions between the local and the global can be discerned in the responses to *Satanic Verses* which again, while superficially uniform, were composed of a diverse range of motivations and objectives. These too, like responses to the Gulf War, were played out according to the parameters and concerns of localized and often very different national political arenas (see Fischer and Abedi 1990: 389–400). Thus the response in Britain, for example, differed in important and significant ways from that elsewhere, because of the particular configuration of relationships there, both between Muslims and non-Muslims, and among Muslims themselves (see Modood 1990; Asad 1990: 257–60; Samad 1992). If wider political events have led to a greater sense of polarization in the Muslim world, the resiliency and intensity of this feeling can therefore only be understood by examining the play between these global developments and the circumstances of each local setting.

To some extent this tension between the local and the global was reflected in the Western media who, while exacerbating and facilitating the sense of polarization among Muslims by apparently being intent on delivering a message of a monolithic East versus West (during the Gulf War and Rushdie affair), simultaneously broadcast evidence of the diversity of the Muslim response which belied that interpretation of events. Thus while many news headlines tended to cast these confrontations in fairly stark terms, a number of television panel discussions and broadsheet leaders were informed by more moderate Muslim voices. This raises the whole question of the powerful Western media and their relationship to Islam.

The media

The Western media are largely seen by Muslims as a negative influence. This view is perhaps not without foundation. The traditional Orientalist stereotypes of Muslims as political anarchists and as tyrants at home subjugating their women have been disseminated in the media as caricatures and stereotypes. Very often the news that is shown about Muslims centres around negative stories.

It is this negative collage of images that allows the idea of Islam as the new enemy after Communism to circulate and take hold in the popular imagination. Popular surveys in the West indicate that the majority of people feel that Islam will be the main villain in the coming time. In turn, Muslims feel that the suffering of their community – in Bosnia, in Palestine, in Kashmir – is ignored by the world, although it has the law and UN resolutions on its side, simply because of hostility to Islam. Many Muslims talk of a new crusade against them; of the need for *jihad*.

However, there is an element of simplification in this. The media by their nature tend to select stories that are sensationalist. They do not pick only on Muslims. Jews in Israel or Hindus in India often complain of bias against them. Besides, the iconoclastic nature of the media encourages them to focus on celebrities and then spoil their image. Examples of Princess Diana or John Major in England support this. Nonetheless, the perception of hostile Western media affects the way Islamic studies are perceived both by Muslims and non-Muslims.

The role of the media is crucial in understanding and appreciating Muslims today. Although Muslims are highly critical of the media and see them as inimical, there are examples when the media have worked in their favour. But first an example in which the media developed a climate of hostility towards Muslims: this is provided by the destruction of the mosque in Ayodhya and the subsequent communal killings in India. In December 1992, a well-planned campaign to destroy the Ayodhya mosque culminated when the structure was razed to the ground. This was the result of a cultural milieu that was spear-headed by the media in the 1990s. In particular, the popular television series *Mahabharata* and the *Ramayana*, although themselves not directed against Muslims, nevertheless created a highly charged religious atmosphere in India.[5] The series was watched by six to seven hundred million people and ran for years. The revivalist, communal political party, the BJP, was the direct beneficiary of the cultural revivalism. From only two seats in Parliament it secured over one hundred and twenty seats in a couple of years. Many of its candidates were the actors and actresses from these two television series. The BJP's demand to destroy the Ayodhya mosque and then many other mosques built by Indian Muslims – because, they argued, these mosques had been built on Hindu sites – struck a chord. The government of India had little political will to resist. Indeed, we saw on television and in other Western media how the Indian police stood aside while individual policemen went up to pay their homage to the Hindu deities.

In contrast, we have the example of Bosnia. It has been the courageous reporting of Western media people, many of whom have been injured and lost their lives, which has brought to the notice of the world the horrors of the Serb rape, death and torture camps. This in turn has helped to create a climate in the West of acknowledging the horrors perpetrated against Muslims. It is not the failure of the media in this case which has prevented the West from taking action against the Serbs to prevent the killing of Muslims. There are many other factors. One of them, no doubt, is the reluctance to see a fully fledged Muslim state emerge in Europe. That is, at least, how some Muslims interpret events.

This apparent ambivalence towards Muslims in the Western media, and their apparent willingness to credit Muslims with the moral high ground in one case but not in another, has raised suspicions and doubts about the media's overall credibility in the minds of many Muslims (cf. Said 1981). Some Muslims seem to be supported, others not. Such ambivalent and even contradictory messages, while obviously reflecting the realpolitik of geo-political relations, sometimes seem to be the very stuff of the postmodern age in which we live, as we shall see in a moment.

First, however, we should emphasize that once again studies of specific Muslims in particular locales are required to fully grasp how media products – television programmes, advertisements, rock concerts – are received and interpreted. As we mentioned earlier, the very fact that media images reach a range of cultural contexts means that audiences are unlikely to respond in identical ways. Instead, like other cultural imports, these images are 'indigenized' (Appadurai 1990: 5), and fitted around local concerns. Yet while there is much talk in general terms about the likely impact which television programmes such as *Dallas* and *Dynasty* might have in the African bush or in Middle Eastern shanty towns like Cairo's City of the Dead, there is not the corresponding empirical evidence which would allow us to comment confidently on how these Western-generated media images are actually integrated into and influence people's everyday practices (cf. Hannerz 1989b: 72). The evidence which does exist, especially that on Muslims, is often anecdotal (though see Stauth and Zubaida 1987). But even this suggests that we should exercise some caution. If television programmes, for example, are viewed not in domestic isolation as they tend to be in much of the West, but as the focus for neighbourhood sociability as in many parts of rural Pakistan, might this not have an influence on how broadcasts are understood? The evidence on divergent viewing practices in the West itself (which vary with class, age and gender; see Featherstone 1991: 57–58) should lead us to be particularly wary when discussing television viewing in contexts where cultural understandings vary widely. In such situations meanings seem almost to multiply and fracture faster than we can accommodate them.

Postmodernism

Finally, elements of postmodernism – although a vague and even slippery concept to define – may prove important in helping us to focus on Islamic studies. Like globalization, not everyone is agreed on precisely what is meant by postmodernism. Indeed, that is part of its allure. Postmodernism encompasses a variety of forms and definitions and this in itself seems to some to be 'postmodern'. While a number of good guides exist to lead us through the dense foliage which has now sprung up around this notion (see, for example, Harvey 1989; Turner 1990b), even these can provide no single understanding; any attempt to 'fix' the meaning of postmodernism seems necessarily self-contradictory, with those who have tried being accused of constructing the very kind of grand narrative that postmodernism sets out to attack (see the summary of Kellner's [1988] critique of Lyotard in Featherstone 1991: 9). If there is agreement, then, it is that the term is impossible to pin down definitively (Featherstone 1991: 1; Boyne and Rattansi 1990: 1).

Some sense of the breadth and 'breathlessness' of what is included under the heading of postmodernism is given by Fardon, who cites the following lengthy (though given the task in hand, succinct) quotation:

> the inventory of features assigned to post-modernism includes: self-referential discourse, heterodoxy, eclecticism, marginality, death of Utopia (read: communism), death of the author, deformation, disfunction, deconstruction, disintegration, displacement, discontinuity, non-lineal view of history, dispersion, fragmentation, dissemination, rupture, otherness, decentering of the subject, chaos, rhizoma, rebellion, the subject as power, gender/difference/power (probably the most positive as a revision of patriarchy), dissolution of semiotics into energetics, auto-proliferation of signifiers, infinite semiosis, cybernetics, pluralism (read: freedom versus 'totalitarianism'), critique of reason, procession of simulacra and representations, dissolution of legitimizing 'narratives'

(hermeneutics, emancipation of the proletariat, epic of progress, dialectics of the spirit), a new episteme or sign system.

(Zavala [1988] cited in Fardon 1992: 25)

Since many of these elements are also typical of modernism, 'postmodernism' can be understood only as one of a relational pair. 'Both terms feed off each other and often seem propelled by a binary logic of opposition which sharpens the differentiation' between them and between the family of terms to which they belong – post(modern), post(modernity), post-(modernization) (Featherstone 1991: 144; see also Harvey 1989: 43). So though, as its prefix indicates, the postmodern comes after the modern, their boundary is blurred and each is mutually implicated in the other (on the difficulty of arriving at an adequate periodization, see Turner 1990a). This makes it rather difficult to determine just how 'new' the changes allegedly typical of postmodernity are and whether they must be subjected to a new (postmodernist) form of analysis.

It was sometime during the 1980s that postmodernist developments in sociology, literature and the arts most visibly began to create an intellectual milieu in counterdistinction to the modern. In addition to those mentioned above, its characteristics were: the juxtaposition of the high and the low, the serious and the frivolous, the historical and the contemporary; the deliberate breaking down of traditional ideas and thought patterns; the notion of 'magical realism'; a cynicism regarding religion and a conscious abandonment to the consumerist society of our times. All these have helped to challenge the traditional method of looking at Islamic studies.

While postmodernism – seen as a term that characterizes a 'series of broadly aesthetic projects' (Boyne and Rattansi 1990: 9) – is probably unknown to all but a small band of artists and intellectuals, postmodernity – as a 'social, political and cultural configuration' (Boyne and Rattansi 1990: 9) – affects everybody to varying degrees, Muslims included. This raises a number of quite different questions. How would a postmodernist perspective affect Islamic studies? Does it herald a new manner of studying Islam? Are these developments making an impact upon Muslims themselves? How have Muslims responded to postmodernity? Although the preoccupation with Euro-American analysis has so far largely precluded asking what postmodernity might mean to Muslims, or what it might mean elsewhere in the globe (cf. Fardon 1992: 37), such questions will need to be asked in the coming time. This book and its contributors do not pretend to answer all of these questions, but we do hope that it will give some sense of how Muslims have been inescapably touched by postmodernity, as well as an insight into how and why they have responded as they have.

Islam, globalization and postmodernity

Of course, as social scientists we accept that there are serious problems in traditional societies – not only Muslim, but also Hindu or Buddhist or indeed, even Christian – confronting and coping with the postmodern age. It promotes a culture based on youth, change and consumerism. It emphasizes noise, movement and speed. Traditional religions emphasize quiet, balance and discourage change. There are thus intrinsic points of conflict. This particular area of conflict is causing concern and anxiety among traditional people throughout the world. In Muslim societies one aspect of this is the so-called Islamic fundamentalist response: people concerned about the pace of change and what this will do to the next generation, people genuinely worried that their culture and traditions which have held for a thousand years will now be changed and even be in danger of being wiped out.

All the contributors to this volume focus to some extent on how Muslims have formulated and responded to these anxieties. However, only some of them dwell particularly on fundamentalism as a response. Fred Halliday in Chapter 5, for example, examines at length contemporary fundamentalisms in Iran and Tunisia, arguing that these can be understood only within their historical context and by using the traditional tools of social and political analysis. He thus questions whether there is, or need be, a distinctively postmodernist approach at all to Islamic studies, and seriously wonders about its applicability and appropriateness in this case. Nevertheless, he recognises that the 1990s are a particularly critical and potentially instructive vantage from which to examine what he calls 'Islamism', with more than a decade of successful Iranian revolution now completed, and the melange of emotions and passions whipped up by the Rushdie affair and the Gulf War leading the way to new Muslim definitions of the self.

This search for identity and distinctiveness in a shifting world has, in some Muslim countries, taken the form of demands for a Muslim state. For an existing regime, these demands raise all kinds of questions and difficulties, especially if the country concerned is both polyethnic and multi-faith. The course pursued by the Malaysian state in the face of such demands, as Judith Nagata demonstrates in Chapter 4, has been one of trying to achieve a workable 'balance' between as many of the interests involved as possible: the various Malaysian Islamic parties, other local political interest groups, and investors from abroad. As Nagata indicates, the task is fraught with contradictions, and the outcome in Malaysia has been a fragile compromise – characterized by the pursuit of modernity under what Nagata calls the 'cloak of Islamic correctness' – which juxtaposes the 'modern' Islam espoused by the state to more fundamentalist versions. Moreover, it is a compromise always susceptible to the perturbations of both the global and local arenas.

Abubaker Bagader's contribution (Chapter 6) provides an interesting counterpoint and complement to Halliday's and Nagata's analyses by offering a glimpse of the new Islamic movements from a Muslim point of view. Bagader both extends the historical and geographical scope of Halliday's discussion of fundamentalist Islam, and identifies the dependence of the new Islamic movements in the Arab world on reciprocal cultural flows between different Muslim nations (cf. Roff 1987). In the world media fundamentalism has become a shorthand for fanaticism and intolerance. It is a word taken from Christian Europe and applied to Muslim revivalist movements. It tells us little and does not clarify. On the contrary, it obfuscates and confuses. Certainly there have been Islamic movements in the modern era before the word became fashionable. But although we know of those in the last century – the great movements among the Sanusi in North Africa and of the Mahdi in Sudan and the Akhund in Swat in northern Pakistan – in the context of current Western media (mis)representations of revivalist Islam, it is particularly important that we also hear the voice of a Muslim academic who has studied them.

Muslim women in particular seem to be squeezed between Islamic fundamentalism and modernity, and between modernity and postmodernity (see Baykan 1990). The chapters by Weiss and by Watson (Chapters 7 and 8 respectively) suggest that, partly as a consequence of the special place which women occupy in Islam, and partly because of the ways in which religion is embedded in local social values (cf. Delaney 1991), Muslim women are frequently perceived as the most vulnerable to radical change and outside influence, the more so since the front door and compound wall are no longer effective barriers to such forces. Indeed, it is now often *behind* such barriers that these influences are strongest through television and the VCR. But, as Weiss reminds us, we should be careful of over-generalizing the impact which such influences can have. Thus class, for example, filters the female response to global processes. In contrast to the women of the Pakistani élite, many of whom lead lives like those of wealthy and professional women everywhere, it is the poor women studied by

Weiss in Lahore's walled city who experience most acutely the contradictions thrown up by contemporary demands. Among these women modern demands for educated brides sit uneasily with conservative notions of respectability which require a woman to stay at home. But this is true only for the moment. These very same women predict that in a decade none of them will be wearing the full body veil (*burqa*) typical of Pakistan.

This prediction is particularly interesting in the light of Watson's account of how the veil has recently been 'revived' by Muslim women living in Britain, France and Egypt as a way of coping with the challenges of contemporary life in these countries, and of emphasizing an Islamic identity.[6] This difference between the women described by Weiss and Watson both underlines the polyvalency of the veil and – at least in the case of the Asian women in Britain and perhaps also the Algerian women in France – recalls the point made earlier about the potentiality for cultural disjuncture between diasporic Muslims and those they leave behind. Above all, though, Watson emphasizes how the practice of veiling has become a politicized act whose meaning shifts depending on the articulation of the local with the global in any particular setting. In short, the perpetuation of the practice of veiling is no unreflective continuation of 'tradition', but is a considered response to the way the world is changing (cf. Baykan 1990: 136). Only by looking at veiling in these terms, Watson argues, can we transcend the polarized views of those Western feminist writers who see all veiling as oppression and those Muslim apologists who claim that it is liberating.

The richness and diversity of forms evoked by the notion of postmodernity is a central concern of the chapters by Martin Stokes and Gustav Thaiss. Drawing on his analyis of 'arabesk', Stokes (Chapter 2) sets out to trace how wider national and global cultural and political forces have been inscribed on this particular form of popular culture among Turkey's displaced urban migrants. He suggests that this has resulted in the use of 'global' metaphors, such as East–West, as a form of social and spatial practice. This is best seen in relation to belly dancing and social dancing, two practices which Stokes argues reveal with special clarity the conflation of global, urban, bodily and moral spaces. Though not discussed in these terms, Gustav Thaiss (in Chapter 3) is similarly concerned with the marking out of global, urban and moral spaces through performative behaviours of a different kind – in his case by analysing how the central Shi'a ritual commemorating Husain's martyrdom is enacted in Trinidad.

This ritual centres on a major tragedy – the death of the grandson of the Holy Prophet, Husain, at the battle of Karbala in 680 AD. It is one of the most important events in Muslim history. For Muslims it signifies the need to stand up to tyranny and injustice. For the Shi'a sect it could be described as an umbilical ritual which both links them to their past and defines who they are. They perform it annually wherever they live, especially in Iran, India and Pakistan. In Trinidad it is transported across the world to a different cultural and political setting, where it is influenced by local colour and rhetoric – now called 'Hosay' rather than 'Husain'. Non-Muslims participate in the Hosay ritual alongside the Shi'a, bringing to it a set of meanings that transform it (for them if not for the Shi'a themselves) from a solemn ritual reminding participants of the terrible events at Karbala into a carnival of fun. For these non-Muslim participants, the Hosay is merely another event in the carnival calendar, and the sorrow is converted into celebration. The symbolism of death (the colour black dominates among the Shi'a because of memories of Karbala) is overwhelmed by the exotic colours of the Caribbean. Drums and dancing characterize the Hosay festival. Competing and antithetical messages thus co-exist. Trinidadian Shi'a are aware that they now have little control over the Hosay and that, because of its wider popularity, its original meaning and structure have been transformed and extended.

If the aims of postmodernism are to seek and celebrate the rich variety of local styles and practices, and to grasp the development of cultural hybridity, then some might see these two chapters by Stokes and Thaiss as suggesting what a postmodernist version of Islamic studies can offer. Both Stokes and Thaiss raise questions about the globalization of culture and its 'creolization' (Hannerz 1987). These themes are amplified in the contribution by Pnina Werbner (Chapter 11), whose finely detailed account shows how Western media representations of the Gulf War were reworked as a locally meaningful narrative among British (mainly Pakistani) Muslims. This is no recently arrived community having to work through the first difficulties of contact with another culture. British Muslims are well-established, with a complex and elaborate culture which draws from the area in which they now live, as well as from their place of origin. Many of them have been formed from birth by 'creole systems of meaning' (Hannerz 1992: 264). Only an account which constructs global events like the Gulf War in terms of local experiences speaks persuasively to such people, and is likely to contribute towards a resolution of the predicaments which persist even among this long-established diaspora. The term 'fabulation' which Werbner uses to capture the manner in which local Muslim preachers interpreted events in the Gulf (and their media imaging) to their congregations thus seems very apt, with its implications of telling a tale of legendary and mythological proportions.

Similar processes can be discerned at work in different ways among other elements of the Muslim diaspora who must also negotiate identity and define Islam in different cultural contexts. In a contribution which usefully focuses on the lives and views of a type of Muslim traveller largely ignored in the literature, Richard Antoun (in Chapter 9) documents the experiences and perceptions of three Jordanian Muslims who left the Middle East to pursue higher education in Britain, Germany and the USA. Antoun argues that, surprisingly perhaps, the desire for secular education continues to have important religious dimensions, even when this education is sought in a non-Muslim country, and even when these religious dimensions are confronted by ways of living which directly contradict them. Such contradictions generate different responses and Antoun evaluates the usefulness of a range of concepts, such as 'compartmentalization' and 'exclusionary closure', for understanding the solutions which these Muslims have arrived at for the predicament of living abroad, as well as for understanding the less frequently remarked predicament of returning home.

Antoun's account of how ordinary Muslims manage their identity and religion while pursuing a university education overseas provides a useful backdrop to Tomas Gerholm's chapter (Chapter 10) on how Muslim intellectuals, through their written texts, elaborate (or fabulate?) their personal visions of Islam. In some respects, Gerholm's intellectuals might be Antoun's students ten or twenty years further on. Similar problems remain of how to follow an Islamic life-style when, in a predominantly Christian country, the institutions and the ethos are not there to meet the particular and often pragmatic needs of the practising Muslim. However, the difficulties of maintaining an Islamic identity are perhaps especially acute, Gerholm suggests, for the Muslim academic or intellectual who must deal with and engage the scientific arguments of their Western and often Christian counterparts. Whereas the traditional Islamic scholars like Allama Iqbal and Maulana Maududi wrote in Persian, Urdu and Arabic, contemporary Muslim scholars like Hossein Nasr, Ismail Faruqi and Ali Ashraf, as well as those discussed by Gerholm, write primarily in English. This lays their work open to a wider, critical and even antagonistic audience. Gerholm focuses mainly on two Muslim intellectuals, and since one of them is Akbar Ahmed, Gerholm's concerns might in some sense be said to encompass the present collection in a reflexive loop that incorporates his own contribution.

Gerholm's chapter, and the volume as a whole we feel, thus suggest that it is a critical moment in Islamic studies. We are at a cusp. It is time to point out the different features on the landscape – to point out where we were in the past and where we are heading for in the future. In the spirit of the age, although we are writing for a traditional scholastic and academic audience, we also wish to address a far wider audience of those interested in Islam and Islamic studies — journalists, writers, media commentators, indeed the average person who now has to grapple with words like *fatwa, jihad* and *ayatollah.*

Events in the last decade or so have transformed and shaken the Muslim world: the Iranian Revolution, the Rushdie affair, the Gulf War. Other influences on Muslim society have been more insidious but have resulted in no less significant transformations. The outside world now reaches into even the most guarded Muslim home, most obviously through television and the VCR. The processes of globalization have influenced traditional cultures and in such a dramatic way that they have raised issues for Muslims which can no longer be ignored. Muslims are forced to engage with these issues and to formulate a response to them. The response has not been slow in coming, but so far it has been a response more based in anger and passion as we saw in the Rushdie affair. Matters which in the past were considered only by the well-informed few are now debated in markets, at village wells and in tea houses — in short, at all those meeting places frequented by ordinary Muslim men and women of whatever level of society. One result seems to have been a more pronounced polarization in the Muslim world, one which creates a disjunction between radical Islam and the West.

This has also resulted in the populist response of Muslims to the world. It is a response formed and fed by the emotions of the bazaar. It reduces the Muslim response to the anger and passion of the spokesmen at the level of the bazaar. And through television this particular response dominates the response of the more reflective, more sophisticated Muslim scholar and statesman or stateswoman. This again is a legacy of the postmodernist era.

We are therefore suggesting that the challenge of understanding Islam in an age of postmodernity will demand all our powers of analysis, old and new. Neither the Orientalism that Said so passionately denounced, nor indeed the anti-Orientalism that Said himself has set in motion, are of much help. We point to a much more complex and more diverse situation, one that requires looking ahead and the forging of more nuanced ways of thinking about Muslim society. We hope that this volume will offer an introduction to that path.

Notes

1   This is not to deny that there is a 'world culture', but it is a 'world culture' marked 'by an organization of diversity rather than by a replication of uniformity' as Hannerz has suggested (1990: 237; see also Hannerz 1989a: 208).

2   Not everyone is agreed on the kinds of people who might properly be considered agents of globalization. Thus, for example, while both Appadurai (1990: 7) and Cheater (1993: 10) regard tourists as such, Hannerz (1990: 241) does not. Hannerz argues that since tourists — like exiles and most ordinary labour migrants — encapsulate themselves in a circle of compatriots, this usually precludes any sustained engagement with alien systems of meaning (1990: 241–43).

3   Although there is not space to dwell on them here, it is nevertheless worth pointing out that the displacement of culture from its territorial base has given rise to a number of conceptual and methodological problems for anthropologists. The (post)modern age seems to have rendered the notion of the bounded society obsolete (compare Kuper 1992 *passim*), and Paine wonders whether or not participant observation will be able to handle the new 'polycultural kaleidoscope' of the 'compressed world' of the twenty-first century (1992: 201–3).

4   Unfortunately, however, we do not deal, except in passing, with the global dispersal of religious scholars. Many religious groups, such as the Jamaat-i-Islami, the Tabligh, the Deobandis, and the Barelwis, have long-standing networks both in the West and throughout the Muslim world. Nor are we able to discuss those pan-Islamic, globalizing movements, such as the World Muslim League and the Islamic Conference, which have sought to organize the *umma* on a formal basis.

5   And to a lesser extent elsewhere, since these series were also screened outside India. It is sometimes forgotten that the global media flow is not always in the same direction, even if it does have recognizable asymmetries. As Hannerz points out, there is not only the question of to what extent the 'peripheries' talk back, but also the question of the extent to which they influence one another. The Indian film industry, which offers entertainment for many parts of the third world, is a good

example of the latter (Hannerz 1989b: 68, 69). Thus Stokes (this volume) remarks on its influence on the development of popular culture in Turkey.

6   This, of course, is not the only time that Muslim dress has come into conflict with westernization. One of the 'less well-known crises of modernisation' was that of the Tunisian soldiers' trousers (see Gellner 1981: 177).

References

Ahmad, M. (1991) 'The politics of war: Islamic fundamentalisms in Pakistan', in J. Piscatori (ed.) *Islamic fundamentalisms and the Gulf Crisis*, Chicago: The Fundamentalism Project, American Academy of Arts and Sciences.

Appadurai, A. (1990) 'Disjuncture and difference in the global cultural economy', *Public Culture* 2 (2): 1–24.

Asad, T. (1990) 'Ethnography, literature, and politics: Some readings and uses of Salman Rushdie's *The Satanic Verses*', *Cultural Anthropology* 5 (3): 239–69.

Baykan, A. (1990) 'Women between fundamentalism and modernity', in B. S. Turner (ed.) *Theories of modernity and postmodernity*, London: Sage.

Boyne, R. (1990) 'Culture and the world system', in M. Featherstone (ed.) *Global culture: nationalism, globalization and modernity*, London: Sage.

Boyne, R. and Rattansi, A. (1990) 'The theory and politics of postmodernism: By way of an introduction', in R. Boyne and A. Rattansi (eds) *Postmodernism and society*, London: Macmillan.

Breckenridge, C. and Appadurai, A. (1989) 'On moving targets', *Public Culture* 2 (1): i–iv.

Cheater, A. (1993) 'Globalisation and the new technologies of knowing: Anthropological calculus or chaos?' Paper presented to the Association of Social Anthropologists' Decennial Conference, St Catherine's College, Oxford, July 1993. Cited with the permission of the author.

Delaney, C. (1991) *The seed and the soil: Gender and cosmology in Turkish village society*, Berkeley: University of California Press.

Donnan, H. and Werbner, P. (eds) (1991) 'Introduction', in H. Donnan and P. Werbner (eds) *Economy and culture in Pakistan: Migrants and cities in a Muslim society*, London: Macmillan.

Eickelman, D. F. and Piscatori, J., (1990) 'Social theory in the study of Muslim societies', in D. F. Eickelman and J. Piscatori (eds) *Muslim travellers: Pilgrimage, migration, and the religious imagination*, London: Routledge.

Fardon, R. (1992) 'Postmodern anthropology? Or, an anthropology of postmodernity?', in J. Doherty, E. Graham and M. Malek (eds) *Postmodernism and the social sciences*, London: Macmillan.

Featherstone, M. (1990) 'Global culture: An introduction', in M. Featherstone (ed.) *Global culture: Nationalism, globalization and modernity*, London: Sage.

—— (1991) *Consumer culture and postmodernism*, London: Sage.

Fischer, M. J. and Abedi, M. (1990) *Debating Muslims: Cultural dialogues in postmodernity and tradition*, Madison: University of Wisconsin Press.

Gardner, K. (1993) 'Desh-bidesh: Sylheti images of home and away', *Man* 28: 1–15.

Gellner, E. (1981) *Muslim society*, Cambridge: Cambridge University Press.

Giddens, A. (1990) *The consequences of modernity*, Cambridge: Polity Press.

Hannerz, U. (1987) 'The world in creolisation', *Africa* 57: 546–59.

—— (1989a) 'Culture between center and periphery: Toward a macroanthropology', *Ethnos* 54: 200–216.

—— (1989b) 'Notes on the global ecumene', *Public Culture* 1 (2): 66–75.

— (1990) 'Cosmopolitans and locals in world culture', in M. Featherstone (ed.) *Global culture: nationalism, globalization and modernity*, London: Sage.

— (1992) *Cultural complexity: Studies in the social organization of meaning*, New York: Columbia University Press.

Harvey, D. (1989) *The condition of postmodernity: An enquiry into the origins of cultural change*, Oxford: Basil Blackwell.

Kellner, D. (1988) 'Postmodernism as social theory: Some challenges and problems', *Theory, Culture and Society* 5: 2–3.

Kuper, A. (ed.) (1992) *Conceptualizing society*, London: Routledge.

Lash, S. and Urry, J. (1987) *The end of organized capitalism*, Oxford: Polity Press.

Lodge, D. (1985) *Small world*, Harmondsworth: Penguin Books.

Luhrmann, T. M. (1994) 'The good Parsi: The postcolonial "feminization" of a colonial elite', *Man* 29(2).

Malkki, L. (1992) 'National geographic: The rooting of peoples and the territorialization of national identity among scholars and refugees', *Cultural Anthropology* 7 (1): 24–44.

Mandel, R. (1990) 'Shifting centres and emergent identities: Turkey and Germany in the lives of Turkish gastarbeiter', in D. F. Eickelman and J. Piscatori (eds) *Muslim travellers: Pilgrimage, migration, and the religious imagination*, London: Routledge.

Modood, T. (1990) 'British Asian Muslims and the Rushdie Affair', *Political Quarterly* 61(2): 143–60.

Paine, R. (1992) 'The Marabar Caves, 1920–2020', in S. Wallman (ed.) *Contemporary futures: Perspectives from social anthropology*, London: Routledge.

Parkin, D. (1993) 'Nemi in the modern world: Return of the exotic', *Man* 28: 79–99.

Piscatori, J. (1991) 'Religion and realpolitik: Islamic responses to the Gulf War', in J. Piscatori (ed.) *Islamic fundamentalisms and the Gulf Crisis*, Chicago: The Fundamentalism Project, American Academy of Arts and Sciences.

Robertson, R. (1987) 'Globalization theory and civilizational analysis', *Comparative Civilizations Review* 17: 20–30.

— (1990) 'Mapping the global condition: Globalization as the central concept', in M. Featherstone (ed.) *Global culture: nationalism, globalization and modernity*. London: Sage.

Roff, W. R. (1987) 'Islamic movements: One or many?', in W. R. Roff (ed.) *Islam and the political economy of meaning*, London: Croom Helm.

Said, E. (1978) *Orientalism*, Harmondsworth: Penguin Books.

— (1981) *Covering Islam: How the media and the experts determine how we see the rest of the world*, London: Routledge and Kegan Paul.

Samad, Y. (1992) 'Book burning and race relations: Political mobilisation of Bradford Muslims', *New Community* 18(4): 507–19.

Stauth, G. and Zubaida, S. (eds) (1987) *Mass culture, popular culture and social life in the Middle East*, Boulder, CO: Westview Press.

Turner, B. S. (1990a) 'Periodization and politics in the postmodern', in B. S. Turner (ed.) *Theories of modernity and postmodernity*, London: Sage.

— (ed.) (1990b) *Theories of modernity and postmodernity*, London: Sage.

Wallerstein, I. (1974) *The modern world-system*, New York: Academic Press.

— (1984) *The politics of the world-economy*, Cambridge: Cambridge University Press.

— (1990) 'Culture is the world-system: A reply to Boyne', in M. Featherstone (ed.) *Global culture: nationalism, globalization and modernity*, London: Sage.

Worsley, P. (1990) 'Models of the modern world-system', in M. Featherstone (ed.) *Global culture: nationalism, globalization and modernity*, London: Sage.

Chapter 79

Rebecca L. Walkowitz

THE LOCATION OF LITERATURE

The transnational book and the migrant writer

It is fitting that the final extract in this anthology, opens with a question (from critic Gauri Viswanathan), that asks: "Precisely where is English literature produced?" This rhetorical question neatly brings together the topics of immigrant literature, postcolonialism, and globalization, not just to point out the contradictions in the term "English literature"—such as the fact that many languages contribute to this nationalistic unifying name for a diverse body of work—but also the new spatial networks that function quite differently in a globalized sense from past migratory movements. In other words, while people, and writers, have always travelled and have always written across nations, new technologies of communication and inexpensive intercontinental travel have led to transcultural networked modes of being and literary production. Books are written and produced via such transcultural networks, and simultaneously occupy multiple "literary systems", and this includes being rewritten to create different versions sensitive to different cultural audiences or markets. Rebecca L. Walkowitz, a world literature critic with a specialization in cosmopolitanisms and transnational modernisms, sketches some of the ways in which literature emerges from non-Anglophone contexts, yet is integrated into Anglophone markets through translation and cultural transposition. Literature then, at the level of production, circulation and reception, is already "a comparative literature." Walkowitz points out that immigrant literature thus functions across communities, and the new hybrid values explored may be challenging to any one national culture. After summarizing some of the authors explored in the essay collection that follows this extract, Walkowitz focuses on the implications of the new globalized "transnational models" of writing, drawing upon critic Susan Stanford Friedman's observation that immigrant authors don't only exist statically in this new hybrid space, since it is one of continual movement, traversing nations, time zones, languages, and cultures. Such a conception of immigrant, or perhaps more accurately "migrant", writing (more accurate because within globalization this networked movement is not one-way only), leads to a reassessment of contemporary globalized writing per se, since many "non-immigrant" authors function in an identical way, creating what critics have called "the transnational book." Walkowitz focuses on an exemplary writer of transnational literature, the "Caribbean-British-US" author Caryl Phillips, especially his creative engagement with the anthology format, that is to say, reworking this mode of collecting literary texts so often used in the past to homogenize and unify literary voices along nationalistic lines. Phillips explores new hybrid transnational categories of writing to disrupt previous stable formations, such as his anthology *Extravagant Strangers* (1997) which foregrounds sites of literary production rather than older codes and symbols of belonging, and creates what Walkowitz calls in a neat phrase "a proliferation of overlapping groups." Analogies that Phillips creates in his fiction and anthologizing are sometimes troubling and deliberately provocative; Walkowitz examines a number of these, such as the comparative approach to being a stranger in an English village versus being a refugee and a stranger "in a nation". Walkowitz points out that this uncomfortable analogy allows Phillips to ask deep questions concerning cultural heritage, nationalism, hospitality, and personal experiences of cultural difference.

"PRECISELY WHERE IS ENGLISH LITERATURE PRODUCED?"** This is Gauri Viswanathan's question, from an essay about the transformation of English studies in the wake of postcolonial theory (22). Her answer—not only "in England, of course"—focuses on the genealogy of the discipline, its development within the British Empire and other dominions outside England through the education of colonial subjects and the efforts of strangers such as "Jews, Dissenters, and Catholics" (23). But her answer also focuses on the dynamic relationship between "sites of cultural production and institutionalization," the way that "English literature" names a mode of analysis and a collection of works as well as the way that modes of analysis establish collections. In fact, she suggests, there is no "English literature" before institutionalization: only with disciplinary protocols do cultural products become a field (20). "Where is English literature produced?" thus asks us to consider that the location of literature depends not only on the places where books are written but also on the places where they are classified and given social purpose.

In its emphasis on critical geographies, Viswanathan's question remains important to continuing debates about the "national attributes" of literature (21). Yet today we would be likely to ask several other questions as well: *In what language* does English literature circulate? *Where* is English literature read? *Who* counts as a producer (writers, but also editors, printers, designers, publishers, translators, reviewers)? And *how* has the global circulation of English literature shaped its strategies and forms of appearance? These questions turn from production to circulation, and back again, reflecting a new emphasis on the history of the book and what Leah Price calls "the geography of the book" within postcolonial studies and world literature ("Tangible Page" 38). This work reinvigorates and reframes Homi K. Bhabha's claim that disciplinary models of comparison and distinction will have to be tested by new ways of understanding community. In *The Location of Culture*, published in 1994, Bhabha argued, "The very concepts of homogenous national cultures, the consensual or contiguous transmission of historical traditions, or 'Organic' ethnic communities—*as the grounds of cultural comparativism*—are in a profound process of redefinition" (5). A decade and more later, essays and reports about the future of literary studies assume the heterogeneity and discontinuity of national cultures, and many scholars now emphasize "networks" of tradition and the social processes through which those networks are established (Damrosch, "What Is World Literature" 3; Greene 216–21). Haun Saussy's essay on the state of comparative literature, published with replies as *Comparative Literature in an Age of Globalization*, marks and elaborates this turn. Like Saussy's volume, *Immigrant Fictions* suggests that literary studies will have to examine the global writing of books, in addition to their classification, design, publication, translation, anthologizing, and reception across multiple geographies. Books are no longer imagined to exist in a single literary system but may exist, now and in the future, in several literary systems, through various and uneven practices of world circulation.

Consider, for example, the literary systems represented on the cover of this volume, which displays in miniature the covers of five contemporary works of fiction in English—or, really, the covers of five editions of those works: they are, from left to right, the U.S.

paperback reprint of George Lamming's *Season of Adventure* (1999; first edition, 1960), the U.S. paperback reprint of Theresa Hak Kyung Cha's *Dictée* (2001; first edition, 1982), the British paperback translation of Iva Pekárková's *Gimme the Money* (2000; first edition, 1995), the Japanese paperback translation of David Peace's *Nineteen Seventy-Seven* (2001; first edition, 2000), and the U.S. paperback reprint of Monica Ali's *Brick Lane* (2004; first edition, 2003). These editions (as well as several others) are discussed in the volume's essays, which follow *Contemporary Literature's* stated mission by focusing only on literature in English. But as I have been suggesting, it has become more difficult to assert with confidence that we know what literature in English is. Some of the books depicted on our cover were produced while their authors were living in a place whose principal language is English; but at least two (*Gimme the Money* and *Nineteen Seventy-Seven*) were not. Some of the books are original-language editions, while others are translations of several sorts: a translation into English (*Gimme the Money,* from Czech), a translation into Japanese (*Nineteen Seventy-Seven,* from English), and a multilingual text (*Dictée*, which moves among several languages, including English, French, and Korean). As the essays in this volume attest, Anglophone works of immigrant fiction are not always produced in an Anglophone country; some immigrant fictions produced in an Anglophone country are not originally Anglophone; and some do not exist in any one language at all. These variations test the presumed monolingualism of any nation, whether the U.S. or England, and remind us that there is a (largely invisible) misfit between the national and linguistic valences of the tradition we call "English literature." That misfit is not new, of course: for many centuries, works of Anglophone literature have been produced outside of England (think of Scotland, Ireland, Wales, India, Nigeria, Antigua, the U.S., Canada, and so on); works produced within England have not been uniformly Anglophone (think of Marie de France's lays and Thomas More's *Utopia*); and other important English works have mixed languages (think of James Joyce's *Finnegans Wake* and T. S. Eliot's *The Waste Land*) or were translated from other languages (think of the King James Bible and Rabindranath Tagore's *The Home and the World*). Is today's literary multilingualism different in kind from the literary multilingualism of the past? My account of our volume's cover suggests that contemporary literature in an age of globalization is, in many ways, a comparative literature: works circulate in several literary systems at once, and can—some would say, need—to be read within several national traditions.

The transnational book

The contributors to *Immigrant Fictions* affirm that thinking about the migration of writers and about the effects of migration on literary culture will benefit from thinking about the migration of books. They approach this project variously. In his interview with Tokyo-Yorkshire writer David Peace, Matthew Hart asks what it means, in terms of research and career, to produce strongly regional and historical novels about England while living in Japan. Peace relates that his émigré experience has led him to think all the more carefully about the production and reception of regional texts. In addition, he explains with equanimity the changes he allowed in the recent French translation of his novel about the 1984–85 miners' strike, *GB84*. These changes involved switching the narrative voice of an anti-Semitic character from third person to first, in order to accommodate "the cultural and historical context of anti-Semitism within France" (567). By making substantial textual changes, Peace enters into several literary traditions, French as well as Japanese and English. Strategies of translation are also a concern in Wen Jin's article about *Fusang*, a novel first published in Chinese (1995) and later in English (2001) by the U.S.-Chinese writer Geling Yan. Well-known in mainland China, Yan now writes directly in English as well as in Chinese; she published her first Anglophone novel (not from translation) in July 2006. Examining the textual differences between the Chinese and English versions of *Fusang*, Jin argues that the multilingual circulation of immigrant fiction destabilizes nation-based conceptions of literary culture. She suggests that Asian American studies will need to adopt a more transnational perspective if it is to accommodate the several communities in which cultural products are produced and received. Jin's reading strategies allow us to see that the sexuality of the novel's eponymous character operates differently in Chinese and U.S. literary culture, and that readers' conceptions of the book's achievement often depend on local assumptions about the desires of Chinese women.

Eric Hayot's article about translation and mediation in *Dictée*, by the U.S.-Korean writer Theresa Hak Kyung Cha, and *Becoming Madame Mao*, by the U.S.-Chinese writer Anchee Min, suggests that immigrant fictions often mobilize two or more cultural vocabularies. In the case of Min's novel, this involves Chinese theatrical practice and Euro-American melodrama. Hayot argues that *Dictée* and *Becoming Madame Mao*, despite significant differences in genre and style, can be seen to share in the resistance to what he calls the "ethnic bildungsroman," the novel of successful assimilation. They resist this genre, Hayot contends, by bringing their readers into contact with the media of immigration, both the processes of fiction-writing and those of cultural pedagogy such as dictation and social performance. Directly, as in the case *Dictée*, and indirectly, as in *Becoming Madame Mao*, these texts reflect on the literary and political activities of making, translating, and becoming a work of art.

From the emphasis in the first three contributions on the cultural and linguistic translation of books, the volume shifts to an analysis of mobility's tropes. Věra Eliášová's essay takes up Iva Pekárková's *Gimme the Money*, a novel about a Czech woman who works as a taxi driver in New York City. Pekárková wrote and published *Gimme the Money* in Czech while she was living in the U.S.; she later translated the novel into English after returning to the Czech Republic; she now lives in London. Eliášová presents Pekárková's novel as a book that theorizes its own cultural mobility: she argues that the novel figures migration as a circular movement, like the itinerary of a taxi, rather than as a single journey. In addition, she suggests, *Gimme the Money* has its own complex "multidimensional mobility" because it operates within several literary genres, including the Eastern European immigrant autobiography, the modernist novel about women in the city, and the new writing from postcommunist Europe. The mix of genres and traditions in Pekárková's work, Eliášová suggests, complicates efforts to place her novels within a national geography: because she wrote *Gimme the Money* as a Czech expatriate in New York but now lives in London, Pekárková fits imperfectly in both U.S. and Czech literary cultures.

Like David Peace and Anchee Min, who live in one place but write about another, George Lamming helped to establish the modern Caribbean novel while living in metropolitan London. J. Dillon Brown argues in his essay that the disjunction between the geography of Lamming's production and initial circulation (England) and the geography of his origin and themes (Barbados) helps to explain his work's infamous "difficulty" and its relationship to modernist precursors. Brown argues, moreover, that any analysis of the post-colonial novel needs to take into account its metropolitan development. He suggests that readers must see Lamming in the context of British literary history, as well as in the context of Caribbean literary history. But more specifically he proposes that Lamming's presence within the literary history of Britain gives a different shape to the literary history of the Caribbean. It is not simply a matter of acknowledging Lamming's participation in one more tradition but rather of examining the transnational context of publishing in the 1950s. "Placing Lamming's work into its metropolitan contexts," Brown writes, "allows more space for emphasizing how his novels foreground the practical impossibility of claims for pure cultural absolutism or an unproblematically static, rooted cultural identity." His essay asks, in both literal and figurative registers, what is the *source* of Lamming's fiction and especially of his literary style?

The final essay in the volume, Alistair Cormack's analysis of Monica Ali's blockbuster, *Brick Lane*, asks whether migration has a proper literary form, and whether migration transforms realist fiction. Taking Ali's novel as his test case, Cormack suggests that the struggle with language and subjectivity at the center of many immigrant novels does not fit well with realism's emphasis on individual agency. Cormack argues that scenes of translation in *Brick Lane*, which involve the interpretation of manners as well as of writing, draw attention to the narration's seamless movement between English and Bengali, and between a sense of estrangement in England and a sense of knowledge about that estrangement. For all its *Bildung*, Cormack proposes, Ali's novel fits uneasily within the bildungsroman tradition. "The demands of representing different cultural signifying systems," Cormack writes, "render unstable the novel's transparency." Cormack concludes that the experience of immigration, once it is represented in fiction, alters the way that mimetic genres function. At the same time, Cormack suggests that novels such as *Brick Lane* are exceptionally popular as immigrant fictions in good part because they mostly avoid the analysis of transnational writing and circulating that Hayot, Eliášová, and Brown see in works by Cha, Pekárková, and Lamming.

The migrant writer

Not every book that travels is produced by a writer who travels, though today it is common for writers whose works circulate in many areas of the globe to participate in book fairs and tours that take them beyond their original continent and hemisphere. In this limited sense, most successful writers are also migrant writers. The globalization of publishing, which generates immigrating books as well as immigrating writers, is discussed in several of the essays in this volume. But contributors also investigate a kind of immigration that is more familiar and in some ways more old-fashioned: they look at writers who have belonged or who continue to belong to more than one nation, region, or state and who now participate in a literary system that is different from the system in which they were born, educated, or first published. Of course, even this understanding of immigration is relatively new, as Susan Stanford Friedman has argued in a survey of the field, because it reflects a shift from nation-based paradigms to "transnational models emphasizing the global space of ongoing travel and transcontinental connection" (906). Several contributors suggest that it is not simply a matter of leaving one system for another, both because most literary systems rely on networks of publishing and distribution that are international if not global and because one is not always welcomed in new systems; one may not fit comfortably in any system; and one does not necessarily give up past affiliations while forging new ones.

These ways of thinking about the varieties and complexities of literary participation correspond to new ways of thinking about whose lives and which objects are transformed by migration. One of the important turns in the analysis of what this volume calls "immigrant fiction" has been a new emphasis on disciplinary paradigms of tradition, language, and classification. That is, scholars have argued that the political and social processes of immigration shape the whole literary system, the relationships among all of the works in a literary culture, and not simply the part of that system that involves books generated by immigrant populations. This means that "the literature of migration," to use Leslie Adelson's term of art, would have to include all works that are produced in a time of migration or that can be said to reflect on migration. Whether one privileges social contexts or literary content, it is no longer principally a matter of distinguishing immigrant from nonimmigrant authors. "The literature of migration," Adelson argues, "is not written by migrants alone" (23).

Conversely, Carine Mardorossian proposes, being a migrant writer or even writing about the experience of migration does not guarantee that one will produce migrant literature. Mardorossian associates migrant literature with an aesthetic program rather than an origin or topic; for her, that program involves rejecting the "opposition between the modern and the traditional, the country of destination and the country of origin" (21). Accordingly, nonimmigrant writers who are engaged intellectually with the movement of people and objects across geographies and cultures, and who articulate in their work a "cosmopolitan, transnational, and hybrid vision of social life," could be producers of immigrant fiction. Likewise, this volume queries the genre it names. Is the immigrant in *immigrant fictions* like the English in *English studies*? Does it name a kind of writer? A kind of book? A kind of writing? A kind of criticism?

Adelson's and Mardorossian's arguments overlap to some extent but not entirely: while Adelson focuses on the transformation of a literary culture, Mardorossian is more concerned with the arguments of individual texts. Both, however, assert that changes in thinking about migration require changes in thinking about belonging, community, and civic recognition. They reject two assumptions: that migrants move "between two worlds" that are distinct and coherent, and that migrants bring with them or enter into literary systems that are unique and strictly local (Adelson 4, 7). These arguments about migration suggest that literary classification might depend more on a book's future than on a writer's past. What has happened to the writer is less important, in these accounts, than what happens in the writing and in the reading, though the biography of the writer may influence the way that books are written and received.

The contributors to this volume also emphasize analytic paradigms of migration and migration's transformation of literary cultures. And the range of authors they consider points to a broad conception of our eponymous term. All of the writers considered in this collection have moved from one place to another at some point in their lives, but the causes and processes of those movements are remarkably different, as are the ways that the writers display mobility in their work. All may respond to immigration, but some do so in a direct manner, by writing about characters who have been transplanted; others treat immigration much less directly, by writing about characters who believe themselves to be very much at home.

Reading beyond the nation

What happens when the migrant writer reflects on the transnational book? My own approach to this question leads me to look at a range of literary and paraliterary texts—anthologies, essays, memoirs, public lectures, interviews, as well as fiction—and at those examples of *comparative writing* that have sought to preempt or replace national models of literary culture. I share with Franco Moretti, David Damrosch, and other scholars of world literature an interest in the circulation and reception of books, but I examine in addition how writers, translators, and anthologists have helped to shape the field. Consider, for example, Caryl Phillips, who was born in Saint Kitts, raised in Leeds, and now lives and works in New York, London, and New Haven. Phillips mentions these locations on his professional Web site and in the biographies that introduce each of the U.S. paperback editions of his work. The language of the biographies varies slightly, but there are some constants: he emphasizes cities and smaller regions rather more than continents, empires, or nations. Here are a few samples:

> Caryl Phillips was born in 1958 in St. Kitts, West Indies, and went with his family to England that same year. He was brought up in Leeds and educated at Oxford.
>
> (*Higher Ground*)

> Caryl Phillips was born in St. Kitts, West Indies. Brought up in England, he has written for television, radio, theater, and cinema. . . . He divides his time between London and New York.
>
> (*Extravagant Strangers*)

> Caryl Phillips was born in St. Kitts, West Indies. Brought up in England, he has written for television, radio, theater, and film. . . . Phillips lives in New York.
>
> (*New World Order*)

In each biography, Phillips suggests that the book we are about to read has many sources and has been shaped, like Lamming's work, by the interplay among several literary cultures.

A Caribbean-British-U.S. writer, Phillips presents his books both as products and as philosophies of migration. In this doubling, they can seem to stand at once inside and outside the immigrant fiction tradition. His books are products of migration because they are built on literary and political histories that correspond to the several places Phillips or Phillips's family has lived. Building on these histories, they make Anglophone literary culture more inclusive of writers born outside of England. Yet they are philosophies of migration because they seem ambivalent about the process of equating culture with community (literary inclusion as national inclusion) and about the ways that cultural expressivity has been used both to justify and to resist anti-immigrant violence. In his work, Phillips tries to make cultural institutions responsive to migration without simply reproducing the forms and strategies of the nation. What new shapes of collectivity, he seems to ask, can histories of migration help us to imagine?

Phillips's novels, anthologies, and essays offer compelling examples of the new world literature and of what I call "comparison literature," an emerging genre of world literature for which global comparison is a formal as well as a thematic preoccupation. By using the term *comparison literature*, I mean to consider the relationship between the writing of world literature and the protocols of reading we bring to those texts. And I mean to draw our attention to the traditional distinction between the disciplines of national literature, which typically refer to what books are, who wrote them, or where they were produced, and the discipline of comparative literature, which typically refers to what we do with books. Comparison literature implies both of these projects, asking us to understand comparison as the work of scholars, to be sure, but also as the work of books that analyze—as Phillips's do—the transnational contexts of their own production, circulation, and study.

As objects and as containers, Phillips's books function as world literature in several respects: they are written, printed, translated, and read in multiple places; and they analyze the relationship among multiple instances of global travel, not only sampling and collating an array of migration narratives but also rehearsing different strategies of sampling and collating. Phillips's work offers an opportunity to consider the relationship between the production and circulation of world literature because—apart from being read within several literary systems—it is written to make those systems less unique. In his concern with uniqueness, Phillips is engaged with debates about *historical* distinctiveness, such as whether the Holocaust can be usefully compared to other examples of racism and genocide; and he is engaged with debates about *national* distinctiveness, such as whether works of literature or other cultural products can be usefully classified by the national origin of their makers, however that origin is defined. It would be possible to look at works of contemporary literature that reflect on the geography of their circulation and translation (Walkowitz, "Unimaginable Largeness"), but here I will focus on works that reflect on the geography of classification and promotion.

Over the past two decades, Phillips has published in an extraordinary number of genres, including the stage play, the screenplay, the radio play, the literary review, the memoir, the anthology, and the novel. Even more striking than the variety of his publications, however, is their consistent borrowing from a single genre—the anthology—whose structure and strategies Phillips uses to shape each of his novels and many of his nonfiction works as well. Patently, the anthology form is an odd choice for a writer committed to literary classifications that exceed or abjure the nation. As Phillips well knows, literary anthologies have been used throughout the twentieth century to affirm the expressive cultures of national or micronational communities (Walkowitz, "Shakespeare"). Given this history, the anthology offers an unlikely fit for the discontinuities of migration, and for ideas of community based on social contact and hospitality rather than on collective memory or cultural sameness.

And yet, for Phillips, the anthology is useful because it articulates at the level of form the problems of order, inclusion, and comparison that migration narratives articulate at the level of content. Put another way, thinking about the anthology and migration together allows Phillips to reflect on the intersection between literary and political histories of belonging. Of course, Phillips is not alone in his effort to accommodate migration within the tradition of the anthology. The sheer proliferation of new anthologies of world literature and the new debates about anthologies of national literature are telling. Indeed, one might observe that Phillips has been rethinking world literature through the anthology at the very same time that many editors, including Phillips, have been rethinking the anthology through world literature.[1] Since the 1980s, when Phillips began writing his novels, trade publishers have been producing anthologies devoted to writing by women, writing by African Americans, writing by Jewish authors in Britain and Ireland, and so on. But the substantial revision and diversification of the major anthologies—English literature, American literature, world literature—is a much more recent trend, and it coincides with a critical turn to multilingualism, micronationalisms, postcolonial writing, and migration. In the Norton anthology series, the addition of an anthology of "world literature" to the anthology of "world masterpieces" suggests a new self-consciousness about the rhetoric of timeless value and about the relationship of that rhetoric to histories of imperialism. New thinking about migration has had an effect, too, on anthologies that do not seem to be about language or geography at all: the landmark *Norton Anthology of Writing by Women*, which arguably started the minor anthology trend within major anthology publishing in 1985, now carries the subtitle *The Traditions in English*, a feature that is surely related to a greater awareness about the uneven geography of women's writing. Within the African American literary tradition, which constitutes one of Phillips's touchstones, many writers have also been anthology-makers and have been wary at times of the logic of cultural nationalism that the anthology's tone of celebration often serves.[2]

Ambivalent about the social function of the anthology while relying on its form, Phillips generates a kind of collectivity in his work—but it is a collectivity of negative belonging, what Virginia Woolf famously dubbed a "Society of Outsiders." One of his anthologies brings together nonnative British writers in a book called *Extravagant Strangers*. In that volume, Phillips creates a tradition of very loose affiliation: his contributors have different ways of being "strangers" in Britain, and some only seem to be strangers by technicality, like William Makepeace Thackeray, who was born in Calcutta before moving to England at the age of five. One might say that *Extravagant Strangers* does more to deflate the coherence of other anthologies than it does to assert its own. It includes not only famous English writers who are in some ways strangers in England but also less famous strangers, such as Ignatius Sancho, who made contributions to English prose. Phillips's anthology, from 1997, creates a new order of literary belonging. That belonging is defined by the geography of production, and thus Phillips's collection follows the path of the Longman and Oxford anthologies, which privilege places of making over language and cultural origin.

Phillips's novels and nonfiction works are like anthologies in that they sample and collate stories of racism, slavery, European anti-Semitism, and recent violence against immigrants.

But unlike other anthologies, which create a single series, Phillips's books tend to promote various microseries within them. In addition to collating the lives of several migrants, his books also represent the life of any single migrant, including their author, as yet another collated account. In the short biographies that preface each of his books, Phillips mentions the places through which he has moved and continues to move. In a 2001 anthology of his own essays, called *A New World Order*, Phillips describes his collated self as "one harmonious entity" (6). And yet there is something not especially harmonious about the relationship among the parts he names—Africa, the Caribbean, Britain, and the United States—or about the collective stories that these places are meant to represent. Phillips intimates this discord by emphasizing what Theodore Mason has called the "historicity" of anthology production—the procedures of selection, arrangement, and framing that allow one series to emerge rather than another (191). Instead of a single progression through places whose meanings are fixed, Phillips presents multiple progressions through places whose meanings vary according to the framework he establishes for them.

For example, the structure of Phillips's introduction to *A New World Order* presents an autobiographical story of migration that is rather different from the one in his paratextual biography. Emphasizing fantasy and memory rather than legal homes, the introduction begins and ends in different parts of Africa, where in one case Phillips is hosted by a British official eager to display his graciousness toward an African porter; and, in another, he is served by an African waiter who assumes that Phillips, like any other loyal subject of the British Crown, must be mourning the death of Princess Diana. Each of these anecdotes serves to register Phillips's discomfort both with British attitudes toward Africa and with African attitudes toward Britain. And Phillips seems to be acknowledging that there is something limited and perhaps false about identity claims based on a distant past: the slave trade may have transported his family from Africa, but an African local treats him simply as a patriot of Britain. Within the book's introduction, there are additional collections: the collection constituted by classmates from Phillips's childhood school, whose surnames a teacher matches to various geographic origins, though not in Phillips's case; and the collection constituted by new technologies of migration, such as worldwide CNN broadcasts, inexpensive airplane travel, and a tourism industry in the former slave ports of West Africa. These different ways of arranging geography and of arranging the ways that people move through geography today suggest to us the several different anthologies in which Phillips's story takes part. The structure of the chapters of Phillips's book follows yet another order, beginning in the U.S. and moving to Africa, to the Caribbean, and then finally to Britain. Taken as a narrative, the chapters seem to tell the history of Phillips's professional life, whereas the series in the biography and in the introduction display the history of his postcolonial consciousness, the history of his passports, and the history of the African diaspora. *A New World Order*, despite the singular name, offers up many orders of migration. With its multiple framings and allegorical constructions, Phillips's anthology aspires to the ingenuity and artifice of fiction.

His fiction, in turn, hews to the anthology but unsettles the logic of representativeness by introducing comparisons among several narratives and by emphasizing regions and cities rather than nations and continents. Reading beyond the nation in the way that Phillips suggests means recognizing literary cultures and political histories that exceed the nation, and also recognizing those that are narrower than the nation, or those that emphasize alternative grounds of collectivity. Phillips's most recent book, *Dancing in the Dark*, is a fictionalized history of the Bahamas-born, Southern California-raised minstrel performer Bert Williams, who traveled across the U.S. and throughout England, and who died as a resident of Harlem in upper Manhattan. Presenting Williams as an Afro-Caribbean performer who is taken for an African American performer who is taken for the racist stereotype of a Southern "coon" that he imitates so well, Phillips wants us to understand the regional and international migrancy that complicates the geography of African American culture, which includes not only the story of Bert Williams but also the frame of that story—a novel by Caryl Phillips. *Dancing in the Dark* emphasizes the international and regional journeys that make up the typical artifacts of national culture. In this case, the African American minstrel performer *par excellence* turns out to be a native not of the American South or of a Northern city, but of the Caribbean and the Pacific coast.

Phillips's novel-anthologies eschew two aspects of the anthology tradition: its claim to express a distinctive literary culture based on race or national origin; and its tone of celebration, which has tended to affirm a group's expressivity without acknowledging the violent history of such affirmations. This ambivalence about the celebration of cultural heritage helps to explain Phillips's choice to put a black minstrel performer at the center of a story about the history of African American theater. Phillips's anthologies tend to emphasize violence rather than creativity, and they use various devices of comparison to create a proliferation of overlapping groups. Phillips values the collective, but his communities are made up of strangers whose affiliation is fragile, provisional, and often temporary.

If *Dancing in the Dark* serves to display the international history of African American and U.S. cultural traditions, Phillips's previous novel, *A Distant Shore*, counters stereotypes about British natives and non-British strangers by sounding national histories of violence in both regional and international registers. Engaging with debates about Britain's treatment of refugees and immigrants, *A Distant Shore*, from 2003, sets a story about the strangeness of an English woman in a new housing development beside a story about the strangeness of a man, also new to that development, who is a refugee from genocidal violence in an African country, perhaps Rwanda. By comparing the condition of being a stranger in a village to the more expansive condition of being a stranger in a nation, the novel asks us to think from the beginning about several scales of belonging. The first line of the novel, "England has changed," turns out to refer not to the arrival of immigrants like the man from Africa but to the arrival of gentrification and of people, like the woman from the town, who buy new bungalows outside small, traditional villages (3). It is in some ways disturbing that Phillips would compare the man's experience of racism in this town with the woman's experience of loneliness and ostracism, but this comparison allows Phillips to suggest that the town's exclusion of strangers like the woman is motivated by nativist values that are similar to those that motivate, or at least excuse, the attack on strangers from other nations and other cultures. The novel also seeks to question the cultural heritage that the villagers think they are preserving. Our only initial hint that national histories may have regional variations and that regional variations can complicate assumptions about ethical superiority comes in the novel's first description of the town: a place "twinned," we are told, with a town in Germany that was utterly destroyed during World War II and a village in the south of France where in those same years Jews were deported to extermination camps (4). The identity of the English town seems to depend on its status as a place where bombing and deportation did not take place. But the descriptions of the French and German towns hint at an incongruity that reflects on England. By selecting a victimized town to represent Germany and a victimizing village to represent France, Phillips asks us to consider the difference between what we assume about English hospitality—its comparative liberalism, for example—and what we might learn about the local treatment of strangers.

In *A Distant Shore* and *Dancing in the Dark*, narratives of migration violate the epithets of place ("liberal England," "fascist Germany," and so on) that have allowed us to classify books and, in turn, to classify writers. By creating new anthologies, Phillips tries to modify the way his books will be contained. He does this by troubling the distinction between container and object: his books may seem like objects, but they are full of containers: comparative frameworks that impose new classifications and ask us to question what we know about the location of literature. Within his novels and nonfiction works, embedded anthologies give dynamic form to the history of migration. Instead of suggesting that books by new arrivals expand or simply disable literary histories based on the nation, Phillips suggests that these works can help us to imagine new literary histories, ones whose scale includes the town, the region, and the housing development, and whose object includes not only the production of books but also their translation, circulation, and comparison. It is these multiple scales and multiple objects that reading beyond the nation, if we are to take up such a charge, will have to accommodate.

In the essays that follow, the contributors to this volume examine multiple ways that works of immigrant fiction travel and make their home today. For books, making a home can refer to processes as different as production, translation, circulation, reception, allusion, and curricular adoption; and these kinds of home-making are not necessarily, or now even principally, exclusive or permanent. By thinking about the migration of books, in addition to the migration of writers, this volume urges readers to imagine that the location of any literary work is achieved and unfinished, indebted to a network of past collaborations and contestations, and to collaborations and contestations that have not yet taken place. In this age of globalization, a new work of English literature has its life in many places. The essays collected here show how contemporary writers such as Caryl Phillips, David Peace, Geling Yan, Theresa Hak Kyung Cha, Anchee Min, Iva Pekárková, George Lamming, and Monica Ali have helped to imagine and create that condition.

Notes

1   See Bate, Damrosch, Greenblatt, and King, who engage with this issue in their prefaces. Leah Price offers further discussion in two reviews.
2   See the discussions in Edwards and Mason. See also Walkowitz, "Shakespeare."

Works cited

Adelson, Leslie A. *The Turkish Turn in Contemporary German Literature: Toward a New Critical Grammar of Migration.* New York: Palgrave-Macmillan, 2005.

Bate, Jonathan. General Editor's Preface. *The Internationalization of English Literature.* Oxford: Oxford UP, 2004. Vol. 13 in *The Oxford Literary History.* Gen. ed. Jonathan Bate. Oxford: Oxford UP, 2003. viii–x.

Bhabha, Homi K. *The Location of Culture.* New York: Routledge, 1994.

Damrosch, David. Preface. *The Longman Anthology of British Literature.* Vol. 2. Ed. David Damrosch. New York: Longman, 1999. xxxiii–xxxvii.

——. Preface. *The Longman Anthology of World Literature.* Vol. F. Ed. David Damrosch. New York: Longman, 2004. xvii–xxi.

——. *What Is World Literature?* Princeton, NJ: Princeton UP, 2003.

Edwards, Brent Hayes. *The Practice of Diaspora: Literature, Translation, and the Rise of Black Nationalism.* Cambridge, MA: Harvard UP, 2003.

Friedman, Susan Stanford. "Migrations, Diasporas, and Borders." *Introduction to Scholarship in Modern Languages and Literatures.* Ed. David Nicholls. New York: MLA, 2006. 899–941.

Greenblatt, Stephen. Preface. *The Norton Anthology of English Literature.* Vol. 1. Ed. M. H. Abrams. New York: Norton, 2003. xxxiii–xlii.

Greene, Roland. "Not Works but Networks: Colonial Worlds in Comparative Literature." *Comparative Literature in an Age of Globalization.* Ed. Haun Saussy. Baltimore, MD: Johns Hopkins UP, 2006. 212–23.

King, Bruce. Introduction. *The Internationalization of English Literature*. Oxford: Oxford UP, 2004. Vol. 13 in *The Oxford Literary History*. Gen. ed. Jonathan Bate. Oxford: Oxford UP, 2003.1–13.

Mardorossian, Carine M. "From Literature of Exile to Migrant Literature." *Modern Language Studies* 32.3 (2003): 15–33.

Mason, Theodore O. "The African-American Anthology: Mapping the Territory, Taking the National Census, Building the Museum." *American Literary History* 10 (1998): 185–98.

McDonald, Peter D. "Ideas of the Book and Histories of Literature: After Theory?" *PMLA* 121 (2006): 214–28.

Moretti, Franco. "Conjectures on World Literature." *New Left Review 1* (Jan.-Feb. 2000): 54–68.

The Norton Anthology of World Literature. Ed. Sarah Lawall. 6 vols. New York: Norton, 2003.

The Norton Anthology of World Masterpieces. Ed. Maynard Mack. Exp. ed. New York: Norton, 1997.

The Norton Anthology of Writing by Women. Ed. Susan Gubar and Sandra M. Gilbert. New York: Norton, 1985.

The Norton Anthology of Writing by Women: The Traditions in English. Ed. Susan Gubar and Sandra M. Gilbert. 2nd ed. New York: Norton, 1996.

Phillips, Caryl. *Dancing in the Dark*. New York: Knopf, 2005.

—. *A Distant Shore*. New York: Vintage, 2003.

—. *Extravagant Strangers: A Literature of Belonging*. New York: Vintage, 1997.

—. *Higher Ground: A Novel in Three Parts*. New York: Vintage, 1989.

—. *A New World Order: Essays*. New York: Vintage, 2001.

Price, Leah. "Elegant Extracts." *London Review of Books* 3 Feb. 2000: 26–28.

—. "The Tangible Page." *London Review of Books* 31 Oct. 2002:36–39.

Saussy, Haun. "Exquisite Cadavers Stitched from Fresh Nightmares: Of Memes, Hives, and Selfish Genes." *Comparative Literature in an Age of Globalization*. Ed. Haun Saussy. Baltimore, MD: Johns Hopkins UP, 2006.3–42.

Viswanathan, Gauri. "An Introduction: Uncommon Genealogies." *ARIEL: A Review of International English Literature* 31.1–2 (2000): 13–31.

Walkowitz, Rebecca L. "Shakespeare in Harlem: *The Norton Anthology*, 'Propaganda,' Langston Hughes." *Modern Language Quarterly* 60 (1999): 495–519.

—. "Unimaginable Largeness: Kazuo Ishiguro, Translation, and the New World Literature." Work in progress.

Bibliography

Adams, Ian and R.W. Dyson. *Fifty Major Political Thinkers*. London & New York: Routledge, 2003.

Adorno, Theodor and Max Horkheimer. *Dialectic of Enlightenment*. Trans. John Cumming. London: Verso, 1992.

Adorno, Theodor W. *Aesthetic Theory*. Trans. Robert Hullot-Kentor. Minneapolis: University of Minnesota Press, 1997.

Ahluwalia, Pal. *Out of Africa: Post-structuralism's Colonial Roots*. Abingdon, Oxon & New York: Routledge, 2010.

Ahmed, Aijaz. "Jameson's Rhetoric of Otherness and the 'National Allegory'." *Social Text* 17 (Autumn 1987): 3–25.

Anidjar, Gil. "Introduction: 'Once More, Once More': Derrida, the Arab, the Jew." *Acts of Religion*. Jacques Derrida. Ed. Gil Anidjar. London & New York: Routledge, 2002.1–39.

Appadurai, Arjun. "Grassroots Globalization and the Research Imagination." *Globalization*. Ed. Arjun Appadurai. Durham, NC: Duke University Press, 2001. 1–21.

Appiah, Anthony and Henry Louis Gates, Jr., eds. *Identities*. Chicago & London: University of Chicago Press, 1995.

Arac, Jonathan, Wlad Godzich and Wallace Martin, eds. *The Yale Critics: Deconstruction in America*. Minneapolis: University of Minnesota Press, 1983.

Ashcroft, Bill. *On Postcolonial Futures: Transformations of a Colonial Culture*. London & New York: Continuum, 2001.

Ashcroft, Bill, Gareth Griffiths and Helen Tiffin. *The Empire Writes Back: Theory and Practice in Post-Colonial Literatures*. London & New York: Routledge, 1989.

Ashcroft, Bill, Gareth Griffiths and Helen Tiffin. *Key Concepts in Post-Colonial Studies*. London & New York: Routledge, 1998.

Badiou, Alain. *Saint Paul: The Foundation of Universalism*. Trans. Ray Brassier. Stanford, CA: Stanford University Press, 2003.

Baldick, Chris. *The Social Mission of English Criticism 1848–1932*. Oxford: Clarendon Press, 1987.

Banton, Michael. *Racial Theories*. Cambridge: Cambridge University Press, 1998.

Baudrillard, Jean. *Utopia Deferred: Writings for* Utopie *(1967–1978)*. Trans. Stuart Kendall. New York: Semiotext(e), 2006.

Bhabha, Homi K. "Foreword: Remembering Fanon, Self, Psyche and the Colonial Condition." *Black Skin, White Masks*. Frantz Fanon. Trans. Charles Lam Markmann. London: Pluto, 1986. vii–xxv.

Bhabha, Homi K. *The Location of Culture*. London & New York: Routledge, 1994.

Belsey, Catherine. *Critical Practice*. London & New York: Methuen, 1980.

Bentley, Jerry H. "Globalizing History and Historicizing Globalization". *Globalization and Global History*. Barry K. Gills and William R. Thompson, eds. Abingdon, Oxon & New York: Routledge, 2006. 18–32.

Birch, Keith. "A Community of Interests." *Radical Records: Thirty Years of Lesbian and Gay History, 1957–1987*. Bob Cant and Susan Hemmings, eds. London & New York: Routledge, 2010. 32–37.

Bonnett, Alastair. "Constructions of Whiteness in European and American Anti-Racism." *Debating Cultural Hybridity: Multi-Cultural Identities and the Politics of Anti-Racism*. Pnina Werbner and Tariq Modood, eds. London & New Jersey: Zed, 1997.173–92.

Borch-Jacobsen, Mikkel. *The Freudian Subject*. Trans. Catherine Porter, London: Macmillan, 1989.

Brennan, Timothy. "From development to globalization: postcolonial studies and globalization theory." *The Cambridge Companion to Postcolonial Literary Studies*. Neil Lazarus, ed. Cambridge: Cambridge University Press, 2004. 120–38.

Buck, Claire, ed. *Bloomsbury Guide to Women's Literature*. London: Bloomsbury, 1992.

Busa, Roberto A. "Foreword: Perspectives on the Digital Humanities." *A Companion to Digital Humanities*. Susan Schreibman, Ray Siemens and John Unsworth, eds. Oxford: Blackwell, 2004. xvi–xxi.

Butler, Judith. "Sex and Gender in Simone De Beauvoir's *Second Sex*." *Simone de Beauvoir: A Critical Reader*. Elizabeth Fallaize, ed. London & New York: Routledge. 29–42.

Butler, Judith. *Gender Trouble: Feminism and the Subversion of Identity*. London & New York: Routledge, 1999.

Caputo, John D. and Michael J. Scanlon. "Introduction: The Postmodern Augustine." *Augustine and Postmodernism: Confessions and Circumfession*. John D. Caputo and Michael J. Scanlon, eds. Bloomington and Indianapolis: Indiana University Press, 2005. 1–15.

Castle, Gregory. *The Blackwell Guide to Literary Theory*. Oxford: Blackwell, 2007.

Cavell, Richard. *McLuhan in Space: A Cultural Geography*. Toronto: University of Toronto Press, 2003.

Childs, Donald J. "New Criticism." *Encyclopedia of Contemporary Literary Theory: Approaches, Scholars, Terms*. Irena R. Makaryk, ed. Toronto: University of Toronto Press, 2000. 120–24.

Chodorow, Nancy. *The Reproduction of Mothering: Psychoanalysis and the Sociology of Gender*. Berkeley and Los Angeles: University of California Press, 1978.

Clarke, George Elliott. *Odysseys Home: Mapping African-Canadian Literature*. Toronto: University of Toronto Press, 2002.

Clarke, J.J. *In Search of Jung*. London & New York: Routledge, 1992.

Colebrook, Claire. "On the Very Possibility of Queer Theory." *Deleuze and Queer Theory*. Chrysanthi Nigianni and Merl Storr, eds. Edinburgh: Edinburgh University Press, 2009. 11–23.

Colman, Andrew M. *A Dictionary of Psychology*. Oxford: Oxford University Press, 2009.

Culler, Jonathan. *Literary Theory: A Very Short Introduction*. Oxford: Oxford University Press, 2000.

Darby, Phillip. *The Fiction of Imperialism: Reading Between International Relations and Postcolonialism*. London and Washington, DC: Cassell, 1998.

Deal, Michelle L. "Wollstonecraft, Mary", Elizabeth Kowaleski-Wallace, ed. *Encyclopedia of Feminist Literary Theory*. New York & London: Garland, 1997. 429–30.

De Beauvoir, Simone. *The Second Sex*. Trans. H.M. Parshley. New York: Alfred A. Knopf, 1968.

De Berg, Henk. *Freud's Theory and Its Use in Literary and Cultural Studies*. Rochester, NY: Camden House, 2003.

De Man, Paul. *Allegories of Reading: Figural Language in Rousseau, Nietzsche, Rilke, and Proust*. New Haven & London: Yale University Press, 1979.

De Vries, Hent. *Philosophy and the Turn to Religion*. Baltimore & London: the Johns Hopkins University Press, 1999.

Drucker, Johanna. *Speclab: Digital Aesthetics and Projects in Speculative Computing*. Chicago & London: University of Chicago Press, 2009.

Eagleton, Terry. *Literary Theory: An Introduction*. Minneapolis: University of Minnesota Press, 1983.

Eagleton, Terry. *The Significance of Theory*. Oxford: Basil Blackwell, 1990.

Eagleton, Terry. *After Theory*. New York: Basic Books, 2003.

Empson, William. *Seven Types of Ambiguity*. London: Penguin, 1995.

Eribon, Didier. *Michel Foucault*. Trans. Betsy Wing. Cambridge, MA: Harvard University Press, 1991.

Felman, Shoshana. *Writing and Madness: (Literature/Philosophy/Psychoanalysis)*. Trans. Martha Noel Evans and Shoshana Felman. Palo Alto, CA: Stanford University Press, 2003.

Fenton, Steve. *Ethnicity: Racism, Class and Culture*. Lanham, MD: Rowman & Littlefield, 1999.

Ferraro, Gary and Susan Andreatta. *Cultural Anthropology: An Applied Perspective*. Belmont, CA: Wadsworth, 2010.

Ffrench, Patrick. *The Time of Theory: A History of* Tel Quel *(1960–1983)*. Oxford: Clarendon Press, 1995.

Foucault, Michel. *The History of Sexuality, Volume 1: An Introduction*. Trans. Robert Hurley. New York: Vintage, 1990.

Fox, Alistair. "Sir Thomas Elyot." *Dictionary of Literary Biography Volume 136, Sixteenth-Century British Nondramatic Writers: Second Series*. David A. Richardson, ed. Detroit: Gale Research, 1994. Electronic version.

Gallagher, Catherine and Stephen Greenblatt. *Practicing New Historicism*. Chicago & London: University of Chicago Press, 2000.

Gasché, Rodolphe. *The Tain of the Mirror: Derrida and the Philosophy of Reflection*. Cambridge, MA & London: Harvard University Press, 1986.

Gates, Henry Louis Jr. *Figures in Black: Words, Signs, and the "Racial" Self*. Oxford & New York: Oxford University Press, 1987.

Gates, Henry Louis Jr., ed. *Black Literature and Literary Theory*. London & New York: Routledge, 1990.

Gendzier, Irene L. *Frantz Fanon: A Critical Study*. New York & Toronto: Pantheon, 1973.

Germon, Jennifer. *Gender: A Genealogy of An Idea*. New York: Palgrave Macmillan, 2009.

Gills, Barry K. and William R. Thompson. "Globalizations, Global Histories and Historical Globalities." *Globalization and Global History*. Barry K. Gills and William R. Thompson, eds. Abingdon, Oxon & New York: Routledge, 2006. 1–17.

Gilroy, Paul. *"There Ain't No Black in the Union Jack": The Cultural Politics of Race and Nation*. Chicago: University of Chicago Press, 1991.

Gilroy, Paul. *The Black Atlantic: Modernity and Double Consciousness*. Cambridge, MA: Harvard University Press, 1993.

Glotfelty, Cheryll. "Introduction: Literary Studies in an Age of Environmental Crisis", *The Ecocriticism Reader: Landmarks in Literary Ecology*. Cheryll Glotfelty and Harold Fromm, eds. Athens & London: University of Georgia Press, 1996. xv–xxxvii.

Goldman, Jane. *The Feminist Aesthetics of Virginia Woolf: Modernism, Post-Impressionism and the Politics of the Visual*. Cambridge: Cambridge University Press, 1998.

Gregg, Robert. "Afterword." *The Negro.* W.E.B. Du Bois. Philadelphia: University of Pennsylvania Press, 2001. 245–72.

Guha, Ranajit. "Introduction." *A Subaltern Studies Reader, 1986–1995.* Ranajit Guha, ed. Minneapolis: University of Minnesota Press, 1997. ix–xxii.

Gupta, Suman. *Globalization and Literature.* Cambridge: Polity, 2009.

Haeri, Shahla. "Obedience versus Autonomy: Women and Fundamentalism in Iran and Pakistan." *The Globalization Reader.* Frank J. Lechner and John Boli, eds. Oxford: Blackwell, 2004. 348–56.

Hall, Donald E. *Queer Theories.* Houndmills, Basingstoke & New York: Palgrave Macmillan, 2003.

Halperin, David M. "The Normalization of Queer Theory." *Journal of Homosexuality* 45.2/3/4 (2003): 339–43.

Held, David. *Introduction to Critical Theory: Horkheimer to Habermas.* Berkeley and Los Angeles: University of California Press, 1980.

Hepworth, Candida N. "Chicano/a Literature: 'An Active Interanimating of Competing Discourses'." *Post-Colonial Literatures: Expanding the Canon.* Deborah Madsen, ed. London: Pluto, 1999. 164–79.

Hockey, Susan. "The History of Humanities Computing." Susan Schreibman, Ray Siemens and John Unsworth, eds. *A Companion to Digital Humanities.* Oxford: Blackwell, 2004. 3–19.

Homans, Margaret. "'Women of Colour': Writers and Feminist Theory." *New Literary History* 25.1 (Winter 1994): 73–94.

Jakobson, Roman. *Language in Literature.* Krystyna Pomorska and Stephen Rudy, eds. Cambridge, MA & London: the Belknap Press of Harvard University Press, 1987.

Jameson, Fredric. *Marxism and Form: Twentieth-Century Dialectical Theories of Literature.* Princeton, NJ: Princeton University Press, 1971.

Jameson, Fredric. *The Political Unconscious: Narrative as a Socially Symbolic Act.* London: Methuen, 1981.

Jameson, Fredric. "Postmodernism and Consumer Society" *The Cultural Turn: Selected Writings on the Postmodern, 1993–1998.* Fredric Jameson. London & New York: Verso, 1998. 1–20.

Johnson, Barbara. *A World of Difference.* Baltimore, MD: the Johns Hopkins University Press, 1989.

Joseph, John E. "The exportation of structuralist ideas from linguistics to other fields: An overview", *History Of The Language Sciences: An International Handbook On Evolution Of The Study Of Language From The Beginnings To The Present.* Sylvain, Auroux, eds., et al. Volume 2. Berlin: De Gruyter Mouton, 2001. 1880–1908.

Karcz, Andrzej. *The Polish Formalist School and Russian Formalism.* Rochester, NY: University of Rochester Press & Kraków, Poland: Jagiellonian University Press, 2002.

Kearney, Richard. *The God Who May Be: A Hermeneutics of Religion.* Bloomington and Indianapolis: Indiana University Press, 2001.

Kerridge, Richard. "Environmentalism and Ecocriticism." *Literary Theory and Criticism.* Patricia Waugh, ed. Oxford: Oxford University Press, 2006. 530–43.

Kesselman, Mark, ed. *The Politics of Globalization: A Reader.* Boston & New York: Houghton Mifflin, 2007.

King, Thomas. "Godzilla vs Post-Colonial." *New Contexts of Canadian Criticism.* Ajay Heble, Donna Palmateer Pennee and J.R. (Tim) Struthers, eds. Peterborough, ON: Broadview, 1997. 241–48.

Kurzweil, Edith. *The Freudians: A Comparative Perspective.* New Haven & London: Yale University Press, 1989.

Lane, Richard J. *Functions of the Derrida Archive: Philosophical Receptions.* Budapest: Akadémiai Kiadó, 2003.

Lane, Richard J. *Reading Walter Benjamin: Writing Through the Catastrophe*. Manchester & New York: Manchester University Press, 2005.

Lane, Richard J. *The Postcolonial Novel*. Cambridge: Polity, 2006.

Lane, Richard J. *Fifty Key Literary Theorists*. London & New York: Routledge, 2006.

Lane, Richard J. *Jean Baudrillard*. London & New York: Routledge, 2009. Second edition.

Lane, Richard J. "Culture." *The Baudrillard Dictionary*. Richard G. Smith, ed. Edinburgh: Edinburgh University Press, 2010. 44–46.

Lane, Richard J. *The Routledge Concise History of Canadian Literature*. Abingdon, Oxon & New York: Routledge, 2011.

Laplanche, Jean. *Life and Death in Psychoanalysis*. Trans. Jeffrey Mehlman. Baltimore: the Johns Hopkins University Press, 1976.

Lawhill, Sarah. "Wellek René." *Encyclopedia of Contemporary Literary Theory: Approaches, Scholars, Terms*. Irena R. Makaryk, ed. Toronto: University of Toronto Press, 2000. 484–86.

Lechte, John. *Fifty Key Contemporary Thinkers: From Structuralism to Postmodernity*. London & New York: Routledge, 2003.

Lemon, Lee T. and Marion J. Reis. "Introduction." *Russian Formalist Criticism: Four Essays*. Trans. and ed., Lee T. Lemon and Marion J. Reis. Lincoln: University of Nebraska Press, 1965. ix–xvii.

Loomba, Ania. *Gender, Race, Renaissance Drama*. Manchester & New York: Manchester University Press, 1989.

López, José and Garry Potter. "General Introduction", *After Postmodernism: An Introduction to Critical Realism*. José López and Garry Potter, eds. London & New York: Athlone, 2001. 3–16.

Lyotard, Jean-François. *The Postmodern Condition: A Report on Knowledge*. Trans. Geoff Bennington and Brian Massumi. Minneapolis: University of Minnesota Press, 1989.

Madsen, Deborah L. "Beyond the Commonwealth: Post-Colonialism and American Literature." *Post-Colonial Literatures: Expanding the Canon*. Deborah L. Madsen, ed. London & Sterling, VA: Pluto, 1999. 1–13.

Marcus, Steven. "*Culture and Anarchy* Today." *Culture and Anarchy*. Matthew Arnold. Samuel Lipman, ed. New Haven & London: Yale University Press, 1994. 165–85.

Marinucci, Mimi. *Feminism is Queer*. London & New York: Zed Books, 2010.

Marx, Karl and Friedrich Engels. *The Communist Manifesto*. Trans. Samuel Moore. London: Penguin, 1988.

Mason, Travis V. "Lick Me, Bite Me, Hear Me, Write Me: Tracking Animals between Postcolonialism and Ecocriticism." *Other Selves: Animals in the Canadian Literary Imagination*. Janice Fiamengo, ed. Ottawa: University of Ottawa Press, 2007. 100–124.

Mattison, David. "The Digital Humanities Revolution." *Searcher* 14.5 (2006): 25–34.

McIntosh, Mary. "The Homosexual Role." *Social Problems* 16.2 (Autumn 1968): 182–92.

McLeod, A.L., ed. *The Commonwealth Pen: An Introduction to the Literature of the British Commonwealth*. Ithaca, NY: Cornell University Press, 1961.

McLeod, John. *Beginning Postcolonialism*. Manchester & New York: Manchester University Press, 2000.

Mitchell, Juliet and Jacqueline Rose, eds. *Feminine Sexuality: Jacques Lacan and the École Freudienne*. Trans. Jacqueline Rose. New York: Norton, 1985.

Moi, Toril. *Sexual/Textual Politics: Feminist Literary Theory*. London & New York: Routledge, 1989.

Moore-Gilbert, Bart. *Postcolonial Theory: Contexts, Practices, Politics*. London & New York: Verso, 2000.

Moore-Gilbert, Bart. *Postcolonial Life-Writing: Culture, Politics and Self-Representation*. Abingdon, Oxon & New York: Routledge, 2009.

Nigianni, Chrysanthi. ". . . so as to know 'us' better Deleuze and Queer Theory: two theories, one concept – one book, many authors . . ." in *Deleuze and Queer Theory*. Chrysanthi Nigianni and Merl Storr, eds. Edinburgh: Edinburgh University Press, 2009. 1–10.

Nordau, Max. *Paradoxes*. Trans. J.R. McIlraith. London: Heinemann, 1896.

Nothof, Anne. "Resonant Lives: The Dramatic Self-Portraiture of Vincent and Emily." *Theatre and AutoBiography: Writing and Performing Lives in Theory and Practice*. Sherril Grace and Jerry Wasserman, eds. Vancouver, BC: Talon, 2006. 37–151.

Olney, James. "Autobiography and the Cultural Moment." *Autobiography: Essays, Theoretical and Critical*. James Olney, ed. Princeton: Princeton University Press, 1980. 3–27.

Pieters, Jürgen. *Moments of Negotiation: The New Historicism of Stephen Greenblatt*. Amsterdam: Amsterdam University Press, 2001.

Ragland-Sullivan, Ellie. *Jacques Lacan and the Philosophy of Psychoanalysis*. Urbana & Chicago: University of Illinois Press, 1987.

Raglon, Rebecca and Marian Scholtmeijer. "Heading Off the Trail: Language, Literature, and Nature's Resistance to Narrative." *Beyond Nature Writing: Expanding the Boundaries of Ecocriticism*. Karla Armbruster and Kathleen R. Wallace, eds. Charlottesville & London: University Press of Virginia, 2001. 248–62.

Reiss, Timothy J. "Revolution in Bounds: Wollstonecraft, Women, and Reason." *Gender and Theory: Dialogues on Feminist Criticism*. Linda Kauffman, ed. Oxford & New York: Basil Blackwell, 1989. 11–50.

Rivkin, Julie and Michael Ryan, eds. *Literary Theory: An Anthology*. Oxford: Blackwell, 2004.

Robbins, Ruth. *Literary Feminisms*. Houndmills, Basingstoke & London: Macmillan, 2000.

Rose, Tricia. *Black Noise: Rap Music and Black Culture in Contemporary America*. Hanover & London: Wesleyan University Press, 1994.

Roudinesco, Elisabeth. *Jacques Lacan*. Trans. Barbara Bray. Cambridge: Polity, 1999.

Said, Edward W. *Orientalism*. New York: Vintage, 1979.

Said, Edward W. *The World, The Text, And The Critic*. London: Faber and Faber, 1984.

Said, Edward W. *Culture and Imperialism*. New York: Vintage, 1993.

Sedgwick, Eve Kosofsky. *The Epistemology of the Closet*. Berkeley & Los Angeles: University of California Press, 1990.

Sellers, Susan. *Hélène Cixous: Authorship, Autobiography and Love*. London: Polity, 1996.

Sellers, Susan. "Virginia Woolf's diaries and letters." *The Cambridge Companion to Virginia Woolf*. Hermione Lee, ed. Cambridge: Cambridge University Press, 2000. 109–26.

Showalter, Elaine ed. *The New Feminist Criticism: Essays on Women, Literature and Theory*. New York: Pantheon, 1985.

Silver, Brenda R. *Virginia Woolf Icon*. Chicago & London: University of Chicago Press, 1999.

Slemon, Stephen. "Monuments of Empire: Allegory/Counter-Discourse/Post-Colonial Writing." *Kunapipi* 9.3 (1987): 1–16.

Slemon, Stephen. "Post-Colonial Allegory and the Transformation of History." *The Journal of Commonwealth Literature* 23.1 (1988): 157–68.

Spicer, Jakki. "The Author Is Dead, Long Live the Author: Autobiography and the Fantasy of the Individual." *Criticism* 47.3 (Summer 2005): 387–403.

Strinati, Dominic. *An Introduction to Studying Popular Culture*. London & New York: Routledge, 2000.

Svensson, Patrik. "The Digital Humanities as a Humanities Project." *Arts and Humanities in Higher Education* 11.1–2 (2011): 42–60.

Tew, Philip. "Reconsidering Literary Interpretation." *After Postmodernism: An Introduction to Critical Realism*. José López and Garry Potter, eds. 196–205.

Tolan, Fiona. "Feminisms." *Literary Theory and Criticism*. Patricia Waugh, ed. Oxford: Oxford University Press, 2006. 319–39.

Tyrrell, Heather. "Bollywood versus Hollywood: Battle of the dream factories." *Culture and Global Change*. Tracey Skelton and Tim Allen, eds. London & New York: Routledge, 2000. 260–73.

Waters, Malcolm. *Globalization*. London & New York: Routledge, 2001.

Waugh Patricia. *Literary Theory and Criticism: An Oxford Guide*. Oxford: Oxford University Press, 2006.

Weeks, Jeffrey *Sexuality*. Third Edition. Abingdon, Oxon & New York: Routledge, 2010.

Wisker, Gina. "Locating and Celebrating Difference: Writing by South African and Aboriginal Women Writers." *Post-Colonial Literatures: Expanding the Canon*. Deborah L. Madsen, ed. London: Pluto, 1999. 72–87.

Wyile, Herb. *Anne of Tim Hortons: Globalization and the Reshaping of Atlantic-Canadian Literature*. Waterloo, ON: Wilfrid Laurier University Press, 2011.

Young, Robert. *Postcolonialism: An Historical Introduction*. Oxford: Blackwell, 2001.

Zimmermann, Bonnie ed. *Lesbian Histories and Cultures*. New York: Garland, 2000.

Zimmermann, Jens. "Suffering Divine Things: Cruciform Reasoning or Incarnational Hermeneutics." *Through A Glass Darkly: Suffering, the Sacred, and the Sublime in Literature and Theory*. Holy Faith Nelson, Lynn R. Szabo and Jens Zimmermann, eds. Waterloo, ON: Wilfrid Laurier University Press, 2010. 377–99.

Žižek, Slavoj. *The Puppet and The Dwarf: The Perverse Core of Christianity*. Cambridge, MA: MIT Press, 2003.

Index

Also available...

The Routledge Concise History of Literary Criticism and Theory

Pelagia Goulimari

Series: Routledge Concise Histories of Literature

This volume offers an introduction to the history of literary criticism and theory through the texts themselves. Pelagia Goulimari examines:

- a variety of key thinkers from Plato and Aristotle through to Foucault and Derrida
- topics and themes in the history of literary criticism such as mimesis and creation, inspiration, the emotions, reason, aesthetic, history, morality, ethics, culture and discourse
- the main genres and movements in the history of literature including the epic, tragedy, comedy, romanticism, realism, modernism and postmodernism
- cross-historical connections between theories and theorists and the dissemination, appropriation and creative misunderstanding of concepts, ideas and arguments.

With features such as a glossary, annotated further reading, descriptive text boxes and instructive marginalia this book is the ideal introduction for anyone approaching theory and criticism for the first time.

2013: 234 x 156mm: 320pp
ISBN: 978-0-415-54431-3 (hbk)
ISBN: 978-0-415-54432-0 (pbk)
ISBN: 978-0-203-48719-8 (ebk)

For more information and to order a copy visit
www.routledge.com/9780415544320

Available from all good bookshops

www.routledge.com/literature

Also available ...

Routledge Critical Thinkers Series

Series Editor: **Robert Eaglestone**, Royal Holloway, University of London, UK

Routledge Critical Thinkers is designed for students who need an accessible introduction to the key figures in contemporary critical thought. The books provide crucial orientation for further study and equip readers to engage with theorists' original texts.

The volumes in the Routledge Critical Thinkers series place each key theorist in his or her historical and intellectual context and explain:

- why he or she is important
- what motivated his or her work
- what his or her key ideas are
- who and what influenced the thinker
- who and what the thinker has influenced
- what to read next and why.

Featuring extensively annotated guides to further reading, *Routledge Critical Thinkers* is the first point of reference for any student wishing to investigate the work of a specific theorist.

<u>Titles include:</u>

Martin Heidegger
Franz Fanon
Hans-Georg Gadamer
Paul Gilroy

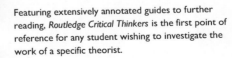

For more information and to order a copy visit
www.routledge.com/literature

Available from all good bookshops

An environmentally friendly book printed and bound in England by www.printondemand-worldwide.com

PEFC Certified

This product is
from sustainably
managed forests
and controlled
sources

www.pefc.org

This book is made entirely of sustainable materials; FSC paper for the cover and PEFC paper for the text pages.

#0240 - 030615 - C0 - 254/178/52 [54] - CB - 9780415783019